THEATER DIRECTING
ART, ETHICS, CREATIVITY

THEATER DIRECTING
ART, ETHICS, CREATIVITY

Kazimierz Braun

Studies in Theatre Arts
Volume 10

The Edwin Mellen Press
Lewiston•Queenston•Lampeter

Library of Congress Cataloging-in-Publication Data

Braun, Kazimierz, 1936-
   Theater directing-- art, ethics, creativity /Kazimierz Braun.
      cm. -- (Studies in theatre arts ; v. 10)
   Includes bibliographical references and index.
   ISBN 0-7734-7828-0
   1. Theater--Production and direction. 2. Theater--Production and direction--Poland. I.
Title. II. Series.

PN2053 .B628 2000
792'.0233--dc21

                                                                        99-053748

This is volume 10 in the continuing series
Studies in Theatre Arts
Volume 10 ISBN 0-7734-7828-0
STA Series ISBN 0-7734-9721-8

A CIP catalog record for this book is available from the British Library.

The Edwin Mellen Press   The Edwin Mellen Press
Box 450   Box 67
Lewiston, New York   Queenston, Ontario
USA 14092-0450   CANADA L0S 1L0

The Edwin Mellen Press, Ltd.
Lampeter, Ceredigion, Wales
UNITED KINGDOM SA48 8LT

Printed in the United States of America

Contents:

Introduction: Towards Creative Directing

Part 1: My Way of Directing

PART 2: Teaching Creative Directing

List of Photographs

1.8. *Intensifying the emotions through direct personal contact.* With students of a directing workshop in Dublin, Ireland, 1983. (Photo by K. Joseph Romanowski)

1.9. *Speaking with theatergoers before the production starts.* A meeting just before the start of *Birth Rate.* The Contemporary Theater, Wrocław, Poland, 1979. (Photo from the author's collection)

1.10. *Staying focused.* Author during directing workshop at Poznań Visual Arts Academy, Poznań, Poland, 1997. (Photo by Przemysław Graf)

SECTION 2. DIRECTOR AND ACTOR SEEK TO EXPRESS THE HUMAN CONDITION

2.1. *Compassion.* Eugeniusz Kujawski (Father Peter) and Krzysztof Bauman (Konrad) in *The Forefathers' Eve.* The Contemporary Theater, Wrocław, Poland, 1982. (Photo from the author's collection)

2.2. *"Come, woo me, woo me, for now I am in a holiday humor..."* Melissa Murphy (Rosalind) in *As You Like It.* Shakespeare in the Park Festival, Buffalo, NY 1991. (Photo from the author's collection)

2.3. *"Is it possible dat I should love the ennemie of France?"* Monika Braun-Bereś (Princess Catherine) and King Henry in *Henry V.* Shakespeare in the Park Festival, Buffalo, NY 1987. (Photo from the author's collection)

2.4. *Deep in thought.* Joan O'Hara in the leading role in *The Old Woman Broods.* The Arts Project Theater, Dublin, Ireland, 1983. (Photo by K. Joseph Romanowski)

2.5. *Philosophical dialogue.* From left to right: Ferdynand Matysik (Ambassador) and Igor Przegrodzki (Writer) in *The Pulp.* The Polski Theater, Wrocław, Poland, 1990. (Photo by Adam Hawałej)

2.6. *Courtly dialogue.* Adèle Leas and Thomas Martin in *As You Like It.* Shakespeare in the Park Festival, Buffalo, NY 1991. (Photo from the author's collection)

2.7. *An erotic encounter.* Halina Rasiakówna (Greta) and Zbigniew Górski (Maks) in *The Trap.* The Contemporary Theater, Wrocław, Poland, 1984. (Photo by Marek Grotowski)

2.8. *Fear.* Tomasz Lulek and Ryszard Jabłoński (Passengers) in *Birth Rate,* The Contemporary Theater, Wrocław, Poland, 1979. (Photo by Marek Grotowski)

2.9. *Brutality.* Stanisław Banasiuk and Tadeusz Galia (Passengers) in *Birth Rate,* The Contemporary Theater, Wrocław, Poland, 1979. (Photo by Marek Grotowski)

2.10. *Anger.* Prisoners sing a song of protest. From left to right: Edwin Petrykat, Zbigniew Górski, Maciej Korwin in *The Forefathers' Eve.* The Contemporary Theater, Wrocław, Poland, 1978. (Photo by Jan Bortkiewicz)

2.11. *Pain.* Marlena Milwiw (The Old Woman), with Zbigniew Górski (Waiter) and Magdalena Kumor (Dancer) in *Birth Rate.* The Contemporary Theater, Wrocław, Poland, 1979. (Photo by Marek Grotowski)

2.12. *Madness.* Eugeniusz Kujawski (Father Peter) and Krzysztof Bauman (Konrad) possessed by the devil in *The Forefathers' Eve.* The Contemporary Theater, Wrocław, Poland, 1982. (Photo from the author's collection)

2.13. *Dangerous stunts.* From the left: Jan Blecki, Kazimierz Wysota, Kazimierz Zadrożny, and Tomasz Lulek fight in *The Plague.* The Contemporary Theater, Wrocław, Poland, 1983. (Photo by Marek Grotowski)

2.14. *Risky hand-to-hand combat.* Michael Karr (Orlando) wrestles with Steve Vaughan (Charles); Thomas F. Higgins, Jr. (Le Beau) and Erin Markle (Chorus) observe. *As You Like It* performed at Shakespeare in the Park Festival, Buffalo, NY, 1991. Fight choreographer: Steve Vaughan. (Photo from the author's collection)

2.15. *A grotesque choir.* Wiktor Grotowicz (Prince Himalay), Grażyna Krukówna (General's Wife), Marlena Milwiw (Chairman's Wife), Teresa Sawicka (Princess Himalay), and Eugeniusz Kujawski (General) in *Operetta.* The Contemporary Theater, Wrocław, Poland, 1977. (Photo by Jan Bortkiewicz)

2.16. *Grotesque lecture.* An ensemble scene in act 1 of *Rhinoceros.* From the left, first row: John Lewin (Logician) lecturing, with Richard Hicks (Student), Richard Levine (Beranger), Steven Yoakam (The Café Proprietor), Robert Breuler (The Grocer); second row: Cathryne Nash (The Waitress), Mary Beth Fisher (The Grocer's Wife), and Marc Crayer, James Richard, Roger Gouenveur Smith (Firemen). The Guthrie Theater, Minneapolis, 1986. (Photo by Joe Giannetti)

2.17. *Playing animals.* Debra Sperling (Pig Squealer) and Johnny Mendez.(Young Pig) in *Animal Farm.* State University of New York at Buffalo, 1990. (Photo by Debbie Hill)

2.18, 2.19, 2.20, 2.21, 2.22, 2.23. *Reaching the depth of darkness at high noon.* Chris O'Neill rehearsing the role of King Lear. Shakespeare in the Park Festival, Buffalo, NY, 1989. (Photo from the author's collection)

SECTION 3. THE DIRECTOR WORKS WITH SPECTATORS

3.1. *Characters mirror the audience.* The prologue of *The Pulp.* The Polski Theater, Wrocław, Poland, 1991. (Photo by Adam Hawałej)

3.2. *Spectators on stage.* Spectators surround the central playing area on the proscenium stage in *Birth Rate.* On the swing: Elżbieta Golińska (the Dove). The Contemporary Theater, Wrocław, Poland, 1979. (Photo from the author's collection)

3.3. *Spectators on stage.* Spectators surround the central playing area on the proscenium stage in *The Plague.* From the left: Kazimierz Wysota (Rat), Tomasz Lulek (Rat), Teresa Sawicka (Porter's Wife), Elżbieta Golińska (Nurse), Zdzisław Kuźniar (the Porter), Jan Blecki (Rat), and Kazimierz Zadrożny (Rat). The Contemporary Theater, Wrocław, Poland, 1983. (Photo by Marek Grotowski)

3.4. *Spectators in a courtyard.* Spectators around the central playing area in the courtyard of the theater building in *The Old Woman Broods.* In the center: Zbigniew Górski (the Poet) and Ludwik Paczyński (Militia Man). The Osterwa Theater, Lublin, Poland, 1973. (Photo by Wanda Parys)

3.5. *Spectators on the street.* Spectators and actors observe the departure of the newlyweds on the street near theater. *The Old Woman Broods.* Opening the car door: Zbigniew Gorzowski (First Man). The Osterwa Theater, Lublin, Poland, 1973. (Photo by Wanda Parys)

3.6. *Spectators visit an actor on stage.* Spectators visit Victor Talmadge (Hunger Artist) in his cage, situated on the thrust stage at the beginning of *The Hunger Artist Departs.* Pfeifer Theater, Buffalo, NY, 1987. (Photo by Irene Haupt)

3.7. *Spectators in the rehearsal room.* Part of the production of *The Plague* staged in the rehearsal room. The audience sit on three sides of the playing area. In the center: Kazimierz Wysota (Rat). The Contemporary Theater, Wrocław, Poland, 1983. (Photo by Marek Grotowski)

3.8. *Spectators in the basement of the theater.* Part of the production of *The Plague* staged in the basement of the theater. The audience sits on three sides of the playing area. From the left: Kazimierz Wysota and Kazimierz Zadrożny (Rats) and Zbigniew Górski (Father Gustaw). The Contemporary Theater, Wrocław, Poland, 1983. (Photo by Marek Grotowski)

3.9. *Spectators outdoors.* Audience before the outdoor production of *Henry V* in Delaware Park, Buffalo, NY. Shakespeare in the Park Festival, 1987. (Photo from the author's collection)

3.10. *Spectators in church.* Spectators mixed with performers in *The Passion Play*. In the center: Stanisław Baltaziuk (Christ). Corpus Christi Church, Buffalo, NY, 1994. (Photo from the author's collection)

SECTION 4. CREATING THEATER SPACE

4.1. *Creating images through the use of characters, sets, and lights.* Group scene in *Anna Livia,* act 1. From left to right: Jan Blecki, Edwin Petrykat, Stanisław Jaskułka, Zdzisław Sośnierz, Teresa Sawicka (Anna Livia), Marlena Milwiw, Zbigniew Górski, Maria Zbyszewska. The Contemporary Theater, Wrocław, Poland, 1976. (Photo by Marek Grotowski)

4.2. *Playing with shadows.* Krzysztof Bauman (Konrad) in his prison cell. *The Forefathers' Eve.* The Contemporary Theater, Wrocław, Poland, 1982. (Photo from the author's collection)

4.3. *Playing in real space—outdoors.* An actor on the roof of a building. Zbigniew Górski (The Poet) in a scene from *The Old Woman Broods.* The Osterwa Theater, Lublin, Poland, 1973. (Photo by Wanda Parys)

4.4. *Playing in real space—indoors.* Production in the Museum of Architecture. *Cleopatra and Caesar.* The Contemporary Theater, Wrocław, Poland, 1976. (Photo by Zdzisław Mozer)

4.5. *Environment created in the black box.* Model of the environment for *Antigone in New York* built by Madeleine Sobota. Department of Theater and Dance, State University of New York at Buffalo, 1995. (Photo by Madeleine Sobota)

4.6. *Environment created in the black box.* Environment for *Antigone in New York* built by Madeleine Sobota. In the center from left to right: Robert Manning (Flea), Ecstasy Seaton (Anita), Damon Kupper (Sasha); far: Owen Muirhead (The Indian) and Gretchen Meyerhoefer (The Newcomer). Department of Theater and Dance, State University of New York at Buffalo, 1995. (Photo by Madeleine Sobota)

4.7. *A daytime performance in a theater modeled on the Elizabethan stage.* The opening scene of *Julius Caesar* in Delaware Park, Buffalo, NY. In the center: Joseph Natale (Julius Caesar). Shakespeare in the Park Festival, 1989. (Photo from the author's collection)

4.8. *A nighttime performance in a theater modeled on the Elizabethan stage.* A scene from act 5 of *King Lear* in Delaware Park, Buffalo, NY. On the platform: Joy Parry (Cordelia). Shakespeare in the Park Festival, 1989. (Photo from the author's collection)

4.9. *Use of height and depths on a proscenium stage.* Bogusław Kierc (Franz K.) and Zdzisław Kuźniar (Father) are on the balcony, with the ensemble situated in two groups center-stage and up-stage in *The Trap.* The Contemporary Theater, Wrocław, Poland, 1984. (Photo by Marek Grotowski)

4.10. *Playing with various heights.* Halina Rasiakówna (Albertine) is standing on a small platform, while Stanisław Jaskułka (Hufnagel) is carried by the group of Lackeys and Maids, from the left: Zuzanna Helska, Zdzisław Sośnierz, Bogusław Parchimowicz, Maria Zbyszewska, and Barbara Pijarowska in *Operetta*. The Contemporary Theater, Wrocław, Poland, 1977. (Photo courtesy of the author)

4.11. *Exploring the depth of the proscenium stage with individual characters.* Upstage: Magdalena Kumor (Young Woman); centerstage: Maria Zbyszewska (Old Woman); downstage: Zbigniew Górski (Young Man) in *Birth Rate*. The Contemporary Theater, Wrocław, Poland, 1979. (Photo from the author's collection)

4.12. *Exploring the depth of the proscenium stage with an ensemble.* A crowd scene in *The Pulp*. Downstage: Igor Przegrodzki (Writer). The Polski Theater, Wrocław, Poland, 1990. (Photo by Adam Hawałej)

4.13. *Exploring the depth of the thrust stage.* The final scene in *The Hunger Artist Departs*. In the center: Victor Talmadge (Hunger Artist) and, from the left, Barbara Gołaszewski (Mother), Richard Hummert (Impresario), Christopher Redfern (Butcher), Molly Heller-Wagner (Journalist), Josh Brewster (Butcher), Colleen O'Mara (Ola), Monica Sosa Backman (Monica), John Kiouses (Butcher), Caitlin Baeumler (Journalist), Susan Sorensen (Mayor). Pfiefer Theater, Buffalo, NY, 1987. (Photo by Irene Haupt)

4.14 *Closing the proscenium stage with bars.* HAMLET: Denmark's a prison. ROSENCRANTZ: Then is the world one. (*Hamlet*, Act II, sc. II). Comparing the theater stage to a prison was a powerful metaphor in communist-ruled Poland. In the photograph: the stage closed off in the final scene of *The Forefathers' Eve*. The Contemporary Theater, Wrocław, Poland, 1982. (Photo from the author's collection)

4.15. *Closing the proscenium stage with barbed wire.* Another example of the same metaphor: the stage closed off in a scene from *The Plague*. Behind the fence: Andrzej Wilk (Teacher) and Bogusław Kierc (Doctor). The Contemporary Theater, Wrocław, Poland, 1983. (Photo by Marek Grotowski)

SECTION 5. CREATIVE USE OF OBJECTS IN THEATER

5.1. *Paintings in a production.* A scene from *Tamara L.* by K. Braun, a play about a painter, Tamara Lempicka, in which copies of actual paintings were used, as well as easels, brushes, etc. From the left: Agata Pilitowska-Borys (Daughter) and Maria Nowotarska (Painter). Right bottom: a picture damaged in action on stage. The Maria Nowotarska Company, Toronto, 1999. (Photo by YOYA Communications)

5.2. *Marionettes.* The Four Angels of the Apocalypse and the Archangel Michael in *The Interrupted Act*. The Osterwa Theater, Lublin, Poland, 1970. (Photo by Wanda Parys)

5.3. *A full size rhinoceros on stage.* Richard Levine (Beranger) in a scene from *Rhinoceros*. The Guthrie Theater, Minneapolis, 1986. (Photo by Dennis Behl)

5.4. *A real car on stage.* Keith Calaman (Mr. Arnaux) and Devon Wyman (Angelique Arnaux) in *Dummies' Ball*. The Black Box Theater, State University of New York at Buffalo, 1997. (Photo from the author's collection)

5.5. *Bicycles in the playing area outside the theater.* Bicycles on the sidewalk in the prologue of *The Old Woman Broods*. Daire Brehan (The Bride) and Joan O'Hara (The Old Woman) approach the entrance of the theater. The Project Arts Center Theater, Dublin, Ireland, 1983. (Photo by K. Joseph Romanowski)

5.6. *Bicycles on the stage.* In the center: David Collins (Son) with a broken bicycle in *Bullai Mhartain*. Deilt Company, Dublin, Ireland, 1989. (Photo from the author's

Foreword

Early in my life, theater appeared to me both as art and as service. The theater about which I heard and with which I was confronted had a definite artistic and ethical dimensions. This vision of theater came to me as a part of my familial and national traditions; I was introduced to it by my theater masters.

During World War II, under Nazi occupation, theater in Poland was prohibited, since it was considered an expression of Polish national spirit. Thus, to do theater against the Nazis' will was an act of bravery and patriotism. During the Stalinist era, theater was treated by the communist regime as a tool in the social and political engineering of the nation. To do a different kind of theater was an act of resistance. During the long years of communist captivity (1945-1989), a highly artistic and definitively ethical theater was a refuge from the unacceptable and unbearable everyday reality; a weapon in the struggle with the devastating culture and mind-corrupting system; it was a strong thread of Ariadne winding through dark and dangerous world "out of joint" (*Hamlet* I. v, 189). This kind of theater was at the side of human dignity. It gave hope.

Stanisław Wyspiański, father of Polish modern theater, introduced the notion of "theater-the temple of art." Adolphe Appia put forth the idea of the "theater-cathedral." Juliusz Osterwa proclaimed that theater is a "sacrificial act." I came to know their works early in my theater life. Under their spell and guidance, I started to understand and practice theater that way. Arduously, for sure. Clumsily, no doubt. Gradually, perhaps, more and more skillfully.

Early on, I was also challenged to consider seriously the ethical aspects of the theater profession. I belonged to a group of university students whose spiritual and academic mentor was a professor at the Catholic University in Lublin, Father Karol Wojtyła, a man of prayer, wisdom, and charisma. One of my early professional assignments, while I was still a student of directing, led me in 1961 to Cracow, where, at that time Karol Wojtyła was a newly appointed bishop. I visited him. A former actor and playwright, he was always interested in theater life and followed its developments. He wanted to hear about new premières, as well as the situation of the theater milieu. Towards the end of our meeting, he asked me to write for him a paper on the ethical problems which a young director encounters in the theater. On one hand, I was not surprised. It was Wojtyła's way of teaching and spiritually guiding people: to let them identify their personal, moral, scholarly, or professional problems and freely search for just, honest, and proper solutions; as a university professor he habitually asked people to express their problems and views in the form of a paper; then, he would offer evaluation, advice, encouragement. Summer vacations with Father Wojtyła always had three components: prayer, tourism, and an academic program of seminars. On the other hand, I remember that I was stricken by that assignment: a director asked to reflect not on art or craft of theater, but on his morality and attitude within the context of theater. I wrote the paper, which cost me more effort then the usual academic homework. I brought it to the professor-bishop. He called me back for discussion. I remember his question: how do you want to combine art with ethics in your theater work? Soon—submerged in everyday theater rehearsals, experiments, tensions, stage catastrophes and victories—I forgot that meeting. Later in my work, I know, I practically answered Father Wojtyła's question in a way he would disapprove.

Yet, gradually, more and more recurrently, the fundamental questions about theater work ethics returned to me. I could not help but recall them when my mentor became the Pope, when I listened to his sermons and read encyclicals, and when I had the joy to see him again.

Towards the end of my way, with increasing clarity I see how profoundly and directly human the theater art is. Only the inseparable union of the artistic and ethical dimensions of theater can give a production meaning and energy, and express the abundant and inexplicable richness of the human being.

I see directing, and I write about it on these pages, as an art of helping actors and spectators to live their lives to the fullest.

Acknowledgements

I want to express my thankfulness first to my teachers of directing, Erwin Axer and Bohdan Korzeniewski, and to all theater artists and scholars from whom I have learned directing through seeing their productions or reading their books. I owe gratitude to all those who allowed and encouraged me to direct, to teach directing, and to write on directing. Among so many of these generous and helpful people I must acknowledge in particular—in Poland: my daughter, Monika Braun-Bereś, Maria Budzyńska, Zygmunt Duczyński, Andrzej Kapela, and Juliusz Tyszka; in Canada: Maria Nowotarska; in Germany: Hans Jürgen Jenssen; in Greece: Maria Panoutsou; in Ireland: Michael Scott; in The Netherlands: Arthur Sonnen; in the United States: Gary Casarela, Thomas Cooke, Andrew Doe, Zygmunt Dyrkacz, Saul Elkin, Ron Engle, Daniel Gerould, André Gregory, Rick Hellweg, Steven Henderson, Nagle Jackson, Larry Jaquith, Stephen Kanee, Thomas Leff, David Lamb, Mitchell Lifton, Thomas Martin, Richard Mennen, Jerry Rojo, Richard Schechner, Ron Sossi, Jarek Stremen, Linda Swiniuch, John Ransford Watts, Max Weber, and Jon Whitmore. I am in debt to a multitude of my former students; among them I especially vividly recall my work with Małgorzata Bogajewska, Anthony Cardinale, Juliett Carillo, Lisa DeRensis, Patti Doyen, Adam Gertshacov, Barbara Jiang, Thomas Kazimierczak, Richard Kramer, Ed Menta, Ewa Mruk, Richard Lambert, Meron Langsner, Gretchen Meyerhoefer, Gloria Pena, Mark Pizatto, Chester Popiolkowski, Rich Tylor, Fabian Wagmister, Ian Watson, Donald White, Jacek Weksler, and Aleksandra Wolska. I remember well, and I will remember for ever, how much I owe to all actors I have and opportunity and privilege to work with. I keep them in my grateful memory. I kindly thank the following photographers for being able to use their photos: Dennis Behl, Jan Bortkiewicz, Cezary Chrzanowski,

Tadeusz Drankowski, Joe Gainetti, Przemysław Graf, Marek Grotowski, Irene Haupt, Adam Hawałej, Debbie Hill, Cliff Moore, Zdzisław Mozer, Wanda Parys, K. Joseph Romanowski, Madeleine Sobota, and YOYA Communications. For professional editing of the book I thank Alayne MacArthur and Charlotte Pressler; for her editorial and translating help I thank my daughter, Justyna; and Mariola Szydłowska for preparing the bibliography and the indexes. For invaluable, loving, and unconditional support of my work I am grateful to my wife, Zofia, and to my children, Monika, Grzegorz, and Justyna.

Preface by Jan Kott

My friend, not too much younger than I, Erwin Axer, an excellent director, and for many years the head of one of the best theaters in Warsaw, used to say: "acting can be taught, directing can't." Yet he had been a directing student of Leon Schiller, and for about forty years he himself taught directing at the Warsaw Theater Academy. Kazimierz Braun, Axer's student, who has directed everything from the classics to the most contemporary works in many countries, and who has taught theater in several prestigious universities, thinks that directing, and what is more, "creative directing," can be taught. He has written a book on it. However, there is no easy answer to the question: can directing be taught or not?

Beginning in the early Renaissance, or perhaps the late Middle Ages, a student of painting began by mixing colors and preparing the canvas for his master. Soon, the master might allow that apprentice to draw a leg or a tree. From the middle of the 18th century on, painting was taught at fine arts academies. Under the guidance of a professor, the student copied plaster figures, then learned acts, and still later he was taken out into the open air. The professor waked from easel to easel making corrections. Many painters, some with renowned names, went through such schools. This schooling brought good results. But was it schooling in creative art?

In France, beginning in the high schools, students are taught to write poetry. To be exact, they are taught to write in classical Alexandrine verse. The tradition of *belles letters* maintained that the mastery of language should include the practical skill of writing in rhymes and meters. In America, there's a mandatory English Composition class in all colleges, for all students, not only for those who are humanistically oriented. Of course, students are taught not only spelling, rules of usage, and principles of composition. My university teaching experience tells me that this writing skills requirement is not only desirable, but necessary. Moreover, for a good ten years now there have also been, in America, weekly, biweekly, or monthly classes and workshops on writing novels, plays, and even lyrical poems. Classes, sometimes quite expensive ones, are taught by writers, poets, and playwrights, whose names are not on the top of the bestsellers list, but are still respectable. Several young people who have made their names by writing for magazines, or have published books have finished these classes, which are advertised as "creative writing."

Singing, violin playing, piano, and trombone are taught at the music academies, as well as composition, solfeggio, and instrumentation. Craft is taught, and performance for the public is taught. But where is the border line, a probably delicate and obscure one, between the craft and the art in singing, in a violin concerto, in virtuosity?

Hence, I repeat once more, can directing be taught? It is a rhetorical question. We are teaching directing in America and in all European countries, except, as far as I know, in England. Peter Brook and Peter Hall did not take directing courses. They begun by directing at their schools at the student theaters; Brook at Oxford, Hall at Cambridge. Did they learn the craft of directing? Did they learn, scene by scene, the art of directing? On the other hand, Ingmar Bergman, Jerzy Grotowski, and Andrei Serban finished theater schools. What did they learn?

Kazimierz Braun, a great magician and master of directing, has written a book on creative directing and seems to positively hold that directing is essentially creative. For directing transforms the written text into spoken words, gives these words to actors to deliver, puts the text within a space closed or open, adds light, a light from dawn to dusk, and selects the entire orchestration of the production.

Braun's work is not only a directing textbook. The artistic and creative directing of which Braun writes also beckons to his own biography and personal experience, and this is the special value of his book.

In the Warsaw Theater Academy, Leon Schiller, one of the greatest creators of the 20th century theater, alongside the teaching of directing, introduced a separate program, called "the knowledge of theater." Braun not only has long years of directing experience, but also has written several books and essays on the history of theater in Poland and in the world. He is not only a director but a theater historian as well. His last book is based not only on his own directorial and scholarly experience, but also on the whole tradition of the Polish and the European theater; it brings to life the famous masters of European theater: Craig and Appia, Copeau and Meyerhold, Brook and Barrault, Beckett and Ionesco; and the Polish artistes: from Mickiewicz and Norwid, through Wyspiański and Osterwa, to Kantor and Grotowski.

This book is not only for directing students and young professional directors, but for all who love theater. It opens eyes.

Jan Kott

Author of *Shakespeare Our Contemporary*
Professor Emeritus, SUNY at Stony Brook

Santa Monica, Summer 1999

INTRODUCTION: TOWARDS CREATIVE DIRECTING

The method of *creative directing*

Participants in my classes and workshops on directing in America, Poland, Ireland, and other countries have often suggested that I should write a book about the method of *creative directing* which we explored and used. This book is an answer to their wishes. All of them—students and young professionals—through their active, imaginative, and inventive participation in our collective work became real co-creators of this method. Many of them are living proof that it works.

The method of *creative directing* is a way of directing in which the director creatively calls into being, articulates, builds, structures, and shapes all elements of a performance. Consequently, the director creates the totality of the performance. The method of *creative directing* enables the director both to work as a creative artist and to foster the artistic creativity of everyone else involved in the preparation of a performance.

Two basic premises are at the core of this method.

The first is the conviction that directing is an act of creating—in the truest sense of the word: making something out of nothing. Directing is indeed an act of giving birth and calling to life, converting the spiritual into the material, transmuting the prosaic into the poetic and the common into the artistic. Seen from this perspective, every aspect of a performance is an infinite, vast field open to the director's creation.

The second is the awareness that directing is both a creation and a craft: as a craft, directing requires skills, techniques, methods, and tools which express the artistic energies and spiritual abundance of human life: life as experienced by the director, lived by the actors on stage, and perceived by the spectators during the show.

Directing, treated and practiced as an art, appeared in Europe at the end of the 19th century. In the 20th century it emerged as a leading force in theater. Many outstanding directors were total creators of their shows. I was introduced to directing as an art during my studies at the Warsaw Theater Academy. I absorbed it also through study of the history of theater and through seeing the works of the best directors of the time. During my years of directing and teaching directing, I gradually transformed a creative *approach* into a *method*. With each new show directed and each new directing class taught, I have been developing, clarifying, articulating, and simplifying it, until it has attained the profile of a distinctive directing method, which I dare to call *creative directing*.

As a student of theater history and participant in theater life, I have learned much from my esteemed precedessors and fellows. I am well aware that there are, and have been, many different directorial methods successfully used in directing and in teaching directing. There are many examples of splendid and dynamic productions that prove the effectiveness of these directorial practices. Some of them are described and explained in books and manuals for directors, which provide directing "know-how," emphasizing the functional, practical, and technical aspects of directing; they are comparable to "how to" books on gardening, fishing, cooking, and other areas of human activity. One can find in these practical advice on how to block a sit-com stunt or a crowd scene in a tragedy, along with recipes for casting actors or building a rostrum. I enormously respect the professionals and teachers who wrote these books. The method presented here, however, has little in common with those approaches and only rarely refers to them. My approach is a *creative* method that strives to enable the director to create artistically. It is an *open* method that provides points of departure for individual creation, rather than prescriptions. This method does not prompt and substitute, but guides and counsels towards a discovery of one's own world. It strives to inspire and to give a young director wings to soar above the theater landscape.

I should make clear that the method of *creative directing* presented in this book is primarily oriented towards the "dramatic theater" (or "straight theater"); that is towards a theater in which an important component is the actor's expressive use of the spoken word. The "dramatic theater" is at center stage in this book as is the director of the "dramatic theater" production. I take my examples from this kind of theater and I prepare the students to work in it. I know from my former students that this method works well also for the opera, the musical, the pantomime, and multi-media shows. Additionally, it is useful in directing (or rather preparing) various artistic, social, political, and religious events, such as concerts, convocations, congresses, meetings, demonstrations, ceremonies, sport events, liturgical services, and others. Some elements of this method, especially the analysis of the text and the work of a director with actors, are applicable to television and film directing.

Definition of theater art

My method of *creative directing* is based on a specific understanding of theater and it functions within its context. The definition of theater which has emerged from my own years of practice and studies of theater history is as follows: "Theater is an interhuman process of communication artistically conditioned and structured."

Theater is what occurs between actors and spectators. Theater is always embedded in the real, concrete, biological and spiritual life of human beings and their direct communications with one another. Theater transforms everyday and mundane interhuman contacts, activities, and acts into art. Theater is born when "art" is added to "life," or rather when "life" is transformed into "art." Theater is life itself, but a life intensified, made expressive, structured, public, and converted into art.

The interhuman process in theater has the basic structure of communication. It involves a sender, a message, and receiver. The actor is the sender. The spectator is the receiver. Performance is the message. In an everyday communication process the message has various human values and functions. It contains information, signs, meanings, warnings, orders, and so on. In theater the messages having all these functions have become endowed with aesthetic values: with the beauty of human existence expressed vocally, physically, visually, and emotionally.

The basic means of communication between people in theater are those used in everyday life: presence, activity, movement, voice, sound, image, and story telling. While in ordinary life these means are used directly, functionally, practically, and on many occasions spontaneously, in theater they are always selected, measured, shaped, structured, and made artistic. Thus, the whole communication process in theater retains the characteristics of life, while transforming life into art.

The essence of theater is action. Action unites all the means of expression and is the primary vehicle of communication between actors and spectators. The greatest mystery of theater is the transformation of an everyday human action into an artistic action. Human deeds become inseparably fused with symbols, metaphors, visions, and dreams. The real is enriched with the unreal. The particular becomes the universal.

Definition of *creative directing*

Directing is the art by which the interhuman process is shaped artistically. The performance is the result of this process of communication between actors and spectators. The director transforms real life processes into artistic processes. The method of *creative directing* achieves this transformation through the use of five general principles.

The first involves creation of the text of the performance, through editing an existing drama, writing an adaptation, or arranging the results of improvisation of actors.

The second is the creation of the human matter of the performance, by shaping and structuring the activities of the actors, their behaviors, movements, and their voice. Included in this principle is the preparation of circumstances for the active involvement of the spectators. Human acts, deeds, and activities create the network of interaction between actors and spectators in performance. The most desired directorial skill is to creatively pilot both actors and spectators through the uncharted lands of theater art.

The third involves creation of the space of the performance. Here, consideration is given to the theater architecture, the playing area for actors and the observation area for spectators. Sets, costumes, props, and lights are all components of the visual aspect of the performance which the director creates usually in collaboration with the designers.

The forth involves creation of the temporal aspects of the performance. They include such aspects as the speed, tempo, pace, and rhythm, as well as musical, sound, and acoustic elements of the performance. The director usually creates these in collaboration with a composer or sound person.

The fifth includes creating (or at least controlling) all the technical, organizational, and production aspects of a performance, usually in collaboration with producers, technicians, and administrators.

A look at the history of directing in Western Culture

Directing, as a set of preparatory practical activities and functions leading to a public production, was a part of theater from its beginnings. Usually the people who fulfilled those functions also participated in the show in various capacities.

The author of a tragedy or comedy prepared its performance in ancient Greece; such was the role of Sophocles, Aristophanes, and many others. For centuries of theater history, playwrights have personally staged their plays. In Western Culture, this tradition has been strong. It included the authors of the scenarios ("sogetti") of Commedia dell'Arte and was continued by such great playwrights as Molière in the 17th century, and Goethe at the beginning of the 19th. In the 20th century, August Strindberg in Sweden, Luigi Pirandello in Italy, Jean Anouilh in France, Helmut Kajzar in Poland, and Sam Shepard in the United States can be cited as examples of authors who directed their own plays.

An actor has often taken the role of director. This actor might be the head of an acting company, the "leading man" or the "leading lady," the father or mother of a family troupe of actors (as was Caroline Neuber in 18th century Germany), or the most experienced member of a traveling company. In the 19th century, Charles Kemble, William Macready, Charles Kean, and Henry Irving in England, Sarah Bernhardt in France, Helena Modjeska in Poland and America, and Eleonora Duse in Italy were but a few of the great actors who took on the role of director. Until today multitudes of actors have prepared productions as directors and frequently also performed in them.

A designer, painter, or scènographer was also often in charge of preparing shows. Leonardo da Vinci in Italy and Inigo Jones in England were director-designers in the European Renaissance courts. This tradition was continued in the French Romantic theater by Louis-Jacques Daguerre and Pierre-Luc-Charles Ciceri. In the 20th century, painters-designers put their decisive mark on the productions of the Ballet Russe of Serge Diaghilev. Andrzej Pronaszko and Józef Szajna were a very powerful force in the Polish theater, as were Emil Burian and Josef Svoboda in the Czech theater. Two leading avant-guard directors of the second part of the century were visual artists. Tadeusz Kantor in Poland, who was a painter, designer, and happener; and Robert Wilson, an architect, painter, and designer in the United States.

A producer (as we would call this person today) was in charge of preparing productions in many countries throughout the long ages of theater history. These people were entrepreneurs, patrons, or sponsors of productions. In Medieval Europe, a town council commissioned the head of a guild of carpenters, masons, or bakers to make all of the necessary preparations and assume all of the costs of putting on an annual passion play. This man would hire and instruct actors, build *mansions*, and negotiate the schedule of the shows with the clergy and town police. Renaissance princes or cardinals personally devised and supervised the productions at their courts. Until the end of the 19th century, noble and rich theater owners liked to personally stage plays. The creator of modern American directing, David Belasco, was a producer, and remained a producer during his entire directorial career.

Authors, actors, designers, and entrepreneurs preparing productions tended to focus on their specific areas of interest and expertise. The consequence was that they did not creatively shape the totality of a performance. Authors as directors centered their attention on the text, disregarding the action. Actors as directors put their hearts and skills into the acting aspects of the show and disregarded the visuality of the mise-en-scène. Designers as directors emphasized the visual, but were unable to build a strong acting component into their productions. Directing producers were interested primarily in the external attractiveness of a show, its ability to lure crowds, and its profit-making potential; they were less interested in the intellectual or aesthetic values of a production. In one way or another, each group was concerned with only one area of performance and usually did not grasp the performance in its entirety.

Creative and artistic directing, encompassing and shaping the whole production, appeared when one person—who was neither an author, actor, designer, nor producer—obtained unified control over all of the elements of performance. One person took charge of editing, cutting, or adapting the text. He made casting decisions and rehearsed the actors. He was also the chief designer, conceiving the visual style, the mise-en-scène, and the sets. Finally, he had control over the production process, being responsible for the planning, scheduling, and organizing of the work.

The first modern director of this kind in Western theater was Ludwig Chronegk. He was appointed director in the court theater in Meiningen, Germany, at the beginning of the 1870s, by the owner of the theater, Duke Georg

II von Meiningen. Chronegk took control over every aspect of the production from preparation to performance. He was not an author. Yet, with the help of Ellen Franz, the Duke's wife and a former actress, he gave the final editorial shape to plays. He was an actor by profession (rather a mediocre one, in fact) but he did not act in his shows. He was not a designer. His boss, the Duke, was an amateur painter and historian who liked to draw historical scenes based on Shakespeare or Friedrich Schiller. Using the Duke's drawings and working with the carpenters and painters, Chronegk transformed them into sets. He was not a producer, having no money besides his modest salary. He was, however, empowered by the Duke to make decisions about all the production expenses of the theater. He controlled and unified all areas and aspects of the production. The modern craft of directing was born.

Chronegk directly inspired and influenced André Antoine in France, Konstantin Stanislavsky in Russia, and Tadeusz Pawlikowski in Poland. These men, with Otto Brahm in Germany, Jacob Green in England, and others, formed a generation of naturalistic directors concerned with creating theater productions that had integral and coherent artistic unity. The foundations of 20th century artistic directing were laid by Gordon Craig in theory, Max Reinhardt in stage practice, and Stanisław Wyspiański in the mise-en-scène. Later on, Adolphe Appia formulated a vision of directing as an art and as a communal interaction. The appearance of these artists at the beginning of the 20th century created a critical mass that advanced the theory and practice of directing as an art.

Gordon Craig, an Englishman, in his book *The Art of Theater* (1905), was the first in the history of theater to declare that theater is a distinct "art" and that the director is a "theater artist," who summons to being "a work of the art of theater." The director, as envisioned by Craig, had training, knowledge, and skills in all of the theater disciplines. Craig believed that this "theater artist" should have sovereign power over all the elements of the performance. Craig's ideal performance, the "work of theater art," is a coherent artistic unit with all its parts—text, acting, and space—transformed and integrated by the director.

The integration of the parts results in a universality which elevates the whole to a level higher than the separate parts. The "work of theater art" exists and functions, according to Craig, within the realm of aesthetics and can be existentially compared to the fine arts. Craig, who began as an actor and evolved into a designer, rarely directed, focusing instead on explaining his theories and ideas in articles and books. He deeply influenced European theater of the 20th century.

Max Reinhardt, who in his youth was an actor in Austria, and later became an internationally recognized director, built rich and complex mise-en-scènes, which achieved a tremendous expressive power through a coordinated use of various means: acting, pantomime, crowd scenes, large-scale sets, and complex music scores. He heavily edited and adapted dramas, or commissioned them from playwrights who wrote scripts especially for him. He strove for harmony between the performance's style and its space, and, according to the character of a play, he put on shows in small or huge theaters, in the circuses or in open-air venues. He unified all elements of his productions with his titanic will and powerful personality. He dominated theater in Germany and Austria from the beginning of the 20th century until the 1930s; and his productions toured throughout Europe and North America. In the late 1930s, he fled to the United States as a refugee from Nazi Germany. He challenged the American theater industry with his insatiable pursuit of high art on stage.

Stanisław Wyspiański, a Pole, was the first European theater artist who personally created all elements of a performance: he was a painter, poet, playwright, designer, and director; he became the first "total theater artist." Beginning with his play, *The Wedding,* which he personally staged in the Cracow City Theater in 1901, Wyspiański wrote several dramas in which text, vision, action, and music, the rhythms of dialogues, and movements of characters described in stage directions, were integrated into total projects of complex and rich productions. He inspired many generations of Polish directors in the 20th century.

Adolphe Appia, a Swiss critic, musicologist, designer and theoretician, in his book *The Work of Living Art* (1921) put forth a concept of a "theater-cathedral"— a communal and interactive process in which artists (representing the different mediums of theater, music, dance, and poetry) and the spectators participate as one group in the creative process. Appia's is a theater of participation. Divisions between senders and receivers, artist and public, actors and spectators are broken down and no longer valid. A production is a collective effort, and directing is transformed into the artistic and spiritual animation of the community.

The art of directing flourished in Europe in the 1920s and 1930s, becoming an indispensable element of theater and an important factor in The Great Reform of Theater (1890-1940). Many excellent professional actors, such as Firmin Gémier in France, Leopold Jessner in Germany, Harley Granville-Barker in England, Theodore Komissarzhevsky in Russia, and Aleksander Zelwerowicz in Poland, adopted a comprehensive and artistic approach to directing, striving to bind together all elements of production and achieve stylistic unity. At the same time, such artists as Oskar Kokoschka in Austria and Tomasso Marinetti in Italy were more interested in theater aesthetics than in theater craft. Their contribution was to the development of directing as a purely artistic activity. Georg Fuchs in Germany and Nikolai Evreinov in Russia tried to enrich theater by returning to the old traditions of Greek tragedy, Medieval morality plays, or Italian Commedia dell'Arte. They sought to connect these traditions with modern artistic movements, and experimented with exaggerated stylization and intensive visualization of a performance.

The next generation of directors to practice "total" and "artistic" directing became the leaders of theater in Europe in 1920s and 1930s. Among these artists were Vsevolod Meyerhold and Alexandr Tairov in the Soviet Union, Jacques Copeau and Gaston Baty in France, Leon Schiller and Wilam Horzyca in Poland, Erwin Piscator in Germany, Emil Burian in Czechoslovakia, Les Kurbas in the Ukraine, and others. They were followed by a group of actor-directors and masters of teaching acting who also based their directing on the principles of totality and comprehesivness in production. Among them were Konstantin Stanislavsky and Evgeny Vakhtangov in Russia, Juliusz Osterwa and Edmund Wierciński in Poland, Lee Strasberg and Harold Clurman in America, Michel Saint-Denis, who worked in France, England, Canada, and the USA, and Michael Chekhov, who moved from Russia through Western Europe to America. Antonin Artaud challenged directing with his vision of a total theater of direct, biological and psychological interaction.

The same total approach to the art of directing has been characteristic of the most influential directors of the second part of the 20th century. The giants of this approach were: Bertolt Brecht and Pina Bausch in Germany; Jean-Louis Barrault, Jean Vilar, Roger Planchon, Ariane Mnouchkine and Jérôme Savary in France; Luca Ronconi and Giorgio Strehler in Italy; Andrzej Wajda, Konrad Swinarski, Jerzy Jarocki, and the pantomime master, Henryk Tomaszewski, in Poland; Joan Littlewood, Peter Brook, and Peter Hall in England; Juri Lubimov and Anatoly Vasiliev in Russia; Karolous Koun in Greece; Tom O'Horgan, Peter Sellars, and the Rumanian émigré Andrei Serban in America; and scores of others.

The leaders of the many theatrical communities who participated in the Second Reform of Theater (ca. 1955-1985) used collective creation, improvisation, and other new methods of theater work to generate complex, multi-layered productions in which all elements were created by the group. The result was a unique, expressive physicality merged with a profound exploration of the actor's subconscious. Space was invented and built exclusively for a given show. Original sound and music for the performances were developed during rehearsals. The list of these directors is long and includes names from all continents and countries: among them are Jerzy Grotowski, Lech Raczak, and Włodzimierz Staniewski in Poland; Julian Beck, Judith Malina, and Peter Schumann in America; Tadashi Suzuki, Shuji Terayama, and Juro Kara in Japan; director-anthropologists Richard Schechner and Eugenio Barba; and director-deconstructivists Richard Foreman and Joanne Akalaitis. In spite of the changes and mutations of modern directing the principle remained the same: all these artists created the totality of their performances. They did not merely put on plays, they did not reuse old styles, and they did not allow any element of the show to remain off-limits to their artistic curiosity and will. Text, acting, space, music, communication between actors and spectators, indeed every aspect of the production was created anew.

Various directing styles

Though adherence to the principle of directorial control over the whole production unifies their work, there are considerable differences among the many directors who have left their mark on the 20th century theater. Modern directors have practiced diverse styles and emphasized various elements of theater in their work. Brecht employed Chinese theater techniques in politically-oriented epic critiques of society. Grotowski investigated acting. Staniewski explored the relations between actors and spectators. Wilson worked with the concept of space. Kantor materialized Craig's dream of a super-marionette in shows where actors turned into mannequins and mannequins were animated by actors. Suzuki trained actors to have rigorous, almost unbelievable control of their minds and bodies, using methods founded on the old Noh techniques.

From the practical and professional point of view, all director-artists took an individual approach to the process of directing, used different methods of directing, and focus on different directorial problems. Each of these various approaches had its advantages and perils.

Some directors can be described as pragmatists. They clearly see in their imagination the general, final shape of the performance they want to build. They work with actors as though with mechanisms for producing stage effects, movements, and sounds rather than with human beings. Such directors never develop personal ties with actors and they do not motivate them to call upon their own private, intimate, or subconscious experiences. Consequently, they are not able to help actors to connect their roles with their own human impulses and motivations, nor to reach the human feelings and emotions of the spectators. Even fascinating directorial projects and ideally functioning productions, if played by actor-dummies, are rarely convincing to the public. On the other side of the spectrum are directors who work as sensitive teachers, untired helpers, understanding confessors, full of empathy and understanding fellows, who communicate perfectly with actors on the private, personal, and emotional level. Yet, they are not able to objectively analyze an actor's work, look at the actor from a distance, shape an actor into an artistically defined character, or build roles as definitive aesthetic structures. Other directors are dreamers. They are guided by inspiration and try to inspire actors using cryptic, metaphorical language during rehearsals. Sometimes they fail at being able to translate their volatile visions into the practice of production. On the other hand, they sometimes lead their companies to a refined and subtle show, which moves the public and leaves a shadowy, incomprehensible, and mysterious impression; such productions often have a lasting impact on the spectators. There are also directors who, like military commanders, lead their casts to risky and dangerous tasks. Others direct as hypnotizers, casting spells on their actors during rehearsals. Some prefer to verbally explain the problems. Conversely, some prefer to play for actors and ask for imitation.

These are only a few, selected examples of possible approaches to directing. It is neither the subject of this book nor my objective to classify various directing styles or methods. It is also not my intention to opt for one or the other of these styles, methods, and ways of directing. I will rather try to present and explain my own method, being aware that even if I described it and explained clearly it would still remain an elusive ideal.

This ideal, which I personally have been pursuing my whole life in theater, is situated in the region of high art. In this region directors express themselves with full artistic freedom, they create all the elements of the production, and as a result, they give birth to works of art of theater. At the same time, they enable their collaborators to achieve an equally free, open, and intensive creative expression. This refers in particular to the work of a director with an actor, the essential layer of the theater creation, which should harmoniously encompass both work with the actor as a human being and as an artist. The first requires courtesy, empathy, motivation, and nothing less than love; while the second must use certain skills, techniques, tools, and methods.

The fact that I have failed so many times to achieve this ideal does not dissuade me from searching for it nor from teaching it to others. This is how I understand my duty to the readers: to help them to create freely and fully on their own.

The foundations of teaching the art of directing

Gordon Craig opened the world's first school of directing in 1913, in Florence, Italy. His objective was to teach "theater artists" and formulate the language of "theater art." The program began by experiments with a "super-marionette"—an utopian yet inspiring ideal. The school was conceived as a workshop in which a small international community of apprentices worked under the master's guidance. Unfortunately, the work was interrupted in 1914, by the outbreak of World War I. Some students joined the armies, some died at the fronts, and the school never reopened.

In 1933, Schiller, an apprentice of Craig's in Paris in 1909, organized a department of directing in the Warsaw Institute of Dramatic Art. It was the first directing department on the academic level. It had a very ambitious curriculum which comprised five directing seminars taught by professional directors, as well as classes in acting, voice, movement, dance, set and costume design, the history of theater, the history of literature, including drama, the history of music, including opera; and classes in philosophy, culture, sociology, psychology, and aesthetics. In addition to their course work, students were assigned to various Warsaw theaters as assistants to directors.

Earlier, some American universities had offered individual courses in directing. Later, directing departments were organized in Moscow, Leningrad, and Prague. After World War II, directing departments surfaced all over the United States and Europe. Classes on directing appeared in the curriculum in many more universities and colleges, and master directors started to offer directing workshops.

The almost century-long experience and tradition of teaching directing in many countries has established that an effective model for teaching directing has three segments. They are: (1) practice at school, (2) history/theory study, and (3) practice in the theater.

The first part consists of practical instruction carried in the classroom. A directing program should have classes, seminars, and/or workshops on directing taught by professional directors. Additional classes should give practical instruction in stage design, costume, lighting, and acting; acting for directors, offered at the directing department, should be oriented towards the work of the director with the actors.

The second part is a broad-based liberal arts education which includes courses in theater and drama history, art history, architecture, music and literature, in addition to philosophy, aesthetics, sociology, social communication, anthropology, psychology, and management.

The third part should offer to students apprenticeships and assistantships with professional directors in both professional and academic theaters. Students should follow up with independent projects of directing skits, scenes, one-acts, and, finally, whole productions under the mentorship of teachers of directing.

The student reader of this book will find here an equivalent to the first component of a director's education—a comprehensive course on creative directing. The second component, the historical and theoretical foundations, as described above, should be built by students themselves; the bibliography in this book will help them. The third segment, that is assistentships and independent work, cannot be replaced by any amount of reading. However, this book does offer a detailed insight into all the phases of the actual process of directing a play.

What you will find in this book

This book begins with a comprehensive introduction which you are now reading. Next you'll find three main topics: my own way of directing, teaching directing, and the actual directing of a production.

Part 1 describes the paths that lead me to directing and to my development of the *creative directing* method. I was drawn to theater at the Poznań University where I studied Polish literature. I became an actor, director, and eventually artistic director of a student theater. During my studies I learned the basics of the history of Polish and world theater and drama. I soon became a "theater addict." I tried to see all the shows possible at home as well as the foreign companies visiting Poland. Travels abroad allowed me to get acquainted with French, English, Italian, and Greek theater. Just after completing my master's in literature in Poznań, I entered the graduate directing department at the Warsaw Theater Academy. The curriculum was rich and demanding; directorial seminars conducted by outstanding directors were at its core. From Erwin Axer I learned the realistic and psychological method of directing based on Stanislavsky. Bohdan Korzeniewski inspired his students with cosmic visions of the "staging theater" within the tradition of Craig, Wyspiański, and Schiller. At the scenography seminar, the leading Polish designer of the time, Andrzej Pronaszko, introduced me to the secrets of using fine art styles in designing sets and costumes. The directing students of the Theater Academy also worked in the Warsaw professional theaters as assistants to prominent directors. I was fortunate to get an assistantship with Axer. In 1961 I directed my first professional production, three one-act plays by Sławomir Mrożek, *Karol, Out at Sea* and *Striptease.* I set out on a fast-track directorial career in theaters in Gdańsk and Warsaw. I also started to direct dramas for public television. In 1967 I was appointed the artistic director, and later also general manager, of a city theater in Lublin, The Osterwa Theater. I began to collaborate with a leading Polish playwright, Tadeusz Różewicz; I staged several of his plays. I reached my directorial maturity in the mid 1970s when I moved to Wrocław. It was there that I was appointed the artistic director and general manager of the Contemporary Theater (Teatr Współczesny). I was not a member of the Communist Party and, therefore, my work was constantly hampered in communist-ruled Poland. Despite that, and despite my struggles with censorship, as well as the pressure from the authorities, I managed to direct a series of productions in which I formulated and demonstrated the principles of my directing method and style. Among them, *Birth Rate* by Różewicz was a manifestation of the modern poetic theater. *Anna Livia*, based on Joyce, was a search for a universal language of theater. *The Forefather's Eve* by Adam Mickiewicz was a saga of climbing the highest peak of Polish drama, in search of the most precious national values, traditions, and hopes that resulted in a production played in four different venues and lasting about nine hours. *The Plague*, based on Albert Camus and Daniel Defoe, was—probably—the clearest example of my approach to directing: I wrote the text of the adaptation, built the space, designed both sets and costumes, directed the actors, and made audience participation vivid.

Part 2 of this book describes and explains the principles and the process of teaching creative directing. It is based on directing classes and workshops I have taught at Polish schools of drama, and universities in America and other countries. This part of the book has five chapters. The first discusses creative analysis of the text. The second, the creation of the human dimension of the performance, including the creative work of the director with actors. The third, the creation of the performance space, including sets, lights, costumes, and props. The fourth, creation of the temporal elements of the performance. The fifth, the creation of the action of the performance. In each of these parts, the reader will find both theoretical analysis and practical exercises which help to develop a specific technique or method. This part of the book includes many *directorial exercises* to be used in classes and workshops. They should foster the students' creativity. The exercises pertain to all major elements of the directorial artistic palette. They explain how to create the human, the spatial, the temporal, and the actional layers of a production. The director, as I see him/her, is an artist who possesses and is able to employ various tools, methods, and techniques to practically, physically, emotionally, and visually express his/her ideas, dreams, emotions, and the uniqueness of his/her personality. The *directorial exercises* are the crux of my book, because they help students to acquire creative directorial skills. They show how one can create—not how one should. They are open and they serve as examples, not as models; they should be reinvented, not repeated; they show possible ways, not unique solutions. Students and teachers can use these exercises to explore and investigate various directorial problems. The exercises serve as starters for further, independent, and original work by a group or class. I developed all of the exercises introduced and described in the book during many years of my directing, teaching directing, and working with students in various countries. Many groups, and, indeed, generations of students, have contributed to the development of these exercises and have verified their usefulness.

Part 3 investigates the actual process of creatively directing a theater production. It discusses the preparations for directing a show and the rehearsal process. The first phase includes selection of the play, analysis of the play, directorial stylistic decisions, casting decisions, planning the finances, devising the timetable of the production process, and preparing the directorial "book." This phase includes also collaboration of a director with playwrights, designers, composers, choreographers, and other specialists. Preparations require creativity and inventiveness on the part of the director, as well as openness to all his/her collaborators. The director should foster and nurture creativity in other people involved in the preparation of the show. The creative approach and attitude is crucial in the rehearsal phase, when the director works, first of all, with the actors. At this stage of the work, creative directing means maintaining the director's own creativity and readiness to look for new solutions, as well as helping actors to create. The director should follow earlier artistic and practical decisions but not be enslaved to them. The director should guide the actors towards the desired goals, but not deprive them of their artistic freedom, always requesting and inspiring their active participation, alertness, and readiness to take risks and strive for perfection. The book provides certain techniques, methods, and tools useful in rehearsing. Remarks on the ethics of the work in the theater close this part.

I will use Anton Chekhov's *The Cherry Orchard* to illustrate the principles of script analysis and rehearsal preparation. Other problems will be demonstrated through descriptions of the improvisations. It is impossible, of course, to improvise in the pages of a book. It is possible, however, to describe improvisations as they happened during my classes and workshops; these might be used as examples for a group's own work.

Applications of this book

This book has the following applications:

First, it is a general guide to classroom-based work, or independent directing studies. *Part 1* describes the major problems a young director could work on. *Part 2* and *Part 3* provide a general overview of the materials that are the subject of directing studies.

Second, it is a practical textbook for students of directing at the undergraduate and graduate levels. *Part 2* and *Part 3* guide the students—led by their instructor—through all of the stages of the director's work in creating a performance. Used as a textbook, the material can be broken into approximately 120 two-hour classes.

Third, it is a collection of directorial exercises, which could be used in classes and in workshops.

Fourth, the chapters on creating the performance space can be useful to directors and designers alike.

Fifth, the book can be a source of information for theater historians on the curriculum of studies and career path of a director in Poland; a country with a vivid and intensive theater life, and the birthplace of many great directors.

Teaching and learning *creative directing*

Finally, teachers and students of directing must ask themselves whether it is possible to teach and to learn creative directing. On one hand, it is impossible to teach and learn creative directing because it is an art and a gift. As any other branch of art, directing is based on one's own talent and inspiration. It requires a special type of imagination and sensitivity, and it needs specific predispositions for one's own work and for work with others. In truth, these gifts cannot be taught or learned. Yet, if someone has talent, imagination, sensitivity, vivid empathy, and social awareness, it is possible to help him/her to discover, recognize, and develop their own directorial energies. On the other hand, it is possible to teach and learn directing, because, in addition to being an art, directing is also a craft. As with any craft, skill, or knowledge, it is based on certain practical abilities, techniques, and methods; and it uses certain tools. All of these can be taught and learned. As the German poet Johann Wolfgang von Goethe stated: "even masterpieces of art are made of 10% of talent and 90% of hard work." This book is addressed to those who have talents and, at the same time, are ready to work hard. These pages will help them become both artists and craftsmen.

The more subtle the work of a craftsmen is, the more specific are the tools required. The tools, however, do not make the craftsman. It is the final work which manifests mastery. A tool, even the most perfect and precise, is dead without a skillful and loving hand. Let's consider an example. In 1987, during his visit to Poland, Pope John Paul II celebrated a mass at the Gdańsk port city on a huge and high altar built in the shape of a ship. The altar was designed by the theater scènographer, Marian Kołodziej, (a master with whom I had the privilege to work years ago.) The Pope and the congregation of several hundred thousand did not care what saws, drills, chisels, and hammers the carpenters used to build the altar-ship. However, without these tools it would not have been erected, and it would not have been so beautiful and uplifting. The same is true of directorial tools, and the tools used by all other artists involved in the production of a show.

The tools are necessary, and they must be highly specialized and effective. But the spectators are not led to the stage shops. They go directly to the auditorium to enjoy the production.

There's another question. Why should we teach or learn directing, in the first place? The simple answer is: in order to be able to effectively direct, of course! But this is too narrow and too utilitarian an answer. Directing has its full meaning only if seen within artistic, ethical, philosophical, and social perspectives. As with other arts, directing has metaphysical and transcendental objectives. As with other social sciences and techniques, directing should be understood and practiced as human service, because, indeed, directing is always service to others.

Directing, indispensable during rehearsals, disappears and dissolves in the production. A director will not star on a stage as an actor; will not enchant the spectators as a designer; will not listen, hidden in the wings, to his own words delivered by the performers, because that is the privilege of the writer; the directors will not hear their music from the orchestra pit, as composers do. It is the director, however, who can prepare the actor to cast a spell on the audience, who inspires a playwright to write powerful words, who motivates the designers to explode their palettes, or composers to create unforgettable tunes. It is the director who catches up the audience "in the clouds," as St. Paul says in the letter to Thessalonians (4, 17)—into the heaven of the magic and mysterious world of theater.

Directing is an art of creating from people, with people, and for people. The human being is the matter, giver, receiver, and objective of the work of a director. A human being with his or her complexity and richness, flesh and spirit, dignity and individuality, desire for freedom and pursuit of happiness; human being who—contrary to the thesis of some philosophers and ideologues—can not be understood apart from the categories of good, truth, justice, and love. Directing, therefore, is situated within the realm of morality and is always morally oriented. Directing might be practiced morally or immorally. Directors should be aware of the moral responsibility and consequences of their productions.

Lastly, seen within artistic, professional, human, aesthetical, and ethical perspectives, directing appears as a vocation. And as such, it might be compared to the vocation of a priest, physician, or psychotherapist. The director is able to give people good or evil, direct them to good or evil ends. Let us hope that students undertaking the study of directing will be motivated only to good works.

PART 1. MY WAY OF DIRECTING

CHAPTER 1. A WAY TO DIRECTING

First theatrical experience

When I entered the drawing room it was already full of people. I ran to my mother's feet and sat on the floor. My parents, my grandmother, my older and younger sisters were there, along with a dozen cousins and guests. People were occupying chairs and benches. Uncle Anthony was sitting on a stool at the piano in the corner of the room, softly playing variations on a motive of one of his own compositions. Two candles were burning on the piano mantle. Without interrupting his playing, uncle Anthony asked my mother:

"Lily, should we start?"

I remember her face in the candlelight, with a bright smile, radiating as always in her eyes when she listened to music or poetry. She looked around, as if checking attendance, and contacted my father; a small gesture of their mutual respect and love, as I understand it now.

"Everybody is here," he said. "We are ready."

Mother turned to uncle Anthony.

"Yes, we can start, Tony. Please..."

Uncle Anthony stood up and waked to the curved side of the piano. From my perspective on the floor, he was tall and slim. He had an aureole of long white hair around a sharply sculpted face with a classical profile and burning eyes. He wore his usual old-fashioned white summer suit, supplemented with a blue bowtie. He said:

"Ladies and gentlemen, I am going to give you a few soliloquies of Konrad, the hero of *The Deliverance* by Wyspiański. The music is mine."

He returned to the keyboard, waited a moment with closed eyes, as if accepting inspiration from above, and started to play. After a few bars he added poetry to the music:

"I want to see a summer day... I want to see a harvest... I want to see the future bread..."

He delivered the soliloquy in an ecstasy. He had a reverberating, deep, tenor voice. The words, coinciding with melody, sounded like an opera recitative. I did not understand the sense and content, but I listened fascinated and enchanted. I felt united with him and everybody else in the room, as all of us were enveloped by this melody and poetry. I knew that I was participating in a family event, but, I suppose, I instinctively felt that I was also involved with something unusual, drawn into a reality higher and larger than this evening, beyond my home, beyond the forest surrounding it, even beyond the war raging in the country and all over the world.

This was my first theater experience. My uncle was an actor and composer. (To be exact, though we called him "uncle," he was my mother's cousin.) Before the war he performed in the Słowackiego Theater in Cracow. But now, it was wartime, his theater was closed by the Germans and only used from time to time for Nazis' galas or rented by a Berlin or Munich touring company playing for the German troops in occupied Poland. Uncle was earning his life as a piano teacher and came to spend summers in my family country house in the Świętokrzyskie Mountains in central Poland. This country house was the only place we had to live, after being expelled at the beginning of the war from our home in Sosnowiec, a city in Silesia, where my father was a lawyer. Staying with us, uncle recited soliloquies from classical Polish plays and played music—Chopin,

Szymanowski, Paderewski, and his own pieces.

It was a real theater. Uncle was the professional actor. We, the family, were the audience. The setting was the black piano at the corner of the room and the huge golden frame carrying the dark paintings of my ancestors which hung over it. Two candles provided the lighting. Uncle was in his own clothes, but his unusual blue bow-tie turned his attire into a costume. The fragments of a poetic drama and a musical score united all of us in the contemplation of beauty. It was a minimal theater, but it had all the necessary theater elements: the actor and the public, word and sound, and all-embracing space and time. So, I learned as a child that theater is something which connects people as they are, and, at the same time, carries them somewhere else, into the realm of poetry and mystery. It may happen anywhere. No stage or auditorium is needed. No elaborate lighting or costuming. Only people and an art connecting them.

I remember many performances given by uncle Anthony Żuliński during the war. Today, I should call them "one-man shows." We, the children, were also frequently asked to stand up at the piano and recite poetry for the family and the guests. Before the war I was too young to go to the theater. During the war, we lived in that country house and I only heard about theater. I heard a lot. My uncle was an actor, but my aunt, Jadwiga Domańska, was also an actress. During the war, uncle Anthony, whose theater was closed, was involved with the underground performances given by the company of The Rhapsodic Theater in private homes in the city of Cracow, performances like the ones in our mountain house. These shows were illegal. Possible punishment included deportation to Auschwitz or even shooting on the spot, if the Germans broke in. My aunt, Jadwiga, an actress before the war, found herself during the war in the Polish army in the West. She organized the theater there, she became its manager and commander, and she played for the troops. Moreover, my uncle Jerzy Braun (the older brother of my father, Juliusz) who was a poet, playwright, composer, philosopher, and politician, used to visit us during World War II in our country house, and he also played his compositions for us, sung songs, and recited poetry at the piano. He was a great artist and a brave man, one of the leaders of the underground Polish government during the war. Both my parents were well-educated and knowledgeable in literature and theater, about which they frequently spoke. They emphasized the role of theater in a person's upbringing and the nation's culture.

Thanks to all of them, very early in my life, I learned another lesson about theater: it is an uplifting and patriotic thing to perform, even when threatened by a Gestapo raid, as we all were in our house, and as uncle Anthony was in Cracow, or even while being shelled by the enemy close to the front lines, as my aunt, the actress-soldier did. These were more lessons in theater. You have to have courage to do theater. You have to be bold to be an actor.

Just after the war, in 1946, I saw uncle Anthony on the regular stage in a production of The Rhapsodic Theater in Cracow. He was in costume but I recognized him at once. Of course, it was him! The proscenium did not separate us. I felt as if I was sitting at his feet on the floor in our drawing room. Since then, an actor on stage has always been for me someone close—a relative, a neighbor, a friend, a brother in the profession. I did not see my aunt on stage at that time, because after the war she could not return to a country ruled by communists and she remained in England. It was a bad, harsh, and cruel time. Perhaps even worse then the war-years. During the war my father was three times arrested by the Germans: once he escaped, and twice he was almost miraculously released. After the war he was arrested again, this time by the communists. He was sentenced to a long prison term because of his anti-communist stand. Other members of my family, including uncle Jerzy Braun, were also imprisoned.

During the years of my schooling I subconsciously pursued my early enchantment with theater. I liked to recite poetry and I read a lot of dramas, but belonging to a family marked as "enemies of the state" meant that I could not even think about any career in public life; theater was out of the question. As it turned out, university studies were also closed to me. Stigmatized as the "son of a political prisoner," I was not accepted at the Poznań University where I applied.

I had to support myself. I found a job as a construction worker.

The political situation in Poland started to change gradually in the mid 1950s. My father, and later also my uncle Jerzy, were released from prison. Applying again, I was accepted at the Literature Department of the Poznań University. My theater interests grew, and I joined a student theater. As it turned out soon, it was the threshold which led me to the theater world.

Theatrical beginnings at the Poznań University

My theatrical initiation was painful, funny, and amazing. The University student theater announced auditions for a play. It was a very bad "socrealistic" play. There was no choice. I auditioned. I was not casted. End of the dream, I thought. So, to be very clear and honest—this was the beginning of my theater career: a rejection.

But there were so many of us who were not casted that the student theater decided to produce another play at the same time, and certainly a better one: *Twelfth Night* by Shakespeare. A young professional actor, Ireneusz Kanicki, from the Polski Theater in Poznań, was hired to direct. I auditioned again. He casted me. I got the role of Feste, a wise and funny jester. The whole cast was made up of those rejected from the first play. It was, therefore, a second-rate cast and second-rate production. Rehearsals went on. The first play, that socrealistic one, opened to good reviews from the Party critics. We had our opening too, but it went unnoticed.

Poznań was a large academic center with about ten universities. Every year a regional festival of student productions was held. It had the format of a competition. A prize was awarded to the best production. The University was represented by its "number one" production of that socrealistic play, but our *Twelfth Night* was somehow included too. And here starts the amazing story which affected the rest of my life: we won the Poznań festival. Absolutely unexpectedly, we got the first prize. As winners of the regional competition, we were sent to the all-Poland festival of student productions. We won it. The first prize again. We, the "second-rate" cast, we, the "rejected." Not surprisingly, I got the "theater bug." I haven't been cured yet.

So here I was— a university student infected by theater. Torn in between classes and rehearsals. I had to be a good student in order to earn good grades and be eligible for the scholarship. My father, after his release from prison, was still persecuted and jobless for years; the situation of the family was desperate. I kept up with classes, but I gradually plunged deeper and deeper into the theater world. During my sophomore year, I got the artistic directorship of the student theater. Soon after, I was invited to play on the professional stage. The role was minor, but the satisfaction was major. For the record: my professional acting debut was in the character of the Citizen of the Town of Güllen Number 3 (there were four of them) in *The Visit* by Friedrich Dürrenmatt in the Polski Theater in Poznań in 1957. As a somehow noted student-actor I also got other professional jobs. For some time I was a news presenter in the television, a real adventure, because at that time television in Poland was just beginning. Everything was not only live—everything was always malfunctioning. I also played some minor roles in televised plays. I worked as lector for the local radio station. All that built my acting experience and, of course, was an asset to my always empty student pockets.

Looking back at my university years, I recall it as a time of very intensive learning in theater, composed of four main segments. First, I studied the history of world and Polish drama, which was a part of the university's curriculum. Second, I studied by myself the history of Polish and world theater. Third, I got the beginnings of stagecraft, playing both in the student and the professional theaters, listening to directors and peeking at actors. Fourth, I consciously tried to see as many theater productions as possible in Poznań, in Warsaw, where I frequently traveled (an expensive extravagance for a student), and, also abroad, an opportunity which suddenly opened up during my junior year.

The Literature Department at Poznań University provided a broad background in literature and language. I made drama the most important subject of my studies. During the four years of the program, I took several classes in the area of drama and I read hundreds of plays. My reading included the Greeks, the Romans, the Medieval and Renaissance authors, the Romantics and the Realists of the 19th century, and the 20th century's playwrights. In modern drama, besides the Polish, I was most interested in the French and Scandinavians, devouring Hugo, Claudel, Montherlant, Giraudoux, as well as Ibsen and Strindberg. Theater history classes were not offered at that time at Poznań University, so I had to study this subject by my own. I spent hours in the University library reading books and old newspapers in which I tracked down reviews, interviews with artists, and photographs of productions. At that time, I had a good foundation in French and the beginnings of German and Italian, so I could supplement Polish sources with foreign. All in all, I built for myself the fundamentals of theater history knowledge. It had many blank spots, but at least I knew what were the most important facts and what direction to go next. I wrote my master's dissertation on the 19th century Polish poet and playwright, Cyprian Norwid, and in the process learned more about the drama and theater of the time.

First glimpses of the craft of directing

Working under the direction of professionals in my student theater and then on the professional stage gave me my first glimpses of the craft of directing. I recall my first directors tenderly, but at the same time, I am aware that their skills were limited. One of them, Roman Sykała, was a graduate of the Leningrad School of Drama. In communist Poland, outstanding theater students got stipends to study directing either in Moscow or in St. Petersburg, at that time called Leningrad. These people got a solid education in Stanislavsky which they used advantageously in their work. They were also brain-washed in socrealistic style, which they usually rejected as soon as they returned to Poland.

Observing Sykała, fresh from Russia, at work with actors, and reading Stanislavsky's books, published at that time in Polish translations, I got my first encounters with the Russian master. His method was never fully internalized by

Polish theater and his reception in Poland has had a long and bumpy history. Long, because Stanislavsky was known and respected in Poland very early. Polish theater artists and critics knew a lot about him and saw his productions both in Russia and on tours abroad. One of Stanislavsky's closest collaborators was a Pole, Ryszard Bolesławski (Richard Boleslavsky), actor and director, responsible for teaching Stanislavsky's method in the United States in the 1920s. Bumpy, because Stanislavsky was Russian and early in the 20th century, his theater was perceived in Poland as representative of the oppressive tsarist state. (From 1795 until 1918 parts of Poland were under Russian rule, others under Austrian and Prussian.) Consequently, when the Moscow Art Theater came to Warsaw in 1906 and 1912 it was boycotted by the patriotic public. During World War I, some Polish actors and directors interned in Russia met Stanislavsky and established good working relations with him. Later, between the two wars, some others traveled to Moscow to see his productions. After World War II, Stanislavsky's situation in a Poland ruled by communists was paradoxical, thanks to the peculiar connections between theater and politics in the country. As the corner stone of socrealism, "the Stanislavsky System" (as it was called) was the only officially accepted acting method taught in Polish schools of drama and was recommended in all theaters. It was politically correct to talk loudly about Stanislavsky and people doing so were rewarded by the regime. But there were not many who did it. At the same time, Polish theater people perceived Stanislavsky's method as an expression of "Russian soul," much different to the Polish one, and treated it as one more part of Soviet culture imposed on Poland in order to annihilate the native culture. So, the majority of both teachers in drama schools and directors in theaters deep in their hearts rejected Stanislavsky. I felt this hostile climate surrounding him. Professionally, I was attracted to his recommendations, but emotionally, I was disposed against using them. A paradox characterizing my own first acting and directing steps.

The heritage of Juliusz Osterwa

From the practical and political points of view, Stanislavsky's reception in Poland was even more complex, because his method was in many points similar to that developed by a master of Polish theater, Juliusz Osterwa.

An actor, director, pedagogue, and founder of the Reduta Theater, Osterwa was a towering figure in Polish theater in the first half of the 20th century. He practiced and taught a realistic and psychological acting, emphasizing imagination, empathy, and the circumstances in the actor's building of character. He strongly stressed the actor's spirituality and his/her personal motivation in performing.

Osterwa was extremely popular in Poland before the war. But after the war, he was denounced by communists and Marxists as a representative of "bourgeois culture," a nationalist, and idealist; his heritage was suppressed. Precisely for the same reasons for which the communists tried to bury him in oblivion, he was a role model for me and a source of inspiration. The direct collaboration of my uncle Anthony Żuliński with Osterwa before and during the war also played an important role in my attitude towards him.

Just as it was politically correct to quote Stanislavsky, it was dangerous to refer to Osterwa. In the cast of *The Visit* in the Polski Theater was an older actress, formerly a Reduta member, Osterwa's student and friend. From her few words in the theater cafeteria and the expression of her face when she recalled Reduta, I could guess how much she was still under Osterwa's spell, although he had passed away ten years ago, and how much she detested Sykała, a director educated in Leningrad who overtly praised the Soviets, and pushed Stanislavsky's terms on actors. But she never publicly spoke fondly of Osterwa, nor contradicted Sykała on Stanislavsky.

Thus, very early, I was somehow torn between Stanislavsky and Osterwa. Instinctively, from the point of view of craft, I felt that both of them would help me. Also instinctively, on the level of national and cultural feelings, I felt close to Osterwa and distant from Stanislavsky. As a result of the complexity of these different traditions and currents—distorted and suppressed, foreign and domestic—as a young actor and director, I tried to build the acting work process on the attitudes taught by Osterwa, and I used his stress on imagination and empathy. At the same time I utilized a selected number of Stanislavsky's tools, such as "motivations," "objectives," "goals," and "circumstances."

Looking back on my whole work, I think that Osterwa enormously enriched my directing and later my teaching in the areas of stressing the personal and moral aspects of theater work, and shaping open, artistically and spiritually oriented attitudes in my actors and students. Stanislavsky provided me with strong and stable foundations and principles of craft, including terminology and means for structuring rehearsals and class work into logically developed and connected stages. The Stanislavsky heritage is well known in America, thanks to his own visits and books, as well as the teachings of his students, such as Richard Boleslavsky, Maria Uspienskaya, and Michael Chekhov. Americans who used and transformed his method, like Lee Strasberg, Cheryl Crawford, and others, further promoted Stanislavsky here. Osterwa could reach America only indirectly, through Grotowski, or my own scattered writings. I feel it necessary to introduce Osterwa more thoroughly to the reader, not only because of my preferences, but because of his impact on Polish theater in the 20th century, within which I grew up, and of which I became a part.[1]

Juliusz Osterwa (1885-1947), was born to a very poor family and orphaned at an early age. He did not finish high school. Instead, he joined a semi-amateur theater (the Teatr Ludowy) in Cracow. He made his acting debut in 1904 and embarked on a fast and glamorous career, passing through theaters in Cracow, Poznań, Wilno, and Warsaw, where he was engaged by the Teatr Rozmaitości, the leading country's stage in 1912. In the meantime (1907-1909), he also

---

[1] In the following paragraph on Osterwa, I use parts of my book, *A History of Polish Theater, 1939-1989: Spheres of Captivity and Freedom.* Westport, Connecticut and London: Greenwood Press, 1996. I do the same, while writing in the present book on Erwin Axer, Jadwiga Domańska, Bohdan Korzeniewski, Mieczysław Kotlarczyk, and Leon Schiller.

traveled extensively in Western Europe, watched eminent actors, and learned the newest theater trends. In 1907 he made his directing debut with *Horsztyński* by Juliusz Słowacki in Poznań, but his first directorial success was *The Wedding* by Wyspiański in Warsaw (1915), which served as a springboard for his assuming the position of artistic director of the Teatr Rozmaitości. Before actually starting this job, however, he was interned in Russia during World War I. In exile, Osterwa organized Polish productions in Samara, Kiev, and Moscow, where he met Stanislavsky. After the war, he returned to Warsaw, and in 1919 established the Reduta (Redoubt), an experimental theater-laboratory for new acting and playwriting. In 1922, he opened an acting school, called the "Reduta Institute," with a demanding program of acting training, communal life, and a new system of theater ethics, based on the notion of service to the public and the nation. The Reduta functioned first in Warsaw (1919-1925), as a theater and an acting school, next in Wilno (1925-1931), as both a stationary and a touring company, and again in Warsaw (1931-1939), as an experimental theater and acting school. While with the Reduta, Osterwa also served as the artistic director of the National Theater (Warsaw, 1923-1925) and the Teatr Słowackiego (Cracow, 1932-1935). He directed and guest-starred all over Poland. Both Osterwa's home and his Reduta venue in Warsaw were bombed at the beginning of World War II in 1939, which prompted Osterwa to move to Cracow. Unemployed, he taught acting and speech there, appeared in clandestine one-man shows, and participated in the underground anti-Nazi cultural movement. In his essays and notes, he formulated the project of two theatrical-religious orders, Dal and Genezja. After World War II, Osterwa directed and acted in Cracow, Łódź, and Warsaw. He was not trusted by the communist regime, but, thanks to his popularity, he was nevertheless appointed artistic director and general manager of the Teatr Słowackiego and head of the School of Drama in Cracow (1946-1947). He died of cancer in 1947.

Osterwa influenced Polish theater enormously, and he was considered one of the prominent artists in its history. His impact was strong during his lifetime. After his death, the Marxists tried to erase Osterwa's memory and heritage from the Polish theater. Since the 1960s, however, Osterwa has again been an inspiration for many Polish directors, actors, teachers, and reformers. As an actor and a director, Osterwa worked in three major domains: classical tragedy, classical comedy, and contemporary, realistic, psychological drama. He played leading roles in all of his major directorial works. As a young actor, handsome and possessing a mellifluous voice, personal charm, and the ability to play different roles, he was at first inclined toward comedy and farce. In his maturity, he turned to drama and tragedy, yet still returned to the lighter repertory from time to time. The best of Osterwa's tragic roles and direction appeared in *The Constant Prince* by Słowacki, based on Pedro Calderón de la Barca (1917, and four subsequent stagings). Osterwa staged this as a religious ceremony and interpreted the role of the Constant Prince (Don Fernand) as a martyr, playing it in a state of ecstasy.

"Truth," in Osterwa's view, was the foundation for theater work, having both theatrical and moral aspects; acting, therefore, was a process of revealing the truth of a character through the revelation of the actor's own truth as a human being. Osterwa treated acting as a "sacrifice" or an "act of redemption." The performance was for him a "sacerdotal sacrifice for the congregation." He referred to spectators as "witnesses." The "communion" between the actors/priests and the public/congregation was his goal, and the "actor-saint" was his ideal. He searched for methods to break the barriers between actors and spectators. During his tours with *The Constant Prince* (beginning in 1926), he invited people from local communities to play as extras. Directing *Outward Bound* by Sutton Vane (co-director Ryszard Ordyński, 1932), in which the action takes place on a boat, Osterwa staged the play on a real riverboat sailing the Vistula river; the actors merged with the public. Osterwa enjoyed utilizing natural spaces and architecture for open-air productions and used live fire for lighting. He believed that moral, spiritual, social, and patriotic values should be at the core of theatrical creation. He treated theater as communion, service, and holy act.

I owed my early encounters with Osterwa to uncle Anthony. I started to study his work at the university. I continued my pursuit of his methods and teachings in the school of drama. I used them a lot in my directorial and pedagogical work. I wrote on him in articles and books. I know that I will never repay my debt to him.

Learning theater as a spectator

My theater experiences as a spectator were abundant in my youth. In Częstochowa, where my family lived after the war, there was a solid professional city theater with two stages. Its repertoire was supplemented by the shows of visiting companies. I saw there national classical plays for the first time, such as *Kordian* and *Balladyna*, tragedies by Juliusz Słowacki, and *The Revenge* and the *Virgin Vows*, comedies by Aleksander Fredro. Uncle Anthony would come to visit Częstochowa with his Rhapsodic Theater from Cracow, or the theater company from Łódź which featured a star, a legend of the pre-war theater, Józef Węgrzyn. Then, during my high-school years, "socrealism" dulled the stages. The Częstochowa theater started to produce contemporary so-called "production" plays which discussed industrial or agricultural problems, "anti-imperialistic" plays in which the notorious character of the Western spy tried to disrupt the happy life of the people in the Soviet bloc; "educational" plays dealing with Poland's history in Marxist terms; and many both Russian and Soviet plays. For a high school student there was no difference between them—they all came from the detested East. At the same time, the majority of national classics, all domestic plays not having an explicit propaganda message, and all Western authors were banned.

The socrealistic scourge was still going on when I moved from Częstochowa to Poznań, but soon, in 1955, the "thaw" (as Ilia Erenburg named it) started to melt the Stalinist ice. The political turmoil of the "Polish October 1956" resulted in a complete change in theater life. Socrealism was at first pushed aside, and then swept away. By the 1957-1958 theater season it had been totally replaced by a new repertoire and new styles. New plays questioned communist rule in Poland.

Old classical dramas, prohibited until then, were brilliantly staged and heralded national values. A whole wave of foreign plays broke the dams of censorship and inundated Polish stages. I was there during that time of the flourishing of the Polish theater. I saw these shows and felt these emotions. I started to write about them as a reviewer for the university weekly. I was young and hungry for theater. And theater provided me with a lot of nourishment.

I was able to see sunset productions directed by the old masters of the Polish theater Schiller and Edmund Wierciński, who at that time were passing away. I saw *The Emergency Ward* by Jerzy Lutowski in Poznań in 1955, which contained a hidden, yet strong, critique of political persecutions in the country and warned that the communists didn't have a moral mandate to rule it. I saw *A Tall Wall* by Jerzy Zawieyski in Cracow in 1956, a new play by the Catholic writer, prohibited until then, who wrote a moral parable about the devastating impact of the past on our present life, a problem very much discussed in a Poland emerging from the Stalinist totalitarian darkness. I saw *The Winkelrid's Feast* by Jerzy Andrzejewski and Jerzy Zagórski in Łódź in 1965, which, in the guise of a medieval Swiss story, mocked the corrupted rulers of the present Poland. I saw in Warsaw the recuperations, that is the first productions following years of banishment, of the national classics: *The Wedding* by Wyspiański in 1955, *The Forefathers' Eve* by Mickiewicz in 1955, and *Kordian* by Słowacki in 1956. I went to Cracow to see the very first production of Tadeusz Kantor in his Cricot 2 Theater, *The Cuttlefish* by Stanisław Ignacy Witkiewicz (1956). I saw for the first time in my life Brecht's epic dramas, as well as some Western plays until then kept off the of Polish stages. Plays by blacklisted Polish writers emerged too: Bruno Jasieński, a disillusioned leftist, executed in Moscow in 1938 where he had gone in search of the communist paradise; Witkiewicz, who committed suicide in 1939, on hearing the news that the Soviets had attacked Poland; and an émigré, Witold Gombrowicz.

Having dumped the socrealistic style into the dustbin of history (as the

Marxists used to say about the art of the past), Polish designers again produced works of incredible beauty. The tradition of modern artistic and imaginative stage design was long and strong in Poland. In the 20th century it was started by Wyspiański and was carried on by many artists who were both excellent painters and innovative designers. The best of all of them, Andrzej Pronaszko, was still active in the 1950s. Many others, such as Jan Kosiński, Józef Szajna, and Andrzej Sadowski, followed suit. In their sets they provided necessary functions and playing areas, but always expressed them with highly artistic and profoundly symbolic means.

I was stunned by the explosive energy and universal dimension of the directorial total theater in the tradition of Schiller, practiced at that time by Wilam Horzyca, Ludwik René, Kazimierz Dejmek, Bronisław Dąbrowski, and others. I got tremors from the wit and subtlety of productions directed by Erwin Axer, Jerzy Kreczmar, and Irena Laskowska. I didn't know how these directors were doing these theater miracles. I only knew that I wanted to follow them into theatrical heaven.

First trip abroad

A real breakthrough in my theater formation occurred when, for the first time in my life I could travel abroad in the fall of 1957, something that before "October 1956" had been simply impossible. As a student-actor and leader of student theater I was included in a Polish student delegation attending a student theater festival in Paris. Thanks to a grant given to me by a Polish émigré organization, I could extend my stay in Paris, go to Italy, and visit my aunt Jadwiga Domańska in London. Everywhere I was hunting for theater. Additionally, every night I devoured tons of books prohibited in Poland, especially on recent history, but also the literary works of the exiled writers.

In Paris I ran across the peak of the theater of the absurd, as Martin Esslin lucidly called it. I am proud that I attended the opening, indeed, the world premiere of Beckett's *Endgame* followed by *Act Without Words* in the Studio

Champs-Élysées. I saw *The Bald Soprano* and *The Lesson* by Ionesco in Théâtre de la Huchette. On the small stage in the Alliance Française, I saw *How to Get Free* by Adamov. What are these playwrights telling me? I asked myself. Are they trying to convince me that life is absurd? I could not agree with them. For me, life was a wide-open field of opportunities. And what about the audiences surrounding me? This was, for sure, a theater for the elites, for a select group of intellectuals, artists, students, and snobs. For whom do I want to do theater? With wide open eyes I watched spell-binding, imaginative productions directed by Jean Vilar, Jean-Louis Barrault, and Roger Blin. I spent many evenings listening to the declamatory productions in the Comédie Française. I was struck by the bad taste of the shows in the Parisian boulevard theaters, another theater lesson. In Italy, I saw Pirandello, played with an incredible verism. In England it was Shakespeare, of course, but also the magician of the pantomime, Marcel Marceau. Each of these event was a "first" in my life experience—fascinating, astonishing, enlightening, opening theatrical horizons. I jotted down notes on the programs in the darkness of the auditoriums. I ran to the libraries to read new plays. I memorized the names of the directors.

In London, I hugged aunt Domańska. She remembered me as a child. I did not recall her at all. A tall, beautiful lady, with regular features and big blue eyes. Her face combined child-like softness with a rock-hard determination. Her voice was deep and melodious. Her smile was gleaming. The army theater which she organized and headed during the war had been disbanded a long time ago. The aunt and her husband Ludomir, an engineer and soldier, who was wounded in the Warsaw Uprising in 1944 and then escaped to the West, were living in a tiny apartment and supported themselves by taking odd manual jobs. My aunt made an incredible impression on me: the great artist amidst the émigré poverty, maintaining her impeccable manners, unbroken dignity, and unshaken optimism. She told me her war theater Odyssey. I had known only a few scraps of it. And now I learned it all. I heard it for the first time. Because of her influence on my life and theater work, her story should be told to readers of this book.

Jadwiga Domańska (1907-1996) was an actress, director, manager, and animator of theatrical life. She was born in the small town of Dąbrowa (near Cracow) in a family devoted to national and social service, and dedicated to the fine arts. Her father Karol (my grandfather) was a respected notary and her mother Henryka (my grandmother) a pianist and leader in girl scout and women's organizations. Domańska studied acting in the Drama School in Warsaw and graduated in 1932. For the next seven years she worked in the theaters of Wilno, Łódź, Bydgoszcz, Łuck, and Katowice, playing many leads. She was first an "ingenue," later moving to leading ladies. "Her classical beauty, Slavic flair, statuesque posture, captivating facial features, and melodious, deep voice predestinated her to playing the roles of heroines, tragic and full of dignity," wrote a critic. She appeared in plays by Słowacki, Wyspiański, and Shaw, and later on in Gozzi, Mickiewicz, and many others. During World War II and immediately afterwards, she acted less frequently, busy with her managerial duties, but she splendidly created the role of the Princess in *Princess Turandot* by Gozzi and acted in Wyspiański's and Szaniawski's plays.

In September 1939, just as she was about to open a new theater season in Katowice, acting the lead in *The Defense of Xanthippe* by Ludwik H. Morstin, the dress rehearsal was interrupted by the outbreak of World War II. Domańska went to Warsaw, where she joined the patriotic underground, volunteered for the underground military organization, and was sworn in as a soldier. Her duties included dispatch-travel between Warsaw and Wilno as a courier across the newly established border between Germany and the Soviet Union. In March 1940, Domańska was arrested by the Soviets while illegally crossing the border, sentenced to eight years, and sent to a detention camp near Novosibirsk in Siberia. In October 1941, thanks to the Polish-Soviet treaty, she was released and immediately joined the Polish troops being organized in the Soviet Union under the command of the London-based Polish government-in-exile. While in the army, she organized and prepared theater productions, first on Soviet soil and then in Iraq, to which the Polish troops were evacuated in 1942. In the spring of

1943, Domańska organized an army theater and was nominated as its manager; after appropriate training, she also earned the rank of lieutenant.

The Dramatic Theater of the Second Polish Corps under Domańska's management played for troops and civilians, accompanying the army into Palestine and throughout the campaign in Italy. This theater performed at improvised venues in the closest proximity to the front lines. The Dramatic Theater was a huge establishment that moved with the troops, with a company of about 60 professional actors, and technical and administrative staff. At the end of the war, the theater settled temporarily in Italy. Domańska and the majority of her company decided not to return to a Poland under communist rule but moved instead to London in 1946, where the Dramatic Theater was disbanded in 1948. Domańska continued to play in professional productions organized in London by the Actors' Union (ZASP), directed both professional and amateur shows, and created theater for children. In 1960, she moved to Canada with her husband, where she continued her artistic and community work within the Polish emigre circles. Respected and celebrated by Polish emigrants, she was erased from theater history in her native country because of her involvement with the army of the Polish government-in-exile and her steadfast anti-communist stance.

After the fall of Communism, Domańska's wartime contribution to the survival of the Polish theater was finally recognized in the country. A charismatic leader, she wrote: "I strove to preserve the distinguished tradition of Polish actors, originated by Wojciech Bogusławski in the 18th century—the tradition of being, first of all, citizens. I value most the attitude of the majority of my fellow theater artists, which I would call 'an attitude of service' by theater to the common national cause."

So I heard the life and theater story of a brave woman and a theater artist. It was a history of an actress reciting poetry for the Polish soldiers in Russia, who had only recently emerged from the Soviet prisons and camps, malnourished and sick, yet yearning for the opportunity to fight and to listen to the Polish word. It was a history of a director of mass productions for the troops staged on the desert in Iraq, on their hasty way from the inhuman Soviet soil to the Western fronts. It was the history of a manager of productions played for the exhausted yet enthusiastic troops close to the battlefields in Italy at the foothills of Monte Cassino, a Polish memorable victory in May 1944. Finally, it was the history of an animator of Polish émigré productions in London, played for the crowds of demilitarized compatriots, who had decided not to return to a country ruled by the communists, a decision she and her and her husband also made. So, theater might be more important then bread? I asked myself. So, theater might help people live bravely and die happily? I thought. So, theater might actively participate in the struggle between the forces of good and evil? I reflected.

Thanks to that first theatrical journey abroad, my view of theater was enlarged, and my curiosity as to what theater is, and can be, was increased. My experience was stretched between the sophisticated, avant-garde productions in Paris and my aunt's stories about the rudimentary human dimensions and functions of theater. I returned to my university studies, to my follies in student theater, and to my professional beginnings, seeing clearly that all this was only the first step in a long way. I learned how much more I had to learn.

The Warsaw Theater Academy

Acting in the amateur student theater and in the professional Polski Theater was not enough for me. Just after having finished my Master of Letters degree at Poznań University, I applied to the graduate Directing Department of the school of drama in Warsaw. (This school has been renamed a few times and is currently officially called "The Warsaw Theater Academy"—I am using its latter name.) The candidates had to submit a written project of a production. Its acceptance was a condition for being granted an entrance exam. As my project I selected a poetic drama by Norwid, *Behind the Wings*. I prepared a detailed directorial book. Upon my request, a painter friend drew stage designs and costume projects. I sent the whole package. It was accepted.

The exam had four parts. First, a defense of the production project. Second, a comprehensive oral exam on the history of world theater and drama. Third, an interview, testing the communicativeness and imagination of the candidate. Fourth, the rehearsal of a scene from the play submitted as the directorial project. There were rumors that the exam was a very difficult enterprise and that not too many candidates passed it every year.

I remember sitting in front of a committee of about fifteen people, the whole faculty of the Directing Department. I know their names, all of them are famous directors, actors, and academics. I recognize the faces of actors whom I've seen in the leading roles on stages, but others are frightening strangers. I only heard stories about them or read their books. They question me for about an hour. I'm terrified and overwhelmed. Next, I have to get on my feet and direct impromptu a scene from my directorial project on a school stage. Professional actors are available. I talk to them and immediately go to blocking. It does not work well. The stress is unbearable. It mounts, when only a small group of candidates is called back to take a written test. I am one of them. Four hours to write an essay. My hand hurts like hell, but I keep scribbling until the last minute. The results are to be announced on the board in three days. The torture of waiting. I go there trying to downplay hope. But I can't control my heartbeat when I look on the board. All's well that ends well. They accepted me.

So, I got to this famous school of directing. Created by Schiller in the 1930s, it had stayed on the course he set. He himself headed it before and after the war, until his death in 1954. When I entered the school in 1958, his spirit, his teachings, his almost personal presence were still felt everywhere. I already knew a lot about him. I thought that I would have to learn more, being a student there. I continued studying his life and productions for many years. Schiller's work, and the way he envisioned and ran the directing instruction, are necessary contexts for my account on studies in the Theater Academy.

Leon Schiller (1887-1954) was a director, composer, teacher, artistic director, and manager of theaters. He was born to a wealthy bourgeois family in Cracow. He studied theater at universities in Cracow and Paris (1906-1911) and musical composition in Vienna (1916-1917). He was a theater critic and also organized an exposition of modern stage design. From 1917 to 1920, he was literary adviser at the Teatr Polski in Warsaw, where he made his directorial debut in 1917 with the folk-tale *Princess Lelijka*. From 1924 to 1926 he served as artistic director of the Teatr Bogusławskiego in Warsaw. Between 1926 and 1939 he directed in Warsaw, Lwów (1930-1931, as artistic director,) Wilno, Łódź, and abroad in Sofia and Paris (a ballet production.) In 1933, he founded and became the dean of the Department of Directing at the Institute of Theater Art in Warsaw. During World War II, he was imprisoned and sent to the Auschwitz concentration camp in 1941. After his release in the same year, he returned to Warsaw and became active in the ruling body of the Clandestine Theater Council. Following the war, he served as an artistic director of the Theater of the Polish Army in Łódź and then of the Teatr Polski in Warsaw, as rector of schools of drama in Łódź and Warsaw, and as dean of directing departments at both of them. He joined the Communist Party (1946), was a communist deputy to Parliament (1947-1952), and was awarded several official prizes. In 1950, he was disgraced by the communists and fired from his managerial positions. He was allowed to guest-direct only occasionally and to work as the editor of the quarterly *Pamiętnik Teatralny*. He died, expelled from mainstream theater activity, in 1954.

Both artistically and personally, Schiller was a dynamic "Baroque Man" (as Korzeniewski used to call him), as well as a man of sharp contradictions. An intellectual from the upper class, he nevertheless became involved with Communism. In his youth, he was a militant leader of the avant-garde, but in old age he accepted the dogmas of socrealism. He oscillated between Catholicism and Marxism, between mysticism and materialism. In spite of all these contradictions, he had a significant impact on the theatrical life of Poland from the 1920s until the 1950s, and also influenced it posthumously.

As director, Schiller prepared about 150 theater productions from 1917 to 1954. In the preparatory phase (1917-1924), he directed mainly his own scenarios based on old religious dramas and "song-plays": *Christmas Carol* (1922) and

Easter, based on *The History of Our Lord's Miraculous Resurrection* (1923). In his most creative phase (1924-1939), he specialized in productions of the dramas of the Polish Romantic poets of the 19th century, which constituted the core of his work: *The Undivine Comedy* by Zygmunt Krasiński (1926, 1938), *Kordian* by Słowacki (1930, 1935, 1939) and *The Forefathers' Eve* by Mickiewicz (1932, 1933, 1934, 1937). Additionally, he directed neo-Romantic plays by Polish writers of the 20th century: *Prince Patiomkin* by Tadeusz Miciński (1925), *Achilleis* by Wyspiański (1925), and *The Rose* by Stefan Żeromski (1926). Schiller also successfully directed Shakespeare (eight productions) including *The Winter's Tale* (1924), *As You Like It* (1925), *Julius Caesar* (1928), and *King Lear* (1935). Among contemporary plays, he directed works by Brecht, Friedrich Wolf, and Arnold Zweig; adaptations of *The Good Soldier Schweik* by Jaroslav Hašek (1929, 1930) and *Cry China* by Sergey Tretiakov (1932, 1932, 1933). After World War II (1945-1954), because of the official ban, Schiller was no longer able to direct his favorite repertory. He repeated his old scenarios and directed only a few larger scale productions (e. g. Shakespeare's *The Tempest*, 1947), and some operas.

Schiller was inspired by the Polish Romantic tradition of poetic theater, as well as the European movement of the Great Reform of Theater. In his youth, he was especially influenced by Wyspiański. From 1909 to 1911, he was a keen apprentice of Craig in Paris. He was also fascinated by Reinhardt, and, later on, he was compared to Vsevolod Meyerhold and Erwin Piscator. Schiller's artistic power was expressed in three major styles: the "staging theater," a "neo-realistic theater," and "song-plays," his own genre of music theater. The "staging theater" (he called it a "monumental theater" or "theater greater then life"), as practiced by Schiller, was based on the Romantic vision of the universe and history. Schiller's directorial innovation in staging Romantic, poetic dramas consisted of using modern, anti-illusionistic means of expression. His stagings were indeed "monumental," grand-scale, rich spectacles. They utilized modern fine arts styles in stage design (for example, cubism) and used elaborate lighting. Their important component was rhythm, created mainly by the movement of crowds and protagonists, and they introduced an abundance of music. Schiller handed down the "staging theater" to his students, followers, and heirs. In his "neo-realistic theater," Schiller explored contemporary political and social problems, following the German "Zeittheater," combining in the mise-en-scènes real elements with expressive (sometime expressionistic) theatrical means. Schiller's "song-plays" were his original invention. He scripted, provided musical settings, and directed several productions based on old Polish songs (folk, religious, love, military, or "Bohemian") as well as on medieval and Renaissance religious dramas.

In his teaching directing, Schiller stressed the necessity for a director to have a humanistic education, to control all major components of theater, and to approach theater as an art. He wanted to turn directors into "theater artists." So, I faced the challenge to become a "theater artist." How can I make it? I thought to myself.

When I entered the department, it had a limit of 10 places the freshman year, but usually fewer than that were accepted and there were on average about 15-20 students at the department. I got there along with four others only. Not too rarely people were dismissed for lack of progress and never got the professional directing diploma, which—by the way—was needed to get a directing job in a professional theater in Poland at that time, within the system of the totalitarian state's full control of employment.

The program took three years. During the last year, the student, still attending classes, had to direct a production of a play in a professional theater, anywhere in Poland (for this the student would get leave from the school) under the supervision of a professor. It was a "directorial workshop" and its acceptance by the departmental committee was a condition for finishing the study and getting a "permit" to direct in professional theaters. It was not the end of the road, though. The next step was a professional directorial "diploma" exam. To be eligible for the exam the candidate had to independently direct a play in a professional theater and write a dissertation on the same play. The production was seen by a departmental committee and the dissertation evaluated by another committee. Based on the acceptance of the production and the dissertation, the candidate was (or was not) invited for the exam, facing again the departmental committee. The long and thorny path was crowed by the diploma and the Master of Fine Arts in Directing degree.

The curriculum was divided into three parts: (1) seminars in school, (2) assistantships in professional theaters, and (3) self-study. All this was complemented by constantly seeing shows in Warsaw and, if possible, elsewhere. The schedule was intensive. In the morning (traditionally between 10:00 AM and 2:00 PM) we worked in the theaters as assistants, participating in rehearsals. In the afternoon (between 3:00 and 6:00 PM) we had seminars in school. In the evening, the majority of us came back to theaters (shows started at 7:00 or 7:30 PM) and either acted or supervised the shows as assistants. Seminars at school were held from Tuesday to Saturday, workdays in theaters were from Tuesday to Sunday. Only Mondays were free. All students got scholarships on the level of about two-thirds of the lowest acting monthly salary in a Warsaw professional theater. It was really meager pay and barely allowed us to survive. Students of directing who were professional actors were employed for the duration of their studies in a Warsaw theater and they, of course, had higher pay. I supplemented my scholarship by writing for the theater and literary magazines.

Seminars in the Theater Academy

All seminars were practice-oriented. Today I would call them workshops. All students in all years of the program participated in them as one group. Promotion from year to year was based on fulfilling the requirements in seminars and individual evaluation. Every year, a group of graduating students would leave and their places would be filled by the newly-accepted. So, there was a rotation of participants, but the freshmen had to immediately work together and compete with the seniors. Indeed, a fierce competition between students was one of the characteristics of the department's ethos. It was an artistic and intellectual rivalry, very healthy, I think, but extremely stressful, I admit.

The most important parts of the program were two directorial seminars led by two leading personalities of the department and the Polish theater of the time, Bohdan Korzeniewski and Erwin Axer. Both of these directors influenced me strongly at the outset of my theater way. Both of them were formed in the theater of free Poland before WWII. Both joined the communist regime after the war: Axer, as a Communist Party member; Korzeniewski, as a "left oriented" intellectual. Both of them at one time or another were heads of the National Theater in Warsaw, a top position within the theater milieu. But by the time of the "October 1956" revolution, both were disenchanted with communism. Axer, a notorious conformist, preserved his Party membership and all the privileges of the "nomenklatura" elite, but detested propaganda activities. Korzeniewski, never the Party member, gradually drifted towards opposition. Not only politically, but more importantly artistically, Korzeniewski and Axer were radically different. When I got to the directing department, Korzeniewski was the dean. I owe him a lot.

Bohdan Korzeniewski (1905-1992) was a scholar, director, teacher, critic, editor, literary manager, and artistic director. Born to a family of the gentry in central-eastern Poland, he studied literature and philosophy at Warsaw University, graduating in 1931 and receiving his doctorate in 1937. Until World War II, he was a theater critic and historian, as well as a professor at the Institute of Theater Art in Warsaw, where he collaborated with Schiller. During WWII, he worked as a laborer and librarian, and was active in the political and theatrical underground as a member of the ruling body of the Clandestine Theater Council. For half a year in 1940, he was a prisoner in the Auschwitz concentration camp. After World War II, he taught theater history at the Schools of Drama in Łódź and Warsaw, serving also as literary manager of theaters in Łódź from 1945 to 1949. In 1947, he made his directorial debut with *The School for Wives* by Molière and soon he embarked on a fast-moving directorial career in Łódź and

Warsaw; he directed also in Cracow, Wrocław, and Gdańsk. From 1952 to 1954 he headed the National Theater in Warsaw. Between 1956 and 1975, he was dean of the Directing Department in Warsaw. From 1948 until the end of his life, he also published several books and edited theater journals.

Korzeniewski was independent and bold. His strong individuality and personality, his brilliant intellect, his profound wisdom, his pedagogical talent, and his directorial skills blended in a unique amalgam. He was an artist, teacher, sage, leader, and moral authority—one of the outstanding personalities in the history of Polish theater. As a director, Korzeniewski followed Schiller's "staging theater" which was manifested most clearly in his productions of the Romantic dramas by Krasiński (*The Undivine Comedy*, Łódź, 1959) and Mickiewicz (*The Forefathers' Eve*, Cracow, 1963). He exposed their philosophical, universal, and transhistorical dimensions, providing them with perfectly clear structures. Connected strongly with French culture (he spoke perfect French and frequently traveled to France), he concentrated his attention on Molière and Giraudoux, staging both of them in his own translations in contemporary, vivid language. His best production of Molière was his *Don Juan* (directed in Warsaw, 1950; repeated in Cracow, 1962), in which the philosophical and moral contents blended perfectly with highly theatrical spectacle: The skeletons danced, the actors switched between playing masked and unmasked, and the contemporary costumes were merged with period ones. Korzeniewski's Molière productions also included *Tartuffe* and *Scapin's Follies*. His other preferred French playwright was Giraudoux and he staged *The Trojan War Shall Not Take Place* (Gdańsk, 1958) and *The Madwoman of Chaillot* (Warsaw, 1958). Additionally, Korzeniewski translated and directed Shakespeare's *Macbeth* (Warsaw, 1960) and *Troilus and Cressida* (Cracow, 1960), for which, as in his Romantic productions, he built large-scale, elaborate spectacles.

As a teacher of directing, Korzeniewski considered himself both Schiller's heir and the guardian of his testament. He strictly followed Schiller and taught the "staging theater" style, strongly emphasizing the leading and decisive role of the director as the "theater artist" in the whole process of preparing production. He treated each performance as a united, coherent, independent work of art, whose "author" is exclusively the director. The sovereign control of the director over all the aspects and elements of the show—textual, acting, designing, lighting, and musical—was Korzeniewski's fundamental principle. In his thirty years of teaching directing and his twenty years as dean of directing at the Warsaw School of Drama, he became the mentor, master, and adviser to dozens of Polish directors of the second half of the 20th century. He formed their attitudes and approach to theater by opening their minds to the world's theater developments and by frequently sending them abroad (by providing them with grants). He emphasized the value of the national theater tradition and taught his students to treat theater as a sublime art, to think and act independently and critically, and to question the authorities and the rulers. An unbending opponent of the Nazi-controlled theaters in the 1940s, and an enforcer of the boycott against them, Korzeniewski was the major force behind the boycott of the state mass media under martial law in the 1980s. In his old age, Korzeniewski became an unchallengeable artistic, moral, and political authority within the theater milieu. He was an example of intellectual integrity and artistic consistency. He lived to see the restoration of Poland's freedom.

Korzeniewski required students to prepare total projects of productions—"staging theater" works of art. They had to have a written form and be accompanied by models of the sets. We had an absolute freedom what play to choose and how to stage it. Anything was acceptable, under the condition that the whole project would have internal consistency and logic. During the weekly seminars we presented our concepts and elements of the projects, which were subject to the professor's critique. Korzeniewski was a very sharp intellectual and sometimes his polite comments were devastating. At the end of every semester there was an exam—a presentation and defense of the total production project. The professor, accompanied by his assistant and other members of the faculty were sitting at one side of a large table. The students occupied the other side of the room and were called one by one to the table. They brought their models and displayed them on the table. They went on explaining the general idea of the mise-en-scène and the production's style, and then, they demonstrated on the model the movements of protagonists and crowds.

The preparation of a model was time consuming. The exam was tense and draining. I remember once we were waiting for the exam, everybody with their big models in boxes or suitcases. One fellow, his name was Lech, did not have anything like that. He had only a thin file folder with him. "Don't you have your model?" I asked. "I did not have time. But I'll try to get by without it. You'll see," he answered. So the exam went on with students one by one placing their elaborate models on the table in front of Professor Korzeniewski. Some models were magnificent, with stairs, platforms, posts, and furniture in them. Some even had small human figures made of clay or plasticene representing characters on stage. Students laboriously explained how they saw their mise-en-scène developing, how they planed to choreograph crowd scenes, what music they were going to use, and so on. They were moving their figurine-actors around inside their models. The professor was nodding with approval and satisfaction. Time came for Lech. He calmly sat in front of the professor, pulled a circle cut of a white paper sheet out of his filefolder, and put it on the table.

"This is my directorial project of the mise-en-scène for *The Trojan War Shall Not Take Place* by Giraudaux." He said.

"And where's your model?" The professor asked with a smile.

"Here," said Lech, pointing to his paper circle. "I want to play it on a bare circus arena. Here it is."

There was a long silence in the room. It was a gamble. Nobody knew what the professor's reaction was going to be.

"Only this arena?" he asked without expression.

"Precisely," answered Lech. "And because I have this idea of staging the play on the arena, empty, except for sand, I could not prepare anything beyond this circle."

There was silence again. The chutzpah of my colleague was evident. Everybody expected a storm. But for a while, it looked like the professor had been beaten at his own game: if any directorial concept could go, certainly, the arena production of the Giraudoux play would be acceptable too. Korzeniewski finally said:

"A very interesting concept, indeed. But, who is going to play in your mise-en-scène, Lech?"

"It should be an excellent cast," said Lech.

"You mean, actors?" asked the professor again without expression.

"Sure, the best actors," replied Lech impulsively, unaware that the professor was setting the trap. "Oh, actors," said Professor Korzeniewski, somehow concerned. "This would not make a consistent mise-en-scène. I thought that you wanted to cast horses, lions, or elephants." There was a thunder of laughter in the classroom. It was impossible to outwit Korzeniewski.

Professor Axer headed the second directing seminar. His style and way of teaching were completely different from Korzeniewski. As a director he was focused on actors, not the on mise-en-scène. He obviously esteemed Stanislavsky, but avoided using his terms. He never mentioned Osterwa, yet, I suspected that, though he rejected Osterwa's spirituality, he followed many of his techniques in work with actors.

Erwin Axer (born in 1917) was a director, teacher, essayist, artistic director, and manager of The Contemporary Theater in Warsaw. Born to a bourgeois Jewish family in Vienna, Austria, and educated in Lwów, Poland, Axer became acquainted with the theater milieu at a young age, for his father was an attorney for the Lwów theater. Axer studied directing in Warsaw under Schiller, graduating in 1939. His directorial debut, delayed by the war, took place in Lwów in 1941, but his theatrical activities were soon interrupted by the war. In 1946, he became the artistic director of the Teatr Kameralny in Łódź which prospered under their leadership; the theater was transferred in 1949 to Warsaw, changing its name to the Teatr Współczesny (the Contemporary Theater). Axer headed it until 1981. In the meantime, he was also the artistic director and general manager of the National Theater in Warsaw (1954-1957). From 1949 to 1981, he was professor of directing at the School of Drama in Warsaw. Since the 1960s, he has frequently directed abroad, mainly in Austria and Germany (he was bilingual).

A rationalist and atheist, a bon vivant and connoisseur, an opportunist and diplomat, a European and cosmopolite, he steered his course skillfully between Communist Party directives and the public's expectations. He was guided by his subtle taste, common sense, and realistic pragmatism. A member of the Party, he was nevertheless no political activist. He lived and created as if everything in Poland was normal. It is not clear whether he ignored the political situation perfectly, or if he was its perfect creation. The winner of several artistic awards and a favorite of the official press, he was respected by actors for his professionalism, by his students for his broad artistic horizons, and by the international theater milieu for his refined culture and personal charm.

Teaching directing, Axer gave students a solid introduction to the professional theater world and allowed them to assist him in his works. Axer's theater was literary, intellectual, and philosophical; his directing was internal and discreet; and his productions were based on acting, though not deprived of various aspects of theatricality. The stage designs in his shows were functional and equipped with selected realistic yet synthesized elements. Carefully chosen and well-written plays that contained intellectual and philosophical insights were the foundation of all of Axer's shows. He was in constant contact with authors and translators; the editors of influential theater journals were on his payroll as advisers. He had a strong acting company, which included the stars; during rehearsals, he patiently taught less experienced players. Directing a play, he cast prudently and then spent long days working on the script and making a deep analysis, always emphasizing the psychology and the social environment of the characters. He used to rehearse blocking for weeks (sometimes several months), searching for the most natural and effective way to stage the events and the movements, relationships, and contacts between the characters. His directorial objective was to reconcile "the truth" with "the expression." He guided his actors discreetly, motivating them internally, encouraging them to improvise during the rehearsals; he used to spend hours giving actors notes and repeating scenes again and again. Long "montage" and "editing" rehearsals were followed by the previews, closed to all but a few friends and advisers. Only after new corrections, cuts, and changes were made could the show open, in most cases to a success at the box office and in the press.

Stylistically, Axer was a realist with a touch of the theater poet. He was not interested in extravagant experiments, nor did he want to subjugate theater to service as propaganda. The first stance made him an artistic traditionalist, while the second allowed him to attract large audiences from the capital's ideologically indifferent middle class. Axer's theater was wise and at the same time, easy to accept. It provided intelligent entertainment and aesthetic sensations, but did not bother the public with difficult moral questions or political statements. It was never impassioned, but it was always attractive. All Axer's productions were perfectionistic, reliable, tasteful, and cultured. Without the risk of madness, they diverted and enchanted.

For Axer's directing seminars we had to prepare short scenes from the plays he was directing in his theater, in which we casted ourselves or invited students from the acting department of the Academy. He expected us to build action on subtext, establish strong contact between characters, and contrast words with behaviors. He observed our scenes attentively and then gave long, very detailed, analytical monologues commenting on them, of the kind I heard years later from Strasberg, during my visit in Actors Studio in New York.

The third most important seminar was that of the stage design. I was fortunate to be taught design (both stage and costume) by the master, Andrzej Pronaszko (1888-1961). Educated as a painter and practicing painting until the end of his days, he became a scènographer and had a long and brilliant carrier in leading Polish theaters, beginning in 1915. His sets were usually architectural, combining precisely defined functions with a highly artistic overall expression, including unrealistic, imaginatively used colors. In his youth he was a cubist painter and he imposed this style not only on sets, but also on costumes, which he stiffened, thus transforming actors into living sculptures. Later in his career, he moved freely from style to style, according to the meaning of the play and the message of the production. His masterpiece was Mickiewicz's *The Forefathers' Eve,* prepared with Schiller as director in the 1930s, for which Pronaszko designed sets, costumes, and the general concept of mise-en-scène. Pronaszko's other interest was in the design of theater architecture. In the 1930s, he proposed several revolutionary designs for theater space in which he abolished the proscenium and experimented with spatial relations between the playing and the observation area.

In his seminars, and his critiques of our projects prepared at home, Pronaszko always required us to base our work on this difficult combination: to design a decor which would have a universal and symbolic meaning, be imbued with mood, metaphor, and a fine arts style and, at the same time, provide a functional space for action and for characters' movements. I remember the tasks he gave us while teaching set design: "Design an interior without using walls." Or: "Design an exterior using only a limited number of set elements." Or: "Design a one-piece multi-functional set for a play with several scene changes." Or: "Using a small proscenium stage, design an outdoor scene giving the impression that space is unlimited." Or: "Use a large proscenium stage create an intimate interior employing only lights and furniture." For the costume projects he would give us such tasks as: "Design the costume for Achilles in *Troilus and Cressida* by Shakespeare so the public would be afraid of him." Or: "Select a painting style. Design a costume for a realistic play (he would give a specific example) which would be both functional and be based on the principles of that painting style." In his critiques of our projects he often digressed and went back to his various stage design and architectural projects, as well as the history of fine arts. He was a living part of it.

Pronaszko taught me several important principles in the area of space, set, costume, and light design. First, to be open and creative and to go beyond the limits of a given stage. Second, to think not only about a specific stage design but about the totality of the spatial conditions of the production. Third, to integrate the design of the sets, costumes, and lights. Fourth, to infuse realistic and functional design with fine arts styles.

Other seminars covered the director's work with actors, instruction in play analysis, the skills of a dramaturg or literary adviser, introduction to music in the theater, and general knowledge of the history of art, architecture, literature, and drama.

The seminar on the director's work with actors was—rightly—taught by an eminent actor, Jan Świderski (1916-1988). He was the leading man in The Dramatyczny Theater in Warsaw and a member of its artistic board. I remember seeing him in a variety of roles: Shakespeare's Macbeth, Willie Stark in *All the King's Men* by Robert Penn Warren, John Proctor in *The Crucible* and Quentin in *After the Fall* by Williams; leads in Dürrenmatt's *Romulus the Great* and *The Physicists;* and Ionesco's *The Chairs*; as well as in Polish contemporary and classical plays. He approached the role primarily from the psychological and sociological sides. He was a realist, but had a strong sense of form and rhythm, and pushed his performances sometimes almost to the edge of the grotesque. Direct, professional, and blunt in his speech and behavior, he taught us how to talk to actors during rehearsals using just a few, concrete and clear sentences referring to objectives, goals, and activities. He would not allow for philosophical and literary digressions, or cryptic and metaphoric directorial language. He wanted the director to be a practical guide and helper for actors, not an esoteric guru. I learned from him to bring down to earth any directorial idea.

Play analysis and writing adaptations of prose, were the subjects of a seminar taught by Jerzy Kreczmar (1902-1988). He was first of all a scholar, but also a director. He used to work as a literary adviser in theaters, and he was an artistic director of The Polski Theater in Warsaw in 1966-1967. Kreczmar earned a doctorate in philosophy at Warsaw University in 1930. He then studied directing in Warsaw with Schiller and graduated in 1937, but he did not make his directorial debut until 1946. He directed on leading stages in Warsaw, Cracow, and Katowice. He published many historical and analytical essays on theater and drama, and a few books. Considered one of the finest minds in Polish theater, a philosopher and rationalist, he was respected as an outstanding intellectual—a rare species in theater—and the director of some brilliant productions, especially of contemporary plays. He made history in the Polish theater by directing *Waiting for Godot* by Samuel Beckett (1957), the first production of a work by the master of the absurd. The production was a manifestation of pure theatricality; the directorial concept turned it into a "philosophical circus." His second memorable feat was *Who's Afraid of Virginia Woolf?* by Edward Albee (1965), a profound interpretation of the cruel psychological abyss of the play. Kreczmar's other directorial masterpiece was *The Birthday Party* by Harold Pinter (1966). His style was that of the intellectual grotesque, based on solid psychological and realistic analytical foundations, conveyed through rich yet formalized acting, enveloped in precisely structured mise-en-scènes, and using nonrealistic stage design. The philosophical and aesthetic functions of the productions were the most important for him. A thinker, an ironic and sarcastic mind, and a critical and sober intellect, Kreczmar set the model for a cerebral approach to theater which he taught us. I learned from him that the analysis of a play must be done with rigidity and lucidity. It must be intellectually sharp and psychologically profound. It must clearly reveal the structure of the play and the same structure should be then imprinted in the production.

The elements of literary management was another subject. The seminar was taught by an excellent professional and specialist, Edward Csató, the editor in chief of the principal Polish theater magazine, a biweekly, "Teatr" ("Theater"), published in Warsaw. A theater critic and theater historian, literary adviser in theaters and insider to the editing process, he was a perfect teacher of literary management. He emphasized that the publicity, the contents of the program of the production, and even what is said in the interviews before the opening, should all be a director's concern and must be consciously prepared. He taught us the practical skills of editing programs, writing directorial notes, cooperating with literary staff, and talking to journalists.

A friendly fellow and experienced editor, Csató was also looking for new authors for his magazine. After a few weeks of classes, he proposed to me that I write for him. Of course, I jumped on it. He accepted my first piece with only a few editorial suggestions and corrections. This established our long-lasting cooperation. I kept publishing in "Theater" for years. Being a directing student and then a director, I did not want to write straight reviews on the shows because I thought it wouldn't be the right thing to do—to evaluate my colleagues' work. Instead, I developed a special kind of writing on theater, a sort of "theater reportage," as I called it. Seeing productions in the country and abroad, I did not critique them, but rather, I reported on them, I described them, I wrote about companies and theater artists, about theater culture in general, and on various historical, theoretical, aesthetical, and craft problems of theater. I published in "Theater" a lot. Csató wrote himself and published critiques of my early shows and promoted me as a director. He died suddenly of a heart attack in 1965. My cooperation with his successors at the "Theater" outlasted the death of my teacher and mentor, whom I recall very fondly.

Assistantships in The Contemporary Theater in Warsaw

The second pilar of the curriculum of the directing department was assistantships in Warsaw professional theaters. All students had to have at least two assistantships per academic year, which meant practically that they had to work in the theater all year round. We assisted our professor-directors and other prominent directors in Warsaw. I was extremely lucky to get an assistantship with Erwin Axer. Usually, as I heard, he picked up his assistant during the entrance exam. If he was pleased with the student, he would keep him/her for another show. The next year, he would choose a new assistant. In this way many students had the opportunity to assist the master-director. But Axer was not present at my entrance exam, as he was recovering from a serious car accident, and I did not meet him until a few weeks later, when the academic year was already under way. It was the dean, Korzeniewski, who assigned me to the Contemporary Theater. Korzeniewski knew that students would profit the most from working as assistants to Axer, so, it was probably an award for a good entrance exam.

The assistant's job was a professional experience, an educational opportunity, and a time-consuming mission. The assistant participated in the meetings of the director with the designers, composers, and technical people, as well as in all production meetings. Then there were the rehearsals, lasting on average about three to four months. In the Contemporary Theater there was a rule that the assistant observed twenty performances after the opening and reported on them to the director. Later, for the whole run of the show, the duty was to watch two performances per week. Productions of The Contemporary were usually successful. Runs were unlimited and frequently topped the one hundred number. After the opening, plays were kept on stage for about a month every night, and then included in the rotating repertoire. That meant that I had to be in theater almost every night.

In Axer's absence, I was casted as assistant to Stanisława Perzanowska, a director and actress of the older generation. A charming lady and a one-hundred-per-cent professional, Perzanowska was a woman star director in Poland between the wars; a rare species at that time. In the fall of 1958 she directed *The Nativity Play* at the Contemporary. It was a religious scenario based on traditional Christmas rituals and carols, put together in 1922 by Schiller and produced at Osterwa's Reduta Theater. Perzanowska played Eve in the world premiere of the play and here, thirty six years later she was directing it, based on the same Schiller mise-en-scène. Plays like this had been prohibited during the Stalinist peak of repression but they returned to the stages thanks to the "October 1956" break-through. Thus, a customary production for Christmas time, *The Nativity Play* was my first assistantship in The Contemporary. The directorial concept of Schiller, as repeated by Perzanowska, was based on "a play within a play" structure, like the play performed by the actors in Elsinore. A company of peasant players from a small village puts on a production depicting the birth of Jesus Christ for other villagers. The professional actors had to play amateurs playing characters in the nativity story—a sort of "double acting." The director had to set two levels of action—a sort of "double staging." It worked very effectively. Perzanowska directed actors with an iron fist, and during breaks told stories from the world premiere. It was as if the pages of the Polish theater history book were turning in front of my eyes. She somehow got to like me and regaled me with more anecdotes. The entire first assistantship was for me a multi-level experience. I was able to sit at the side of one of Polish theater's legends, to observe her pure professionalism, and to listen to her insider's stories.

In the late fall of 1958, Axer returned from the hospital. It was up to him to decide whether I would stay longer at The Contemporary or not. Perzanowska, apparently, recommended me, and Axer casted me as assistant in his own production. When that work was over, to my surprise, he not only kept me in the Contemporary Theater for the next academic year, but for the rest of my studies. Other assistants would come and go. Some assisted him on a single occasion. Usually he had two or three assistants in each play. But I was appointed as assistant in all productions he directed at that time. It was an invaluable learning opportunity and life experience.

Axer's Contemporary Theater in Warsaw was considered one of the most prominent Polish stages. It was focused on the 20th-century world drama and had the most Western-oriented repertoire in Poland, continually producing plays of outstanding literary quality by authors including: the Americans—Albee, Archibald MacLeish, and Thornton Wilder; the British—Edward Bond, Aldous Huxley, John Osborne, Pinter, and George Bernard Shaw; the French—Cocteau, Ionesco, Montherlant, Armand Salacrou, Françoise Sagan, and Georges Schéhadé; the Swiss—Frisch and Dürrenmatt, and many other foreign authors, among them the Irish-French master Beckett. Axer's directorial masterpiece was Brecht's *The Resistible Rise of Arturo Ui* (1962). He also directed a number of renowned Polish playwrights: Szaniawski, Mrożek, and Bryll. Sometimes he would reach for an author a little too extravagant for him (like Witkiewicz), a contemporary Polish writer of lesser quality but of greater political influence (like Kruczkowski), or a Soviet socrealist, like Aleksey Arbuzov. He mounted the classics only occasionally: *Kordian* by Słowacki (1956, 1977), *Iphigenia in Tauris* by Goethe (1961), and Friedrich Schiller's *Maria Stuart* (1969). The renown of his theater was based on its repertoire, on the level of acting performances in each production, and on the directorial mastery of Axer himself who set the tone. Only occasionally other directors, such as Jerzy Kreczmar or Konrad Swinarski, were invited.

The Contemporary gave only a few productions per season, usually not more then five, and sometimes merely two. Every production was meticulously rehearsed for a long time. Table rehearsals weeks long were followed by months of careful blocking and reblocking, searching and wandering, until the perfect solution, interpretation, and form were found and firmly established. Axer sought to express both the author's meanings and his directorial ideas in the acting matter. He had an excellent permanent company led by stars, such as Zofia Mrozowska, Aleksandra Śląska, Irena Gordon-Górecka, Tadeusz Łomnicki, Andrzej Łapicki, and Kazimierz Opaliński. The level of ensemble work was always extremely high. All actors masterfully combined the deep internal psychology of their characters with high external expressiveness. Axer used to spent hours, even days, rehearsing one scene. He worked patiently and tirelessly, both sensitively guiding actors and stubbornly insisting on their progress. Observing him at work was an ultimate learning experience. The assistants, sitting just behind him and taking notes, had to be alert all the time and actively follow the work, because he asked us from time about our reaction or opinion of an actor's interpretation of a line, or performance in a scene. During a rehearsal he turned to me suddenly and quizzed:

"How do you like it?"

It was about Łomnicki's performance in a scene of *Iphigenia in Tauris*.

Accidentally, I had not been paying attention at this moment. I got red. I replied precipitously:

"I like it very much."

He got sour: "I think that it is awful."

I was ashamed and said nothing. The rehearsal went on. New variants of the interpretation. Repetitions. A new approach. And again a return to the first version. After the rehearsal we went to the cafeteria and Axer said: "You were right. That first version was the best one."

I said nothing again. I did not tell him that my reply was correct only by chance.

Rehearsals were exhausting, sometimes very tense, and even dramatic. There were stages of the tension. Usually all actors, not rehearsing on stage, were allowed to watch from the wings or from the auditorium. A first degree alert was sounded when Axer ordered the stage manager not to allow anybody around the stage or the room, and worked with the cast of a given scene, having assistants with him. A second degree alert happened when Axer ordered the others assistants to leave and I, as a sort of "personal assistant," stayed. The third degree of tension arose when Axer decided to stay on stage with one actor only, while the other actors along with myself were kicked out.

I assisted Axer in five consecutive productions. First was *Biedermann and the Firebugs* by Max Frisch, a contemporary Swiss author, which opened on April 23, 1959. It was the Polish premiere of a play with a philosophical, political, and social message: the upper classes of the bourgeois society at the West, through their stupidity and lack of imagination, unconsciously help the lower classes to turn the social order upside down. Or, as the author suggested in the epilogue, it is the hell and the devil himself who destructively operate within our secular world. The Chorus of Firemen helplessly watched the gradual burning of a city—a symbolic end of civilization. Any play debating relationships between the "haves" and the "have-nots" at the West could be easily interpreted by the Polish public as referring to the situation in their country in which the privileged communists ruled over the destitute masses, and these masses waited only for an opportunity to revolt. This was enough for the audience in Warsaw to get exited, but not too much for the censors; the play did not directly and overtly challenge the regime. As usual, Axer steered a safe middle course in taking on this play. Perzanowska, who at that time mothered me in The Contemporary, played the female lead. Łapicki, a dashing star, topped the male ensemble.

My second assistantship came in *The First Day of Liberty* by Leon Kruczkowski; it opened on December 12, 1959. Kruczkowski was a communist writer and official of influence, whom Axer probably courted for years. At that time, thanks to the "October 1956" changes, Kruczkowski had been removed from his public positions but remained a powerful figure behind the scenes of the Party leadership. Every new play of his was blown up to the dimension of an event of utter importance by the press steered from above. Axer, who liked to be in the spotlight, had years earlier directed the world premiere of another Kruczkowski play and was praised for it. He decided to repeat the trick. He also planned to go with the production of *The First Day of Liberty* to Paris, to represent Poland at the Festival of Theater of Nations, an ultimate honor. Axer thus took on *The First Day of Liberty,* a mediocre play with pretenses to philosophical profundity. The plot was supposedly based on the true story of a group of Polish officers, liberated from a German P.O.W. camp at the end of the war, returning home. But—without going into details—historically and ideologically the play was a lie, distorting the notion of freedom precious to all Poles. The cast was excellent and experienced, with Tadeusz Łomnicki, one of the best Polish actors of the time in the lead, partnered by another star, Aleksandra Śląska, a heroine of unusual beauty and energy. Years later, I had the privilege to direct her in my own productions.

Rehearsals were long and full of tension, because the play did not provide too much material for actors. It was still an educational occasion for me. I saw for the first time Łomnicki and Śląska in action. I observed Axer's directorial methods of working with them. He combined subtle piloting of actors towards desired interpretations with leaving them full freedom to create. Rehearsals were a process of constant searching and insatiable perfecting. Eventually, the acting fabric of the production was highly expressive. The premiere was pronounced a success by the press.

Meeting Kruczkowski at the rehearsals, the opening, and at the reception after it, was for me an especially disgusting experience. He was one of those communist officials who were not only responsible for imposing the Soviet system on Poland and attacking national culture, but, more specifically, as a deputy minister in the communist government, he was directly responsible for persecutions of people like my father Juliusz, and my uncle Jerzy. Moreover, Kruczkowski came from the same small town in Southern Poland and he had personally known my father and uncle for years. Yet, being in power, he did nothing to help them, even though he knew that they were not guilty of the crimes of which they had been accused, and spent years in prison, though completely innocent.

To make things worse, immediately after the Warsaw opening of *The First Day of Liberty* I was summoned by Axer and told that he had an offer to direct the play again, this time at The Słowackiego Theater in Cracow, one of the country's top stages. He accepted the offer, he said, or rather, he could not refuse it (I understood that the author was behind that), but as he couldn't do it personally he was sending me to direct it in his mise-en-scène and under his supervision. He would start rehearsals at the table, then leave me in Cracow for the blocking, and return before the opening for necessary corrections.

I was stunned. It was a big news. To direct under Axer's mentorship, not only to assist him, was the impossible dream of a student of directing. It was an honor and an opportunity. At the same time, I had serious problems with the play and the author, and I internally froze anticipating that I would have to work on the same material again. I kept my thoughts to myself, of course. Besides, Axer didn't ask me whether I would go. He simply told me to go.

We went to Cracow. The artistic director and general manager of The

Słowackiego Theater, Bronisław Dąbrowski, was a legendary figure, I feared him. The cast was composed of old masters and young, ascending talents. I felt lost and confused when they stared at me. Some of them took me for nothing. Some were friendly and supportive, like the young ingenue, Maria Nowotarska, later the leading lady of the same theater, and still later, my favorite actress who played in three of my plays.

I did my best to recreate both the external blocking and the internal processes from the Warsaw production. It was hard. For the first time—and still a student of directing, and only twenty five years old—I directed a cast of brilliant professionals in a big theater. I felt the pressure of the stage on which sixty years earlier Wyspiański put on his memorable *Wedding,* where Osterwa played the Constant Prince, where the famous actors performed their historic roles and the best directors staged their never-to-be-forgotten productions. And there was I, green, stupid, and inarticulate. Some of the rehearsal were nightmares. Some brought sparks of satisfaction. I was learning every minute, mostly from my mistakes. I saw how different it is to repeat even the most precise and acute directorial remarks which I recalled from Axer, and to find my own words to influence the actors during rehearsal. The first usually did not work, to my surprise. The second sometimes made an impact, but sometimes did not bring any effect. Why? Only rarely could I tell. But I tried. I was painfully discovering ways of communicating with actors.

After about two months of rehearsals Axer came back. To this day I remember the emotion with which I was sitting, again behind him, as he watched the poor results of my wretched efforts. I thought that he was going to decide this thing should never be played and cancel the opening. I thought that it was impossibly bad. But it turned out that it was not so bad after all. Axer had a few additional rehearsals. He suddenly and miraculously transformed my directorial skit into his directorial work of art. To my surprise, on the poster and in the program I was not called "assistant to the director" but "an associate director." An associate director to Axer! I remember walking through Cracow's streets and looking at the posters on the billboards. The opening, on February, 27, 1960, attended by the author, was again a success, at least, according to the press.

But Axer's scheme to get a boost from producing Kruczkowski's play misfired. A week before the Cracow premiere the Wybrzeże Theater in Gdańsk put on the same play. Andrzej Wajda, a brilliant and rising filmmaker, directed it in cooperation with Zygmunt Hübner, the talented artistic director of the Gdańsk theater. They had a company of young actors, led by the movie stars Zbigniew Cybulski and Bogumił Kobiela. Kruczkowski apparently preferred the Gdańsk production over the Warsaw and Cracow. That production, Wajda's, not Axer's, was sent to Paris, on a decision by the central committee of the Party as advised by the author. Axer was mad and promised never again to produce Kruczkowski.

Back in Warsaw, my fourth work with Axer was in *Knock, or the Triumph of Medicine* by Jules Romains, which opened on June 30, 1960. It was a French grotesque and philosophical comedy about the cynicism of the medical milieu and the manipulation of the patients by the doctors. A play disclosing the secrets of manipulation was metaphorically revelant to the situation in Poland. Again, as with *Biedermann,* it was a text acceptable for the censors and exiting for the public. *Knock, or the Triumph of Medicine* was a triumph for Louis Jouvet in Paris in 1923. Axer produced it for the first time in Poland and he borrowed from Jouvet the mise-en-scène concept in the first act. The action takes place around a car sitting in front of a railway station. At the end of the act, the passengers take their seats and the car starts to drive across the countryside: the car's wheels were turning and a horizon gradually moved behind it. Of course, the car was motionless, but the horizon was slowly unrolling—a huge painted ribbon stretched upstage and pulled from one side to the other. A triumph of theatricality.

Observing how Axer directs a comedy, how he strikes a perfect balance between wild situational comic stunts and witty dialogue was one more lessen for me. The production was extremely funny, yet intelligent and tasteful.

For the fifth consecutive time Axer casted me as his assistant in *Iphigenia in Tauris* by Goethe. It opened on February 1, 1961. After the comedic *Knock,* Axer took on a neo-classical serious drama written by a romantic poet. *Iphigenia* was a poetic and uplifting story of faith, virtue, and love. The play, written in verse and translated by Edward Csató, was composed almost exclusively of long soliloquies, with only a few dialogues.

It was absolutely new material for me. I was so fortunate to have such a broad range of plays in which I could assist Axer. Again, I was lucky to observe Łomnicki at work on the role of Orestes. Iphigenia was played by the subtle and gentle, yet strong heroine, Zofia Mrozowska. The objective, set by the director, was to combine literature and abundance of words with true and passionate acting. Lofty, rhythmic verse, long poetic passages, and speech full of metaphors posed special acting problems. During the rehearsals Axer would order everybody to stay away from the stage and would work for hours with one actor only. These instances were for me an especially meaningful lesson in a director's individual and personal work with an actor, of directorial care, directorial pain, and directorial love for the actor. It was obvious that the director suffers with the actor, compassionately shares his or her efforts, and searches along with them. Unlimited time for such work sessions, along with unrestricted energy expenses, provided circumstances in which powerful acting eventually started to sprout and flourish. I recall rehearsals of *Iphigenia* as the most penetrating experience of directorial sharing with actors. After about five month of rehearsals with the cast of only five actors the director succeeded. Characters truly lived, suffered, longed, and loved while delivering long poetic soliloquies. The production had a strange beauty and incredible energy.

During the years of my directing studies I started to direct myself. I staged a few productions in Warsaw's student theaters and prepared several readings of poetry and drama in the Institution for the Blind run by the Carmelite Nuns in Laski, near Warsaw. It was a special experience. The reading for the blind had to be especially articulate and diction was the primary concern. It was, for me, the discovery of the might of the well-delivered word alone, not supported by image, gesture, or movement. Action had still to be found in a drama, but conveyed with only audible means by actor-lectors. As a director, I was always focused on action and liked physical theater. But after that experience with readings for the blind I more consciously and respectfully approached the word in productions.

I had one more experience in The Contemporary. Axer accepted for production *The Story of the Barber Vasco* by Georges Schéhadé, a play which I translated from French, after having seen it in Paris directed and performed by Jean-Louis Barrault. It was a poetic play about a good, common man lost in a world submerged in cruel war. The action was fairy-tale like. The characters reminded me of archetypes in a morality play. This time Axer did not direct nor I assist. Jerzy Kreczmar directed *The Story of Vasco*, and invited an outstanding painter, Piotr Potworowski, to design. As the translator, I had open access to the rehearsals. Kreczmar consulted me many times. I got two new lessons. First, how a wise director cooperates with a translator. Second, how a director integrates the work of a painter into the totality of a production. Kreczmar, who knew French probably better then I, proposed many corrections of my translation. But he did not simply change the text. Instead, he imposed nothing, kindly checking and discussing with me all of the editing. He asked me to speak about the author and about the Paris production to the cast. Observing Kreczmar's work with Potworowski was also an instructing experience. I participated in some of their meetings. Kreczmar spoke about the problems of the play, about the action and characters, but left the designer freedom as to how to translate that into his visions. The projects for sets and costumes prepared by Potworowski had the character of paintings, works of fine arts, not design projects. They were beautiful, with vivid, nonrealistically used colors, and presented distorted objects and body shapes. I was enchanted, but also terrified that they would be impossible to transpose into three-dimensional sets and costumes. Kreczmar accepted Potworowski's works without any changes and then spent long hours with the technical director searching for the means to turn the paintings into stage designs. It worked. It resulted in one of the most unusual designs I ever saw and, probably, some of the best painted scenery in modern theater, certainly comparable to the designs of Pablo Picasso or Fernand Léger. The action of the play was divided into several scenes. In each, the stage was closed by a huge painted backdrop, precisely recreated from Potworowski's painting. The backdrop was supplemented by objects painted on flat canvas with frames of necessary shapes. Costumes and wigs, distorting the bodies' contours, but still allowing for movement, had Potworowski's vivid colors. All together it was a cohesive and unique world created by a poet-playwright and a painter-designer. The director allowed both of them to reach the peak of expression and masterfully combined the literary and visual elements. The opening on March 22, 1961 was my last contribution to the Contemporary and it happened towards the end of my directing studies.

Simultaneously with *The Story of the Barber Vasco* I rehearsed my own production, the "directorial workshop," *The Cooks* by Nora Szczepańska. Axer selected it for me and was so generous as to allow me to do it at the Contemporary, so I did not need to shop around for a spot in the provincial theaters to do my final project. He gave me also an excellent cast, including Łomnicki. The author had an interesting concept: three women, working in the kitchen, look, as if from behind the scenes, at the characters of *Antigone, Hamlet,* and *Waiting for Godot*. The concept was good but the play was not. Antigone and Ismene, Hamlet and Horatio, and Estragon and Vladimir, would drop by the kitchen and interact with the cooks. It resulted in nothing more than shallow small talk. Axer probably wanted to help a young female author by accepting her play and giving her the opportunity to see it rehearsed. But he did not help me. The actors were very critical of the play and reluctant to work on it. The rehearsals were for me one long headache, and I was many times at the brink of resigning. I bitterly promised myself that I would rather never direct then direct a bad play. But I also had to think that perhaps the play was not that bad after all, and I was a bad director instead, who was not able to do the play justice. I lost faith in ever opening the play. But a miracle happened. *The Cooks* was ready on April 23, 1961. The production was accepted by the departmental commission. Instead of joyfully marking my graduation, it brought me doubts about my directorial future. In any case, I had learned one more simple, important lesson: the road towards an opening is always bumpy, thorny, sweaty, and dusty. Don't allow yourself to lose hope and keep trying.

Self-study

The third pilar of the curriculum at the directing department was self-study in a broad range of areas in the history and aesthetics of literature, including drama; fine arts and architecture; and music, including opera and ballet. We had a separate seminar on the history of music. None of the other topics were taught systematically in school; instead, they were the subjects of our self study. We had to read entire shelves of books at the academy's library and browse through hundreds of albums on painting and architecture. Our progress was checked weekly at a seminar led by professor Henryk Szletyński, and at the end of every semester there was a comprehensive oral on all this historical stuff. Szletyński, accompanied by other faculty, would question us on the strangest and most obscure details: What is the architectural style and who built this or that church or palace in Warsaw? What was the title of the first play ever written by Goethe? Whom did Michelangelo portray on the ceiling of the Sistine Chapel? Where and when did Caroline Neuber made her acting debut? What was Molière's itinerary on his tour of the French provinces in 1645-1658? What was the repertoire of the Bogusławski second management of the National Theater in Warsaw in 1790-1794? (Wojciech Bogusławski, was known as the "father" of Polish modern theater; he lived from 1757-1829). Who were the painter-designers in Diaghilev's *Ballets Russes*? Which architectural theater designs came from the Bauhaus? And so on, and so forth. It was sheer torture.

I wanted to go beyond Szletyński's interests, and make this general self-education as broad as possible. I imposed on myself a strict program of reading and seeing shows. This was a journey to lands about which I had already heard but never visited. For the first time I read books and essays by Craig, Appia, Fuchs, Copeau, and Piscator. I studied the records of productions and read about the directorial methods of Alexandr Tairov, Evgeny Vakhtangov, Louis Jouvet, Charles Dullin, Bertolt Brecht, Jean-Louis Barrault, and many others. I attended literally all opening nights in the Warsaw theaters; students of the Theater Academy got comps which made it easier. I traveled to Łódź, to see my dean Korzeniewski's imposing production of *The Undivine Comedy* by Zygmunt Krasiński, one of the Polish Romantic plays which had been prohibited by the regime for years. I went to Cracow to attend Kreczmar's opening of another Krasiński drama, *Irydion*. I saw the first Grotowski production, *Orphée* by Jean Cocteau, in the Thirteen Rows Theater in Opole. My professor and editor of "Theater," Edward Csató, sometimes sent me to see productions all over Poland, paying for travel and then for my reportage. I started also to publish in other theater and literary magazines.

Among others, I wrote about productions of Kotlarczyk's Rhapsodic Theater in Cracow. It was the same company with which my uncle Anthony Żuliński had played during and after the war. When, later on, I occasionally visited the Rhapsodic, I always inadvertently succumbed to its peculiar style. When I went to see it again, as a student of directing and a theater reporter, I tried look at it consciously and analytically. Again, it made a deep impression on me. I feel that the Rhapsodic influenced my work and attitude in two ways. First, it demonstrated and proved the power of an non-realistic, highly stylized production. Second, it exemplified the attitude of bold artistic and political independence. I owe the Rhapsodic, and Kotlarczyk, a lot.

Mieczysław Kotlarczyk (1908-1978) created the Teatr Rapsodyczny (Rhapsodic Theater) in Cracow as an underground, and, therefore, illegal organization during the war, in 1941, which performed in private homes. The Rhapsodic was a theater of the word. The basic means of expression was the recitation of poetry with restrained acting, minimal stage accessories, simple, stylized costumes, and music, usually played on the piano only. During the war the Rhapsodic had among its actors a student of the clandestine Jagellonian University, Karol Wojtyła, who later became Pope John Paul II. The theater functioned from 1941 to 1953, when it was closed during the peak of Stalinist repression for its patriotic, Catholic, and anti-communist stand. Resurrected in 1957, after the "October 1956" thaw, it soon came under attack again from the united forces of the Party, the censors, and the secret police.

Material for the scripts was invariably taken from major literary works, and the objective of the theater was to extol spiritual and national values. Kotlarczyk always prepared his own scenarios, based on national and world epics by Mickiewicz, Homer, Ariosto, Byron, and Pushkin, as well as plays, montages of modern poetry, and adaptations of novels. Most memorable among Kotlarczyk's productions were: Słowacki's *King-Spirit* (1941) and *Samuel Zborowski* (1943), Mickiewicz's *Pan Thaddeus* (1942, and four later versions) and *The Forefathers' Eve* (1961), *The Attic Salt* (an adaptation of Aristophanes' works, suspended by the censors before its opening in 1953, and eventually performed in 1963), Homer's *The Odyssey* (1958), *The Forefathers' Eve* by Mickiewicz (1961), *Faust* by Goethe (1965), and *Acropolis* by Wyspiański (1966). In all of these, Kotlarczyk emphasized the universal and poetical dimensions of the plays. In *The Forefathers' Eve* he stressed the dialogues between heaven and earth; in *Faust*, he focused on the dramatic struggle of a hero who opposes the established state of things and desires to acquire power over nature in order to minister to humanity; and, in *Acropolis*, he eulogized the forces of culture, hope, and freedom.

Aesthetically, the Rhapsodic productions had an non-realistic and metaphorical style. They emphasized the word (the spoken text)—pronounced, celebrated, and proclaimed—as its principal means of expression. The word was treated actively as a vehicle of action. It was a creative word, *Logos*, in the Biblical sense: The word, pronounced by God, held creative power. The word in Kotlarczyk's productions had might and power, expressing both human spirituality and activity, conveying values and generating events. It appealed to the spectators' imagination, forcing them to co-create. As the deliverer of the word, the actor was the center and the focus of Kotlarczyk's style and method. The actors expressed themselves both as characters and witnesses to the characters' deeds, as commentators, narrators, communicators, as well as the spectators' guides or mentors. Strong and direct contact between the actors and the spectators was maintained during the entire performance. Declamation, diction, and delivery of the word were of primary importance in Kotlarczyk's productions. He precisely orchestrated group recitations. The objective of the productions was to share spiritual, aesthetic, patriotic, and literary values with the public, to teach and to moralize. In all his works Kotlarczyk sought to reveal theater's sacred sources and spiritual powers, and to convey them to the audience.

I visited Kotlarczyk for the last time after seeing *The Forefathers' Eve* in 1961. Later, I closely followed his story. I feel it's right to tell it now, even though it happened after my school years.

Kotlarczyk's shows were continually offensive to the regime. He was accused of "mysticism," "clericalism," "idealism," and disregard for the "Party leadership." The official press called for closing his theater. Nevertheless, constantly under fire, he managed to navigate the rough seas of theater life in a totalitarian state. But a catastrophe came. In 1966, the twenty-fifth anniversary of the Teatr Rhapsodic approached. On this occasion, Kotlarczyk produced *Acropolis* by Wyspiański and published a booklet that documented the theater's history, including a factual note that one of the actors in the original company of the Rhapsodic in 1942 was a certain Karol Wojtyła, a student from a clandestine university. By 1966, that same student had become the Archbishop of Cracow. Not considering the possible consequences, Kotlarczyk asked his former actor to say a mass at the Cracow Cathedral for the Rhapsodic on its anniversary, and he also invited him to attend the opening of *Acropolis*. In his sermon, the Archbishop congratulated Kotlarczyk and his company for their long-continued efforts, stressed the importance of their work for the preservation of the national culture and the spiritual life of the nation, and publicly accepted Kotlarczyk's invitation to the *Acropolis* premiere. The authorities went mad. They launched an unprecedented attack on Kotlarczyk for his close association with the Church. (Indeed, Kotlarczyk enjoyed the friendship of his former actor, now the Archbishop, and maintained close ties with other clergymen, including Cardinal Wyszyński, the Polish Primate.) By coincidence, the year 1966, the twenty-fifth anniversary of the Rapsodyczny, was also the millennium of Christianity in Poland, which was converted in 966. The Communist Party, and its leader Gomułka, tried to overshadow the Church's religious millennium ceremonies by organizing noisy rallies marking "1000 Years of the Polish State." Within this context, the Rapsodyczny's anniversary and Kotlarczyk's activities were deemed "subversive" and "detrimental to the state." Kotlarczyk was questioned several times, reprimanded, and "advised" to cancel his invitation of the Archbishop to the opening of *Acropolis*. The Archbishop himself understood the delicate situation and informed Kotlarczyk that he would not attend. The repressions continued anyway. The anniversary's booklet, (previously approved by the censors) was confiscated, and the production of *Acropolis* was defamed by the critics in a campaign orchestrated from above. Then, without notice, on April 11, 1967, Kotlarczyk was dismissed from his position as the general manager and artistic director of the Teatr Rapsodyczny.

In spite of his own appeals, protests by several renowned artists and scholars, the objections of the majority of the acting company of the Rhapsodic (though all fourteen Party members in the theater supported the fatal decision), and, finally, even an official letter sent by Karol Wojtyła, now a Cardinal, to the Minister of Culture, the dismissal of Kotlarczyk was sustained. On July 18, 1967, a small note on the announcement board in the green room in the theater read: "The last performance of the Teatr Rhapsodic is being played today." The note was not signed. No one wanted to take personal responsibility for the final blow. The

Rhapsodic was closed and the company disbanded. It was probably the saddest day in the history of postwar theater in Poland. An important center of national spirit and art had been destroyed. The totalitarian communist regime celebrated its victory over culture.

The Rhapsodic nevertheless remains a bright spot in the annals of Polish theater, as a stronghold of high artistic values and moral principles. Kotlarczyk is remembered as an innovative, original, and creative artist, a constant opponent of the captivity of his country, and a man who paid the highest price for his ideals, which, for an artist, is to be deprived of the right to create. Following the closing of the Rhapsodic, Kotlarczyk taught speech in Church seminaries and was employed temporarily at the Lublin Catholic University. He also wrote his memoirs, which he smuggled to the West and published beyond the reach of the communist censors. He contracted a terminal illness and died in 1978. In the history of the captive theater in his captive country, Kotlarczyk set the highest aesthetic and moral standards. He never yielded to the communist ideologues' pressure, never produced or directed any work of dubious value, and never accepted theater's subjugation to propaganda purposes. Bold during the war, when his activities were subject to the death penalty, and defiant under the communist rule, under fire the whole time and endangered by the closing of his theater, he did not stop expressing his predilections and convictions. Catholic and anti-communist, constant and untiring, a noble human being and a zealous creator, Kotlarczyk vividly and tragically personified the fate of the theater artist in a totalitarian state. He was an artist with a idea. A creator of a style. A man of principle. A role model to follow.

My years in Warsaw's Academy fell in one of the most exiting period of theater history in Poland in the 20th century. After "October 1956" three types of repertoire, until then prohibited, started to dominate. First, the world and national classics, second, the modern Western plays, and third, contemporary domestic dramas. A lot of debate provoked the "power tragedies"—an appropriate choice in the post-Stalinist times. *Richard III* was produced in the Ateneum

Theater, with a stunning Jacek Woszczerowicz; *Macbeth* with my professor Jan Świderski and *Oedipus Rex* with Gustaw Holoubek in the Dramatyczny; *Don Carlos* by Friedrich Schiller, *Erik XIV* by Strindberg, and *King Lear* in the Polski; *Hamlet* in the Powszechny. All of these plays debated power and morality—problems which were previously unwanted on the stages, because the principles of totalitarianism were obeying the authorities and accepting the Party line, not posing questions or seeking truth. In addition to power tragedies, I remember a wide selection of Shakespeare played at that time in Warsaw: *Henry IV, Part I* in the Ateneum, *Othello* in the Klasyczny, and *Twelfth Night* in the National.

Productions of national classic resulted in large scale, imaginative stagings of romantic and neo-romantic dramas, especially those of Słowacki (*Beatrix Cenci, Mazepa, Fantazy, Mary Stuart, Lilla Weneda*) and Wyspiański (*The Wedding, November Night, The Deliverance*). The Western repertoire flooded the stages. There was a large selection of outstanding American plays: *Desire Under the Elms* by O'Neill, *The Time of Your Life* by Saroyan; all Miller's best: *The Crucible, Death of a Salesman, A View from the Bridge,* and *After the Fall;* Williams' *The Glass Menagerie, A Streetcar Named Desire* and *Rose Tattoo.* Brecht was played without restrictions: *Caucasian Chalk Circle, Galileo, Mr. Puntila and His Man Matti, Mother Courage, The Threepenny Opera, Fear and Misery of the Third Reich,* and *The Resistible Rise of Arturo Ui.* The French authors: Beckett, Ionesco, Genet, and Sartre; the British: Osborne, Pinter, and Wesker; along with Italians, Germans, Swiss, Argentinians, and others, were played in all theaters. New Polish playwrights, encouraged by the change of political climate, made their debuts: Tadeusz Różewicz, Sławomir Mrożek, Tymoteusz Karpowicz, Janusz Głowacki, and Krzysztof Choiński. The world premiere of Różewicz's *The Card Index* in The Dramatyczny Theater (March 25, 1960) made history. It was a true resurrection of Polish theater. I saw all these productions—listening, watching, taking notes, learning. Learning a lot.

Foreign productions started to pour into Poland. Another thrill. I was still in high school when Bertolt Brecht visited Poland with his Berliner Ensemble in 1952, and did not see it. I heard that Brecht, a Marxist turned anticommunist, enormously helped the Polish theater people to fight socrealism with his anti-realistic performances. I saw original productions of that famous theater later on, both in Poland and in Berlin. In the years of my university studies, Brecht started to be played all over Poland and was treated as an ally. It was still too early for me to see the beautiful shows brought to Warsaw by the Paris' Théâtre National Populaire of Jean Vilar in 1954. It was a theater based on masterful delivery of the word and expressive acting, as well as aesthetic stylization, literary poetry, and moral principles; another ally in the struggles for authentic Polish theater under the socrealistic attack.

I was grown up enough to profit from the next visits of foreign theaters. First, I stretched to the limit my student budget and took night trains to from Poznań to Warsaw to watch them. In 1957, the Royal Shakespeare Company brought to Warsaw Shakespeare's *Titus Andronicus* directed by and starring Laurence Olivier; a piece of theater of an intensity unknown to me before. In 1958 Carlo Goldoni's *The Servant of Two Masters* was performed in Warsaw by the Piccolo Teatro from Milan, directed by Giorgio Strehler and with Marcello Moretti in the lead; a delightful piece of pure acting theater. When I moved to Warsaw, I had these famous visiting theaters within the reach of my hand.

Subsidized and supported by the authorities, theaters from the Soviet Union kept coming. It was interesting to see how far behind the Polish theater they fell in the late 1950s. Their repertoire, style, and means of expression were still restricted by the official doctrine of socrealism, which had been abandoned in Poland by that time. It was, in a way, a negative learning experience and a reminder what a devastating effect on theater control from above can have. The companies coming from the West did not surpass Polish productions in terms of staging or acting, but were a proof how powerful theater can be. They provided the young director with a vast field of study. Théâtre du Vieux Colombier (a successor of the famous Copeau company) from France showed *The Lark* by Jean Anouilh directed by the author and *The Trojan War Shall Not Take Place* by Giraudoux. Only a few month after Vieux Colombier, the Old Vic from London presented *Macbeth* and Shaw's *Saint Joan*. What an opportunity for a directing student it was to compare two plays on Saint Joan, one written by a British and one by a French playwright. It was a vivid "comparative theater" class. I found the French approach more appealing. Anouilh freely played with time, space, stylization, and symbolism, while Shaw's drama seemed to be heavy handed, developing logically yet somehow dully, with devastatingly long monologues in the court scene. I remember also the visits of the Théâtre National Populaire from Paris with productions directed by Jean Vilar; and the Teatro di Eduardo from Naples, Italy, who brought plays directed by the founder of the company, Eduardo de Filippo himself. Vilar's productions had wide breath and impeccable delivery of text. De Filippo stunned me by his verism, so different to the stylization widely practiced in Poland. For the first time, I saw original Brecht productions performed by his Berliner Ensemble company, and got a Brechtian class of alienation in both mise-en-scène and acting. I remember also the excitement of a discovery when I saw a kind of performance completely new to me: a dance production brought to Warsaw by Jerome Robbins. Later on, the Royal Shakespeare Company came with *King Lear,* directed by Peter Brook and performed by Paul Scofield. It was an overpowering theater experience: such power of acting, such power of directing.

During my first two years at the Theater Academy I was prohibited from traveling abroad by the authorities. I could not get an exit visa or obtain passport—same thing. It was a political punishment for my publication of an article in the émigré monthly "Kultura" ("Culture") in Paris, during my stay there in 1957. To publish abroad, and especially in a journal known for its anti-communist stand, was considered a crime by the regime. Naively, I had thought that all totalitarian restrictions were abolished after the "October 1956." It was not so. In spite of the enlargement of freedom in artistic creation, the regime and its police were firmly in control. I learned it the hard way, when I got a grant to study abroad in 1959. The reply to my application for the passport was negative. This was repeated the next year. Only upon intervention of my mentor, Axer, who had good connections with the officials, did I finally get the passport in 1961, and could accept the award for young director bestowed on me by the International Theater Institute in Paris. It was my other mentor, dean Korzeniewski, who nominated me for this award and saw that I got it.

What an unforgettable experience it was! I first went to Avignon, France, where Jean Vilar every year held a theater festival as well as workshops for young theater people. The open-air productions of Vilar in the courtyard of the Papal Palace and the meetings with him enlarged my knowledge of French theater and introduced me to good working methods of animating large groups of youth. An international multitude from France, Italy, Spain, Germany, England, and other countries talked constantly about theater, exchanged opinions on the shows, and shared their theater cultures. Towards the end of the workshop, each national group had to prepare a short production and perform it for all participants, a throng of about a thousand. In our small Polish group we had excellent actors. I directed the show, composed of pantomime skits, and a few scenes from Polish plays translated on the spot. The crowd loved it.

The award of ITI allowed me to travel to London, to see my "theater aunt" Domańska. I also called upon my "theater ancestors," Shakespeare, Marlowe, and Ben Jonson, whose plays I saw. Then I stayed in Paris for a month and went to theater every night. Additionally, I participated in a workshop in the French National Television. From France I went to Italy. I saw performances, but most of all I visited museums and walked through architectural wonders. From Italy I went to Greece, where I spent hours in ancient theaters and amphitheaters. A production seen in Epidauros was like a trip back in time to the holy and ritualistic sources of Western theater. In shocking contrast, the majority of productions in Athens were shallow and oriented towards entertainment. There was a significant exception, though: Karolous Koun, the leading personality of

Greek post-war theater, and head of Teatro Texnis (The Artistic Theater) in Athens. He showed me a highly artistic production of Lorraine Hansberry's *A Raisin in the Sun,* and explained to me his program. He sought to use classical theater principles in work on contemporary plays. He did it, by searching for deep philosophical content in every play and then exposing it by the use of universal means of expression, like stage symbols and metaphors. I recall my meeting with him as one of the formative moments in a young director's education.

This education was certainly not finished then, but the first stage of it was completed. I returned home in the fall of 1961.

My first real, professional theater job was waiting for me.

CHAPTER 2. SHAPING A THEATER STYLE

Early directing in professional theater

The job which was waiting for me was in the Wybrzeże Theater in Gdańsk. Before I had finished school, Axer had recommended me to them. It was one of the top theaters in Poland, located in a big metropolis, composed of three cities—Gdańsk, Gdynia, and Sopot; also called the "Triple City." The theater had two stages: a big house, shared with the opera in Gdańsk, and a smaller stage in Sopot. Construction of a new theater was under way, in order to get a second stage for the exclusive use of drama and leave the existing big theater to the opera. The new building was finished in 1966. The Wybrzeże was a big organization producing about 12 plays per theater season. It had its shops, administration, and rehearsal spaces. There was a permanent company of about 50 actors, plus directors, designers, and stage managers, as well as literary and musical advisers. The artistic director was a young, energetic, and talented Jerzy Goliński, smoothly cooperating with an experienced general manager, a man of late middle age, Antoni Biliczak. Gdańsk and Gdynia were port cities, with shipyards, fuel refineries, and factories, and, consequently, a large working class population, which made them a sensitive and important political centers. It was historically logical then, that in this very place calls for Poland's independence and for economic reform would be strongly voiced. They led to strikes, demonstrations, and bloody clashes between the workers and the police and army in 1970, and, eventually to the birth of Solidarity in 1980. Lech Wałęsa, the

Solidarity leader, was an electrician in the Gdańsk shipyard; in the 1990s he became the president of Poland. The "Triple City" was also a big cultural center with a renowned Polytechnic School and the Medical School, along with a University, an Academy of Fine Arts, and a Music Academy. The mix of working class and academic populations, along with an international flair typical for a port city, provided theater with both popular and sophisticated audiences. The Wybrzeże theater was meeting the challenge by producing an amalgam of classical and contemporary plays, as well as comedies and dramas with music. It was a good and demanding place to start.

I stayed with the Wybrzeże Theater for two seasons, 1961-1963, and 1963-1964. In 1962 I also got a job in Warsaw. I returned to Gdańsk for another season in 1966-1967. For the record I have to put down my professional directorial debut: it was the world premiere of three one-act plays by Sławomir Mrożek, *Karol, Out at Sea,* and *Striptease* which opened December 31, 1961. Axer came to see it and, I think, he liked it. I felt that I had made up for my disappointing "directing workshop," *The Cooks.* As required, I submitted one of my next productions for the directorial "diploma" exam. It was *The Ring of the Great Lady* by Norwid, produced in the Polski Theater in Warsaw in 1962, which opened to favorable reviews. One of them was written by Jan Kott, the famous Shakespearian scholar, professor of Warsaw University, and, at that time, the oracle of Warsaw critique. My production was accepted by dean Korzeniewski and the departmental committee. I wrote the dissertation. I passed the exam. I got my M.F.A. in Directing. I was a professional director.

Painting backdrops for my work

In *Karol, On the See,* and *Striptease* I consciously used Axer's psychological and realistic approach to acting which, in collision with Mrożek's absurd dialogue and grotesquely shaped characters worked very well. In one of my next shows, *Two Theaters* by Jerzy Szaniawski in the Polski Theater in Warsaw (1962), I purposely used the "staging theater" style which I learned from Korzeniewski. Balancing between these two approaches, and trying to combine them, I slowly started to forge my own style. It began to appear in productions of poetic plays by Norwid and then of Różewicz. Work on Brecht's epic dramas (*Caucasian Chalk Circle, Mother Courage, The Good Woman of Setzuan*) as well as on Wyspiański's stage visions (*The Wedding, November Night, The Deliverance*) helped me further to discover it. Seen in many of my productions, it acquired the most clear form in *Anna Livia, Operetta, Birth Rate, The Forefathers' Eve,* and *The Plague.* Years later it was well manifested in my American productions, among others, in *Rhinoceros, The Hunger Artist Departs, A Man for All Seasons, Antigone in New York,* and *Dummies Ball.* It took me years to articulate it and I am still working on it. It turned out to be, eventually, an amalgam of realism and symbolism, with a solid psychological foundation in the acting and unlimited imaginary horizons in the mise-en-scène. It incorporated text as one of—many equal—elements of the show and used space in an innovative way. It was my *creative directing.*

I should not tell, however, one by one, the story of all my productions. This book is not about me. It is about you. What matters is how you can make it in artistic directing. My way to directing, and major steps in directing, are only examples of how one can learn and practice this beautiful and difficult art. On the following pages I will present and explain a few of the important directorial problems which I encountered and tried to solve. They may serve you to solve your own.

But first, let me paint briefly a backdrop—or rather three of them—of my theater way, which will serve as general reference and context for the specific topics we are going to discuss.

First is the historical backdrop. It depicts the general political situation in Poland and my own predicament there, and later on in the US. The beginning of my theater way, including directing studies and first steps as director, fell into a relatively favorably political climate in Poland. After the "October 1956," theater experienced a period of flourishing; many restrictions previously fettering artistic creation were lifted, or at least temporarily suspended. The international theater exchange provided challenge for Polish theater. I personally learned a lot from foreign masters. But in the mid 1960s, the political, social, and economic situation in Poland worsened, and that led to violent confrontations between the society and the regime in 1968, 1970, and 1976. The fact that I refused to join the Communist Party gradually started to put me in the position of an outsider. In spite of that, my theater way had an ascending tendency. It was marked by good responses from the audiences and (often enough) by good reviews; directorial prizes marked some of my productions. In the 1970s, I could still work effectively, but my conflicts with the regime increased. What I did achieve was in every instance done against the political odds. The tension was sometimes unbearable. But this very tension provided me with energy to create, and supplied both my companies and the public with incredible enthusiasm and vigor. It was a time of fiercely bold and explosively vivid theater in Poland. I am happy that I lived and worked there at that time. My clear declaration on the side of Solidarity in 1980, and my taking part in different underground, illegal activities during martial law in the 1980s, set me on a collision course with the regime. In the summer of 1984, I was dismissed from my job in the theater for political reasons. At the same time, my work at the university was made impossible by the communist authorities, and the same was threatening at the school of drama. It was a complete breakdown in my life, as well as that of my family. There was no place for us in Poland. My wife and children faced that bravely. My good American friends, whom I always remember with gratitude and fondness, offered me a job here. I found in America a home and freedom, along with a multitude of new opportunities, difficulties, and challenges. Both the professional and university productions which I directed in the United States provided me with new experiences and enriched my directing, as well as my teaching of directing.

The second is the professional backdrop showing the major steps in my theater way. From 1961, until 1967, I worked as a full or part-time director, in the theaters of Gdańsk, Warsaw, Lublin, and Toruń. It should be explained that within the system of socialist state control of employment, every director had to have a permanent job. The contract was one season long, and carried with it the duty to direct from two to four productions per season (depending on experience) for a monthly salary. Only after fulfilling this obligation, could one freelance in other theaters. Besides theater, I started to direct plays for television in 1962, and I continued to do so until 1984. In 1967, I got my first artistic directorship, and soon after, also the general management of the city theater, the Osterwa Theater, in Lublin. In 1975, I moved to Wrocław where I assumed the artistic directorship and the general management of the Contemporary Theater. (Note: as assistant I worked in the Contemporary Theater in Warsaw. In Wrocław I headed a theater under the same name: the Contemporary Theater). I worked in Wrocław's Contemporary, until my dismissal by the authorities in 1984. Simultaneously with my theater work, I competed a doctorate in philosophy at Poznań University in 1971, and a second doctorate in theater (in Poland: "habilitacja") at Wrocław University in 1975. In between 1974 and 1985, I taught at Wrocław University and the Wrocław and the Cracow schools of drama. In 1985, I left Poland and came to the United States. I directed professionally in The Guthrie Theater in Minneapolis and some other places, but I chose to focus on university work. After short-term employment at New York University, Swarthmore College, and University of California Santa Cruz, I settled down at the State University of New York at Buffalo.

The third backdrop is a map of my various works and areas of interest. There are many of them, but I can arrange them in clear compartments, like those pure squares and rectangles on Piet Mondrian's paintings—they have individual colors and sizes but are continually integrating themselves. The same is true with my work. For years, it has had two main compartments: theater praxis and scholarship. The praxis was divided into directing and managing theaters. The scholarship had the form of researching, writing, and teaching. These main segments were separate, in terms of the daily or yearly schedule, but they were also integrated, mutually influencing each other. Directing, I understood theater history better. Researching old productions, I enriched my directing. Directing was motivated by the need to express the ideas and values I wanted to proclaim. Research was prompted by curiosity and a desire to share my findings with others; this resulted in writing and teaching. Eventually, my entire work was compartmentalized into four disciplines. First: directing. This was professional directing in theaters in Poland and abroad, directing plays for television, and directing in schools of drama in Poland and at the universities abroad. Second: managing. My artistic and administrative management of theaters in Poland lasted for seventeen years. Third: writing. My writing on theater has resulted in hundreds of articles and twenty three books. I have written on theater history, but also poetry, prose, and drama. Fourth: teaching. I taught acting and directing, as well as history and theory of theater, playwrighting, history of world civilizations, and other subjects.

I have to stress again, that all these compartments are connected. They are all the cords and knots of one net. I would select out of that net only these problems which strictly refer to directing.

Creating the performance text

The postulates of the "staging theater" style provided for the director's creative control over the text. The director was expected to actively work on the text—adapting, editing, or correcting the translations. The director could also write his/her own adaptations or scenarios, which was widely practiced. To write a play was another option, but only those with special talents and skills could successfully combine directing and playwriting. Truly, only Bertolt Brecht was the undisputable master of both trades in the 20th. But many excellent directors practiced writing adaptations of prose and poetry for their own productions. The custom of directors preparing adaptations for their own shows emerged at the beginning of the 20th century. It was practiced first by Copeau. Later on most celebrated examples included Piscator's *War and Peace* by Leo Tolstoy, Leon Schiller's *The Story of Sin* by Stefan Żeromski, Gaston Baty's *Madame Bovary* by Gustave Flaubert. Meyerhold, Burian, Jean Littlewood, Arianne Mnouchkine, Jerzy Jarocki, Jérôme Savary, Yuri Lyubimov, and many other directors also authored competent stage adaptations. I myself have prepared adaptations of several prose and poetry works which I then directed.

The emerging new theater of the Second Reform also provided hundreds of examples of the performance text created by a director in the 1960s and 1970s. On some occasions directors prepared their own scenarios, on others they articulated the text of the show through improvisational rehearsals with actors. Grotowski with his Laboratory, André Gregory with his Manhattan Project, and scores of others, did it. In the Open Theater, playwrights cooperated with Joe Chaikin in the collective creation process.

Thus, in the 20th century theater tradition, directorial control over the text was a matter of principle. Baty exclaimed: "We have to liberate ourselves from the slavery of the Lord Word" ("Sire le Mot"). It was a directorial battle-cry. Of course, nobody really wanted to expel the word from the theater; all modern directors loved masterpieces of drama, old and new, poetic and prosaic, and often staged them. But the artistic freedom of directing had to be expressed also through the control of the text. This was expected from a director in Poland in the 1960s.

The first step was analysis. I was taught by Kreczmar in school, and by Axer in the theater, that an attentive and deep analysis is the foundation of directorial work on drama. The thoroughly examined and profoundly understood text could be used in many different ways during rehearsals. Its contents, not the letter, mattered. Following the analysis, the director had to prepare his/her version of the play. From Korzeniewski, and through my own study of the methods of Schiller or Meyerhold, I learned that the directorial version of the text used in performance might differ significantly from the author's original.

Early in my work I encountered another problem. Many of the plays by

Cyprian Norwid (the 19th century poet and dramatist) which I laboriously studied, were in his life time unpublished and, when posthumously discovered in his crates, turned out to be severely damaged. In order to stage them I had to reconstruct lines and scenes, establish structures, and come up with whole adaptations of the plays. In this way I was entering into the author's field of competence. These works additionally prompted my active attitude towards the dramatic text.

Then, an event of utter importance for my whole directorial carrier happened. I started to collaborate with an acclaimed playwright, Tadeusz Różewicz. At the time we met, he was already a poet of world renown and an experienced playwright, while I was young and green.

His works give an extraordinary insight into the existential, cultural, and civilizational situation of humanity and the individual human being, they contain unusual images, and have wide poetical breath.

I found in him a playwright who could both challenge and enrich me. He, I guess, found in me a receptive reader and listener, and a director who wanted not only to repeat verbatim the playwright's lines and recreate stage directions, but to search for their theatrical rebirth as a "new creation," as St. Paul says.[2] Being a poet, Różewicz wrote plays in which realistically drawn characters were involved with mundane actions, but, at the same time, these actions had universal meaning and the characters reached the level of archetypes. Moreover, many plays by Różewicz had open and undefined form, purposely chosen by the author. They called for the director's cooperation. A poetic vision had to be transformed into a poetic production.

Over time I have staged eighteen productions of Różewicz's twelve plays.[3] Working with him, I learned two lessons. First, you have to attentively listen to

---

[2] Compare Rm 8, 19-22.

[3] My collaboration with the poet/playwright resulted also in a book, *Languages of Theater,* by Kazimierz Braun and Tadeusz Różewicz. Wrocław: Wydawnictwo Dolnośląskie, 1989.

the author and to work as hard as possible to get to the bottom of his text. In case of the Greeks, Shakespeare, Claudel, or Różewicz, it is never possible to get to this bottom, because it is always deeper than you think, and their horizons are continually expanding. Yet, you have to make an effort to follow these writers to the ultimate frontiers. Second, you have to create along with the author. You have to respond with your creativity to his. He has his far-reaching, universal goals. You also have to shoot for the stars.

Work on Różewicz's plays was always a journey to unknown lands. This was true when I worked on more strictly written plays—in terms of their form—such as *White Marriage, The Trap, The Hunger Artist Departs,* and *The Old Woman Broods.* His other texts, such as *The Card Index, The Interrupted Act,* and *Birth Rate* had open structures and demanded the director's input.

The Card Index posed a special quandary. The play was produced and published in 1960. But several years later Różewicz published an additional set of scenes of *The Card Index.* Some of them were previously cut by censorship and some pulled out of his files. The author himself did not combine the first body of the text with a new one, leaving that to the director. I took on the task of composing one play of the two existing parts. The author accepted my adaptation. Based on it, I staged *The Card Index* several times.[4] I adapted the text slightly differently every time, depending on with what actors and for what audiences I was working.

Interrupted Act and *Birth Rate* are, smilingly, only dramatic sketches. They contain philosophical essays. Dialogues are minimal. Stage directions vague. But still both these texts have the potential for full scale productions. My work, in consultation with the author, was to transform his sketches into stage events.

---

[4] I staged *The Card Index* several times: in Lublin (1970), in Sofia, Bulgaria (1978), in school of drama in Cracow (1979), at the University of Connecticut in Storrs (1980) and at Notre Dame University, Indiana (1982). I directed *Birth Rate* in Wrocław's Contemporary (1979) and Chicago's Actors Ensemble (1989), and showed it also in Dublin, Ireland (1980) and on tours in Poland, Spain, and Germany.

Różewicz visited me during rehearsals frequently. We spoke. I remember these talks as a competition in listening. Sure, I wanted first of all to hear what he told me. I listened most attentively. But he listened too. He echoed what I did on stage and delicately sorted that out. It seems to me that this is the best possible dialogue of two artists: to listen to each other.

I prepared *Interrupted Act* in Lublin in 1970 and for the television, also in 1970. The text is brief, yet full of incentives to go beyond it. I developed the concept of playing the same text four times, as four stages of theatrical work on a play. The first was the table rehearsal, with discussions between actors, director and author; I introduced the characters of the director and author while adapting the play. The second was a blocking rehearsal, with many variant ways of playing the same scenes. The third, was a technical rehearsal with elements of sets which functioned and malfunctioned, with corrections of cues. The fourth was the stage-ready show. The director, a Pirandellian figure, was running back and forth from the auditorium to the stage. The whole production was based on the principle of "theater within theater." It depicted the process of creating a production, and thus, had a double, intertwining action: the action of *Interrupted Act* as it develops, and the action narrating the theater artists' struggles to put on a show, with their failures, sometimes hilarious, and their bursts of inspiration.

Birth Rate posed yet another problem. There were almost no characters, no lines, no specific stage directions. Only a philosophical essay on the demographic explosion and its consequences, and several descriptions of apocalyptic visions. I prepared a script based on four components. First, scenes with action based on visions from *Birth Rate* (without dialogues). Second, some of Różewicz's poems. Third, a few dramatic fragments from his other plays. Fourth, blank spots which I planned to fill in through improvising with the actors. With the author's approval and frequent visits to the theater, an aleatory production started to emerge. A long scene was improvised first in real space—a train compartment in the railway station. It practically and metaphorically expressed the growth of population: a compartment for six passengers was gradually flooded by other compartment sitting and hanging everywhere. Their relationships oscillated between politeness to hostility, and finally turned into a ruthless fight for breathing space. Other elements worked too, providing for strange images and fascinating actions.

My second crucial experience in collaboration with the author was with James Joyce. No, no, no, not the famous Dubliner. He died many years before I took on his works. He was represented by his Polish alter ego, Maciej Słomczyński, a translator with absolute pitch when it came to Joyce's prose. Upon my request, Słomczyński prepared a stage adaptation of *Ulysses* combined with elements of *Finnegans Wake*. It was a good, interesting, and a very long play. It had about 300 pages. It would result in a production several hours long. I wasn't afraid of that, but I had a feeling that it did not transform *Ulysses*—the best novel of the 20th century, and probably in the history of world literature—into the project of a production which would be the only way to match the original. Even if not fully satisfying, though, it was certainly a good piece of playwrighting. I made the cast and started rehearsals. But nothing worked. After about two month of rehearsals, I found that we were at a dead end. I decided to stop rehearsal, one of the luxuries of having a well-subsidized theater, with a rotating repertoire of successful productions. I went to Cracow and spent three days in almost round-the-clock talks with Słomczyński. He was receptive. He also knew how to listen. I asked him many questions and I listened to his answers. It was during that Joycean work session—memorable for me—when I came up for the first time with the idea of an analytical "graph." It was a drawing which visually presented the structure and some aspects of the action. Working with Słomczyński, I drew graphs of many different possible versions of the adaptation, showing how various parts of *Ulysses* and *Finnegans Wake* could be connected. I left these drawings with Słomczyński.

They were certainly a useful means of communication between a director and a playwright discussing Joyce. But it occurred to me that they might serve in the analysis of any play. I started to use this type of drawings when analyzing plays

I was preparing for direction. Next, I discovered that this kind of graphical analysis works, or more, is absolutely necessary, when I work on any prose or poetic material which I want to transform into a script. Later, I found that it also helps me as playwright. The graph presents the action of the play as a strip divided into scenes. Each scene has a title summarizing the action and is accompanied by information about the characters participating in it, the location, and the time. Teaching directing in the Cracow school of drama in 1978, I had fully developed my graph and I shared it with students. In America, I used it for the first time in the directing class at the University of Connecticut in Storrs in spring 1980. Later, I came up with an additional use of it, not only for analysis, but also for preparing the directorial project. I also used the graph while collaborating with first-time playwrights and while teaching playwrighting.

But let's return to my work on Joyce. Only two weeks after our work session, Słomczyński, who was a dear fellow workaholic, (as I am), sent me the script. This time it had about 50 pages. It was a masterpiece. It had a new title, *Anna Livia*. It did not have anything to do with the linear action of *Ulysses,* and it did not attempted to decipher *Finnegans Wake's* linguistic hieroglyphs. Yet, it was the essence of Joyce: a story of birth, love, life, death, and resurrection expressed in metaphoric theater language, in poetic dialogues and songs, accompanied by unusual stage images. I immediately made a new cast. We threw ourselves into rehearsals. It was an exhausting, yet joyful time. The opening was a thrill. We got a marvelous response from the public. The reviews were so good that they were almost humiliating for me, for I knew that the credit went to Joyce and Słomczyński, and to the actors, lead by Teresa Sawicka. We got the ultimate honor: an invitation to come to Joyce's Dublin for the Festival celebrating the one hundredth anniversary of the birth of the author in 1981. The standing ovation of the public in the overcrowded Olympia Theater is one of my most precious theater memoirs.

Specialists appreciated the production for its coherent combining of refined literature with visuality and expressive acting with the inventive use of space. I am tempted to quote a description of this production—one of my most important works. As elusive as the flow of the scenes/images/dreams was, it rendered the style, form, and content of the production: "The play is a fusion of two intertwining motifs: femininity and reincarnation, or to put it a different way: love and death. Anna Livia comes from *Finnegans Wake* where she is both a woman and a river. (In psychoanalysis water symbolizes sex or fertility; Anna Livia personifies both.) She is an eternal woman, any woman, and a specific one. . . . She is real, and reminiscence, and a daydream. Relations between Shaun and Shem, Anna Livia's sons from *Finnegans Wake*, and herself, constantly change. They are father and son, or husband and lover, sometimes they become one person for her. Each of them seems to represent one of the two versions of man as seen by a woman. Moreover, the director differentiated their appearances and manner of acting. Shem is Romantic, young, slim, a bit unreal and faded like a figure in a dream. Shem is dead but for Anna Livia he is the only real lover. . . . Shaun is older, portly, slightly bourgeois, a rationalist. Most often he appears as Bloom while Shem assumes the features of Stephen Dedalus. Generally they assume the appearances of the figures Anna Livia sees in them. It is she, an existence-controlling element, who can bring them to life or send them into oblivion. . . . Kazimierz Braun's production appears to follow the style of Joyce's works. ... Diversified narration has been replaced by the varied theatrical idiom: cabaret, lyrical monologues, everyday conversations, prayers, and recitations, as well as sex, nudity, and comicality. . . . Amid the noise of battledores and splashes of water (there is a hole filled with water on the stage), the Washerwomen talk about Anna Livia. They speak a strange, distorted but pointed language full of newly coined ambiguous words. They look and behave like lewd country girls. . . . Anna Livia slowly emerges from below the ground or rather, like Venus, from the water. . . . Anna Livia brings a man lying face down to life. It is Shem. . . . A bedroom seen from above. Anna Livia-Molly is asleep beside her husband. Looking at them from above, we feel like Alice in Wonderland, seeing people and objects from a different side than usual. The difference between background and foreground disappears; everything is at an equal distance from the spectator. Molly is dreaming of a great, Romantic, fulfilled and true love. . . . Shem-Stephen enters Molly's dream. We see him below, under her feet. Other men appear. The dream turns into a frivolous revue. . . . Shem-Stephen, dancing in Anna Livia-Molly's dream, is her son. Next moment, he is no longer her vision and a dream but, in turn, she becomes his recollection, the picture of his dead mother. The Washerwomen lead a very old woman onto the stage. Now, two images of his mother speak simultaneously to Stephen: one who has just died, the old woman standing behind the white sheet of the Washerwomen, and the young and beautiful Anna Livia miraculously suspended over the ground. . . . Twilight. A graveyard in the background. A funeral procession. It is the funeral of Anna Livia's son-husband-lover. A crowd of mourners in black."[5]

Encouraged by collaboration with Słomczyński in writing the Joyce adaptation, I moved to write my own adaptations. Before *Anna Livia* I had made a couple of works of that kind. They left the heartburn of artistic dissatisfaction. The next ones aimed higher and bore fruit abundantly. Among them I should list *The Iliad,* based on Homer, which I did in collaboration with the poet Bogusława Miłobędzka, *The Plague,* based on Camus and Defoe, and *Animal Farm* based on Orwell. Two principles guided me in these works. The first was negative: an adaptation of a literary material for the stage should not be an attempt to write a play based on the original and it should not use the original verbatim. The second was positive: to write the adaptation as the director, right away jotting down a project of the production and coming up with theater means to express the ideas, the content, and the overall nature of the literary material. Adaptations which I prepared this way were not plays, but rather theater scenarios. They included actions, envisioned images, and used space extensively. They introduced characters sometimes different than in the original. In every case, they were

---

[5] Małgorzata Dzieduszycka. "Anna Livia." *The Theater in Poland.* 1 (1977): 8-11.

fundamentally true to the original, but they were new theater creations. They strove to match literary works, from which they were born, with works of theater art. My other adaptations also followed the fundamental principle of directly transforming the literary material into a production project.

Working with actors: between human and artistic values

I got the foundations of the directorial work with actors studying the methods of Osterwa and Stanislavsky, reading biographies of the distinguished actors of the past, and pondering over essays by Copeau and Craig, including his notorious *The Actor and the Super-Marionette* in which he provocatively proposed to chase actors out of theaters and replace them by super-marionettes. I got a taste of what it means to be directed, when as a student-actor I had to obey terse and dictatorial instructions from my director-professionals. Then I listened to Axer's inspirational and psychotherapeutic notes to actors in the theater, and to Świderski's practical and blunt remarks at seminars on directing actors at the Theater Academy. It was a palette of different approaches—from sensitive, compassionate and delicate whispering to actors, to shouting at them like a drill sergeant. Communicating with my fellow students, whom I directed in student productions, I imitated this or that approach of my directors and teachers. When, lonely and confused, I started to face professional casts, I soon discovered how different reading and listening about directing actors is from actually doing so.

After so many years of directing, I know for sure that the director's work with actors is the most important of all directorial skills. In this area in particular, I learned the most from my own mistakes. I am sorry that these mistakes were made in the living matter of the psyches and the bodies of actors. I deplore the fact that many times I wounded them, misguided them, or neglected them. I also found that there's no bigger satisfaction for a director than to observe an actor performing an unusual artistic feat that was prepared during rehearsals, and no more precious reward than an actor thankfully hugging the director after the opening.

For sure, directing actors is the most difficult of all directorial skills. Why? Because all the time it is a twofold process. It has a human dimension, in which one person interacts with another person. Both of them are human beings, they are friendly or aggressive, open or narrow-minded, eager to work or lazy, inventive or passive. It has also an artistic dimension, in which the director and the actor create in the realm of the aesthetic. They try to overcome earth's gravity, the literariness of words, and the languidness of action. How to push a sensitive, delicate, and fragile person into that blinding and hurting world of the character? How can a director be at the same time strict and hard, and kind and good? How it is possible to combine uncompromising aesthetical standards with love and forgiveness?

The artistic reality of the production is based on the human reality of its creators. The director—I believe—should be a person of principle in the work with actors. These principles, as I learned, must have both aesthetic and ethical dimensions. Aesthetically, the director needs to develop and use during rehearsals a set of solid techniques and methods in order to precisely and effectively communicate with actors. That provides actors with a sense of professional security. Ethically, the director must be trustworthy and deserve to be trusted. That provide actors with the sense of personal security. Actors should know that the director is a person who keeps his/her word, who never deceives, who takes full responsibility for his/her actions and words, and allows others to take their responsibility for their share in work. Theatrical rehearsals based on those principles are processes of establishing a covenant between the world and the theater, between human beings, which we are, and theater artists, which we strive to be.

I have been gradually learning to work with actors. I made small discoveries one by one. My first, most important and simple experience was that to learn how to work with actors you have to actually do so. Having a knowledge of theater history, I realized every time that my latest discovery had already been made centuries ago, many times, by others; but I still had to make it again, personally, practically, and painfully. For in the matter of working with actors, it is only your personal experience which really gives you the directorial skills. You have to feel a certain type of contact with actor, you have to see the impact of your particular directorial remark, you have to understand how a specific word or gesture of yours results in the actor's behavior, and you have to live with your actors through all the ups and downs of the rehearsals. It cannot be found in books, although they may help. It cannot be taken from others, although they may provide guidance. It must be learned personally through living contact with actors.

The art of acting is a integral art of the entire human being. All elements of acting, all acting means of expression, are interconnected and they interact all the time. For practical reasons, it is legitimate, however, to dissect acting into a few major, and a multitude of smaller regions. The major ones include performing actions, the use of the word, and the use of movement, including body and face language. An example of the smaller ones can be a "mudra" in the Hindu theater, an acting position and expression of the body, hand, or eyes having specific meaning. There are dozens of "mudras" and Indian actors spend years perfecting each of them. Examples of small, specific, and concrete means in Western theater might be found in the art of walking (Stanislavsky has a long paragraph about it), eating, shooting, kissing, and so on, and so forth. I can't enter into that fascinating thicket. I would only mention that each acting means has sense only within the totality of the acting performance. But let's at least briefly talk about those major areas of the art of acting: performance, word, and movement.

We, the directors, have to help actors to perform. It is obvious that in explaining the character to an actor you have to talk about the character itself and its actions, as well as about all circumstances—social, spatial, temporal, and others. What really helps, according to my experience, is to connect all these data with the actor's personal life experience. It is not an easy thing to do, because you do not always know your actors well. Yet, you can and should help them to be themselves, to reach to their own, personal, private, and authentic sources of energy while playing roles; to free themselves from conventional behaviors and cultural patterns; to take off their masks and armors.

We have to remember that almost all most memorable productions in the history of theater were prepared by teams of people who knew each other, who had been working together a long time, who shared their craft, their culture, and their life. This bond between theater work and everyday life, which provides a strong foundation for effective rehearsals and ensemble based productions, struck me first when I read about the vacations Stanislavsky and Vladimir Nemirovich-Danchenko took with their actors in the Crimea. The same ethos prevailed in the Copeau company and in Osterwa's Reduta community. I experienced the same with my student Poznań group. I always touched it visiting Grotowski and his actors. I felt that seeing Chaikin's Open Theater or Beck's and Malina's Living Theater productions. My Wrocław company had been gradually developing this kind of bond, through every-day work interactions, as well as tours abroad and oppositional activities during martial law years. When recently, in 1998, I saw again the brilliant Gardzienice Company from Poland, with its leader Włodzimierz Staniewski, I realized that they constantly make such tremendous progress in their art because some of them have worked and lived together for up to twenty years. It is a foundational principle of their work: to share both theater and life.

It seems to me, that it is a worthwhile effort to break through professional or academic barriers, and connect with people on the personal level, even if it is a-one-time work with a cast gathered for a particular play, which you know will never be assembled again. (The lack of permanent acting companies, staying together for longer time is for me the deficiencies of American theater; there are too few exceptions to this rule.) Some actors strongly resist any private connection with directors, some don't care for them. Yet, the personality of the actor must be engaged in building a role, for it is impossible for a director to build a deep performance of an actor only on the craft level. It is equally impossible, of course, to achieve truly artistic acting performance if the director-actor interaction happens only on the personal plane and does not aim towards finding the artistic structure of the role. Both these levels—the professional and the private—are like two wings which allow the bird to fly, or two lungs which enable healthy breathing. In the director's work with actors they supplement each other.

Let me give you an example. In *The Plague,* to which I often return as my "model production" (in Brechtian terms) I casted in the role of Teacher an excellent actor and a good friend, Andrzej Wilk. I knew that he was an underground Solidarity activist very strongly involved in the opposition to the communist-military regime in Poland in the 1980s. In one of the scenes of *The Plague,* Teacher had a monologue in which the key moral and political message of the production was revealed. The Teacher said that sometimes in history a time comes, when to say that two plus two makes four is punished by death. But maintaining that two plus two makes four is the basic moral duty, a testimony to a person's humanity. Similarly, in times of plague, a human being must make a simple, basic choice: to call it "plague," or to deny that plague is plague. The Teacher continued, that for him and his friends the choice was clear. They had to state that "plague is plague." It was a crucial statement, because the whole action up to this point had suggested that in this production, plague functions as a metaphor for the moral and political situation of the country under communist martial law; Camus' point of reference in *The Plague* was the Nazi's rule in France during World War II.

Wilk's delivery of the monologue had penetrating power and startling impact. For he delivered it with acting mastery and, at the same time, he spoke from his heart and mind. He was the character of Teacher fighting the plague in the production. And he was an underground Solidarity activist fighting the military junta in real life. It was a case of an absolute identification of the actor with the character. The personal motivation of the actor as a person having his political views and moral standards, was identical with the character's political and moral position. The character's motives were indistinguishable from the actor's. The unity of the artistic acting means of expression with the personal psycho-physical disposition of the actor was complete. It was perfect acting. Absolutely personal and impeccably artistic. The actor's ego was united with the character's. The actor stood fully behind the character, and the character enabled the actor to express his ideas and feelings. The proclaimed truth and beliefs of the actor were those of the character and vice versa. Wilk's performance had an absolute and pure truth both on the personal and artistic levels. It was an acting of incomparable, unlimited, explosive energy, because it was a perfect blend of the personal and the professional sides of acting. I expected that, casting Wilk in the role of Teacher. We worked on it. He made it.

The actor's speech, the delivery of lines and monologues, the diction and the interpretation of text, especially if it is verse, are another vast field of directorial care. I had good examples to follow, first off all, the Rhapsodic Theater shows. I personally practiced declamation of poetry and I had a good sense of the vocal, rhythmic, and emotional value of the word. Early on, I learned that in the theater the word must be delivered in action and be a part of action. Otherwise, it simply doesn't come across to the spectator. It is one of the principles of theater and whatever might be the explanation—it is a fact: in theater, action is a vehicle for the word. If so, the word on stage must always be transformed in "the actional word," as I call it. Good playwrights know that. Shakespeare is the best example. His words burn, pierce, sweep, excite, kill, and uplift.

Whether it's Shakespeare or not, however, the major directorial problem in work on the textual aspect of a production is to integrate speech with action. We encounter this problem in both prose and verse plays. It is easer to solve it when actors lines' use the vernacular and include everyday idioms or slang. It is more difficult in verse plays, with metaphoric, lofty language. Combining speech with behaviors and stage business is a remedy in the former. Infusing speech with passion is the way to go in the latter. I observed the use of both remedies while assisting Axer. In Frisch's *Biedermann* there is a scene of a family dinner with continuous dialogue between four characters. After several weeks of rehearsals, plates, glasses, bottles, forks, and spoons were literally dancing in the actors hands while they were flawlessly conversing. In Goethe's *Iphigenia* the infernal passions of Łomnicki or the angelic gentleness of Mrozowska carried the long, wordy, verse soliloquies with volcanic energy to the audience. Quite early in my own directorial career, I worked on another play by Frisch, *Andorra* in the Wybrzeże Theater in 1964. There was also a family dinner scene. The task was, as in *Biedermann,* to inseparably combine a quartet dialogue of characters with their uninterrupted eating and drinking. Directing plays written in verse by Norwid I was learning ways of infusing fragile, poetic words with true human emotions. In *Romeo and Juliet* (Teatr Polski in Warsaw, 1963) and *Hamlet* (in Lublin, 1968) I got my first lessons in Shakespeare. I had the feeling that I was faced with an impossibly difficult challenge, and, at the same time, that the author was taking me by the hand, like a little child, and leading me safely through the labyrinth of the play. Trusting him was the best way to go. Unmistakably, he permeates the dialogues with the energy of action. I had the same experience every time I directed Shakespeare.

Movement expressing action seemed to me an especially effective directorial tool. Blocking, therefore, was for me always of primary importance. I got additional incentive and encouragement to use vivid movement on stage, when I saw the pantomime masters Marcel Marceau's and Jean-Louis Barrault's non-realistic and expressive skits. I learned about the past of pantomime, reading about Deburau's shows in the 19th century, and studying the exercises of the 20th century's Etienne Decroux. My experience in the area of movement was enhanced by directing plays for television, where close-ups had to have restricted movement and required utter precision in blocking. Television was for me a school in blocking minute details. Early on, I also faced the task of choreographing crowd scenes. In *Two Theaters* by Szaniawski (1962) I had a group of 50 young boy-fighters from the Warsaw Uprising of 1944. In *November Night* by Wyspiański (1967) I had a troop of 40 marines playing cadets at another Polish uprising, that of 1830. Working on *Two Theaters*, I tried to meticulously and specifically prepare the complete choreography beforehand and put the boys into it during rehearsals. The result was dull. I learned that within a certain framework of movement, I have to give performers freedom to improvise. Working on *November Night* I knew that. The cadets had certain drills which they performed in absolute unison, but in the scene of the attack on the Russian cannons I asked them to improvise movement and they were unbelievably expressive. The crowd scenes with the cadet troop brought applause from the public every time during the action, a rare occurrence.

But movement for the camera, as well as in crowd scenes, was usually focused on the external expression. Searching for an internal focus for the characters, I turned to yoga. I started to practice it personally and added yoga-type exercises into the usual warm-ups with actors. Then, I befriended one of Grotowski's actors, Zbigniew Cynkutis, and with his help I introduced elements of physical and psycho-physical training of the Lab Theater in my work. I twice invited Cynkutis to my Lublin theater to have a workshop with my actors, and again twice in Wrocław, where he collaborated with me during rehearsals of *Anna Livia,* and directed Ibsen's *Peer Gynt* (1976). Cynkutis' work enhanced the movement abilities and the movement awareness of some members of my companies both in Lublin and in Wrocław. In addition to Cynkutis', we had voice and diction workshops in Wrocław, led by a renowned specialist and professor of Warsaw Theater Academy, Krystyna Mazur. We also invited choreographers and pantomime masters to heighten the company's skills.

With the passing time, I discovered that something more is expected from the director besides techniques and skills. I would call it "directorial virtues." Every human being has weak and strong points in his/her character. It is a private matter. I will explain what I mean by "directorial virtue" in an example. We were rehearsing *The Old Woman Broods* by Różewicz in Lublin in 1973. We were working on a scene in which a soldier leaves home for war and is wounded in combat. His mother finds him on the battlefield, he dies in her lap, and she buries him. It was a poetic scene with a lot of movement but little dialogue, and containing a lullaby sung by the mother for her dying son. We used improvisation. After talking about the characters, objectives, circumstances, and possible first steps of the action, I asked the actors to take their places, and went to the other side of the rehearsal room. Very slowly, they started to improvise something like a game involving a mother and a child, about which we had not spoken before. Then, the improvisation gradually died down. Actors lay on the floor as if asleep and appeared as if they were having dreams, but showed no vivid physical expression. I watched impatiently and was at the brink of interrupting them, because the improvisation did not take the direction about which we had spoken. But after weighing the decision whether to interrupt or not for a while, I decided to wait. I waited for a long time. Long, indeed. When you wait for something to happen and it does not happen—time is moving really slow. So I wait and wait. Suddenly, as if it was a development of the mother's dream, the mother and son improvised the scene of the soldier's departure. Others started to beat a rhythm on the floor. It was a battle. The young man participated in an attack. He was wounded. He fell. The mother observed this from a distant slope. She rushed to the battlefield. The improvisation went on. It was penetrating, fresh, imaginative, creative acting. At the end, after the burial, the mother sat helplessly at the grave and started to hum the lullaby. Heartbreaking acting. The actors finished and were sitting on the floor exhausted. I approached them, but was speechless. Then, the actress playing the mother, whose name was Wanda, said: "I thank you for not interrupting us after the sluggish start. Thank you for your patience." This is what I mean by "directorial virtue." That time it was instinctive. In the following years I have consciously worked on that important directorial virtue, or simply skill: to be patient working with actors. There are other directorial virtues. Their identification and development should be a secret of every director.

In the director's rapports with actors there is also something like a need to offer sometimes a "life support." This is support which a director offers actors beyond intellectual notes, professional advice, or psychological help. In 1971, I directed a television production of my own adaptation of Żeromski's novel *Ashes*. In the leading role I casted Eve, a very young and very talented actress. The recording of a scene had been interrupted by a camera malfunction. We were waiting for the camera replacement to shoot the same scene again. Looking down into the studio from the window in the directorial control room, I spotted Eve in a corner of the studio, behind the sets, as if in a small cage. She was unplaiting and plaiting again an artificial braid. Her fingers were moving mechanically. I realized that she was in trouble.

"Wait, for me, please," I said quickly, to my assistant, "I'll be back soon."

I ran down to the studio. I stumbled on some cables. She did not hear me when I approached her. I touched her shoulder. She moved nervously.

"Are you O.K., Eve?"

"I'm trying to focus. Is this break going to be long?"

"No. We are about to run."

"How was my scene?" She asked. In her eyes I saw an actor's cry for help. The cry of an actor confused by the directorial notes, by the blinding lights, by the constant movement of cameras, by the technicians milling behind the sets. She was tense and terrified. She wanted so much for her first leading role in television to be a success. It was her big chance. And my responsibility. During that interrupted recording, she had been bad. She had lost everything she had achieved at the rehearsals; it was as it she lost herself. She did not hold pauses, contacts, smiles. She had stiffened her spine and blocked her veins. She was in a hurry. She was shallow and technical. She played as if she wanted to do it as fast as she could, and run away from the studio. I knew that I would have to tell her something which will bring back her warmth, delicacy, and that unusual smile of hers, so necessary in this role, a smile which was a mix of surprise, almost sad and almost close to weeping, and, at the same time, open, bright, and hopeful. It was for that mysterious smile, besides her obvious talent and skill, that I casted her. This role had to make her a young star. Right now she was far from that. What could I tell her? Nothing, in terms of directorial technical advice, I knew. It needed to be something which would transform her internally and allow her to be herself again. What? I wanted her to cross the border, to break the barrier. How to do it? I was filled with a true, overwhelming, unlimited tenderness to her, and wished her all the good in the world. I wanted her to play her role eminently well. I wanted her to fly. I loved her as God loved the first woman as He was creating her in paradise. I wanted to create her. I was moved and determined. I gathered my whole energy, will power, and, yes, love, and I wanted to breathe all that at her, but I said only:

"Listen, Eve, all that is not important..."

"Not important?" She interrupted me.

"Not important. The cameras. The crew. Your wig. Your career. My directorial notes. The blocking."

"What? The blocking is not important?" She was even more terrified.

I continued: "No. Not at all. Nothing matters beyond one thing. You know what to do in this scene? Do you?"

"Yes." She said.

"Do it. Do only this. This. Nothing else."

I rushed back to the control room. The studio was ready. The actors took places. The shooting went on. She was brilliant.

Timing the space

My first encounters with performance space in my family's "home theater," as well as the stories about my aunt's war productions mounted in the desert, taught me that theater can simply happen anywhere.

It was an irony of the history that my theater initiation happened in a "home theater" in my family home, and one of my last productions in Poland also took place in a "home theater." During martial law in Poland in the 1980s, an important element of resistance against the communist military regime was the boycott of the official mass media, first of all television, organized by theater artists, joined by scholars, virtuosos, and intellectuals. At the same time, theater people performed in churches and in private homes, thus avoiding censorship. I participated both in the boycott and in the underground theater. In the fall of 1982, I prepared the staging of my own play *Valesa,* in the home of my friends, and in spring 1983, of my other play, *Before I Conclude* (later published under the title *The Boycott*). It was impossible to produce these plays in public theaters since they referred to moral and political choices facing the Poles during martial law and contested the regime. The censorship would not allow that. In both cases actors sat in a corner of the room at a table facing about 60 spectators sitting on chairs and on floor, hanging wherever they could. These people were invited only by word of mouth—the telephones were bugged. Interacting as characters, actors stood up and moved in a tiny space, almost waking on the spectators toes. Both actors and spectators were threatened by the possibility of a police raid. They shared the same values and views. They wanted to be together. They created a strong community. As in my youth, I experienced physically and emotionally the perfect unity between the performance and its space.

During my first year at the directing department, Axer asked all students of his seminar to prepare a project for a theater of their dreams. I proposed a theater architecture which I would call today simply a black box—a flexible theater space in which actors and spectators could freely mingle. When I presented it in class, Axer, a born and practicing traditionalist, listened to me with abomination. He told me that actors would be too distracted by the closeness of the spectators and they could not fully develop their roles. I kept this remark in my memory as a warning, but did not abandon my interest in non-proscenium spatial structures.

Pronaszko explained to me the practical and technical means of transgressing the proscenium. Jean Vilar showed me an open-air theater of an incredible power in the Papal Palace yard in Avignon. Greece offered me productions in ruined and also in newly restored ancient theaters. Robert Wilson's *Prologue,* which I saw in Paris, was played in several locations in the theater building. The study of ancient, Medieval, and Elizabethan theater architecture, as well as Far Eastern and African theaters, opened up for me the richness of theater spaces in various times and cultures, and gave me insight into a plethora of ideas and achievements in the matter of performance space.

I learned that the proscenium, an invention of the Italian baroque court theater in the 17th century, which worked well for illusionistic moving sceneries and opera productions, has been repeatedly contested. Early in the 19th century, romantic shows used theater-circuses, which were large prosceniums having a circus arena in front of the stage, allowing huge crowd scenes and horse riding. During the 19th century, German artists, including Ludwig Tieck, Gottfried Semper, Egon Putlitz, and Karl Leutheschläger, tried to reconstruct the Elizabethan theater structure and stage in it Shakespeare's plays. In the 20th century, Shakespearian stages were built in Stratford, Canada, in Chichester, England, and elsewhere. In his Bayreuth Festspielhaus, built in 1876, Richard Wagner attempted to use the Greek amphitheatrical *theatron* in order to situate audiences closer to the stage and to ease the division between the playing and observation areas of the traditional proscenium. At the end of the 19th century and at the beginning of the 20th century, directors put on productions in the ruins of old Greek and Roman theaters and amphitheaters. Copeau, Firmin Gémier, Osterwa, and others remodeled their theaters in order to allow easier contact between actors and spectators. Reinhardt, Nikolai Evreinov, Teofil Trzciński, and, again, Copeau and Osterwa, put on shows in real architecture. Meyerhold, Piscator, Burian, Pronaszko, and others came up with projects for a completely new theater architecture. Schiller in Warsaw, and Nikolai Okhlopkov in Moscow actually staged productions in a non-traditional spatial manner in the 1930s. I started to feel that the proscenium was not the best theater architecture for the shows of the second half of the 20th century.

As a young director, however, I usually worked on proscenium stages and I did not question them at first. Through my work on models, and in collaborating with designers, I was learning how to effectively use the proscenium. I treated the stage interior as a canvas for painting. With sets, lights, costumes, and movements, I built entire pulsating images. The proscenium was a serviceable space for them, but later I found that theater images and visions might be created in any space. Intensive visuality emerged as one of the dominating characteristics of my work. More and more actively I participated in the design process, and eventually started to design on my own. Prosceniums were available everywhere. I mounted productions on huge proscenium stages, such as the Polski Theater in Warsaw, the Słowackiego Theater in Cracow, the Wybrzeże Theater in Gdańsk, the Polski Theater in Wrocław, as well as the Olympia Theater in Dublin, Ireland, the city theater in Jassi, Rumania, and on some German stages. There were also numerous smaller proscenium theaters in which I directed. In some of them I made temporary or permanent architectural adaptations in order to somehow ease the rigidity of the proscenium structure. In the Osterwa Theater in Lublin, the stage was connected with the auditorium by steps. In the Contemporary Theater in Wrocław I installed a wide forestage enlarging the whole playing area and acquiring the ability to move action back and forth between the stage proper and the forestage. From time to time it was necessary to made additional constructions. Some of my productions were played on a stage used as a black box, usually with a central playing area around which the public sat or stood on bleachers. For *Mother Courage* I covered the whole stage as well as the walls of auditorium with white drapes, giving an impression of an unified space, an outdoor winter landscape. (*Mother Courage's* action always takes place outdoors.) Across the auditorium I built a platform, a sort of a *hanamitchi,* which gave more options for the movement of Mother Courage's wagon. In Galați, Romania, I had an arena stage in the center of the proscenium theater auditorium. By putting one section of chairs on stage and use the proscenium boxes the audience was situated on all four sides of the round platform. Directing *The Card Index*, I needed a playing area representing a street, with spectators on both sides, as if on the sidewalks. Thus, I built a rectangular platform in front of the proscenium, covering the first rows of chairs, and put one section of seats for the spectators on stage with the audience seated in the auditorium. This spatial arrangement was used in Sofia, Bulgaria, in Storrs at the University of Connecticut, and in South Bend at Notre Dame University, among other places.

Being involved as a consultant in the construction of a new theater in Lublin (a promising project which failed to materialize) I felt that I had to learn more. Extensive research resulted in writing a book, *Theater Space;* one of these instances when as I was learning, I wrote a book in order to share my findings with others.

In America I got two excellent tools—the thrust stage and the black box. I worked on thrust stages in The Guthrie in Minneapolis and in the Pfeifer Theater in Buffalo. I tasted and tested the black box advantages first in SUNY at Buffalo's Harriman Hall, where an old and dilapidated proscenium theater could be transformed into a very handy black box. I mounted *The Time of Your Life* there, designed as an environment, with a jukebox, piano, small performance platform, bar, and tables and chairs, with spectators in several small sections of chairs all over the interior of the Nick's bar. A door, leading directly to the parking lot, served as powerful *coup de théâtre* when police burst into bar. In *Largo Desolato* by Vaclav Havel, which I prepared in the black box at the Kalamazoo Theater Festival (1990) I built a total environment of the interior of the Prague apartment of a Czech dissident. It was composed of two connected rooms, a kitchen, a bathroom, and a balcony. Spectators were placed inside the environment in small sections of chairs on bleachers. They could feel as if they were invisible guests of the owner of the apartment, or as if they were subletting it. Later on, I used the Black Box Theater in the Center for the Arts at SUNY Buffalo with delight.

Another opportunity to stage productions in an unique theater space was provided in a replica of the Elizabethan theater structure in Delaware Park in Buffalo. It is situated in a small valley and the public sits on the slope in front of it. It's an efficient performance space. In *Julius Caesar* and in *King Lear* I added a runway across the slope, connecting the main stage with a platform on top of the hill. The traffic up and down the hill on the runway energized movement in both shows.

Productions in real spaces

Curiosity as to how other performance spaces may function drew me to further experiments. I made my next step using natural spaces and locations for productions or parts of them. The real, natural, or "found" space has a multifaced impact on production, influencing actors' performance and spectators' perception. Actors dealing with real space can plunge deeper into the inner layers of their souls, focusing on the characters' deeds. They are neither disturbed by the artificiality of the sets nor required to imagine the space they supposedly are in. From the audience's point of view, real space both alienates spectators from the show, influencing them intellectually, and, at the same time, it draws spectators deeper into the show emotionally. It is a paradoxical mechanism, which I have observed several times, and every time it worked to the advantage of the show.

In 1968 we went with the Lublin theater on tour to Macedonia, with *Hamlet* and *Cleopatra and Caesar* by Norwid. I had a fabulous opportunity to stage it in the ruins of the ancient Roman theater in Stobi near Skopje. Roman troops, marching on two thousand years old stones, or Caesar meeting Cleopatra amidst white marble broken columns, provided me with unforgettable memories. In Wrocław, I staged the same tragedy by Norwid in the Museum of Architecture, which also provided a fitting environment for the ancient action. A comedy by Fredro, *Litta and Company,* a popular and funny entertainment, was played on a platform put on in the town square in Wrocław, near the monument to the author, which was ironically referred to during the action. A part of *The Forefathers' Eve* was played in a Wrocław church. Later, both in Poland and in America, I had an opportunity to stage whole shows in churches. Directing in the shadowy naves and in soaring sanctuaries I was traveling in my thoughts back to the medieval cathedrals, where the nativity, the morality, and the passion plays were staged for enraptured congregations of believers.

The "Walking Theater"

Setting productions in real spaces, I soon found that the expression and impact of the show may be enhanced by the use of several different venues in the same production. This resulted in moving the audience during the show. Spectators went from one venue to another.

Moving the public from location to location or asking spectators to walk along with the actors is an old tradition in many theater cultures, extensively used in the Medieval theater all over Europe, in the Spanish Golden Age Corpus Christi pageants, and elsewhere. Contemporary street productions use this device too. In many productions I provided circumstances for the public to move from scene to scene, from a venue to a venue. It happened as early as 1973, in my *Old Woman Broods*, in Lublin. We played various parts of this production in different locations. First, in the theater, but not on stage—the stage and the auditorium were unified by a large platform equipped with rows of benches on two sides for the public, with the playing area in the center. Second, in the theater's yard, where the playing area was on the roof, and then in the parking lot. Third, on the street, as a procession of actors and spectators. And, fourth, back in the theater, in the rehearsal room. Visiting Warsaw with the same production, we played in a black box theater, and then on the street. Instead of the roof, an actor used a fourth floor window, and a fire brigade with a huge truck and ladders helped him down—a happening-like part of the show. *The Old Woman Broods* in Dublin, Ireland had its prologue on the street in front of the theater, the first part was played in the art gallery in the theater's lobby, and the second in the theater proper in which an environment was built.

Walking the public was the principle behind the use of space in both of my productions of *The Forefathers' Eve* (in 1978 and 1982). In the 1978 *Forefathers'* production, the first part of the show took place in the theater, the second in a church, the third, back in the theater, and the fourth in a museum. Spectators waked from venue to venue through a modern city, which, I thought, had an alienating effect for them and allowed for historical reflection, comparing the time of the action with that of their own lives. In the 1982 version of the same play, we used only the theater, for under martial law a large group of spectators would not have been allowed on the streets; it would have been considered a political demonstration and attacked by the police. We performed first in the theater basement under the stage, then on stage, used as a black box with the public standing around the playing area, and then on stage with the public sitting in the auditorium.

Birth Rate (1979) in Wrocław was performed also in several venues. First, in the rehearsal room, where the director held a workshop for a group of audience members. Second, the public participated in a series of scenes played in our small theater, called the "Prop Room," next door to the main theater building. The scenes were staged in different corners of the Prop Room for small groups of spectators guided by actors. From there, the public was walked to the main theater. The third part of the show was played in the lobby with the public standing and the actors using a staircase as the playing area. The fourth part was done on stage with the public sitting in the auditorium. For the fifth, the public was asked to enter onto the stage used as a black box, with a central playing area surrounded by bleachers for the audience standing around. On tours in Poland, Germany, Ireland, and Spain we have always used different venues in the theater building and the city surrounding it. In Dublin some scenes were played in the hospital next door to the Gate Theater in Dublin (1980). In Sitges, Spain (1980), participating in the International Theater Festival, we staged one scene on the seashore; another one was played as a parade in the old port, and the next at the railway station. I used the device of walking the public in *The Iliad,* performed in Poland and in Japan. My "model production," *The Plague,* was also played in a non-traditional space with the public moving from venue to venue. I will talk more about that production later on.

In America, my "Walking Theater," as some people called it, was used in productions of *The Hunger Artist Departs* (1986), *The Time of Your Life* (1988), *Antigone in New York* (1995), and *Dummies Ball* (1997). In *The Hunger Artist* spectators first visited the Author writing in his studio, a character created in the adaptation, and then his creation, the Hunger Artist, fasting in his cage situated on the thrust stage. Eventually, spectators took their seats in the auditorium. In *The Time of Your Life,* almost the entire action takes place in Nick's bar, except for one scene which is located in a hotel room. The bar was an environment with spectators inside. For the hotel scene, the public was asked to move within the same building to a hallway, where they could observe action in the hotel room through a glass door and a window. The scene was staged in an a department conference room; microphones allowed for hearing the lines. After that scene, spectators returned to the first environment. In *Antigone in New York* (1995), collaborating with the excellent stage designer Madeleine Sobota, we used two adjacent black boxes. In the first, Madeleine built the environment of Tompkins Square Park in New York, with trees, bushes, grass, alleys, benches, lamps, trash cans, and several *mansions* of the homeless; the observation areas were scattered inside the park. In the other black box we had the pier in the port, with many coffins in a large playing area, with the public standing at one side. After the pier scene, the public returned to the first environment. *Dummies Ball* (1997) was performed in two theaters in the Center for the Arts at SUNY Buffalo. The first part was played in the proscenium theater and the second in the black box theater. The action on stage took place in the fashion magazine and was seen by the public as if through a window display. The black box was set as the environmental interior of a wealthy automaker's mansion.

If I were to be asked: why all that? Why not quietly and politely use the old-fashioned and safe proscenium only? Why give the technical director a headache, and the public discomfort? (I have sometimes been asked such questions.) My answer is simple. I do it, first, in order to establish a covenant between the action and the space; and, second, to freely create in the domain of theater space, as I try to do in all other areas of theater. I advise my students to do so too. I don't want to prompt them about how to solve certain space problems. I want to share with them the attitude of searching. So, here's my advice: be free in creating space. Only this, and as much as this. Choose, use, and build theater space as necessary for each particular production you direct. Be free. Be creative.

Audience freedom

It seems to me that there's a certain "freedom syndrome" in the theater. The more freely you create, the freer is the public. Being free in the case of the theater public means being active, imaginative, eager to think, and ready to offer compassion. The creativity of director is reciprocated with audience creativity.

Spectators, along with actors, make theater. It is a fundamental truth and I wonder why so many directors disregard spectators, preparing productions as if for themselves only. Observing dozens of performances of the same play as an assistant in the Contemporary Theater in Warsaw, I had the chance not only to see actors performing for different audiences, but most importantly, to listen to, and feel, the very different reactions of audiences to the same production. In my first season as professional, I directed *Tonight We Improvise* by Pirandello in the Wybrzeże Theater in Gdańsk (in 1962), a play which I translated from Italian. The character of the Director, according to the author, occupies a seat in the auditorium, and from time to time intervenes in stage events. It was fascinating to observe how excited spectators were that one of them was taking an active part in the action, even if they knew, of course, that he was an actor. I have been finding vivid public reaction and participation literally on every page of the theater history books. As a student, I wondered why the public was so passive in Poland in the 1950s.

It was different when Polish productions started to be loaded with political content and political allusions to which the public reacted hysterically after "October 1956." It was different in some experimental productions that I saw abroad and in the Wrocław alternative theater festival. I personally was a spectator ready to interact at early *happenings,* like those created in Lublin in the 1970s by Tomek Kawiak (later an internationally acclaimed sculptor). Directing in television, on the other hand, I felt the lack of a live audience and I helplessly tried to imagine how people would react at home seeing my shows; it was very frustrating. Perhaps because of this feeling of emptiness and longing for a live audience, I gradually lost interest in directing for television. I had another experience with the public, when, as artistic director of the Lublin theater, which toured extensively in the surrounding small towns, I could see and sense different reactions of different audiences for the same play.

Audience participation might be emotional, physical, mental, or spiritual. It is worthwhile to reflect on how it happens and use it, or, if we prefer so, to consciously avoid it. Involving the audience is a matter of the attitude of the theater artist and the result of the production's structure.

In terms of attitude, spectators must get clear signals that the actors respect them and anticipate their being a part of the show. This attitude has an internal and external side to it. Internally, even if hidden, it is felt by the public. I expect that scholars will some day describe how bio-currents and psycho-waves circulate between actors and spectators in theater. Without such research, we still can tell that the actors' attitude towards the public is readable either consciously or unconsciously by the public. Spectators can tell how an actor treats them. The actor's attitude manifests itself in the level of the energy expenditure, in terms of voice, movement, and overall performance (I'm not talking of course about loudness, for instance!), in the firmness of the focus, in the ability to pause, in the personal truthfulness; yes, spectators can tell if the actor is "telling the truth," or if the actor "lies." Having seen thousands of productions in my life, after the first scene of a play I can relate if the actors like to play for me or not, if they are thrilled to be with me this very night or they are bored to death, if they are playing for fun or only because they are getting paid for it, if they are sincere with me or want to deceive me.

Actors, if prepared to do so during rehearsals, might internally and externally express a special care for the audience. Travelling with my productions abroad, at first I did not make any special efforts to reach out to foreign audiences. It was a mistake. One of the many from which I learned. In order to communicate with foreign audiences, it was not enough to play as well as at home, and provide a translated synopsis of the play in the program. By the way, the headsets allowing for simultaneous translation during the show are for me beneath theater's dignity. They are helpful at conferences. In theater they destroy the magic. I have never used them in my productions.

I remember standing in the back of a dark auditorium during my theater first foreign tour, I was astonished how differently the public reacted. Why? It was stupid of me, but I suddenly realized that these people did not understand the words. What a discovery! They saw images, they felt the energies of the actors, but they did not comprehend the words. This meant that for them the production should be prepared in a different way. How? Next time, planing a tour abroad, I decided to translate some soliloquies, dialogues, or songs into the language of the public of the country we were going to. The actors learned their texts with tutors. It worked. The audiences were enthusiastic. I realized that it was not so much the matter of translating parts of the show into language which the public understood—this might have been achieved by selling scripts of the play in the foyer. It was for sure the matter of manifesting the attitude. Speaking or singing in Greek, German, English, French, Spanish, Russian, or Japanese, even mispronouncing the words, the actors sent an unmistakable message: we want to communicate with you! We are making a special effort to reach you! We need to be with you! It was reciprocated with warmth and love. When I planned a tour with a Polish production to Japan I decided to translate some songs and soliloquies into Japanese, as we previously did with the European languages. The actors learned their texts by heart not knowing Japanese a bit. It worked. They were understood by Japanese audiences. People in Tokyo, Kanazawa and Sapporo cherished the efforts of Polish actors to speak their tongue and loved the show. There were endless standing ovations and communication was very strong. When during our Dublin visit with *Anna Livia,* Teresa Sawicka delivered the final, long soliloquy in English, the applause was wild. An additional way to communicate with foreign audiences, was the director's interaction with audiences, critics, and theater people before the show: not in a form of a press conference or lecture, rather as a workshop and discussion on the major artistic and intellectual problems of the production.

In terms of the structure, the production has to be open to the public and include certain spots or segments which would be filled by spectators. In order to allow space for the audience, the production's structure should be somehow loose. Events should leave unlighted corridors of mystery. The interpretation should not be so definitive as to leaving spectators no room for their own conclusions. The space should allow audience activity; with some effort this might be done in proscenium theaters, and is easier in black boxes, real spaces, or in open-air venues. In any case, contact between spectators and actors should be possible, exchange assured, participation—of any kind—facilitated, and community encouraged.

There are also problems stemming from the public's makeup. You can usually know who is coming to see your show in general terms—what social, age, or cultural group. But you cannot always control the public behavior or reaction. Only rarely can you have any impact on the reviewers. But it's always worthwhile to anticipate both who is coming and how the spectators will react. As a speaker should be prepared for friendly, neutral, and hostile questions after the talk, a director should prepare actors for different kinds of public reception. In my directing journey I encountered many different types of public. When I was unprepared, and my actors were caught off guard, it usually ended in disaster. Conversely, efforts to accommodate specific audiences usually paid back, both at home and abroad. The example of productions prepared especially for foreign audiences showed it clearly. Their gratitude for our playing especially for them was always infinite. They sent true love to actors after the shows.

Playing for foes

Sometime it is impossible to communicate with the audience, or some members of it. Critics might come with their prejudices ready to sentence the show to death before it started. Some political groups might come with their agendas and try to disrupt the show. You can do nothing, except to maintain your calm and pride, and stick to your principles. It happened to me in Poland and it happened to me in America. In Poland it was the humiliating ritual of playing for censors, repeated before every opening . Each production had to be censored. The permit to play for the public was granted, or not. There were two stages of theater censorship: first, the censorship of the play, and second, the censorship of a ready production. Censors came to see a ready show during the second general rehearsal. If they ordered cuts or changes, the theater had one more general rehearsal to dress the wounds inflicted by censors in the body of the production before the opening.

I vividly remember those general rehearsals attended by censors. Sometimes their verdict was uncertain. Sometimes, I anticipated a fight. A Siberian wind blew through the empty auditorium with a few gloomy and tense figures sitting in the third or fourth row in the center; sometimes there was a whole commission of several officials. I took my place somewhere in the corner.

I had my first personal encounter with the censors at the first general rehearsal of the very first show I directed in professional theater. I have already mention that production of three one-acts by Mrożek, *Karol, Out at Sea,* and *Striptease* in the Wybrzeże Theater in Gdańsk. In *Karol* Mrożek portrayed three typical characters—at that time in Poland: Grandpa, a stubborn old-timer, supposedly a representative of the Party "concrete" as they were called; his Grandson, a young, stupid, boorish, narrow-minded, and power-hungry activist; and an Optometrist, an intellectual, terrorized by those two, afraid to the point of servility. The play, along with other two one-acts, was permitted by the censors probably only because its contents was expressed in Mrożek's witty, subtle, allusionistic, and metaphoric way. The censors must have been sensing a political perversion, but could not point out any specific line or action which would undermine the system. It came out on stage. My costume designer, Ali Bunsch, an excellent artist and a staunch anti-communist, gave Grandpa a red scarf. Not a typical red tie, which would be too obvious, but, still a red wool scarf. The censors jumped on it after the show. "We know who the author wanted to ridicule here!" shouted the senior censor. "And you, comrade young director..."—they called me comrade, even though I did not belong to the Party—"...you comrade young director, you associate yourself with this attack on the old guard of the Revolution." As so forth, and so on... On the orders of the censors, the red scarf was changed into a blue one. Even in the blue—the public knew who Grandpa was.

A few years later in Gdańsk, I directed *November Night* by Wyspiański, a poetic, imaginative tragedy with a great mise-en-scène potential, which I tried to use to its fullest. A classical national masterpiece passed the initial stage of censorship without a problem; the production seen by censors at the general rehearsal was accepted without discussions. Watching the opening was an unforgettable experience for me. The overwhelming majority of the public was enthusiastic, while a few gloomy faces in the first rows indicated the critics and Party officials. Just after the opening a bomb shell exploded. A reviewer from the Party newspaper wrote that the production was "anti-Soviet" and, therefore, was an unacceptable offense to the everlasting Polish-Soviet friendship. It happened, from time to time, that the censors were not vigilant enough, and the Party reviewers had to correct their errors. This was precisely the case. Of course, *November Night* is an anti-Russian play—a history of the Polish uprising against Russians. But, though having a clear political and historical sting, it is also an universal, poetic metaphor about death and resurrection, a parable about the seed which must die in the ground in order that the grain can grow and crop may abound. For the communist critic, however, "anti-Russian" was simply equal to "anti-Soviet." The censorship revoked the permit and the show was taken off the bill.

Still further on in my directorial work, I prepared in Lublin, with my young, energetic and talented company, a production based on contemporary poetry, mostly Różewicz's, under the title *Penetration* (1971). It was a chain of stage visions revolving around conflicts between the young and the old, between freedom and oppression, between artistic creation and the dull reality of life. Both the stage and literary language was symbolic, metaphoric, and purposely hazy. For my company and myself it was an extremely important statement. But for the censors? They approved the collection of poems for production. But when they saw what we did with them on stage, they were stunned and terrified. They observed the general rehearsal with growing dismay, then banned the production on the spot. I had several confrontational discussions with them and finally they gave me the permission to play under the condition that several cuts would be made. It was presented to me as an ultimatum: either I accepted the cuts or the show would not be played at all. In order to save the show, I consented. We gave the première. The reception of the public was ecstatic. What a difference: a difference between two completely different receptions of the same production. One was attended by a hostile public—the censors; the other one by friends. The ovation after the opening alarmed the censors again. At every production, in every theater in Poland, every night two free seats had to be reserved for the censors. They were coming to see every performance of *Penetration*. They ordered new cuts. I opposed them. A sort of arbitration was decided upon: a dignitary from the central committee of the Party would come and evaluate the show. The man came and saw it. He presented to me a new ultimatum: either I would quietly remove the play from the repertoire or I would be removed from the artistic directorship of the theater. If I would not agree to take the play off the bill and therefore was dismissed, the play, of course, would not be performed anyway. It was a tough choice. I discussed it with trusted members of my ensemble. We decided that it was not—not yet—the time to pay the ultimate price. *Penetration* was played never again. The time to pay that ultimate price came later.

Before it came, I had several other fights with the censors. Every time I experienced that radical difference in the reception of the production. During the general rehearsal played only for censors the actors encountered reserve, suspicion, and rejection. During the opening and the following performances, it was like running towards a friend's open arms, ready to hug you.

When finally, thanks to the pressure and efforts of many directors, including myself, plays of the émigré Witold Gombrowicz, unwanted by the communist regime, were allowed to be produced in Poland, I took on *Operetta*. It was in 1977 in Wrocław. Alert censors came to see the rehearsal, and strictly observed the action. One of the characters, Hufnagel, the leader of the revolution, wore a leather cap in the style of a Bolshevik commissar. The censors spotted it. They ordered us to change the cap to a bowler. They did not understand that this was a double irony: a leader of a popular revolution wearing a bowler hat.

The Hunger Artist Departs by Różewicz had its world premiere in my Contemporary Theater in Wrocław in the same year as *Operetta*, 1977. The production, directed by Helmut Kajzar, was sharp, beautiful, and wise. But the censors did not like it. After the general rehearsal they put forth several accusations against the author, the director, and, of course, myself, who, as artistic director, allowed such a subversive production to be prepared. Among the many accusations, two were most severe. First, in the play the Butchers watch the Hunger Artist, making sure that he doesn't eat during his forty-day fast. They, themselves, eat and drink all the time. They eat meat. And there are shortages of meat at the market. "It's a provocation!" Second, there is a scene in which people are waiting in line to buy tickets for the show of the Hunger Artist's release from the cage after his fast. People are complaining and fighting while waiting in the line. "But it doesn't read as a line for tickets for the show, comrades! It's a nasty allusion to all lines in front of all stores in Poland! It's also a provocation!" Among others cuts, the censors ordered us not to form a line for tickets at all, and to replace meat by fish.

The Plague—my "model production"

Finally, came my last battle with the censors, and, indeed with the whole system of control of the theater in a Poland ruled by the communists. My last stand was *The Plague*. After martial law was imposed in Poland on December 13, 1981, we—the whole company of the Contemporary Theater in Wrocław—had been thinking what our artistic response to the situation should be. We prepared several productions which expressed both ours and the nation's opposition to the regime.

The most important of all of those productions was *The Plague*. During the general rehearsal the censors were milling impatiently and exchanged loud remarks. Immediately after the end of the show, the head of the commission announced the sentence to me: performances of *The Plague* were prohibited. They told me that the production undermined the political order in the country and attacked the authorities. If performed, it threatened to instigate riots and street demonstrations. By no means would it be permitted. I did not give up. After several hours of discussions and negotiations the permission was given for two "closed" performances under the conditions that some lines and mise-en-scène elements were cut. Ads and any information about the opening in the media were banned. But the word of mouth was enough for the theater to overflow with the public. Two productions were given on May 6 and 7, 1983. And again we experienced the night and day difference between the show for the censors and for the theater goers.

It's time to say more about *The Plague*. I have already referred to it on some occasions, especially talking about the aesthetic and ethical dimensions of acting. *The Plague* was indeed my "model production" in terms of acting, writing an adaptation, and creating the space.

In terms of acting, I have already described the perfect unity of the character of the Teacher and the person of the actor playing this role. Similar phenomena typified the entire cast. All the actors who performed *The Plague* created profound and expressive roles, and, at the same time, put their personalities behind the characters with ultimate determination. They believed in what they were doing and saying. The spectators believed them. An extraordinary sense of community and cohesion was the foundation of both the production and its reception.

From the textual point of view *The Plague* was based on Albert Camus' novel and *The Journal of the Plague Year* by Daniel Defoe. In writing the adaptation, I used almost none of the elements of either works in a direct way, but, at the same time, I reconstructed their meaning and message in the theater material. Defoe described the plague in London in the 17th century. Camus, writing in the 1940s, metaphorically referred to Nazism. I added to that my personal knowledge of the communist rule in Poland since 1945, and especially under the martial law of the 1980s. How did the plague operate? How did the English society react to the fatal disease? How did the French nation cope with the universal disease of Nazism? How did the Poles face the communist scourge?

By studying Camus' and Defoe's works and examining my own experience, I was led to the conclusion that the plague—both practically and metaphorically—works by breaking ties, destroying communication and contact between people. The plague performs an act of separation and exile. Everybody is alone in the presence of the plague. Everybody dies alone when infected by the plague. Everybody living in the time of plague has to chose whether to face it with either dignity or lowliness. Everybody individually makes a moral choice as to what is his/her attitude towards the plague. The human attitude of dignity is based on recognition that the plague is evil—an evil outside, as well as inside the person. The attitude of lowliness presumes fear. It is a denial of the fact that plague is plague, and, therefore, that evil is evil. Dignity means truth. Lowliness means the lie. We cannot control plague, when it rages, but we can control our own choices towards it. Consequently, denying that we are facing the plague, we participate in culture of death. Contradicting the plague, we create a culture of life, no matter if we personally survive or not. We can fight the plague telling the truth; not allowing the societal ties and structures to disintegrate; maintaining them even under mortal danger; and restoring them when they are destroyed by plague. The question for me was how to express these mechanisms and problems in theatrical terms.

I decided to strip the action from the text. I disconnected them. There was no dialogue between the plague representatives and their victims. Only those united in the fight against the plague were allowed to have interactions. The social group represented by the spectators was also broken and divided, to express that every spectator is alone in the presence of plague as the characters are. Both actors and spectators at that time in Poland faced the plague on an equal basis. Technically, the whole script was composed only of soliloquies which were usually narrated by the characters using the third person and the past tense, and addressed the audience directly, not the partners, thus additionally alienating the text from the action. The character of the Teacher, for example, would neither speak directly to the partner, nor, in talking to a spectator, would use the form: "I think..." Rather, the Teacher would say: "The teacher thought that..." Not before the final scene was the awareness of unity and solidarity restored and communication allowed. The action either mirrored or contradicted the monologues. New characters, not existing in the originals, were introduced, such as the Doorman's Wife, the Nurses, and the Rats, the representatives, carriers, and guardians of plague. The fundamental disconnection between the words and actions seemed to be the clearest expression of what the plague is, how it operates, how it confronts people, and, ultimately, how one can take a stand against it: by siding with truth and life, and thus uniting the broken world.

The Plague's spatial structure reflected the philosophical decomposition of the world shown in the action. The production was played in several venues. Spectators waked from one to another.

The first part, called *The Entrance of the Rats*, was played on the stage, with the playing area in the center and the public standing around on graded platforms. The curtain was closed. The whole space was transformed into a black box.

Then, the action spit into three simultaneously performed episodes, played in three separate spaces, for three groups of the public. The public was led from space to space and each episode was played three times. *The Fight Against the Plague* was played in the rehearsal room which was decorated and equipped like a hospital ward, with beds for dying patients, served by doctors and nurses; the audience was seated on three sides of the playing area. The next episode, *Escapism,* was staged in the theater's foyer; a writer's study was set on a platform and standing spectators surrounded it from three sides. The third episode, *Spiritual Resistance,* was in the theater basement, in a huge empty space below the stage. In the center was an altar and the public sat on benches against three walls. That venue represented an internment camp, and its concrete walls provided with the mood of a real prison. Spectators, led from space to space, encountered in many different places the Journalist, who was trapped in the closed city, appealed for an exit permit in several offices to no avail, and finally was put into prison. The second act of the production was played in the traditional proscenium format.

Because of the media blackout there were no reviews of the show. Only one well-established critic from Warsaw, Tomasz Raczek, got the permission to publish a description of the show and a review of it. I'll quote him below in order not to portray *The Plague* by myself. Here's a witness testifying.

"We are inside the Contemporary Theater in Wrocław. The audience, a strangely embarrassed procession, enters the stage through a narrow passage, stops behind the raised curtain, surrounding the square area amphitheatrically. The center is furnished with a table, four chairs, a vase of flowers; beside, there is a gas oven with a few pots on it. They contain the doorman dinner. The are evidently hot and they smell delicious. The curtain falls behind our backs and blocks the view of the empty seats in the auditorium. The doorman sits down at table, and his wife takes her time serving potatoes, meat, and then jelly from the aromatic saucepans. A doorkeeper's usual peaceful dinner. And yet, there is something unusual about it as it is interrupted with the news that a dead rat has been found in the cellar. Every bit of food brings new information. The number of rats grows and THE PLAGUE enters the doorkeeper's room with the dessert. At first one rat emerges from under the table, sits down on the doorkeeper's chair and makes a dash for his food. It is followed by others who sit down to the feast. The doorkeeper dies. The rats mix with the crowd and fight their way among us. They stop behind our back. The rats, the carriers of the plague, are carefully dressed waiters with napkins over their arms in Kazimierz Braun's production in Wrocław. It soon turns out that the waiters/rats are also masters of ceremony who engage us in their rite. ... Suddenly, the table, still steaming with the doorkeeper's unfinished dinner, transforms into an operating table. The doctor stands beside and write death certificates with growing trepidation. Neither he nor the other doctor know yet that the newly-arrived patients are under sentence: they certainly cannot tell how heavy the sentence is. How many corpses does one need to embrace the dimension of the imminent horror? A few dozen to be able to give it a name. Thousands in order to understand, though one cannot tell for certain. The Doctor has realized that the city is pervaded by the plague. ...

The waiters/rats divide the public into three groups. They make imperious gestures to show the people which way to go. The three crowds separate, ushered by the rats towards their experiences. In the corridor, a boy in blue jeans stops them on their way. He shouts: "He was not from here, he was a foreign journalist, he had the right to leave..." The outcry is irrational as it calls for individual rights when the plague has deprived the community of any rights. This is the first introduction of the ghastly atmosphere. Genuinely ghastly, just as the teenager's outcry in an empty corridor. We follow a rat in our way through the theater passages, corridors, cellars. The remaining two crowds of spectators move as silently as ourselves somewhere near.

We are ushered into the room of the writer. A bed, a bedside table with a lamp and alarm clock, a desk, a kettle, a mug—these are objects of the writer's daily existence. ... The rat who has brought us here makes himself comfortable in an armchair. He looks derisively at the sleeping writer. In a minute, he will bring destruction upon his world. He sets the alarm clock running. The radio, the telephone, a record, and the loud-speaker bring the news of the ever more stringent rigorous of the time of the plague. [The TV set was banned by the censorship as directly connecting action with contemporary Poland.] The world of order and work, the world of systematic civilization principles begins to crumble and disintegrate. Though in distress, the writer does not give up. He separates himself from the world. He draws the curtains, turns off the radio, sits at his desk and for the hundredth time moves to the world of the lovely horsewoman who rides a beautiful horse through the lanes of forest of Boulogne. He is determined to go on writing. ... So as not to yield to the plague which in the writer's room turns out to be a barbarian force which bluntly claims to be able to suppress order, culture, civilization.

The rat tells us to move on, however. For a while he looks us sneeringly in the eyes, flicks the dust of the desk, and almost imperceptibly, which makes it all the more painfully humiliating, shows us the direction of further march. In the corridor, we hear the crying journalist in blue jeans again. ... We climb down the stairs to the basement. Here, under the stage ... in semi darkness we find places for ourselves by the walls. The rat approaches a movable spotlight with which he illuminates our faces. Sharp light straight in the eyes inspires fear and instinctive rebellion. ... We are in a camp for rebels. For the sake of the remainder of society, for the sake of all the healthy and the sick, they have been locked up ... The priest descends narrow metal stairs to meet them. The rat once again throws a beam of light at our faces which makes us suddenly realize that the priest is speaking to us, that we have filled the stadium for the undisciplined. The priest speaks beautifully for a long time ... to extol the value of eternal life. At that point, in the dusk of the cellar, in the atmosphere of uncertainty and threat, a second thought occurs to us: here, the plague has also become a symbol of evil inherent in ourselves which can be so easily stirred to life. A symbol of mutual enmity, the desire to prove one's own superiority, the littleness that magnifies the impact of real evil. ...

The rat tells us to move on again. Again we hear the journalist who cries that someone "has found himself here quite by chance." There are other corridors, stairs, and rooms. Finally, we enter the hospital ward. We see four carefully made beds, nurses, and doctor. The Teacher also comes here to have an important talk with doctor. Only at the beds of the plague's successive victims, when yet another death is announced, one every few minutes, can we see the plague's third face and understand that both locking oneself in the castle of one's own home and locking others in the camps for the undisciplined is futile task. The only creative interpretation of the plague consists in the statement that ... it can be overcome only through our action. ... Hence ... we should fight not only for the destruction of the plague, but for the salvation of man. The rat/waiter dashes to strip the pedantically spread sheets from the successive beds, which marks successive demises. He turns to us once again and makes a barely precipitable, slighting gesture to order us out of the room.

The next part is enacted in the theater proper. The three united crowds take seats in the auditorium. Transformed into spectators proper, they will be "cheered up" with a comedy by Molière. After a few lines, however, an actress falls ill, another victim of the plague. A double takes her place. She too grows weak, and so does her partner. To "cheer us up" ever new doubles enter the stage. They are older and older, and barely know their lines. The artificially reanimated theater crumbles and faints because the plague does not save the actors. The rats/waiters are about to serve us the final dish. Our ultimate humiliation. They remove the waiter's napkins from their arms and give them away to the survivors. Dismayed and confused, people begin to compete for the rats' affections. They coax the rats and tidy things up, and finally build barbed wire entanglements in the front of the stage. ... The rats go away in the end. They grow bored and sneak away leaving the wire entanglements and people free from fear. The plague stays behind among them. It is no longer dangerous or lethal, but it has taken a much more powerful grip on them than one could expect. They will not be strong enough to dismantle the entanglements."[6]

"The production ... is remarkable, the unquestionable success ... Both the adaptation itself and the show are marked with clarity, concision, and purity of construction. To find such an accurate choice of truly theatrical means of expression (as for instance the idea of rats/waiters) instead of servile reproduction of traditional devices, so rightly and successfully relinquished here, is not a common occurrence. The utter discipline of the cast and the construction of the performance, (partially simultaneous, partially successive,) combine to give a genuine artistic achievement."[7]

After each of the two productions the public stood up and applauded for long, long minutes. Some faces were in tears, some were grim, all ecstatic. But people were calm. They knew that the production was banned and could be not played anymore, so they manifested their support univocally, yet quietly and gently. At the same time, they wanted to let us know how much they appreciated our efforts to say something even with a gag in our mouths. After the ovation, spectators approached the stage and shook hands with the actors, another meaningful gesture of support and oneness. The mise-en-scène provided that at the final scene the stage was closed by a barbed wired fence. So actors and spectators shook hands reaching through the barbed wire. A symbolism impossible to describe.

So there was enthusiasm and support, but no riots, no street protests as predicted by the censors. I used that as an argument in further negotiations with authorities. With a lot of pain, I got permission for six more performances. This, I was told, was the limit. But the fame of the production spread. Interest and pressure from intellectuals, artists, and scholars in Poland, as well as from foreign critics, resulted in one more presentation, and, eventually permission for the production to be performed in the theater's repertoire. With additional pains, in response to invitations pouring in from abroad, I got a permit to show *The*

---

[6] Tomasz Raczek. "The Plague." *Theater in Poland,* Number 1-2, 1984, pp. 26-29.

[7] Tomasz Raczek. "The Plague." *Polityka,* August 6, 1983.

Plague at the West Berlin Theater Festival, in September 1983, and at the Holland Festival in Amsterdam in June 1984. However, permission was not given to play *The Plague* at Belgrade's BITEF Festival in 1983; a BITEF presentation in 1984, as well as a planned tour in Greece in September 1984, and two-week run in London in December 1984, were canceled, because in order to stop the production, its director was fired by the authorities and the theater closed. It happened July 4, 1984.

But the image of actors and spectators shaking hands through the barbed wire stayed with me forever.

My long journey into American theater

I have been traveling to American theater for about 30 years.[8] I'm still on the road. My first contact with American theater came in 1970 when I saw early Wilson's productions in Paris. Later, in Poland I saw the Bread and Puppet Theater, the Performance Group, and the Manhattan Project. Visiting the US, I saw lots of Broadway and off-Broadway including the productions in Open Theater, Mabou Mines, Richard Foreman's Ontological-Hysteric Theater, and Andrei Serban magic rituals in LaMama. Also, I saw Schechner's environmental actions and Wilson's stage dreams again. I saw many regional and university productions. I studied the history of American theater in books by foreigners such as Françoise Kourilsky and Franck Jotterand (whose book I translated into Polish collaborating with my wife Zofia[9]). And, of course, I read books and essays by Americans scholars, critics and artists such as Eric Bentley, Oscar Brockett, Robert Brustein, Robert Corrigan, Margaret Croyden, Robert Findley, Michael Kirby, Arthur Seiner, Richard Schechner, and many others. I became a subscriber

---

[8] In this subchapter I use a bit of my article, "My Long Journey into the American Theater," published in *The Drama Review,* Volume 34, Number 2 (T 126), Summer 1990.

[9] Jotterand, Franck. *Le nouveau théâtre americain,* Editions du Seuil, 1970. Polish translation *Nowy teatr amerykański.* Warszawa: WAiF, 1976. Przekład Zofia i Kazimierz Braun.

of *The Drama Review,* I read every issue of *Yale/Theater.* I met many American theater legends, starting with Ellen Stewart. I had discussions with Daniel Gerould and Michael Kirby. I listened to the lectures of John Cage and Allan Kaprow. I watched Lee Strasberg teach in his Studio.

It was indeed many years of learning, observing, admiring. The productions were imaginative, innovative, and full of energies. The people were open, kind, hospitable, and avid to meet a theater person from Poland. During those years I wrote a lot about American theater. I was the first in Poland to write about Wilson. I analyzed the works of Schumann, Schechner, Foreman and others. I knew that my view was that of a foreigner, but I tried to understand, to describe objectively, to present all the most important aspects and values of American theater.

I began to lecture, direct, and teach directing workshops in America in 1975, when Edward Czerwiński invited me to the Slavic Culture Center in Port Jefferson, New York. Later, I was a guest of Daniel Gerould at CUNY, Mitchell Lifton at Notre Dame, and Ron Engle at University of North Dakota.

When I lost my theater in Poland, some my American friends invited me to the States and I came here in 1985. Thomas Leff offered me a year-long academic job at Swarthmore College; Richard Schechner a semester at NYU; Andrew Doe a semester at University of California, Santa Cruz. I made my professional "debut" in America in The Guthrie in Minneapolis where I directed *Rhinoceros* in 1986. How strange it was to hear and read that it was a "debut"... by a director of 50, who has already staged more then 100 professional theater and television productions.

The same year, 1986, I got a position at the Department of Theater and Dance, at University at Buffalo. This was like starting a home run. I am still on my way. But I am running home. My home base is now in America.

For years I have taught at Polish universities and schools of drama. I had also directing workshops in Poland, Ireland, Great Britain, the Czech Republic, and other places. In America, teaching directing gradually emerged as my focus. I

132

taught classes and had directing workshops at many universities[10]. Interaction with both American actors during rehearsals and students in classes helped me to further articulate my method of *creative directing*.

It is based on three pillars. First, on my own long-lasting directorial work. Second, on my study of the history of theater in various cultures, including the history of directing. Third, on my experience as a teacher of directing who continually tries to perfect his method.

I am proud of my many talented students. It is for them, and for the next generations of students of directing that I wrote this book.

---

[10] I had directing workshops at the following: New York University, University of California, Berkeley, University of California, Santa Cruz, Stanford University, University of North Dakota, Grand Forks, University of Pennsylvania, Philadelphia, De Paul University, Chicago, Kansas University in Lawrence, Catholic University in Washington, D.C., University of Tennessee, Knoxville, University of Wisconsin, Milwaukee, University of Southern Illinois, Carbondale. I had also lectures on theater at the above, as well as at: Harvard University, CUNY, Graduate Center, University of Ottawa, SUNY Stony Brook, and others.

PART II. TEACHING CREATIVE DIRECTING

Introduction

In this part of the book I will lead you through the practical process of teaching creative directing. I will demonstrate a method of creative analysis of the text, (very much different from the literary one), and then I will work with you on the four basic elements of a performance: the human layer of it, the space, the time, and the action. We will explore all of the elements of a production, learning creative directing through a series of practical exercises which serve as both theoretical and practical explanations of specific directorial problems; and they demonstrate and teach ways to solve these problems.

The exercises refer to the creative work of the director with actors, to the creation of space and time, and, finally, to the action of the production. They are based on the following premises:

(1) Our focus is on theater directing, though the exercises are useful also for film and television directors, for designers and playwrights, as well as for organizers social events or masters of ceremonies.

(2) The students participating in a directing class or workshop personally play in all of the actions or scenes provided in this book. We don't need and don't plan to use outsiders to play for us. All of the practical work, not only the acting, but also the design, lighting, and music or sound is be done by the students of our class or workshop. Everyone profit from this: directors get an introduction to the

acting experience by wearing the "actor's shoes," actors get a better understanding of what directing is all about, and all others have an opportunity to participate in and contribute to the creation of every element of the production.

(3) We improvise. We create actions, exercises, short "dramas," scenes, or skits by ourselves. We play them by ourselves and for ourselves.

(4) The exercises provided in this book are examples; students should also create exercises on their own.

(5) I call the leader of the group (the teacher, instructor, professor, a director) the "master", in order to emphasize that as teachers and learners we are in a relationship of masters and disciples. The class or company of student/participants is called the "group," to emphasize group effort. Individual members are called simply "students," to emphasize that they are learning. Mutual help, respect, and understanding is the foundation of our work together.

(6) In class or workshop situations, the master always explains and then practically demonstrates every exercise: he/she always does it first. The master's explanation and demonstrations can be taken directly from this book.

(7) We always divide work on every exercise into the same segments and we always use universally accepted, professional terminology. This develops within a working group certain habits, rules of the game, and even rituals. It helps to build team spirit, ease communication, structure work, and provide every member with a sense of security. Simply put, if people know the order of the work, the procedures used by the master, and what certain terms mean, they focus on the work itself, not on decoding the master's messages.

(8) You can use this book while working as a group without a master. In this case, however, you should select a leader, acting as "master" during the whole process or at a single work session.

(9) If you are only going to read this book, not use it for practical work—that's fine. But when reading descriptions of exercises, please, engage your imagination and try not only to read, but also to see what is going on, what people are doing, what kind of space they are using.

(10) The exercises are divided into four phases that describe and explain what they are composed of and how to use them. These stages are: situation, action, discussion, and development.

Situation. The situation contains a general introduction and exegesis of a problem, topic, exercise, action, or scene. It is followed by casting, giving tasks, explaining the circumstances, and describing the space. If an action should be improvised (which is the most frequent case), the situation will provide the start, and include what is necessary to begin an improvisation, but not disclose or anticipate the outcome. We should remember that the more precise the explication of the situation, the better and smoother the exercise will go.

Action. Action is the central element of each exercise. Members of the group play the action. In the section on action, you will find a short description of the events as they actually developed during my classes and workshops. They are accounts of real actions done by my students; they are feasible! You can recreate them, or use as incentive for your own work. Naturally, the results of an exercise conducted by a creative group may vary from those described in this book.

Discussion. Discussion is the closing part of the work. It is absolutely necessary for its success. The master should always provide students with an analysis of what they did, along with an evaluation of what went well and what needs improvement. Decisions, oriented towards further work, must be included. The master should allow for discussion and summarize it. The session will not be over before students, like actors in the theater, take notes on the work.

The habit of taking notes during exercises or rehearsals, as well as at the end of them, is crucial both for efficient use of time and for consciously absorbing material. If, for example, a scene has been blocked during a rehearsal, all of the actors should write down the blocking, as well as its interpretation and contacts, so that they are able to reenact them next time. Notes are absolutely necessary to the effective progress of work. They remind us of what was done yesterday, and they help to summarize what was done today. Keeping notes should be a requirement in the university setting and is a good habit for professionals. Notes help actors begin each new phase of the work where they have finished the old one—rather than having to start from scratch. On the one hand, work notes should facilitate fast progress; but on the other hand, they should not inhibit actors from improving or changing anything in the future.

Development. This paragraph in the book describes how the practical work on an exercise or scene can be pushed farther or transformed. These suggestions can be used by the master for the next stage of work, but it's better for students to develop exercises or scenes on their own. The development phase is provided when an exercise should be continued, but is not necessary when the work is finished.

CHAPTER 1. CREATIVE TEXT ANALYSIS

Introduction

In a practical and literary sense, the "text" used by a director is a play, adaptation, scenario, or collection of lines articulated by actors during improvised rehearsals. A playwright sometimes participates in the process of collective creation, puts down words developed by actors, and helps to structure them into a coherent script. Meghan Terry and Jean-Claude van Itallie worked that way. Sometimes the directors are at the same time the authors of the play, as were Stanisław Wyspiański, Bertolt Brecht, and Richard Foreman, or they may have written adaptations of novels which they personally direct.

In a communicational and linguistic sense, the term "text" in the theater denotes the totality of means of expression used by the actors in communicating with spectators, and vice versa. These means include: the actions and activities of people; their spoken language in dialogues or soliloquies; the movements of people, objects, and sets; images, whether created by actors' bodies, sets, costumes, lights, or projections; music and sound; and finally, an array of miscellaneous ways of communication within a theater, such as the ushers' rituals, the contents of playbills, advertisements in the media, interviews given by director and actors, and so on. In this chapter we will understand "text" as "literary text," thought we should be aware of this second, broad comunicational meaning of the term "text" in theater.

The work of a director on the literary text is composed of three stages. First, the director studies, analyses, and eventually takes full responsibility for a text written by an author. Second, the director uses this literary text for building the project of a theater production. Third, the director utilizes the text during rehearsals, transforming a written text into a spoken text, and integrating it with all other means of expression.

The theatrical analysis of the text is the beginning of the work of a director. It is an analysis exploring the theatrical potential of a play and is oriented towards theater. It serves to build a production. The theatrical analysis of the text results in notation of the characters' actions, a description of spaces, and a scenario of movements, rhythms, and sounds. The director decodes the text, discovering all the production's elements in it. Digesting and absorbing the text leads the director to a "reading" of the text. Based on this "reading," the director makes interpretational decisions. Next, the director edits the text. Editing includes making cuts, changing the sequence of the scenes, rewriting words or entire sections, or asking the author to rewrite, if the author is alive and willing to do so. In case of an old play the director may make necessary modernization of the text. In case of a translation he/she decides which translation to use. If the director knows the language of the original text he/she may edit it; otherwise, the help of a translator is needed. Thus, the director transforms a text written by someone else into his/her own text, and transmutes the literary text into a theatrical one. This is the process of changing literature into the material for a production.

Most frequently the text used by a director is a drama—so we will discuss the method of creative analysis of a drama. This method, however, can also be used for the analysis of a stage adaptation, scenario, screen play, or any kind of social event script. It might serve as well in theatrical analysis of novels, poems, or documents which one would like to use to write plays, screen plays, or stage adaptations. It is relevant to all kinds of texts, both realistic or unrealistic, both literary or non-literary, and dramatic or non-dramatic.

The directorial analysis ought to be objective, unbiased, and honest, as well as attentive, open, and sensitive. We, the directors, should assume that the authors are better writers than we, and that we can always learn from them. We should listen to the author and learn about his/her intentions. It is equally important not to confuse the text analysis with the project of the production. The project comes after the analysis of the text. An arduous, patient, and humble analysis allows us to detect the creative impulses in the text, explore its complexity, identify its production possibilities, discover its potential for building characters, creating stage events, structuring the space, and influencing the audience. We should allow ourselves to reach into the text's depths. Obviously this approach is fruitful when working on the masterpieces of world drama, but it should also be applied to the analysis of plays of any caliber. Sometimes we are tempted, even at the early stages of work, to cut certain lines, or nervously call the author with a request to rewrite scenes. We might end up doing so. But authors will listen to our ideas only if we prove that we know their scripts well. We should establish a strict rule that, without exception, a comprehensive, deep, systematic, and objective analysis of the text comes first. This is the foundation for any further step in working on the text itself or building a production based on it.

Of course, during the analysis we are already developing our fantastic (and also not so fantastic) directorial concepts. We see the spaces, we hear the music, we feel the characters squabble, and we start building the show in our imagination. This is expected and natural. We can write down all our thoughts, visions, and ideas. We will return to them later, while building the project of the show and during the rehearsals. But they should be temporarily moved aside—in order not to overshadow and obscure the analysis or to block free access to the text. Our focus should be firmly on the text itself.

We read the play several times. A Polish master, Leon Schiller, used to tell his directing students that before they even start the analysis they should read the play "seventy-seven times." In the Biblical sense it means "an infinite number of times." It is good counsel. Indeed, we need to read the play many times in order to really get to know it. Let's read the play with openness and sensitivity. Let's read the dialogues and stage directions, the author's own forewords (sometimes long and analytical, as in Shaw's plays), and let's even pay attention to the author's special editing habits. Vladimir Mayakovsky, for example, was notorious for using typographical tricks in order to emphasize his own interpretation of the lines. While reading the play "seventy-seven times" we should also study the author's biography, all his/her other works, get acquainted with the production history of his/her plays and research the practices of the theater of the time. Indeed, a director working on a Calderón moral tragedy must study the religious tradition of the Spanish Golden Age theater. When preparing ourselves for the analysis of *Rhinoceros* by Eugène Ionesco, we should realize that it is a play written by a political refugee who had a first hand knowledge of totalitarianism. Getting ready to direct a play by Tennessee Williams, we have to familiarize ourselves with the deep-seated cultural conflict between the North and South of the United States. All such study and research should be done during the preparatory, pre-analytical work. It pertains to the general cultural, civilizational, historical, literary, artistic, philosophical, social, and political context of the play and to the play itself, glossing its plot, characters, environment, language, and ideas. Moving to the analysis proper, we use this data when necessary, but the play should be still treated as unknown territory, open to non-dogmatic exploration.

General guidelines for a creative analysis of a text

The theater, as we established, is an interhuman process of communication artistically structured. People participating in this process are actors and spectators. The process itself is the action. An action is composed of events occurring between actors and spectators; usually the actors play the events, but sometimes the spectators provoke them as well. The action happens in a space and in a time, the two basic categories of human existence. The analysis of a text must, therefore, encompass these four elements: (1) People taking part in the theatrical process: actors and spectators. (2) Space: the space in which the action takes place. (3) Time: the time in which the action occurs. (4) Action: actions of the people involved in the theatrical process.

People in theater

Each of the above elements has at least three levels or dimensions. Let's have a closer look at them. People in theater are, first, human beings as they are—actors and spectators. Second, they are characters played by actors. Third, they are characters elevated to the level of archetypes. The people in the theater are truly all who meet during the show in the theater. Both actors and spectators are unique, individual human beings and distinctive persons, with their own personal and private characteristics. At the same time, each belongs to a group, nation, social class, and culture.

In the case of an actor, his or her personality, age, sex, professional training, human experience, beliefs, morality, and political views are the "baggage" they bring on stage. For example the Polish actor, Jacek Woszczerowicz, could portray the character of Shakespeare's Richard III, a grand dictator, manipulator, and malefactor, so convincingly and profoundly because of his excellent acting training and long years of stage experience, but also because on a personal level he had first-hand knowledge about the characters of such dictators, having lived for years in a country ruled by Hitler and Stalin.

In the case of each spectator, as well as for the audience as a whole, participation in the show is conditioned by cultural background, artistic taste, attitude towards theater, education, emotional involvement with the production, and even individual experiences just before the show. There is a profound difference, in terms of participation in a show between various individual spectators and groups. A professional critic in New York could sit in the orchestra, mad and gloomy, having had to come to the theater in spite of flu, headache and runny nose, because he has a midnight deadline for submitting his review; he could hate the show, no matter how good the actors are. A student of

Belgrade University could come to the theater directly from a political demonstration against Slobodan Milosević's regime and bring her excitement and adrenaline with her, happy that this time the protesters have outwitted the police and hopeful that they are finally going to win; she loves the show even if it is not so good. How differently these two spectators would participate in a show! Theatrical communication during the show would be completely different! A world of difference separates communication between the actors and theater-goers during an experimental production at the Edinburgh Festival or at a matinee for tourists at the Comédie Française in Paris. Similarly, a different kind communication occurs at a free performance of Shakespeare in Buffalo's Delaware Park; at the opera in Bayreuth, where ticket prices are in the hundreds of German marks; at an off-off-Broadway production in Greenwich Village where five actors in jeans play for fifteen friends in jeans; during the black-tie opening of a Broadway musical; at an open-air mass spectacle at Spoleto marketplace and in the noble baroque interior of the Milan's Teatro alla Scala.

We have to see clearly that the first and most basic level of communication in theater is communication between actors and spectators as they are. This communication is always present—it is the foundation of every production. Theatrical communication takes place first of all on the basic, human level. Directors can disregard it, but in doing so, they deprive themselves from exploring a vast territory on which the production can be shaped. Conversely, calling to what is personal, private and individual in each actor during the rehearsals and in each spectator or audience group during the show, opens enormous creative and artistic horizons.

Characters played by actors belong to the second level of communication in production. Actors play actions as characters; spectators perceive actors as characters. Actors may chose from many conventions and styles to play characters: they may hide themselves behind them, change themselves into characters, or they may play themselves, exposing their own personalities. Communication between characters connects a character with a character, and a character played by an actor with a spectator. The spectators decode the messages sent by the characters and they, in turn, address messages to spectators. The actors' messages are spiritual, biological, emotional, vocal, or movemental. The spectators also send messages: they freeze, sweat, laugh, cry, clap, whistle, throw flowers or tomatoes; they approve or protest; sometimes they leave the theater. During the show they either forget themselves and allow the magic to overwhelm them, or, conversely, they consciously and ostensibly "play" certain "roles," such as "the enthusiast," "the enemy," "the friend," or "the outraged citizen"—expressing their political, moral, social, or artistic views, attitudes, and opinions. Theater historians delightfully describe vivid public reactions, and even disturbances before, during, and after the shows. For example, the patriotic Poles demonstrated their national feelings after the production of *Cracovians and Mountaineers* by Bogusławski in Warsaw in 1794. The Romantics and the Classicists used their fists during the 1830 opening of Victor Hugo's *Hernani* in Paris. The public fought before the 1911 New York opening of the Dublin Abbey Theater's production of Synge's *Playboy of the Western World.*

Archetypes function on the third level of communication in the show. Special artistic figures and means of expression, used in the performance by directors, designers, and especially actors, imbue a character with general and universal meaning. As a result, a character becomes an archetype, a mythical hero, or an "everyman." The scene of Mother Courage mourning the death of her daughter Catherine was modeled by Irena Eichlerówna in Warsaw National Theater in 1962 as the *Pieta*, the famous sculpture of Michelangelo in which Mary, Mother of God, mourns her son, Jesus, carrying him on his lap. Eichlerówna purposely used this icon and thus she achieved an archetypical generalization by connecting the Brechtian character with the sculpture of a mourning Mother of God. She became "every mother" mourning her child murdered, fallen on the battlefield, or lost.

In summary: there are three levels of communication between actors and spectators. First, the level of "us": people—as we are. Second, the level of "they": characters—as played by actors and sometimes the spectators who play certain roles as well. Third, the level of "everybody": archetypes—the highest, universal and general form of playing a character.

During the analysis of a drama we focus on the characters. In making the project of a production we must consider what actors should play the characters and for what audiences we are going to prepare the show. Rehearsing, we can orient actors towards playing archetypes, elevating the whole production to a high level of generalization, universality, and poetry.

The space of the performance

The space in which a theatrical action develops is, first of all, a real space. The real space may be transformed by sets, functional or descriptive into a space created for performance. The use of symbols, artistic composition, and fine art styles may further transform a theater space into a universal and mythical space. Space in theater can, therefore, exist: first, as real; second, as created; and, third, as transcendental.

The real space in theater is the space of a specific stage or other playing area, along with the auditorium and the architectural totality of a theater building in which the show is performed. All entrances, foyers, staircases, as well as architectural structures in the surrounding area are also included. In the case of open-air productions, the space is also specific and real. Examples of these include a castle yard, a clearing in a forest, a parking lot at a university, or a street in a modern city. The characteristics of the existing space, such as structure, dimension, lighting, visibility, and audibility impose specific means of expression on the actors, and have an impact on the perception of the public. Consequently, space as it is decides the general character and nature of the theatrical interaction. The reality of a space conditions the production even if neither the actors nor the spectators are aware of it. Indeed, the space decides the meaning, message, style, and form of a production. It proscribes and requires certain means of acting, designing and costuming.

In classical Greek theater, the vastness and openness of the space imposed the use of hieratic gesture, singing, chanting, dancing, as well as the wearing of an *onkos*, *kothornos* and mask. The small interior of a Twentieth century proscenium theater with its realistic sets both allows and requires the actors to use whispers, every-day behavior, and life-like make-up. Space also influences the behaviors of an audience. People feel, dress, and behave in one way in an opera theater, amidst golden columns, crystal mirrors, and red carpets, and in a completely different way in an avant-garde street production, where actors on stilts mingle with a crowd of passers-by.

Real space encompasses both actors and spectators. It affects both their consciousness and unconsciousness. Its true and basic purpose and function influence all present in it during the show. A space which originally is a home of tradition, a place of worship, or a crossroad of civilization identifies those using it as partakers in a religious ritual, as members of a cultural community, witnesses to a political demonstration, or participants in a civilizational experience. Real space (also called "found space") has enormous myth creating energy. Its reality, confronted with the created action, elevates a production to the level of symbolism, universality, and mythology. The power of a real space has been one of the major energies in the theater of every culture. In the 20th century, theater artist have rediscovered it. Reinhardt produced *Everyman* on the huge stairs leading to the entrance to the Salzburg cathedral (1920). Trzciński put on the Renaissance tragedy *The Dismissal of the Greek Envoys* by Jan Kochanowski at the royal castle courtyard in Cracow (1929). Jerzy Jarocki staged *Murder in the Cathedral* by T. S. Eliot in the Roman Catholic Cathedral of Warsaw (1982). For the same reasons, drawing on the power of real space, I situated several of my productions in various existing spaces. As I have already mentioned, I played a parts of the productions in real spaces, such as the street in *The Old Woman*, the church in *The Forefathers' Eve*, the hospital and the railway station in *Birth Rate*. I have situated whole productions in a factory in Lublin, in museums in Wrocław, and in churches in New York and Buffalo. In all these, and many other instances, the real and existing space was chosen by the director knowing its mighty impact on the theatrical communication process.

Space intentionally and artificially created for the production's purposes has two major functions. First, it invalidates or masks the real space. Second, it establishes another space—the location of the fictitious action. The created space is usually built only on the playing area, for example on the stage of a proscenium theater, but sometimes it also embraces the observation area, for example by special decorating of the auditorium. In many productions the observation area (the auditorium) itself has been used as a playing area, as in Konrad Swinarski's staging of *The Forefathers' Eve* by Mickiewicz in Cracow in 1973. The created space is made of sets and lights. The sets can have endless variety. They can be realistic or unrealistic, illusionistic or abstract, minimal or abundant. They always fulfill two major tasks: functional and aesthetic.

Functionally, the sets impose and allow certain movements, provide entrances and exits, structure the whole playing area horizontally and vertically, and provide actors with furniture and objects to use in the course of action. In many productions the sets are exclusively functional and descriptive, representing certain spaces, most frequently interiors, as we see them in everyday life. The notorious, boring, middle class "living room" has been reproduced in thousands of plays and productions with mortifying mediocrity and lack of imagination, without even a bit of naturalistic dread or an iota of heaven-opening symbolism.

Aesthetically, the sets, along with costumes and lights, create the visual layer of the show. Sets and costumes may belong to a specific historic period or aesthetic style of fine arts. The discipline of set design was enriched when renowned painters, such as Pablo Picasso, Fernand Léger, Joan Miró, Enrico Prampolini, Oskar Schlemmer, along with scores of Futurists, Dadaists, and Surrealist brought their styles on stages and offered their fine arts styles to theater design. In between the purely functional and descriptive sets, on the one hand,

and the ambitious, artistic sets, on the other, there is a vast middle ground where sets fulfil necessities of the action and have the aesthetic qualities of fine arts.

Real or created theater space becomes transcendental when it carries the action of the play into the realm of myth, universality, or transhistorical generalization. The space of a performance transforms into the space of transgression and transfiguration. The barriers of reality are broken. The performance space expands, metaphorically embraces other spaces, and becomes ubiquitous. For example in Mickiewicz's Romantic play *The Forefathers' Eve,* the martyrdom of the Polish nation is compared to the passion of Christ. Poland suffers under foreign rule, as Christ suffered on the cross; Poland has been crucified and, therefore, like Christ, will be resurrected. The action occurs in several places in Wilno and Warsaw, as well as in heaven and hell; a cosmic and poetic vision. In the 1932 production of this play, directed by Schiller and designed by Pronaszko in Lwów, the whole action was performed on a vast, multilayered, mountain-like platform, crowned by three crosses. It was an obvious allusion to the Golgotha, the mountain of the death of Jesus Christ. It was, as Mircea Eliade writes: a mountain—center of the universe, both the concrete location of the action and a symbolic, transhistorical icon. The platform-mountain remained on stage all the time, while the specific locations of different scenes were temporarily set on its slopes. The central metaphor of the play—the comparison between Poland's fate and that of Christ—was achieved by spatial and visual means of expression. The space design elevated the whole production on the plane of transhistorical universality. In the staging of *King Lear* directed by Zygmunt Hübner in the Polski Theater in Warsaw (1962), the designer Krystyna Zachwatowicz built a huge skull on stage and the subsequent scenes were played in its caves and cracks. The Shakespearean tragedy acquired the eschatological dimension of a morality play about the final judgment on every human being. In his play *The Old Woman Broods*, Tadeusz Różewicz describes in a stage direction a space as a beach (a place of biological exuberance of life), a trash dump (a place of refuse and decay), a battlefield (a place of killing) and a graveyard (a place of eternal rest and peace)—it is the transcendental space of a human destiny from the cradle to the grave.

To summarize, a theater space has three dimensions. They are: first, real space, a space of a given theater architecture or an outdoor theater ground. Second, created space: a space made by sets, costumes, and lights. Third, transcendental space: a space which is transhistorical, transcultural, and universal.

The time of the performance

Every performance spans three levels of time. The first level of time in theater is real. It is the time "now." The second is the historic time of the action; past, present, or future. It is the time "then." The third, is a mythical, eternal time without time. It is an "every time" time.

The "real time" of the performance is simply the time measured by the watches of the actors and spectators. Time is an abstract notion. Humanity has established ways of counting it, and, consequently, each production can be measured in minutes and hours. Real time determines if a production is played during the day or night, if it starts "early," as shows for school students should, or if it ends "late," like cabaret shows, if it is "short," like some Samuel Beckett's plays, or "long," like some of Wilson's productions. "Real time" impacts the theatrical interhuman process. It influences the actors' performance and the spectators' perception. Specific kinds of interhuman relations are born during a short street action; very different ones arise during the evening-long production of an opera. However, "real time" is also relative, and is perceived within a given cultural context. In contemporary America, a two and a half hour production is standard, as is a five-hour Noh production in Japan.

The time of the action is the historic and structural time within which the dramatic events of the play take place. From the historic point of view every action takes place in a specific time. We decipher that time by analyzing the play, or by arbitrarily imposing it on the production. In general, the play will tell us when the action takes place. Alternatively, a director may decide when to situate the action. For example, Shakespeare's *Richard III* historically takes place in the 15th century, but its 1991 production in the National Theater in London set the action in the 1930s. In any case, we must know whether the play is ancient or contemporary. Does it take place in the past or in the future?—as does the drama about a future society of robots, *R. U. R.,* by Karel Čapek. The text analysis often allows to find the precise date, time of day, or even the exact time of a scene, act, or whole play. From the structural point of view, an analysis of the time of a play's action reveals whether the time flows continually or is broken into segments. Do the events develop over a span of a year or perhaps over many years? Does the author follow the classical rule of "time unity" and puts the totality of action within twenty-four hours? Are there flashbacks? For example, *Who's Afraid of Virginia Woolf?* by Edward Albee takes place during one night. In *The Wedding* by Stanisław Wyspiański the first act takes place in the evening, the second at night, and the third in the early morning next day. In *The Cherry Orchard* by Anton Chekhov, the first act happens in spring, the second in summer, the third in fall, and the fourth at the beginning of winter. In Shakespeare's *The Winter's Tale*, sixteen years pass between act III and IV. Shakespearian chronicle plays, on the other hand, reflect more or less precisely the true historical events, including the duration of time passing in between them. Similarly, the epic plays by Paul Claudel and Bertolt Brecht indicate how much time separates particular events. Some authors allow time differences between acts, while others insist on the continuity of the action, even if there is an intermission for the public between acts, as Shaw does in *Heartbreak House* between act II and III. In *The Front Page,* authors Ben Hecht and Charles MacArthur indicate that there is only a five minute span between acts 2 and 3, though if the real-time intermission between them is probably the usual fifteen minutes. Most frequently the time of the stage action is somehow compressed and condensed in comparison to real time. During about one hour of real-time production, an author can depict about three hours' worth of stage events. This is the case in the last act of Pinter's *The Homecoming*. On other occasions, authors (and directors who follow their directions) suggest that the duration of stage events be identical with real events. The Polish writer of Romantic comedies, Aleksander Fredro, usually used this technique. Authors can also suggest that certain events take place simultaneously. In *The Deliverance* by Wyspiański, the second part of act 1 and the first part of act 3 happen at the same time as act 2. Directors have rarely been able to solve that difficult challenge of Wyspiański's construction of time in *The Deliverance*.

The mythical time of the production transports events taking place "now" into "every time." Eternity embraces and devours the present. Time is both lost and suspended. The mythical time in theater is the most difficult to describe and explain. The transformation of the specific time of stage action, real or historic, into a timeless, mythical time is impossible to document. Nevertheless, it's clear that both playwrights, especially those who are poets, and directors, especially those inclined to poetic theater, use particular means of expression in order to suggest the timeless, transhistorical, and mythical dimension of the events. The mythological suggestion in terms of time usually coincides with a similar myth-enriched treatment of characters, space, and action. Indeed, mythical heroes act in mythical time and space. In spite of the elusiveness of mythical time in a production it is possible to point out ways in which authors and directors call on and refer to existing myths, or create new ones. For example, many 20th century dramas that discuss contemporary problems are situated, costumed, and modeled on ancient mythical stories. We find this technique in plays by Jean Giraudoux (*Amphitrion 38, Electra, Judith, Sodom and Gomorrah, The Trojan War Shall not Take Place*), Jean Anouilh (*Antigone, Eurydice*), Eugene O'Neill (*Mourning Becomes Electra*), Janusz Głowacki (*Antigone in New York),* and many others.

In summary: there are three types of time in a production. They are: real time—"now;" time of the action—"then;" and mythical time—"always," "ever," a "timeless time."

The action of the performance

The action of the production also has three main levels. The first level is the direct, interhuman, and real communication between actors and spectators. The second level is the action created, fictitious and invented, performed by the characters; this is the "story" or the "plot" of a play. The third is the level of generalization and universalization on which the story acquires the dimension of myth.

Interhuman communication is always the real, true, and concrete foundation of the totality of the processes occurring during the show. Human interaction is composed of behaviors, manners, lifestyles, ways of communicating, and the attitudes of actors towards spectators and vice versa. For example in ancient Rome free citizens sat in the theater auditorium while on the *pulpitum* (playing area) slaves appeared. The masters were entertained by their slaves. It horrifies, yet does not surprise, that these relationships of radical social separation and subordination allowed the slave-performer to be killed for the owner's fun. Indeed, just as Christians and gladiators died in the amphitheaters, actors in Roman theaters actors were sometimes killed when the action called for the characters they played to be murdered. A radically different interaction, one of partnership and brotherhood, occurred in a production prepared by Meyerhold in Moscow during the Bolshevik revolution. Revolutionary-actors played for revolutionary-spectators, singing *The Internationale* together at the end of Emile Verhaeren's *The Dawns* (1920). A warm, supportive, and friendly mood characterized underground productions held in private homes in Poland under martial law in the 1980s: both actors and spectators were committing a crime from the point of view of the military junta, both could be persecuted and penalized, both manifested their defiance towards the regime, and both wanted to share their spiritual and human values. Conversely, a critics' decision to pan a play, made prior to the opening night, could send a freezing cold wind through a theater; this happens sometimes in theatrical capitals, such as New York, Paris, or Warsaw.

The fictitious action played by the characters—the "story" or the "plot"—is the customary vehicle of theater interaction. Action consists of stage events, conflicts, and characters' deeds. It is communicated to the audience by the actors' use of various means of expression, such as movement and voice. Spectators perceive action consciously and subconsciously, as well as intellectually and emotionally. Sometimes action stimulates vocal or even physical reactions in spectators. The hotter, more dynamic and vivid the action is, the stronger the communicational process during the show. There are directors who infer from this that if the speakers around the stage vibrate loudly, and special effects, such as smoke, lasers, and stage mechanics, are frequently used, the impact of the show on the spectators will be more powerful. Of course, they are wrong, because the intensity of action is not measured by decibels and frequency of light changes. Action might have the impact of a tornado even if developed in silence, semi-darkness, and slow motion.

The mythical action is born when the story played on stage acquires the dimension of universality and generalization. The play does not lose its immediate meaning but transforms: it somehow enlarges and opens, it embraces other similar stories, it incorporates other comparable characters, and refers to analogous events in different times and places. The mythical level of stage action can be attained by playing and/or staging certain actions, or the whole play as a parallel to an ancient myth, fairy tale, or grand historical event. In *The Trap,* whose action takes place in the 1910s and 1920s, Różewicz compares the conflict between father and son to the Biblical story of Abraham and Isaac. In my production I staged the scene of a father-son quarrel aroud an ancient, sacrificial, stone altar which was built in the courtyard of an otherwise average and realistic twentieth century Vienna apartment building. The Biblical metaphor worked strongly. The director Lidia Zamkow modeled the scene of the meal of the homeless in *The Lower Depths* by Maxim Gorky (Cracow, 1960) exactly as the *Last Supper* is depicted in the famous painting by Leonardo da Vinci. It tremendously widened the breadth of the scene.

TABLE: BASIC ELEMENTS OF THEATRICAL PROCESS

PEOPLE	SPACE	TIME	ACTION	CATEGORY
WE actors and spectators	**HERE**	**NOW**	**INTERHUMAN PROCESS**	**LIFE**
THEY characters	**THERE**	**THEN**	**STORY** told in a play	**ART**
EVERYBODY heroes of myth legends histories archetypes	**EVERY-WHERE**	**EVER**	**MYTH**	**TRANSCEN-DENCY**

In summary, there are three levels of action in theater. First, the level of real, true and practical interhuman communication between actors and spectators. Second, the level of the communication through the action presented or the story told. Third, the level of communication within a myth when the action acquires general, universal, and transhistorical dimensions. Combinations of these three levels are infinite and offer unlimited creative possibilities. We can show these three levels in the form of a table. The analysis of a play reveals all these elements, the project of a production establishes the means for expressing them, and the actual production conveys them to the audience. Aware of all these options, we will be searching for them during the analysis and, later on, during rehearsals. The analysis itself will be held primarily on the level of the story as told in the play by the author. The story is played by characters living in a certain space and time. It is the level of "they" (the characters of a play)—"there" (the space of the action of the play)—"then" (the time of the action of a play)— and "story" (told in the play.)

Sequence of the analytical procedure

The core of the analysis consists of questions about the person and her/his actions, and about the person's conditions of life, such as space and time. During the analysis we investigate these four elements; they are connected and influence each other. We start the analysis by asking questions about the person. We proceed by investigating space and time. We finish by investigating the action.

People in theater (actors and spectators) and their actions are always inseparably linked: people act and actions are executed by people. Theater is the art of living human beings; we ought to always remember this basic truth. We should, therefore, begin every step of theater work with a human being, a person—alive, present, active, and creative. Hence, in analytical work we have to start by asking questions about the people: who are they? what they do? what is happening to them? where they are heading? what are their objectives, goals, dreams?

To analyze a character we first ask simple questions about his/her name, sex, age, occupation, and societal ties. We continue the investigation by delving farther and deeper with questions about the character's hidden and internal self—feelings, emotions, motivations, thirsts, hungers. Because a character in a play is usually not alone we have to immediately ask further questions about the social environment of a character: to what social, political, generational, or cultural group does it belong? What is the character's status within a society, nation, family, and humanity?

A character in a play, likewise a person in real life, exists always within the categories of space and time. These two dimensions, conditions, or "circumstances" (as Stanislavsky called them) are, therefore, the next two areas of investigation. We have to ask questions about space and time: where does a person live and act? Where is he/she in terms of space, venue, location? When does he/she live and act? What is the date, hour, and minute of the character's activities? We finish our inquiry on the action with questions about the character's acts, deeds, and activities. Once we know the character and the circumstances of space and time, we can fully understand and diagnose his/her action. This sequence (or order) of our analytical investigation allows us to logically reveal one by one all of the major elements and to proceed from what is external to what is internal, and from what is easily given to what is difficult to expose. The analysis of the action is certainly most difficult, so we make it at the end of the whole procedure. Generally, the most helpful and useful sequence of analysis is this: to start by characters, to continue with space and time, and to finish with action.

The graphical method of text analysis

As I have just indicated, all analytical data should be collected and noted in a specific order. This results, first, in a clear presentation of the analytical findings; and, second, it makes all the data easily accessible and useful in working on a project of a production, and later during the rehearsals. Four major elements (people, space, time, action) should be put into a directorial "diagram," "model," or "graph." My American students used to call it a "Kazograph" linking my first name (in its shortened version, Kaz) with the word "graph." Below, I will use the term "graph."

The analytical graph structures, arranges, and visually presents the analyzed text. The graph might be compared to a musical score. Looking at it, the conductor sees simultaneously various instruments' melodies and at the same time their interactions. Similarly, looking at the graph, the director sees how action is carried on by various characters within the circumstances of space and time. I guess that all directors have—to a higher or lesser degree—a visual imagination, necessary to build stage images. All of them can profit from seeing the whole play displayed in front of their eyes. Graphical presentation of the play should be useful for all kinds of directors, theatrical or film, professional or amateur. The graph, which I am going to show and explain, is simple, clear, and easy to make. It is based on the simultaneous visual presentation of the four major elements of a play (characters, space, time, and action). It also includes additional notes about sound, music, lighting and special effects. We should avoid overloading the graph with other notes in order not to lose its clarity.

Even though the following description about how to begin constructing a graph may sound childish and simplistic, it contains important fundamentals that is necessary to master more complex tasks. Indeed, we will soon be confronted as high-level specialists with difficult and sophisticated intellectual and artistic problems, dilemmas, choices and decisions. But let's start on the apprentice plane. In order to make the directorial graph we need a simple sheet of paper and markers or crayons of four colors: red, green, blue, and black. Additionally, purple and yellow markers, along with a pencil, will come in handy. Let's go step by step: (1) Put a sheet of paper horizontally in front of you. (2) Fold it in half and again in half. (3) Draw a thick black line on the fold mark in the center and two dashed lines on the fold marks below and above it. The page is now divided horizontally into four parts. In the middle we have an uninterrupted line, and two dashed lines below and above. These four parts of the sheet will be used to take notes on the four major elements of the analyses. Let's continue. (4) Using the upper case letters, please, write: In red—below the uninterrupted line: CHARACTERS. In red—above the uninterrupted line: ACTION. In green—at the bottom of the page: SPACE. In blue—at the top of the page: TIME. As a result, in the middle of the page we have an axis of the analysis shown in black and two main categories, CHARACTERS and ACTION, in red. Below we have SPACE noted in green, and above TIME in blue. (5) Now, after these four words (CHARACTERS, ACTION, SPACE, TIME), we draw a vertical black line. These words are now titles of the four categories we are going to look for and put down in the graph. (6) Just after the vertical line, let's write on top of the page, using the black color: "Scene 1."

TABLE: A GRAPH READY FOR THE ANALYSIS

[The top of the page]

	Scene 1
TIME [blue]	
ACTION [red]	
CHARACTERS [red]	
SPACE [green]	

[Bottom of the page]

We are now ready to start the analysis of the first scene of the play. We will use the vertical lines for the subsequent scenes (which we can also call "segments," or "parts") and we will number them. The criterion for dividing the action of the whole play into scenes is the presence and/or participation of the characters. When a new character enters, or one of the present characters leaves, the action changes and a new scene begins. Playwrights themselves sometime divide the play not only into acts but also into scenes. If this is the case, we can follow them. There are many plays, however, that do not have these partitions; for these a director making an analysis should divide the acts into scenes. The nature of the connections between scenes is a matter of the playwrights' technique. Some authors like "soft" connections when the action of one scene dissolves into the next. Some use "hard," or "sharp" editing and colliding scenes, abruptly introducing new characters, and changing the course of action, moods, and tempos. For example, Chekhov usually employed "soft" editing, while Brecht used "hard." We will discover all of this during the analysis.

One page of the graph should suffice for an analysis of two or three scenes. We should attach new pages—as needed. We should not write on each new piece of paper the titles of the four fields (CHARACTERS, ACTION, SPACE, TIME). We simply glue or staple the next page to the previous one. Eventually we are going to produce a continuous graph strip that may be two or three yards (or more) in length.

We begin the play analysis by working on the characters, then we proceed to space (going down), followed by time (going up), and finish on action (jumping down). In the four fields of the graph we put our notes using colors of the respective titles (people and action—red, space—green, time—blue). If it is necessary to note music or sound effects we put them in the time field (for music is a temporal art) and we use the color purple. For any special technical requirements or effects we use brown and put them in the space field. Special lighting notes should also be made in the space field, as they usually correlate with sets. Lighting notes should be made in yellow. Of course, all my suggestions about colors—are suggestions only. For me, they have a simple logic. Red is a color of life and love, a color which is always "active," and is in the center of attention. So, I use red for notes about people and action. Green is the color of the grass on which we walk, so, I use it for the space. Blue is the color of an unlimited sky above our heads, so, I use it to indicate time. Purple is an intense and dramatic color. It seems to me suitable for taking notes about music and sound, because they always intensify the stage action. Brown is—for me—practical. It serves well to note technical effects and requirements. Finally, yellow is a bright color, good to note lighting. Everybody may use their own colors, under the condition that they are used consistently.

In the following analytical work we are going to utilize as an example *The Cherry Orchard* by Chekhov. There are many reasons for choosing this play. First, is a masterpiece of world drama. Second, it has a strong realistic and psychological layer. Third, it also has powerful symbolic and universal dimension. All together, it is a rich and complex, yet accessible material. *The Cherry Orchard* is a play about the collision of two epochs, about the passing of generations, ways of life, social classes and economic systems, about the destruction of old values and the emergence of new ones. Are the new values finer and better than the old? Is the new world emerging in the play happier than the old one? I always read and study *The Cherry Orchard* with emotion. It seems to me that it is one of the most profound and prophetic plays ever written in the twentieth century. *The Cherry Orchard* will be used only as an example, though. We will make an analysis of the first act of *The Cherry Orchard* to clearly demonstrate the method of graphing. We will work only on the first act, but readers are advised to continue the analysis until the end of the play. I, personally, do the graphical analysis of each play I work on.

I assume that before we start the analysis we have already read the play "seventy-seven times". Working on the analysis, we have to read every scene again. Chekhov does not divide *The Cherry Orchard* into scenes, so we shall decide when one scene ends and a new one begins. Remember, the criterion for dividing action into scenes is the appearance or disappearance of a character. After we are done with one scene, we will move to the next one. In this way we gather the analytical material of the whole play.

Analysis of the first act of *The Cherry Orchard*

Scene 1. Characters. We start with the characters. In the field titled CHARACTERS (below the horizontal axis of the page) we write down in red the names of the characters in a column. The order of these names should not be accidental, but rather must reflect the importance of a character from the point of view of its participation in the action of a given scene. *The Cherry Orchard* begins with the entrance of Lopahin and Dunyasha. Later, Epihodov joins them. He then leaves, and Lopahin with Dunyasha continue their scene. Using the criterion of the presence of characters, we can recognize three short scenes at the beginning of the play: #1 Lopahin and Dunyasha, #2 Lopahin and Epihodov, and #3 Lopahin and Dunyasha. Scene #2 is a kind of interlude between the two scenes of Lopahin and Dunyasha. Let's work on the first scene: Lopahin and Dunyasha.

Lopahin, along with Lyubov Ranevskaya, is one of two protagonist in the play. He tries to get the cherry orchard—she defends it. Lopahin is an important character in the first scene. I would put his name on top because of his eminence, not because he has more lines or because, as indicated in the stage direction, he enters the stage first. Second on the list of characters is Dunyasha. She is a very distinctive character, but does not participate directly in the main conflict of the play.

I would suggest putting also "the cherry orchard" on the list of the characters. Why? Because it is a symbolic character in the whole play. It "plays" a role. It is always present—near or far. The cherry orchard is—almost—a partner for many characters, including Dunyasha in the first scene, Ranevskaya later on, and others. During the whole play the cherry orchard is talked about, is a subject of dreams and worries, it appears in the text and subtext, and it is the focal point of the whole story. We have to establish clearly from the very beginning of our work that the cherry orchard is extremely important. We have to find out what is its impact on the actions of the other characters, or even "who" the cherry orchard is in the play? For these reasons I suggest putting the name "the cherry orchard" on the list of characters in the first scene. In order to indicate that the cherry orchard is, after all, not a person, but a thing and a symbol, we can put this name in brackets. We should repeat this notation in the following initial scenes and we can drop it from the list of characters later on, still remembering that the cherry orchard is present all the time as a true participant in the action.

I would also suggest putting the dogs on the list of the characters of the first scene. Dunyasha mentions them. Are they around? Will they start barking like mad when the arriving party nears? Building the project of the show, we may or may not choose to have live dogs on stage. In a film version of *The Cherry Orchard* I would love to have them. On the theater stage—rather not. The point is, that in making an analysis we dig for all the data and options that exist in the play. The dogs are an option. In our graph we don't have a special and separate field for the orchards, animals, specters, or robots. We have to allow them a little space in the field of the human characters. It is worth while to put them down because they sometimes play a pivotal role in the action. In *The Cherry Orchard* it is the cherry orchard. In Molière's *Don Juan* it is the stone monument. In *The Wedding* by Wyspiański "the Mulch," a rose bush covered by straw for winter protection, is an important character; the Mulch is an object, but it speaks, moves, and acts. In Ionesco's *Rhinoceros* it is the rhinoceros. In *Striptease* by Sławomir Mrożek there is a mysterious and threatening "Hand," a symbol of totalitarian control, which has a crucial role in the play. The list goes on. So, there are reasons to include "the cherry orchard" as well as "dogs" to the list of characters. Eventually, the analysis of the characters in the first scene of *The Cherry Orchard* goes like this:

CHARACTERS: Lopahin
                  Dunyasha
                  [The cherry orchard]
                  [Dogs]

Space. We have already read the author's initial note several times. Chekhov tell us that "The action takes place on the estate of Madame Ranevskaya"[11] The first stage direction describes the interior of a room, called "the nursery." I recommend writing these data in a column on a separate sheet, starting with the most general information and ending with the details. We will evaluate them, and then move to the field titled SPACE in the graph. At the beginning of a play we usually find quite a lot of data about space. As the play progresses, we usually encounter new and additional descriptions of the space. It is useful to put all of them down, but, if the space does not change, it's not necessary to repeat them with every new scene. Later on we can take note of certain elements of space as they are emphasized or changed, as the action develops. An attentive analysis of the space serves the director's analysis of the play, his/her building of the production project, collaboration with designers, and rehearsals with actors. The data on space we are looking for comprise geography, environment, and

---

[11] Translation of all quotes from *The Cherry Orchard* is done by myself.

architecture, including specific features such as entrances and exits, windows, staircases, as well as objects, such as furniture, musical instruments (for example, a piano), lighting fixtures, appliances (for example, a stove), and many more.

The space of the first scene (and the whole of the first act) of *The Cherry Orchard* is well described both in stage directions and in the dialogues. Let's compile the data. We learn that:

(1) The action of the whole play takes place somewhere in southwestern Russia. (2) There is a country estate with an old manor. (3) The manor is surrounded by a cherry orchard, currently in bloom. (4) There are several rooms in the manor. (5) One of the rooms is the nursery—the first scene, like the whole of the first act, takes place in it. (6) The nursery has a door leading to the interior of the house, and another door leading, through a vestibule, to the outside. (7) The windows of the room have shutters, which are now open, allowing a view of the cherry orchard. (8) There is furniture in the room: an armchair, chairs, table, children's beds, and other objects. These data may be summarized and simplified into the following concise notation:

SPACE: A nursery room in a country manor
             A cherry orchard visible through the windows
             The orchard on an estate in southwestern Russia

Time. We know, from previous studies, that *The Cherry Orchard* was written in 1903 as a "contemporary play." Both the lines and the stage directions precisely indicate the time of the action at the beginning of the play. Dunyasha says: "It is about two in the morning" and continues with: "It's almost daylight." Epihodov states: "The trees are covered by morning frost." In a stage direction we read: "Dunyasha blows out the candle." All of these data clearly show that it is very early morning, spring, probably late May. We can, therefore, put on our graph:

TIME: The beginning of the 20th century
            Spring, late May
            Very early morning, about 2:00 AM

Action. At this point, we understand the characters' activities and words, we realize what is going on, and know where and when all this is happening. Now we should be able to clearly define the action. This definition should have the form of a concise title. The title should be dramatic and call to the imagination. It is a directorial key to the action. It gives insight into the stage events and characters' deeds. It logically ensues from the action and expresses its essence. It should be easy to grasp and remember, as well as being useful and handy for both director and actor. It must be dynamic, pointing out to the major conflict of the scene and providing information about the characters' motivations, goals, and objectives.

Meyerhold was the first to give titles to particular scenes of a play for analytical purposes. In his 1922 production of *The Forest* by Alexandr Ostrovsky, he even communicated the titles to the audience by projecting them on an upstage screen. Meyerhold's contemporary, the film director, Sergei Eisenstein, taught his students to find a title for every section of a screenplay being prepared for shooting. Later on, Brecht borrowed this method from both Meyerhold and Eisenstein and gave titles to every scene in his plays. In the productions he directed, the titles were shown on banners on stage. Tennessee Williams in the text of *The Glass Menagerie* introduces frequently a "LEGEND ON SCREEN" or a "SCREEN IMAGE," as he puts it. These are titles of songs, titles of scenes, names of characters who lead the scenes, quotes of lines, old photographs, magazines covers, and so on. The author expects that these "legends" and "images" be produced on stage. Indeed many directors followed his wish.

The title of a scene summarizes and interprets the action realistically, symbolically, and mythically. Sometimes it is useful to come up with two titles, one expressing the action on the realistic and "life-like" level; the other reflecting the universal and metaphorical plane. The title works best if it uses a verb and refers to a character (or characters') activities or deeds. A verb based, active title helps the director to give actors precise tasks.

How should we title the first scene in *The Cherry Orchard*? We find the answer both in what is given directly: the dialogue and stage directions, as well as what is hidden in the subtext and psychology of the characters. We should be aware that sometimes (very often in Chekhov!) the subtext contradicts the text, and only the summary of both allows us to discover the true meaning of a scene. We already know who appears in the first scene (what characters), where they are (in what space), and when the action takes place (what time it is). But what do these characters do? What is their action? What do they want? What is happening to them? We should ask them: "What do you do?" "What do you want?" "What is your aim?"—not "What are you talking about?" Usually, the characters' acts and desires are directed to other characters, whether present on stage or not. The characters influence other characters, trying to get something from others, or expecting something from them. These wishes and acts collide with others' wishes and acts, and either annihilate or amplify them. In a constant struggle of wills there are winners and losers; and their roles frequently change. In the first scene of our play we have Lopahin and Dunyasha. Let's ask each of them: "What do you want?" "What is happening to you?" Both of them are waiting for the arrival of Madame Ranevskaya and her party. Both are waiting anxiously and impatiently. Dunyasha almost faints. Lopahin is nervous and tense because he does not know how Ranevskaya will react to him, a former peasant, the son of a serf, and now a businessman and a potential buyer of the estate. What, therefore, is the action? What title should we give it? What about *Waiting*? Yes, these people are waiting. But it is not enough. There's something more to it. What kind of their waiting is it? Is it impatient, uncertain, nervous, full of anxiety or full of hope? What are these two waiting for? For a change in their lives? For someone who will provide sense to their lives? For something which would fill the emptiness of their existence? More practically, Lopahin is waiting, as he will be doing until almost the end of the play, for the fulfillment of his deepest dream—buying the cherry orchard. At the same time, he knows that not even acquisition of the orchard can change the fact that he is neither an aristocrat, nor the owner of a hereditary estate, but a peasant and parvenu. Dunyasha is waiting for a fairy-tale prince to propose to her and whisk her away to a different life, but instead, it is Epihodov who has proposed to her, and he is far from being Prince Charming. Later on Dunyasha will take Yasha, a valet arriving from Paris, for a prince. She'll fall in love with Yasha so easily precisely because she has been waiting for a change in her life from the very beginning of the play.

After having asked these questions and thinking about the answers, we can say that *The Cherry Orchard* begins with a painful and unclear expectation. From reading the whole play (remember?—seventy-seven times) we know that virtually all the characters in this play are waiting, expecting, and longing for a change. From reading other plays by the same author (remember?—I recommended that) we know that an existential waiting is a general Chekhovian motive permeating all his works. The expectation of something, or waiting for something, not clearly articulated, vague, dreamy, alluding to a change in life, a change which probably will never happen, is the state and the action characterizing many (if not all) characters in Chekhov's plays, including, of course, *The Cherry Orchard*. It is a uniquely Chekhovian "passive activity" which has both realistic and symbolic dimensions, as well as both historic and metaphysical ones. It describes the fates of characters, indicating that they have archetypical scope. It refers to actual historical processes, class struggle, political transformations, family, and cultural changes and it has philosophical and universal proportions.

The general and contextual data confirms our findings about the first scene of *The Cherry Orchard*. Indeed, Lopahin and Dunyasha are waiting—each in their own way—for a change, a transformation. Both are tired, nervous, anxious, sleepy, their eyes are hurting, their bones are aching. They are listening and looking through the windows. They are preparing themselves for meeting the arriving party. They are in the nursery, which is foreign territory for both of them, adding to their anxiety. A proper space for Lopahin would be either a business office, or a spot outdoors where he would stand barefoot, a peasant boy. Dunyasha's proper space would be the kitchen. They have been waiting since yesterday and it's already morning. They are exhausted. So, what is the action?

And, consequently, what is the title of the scene? The criteria for selecting a scene title are not absolutely clear. We only know that it should logically emerge from the action, be based on the text and subtext, and be useful in practical directorial, designing, and acting work. Let's take a risk and propose the title: *Awaiting a Great Change.* I would not insist that this title is the best or the only one possible for the first scene of *The Cherry Orchard* but it sounds convincing and interesting. It appeared several times in my classes and workshops based on *The Cherry Orchard.* Alternative titles were: *Waiting for the Overseas Guest, A Painful Waiting, An Anxious Waiting, Morning After a Night Watch* and others. Let's stick to *Awaiting a Great Change.* We put it into the graph. Summarizing: the analysis of the first scene of *The Cherry Orchard* may be presented as follows:

<table>
<tr><td colspan="2" align="center">**TABLE: THE ANALYTICAL GRAPH**
OF THE FIRST SCENE OF *THE CHERRY ORCHARD*</td></tr>
<tr><td>TIME:</td><td>The beginning of the 20th century
Spring, late May
Very early morning, about 2:00 AM</td></tr>
<tr><td>ACTION:</td><td>*Awaiting a Great Change*</td></tr>
<tr><td>CHARACTERS:</td><td>Lopahin
Dunyasha
[The cherry orchard]
[Dogs]</td></tr>
<tr><td>SPACE:</td><td>A nursery room in a country manor
A cherry orchard visible through the windows
The orchard on an estate in southwestern Russia</td></tr>
</table>

Scene 2. We continue the analysis of the following scene precisely the same way as the first one. We will read, study, investigate and evaluate all the data pertaining to the characters, space, time, and action, and we will put them in to the graph.

Characters. A new character, Epihodov, enters and interrupts the previous scene. Dunyasha soon leaves to fetch *kvas* (a soft drink) and Epihodov stays with Lopahin. After a while Dunyasha returns and Epihodov exits, ending this short scene. Epihodov is the central character—it is his scene. From the point of view of the analysis, and in the work of a director with an actor, the first appearance of a character is a very important moment. It is when a character introduces himself/herself to the audience. As in real life, the first impression is crucial and leaves a lasting impact. The director ought to identify all first appearances of all characters, to decide consciously how a character should be presented to the public, and determine what aspects of the role should be emphasized. We may discover that the very first appearance of a character should be a *coup de théâtre*, or, alternatively, that there are reasons not to underline the first entrance and, in a way, "hide" it, postponing the character's "grand" entrance. There are thousands of ways to stage the first entrance and first scene of a character. In any case it is an important moment for an actor and it is a significant point of the action. Chekhov wants to present Epihodov from the very beginning in his whole theatrical grandeur. His short scene is an acting "solo," a skit in which the actor should present all of Epihodov's psychological and physical characteristics. An actor should show Epihodov's state of mind: he is timid and afraid. All his other traits should be exposed too: how he moves—his steps are awkward in his squeaking boots; how he speaks—he expresses himself pathetically and unnaturally; how he behaves—he commits gaffes all the time. It is probable that he brought the bouquet for his fiancée-to-be Dunyasha, but he is afraid to give it to her, so he lies, telling her that it is for Madame Ranevskaya from the gardener.

Space. The space in the second scene does not change. However, in the first scene an entrance from the interior of the house was employed, and in this scene an entrance from the exterior (through a hallway) is used. In a way the set enlarges, reveals more functions, and suggests the adjacent spaces. The cherry orchard, seen through the windows, still plays an important role.

Time. The time analysis in the second scene reveals Chekhov's general treatment of time. The second scene immediately follows the first with complete continuity. Working on the subsequent scenes we learn that Chekhov uses "real" time in each of the acts of the play, and suggests that the duration of the stage events is as long as it would be in real life. (He does that in other plays too.) It is a simple, yet significant analytical discovery. The watches of the characters and the spectators move at the same rate. This approach to the stage time makes the action believable and natural, and it merges the lives of the characters into the reality of the life of the audience.

Action. The action of the second scene, as well as of the first, is based on waiting. Epihodov interrupts the waiting of Lopahin and Dunyasha, but he himself is also waiting for the arrival of Madame Ranevskaya as well as for Dunyasha's answer to his proposal. Epihodov's entrance and his interaction with Lopahin expose a nasty trait in the character of the latter: Lopahin awaits the arrival of Ranevskaya and, feeling inferior to her, compensates by boorishly showing his superiority to Epihodov. Dunyasha, confronted with Epihodov, who wants to marry her, is perplexed and runs away. As a result, Epihodov, who obviously came to see Dunyasha, is left with Lopahin. What is Lopahin doing? He humiliates Epihodov in order to boost his own ego. What is Dunyasha doing? She tries to cover her emotions. What is Epihodov, the central character of this scene, doing? He courts Dunyasha in her presence and her absence. He mumbles nonsense. He moves like an elephant in a china shop. It's Epihodov's scene. How should we title it? *Awkward Love's Labors*? (as an analogy to *Love's Labor's Lost*) or *The Courtship of a Hundred Misfortunes*? (using a quote from the play—Epihodov is called around "one hundred misfortunes.") Let's take the first one. The analysis of the second scene is as follows:

TIME:	[Immediate continuity]
ACTION:	*Awkward Love's Labors*
CHARACTERS:	Epihodov
	Lopahin
	Dunyasha [exists and returns]
	[The cherry orchard]
	[Dogs]
SPACE:	[As before] Emphasis on the entrance from the outside

Scene 3. The third scene is linked with the first one on all levels: there are the

same characters (Lopahin and Dunyasha), the same space, the time is running continuously, and the action continues from the action of the first scene: Lopahin and Dunyasha are waiting for a change. Putting this into our graph shows:

TIME:	[Immediate continuity]
ACTION:	*Awaiting a Great Change* (second part)
CHARACTERS:	Lopahin
	Dunyasha
	[The cherry orchard]
	[Dogs]
SPACE:	[As before] Emphasis on the exit

Scene 4. Scene 3 scene ends with the exit of Lopahin and Dunyasha. They go to meet the guests. The author wants the stage to be "empty" for a while, indicating that the first three scenes were a kind of prologue. Now the action of the play will start for good. We established that the presence/activity of a character (or characters) is a criterion for identifying separate scenes. From this point of view, Scene 4 of *The Cherry Orchard* is a short, yet individual segment of action, introducing the old servant Fiers. He is alone on stage. His entrance is certainly important for the author, because it is Fiers' first appearance, and he is (as we already know from reading the whole play) a symbolic character, one of the keys opening the universal and mythical layer of the story. Fiers's approaching death at the end of the play symbolizes the death of the cherry orchard, the passing of the old social and political order, and the destruction of both the family and the estate. It is the tragic perspective in a drama that otherwise contains comedic aspects. We can say that Fiers is, from the very beginning, the symbol of death, that he carries the death virus. (One of my students, Jill, proposed a hypothesis that Fiers is death incarnated and in her project of the production she gave Fiers a tragic mask of death. It was a very interesting directorial concept.) What is Fiers, an old servant, or butler, doing in his scene? He left early for the railway station, not oversleeping like Lopahin. At the station he met his mistress with reverence and joy, and now he greets her at home, after so many years of absence. Maybe, appearing on stage, he makes a last minute inspection checking whether everything is in order? Or he hurries up

to correct something (furniture? china? samovar?) which, as he recalled on the way from the station, needed to be fixed? Maybe he runs away to hide his emotions and weeps in a dark corner? Perhaps he feels and smells the death of the house and tries to exorcise it? Or does he, himself, foresees the death of the house, the orchard, the family? We don't know for sure. The author does not explain this in the stage directions and he does not give Fiers any lines in the scene. The director and the actor playing Fiers will determine this. But the material for their work should be prepared in the graph.

TIME:	[Immediate continuity]
ACTION:	*Last Inspection* [on the realistic level]
	Death's Foreboding [on the symbolic level]
CHARACTER:	Fiers
SPACE:	[As before]

Scene 5. Voices of the guests and the hosts are heard before they all enter the nursery. Three groups appear: the party from Paris, those who met them at the railroad station, and those who greet them at the entrance to the house. The characters' actions include their own individual activities, the relationships among them, and their correlation with the space. People coming from abroad tenderly acknowledge the home and the orchard. The locals interact with newcomers. Additionally, it should be noted that this is the first group scene of the play. In further analysis we should always identify a general nature of a scene: is it intimate, with only two or three characters? Or is it a group scene with several of them? Or is it a crowd? Or even a mass scene? It is worth while to indicate group (crowd, mass) scenes in the graph. It helps to see and understand the structure of the whole play. In my graphs, to point out group scenes, I put a capital "G" in the action field. The analysis of the arrival scene in *The Cherry Orchard* gives the following results:

TIME:	[Immediate continuity]	
ACTION:	G [group scene] *Tender Greeting of the Old Home* [on the realistic level] *A Home Coming* [on the mythical level]	
CHARACTERS:	Coming from abroad:	Ranevskaya Anya Charlotta (with a dog)
	Meeting them at the station:	Gayev Varya Servants (with luggage)
	Meeting them at the entrance:	Lopahin Dunyasha Pishtchik
	[The cherry orchard] [Dogs]	
SPACE:	[As before] Emphasis on the windows and doors	

Scene 6. The whole party leaves the nursery. The group scene ends and an intimate scene follows, with only two characters: Anya and Dunyasha. They exchange confessions but somehow fail to understand each other. What do these two women do? What do they want to express and what do they fail to communicate? Dunyasha mentions Trofimov—why? How does Anya react to the news that he is here? Below I shall present the results of my analysis of this scene. Later, as the analysis progresses, scene by scene, I present only my conclusions. I suggest that the reader first go over my conclusions, and, second, make his/her own analysis and compare it with mine. The analysis of the whole play should follow, using the method presented here.

The graphical analysis of scene 6 of *The Cherry Orchard* is as follows:

TIME:	[Immediate continuity]
ACTION:	*Unreciprocated Confessions*
CHARACTERS:	Anya Dunyasha
SPACE:	[As before] Emphasis on the windows and furniture: Anya, former occupant of the rooms greets them

Scene 7.

TIME:	[Immediate continuity]
ACTION:	*Dreadful Future*
CHARACTERS:	Anya
	Varya
	Lopahin [a short appearance]
	Dunyasha [at the beginning and at the end of scene]
SPACE:	[As before]

Scene 8.

TIME:	[Immediate continuity]
ACTION:	*French Courtship*
CHARACTERS:	Yasha
	Dunyasha
SPACE:	[As before] A hidden corner in the sets

Scene 9.

TIME:	[Immediate continuity]
ACTION:	*Building Bridges to the Past* [Yes: to the past!]
CHARACTERS:	Dunyasha
	Varya
	Anya
	Fiers
SPACE:	[As before]

Scene 10. In this scene we have the first confrontation between Madame Ranevskaya and Lopahin. It is the "first battle of the cherry orchard." A similar battle will occur in the second act. The third act will culminate in the triumphant dance of Lopahin who has finally bought the orchard. Scene 10 is—from the point of view of the structure of the whole play—the key scene of act one, and one of the key scenes of the whole plot. This "battle of the cherry orchard" is a very strange combat: there are more evasions than attacks, more allusions than clear statements, more hidden subtexts than open texts referring to the conflict over the cherry orchard. The analysis of this scene is as follows:

TIME:	[Immediate continuity; morning still brighter]
	G
ACTION:	*The Battle Over the Cherry Orchard # 1*
CHARACTERS:	Ranevskaya
	Lopahin
	Varya [she exits and soon returns]
	Anya [she exits early in the scene]
	Fiers
	Gayev
	Pishtchik
	Yasha [enters during the scene]
	Charlotta [enters and soon exits]
SPACE:	[As before] The focus is on the cherry orchard

Scene 11.

TIME:	[Immediate continuity]
ACTION:	*Dreams About a Miraculous Saving of the Cherry Orchard*
CHARACTERS:	Ranevskaya
	Gayev
	Varya
	Fiers
	Pishtchik
SPACE:	[As before] The focus is on the cherry orchard]

Scene 12.

TIME:	[Immediate continuity]
ACTION:	*The Past Resurrected*
CHARACTERS:	Trofimov [he appears for the first time and is the most important character in this scene]
	Ranevskaya
	Gayev
	Varya
	Fiers
	Pishtchik
SPACE:	[As before] Look into the cherry orchard

Scene 13.

TIME:	[Immediate continuity]
ACTION:	*The Incurable Sickness of Will*
CHARACTERS:	Gayev
	Varya
	Yasha [soon exits]
	Anya [exits during the scene]
	Fiers [comes and takes Gayev]
SPACE:	[As before]

Scene 14.

TIME:	[Immediate continuity; it is now bright morning]
	MUSIC: A tune from the shepherd's flute
ACTION:	*Anxiety and Hope*
CHARACTERS:	Varya
	Anya
	Trofimov [at the end of scene]
	[Shepherd—either on or off stage]
SPACE:	[As before] Focus on the cherry orchard in bloom

Summary of the analysis of the first act of *The Cherry Orchard*

Now, that we have finished the analysis of the firs act of the play, let's review the results.

Characters. Our analysis of the characters identified who they are from the sociological, familial, professional, economic, and generational points of view. We learned a lot about their souls, personalities, and ways of life. For example, Madame Ranevskaya's constant drifting and lack of will contrasts with Lopahin's steely will power. We know how the characters behave, move, and speak. For example, Epihodov behaves awkwardly, Fiers hobbles, and Yasha is expressing himself in a caricatured "Parisian" way. We found the means of expression the author envisages for every character. For example: Madame Ranevskaya very often bursts in tears; Anya is emotional; while Varya is composed and cold. "The cherry orchard," treated as a character, is always present, and from time to time it is "enlarged," shown like a film close-up. We almost have the feeling that it steps down stage and directly addresses the public. The cherry orchard draws people in and delivers them out, as they emerge from it and dissolve into it. It is a constant point of reference, a springboard for discussions, and an inspiration for dreams and desires. The cherry orchard is both the subject and the object of actions and dialogues. It is also a symbol of the old Russia, of the old social system, of the old values, and of a world now passing away, and of life. At the end of the third act Trofimov says: "Russia is our orchard." Leaving the estate Ranevskaya says: "Oh my beautiful, lovely orchard! My youth, my happiness, my life..." Indeed, the cherry orchard continually affects all the characters in the play with force. It is a true character.

Space. The analysis revealed the space's structure, functions, traits, and appearance. In the first act of the play the whole space has two parts. It is, first, an interior equipped with furniture, windows and doors; and, second, it is the exterior—the cherry orchard—all the time visible and accessible.

Time. The analysis of time reveals how the author treats it. In *The Cherry Orchard* time passes continuously and realistically within each of the four acts. The present time also includes the past and the future—in the form of memoirs, recollections, dreams, and plans. The past is evoked, for example, in the story of Grisha's drowning. The future appears in Trofimov's fantasies. Additionally, the author introduces strange sounds which play a symbolic role and push the realistically running time onto the universal level; at the end of the first act it is the Shepherd's flute. In general, an analysis of time in *The Cherry Orchard* suggests that the play, conditioned historically and situated within very specific time spans, changes of seasons, and even up to the minute time-frames, is oriented towards timelessness and universality.

Action. The analysis discovered the action's events, structure, and rhythm. We found that Chekhov uses soft, easy flowing edits, comparable to the film figure of "dissolving." We learned that the author divides the action of an act into short (sometimes very short) and long scenes, and that he likes to clash intimate and group scenes. Finally, the analysis taught us that the conflicts in this play are usually built on the level of subtext (not text) and that the mood or "atmosphere" is the author's most cherished means of expression.

The analysis of the play conducted objectively, attentively, humbly, and honestly, as well as passionately and keenly, allows the director to find the creative impulses for further work, and to collect abundant data for building a project of the production. These are necessary to productive rehearsals of the play. The production project, and work on the actual show, however, are different problems. We'll deal with them later.

CHAPTER 2. CREATING THE HUMAN LAYER OF THE PRODUCTION

Introduction

The people in the theater are actors and spectators. Both of them have helpers during the show: on the side of the actors it is the technical and administrative staff, on the side of the public, the box office people, ushers, and receptionists. But a theater process will take place even without anybody besides actors and spectators. An actor and a spectator are the only ingredients necessary to create the human matter of performance. The creative shaping of this matter is the director's most important task. It begins with work with actors.

A director's acting experience might be helpful in his/her work. It is not a condition, though, as many 20th century directors have proved. Absolutely indispensable is the director's understanding of acting's creative mechanisms, an openness to other people, an attitude of service to others, and the realization that in the actual theater production there's no place for the director. The director simply disappears and is no longer needed when the show is played and the actors interact with the public. The responsibility of the director is to prepare this interaction. And not only to prepare it, but to creatively structure, shape, and define it.

In this short course on directing there is not enough space for a detailed discussion of acting. Likewise we can't give in-depth consideration to the problems of design, music, or the technical aspects of theater work, yet all are directorial concerns. In this chapter on creating the human layer of the show, we are only going to discuss the basic problems of acting, which are of particular interest and importance for directors. At the same time, I strongly recommend that all practicing or potential directors deepen their knowledge and experience in the domain of acting. The same refers to the problems of audience and its participation in the show, including the role and function of spectators in the production from the artistic, psychological, and sociological perspective.

The director's work with actor

Acting is the basic matter of the performance. An actor is a human being artistically structuring his/her life and sharing it with an audience. Hence, the two dimensions of acting are human and artistic. An actor is, first, a living human being, and, second, an artist.

As human beings, actors are persons with spiritual, physical, biological, and psychological characteristics; human beings as they are in their truth, privacy, and individuality; human beings conditioned by their sex, age, appearance, experience, education, profession, way of speaking and moving, manners, aspirations and dreams.

As artists, actors purposely and consciously create, shape, and structure their activities. They are artist who publicly express their personalities; artists who share with others their aspirations and wishes, beliefs and ideas, opinions and values, feelings and thoughts; artists who communicate to others their spirituality and physicality. Actors do all this through "acting," "playing," or "performing," a craft subject to certain rules.

Directors should know and understand that acting is a twofold phenomenon composed of the human and personal, as well as the artistic and public, because during the rehearsals they work with people as they are—human beings personally and culturally conditioned, as well as with artists—craftspeople, creators, and professionals. The director influences people and shapes these people's art. A director's work with actors is a constant interhuman interaction of sharing and exchanging. It is based on empathy and understanding, and it requires personal cooperation. At the same time it is an artistic and creative process, which has methodic foundations and aesthetic goals.

Rules of the director's work with actors

The personal and private life of an actor, and his/her public and artistic expression of that life are two, inseparably connected spheres of acting. The most difficult and necessary skill of a director is to combine the ability to communicate and work with an actor on these two levels: the human and the artistic. The experience of many directors, including myself, teaches that both of these levels are important; they should be activated simultaneously or in turns, but none of them should be neglected. The most desired ideal in the work of the director with the actor is a blend of delicate and friendly interaction on the human level, with a systematic and strict collaboration on the artistic level. Proper interhuman relationships are the condition for artistic effectiveness; difficult artistic problems are most solvable in an atmosphere of trust, tolerance, and understanding.

There are several fundamental rules on which the work of a director with an actor should be based. They refer to both human and artistic aspects of director-actor work. They should be integrated through each stage of the rehearsal process.

A table concisely presents these matters:

TABLE: DIRECTOR'S WORK WITH ACTOR

Principles of the director's work with actors on the human level

(1) Actors are human beings—as you are. Respect their dignity and pride. Spare their sensitivity and nerves. Love and accept them as they are.

(2) Treat every actor as an individual, unique, and sovereign person—which he/she is. Even working with a large cast you have to treat each actor as an individual.

(3) Allow the actors to be open and be open to them.

(4) Return frankness with frankness.

(5) Always tell first and underline what was good in an actor's work. Criticize with caution and sympathy, and only when necessary. Remember: you are praising or criticizing a living human being, not a tool or machine.

(6) Develop an atmosphere of mutual trust and understanding during rehearsals.

(7) Respect actors' fear and shame. Assure them—in words, attitude, and deeds—that they are safe with you.

(8) If a difficulty arises, try to solve it privately and individually, not publicly in front of the whole cast.

(9) The more delicate you are in working with an actor—the sharper, bolder, and riskier the acting he/she is going to propose.

(10) Between fraternization and coldness there is a vast territory for friendship and partnership between a director and an actor.

Principles of the director's work with actors on the artistic level

(1) Remember, only the actors will play the show, not you. Let the actors know from the very beginning of the work that they are responsible for the final shape and expression of the show.

(2) Expand actors' artistic self-esteem and independence. Help their individualities to grow.

(3) Allow actors to improvise, propose, invent, and create. The more freedom and improvisation during rehearsals the firmer the production will be. A paradox: the more actors invent themselves—the more control over the show the director has.

(4) The deeper the internal motivation of an actor—the more expressive his/her external expression.

(5) The more individually you work with an actor—the more individual, unique, and special the character he/she will create.

(6) Speak to actors concisely and to the point. Never waste actors' time. If you can't help—don't hurt.

(7) Be systematic in your work—the actors will reciprocate with the same.

(8) "Play" for actors and "show" how to play during rehearsal only as the last resort. If you play for actors—play as a director, not as a "better actor."

(9) Use various techniques and methods of work as a creative artist, and create dreams and visions as a rigorous and strict practitioner.

(10) Teach actors humility towards the art of theater, and yourself humility towards the art of acting.

Ways for the director to communicate with actors

Working with actors, the director must clearly and efficiently communicate with them. Some ways of communication are effective and some frustrate understanding. Various means of communication between directors and actors can be distinguished and described separately, but usually all of them are used in combinations.

TABLE: DIRECTOR'S COMMUNICATIONS WITH ACTORS

(1) Informing actors—communication on the level of consciousness and intelligence.
(2) Inspiring actors—communication on the level of subconsciousness, emotions, imagination, and fantasy.
(3) Instructing actors—communication on the level of will.
(4) Giving notes to actors—communication on all the levels.

Informing actors is communicating—usually by words—certain data or facts concerning characters and action. Information is always the basic and substantial part of a director's communication with actors. Actors should be informed about the character, partners, and various circumstances. Directors inform actors about their characters' personalities, background, motivations and objectives. They discuss who the characters are, what they do, and what they want. It is necessary also to talk about the circumstances of characters' actions; be they social, spatial, or temporal. Informing is communication on the level of intellect; it is sharing knowledge; it is appealing to actors' consciousness, expertise, and personal experience. For example, informing an actress about Madame Ranevskaya (in *The Cherry Orchard*), a director would speak about her age, family situation (failed marriage), social position (she belongs to the aristocracy) means (she has lost her fortune), habits (she likes throwing money away), behaviors (she cries very often), and about her personality (she is very emotional). The circumstances of her social environment would be discussed as well. She is very lonely—her brother lacks volition, her adviser Lopahin is in reality her opponent, and the younger generation does not understand her at all. The actress should be also informed about the circumstances of space (her visceral connection with the cherry orchard) and time (time is running out fast: there's a deadline for the auction of the cherry orchard). Directing a Shakespearian chronicle, a director might discuss with the cast certain historical facts. Working on a Restoration comedy, he/she might talk about the manners of the late 17th century English gentry. While preparing a Sam Shepard play they could explore the memories of a destitute child in rural America.

Inspiring actors is communication that calls on their subconscious (or unconscious)—a vast territory beyond logic and knowledge. A director can inspire an actor in many different ways. We can present this in a table.

TABLE: EXAMPLES OF INSPIRING ACTORS

(1) Giving a task practically impossible to do: "Jump to heaven."
(2) Surrounding them with fantastic or dream-like circumstances: "You fly with a flight of cranes."
(3) Suggesting feelings analogous to their stage activities: "It's as of you were on the roof of a skyscraper."
(4) Comparing their stage business to an animal's: "Attack her like a tiger."
(5) Recalling fears: "Your house is surrounded by flood waters."
(6) Hinting at desires: "You want this terribly..." (candy, drink, sex.)
(7) Remembering dramatic experiences: "A branch of a tree broke under your foot. You are falling!"
(8) Using symbols: "Carry this box as a priest would carry a reliquary."
(9) Implying metaphors: "You approach her as a wounded bird."
(10) Alluding to experiences: "It is as cold as a bus stop in a North Dakota winter."

Generally speaking, calling on the subconscious and the imagination is always based on transforming an existing situation, realistic task, or everyday activity into a situation, task, or activity which is unrealistic, paradoxical, mysterious, or impossible. In this way the actor is submerged in a different world—a world of dreams, terrifying images and recollections, or soothing visions and memories. Finding him/herself in such an unusual world he/she is forced to call on unusual reflexes, impulses, reactions, or behaviors. Consequently, he/she finds new, fresh, and unexpected means of acting.

Instructing actors is communicating with them using orders, commands, or directives. These may refer to movement ("stand up," "go," "stop"), to activities ("help her to sit," "open the book"), to speech ("speak louder," "scream"), and to various means of expression ("laugh," "close your eyes"). In certain predicaments a short instruction is effective and expedient. It saves time and spares unnecessary explanations. It might serve an actor as a springboard for further independent work. For example, if during the scene of Catherine and the peasants in Brecht's *Mother Courage* the director suddenly shouts: "Take the ladder up, now!"—the actress gets a strong, unequivocal impetus. It is a help for her. She (hopefully) follows it without hesitation, and after having done this, she goes on with her major task: to wake up the villagers in the valley settlement. This sharp, brief, and closed instruction given at the right time by the director would help the actress fulfill her necessary physical activity at the right moment.

Instructing, ordering, or commanding may be closed or open. An instruction is closed and definitive if it leaves little or no margin for interpretation. Indeed, "Take the ladder up, now!" is clear, definitive, and closed. Similarly, commands such as: "Hit the dirt!" or "Get out!" are certainly closed. Closed orders are sometimes useful, but they do not inspire the actors to create and leave them passive. For these reasons closed orders should be used only rarely. On the other hand, an instruction can be open and leave the interpretation to the actor. For example, if a director says: "Hide yourself!" an actor can use many different ways and speeds, as well as places to hide himself/herself, making his/her own choices about how to fulfill the order. Open orders set actors' creativity in motion, demand their activity, and enhance their independence. Generally speaking, instructing may be useful and effective, but it should not became the only way of directing. If this happens, the directing changes into boot camp training, with the director as drill sergeant. Shows prepared this way may be well functioning mechanisms but usually there is no life in them. Below you'll find the most important elements of directorial notes.

TABLE: DIRECTORIAL NOTES

(1) First, thank the actors, praise their efforts, underline their accomplishments, tell what was good in their work. This is the most important principle of director's notes.

(2) Second, suggest developments, changes, corrections, or modifications.

(3) Third, advise what did not work, what should be dropped, what went wrong and should not be repeated.

(4) Be affirmative. Don't ever fail to tell the actors what was good in their play and always expect them to make progress.

(5) Be specific. Address the details of acting in terms of lines, bits, movements, gestures.

(6) Be analytical. The analysis should be objective, descriptive, and practical. If you are either commending or criticizing, explain and justify why your are saying something, why you advise keeping or dropping something.

(7) Be evaluative. And don't be afraid to evaluate! The actors expect you to tell them truly and professionally what is good in their play and what is not so good. Evaluation, however, must be always tactful, professional, and constructive. If you have to really tell someone something which might hurt them—do it individually in a dark corner.

(8) Be future-oriented. Never stop on a negative. Always demonstrate to actors the perspective of improvement and progress. In talking about future tasks, first, explain them clearly, second, say why are they needed, third, illuminate their internal motivations, and, fourth, advise what might be the external means of expression to materialize these tasks.

(9) Be enthusiastic and encouraging. This refers both to evaluation of what was done and to setting new objectives.

(10) Giving notes allow and require the actors to take written notes; this is also necessary during actual rehearsals. After the notes, discussion and questions should be encouraged. Discussion must be clearly summarized and closed by the director, not leaving any doubts as to the conclusion. Questions must be frankly and specifically answered. It is the director who "chairs" the meeting.

Giving notes to actors after they played a bit, a scene, or the whole play is an absolutely necessary element of directing. The actors must hear from the director how the work went, what was good (this always goes first!) and what was not so good; what could, or should, be corrected, changed, or improved. Regardless of which method of communication we use during the rehearsal (informing, inspiring, or instructing) the notes should be multi-layered and include both intellectual and emotional exchange; they must be intellectually clear and emotionally convincing. The director can be enthusiastic and can disapprove. The former is uplifting, the latter should never be offensive; if it is necessary, it must be delicate and encouraging. Notes are, in a way, the director's performance. Giving notes we can sometimes "play" something for actors; it is appropriate to not only comment verbally but also demonstrate physically; directorial "playing," as I said, should not be overused. There are three basic steps in giving notes: first, say what is good, second: discuss what should be changed, third: say what is bad. It goes like this: good—changeable—bad. In other words: keep what is good; change what should be developed; throw away what is bad.

The technique of "Five questions about the character"

The director works with an actor-person and with an actor-artist. During rehearsals the director is the actor's teacher, guide, leader, adviser, inspirer, friend, helper, care-taker, and (sometimes) baby-sitter. It is extremely important that the process of work of the director with the actor is a two-way exchange of creative energy: from the director to the actor, and from the actor to the director.

We know that the levels of communication between the director and the actor, and vice versa, include consciousness and subconsciousness, intellect and imagination, emotions and will. We also established that ways of communicating embrace information, inspiration, orders, and explanations. The director discusses with the actor his/her character's actions and deeds, motives and goals, and circumstances. Based on the material gathered during the text analysis and prepared in the project of the production, the director gives the actors tasks to fulfill. The various aspects of each task should be explained in a certain order. Always using the same pattern/sequence of informing, inspiring, explaining, and discussing, we organize and sequence the communication between director and actor. This pattern/sequence might be called the "Technique of five questions about the character." The questions refer to: (1) the character, (2) the character's partners, (3) space, (4) time, and (4) the character's action. We ask (and answer) five specific questions: (1)who? (2)with whom? (3)where? (4)when? (5)what? Of course, it might be necessary to ask more questions, or to modify these listed here. But the general technique remains the same. Altogether, we address five subjects and five areas of problems.

TABLE: TECHNIQUE OF FIVE QUESTIONS
ABOUT THE CHARACTER

(1) Character: Who? Who is the character? Who is he/she in terms of age, occupation, profession, social environment, family ties, culture, psychology, etc.?

(2) Partners: With whom? Who are the character's partners? With whom does the character interact? What are the social, familial, professional, and other circumstances of the character's actions?

(3) Space: Where? Where is he/she? Where does the character act? What are the spatial and environmental circumstances of the character's actions? What is the exterior or interior of this space? What is especially important for the character from the point of view of space?

(4) Time: When? When does the character act? What are the temporal circumstances of the character's actions, including history, date, season, time of day or night?

(5) Action: What? What is the character doing? What is happening to him/her? What does the character want? What are the character's objectives, wishes, or dreams?

The "Technique of five questions about the character" is necessary for the work of a director with an actor, but is it also useful for the director's communication with other people involved with the preparation of a show, for it always situates the person, the human being, in the center of the whole theater work. It focuses on the person and, simultaneously, it helps to see this person within a context/environment: social, spatial, and temporal. It also allows us to discern the action in which this person is involved. Let's use this technique working not only with actors, but also with designers, authors, literary managers, or producers, always beginning with the human aspect of the production, not with objects or money. Talking with a set designer, for example, we should first explain who the characters are, what they are doing, or what they are fighting about; only then should we turn to the space where the action takes place. The same is true in our work with costume designers. We have to first establish who the characters are, and only then how they should be dressed. Talking to the author of the play, whom we might need to ask for some rewriting, we also have to speak first about the characters—who they are, what they do, and so forth—not about their words; the words are secondary. Similarly, this is the concrete sequence for talking with composers, technical directors, producers, and others. The "Technique of five questions about the character" always guides us to the core of the problems of our work and allows us to navigate the complex, and sometimes perilous waters of the theatrical process.

Exercises for the director's work with actors

We are going to get on our feet now. In a series of practical exercises we will study and practice two directorial skills: the various ways of directorial communication with actors and the "Technique of five questions about the character." Investigating various ways of communication we will purposely make sharp distinctions between them. In real work with actors they are sometimes combined or used alternately. Using the "Technique of five questions" should become "second nature" to a director and I strongly recommend its use every time we work with actors, especially when we take on a new action or scene. Of course, sometimes we don't need to ask or answer all five questions, but we should be aware that access to all five of them creates a solid web of data which allows an actor to safely rehearse, improvise, and create. From now on, I will call the "Technique of five questions about the character" simply the technique of "5Q."

Exercise: *Informing actors*

As I have explained, the director can communicate with actors on the level of consciousness and intellectual exchange, sharing with them information about their characters, circumstances, and actions. An exercise under the title *If I Had a Cap of Invisibility* provides an insight into informing actors. It is a short "play" about a student who came late to the class and tries to avoid being caught by the teacher. In terms of space we need: a teacher's desk with a blackboard behind it, and chairs for students in front of it. Places for spectators should be set at two sides of the room.

Note: see the chapter on space for more information on structuring the performance's space. All parts of this book are connected and complement each other.

Situation. The master casts a student as "The Late Comer" (for brevity's sake will call him "A"), another student as "The Math Teacher" ("B") and the rest of the group as other students. The master informs "A" about his character using the technique of "5Q."

(1) Character—Who? The Late Comer is a student at a high school. He is timid and meek. He did not do his homework. He comes ten minutes late for the class. (2) Partners—With whom? The partners are a teacher, (known for his severity), and the classmates. (3) Space—Where? In a classroom. (4) Time—When? The present, early morning, ten minutes after the beginning of the first class. (5) Action—What? "A" enters the classroom and tries to get to his seat unnoticed by the teacher. He is motivated by his shyness, lateness, and failure to do the homework. His objective is not to be caught by the teacher.

The teacher and other members of the group (playing students) should be separately informed with the use of the technique of "5Q" and advised to react to "A's" actions.

Action. "A" enters the classroom on his toes. "B" is writing geometrical models on the board and does not see him. Other students attentively follow "A's" movements and—silently—cheer his efforts. Just before reaching his seat "A" stumbles, makes noise, and is spotted by "B" who stares at him. All freeze. End of action.

Discussion. Actors were informed who their characters are, what the circumstances are, and what is the action. The master gave them their acting tasks and they were asked to react to others' actions. Informing the leading characters separately from the group, we provided grounds for true improvisation.

Development. Each of the students may now prepare another version of the same scene with "A." "B" and others should be prepared to react to "A's" new actions. For example: the entering student takes off his shoes in order to walk quietly—certainly the teacher seeing him barefoot will be very surprised!

Exercise: *Inspiring actors*

Situation. We create an action titled *A Sheep and the Wolves*. The master casts one student as a smuggler at a border ("A"), and five students as customs officers ("B"). The rest of the group are spectators. We inform both "A" and "B" using an animal metaphor—influencing their imagination, fantasy and subconsciousness. We don't expect the actors to imitate animals, to reproduce their movements, behaviors, or sounds, but we inspire them internally by comparing their characters to animals. Space-wise it would be best to play this scene in a park or forest. If this is too difficult, we use any room full of furniture—it might be a classroom—which we will turn into a dilapidated and disarrayed place. The playing area is a narrow way across the bushes (or the furniture) and the observation area is situated in a few "islands" on both sides of the way.

We talk to "A" and "B" separately (as in the previous exercise) in order to prepare them for improvisation and solicit fresh reactions to each other's actions. We use our technique of "5Q," but this time, instead of informing actors, we inspire them. The master's talk to the actors might be:

(1) Character: Who? Who is your character? "A"—you are smuggling drugs across the border. No! You are a sheep. You are afraid of wolves. Your skin is white, without blemish, and very precious. You know that wolves can see and smell you from a distance. Imprudently, you stayed behind the flock, gorging yourself on that delicious grass in the valley, and now you have to follow the flock alone to the enclosure on the other side of the forest. You are afraid, but you make your living by smuggling, so, you have to go. No! You are a sheep. Your instinct forces you to go. "B"—you are custom officers. No, you are wolves. Your instinct tells you to hunt a sheep. You have to catch it and devour

it. Additionally, you are paid for each smuggler caught. No! You are wolves—you are simply hungry. (2) Partners: With whom? "A"—you are alone. But at any time you may run across a pack of wolves who are somewhere in the dark bushes and are hungry. "B"—your are a pack of hungry wolves. You hunt as a team. Anything living, especially a lonely sheep, is a target and should be your prey. (3) Space: Where? "A"—you are returning from a pasture to your home, passing by a forest, full of wolves. It is a dangerous, foreign, and frightening territory. "B"—it's your territory. You are in your kingdom. You know all bushes, trees, and paths. You know how to move and hunt here. (4) Time: When? The same circumstances in terms of time exist for "A" and for "B:" it's late night and dark, from time to time a full moon appears from behind the clouds. (5) Action: What? What are the characters doing? What is happening to them? "A"—you are hurrying home. You have to cross this forest unnoticed and unspotted, and, most importantly, whole, that is, not eaten. You must return home—your instinct orders you to go even if you are terrified. You'll not resign. There is only one direction for you: home. "B"—you hunt. You have to hunt. If you don't hunt anything you'll go on starving and soon perish.

Action. A smuggler is trying to cross the forest, under cover, moving silently, waiting from time to time for the moon to disappear behind the clouds. The customs officers comb the forest. Suddenly they see the smuggler. He flees. There is a chase. He's caught. End of action.

Discussion. The master inspired the actors by appealing to their imagination. The actors were surrounded by unusual circumstances. Their tasks were based on instincts.

Development. Let's now try to use the same kind of animalistic inspiration to motivate actors to create other simple actions. Again, we are not looking for animal-like external behavior, but for animal-like internal motivations in acting: for example, hastily searching for a hidden object, running away for dear life, or entering a dark room. In the subsequent scenes these might be done "as a mouse," "as an elephant," "as a lion," "as a snake," etc.

Exercise: *Ordering actors*

Situation. Let's create an action, *Crossing a Mountain Creek*: a squadron of paratrooper commandos braves a mountain creek, initially in silence, trying to avoid detection, and then, under the enemy's fire. The actors will get information that allows them to start improvising, but then the master will give them orders to which they should react spontaneously and instantly, continuing the improvisation. We'll set the playing area in the center of our room and the observation areas on both sides of it. It would be better, if possible, to set the playing area below the observation area—for example, to play in a courtyard and to observe from second floor windows.

We cast a group of five paratroopers and give them names: "A," "B," "C," "D," and "E." We inform them, as usual, using the technique of "5Q." This time the information is identical for all characters, but we'll ask all members to react to the master's orders in their own way and, at the same time, to also react to what other paratroopers are doing. We can give paratroopers props that function as rifles, backpacks and other military gear, or we might use pantomime in which objects are imaginary. The master talks to the cast:

(1) Character: Who? Who is your character? You are a paratrooper, an experienced soldier, and you are on a dangerous secret mission. (2) Partners: With whom? You are a member of a troop. You're bound with other soldiers by absolute solidarity and unequivocal friendship; everybody is helping, covering, and fighting for everybody. You are threatened by the enemy who might attack you any second and later on you come under fire. (3) Space: Where? You are behind enemy lines. You are crossing a mountain creek which is cold and swift; it makes whirlpools and its bed is full of loose rocks; the enemy is on the other side of the creek. (4) Time: When? It's war time. Early morning. Fog. You left the base yesterday afternoon, so you have already been on your feet for about twelve hours—you are very tired. (5) Action: What? What are the characters doing? What is happening to them? You have to cross this creek. You have to do it in spite of the enemy's fire. You must not lose your gear—you carry explosives

to blow up a bridge in these mountains. You must always help your buddy.

Action. Paratroopers cross the creek. The enemy starts firing at them. The paratroopers move on, fire back, and finally reach the other bank. Their actions are steered by the master's orders:

"A!—You tripped over a stone and went under water!"

"B!—Drag him out!"

"C!—You got hit in your neck. Your backpack slipped into the water."

"D!—Fire at the target on the other bank!"

"E!—Pick up C's backpack."

And so on, and so forth.

Discussion. In this exercise we studied the effectiveness and results of short orders given by master during group improvisation. The orders were simple and brief, either closed ("Drag him out!") or open ("Fire at the target on the other bank"). They did not contain motivations, explanations, or inspirations. They had to be obeyed immediately. They allowed the improvisation to go on without interruptions. This kind of work of a director with actors—giving orders—might be used as the only method or in connection with others (informing, inspiring), but should not be overused.

Development. Let's create another simple action. First, we'll give actors material for beginning an improvisation and than we'll steer it by giving short orders.

Basic types of acting

Acting ("stage acting," "playing," or "performing") is the art of publicly living one's life. Acting can be analyzed, explained and studied in terms of styles, conventions, techniques, and methods. Playing on stage, an actor uses himself/herself as a human being and, at the same time, he/she artistically shapes his/her actions. Consequently, stage acting and acting training (classes, workshops, rehearsals) embraces these two spheres of acting: the personal and the artistic. These two spheres have been present in acting throughout the history of theater in all cultures. One or the other was accentuated and provided for either "personal acting," or "character acting," both of them having unlimited variations.

"Personal acting" stresses the person, the individuality, the uniqueness of an actor as a human being. There's no place for the actor—character dualism in it. The actor does not change into a character but remains as he/she is. This kind of acting has two basic types: private and professional. The private (or unprofessional) acting of personality was characteristic of endless productions in which performers were not able and did not even try to play characters. Rather, they demonstrated or operated them, as was the case in early Greek, in medieval European theater, at Renaissance university shows, and Baroque court productions. Similarly, many avant-garde companies of the 1960s pronounced the slogan: "Don't act—be!" and treated their public appearances as tests of their private and personal sincerity, openness, shamelessness, and boldness. The professional acting of personality has been, and still is, first of all, "star acting." Acting stars appeared on Roman stages, were pillars of the Commedia dell'Arte troupes, flourished in the Far Eastern theater, and influenced the Western theater in the 19th century. Some historians have called the 19th century Western theater the "age of theater stars." (The 20th century is certainly the "age of film stars.") Acting stars do not identify themselves with characters, rather they subordinate characters to their own personalities, reduce characters to their own shapes, and while they use the characters' lines and actions, they do not suggest that they are those characters. They remain themselves. The character (or "role") is for them only a pretext for presenting themselves—as outstanding personalities, virtuosos, indeed, stars. A certain amount of the "acting of personality" is, of course, always present in acting, but in many styles and schools of acting, the actor's personality is covered by character.

"Character acting" (or "acting of role") is based on playing a character (a role) by an actor. Its principle is the dualism of actor and character. In the many styles and techniques of this kind of acting, there are two basic tendencies, though there are a multitude of variations: the realistic acting of the character, and the non-realistic acting of the character.

"Realistic character acting" (or "acting realism") is a style in which an actor builds a character based on his/her real and true feelings, emotions, and thoughts. The actor draws on his/her real life experience and uses his/her surrounding social and physical reality. The actor builds his/her character based on his/her own true background, knowledge, emotions, and observation of others, as well as imagining and figuring out how someone else would feel, think, or behave in a given situation. At the same time, an actor tries to reproduce external features of the character. Acting realism is usually connected with psychologism, that is with building a role based on the psychology of a given character. Endeavoring to realistically and psychologically build a role, an actor desires to "live through," or even "incarnate" into a character. The Stanislavsky Method, as well its variations, the Michael Chekhov Method and the Strasberg Method, are methods of realistic, psychological, and sociological acting, in which the main objective of an actor is to create a true character, to hide himself/herself behind the character, or to identify with it. A variant of acting realism is acting naturalism, which is focused on details of speech, movement, or behavior.

"Non-realistic character acting" (or "formalistic acting," "grotesque acting," "alienated acting," or "presententional acting") is a style in which the actor builds a character based on the external features and behaviors of the character. This kind of acting usually uses exaggeration, expressive movement, stylized gesture, dance, gymnastics, or pantomime, with disregard or lack of interest in the psychological processes of character. This approach has existed in acting throughout the ages. In the 18th century, Denis Diderot in his *Paradox of Acting* identified it as "cold acting," or "calculated acting." In the 20th century it produced two distinctive acting styles: the Biomechanics of Meyerhold, and the Alienated Acting of Brecht (called also Presentational Acting). According to both of these artists, the actor should not create a realistic and psychological portrait of a character, instead, he/she, using his/her own personality, body and voice, composes an artistic image of a character, sometimes close to a caricature or cartoon. Meyerhold's Biomechanics is based on the actor's biology and uses strictly choreographed movement perfected through rigorous training. Its objective is to display a character through movement, gesture, and physical activities. Brecht's Alienated Acting is based on the actor's intellect and critique of the character played. It uses elements of realism, but as quoted in selected segments or traces. The goal is to show only certain aspects of a character and leave the rest to the audience's critical thinking. Brechtian training embraced both acting exercises and ideological lectures—both in Brecht's own Berliner Ensemble and in many political theater groups, especially in Latin America.

Various acting methods, based on different techniques of training and performing, have always been connected with specific cultures, types of drama, and production trends. Today, in the theater of the "global village" (as Marshall McLuhan says) and in the age of intensive international exchange, many acting styles and training methods coexist and interplay. Preparing a production project and rehearsing the show, a director should consciously select the proper acting technique for a given production.

Exercises in basic types of acting

In a series of exercises we'll study and demonstrate the fundamentals of various types of acting in Western culture. The exercises serve three objectives. First, they introduce prospective directors to major problems of acting. It should be absolutely clear though, that they are only an introduction; further work and study on acting is indispensable for every director. Second, they demonstrate the ways of communication between director and actor. Third, they explain, describe and teach the "Technique of five questions about the character" ("5Q"), helping readers/students to practice it. We'll work on: (1) the basic interhuman process of communication (the pre-theatrical or non-theatrical process),(2) acting of personality, (3) realistic acting, and (4) non-realistic acting.

Exercise: *Creating the basic interhuman process of communication*

This exercise is a practical demonstration of the basic, real, and everyday interhuman process of communication—a process which is not yet theatrical, nor artistic.

Situation. The master and students sit in a circle. The master asks students—one by one—to tell a story. Each story must strictly fulfill the following conditions: (1) It must be a true story. (2) It must be something which happened to the storyteller. (3) It must be dramatic—based on a dramatic, unusual, or extraordinary event, experience, or accident. (4) It must be closed: something which had a beginning, development, and conclusion. (5) It must be a short, concise, and pithy story.

Action. Students tell their stories one by one. The master takes notes, writing down the titles or themes of the stories along with the names of the story tellers—for use in future exercises. The master selects one of the stories. Let's assume that it is as a story about a car accident in which the teller—a young man—was injured. That's it for the action. Yes! Here is the point: the whole action was telling the story. We are going to explain this at once.

Discussion. Indeed, the action in this exercise was the process of telling the story. It was a process of interhuman communication: someone told a story to others. That what happened in the classroom and that is what the action was. It was a direct, simple, ordinary story telling. Now let's make an analysis of this event which will lead us to interesting findings. The technique of "5Q" is useful for this analysis.

(1) Character: Who? Who is the character? There was no character. This is the point! A student, personally and privately, told other students a story. He didn't play any character. It was him. It was his own, true story. (2) Partners: With whom? One student told the story to other students. To whom was he addressing his story? To other students. (3) Space: Where? Where was the story told? Here, in our room—as it really is, without any built or imagined sets. (4) Time: When? Now. Oh, a few minutes ago. Anyway, during our class or

workshop. In real time. (5) Action: What? What is the character doing? What is happening to him? Again—there was no character. What was the student doing? He was telling the story. He shared with others his own real experience about a car accident.

The analysis shows, that one student told other students a true story, here and now. This story telling, this sharing, occurred on the basic interhuman level, between people as they are. It was an everyday, real, true, and simple interhuman communication process. It was not theater.

Exercise: *Personal acting*

Let's see now how an everyday, real, true, and simple interhuman process of communication transforms into a theatrical communication process based on personal acting.

Situation. The master works with the student—"author" of the story. The master may work with the "author" separately and individually, and then show the result to the group and explain what happened, or they may work publicly, explaining every step to the whole group. (It seems to me that the first approach is better—but I leave it to the reader/user). Working with the "author" the master transforms the storytelling into a one-man show and the storyteller into a performer. The master again makes an analysis of the story. This time he/she focuses not on the simple process of communication between the student and his fellows, but on the story itself as it happened to the "author" (and other people), somewhere else, sometime ago. In this way material for the one-man show is amassed and prepared. The master does not ask what happened in our room (as in the case of simple storytelling) but what happened to the storyteller then and there, when he actually had his car accident.

(1) Character: Who? Who was the character? Let's call him "A." "A" was a seventeen year old high school student, who had just got his drivers license, and was very proud that he could drive. (2) Partners: With whom? Who was in the car besides the driver and who was involved with the accident? His whole family:

parents and older sister. (3) Space: Where? Where did the accident happen? On the road. It was a narrow, slippery road in the mountains, with snow and trees at both sides. (4) Time: When? It happened three years ago. It was winter, late evening, after sunset. (5) Action: What? What happened? The family was going to a mountain resort to celebrate New Year's Eve. "A" was at the wheel and he drove too fast in spite of his father's admonitions. On a curve the car suddenly slipped off the road and landed in deep snow. The air bags went off. There was a terrible bang, a moment of dread, complete darkness, and then, deafening silence, because the engine stopped. The car was covered with snow. After a while, using a flashlight, which they found in the glove compartment, they realized that they were all alive and no one was injured. They were not able to open the door. The power windows did not work without the engine running. They were stuck. And then, mom, with her magnificent sense of humor, proposed a New Year's Eve toast. Bending the back seat, she was able to reach to the trunk and get a bottle of French champagne they were carrying. "We'll be late for the party anyway. So, let's drink! We'll try to dig ourselves out later," said mom. Everybody responded enthusiastically. They drank. There was another bottle of champagne in the trunk, and even a third one. They sang. The "author" does not remember when someone came along to pull them out.

We have to give the story a title and transform it into an action. What about *New Year's Eve Party in a Snowdrift*? The action will be played by the "author" of the story. He is going to play the character of a careless driver. Yes, he is going to play a character—not himself. He will, of course, use his own experience for building the character. Having gone through a car accident he is well prepared to play the character of a driver who had a car accident. This helps him as an actor—but does not matter for the audience.

Let's consider an example. The Captain, a character in August Strindberg's *The Father*, is involved in a cruel marital conflict. The spectators in the theater do not necessarily know or care whether the actor playing the character of the Captain has been married or what marital conflicts he has had. Yet, if the actor has had, let's say, three failed marriages, he might play this character with more understanding and more subtle nuances. The point is that a personal experience of an actor with a character's situation, while not required, certainly helps to equip an actor for playing the character.

The creative acting process in our work goes like this: (1) An actor had a car accident. (2) An actor plays a character who had a car accident. (3) An actor playing a character who had a car accident uses his own experience from having a car accident.

Now, based on the analysis of the story, the master, working with the student "author," prepares a one-man show. All elements of the story can be used: events, partners, words, and circumstances, but all of them should be purposely arranged, condensed, contrasted, etc. Besides text and movement, stage business and behaviors should be introduced, as well as interaction with the audience. Music or sound effects might be developed—what about other students vocally producing sounds and tunes? Space should be built and equipped with necessary objects—what about a small, matchbox model of a car and books representing mountains on a table? Lighting, even the simplest, must be created too—what about the flashlight mentioned in the story? Finally, the show should get a clear structure, including a beginning, a development, and an ending. The title should be somehow communicated to the audience—we can quickly draw a poster or the "author" might announce the title to the spectators.

Action. "A" (both the "author" of the original story and now the actor playing the character of a young man) shares his New Year's Eve experiences with spectators. He lives through the events again, he plays them, demonstrates them, illustrates them, materializes them, makes them actual, real, happening here and now. A theatrical interaction between an actor and the audience is born. Indeed, it is no longer a student telling fellow students his own story—it is now an actor playing the character of a careless driver who provoked an accident on a mountain road.

Discussion. Let's consider what we have done. During a brief rehearsal with the master, a student became an actor playing a character. A true story was transformed into material for a production and the production was actually played. It was a simple and humble one-man show, but it had all the elements of a performance: a developed character, action, space, rhythm, music, light, etc. The actor used "personal acting" because he played a character very close to himself, he drew on his own memory, experience, feelings, emotions, and he was even able to use words which he—once upon a time—used himself. His personal closeness to the character allowed him, in a natural and obvious way, to use "personal acting."

Exercise: *Realistic and psychological acting*

The same story told by a student is now used for an elaborated action in which we employ material from the original story, but we change the characters, the course of the events, and all the circumstances. We do this to move from personal acting to realistic and psychological character acting. When a member of our group played the character of a careless young driver he was using his own experiences and his acting was based on the mechanisms of personal acting. Now, the same student is cast as a different character, somehow parallel to himself, but not identical, or even close. It is impossible for him directly to use his own life experience in building the character, but he is able to use it indirectly in building a character. The original story is used as material for a new chain of events, the original words (previously developed and used by one person only) are distributed among many characters, and the space and time are totally changed. Generally, we use the original story as material for a completely new action, with a different plot, characters, and circumstances. The distance between the original story and the "play" we create stretches. This also require us to build a new performance space, with newly articulated playing and observation areas. The play, and the production based on it, is neither a staging of the original story, nor a development of the one-man show, but it contains a similar fundamental human experience, similar events, and the basic material of feelings and thoughts which first appeared in the story told by the student in the class/workshop situation. The analogy between the original story and the newly developed drama helps the actor (the "author" of the story and the performer in the one-man show) to play the new character involved in a new action, in new circumstances. This new action should have a new title—would you agree to *Racing into a Snowdrift*?

Situation. Let's assume that a car accident happened not to a family driving to a New Year's Eve party, but to a group of fans of a hockey team from Connecticut going by bus to Boston. Their bus, driven too fast, slipped off the road in a heavy snowstorm. The snow on the ground was so thick that it absorbed the collision. Some people were cut by glass and some had bruises. Most seriously injured was the bus driver, who hit the steering wheel because his seat belt was not fastened. A few of his ribs were broken, he had some internal injures, and he was bleeding. One of the passengers used a cellular phone to call for help. When the ambulances arrived, everyone was helped out of the bus and attended to on the spot. Meanwhile the bus company was sending another bus to pick them up. Only the bus driver had to be taken to a hospital, where he was rushed by the ambulance attendants to an operating room.

We cast the bus driver (A), ambulance attendants (B), nurses (C), and doctors (D). In the role of the bus driver we cast the same actor who told the original story and who was the one-man show performer. He now plays a different character, but his true experience (as told in the story) helps him to play this new character. Let's first work with A using "5Q" technique. Other actors should be also informed, but now we explain only the work process of the master with A.

(1) Character: Who? Who is the character? He is a bus driver. He is about thirty years old and overconfident. He did not care to fasten his seat belt and drove too fast in a heavy snowstorm. An important fact from his past is that he was a race driver, but his professional license was revoked for recklessness. When applying for a job with the bus company he did not disclose his record. (2) Partners: With whom? His partners are: the ambulance attendants, nurses, and doctors. (3) Space: Where? Action takes place in the hospital arrival area, in a

hallway, and in the operating room. The playing area extends from the entrance to the operating room. The performing area is first, on and around the stretcher, and, second, on and around the operating table. The observation area is movable: the spectators move along with the stretcher, and then stand at the open operating room door until a nurse closes it in front of their faces announcing the end of the show. (4) Time: When? Last year, in winter, late evening. (5) Action: What? What happened? We are talking now, of course, about the action of our play. It is a new action. It develops as follows:

Action. The injured bus driver is driven to a hospital. Upon arrival, the ambulance attendants wheel his stretcher off the ambulance and rush him to the operating room. While on the stretcher, the bus driver, obviously in shock, tells the ambulance attendants how the accident happened, boasting that he saved the lives of all the passengers by his masterly maneuver. He repeats his story to the nurses preparing him for surgery and to the anesthesiologist giving him a shot, until he suddenly loses consciousness.

Discussion. A true story, at first told personally and directly by a student to a group of students, was then transformed into a soliloquy performed by the same student, and eventually used as an inspiration for writing and performing a play, in which the same student played the character of a bus driver. When telling the story he was himself. When presenting a young man he portrayed a character different than, but very close to himself. When playing the bus driver he performed someone different than himself; yet he was able to draw on his own experience as someone who in reality was once involved with a car crash. This experience allowed him to realistically, truly, and convincingly play the role of a bus driver. In this way we have demonstrated the basic creative mechanisms of realistic character acting.

In summary: first, we had an original true story told by a student. Second, we transformed it into material for a one man-show. Third, we went one step further and transformed it again into a short play which we produced. The one basic and central event to all these stages remained the same: a road accident. A student, first, told a true story, second, used it as a material for a soliloquy by a young man, and, third, used it as an inspiration for playing a bus driver. These stages and transformations can be shown as follows:

TABLE: TRANSFORMATIONS OF INTERHUMAN PROCESS INTO ONE PERSON SHOW AND A PLAY/PRODUCTION

TRUE STORY	ONE MAN SHOW	PLAY/PRODUCTION
Title: (no title —a real interaction)	*New Year's Eve Party in a Snowdrift*	*Racing Into a Snowdrift*
CHARACTERS: Student (inexperienced driver) Members of his family	A young man	Bus driver (former race driver) Ambulance attendants Nurses, Doctors
SPACE: A mountain road A passenger car	Empty stage A few props	Hospital: entrance, hallway, operation room
TIME: Time of telling the story: now	Time of the events: contemporaneous	Time of the events: a year ago
ACTION: Student had a car accident while driving with his family in the mountains	A young man has a car accident while driving with his family on the mountains	A bus driver is rushed to a hospital for surgery

---

Development. Let's use another story told by another student. The master asks this second student to repeat his/her story in order to refresh our memory. As result we are getting a direct interhuman interaction, a real act of social communication. There are no performers or spectators—simply students listening to one of their own. Next, we use this story as material for a one-person show and ask the "author" to play it. Eventually, we use the same material for writing a "play," introducing new characters, creating different yet analogous events, replacing circumstances of space and time, and producing this new performance.

Exercise: *Non-realistic and antipsychological acting*

Let's use our first story again, as well as the "play" we built on it, but the production will be completely different. This time, instead of realistic and psychological acting, let's use non-realistic and antipsychological acting. The change in the acting style will be based on a change in the acting means of expression. This will result in a general change of style in the whole production.

Situation. We will begin our "play" as it was previously devised: a bus driver is rushed to a hospital. On a wheeled stretcher, he repeatedly tells his story, and he is directed to an operating room where he gets an anaesthetic. The ambulance attendants, nurses, and doctors interact with him. This time, instead of realistic acting based on the psychological background of the characters, let's use non-realistic acting, not psychologically motivated. Let's assume that the injured bus driver, carried to a hospital, is extremely agitated. Instead of telling his story—he sings it, imitating an opera singer. The ambulance attendants, the nurses, and the doctors instead of fulfilling their regular and realistic functions, perform several grotesque activities, such as giving the patient dozens of shots, examining him in an absurd way, singing as a choir, etc. The master uses the "5Q" technique to give the actors information referring to the interior of the characters in the same way as it was for realistic and psychological scene. Actors are ordered, however, to change the external expression. External, physical, and grotesque means are suggested.

Action. The arrival of the injured bus driver at the hospital and his travel to the operation room is now played like this: the ambulance attendants take the bus driver off the ambulance singing a lullaby; the bus driver, carried on the wheeled stretcher sings the melody of the Toreador's aria from *Carmen*; nurses perform a complicated choreography giving him dozens of shots; the anesthesiologist dances an Argentinean tango with the patient until the latter falls asleep; and the doctor throws him on the operating table.

Discussion. We used the same material, same characters, same space and time, same text, and we played the same action as in the realistic scene. We also used the same title, *Racing Into a Snowdrift*. But this time we changed the means of acting expression from realistic to non-realistic. Consequently, the style of the whole production changed, as well as the communication among actors, and between actors and spectators.

Development. Transform the second story, of the second student, into an non-realistic and antipsychological scene, following the model provided above.

The director's work with the audience

The spectator, along with the actor, is one of the two basic theater components and theater creators. Without spectators—present, alive, reacting, participating, and, indeed, creating—there's no theater at all. Actors and spectators exchange their biological energies, they communicate viscerally sharing feelings, emotions, moods, attitudes, and cerebrally exchanging meanings and ideas, as well as denotations and connotations of the words. They also communicate through images and sounds. Usually actors are senders of messages and spectators are receivers. The theatrical process of communication depends not only on how the actors send their messages, but also on how the spectators receive them. Spectators can be open, warm, receptive, sensitive, sympathetic, or friendly, and they can be closed, cold, prejudiced, indifferent, presumptuous, or hostile. The spectators might also be senders in the theatrical process—when they applaud, whistle, boo, leave the show, throw objects on stage, or physically interact with the actors.

In some eras of theater history, audiences were especially alive and active: in ancient Roman theater, in the Medieval European theater, during the Commedia dell'Arte performances, and in the Elizabethan theater's "wooden O" (as Shakespeare calls the theater building in *Henry V)*. Strong political and patriotic reactions from the public were characteristic of romantic theater in Germany, Poland, or Belgium. Italian, Russian, and Polish Futurists purposely provoked riots in theaters and fights with spectators during their *serati* which often ended in the mutual throwing of tomatoes, rotten eggs, or chairs. At the Bolsheviks' shows of the *Blue Shirt,* spectators and actors frequently sung revolutionary songs together. Physical involvement was both expected and encouraged by many avant-garde companies of the 1960s, such as the Living Theater or the Performance Group. Extremely active, yet discreet emotional participation characterized Polish underground productions both during World War II and the martial law of the 1980s. In all these instances the audience's participation occurred spontaneously, or was purposely provoked by actors. Such provocation would have been prepared during rehearsals under the director's supervision as a "directed participation."

The very structure of a show, the selection of means of expression and the performance space result in the mode and format of communication between actors and spectators. Working directly with actors, the director indirectly influences spectators. The director himself/herself is a spectator for actors during rehearsals. He/she tests, verifies, checks, and foresees how a spectator will react to the actor's performance in the future, during the show. Communicating with actors, the director prepares the communication of actors with spectators. Similarly, an actor working with a director during rehearsals prepares for his/her communication with the audience when the curtain goes up. A director either opens and widens lines of communication of actors with spectators, or blocks and closes them. He/she can prepare a production which develops as a friendly encounter or a hostile confrontation. He/she can situate communication between actors and spectators on the level of subtle spiritual exchange or on the level of a noisy Disney World fair. In selecting the artistic style of a performance the director inevitably also selects the cultural and social conventions which are going to function in the theater when the performance will be played for the public.

Besides the indirect contact of the director with the spectator—via actor—there is also an immense sphere of the director's straight influence on the public. Sometimes the director personally participate in the shows: it was a custom of Tadeusz Kantor in Poland and Richard Foreman in America. There are directors who like to meet the public, or groups before the show (I did it every night before the production of *Birth Rate* by Różewicz) or after the show (as Staniewski always does in his Gardzienice Theater). The director also has at his/her disposal such means of contact with spectators as interviews and notes in the programs. His/her dependable tool of directly influencing the public is theater space. Consciously and purposely arranging, structuring, or building the space of a performance, the director establishes specific relationships between actors and spectators and shapes their communication on both artistic and social levels. (The problem of building the production space, including relations between playing and observation areas, will be discussed in the chapter on creating theater space.)

Identifying the public

Before starting rehearsals, we have to cast the show. When this is done, we know who the actors are. In order to establish communication between actors and spectators during the production, we have to also know who the potential spectators are. In a way, we have to "cast" spectators too. We must ask ourselves a few simple, yet fundamental, questions: for whom are we preparing this production? Is there anybody out there who is ready to listen to what we want to say? What is a favorable and proper environment for it? Such questions help us to identify our public.

We may, for example, find out that a philosophical play by Samuel Beckett will not find spectators in a tourist and entertainment center, while a musical would do well there. We can expect that a metaphysical and poetic play by Paul Claudel will not be well received in a regional theater located in a working, middle class city, but it might attract the public to a university stage. We can presume that an open-air production for the masses will be well received and communication with audience will prove strong, if we create many crowd scenes and, perhaps, give actors torches in the grand finale of the show. We can suppose that a national classical tragedy will be appreciated by the audience in a National Theater in an European capital. We can be sure that actors on stilts will attract the attention of the spectators of a street show. Generally, we have to assess what kind of communication between the actors and spectators will occur during the show: visceral? cerebral? visual? And what about language? Producing Shakespeare, even in England, we can run into a problem today, because some spectators may not understand the archaic language. And what about touring abroad and playing for foreign audiences? We can safely take an American show to the Edinburgh festival, especially if we have a highly visual performance; a street action can travel to Poznań Malta International Festival in Poland, and an experimental performance will go to Avignon in France.

Only after we have studied the future potential audience can we make an educated and prudent decision about whether to go ahead with the project or abandon it. Evaluation of the potential audience leads us also to conscious choices of means of expression. What means should we use to reach a specific audience in a specific theater? The more attentively the director examines the potential public, the more alive and intensive the theatrical interaction will be. It might be hard sometimes to predict who all of the potential spectators will be, but it is always possible to predict which spectators will form the core, the majority, or the most influential group—a group to which we are going to address the show in a special way.

The directorial decisions—as far as the audience is concerned—should be based on culture, manners, values, and artistic and social conventions functioning at the place and time of the show. The director might accept and follow them, or, for his/her reasons, oppose or disregard them. Any directorial decision affecting the audience can be good and work well—but it should be conscious. The director might chose to play a production in complete separation from the public, or to open it and make it easily accessible. He/she might show the events as being alienated from the spectators, or include the audience—emotionally, intellectually, or physically—in the very midst of the action. Each of these can be done with the use of acting, space structuring, lighting and other means of expression. For example a baroque, proscenium stage might provoke the feeling of a closed and guarded castle, or might be open and connected with the auditorium by an apron and wide stairs. An actor can play "asides" as a character's own thoughts closed to the public, or can share them with the spectators, turning an "aside" into what is almost a dialogue with the audience. Actors playing on an elevated stage create a rather distant relationship with the audience, while sharing the floor with the spectators helps to instigate an easy and warm exchange. A director can put up or dismantle barriers between actors and audiences, can consciously measure the span between stage and seating, can even "cast" the whole audience, or some spectators, in specific "roles," imposing on them certain feelings, modes of perception, or even behaviors. For example, in *The Commune* (1973), a production by Richard Schechner, a group of spectators at one point in the show was asked to move to the platform in the center of the playing area and "play" the roles of Vietnamese peasants. In my production, *The Plague*, spectators in one scene were treated as prisoners in an internment camp.

Exercises: *Exploring interaction with the public*

In the series of exercises we will study fundamental factors influencing interaction between actors and spectators. In this way we are going to find how a director can influence and structure this interaction, and, consequently, the audience's perception. Of course, we are going to use our technique of "5Q." In particular we will ask—and try to answer— such questions as: (1) Who are the spectators? (2) What is their attitude towards actors? (3) How does the audience react? Is it active or passive? Involved or disinterested? Supportive or hostile? (4) How does space influence the interaction between actors and spectators?

Let's use material from another story told by another student. As we have already learned, we can transform it into a one-person show, and even into a "play.".

Situation. The story goes like this: Juliett (it is her real story—as she told it in my class) had a quarrel with her boyfriend. She was angry at him and at herself. They parted. "It's all over!" she shouted. Why? What happened? They set a date to go to see a movie. He was supposed to pick her up. But he was terribly late. When he finally arrived, he simply blew his horn in the driveway, not even coming inside, not apologizing. She got furious. She opened the door, scolded him, and shut the door. She would not open the door when he came back and rang the bell, knocked, and begged her. Eventually, he left. She sat in the kitchen and cried. And then, she started to imagine that he gently knocked at the door again. She opens it, he enters, she asks him to sit without a word, he sits at the other side of the kitchen table, they are quiet, they gaze at each other, they forget the movie and the quarrel, and dusk slowly falls down and embraces them.

This story can be easily staged as a one woman show: a young woman telling the audience her experiences and dreams, addressing her absent boyfriend in her imagination, seeing him parked in the driveway, entering the kitchen, sitting in front of her, and smiling. Indeed, Juliett prepared a beautiful one woman show under the title, *Go and Return*. She played it for the class.

We are going to use her story now, but we'll go one step further, and transform the story into a scene with two characters: Juliett and the man—let's call him Raoul.

Action. The action of our "play" (based on Juliett's story) has four scenes.

Scene 1: Juliet is on the phone. She screams at Raoul. He is supposed to pick her up but he is late. He is always late. They will miss the movie. She tells him she doesn't want to see him anymore. At this moment Juliett stops talking only to understand that Raoul is calling from a gas station. He is late because his car broke down. Juliett is ashamed and sorry. She offers to come and pick him up. "What's the address? Mobil? Where? I don't hear you...", she says. There is a knock at the door at this moment. Juliett runs to the door with her cordless phone still in hand, helplessly yelling: "Where are you? Are you still there? Hello..."

Scene 2: Juliett opens the door. Raoul is on the porch with a cell phone in his hand. He is really late. But his car wasn't broken down. He wasn't calling from a gas station. He called from his car, sitting in her driveway. A joke. "A joke?", Juliet says in anger. She doesn't want to talk to him. She shuts the door in his face.

Scene 3: Juliett is furious. She throws the phone on the stand. She sits on a chair. She cries, mumbling some words of anger, disappointment, and regret. She starts to imagine that he returns. She switches on the radio. Soft, classical music is heard. It is Yehudi Menuhin playing Brahms. Juliet slowly improvises a dance. She takes off her shoes. She tiptoes to the door dreaming that Raoul is there. She opens the door. Yes! He is still there, standing on the porch.

Scene 4: Without a word, Juliett invites Raoul to the kitchen. They sit at the table. Music is playing. They stare at each other. End of the show.

We now prepare the production of this "play," instructing/informing both actors using the "5Q's" technique. Juliett is already well prepared to play the female's role—it is her story and her personal background helps her to play the character of an ill-tempered girl. The student playing Raoul might also have relevant experiences to draw on, but it is not a condition. When the production, hastily rehearsed, is ready we play it for various audiences. We cast all other students in the roles of the spectators and we also instruct/inform them using the technique of "5Q." We should work with actors (students playing characters) and spectators (students playing spectators) separately in order to prepare them for improvisation. The actors should not be given information about the spectators' reactions or activities.

We will create five different scenes with five different types of audiences in five different spaces. The spaces should correspond with a given type of audience. In each performance we will define (1) the audience, (2) the space of the performance, and (3) the interaction between this specific audience and actors.

Playing for a friendly audience: (1) Audience: the audience is a group of members of an association of theater fans at a high school in our town. (There are associations or clubs of theater fans all over the world.) All of the members love theater, enjoy seeing shows, personally know the actors, collect programs, and organize discussions about productions by inviting directors and actors to their school. They love to applaud actors at the end of the show. (2) Space: the small playing area directly on the floor in the corner of our room, with a few rows of chairs in front of it, close to the playing area which is equipped with minimal furniture. The door to Juliett's house is imaginary (physically nonexistent) and is situated in between the playing and observation area. Hence, Raoul enters through the audience. (3) Interaction: actors use realistic/psychologic, delicate and shadowy means of expression. Juliett, talking in her dream to Raoul, addresses the audience. Spectators are silent and focused. During the show they clap or laugh when appropriate. After the show they applaud loudly and leave enchanted, exchanging favorable comments.

Playing for a participatory audience: (1) Audience: participants in an international theater festival who came to see a production given by their friends from another country. (2) Space: a playing area on the floor. The spectators sit in the floor in a circle, around the playing area. No furniture or props. All props should be pantomimed, except for the radio—a necessary music source. (3) Interaction: Actors are playing expressively and vehemently. Spectators are focussed and supportive. There should be an audience participation scene: Juliett dreams about Raoul's return; she sits on the floor, facing the imaginary door, and starts whispering: "Return.... Return..." She repeats this several times. She develops this word into a chant, a song, a dance, and a whole ritual of spellbinding on the absent man, ordering him to return. Juliett's words and actions, persistently repeated, gradually affect the spectators, who join her in the ritual: they chant, sing, and dance with her; and they quietly return to their places on the floor. When the show is over the audience does not leave. They stay, sitting in the circle. After a while the actors join them. Somebody has a guitar. They all sing.

Playing for an unfriendly audience: (1) Audience: the audience is now a small group of hostile people. Let's identify them as the censors, who, years ago in all the countries ruled by communists, controlled shows before the opening, watching for political references or allusions, ready to cut lines, scenes, stage business, or even to prohibit the entire production. The censors appear at theater rehearsals all over the world in all sorts of guises. They are a typical example of an unfriendly audience. (2) Space: a large proscenium theater. On the stage is a set representing a kitchen. The censors are sitting in the center of a spacious, empty auditorium. (3) Interaction: actors play the show as before, but in a large theater they have to speak loudly, which kills the intimacy and delicacy of their feelings and exchanges. Spectators react negatively: they whisper nasty remarks, they mill in their seats, and they laugh at inappropriate moments. After the curtain they do not applaud and leave theater discussing which lines they are going to cut.

Playing for an indifferent audience: (1) Audience: a group of people completely uninterested in the show. For example: a tour group of American senior citizens in Paris. A visit to the Comédie Française is included in their tour package. After having seen, in the foyer, the armchair in which Molière died in 1673 just at the end of *The Would-be Invalid*, they go to the auditorium and promptly fall asleep as soon as the curtain rises. (2) Space: a traditional proscenium theater. It might be the same as for the "unfriendly audience." (3) Interaction: action is played by the actors realistically, behind the "fourth wall," without any contact with spectators. The public sits motionlessly and doesn't react at all. Some people doze. One person might snore from time to time, but it should not be funny and no one should laugh. After the show the audience claps very briefly and leaves the theater talking abut matters unrelated to the show, such as shopping, sight-seeing, French cuisine, and so forth.

Playing for hostile audience: (1) Audience: the audience is now composed of a few drunk individuals, who behave aggressively towards actors. They attempt to interrupt the show. (2) Space: a café theater—a small playing area with tables and chairs in front of it. Our play is now presented as a Lunch Show during a lunch break in a big city. (3) Interaction: actors try to ingratiate themselves with the public and make them laugh, they overplay gestures and lines. The spectators don't care for the show and treat it as an unwanted offer of the establishment. They speak loudly, shout, boo, whistle, and clap at inappropriate moments.

Finally, they manage to interrupt the show. The actress playing Juliett leaves stage in tears. Raoul starts screaming at the unruly spectators and a fight erupts.

Discussion. The series of exercises showed that the same production might change when played for various audiences. Indeed, the audience, along with the space, influences actors, who play differently for different audiences. Depending on the audience, actors have to change their means of expression and even their lines. The interaction and the show itself is different every time because the audience is different. The audience has a powerful role and responsibility. The spectators, by their behaviors, reactions, and activities can change the production. They can participate intellectually, spiritually, emotionally, and physically. They can also be indifferent, they can hide themselves behind the "fourth wall," they may be so cold as to freeze the actors. The director can creatively—consciously and purposely—use the potential of the audience. He/she can steer, influence, and manipulate the public. Usually, the director does not directly command or instruct the spectators (as in our exercises above), but he/she has means to influence spectators indirectly. It can be done through shaping the interaction between the actors and spectators, by providing the spectators with specific perceptual conditions, and by structuring the space in which an interaction between actors and spectators occurs.

CHAPTER 3. CREATING THE PERFORMANCE SPACE

Terminology

One of the most important directorial tasks is to create the performance space. The space must provide actors with a playing area and spectators with an observation area. It should facilitate interaction between actors and spectators, and unite them in common emotions, tensions, or reflections. A purposely shaped space for the performance expresses the nature, quality, and structure of theatrical action. It conveys meanings, ideas, values, and opens up the spectators to the inside of stage events and characters' souls. Conversely, a theater space left unstructured, accidentally shaped, or with qualities that are contradictory to the action works against the sense and message of the show. The director can and should always actively approach problems of theater space and create it new every time, for every production.

Terminology that refers to theater space and theater architecture in particular is rich, but rarely used consistently. We have already used some of the terms. Now we have to explain them. Defining those terms allows us to communicate clearly and precisely.

TABLE: THEATER SPACE—TERMINOLOGY

1. BASIC TERMS

Theater space: the totality of architecture of a theater or any other space used for a performance, whether natural or civilizational. Theater space includes the performance space (see below), as well as all venues, places, rooms, facilities, spatial elements, and the near and far spatial environment of a theater or the performance site, which condition interaction between actors and spectators.

Performance space: both playing and observation areas during the performance.

Playing area: the space used by actors; the space where theater action is played. There have been many kinds of playing areas throughout the ages of theater history in various cultures. In Western culture, since the 17th century, a playing area situated inside a theater building has been called a "stage."

Observation area: the space occupied by an audience during the performance. The observation area is usually called the "auditorium," or simply the "theater."

2. TYPES OF THEATERS

Proscenium theater: a theater equipped with a proscenium stage.

Theater in the round: theater with the playing area having a round shape, usually situated in the center of the performance area and surrounded by the observation area on all sides.

Black box theater, adaptable theater, flexible theater, variable theater: a theater space equipped with a performance space which allows both playing areas and observation areas to be set in any spot to establish various relations between them.

True space theater, real space theater, natural space theater, found space: a performance space set in any existing space, whether natural or civilizational. The performance is played in existing architectural or natural environments, or structures that are real, not changed or disguised, in which everyday human activities otherwise occur. Examples are churches, public buildings, palaces, castles, streets, parks, parking lots, etc.

3. TYPES OF PLAYING AREAS

Proscenium, or proscenium stage: a stage with a frame separating it from the auditorium. This type of stage was first introduced in Italy in the 17th century; hence, it is also called the "Baroque Stage," or "Italian Stage;" other terms include: "Picture Frame Stage," or "Picture Framed Stage." Its major principle is to divide the universe into the world of the actors and that of the spectators. Its major aesthetic objective is to produce illusion.

Arena stage: playing area situated in the center of the performance space and surrounded by the observation area on all sides.

Open stage: playing area (or many playing areas) not separated from the observation area and situated in any place within the performance space.

Thrust stage: playing area surrounded by observation area on three sides.

Pictorial thrust stage: same as thrust, but having a proscenium stage behind the thrust stage.

Basic configurations of theater space

Theater space is human space. It is a space in which the interhuman theatrical process of communication develops. It is a space of actors and spectators. These two groups of people might be situated within a space in many different ways. Their positioning imposes and dictates the character, nature, intensity and other features of the theater process. By creatively shaping theater space, we creatively shape the entire theater process, and hence, the performance and its perception by spectators.

The two basic types of mutual positioning and situating of actors and spectators within a theater space are: unification and separation. Theater space makes actors and spectators either a consolidated community or two confronted armies. The history of theater knows both of them. Early Greek theater and Christian medieval theater, as well as Renaissance popular shows, used a space strongly uniting actors with spectators. In ancient Greece they all shared the same space carved into nature and surrounded by nature, with the same sky about their heads. Playing and observation areas were distinct, but both were open and without sharp barriers. The *orchestra*, which was used by the chorus, was the middle ground, the space that connected the playing area for actors (called *proskenion*) in front of the *skene* building, with the *theatron*, the observation area for spectators. The chorus consolidated the whole space from the spatial point of view, for it entered onto the *orchestra* directly from the natural environment of the *theatron*, using entrances (*parodoi*) situated between the *skene* and the *theatron*. From the political and societal points of view, the chorus also unified the performers with the public. The audience that gathered to see a show represented the whole population of the city-state, including men, women, boys, priests, city officials, visiting dignitaries, and slaves (accompanying their owners). Statistically, not all attended, but theater was a matter of interest and care to everybody. The context of the Greek democratic system, with its elections and voting, provided that the Chorus members were figuratively perceived as representatives of all citizens. In this way the spectators had their representatives in the show. Finally, from the religious point of view, taking part in the production for all performers (actors and chorus members) and for all spectators was synonymous with joining in a religious ceremony with its universal and social connotations and consequences. Thus, Greek theater was spiritually and spatially unified.

Religious faith, socio-political conditions, and space played the unifying role in early medieval European theater. Barriers between the show and the audience were blurred by the fact that the actors were recruited from the local people. The community members played for their own community. The decisive unifying force was space: in a church, in a city place, or on the streets. Both performers and audiences shared the same space. The playing areas for actors (*mansions*), were erected on the church floor or in the dirt of the street. The congregation had easy and direct access to them. Spectators from different social classes mingled freely with actors; only bishops, nobility, and city council members would have separate boxes. Similarly, the compact Elizabethan theater, with its large front playing area, surrounded closely on three sides by a crowd of mostly standing spectators, did not impose strict spatial divisions on either actors or audiences. Space in the popular Italian productions of the Renaissance did not distance actors and spectators, for a simple platform and a booth for actors behind it were put on in a town square and were easily accessible to the public. The principle of mingling actors with spectators is used in many modern street productions where the space is common, and neither playing nor observation areas are strictly defined. The movability of such shows enhances the feeling that space is being shared on an equal basis by everybody involved: actors, spectators, and accidental passers-by.

The sharp and austere division of theater space into two sections, the playing and the observing areas, appeared in the Hellenistic theater, was a principle in Roman theater, and also characterized major theater forms in China and Japan. From its very beginning, the Baroque theater of 17th and 18th century Europe, with its proscenium frame, its trench of an orchestra pit, and fence of front footlights, divided the theater space into a playing area restricted to actors and an observation area that confined the spectators. The spatial partition of Baroque theater was contested as early as the beginning of the 19th century. In the 20th century, attempts to abolish the monopoly of the proscenium multiplied and many alternatives were introduced: return to ancient Greek and Roman theaters and amphitheaters, open-air productions in parks or castles, and, finally, the flexible space; black box theaters were constructed all over the world. At the end of the 20th century, when I write these words, the proscenium stage is still the most popular in Western culture. It has, however, lost its royal status and become only one of many possible alternatives for structuring theater space. A perfect example of this situation can be found at the State University of New York at Buffalo, where the new Center For the Arts (1995) is equipped with two proscenium and two black box theaters. Avant-garde productions rarely use the proscenium at all, and, as a rule, devise the space anew for each production.

In between these two poles—a theater space united or divided—there reside, in the middle ground, an endless number of ways of establishing spatial relations between actors and spectators.

Space as a major field of theater creation in the 20th century

The creative shaping of theater space by directors was one of the major developments in the art of directing as it emerged at the dawn of the 20th century. Directors reinvented spatial relations between actors and spectators, imaginatively collaborated with set designers, and designed productions, or even whole theater buildings by themselves. A director's creativity in the field of theater space was one of the foundations of both the Great Reform of Theater and the Second Reform of Theater. New principles in creating theater space were formulated in the first part of the 20th century with a special vigor by Appia, Copeau, Artaud, and Osterwa.

Adolphe Appia decisively advanced the reform of stage design. His contributions included the abandonment of illusion and the promotion of symbolism. Instead of painted flats, he introduced almost abstract three-dimensional structures organizing the stage space vertically and horizontally, through the use of platforms, pillars, and stairs. Later on, Appia proposed the revolutionary postulate of using a homogenous and communal space, not divided into playing and observation areas, abolishing distinctions between actors and spectators. Appia wanted to create performances in a new space, which was not a traditional theater. He called this new space "the cathedral of the future."

Jacques Copeau experimented at first with performance space inside the proscenium theater. He remodeled his Paris' theater (Théâtre du Vieux-Colombier) by tearing down the proscenium frame, stripping the stage of the wings, adding a stepped forestage, and installing a fixed structure of platforms and stairs in the center of the stage. He called this playing area a "bare stage" (or "naked stage.") Later, he left the theater building altogether, and created open-air shows on platforms put on ad hoc in meadows or villages squares. He also staged large scale spectacles in real architectural environments. Copeau's objective was to guide actors and spectators to spiritual and religious experiences in a homogenous and communal space. He was the first of the great European directors in the 20th century who practiced an "exit from the theater building."

Antonin Artaud in a series of essays and manifestos also demanded that the theater artist abandon theater buildings and create performances in ad hoc, real and natural places in which both actors and spectators would share the space on an equal basis. He envisioned theater production as a process of direct human experience and interaction.

Juliusz Osterwa while continuing to direct in closed interiors, tried to abolish the divisions between playing and observation areas by enlarging the forestage, building stairs connecting stages with auditoriums, or playing directly on the hall floor. He staged outdoor shows in natural venues in which actors merged with spectators. In his most famous open-air production, *The Constant Prince*, by Calderón/Słowacki (1926) he played on a platform shaped like an sacrificial altar;

spectators were treated as the congregation of faithful.

Appia proposed a space of communion; Copeau, an open, anti-illusionistic, performance space; Artaud, a real space; and Osterwa, a sacred space. All of them treated theater as a complex, human, and artistic communal process significantly conditioned by space. Their objective was to find a space in which communion and art, as well as the creativity and spirituality of the people involved with the theatrical process, could be made intense, penetrating, and uplifting. These most radical approaches to theater space were accompanied throughout the whole of the 20th century by an abundance of various experiments and achievements in the field of theater space. The symbolic and monumental visions of Appia and Craig fought successfully (at least in Europe) with naturalism. Designer Emil Pirchan and director Leopold Jessner treated stairs as a major space-organizing element; stairs replaced the descriptiveness and illustrativeness of old-fashioned, painted stage design by sheer functionalism. Vsevolod Meyerhold, collaborating with constructivist painters, built sets that were "machines for playing." The designer Pronaszko, collaborating with directors Schiller and Wacław Radulski, created sets that were cubist sculptures. Numerous directors of the Second Reform of Theater emphasized the importance of theater space and used it in endless creative ways. They turned old proscenium theaters upside down, putting spectators on stage and playing in the auditorium, or using the entire theater building for their shows, with all rooms, offices, halls, foyers, and basements made into performance spaces. Some of them left theater buildings and put on shows on streets, in parks, on parking lots, and forest clearings. They shaped the relationships between playing and observation areas as required for particular productions. They claimed that space has such an impact on the production, that the very order of theater creation should be reversed: we should not put on our new shows in the existing theaters, rather we should build new theaters for our shows. Yet, if building a new theater every time might prove to be too expensive and impractical (I guess the reader gets the irony of this statement), we have to be able to build anew theater spaces within existing theaters. As a result of all these innumerable works, both failed experiments and astonishing achievements, a new principle in treating space in theater has emerged: a theater space should be created anew for every production.

Creating theater space

Theater space functions according to a few basic principles. We can find them in the history of theater and detect them in the works of major directors and designers. A space becomes a theater space when a human being starts to communicate with another human being in it using the means of theater action. Because these two, actor and spectator, are needed for theater to be born, theater space always has a social, communicational, and interactional character. It must fulfill the conditions necessary for direct communication and interaction. It must provide mutual visibility and audibility: live people communicate directly with live people. This is a specific theater condition. Film, television, and other mechanical arts do not require direct interhuman communication. The fact that people in theater must communicate directly, including seeing and hearing each other, sets limits on theater and reveals its uniqueness. Screens with close-ups of actors' faces and personal microphones might overcome the spatial distance between actors and spectators, but at the same time change the production from theater to mixed media. We are not going to discuss here the aesthetics of various kinds of modern art; we should only understand that theater is, indeed, unique: it is—as I have already stated many times—a purely human art, based on direct interhuman contact.

The basic necessity for visibility and audibility in theater may be satisfied in many different ways. They may be consciously shaped in order to express and carry certain meanings, values, and energies. The mutual positioning of actors and spectators, their number (on both sides), and the space in which they interact, along with its lighting and acoustics, have a decisive impact on the whole theater process.

The actor is the energy-radiating center of theater. The presence and activity of the actor articulates the space around him/her. The playing area of the actor is, therefore, the primary element of theater space. Its shape, dimensions, character, architecture, and equipment are defined by the needs and requirements of the actor. During the show an actor's actions are transformed into interactions with the audience. Hence, the playing area articulates and emits the observation area. The observation area is always inseparably connected with the playing area and does not exist without it. Each is indispensable to the fulfillment of the other.

Creating theater space we do not work on architecture, buildings, technologies, or equipment—we work on a place for the interaction of living human beings. As Appia once said, we work on a "living space."

As always in theater work, we begin with a living human being, an actor. This human being, this actor, acts within a space. We create that space—it is the playing area. Next, we identify another human being, the spectator. These two, actor and spectator, should communicate. We have to provide the spectator with a space—it is the observation area. The playing and the observation areas together make up the performance space. We should now understand that the process of creating theater space must always have a precise, logical, and casual sequence:

(1) we create and define the playing area for actors;

(2) the playing defines the observation area for audience;

(3) we specifically define the observation area.

Consequently, the performing space can be both homogenous and hierarchical, as well as communicational and human. It is homogenous because it allows the birth of community and theatrical interaction. It is hierarchical because it situates the actor in its center. It is communicational because it allows actors to communicate with spectators. It is human because it provides conditions for live and direct interhuman contact. We can summarize these findings in a table:

**TABLE: PRINCIPLES OF THEATER SPACE
EXISTENCE AND CREATION**

Principles of existence
(1) Theater space is always a human space.
(2) Theater space is always a space of interhuman communication.
(3) Theater space is always a space of direct interaction between
    actors and spectators.
(4) The playing area is the core of performance space.
(5) The observation area is a function of the playing area.

Principles of creation
(1) The human being is always in the heart of theater space.
(2) We first build the playing area for actors.
(3) We follow by building the observation area for spectators.
(4) We continue by aligning and balancing the performance space
    (which consists of playing and observation areas).
(5) We finish by shaping the totality of the theater space.

Basic elements of theater space

From the point of view of theater art[12], any theater space has four basic elements: (1) The human being in space. (2) Space as is; its characteristics, dimensions, construction, material, architecture, etc. (3) The structure of the space; its design, divisions, equipment, furniture, objects, entrances and exits, windows, etc. (4) The lighting of the space.

These four elements are always there and are always inseparably connected. They have an infinite number of combinations, influence each other, and offer an inexhaustible source of creative energy for a director who can actively shape them. It is striking, however, that so often these energies and options are neglected by directors and sometimes not used at all. There are many directors who accept a theater space as given and find it impossible to either build anew, or at least change it. They passively and mindlessly approach the spatial aspect

---

[12] I write on theater space only from the theater's point of view. I don't mean to encroach on the fields of expertise of architects, physicists, or mathematicians.

of the production and neglect the social and aesthetic relations between the playing and observation areas. They do not appreciate the tremendous power and energy of theater space. Indeed, it has the power to shape the whole production.

Let's embark on a journey during which we will free ourselves from the slavery of the mental clichés about existing theater architecture and spatial structures. Let's experience the joy of finding new spaces and building them. We will actively search for theater spaces, create them, structure them, light them, and populate them. We will create a new and unique theater space for every single production.

The human being in space

As we already know, theater space always emanates from a human being. A person, by his/her sheer presence, position, behavior, movement, and activity defines, shapes, and structures the theater space. The process of building a theater space begins with a person, an actor, in a space. The goal of this process is to articulate a space for that person—the actor, or for a group of actors. Next, we articulate the space for an interaction of actor/actors with spectator/spectators. In order to do so, we investigate human beings in a space, their activity, and their interaction. We ask such questions as: who is in the space and why are they there? What are they doing there? How are they using the space? Who communicates with whom in a space? What is going on in a space? How does the activity of people occupying a space influence newcomers? And so on, and so forth. In the following exercises we will study how the use of a space by a group of people influences other people in the same space.

Exercise: *Creating communion in space*

Situation. The group divides into two equal parts. One part stays in the room. The other leaves. These who stayed are asked by the master to sit in a circle on chairs in the center of space. There should be some distance in between the chairs and half of the chairs should be left unoccupied. Those who left the room are instructed to make a line at the closed doors and wait. Upon a signal from the room—for example, clapping hands—one student enters. The rest wait. Another call is given and the next student enters, until all those who were waiting in line are in the room. The student entering must close the door behind himself/herself, stop for three seconds (counting them mentally), decide what to do, and fulfill the decision. Absolutely no talking allowed during this exercise!

Action. The first student (let's call her "A") enters and stops. All of the students sitting in the chairs turn their heads towards her and smile. (No words or gestures!) "A" sees, feels, and realizes that the group invites her to join the circle. She sees the circle as an easily accessible space for her. She goes towards the group and takes one of the unoccupied seats. She joins the community. The same actions are repeated with other entering students.

Discussion. The group prepared a place for the newcomer and encouraged her to take it. The free chairs and the inviting attitude of the group conveyed the message to the newcomer that she was welcomed. On the basis of this spatial and social message, she decided to join the group.

Development. The group uses the space in various ways to let each newcomer know that there is room for them and that they may join the community. For example, if everyone present danced individually all over the room—the newcomer would feel free to join, especially if greeted with a friendly smile.

Exercise: *Prohibiting communion in space*

Situation. The group divides into two equal parts. One part stays in the room. The other leaves. The group inside the room sits in a tight circle in a corner and motionlessly waits for the entrance of the newcomer. The group outside is instructed to wait for the call and enter individually. Every entering student must close the door behind himself/herself, stop for three seconds (counting them mentally), decide what to do and fulfill the decision—all as in the previous exercise.

Action. "A" enters. Nobody reacts to her appearance. "A" sees, feels, realizes that there's no place for her in the group and on the territory occupied by this group. Out of necessity she takes a seat, or remains standing, somewhere outside the group; she remains alone and does not join the community. It may happen that "A" is an assertive individual and she breaks into the group, forcibly making room for herself inside the circle. She still does not became a member of the group; she is, perhaps, even more lonely sitting alone inside the circle of unfriendly people coldly staring at her. It is their circle—she is a stranger, an intruder. The same repeats with other newcomers.

Discussion. The group annexed part of the space exclusively for themselves and did not want to share it with anybody else. This use of space excluded newcomers from the territory occupied by the group. The newcomer was not invited to join and had to remain an outsider. If more people would enter the room at the same time—we may try this variant of the exercise—they would also be automatically excluded from the community occupying the corner of the room. The group occupying part of the space did not want to share it with anybody. Others were excluded and could not join the group. This resulted in the relationship of separation or even hostility between those in the room and the newcomers. Let's discuss how often such a situation happens in a waiting room, in a night bus, even in a church.

Development. Let's invent other ways of using a space by a group who will not allow the newcomers on their territory. For example: members of the group in the room are busy with some work which precludes newcomers from joining. Going further, we can instruct newcomers to try to force themselves into the group activity which will result in conflict, or even a fight. A whole chain of improvised actions may occur.

Space as is

Theater space as is, or space as it is given, is conditioned by: the space's dimensions, its construction, material and architectural style, as well as its surroundings, which may be natural or civilizational. Theater space always has certain general characteristics: it may be small or large, open or closed, situated inside of a building or outdoors, made of wood or concrete, public or private, accessible to everybody or restricted, visible or hidden, etc. Productions take place in a variety of old or new theaters, in ancient ruins, in the parks, or on the perking lots. Each of these spaces imposes a specific character on the interaction of actors and spectators, each demands definite means of expression from actors and ways of perception from spectators, each allows and encourages particular social behaviors and prohibits others. We know that performance space is always divided into the playing area and the observation areas; that there may be multiple playing areas and observation areas in one show; that playing and observation areas may be interchangeable or merged.

In the following series of exercises we will investigate how space influences the people using it, how it defines their actions, movements, and the positions they take within the space. For these exercises we'll need many different spaces. We can easily find them inside or outside the building we currently use, in a nearby park or forest, in a store, cafeteria, the waiting room of an office, in a church (under the condition that we'll respect its sacred character), or in any other place. Finding and identifying the spaces may be a home-work assignment given to all students. They should work as two-person teams. The master instructs them: "First, look around in this building and in its vicinity. You may go farther, but it should be only a short walking distance. Second, find a space which is particularly attractive, appealing, or interesting for you. Don't tell anybody that you selected that space. If, by chance, two teams run across each other in a space, the second team to arrive should leave and look for another space." At the next class/workshop, when the assignment has been done, the master informs students of the "rules of the game." They are as follows:

(1) Each team of two people prepares an action (a scene) in the space they have found. The members of other teams should not observe their work. (2) Work in your spaces without changing or rearranging anything in them and don't

change the lighting either. The space should remain as you found it. (3) In some of these spaces you'll encounter people. Acknowledge their presence, but do not interfere with their activities or work and do not interact with them. Surely, the presence of these people will influence you somehow, but you should interact with the space as is, not with the people present in it.

Each team is given the master's instructions and goes to its space where it works on its assignment. (The assignment is explained below.) After that, all teams return to the classroom but do not talk about their work with others. When all teams have done their work and returned to the classroom, the master decides on the sequence of presentations of the scenes, then asks the group to accompany him and the first team to its space. In that space the team performs the scene. Other members of the group are spectators. After that, the group follows the next team, and so on, until all teams have done their scenes. When all scenes have been played, the students return to the classroom where the master explains the whole project and discusses it with the group. Now we are ready to begin the exercises.

Exercise: *Space conditions human behaviors*

Situation. The beginning of the scene is the same for all teams. In order to allow them to work independently, instructions for the exercise should be given separately to each team. The scene begins with a meeting between two people. They interact without words. In every scene these people are different: lovers on a tender date, conspirators meeting secretly, spies exchanging messages in a smilingly casual manner, stockbrokers comparing notes from the morning session during a lunchtime break, students hastily reviewing a textbook just before a test, and so on, and so forth. The choice should be the students'. We assume that "A" and "B" know each other and want to meet. One of the characters, let's call him/her "A," comes for the meeting earlier, perhaps, even very early, and the other, "B," comes later, or is even very late. The master informs students about their characters using our "5Q" technique. The general information is similar and the details depend on the characters the students have chosen. Let's consider one example: the characters are two young people in love. The master's information can go like this:

(1) Characters: Who? Who are the characters? "A" is a young woman, she's an American, 22 years old, a student at the school of drama. She comes from a lower middle class, an Italian family in Chicago. She is a talented and outgoing actress but privately she's shy. "B" is a Basque, 25 years old, a professional soccer player, who successfully played in the Spanish national team at the last World Cup in Paris. He got an offer to play for an American club, the Chicago Fire. He arrived two months ago and joined the rest of the team in the training camp. He's physically strong and emotionally fragile. The two of them met accidentally a week ago in a hangout near to both the school of drama and the soccer stadium. (2) Partners: With whom? Who are the character's partners? "A" and "B" are partners for each other. They are the only participants in the action. (3) Space: Where? Where do the characters act? What are the spatial and environmental circumstances of the characters' actions? They are in America, in Chicago, in a public park, in a secluded spot hidden in the bushes, where they discovered an old bench. The park is situated half-way between the university campus, where "A's" school of drama is located, and the recreational grounds with a soccer training field where "B" sweats. Note: this scene should be played in a real park! (4) Time: When? When do the characters act? What are the temporal circumstances of the characters' actions? It is happening today. The season, date, and hour of the action occur in the present, precisely at the time we are working on this exercise. (5) Action: What? What are the characters doing? "B" comes too early for the date. He has a break in the training camp. "A" is not yet there. "B" sits on the bench, but he is not able to wait patiently. He's angry. He decides to punish "A" (if she comes at all) and he hides himself in the bushes behind the bench. "A" comes in a hurry—she's late. Her rehearsal was extended by the director. She thinks that "B" has already left. Upset, she sits on the bench and waits for him anyway—a good material for actress' improvisation. "A" sees

her, but does not appear from the bushes for a long time. Finally, "B" decides to leave. When she is about to exit the spot, he produces a sound from the bushes; it may be a bird or animal sound. She hears and recognizes the sound. She stops. He appears. She is surprised, angry, happy, etc. The continuation of the scene should be left to actors' improvisation.

Action. The structure of action should be identical for all scenes of all teams and divided into similar episodes. Except for this, actors should be free to improvise, according to what characters they play, the relationships between characters, and the specifics of space and time. The action of all scenes, despite variations in content, should consist of the following episodes:

Episode 1: One of the characters enters the space, finds out that the space is empty (the other character did not come yet) and decides where and how to wait.

Episode 2: The second character arrives and meets the first character.

Episode 3: They interact—according to who they are and what they are supposed to do.

Episode 4: They both leave the space, either together, or separately.

Discussion. Student teams chose several different spaces, for example: a vast and empty public park, a small, cramped room in a dormitory, a noisy cafeteria, a quiet library, a department store full of shoppers in a shopping mall, a bus stop with commuters standing in line, a subway platform with passengers constantly milling about, a waiting room at the dentist's where classical music is played (supposedly soothing patients' pain and anxiety), a squeaky, revolving door at the entrance to a gym, etc. The actors prepared, rehearsed, and played their scenes in those spaces. The scenes were conditioned by the space they used. Every space imposed its general mood, qualities, dimensions, features, and functions on the action and characters. Characters acted, behaved, and moved in concert with the conditions of the space. The very nature of the meeting between two people was significantly affected by the conditions of the space in which they met. Of course, as we warned students, the presence or absence of other people, as well as the structure and lighting of the space played an additional conditioning role, but most important was the impact of the space as it was provided.

Development. The same exercise can be repeated with bigger teams, composed of three, four, or more students. New spaces can be found and new characters may be introduced. Every time a team should be divided into two groups—"hosts" and "guests." "Hosts" enter a space and initiate an action in it. "Guests" arrive and respond to the action of "Hosts," who, in turn, interact with "Guests," thus building up a chain of improvisations. Each team should have a leader, who functions as director. He/she should inform actors (using the "5Q" technique) and take charge of the spectators, leading them to the space, indicating what position or place they should take, and opening and closing the show.

Exercise: *Space names characters*

Space has power not only to condition people's actions in general, but also to "name" (describe, articulate, or characterize) people acting in it, or cast them in specific roles. Before we move on to an exercise which will help us to understand and experience the specific impact of space on characters, I'd like to tell you a story which clearly explains the problem we are working on now. It is a true story. It happened in one of my workshops. Robert had the task of creating an action in which the space would be used according to its general characteristics and functions, supporting peoples' activities, and describing them—telling the spectators (without words, of course!) who these people were that were using this space. The space was supposed to "name" people. Robert chose a spacious plaza in front of the university theater, dominating the whole architectural environment, with vast steps leading up to it from the sidewalk level. He created an action in which people formed a picket line and waked in a circle, waving hastily improvised banners, with only one word on them: "No," and chanting: "No-No-No!" Spectators, including myself, were situated on the steps to the theater and had an excellent view of the playing area below. It was an expressive scene, with characters clearly defined as protesters and their action as a protest. Obviously, for me, they were protesting students. During discussion after the show, I asked

Robert who the protesters were and he answered: "GM workers. There is a strike in Detroit going on. That inspired me." I asked other students how they read the characters. For all of them the protesters were, as for me, simply protesting students. "But I saw them as GM workers!", argued Robert. "They weren't GM workers,"—I explained—"because the space they were using was a part of the university campus, it was a university plaza in front of the university theater. These spatial conditions articulated—or, we can say, named—young people using that space as students."

This was so, not because the performers playing the protesters were in reality students, and we knew that. We would have read this scene in the same way even if it had been played by a cast of professional actors playing people protesting at a university. If their costumes and banners did not specify otherwise, they would be taken for students, precisely because the space was a students' space, a university space. Yes, indeed, the space named and articulated the characters as students. On the other hand, if the same action took place on the GM premises in Detroit, the people walking a picket line would surely be taken for GM employees. The space would describe them as such. Let's now create an action to study this problem; the same action will be played in several different places.

Situation. The sole character in the scene is a man going to sleep. Let's call him "The Sleepy Man" ("A"). He must find and prepare a sleeping place for himself. We should, first, find those places, and, second, articulate the playing and observations areas there. The spaces are:

(1) The single room. The room is small; there is a simple bed, a pillow, a blanket, and a night light. We can find such a room in a dorm or set it in the corner of our classroom. A few chairs for spectators in front of the bed will do for the observation area.

(2) A quiet alcove in our building. The playing area: an armchair or sofa. Observation area: the public may sit on the floor. For playing this scene "A" should have a bag and use it as a pillow.

(3) A remote quarter of a public park. Playing area: a bench. Observation

area: the grass in front of the bench. If the weather is good "A" doesn't need any props. If it is cold "A" must have a jacket, gloves, scarf, and hat.

(4) A secluded spot in a forest or any other hidden place. Playing area: the interior of a clump of bushes or other natural features. Observation area: a place from which the audience may secretly observe action. "A" needs a sleeping bag and some other equipment.

(5) An infrequently-used staircase in a building. Playing area: a platform of the staircase. Observation area: the flight of stairs above and below the playing area. "A" needs a sleeping bag and some equipment.

Action. "A" performs the same (or similar) action in each space: he enters a space looking for a place to sleep. He finds the place. He prepares himself a bed (or nest) and quickly goes to sleep. He has a nightmare—this part of the action should be left open to actor's improvisation. Activities of "A" should be similar, if not identical, in each space, modified only slightly in order to better accommodate the character's activities in the space. For example: In his room the man takes off his clothes, goes to bed, and covers himself with a blanket. In the alcove or in the park (if it is summer) the man simply lays down on the floor or grass, putting something under his head. In the forest he crawls into a sleeping bag. In the unused staircase he puts something under himself to make the sleeping spot softer and covers himself with all his possessions.

The action ends the same way every time. This ending might be surrealistic. A second actor appears and introduces himself to the audience: "I am the Guardian Angel of this tired traveler..." After this beginning, the actor should improvise an few sentences, informing the audiences that he, the Guardian Angel, is going to watch over the sleeping man, defending him from nightmares obviously sent to him by Satan. The Guardian Angel will wake him up when the time comes or in the event of danger. For example, in his room he might oversleep and be late for work in a factory; in the school, the campus police night patrol might find him, with unpleasant consequences; in the park or forest a thief might take advantage of him. The Guardian Angel closes the show, thanking the audience for coming.

Discussion. The same action, performed by the same character (a sleepy man), took place in various spaces. Each different space named (defined, articulated) the character. He was someone else because he was in a different space. In discussing this exercise with students, the master should ask them to establish who the character was in different spaces. For example:

(1) In a small room he was an immigrant returning to his shabby room after a long day of hard labor, and falling into bed almost unconscious with fatigue.

(2) In the university alcove, he was a student who partied all last night and is too sleepy to attend morning class.

(3) In the park he was a sick person, who suffered a sudden attack of high blood pressure; when this happens, as his doctors instructed him, he must lay down quietly and try to sleep.

(4) In the forest, he was a tourist who likes to hike on his own and sleep under the stars.

(5) In the unused staircase, he was a homeless man.

Development. Students should create their own scenes in which the same character performs the same action in different spaces. They should not forget to articulate the playing area and the observation area. After each scene the master should lead a group discussion about the work the students have done.

Structure of space

We structure space in thousands ways. We plan cities and neighborhoods. We design the interiors of our homes. We throw highways and railroads over land. In churches we reserve some special areas for what is holy, others for the priest, and still different ones for the congregation. In airports and banks, we set up barriers that channel customers' movements. In consulates, we put officers behind bulletproof glass, separating them from the applicants. We put barricades on the roads and police lines on the streets. We plant islands of shrubs and rows of flowers, structuring the space of our yards and gardens. The structure of space is created by vertical and horizontal divisions; by levels, stairs, and pillars; by internal equipment, furniture, and objects; by the functional design of entrances and exits, work areas, windows, or skylights; and by lighting—what a difference a focused lamp over a desk of a writer, or the diffuse of lighting of a ballroom, can make! Each space has a specific structure. A completely empty space has a homogenous structure. Inside theater buildings, space is divided by permanent architecture, which separates the stage from the auditorium and structures foyers, lounges, and all other facilities for the audience. The space of the stage is an area structured by sets. In an open-air theater, the structure of space is imposed by the surrounding mountains and valleys, or buildings and streets, and by our decisions about how to arrange performance space within the natural or architectural contexts and how to situate actors and spectators within it.

As we know, theater space has two major structural elements: the playing area and the observation area. From the structural point of view the playing area may be on a proscenium stage, on a platform, on the floor, or it may be simply a circle in the earth or grass. The observation area may be equipped with golden boxes, armchairs, or benches, or might be set on the ground; the public may sit or stand.

Ways of access to their areas, for both actors and spectators, are an important structural element of theater space. Actors must always somehow reach the playing area, find themselves behind the closed curtain or enter on the thrust at the beginning of the show. The arrival and departure of the audience must also be planned and is conditioned by the space's structure. In a series of exercises we'll investigate relationships between the structure of a space and the human activities in it.

Exercise: *The structure of space identifies the users*

Structures and, more specifically, the functions of structures of space, define the people who use them. They specify people's social or professional status, occupation, place within a military or corporate hierarchy, position within an institution, church, convent, school, and so forth. It is natural for a priest to stand at the altar. In the court of law we expect that the judge sits in the large chair behind the bench. The president of the corporation occupies a central armchair at a conference table. It is obvious that the professor uses a podium with a microphone in a large lecture hall. The very use of certain structural elements in a space identifies the users. Let's examine these matters with a practical exercise.

Situation. We set a large table directly in front of the entrance to our room. Three students sit on chairs behind the table on one side, facing the door. The other students, all but one, stand at two sides of the room perpendicular to the table—they are spectators. One student ("A") is asked to leave the room while preparations are made inside. She returns when called and fulfills a simple physical task (without getting complete "5Q" information): "Enter the room. Stand in front of the table, keeping distance from it."

Action. "A" enters and stands in front of the table. (This is it!)

Discussion. The master asks the students: who are the people at the table, and who is the person standing in front of the table? Is it a panel composed of director, producer, and casting agent auditioning an actor? Is "A," thus, an auditioning actor just about to open her mouth? Or maybe these people at the table are army officers and "A" is a candidate about to be interviewed? Or are these three the panel of judges and is "A" the defendant? All these options, and many more, are plausible. The point is that the a particular structure of the space (in this case made only with one table and three chairs,) and a particular use of it by people (three persons sitting and one standing in front of them,) imposed on all of them quite specific roles and relationships. The structure of a space, the use of furniture, and the taking of certain positions within the space always imposes on people specific roles and relationships, establishes a hierarchy, suggests who they are and what is going on. The very structure of the space casts people in roles.

Development. We may make a number of alterations to the initial situation.

(1) We add two persons standing behind the three sitting. Are they guards,

deputies, police, or a retinue?

(2) We add a small table at one side and seat one person at it. Is this new person a secretary, a clerk, or an assistant?

(3) Instead of heaving only one person in front of the table, we set a whole group of them in a row. Perhaps they are a group of illegal immigrants caught at the border and being interrogated by the border guards?

(4) We put a chair on the table and seat one person on it, with two others standing below. "A" is now kneeling in front of the table. Is the elevated chair a throne? Is the person using it a king or queen? Is "A" a suppliant at a medieval court?

Exercise: *Creating an action concordant with the structure of space*

Usually, in everyday reality, people use a space in accordance with its structure, function, or equipment. We do it automatically and unconsciously. It is obvious to us. In so doing, we assume certain social roles and undertake certain activities imposed on us by the space's structure. We may consciously use this mechanism in our directorial work. We can—without words or lengthy explanations—send clear signals about the characters, their relationships and actions to the spectators.

As in the above exercises with space itself, we have to stage a series of scenes in various places—in interiors or exteriors, in private spots or public venues, and in small or large spaces. We may use a college hallway, a dorm room, a park, a department store, etc. We can even use the same places as before in our exercise with a "sleepy man." Of course, it would be more interesting to discover new spaces.

Situation. For their homework, students chose various spaces which must be clearly defined in terms of their function, use, and character. All students together with the master visit all these spaces, guided by the students who found the given space. The master divides the group into small teams of 2-4 people, and assigns spaces to them. Each team gets a task: "Go to your space, and discover intellectually, emotionally, and experimentally what is the proper/natural/normal use and function of this space based on its internal structure. Prepare a short action which confirms your discovery, i.e. make practical use of your space in accordance with its structure.

Action. Each team goes to its space. As instructed, students discover the proper/natural/normal use and function of the space and prepare an appropriate action—a short scene. For example: in a store, they shop and then get in a line to check out; in the doctor's waiting room they register and sit quietly in the chairs, waiting; in a classroom they cast themselves as teacher and students and start working on a topic; in the park they can walk; in a church they pray; on a playground they play; in a swimming pool they swim; encountering a trash can they throw trash into it; and so forth. After they have discovered and explored their space they stage a simple scene in it. Next, all teams, one by one, lead other students and the master to their spaces where they repeat (play) their scenes. The other students and the master are the spectators.

Discussion. In each space, its internal structure, function, equipment, furnishings, and objects—that is, everything which usually and normally is there—encouraged, made possible, or even imposed on users certain specific behaviors and activities. The students used a space in accordance with their experience, knowledge, and habits. Indeed, this is the way we usually use furniture or tools in real life, as well as sets or props on stage: we sit on chairs, we eat at a table, we put gloves on our hands and hats on our heads. Within a given space we usually do what is normal, natural, everyday, functional, and expected. The exercises confirmed that.

It should also be noted that this normal use of a space casts the users in a certain social role: shopping in a store, we are customers, waiting at a doctor's, we are patients, praying in a church, we are believers, playing on a playground, we are happy children.

Development. Let's look again in and around our classroom, building, and the vicinity. Let's discover the normal, natural, everyday, or natural functions of various spaces in terms of their internal structure and equipment. Let's use those space as they should be practically used. But let's also experiment and play with our imagination. For example, so many times we pass by a fire alarm hose in a red box in our school hallway. Let's stage (not making a false alarm and not damaging any equipment!) an action in which firemen arrive at the building and put out a fire in our classroom. Another example: the stairs, which we use several times a day, can serve in so many different ways. We can walk, run, jump up and down, we may rush, or we may slowly climb like a person having heart problems.

Exercise: *Creating an action which conflicts with the structure of a space*

The structure of a space may be in accord with people's actions in it, as in the previous exercise, or they may be in conflict. The latter—the conflict, argument, or fight between a space's structure and people's actions is a treasury of creative, interesting, unexpected, revealing, and surprising dramatic effects. History, social life, art, and theater is full of such uses of space. What am I talking about? I'll explain this with a few examples:

In 1807, during their campaign against Spain, the cavalry troops of revolutionary, anti-Catholic, and secular France used to use churches as stables. The invaders not only found good shelter for themselves and their horses in every village or town on their way, but in addition, they humiliated and terrorized the Spanish, who were devout Catholics. The French used the churches against their normal function. The sacrilegious employment of the churches deeply offended the Spanish, and, contrary to the French expectations, it hardened their resistance.

In Beckett's *Endgame,* we read in the initial stage direction that there are on stage two ashbins sitting next to each other. It turns out that the ashbins contain two people, an old couple, Nagg and Nell, parents of the hero, Hamm. This absurd vision is based on the conscious misuse of space: the ashbins function against their original and normal purpose, alienating action and characters from space, and providing a profound insight into the existential situation of the old couple and the generational relationship between the son and his parents.

The alienation effect (*Verfremdungseffekt*), a significant part of Brecht's aesthetic, is based on the collision of two or more stage elements which would not normally be used together. Brecht confronted moments of realistic acting with pantomime, dialog with song, real objects with stylized sets, and emotional exchanges between some characters with dull Marxist lectures given by others. In Brecht's own mise-en-scène of *Mother Courage*, the Cook propositioned Mother Courage while changing his worn-out shoes and socks, full of holes.

In my production of *The Story of Blok* by Alexandr Stein, I put the audience on a proscenium stage and some scenes were played in the auditorium. This reversal of the normal use of theater architecture—to situate the playing area in the auditorium and to set the observation area on stage—was widely used by many directors in the 1960s, 1970s, and 1980s. It helped to establish new relationships between actors and spectators, between text and subtext, and between action and space.

Situation. Student teams (the same as in the exercise on the accord between space and action) work in their respective spaces. They have already found and know the normal use of their space. Now, their task is to discover, imagine, and invent an abnormal, unusual, or illogical use of the same space. Each team has to create a scene in which they demonstrate this completely new use of their space.

Action. Teams go to their spaces, make their discoveries, and create their scenes. The scenes might be realistic or stylized, acted, or mimed. All means of expression are allowed. For example: a team discovers that a telephone booth can serve as a shelter when a sudden rain shower surprises people on a street; a bench in a park can transform itself into a canoe in which a couple of tourists slowly paddle on a lake; a display window may serve as a mirror; a Coca-Cola dispenser in a college hallway might be an object of worship. After they have created their scenes, all teams return to the classroom. Next, all teams, one by one, lead other students and the master to their spaces where they play their scenes.

242

Discussion. In each space, its normal internal structure, function, equipment, furnishing, and objects were used this time in an abnormal, unusual, illogical, and nontraditional way. The space was, in a way, rediscovered: it revealed its hidden potentials and energies, and it metaphorically acquired a new character and a new dimension. This new use of a space cast the users in new roles. In the same way, French soldiers in Spain became for the Spanish not only invaders but also Antichrists, because of the sacrilegious use of the churches. People worshiping a Coca-Cola machine would seem to passersby to be members of some crazy cult. Students coming to an art gallery, taking off their clothes and lying on the floor wearing sunglasses instead of looking at the paintings would be taken for anti-cultural barbarians. (The gallery's management would probably call the police—to prevent that we should in advance ask for permission to conduct our experiment in the gallery.)

Development. Let's try to stage several short actions in our building, turning it upside down (don't treat this literally, please!) in order to rediscover the unexpected potential of different locations in our school.

Creating light

Light is one of the decisive elements in the theatrical process. Lighting techniques have developed along with the changing aesthetics of theater and the advances of technology. The history of lighting in theater begins with the use of natural light, then moves to torches, to oil lamps, to gas light, after ca. 1820, and then to electricity, after ca. 1870. In the 20th century, precise spotlights, projections, lasers, and strobe lights, as well as computerized boards have been used.

Many directors treat light as one of their favorite and most effective means of expression. In the works of some modern theater artists (such as Wilson or Strehler) lighting is an intrinsic and striking element of their shows. At the same time, in numerous productions, especially in Western culture, lighting is neglected and supports neither the mise-en-scène and the sets nor the actor. Our objective—in this section of the book—is to attract the attention of potential directors as well as practicing directors to the power and unlimited artistic potential of light in the theater.

Lighting can enhance the structure and expression of space, or it can obliterate them. Indeed, lighting and structure are always connected and either support or contradict each other: proper lighting makes the structure clearer and its impact stronger, while improper or accidental lighting may hide some parts of the structure or not allow the structure to function at all.

The lighting of the performance space, and especially the playing area, may be live or artificial. Sources of light may include: candles, lamps, torches, burning fuel, and electric lights of various types. Lights may be operated with the use of lighting boards or directly by actors moving spotlights on stage or handling lamps or candles. Human ingenuity and technical possibilities have no borders—and this is true with theatrical lighting too. There are, however, certain basic and universal principles of the functioning of light in a theater production. It is worthwhile to know them. My own experience, as well as that of many contemporary directors, confirms that these principles (almost like laws of physics) are applicable to any space, any decor, and any action, in any show.

TABLE: PRINCIPLES OF LIGHTING A THEATER PRODUCTION

Light and human beings in theater

(1) Light in theater serves the present, active, and moving human being.

(2) Light in theater serves, first of all, people, and secondly, objects. Remember: the human being is always in the center of theater, and he/she must get light first. Objects, including sets and costumes, should get light only as they are used by actors and as they enhance actors' actions.

(3) A human being creates a theater space around himself/herself and light should follow this process of creation.

(4) The logical procedure for working on lights in theater is to move from lighting a human being to lighting the space.

Live light in theater

(1) Nothing matches the power of live light: a torch, a candle, a lamp, a burning barrel of oil, a camp fire, or a single match.

(2) Live light can be easily operated by an actor, which makes lighting humane and personal.

(3) Live light is both natural and effective, as has been proven by a multitude of both open air and indoor productions throughout the history of theater.
Note: the use of open fire is easier and safer in outdoor production.

(4) Live light in closed spaces is even more powerful then outdoors, for it is aesthetically alienated, psychologically unexpected, and perceptually unusual.

Artificial light in theater

(1) The fewer lights used, the stronger the effect of lighting. The fewer colors, the stronger impact of those used.

(2) There's no more dynamic and dramatic lighting than that hitting an actor from behind and from the side.

(3) An actor's face must get light from two angles, otherwise it is either flat or dark.

(4) Shadows invest life in the space and the sets, and intensify actors' movement.

Note: local fire regulations must always be fully respected.

In a series of exercises we are going to check these principles and observe how they work. We'll study the impact of lighting on human actions, as well as the basic relationships between lighting and space.

Exercise: *The attracting power of light*

This exercise demonstrates how source, kind, and position of light influence people, including their use of a space, the positions they take within it, and their behavior.

Situation. We need an empty room which can be darkened. All students leave the room and wait behind closed doors. The master, alone in the room, makes it dark, sets a candle in the center of the room and lights it. He/she leaves the room, closes the door, and gives the following instructions to the students waiting outside: (1) One student plays the role of the starter (as at a field and track competition)—he/she is going to let all other students into the room, one by one, at fifteen-second intervals. (2) Students wait in line. Upon the starter's sign they individually enter the room, closing the door behind themselves. While they are in the room, they stop for three seconds, decide what to do and where to go and do it—that is, to go somewhere and take a position. Then, they should freeze and remain frozen until the end of the exercise is announced by the master. (3) The starter enters fifteen seconds after the last student. The master enters fifteen seconds after the starter. Note: The master gives students only the above instructions and does not tell them what to do, where to go, and whether to sit or stand.

Action. Students enter the room one by one and take their positions inside. On entering, everyone is confronted with the light of the candle sitting in the center of the room. Everyone chooses a place based on the fact and position of the candle light. The master enters last and also takes a position.

Discussion. The master explains the exercise: (1) Everybody, please, don't change your places, stay where you are. Now, look around and see who is where. How are you sitting or standing? What direction are you facing? (2) Now, let's reconstruct the order of entrances. Who was first, second, and so on? (3) Now, think what motivated you to take your place and your position? Could everybody, please, explain their choice to the group?

Listening to the answers we discover that everybody—indeed, everybody—was motivated first of all by light. Students chose their positions because of the light. In a way, the light imposed their positions on them and prescribed to them where to go and how to sit or stand. Looking around, we will see that everybody, or at least the majority of students, will be sitting on the floor and facing the light. What is more, everybody, or at least the majority, will be sitting in a circle around the light. If there are some students who are not facing the light and not in the circle, discussion with them will reveal that they were heavily influenced by light too. They had the impulse to face it and join the circle, but they decided to suppress this initial impulse and, in a way, fight the attracting power of light. The presence of other people in the space was an additional factor conditioning the participants' behaviors. Those entering the room later were strongly drawn into the existing circle.

The master should also remind students that in giving instructions at the beginning of the exercise he/she did not specifically tell them what to do in the room, where to go, or whether to sit or stand. The choice was entirely left up to each individual student. We discovered that the call of light is so strong that it motivates everybody with almost equal force. A single, weak, small flame had the power to steer the behavior of the whole group of people, shaping them into a community sitting in a circle on the floor around a tiny candle.

Development. The same exercise might be conducted at night in a meadow or in the woods where the master would prepare a camp fire and sit at it waiting for pupils. Students should be told the time at which they should arrive at a location (for a example a parking lot or bus stop) and be given directions where to go from there to meet the master. They should not be informed, though, that there will be a camp fire, nor of what they should do when they see the master, except that they should not talk to him/her or among themselves. It is almost a certainty that the students, arriving gradually at the spot, will create a circle around the camp fire. A similar exercise can be conducted in an empty room, having windows at one side through which light is pouring. Participants, asked to enter the room individually and take whatever positions they want, would most likely sit facing the windows. If not, after analyzing their motives, we'll find out that they were attracted by the light, but decided to oppose its call. Another idea for an exercise on the attracting power of light is to use a dark corridor with many doors leading to many rooms with only one lit. Let's experiment and see which room students are most likely to enter. It should not surprise us when students choose the room with the light.

Exercise: *The rejecting power of light*

Light may attract and bring people together, as well as unify a space, but it may also separate and divide both space and people. Let's verify this.

Situation. As in the preceding exercise, the master prepares the room while students wait outside, behind closed doors. The master sets a single, strong spotlight in the center of the room and directs it on the door. Then, the master instructs students outside the room to proceed as before: upon the sign given by the starter, who allows students to enter the room every 15 seconds and closes the door behind them, they are to enter, stop, decide what to do and where to go, go there, sit or stand, and freeze. Then they are to wait until the end of the exercise. The master enters the room first and stands behind the light. He/she gives a vocal sign to the starter.

Action. The first student enters and is blinded by the light. He/she stops and then escapes from the light, going somewhere into the darkness. After the last student makes his/her escape, the master directs the spotlight onto the ceiling of the room, filling the entire space with light, and explains the exercise.

Discussion. Blinded by the strong light, all participants tried to escape and hide themselves somewhere in the darkness. Some, the most courageous, attacked the light, went straight to it, passed it, and took their positions behind the light, but still in the dark areas of the room. It rarely happens that someone sits in the light in a gesture of surrender to its power. In each case, the light strongly impacted people's behaviors, dictated their movements, and their use of space. Coming from one direction, the light dispersed the participants and did not allow them to form a community. On the contrary, they were alienated and separated from each other because everybody felt individually intimidated and threatened by the light.

Development. Let's set a light instrument on the floor, just in front of the back wall at the opposite side from the door leading to the room. The light should be widely spread all over the room. There should be no space left behind the light and, consequently, no way to escape from the light. As a result, participants will be scattered all over the room sitting with their backs to the light. They couldn't escape from the light, so they tried at least to protect their eyes from being blinded. The light imposed on people a specific use of space, and made them isolated in it.

Exercise: *The relationship between light and character*

Light not only has the power to direct people's behaviors and movements, but also to "cast" them as specific characters, or, in other words, to impose certain roles on them. We will use an exercise to study the phenomenon and discern the interdependence between light (including its sources and instruments used), people, and their actions.

Situation. We set a small playing area in a corner of our room: a table and four chairs. We seat four students on the chairs and give them playing cards. They are instructed to play a card game such as bridge, poker, or another one, using the appropriate rules and words for bidding or betting. All other words should be excluded. The rest of the group should be seated as the audience on chairs in front of the playing area, leaving an aisle in the center. We will repeat the same exercise four times, so there should be four different games played. We'll set a different light for each game. The master does not instruct players who they are, what to do, and so on—they are asked only to play the card games according to the rules. Players are also asked to choose a game they deem appropriate to play in a given light. Each of the four scenes, though including four different games, has the same general structure of action:

Episode 1. The light comes on, or is set by the master. Four players wait behind the audience. Seeing the light, they decide what game they are going to play. They enter from the audience's side through the aisle and sit at the table.

Episode 2. Players prepare themselves for the game: sit comfortably, shuffle cards, roll up their sleeves, and so on.

Episode 3. Players play the game—one round of it, which shouldn't last more than a few minutes—using appropriate bids. When they are done, they leave the playing area the same way they have entered.

The four games/scenes each have, as I said, different lighting, each of which conditions the players' behaviors. These four kinds of lighting are as follows:

First game: a candle only, sitting in the corner of the table. This light forces the players to search for enough light to look at their cards. Perhaps they will even stand up from time to time and hold their cards close to the candle, or move the candle around on the table, which might provoke protests by other players—a good source of material for improvisation. (Remember, no words!)

Second game: a lamp hanging high over the table—a student "plays" a lamp on a stand, extending an arm over the table and gently holding a flashlight or an office lamp.

Third game: a wide-open and strong light is set in front of the table close to it on the floor. The light blinds the players and projects their sharp shadows onto the back wall. Coming from one direction, it forces them to search for light, though of course, differently than in the first game.

Fourth game: the same wide-open and strong light is set on the floor behind the table and behind the players; additionally a fan is positioned in front of the light. Again, the direction of the light forces the players to search for light.

Action. Players enter the playing area, sit at the table, and play their game. When they have finished—they exit. They wait until a new light is prepared and they enter again. This is repeated four times. The light is different every time.

Discussion. The different kinds of lighting provided different atmospheres, but what's more, they completely changed the playing area and named the players. The master provokes students' discussion, asking several questions: (1) How would you describe each space with its four different kinds of lighting? (2) Can we say that it was a different space each time because of its different lighting? (3) What was the mood of the same space with different lighting? (4) What was the character of the game? (5) How did the players behave in different lighting? (6) How did they contact other players in different lighting? (7) How can we title these four scenes? (8) What roles did the players assume in these scenes?

There may be many answers to these questions, but all of them will point out that each kind of lighting completely changed the meaning, expression, and mood of the scene. On a practical level, it also changed the space. It named the characters differently every time. The following responses were given by students from one of my workshops:

First game—light from a candle: it was a play titled *Poker in a Gold Stampeders' Cabin*. The players were tenacious gold miners.

Second game—soft light from a lamp: *Bridge on Board a Cruise Ship*. Players were wealthy vacationers.

Third game—strong light set in front of a table with players' shadows on back wall: *Twenty-one in the Cabinet of Doctor Caligari* (an expressionist movie). The players were patients in Dr. Caligari's clinic.

Fourth game—light from behind with rays shooting through the fan and the players' silhouettes, blinding the audience: *A Gambler's Ballet*. The players were professional gamblers.

Of course, the students in our group can come up with different titles for the scenes and different readings of the characters. We see that changes in lighting, even those achieved with very simple means, can radically change the action, the space, and the characters, including their activities and contacts. We should also note that in changing lights for each scene we were true to one of the principles of lighting—the one which says: "The fewer lights used—the stronger the effect of lighting." Indeed, in each scene we had only one source of light, but this single light was extremely expressive and had tremendous theatrical power.

Development. Let's create another action in a space. Then, let's repeat the same action in the same space changing the lighting every time. In talking it over with students, let's make clear how the lighting of a space changes the action, the space, and the characters.

Creating the performance space

Actors and spectators articulate the space and, at the same time, are conditioned by space, including its structure and lighting. We have to further investigate the theatrical processes of communication from the point of view of space, creating various relationships between the playing and the observation area. We shall see how their mutual positioning influences both actors and spectators.

Exercise: *Creating a homogenous and communal performance space*

We shall create a space which unites all present, that is both actors and spectators, transforming them into one community. This will be a space of encounter, cooperation, and common creation—a modest fulfillment of Appia's dream of "the cathedral of the future."

Situation. Let's set a circle of chairs (not tightly connected) in the center of the room. The playing areas are inside and outside of the circle. The observation area is the circle of the chairs. Students will play roles in a wedding: groom and bride, a priest or minister, parents, best man and maid of honor, assistant, and master of ceremonies. Simple costume elements and a few props would help. Other students will be spectators. Lighting should be soft and focused in the center of the circle. It would be very helpful to secure music: a live instrument (or instruments), a disc, or tape. Ideally, an instrumentalist should be a part of the wedding party and walk with it. We instruct actors using our "5Q" technique and we invite spectators to the room and ask them to sit in chairs.

Action. The wedding party enters the room, goes around the circle of chairs and enters the center of the circle. A wedding ceremony is performed. It should be a non-denominational, simple ritual, with only a few words improvised by the priest or minister and the young couple exchanging vows. The movement of the wedding party should be blocked on the round. Spectators should be gently (not forcibly!) invited by the master of ceremonies to participate—for example to carry the bride's train or candles, to hold a sacred book, to stand as witnesses during the exchange of vows, and to repeat certain lines or incantations of the priest or minister. After the ceremony, the party leaves the circle, goes around the chairs and directs itself to the exit while the master of ceremonies encourages spectators (gently!) to join the group. Everybody leaves the room.

Discussion. Both actors and spectators shared the same space and were all conditioned by its structure and lighting. In terms of structure of space, there were no strict divisions between the playing and the observation areas, which allowed the spectators to join the actors in the action without the feeling that they were crossing a border and entering a foreign territory. The feeling of breaching a barrier would be obvious and strong if spectators were invited to join the wedding party on a proscenium stage. Explaining the exercise, the master should ask the student-spectators: "Was joining the wedding party difficult? Or easy? Did the space (including its structure and lighting) encourage you to do so? Why?" Students who played roles in the wedding should be asked: "Was the inclusion of spectators in the ceremony acceptable? How did you feel about their presence as members of the wedding party?"

Development. Let's play the same scene again from the very beginning until the exit of the wedding party. It will consist of both actors and spectators—as before. Right? Yes! Students who formerly were spectators are already members of the wedding party, and, therefore, actors. Their status has changed, but it has changed in a smooth and natural manner because there were no strict boundaries between the playing and the observation areas. Now, the wedding party continues down a hallway, and then on a sidewalk across the campus. The master of ceremonies and all wedding party members invite accidental passersby to join. Some will! Let's continue walking to a spot where a car for the newlyweds is waiting (if we can't afford the limousine...) and there, let's ask everybody (actors, former spectators, and newly recruited participants) to form a group for the wedding photograph. After a snapshot is taken, the master of ceremonies thanks all present and the newlyweds drive away.

Continuing the same kind of work, let's find or build other spaces which will have interchangeable and not divisive playing and observation areas that induce community. The internal structure of space and lighting should facilitate these too. For example: a conference room with a large round table in the center, a dance floor in a restaurant, a gym, etc. What is the result of actors and spectators sharing the same table? What will happen if spectators dance on the floor and a few actors (playing characters) start a fight in the midst of them? How people interact in a gym?

Exercise: *Creating a divided and dividing performance space*

We are going to examine how a space which is internally divided by structure and lighting can have a dividing impact on both actors and spectators. The use of such space results in confrontation between actors and spectators. As directors, we must be aware that certain spaces have such an impact and we should either avoid using them, or use them purposely, if our objective (as rare as it might be) is to make antagonists our of the actors and the audience.

Situation. Let's divide our room into two parts by setting a barrier across it; the barrier may be simply made of chairs. In the middle of the barrier we leave a narrow passage equipped with some sort of gate or closure; a string attached to two chairs will do the job; a chain would be, of course, better. On one side of the room we set chairs in rows, with an aisle in the middle, leading to the gate. On both sides of the aisle we put a string, cord, rope, or chain, thus blocking access to the chairs from the side of the aisle; the chairs are accessible only from the sides of the walls. The other part of the room, in front of the chairs and behind the barrier, is left empty. Light should be focused only on the empty part of the room. We use the same wedding party and the same group of spectators. The wedding party waits outside the room while the master invites the spectators to take seats in the chairs.

Action. The music plays and the wedding party enters the room. The party proceeds down the alley towards the empty area. The master of ceremonies unties (or unlocks) the blocking string (or chain) letting the party enter the empty space and closes the passage after them. The wedding ceremony, identical to the one in the previous exercise, now takes place on the area restricted, barred, closed, and cut off from the rest of the room. When the ceremony is over, the master of ceremonies lets the party exit, closes the passage again, and leaves the room.

Discussion. In this exercise the space was divided; its structure and lighting broke it into two separate parts. It radically divided the users, prohibiting any direct contact between actors and spectators. Barriers, closures, and ropes or other blocking devices, along with lights, split the whole space into two different areas. Community was not established and interaction was not allowed. The spectators were passive observers of the actors' actions.

Development. Using simple furniture and lights, let's create other divided spaces. For example: a classroom with chairs confronting the professor's desk; the office of a high official, with a huge and domineering desk and armchair for the boss, and two small chairs in front of it for the visitors; or a public office with a counter barricading the clerks from the clients. Let's also look around in our building and its vicinity, and identify all the divided spaces which have always been there but which we haven't noticed before. Next, let's analyze and discuss all these spaces, asking the following questions: what specifically divides these spaces? Which of them are divided sharply and obviously, and which have their divisions disguised and hidden? How do we feel in these spaces? How do they impact our mood, behavior, attitude, and activities?

Creating the playing area

We already know that the playing area is a part of the performance area that must be accessible to the audience and from which actors must be seen and heard by spectators. In various cultures, throughout the history of theater, playing areas met these conditions in thousands of different ways. The playing areas had the character of temples (as in Japanese Noh theaters), sandy village yards (in various Indian theater forms), aristocratic mansions (as in early Baroque Italian theaters), meeting halls (as in Piscator's productions in the Germany of the 1920s), or public playgrounds (as in Peter Schumann's shows in the 1980s). The architectural, aesthetic, and functional characteristics of the playing areas have always depended on various historical, cultural, and social determinants, including the culturally specific conventions of communication and the technology available. The history of theater architecture is a worthwhile, even necessary, subject of study for a director. This book is not able to enter into its fascinating labyrinth. We should, however, make our directing students aware of the major principles of creating the playing area.

TABLE: PRINCIPLES OF CREATING THE PLAYING AREA

(1) The playing area is a space where people (actors) live their lives; it is a living space.
(2) The playing area conditions the character, style, meaning, and message of the show.
(3) The playing area must allow interhuman communication between actors and spectators during the performance.
(4) The playing area must provide visibility and audibility to the actors and their actions.
(5) The playing area must fulfill the functional and technical needs of the action.
(6) The playing area allows the use of the energy and style of the fine arts to enrich performance.

In a series of exercises we'll test the above principles. We'll create a scene based on the same (or similar) action, and will perform it in many different playing areas, asking ourselves which is the best playing area for a given action and how it may fulfill all the principles of its creation. Each time, it will be necessary to create an observation area also, but we'll keep our focus on the playing area itself.

Exercise: *In search of the perfect playing area*

Situation. As I said, we create a series of scenes. The core action—the same every time—centers on a young actor/actress preparing for an audition, actually auditioning, and then waiting for the announcement of the cast. The title of the whole serial is: *Audition Odyssey.* The characters in every scene are: a young actor/actress ("A") and his/her various partners. The audition piece is the famous Shakespearian monologue of Jaques from *As You Like It* (act II, scene VII, verse 138-165), which begins with these memorable words: "All the world's a stage,/ And all the men and women merely players." One of our students should prepare this monologue beforehand, even if the whole monologue will not be used in our scenes. Let's assume that both young men and women were invited to audition for the role of Jaques in an experimental production of the play. To prepare the actors we'll instruct them using our "5Q" technique.

Action. Action of our serial is divided into six episodes as follows:

Episode 1. At home."A" and his/her mom. "A" hastily repeats the audition piece while eating breakfast. He/she is late for a workshop. Mom serves coffee, cereal, and milk. At the same time she helps "A" to put on his/her shirt or comb his/her hair and corrects his/her interpretation of the monologue. "A" rudely rejects mom's help and hurries out.

Episode 2. In a workshop room. "A" and his/her teacher. "A" delivers the monologue. Teacher corrects him/her. Nothing works.

Episode 3. In a living room. "A" is alone. He/she watches a video tape of a Royal Shakespeare Company production of *As You Like It.* "A" plays the tape back and fast-forwards it many times. He/she tries to imitate the actor playing Jaques, in vain.

Episode 4. In a theater—on stage and in the auditorium. "A" and the director auditioning for *As You Like It.* Director listens only to the beginning of the monologue and interrupts, ordering a change in "A's" interpretation. This is repeated several times.

Episode 5. At home. Mom, dad, and "A" eat dinner at a table. "A" is making fun of his/her monologue, eating and drinking pop. Parents say nothing. Suddenly "A" throws up and runs away.

Episode 6. In the bed. "A" has nightmares about his/her audition. He delivers the monologue in a horrible way.

We will use the principles listed above in our search for an appropriate playing area for every episode. The episodes could be staged in the following spaces:

Episode 1. A real kitchen in a real home with spectators standing in the entrance to the kitchen.

Episode 2. Our classroom, in which we might leave nearly all of the space for actors and place spectators discreetly in the shadows in two, or all four corners of the room.

Episode 3. A real living room might work, but we can also create the playing area on the floor of our classroom, putting the TV set against a wall and a sofa for "A" in front of it, with observation area on two sides of the square playing area.

Episode 4. The best playing area for this episode would be a proscenium stage for the auditioning actor with the director sitting in the auditorium. The best observation area would be the side boxes and the first row of the balcony, or, if there's no balcony, the seats in the auditorium around the director.

Episode 5. Again, this scene would work best in a real kitchen with standing spectators observing from the door.

Episode 6. The playing area should consist of a bed, sofa, or sleeping bag put on the carpet. Because it is a nightmare scene we should try to provide for an unusual visual environment. We might think about using a proscenium stage, put the bed in the center of it and set expressionistic lighting, or ask the university fine arts gallery to allow us to stage this scene in an exposition hall. The observation area should be determined based on where the playing area is.

Discussion. In a series of scenes we tested the principles of creating the playing area. Performing the breakfast and the dinner scenes in a kitchen would provide a believable living space. The actors could easily communicate, and all of the necessary facilities (table, stove, toaster, fridge, coffemaker etc.) would be at hand. Spectators (a small group) placed in the door to the kitchen, would have good visibility and audibility and a feeling of "being there." The scene would convey a mood of family life, mother's love, and child's ingratitude. Stylistically a scene like this would be hyper-realistic. The effect of the use of the classroom for a workshop scene, and a proscenium theater for an audition, would be obvious. It would fulfill all principles of creating the playing area, except for a clear reference to a fine arts style. Still, using objects and light, we can purposely stress the modern character of our classroom (if this is true). If we use a proscenium theater for the audition episode, we can accentuate its architecture, making it as theatrical as possible. Finally, the nightmare scene played on a proscenium stage or in a fine art gallery would fulfill every principle of creating the playing area, and would offer a unique opportunity to enhance its aesthetic, visual value.

Development. A student volunteer may create an action in several similar episodes, based on the above principles.

Creating the observation area

We already know that theater space is a space of interhuman interaction and it may also be a territory of confrontation. In both cases the director (working with an architect and/or a designer) has to create not only the playing area but also the observation area. In consciously creating the observation area, the director either allows interaction to happen or blocks it. The former is a common concern for a director who wants the energy from the stage to flow freely to the auditorium. Blocking interaction is purposely used only sporadically by directors, but it may occur against their will if they do not control the possible obstacles to theatrical communication.

In previous exercises we created actions situated in a space in which we articulated, first, the playing area, and, second, the observation area. This sequence was correct and we should always proceed in this way. Now, we'll try to take the next step, building the observation area not only as a simple derivative of the playing area but as a creatively shaped and structured component of the entire performance space. We'll study how the observation area not only evolves from the playing area, but how it influences the playing area and the interaction of actors and spectators. Creating the observation area finishes our conquest of the kingdom of theater space.

Exercise: *Observation area influences the playing area*

In four exercises, we'll focus on the impact of the observation area on the playing area. In every exercise we'll have the same beginning and the same action will be performed in a generally similar space, but we'll be changing details of the playing and observation areas. We'll observe how the observation area, its dimensions, structure, character, and relationship with the playing area, influences the meaning of action and even casts spectators in certain roles.

Situation. The beginning is the same in all four scenes: a group of prisoners is imprisoned in a prison (I purposely play with redundancy!) It is not, as one could think, a passive and dull situation without dynamic action, because a prisoner always dreams about freedom, tries to escape from prison in his/her imagination or even works out a practical plan of escape (such is the plot of several movies), builds relationships with other prisoners, obeys or challenges the guards, and so on, and so forth. The performance space, in all four scenes, is a prison. People may be imprisoned in many different places. In our exercises we use as a prison: a cell (built on the proscenium stage), a real basement (in our school or someone's house), an empty classroom, and a sporting arena (or any other indoor space with defined borders). We'll symbolically and practically express and describe the prison by using only bars. A few sticks from a carpenter's shop, or broomsticks which we easily find in a janitor's closet, connected to a cross, will do the job. We may also use a section of a light fence or wire netting, or anything else that is handy and which can stand for prison bars. We are going to set the bars in various places, installing them, or using "invisible" operators (as in the Japanese Kabuki shows), to hold them. As characters we need a few prisoners and a few guards. Before each scene they should be instructed using our "5Q" technique.

Action. The action is basically the same in all four scenes. A guard leads prisoners to the prison and leaves; the prisoners sit on the floor for a long time; they start a protest by taking off their shoes and banging them on the ground; the guard appears and whistles but this does not interrupt the protest; a second guard arrives and shoots in the air but this does not help either; the first guard whistles again and points his gun at the prisoners; they stop the protest and stand up in a line with their hands behind their necks; the guards leave; the prisoners sit. (We have the option to repeat this chain of events over and over again several times—if we want to.) We are going to play the same action using the same characters in four different spaces. The observation area will drastically change every time.

First scene: the observation area is clearly separated from the playing area; the actors and spectators occupy separate areas.

We set the bars downstage on a proscenium stage. The prisoners are led behind the bars and sit on the bare stage floor while the spectators sit in comfortable chairs in the auditorium. The observation area is separated from the playing area by the theater architecture (the proscenium) and by the set (the bars). The spectators are psychologically and emotionally alienated from the actors playing the characters. Sitting in the auditorium the spectators are safe and can observe the prisoners as though they were watching animals in the zoo. The spectators are not physically involved in the action, and nobody bothers them by inviting them to participate. Certainly, actors may play their characters very expressively, and their actions might engage and fascinate the spectators, but the point is, that the spectators remain spectators—independent observers of the events taking place on stage. Generally, thanks to this kind of spatial arrangement, and, specifically, because the observation area is separated from the playing area, we have no doubt who is who: the characters are prisoners—perhaps they are playing the Shoemakers imprisoned in act 2 of *The Shoemakers* by Witkiewicz— while the spectators are free people. The observation area makes them free.

Second scene: the observation area is situated in the same space as the playing area; actors and spectators share the same space but are separated within in.

This time we set the bars in a basement, leaving only a narrow space behind the bars for the prisoners who are sitting on the floor. We reserve some room for the spectators to stand at the opposite side of the basement. The prisoners are already behind the bars when guards let the spectators into the basement and show them where to stand. Then, guards take a position in between the bars and spectators, all the time controlling them. The spectators are permitted to have a glimpse of the prisoners, but are kept in the distance and prohibited from communicating with them. Perhaps the characters are hostages kept in a basement by terrorists. The spectators are, perhaps, their families, allowed to see their loved ones alive, and subjected to ransom demands. Or, the prisoners are three American soldiers captured in Kosovo and the spectators are a delegation from the International Red Cross. Setting the observation area in the same space as the playing area we imposed specific roles on the spectators: they share not only the space with the actors, but also their fate. Both the characters and spectators are controlled and manipulated.

Third scene: there is no separation between the playing area and the observation area. Both are situated in one space, shared by actors and spectators.

Guards lead the spectators to a room (it may be our classroom) and show them a place to sit on the floor by the walls. Next, guards lead the prisoners into the same room and order them to sit in the center of the room on the floor. Then, the guards put the bars in the open door of the room and stand outside, in the hall. The bars have transformed the room into a prison. Both the actors and the spectators share the same space: all are in prison, all are in the situation of prisoners, all are locked and guarded. The spectators find themselves in the same situation as the prisoners. What is this prison? If it was in a totalitarian country, it might be our school, being used as a temporary detention center. Who are the prisoners? They might be students arrested during a street demonstration against that totalitarian regime, temporarily detained at their own university, before being transported to a regular prison. Who are the people sharing the same space and the same human situation with the prisoners? We were seated separately, but in the same room as the prisoners. Perhaps we are also detained? A strange feeling. We, the spectators, sharing the same space with the actors, not having a clearly separate and different observation area, are cast in the same roles as those played by the actors. The lack of separation between the playing and observation areas unites actors and spectators not only spatially and physically but also emotionally and psychologically. Perhaps, when the prisoners stage their protest, taking off their shoes and banging them on the floor, we, the spectators, will join them?

Fourth scene: the observation area is a mirror of the playing area; the spectators mirror actors.

The bars are positioned precisely in the middle of a sporting arena (a basketball parquet would be best because it is not too big and not too small) or any other strictly defined space (a large hallway, a rectangular large room). Guards (we need four) lead in the prisoners and seat them at one side of the bars in a tight group (we would need more prisoners for this scene). Next, guards lead in the spectators and seat them on the other side of the bars, also as a tight group. Then, the guards stand at the four corners of the space. As a result, we have two groups of people sitting on two sides of the bars in the same guarded space. The playing area is an exact mirror of the observation area, and so are the actors and spectators. This arrangement makes both actors and spectators prisoners in two compartments of the same prison. To tell the truth, the bars are not even necessary. It would be enough to instruct the two groups of people to sit or kneel—yes, some brutal police do that—in identical clusters. The playing area embraces the observation area and the observation area is incorporated into the playing area. The performers do not differ from the spectators and the spectators are identified as performers. If, in this arrangement, the prisoners start their protest, we can expect that spectators will soon join them. When the whistles and shots interrupt the protest, we can expect that not only prisoners but also spectators will stand at attention with their hand behind their necks.

Discussion. A study of the various relationships between playing and observation areas leads us to the conclusion that the setting and positioning of the observation area decisively influences the meaning of the action and its perception by the spectators. It also casts the spectators in certain roles. The observation area's nature, shape, equipment (chairs or no seating), its distance from the playing area, and its division (or lack of it) from the playing area, changes the spectators, influences them psychologically and physically. Depending on the use of various playing areas (stage, basement, room, arena), the position of the bars, and the general character of the observation areas (an auditorium with seats, a basement without seats, the floor of a room or, an arena), the spectators' perceptions, feelings, and attitudes towards the characters will vary. In our exercise they were neutral observers, in the theater; involved observers, in a basement; participants emotionally identifying themselves with characters, in the room; and participants physically identified with characters, at the arena.

Development. Let's create another simple action in a space in which we articulate both playing and observation areas. Next, let's manipulate the observation area in order to induce different relationships between the playing and observation areas, and, consequently, between actors and spectators. Let's observe and discuss how the spectators feel, behave, and are cast in various roles depending on what and where the observation area is.

CHAPTER 4. CREATING THE TIME OF PERFORMANCE

Introduction

Every theater production, every interaction of actors with spectators takes place in time. We have already established that time in theater, being itself an abstraction, has three layers: (1) Real time. It is the time measured by the watches of the participants (actors and spectators) in the theater process. We can call it the time "now." (2) Time of the action/story. It is the time that measures the events of the action. It may run at the same speed as "real" time, but is usually slower or faster: for example, the events of a play may extend over many years. It is a time "then." (3) Mythical time. It is a universal, transhistorical, eternal, and timeless time. It is a time "ever."

There are three factors that affect our experience of time in theater: (1) Length, duration, or passage of time in the entire show, particular scenes, or single bits. (2) Speed, tempo, or pace of action, which are expressed through movement, speech, changes of light, and other elements of a production. (3) Rhythm, which results from combining various speeds, tempos or kinds of pacing and may be found in a production in the areas of action, movement, speech, music and sound, light, and space.

We discussed these matters a little bit while working on text analysis. Now, we are going to have a closer look at them and study them in a series of practical exercises. We immediately run into the problem of terminology pertaining to the temporal aspects of performances. Such terminology has never been firmly established nor universally accepted by theater artists. Directors, including myself, use various terms, depending on what feels right and as common sense guides them. To properly and clearly communicate with our students, we have to discuss these matters with them, decide what terms we are going to use in our work, and agree on their meaning.[13] The scope of our interest can be shown in a table.

TABLE: TIME IN THEATER PERFORMANCE		
TERM	**ASPECT**	**LAYER**
REAL TIME	LENGTH, DURATION, PASSAGE	NOW
ACTION TIME	SPEED, TEMPO, PACE, RHYTHM	THEN
MYTHICAL TIME	ALL ASPECTS	EVER

The temporal side of directorial work—obvious in opera, operetta, and musical—is often disregarded in straight theater, to the detriment of the artistic results. We should be fully aware that time is an extremely powerful element of a production. Directors can and should creatively shape all these layers and aspects of time in the production.

Length, duration, and passage of time in production

Each production, each part of it, every scene, or even a brief bit, always has a specific length which might be measured in terms of real time. An important conclusion comes from this simple observation: the director is responsible for the decisions about the length of the production, including all its parts and elements. These decisions have a strong impact on the artistic expression of the show, on its perception by the audience, and on the totality of interaction between actors

---

[13] As in the case of space, we do not want to encroach on the territory of the various specialist on philosophical, musical, psychological, or physical aspects of time. We are working in theater and we speak of time as one of the aspects of theater production.

and spectators.

The length of a production is measured in minutes, hours, or days and is determined by the conventions of a milieu, society, or country. For example, a religious production in the Middle Ages could go on for days. The duration of the show had a decisive influence on the participating communities, allowing them to submerge deeply and spiritually into the sacred stories slowly unfolding before their eyes. On the contrary, the fast moving and poignant productions of the Commedia dell'Arte captivated their audiences' attention thanks to their vivid acting, but also its brevity. The public reacted differently to a short royal court masque than they did in the endlessly dragging production of a Chekhov play as staged by Stanislavsky. Today, our perception of a lengthy opera is different from that of an off-off Broadway short production.

The same impact of real time is reflected in the customary hours for the beginning and ending of a show. Looking at my watch, I see what time it is when the curtain goes up and when it finally comes down after the applause has faded. Currently, western culture it is an unwritten law that an evening show shall last two-and-a-half to three hours. This length is a simple consequence of the hours of operation of public mass transportation in the cities of Europe and Latin America and of the commuting time from American suburbs to the downtown areas where theaters are usually located. In New York, a Broadway production usually runs for about three hours. Producers nervously consult their platinum watches at the dress rehearsals of a new show. If it drags on longer than three hours, they mercilessly order cuts. Cultural eating habits also come into play. In the United States, people usually eat dinner before the evening show, so the show should not start too early. But in France, for instance, people dine after the show, so consequently it should not start too late. The length of a production fits it into a culture. If it does not, it may be either rejected or attract special attention. In 1978 in Poland, two productions made headlines because of their length (if not for other reasons): *As the Years, As the Days Go,* a scenario by Joanna Olczak-Roniker directed by Wajda in Cracow, and *The Forefathers' Eve* by Adam

Mickiewicz, directed by myself. Both of them lasted for about nine hours. On the opposite side of the scale, illegal and secret productions played in Poland in private homes during the martial law period of the 1980s could not be longer than about an hour and a half. The nerves of both actors and spectators, threatened by a sudden police raid, would not bear a longer show.

In various cultures there are also certain rules and habits pertaining to intermissions in theater productions. For example, a long Kabuki evening, composed of several loosely connected segments, must have a long intermission allowing audiences to have their dinner in the theater or its vicinity. A long intermission in the National Theater in London would be unacceptable for the public, because it would break the cohesion and spell of the production.

There is also the problem of the time span of human attention. It is known that kindergarten kids cannot focus on one thing for more than a few seconds. By the end of elementary school they can keep their attention on one subject for about fifteen minutes. An adult can remain attentive for as long as 45-60 minutes; this explains the standard length of time for a school and university class. These conditions (there is a specialized literature on the subject and I highly recommend it) must be taken into account by a director preparing shows for children, students, adults, or senior citizens.

There are, finally, architectural, weather, and climatic factors. We must know if the building in New York in which we are planning to put on a show in summer has an air conditioning system. Preparing an outdoor production for nights in August, we'll choose a different hour for its beginning and ending depending on whether we are in Boulder, Colorado, or in Spoleto, Italy: in the former, the early evenings are already crisp; in the latter, the summer heat does not ease until 10:00 PM. To be able to attend a production on a Sunday night in winter is a safe bet in Latin American cities. On the other hand, we usually schedule Sunday shows in Anchorage, Edmonton, or Bergen between November and April only as matinees. In the event of a heavy snow, we must give the public time to return home safely and have enough sleep before going back to work on Monday morning.

All these are obvious, even banal, conditions that have a bearing on the scheduling of theater productions. They are important, however, because theater is a part of the culture of a given society. Directors must be aware of the cultural conditions of their work. They may wisely accept them, or purposefully defy them. In any case, they must know them and take them into account when preparing a production. Each director must consciously decide what time the show will begin and how long it will last, including the length of each act and the intermissions.

Speed, tempo, pace

The words "speed," "tempo," and "pace" are sometimes used interchangeably but each has certain semiotic nuances. "Speed" has practical applications, for example, when referring to motion; speed can be precisely measured, as indicated by a car speedometer, and compared, as when one runner runs faster than the other. "Tempo" refers to constant or repeated speeds: a crew of an eight-oared boat rows in a tempo of 32 strikes per minute; musical pieces use certain tempos. "Pace" refers not only to speed, but also to force or rate. Both tempo and pace usually describe the degree of speed, or intensity of action, speech, and movement.

The simplest and most obvious of these terms is speed. It is the one I prefer to use in my theater work, to refer to the entire show and to particular scenes, as well as to speech, movement, activity, and technical effects in the production. We can safely state that a show was played fast or slow. We can observe that the scenes of a production have different speeds. An actor may speak fast—we hear this typically on French and Italian stages, or slow—enjoying the beauty of a Slavic language. A stage movement might be as fast as lightning—as traditionally Puck's is, in *Midsummer Night's Dream,* or unbearably slow—as are the motions of some Noh characters. A thirsty character might swallow a cup of water in no time, while a connoisseur might endlessly sip a glass of champagne. A blackout may suddenly strike the stage, or a horizon may gradually change color. A speed is usually proposed by the author in the play. It should be discovered by the director during the analysis and either accepted or altered.

Let's consider an example. Molière's early plays were traditionally performed at tremendous speed. This was justifiable because they evolved from Commedia dell'Arte scenarios; their actions are swift and the characters' activities are comprised of rapid movements, along with kicking, beating, running, and hiding. Line exchanges are brisk, they seem to gallop, and words sound like notes played *stacatto*. There's no time for deep psychology or nuances of interpretation. The play runs like mad—and so must the production. But, if a director purposely changes all that into a slow speed and solemn interpretation, and orders actors to protract their activities and prolong lines—the farce changes into a drama, verbal duels into psychological debates, and characters change from Commedia dell'Arte types into complex persons. This was Roger Planchon's directorial interpretation of Molière's *Georges Dandin* in Lyon, France (1958). The hero, a betrayed husband, instead of being a stupid, helpless, and funny object of manipulation, was transformed into a suffering, wounded man, conscious of his situation—a stunning reinterpretation and rediscovery of the old play. It was achieved almost exclusively by changing the speed of action. Conversely, a directorial decision to play all the hesitations, digressions, and wandering thoughts of Hamlet at machine gun speed, together with drastic cuts in the text, transformed the philosophical tragedy into a contemporary cabaret skit. This was Charles Ludlam's interpretation of *Hamlet*, titled *Stage Blood,* produced by his Ridiculous Theater in New York (1977). Those of us who saw André Gregory's production of *Alice in Wonderland* were absolutely stunned, not only by its beauty and energy, but also by its incredible speed. And those of us who have ever seen a Jerzy Grzegorzewski work in Poland have always been carried away into a different dimension of time by the dream-like, endlessly flowing slow speed of his shows.

Contrasting the speed of a climactic scene with that of the rest of the play is a technique which has been consciously used by a multitude of playwrights and directors. For example, the final scene of John Osborne's *Look Back in Anger* is slow and delicate, marvelously contrasting with all the previous rapid quarrels. Conversely, Chekhov's slow development in *The Cherry Orchard* is given a sudden contrast in the mad dance of a happy Lopahin who bought the cherry orchard at the auction and now celebrates the fulfillment of his dream. After that rapid climactic scene, the action slows down again. These are only a few examples of the distinct and creative use of speed in plays and productions. Certainly, we could list many more cases through analyzing dramas or attentively observing the stage works of master directors.

Rhythm

Rhythm is a sophisticated and powerful means of expression for playwrights, directors, stage and light designers, and, of course, composers and sound designers. Rhythm—in theater—is a certain repeated, recurrent, regular, pattern, unit, or structure of activities, phrases, words, sounds, melodies, quantities, volumes, or images. Rhythm arises from composing, colliding, and contrasting various speeds, volumes, colors, or shapes. Rhythm in a production appears in the areas of action, speech, movement, sound, and music, as well as space and light. It is an organizing and structuring factor. It functions aesthetically (in terms of music and fine arts), has an emotional appeal (because it brings certain moods and provokes sentiments), helps to disseminate information (by purposely used repetitions), and it may contribute to cultural denotation of certain means of expression used in a show (music, dance, gesture, or imagery). We can speak about various kinds of rhythms in theater, such as:

Rhythms of actions. A rhythm in actions is created by repeated events or situations. Examples: the consecutive deaths of characters in the final scene of *Hamlet*; the bribing of Chlestakov by city officials in Act 2 of *The Inspector General* by Nikolai Gogol; Wang's encounters with the three gods in *The Good*

Woman of Setzuan by Bertolt Brecht; transformations of people into rhinos in the *Rhinoceros* by Ionesco.

Rhythms of characters' stage deeds. In many plays (and in many productions too) we may discover rhythm based on the characters' appearances and disappearances, their activities, soliloquies, or physical feats. Examples: in every Greek tragedy or comedy the Chorus appears at carefully measured intervals, thus creating the rhythm of its interventions; in *Inadmissible Evidence* by John Osborne, the partners, one by one, abandon the hero, Bill Maitland and their exits create a strong line of rhythm in the action of the play; Hamlet's monologues are pillars of action in the tragedy and they create its most distinctive rhythm; Saint Joan in Shaw's play hears the voices of saints and prays to them and to God—these moments create the rhythm of her supernatural contacts.

Rhythms of speech. Rhythms of speech are introduced, first of all, by verse. Whether it is Sophocles, Shakespeare, Molière, Calderón, Lope de Vega, Byron, Mickiewicz, Słowacki, Hugo, Pushkin, Fry, or T.S. Eliot, the director must identify a specific type and measure of verse used in the play and build the rhythmical value of the production on it. There are plays which use verse and prose in turn, and plays written in a special rhythmical prose. Speech rhythms must always have an impact on the overall rhythmical structure of the show.

Rhythms of dialogues and single lines. Each play (well written, of course) has a certain specific rhythm to its dialogues. Some playwrights' dialogues, even if technically written in prose, are close to music, like those of Samuel Beckett. Strindberg's characters speak as though allowing us to listen to their thoughts. Oscar Wilde's heroes converse as they would in a living room. Brechtian figures deliver eloquent speeches and lectures. All of this is material for crafting a production's rhythm. There are also plays in which authors purposely introduce and repeat the same line: "You wanted it, Georges Dandin"—repeats Molière's comedy hero. In *The Revenge*, Aleksander Fredro gives the character of the Notary a recurring line: "Let Heaven's will on earth be done—Acclaimed by all, opposed by none!" Solony's "Chick! Chick! Chick!" in Chekhov's *Three Sisters,* an apparently nonsensical and hilarious saying, is repeated many times, creating an ominous rhythm like an *ostinato* running through the whole play.

Rhythms of movement. They can be especially expressive and captivate the audience's attention, exposing the structure of action and identifying characters. Rhythms of movement are most evident if in a straight drama we suddenly have a dance (as Nora's famous scene in *A Doll's House*), or if a character moves in dance-like movements (as Barrault's approach to Beranger in a few of Ionesco's plays). Individual characters very often have their own specific movement patterns. The hobbling of Richard III, if properly explored by an actor, can create a physical and aural rhythm present throughout the production. In Büchner's *Woyzeck,* the clumsiness and confusion of Woyzeck's steps is contrasted with the military precision of the movements of his two opponents, the Captain and the Doctor. Movement of the sets can also be a powerful source of rhythm. Most obviously a revolving stage, if it is used not only to transport sets, but to emphasize the movement of individuals and groups, can express the rhythm of a production in a unique way. I remember how happy I was when I discovered an extremely dynamic way of amplifying the movement of young Polish young soldiers attacking Russian cannons and falling wave by wave—by setting it on a revolving disc in my production of *November Night* by Stanisław Wyspiański in Gdańsk in 1967. Of course, I knew to what excellent effect Reinhardt used the revolving stage in his production of *A Midsummer Night's Dream* in Berlin in 1905; I always tried to learn from masters.

Rhythms of music and sound. Music and sound purposely and effectively used in a straight drama are an always fresh and open source of rhythms. Claudel knew this when he introduced singing psalms in his *Satin Slipper.* Brecht introduced songs, thus breaking from time to time the action. Gombrowicz wrote *Operetta,* a philosophical play in the guise of a musical. Surely all the composers, writers, and directors of musicals, operas, and operettas know the profound effect of music. Sounds or shots, thunders, trumpets, or drums can also create the rhythmical line of a show. In my production of *Richard III* the penetrating, infernal sound of a huge and massive gate closing behind the king's victims created a rhythm that underscored the action.

Rhythms of space. Rhythms of space are created by visual means: shapes, masses, verticals, horizontals, colors, and lights. Sets designed by designers who are painters or sculptures introduce rhythms of columns, stairs, and platforms, as well as colors. To understand the rhythm of space in theater, let's recall Appia and his *Rhythmical Spaces* or Peter Schumann's huge puppets towering over the heads of performers and spectators in a production-pageant, such as *Cry of the People for Meat* or *Crucifixion of a Young Tree*.

Generally speaking, rhythm is a strong, yet hidden and challenging means of expression in theater. It structures action on stage and influences the perception of the audience. Many directors, whether musically sensitive or fine arts-oriented, use rhythm to the advantage of their work. All of us should try to use the power of rhythm in performance.

Let's practice applying the elements of time in performance with a series of exercises.

Exercise: *Setting the length of the performance*

Situation. Let's create a scene titled *Search*. The action is based on the activity of searching by someone who either has lost something, or is looking for something. This action is performed by various characters and takes place in any room. The playing area encompasses the entire space and the observation areas are situated as small islands of a few chairs, here and there. We will measure the duration of each action.

Action 1. A student enters an empty lecture hall and looks for something left in a class he/she attended an hour ago. The actor should decide what he/she is searching for (a book, an apple, a bag, a purse, etc.) When the student finds the lost object, he/she reacts to his/her successful search. The reaction depends on what the object was. He/she leaves. This scene should last about one minute.

Action 2. We repeat the same action, but this time we add more nooks and crannies for the student to search in and more lost objects—as if he/she had a hole in his/her bag and was dropping one thing after another. The use of an actual old bag would help to play this action. We do not change the speed of the student's movement and activities. This scene lasts about two minutes.

Action 3. We add a second person searching for objects in the same room. Each of them should search for their own lost objects. The first character should move slower than in the previous scenes. The new character should move faster and have more objects to find. This scene lasts about four minutes.

Action 4. We add a third person, but this time the searchers should work as a team; they are now customs officers, or soldiers of an anti-terrorist brigade inspecting a suspicious location and suspected people at a border crossing between two hostile countries. (Unfortunately, there are many borders like this all over the world.) Spectators should be included in the search as travellers at the border. The team of searchers systematically and slowly runs through all the objects in the room and all the pockets of the travellers. The search may include verbal interactions between searchers and searched. The searchers could use lines such as "Open"— "Close"—"Turn" and so on. (This action reminds me of the endless searches to which I was always subject when crossing by car the border between Poland and Communist Eastern Germany, the so called German Democratic Republic, or DDR. The search was repeated twice: once upon entering the DDR and again before leaving it.) This time the whole action lasts longer—let's say eight minutes.

Discussion. In the four scenes we had the same basic action, but we added characters, objects, and finally also people to be searched. More characters, more objects, more episodes, and more interactions resulted in prolonging the time of the scene. Certainly, we sometimes had the impression that it was all dragging on too slowly. Great! This is the point. We are now aware of the main elements of the duration of a scene. These are the number of characters, objects, and activities. If we would like to shorten our search scene, we should reduce the number of objects searched for and people subjected to the search. We may also achieve that by accelerating the speed of search. This leads us to the next exercise.

Exercise: *Setting the speed of the performance*

Situation. We use the same action as before—the scene under the title *Search*—in its final version with a team of custom officers and travellers at a crossing point.

Action 1. We play this scene very slowly, lasting about eight minutes. (Don't cut corners, please! We have to really feel the length!) Next, we play the same scene as fast as we can, but—this is extremely important—all the activities should be precisely repeated, all objects and people's pockets searched as before. The only change is in speed. The whole scene should now last only about two minutes.

Action 2. To really see and feel the differences and effects of employing different speeds, let's play the same scene about searching one more time—this time unbearable slowly. It should last about 15 minutes or twice as long as in the previous slow version.

Discussion. Let's observe how meaning, expression, and the type of interaction in the same scene has been changing along with the changing speed. It is also extremely important to note that the characters also changed because of the changes in speed. A person searching for something slowly is unlike a person searching with swiftness and alacrity. These two persons are obviously different in the way they think, move, operate objects, and use the space. Various speeds of actions also result in various attitudes towards partners.

The master discusses all these mutations with students, accentuating the effects of using different speeds. We see that change in the speed of action (including the characters' movements) results in changing our perception of the action and our decoding of the characters. Next, the master proposes to give titles to the scenes which were played and to name the characters appearing in them. The titles will summarize the meaning and expression of the scene, while the names will emphasize the relationship between speed and characters. For example, in the exercise *Setting the length of a performance* we can have:

Action 1. Title: *Absent-minded Student*. Character: Student

Action 2. Title: *Even a Scrupulous Soul Can Lose an Elephant* (one of my bright students' inventions.) Character: Scholar.

Action 3. Title: *The Menaechmi in Search of their Possessions* (as an allusion to Plautus' play, another student's bright proposal). Characters: Lazy Menaechmus, Active Menaechmus.

Action 4. Title: *The Boredom of the Border's Rituals* (in memoriam of the DDR customs officers who were concerned only about their orders, and were never in a hurry, disdaining and disregarding all travellers.) Characters: East German customs officers and travellers at the border crossing.

In exercise *Setting the speed of the performance*:

Action 1. Title: *To Be in Time Before the Bomb Explodes* (assuming that the team in a hurry is an anti-terrorist brigade acting on a tip that there's a bomb in the waiting room at the airport). Characters: Anti-terrorist team and travellers at an airport.

Action 2. Title: *Traveller's Nightmare*. Characters: Nightmarish custom officers and travellers who are terrorized by them.

Development. One of the students creates an action and, under his/her direction, the actors playing it change the speed of their activities and movement. We observe and then discuss how speed changes affect the whole action and the characters.

Exercise: *Setting the rhythm of the performance*

Situation. Let's create a scene which has at least five episodes/segments/events. We need this many episodes in order to establish a rhythm, based—as we know—on contrasting speeds, volumes, quantities, etc. It is a scene titled *Guests' Greeting*. The President and the First Lady greet arriving guests at the entrance to their residence. We need to cast the following characters: President, First Lady, bodyguards, police, and at least five guests. The arrival of a guest will function as one episode in the scene. The playing area is the entrance to the mansion. The President and First Lady are standing at the door inside of the house; the bodyguards are behind them and at two sides of the entrance; and the guests arrive from outside. The observation area for spectators is provided in front of the door; spectators are kept at a distance by the police. Guests pass through the audience and are allowed to proceed to the door by the police. Our task is to differentiate the speeds of movement and speech of each character—from very slow to very fast. Purposely mixing up these speeds, we create a rhythmical structure of the scene. We are going to create four variants of the same action playing it: (1) realistically, (2) grotesquely, (3) as a musical, (4) as an opera.

Variant 1. Realistic action. Body guards open the door and the President and First Lady appear inside. Guests arrive, are checked by the police, and approach the presidential couple. The hosts greet them and invite them inside. Body guards watch attentively. Actors may use simple improvised lines, such as:

PRESIDENT AND FIRST LADY (*greeting their guests*): "Mister Ambassador..."—"Madam Secretary..."—"Hey, Old Bob..."—"General, welcome, sir..."—"Nice to see you, Monica..." and so on, and so forth.

GUESTS: (*arriving*) "Mister President..."—"First Lady..."—"Hallo neighbor..."—"It's an honor..." and so forth.

Let's have a sudden twist in the action. One of the guests is unexpectedly attacked by two bodyguards who swiftly twist his/her arms and drag him/her away, while the other bodyguards push the President and First Lady inside and slam the door. Seeing this, the police order both waiting guests and spectators to disperse.

Variant 2. Grotesque action. Let's develop the same scene, without changing anything but strongly intensifying and exaggerating the differences between speeds, amplifying the volume of the lines, and adding other elements that would further augment differences between various activities and lines. In this way, we'll emphasize the rhythm. For example, one of the guest may get crutches and another a can; someone may whisper their lines and someone may deliver them very loud. Simple costume elements, such as hats might help; we can easily make funny hats of newspapers. We my also introduce repeated physical activities: some people might fix their hair, or take off their gloves (if it is summer—pantomime will do the job), and so on.

Variant 3. Musical. Next, let's play the same scene again, stressing the rhythm even more. Instead of speaking, the characters are going to sing. Instead of moving, they are going to dance. We need music with a strongly felt rhythm; a tango would be best. All of the characters should be in constant motion, dancing individually, and as couples or groups. Their movement should be choreographed.

Variant 4. Opera. Let's play the same action, but, instead of a tango, we will use a military march with appropriate choreography. All the lines should be sang in Wagnerian operatic style.

Discussion. The master explains how rhythm worked in the four mutations of the same action. First, it was a discrete element hidden in the realistic style of acting, helping to individualize the characters. Second, it was a means of making very clear who was who and how each behaved, and the scene acquired a grotesque style. Third, the use of singing and dance transformed the scene into a musical. Fourth, the use of a military march, marching choreography, and operating singing, transformed the scene into a militaristic nightmare. In this scene the President was a military junta leader and all of his and the First Lady's guests were generals or admirals.

Changes in the means of expression, including singing and dancing, were provoked by our search for ways to strongly underscoring the rhythm. The action of the scene was the same each time. The rhythms were different, however, transforming the action.

CHAPTER 5. CREATING THE ACTION OF PERFORMANCE

Action as the vehicle of communication

We spoke about action when we were making an analysis of the play. Let's recall: an action is created by acting people. Action has three layers: (1) The layer of life—a real and true interaction between living people (actors and spectators). (2) The layer of art—a fictitious interaction between characters (played by actors) who perform a story for spectators. (3) The layer of myth, universality, and generalization. All of them are interconnected and conditioned by the others. The first and second layers are always elements of theatrical process. The third appears only in masterpieces of theater. A director's work is to creatively shape each of these layers and interconnect them.

Theater action has the capacity to communicate. It is a tool and means for conveying ideas, meanings, and aesthetic values. Action transmits information, feelings, emotions, and energies. Action is an expression of human values and spirituality. Every action in theater *is* both a process of communication and a process of transformation. It is a process of communication, because it unites actors and spectators in the mutual exchange of human and artistic riches. It is a process of transformation, because it turns the ideas, values, feelings, energies, and other matters of theater into real and practical human acts.

Every human act has an internal and external character. The act is based on internal spiritual, psychic, and biological processes and it has an external expression of activity, speech, and movement. The internal transmutes into the external during performance thanks to the actor-spectator interaction. This is precisely *the* creative, decisive, mysterious moment of the birth of theater, its life's conception, and its energy's eruption. In this moment volatile thought changes into the concrete act of a real person; effervescent emotion alters into a human deed; a word, which is nothing more than a vanishing sound, energizes the movement of a living body; and, a gesture, brief as lightning, converts into a lasting symbol. At the same time, human movement, speech, sweat, and tears become the breath of poetry and the flight of the spirit. The director furnishes the human, spatial, and temporal conditions for these miraculous transformations.

Human actions are basic and primary in theater art. They have the power to instigate the theatrical interaction. Words alone, if not carried by action, are shallow and hollow in theater; they may convey meaning but they do not convey life. A play's text would not come across to the spectator if it wasn't carried by action. This is why when working on a play, we first read and analyze the text; second, we discover the action beneath it; third, we reconstruct and set this action in motion; and fourth, we return to the text, as one of the many means of expressing action. Eventually, the engine of action drives the words. Actors speak while acting, and acting supplies their words with energy which transmits the words to the spectators. As a result, words are integrated with action, and action is enriched by words. Movement alone in performance, if not tied into action, is either trivial, physical work, or meaningless, artistic gymnastics. It is only action which gives both words and movements, as well as all other means of expression, a theatrical puissance. Action is the practical and magical force of theater.

Creating actions—the task which we are now undertaking—begins with generating human acts and activities. We will add words to acts only when necessary. We will be treating words (lines, dialogues, and soliloquies) as secondary to action, and, at the same time, inseparably connected with action. In order to develop the necessary skills in building actions, we will break our work on action into two divisions: creating actions without words and with words. First, creating actions without words, we'll find our material in ideas, thoughts, memories, experiences, wishes, and feelings. Action provides them with structure and substance, transforming what is internal, mental and spiritual into what is external, physical, and real. Second, creating actions with words, we'll use the same mechanism, but we'll enrich silent, human acts with speech. We'll pay special attention to the various relationships between action and text, such as: how words complete and crown action, how words set up action in motion, and how action changes the meaning of words.

As in all previous exercises where our work was based on scenes, the master will first explain the problem and create a practical scene. The master may use exercises from this book or invent his/her own. Then, students will create their scenes, following the same procedures as the master. Each scene should be structured as a comprehensive and finished production—even if it is very short. As before, the exercises are divided into four stages, and described in four sections on situation, action, discussion, and development. In the situation section we must include and explain the following elements: title, action and its structure (including specific episodes, the beginning and the ending of the show), characters, and space.

Each scene must get a title. Working on the analysis of *The Cherry Orchard* we learned how to develop titles for particular scenes. You will recall that the scene's title results from revealing the action and discovering the conflict between characters, within given circumstances of space and time. The title, directly or metaphorically, points to what is most important in a scene. The titles we create must be communicated to the audience. The title is the most important part of the information about the production. The public must be informed that a show is going to be played, where it will be played, and when will it start. The director should decide how to communicate this information—posters? ads? announcements? drummers marching through the campus? The choice of how to disseminate the title of the show should be left to the individual director's decision. The public must be somehow gathered before the show and led into the observation area. For example (this is a preferable way to do it in our scenes) the director meets the audience at the entrance to the theater or other venue, greets people, announces the title of the show, invites the audience into the performance space, and informs them where to sit or stand. We should understand that spectators start perceiving the production upon entering the theater. The director should be aware of this, and should creatively use it to the avail of the production, steering the audience's perception from the very beginning.

The action should have clear structure and development, and contain precisely shaped episodes, each based on the characters' activities. The beginning and the ending of the show—seemingly obvious and simple—are also directorial concerns. The show must somehow start (curtain? blackout? clap of hands? or with a line from the director: "Action!") and it must somehow end (again—curtain? light? director's information?). We should know that the ending of the show is not always obvious where a new play is concerned (which is always the case in our work). Eventually, the audience must be thanked, excused, or dismissed.

Specific characters take part in each scene. They must be identified, defined, and cast with students. The director makes casting decisions. When we have the cast, we instruct actors using our "5Q" technique and immediately move to rehearsing the scene. In our class/workshop situation two or three rehearsals of a short scene will do.

We have to find or build a performance space for our scene, structure the venue into the playing and the observation areas, provide sets, and lighting. Space is created based on the principles and techniques we have worked on in the section on space in this book. All members of the group should help provide technical and physical help in building the space.

Exercise: *Creating an action without words*

Let's sit in a circle. The master asks students to think about a simple, single, concrete, and practical wish—but not to tell it. Instead, each student puts it down on a piece of paper, adding his or her name, and hands it over to the master.

Based on this wish, each student is going to create an action. But in order to explain the task practically, the master should create his/her action first. Let's assume that the master wrote on his own slip: "To remain alone." (If I'm not mistaken, many teachers, from time to time, have this wish.)

Situation. The ambiguous, general, and vague wish—"to remain alone"—is going to be expressed in the practical and physical activity of an individual who wishes to remain alone—he/she is escaping, hiding, distancing, flying from a group in order to do something which he/she does not want others in the class, team, or other group to know or see. The title of the scene is: *Give Me a Break.* The action of the scene expresses the wish of the individual wanting to escape the crowd. It is a simple and prosaic story about a glutton who likes and needs to eat constantly, but tries to hide this habit. Characters participating in the action are: Glutton, ("A", a student), a tutor, a graduate student, and other students. Glutton is a compulsive eater who can't resist digging into his/her bag, taking a bite, and constantly chewing. Glutton has the task of secretly eating a whole box of cakes or chocolates (or fruits—which would be healthier). Tutor is a graduate student who tutors students after classes. He supervises the study room in a dorm, enforces silence and order, and advises students on their homework as needed. Students are fellows of Glutton from the same class. They do their homework, but, knowing Glutton's addiction, they try to prevent him from eating, or steal his sweets. Other members of our group will be spectators. As space for the scene we use our classroom, which will work as a study hall in a dorm. We need a large table which we can put in the center of the room. The tutor, students, and spectators sit around it, leaving a few chairs free. We also need a few chairs dispersed in the room.

Action. The master (who directs this scene) informs spectators at the entrance to the room about the title of the show, asks them to follow him inside, and to sit around the table, leaving some empty chairs in between. The master gives the sign to the actors to start. The tutor enters, and, after a while, he is followed by the students, including "A." The tutor uses his/her time to correct a pile of quizzes—all of them are very bad, which is good material for the tutor to improvise his/her reactions while reading, correcting, and grading. Students do their homework—they should be advised to work on their assignments in a way that individualizes their characters (a lazy student, a hard-working student, a sleepy student, etc.). "A" reaches into his/her bag and feeds himself/herself. A student sitting next to "A" tries to steal some of the sweets. "A" closes his/her bag. Another student attacks him/her. "A" escapes to a chair in a corner of the room. He/she is followed by other students who try to pilfer his/her goods. This is repeated many times in different variants. "A" runs away and tries to feed himself/herself secretly, while other students discreetly follow him. The major circumstance conditioning the behaviors of all students, including "A," is the tutor's presence, his forbidding glances, and his sharp knocking on the table to bring the room to order. The pinnacle of the action occurs when, during yet another escape, "A" stumbles and all his cookies (or whatever it is) spill all over the floor. "A" and the other students are petrified and look at the tutor who suddenly stands up and stares at them. The master's voice or clap ends the action. Audience is thanked and excused.

Discussion. An ambiguous and vague wish "to be alone" was expressed in the realistic activities of a gourmand student who wanted to be alone in order to satisfy his/her compulsive eating. His/her activity was hindered by the activities of other students and a tutor. A chain of activities and counter-activities was set in motion. They created an entire action.

Development. Students should now be asked to create their own scenes, based on the wishes they have already expressed. Everyone selects casts, builds spaces, and rehearses their scenes. The master helps them with all stages of their work. When a scene is ready to be played, the student-director takes care of the audience, starts and ends the show, and dismisses the audience. Note: to effectively use time, two or more scenes might be prepared simultaneously and then played one after another. After each scene there should be a discussion.

Exercise: *Creating an action with one word or one sentence*

We are going to work now on scenes containing text. Words or sentences may be grammatically modified and/or repeated; they also may be connected with (or addressed to) various characters and used by one or many characters. Text may be used in any way we want: realistically, directly, paradoxically, metaphorically, or as nonsense. It may be spoken, sung, or chanted. It may appear at the beginning of an action, during the action, or at the end—summarizing or explaining the action. First, we are going to use only one word or one sentence containing a verb. For example, a word: "Leave!"—"He stopped!"—"They begun" or a sentence: "We'll take off any minute"—"You came too late"—"I can't stand it!" Second, we will create actions containing two words or two sentences locked in conflict, contradiction, or opposition. For example: "Approach!"—"Get away!" or "His judgment was right"—"His judgment was wrong." Third, we'll eventually work on a short dialog based on the exchange of two lines (two sentences). For example: "Sit with me."—"I don't want to." Or "I miss her."—"Call her."

As usual, let's begin in a circle. The master asks students to propose a brief text which will be used for creating an action. (Remember, it must contain a verb.) Many concepts fly and are discussed. Let's assume that the group chose a text containing one sentence: "I see a blank wall." (This sentence was actually proposed by the playwright Anthony Cardinale, participating in one of my workshops). The master creates a scene with the use of this sentence.

Situation. The scene title is: *The Return of the Secret Agent.* The text—"I see a blank wall"—will function as a password allowing the agent to cross check points and various guarded entrances in a restricted access building. The action goes like this: the agent returns from a mission to his/her headquarters (CIA in Washington, D.C., KGB in Moscow, or a ministry of interior affairs somewhere in the world) and has to report to his/her boss. But, to get to the boss's office he/she must give the password to several guards, to the secretary, and, finally to the boss himself. All of them know the password ("I see a blank wall") and when the agent delivers it, they let him/her go; the boss greets him/her cordially.

We need to cast the following characters:

AGENT
GUARD 1, at the entrance to the building
GUARD 2, at the doors or elevator downstairs
GUARD 3, at the beginning of the hallway or at the elevator upstairs
SECRETARY
BOSS

Next, we need to find or build the space. Playing areas should be:

Entrance to the building
Hallway (or elevator stop) at the first floor
Hallway (or elevator stop) at the highest floor
Office of the secretary
Office of the boss

Observation areas will be in motion: spectators will accompany the agent, stop when he/she stops, and move along with him/her.

The master instructs students/actors using the "5Q" technique. He/she asks students/spectators to go to the entrance of the building and wait there for the beginning of the show. When the actor playing the Agent is ready to start, the master informs audience that they are going to participate in the play *The Return of the Secret Agent* and ask them to follow the agent as he/she moves. Of course, the development of the action remains unexplained to the audience.

　Action. The Agent, carrying a briefcase or bag, arrives at the building (by car, by motorcycle, by limousine, by bike, or simply on foot). He/she approaches the Guards, salutes and says the password, "I see a blank wall." Each Guard returns the greeting, repeats the password, communicates with a superior (using a phone, a cell phone, or a radio) saying the line, "I see a blank wall," gets confirmation (not heard by spectators), salutes the agent, and lets him/her pass. The last Guard gives the password verbally to the Secretary. She calls the Boss and exchanges the password with him, then invites the Agent into the Boss' office. The Agent and the Boss repeat the routine, exchanging the password. After that, the Boss invites the Agent to sit. When the two of them sink into the armchairs, observed by spectators standing in the open door to the office, the master shuts the door and thanks the public for coming. This is the end of the scene.

Discussion. A text, accidentally proposed during a workshop, became a line in a scene, functioning as password, permitting movement through a restricted and guarded building. Characters were using the sentence in a an abstract way, totally disregarding its true and real meaning—there was no "blank wall" and nobody was looking at any "blank wall." But the text worked perfectly as a part of the entire chain of logical and realistic events, creating the action of the scene.

Development. Every student creates his/her own scene using precisely the same text—"I see a blank wall." The sentence may function in many different ways in many different actions, as my students many times found. For example, it may be the line of a patient in the optometrist office (a scene created by Mary); it may serve as an ecstatic exclamation by dancers in a disco (a scene by Patti); it may be a time-killer dully repeated by two prisoners (scene by Gene); it may be whispered by a scholar working at the university library (scene by Michelle). It also worked perfectly in a scene created by the author of the line, Anthony Cardinale. He staged an action of graffiti painting. An insatiable artist steals into his school at night and covers the walls with graffiti. Every time, he sees a clean wall or free space which he can use for his hieroglyphs, he whispers: "I see a blank wall" and covers it with a fountain of colorful spray.

Exercise: *Creating an action with two words or two sentences*

Situation. Let's work on an action in which we use two words or two sentences. One of my students (Joshua) proposed two short words: "lose" and "find." Using these words we create a scene titled *Where are You?* The scene is composed of several episodes in which "to lose" and "to find" will be repeated in many variants in connection with various actions. It is a story about parents whose child was abducted, then was found, but passed away in a hospital, apparently of wounds received in captivity. The parents, devastated, try to get help from a psychotherapist who is not able to assist them. They finally find solace in love for the deceased child which still unites them. A sad story and good material for a scene.

Characters:

MOTHER
FATHER
DAUGHTER, a child
SHERIFF
DOCTOR
PSYCHOTHERAPIST

Spaces: playing areas situated in various places where action of "losing" or "finding" is performed—as indicated below in description of the particular episodes. We can set them simultaneously in our classroom, in the same way the Medieval *mansions* were dispersed around a town place. Each playing area should be equipped with minimal sets and props; we would need some costume elements too. The spectators may sit on the floor in the center of the room and turn to the respective playing areas around them as the action progresses.

Action. Action is divided into six episodes as follows:

Episode 1. Mother and Daughter in the park. Mother reads a book. Daughter plays by hiding herself in the bushes, from where she extends only her hand and waves until Mother spots her and calls: "I've found you!" The Daughter runs to a different bush and hides herself again, shows her hand, and waves. Mother raises her eyes from the book, sees her, waves, calls, "I've found you"—and the game goes on several times. But after hiding herself again, Daughter does not show her hand. After a time, Mother realizes that Daughter interrupted the game and starts looking for her. She does not find her.

Episode 2. Mother and Father at the Sheriff's office. All three are going through an album with photographs, apparently of the daughter. The telephone rings. Sheriff picks up the receiver. He says: "We've found her!"

Episode 3. Mother and Father at the hospital in the surgical waiting room. Doctor appears from the operating room. He says: "We lost her."

Episode 4. Mother and Father in their bedroom. Mother sits at the edge of the bed and cries. Father tries to console her. Mother screams: "We lost her!" She repeats the line several times.

Episode 5. Mother and Father at the Psychotherapist's. The three of them sit in silence. Suddenly Mother jumps up and runs away. Father sits still. After a long pause he says: "I'm losing her."

Episode 6. Mother and Father in bed. They sleep. Mother gets up quietly, takes a flashlight and starts looking for Daughter all over the house. She directs light on the mirror. Sits on the floor in front of the mirror. Father finds her. He sits at her side and delicately hugs and rocks her. Daughter appears in the mirror. Mother whispers: "I've found her." Father whispers: "I've found you." The end.

Discussion. In individual episodes, the words "to lose" and "to find" (or their variants) were connected with various events, activities, and persons. The exercise showed how the same (or similar) lines acquire completely different meanings and functions within the context of different actions, interhuman situations, spaces, and speakers who use that line.

Development. Let's invent/choose other conflicting/opposing words or sentences. Following the above example, students create their own scenes in which these texts should be used within the context of different actions and by different characters.

Exercise: *Creating action with a dialog of two lines*

Our task is to create a scene with a short dialogue, composed of two lines. Carefully examining the options provided by only two lines—we prepare ourselves to direct longer scenes with text and eventually entire plays.

Situation. Let's assume that discussion with the group resulted in formulating a simple dialogue: "Oh, how nice that you've come."—"I had a lot of work today." In order to explore the possible uses of these lines, let's create an scene titled *A Marriage Textbook*. (Elements of this scene were proposed by Gerald.)

We are going to use this dialogue in a series of episodes involving a young couple. The action will depict how their relationship changes, how it deteriorate and ameliorate. The same dialogue will function differently depending on the context of the action. The master should direct the scene first. Here's is a proposal for how it might go.

Characters:

> WIFE
> HUSBAND
> KRONOS, god of time, invisible to the humans

Space: the action takes place in the dining room in the couple's home. There are three doors leading to the room—to/from outside, to/from the kitchen, and to/from the bedroom. We need to put or hang a calendar somewhere. The playing area is in all three rooms and three doors. The observation area should be very close to the playing area, possibly on two or three sides of it, giving the audience the impression that they are peeking into the private space and life of the characters.

Music: it would help to have some music from a disc player operated by actors on stage. Music—choosen by the director—would help to indicate the artistic preferences and social status of the characters, as well the time of action.

Action. Action is divided into five episodes.

Episode 1. (*Kronos is in the corner. Wife prepares dinner in the kitchen. She brings plates, a bottle of wine, glasses and dishes from the kitchen to the dining room. She is joyful. Finally, she brings candles and lights them. She sits at the table and waits. She waits for a long time. Husband enters in a hurry. Wife rushes to meet him at the door and hugs him.*)

WIFE: Oh, how nice that you've come.

HUSBAND: (*As asking for forgiveness and happy to she see her*): I had a lot of work today. (*They kiss, embrace, and go to the table. Wife starts the disc player. They sit face to face. The Husband reaches for the wine bottle. The Wife smiles. They freeze.*)

KRONOS: (*Goes to the calendar, rips the date page off the calendar and shows it to the public. He goes to the table and blows out the candles. He switches on the work light and switches off the stage light. In the work light the Wife picks up all the dishes, plates, knifes, forks, spoons, glasses and bottle, and takes them to the kitchen. The Husband leaves. Kronos stops the music, switches off the work light and switches on the stage light, goes to the corner, and stands there as at the beginning.)*

Episode 2. *(As at the beginning. Kronos in the corner. The Wife prepares dinner in the kitchen. She brings plates, a bottle of wine, glasses and dishes from the kitchen to the dining room. Finally, she brings candles and lights them. She sits at the table and waits. She waits for a long time. Husband enters staggering, obviously drunk.)*

WIFE: *(From the table, ironically:)* Oh, how nice that you've come.

HUSBAND: *(Mumbling unintelligibly:)* I had a lot of work today. *(He approaches the table and sits. The Wife starts the disc player—a new musical piece. The Husband reaches for the wine bottle. The Wife pulls it out of his hand. Both freeze.)*

KRONOS: *(Goes to the calendar, rips off another page and shows it to the public. He goes to the table and blows out the candles. He switches on the work light and switches off the stage light. In the work light the Wife picks up everything from the table and takes it to the kitchen. The Husband leaves. Kronos stops the music, switches off work light and switches on the stage light, goes to the corner, and stands there as at the beginning.)*

Episode 3. *(As before. Kronos in the corner. Immobile. The Wife prepares dinner in the kitchen. She brings plates, a bottle of wine, glasses and dishes from the kitchen to the dining room. Finally, she brings candles and lights them. She sits at the table and opens the wine bottle. She pours herself wine. She sits for a long time. She stands up, takes the glass of wine and goes to the bedroom. Husband enters without a word and sits at the table. He pours himself wine.)*

WIFE: *(From the bedroom)*: Oh, how nice that you've come.

HUSBAND: *(Without expression)*: I had a lot of work today. *(He eats for a long time in complete silence. Then, he freezes.)*

KRONOS: *(Goes to the calendar, rips off another page and shows it to the public. He goes to the table and blows out the candles. He switches on the work light and switches off the stage light. In work light the Wife picks up everything from the table and takes it to the kitchen, while the Husband leaves. Kronos switches off work light and on stage light, goes to the corner and stands there as at the beginning.)*

Episode 4. *(As before. Kronos in the corner. Immobile. The Wife prepares dinner in the kitchen. She brings plates, bottle of wine, glasses and dishes from the kitchen to the dining room. Finally, she brings candles and lights them. She is without feelings. She sits at the table and opens the wine bottle. She pours herself wine. She systematically eats and drinks. Husband enters. He's contrite.*

He sits a the table and starts eating. She does not look at him.)

WIFE: (*Not interrupting eating, indifferently*): Oh, how nice that you've come.

HUSBAND: (*Asking for forgiveness*): I had a lot of work today. (*They eat for a long time. The Husband goes to disc player and starts the music—new piece. Then, the Husband returns to table, pours himself wine and extends the glass towards the Wife, as if proposing a toast. She doesn't react. They freeze.*)

KRONOS: (*Goes to the calendar, rips off another page and shows it to the public. He goes to the table and blows out the candles. He switches on the work light and switches off the stage light. In the work light the Wife picks up everything from the table and takes it to the kitchen, while the Husband leaves. Kronos turns off the music, switches off the work the light and switches on the stage light, goes to the corner and stands there as at the beginning.*)

Episode 5. (*As before. Kronos in the corner. Immobile. The Wife prepares dinner in the kitchen. She brings plates, glasses and dishes from the kitchen to the dining room. Finally, she brings candles. She is ill. She starts lighting candles. Husband enters in a hurry. He rushes to her, takes the matches from her fingers and lights the candle. He goes to the kitchen and brings wine. He turns on music—another piece. He pours wine. They both look at their glasses and sit in silence.*)

WIFE: (*Whispering:*) Oh, how nice that you've come.

HUSBAND: (*Whispering:*) I had a lot of work today. (*They move glasses on the table towards each other. They freeze.*)

KRONOS: (*Goes to the calendar, rips off another page and shows it to the public. He goes to the table and blows out the candles. Then, he tears many more pages from the calendar and throws them in the air, if showering the couple sitting at the table with rice thrown on the newlyweds at the church door. Now Kronos sits with them at the table. He delicately takes the glasses out of their hands and joins their hands together on the table. He blows out the candles. After a while, all three get up and bow to the public.*) The end.

Discussion. We've examined how the same dialogue has different meanings and subtexts, as well as different dramatic functions, depending on the context of action. In this series of episodes the same dialogue expressed love, hatred, indifference, separation, and reconciliation. Respectively, using the same dialogue within the different circumstances the characters were to each other lovers, enemies, strangers, loners, and peacemakers.

Development. Let's invent other two-line dialogues and use them in scenes.

Students should direct them, colliding the same dialogues with various actions and characters. We'll see how the meaning and function of the dialogue change depending on the action, circumstances, and characters involved.

Exercise: *Creating a multilayered action with unlimited dialogue*

We are going to try to integrate our training in creating action without words and with words, along with our previous experiences in creating the human layer, the space, and the time of the show. We'll create a complex, multilayered action with dialogue—a full scale production, although its length may not exceed a few minutes. The production must fulfill all the previously established and explained conditions. It must have title, action, characters, and space (including playing and observation areas). Additionally, we'll pay special attention to the style of the performance—reflected in acting, space, and interaction with audiences. We shouldn't neglect to purposely use rhythm and provide every production with music/sound effects. Our productions should have text—either verbally improvised in class or written at home by students. They should be brief, having a clearly developing action and sharply defined characters who use poignant dialogues. We will make an analysis of the text, cast the play, build the space, make other preparations, and go on to rehearsals.

As we see, there are many different things to prepare and create before the rehearsals. All of them make up the "directorial take-off checklist"—as I call it, using an analogy to the checklist a jet pilot must use to inspect readiness of the aircraft before take off. Two pilots sit in the cockpit, the second pilot takes a plastic-bound "Checklist" and reads out loud, point by point, all the items which must be checked; the first pilot repeats each item and looks at, or tests each of the instruments, buttons, switches, controls, or handles. Only after the whole list has been meticulously covered are the plane and the crew ready to take off. The same is true with a theater production. The director must do certain preparatory steps before the beginning of the rehearsals. Indeed, working on every show—short or long, simple or complex— the director must check, like the jet pilot, to see if everything is ready for take-off. At this stage of our work we are going to use a short directorial checklist. It is sufficient for creating short scenes and exercises. We're going to use this list to create a scene with multilayered action and dialogue. Later on, working on entire, longer shows, we'll come up with a longer list.

TABLE: SHORT DIRECTORIAL TAKE OFF CHECKLIST
What must be created, made, prepared, verified, and inspected

    (1) Title
    (2) Action
    (3) Characters
    (4) Text
    (5) Structure
    (6) Beginning and ending of the show
    (7) Space, including playing and observation areas
    (8) Style, including sets, costumes, lights
    (9) Rhythm, including music and sound
    (10) Cast

Situation. Material for this scene should be taken from one of the initial stories told by students, which the master was collecting and had in his/her file. Let's look up this file and find an appropriate story. One of my students (Bianca) told a story about an incident in a zoo. On a high school field trip to the zoo, against the teacher's warnings, she gave her lunch sandwich to a monkey. The monkey gently took the sandwich with one hand and firmly grabbed the girl with the other. The girl was terrified and screamed like hell. Zoo guards were called and only after a long struggle with the monkey were they able to rescue her. Let's try to work on this material, using our directorial checklist.

(1) Title: *A New Zoo Story* (an ironic allusion to Edward Albee's play.)

(2) Action is based on Bianca's story: a group of high school students and their teacher visit a zoo. They pass by several cages with various animals. (It should be determined what animals.) The visitors approach a cage with a monkey. The

teacher attracts students' attention to the sign on the cage: "Do not feed the animals!" and instructs students to obey this rule. (The teacher's line should be improvised.) The monkey makes grimaces at the students, indicating that it is hungry. A girl takes a sandwich from her bag and, hiding this from the teacher, offers the sandwich to the monkey. The monkey takes the sandwich with one hand and grabs the girl with the other. The girl reacts hysterically; she screams and fights with the monkey. The rest of the group panics. The teacher runs to the emergency telephone and calls for help. (Line to be improvised.) Two guards arrive in a hurry. One, after some difficulty with the lock, enters the cage and tries to get the sandwich from the monkey, while the other holds the girl and tries to calm her. After a long struggle the girl is freed and the guard gets the sandwich. The girl faints. Teacher, guard, and other students try to help her, while the monkey hits the other guard on the jaw, reclaims the sandwich, sniffs it and taste it, but does not eat it. At this moment a parrot appears over the cage and its intervention closes the show.

(3) Characters:

> CARELESS GIRL
> MONKEY
> TEACHER
> GUARD 1
> GUARD 2
> PARROT
> OTHER ANIMALS
> STUDENTS

(4) Text: The teacher's lines explaining the "Do not feed the animals" rule and his/her call for help should be improvised. The closing dialogue is as follows:

PARROT: (*Landing on the cage's roof*): Bravo Godzilla! Bravo Godzilla!

MONKEY: Oh, you're very kind, parrot, but I am not a movie star. I'm a modest monkey.

PARROT: You are, you are, you're fabulous. Pardon me, is this a peanut butter sandwich, by a chance? I like peanuts...

MONKEY: No, it is an awful turkey sandwich with horrible mayonnaise and an absolutely distasteful tomato.

PARROT: So, why did you even care for it?

MONKEY: I have a deal with the management. For every visitor I catch feeding animals I get a jar of peanut butter. I love it.

PARROT: The guards don't know that?

MONKEY: The guards are punished for allowing feeding. But I'm smarter. I'll invite you for dinner when I get my jar.

GUARDS: (*Singing and dancing*): The guards are kings of the zoo.

         They dance like the antelope gnu.

         They howl like wolves to the noon.

         The show is closing soon...

(*Entire cast joins the guards and repeats the same verse, singing and dancing.*)

PARROT (*Announces*): End of the show. No peanut butter this time.

(5) Structure: Action is divided into three episodes:

Episode 1: Entrance of the visitors

Episode 2: Illegal feeding and struggle over the sandwich

Episode 3 : Grotesque epilogue

(6) Beginning and ending of the show: action starts with the entrance of visitors to the zoo. The monkey should be in the cage at that time. Spectators may be led in as members of a visiting group. The show ends when the ensemble members stop dancing and take a bow. Animals in all cages applaud. Audience, hopefully, applauds too.

(7) Space, including playing and observation areas: It would be best to play our performance in a real zoo. If not, we need to set cages with different animals scattered around our room. The main playing area is inside of the monkey's cage and around it. The observation area—for the standing public—is in front of the cage.

(8) Style, including acting, sets, costumes, lights: realistic and grotesque in turns.

(9) Rhythm, including music and sound: the normal speed of the realistic activities and lines should be contrasted with the tremendous speed of the grotesque ones. Three distinct collisions of normal versus fast speed will result in creating the specific rhythm of this show and, additionally, will underline the contrast of realism with the grotesque. We may also have constant background music, as from the loudspeakers in the zoo.

(10) Cast: everybody knows everybody in our group, so the master quickly proposes the cast. But now, because the show is going to be a more complex one, we have to divide the whole group/class into four units who will be simultaneously working on different aspects of the show. This is an effective way to speed up the whole process of preparation. These four groups should be: First, the cast, with whom the director rehearses. Second, the design-technical unit preparing the space, set, costumes, and light, as instructed by the director. Third, the music-sound unit preparing whatever is necessary, as instructed by the director. Fourth, the administrative-production unit preparing the posters and programs, and taking care of the reception of the public—we might invite people who happen to be in the hallways to attend our show. The administrative unit's work should also be done in consultation with the director. All units work at the same time. The director makes an analysis of the play and instructs actors using the "5Q" technique. The same technique should also be used with some modifications for the animal roles. The actors playing animals should decide what means of expression (in terms of movement and sound) they are going to use. We should have two or three rehearsals with actors, one technical rehearsal coordinating all elements, and, finally, we should be ready to play the grand opening—which, hopefully, will be a huge success.

Action. The play develops as described above in the Situation section, including events and dialogues.

Discussion. After the show we sit in a circle and discuss the work. It would be beneficial to go through the directorial checklist again and see how it worked, what was good, what was so-so, and what was bad.

Development. Let's pull another student's story from the master's file. The "author" of the story should transform it into a play and direct it. The master will serve as adviser, leaving the director/student as much artistic freedom as is possible and reasonable.

Exercise: *Creating an "impossible action"*

The last stage of our work on action should be to create an "impossible action." I use this term to describe an action which is realistically and practically impossible to stage. However, the creative imagination of a director can overcome all limitations and beget a production against all odds. It is a difficult, and even a strange task, but working on an impossible action gives us a better feeling about what directorial creation really is: an act of trespassing from everyday life into the territory of mystery, a labor of discovery of uncharted lands and seas, a step into the darkness of an unknown universe, and an attempt to make possible what seems to be impossible.

To clearly see what an impossible action is we should use non-dramatic material, such as a story, a dream, a poem, or an idea, Rather then "translate" this material into a play, which we would stage, we will directly transform it into a production. This would better show the difference between the point of departure (the non-dramatic text) and the point of arrival (the performance). The most useful material would be a description of some inconceivable event or deed, an account of a vision or a miracle. The text which I have used several times in my workshops on creating an impossible action was the *Gospel of Saint John,* describing the miracle in Cana of Galilee (2, 1-11). It is a story about transformation: water is transformed into wine, and unbelievers are transformed into believers. Transformation is precisely the problem we are working on now. The text of John is difficult and challenging, but it works very well and on many occasions, young directors have made astonishing applications of it. So, let's try.

Situation. We make an analysis of the text, as usual, and we proceed using our directorial checklist.

Title: *The Miracle of Transformation.*

The action is described in the text: there's a wedding in Cana; the Mother of Jesus is one of the guests. Jesus with his disciples is passing by and they too are invited. They take part in the wedding party. The guests, apparently, have drunk all the wine; they complain, and want more. Upon his Mother's request Jesus transforms water into wine; everybody is happy and the wedding party goes on. The disciples of Jesus realize that he has performed a miracle and believe in him.

Characters:

> JESUS
> MOTHER OF JESUS
> THE GROOM
> THE BRIDE
> THE WEDDING MASTER
> DISCIPLES OF JESUS
> WEDDING GUESTS
> SERVANTS
> MUSICIANS

Text: the Gospel contains lines of the partakers in the story. These lines may be used, if necessary.

Structure: the analysis tells us that the story is composed of several episodes, as follows:

> **Episode 1**. Wedding party going on
>
> **Episode 2**. Invitation of a strange guest, Jesus
>
> **Episode 3**. Discovery of lack of wine
>
> **Episode 4**. Mother's intervention
>
> **Episode 5**. Transformation of water into wine
>
> **Episode 6**. Mother's relief
>
> **Episode 7**. Disciples' act of faith

The beginning and ending of the show: ...now I want to stop my explanations and proposals, because, contrary to our rule that the master takes on any scene first, I think that it is better not to show students possible solutions for this exercise. Rather, the master should allow them to come to their own discoveries completely independently and freely, and to create their impossible action as they wish. It is the last assignment in this part of the book, so, it's time to throw the doors wide open and let directors go wherever they want.

Action. I was stunned several times by the fresh, imaginative, and bold actions based on the *Miracle of Transformation* created by my students. I remember, for example, a hallucinating and dynamic scene (created by Zygmunt) in which the whole action was expressed metaphorically through music, improvised singing and dancing. I remember an almost abstract and conceptual, yet refined philosophic and aesthetic proposal (created by Paula). On a wedding table with a white table cloth, among plates and flowers, sat a large, glass jar full of water with the narrow ray of a spotlight focused on it. The narrator was slowly reading the gospel story about the transformation of water into wine, while enchanted spectators, seated at the table, observed the clear water in the jar gradually changing into red. It was the narrator slowly pouring a red liquid into water. In front of our eyes the water was transformed into wine.

I remember a dramatic and powerful scene (created by Margaret). The Mother of Jesus was kneeling at the foot of the cross in which Jesus was dying and she was seeing in her imagination the Cana miracle with people dancing and drinking. Deep sorrow and pain collided with high joy and jubilation. The hope in miracle was shown through the grim reality of her dying son. If the miracle of water turned to wine was possible there and then, in Cana, the miracle of resurrection will be also possible here, in Calvary. It was a profound and beautiful directorial concept. I remember several creative and innovative directorial concepts, ideas, and solutions devised by young people whom I tried to accompany on their way to creative directing.

I propose that at the conclusion of this part of our work—work on creating action—we have a festival of impossible actions prepared by all students. They have proven that the impossible is possible in theater. This would be a good ending to this part of the process of teaching-learning creative directing.

PHOTOGRAPHS

(All photographs are from productions directed by Kazimierz Braun)

SECTION 1. THE DIRECTOR WORKS WITH ACTORS

1.1. *Dissecting the text*

Author with actress Shirim Divrin Trainer during a rehearsal of *The Hunger Artist Departs*. McCarter Theater, Princeton, NJ, 1986. (Photo by Cliff Moore)

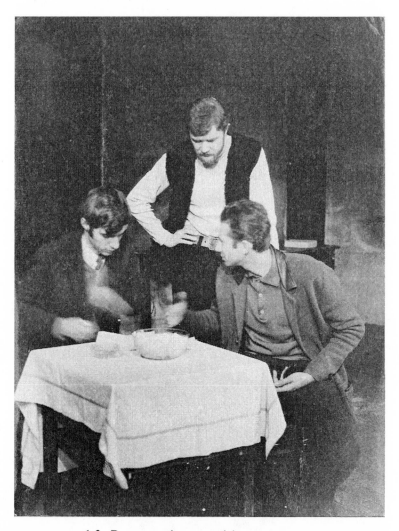

1.2. *Demonstrating an activity on stage*

With actors (from left to right) Zbigniew Sobiechart and Tadeusz Borowski during rehearsal of *The Interrupted Act*. The Osterwa Theater, Lublin, Poland, 1970. (Photo by Wanda Parys)

THE DIRECTOR WORKS WITH ACTORS

1.3. *Listening to the actors*

With actors (from left to right) Bolesław Abart, Tadeusz Galia, and Justyna Moszówna during rehearsal of *Cleopatra and Caesar* performed at the Museum of Architecture in Wrocław. The Contemporary Theater, Wrocław, Poland, 1975. (Photo by Tadeusz Drankowski)

THE DIRECTOR WORKS WITH ACTORS

1.4. *Explaining your ideas to the actors on stage*

With actor Igor Przegrodzki during a rehearsal of *The Pulp*. The Polski Theater, Wrocław, Poland, 1990. (Photo by Adam Hawałej)

THE DIRECTOR WORKS WITH ACTORS

1.5. *Guiding actors during a rehearsal in the church*

With actress Barbara Kogut during rehearsal of *The Passion Play* in the Corpus Christi Church, Buffalo, NY, 1994. (Photo from the author's collection)

THE DIRECTOR WORKS WITH ACTORS

1.6. *Motivating the company during an outdoor rehearsal*

With Chinese student of directing Barbara Jiang at the State University of New York at Buffalo, 1995. (Photo from the author's collection)

1.7. *Interacting with a group during a street rehearsal*

With students of a directing workshop in Dublin, Ireland, 1983. (Photo by K. Joseph Romanowski)

1.8. *Intensifying the emotions through direct personal contact*

With students of a directing workshop in Dublin, Ireland, 1983. (Photo by K. Joseph Romanowski)

1.9. *Speaking with theatergoers before the production starts*

A meeting just before the start of *Birth Rate*. The Contemporary Theater, Wrocław, Poland, 1979. (Photo from the author's collection)

1.10. *Staying focused*

Author during a directing workshop at Poznań Visual Arts Academy, Poznań, Poland, 1997. (Photo by Przemysław Graf)

SECTION 2. DIRECTOR AND ACTOR
SEEK TO EXPRESS THE HUMAN CONDITION

2.1. *Compassion*

Eugeniusz Kujawski (Father Peter) and Krzysztof Bauman (Konrad) in *The Forefathers' Eve*. The Contemporary Theater, Wrocław, Poland, 1982. (Photo from the author's collection)

DIRECTOR AND ACTOR
SEEK TO EXPRESS THE HUMAN CONDITION

2.2. *"Come, woo me, woo me, for now I am in a holiday humor..."*

Melissa Murphy (Rosalind) in *As You Like It*. Shakespeare in the Park Festival, Buffalo, NY 1991. (Photo from the author's collection)

**DIRECTOR AND ACTOR
SEEK TO EXPRESS THE HUMAN CONDITION**

2.3. *"Is it possible dat I should love de ennemie of France?"*

Monika Braun-Bereś (Princess Catherine) and King Henry in *Henry V.* Shakespeare in the Park Festival, Buffalo, NY 1987. (Photo from the author's collection)

DIRECTOR AND ACTOR
SEEK TO EXPRESS THE HUMAN CONDITION

2.4. *Deep in thought*

Joan O'Hara in the title role of *The Old Woman Broods*. The Arts Project Theater, Dublin, Ireland, 1983. (Photo by K. Joseph Romanowski)

DIRECTOR AND ACTOR
SEEK TO EXPRESS THE HUMAN CONDITION

2.5. *Philosophical dialogue*

From left to right: Ferdynand Matysik (Ambassador) and Igor Przegrodzki (Writer) in *The Pulp*. The Polski Theater, Wrocław, Poland, 1990. (Photo by Adam Hawałej)

DIRECTOR AND ACTOR
SEEK TO EXPRESS THE HUMAN CONDITION

2.6. *Dialogue during a dance*

Adèle Leas and Thomas Martin in *As You Like It*. Shakespeare in the Park Festival, Buffalo, NY 1991. (Photo from the author's collection)

DIRECTOR AND ACTOR
SEEK TO EXPRESS THE HUMAN CONDITION

2.7. An erotic encounter

Halina Rasiakówna (Greta) and Zbigniew Górski (Maks) in *The Trap*. The Contemporary Theater, Wrocław, Poland, 1984. (Photo by Marek Grotowski)

DIRECTOR AND ACTOR
SEEK TO EXPRESS THE HUMAN CONDITION

2.8. *Fear*

Tomasz Lulek and Ryszard Jabłoński (Passengers) in *Birth Rate,* The Contemporary Theater, Wrocław, Poland, 1979. (Photo by Marek Grotowski)

DIRECTOR AND ACTOR
SEEK TO EXPRESS THE HUMAN CONDITION

2.9. *Brutality*

Stanisław Banasiuk and Tadeusz Galia (Passengers) in *Birth Rate,* The Contemporary Theater, Wrocław, Poland, 1979. (Photo by Marek Grotowski)

DIRECTOR AND ACTOR
SEEK TO EXPRESS THE HUMAN CONDITION

2.10. *Anger*

Prisoners sing a song of protest. From left to right: Edwin Petrykat, Zbigniew Górski, Maciej Korwin in *The Forefathers' Eve*. The Contemporary Theater, Wrocław, Poland, 1978. (Photo by Jan Bortkiewicz)

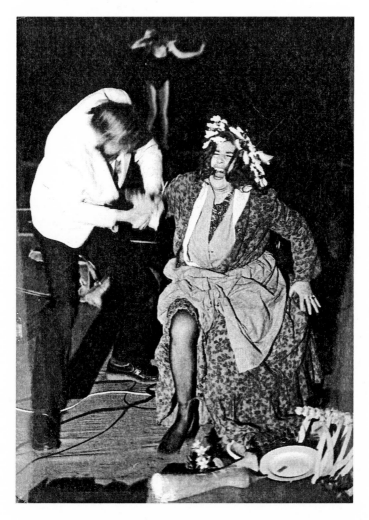

2.11. *Pain*

Marlena Milwiw (The Old Woman), with Zbigniew Górski (Waiter) and
Magdalena Kumor (Dancer) in *Birth Rate*. The Contemporary Theater, Wrocław,
Poland, 1979. (Photo by Marek Grotowski)

DIRECTOR AND ACTOR
SEEK TO EXPRESS THE HUMAN CONDITION

2.12. *Madness*

Eugeniusz Kujawski (Father Peter) and Krzysztof Bauman (Konrad) possessed by
the devil in *The Forefathers' Eve*. The Contemporary Theater, Wrocław, Poland,
1982. (Photo from the author's collection)

DIRECTOR AND ACTOR
SEEK TO EXPRESS THE HUMAN CONDITION

2.13. *Dangerous stunts*

From the left: Jan Blecki, Kazimierz Wysota, Kazimierz Zadrożny, and Tomasz Lulek fight in *The Plague*. The Contemporary Theater, Wrocław, Poland, 1983. (Photo by Marek Grotowski)

DIRECTOR AND ACTOR
SEEK TO EXPRESS THE HUMAN CONDITION

2.14. *Risky hand-to-hand combat*

Michael Karr (Orlando) wrestles with Steve Vaughan (Charles); Thomas F. Higgins, Jr. (Le Beau) and Erin Markle (Chorus) observe. *As You Like It*. Shakespeare in the Park Festival, Buffalo, NY, 1991. Fight choreographer: Steve Vaughan. (Photo from the author's collection)

DIRECTOR AND ACTOR
SEEK TO EXPRESS THE HUMAN CONDITION

2.15. *A grotesque choir*

Wiktor Grotowicz (Prince Himalaya), Grażyna Krukówna (General's Wife), Marlena Milwiw (Chairman's Wife), Teresa Sawicka (Princess Himalaya), and Eugeniusz Kujawski (General) in *Operetta*. The Contemporary Theater, Wrocław, Poland, 1977. (Photo by Jan Bortkiewicz)

DIRECTOR AND ACTOR
SEEK TO EXPRESS THE HUMAN CONDITION

2.16. *Grotesque lecture*

An ensemble scene in act 1 of *Rhinoceros*. First row, from the left: John Lewin (Logician) lecturing, with Richard Hicks (Student), Richard Levine (Beranger), Steven Yoakam (The Café Proprietor), Robert Breuler (The Grocer); second row: Cathryne Nash (The Waitress), Mary Beth Fisher (The Grocer's Wife), and Marc Crayer, James Richard, Roger Gouenveur Smith (Firemen). The Guthrie Theater, Minneapolis, 1986. (Photo by Joe Giannetti)

DIRECTOR AND ACTOR
SEEK TO EXPRESS THE HUMAN CONDITION

2.17. *Playing animals*

Debra Sperling (Pig Squealer) and Johnny Mendez (Young Pig) in *Animal Farm.*
State University of New York at Buffalo, 1990. (Photo by Debbie Hill)

DIRECTOR AND ACTOR
SEEK TO EXPRESS THE HUMAN CONDITION

2.18, 2.19. *Reaching the depths of darkness at high noon*

Chris O'Neill rehearsing the role of King Lear. Shakespeare in the Park Festival, Buffalo, NY, 1989. (Photo from the author's collection)

DIRECTOR AND ACTOR
SEEK TO EXPRESS THE HUMAN CONDITION

2.20, 2.21. *Reaching the depths of darkness at high noon*

Chris O'Neill rehearsing the role of King Lear. Shakespeare in the Park Festival, Buffalo, NY, 1989. (Photo from the author's collection)

DIRECTOR AND ACTOR
SEEK TO EXPRESS THE HUMAN CONDITION

2.22, 2.23. *Reaching the depths of darkness at high noon*

Chris O'Neill rehearsing the role of King Lear. Shakespeare in the Park Festival, Buffalo, NY, 1989. (Photo from the author's collection)

SECTION 3. THE DIRECTOR WORKS WITH SPECTATORS

3.1. *Characters mirror the audience*

The prologue of *The Pulp*. The Polski Theater, Wrocław, Poland, 1991. (Photo by Adam Hawałej)

3.2. *Spectators on stage*

Spectators surround the central playing area on the proscenium stage in *Birth Rate*. On the swing: Elżbieta Golińska (the Dove). The Contemporary Theater, Wrocław, Poland, 1979. (Photo from the author's collection)

THE DIRECTOR WORKS WITH SPECTATORS

3.3. *Spectators on stage*

Spectators surround the central playing area on the proscenium stage in *The Plague*. From the left: Kazimierz Wysota (Rat), Tomasz Lulek (Rat), Teresa Sawicka (Porter's Wife), Elżbieta Golińska (Nurse), Zdzisław Kuźniar (the Porter), Jan Blecki (Rat), and Kazimierz Zadrożny (Rat). The Contemporary Theater, Wrocław, Poland, 1983. (Photo by Marek Grotowski)

3.4. *Spectators in courtyard*

Spectators around the central playing area in the courtyard of the theater building in *The Old Woman Broods*. In the center: Zbigniew Górski (the Poet) and Ludwik Paczyński (Militia Man). The Osterwa Theater, Lublin, Poland, 1973. (Photo by Wanda Parys)

3.5. *Spectators on the street*

Spectators and actors observe the departure of the newlyweds in a street near the theater. *The Old Woman Broods*. Opening the car door: Zbigniew Gorzowski (First Man). The Osterwa Theater, Lublin, Poland, 1973. (Photo by Wanda Parys)

3.6. *Spectators visit an actor on stage*

Spectators visit Victor Talmadge (Hunger Artist) in his cage, situated on a thrust stage at the beginning of *The Hunger Artist Departs*. Pfeifer Theater, Buffalo, NY, 1987. (Photo by Irene Haupt)

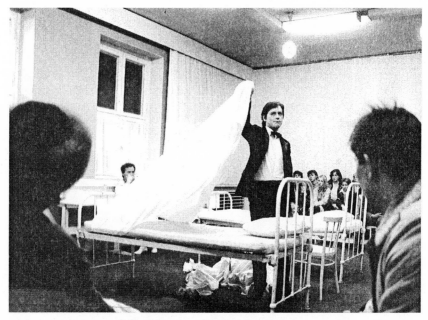

3.7. *Spectators in the rehearsal room*

Part of the production of *The Plague* staged in a rehearsal room. The audience sits on three sides of the playing area. In the center: Kazimierz Wysota (Rat). The Contemporary Theater, Wrocław, Poland, 1983. (Photo by Marek Grotowski)

3.8. *Spectators in the basement of the theater*

Part of the production of *The Plague* staged in the basement of the theater. The audience on three sides of the playing area. From the left: Kazimierz Wysota and Kazimierz Zadrożny (Rats) and Zbigniew Górski (Father Gustaw). The Contemporary Theater, Wrocław, Poland, 1983. (Photo by Marek Grotowski)

THE DIRECTOR WORKS WITH SPECTATORS

3.9. *Spectators outdoors*

Audience before the outdoor production of *Henry V* in Delaware Park, Buffalo, NY. Shakespeare in the Park Festival, 1987. (Photo from the author's collection)

3.10. *Spectators in a church*

Spectators mixed with performers in *The Passion Play*. In the center: Stanisław Baltaziuk (Christ). Corpus Christi Church, Buffalo, NY, 1994. (Photo from the author's collection)

SECTION 4. CREATING THEATER SPACE

4.1. *Creating images through the use of characters, sets, and lighting*

Group scene in *Anna Livia,* act 1. From left to right: Jan Blecki, Edwin Petrykat, Stanisław Jaskułka, Zdzisław Sośnierz, Teresa Sawicka (Anna Livia), Marlena Milwiw, Zbigniew Górski, Maria Zbyszewska. The Contemporary Theater, Wrocław, Poland, 1976. (Photo by Marek Grotowski)

CREATING THEATER SPACE

4.2. *Playing with shadows*

Krzysztof Bauman (Konrad) in his prison cell. *The Forefathers' Eve*. The Contemporary Theater, Wrocław, Poland, 1982. (Photo from the author's collection)

4.3. *Playing in real space—outdoors*

An actor on the roof of a building. Zbigniew Górski (The Poet) in a scene from
The Old Woman Broods. The Osterwa Theater, Lublin, Poland, 1973. (Photo by
Wanda Parys)

4.4. *Playing in real space—indoors*

Production at the Museum of Architecture. *Cleopatra and Caesar*. The Contemporary Theater, Wrocław, Poland, 1976. (Photo by Zdzisław Mozer)

4.5. *Environment created in a black box*

A model of the environment for *Antigone in New York* built by Madeleine Sobota. Department of Theater and Dance, State University of New York at Buffalo, 1995. (Photo by Madeleine Sobota)

4.6. *Environment created in a black box*

Environment for *Antigone in New York* built by Madeleine Sobota. In the center from left to right: Robert Manning (Flea), Ecstasy Seaton (Anita), Damon Kupper (Sasha); far: Owen Muirhead (The Indian) and Gretchen Meyerhoefer (The Newcomer). Department of Theater and Dance, State University of New York at Buffalo, 1995. (Photo by Madeleine Sobota)

4.7. *A daytime performance in a theater modeled on the Elizabethan stage*

The opening scene of *Julius Caesar* in Delaware Park, Buffalo, NY. In the center: Joseph Natale (Julius Caesar). Shakespeare in the Park Festival, 1989. (Photo from the author's collection)

4.8. *A nighttime performance in a theater modeled on the Elizabethan stage*

A scene from act 5 of *King Lear* in Delaware Park, Buffalo, NY. On the platform: Joy Parry (Cordelia). Shakespeare in the Park Festival, 1989. (Photo from the author's collection)

4.9. *Use of height and depth on a proscenium stage*

Bogusław Kierc (Franz K.) and Zdzisław Kuźniar (Father) are on the balcony, with the ensemble situated in two groups in the center and upstage in *The Trap*. The Contemporary Theater, Wrocław, Poland, 1984. (Photo by Marek Grotowski)

4.10. *Playing with various heights*

Halina Rasiakówna (Albertine) is standing on a small platform, while Stanisław Jaskułka (Hufnagel) is carried by the group of Lackeys and Maids, from the left: Zuzanna Helska, Zdzisław Sośnierz, Bogusław Parchimowicz, Maria Zbyszewska, and Barbara Pijarowska in *Operetta*. The Contemporary Theater, Wrocław, Poland, 1977. (Photo courtesy of the author)

4.11. *Exploring the depth on the proscenium stage with individual characters*

Upstage: Magdalena Kumor (Young Woman); centerstage: Maria Zbyszewska (Old Woman); downstage: Zbigniew Górski (Young Man) in *Birth Rate*. The Contemporary Theater, Wrocław, Poland, 1979. (Photo from the author's collection)

4.12. *Exploring the depth on a proscenium stage with an ensemble*

A crowd scene in *The Pulp*. Downstage: Igor Przegrodzki (Writer). The Polski Theater, Wrocław, Poland, 1990. (Photo by Adam Hawałej)

4.13. *Exploring the depth on a thrust stage*

The final scene in *The Hunger Artist Departs*. In the center: Victor Talmadge (Hunger Artist) and, from the left, Barbara Gołaszewski (Mother), Richard Hummert (Impresario), Christopher Redfern (Butcher), Molly Heller-Wagner (Journalist), Josh Brewster (Butcher), Colleen O'Mara (Ola), Monica Sosa Backman (Monica), John Kiouses (Butcher), Caitlin Baeumler (Journalist), Susan Sorensen (Mayor). Pfiefer Theater, Buffalo, NY, 1987. (Photo by Irene Haupt)

4.14 *Closing the proscenium stage with bars*

HAMLET: "Denmark's a prison." ROSENCRANTZ: "Then is the world one."
(*Hamlet,* Act II, scene ii, line 244-5). Comparing the theater stage to a prison
was a powerful metaphor in communist-ruled Poland. In the photograph: the stage
closed off in the final scene of *The Forefathers' Eve*. The Contemporary Theater,
Wrocław, Poland, 1982. (Photo from the author's collection)

4.15. *Closing the proscenium stage with barbed wire*

Another example of the same metaphor: the stage closed off in a scene from *The Plague*. Behind the fence: Andrzej Wilk (Teacher) and Bogusław Kierc (Doctor). The Contemporary Theater, Wrocław, Poland, 1983. (Photo by Marek Grotowski)

SECTION 5. CREATIVE USE OF OBJECTS IN THE THEATER

5.1. *Paintings in a production*

A scene from *Tamara L.* by K. Braun, a play about a painter, Tamara Lempicka, in which copies of actual paintings were used, as well as easels, brushes, etc. From the left: Agata Pilitowska-Borys (Daughter) and Maria Nowotarska (Painter). Right bottom: a picture damaged in action on stage. The Maria Nowotarska Company, Toronto, 1999. (Photo by Jarosław Dąbrowski)

5.2. Marionettes

The Four Angels of the Apocalypse and the Archangel Michael in *Interrupted Act*. The Osterwa Theater, Lublin, Poland, 1970. (Photo by Wanda Parys)

CREATIVE USE OF OBJECTS IN THE THEATER

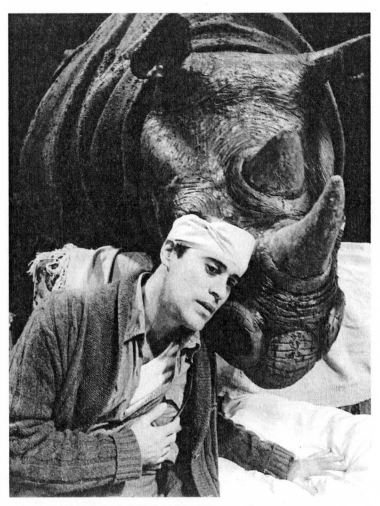

5.3. A full-size rhinoceros on the stage

Richard Levine (Beranger) in a scene from *Rhinoceros*. The Guthrie Theater, Minneapolis, 1986. (Photo by Dennis Behl)

5.4. *A real car on the stage*

Keith Calaman (Mr. Arnaux) and Devon Wyman (Angelique Arnaux) in *The Dummies' Ball*. The Black Box Theater, State University of New York at Buffalo, 1997. (Photo from the author's collection)

5.5. Bicycles in a playing area outside the theater

Bicycles on the sidewalk in the prologue of *The Old Woman Broods*. Daire Brehan (The Bride) and Joan O'Hara (The Old Woman) approach the entrance of the theater. The Project Arts Center Theater, Dublin, Ireland, 1983. (Photo by K. Joseph Romanowski)

5.6. *Bicycles on the stage*

In the center: David Collins (Son) with a broken bicycle in *Bullai Mhartain*. Deilt Company, Dublin, Ireland, 1989. (Photo from the author's collection)

5.7. *Mannequins and a scarecrow*

Actors dancing with mannequins, watched by a scarecrow in *Bullai Mhartain*.
Deilt Company, Dublin, Ireland, 1989. (Photo from the author's collection)

5.8. *Hundreds of shoes on stage*

Shoemakers frantically making shoes. From the left: Steven Barr (First Apprentice), Wane Grace (Master Sayetan), Peter Schreiner (Second Apprentice), and Soldiers in *The Shoemakers*. The Odyssey Theater, Los Angeles, 1987. (Photo from the author's collection)

5.9. *Huge puppets*

Huge puppets dominating the stage in *The Pulp*. In front, from the left: Danuta Balicka (Producer) and Edwin Petrykat (The Dignitary). The Polski Theater, Wrocław, Poland, 1990. (Photo by Adam Hawałej)

5.10. *Immense cross*

A cross carried by Stanisław Baltaziuk (Christ) in *The Passion Play*. Corpus Christi Church, Buffalo, NY, 1994. (Photo from the author's collection)

SECTION 6. THE OPENING

6.1 When the work has been done. . .
The author with wife Zofia before the opening of his
play *Émigrée Queen* in Toronto, 1992.
(Photo Alfred Mrozicki)

THE OPENING

6.2 The director's greatest joy: an actor's success. . .
Maria Nowotarska in the role of Helen Modjeska after
the opening of *Émigrée Queen* in Cracow, Poland, 1993.
(Photo from the author's collection.)

PART III. CREATING THE PRODUCTION

Introduction

In this part of the book—and in this part of this course on directing—we are going to analyze, discuss, and work through all preparatory steps leading to the creation of a production. In the previous part we have learned various creative attitudes and techniques. Now, we have to employ them in the world of practice and profession. We shall also develop additional, new techniques and methods that are necessary to the director's work on a play before and during rehearsals. We are going to demonstrate and work on these problems in class, complementing class work with the assignment of homework.

As in previous class exercises, students will act in the directorial skits and fulfill additional tasks, such as building space or providing music. The master—in this part of the work—should not personally direct or demonstrate exercises, limiting himself/herself to explaining problems and setting objectives for students. The master should provide guidance, support, advice, comments, and evaluation of the students' work, as well as instigate group discussions, but should let the students discover practical solutions by themselves. Of course, the master's emergency help may be needed and, if so, should not be denied. But the rule should be to give students as much creative freedom as possible and teach them to take full responsibility for the result of their work.

The process of practical directorial work on a production (that is preparations and rehearsals) should be based on material provided by this book, but, at the same time, each student/reader should select a play of his/her choice and work on it parallel to the class work, using what they have learned in classes (or by reading this book) to prepare their own projects. The best material for this initial, independent student work is a realistic, well written and clearly structured drama, preferably a one-act, with a limited cast. It would serve as handy learning material and as a spring board for future, more difficult and complex undertakings. After having selected their dramas, students should prepare their productions step by step, and then actually direct them. If mounting a whole play would prove impossible within the given circumstances of the work environment, a part of a play or only a scene will do the job. But the point is that the production, even if it is a very short one, must be fully developed, with all its elements brought to perfection.

If the reader of this books happens to be an established director or a theater scholar or critic, I would suggest that they too select a play and work on it using their imagination, as it unfolds on these pages. If this book serves as a basis for a class or workshop, I suggest using it as follows:

(1) Read in class the selected chapter or paragraph of the book in class and discuss it.

(2) If a paragraph in the book contains practical exercises, work on them in class.

(3) Using the homework assignments proposed in the book, have the students work individually and independently on a given problem, preparing their written and/or verbal responses.

(4) Have the students present the results of their homework in class, followed by the master's comments and a group discussion.

CHAPTER 1. THE DIRECTOR'S WORK OF MIND AND IMAGINATION

Play selection

We direct because we need to or because we have to; we direct for artistic or monetary reasons; we direct because we are addicted to it or because we feel an urge to experiment. There are so many reasons for directing.

We want to express ourselves and/or to express in theater an idea, thought, desire, opinion, judgement. We desire to proclaim or defend a value, a belief, or truth. We assume that directing a particular play is our duty towards a society, milieu, nation, friends, or our own company. Directing might be also our own personal duty, if we have an iota of talent—it cannot be hidden and buried. We sometimes direct for art's sake only, without caring about the possibility of success or disaster, profit or loss. Many times we direct because directing is our profession (or we want it to be our profession) and it is simply our way to earn our living. We also direct because we relish experimenting. So often we are curious about what theater can offer us and what we can offer the world using theater. For some of us directing is an obsession, for, if we have been directing for a long time, we can't live without it. Finally, we direct, because, simply, we love it.

Usually, these reasons are interrelated. In any case, a moment comes, when we decide to put on a show and we start the long—sometimes very long and painful—way to a production and its opening. In this section of the book we'll cover the milestone stages of preparation of a production from the play selection to the first rehearsal.

But how do we select a play? Well, I guess it all starts with a growing, at first unconscious, interest in an area of life or human experience, and culminates with the urge to say something, to share something with others. There may be months or years in between this very first impulse and our selection of a play. In the meantime, we read dozens of plays, we talk to playwrights, or we weigh a decision to write a play, or an adaptation of a novel, ourselves. These initial, personal, private, and intimate stages of directorial creation are so secret that we can't analyze them. What we should realize is that the first impulse to direct is something absolutely individual, totally internal, and entirely spiritual. But then comes the next stage. The project starts to formulate in our consciousness and it eventually emerges from the very depth of our soul, as a choice of our intellect, heart, or instinct. Now we have to evaluate it—objectively, coldly, practically, and realistically. We have to asses if we truly want to work on this particular play or topic devoting to it several month, if not years, of our life. This assessment can be made using a list of criteria of directorial play selection. We list the criteria in a certain order, but they are all interconnected; in a given situation one or another dominates.

TABLE: CRITERIA FOR DIRECTORIAL PLAY SELECTION

(1) Personal
(2) Social
(3) Artistic
(4) Ethical
(5) Practical

---

(1) Personal criteria are the strongest. I simply want, I need, I really must direct this play. The more subjective the personal criteria are, the stronger the director's ego—the stronger is the necessity to objectively asses them. Selfishness

has ever been and always is an important and legitimate motive in all artistic undertakings—but selfishness must be tamed. So we ask ourselves questions. Is my wish to direct this play a stupid and shallow caprice, or it is an authentic, human need? Maybe, at one moment it occurred to me that I have to do this play, but a moment later I wasn't so sure and my enthusiasm vanished? Perhaps, someone asked me, offered me, or even ordered me to work on this play—what is my personal reaction? Would it be honest to do it? Would I be true to myself? Can I really put my name on the poster of this production? Can I sign it as mine? Questions about personal criteria of play selection are always questions of "why?" Why do I want to do it? Why now? Why here? Why me? And why this play?

(2) Social criteria are criteria of service—service to others. It is worthwhile to reflect upon our priorities. Do I want to direct this play for my own satisfaction and profit, or do I want to offer it to others? Whom do I want to serve by my work—myself or others? And if I want to serve—what is this service? What do I want to offer or give others? Is it art? Education? Enlightenment? Do I want to help others to grow? Or, perhaps, what I want to do will harm audiences, corrupt or confuse them, encroach on their freedom? Will my production help people to live honestly? To live an ethical life? Will my production make them happier? Reflections on the social criteria of play selection lead us to specific questions such as: with whom do I want do this play? For whom do I want to do this play? "With whom" means with what actors, designers, other artists. "For whom" means for what public. Hence, examination of social criteria of a directorial choice of a play leads to questions about the acting company and about the audience within a given social, historical, cultural, and political context. Social criteria, if met, embed a production in the social soil.

(3) Artistic criteria might be diverse: a play may be especially suited as a vehicle to convey the director's own style and artistic preferences. A play itself may be new, ground breaking; and this may be a valuable reason to do it. A play may contain a special challenge in terms of means of expression that a director would like to confront himself/herself with. A play might provide material for an

expedition to the unknown, artistic territory that the director is willing to explore. A project may promise the thrill of an experiment and it's tempting to take on it. We reflect here on aesthetic values of a planned production, on beauty.

(4) Ethical criteria, when examined, lead us to questions about the play's spiritual aspect, its place in a moral system, its political appeal, its intellectual meaning, and its human values. Without a play having those aspects—personal criteria would be too narrow, social criteria would not allow a production to reach the level of art, and artistic criteria alone would lead to a shallow production. So, we need to use such standards as truth and justice. We need to simply ask ourselves: is directing this play an honest and right thing to do?

(5) Practical criteria are important not only for the director's own safety, but also from the perspective of a given theater, institution, or organization. Theater work has always had a communal nature, it involves the energy, time, and money of many people, beginning with the producers and ending with the public. Practical criteria of play selection should be examined by asking questions about the means which are necessary to put on the show. First, on what human means may we count? What about actors, designers, composers, choreographers? Examining social criteria we felt a need and desire to work with certain people. But now, practically, are they available? Will they be interested in working with us? Are we going to have adequate technical and administrative staff or should we do everything by ourselves? If we don't see enough able people around to lift the project up, we either have to find them, or, work first on getting them on board. And what about the public? We want to direct our artistic message to certain people, but we have to coldly evaluate whether they would care to see our show. And simply, how many people might be willing to come to the theater? If we don't expect audiences to flock to our show, the entire project gets a big question mark. It should be reconsidered or abandoned. Second, we ask questions about space. Do we have an appropriate space for our project—a theater, a venue? If not, we have to find it, or build it. Third, we consider production and administrative resources. Do we have a proper institutional and organizational

structure which could cope with our project or should we create them first? Fourth, what about money? We have to soberly calculate the cost of the project and match it with available money. If it is not enough, we have to plan on raising money or finding sponsors. In any case, financial matters must be weighed before we go farther.

All the criteria should be carefully examined and bring us to the final decision: I want to, and I will, direct this play. Only if all the criteria are met can we count on a good result for the undertaking. To give the reader a practical example of how it works, I will use my own work. I can say, that deciding to direct my "model production," *The Plague,* I took into account all the above listed criteria of play selection. (Because of its "model" character, I refer to *The Plague* again.) Additionally, it was not only a directorial choice but also a production decision, because I was Artistic Director and General Manger of the Contemporary Theater in Wrocław, Poland, where the show was planned.

(1) My decision was based on personal criteria: I had a strong personal conviction that I need, I want, and I have a duty to prepare this production there and at that time—in Poland under martial law in the 1980s—as a personal statement and a testimony.

(2) I weighed the social criteria, and they led me to believe that by putting on *The Plague,* I'd say publically and loudly what many people—the majority of the nation—could not say, because of the military censorship and virtual non-existence of free speech in the country. I was under the same restrictions, but I counted on outwitting the censors and sending my message across to the audiences anyway. Considering the social criteria of the play selection, I also wanted to serve others, especially those who were at that time deprived of any possibility of expressing themselves, because they were threatened, attacked, or imprisoned. I wanted to speak in their name. Additionally, still thinking about the social context of the work, I knew that I can count an my able, skillful and devout acting company, and that all theater employees (perhaps with only a few exceptions) would fervently participate in preparing this show. I simply thought

that to prepare *The Plague* was a right thing to do.

(3) I seriously considered the artistic criteria. I saw in *The Plague* excellent and useful material to prepare a production in which I would follow my dearest artistic principles and employ my most effective means of expression. Namely, I would be able to prepare a strong, communal interaction of actors and spectators; I could imbue the production with symbolism and poetry based on a strong realistic foundation; I could build a unique theater space, using various locations in the theater building and walking spectators from place to place (stage, auditorium, basement, foyers, rehearsal rooms, and hallways); I could use a lot of visuality, music, and lighting according to my artistic preferences.

(4) The ethical criteria were as important as the others and motivated me, as well as my friends, in our decisions. (Of course, I did not make that decision alone, but I consulted and talked it over with the advisers and the company.) It was a time when the communist military junta based their rule on lies and deception—we felt that our duty was to speak out the truth about the situation in the country. It was a time when human rights were trampled and annulled—we felt that we had an obligation to defend human rights and national values. It was a time when the country was again frozen by eastern winds—it was necessary and honest to underline Poland's ties with the West by staging a production based on masterpieces of Western literature. In a time when a culture of hatred and death was openly proclaimed—it was right, we thought, to uphold a culture of solidarity and life.

(5) Finally, I clearly calculated the practical aspects of the work. I thought that if the project could be pushed through the censorship (which was a risky assumption but it worked) the production would be a huge box office success and would draw crowds (which indeed happened) and would be an unusual artistic success (which also came true). What I did not calculate was my personal risk: putting up *The Plague* in that perilous time in Poland eventually cost me loss of my theater and a complete breakdown in my whole life and theater career. But even now, I am positive that it was worthwhile to pay the highest price for a

production which turned out to be the "production of my life."

Beginning with the problem we are working on now—the play selection—students in our class (or readers of this book) should be getting homework assignments. Assignments will help them to deepen their understanding of a given topic and to develop several directorial skills. Here is our first task of this kind.

Homework: All students should select a play for directing and provide written justification of the choice based on the criteria listed above. It will be worthwhile to spend a few of the following classes on students' presentations of their choices and their defense of them. It is a necessary foundation for the next stages of the work and it must be solid.

Practical preparation for production

After the play selection and decision to produce it—we start practical preparations. We have to do much concrete work. If the production was not commissioned and the director was not invited to do it, the first steps must lead to finding a theater or an organization which would like to put on our project. We can embark on such a search, while still working on the production project. Preparation starts with the individual and solitary work of the director. Next, he/she includes other co-creators and producers, and, eventually, he/she transforms the volatile project into a solid body of performance, working with actors and technical staff.

Setting the directorial take-off checklist (when learning to create an action) we have already pointed out some necessary areas of the director's preparatory work. In the class/workshop environment the director/student personally and individually (with some help from others) created all aspects and elements of the show, both conceptually and practically. Now, working on a show in the real world environment, the director should still create all of the show's elements in his/her imagination, but their materialization is either a matter of his/her own practical work, or is delegated to others. Previously, we put together a *Short Directorial Take-Off Checklist*—now we have to extend it and apply it to the complex process of producing a play in a theater.

TABLE: FULL DIRECTORIAL TAKE-OFF CHECKLIST

First stage: director's work of intellect and imagination
(1) Play analysis—made with the use of the "graphical analysis method"
(2) Decisions pertaining to text (editing, cuts, or changes), interpretation, space, style, rhythm, music, light, and all means of expression, including the mode of beginning and ending the show.
(3) Decisions about the human fabric of the show—cast and audience.
(4) Preparation of the initial production budget.
(5) Preparation of the initial work schedule (date of opening, number and time of rehearsals, time table for technical and administrative work).

Second stage: director's practical preparations
(1) Making the "graphical production project."
(2) Completing the "directorial tool box."
(3) Writing the "written production project."
(4) Preparation of the "directorial book."
(5) Director's preparation for work with designers, composers, and producers; preparations for rehearsals with actors.

Third stage: implementation of directorial projects before rehearsals
(1) Director's work with designers of sets, costumes, lights; with composers and sound specialists; with choreographers, fight masters, and others.
(2) Director's work with literary adviser or manager.
(3) Director's work with producer or producing institution, organization, etc.
(4) Director's work with technical director, stage manager, and craftsmen.
(5) Auditioning and casting.

Play analysis

In the chapter on creating the text of a performance we learned the method of "graphical analysis." Now, it's time to use it in preparation for a real production. As we remember, using this method, we study the human, the spatial, and the temporal layers of a play. We find who are the people (characters) involved in the action, what is the space and time of the action, and, finally, what is the action itself; we try to provide each scene with a title. We also take notes on all practical aspects of the action and put down our directorial concepts. The graphical analysis, along with these various notes, is the foundation for further directorial works and decisions.

Homework: make an analysis of a play which you chose to direct.

Directorial decisions pertaining to text, interpretation, space, style, rhythm, music, light, and all means of expression

Graphical analysis enables us to make all necessary decisions pertaining to text (editing, cuts, or changes) and interpretation (what the play is about). Thanks to the analysis we should now be able to answer fundamental questions about the production: what do I want to say to my audiences with this play? What should my production be about?

For example, the musical *Oklahoma!* (1943) was a story about love and the beauty of the country and its people, a message resounding especially strong during the dark hours of World War II. Jean Vilar's production of *Alcade of Zalamea* by Calderón (1961) was a tale of human dignity winning against all odds. Grotowski's *The Constant Prince* based on Calderón/Słowacki (1965) was a study of the human spirit's constancy and supremacy over the body. Richard Schechner's *Dionysus 69* (1969) was a theatrical song about the unstoppable energy of love and life. Rich Tylor's *Danny and the Deep Blue Sea* by John P. Shanley (1998) was an intimate and personal appeal for gentleness and compassion in a cruel and cold world.

Interpretation leads to decisions about the general vision and concept, as well as the mise-en-scène and style of the show. For example: should it be a lofty and traditional production of a classical play done in period style? Or an experimental, "happening"-like performance that encourages and expects audience participation? Or a psychological-realistic family drama closed behind the "fourth wall"? The choice of space for the show has especially heavy consequences, and the options are virtually unlimited. Should my production be played on a proscenium stage or in the black box? Or, perhaps, I need a natural, found space? Should the space be closed or open, indoors or outdoors? To explain these choices, let's again turn to examples. A proscenium stage is certainly an obvious choice for hundreds and thousands of Western realistic-psychological dramas from Henrik Ibsen, through

G. B. Shaw, Eugene O'Neill, and Tennessee Williams, to Edward Albee, Caryl Churchill, Sam Shepard, David Mamet, and others. A black box is a perfect space to build an environment. I mentioned environments in my black box productions such as: *The Time of Your Life, Largo Desolato,* and *Antigone in New York.* Real architecture suits an open-air spectacle. Preparing, in 1935, a medieval-style production about the Florentine monk and preacher Savonarola, French master, Jacques Copeau, decided to play it as an open-air show in Florence's central city square, within the natural, historical, Renaissance architecture—the same places and streets that Savonarola waked through centuries ago. Andrzej Wajda, the noted Polish film and theater director-dissident, put on *The Upper Room* by the poet and dissident Ernest Bryll (a play about the apostles' reaction to Jesus Christ's crucifixion, metaphorically referring to the communists' attack on Solidarity in 1981) in the natural space of a church in Warsaw which was still under construction—it was realistically a convenient hiding place and metaphorically a spiritual stronghold. The space provided a perfect setting for an illegal show with strong interaction between actors and spectators, opposing and defying the authorities. The action of Adam Ziajski's scenario, *A City Vaudeville,* takes place in a water resort, so when mounting it at the Poznań Malta Festival (Poland, 1996) Ziajski chose as the playing area a waterworks on the city square with the public standing around the fountain; the day was warm and sunny, and many spectators joined the actors in the water. *A City Vaudeville,* a light and funny show, was a perfect example of a natural and easygoing physical interaction between actors and spectators. A production of a national classic on a proscenium stage at the Comédie Française in Paris, with solemnly moving characters delivering lofty speeches, would certainly exclude any direct interaction between the Comédie players and the audience. An experimental, offensive, sexually explicit or politically aggressive show would work well in a small off-off venue, and would create strong emotional bonds between actors and spectators.

As we see, the directorial, aesthetic concept of a show is always inseparably connected with the space choice, and the space choice leads to coining the style of the show, as well as instigating the desired interaction between actors and spectators or blocking it. The ideal seems to be to connect coherently and logically all the performance aspects.

Working on a play analysis, I used the example of *The Cherry Orchard*. I want to return to this play in order to demonstrate how the analysis leads to practical, directorial decisions. I should confess that I have worked on *The Cherry Orchard* several times in classes and workshops but I have never dared to direct it. I wasn't sure if I had an ample cast, suitable space, and enough time for rehearsals. *The Cherry Orchard* is an excellent play: well-written, rich, and profound; its message is both universally and contemporarily valid and appealing; it combines realism and symbolism with finesse. The director should approach *The Cherry Orchard* humbly and respectfully. What I write about this play is based on many hours of analysis and preparations of directorial projects, but it is not a description of an actual production. You, my readers, worked with me on the analysis of it, so you are well prepared to comprehend my directorial decisions pertaining to *The Cherry Orchard*.

Directorial decisions pertaining to *The Cherry Orchard*

Text. *The Cherry Orchard* was originally written in Russian. The first step leading to an English language production is to find the best translation. There are many translations of this 20th century classic and the potential director should gather them, compare them, and select one. The selected translation will certainly be not perfect, so, the next step is to correct it. The director who does not know the language of the original may make edits using other translations, or, as is the most advisable, work with someone fluent in the original's tongue. Editing usually has two objectives: first, to make the text fully understandable to contemporary audiences; and, second, to unify the language with the given directorial interpretation of the play. As for me, working on *The Cherry Orchard*

I use the translation of Stark Young, with some editing checked against the original.

Interpretation. My interpretation of *The Cherry Orchard* can be described as "faithful to the soul of the text and not limited by the author's stage vision." This means that I follow the author's story, action and ideas, but not his stage directions and interpretive remarks. Chekhov tells the story of the fall of a Russian noble family at the turn of the 20th century, which loses its land, including the beloved cherry orchard; the family disintegrates and its members have to change their life styles; the cherry orchard is chopped down. A new societal class, new social and economical orders, and new life styles emerge. On the grounds of the former cherry orchard, a residential quarter will be developed. This story has realistic and historical as well as symbolic and universal dimensions. In my interpretation I use the realistic layer of the play, but I stress universality. I want to embrace in the story of the cherry orchard and the Ranevskaya family the stories of all families forced to leave their land, home, country; of all persecuted intelligentsia and artists; and of all social groups and individuals who represent a traditional and conservative culture with its values, as well as weaknesses. Such people dramatically collide with those who represent the new culture—a culture of force, a culture of demolition of the old world order and the setting up new laws and ways of life. The cherry orchard is a symbol of traditional values, and life's energy and beauty. It is doomed to go. The wheel of history turns inevitably. But what will life without the cherry orchards be? I'd like to put this question to the audience and leave it open. Spectators should answer it for themselves.

Style. Style of the production should be a well-measured mixture of realism and symbolism. Realism should be a solid foundation for the characters' playing; symbolism should carry universality and generalization. The production should have broad transhistorical and transcultural meaning and appeal. Actors and spectators will share the same space (see below) but without direct interaction, perhaps, with the exception of the ball in act four, when spectators could join the dance.

Space. Analyses of the play revealed the following: (1) The cherry orchard is all the time present in the action as a "character." In the graphical analyses of the initial scenes of the play we even included it in the list of characters. The cherry orchard is the most important element of action in terms of both spiritual and physical events. (2) The action of the play takes place in a few different locations which require fulfillment of specific functions, such as entrances and exits to/from interior and to/from exterior, and provision of certain furniture, primarily seats. (3) Most of the crucial events occur in the depths of the character's souls. People's spiritual lives, memories, fears, dreams, desires, and hopes are the basic matter of the action.

If these findings are true, the consequences are as follows: (1) The cherry orchard should always be present and visible. (2) Specific locations (in all four acts) can be structured, and their functional requirements met, by chairs, props, lamps, and other objects. (3) Actors should be close to spectators—in order to be able to play delicately and come across with subtle emotions and soul movements.

Again, if these assumptions are correct, the following practical consequences ensue: (1) The action of the whole production should be played inside of a cherry orchard—if possible real and natural, or built-in as an environment in a black box theater. (2) Inside of the orchard, a central playing area should be set, yet not strictly defined. For example, it might be bordered by garden lamps on stands. Characters would have access to the central playing area from all sides and the paths leading to the center might be used as additional playing areas. The central playing area should be transformed in all four acts with use of the furniture and objects; for example in act 3, a wooden dance floor should be installed. The cherry orchard would remain the same all the time. (3) Both characters and spectators should use identical garden chairs; characters would get them when necessary; spectators would sit on them scattered in the orchard around the central playing area. Generally, it is an environmental approach to the space and mise-en-scène.

This spacial arrangement will work throughout the whole action. The final scene—the beginning of chopping down the orchard—may be staged in many different ways. For example: woodcutters (several dozen of them, if possible) with axes enter the orchard and start cutting trees; or bulldozers start approaching the orchard from all sides fracturing and derooting trees; or only the sound of axes chopping trees could enfold the spectators. The concrete solution to the ending of the production, including all other spatial decisions should be left to talks between the director and the set designer. In any case, I know that the whole play should be played in the cherry orchard with characters and spectators sharing the common environment.

Rhythm, music, and other means of expression. I feel that the whole action should be—as much as possible—played with contrasting and changing rhythms, moods, and lights. A live orchestra playing at the ball of the third act is a must. A most suitable way of playing *The Cherry Orchard* would be to stage it somewhere in the country in a cherry orchard in bloom. I dream about a two day soul searching process of meetings, discussions and workshops in which *The Cherry Orchard* would serve as the Ariadna's thread. Let's imagine: the public arrives to a country orchard on a Friday evening, and has a discussion with actors and director on theater in the changing world; there are rooms reserved in near-by motels. Act 1 is played on Saturday at dawn, act 2, in the afternoon, and acts 3 and 4, at night; interactions, meetings, discussions, and workshops, as well as food and music, make up the program in the meantime.

Homework: write a note on all the above directorial decisions for the play you are working on.

Decisions about the human fabric of the show

Decisions about the human fabric of the show refer to cast and audience. Actual casting may be one of the final directorial tasks before the rehearsals. But general decisions pertaining to both actors and spectators should be made very early, based on interpretation of the play and stylistic approach to the production.

We ask several questions: who should play, what actors? Should we look for established stars? Or would a young and energetic cast better carry our concept? For whom should we play? What spectators do we want to reach? In the United States, for example, there are several distinct and separate theater systems: the theater industry, regional theaters, experimental/avant-garde theaters, and university/school theaters. In each of these systems the audiences are differently oriented, they seek different values and gratifications from attending productions: entertainment, cultural enlightenment, artistic adventure, or intellectual stimulation. We have to appreciate this diversity and be fully aware for whom we are preparing a show. Is our audience enthusiastic senior citizens, unruly high school students, blasé theater critics, enemies, colleagues, or friends?

Another question arises about the human fabric of the planned show—what kind of interaction between actors and spectators do we want to create? It depends who is addressing whom (what actors and what spectators) and how we prepare the production: as an objective work of theater art, or as a communal experience; as a social "show-off" event in which people participate to see others and to be seen and don't care too much for the show; or as a risky and thrilling experiment of trespassing on the boundaries of what is politically correct, culturally acceptable, or artistically known. Preparing a production we should be aware of all these conditions and options, and consciously make all decisions pertaining to the human fabric of the planned production based on how we answer these questions.

Homework: write a statement about "with whom and for whom I intend to prepare my show." Think whom are you going to cast and decide who the ideal audience should be.

Preparation of the initial production budget

These days, the production budget is one of the special concerns of a director. Even if the director is not responsible for the production finances or proposing the budget, the director should be fully aware how much money a theater, an institution, or a university department has for his/her show. The director must personally think about the real and necessary cost of the show and the major items of the budget. I am not talking, of course, about specific calculations of the amount of fabric for a costume or lumber for a platform. I am suggesting that the director should be aware about the general scope and level of the expenses which are required to materialize his/her project. This knowledge indicates whether a play production can even be submitted as a practical proposal. It also tells to whom we can propose our project. The five major elements of a budget for any play are:

(1) Personal costs: honoraria of artists, administrators, and technicians involved with the project; also author's royalties.

(2) Material costs: costs of sets, costumes, props, music, sound, etc.

(3) Administrative costs: theater/venue renting, heating/cooling, light, etc.

(4) Advertising and promotion costs.

(5) Transport costs—if the project includes a tour, trip abroad, etc.

Depending on the circumstances some costs might be very high, such as renting a theater when we don't own one. Some costs may be non-existent: for example, acting salaries for a university production. In an institutional theater all these costs might be a part of a yearly budget, but still this budget is divided among specific productions. Awareness about the costs of the project is the director's practical duty. It is also a moral obligation. We must be conscious that our decisions have not only interpretational, artistic, ethical, or ideological bearing, but also financial, material, and production consequences. Money will be spent, and it will not usually be our money. The director has a responsibility to think about the expenses.

Homework: write a proposal of the initial budget of your production, breaking the expenses into the five categories listed above.

Work schedule

Preparation of the schedule of the entire work process is the next directorial task. The schedule has two stages. First: the artistic, technical and administrative preparations before the rehearsals. Second: the rehearsals with actors.

Preparing the schedule independently, or within the guidelines given by the producer, the director assesses the amount of time needed for the preparatory work before the rehearsals and the time required for the actual rehearsals. Both artistic and financial considerations require that the schedule be carefully planned and then strictly observed. We know that once the date of the opening is set—it is "sacred." These are the rules of the game and we should play by the rules.

The schedule for the preparatory phase of the work breaks into:

(1) The individual work of the director. Its length is flexible. There are projects which mature over years. There are others which require maximum speed: for examples when we unexpectedly get a tempting proposal on very short notice. Speed should never mean haste and superficiality, of course.

(2) The work of the director with his/her collaborators: designers, composers, producers, and others. Here not only one's personal work tempo, but also that of others should be considered. This stage can also be longer or shorter.

(3) The technical and administrative work on the production: building sets and costumes, composing and recording music, advertising the show, and so on. This stage depends mostly on the producer, but the director must understand what jobs other people have to do and be aware how much time they need to fulfill them.

Rehearsals with actors form the second and the most important part of the whole work process. The number and the length of rehearsals depend on the customs and possibilities of a given company or institution. The director should know how much time for rehearsals is an absolute minimum from his standpoint. Based on this, he/she should either accept or reject the amount of time proposed by the producer; of course, the time for rehearsals should be negotiated between director and producer for the good of the show.

Schedule of rehearsals with actors includes:

(1) table/reading rehearsals,

(2) blocking rehearsals,

(3) technical rehearsal,

(4) general rehearsals.

The specific rehearsal schedule will be developed by the director during the next phase of practical preparations.

Homework: prepare a general schedule of all work before the rehearsals and indicate how much time do you need for rehearsals.

CHAPTER 2. THE DIRECTOR'S PRACTICAL PREPARATIONS

Making the graphical production project

The next directorial task is to prepare the graphical production project. It is based on the graphical analysis. It, first, reflects the transformation of the text of a play into a production project, and, second, graphically presents major elements of the production.

Preparing a production, the director may decide to be "faithful" to the author or to stage the play "against" the author. While trying to faithfully render the play on stage, the production project would not differ too much from the analysis. Faithfulness, however, may mean different things, such as faithfulness to the ideas and message of the author, or to his/her stage vision, in terms of space, period, style, and stage directions, or both. Faithfulness may also be achieved (sometimes with better results) by a change of the play's dramatic structures and replacement of the means of expression proposed by the author with different ones. Staging the play "against the author," equates to treating a play merely as pretext for the director's own vision. In this case the play is used ironically or perversely, and turned upside down. In between these two extreme directorial attitudes of following the author or quarrelling with him/her, there are thousands of options combining both positions in different proportions. We should also note that there are many plays whose faithful staging is simply impossible, because, for example, contemporary theater does not have the means of expression, or the cultural environment which defined a production of a Greek tragedy in the fifth century BC or a German passion play in the fifteenth century.

The director prepares the graphical production project in the same way as the graphical analysis was done: as a long strip illustrating, in color, in the same as in the analysis, the major aspects of the production, along with notes on specific mise-en-scène concepts, expressed by notes and/or pictograms. As an example of a graphical production project, I will show you my project of act 1 of *The Cherry Orchard*. Comparing it with the graphical analysis of the same play, you will get a clear illustration of how a director moves from the textual and intellectual analysis to the practical and production-oriented project.

Making the graphical production project of *The Cherry Orchard*

The project is based on two propositions: first, to preserve the Chekhovian dramatic structures, and, second, to express them with the use of contemporary means of expression.

Scene 1. Characters, space, time and action are transported from the analysis into the project. All elements obtain more specific and precise shape. Dogs are dropped from the list of characters. (The analysis identified them, but they seem to me more appropriate for a movie than theater.) Space is united and twofold: internal and external. Internal space must be functionally defined, while external space should open perception to symbols, metaphors, and universalization. The time is specified as "very early morning in spring," conditioning characters' feelings, movements, and speech. Indeed, someone who did not go to bed at all would behave at this hour in a particular way. Anxiety and fatigue should be reflected in the behavior of the characters. Spring should be emphasized as important for the play's dramatic structure: the action runs from spring, through summer and autumn, to early winter.

In our "graph" we see:

TIME:	Very early morning in Spring
ACTION:	*Anxious Awaiting*
CHARACTERS:	Lopahin
	Dunyasha
	[The cherry orchard]
SPACE:	A cherry orchard in bloom
	A nursery room in a manor surrounded by the cherry orchard

Scene 2. The expressive title of this scene (*Awkward Love's Labors*) was found during the analysis and it is good material for the actor playing Epihodov. In terms of space in this scene we have the very first entrance of a character from the outside—we should put a note about this in the graph.

TIME:	[Immediate continuity]
ACTION:	*Awkward Love's Labors*
CHARACTERS:	Epihodov
	Lopahin
	Dunyasha [exists and returns]
	[The cherry orchard]
SPACE:	[As before] First entrance of a character from the outside

Scene 3. Adding a note "Increased anxiety" to the title, *Anxious Awaiting,* will indicate both the continuity of the action and the mounting tension. For a director it will be a reminder that scene 3 is by all means connected with scene 1 and that the intensity of the character's emotions rises.

TIME:	[Immediate continuity]
ACTION:	*Anxious Awaiting* (second part)—[Increased anxiety!]
CHARACTERS:	Lopahin
	Dunyasha
	[The cherry orchard]
SPACE:	[As before] Emphasis on the direction of the arrival of the guests

Scene 4. Analyzing this scene we discovered the symbolic nature of Fiers. Realistically, he makes a last hasty inspection of the manor, but symbolically he introduces the motif of death—which should be emphasized in the graphical production project. This emphasis may have interesting acting and staging consequences and should inspire both costume designer and composer. Having already chosen the environmental mise-en-scène for the whole production, this scene poses two directorial problems. First, the activities of Fiers and the entrance of the guest coming from the railway station are simultaneous. This

simultaneous development of two or more events or movements will be one of the continually emerging problems of the production. The environmental space offers multiple options for blocking simultaneous movement. At the same time, it requires very precise choreography. The second problem which arises in this scene is the integration of the interior with the exterior in terms of action, space, and movement. The exterior, in a way, enters to the interior, and the interior opens to the exterior. This integration should be based on the movement of characters and helped by lighting.

TIME:	[Immediate continuity]
ACTION:	*Last Inspection* [on the realistic level] *Death's Foreboding* [on the symbolic level]
CHARACTER:	Fiers
SPACE:	[As before] Integration of the interior with the exterior. Light unifies the whole space. For the first time the entire environment is revealed and comes to play.

Scene 5. Notation of this scene should be moved from the analysis into the project with only slight changes. This is the first group scene in the production. Certainly, it should contrast with the previous, as well as the ensuing scenes in which only a few characters participate. The tender greeting of the orchard and the house should be both emotional and physical. Also, the universality of the action in this scene—the homecoming, an ever-repeating motif in the history of mankind—should be emphasized. I would suggest that it should not be based on local, Russian folklore and manners, but rather found in the treasury of myths telling the story of homecoming, returning from a long journey, or reuniting with loved-ones after a long absence. Odysseus returning to Ithaca or Terry Anderson returning from his Lebanese captivity come to mind. We should be open and free to include such associations in our mise-en-scène and blocking. In old (and old fashioned) theater the ideal was unity of style of the whole production (connected with the three classical "unities" of action, space, and time). In contemporary theater, clashes of styles, means of expression, and images, as well as sudden leaps in space and time, are perfectly acceptable and they increase the artistic expression of the performance. Don't be afraid to be free, my friends.

TIME:	[Immediate continuity]	
	G [group scene]	
ACTION:	*Tender Greeting of the Old Home* [on the realistic level]	
	A Home Coming [on the mythical level]	
CHARACTERS:	Coming from abroad:	Ranevskaya
		Anya
		Charlotta (with a dog)
	Meeting them at the station:	Gayev
		Varya
		Servants (with luggage)
	Meeting them at the entrance:	Lopahin
		Dunyasha
		Pishtchik
	[The cherry orchard]	
SPACE:	Whole environment!	

Scene 6. Analytical notation of this scene should be used in the project. Working on this scene we must emphasize the contrast between the preceding group scene and this one, which is intimate and has a small scale. A new title, *Unrelated Hopes of Two Dreamers* provides handy material for actresses: both of them thread their own line of action, they talk to each other, but they barely communicate. This scene is extremely subtle, delicate, lyrical, and shadowy. We can enjoy and use Chekhovian mastery in full force: after a noisy, chaotic, and expressive group scene—now we have a soft and personal scene of two dreamers. In terms of space, we focus on the interior—center of the environment and depth of the characters' souls.

TIME:	[Immediate continuity]
ACTION:	*Unrelated Hopes of Two Dreamers*
CHARACTERS:	Anya
	Dunyasha
	[Remember: plunge inside of the characters souls!]
SPACE:	Focus on the interior. Anya, former occupant, greets her home

Scene 7. The delicate mood is broken. From the dreamers' space we return to earth—we stress this adding a second segment to the title of the scene: *Dreadful Future and Hurting Present*. Space again enlarges because of Lopahin's intervention and Dunyasha's movement. We have here a new directorial problem: the space in the entire production should have a certain pulsation—it enlarges and shrinks, it embraces the whole environment (or parts of it) or focuses only on the

328

very center. We have to find a means to achieve this effect through movement, light, and music. Maybe, beside lights, we should use music every time when space "moves." Icons indicating important lighting changes and music (or sound) should be chosen and used consistently in the graph.

TIME:	[Immediate continuity]
ACTION:	*Dreadful Future and Hurting Present*
CHARACTERS:	Anya
	Varya
	Lopahin [a short appearance]
	Dunyasha [at the beginning and at the end of scene]
SPACE:	Space "enlarges" with Lopahin's and Dunyasha's movement and "shrinks"back
	Special light [E]. Special music? [♪]

Scene 8. The project should include notes about two aspects of action in this scene. First, in terms of mood, the "hurting present" grows. The boorishness and bullishness of Yasha sets one of the extreme poles of the production. This mood is contrasted with the delicacy and tenderness of Anya, Trofimov, Varya, and Gayev. Second, Yasha's embrace (and more...) of Dunyasha when he drags her into a hidden site in the environment, reveals for the first time a part of it which was not yet used. The entire environment should contain such corners and spots in which some special events are played.

TIME:	[Immediate continuity]
ACTION:	*French Courtship*
CHARACTERS:	Yasha
	Dunyasha
	[Yasha kissing and fondling Dunyasha!]
SPACE:	A secluded spot in the environment

Scene 9.

TIME:	[Immediate continuity]
ACTION:	*Building Bridges to the Past* [Yes: to the past!]
CHARACTERS:	Dunyasha
	Varya
	Anya
	Fiers—preparing for breakfast in the orchard
SPACE:	A new location in the environment—a breakfast area in the orchard

Scene 10. The transformation of the analysis of the project must stress the first battle over the cherry orchard between Ranevskaya and Lopahin. The cherry

orchard is now a real, participating character—it should be put on top of the list of characters and emphasized in the space description.

TIME:	[Immediate continuity; morning still brighter]
	G
ACTION:	*The Battle Over the Cherry Orchard # 1*
CHARACTERS:	The Cherry Orchard [!]
	Ranevskaya
	Lopahin
	Varya [she exits and soon returns]
	Anya [she exits early in the scene]
	Fiers
	Gayev
	Pishtchik
	Yasha [enters during the scene]
	Charlotta [enters and soon exits]
	[Blocking: movement of Ranevskaya in the orchard!]
SPACE:	Action takes place in the cherry orchard. Special light [E]

Scene 11. Members of the family return from the orchard to the house—from the exterior to the interior. This emphasizes their inability to defend the orchard. They are only able to dream about it. The orchard still plays a crucial role in both action and imagery: the sun is rising in the orchard (what a material for lighting), but in the room it is still grey (which stresses the mood of the family).

TIME:	[Immediate continuity]
ACTION:	*Dreams About a Miraculous Saving of the Cherry Orchard*
CHARACTERS:	Ranevskaya
	Gayev
	Varya
	Fiers
	Pishtchik
	[Blocking: motionlessness of this scene contrasts vivid movement in the previous one]
SPACE:	In the interior. Sunrise in the orchard—shadowy in the interior

Scene 12. Trofimov appears for the first time. It's his scene—which should be noted in the project. Trofimov personifies the deceased Grisha, Ranevskaya's son. One directorial problem is how to identify Trofimov with Grisha at the beginning of the scene. Anyway, Grisha must be included on the list of characters. Another question is how to actually stage Ranevskaya's vision of Trofimov carrying Grisha's dead body out of the river, with water dripping off

his clothes. We could also have Trofimov enter from the orchard's far end with
the sun rising behind him and, because of the blinding light, we could create a
mystery: is it a real person or a ghost? There are many options—let's think
creatively which one to choose.

TIME:	[Immediate continuity]
ACTION:	*The Past Resurrected*
CHARACTERS:	Trofimov [he appears for the first time
	and is the most important character in this scene]
	[Grisha, dead son of Ranevskaya]
	Ranevskaya
	Gayev
	Varya
	Fiers
	Pishtchik
	[Optional: to stage action of Trofimov carrying drowned Grisha]
SPACE:	The entire environment. Sun is rising and blinding [E]

Scene 13. Everything is somehow melting and mixing up in this scene. The
previous scenes were dramatic and confrontational: the struggle for the cherry
orchard, helpless tossing in the face of imminent loss of it, and the heartbreaking
appearance of Trofimov. Now, calm overwhelms all. Everyone discovers how
tired they are. The project should include a note about the tempo of this
scene—very slow and sedate.

TIME:	[Immediate continuity]
ACTION:	*The Incurable Sickness of Will*
CHARACTERS:	Gayev [Acting: slow speed, fatigue, helplessness]
	Varya
	Yasha [soon exits]
	Anya [exits during the scene]
	Fiers [comes and takes Gayev]
	SPACE: The interior only

Scene 14. Transformation from analysis to project is based on the introduction
of the Shepherd who was listed as an optional character in the analysis. Now we
decide to include him and to focus the whole scene on him. There are several
directorial problems with the Shepherd such as: how to costume him so as to
emphasize his symbolic character? Perhaps in all white? What tune should he play
on his flute? Can the actor play the instrument? He should! (This problem should

be also put into directorial notes for auditions.) The space should again be unified and the entire environment used.

TIME:	[Immediate continuity; it is now bright morning] MUSIC: A tune of the shepherd's flute [♪]
ACTION:	*Anxiety and Hope*
CHARACTERS:	Shepherd Varya Anya Trofimov [at the end of scene]
SPACE:	Entire environment. Focus on the cherry orchard in bloom

Summary. The graphical project of the production was based on the graphical analysis of the play. Practical solutions, or problems to be solved, were included in it, as well as some important interpretational, blocking, light, and music/sound notes. According to the choice of faithfulness to the author—the sequence of the events, as well as number of characters in the particular scenes, did not change, except for the option of having Grisha and the Shepherd on stage. Many data were directly transported from the analysis into the project. At the same time, action and space were significantly changed. Action included suggestions of a sort of extension or enlargement of some scenes: Yasha-Dunyasha, battle over the cherry orchard, Trofimov's entrance, possibly with Grisha's body, and the final scene of the act. Space started to live and move because the action moved back and forth from the interior to the exterior, using the whole environment, both the room and the cherry orchard. All these changes or options were put into the graph of the project.

As with the analytical graph, the subsequent scenes, drawn on separate pages, then glued together, result in a long strip (or ribbon) of the production graph. Looking at it, we see that both the realistic/psychological and the symbolic/universal layers of action, discovered in the analysis, were preserved, are now more expressive, and transformed into practical means of expression.

Homework: prepare the graphical project of the play you are working on.

Directorial tool box

The directorial tool box can be compared with that which a specialist from the Bell Atlantic company takes to repair a telephone line broken by an uprooted tree during a storm, or that, which a paramedic takes from the ambulance, rushing to an accident victim lying on the highway's asphalt. The tool box of the repairman contains the necessary tools, materials, and basic spare parts necessary to make a repair. The box of the paramedic has medical instruments, drugs, or injections to allow him to offer first aid. The director must also have a tool box which—both before and during the rehearsals—allows him/her to work effectively, efficiently, and professionally. The directorial tools are lists of various kinds, a rehearsal schedule, and the graphical project of the show. I'm going to list them and then explain them point by point.

TABLE: DIRECTORIAL TOOL BOX

(1) Cast list
(2) List of spaces, venues, or places of action (including sketches)
(3) List of sets, including bigger furniture, objects, and appliances (including sketches)
(4) List of costumes (including sketches)
(5) List of most important props
(6) List of musical pieces and/or sound effects
(7) Lighting project
(8) List of special effects and other extraordinary requirements
(9) Detailed rehearsals schedule
(10) Graphical project of the production

---

(1) Cast list. The director does not copy the cast list from a printed text of the play, but meticulously works on it and comes with his/her own list. Why? Because the format and mode of listing by both authors and publisher rarely reflects the characters' importance and involvement in action. Instead, it is conditioned by various cultural, historical, and editorial customs, rules, or, simply, caprices. To explain this, let's consider a few examples.

Shakespeare (or rather his posthumous editors) usually puts at the top of his cast lists kings and princes, below them the nobility, still lower, town folks, later servants, and usually only at the very bottom of the list— women, even if they are queens or ladies; only rarely is this rule broken. In *Romeo and Juliet* (as published by the reliable Folger Shakespeare Library, 1971) we have on the top of the cast list the Chorus (which is fine, but of no consequence). The register of the characters continues with Escalus, Prince of Verona, followed by Paris, a young count, Montague and Capulet, the heads of two hostile families, an Old Man, kin to Capulet—only then do we arrive at Romeo, who is listed in sixth place. Tybalt is in ninth place. Juliet occupies the second to last position—number 25. But she is the most important character! On the directorial list, based on the characters' involvement with the main conflict, Juliet should occupy first place, Romeo, the second. Tybalt and Friar Lawrence should follow, and then the others. Prince Escalus should fall to the bottom of the register. In *The Three Sisters,* Chekhov puts Andrey Prozorov first on the character list, then his fiancée (and later wife) Natalia Ivanovna, and only after them the three sisters, Olga, Masha, and Irina. Yet the sisters play bigger, more complex, and more difficult roles, and they are more important to the action than their little brother and his narrow-minded and plain partner. In *The Good Woman of Setzuan* Brecht simply lists characters in order of their appearance on stage. (This mechanical and smilingly polite way of listing characters is used by many authors, publishers, and producers.) Yet, it is not Wang, or the three Gods that Brecht lists first, but Shen-Te, who is by far the most important character in the play; her role is decisive, she plays the lead, and she is the heroine. The same Brecht, in his *Mother Courage,* composes the list of characters more logically, putting Mother Courage and her three children first on the list, not, for instance, the two soldiers who begin the action. Różewicz provides a hierarchically composed list of characters in *The Funny Old Man,* while he does not list characters at all before the text of *The Trap.* We see that even the greatest playwrights approach the problem of listing characters in a variety of ways. Directors may, of course, prepare their character list as they like, though under the condition that it will serve their work. A logical, proper, and clear list of characters is one of the more significant tools, necessary to a director's own work and in communicating with producers, casting agents, collaborators, as well as with actors and public.

The directorial cast list must meet several conditions and have a variety of characteristics. First, the cast list is the director's own tool. Work on the development of the proper cast list forces the director to deepen the analysis of the characters, to better his/her understanding of the relationships between them and their place in the play's structure. A well-thought out and structured cast list also helps the director to work on the auditioning and casting. He/she clearly sees which characters are important and which are secondary. Relationships and ties between characters, as well as their groupings, are clearly established, which helps with both casting and rehearsing.

Second, the cast list is the director's means of communication with the producer, artistic director, casting agent, or sponsor. For example, it is the director who should provide a cast list to the casting agent (with the consent of a producer or artistic director, of course). Doing so, the director gives the agent his priorities and objectives in a hierarchical order and, at the same time, he/she directly communicates with the potential pool of actors by the way of ads. Preparing the cast list of *The Shoemakers* by Witkiewicz for the production in the Odyssey Theater in Los Angeles (1987), I put on top of the list the master shoemaker, Sajetan, and his major opponent, the persecutor Scurvy, followed by the "first lady" of the cast, The Princess. Only after these three leads, were the two shoemaker Apprentices listed. It differed from the author, who listed the three shoemakers first. The cast was advertised and then appeared in this order in the program.

Third, the cast list is a necessary tool for the director in working with co-creators of the show, in particular with the costume designer and prop master. The cast list sets priorities for them, establishes not only who gets what costume or personal prop, but also, for example, how many costume changes are needed.

Fourth, the cast list is a directorial message to the actors. It informs them about the hierarchy of the characters, about their relationships as well as their mode and way of involvement in the action. The cast list indicates the social, familial, or professional status of an individual character and groups characters in families, factions, parties, clans, and the like.

Fifth, the cast list sends a message to the audience. It is an important way of suggesting the directorial interpretation of the play and influencing the audience's perception of it. In the case of plays with larger casts it also helps the audience to follow the action, and to focus on the production values, first of all the acting, instead of trying to decipher who's who on stage.

Because of all these reasons the cast list as prepared by the director (not by anybody else) must be published in the program of the show. There are two principles in putting together the cast list: the cast list should enumerate characters according to their importance from the point of view of the main conflict and the action; and, the cast list should assemble characters according to their membership in certain groups. For example, in *The Cherry Orchard* the cast list should begin with Ranevskaya and Lopahin, because these two are the major opponents in the fight over the cherry orchard; they personify the most important conflict of the play. This is different from the order used by the author, who starts his cast list with Ranevskaya, but lists Lopahin in the fifth place. In the spectators' perception this order would obliterate the real importance of Lopahin's role in the story. The actor playing Lopahin, seeing his name somewhere in the middle of the cast, would also not get the unequivocal message that he is playing one of the two leads. Similarly, it is very important to assemble characters in certain groups in order to inform both the audience and the company who belongs to which of these teams and who fights with who on the play's turf.

In the Random House edition of *A Man for All Seasons* (1962), Robert Bolt lists characters in order of their appearance on stage, adding a few words about their age, clothes, and other characteristics. Omitting those additional notes, the author's cast list goes like this:

> The Common Man
> Sir Thomas More
> Richard Rich
> Duke of Norfolk
> Alice More
> Margaret More
> Cardinal Wolsey
> Thomas Cromwell
> Chapuys
> Chapuys' Attendant
> William Roper
> The King
> A Woman
> Cranmer

To publish the cast in this order in the program would be misleading and confusing the audience. It would not express at all that the main conflict of the play is between Thomas More and King Henry VIII. At the same time, the director would lose an excellent opportunity to include in the program important information steering the audience's attention. Therefore, the cast list I prepared and published in the program of The Kavinoky Theater in Buffalo (1996) for my production of *A Man for All Seasons* read as follows:

> The Common Man
> *The Protagonists:*
> > Sir Thomas More
> > King Henry VIII
> *More's Family:*
> > Alice More, More's wife
> > Margaret More, More's daughter
> > William Roper, More's son-in-law
> *State Officials:*
> > Thomas Cromwell, state secretary
> > The Duke of Norfolk, King's advisor
> > Richard Rich, career office holder
> *Church Leaders:*
> > Cardinal Wolsey
> > Cardinal Cranmer
> The Spanish Ambassador
> The Woman

Similarly, in the Folger edition of *Richard III* (1996), the characters of the play are listed in a rather chaotic manner. Richard, Duke of Gloucester, later King Richard III, is on top, but he is immediately followed by Lady Anne; she neither enters on stage just after Richard (it is Clarence and Brakenbury who join Richard), nor is the most important female character from the point of view of the dramatic conflict (it is rather Queen Margaret listed on the 11th position). King Edward IV is listed third, but Clarence is seventh and Buckingham twelfth, while both are certainly very important characters. Altogether, 54 characters are listed, including four children, in addition to ghosts, servants, citizens, bishops, soldiers, and many others. There are, probably, only a few theaters in the world which could cast all of these characters. If all were cast, the need would be even greater to list them in the program in a well-thought-out order. The same is true if a director wants to limit the cast—not only for financial reasons, but most importantly to tell the story clearly, not plunging the spectators into a swamp of too many players. The characters' list for *Richard III* may go like this:

The Kings:
   Richard, Duke of Gloucester, brother to Edward and George, later
      King Richard III
   King Edward IV, brother to Richard and George
   Earl of Richmond, Henry Tudor, later King Henry VII
The Queens:
   Queen Margaret, widow of King Henry VI
   Queen Elizabeth, wife of King Edward IV
   Lady Anne, later Queen Anne
The Princes, heirs to the throne:
   Prince Edward
   Richard, Duke of York
The Lords:
   George, Duke of Clarence, brother to Edward and Richard
   Duke of Buckingham
   Lord Stanley
   Lord Hastings
   Lord Mayor of London
   Bishop Ely
   Sir Ratcliffe
The Commoners, Soldiers, Citizens, Servants and others:
   First Man, Tyrrel
   Second Man, Murderer
   Third Man, Murderer
   Fourth Man, Page

The above was the cast list of *Richard III* developed by myself for a production in The Kavinoky Theater (1999). It reflected the editing of the text, combining roles, the mise-en-scène concepts, and it conveyed the structure of the action and the characters' relationships. Of course, there are exceptions to this rule of structuring the cast list. For example, if a production is a collective creation of the whole company, information about this should be included in the program and all members should be listed alphabetically.

Homework: put together a well-structured cast list of your play.

(2) List of spaces, venues, or places of action. This list should contain the spaces, venues, or locations necessary to perform the play according to the production project. First of all, we should indicate where we want to place our production: in a theater, in a parking lot, or in a basement. This list may contain, of course, only one venue, for example, a proscenium theater. In a brief note we should explain that we need a small theater (as for certain psychological plays) or a large one (for an opera). But it may happen that we plan to use several different venues for one production, and thus, we have to list all of them. Wilson in his *Prologue* (1970) moved the public around and inside the whole theater building. Peter Schumann used to play various parts of his productions/parades in many places at his Vermont farm or on tours all over the world. I, personally have directed many shows in which I used multiple venues, both inside and outside theater buildings, as I indicated in the first part of this book.

Homework: Prepare a list of spaces needed for your production.

(3) List of sets, including large furniture, objects, and appliances. This list reflects the necessities discovered in play analysis and imposed by the production project. Sets should be described on this list from the functional point of view, not their appearance or style, which should be left to the director's talks with the set designer. Notes about sets should specify entrances and exits, stairs and windows, and all of the significant set operations and movements you want to achieve during action (for example, using the trap). If action takes place in many different places, as in dramas by Shakespeare, Goethe, Słowacki, Claudel, Mayakovsky, Brecht, and so many other authors, all these places should be specifically described; again, discussion with the set designer will determine what they should look like. Furniture and objects, based on their function, should also be listed and explained. Certain appliances are necessary to stage specific scenes as imagined by the director. In my production of *Rhinoceros* by Ionesco (The Guthrie Theater, Minneapolis, 1986) I needed four computers for the Act 2 office scene. As a spectator, I saw productions in which scrambled eggs were made on stage, a *samovar* boiled and hot tea was served, and kerosene lamps were lit on stage—all these are examples of working appliances. The set designer, the technical director, and the stage manager should get a list of such appliances ahead of time.

Homework: Prepare the list of sets, furniture, and appliances for your production.

(4) List of costumes. In the past ages of theater history, costumes first of all helped a star shine: Helena Modjeska, playing Shakespeare's Cleopatra, had ten costumes. In contemporary theater, costumes must serve the actors, of course, but they belong to the directorial vision of production. Along with sets and movement, they heavily influence the visual style of the show. An examination of Shakespeare stagings in the 20th century proves this point. We have had it all: *Hamlet* in full dress—a proper costume for an upper class family criminal story; *King Lear* in furs, costumes fitting for a saga of bloody fighting within a barbaric tribe; *Richard III* in 1930s uniforms alluding to both Fascism and Nazism; *As You Like It* in suits and jeans, showing the clash between the urban world of business and the hippies hiding in the Forest of Arden. (All these are examples taken from actual productions.)

The costumes list should contain two sections: (1) General information—how the director sees costumes. For example: are they working gear or formal dresses? Are they for summer or winter? Are they contemporary or period? (2) A detailed list of all costumes with information about their changes, functions, and special uses, for example, whether they will be damaged on stage.

The costume list prepared by the director must be left open to creative discussions with the costume designer. To provide the reader with a specific example of how a costume list should be written, I will quote my own list prepared for *Antigone in New York* by Janusz Głowacki (1995.) Note: in my mise-en-scène there were more characters than in the original play.

TABLE: COSTUME LIST FOR *ANTIGONE IN NEW YORK*

(1) General information
A. Action takes place in winter, in the park (thus, open air), in New York. All characters dress for protection from the cold.
B. All costumes should be realistic. Costumes of homeless are weary and dirty, and, in contrast, costumes of passers-by are new and clean.
C. Police must have authentic gear (uniforms, weapons, flashlights, etc.)

(2) Detailed costume list

CHARACTER	BASIC COSTUME	ADDITIONAL COSTUME
Leads:		
Anita	As in the text—many layers: dress, sweater, two coats, hat, men's shoes, gloves with holes	Wedding dress
Sasha	As in the text—many layers: old suit, sweater, two coats, scarf, hat, gloves, winter shoes	Wedding suit, white shirt, tie, patent-leather shoes
Flea	All jeans: trousers, jacket, coat, hat, gloves; warm scarf	
Paulie:	Typical New York business man	
Police:		
Policewoman 1	Winter uniform and full patrol gear	
Policewoman 2	As above	
Policeman 1	As above	
Policeman 2	As above	

Homeless people:
First Man; Vietnam veteran—uniform
Second Man; Vietnam veteran—uniform
The Blind Violinist; he was a virtuoso—full dress, white shirt, white gloves, etc.
Pixie; she was a hat shop owner—hat, evening dress, fur coat, etc.
The Jamaican; he was a clown in circus—clown's costume and a blanket
The Indian; he was a construction worker—three flannel shirts, jeans, boots, etc.
The Howling Man; he was a clerk in an office—suit, coat, umbrella, etc.
Ordinary New Yorkers:
The Newcomer; a business woman
A Couple; upper class woman and man with a baby in the stroller
A Passer-by; a Wall Street broker
The Professor; old man on a bike—helmet, bike gear, backpack
Students; typical NYU students in mid 1990s
Gang of Three Girls; all dressed in black: leather jackets, mini skirts, boots, etc.

Homework: Prepare the costume list of your production based on the principles explained above.

(5) List of props. Working on the props is an important opportunity for the director to come up with new and creative ideas. In his production of *The Miser* by Molière (1921), the famous French actor and director, Charles Dullin, gave two servants of Harpagon big knives. Of course, there are no knives in Molière's play, but the director had this innovative and thrilling concept to arm the servants. Thanks to these knives they were not only simple servants, but also armed guards, and Harpagon's house was turned into a stronghold under siege. These servant/guards carried knives all the time, and had them ready as they opened the door to visitors. They did not slaughter anybody, they did not even disclose the knives to guests, but the spectators knew that they had them! The story of a paranoid miser, concerned only with his money and its defense, feeling threatened and attacked, came across very clearly. These two knives, which changed the meaning of the whole play, had to make their way from the director's imagination to the prop list. And it was the director (not the stage manager) who put them there.

Usually, a lot of props appear in a play. They are quite obvious and necessary to perform certain actions and functions, such as eating and drinking in a realistic production, fighting with swords in the final scene of *Hamlet,* or climbing a Himalayan mountain using mountain gear in Patrick Meyers' *K2.*

The list of props should be broken down into two parts: (1) Personal props, and (2) Stage props. The personal prop list should be prepared in the same way as the costume list, by character, while the stage props should be broken down according to the succession of the sets. It is typically the stage manager's work to put this list together, but it is not a waste of time for the director to do it first. I strongly encourage directors to work on the prop lists for their shows—it is not only a mechanical job but a creative one. Certainly, the stage manger should make his/her prop list and check it with the director's list. The stage manager's list should in turn be checked (and probably supplemented) by the director.

Homework: prepare the prop list for your production.

(6) List of musical pieces and/or sound effects. Music and sound is another field of directorial creation. It should be envisioned by the director but remain open to further discussions with the composer and sound person. They should be encouraged to work creatively. Yet, it is the director who puts the initial proposals on the table—within the context of the interpretation of the play, the style of the production, the mise-en-scène, and all the other means of expression envisioned. Outstanding composers, with whom I've had the privilege to collaborate, have taught me that I should come well-prepared for our first working session and explain all my expectations, needs, and proposals, both in general and in specific terms. Then, I should allow them to freely create on their own. But it was my duty to set the general direction, speak about scenes' moods and characters' feelings, as well as the functions and applications of music/sound to specific action twists, and to precisely list all points in the planned production where music/sound must be heard.

We found where music and/or sound appear during the analysis and we included these moments in the graphical project of the show. Now, we are ready to put all that stuff on a separate list and take it to a meeting with the composer or sound master. Such a list is also handy during the technical rehearsals.

The list of musical pieces and sound effects, prepared by director, should include: (1) General statement on the nature and character of music/sound in the production. (2) Specific list of all music/sound appearances.

The general statement about music/sound, for example, informs our collaborators that we need to have Gregorian Chant in *Murder in the Cathedral* by T. S. Eliot; that we will choose early 1920s jazz for our production based on the adaptation of F. Scott Fitzgerald's *Great Gatsby*; or that we want to use music instead of realistic sound effects in Williams' *The Rose Tattoo*—once I saw a production of this play in which all sound effects were beautifully rendered in music (The National Theater, Warsaw, 1960). Also, in the general statement we express our basic choices. For example, we note that we can use existing musical pieces, or that we must have music originally composed; we can have taped music, or we desire to introduce a live band on stage. This last question is especially sensitive if we are working on a musical. It should be discussed with both composer and producer—yet,the director must have an articulate opinion on the issue.

The specific list of music/sound effects should entail brief descriptions of all the pieces with reference to the stage event, including the page in the directorial book.

Homework: prepare the music/sound list for your production.

(7) Lighting project. On this territory we are already at home, after having done both the analysis and the production project. Now, it's time to put together a concrete lighting project, and—when the time comes—to share it with set and light designers, the technical director, and the master electrician. The light designer, working with the electrician, will come up with a lighting plot.

Note: We should be aware, that the field of work, position, and function of designers vary in different countries within Western culture. In Europe, one artist usually designs both sets and costumes, and cooperates with the director in designing lights. It is the exception when these functions are divided, when one person designs sets and the other costumes. Also, there's no light designer; the job is done by the director collaborating with the set designer and a master electrician. In the United States and Canada, the situation is different. Typically, there are three designers, for sets, costumes, and lights; major stage props are the concern of the set designer, while personal props are usually the costume designer's headache. In my directing career I have worked in both of these systems and I believe that the European approach better serves the artistic coherence of the show. The North American system requires the director to be an intermediary between the set, costume, and light designers—and himself/herself. Democratic equality, enviable in political and social life, does not work well in theater, which is created and driven not by voting or consensus, but by artistic vision. It's great if four artists (a director and three designers) push towards one direction, but if not, one of them must take command—and it should be the director.

The directorial lighting project contains two sections: (1) General style and convention of lighting. (2) Specific requirements, including special light effects.

The first is a consequence of the general production style. In an outdoor production we may, for example, choose to use only live fire, such as barrels with burning oil and torches. In an indoor show we decide whether we want to use traditional, colored and realistic lighting in an interior, as in a contemporary American living-room drama or, conversely, whether we want to have bright, white floodlights all over the stage, as in an orthodox Brechtian production. We may plan to use only strong spotlights following the characters' movements through darkness, or to have small, hand-operated instruments, focused on characters' faces—Andrei Serban had such lighting in his production of *Medea* at LaMama in 1974.

The second refers to specific lighting requirements. For example, we may want to have only footlights in some scenes, as would be the case in *Cabaret*. In *Rhinoceros* by Ionesco we want a strong light from the open trap in the scene when a rhino rages downstairs, while action is played upstairs in the office; the public should feel the animal's presence below the level of the stage. Another example of a special requirement may be the electric flashlights carried by the two detectives in *Suicide in B-flat* by Sam Shepard, the jukebox lights coming on and off in *The Time of Your Life* by William Saroyan, or, simply, the burning cigarette ends moving in complete darkness in the love scene between Masha and Viershynin in *Three Sisters* by Chekhov. Lightning during a storm is certainly a special light effect—we may need them in *King Lear* by Shakespeare, in *The Good Woman of Setzuan* by Brecht, or in *Kordian,* the Polish Romantic play by Juliusz Słowacki.

Homework: Put together the lighting project for your production. Discuss the general lighting concept and provide a list of specific light requirements.

(7) List of special effects and extraordinary requirements. Here, we are also already prepared. We take from the production project all the special effects—if there are any—and make a separate list of them. The special effects might be: fog, dust, running water or an operational gas stove on stage, a pool with water, a collapsing wall, or a breaking window, etc. Sometimes we need a car on stage, which is certainly a special requirement, and sometime a tank—yes! Let's consider these examples.

Fog? Oh, it is nowadays a popular (maybe overused) special effect and we see it in many productions from musicals to straight dramas.

Dust? The rhinoceros (in my favorite Ionesco play) raises clouds of dust every time it runs across the town. How, technically, to show this? We'll discuss this with the technical director. But we must have this special effect on our directorial special effects list.

Running water or operational gas stoves? Well, the restaurant kitchen in *The Kitchen* by Arnold Wesker must be equipped with them.

Pool with water? Of course, the adaptation of *The Grapes of Wrath* by Steinbeck requires such a facility on stage. It's fun to see actors jumping into a trap and splashing water on spectators in first rows.

A collapsing wall or a breaking window? In the Ionesco play, *Madness for Two,* the apartment of an old couple is subjected to gradual destruction caused by a war ranging in the city—there's shelling, bombing, and the maneuvering of tanks is heard. The glass in the windows breaks, the ceiling falls, the walls, one by one, collapse. In the production by The Contemporary Theater in Wrocław (1982,) directed by Jerzy Bielunas and designed by Ali Bunsch, this was executed with astonishing precision and frightening realism.

A car on stage? Why not! In the above mentioned *Grapes of Wrath* the old truck is all the time on stage—running, turning, and parking. In *Mr. Puntila and His Man, Matti* by Brecht, Matti is Puntila's driver and a luxurious car must be a part of the decor and playing area; as a matter of fact I saw one on stage in the Royal Shakespeare Company's Aldwych Theater in London in 1965.

A tank? Well, in *The Good Soldier Schweik in World War II* by Brecht there's a scene in which a huge tank rolls on stage; I saw It! I also remember a student at the Directing Department in Warsaw who proposed to play *The Trojan War Shall Not Take Place* by Giraudoux on and around a real tank. So, yes, we might need a tank to fulfill either author's requirements or our directorial fantasies. The question remains, whether, or how, they might be fulfilled?

Homework: make the list of special effects and requirements for your production.

(9) Detailed rehearsal schedule. The director must fully control the use of time during the entire work process. Within the parameters provided and agreed upon by the producer, the director should personally prepare the schedule of rehearsals. It should not be left to the stage manager, who, of course, should be involved in this work too. A precisely planned, and then strictly followed, rehearsal schedule provides actors (and everybody else) with the sense of security and respect for their work, prevents wasting time, and mobilizes progress. It guarantees that rehearsal time is used efficiently. The technical and administrative staff of a theater also needs to know the precise schedule of the rehearsals. From the very first rehearsal until the opening, everything should be strictly planned. Certainly, we have to have some windows open to unexpected needs or accidents, such as the illness of an actor or director. Diversion from the schedule should be a rare exception. The rule should be that the schedule is strictly followed.

There are four types of rehearsals and these are: table, blocking, technical, and general. All four segments must fit into the general time grid and lead to the opening. I will show how it works using the example of a play *X*. Let's assume, that it is a straight drama in two acts, with a cast of about twelve actors. Let's also suppose that we have six weeks rehearsal time, plus lighting rehearsals besides the regular schedule. Specifically, we would have five weeks of six work days (from Monday to Saturday) with four-hour rehearsals, one final week of five six-hour rehearsals (from Monday to Friday), and then the opening on Saturday. Within the time given, we have to have a few table rehearsals at the beginning, and technical and general rehearsals at the end. We are going to find immediately that it is a very tight schedule, as a matter of fact, too short. We have to be thoroughly prepared for the rehearsals and take advantage of every minute of every rehearsal to be able to prepare the show on time.

TABLE: REHEARSAL SCHEDULE OF PLAY "X"

DATE	WHAT (MATERIAL)	WHO (ACTORS)
WEEK # 1	TABLE REHEARSALS	
Tuesday	Directorial introduction & First reading	All
Wednesday	Analysis of the first part of the play	All
Thursday	Analysis of the second part of the play	All
Friday	Analysis of characters	All
Saturday	Analysis of characters, cont.	All
WEEK # 2	BLOCKING REHEARSALS	Characters in their scenes
	First part of the production	broken down by hours
WEEK # 3	BLOCKING REHEARSALS	As above
	Second part of the production	
WEEK # 4	BLOCKING REHEARSALS	As above
Tuesday	First part, first half	
Wednesday	First part, second half	
Thursday	First part, walk through, notes	
Friday	Second part, first half	
Saturday	Second part, second half	
WEEK # 5	BLOCKING REHEARSALS	As above
Tuesday	Second part, walk through, notes	
Wednesday	First part, run through, notes	
Thursday	Second part, run through, notes	
Friday	Entire play, run through, notes	All, SETS
Saturday	Entire play, run through, notes	All, SETS & COSTUMES
Saturday night	Lights	SETS
WEEK # 6	FINAL REHEARSALS	
Monday morning	Lights	(No actors)
Monday night	Dry tech	(No actors)
Tuesday	Tech with actors	ALL, EVERYTHING
Wednesday	First general, notes	As above
Thursday	Second general, notes	As above
Friday	Third general (preview), notes	As above
Saturday	OPENING	

The director must be unequivocally, unexceptionably, and absolutely punctual—always on time and always ready. Setting such an example he/she may expect and require the same from others, and, indeed, he/she must strictly enforce absolute punctuality. Punctuality is a matter of practical necessity and of work ethic. It is also the foundation for the artistic discipline of the production which can only be achieved if the rehearsals are based on work discipline.

Homework: prepare the rehearsal schedule for your production—based upon the above format.

(10) **Graphical project of the production**. We have it. It is the graph in the form of a colored ribbon which we've already made. Now, we have to place it in our directorial tool box. We're going to use it frequently. It is the last item which we need to have in our tool box—we have to take it to meetings with designers and all other collaborators before the rehearsals, and then, to actual rehearsals with actors. The directorial tools should not be confused with those which the stage manager needs. They may overlap or be similar, but there is a fundamental difference: all the tools described and explained here are a part and result of the directorial creation.

Written directorial production project

The written project of production is based on all of the directorial preparations up to this point, summarized in a written form. It is founded on the play analysis and on all directorial creative and artistic decisions, in terms of interpretation, style, space, and cast; it encompasses the practical aspects of the planned show, such as money and time, needed for materializing our proposals. The written directorial production project must be concise, brief, essential, and clear. We write it for two purposes: first, to force ourselves to finally translate dreams into practice; and, second, to develop a means of communication with producers, sponsors, and the media. It will also be shared with all collaborators and actors. While the directorial tool box serves for internal communication, the written project is oriented for external use. I have to underline that the written production project is not an essay or paper. It should not be a display of the director's erudition, the profundity of his wisdom, or the exuberance of his/her imagination. Nothing like that. It should be a simple note. Think of it as a memo. It should be no more than two or three pages long and divided into short paragraphs. If we have something to reveal to the world, we are going to do it practically through our production, not by writing about it. All our ideas and concepts should be, of course, in the background of the written project, but center stage must be devoted to the plain and simple presentation of what we want to do and how we plan to achieve our goals. We shouldn't be afraid to be laconic in writing it.

TABLE: DIRECTORIAL WRITTEN PRODUCTION PROJECT
Contents:

(1) General information:
> Title of the play
> Author
> Director
> Designer (Designers)
> Composer
> Choreographer and/or other collaborators
> Cast
> Space
> Time

(2) Note on the play and the author
(3) Justification of the choice of the play from the artistic, ethical, philosophical, social, political, and educational point of view
(4) Style of the proposed production
(5) Sets
(6) Costumes
(7) Major props, furniture, objects
(8) Music/sound effects
(9) Lighting
(10) Special effects and/or requirements

I'm going to fill in the above, using as an example a written directorial project prepared by myself for the *Dummies' Ball* by Bruno Jasieński.

(1) General information:
> Title of the play: *Dummies' Ball*
> Author: Bruno Jasieński
> Director: [Name, address, phone, fax, e-mail]
> Designers/Designers: [As above]
> Composer: [As above]
> Choreographer and/or other collaborators: A movement specialist is needed to

work on the dummies' characters.

Cast: 33 actors, 19 males and 14 females; 15 actors play dummies (7 males and 8 females) and 16 actors play humans. The actors playing dummies must all be young, while some of the human roles are for middle-aged people.

Space: Two theaters: a proscenium and a black box.

Time: Rehearsals should have workshop format and last at least eight weeks.

(2) Note on the play and the author:

Play: *Dummies' Ball* is a play about the clash of two worlds and two cultures: the mannequins and the humans. The mannequins are cruel, stupid, and narrow minded, they have neither ideals nor morality; they are not able to love and they behave stereotypically. The mannequins envy humans and treat them as oppressors, while trying to imitate them. Humans treat mannequins as objects, debase and offend them. Humans are (from the mannequins' point of view) very stupid: they don't understand that mannequins have their own lives too. In the course of the action it turns out that the humans are no better than the dummies. The play ironically and bitterly warns the human race not to turn into "dumb dummies" (a quote from the play). Through *catharsis,* the play offers the hope of a better future for humanity. The action takes place in Paris in the 1930s. There are two groups of characters: dummies from fashion magazines and wealthy industrialists.

Author: Bruno Jasieński (1901-1938) wrote his play in the early 1930s. He was a Pole, temporarily living in France, and then in the Soviet Union. At first, a Futurist poet, he also wrote novels and plays, and was a journalist. Connected with the international communist movement, he settled in Moscow and got a post as editor of a literary magazine. Soon after, during the Stalinist purges, he was accused of spying, arrested, tried, sentenced to death, and shot in prison. His works were published in Poland and France before the war, as well as in the Soviet Union until his death. Later, he was completely banned in the Soviet Union and in communist-ruled Poland until 1957, when he was rehabilitated and *Dummies' Ball* was produced for the first time in Katowice, Poland.

(3) Justification of the choice of the play from the artistic, philosophical, moral, social, political, and educational point of view:

Dummies' Ball is a grotesque play—it is a challenge to any young acting company or acting students, because it requires physically oriented acting, based on movement; it is useful material for training actors. *Dummies' Ball* is also a wise play. It contains an intelligent, ironic and ever valid critique of a society ruled and manipulated by narrowly minded bureaucrats, cynical politicians, greedy industrialists, amoral elites, and confused masses. The play suggests that technologies, robots, automats, and all of civilization's tools and toys are gradually controlling and enslaving living human beings. It is worthwhile to think about these problems and to recognize those threats.

(4) Style of the proposed production:

Dummies' Ball was written as a non-realistic, grotesque play. The playwright's concept should be reflected in the mise-en-scène and acting. Actors playing mannequins should develop means of playing lifeless mechanisms. Actors playing humans should expose the mechanical emptiness of their behaviors and deeds. The performance's space should be based on the conventions of the proscenium and then the environment. In the first part of the play, the action takes place at a fashion magazine with the playing in a central meeting spot of several aisles and rows of shelves and mannequin stands. The observation area should be in front of the playing area and spectators should be treated as voyeurs secretly observing the dummies' annual ball. The second act takes place in the mansion of a wealthy auto maker. The main playing area should be situated in a hallway/entrance to the mansion, with a car of the period displayed in the center, and several doors leading to the adjacent rooms, including a bar and dance floor.

(5) Sets:

Two sets are needed, one in each of the two venues. All elements should be from 1930s France. The first set should include necessary equipment to the fashion magazine with displays, cashiers desks, shelves, stands, dummies, etc. The second set, the interior of a mansion, should contain furniture, pictures, carpets, a bar, and a dance floor.

(6) Costumes:

Like the sets, the costumes should be of the 1930s. The dummies should get a variety of clothes, as representing different departments of the magazine: formal, casual, sport, beach, ski, etc. Guests and servants in the second part are attending an elegant upper class party—all are dressed appropriately. A separate problem is how to clothe the two workers' union dignitaries coming to see their leader during the party. They are well dressed but with a flair of bad taste.

(7) Major props, furniture, objects:

[We list major elements which decide the style of the show and fulfill its most important functions. In this point we repeat what was already stated, but for the production process and technical work purposes this must be a separate list.]
(A) Dummies and their parts in the fashion magazine. (B) An antique car of the 1930s.

(8) Music/sound effects:

Dance music of 1930s. (A) In the first part: American jazz with sharp, wild rhythms—charleston, foxtrot, etc. (B) In the second part: European music, slower and smoother—tango, waltz, etc.

(9) Lighting:

In both sets operational light fixtures are needed. In the second part we need two strong electric flashlights.

(10) Special effects and requirements:

There is a special technical problem. At the end of the first part the dummies cut off the head of a man who accidentally entered their ball. The head is cut off and the dummies play with it like with a basketball. One of them takes off his head and puts on the human's. Then, carrying his head under his shoulder, he leaves, followed by the man without a head. In the second part the same dummy, with the human head on his neck and carrying his dummy head, appears at the humans' party. The man without a head breaks into the party and reclaims his head from the dummy's neck, while the dummy returns his own head. The problem is how to cut off the head of one of the actors, and how to twice exchange heads on actors' necks?

Homework: write the project of your own production—following the above format.

Preparation of the "Directorial Book"

We've been working on "the book" for weeks, months, or even years. We started with the first readings and analyses. We ended with putting together the written production project. Now, the text of the play must be once more reviewed and all the cuts or changes clearly inserted. It is useful to draw horizontal lines in the script, dividing particular scenes, as they were identified in the analysis and then introduced to the graphical production project. In the project, on the other hand, we write down pages of the script on top of each scene. This helps to travel back and forth easily from the script to the project and vice versa.

If the directorial book significantly differs from the author's original version, I'd suggest printing the text again—with changes and without lines which were cut. We are going to use precisely this one—not a full original or any other version of it. This new, final, clean version should be copied for all: for co-creators, producers, technicians, and, of course, for actors. We might, later on, recommend that the actors go back to the whole, unabridged and unedited version of a classical play for enrichment, as well as suggest to them specific readings about the play. However, the book prepared by the director must be the final stage version. It is a work tool. It should be definitive and clean.

Homework: prepare your clean and final book.

Director's preparation for work with designers, composers, and producers; preparations for rehearsals with actors

Paradoxically, this is the shorter volume of our preparatory work, with one exception, which I'm going to explain in a moment. It is short, because we are already prepared to work with all our collaborators. All we have to do is put our notes and tools in order, and select what we need to take to a meeting with a designer, composer, choreographer, or anybody else. Preparation for the work with actors is also done. One more directorial assignment is to prepare the directorial opening statement for the beginning of the first rehearsal—an extremely important task which steers the course of the whole further work. It is one of the preparatory tasks, so we have to work on it now. But it belongs to the rehearsals, so I shall discuss contents and structure of this statement later—in the chapter on the actual work on the production.

Homework: write the opening directorial statement based on the format provided above.

CHAPTER 3. IMPLEMENTATION OF DIRECTORIAL PROJECT
BEFORE REHEARSALS

Collaboration of the director with the co-creators of the production

After having completed his/her own preparatory work, the director will possess a rich store of plans, projects, and ideas about the production. Now, the time has come to share them with others. First, with different artists with whom the director is going artistically to forge the show. Second, with producers, administrators, and technicians who will materialize it. Third, with actors, who are going to play in the show and interact with the audiences.

In many shows, it is the designer who is the most important co-creator of the performance. In others, it is the composer or choreographer. Sometime we need a special help of a fencing master, as in several of Shakespeare's plays, a wrestling coach in *As You Like It*, or a boxing coach in *Golden Boy* by Clifford Odets.

Cooperation with designers, as well as with all other artists and specialists involved with the production, is an extremely important and equally difficult area of directorial work. The ideal seems to be harmony and balance between the director's artistic sovereignty and control over the entire production, on the one hand, and the creativity and independence of the other artists, on the other. We could jokingly say that the director "knows best" regarding everything about the totality of the production, while the designers or composers "know best" within the area of their expertise. The most artistically beneficial relationship is one of mutual inspiration, respect, and the utmost giving of everyone's individual energy, while submitting one's own ambition to the common goal.

Certainly, the work of director with the various co-creators will differ and each relationship has its own nuances. But there are certain general practices, rules of conduct, and work techniques which help the director to communicate and collaborate with all these artists. The director's work with co-creators follows specific stages. We'll discuss them one at a time.

TABLE: STAGES OF THE DIRECTOR'S WORK WITH CO-CREATORS OF THE SHOW

(1) Identifying co-creators and establishing contact
(2) Opening the horizons
(3) Meeting midway
(4) Mooring in the harbor
(5) Nurturing the production process

---

(1) Identifying co-creators and establishing contact. This is an initial stage. Before meeting the potential co-creator, the director has already been working on a production project for weeks, months, or years. He/she knows a lot about the play (or any other material) which he/she wants to put on. The analysis has been done a long time ago. The production project has been drawn and written. The director sees the production in terms of style and means of expression. He/she has a clear sense of where to go. At the same time, there are still some hazy spots and uncharted territories on the map of the future production, especially in the areas of visuality and music. The director has his/her concepts and inklings about how to solve these problems. He/she may plan to personally design the show or compose music—this happens, and it is probably the best option. But if the director needs to have a designer and/or composer on board, he/she needs them not merely as crew members, but as creative artists, who would enrich the production with their mastery and imagination, and as skillful professionals, help to transform vague concepts into artistic facts.

Thus, having set the general direction of the journey, the director looks for people who would like to go with him/her. They may be found in many different ways. A director's invitation to a co-creator may be grounded in an old friendship and previous, common works. Someone may recommend a designer or composer to the director. The director may have personally heard of the other artists' accomplishments and want to work with them, perhaps, to learn from them. In any case, the director and his/her potential partner meet and deliberate whether they are destined to work together. They try to find out if they share an interest in a given play or topic and whether they feel that they can and should set out in the same boat.

It is crucial that during this first meeting the director does not throw all his/her knowledge, ideas, and plans pertaining to the play onto the potential partners. The director should rather speak about general plans, possible interpretation, and the style sought. All that should be open and not definitive. Next, the director asks his/her partner to read the play. Nothing more. The point is that the designer or composer should get general guidelines about how to read the play and what to look for in it, within the larger context of directorial interpretation and the proposed mise-en-scène. At the same time, they should be asked to read the play independently, unimpeded by the director's interpretations, testing their own authentic reactions to the play and to the director's general plans.

Their task is to decide whether or not they want to join the director. It's as simple as that. To join— means to support, to help the director in his/her work, and to contribute to it with full energy. It must be absolutely clear that they are joining the director in his/her interpretation and vision of the play. Neither their own, nor anybody else's, as for example, the producer's. After all, in the case of, let's say, a classical play there are thousands of possible choices in terms of interpretation, style, or approach, and it is obvious that the designer or composer does not start working on the production from scratch, but rather, enters on the track already laid down by the director.

After the designer's or composer's reading of the play, and their own preparatory work, they will be able to formulate their reactions and decisions. First, they should ask themselves whether they reacted to the play at all. Does this play interest them? Is it important for them? Is it alive? Are they willing and eager to work on it? Second, is the director's interpretation acceptable to them? Is the director's project convincing? Or, does it look completely strange? If the play does not interest the designer or composer, or the proposed directorial interpretation does not convince them, they should—kindly—quit. This should be mutually explained and respectfully accepted. In this case the director would continue his/her search for another collaborator. But if there's a spark, and the two artists find that they are in tune with one another—they can immediately start working together. They move to the next stage.

(2) **Opening the horizons**. The designer, composer, or choreographer are artists. The director must respect them as such and allow them to create. The more creatively they work, the more fruitful their contribution to the production is. They should be encouraged and heartened, not frightened and limited. During the first work session, when it is already decided that they are on board, the director should still refrain from introducing them to all the details of his projects. Rather, he/she should talk about the meaning of the play, about the style of the production, and about the type of interaction expected between actors and the public. Next, the director should put several questions to the collaborator, not expecting immediate answers, and describe many possible options, not asking for an on the spot choice. All the pertinent artistic problems should be listed and explained—and left to the collaborator to solve. Of course, all questions, options, and problems are based on the interpretation already established by the director. But they should be left open to the creative response of the collaborator. It is as if the director now sends the collaborator on a solitary journey, providing him/her with food and equipment, and showing the direction—but leaving them alone to walk towards the wide open horizon. The collaborator goes off to work alone.

We have to set a date for the next meeting—a week, a month, or tomorrow (this may also happen.) Naturally, there should be a way to communicate in the meantime. The point is, that the collaborator needs and must have some time for himself/herself.

The first work session should be delicate in mood, general in dealing with material, and full of expectations and encouragement, yet, without decisions, particulars, and results. It should be like the meeting of the Little Prince with the Fox in Antoine Saint-Exupéry's novel: the fox should not be scared, we have to tame it delicately, we must allow the fox to remain the fox.

(3) Meeting midway. The second work session is radically different from the first one. It should be concrete, leading to decisions, and aiming for results. Solutions should be selected, ideas materialized, and expectations turned into firm objectives. Going into this session, the director should take all his notes, graphs, and the directorial tool box. The set designer should have initial plans or a model. The costume designer—initial drawings or examples of cloth taken from fine art history books or contemporary fashion magazines. The composer—the notes of some melodies or discs with proposed pieces. All this should be material allowing and supporting concrete discussions, negotiations, perhaps even quarrels, which also happen, and can be healthy, if constructive. But every discussion must lead to a solution, negotiations must end in signing a treaty, and quarrels should be peacefully resolved.

We have to be sure (if in artistic creation we can be sure of anything) that a given spatial or musical decision will support the interpretation of the play and the directorial project of the show, and, at the same time, be technically feasible and financially possible. For example: do we have a trap for Ophelia's grave? Do we have the money to record music with a big orchestra?. As a result of this work session, the collaborator must be absolutely clear on what to do next, what sets to draw, what costumes to render, what music to compose. At the end of the meeting, we have to make commitments, open our calendars, and set dates for when the final projects, notes, or tapes are going to be ready.

(4) Mooring in the harbor. The third work session is the mooring in the harbor. It is the arrival, the home run, the summary. The designer shows projects and models, the composer sits at the piano and plays melodies or clicks the button on the disc player. If small corrections are still needed, they should be specifically talked over and decided upon. If so, another brief meeting must be set. If not, the projects go to the shops, the purchases are initiated, and the recording studio rented.

(5) Nurturing the production process. It is the designers who supervise the making of the sets, furniture, props, and costumes. It is the composer who oversees the recording, sometimes personally conducting the orchestra. It is the choreographer who gets his/her rehearsals scheduled, and works with the actors or dancers. Every one of these artists works independently and is fully responsible for his/her work sector. But experience teaches, and it is recommended, indeed, imperative, that the director should personally accompany the designer in handing the projects over to the shops, stops by at the beginning of the recording session, and sit in from time to time at the dance rehearsals. Such involvement has multiple benefits. First, it stresses that the production is a group effort: all its elements are equally important, and all working on it are equally dear. Second, it shows all those involved with the preparation of the show that the director has approved all the projects, and that he/she fully supports the designer, composer, or choreographer in their work areas. Third, it indicates that nothing being done is a separate element, but everything belongs to the unified structure, and has an important place in the complex mechanism we are all laboring to set in motion.

Class work: let's work in the format of a psychodrama. We select "directors," "set designers," "costume designers," "composers," and "choreographers" out of the student body. We give them some time to prepare themselves for work in these roles on *The Cherry Orchard*, a play they know well from previous classes. Then the "directors" sit with other co-creators in pairs and talk over *The Cherry Orchard*, as if it was their first, second, and third work meeting.

Homework: the director prepares himself/herself to work with co-creators on his/her play and then, in class, explains how he/she will be sharing their plans with co-creators. At this stage, members of our class/workshop should try to find designers and composers and start working with them on their plays.

Collaboration of the director with a literary adviser

A literary adviser, a literary manager, or a dramaturg is always a part of the artistic team preparing a production in Europe. In the United States this specialist is slowly finding his way into professional and academic theater structures. This person works for the good of the entire production and improves its literary quality; helps artistic directors in selecting plays; helps directors in studying a play's context and doing work on the text (for example, finding the best translation of a foreign play); and helps actors to enlarge their knowledge of the epoch, style, and cultural conditions of their roles. So, collaboration with the literary adviser may be beneficial for the whole team. It's worthwhile to listen to people wiser then us.

Specifically, there are two aspects to the director's cooperation with a literary adviser. First, they can be the director's partners, persons in whom the director can confide his/her findings and plans, asking for critical evaluation, advice and opinion. The literary advice gives the director an opportunity to talk over every aspect of the show, and get feedback, criticism, or flat opposition, which can also be very helpful. Discussion with a literary whiz helps a director to remain in a state of intellectual and artistic alertness during the entire process of work on a play. The literary adviser can be an excellent sparring partner for the director, like those in tennis or boxing. Second, collaborating with a literary adviser, the director works on the content and editorial structure of the production program, poster, press releases, and advertisements. All of them should be the primary concern of the literary adviser, but the director should—as in all other aspects of the production—creatively control them, and specifically approve (or disapprove) the literary adviser's work.

Working with the literary adviser, the director should proceed as with other co-creators: first, to introduce this person to the general project of the production, instigating the partner's activity and creativity; second, to discuss the tasks the adviser will undertake to achieve the goals of the production.

Class work: as with the designers and others, let's work with the literary manager using the psychodrama format. Students should be cast as "directors" and as "literary advisers." They should talk over the literary aspects of *The Cherry Orchard* and come up with specific assignments and questions for the literary adviser.

Homework: directors prepare their lists of topics pertaining to their plays to discuss with the literary person. Again, as with the stage designers and others, it would be good if directing students could establish real cooperation with a literary adviser and work together with him/her on their plays.

Collaboration of the director with the producer or producing institution

In the areas of the budget, administration, scheduling, casting, work space, and the like, the director collaborates with the producer, the artistic and/or managing director of a theater, the chair of a university department and/or its technical director, or a representative of any other producing or sponsoring institution or organization. These people are also co-creators of the show. Working with them, the director should introduce them to all his/her artistic plans, and give them a detailed explanation of his/her motives and objectives. We have to do everything possible to make the producers our partners, to convince them to treat our projects as their own projects, and our objectives as their own objectives. Only then will they fully support our work on the production, and invest as much creative energy and devotion in it as we do. Of course, the producers' priorities may be different from the director's, for they are responsible and interested first of all in the organizational and economic aspects of a project. But they understand better then others that the artistic success of the show, and therefore the success of the director's vision and the actors' performances, are the guarantors of its financial success.

Class work: again, a psychodrama. A "director" and a "producer" sit in front of each other and the "director" presents to the "producer" his/her proposal. The "producer" questions the "director" and evaluates the project. They negotiate.

Homework: write a formal and complete letter to the producer proposing your play. Use as the format, the written production project adding, naturally, the proper salutation and closing for a business letter.

Collaboration of the director with the technical director, stage manger, shop heads, stage hands, and other technical and administrative staff

Theater is a collaborative art. I remind students of that on every occasion.

Here's another example: we have to be fully aware that the technical people (in some schools they are nicely called "techies"), as well as administrators, are as important for the preparation of the show as anybody else, and that they too play a crucial role in shaping its artistic expression. There are usually many of them: technical directors, stage managers, administrators, heads of shops, masters of various skills, set, costume, and prop people, light and set operators, box office employees, house managers, and ushers. All of these people contribute to the building of this complex and magnificent edifice which is the production. They either make things which are seen by the public, such as sets or props, or those unseen, such as the work of changing sets behind the closed curtain. Some of them personally interact with the public, contributing to the spiritual dimension of it, building the work atmosphere during the rehearsals, and the aura surrounding every evening show. We have to be aware how much they can help and how uplifting their work can be. We both have to help them and teach them to positively endow the show. We have to be equally aware that they can easily damage the show, for example, by not properly installing a hinge on a door which could jam during stage action, by delaying a light cue, or by not treating the spectators in the house politely. So, we, the directors, have to treat all these people with respect and kindness, acknowledge their hard work, stress their importance for the artistic result, help them to do their best, and praise their efforts. Personal interaction of the director with all these people should be a daily routine.

On a day-to-day basis, the stage manager is the director's closest collaborator. The director should allot plenty of time for discussing and explaining the project to the stage manger and then consult with him/her about the multitude of practical problems which continually arise.

Class work: at this stage of our work, it is advisable to organize a visit to a good, well equipped professional theater during which the technical director of that theater will guide the students through all the shops, offices, and facilities. If we are working at a university or college, a similar guided visit is a must.

Homework: write an account of the visit to the shops and offices and briefly describe the assignments of all the people you met and observed.

Auditioning and casting

Casting is the work of thought, imagination, empathy, auditioning technique, and diplomacy. It is one of the most important directorial tasks and prerogatives. As a task, it should be systematically prepared and professionally executed. As a prerogative, it should never be relinquished, for it is an artistic, creative work and it decisively influences the artistic result of the show. We can't allow ourselves, or anyone else, to transform this—I wouldn't hesitate to say sacred—directorial enterprise into an administrative and mechanical distribution of roles or into barter for personal favors. The cast conditions the success or failure of the show. A cast adequate and supportive to our project will enormously facilitate the rehearsals, while casting haphazardly and inappropriately might turn the whole work into a nightmare.

Casting is the last decisive step in transforming a volatile dream about a production into solid matter. It's giving body—real human body—to what we have been only thinking and imagining. Casting, as all other directorial preparatory steps, is first of all the director's own responsibility, but, at the same time, it should be open to the advice and opinion of others—artistic directors, producers, literary advisers, professional colleagues. If we work within a permanent company, our own ensemble, or a set group of people we should include them in our casting struggles. They should understand that it is the director who makes final cast decisions, but they should be also encouraged to share with the director their aspirations. It is a difficult ideal, but in working on a cast, the director should be faithful to his/her project and, at the same time open and flexible to other's input.

Work on the production project has included, among other elements, a cast concept derived from the interpretation of the play. For example: we may decide to cast actors in accordance with the characters' features as they appear in the play, which is, probably, the most common case. Consequently, we will try to cast actors compatible with the characters in terms of race, gender, age, appearance, and general psycho-physical portrait. On the other hand, we may choose to have an interracial cast, or to decide that male roles should be played by women, or vice versa. There have been productions in which women played Hamlet, Lear, or the Hunger Artist in Różewicz's play. There have also been contemporary shows based on the Elizabethan tradition in which Rosalind, Viola, and Olivia were played by young men. In contrast, I once saw a production of *Twelfth Night* played only by women. We may decide that the best cast for a production would be composed exclusively of young actors. We may conclude that we have to have a star in the cast, and, therefore, we will build the rest of the cast around this star. Or we feel that have to have an entire star cast—which might be pure fantasy or prove to be an absolute condition.

The cast list sitting in our directorial tool box is the basic tool in our work on the cast. It identifies the characters, groups them, and shows their hierarchy and interdependence. The way we make casting decisions depends on the situation and circumstances: we may have a permanent company and distribute roles within it, we may have a core ensemble to use and look for additional actors, we may have a group of graduate students who should be cast in a university production, we may have a completely free hand and cast based on auditions.

Auditions might either be wide open, or specifically oriented towards the search for a lead or any other particular role. There's a whole market of professional literature about auditions and auditioning, and many libraries contain textbooks, audition pieces, and audition forms. It is worthwhile to study them, and I recommend it to the reader of this book. Most of these materials are addressed to actors. I would like to share some advice with directors.

(1) The rules and parameters of the auditions must be absolutely clear and specifically announced. To organize auditions is usually not the business of the director, but the director must discuss the audition rules with the organizer (casting agent, artistic director, chair of the department, or others). These rules should include an announcement of the list of the roles sought, indicate what the actor should prepare for the audition (monologue, prose, verse, song, etc.), the time allowed for addition, the time-table for call backs, and any other relevant information.

(2) The auditions are an interhuman interaction. Not an impersonal exam, not an objective test, not a cold-blooded evaluation. No, the auditions are an exchange of human energies, feelings, and hopes. The more you give, the more you get. The director conducting auditions must be warm, open, encouraging, helpful, and supportive. It is his/her first chance, and a very important one, to meet people, to get to know them, to include them in the group effort of creating a production. Always be courteous and kind during auditions! Break the ice at the beginning of the audition by exchanging a few words with the actors. Thank them sincerely when they have finished. Be yourself and allow them to show who they really are.

(3) The director should be active during auditions. Of course, we have to allow actors to deliver whatever they have prepared, if it is within the scope and limits of the established parameters. But to get to better know the actor, the director should ask for something additional, for example another interpretation of the same monologue. The director should also test the way the actor takes directions—an indicator of future, smooth rehearsals.

(4) Auditions should be focused on acting. Yes, on acting—not on reading! "Could you read this for me?" is a director's line frequently heard at auditions. All right, you may like to hear how someone reads, but it is not the same as acting. Usually, actors reading "impromptu" give a horrible interpretation which is totally misleading and does not present their true skills and abilities. If you have already heard from the first part of the audition that this actor can speak properly, you shouldn't ask him/her to speak more, that is to read; rather, you should investigate his/her acting. Have the actor do something, to express emotion through an activity without words, to integrate speech with movement, or to speak and perform a physical action at the same time; and so on, and so forth.

After the auditions, the director does his/her homework. Don't skimp on the time for it. Allow yourself several options for casting certain roles and prioritize actors who can play them. It might happen that an actor you had first on the list becomes unavailable. Have an alternate on your cast list. Try to cast after one round of auditions. Don't overuse the call-backs. If you call back too many actors, you are showing your indecisiveness and wasting their time. If you feel that you must have call-backs, limit them to the fewest possible number of actors. If you call back actors to choose for one role, ask them to perform the same scene, or improvise on the same topic. This will allow you to compare them clearly.

Once publicly announced, the cast list should be treated as written in stone. It should be your directorial trademark and a facet of your reputation in the theater circles: you are a director who works hard on the cast, who carefully and attentively auditions, who treats casting very seriously, who keeps his/her word, and who stands behind his/her actors. People will trust you, love to work with you, and give your their best at the rehearsals.

Class work: select a "director" in your group, cast other students as "actors," and ask the "director" to audition "actors" for *The Cherry Orchard*.

Homework: come up with an ideal cast for the play you are working on. It may be composed of the best actors in the world. All the stars are available for you and you have all the money in the world to pay them. It is a good and useful exercise: it allows the director to explain how he/she sees characters in his/her play and it teaches us to aim for the stars—literally and metaphorically.

CHAPTER 4. CREATIVE REHEARSALS

Introduction

In this chapter I am going to discuss the process of rehearsals. This is *the* most important and decisive segment of the whole work of directing. It leads to victory or defeat, to satisfaction or emptiness, and to happiness or despair. Rehearsals are work with people. We, directors, do not express ourselves personally and directly in the theater. We speak through actors. It is one of the directing mysteries: the more expressively and freely the actors perform—the more the directorial energy and vision comes across to spectators. Rehearsals are based on a paradox of freedom: the director must create as freely as possible and, at the same time, allow actors the utmost creative freedom. Rehearsals have human and ethical, as well as artistic and professional dimensions. The major directorial problem during rehearsals is to combine interaction with people, as they are, and work with artists, as they should become. The rehearsals transform actors into characters expressing artistic structures and values. Here's another mystery of theater: the deeper the actors enter into their characters, the brighter their own humanity shines.

There are many directorial techniques and methods of rehearsing. You can find many of them in different books on directing and learn them in directing classes and workshops all over the world. Many of them are useful and helpful, while some of them remind me of prescriptions and medical aids rather then creative inspirations. I recommend those which are open, flexible, and adaptable. I would be careful with those which are closed, rigid, and one-sided. I will introduce you to a few of my own directorial techniques, but only as an inspiration, suggestion, and demonstration of colors on a directorial palette; there are so many different ways to direct. I share with you some of my very firm convictions, and some counsel which you may use as you wish. You can take them from me, but then, you have to continue on you own, independent way. Rehearsing, we employ certain techniques and methods, but it is attitudes, values, and ideals which are most important and should always guide us.

First rehearsal—general remarks

When all preparations are done—after the director's own work, a period of collaboration with co-creators, sending projects to the shops, and casting—comes the big moment of the first rehearsal. I wish I had enough persuasive power and adequate vocabulary to convince the user/reader of this book how important the first rehearsal is. Perhaps, I don't need to persuade you of that at all, because you already know that the first rehearsal is crucial. You know that, don't you?

The first rehearsal is the beginning of transfiguration: thoughts, ideas, and images seen in imagination or on paper in the form of the director's projects, the designer's drawings, the sounds heard in boundless ether or played by the composer on a keyboard, and emotions having only a vague shape of presentiments—all of these start to transform into the life of living people, their deeds, their words, their actions. It is a moment of joy and hope, and it is the beginning of tussle and frustration. Rehearsals are going to be as painful as the labor of birth, but there will be the joy of new life coming at the end.

The first rehearsal sets all these processes in motion. It is like a spacecraft lifting off. The production project, loaded with directorial concepts and plans, tanked with intellectual and emotional fuel, packed with the creative energy of the director, designer, composer, and all the people which have already been working on the show, with actor-astronauts in their seats, is ready to be launched. It has to overcome the gravity of earth and human laziness, it must free itself from our will's weakness, imagination's limitations, and fear's hindrances. Ignition! How terribly slow—at first—the spacecraft lifts off. How hard it is to believe that it will ever fly. But it does! In a few seconds it acquires a tremendous speed and pierces the sky. So should we lift off our production. We have to aim for the sky of theater truth, theater hope, theater beauty, and theater love. We'll fly.

We have to do everything possible to make the first rehearsal a feast, an uplifting moment, a hope-giving experience. And we can take an example from a space craft: our work should immediately acquire speed and intensity. It should be, from the very beginning, alive, hot, and energetic. All company members should treat it as a personal challenge and personal responsibility. All should attend the first rehearsal: actors, co-creators, producers, and staffs. All of them will profit from it individually and the work will acquire the quality of a group effort.

The rehearsal space for this first meeting should be inviting and encourage concentration. Something underlying the festive character of the day would help: flowers, a modest reception at the beginning, good classical music, and so on. We need a large table to accommodate everybody, or (if we don't have one) we should sit in a circle. The first rehearsal has two basic parts: the directorial introduction and the first reading of the play. It may be too elementary to advise, but I have to say it: before the beginning of the work the director should shake hands with everybody—a meaningful, symbolic, and consequential gesture.

First rehearsal—first part

The director starts the rehearsal by greeting all present. After only a brief introduction, the director should ask the host of the house (artistic director of theater, chair of the department, producer) to say a few words. In addition to being civil and showing good manners, it sends the message that the director has the full backing of the host and is empowered to lead the work. When the host has finished, the director takes over.

The director's first task is to introduce all co-creators, adding to each name a warm comment. Following this, the director reads the cast list. It is important that the director does this, not as a mechanical checking of attendance, but as a public and personal ritual, conferring upon every actor his/her role. This act has a double meaning: first, it helps build a bond between the director and the actor, who in this way gets the role directly from the director, and, second, it starts transforming a group of individuals into a team. Additionally, if auditions were wide open, people may not know each other, so announcing their names and roles introduces them to each other. If they did not meet before, they should be encouraged—at this very moment—to meet each other, shake hands, recall former works, etc. This should be an easygoing moment of breaking the ice.

Second, the director makes the directorial statement. It is a very serious task. The statement must be well prepared and may be delivered with the use of notes. It conditions the effectiveness of the beginning of the work. If presented well, it gives the work process energy, purpose, and precision. The directorial statement has five major parts and we will discuss each of them one by one.

> **TABLE: DIRECTORIAL STATEMENT**
> **at the beginning of the first rehearsal**
>
> (1) Opening
> (2) The play—presentation and interpretation
> (3) The production—description and explanation
> (4) The work process—basic information
> (5) Closing

(1) Opening. The director should start with an intimate confession or a startling declaration that immediately draws everyone's attention. This must be, indeed, something personal and emotional, something community building and touching. Just after this first phrase, the director has to clearly, briefly, dynamically, and plainly state the objective facing the company. Examples of objectives include: a world premiere of a new play, a revision of a classical drama, or an artistic experiment in a specific area; there may be others. The statement should be followed by an expression of hope for good results in the work and confidence in the people. This part of the directorial statement must be strong, yet, brief.

(2) The play—presentation and interpretation. The presentation of the play, and then the production project, are two central and crucial elements of the directorial statement. The analysis, made a long time ago, is the foundation for presenting the play. First, the director speaks about the play (or other literary material the company is going to work on). Even if it is an old play, but most importantly if it is a new one, the director has to say what this play is about (problem, conflict), how the action develops (story), who the characters are, where and when the action takes place. These data should be presented as objectively as possible, but immediately after that, the director has to come up with his/her understanding and interpretation of the play.

Second, the director presents the author. In the case of a classic, besides reminding the group of the known facts (dates of life, major works, major productions) it is worthwhile to say something special, intriguing, or personal; perhaps, an anecdote. In this way the director includes the author in the company as a member of the team, someone close and familiar. If the author is still around, it would be fabulous to invite him/her to the first rehearsal and—precisely at this moment—ask him/her to say something, or, if this is not possible, to at least read a few sentences from a letter from the author. If it is an author not known to the cast (a new writer, a foreigner) we have to make a special effort to provide with some bare-bones facts, and perhaps an intriguing story about him/her.

In any case, the author should be incorporated into our work process and included in the working team. Once upon a time, I was delivering my directorial statement at the first rehearsal of a play, *Two Theaters* by Szaniawski. I was a beginner. He was an eminent playwright. I asked him for a meeting before the rehearsals. He was known to be taciturn. Going to see him, I did not realize how strong that habit of his was. When his wife let me into his study, full of books, and we sat at a small table with coffee, I was afraid to say anything to the master, and the master was silent. It lasted for a very—and I'm telling you—a very long time. Then, I asked him a question. He was listening attentively, he nodded, he smiled, then he apparently was about to say something, I kept holding my breath, but after a while, he eventually said nothing. I asked him another question. The process of his brooding, pondering, weighing the response repeated, and when he was at the brink of uttering a word, he halted it. I asked new questions—to no avail. I tried to guess what he wanted to say. It was useless. Finally, his wife kindly reappeared and asked me if I wanted more coffee. I did not. The audience ended. Still, I learned a lot about him, and something important about his play: like the author himself, the play was airy and gossamer, and the subtext was always more important than the text, yet, the text was brilliantly dense and impeccably precise. I remember this conversation without words with the master-writer as a very moving and educating experience. He was a man who communicated with the world only through his writings. Beneath the surface of the words there was an abyss of feeling. I told this story to actors at the first rehearsal of *Two Theaters* and I think that it said something about the author and made him familiar to them.

(3) **The production—description and explanation**. Just after talking about the play and the author, the director should move to presenting the production project. The director explains how he/she is planning to translate the play into a performance. Speaking about the play, we have referred to words and thoughts. Talking about the production we should refer to people and stage matters. The vision, shape, meaning, and message of the show should be presented in general terms, not inundating listeners with details. Hence, the director should briefly address, point by point, the mise-en-scène and the style of the show, the acting style and convention, the space, including sets and costumes, and the targeted audience. All this should be concrete and practical. At this time, we ask the designers to display and explain their projects, models of sets, and costume

renderings.

When this is done we have to close this part of the directorial statement with a summary: this is what we are going to work on (the play) and this is how we are going to do it (the production.) A high note, something about the expected shape and level of the production, should close this segment. Now the tune changes—because the next part will not be about art but about mundane affairs.

(4) The work process—basic information. This section of the opening statement covers information about dates, schedules, regulations, etc.

First, we ask everybody to open their calendars to the present day, and go ahead to find and mark the opening date. It should be almost like a ritual. From this very moment on, time is running to the opening. (I speak here about the real opening, not the press opening, which might fall days or even weeks later.) All are on board. All know when we have to be ready. All are responsible for making the show happen, and happen on time. Second, we distribute (with the help of the stage manager) the schedule of the whole rehearsal process, which should be, of course, ready and copied for everyone. The director should at this moment make a promise to scrupulously follow the schedule—and later he/she should keep their word. It builds confidence and trust between actors and director. Third, we have to clearly and solemnly announce the policy about punctuality, which must be treated as a norm and law. Later, it should be strictly and severely enforced. (Perhaps there's no other field of theater work in which such severity is necessary.) Fourth, we establish communications. At this time the contact sheet (already prepared by the stage manager) should be passed around for necessary corrections, and, after editing, distributed to all. Fifth, the director asks the stage manager to talk about different aspects of contracts, union rules, regulations, such as smoking (or rather no smoking) in the theater, fire routine, telephone use, coffee availability, breaks in rehearsals and so on.

Generally speaking, there should not be too many announcements. Let's not waste precious time. The opening is quickly approaching.

(5) Closing. After the practicalities, we return to artistic matters. The introductory statement must be closed by the director with a brief summary of the artistic goals of the whole work. The director's last statement should be, again, personal, startling, and uplifting. It should contain encouragement and hope. Next, we thank all present for arriving and we invite them for the second part of the rehearsal, the reading of the play, but we don't insist that anyone other than the actors stay. Handing the baton over to the stage manager, we announce the break. The stage manger should inform how long the break is and then strictly observe the time.

Homework: prepare a directorial opening statement for your play—a VERY, very serious and difficult task.

Class work: all students deliver, one by one, their directorial statements. This work may last over a few classes. The development and delivery of the directorial statement is an extremely important skill, so we must allow ample time for these presentations.

First rehearsal—second part

The second part of the first rehearsal should be devoted to reading the play. Immediately—in the roles. After the break, when the actors have returned to their seats, they are asked to sit according to the order proposed by the director. This order must reflect the cast list prepared during analysis. We seat the lead actor (if there's a single lead) at the right hand of the director (which is the place of honor) and actors playing the remaining roles at two sides in the hierarchical order of their roles, at the same time grouped as families, clans, parties, etc. The assistant should be seated at the left hand of the director, and the stage manager in front.

Let's see how it works at a large rectangular table or in a circle of chairs. Working on *Death of a Salesman,* by Arthur Miller, we would clearly have one lead, so, we would seat the actor playing Willy Loman at the right hand of the director. Following Willy to the right, we would seat his family: his wife, his sons, and Uncle Ben. At the director's left hand, we should have the assistant, and then the other characters, beginning with Mr. Howard. In this way, we would have the inner family world at one side and the outer world on the other. The structure of action and characters relationship would be clearly displayed. If it was the first rehearsal of *Romeo and Juliet,* I would seat the two clans (the Montagues and the Capulets) on two sides of the table, with Romeo and Juliet at the top of them. At the bottom of the table, in between the two clans, we would have Friar Lawrence (who is an intermediary between the two clans), flanked by Chorus and the Prince (who is not directly connected with either clan). Rehearsing our favorite, *The Cherry Orchard,* we would do something slightly different. There are two major protagonists and opponents—Ranevskaya and Lopahin. The director would take the place at the top of the table, flanked by the assistant and stage manager. At one side of the table I would sit Ranevskaya, followed by her family (Gayev, Varya, Anya), Trofimov (Anya's fiancé-to be), and the domestic servants (Dunyasha and Fiers). On the other side of the table: Lopahin, followed by the outsiders (Epihodov, Pishtchik, the Station Master, the Post-office Clerk), and arriving servants (Yasha, and Charlotta, the governess); at the bottom of the table I would seat the symbolic character of The Shepherd.

TABLE: SEATING CHARACTERS FOR THE FIRST READING OF *THE CHERRY ORCHARD*

Assistant	DIRECTOR	Stage Manager
RANEVSKAYA		LOPAHIN
Gayev		Epihodov
Varya		Pishtchik
Anya		Station Master
Trofimov		Post-office Clerk
Dunyasha		Yasha
Fiers		Charlotta
	The Shepherd	

The new placement of actors is a conscious directorial technique. It extracts actors from their private and social bonds and transports them into the structure of the play; from social relationships to character relationships; from everyday life into artistic reality; from private chit-chat into reading the lines. The placement of actors based on the characters' relationships conveys practical, physical, and nonverbal information, which is stronger than words, about a character's position within the play and his/her connections to the other characters. A request to change seats may provoke some commotion and ironic comments, but its benefits will show immediately.

When new places are taken—we start reading. We assume that the actors have gotten the final text prepared by the director. We read the totality of the text including the author's introduction (in a Shaw play it would be rather long), the cast list, the space description, the lines, and all stage directions. Longer stage directions may be read by the stage manager or assistant, while actors should read the shorter stage directions, inserted in their lines. The request to read the stage directions out loud is also a conscious, directorial technique. It helps to attract the actors' attention to the movement, interpretation, and activities suggested by the author. In the next stages of work we will not be slaves to these stage directions; sometimes we'll completely disregard them. Reading them at the beginning of the rehearsals (not skipping!) enriches the text and makes it multi-dimensional. It also focuses the actors on action, not only on words. The reading out loud of stage directions such as: "suddenly bursting into tears," "throwing herself on her knees," or "laughing"—may make us laugh—that's fine—let's laugh—and this laughter will alienate the given line, allowing us to hear its full dimension, absurdity, or double meaning. All this provides actors with rich material for work.

During the first reading, the director does not explain or analyze the play. The reading should be interrupted from time to time, however, because this first take on the text is usually dull and boring. It does not yet have—and it can't have—acting fire. It does not carry emotions and thoughts. For this reason, the director should sometimes interrupt, ask for a line to be repeated, or make an à propos anecdote, for example, referring to previous productions of our play.

After having read the whole play we will be tired. We shouldn't prolong the rehearsal. We close it, commenting only briefly on the play. We emphatically thank everybody. The first rehearsal is over.

Class work: let's properly seat the cast of one of the plays currently prepared by students and read a scene or two from it, being sure that we read the entire text: lines, stage directions, and other information.

Table rehearsals—uncovering sources of energy

Table rehearsals can be broken down into two parts: (1) analysis of the play; and, (2) analysis of the characters. We are ready for both. We made the analysis at the very beginning of our work and we came up with the graph of it. Then, we transformed the graph of the play into the graph of the production. We now show the production graph to actors, and, using it, explain the structure of the action, conflicts, and events. The major, or perhaps the only purpose of the text analysis is to open a radiating source of energy for the actors. Of course, discussion of the historical, literary, or sociological context of the play is useful, but the main thing is to allow the actors to see the events, to let them know what the characters do.

Every director establishes how many table rehearsals he/she needs. As we know, one of the breakthroughs of the Great Reform of Theater was a new approach to play analysis and the prolongation of table rehearsals. It was a healthy reaction to the shallow and banal acting of 19th century stars, who were instantly ready to act not caring about the content and message of the play, thinking only how to display their acting tricks. Longer table rehearsals allowed directors and actors to slowly and delicately discover and expose the unique world of the play. The analysis embraced elements of literature and sociology, as well as philosophy, poetry, anthropology, and psychology. Stanislavsky's year-long rehearsals of a Chekhov play are still an example which should not be forgotten. I would strongly recommend, particularly in the university environment, to extend table rehearsals, or (as I always do) to precede the actual academic production with a semester-long workshop on the play which is to be produced.

Even with time and money constraints, it is possible to devote more time to the analysis and there are ways to do it. I usually have only three to five table rehearsals; five is the standard. The first (as already described) is an introduction to the whole work—it contains the directorial statement and reading of the play. The next two table rehearsals serve the analysis of the play. Two others focus on the analysis of the characters. So there are only five table rehearsals at the beginning. But then, during the blocking rehearsals, even in their advanced stage, I return to the analysis. Before every blocking rehearsal, I ask actors first to read the scene in question, or to go through their lines (if they have been memorized), and I again speak about the motivations and objectives, explain the circumstances, and suggest new interpretive options. In this way the intellectual, literary, psychological, historical, and theoretical analysis is not only a part of the initial phase of the work, which could easily be forgotten and ignored in building the action and characters, but is an on-going process, always being integrated with stage practice. Analysis is applied in small doses every day and continued almost until the opening. It works better than long table rehearsals. Still, some table rehearsals at the beginning of the work are needed. From the beginning of the first analytical rehearsal we have to ask actors to keep notes and allow them enough time to do so.

(1) **Action analysis**. We read the play in cast, breaking the reading into the scenes established in the graphical project of the production. After each scene we discuss it, using the title of the scene which we have in the graph. We should propose, not impose, these titles. We should encourage actors to come up with their own titles, which may better express what is going on in a given scene. Reading the play scene by scene, we point out which characters are participating in the scene, its space and time, and we thoroughly explain the action. In this way we cover the whole play during two table rehearsals.

Generally, the analytical rehearsals should be actor-oriented. They must serve actors, introducing them to the secrets and depths of the play. Listening for the first time to the lines read out loud, the director himself/herself understands them better and may deepen the analysis. Indeed, table rehearsals should be treated by the director as an opportunity to continue his/her work on the play analysis, not only to share with others what he/she has already found. This is a matter of directorial attitude: the director must be well prepared for every segment of work, should lead the way, and should definitely set objectives and goals for others, but, at the same time, he/she must not cease searching and must remain open. The work of director during rehearsals should be based on the delicate balance between the stubborn and tireless transformation of the already prepared production project into the production matter, on one hand, and, on the other, a humble openness to the proposals of actors as well as his/her own new ideas. During rehearsals, the director should be both the commander who leads the charge, and a simple private who trails at the end of the troop, helping a wounded buddy.

Class work: The master asks one of the students to conduct the analytical rehearsal of a few initial scenes of his/her play, focusing on action and using his/her graph. Other students should be cast in the play. The master's comments and discussion follow.

(2) Character analysis. At first, we generally explain the characters one by one from the point of view of their taking part in action, conflicts, and mutual ties and relationships. Then, we read the play again, stopping at all first appearances of the characters (we have them precisely indicated in the graph) and talking more specifically and in depth about the individual characters. After a scene of importance to a given character, we further discuss their motives, objectives, accomplishments, or failures. The technique of "Five questions about the character" comes in handy. We have to employ it, and to introduce actors to it. In the following weeks we are going to use this technique to communicate with actors every day. Talking about characters, it is important to underline the connections between the subsequent scenes in which they participate, and explain what they do in the meantime, that is, when they are not present on stage. In the university setting, at this time, we may ask student actors to write biographies of their characters, including both what they do on and off stage, and provide a reconstructed part of the characters' life before the action. To speculate what their fate may be after the play has ended might also help. Of course, this is only applicable if they were not killed in the action of the play, like Antigone,

Haimon, Caesar, Cassius, Cleopatra, Juliet, Miss Julie, Romeo, Tybalt, Hamlet, Laertes, Balladyna, Hedvig (in *The Wild Duck*), Catherine (in *Mother Courage*) and scores of other wretched victims of conflicts in so many plays.

Character analysis must point out the character's involvement in conflicts, as well as actions, and the character's use of space and time. Let's examine these matters using examples.

Conflict: All characters in all plays are involved with conflicts. Working on the analysis with actors, we have to specifically explain and characterize the conflict. For example, Macbeth is fighting for political power. Both on his way to the crown, and while he is struggling to keep it, he enters into conflicts with other characters.

Action: Every character (I should add—in every well written play) has a characteristic, most important, repeatable action which is the core of their stage life. This action must be discerned in the analysis. For example, Iago in *Othello* repeats the same action several time: he tries to convince Othello that Desdemona was unfaithful to him. Finally, he succeeds. Tragic consequences follow.

Space: We know that space strongly conditions a character's actions, behaviors, ways of thinking and feeling. We have to specifically point out to actors what spatial conditions are important for their characters. In Jean-Paul Sartre's *Huis clos* (translated in English either as *Vicious Circle* or *No Exit*), the action takes place in a closed hotel room which turns out to be Hell. In *Six Characters in Search of an Author* by Pirandello, the action takes place in the theater. In *The Constant Prince* by Calderón the space (with the single exception of scene 1, act 3.) is set outdoors.

Time: Every character—as the analysis always reveals—is conditioned by time and uses time in a special way. Beckett's characters always have plenty of time—they wait for death, they know it, and so they are not in a hurry to meet him. In Wilder's small town society in *Our Town*, time runs very slow. Conversely, there are many plays where characters are in a hurry: when the King decides to get Hamlet, his men are chasing the prince all over the castle; Pierre Beaumarchais' Figaro rushes to outwit the Count in *The Marriage of Figaro*; Ill, the hero (or anti-hero) of *The Visit* by Friedrich Dürrenmatt, has a price put on his head at the end of the first act, and runs away, trying outrun death.

Class work: The master selects a student to conduct an analytical rehearsal using characters from his/her play. Again, other students should be cast in the roles and seated at a table in a specific order while the analysis goes on. Comments and discussion follow.

Blocking rehearsals—giving birth to life

The real directorial task during blocking rehearsals is to give birth to life. Yes, life. We have to endow characters with life, then, make the interaction between characters alive, and finally, prepare live interaction between actors and spectators. Blocking rehearsals are the work of weaving the living matter of the performance.

Blocking rehearsals are the core of the whole rehearsal process. Characters' actions, activities, movement, gesture, and speech are integrated in the pulsating matter of the show. Integration of all possible acting abilities and means of expression is indeed the most burning directorial problem. On the pages of this book I have already spoken about various techniques for creating the human matter of the show and on the collaboration of the director with the actors. We used those techniques to work on short scenes and exercises. Now, the time has come to employ them in work on the whole production. In this way, the previous part of the book on learning directing serves this part on building the production, and both of them complement each other. We are going to use various creative techniques we worked on before and add new ones to them.

Blocking rehearsals are a constant process of communication between the director and the actors, and vice versa; it is a constant interaction. Depending on the culture, work habits, professional preparation, and personalities involved, this interaction acquires various forms. That's fine and normal. The point is that everybody participating in rehearsals must be aware that only through wide-open communication and sincere interaction can we prepare a living production.

TABLE: DIRECTORIAL TOOLS FOR BLOCKING REHEARSALS

(1) Principles of the director's work with actors
(2) Ways for the director to communicate with actors
(3) The technique of five questions about the character
(4) The technique of creating real events
(5) The technique of setting camp fires
(6) The technique of establishing a ground plan
(7) Improvisation as a basic technique of blocking
(8) The technique of creating multilayered interaction
(9) The technique of finding an individual in a crowd
(10) The technique of integrating rehearsals into one process

---

In the previous part of the book we worked on the first three in the above list. Now we are going to review them briefly and move on to the remaining seven.

Principles of the director's work with actors

We established that these principles include the director's work with actors on the human and personal level, on one hand, and on the artistic level, on the other. We pointed out that work with an actor on the personal level requires respect for his/her dignity, pride, sensitivity, and nerves. It must be based on actor's individuality and sovereignty; it must be open, frank, positive, compassionate, and loving. On the artistic level, work with an actor should be based on the principles of respect for his/her creative freedom, enhancing their responsibility for the final result, and including improvisation. Working with actors the director should be well prepared and organized, systematic and professional. He/she should teach actors humility towards the art of theater, and teach himself/herself humility towards the art of acting.

Ways for the director to communicate with actors

The four major ways the director communicates with actors include: informing actors, inspiring actors, instructing actors, and giving actors notes. We investigated and learned these ways through several exercises.

The technique of five questions about the character

This technique is based on asking five questions about the character, his/her partners, the space of action, the time of action, and the action as such. We called this technique "5Q" and used it on many occasions.

The technique of creating real events

This technique allows us to create real events based on real human life. So often in the theater we feel and see only artificiality, superficial behaviors, and hollow acting. By all means we have to avoid this. Our objective is to give birth to real life on stage. The process of creating life in theater has three stages. First: at the beginning there's the actors' real life. Of course, appearing on stage they are living human beings. During the rehearsals they should be enabled to live truly and fully as human beings. Second: the life of actors transfigures into the life of the characters. The imaginary circumstances conditioning the characters are no longer imaginary. They acquire authenticity for the actors playing the characters, and become their only reality. Third: the life of the characters reaches out to the spectators and pulls them into the living circle. Now, the characters live truly and fully not only by themselves, but also in the hearts and souls of the spectators, who, in turn, identify themselves with the characters. This multilayered process may come into being through technique of creating real events which also has three stages. First, actors create real events; second, they transform them into stage events; and, third, they include spectators in them. How does it work?

The first stage is the process of weaving in material from real life. We introduce actors to a real space and we situate them in it. The space should indeed be real, or at least structured as such: with real dimensions, distances, functions, entrances, exits, furniture, equipment, etc. Everything should be—as far as possible—as real as in real life. The space is only the playing area. The observation area is not set at all. This is crucial: there's no stage, no auditorium; the actors are alone, there are no observers. The world, in both human and spatial terms, is defined, closed, and homogenous. Is this clear? There should not be any spectators, or any theater! The actors are not performing for anybody, they are not seen, admired or hated. No. They are alone. By themselves. In their own space. Living their own lives. Only the director may (and should) find a spot somewhere in a corner, but he/she too does not represent the spectators, as usually in the theater, and his/her territory does not represent the observation area in any way. It should be as if the director is invisible. Indeed, the director might leave the actors alone for a time!

When actors are alone and in their own space, they play the dramatic event taken from the play, they interact, they quarrel, they kiss (nobody sees it from the outside) they make fun (nobody besides their group is going to laugh), and they speak (nobody should hear it beyond their venue, so it's not necessary for them to raise their voices). As a result, what they do is real, true, and functional; they satisfy real needs; they use only the scale of movement and volume of voice that is necessary for themselves. They don't act. They do only what is essential and nothing more, nothing theatrical. They should not even think about theater. This predicament allows them to get rid of any acting, performing, making believe, pretending or falsifying in terms of their interhuman communications, movements, contacts, and speech. They live real life.[14]

As we know, this technique was first introduced by Stanislavsky in his Crimea rehearsals in 1900; by Osterwa, when he rehearsed a play by Kazimierz Tetmajer, *Judas* (1921) in a secluded spot in a park on real grass and in the middle of trees; by Grotowski, rehearsing *Kordian* (1962) in an environment constructed as a hospital room. I used this technique several times, most effectively, I guess, when in 1979, I rehearsed a scene of *Birth Rate* by Różewicz which takes place in a compartment of a train car—in a real compartment of a

---

[14] The same, of course, is the impact of a real location on actors in film.

train car, sitting on side-rails at the Wrocław central station.

Let's imagine applying this technique, for example, to the scene of the family supper in *The Tidings Brought to Mary* by Paul Claudel. (I purposely propose a scene of a meal because it may be found in many plays.) We find a small room, or build one on the stage—with four walls, or, at least, define somewhere a small square space. We set the table and stools in the center of the room. There should be a stove at one corner, a door, a window. The actors sit at the table, as they would in a country kitchen and talk (using their lines), eat, drink, perform activities, including the everyday ritual of the father breaking bread, a symbol of the Eucharist in Claudel's play. The actors do all this by themselves and for themselves, focusing on themselves. They live the life of a simple peasant family. When they have fully developed their communal real life, they can move to the next stage of their work. On to the theater stage.

The second stage consists of moving real events into the production reality. An event created and grounded in real reality, may now be moved into the theater reality, put on stage and into the sets. At this time, the observation area emanates from the playing area. The place for spectators is established, including the distance, the direction of their observation, and the acoustic conditions. Moving the real event onto the stage (or other playing area) is sometimes possible without any changes. This was precisely the case in my *Birth Rate* production, in which I bought the old train car in which we rehearsed, cut out a compartment, took off a few panels to allow visibility, and placed the compartment in the center of the playing area in the theater. (It was the proscenium stage used as a theater in the round.) During the show, actors played inside the compartment, as they did during rehearsals. The spectators stood around the compartment—visible and accessible from all sides.

The other option is to change the space and the blocking, while retaining the full, internal energy of real life as developed by actors. This is how we wold approach the supper scene of *The Tidings,* if we would like to play it on a proscenium stage. The family would sit at one side of the table with the father in the center (a reference to the medieval *mansion*—a proper stylistic connection for Claudel's play). The direction of contacts, as well the volume of speech should change, and stylized gestures like those seen in medieval illuminations could be used. But the internal, human, psychological, and emotional reality of the actors' actions would not change. They would still live their real, true, intense life. At the same time, their life will become accessible to the public. We can apply the same technique to any other family meal scene, or, practically, for every action.

As we see, this procedure is one hundred per cent different from the usual and "normal" theater work, in which blocking is done directly on stage, and both movement and speech are conditioned from the very beginning by the dimensions of the stage and house, along with the visual and acoustic requirements of the potential spectator. We may say, that the difference is this: in the technique of creating real events the whole process is done by actors, who create their own full, coherent, and closed world; and only secondly this world opens and becomes accessible to spectators. In the "normal" blocking practice, the process is from the very beginning wide open, and, in a way, originated by the spectators as it is being prepared for them. Actors are not creating a reality but preparing a replica to be observed and heard by spectators. In this procedure, actors sometimes don't even have a chance to ignite their internal human energies. As a result, in most productions, instead of real events performed by involved and possessed actors, there are theatrical events performed by indifferent actors for unbelieving spectators. Such shows lack the mystery of real life.

Class work: a student should propose a scene from his/her play and rehearse it using the technique of "creating real events"— as described above.

The technique of setting "camp fires"

Remember our exercise with students coming to a night camp fire somewhere in the country? Here we have a technique which takes its name from the attractive energy of open fire. It is a technique for finding/setting the external and biological expression of internal feelings, wishes, needs, desires, or states of mind.

We have to understand that the expression which we are looking for during blocking rehearsals is simply the external form of what is internal. The proper sequence for the creative process during blocking rehearsals should always be a movement from the internal to the external. (Not the other way around!) During blocking rehearsals we must always be sure that only an internal impulse prompts the external movement of the body or instigates a physical activity. (Never, ever the other way around!) Except for placing actors at certain points at the beginning of an action, and on rare occasions, giving them definitive orders, we shouldn't tell an actor where to go (right or left), whether to take a specific position (sit or stand), or how to say something (softer or louder). Instead, we should tell the actor what to do, what to accomplish, or whom to influence—the actor's will and imagination, consciousness and subconsciousness sets his/her internal energy in motion and results in a deed, movement, or sound.

We set "camp fires" by providing a few (not too many!) points in the playing area which would influence actors. These focal points should draw actors in—as a camp fire draws a wanderer lost in the wilderness at night. They should be attractive, needed for some activities, or necessary to perform certain works; conversely, some should reject and push actors away. "Camp fires" in theater are, therefore, special points in the playing area which either attract or reject actors, influence their senses, emotions, thoughts, and judgments. Consequently, they motivate an actor's behaviors, movements, gestures, and activities.

Structuring a playing area, we situate camp fires like piñadas for children or booby traps for soldiers. They draw in or repel. They send impulses to actors: "Come to me!" or "Stay away!" Wanting to satisfy a need, having to perform an activity, an actor must come to the camp fire and use it. Or, feeling that there's a danger, they must stay away from it. Motivated by a camp fire, an actor (playing a character), has to go somewhere, must do something, is obliged to take a position, or, conversely, doesn't move, abstains from doing something, etc. Thanks to the burning camp fire an internal impulse is born. It brings about external results.

In real spaces, camp fires are equal to certain objects, structures, and functions of space, such as furniture, appliances, machines, and all sorts of architectural settings. In my office in the Contemporary Theater in Wrocław, I remember, I had three main camp fires. First: my desk with its telephones (at that time we did not have computers), along with my armchair and one chair for brief exchanges with employees; second: a conference table with 14 chairs for meetings in larger groups; and, third, a small table with four armchairs for more intimate talks. The fourth camp fire was the door, and the fifth, the book case. Greeting someone, I went to the door, and from there, with the guest, I proceeded to either the small or large table. These two places invited either a chat or a conference. If, during the conversation or meeting, I needed a document, I had to go to the desk, and for a book I had to move to the book case. After a talk, I usually accompanied the guest to the door. Then, I returned to the desk. My movement inside the office was very precisely dictated by the different camp fires.

After all, we always have camp fires on the playing area—but they might be set purposely and consciously, or accidentally and without any sense, hampering contacts between characters and making them almost impossible to perform, authentically, logically, and truly. Controlling camp fires on the playing area—we control the movement of characters, long before they appear.

Let's study the space in which it is most difficult properly to set camp fires—the proscenium stage. Indeed, it is really tricky to block a movement on it which would be both real in terms of acting and accessible (visible and audible) for the public. But even the proscenium may be bridled. For example, if we position the grandfather's armchair (the armchair being the camp fire) downstage left, close to the frame and placed *trois quarts* upstage—we allow the whole family coming to grandpa's eightieth birthday party, entering through the upstage right door, to address him directly. They will look in his eyes, and, at the same time, show their faces to the audience. We'll be even better off if we provide grandpa with a wheelchair and situate him at the beginning of the party at that downstage corner, but later on move him around. (Lillian Hellman uses a wheel chair for Horace Giddens in *The Little Foxes*.) A throne on a platform, positioned upstage center, makes the king sitting on it not only the ruler of the country, but of the stage too. The central upstage place of the king requires that the subjects attending him show their backs to the audience. The king is sole ruler: we see only his face. The throne is the camp fire—it imposes specific behaviors and movements on all present, and it attracts everybody upstage. If we want everybody to be drawn downstage, we situate the "camp fire" in the auditorium, treating it as an—imagined—yard or interior of a hall. In this case the ruler would go downstage to speak to the imagined crowd—as he can do in act 1, scene 2, of *Hamlet,* or in the final scene of *Arturo Ui* by Brecht.

But, as I have done in this whole book, I will refrain from giving prescriptions—where to situate camp fires for action in this or that play. Instead, drawing on examples for world drama, I will provide a brief list of general types of camp fires.

Entrances, exits, stairs, gang ways, and bridges. Entrances and exits may identify the characters using them. A central—usually wide and ornate—door has been for ages the entrance for kings, queens, and all sorts of rulers. In classical Greek theater the central door from the *skene* leading onto the *proskenion* was reserved for monarchs, the right door (*skene*-wise) for foreigners, and those on the left, for citizens. Additionally, the central door was used for the solemn ritual of exposing and honoring the dead. It was equipped with an *ekkyklema* (a wagon) on which the body of the slain hero was brought from the *skene* onto the *orchestra*. In *Tango* by Sławomir Mrożek, the action takes place in a dilapidated drawing-room with several doors leading to it. The entrances from/to each of them indicate who's living where and, in a way, imposes behaviors on their users: the servant Eddy approaches the room of Eleonore, the lady of the house, on his tip-toes, to visit her at night—they are lovers; but when discovered by Arthur, Eleonore's son, he humbly exits to the kitchen where he lives. Indeed, the speed, pace, and expression of your walk depends on where you are going. You anxiously and fearfully enter the boss's office (as in *Angels in America* by Tony Kushner) and you are relaxed and confident returning to your own home (as in *Who's Afraid of Virginia Woolf*). If a designer, like the Czech master, Josef Svoboda, provides you with enormous stairs in *Hamlet,* you have a lot of choices about how to block your movement in the violent scene between the Danish prince and Ophelia. But if the designer, like Jo Mielziner, the famous American artist, builds on stage a house with many rooms assigned to different family members, and you play Biff, you don't have a choice, you have to play the brothers' night scene in the boys' upstairs bedroom.

Observation points— windows, castle walls, mountain peaks, etc. These camp fires strictly impose direction on movement, speech, and/or contact. We find windows in so many realistic plays. Authors love writing entire, long scenes in which a character is narrating what he/she is seeing through the window looking from the inside to the outside (of course, our *The Cherry Orchard* first comes to mind) or from the outside to the inside (as in *The Interior* by Maurice Maeterlinck). The guard in Aeschylus' *Agamemnon* has an observation post on top of the walls of the castle, and from there he sees and relates to spectators the arrival of the king from Troy in the nearby port. Cassius sends Titinius to the top of the hill to better see the battle-field in the final combat scene of *Julius Caesar*; in an Elizabethan theater Titinius would certainly mount the upper playing area.

Furniture belonging to characters. Furniture focuses and blocks the movement of its owners as well as their partners, opponents, or contestants. A comfortable armchair no doubt draws Professor Higgins in Shaw's *Pygmalion,* and he will sink into it for long moments. A kneeler repels an atheist, a French revolutionary, in *Dialogues of the Carmelites* by Georges Bernanos. Macbeth and Banquo's Ghost fight for the throne, as so many other kings and usurpers do. In Havel's *Largo Desolato,* the writer's desk is obviously a major camp fire for the character of the writer. In his study he also has book cases with hundreds of books, an armchair with a lamp, and a sofa—all of them are additional camp fires. And it goes like this: writing, the writer uses the desk, checking something in a book he goes to the shelves, reading, he sits on the armchair and switches on the lamp, fondling a woman admirer of his talent, he, no doubt, does it on the sofa. His entire movement in the study is conditioned by the focal points—the furniture—the camp fires.

Eating places. Eating places strictly impose movement, behavior, and stage business on characters. We find various tables at which people eat and drink in realistic plays by Ibsen *(A Doll's House)*, Gorky *(The Enemies)*, and Shaw *(You Never Can Tell)*, in the absurdist dramas by Witkiewicz *(Jan Maciej Karol Hellcat)*, Ionesco *(The Bald Soprano)* and Pinter *(The Birthday Party)*, in poetic plays by Mayakovsky *(Bedbug)*, Eliot *(The Cocktail Party)*, and Różewicz *(White Marriage)*. In *The Long Christmas Dinner* by Wilder, there's a long dining table on stage with chairs behind it, two of them on two ends symbolically indicating (by flowers and black drapes) birth and death. People are born—they come, eat, drink, talk, and leave—they die. The cycle of life goes on at the Christmas table. The wedding table structures the blocking of a scene in *The Good Woman of Setzuan* by Brecht, and the banquet table is a camp fire at the end of the first act of *The Visit* by Dürrenmatt.

Places of rest, sleep, illness, etc. These places block movement almost by themselves. The functions they offer and behaviors they impose are obvious and unavoidable: a bed in a bedroom, hotel, or hospital, a sofa in the living room, or an office, a sleeping bag in the mountains, or a towel on a sandy beach.

Machines, appliances, gadgets, or tools. These are particularly strong camp fires because they must be used, serviced, set in motion or stopped. Here are only a few examples: a lighter needs a smoker, a bottle searches for a drinker, a coffee-maker lures a coffee lover, a gas stove waits for a cook, a hand hairdryer (in Clare Boothe's *The Women*) serves the beauty-enhancing session of a woman, a cash register (in Robert Sherwood's *The Petrified Forest*) is operated; and so on, and so forth.

Class work: one of the students selects a scene from his/her play and finds what "camp fires" can be set in it, then he/she casts the play and working with actors, tests how the "fires" work. Perhaps they should be reset? changed? replaced? As usual, the master's comments and group discussion follow.

The technique of establishing a ground plan

This technique serves to quickly, simply, and effectively begin a blocking rehearsal, or any new scene, short or long. Using this technique the director, like a mountain guide, decides where to start the attack on the summit, as a starter at track and field competition calls runners to take their places, or as an air traffic controller directs planes to the runway for departure.

At the beginning of a blocking rehearsal, the director has in his hands five pieces of a puzzle: text, action, characters, space, and time. He/she has to decide what material (what part of the text) he/she wants to work on. Action identified in the text of the play must be translated from words into human deeds; action acquires the form of activities, movement, or stage business. Characters take part in an action, so actors playing them must get their initial tasks. Those task are performed in space and time.

The analysis that was done before blocking rehearsals tells us what the action is, what characters take part in it, and where and when the scene takes place. We start blocking by using three obvious and concrete elements: space, actors/characters, and action.

First, we define the space. It must serve the action (here we can use the technique of creating real events), and it must allow characters to act (here we can use the technique of setting camp fires). At home we have prepared a simple ground plan of the space, indicating camp fires—focal points, entrances/exits, furniture, appliances, risers, stairs, etc. At this stage of work all of this is based on the directorial project and the plans of sets which are already being built. In the theater, before the rehearsal, we prepare the space to resemble as closely as possible the finished sets.

Second, we situate actors in space. We ask them to take positions at departure points—the places where they should be at the beginning of an action, or from which they start a movement or activity. We tell them what is in the space, how a tool operates, where the entrances or exits are, and so on. When the actors are at the starting places, we inform them using our "5Q" technique. In this way we explain to them why and for what they were situated in the given places, and we tell them what their next step should be, where they are to go, what they are supposed to do. It is important to inform actors who are already in space and in their starting places (not sitting at the table), because this is practical, and connects them with the space and their partners. It is advisable not to give actors too many tasks over too long a stretch. It's better to proceed by small, yet firm, steps.

Third, we set the actors in motion. We do it by clapping, saying "Action," or simply, "Please, go." They make their first moves fulfilling their tasks. In so doing, they move in space, they use furniture or tools, they make contacts and connect. A web of blocking is being woven. We have to allow the actors to act as long as their actions are creative and make sense. When they run out of fuel we interrupt them. Once again we set all the initial parameters and ask them to start.

To summarize: the director makes three initial steps to start a blocking rehearsal. First, the director builds the space. Second, he/she introduces actors to this space, explains to them how to use it, and gives them instructions, including what their first step in the space is to be. And then, third—they go.

Improvisation as a basic technique of blocking

Improvisation by actors endows rehearsals with openness and freshness. Improvisation is creative and free. But only an internally grounded, well prepared, and disciplined improvisation is effective. What is an internally grounded improvisation? It is improvisation in which the internal impulse governs the external form. Actors should be given internal motives, reasons, and objectives, but not told what the result in terms of movement, gesture, or voice should be. What is a well-prepared improvisation? It is one which has clear and precise points of departure and is oriented towards solving specific problems. What is a disciplined improvisation? It is not, as one can imagine hearing about improvisations, an anarchic technique leading to whatever anybody wants and dreams of. It is an improvisation which has limits and goals (Use only your body! Explore your body's balance! Use only your voice! Explore the space! etc.)

Improvising actors create by themselves the material of deeds, activities, contacts, and movements. Improvisation might be delicately steered by the director but not interrupted too soon. Interruption is necessary only when the creative energies of actors dry up. Improvisation is a search. It is a journey into the unknown. It is based on curiosity. Director should help actors to develop an attitude of constant curiosity, openness, and devotion to searching; he/she should teach actors to believe in improvisation and to enjoy using it. At the same time, director must provide improvising actors a sense of security and confidentiality, and respect their efforts and openness.

Improvisation results in blocking. Rarely it is perfect on the first take. We select what was good and what worked, and we advise the actors to abandon and forget other elements. In this way we set more specific objectives for the next improvisation. We repeat the improvisation, trying to keep it fresh and open, not to make it a mere repetition of the previous one. I strongly recommend using improvisation during blocking rehearsals. Directorial blocking should always focus on the initial phase of a scene, and never include the totality of movement, crosses, activities and so on; these should be left open to improvising actors. If the director comes up with a completely defined choreography for a scene, the result is usually a mechanical ballet, not live theater.

To summarize, blocking with the use of improvisation has four stages. First, the director precisely and comprehensively establishes the beginning of a scene or bit and advises how and where to make the first step. Second, the actors improvise. When the improvisation is done or stopped, the director steps in again.

Third, the director evaluates the improvisation—some elements are accepted, some should be modified, some abandoned. Fourth, the actors take their places of departure, and improvise again, but within narrower boundaries, and come up with a more precise result.

And one more generalization, connected with our work on improvisation: directing should always be first of all internal. The director should refer to internal motives, objectives, wishes, feeling, etc.—not to the external result, shape, or form. It is the actor who transform the internal into the external.

Class work: a student proposes one scene of his/her play and casts it. He/she blocks it using actors' improvisation.

The technique of creating multilayered interaction

The contact between actors is always the foundation of their actions, regardless of the style or type of acting they use, and no matter what they do, whether they fight or collaborate, whether they love or hate each other. In the case of a scene in which several characters take part, contacts among actors results in a dense net of multidirectional actions and reactions. In the case of a soliloquy the actor's partner is the audience. Spectators are obviously an actor's partners in soliloquies if they are addressed directly, as was the case in Elizabethan theater, but they are also partners, even if an actor supposes that he/she is alone and is only thinking out loud.

Contact is always an act of interhuman communication, a stream of energy sent from person to person. Contact may be made in many different ways and its energy may have many different forms: the verbal—when speech is used and actors/characters talk to each other; the physical—when actors use movement, gesture, activity, stage business; the biological—when they use their bodies' energies; the psychological—when they apply psychological pressure on partners; and, finally, the sensual—when they use or target a specific sense (vision, hearing, touch, etc.) of the partner. Certainly, sometimes we select one of the ways or means of contact and use it exclusively or stress it in a special way: we read the Scriptures, we dance with joy, we show old photographs. Usually contact is multilayered. For example, when I talk to you I look at you, and I also affect you by my presence, body language, gesture, and movement. In wordless, real activity, like violence, movement, visuality, psychological and biological pressures may take part. The same is true in theater. Contacts between two or more actors are usually multilayered. The more of these layers, the stronger the contact. Hence, the advice to the director (and to the actor too): use as many layers of contact as you can: speak—in motion, be silent—hearing your internal voice, act—with full energy, be—entirely yourself, live—in body and soul.

TABLE: THE MULTILAYERED CONTACT principles

SPEAK—IN MOTION
BE SILENT—HEARING YOUR INTERNAL VOICE
ACT—WITH FULL ENERGY
BE—ENTIRELY YOURSELF
LIVE—IN BODY AND SOUL

Class work: a student selects a scene from his/her play (not too long, with not too many characters), casts it, makes an analysis of it, and establishes the tasks for characters. Next, he/she asks actors to act the scene using only one contact layer: speech, or movement, or gesture, etc. Let's discuss what the results are. How does it go? Is it at all possible to use only one contact layer? Then, the director asks actors to play the same scene again using multilayered contact. Let's talk again about how it works. How different was it?

The technique of finding an individual in a crowd

Blocking group scenes is a special and especially difficult directorial skill. I love them. Blocking group (or crowd) scenes is one of my favorite directorial fields and I have, probably, a good understanding and feel for how to build them. I was lucky to have the means to use huge crowds on stage when I needed them: in *Two Theaters* by Szaniawski in the Polski Theater in Warsaw (1962), in *November Night* by Wyspiański in the Theater Wybrzeże in Gdańsk (1967), and in the *Forefathers' Eve* by Mickiewicz in Wrocław (1978), where the ritualistic chorus and the ensemble of a ball scene counted forty actors. I have had also the directorial privilege of blocking many group scenes in Shakespeare, in Brecht, in Gombrowicz's *Operetta* and many other plays with large ensembles[15].

At this point—avoiding, as usual, prescriptions—I would like to share a basic technique for building different kinds of group scenes. I call it the technique of "finding an individual in a crowd," because it gives life to a crowd and, at the same time, allows every member of the crowd to live his/her individual life. This technique is based on the following principles:

First, the group scene is a scene of individuals. Any group scene is simply a scene in which many individuals participate. Consequently, the director must treat every one of them as individuals, not as an anonymous and faceless member of the mass. Every one should get coaching and feedback from the director. Based on acknowledgment and respect for their individuality, these individuals may be grouped—depending on the logic of the action—as families, teams, troops, parties, etc.

Second, the group scene require leaders. A large group should be divided into smaller groups and each of those small groups must get a leader. He/she must be the head, commander, captain, foreman/forewoman of a group. The director appoints the leaders the same way as he/she casts all other characters. The leader is responsible for the group, and he/she commands and coordinates the group's activities, movement, etc. He/she should not suppress the creativity and individuality of the members. The leaders of the groups are helping the director and might work as directors with their groups—having special rehearsals. Indeed, while working with a large group of people (and not only on group scenes in

---

[15] I directed Shakespeare's *Hamlet* (twice), *Twelfth Night* (twice), *King Lear, Julius Caesar, Henry V, Richard III,* and *As You Like It*; I directed Brecht's *Mother Courage* (twice), *Good Woman of Setzuan* (twice), *Caucasian Chalk Circle,* and *Fear and Misery of the Third Reich.*

theater) it is advisable to divide the entire group into smaller units and appoint a head for each. It facilitates communication and organization of work. It should not diminish the responsibility of individual members. Rather, some people—the heads of units—have a double responsibility.

Third, camp fires are a necessary device in blocking group scenes. In working on a group scene, we must set clear and strong focal points that attract or repel people, and explain to actors (and extras) what these point are, how they work, and what can we do with them, etc. A clear example of a raging camp fire in a group scene is Caesar's dead body, exposed and addressed by Mark Antony before the crowd of Romans.

Fourth, improvisation should be a part of the blocking of group scenes. Certainly, in blocking a group scene we have to establish departure and arrival points very precisely for both individuals and groups, and we also have to explain the acting tasks using the "5Q" technique. Then, we have to encourage the whole group to improvise, and set the crowd in motion. We have to be aware that when rigid choreography of a group scene is prepared at home by a director and then imposed on actors (and extras), it may result in well orchestrated movement, but rarely provides a volcanic eruption of energy—a potential always present in a group scene.

Class work: a student finds a group scene in his/her play, or, if there's no such scene in the plays on which our students are working, he/she should multiply certain characters, for example: adding retinue to the king, a clique of orderlies to a general, additional staff members in an office. All the characters should be individually cast. Then the student-director directs a group scene. We should allow enough time for discussion.

The technique of integrating rehearsals into one process

Each rehearsal is a link in a chain of a live human process. Rehearsing is not building a machine, adding domino tiles, or erecting a house out of prefabricated segments. It is most like growing a rare flower, taming a wild horse, or raising a child. It is a live process. After each rehearsal the director should ask himself/herself: "Was it life? Was it a process? Was it authentic, true, personal?

Or was it dead at birth, artificial, false?" The elements of work which were unsuccessful and do not pass severe scrutiny should be abandoned. These successful ones should be developed. There are a few conditions which should be met in order to achieve the living continuity of rehearsals. They may be summarized in three points: evaluate—plan—go ahead.

First, evaluate! Every rehearsal should be strictly and objectively evaluated by the director. It is imperative to step back and consciously assess one's own, and others, work. Don't be afraid to evaluate. It's your duty. There are five critical areas to evaluate:

(1) Life—was there life in what I did? Was it a living process?

(2) Material—how much material was worked through, compared to the work schedule? How effective was the rehearsal? If it was a reading rehearsal—did I explain what I wanted to? Was I understood? If it was a blocking rehearsal—was it satisfactory? What needs correction and/or amendment?

(3) My own work—how did I work in terms of creativity, intensity, openness, kindness, handling difficult situations, effectively using time? Was I a martinet or a nurse for actors?

(4) The actors' work—what is the stage of their readiness in terms of acting, lines, movement, special skills? Are they (and every actor should be evaluated individually) making progress? What are their major problems? How can I help them?

(5) Technical preparations—compared to the schedule, are we on time? Are there delays? In what areas? What can I do about it? To whom should I talk?

Second, plan! The next rehearsal should be practically and realistically planned and prepared by the director. The same questions asked above should be asked in preparing the next rehearsal:

(1) Life—how to make the next rehearsal a living process.

(2) Material—what should be done.

(3) The director's tasks, challenges, objectives.

(4) The actors' work.

(5) The technical preparations.

Third, go ahead! Every new rehearsal should start at the point where the previous one ended. We have to enter into the same living stream. To start by reading and talking helps a lot. Some corrections to yesterday's material should be made. Then we have to get up on our feet and take a step forward, into the unknown. We have to make progress, to add something to what was done before.

There are also some simple practical procedures which help to strengthen the continuity of the process:

(1) Just before the rehearsal the director should have a look at the book and at his notes, checking the planned material.

(2) The actor must work on the text at home and use notes taken during rehearsals. In the theater, a time to relax and focus is needed before work.

(3) Ensemble warm-up is a commendable habit.

(4) Silence before rehearsal helps us to enter into the world we are going to create.

CHAPTER 5. FINAL REHEARSALS: LIGHTS, TECHNICAL, GENERAL; THE OPENING

Lights rehearsals

As I have already stated, in the European tradition it is the director who designs lights. He/she collaborates with the set designer and master electrician. This model comes from the Wagnerian tradition of a unified work of art, developed in practice by Chronegk and Reinhardt and aesthetically by Appia, Craig, and Fuchs. It was firmly established throughout Europe by the pioneering directors of the Great Reform of Theater and continues until today. It results in the creation of productions that are coherent and integral works of theater art. In the United States, at the beginning of the 20th century, David Belasco combined directing with lighting designing. He had a special atelier in which he personally experimented with lights. His sunsets or dawns were famous among theatergoers. The director as total theater artist was known in America, and has had brilliant representatives (presently: Tom O'Horgan, Peter Sellars, Andrei Serban, Robert Wilson and others), but has not been widely accepted. In America, the lighting designer usually works almost autonomously and separately from the director. As a result, in many productions the lights are not integrated with the mise-en-scène and do not support the action. Lights frequently and obviously contradict the action. Yet, it is the style of the production established by the director and the requirements of the action which must always determine all means of expression. Regardless of culture, working independently, or collaborating with a lighting designer, the director creates lighting.

Working on lights for the production, it's worthwhile to stress once more that theater belongs to the sphere of culture and within it, to both the human dimension of culture and to the artistic realm of it. This cultural double aspect of theater, human and artistic, is a guide for the whole theater creation, including lighting. Thus, if theater is indeed a cultural phenomenon, it does not tolerate strong doses of technology and mechanization. Theater does not want, and does not need, to be pushed towards the civilizational infrastructure of electronic bliss in which the temptation of playing with electronic, glitzy toys overwhelms real and direct interhuman exchange. This temptation is strong and dangerous especially in large, modern theater buildings, equipped with computers, sophisticated light and sound systems, and all sorts of mechanical wonders. As I suggested before, limiting light sources and their colors increases the efficiency and power of those used. Interhuman contact is always a stronger foundation for a production than any mechanical effects, including lighting. Also, the temptation to focus light only on the human face moves theater close to television and film close-ups, while theater—let's be sure—is the art of the whole human being, and, therefore, of the whole human body. Setting lights for a theater production, we have to understand that on stage the actor acts and is seen in full silhouette. There are no close-ups in theater. (The screen at the side of the proscenium frame changes theater into multi-media; its aesthetic is different from theater.) Another temptation prompted by modern technology is to provide too much light. Television shows are always glowing. A shadow is an enemy in the studio. Computer-generated images usually have neither depth no shadow. They exist in an artificial world in which there's no day or night. Yet, a shadow is the son of the sun, a double of the living human being. In theater a shadow is a messenger of nature and sign of life. I suggest that directors reevaluate their lighting principles (or lack of them), their lighting aesthetic (perhaps borrowed from television), and lighting habits (not caring for them and/or taking a laissez-faire approach to the lighting designers). I propose a return to the natural sources and primeval energies of light in theater. Young directors can simply turn their backs to the old, artificial, and careless ways of lighting and create their own, new, and innovative lighting.

The director collects initial information and hints about lighting during the analysis. He/she draws conclusions about those findings while preparing the production project. In his/her directorial tool box, the director has notes on lights and may complement them with sketches. The director is, therefore, prepared to have a work session with the light designer or master electrician before the beginning of the rehearsals with actors. At that session, the director presents and discusses his/her lighting needs and orders, as well as possible solutions.

Working on light in space, we examined various aspects and energies of it and we came up with a few basic rules of creating light in theater. These rules, or—I would even say—laws, function universally and have broad applications, especially in straight theater. Let's carefully review them. We will follow with a work session in class

Class work: a student selects a short scene from his/her play, casts it, works with actors on the analysis, gives them instructions using the "5Q" technique, and blocks the scene—all in work light. Next, student-director lights the scene using various instruments and types of light: electric projectors, candles, a light coming from an outer space, etc. Evaluation and discussion follow.

406

TABLE: PRINCIPLES OF LIGHTING A THEATER PRODUCTION

Light and human beings in theater

(1) Light in theater serves the present, active, and moving human being.

(2) Light in theater serves, first of all, people, and secondly, objects. Remember: the human being is always in the center of theater, and he/she must get light first. Objects, including sets and costumes, should get light only as they are used by actors and as they enhance actors' actions.

(3) A human being creates a theater space around himself/herself and light should follow this process of creation.

(4) The logical procedure for working on lights in theater is to move from lighting a human being to lighting the space.

Live light in theater

(1) Nothing matches the power of live light: a torch, a candle, a lamp, a burning barrel of oil, a camp fire, or a single match.

(2) Live light can be easily operated by an actor, which makes lighting humane and personal.

(3) Live light is both natural and effective, as has been proven by a multitude of both open air and indoor productions throughout the history of theater.
Note: the use of open fire is easier and safer in outdoor production.

(4) Live light in closed spaces is even more powerful then outdoors, for it is aesthetically alienated, psychologically unexpected, and pereceptionally unusual.

Artificial light in theater

(1) The fewer lights used, the stronger the effect of the lighting. The fewer colors, the stronger the impact of those used.

(2) There's no more dynamic and dramatic lighting than that hitting an actor from behind and from the side.

(3) An actor's face must get light from two angles, otherwise it is either flat or dark.

(4) Shadows invest life into the space and the sets, and intensify actors' movement.

Note: local fire regulations must always be fully respected.

Technical rehearsals

Technical rehearsals serve to coordinate and tune up all of the production elements which by that time should have been provided and operational. The director participates in technical rehearsals, supervises the work, corrects or gives notes, but it is the stage manager who leads them. Tech rehearsals (as they are called) have two stages:

First stage: checking, coordinating, and tuning up all elements and technical operations in the areas of: (1) Stage—scenery changes (scene shifts), the functioning of a revolving stage, fly bars, traps, doors, windows, etc. (2) Lights—assuming that lights have already been set during special lighting rehearsals. (3) Music/sound—recorded on tape. (Live music practice is not a part of technical rehearsals.) All these works and operations are completed by stage technicians supervised by the stage manager. They have to learn and exercise all their assignments. Because of this, actors are usually not called on for the tech rehearsals. Various movements or cues may be shown or read by an assistant.

Second stage: integrating the technical elements as listed above (stage, light, and sound) with acting. Usually, at that time (if not earlier) actors wear costumes for the first time. Specific cues or technical operations must be strictly coordinated with actors' lines and movement, sometimes with costume changes. Often, it is necessary to repeat them several times until everything goes smoothly.

Tech rehearsals are, supposedly, the least pleasant and exciting element of the show preparation. But the director must understand their importance and necessity, and must allow enough time for the stage manager and the entire technical crew to rehearse—whatever they have to. It is the director's responsibility to facilitate the work of the technicians and to surround their efforts with respect. Besides, if the production has been timely and properly prepared, the tech rehearsals should be as smooth as butter.

General rehearsals

They should be treated as shows. All elements of the production should be in place: acting, stage operations, light, and sound. Actors have costumes and for the first time wear make-up. The ideal is not to interrupt the flow of the action and not to allow interruptions during the general rehearsal. Notes, including technical notes, should be given after the end of the play. Again, if the technical rehearsals went well and the actors are ready—this is possible. If not, we have to do our best to limit interruptions and allow the production to run. In practice, the first general rehearsal is sometimes the last technical rehearsal—a last opportunity to correct the coordination of all the elements of the show, and even to repeat a scene shift or sound cue. All right, we may take it easy and allow the first general rehearsal to stumble. But we have to insist on having the second general rehearsal on the level of the production—both artistically and technically.

Before the second general rehearsal the director has to perform an important—I would say—ritual. The whole company and the entire crew should be asked to come and the ethical rules of theater work should be reviewed or announced—reviewed if they have been in place in a theater or company for a long time, announced, if this was not already done. The beginning of the second general rehearsal seems to be the best time for this ritual. Before the first general there might have been to many things to fix, to much worry, too much running around and screaming. But before the second general rehearsal everything should be in place and we have to take time to sit together and speak about the ethical aspect of our work.

The ethical rules or regulations for a show are based on the by-laws of a theater association or union, they may be formulated by the sponsoring or producing organization, or proposed by the director; the director, of course, has been using those rules from the very beginning of his/her work on the production. The point is, that they should exist, they should be clear, they should be announced, and, when announced, they should be enforced. The enforcement authority belongs to the stage manager and the authorized representative of the body which established the rules.

Hence, before the second general rehearsal, the director gathers the artistic, technical and administrative company and personally reminds/informs them about the ethical rules. It's important that the director does it personally, because the ethical dimension of the whole work process and performance are inseparably connected with its artistic dimension.

TABLE: ETHICAL RULES OF THEATER WORK
major guidelines

(1) Priority of the artistic dimension of the production, its artistic level and form, over any other consideration.
(2) Priority of aesthetic and ethical values and ideas expressed in the production over any other aspect of the production.
(3) Requirement of absolute invariability of the artistic form of production, as established during rehearsals.
(4) Requirement of investing full human, creative, and artistic energy in every production.
(5) Necessity and value of cooperation between all people involved with the show.
(6) Necessity and value of observing quiet and silence around the playing area before and during the performance.
(7) Necessity and value of punctuality on and off stage.
(8) High respect for the work of other theater people.
(9) High respect for the audiences.
(10) Obligation to observe safety, fire, smoking, and other regulations.

The third general rehearsal is simply a full and regular performance. It might coincide with the preview. If not, we may privately invite some friends or family members. During every general rehearsal the director takes detailed notes and after the action shares them with the actors, stage manager, and other interested specialists. After the third general rehearsal there should not be too many notes, of course, because everything should go well.

Homework: every student individually writes a set of ethical rules based on the above format, but modified and enriched according to his/her views and needs.

Class work: we read all the ethical rules prepared by students, discuss them, and come up with a list agreed upon by the whole class/group. It would be worthwhile to print it, copy it, and give a copy to every member at the end of our work—which soon will come to a close—as a souvenir.

The opening

The opening ends the process of rehearsals and starts the run of the show. It is a threshold. It always leads to an unknown land, because, until they are confronted with the public the actors fully develop their roles, and the production either works and lives, or petrifies and dies like a bird frozen in flight. The opening is a feast. It crowns weeks, month, or sometimes years, of hard work. It is not a time of repose after work, rather a time of fulfillment in even harder work. The opening finally transforms the project into a reality. The theatrical process acquires its full dynamism. Action changes into interaction.

An opening night celebration, both before and after the show, is a good theater tradition. Before the show, we exchange small gifts, cards, flowers, and wishes; after the show, we thank everybody and socialize. All that is fine. The ethical rules, which we recently reviewed, should not be put on hold the day of the opening because this could harm the production. They must be fully observed, which means, among others, that a festive atmosphere in the theater ought not to disrupt silence and concentration before and during the show; and, that we should refrain from hard partying afterwards, because this might negatively influence the next day's performance.

The director does not give notes after the opening (nobody would be willing to listen to them, or remember them). Detailed notes should be given after the second production and include observations from the opening too. Notes after the show will now have a new part: the director will evaluate not only stage action, but also interaction with the public.

By the way, the ethics of a director's work require the director to watch at least two performances after the opening and to scrupulously give notes to the whole company. Later, the director should monitor the show from time to time and have assistants do it on a day to day basis. An outstanding Polish director and pedagogue, dean of the Directing Department at the Warsaw Academy of Theater, Edmund Wierciński (1899-1955) used to attend every single show of every production he ever directed. Yes, he came to the theater every night during the whole run, and gave notes to actors after each show. His productions were usually successful—certainly in part for their phenomenal artistic discipline—and run for hundreds of nights. Every night Wierciński was there. It was, perhaps, the directorial virtue elevated to the level of heroism, or even directorial martyrdom. But, at the same time, the master was sending an impeccably clear signal to his actors, to his students, and, indeed to the whole theater community: every show of the production is equally important and must be treated the same as the opening. We probably can't rigorously imitate Wierciński, but we have to remember his message.

It is a good directorial ritual to thank everybody after the opening. Everybody: actors, co-creators, stage managers, technicians, administrators, and all others. No one should be forgotten or omitted.

The opening provides one more opportunity: to make peace, to forgive, and ask for forgiveness. Yes, life is sometimes difficult, tensions, especially just before the opening, run high. People are people, and sometimes their nerves crack. Animosities and bad blood taint the atmosphere. The director himself/herself may provoke or participate in clashes and conflicts. The opening, with its festive mood and everybody's aspiration to succeed, to help each other and to do their best, is a perfect opportunity to annul old accounts, forfeit debts, erase offenses, to forget anything bad and dark, and to remember only what was good, bright, beautiful, and uplifting.

As to me, I also—ending this course of directing and presentation of my method of *creative directing*—thank the reader for walking with me that long and sometimes, I know, dusty and steep way. I ask for amnesty, if I did not explain something as clearly as I wanted to, if I did not answer all your questions, and if I did not offer enough help. Forgive me. Take from this book what can be beneficial and helpful to you. I will be very happy if this book turns out to be at least a little bit serviceable to anybody—artistically, ethically, professionally, intellectually, personally, and spiritually.

These are the dimensions of directing about which I wrote.

Afterword by Ed Menta

I first met Kazimierz Braun in the Winter of 1980. I was a second year M.F.A. candidate in the Directing Program at the University of Connecticut. Under the leadership of such men as Jerry Rojo, John Herr, and Jarek Stremien, the Directing Program made a conscious effort to introduce its students to contemporary European directors. (The term before I had studied the work of Andrei Serban and Peter Sellars.) Kazimierz had been invited for a one-semester guest artist residency to direct Różewicz's *Card Index* and teach directing.

I realize now that Kazimierz's seminar was a turning point in my artistic study. I recently discovered I still have my notes from this course in which we dissected the first act of *The Cherry Orchard* using the "Kazograph" method he describes in Part Two of this book. For the past 14 years I have been teaching a similar technique of graph analysis to my own directing students.

The graph analysis wasn't the most important thing I learned from Professor Braun, however. He was the first theater artist I'd ever met in my young life who combined two elements: first, what I would have loosely termed then as a sense of "avant-garde theater" (his production of *Card Index* literally blew me away in its use of space, lighting, and overall imagery); with, second, an absolute iron-clad work ethic. After he learned I would direct Sam Shepard's *Suicide in B-flat* later that Spring, for the rest of the term, whenever he saw me in the hallway, he would ask with genuine surprise in his high pitched English drawl: "But *Ehh-*

hd!... Why are you *here?* Why aren't you *working on your play... hmmm?"*

The book you have just read is a guide for all students and teachers of directing. Rarely have I seen such useful artistic precepts practically described: The Graph, The Directorial Toolbox, The Technique of Setting Camp Fires, and all other directing exercises and techniques that can be found in this volume.

But *Theater Directing: Arts, Ethics, Creativity* is much more than a "how to" book, as Kazimierz himself makes clear in his Foreword. Instead, it exemplifies a way of approaching art, not through a series of exercises, theories, or even a philosophy, but through a courageous life lived in the face of artistic adversity and censorship that most American artists can only imagine. In these pages, Kazimierz recognizes how each artist is a sum total of lifelong mentors and influences. His early exposure to art during the war through his family members and friends such as his uncle, Anthony Żuliński, and his aunt, Jadwiga Domańska, reminded me of reading about Stanislavsky's early artistic life engendered in his family's performances. His teachers at Warsaw Theater Academy, Bohdan Korzeniewski and Erwin Axer, among others, embedded an artistic morality which helped Kazimierz make the ultimate choices he must in 1983 with *The Plague*. (His decision to stage the production led to the closure of his theater in Wrocław, his dismissal as Artistic Director and General Manager, and his eventual departure from his homeland.) In this sense, Kazimierz is part of a long line of East European theater directors (perhaps first established by Meyerhold) who become enemies of the state because of their use of theater as a tool for social progress and means of truth in totalitarian society. And yet through it all, Kazimierz found himself adhering to the moral purpose of art, as he was urged to contemplate early in his career by his Professor-Bishop Karol Wojtyła. What better lesson could we teach our students or learn ourselves in today's theater?

In writing this piece, I stumbled upon a long forgotten memory. Half-way through our semester, Kazimierz returned to Poland (which, as it turned out, would only be his home for less then four more years). Before he left, I asked him to attend a run-through of the Shepard play I was directing. It was my hope to create an atmosphere of a jazz night club for the audience. The next day in his office, he critiqued what he had seen. Though he was polite and graciously complimented me on several aspects of the play, he summarized by saying that, for him, ultimately the production did not work. He had not been transported to the feel of a jazz night club space. To do this, I would have to breake free of the prison of the studio proscenium theater and physically change the relationship of the audience and performers. It is a valuable lesson I remind my own students (and ignore myself all too frequently). But the truest value was in Kazimierz treating me as an artist, not as a student director. He held me to the highest possible standards, the same which he set for his own work.

That is a lesson I have tried *not* to ignore in my own teaching.

Ed Menta

Professor, Director of Theater at Kalamazoo College
Author of *The Magic World Behind the Curtain: Andrei Serban in the American Theater*, 1996 Outstanding Academic Book

Kalamazoo, Summer 1999

BIBLIOGRAPHY

Alberts, David. *Rehearsal Management for Directors*. Portsmouth, NH: Heinemann, 1995.

Albright, Hardie. *Stage Direction in Transition*. Encino, CA: Dickenson, 1972.

Allensworth, Carl, Dorothy Allensworth and Clayton Rawson. *The Complete Play Production Handbook*. New York: Crowell, 1973.

Antoine, André. *Mes Souvenirs sur le Théatre Antoine et sur L'Odéon*. Paris: Bernard Grosset, 1928.

————. *Memories of the Théâtre Libre*. Translated by Marvin A. Carlson. Ed. by H. D. Albright. Coral Gables, FL: University of Miami Press, 1964.

Appia Adolphe. *Essays, Scenarios, and Designs*. Ann Arbor, MI: UMI Research Press, 1989.

————. *Music and the Art of Theater*. Coral Gables, FL: University of Miami Press, 1962.

————. *The Work of Living Art: A Theory of the Theatre* and *Man is the Measure of All Things*. Coral Gables, FL: University of Miami Press, 1960.

————. *Texts on Theatre*. London; New York: Routledge, 1993.

Artaud, Antonin. *The Theater and Its Double*. New York: Grove Press, 1958.

Austell, Jan. *What's in a Play?* New York: Harcourt, Brace and World, 1968.

Bablet, Denis. *Edward Gordon Craig*. New York: Theatre Arts Books, 1966.

Barba, Eugenio. *Beyond the Floating Islands*. New York: PAJ Publications, 1986.

———— and Nicola Savarese. *A Dictionary of Theatre Anthropology: The Secret Art of the Performer*. London; New York: Routledge, 1991.

————. *The Paper Canoe: A Guide to Theatre Antropology*. London; New York: Routledge, 1995.

Barrault, Jean-Louis. *Comme je pense*. Paris: Gallimard, 1983.

————. *Memories for Tomorrow*. New York: Dutton, 1974.

————. *Saisir le présent*. Paris: Robert Laffont, 1984.

————. *The Theatre of Jean Louis Barrault*. New York: Hill and Wang, 1962.

Bartow, Artur. *The Director's Voice: Twenty-One Interviews*. New York: Theater Communication Group, 1988.

Baty, Gaston. *Rideau baissé*. Paris: Bordas, 1949.

————. *Théâtre nouveau: notes et documents*. Paris: Société des Spectacles, 1927.

418

Beacham, Richard C. *Adolphe Appia: Artist and Visionary of the Modern Theatre.*
Chur, Switzerland; Philadelphia: Harwood Academic Publishers, 1994.
————. *Adolphe Appia, Theatre Artist.* Cambridge, New York: Cambridge
University Press, 1987.
Beck, Julian. *The Life of the Theatre.* New York: Avon Books, 1972.
Belasco, David. *The Theatre Through Its Stage Door.* Ed. by Louis V. Defoe. New
York: Harper, 1919.
Bearn, Pierre. *Paul Fort; avec un choix de textes.* Paris: Seghers, 1975.
Berger, Melvin. *Putting on a Show.* New York: F. Watts, 1980.
Berry, Ralph. *On Directing Shakespeare: Interviews with Contemporary Directors.*
London: H. Hamilton; New York: Viking Penguin, 1989.
Besson, Benno. *Jahre mit Brecht.* Willisau: Theaterkultur-Verlag, 1990.
Black, George. *Contemporary Stage Directing.* Fort Worth, TX: Holt, Rinehart and
Winston, 1991.
Black, Malcolm. *First Reading to First Night: A Candid Look at Stage Directing.*
Seattle: University of Washington Press, 1975.
Blanchart, Paul. *Histoire de la mise en scène.* Paris: Librairie théâtrale, 1948.
Blau, Herbert. *The Impossible Theater: A Manifesto.* New York: Collier Books;
London: Coller-MacMillan, 1964.
Boal, Augusto. *The Theater of the Oppressed.* Charles A. and Maria-Odilia Leal
McBride, trans. New York: Theater Communications Group. 1985.
Bradby, David and David Williams. *Directors' Theatre.* New York: St. Martin's
Press, 1988.
Braun, Edward. *The Director and the Stage: From Naturalism to Grotowski.* New
York: Holmes and Meier, 1982.
Braun Kazimierz. *A History of Polish Theater, 1939-1989, Spheres of Captivity and
Freedom.* Westport, CT and London: Greenwood Press, 1996.
————. *Cypriana Norwida teatr bez teatru.* [*Cyprian Norwid's Theater
Without Theater.*] Warszawa: PIW, 1971.
————. *Druga Reforma Teatru.* [*The Second Reform of Theater.*] Wrocław:
Ossolineum, 1979.
———— and Tadeusz Różewicz. *Języki teatru.* [*Languages of Theater.*]
Wrocław: Wydawnictwo Dolnośląskie, 1989.
————. *Nadmiar teatru.* [*Excess of Theater.*] Warszawa: Czytelnik, 1985.
————. *Notatnik reżysera* [*A Director's Notebook.*] Lublin: Wydawnictwo
Lubelskie, 1970.
————. *Nowy teatr na świecie (1960-1970)* [*The New Theater in The World (1960-
1970.*] Warszawa: WAiF, 1975.
————. *Przestrzeń teatralna.*[*The Theater Space.*] Warszawa: PWN, 1982.
———— and Stanisław Bereś. *Rozdarta kurtyna.* [*A Torn Curtain.*] London: Aneks,
1993.
————. *Szkice o ludziach teatru.* [*Essays on Polish Theater Artists.*] Warszawa:
Semper, 1996.
————. *Teatr polski 1939-1989. Obszary wolności — obszary zniewolenia .*[*Polish
Theater 1939-1989, Realms of Freedom—Realms of Captivity.*] Warszawa:
Semper, 1994.

_____. *Teatr Wspólnoty*. [*The Theater of Communion*.] Kraków: Wydawnictwo Literackie, 1972.

_____ and Zofia Reklewska-Braun. *Teofil Trzciński*. [*Teofil Trzciński*.] Warszawa: PIW, 1967.

_____. *Wielka Reforma Teatru w Europie*. [*The Great Reform of Theater in Europe*.] Wrocław: Ossolineum, 1984.

_____. *Wprowadzenie do reżyserii*. [*Introduction to Directing*.] Warszawa: Semper, 1998.

Brecht, Bertolt. *Antigonemodell*. Berlin: Gebrueder Weiss, 1949.

_____. *A Little Organum for the Theatre*, translated by John Willet, in *Playwrights on Playwriting*, ed. by Toby Cole. New York: Hill and Wang, 1960.

_____. *Mutter Courage Modell*. Berlin: Henschelverlag, 1958.

Brecht, Stefan. *Peter Schumann's Bread and Puppet Theatre*. London: Methuen; New York: Routledge, 1988.

_____. *The Theatre of Visions: Robert Wilson*, Frankfurt-am-Main: Suhrkamp, 1978.

Brockett, Oscar and Robert Findlay. *Century of Innovation*. Boston: Allyn and Bacon, 1991.

Brook, Peter. *The Empty Space*. New York: Harper and Row, 1968.

_____. *The Open Door*. New York: Theater Communications Group, 1995.

_____. *The Shifting Point: 1946-1987*. New York: Harper and Row, 1987.

Brown, Andrew. *Drama*. With an introduction by Tyrone Guthrie. New York: Arc Books 1962.

Brown, Gilmor and Alice Garwood. *General Principles of Play Direction*. New York, Los Angeles and London: S. French, 1936.

Browne, E. Martin. *Beginnings in Drama*. Studio City, CA: Players Press, 1998.

Busti, Kathryn Michele. *Stage Production Handbook: Job Responsibilities for All Technical Backstage Crews*. Littlleton, CO: Theatre Things, 1992.

Canfield, Curtis. *The Craft of Play Directing*. Drawings by W. Oren Parker. New York: Holt, Rinehart and Winston, 1963.

Carlisle, Barbara and Don Drapeau. *Hi Concept—Lo Tech: Theatre for Everyone in Any Place*. Portsmouth, NH: Heinemann, 1996.

Carnicke, Sharon Marie. *The Theatrical Instinct: Nikolai Evreinov and the Russian Theatre of the Early Twentieth Century*. New York: P. Lang, 1989.

Carra, Lawrence. *Controls in Play Directing: Types and Styles of Plays*. New York: Vantage Press, 1985.

Carter, Huntly: *The Theatre of Max Reinhardt*. London: F. and C. Palmer, 1914.

Cassady, Marsh. *The Theatre and You: A Beginning*. Colorado Springs: Meriwether, 1992.

Catron, Louis E. *The Director's Vision: Play Direction From Analysis to Production*. Mountain View, CA: Mayfield, 1989.

Cerný, František. *Otázky divadelní režie*. Praha: Melantrich, 1988.

Chabanenko, Ivan. *Zapysky teatralnoho pedahoha: zbirnyk statei*. Kyiv: Mynisterstvo, 1980.

Chekhov, Michael. *To the Director and Playwright*. Westport: Greenwood Press, 1966.

Chilver, Peter. *Producing a Play*. London: Batsford, 1974.

Cioffi, Kathleen. *Alternative Theater and Poland, 1954-1989*. Amsterdam: Harwood Academic Publishers, 1996.

Clark, I. E. *Stagecrafters' Handbook: A Guide for Theatre Technicians*. Studio City, CA: Players Press, 1995.

Claus, Horst. *The Theatre Director Otto Brahm*. Ann Arbor, MI: UMI Research Press, 1981.

Clay, James H. and Daniel Krempel. *The Theatrical Image*. Lanham, MD: University Press of America, 1985.

Clurman, Harold. *The Fervent Years: The Story of the Group Theater and the Thirties*. New York: Alfred A. Knopf, 1950.

————. *On Directing*. New York: Macmillan, 1972.

Cohen, Edward M. *Working on a New Play: A Play Development Handbook for Actors, Directors, Designers and Playwrights*. New York: Limelight Editions, 1995.

Cohen, Robert, and John Harrop. *Creative Play Direction*. Englewood Cliffs, NJ: Prentice-Hall, 1984.

Cole, Susan Letzler. *Directors in Rehearsal: A Hidden World*. New York: Routledge, 1992.

Cole, Toby. ed.: *Acting: A Handbook of the Stanislavsky Method*. New York: Crown Publishers, 1947.

Cole, Toby and Helen Krich Chinoy, eds. *Directors on Directing: A Source Book of the Modern Theater*. With an illustrated history of directing by Helen Krich Chinoy. Indianapolis: Bobbs-Merrill, 1963.

Condee, William Faricy. *Theatrical Space: A Guide for Directors and Designers*. Lanham, MD: Scarecrow Press, 1995.

Constantinidis, Stratos E. *Theatre Under Deconstruction?: A Question of Approach*. New York: Garland, 1993.

Converse, Terry John. *Directing for the Stage: A Workshop Guide of 42 Creative Training Exercises and Projects*. Colorado Springs: Meriwether, 1995.

Copeau, Jacques. *Souvenirs du Vieux-Colombier*. Paris: Nouvelles Éditions Latines, 1931.

Corringan, Robert. *The Making of Theater from Drama to Performance*. Glenview: Scott and Foresman, 1981.

Counsell, John. *Play Direction: A Practical Viewpoint*. New York: St. Martin's Press, 1973.

Craig, Edward Gordon. *Gordon Craig on Movement and Dance*. Ed. and with introduction by Arnold Rood. New York: Dance Horizons, 1977.

————. *On the Art of the Theatre*. New York: Theatre Arts Books, 1961.

————. *The Theatre - Advancing*. Boston: Little, Brown and Co., 1919.

————. *Towards a New Theatre: Forty Designs for Stage Scenes with Critical Notes*. New York: B. Blom, 1969.

Creating Theater: The Professionals' Approach to New Plays: [interviews by] Lee Alan Morrow and Frank Pike. New York: Vintage Books, 1986.

Csató, Edward. *Leon Schiller*. Warszawa: Państwowy Instytut Wydawniczy, 1968.

Dean, Alexander and Lawrence Carra. *Fundamentals of Play Directing*. New York: Holt, Rinehart, and Winston, 1980.

DesRochers, Rick. *Playing Director: A Handbook for Beginners*. Portsmouth, NH: Heinemann, 1995.

Dietrich, John E. and Ralph W. Duckwall. *Play Direction*. Englewood Cliffs, NJ: Prentice Hall, 1983.

The Director in a Changing Theatre: Essays on Theory and Practice, With New Plays for Performance. Ed., with an introd., by J. Robert Wills. Palo Alto, CA: Mayfield, 1976.

The Director in the Twentieth Century. Ed. Alfred G. Brooks and Oscar B. Goodman. Associate editor: Lisbeth J. Roman. Binghamton: Max Reinhardt Archive, State University of New York at Binghamton, 1970.

Dolman, John and Richard K. Knaub. *The Art of Play Production*. New York: Harper and Row, 1973.

Donner, Jorn. *The Personal Vision of Ingmar Bergman*. Bloomington: Indiana University Press, 1964.

Dramaturgy in American Theater: A Source Book. Ed. Susan Jonas, Geoffrey S. Proehl; Consulting editor, Michael Lupu. Fort Worth, TX: Harcourt Brace College Publishers, 1997.

Dudzik, Wojciech. *Wilama Horzycy dramat niespełnienia*. Warszawa: Uniwersytet Warszawski, 1990.

Dullin, Charles. *L'Avare de Molière, mise en scène et commentaries de Charles Dullin.* Paris: Éditions du Seuil, 1946.

_____ . *Souvenirs et notes de travail d'un acteur*. Paris: O. Lieutier, 1946.

Edwards, Christine. *The Stanislavsky Heritage, Its Contribution to the Russian and American Theatre*. New York: New York University Press, 1965.

Efros, Anatoy. *Rehearsals Are My Love*. Moscow: Isskustwo, 1975.

_____ . *Profession: Director*. Moscow: Isskustwo, 1979.

Esslin, Martin. *Brecht: The Man and His Work*. New York: Doubleday, 1960.

_____ . *The Theater of the Absurd*. Garden City, NY: Anchor Books, Doubleday, 1961.

Eynat-Confino, Irene. *Beyond the Mask: Gordon Craig, Movement, and the Actor*. Carbondale: Southern Illinois University Press, 1987.

Farber, Donald C. *From Option to Opening: A Guide to Producing Plays Off-Broadway*. New York: Limelight Editions, 1988.

_____ . *Producing on Broadway: A Comprehensive Guide*, New York. DBS Publications [1969].

Fernald, John. *The Play Produced: An Introduction to the Technique of Producing Plays*, foreword by Flora Robson, London, H. F. W. Deane and Sons; Boston: The Baker International Play Bureau, 1933.

_____ . *Sense of Direction: The Director and His Actors*. New York: Stein and Day, 1969.

Fialko, Valerii. *Rezhissura i setìsenografieia: puti vzaimodeistvieia*. Kiev: Mystetistvo, 1989.

Filipowicz, Halina. *A Laboratory of Impure Forms*. Westport, CT and London: Greenwood Press, 1991.

Fishman, Morris. *Play Production: Methods and Practice*. London: H. Jenkins, 1965.

Flashar, Hellmut. *Inszenierung der Antike: das griechische Drama auf der Bühne der Neuzeit, 1585-1990.* München: Verlag C.H. Beck, 1991.

Foreman, Richard. *Reverberation Machines: The Later Plays and Essays.* Barrytown: Station Hill Press, 1985.

Frejka, Jiři. *Žive divadlo.* Praha: E. Pleskot, 1936.

Frerer, Lloyd Anton. *Directing for the Stage.* Lincolnwood, IL.: NTC Pub. Group, 1996.

Frick John and Stephen Vallillo. *Theatrical Directors: A Bibliographical Dictionary.* Westport, CT and London: Greenwood Press, 1994.

Fuchs, Georg: *Revolution in the Theatre.* Condensed and adapted by Constance Connor Kuhn. Ithaca: Cornell University Press, 1959.

Gassner, John. *Dramatic Sounding.* New York: Crown Publishers, 1968.

————. *Producing the Play.* With the New Scene Technician's Handbook by Philip Barber. New York: Dryden Press, 1953.

Gerould, Daniel, ed. *Twentieth-Century Polish Avant-Garde Drama.* Itaca and London: Cornell University Press, 1977.

————. *Witkacy: Stanisław Ignacy Witkiewicz as an Imaginative Writer.* Seattle and London: University of Washington Press, 1977.

Gielgud, John and John Miller. *Shakespeare: Hit or Miss?* London: Sidgwick and Jackson, 1991.

Glenn, Stanley L. *A Director Prepares.* Encino, CA: Dickenson, 1973.

Glover, J. Garrett. *The Cubist Theatre.* Ann Arbor, MI: UMI Research Press, 1983.

Golub, Spencer. *Evreinov: The Theatre of Paradox and Transformation.* Ann Arbor, MI: UMI Research Press, 1984.

Gorchakov, Nikolai M. *Stanislavsky Directs.* New York: Limelight Editions, 1985.

————. *The Vakhtangov School of Stage Art.* Moscow: Foreign Language House, 1959.

Granville-Barker, Harley. *The Exemplary Theatre.* Freeport, NY: Books for Libraries Press, 1970.

————. *On Dramatic Method.* New York: Hill and Wang, 1956.

Green, Amy S. *The Revisionist Stage: American Directors Reinvent the Classics.* Cambridge and New York: Cambridge University Press, 1994.

Gregory, William Alfred. *The Director: A Guide to Modern Theater Practice.* New York: Funk and Wagnalls, 1968.

Grote, David. *Play Directing in the School: A Drama Director's Survival Guide.* Colorado Springs: Meriwether, 1997.

The Grotowski Sourcebook. Ed. by Lisa Wolford and Richard Schechner. London, New York: Routledge, 1997.

Grotowski, Jerzy. *Towards a Poor Theater.* New York: Simon and Schuster, 1968.

————. *Teksty z lat 1965-1969: Wybór.* Wrocław: Wiedza o Kulturze, 1990.

Guthrie, Tyrone. *A Life in the Theater.* New York: McGraw-Hill, 1959.

Henze, Herbert. *Otto Brahm und das Deutsche Theater in Berlin.* Berlin: E. S. Mittler und Sohn, 1930.

Hiss, Guido. *Der theatralische Blick: Einführung in die Aufführungsanalyse.* Berlin: D. Reimer, 1993.

Hodge, Francis. *Play Directing: Analysis, Communication, and Style.* Englewood Cliffs, NJ: Prentice Hall, 1994.

Horzyca Wilam. *O dramacie*. Warszawa: Wydawnictwa Artystyczne i Filmowe, 1969.

Houghton, Norris. *Moscow Rehearsals: An Account of Methods of Production in the Soviet Theatre*. New York: Octagon Books, 1975.

Hübner, Zygmunt. *Sztuka reżyserii*. Warszawa: Czytelnik, 1981.

Innes, C. D. *Erwin Piscator's Political Theatre: The Development of Modern German Drama*. Cambridge: Cambridge University Press, 1972.

Jessner, Leopold, *Schriften: Theater d. zwanziger Jahre*. Berlin: Henschelverlag Kunst und Gesellschaft, 1979.

Johnson, Albert and Bertha Johnson. *Directing Methods*. South Brunswick, NJ: A. S. Barnes, 1970.

Jones, David Richard. *Great Directors at Work: Stanislavsky, Brecht, Kazan, Brook*. Berkeley: University of California Press, 1986.

Jones, Edward Trostle. *Following Directions: A Study of Peter Brook*. New York: P. Lang, 1985.

Jouvet, Dullin, Baty, Pitoeff: le Cartel. Paris: Bibliotheque Nationale, 1987.

Jouvet, Louis. *Témoignages sur le théâtre*. Paris: Flammarion, 1952.

Kahn, David and Donna Breed. *Scriptwork: a Director's Approach to New Play Development*, with a foreword by Lanford Wilson. Carbondale, IL: Southern Illinois University Press, 1995.

Kantor, Tadeusz. *A Journey Through Other Spaces: Essays and Manifestos, 1944-1990*. Edited and translated by Michał Kobiałka. With a *Critical Study of Tadeusz Kantor's Theater* by Michał Kobiałka. Berkeley: University of California Press, 1993.

Karpiński, Maciej, *The Theatre of Andrzej Wajda*, Cambridge: Cambridge University Press, 1989.

Kazan, Elia. *An American Odyssey*. Ed. Michel Ciment. New York: St. Martin's Press, 1989.

Kiebuzinska, Christine. *Revolutionaries in the Theater: Meyerhold, Brecht, and Witkiewicz*. Ann Arbor, MI: UMI Press, 1988.

Kirby, Michael. *Futurist Performance*. New York: Dutton, 1971.

————. *Total Theatre*. New York: Dutton, 1969.

Knapp, Bettina Liebowitz. *Louis Jouvet, Man of the Theatre*. With a foreword by Michael Redgrave. New York: Columbia University Press, 1957.

Komissarzhevsky, Theodore. *Myself and the Theatre*. New York: E. P. Dutton and Co., 1930.

———— and Lee Simonson. *Settings and Costumes of the Modern Stage*. New York: B. Blom, 1966.

Korzeniewski, Bohdan. *O wolność dla pioruna... w teatrze*. Warszawa: PIW, 1973.

Kotlarczyk, Mieczysław. *Podstawy sztuki żywego słowa*. Warszawa: Wydawnictwo Związkowe, 1961.

————. *Reduta słowa*. London: Odnowa, 1980.

Kott, Jan. *Shakespeare our Contemporary.* Garden City, NY: Anchor Books, Doubleday and Co., 1966.

————. *The Theater of Essence.* Evanston, IL: Northwestern University Press, 1984.

Kozelka, Paul. *Directing.* New York: Richards Rosen Press, 1968.

Krasiński, Edward. *Edmund Wierciński.* Warszawa: Państwowy Instytut Wydawniczy, 1960.

Krull, Karena. *Drama Made Easy: A Complete Step by Step Handbook for Producing Skits and Plays.* Colville, WA: Eternal Hearts, 1995.

Kumiega, Jennifer. *The Theatre of Grotowski.* London and New York: Methuen, 1985.

Kurbas, Les. *Spaglady Souczasnikiv.* Kiev: Misterstwo, 1969.

Kurtz, Maurice. *Jacques Copeau.* Paris: Nagel, 1950.

Law, Alma and Mel Gordon. *Meyerhold, Eisenstein and Biomechanics: Actor Training in Revolutionary Russia.* Jefferson, NC and London: Mc Farland and Co. Publishers, 1996.

Leiter, Samuel L. *From Belasco to Brook: Representative Directors of the English-speaking Stage.* New York, Westport, CT, London: Greenwood Press, 1991.

————. *From Stanislavsky to Barrault: Representative Directors of the European Stage.* New York, Westport, CT, London: Greenwood Press, 1991.

Lermimier, Georges: *Jacques Copeau.* Collection "Les Metteurs en scène". Les Presses Littéraires de France, 1953.

Les Voies de la création théâtrale. Etudes de Odette Aslan [et al.] Réunies et présentées par Jean Jacquot. Paris. Éditions du Centre national de la recherche scientifique, 1970-1997.

Levy, Shimon, ed. *Theater and Holy Script.* Brighton: Sussex Academic Press, 1999.

Lewis, John, Laura Andrews and Flip Kobler. *The Complete Guide to Church Play Production.* Nashville, TN: Convention Press, 1997.

The Living Book of the Living Theatre. With an Introductory Essay by Richard Schechner. Greenwich, CT: New York Graphic Society, 1971.

Lorda Mur, Clara Ubaldina. *Jean-Louis Barrault: teatre i humanisme.* Barcelona: Institut del Teatre, 1992.

Lubimov, Jurij. *Le feu sacré: souvenirs d'une vie de théâtre.* Paris: Fayard, 1985.

Lugné-Poë, Aurelien: *Sous les étoiles, souvenirs de théâtre, 1902-1912.* Paris: Gallimard, 1933.

Mainusch, Herbert. *Regie und Interpretation: Gespräche mit Achim Benning, Peter Brook, Dieter Dorn, Adolf Dresen, Boy Gobert, Hans Hollmann, Takis Mouzenidis, Hans-Reinhard Müller, Claus Peymann, Peter Stein, Giorgio Strehler und Georgij Towstonogov.* München: W. Fink, 1985.

Mantegna, Gianfranco. *We, the Living Theatre.* New York: Ballantine Books, 1970.

Marinetti, Filippo Tommaso. *Selected Writings*. Ed., and with an introd. by R. Flint. New York: Farrar, Straus and Giroux, 1972.

Marker, Lise-Lone. *David Belasco: Naturalism in the American Theatre*. Princeton, NJ: Princeton University Press, 1974.

Marowitz, Charles. *Directing the Action: Acting and Directing in the Contemporary Theatre*. New York: Applause Theatre Books, 1991.

————. *The Other Way: An Alternative Approach to Acting and Directing*. New York: Applause Theater Books, 1998.

Marshall, Norman. *The Producer and the Play*. London: Davis-Poynter, 1975.

Martin, Jacqueline. *Voice in Modern Theatre*. London, New York: Routledge, 1991.

McCaffery, Michael. *Directing a Play*. New York: Schirmer Books, 1989.

McMullan, Frank Alonzo. *Directing Shakespeare in the Contemporary Theatre*. New York: R. Rosen Press, 1974.

————. *The Director's Handbook: An Outline for the Teacher and Student of Play Interpretation and Direction*. Hamden, CT: Shoe String Press, 1964.

————. *The Directorial Image: The Play and the Director*. Hamden, CT: Shoe String Press, 1962.

Meiler, Gisela. *Kunst und Kult im Werk von Gaston Baty: Motive, Probleme und Tendenzen einer Theaterreform*. Munchen: Kitzinger, 1984.

Meldolesi, Claudio. *Fondamenti del teatro italiano: la generazione dei registi*. Firenze: Sansoni, 1984.

Menta, Ed. *The Magic World Behind the Curtain: Andrei Serban in the American Theater*. New York: Peter Lang, 1995.

Meyerhold on Theatre. Translated and edited with a critical commentary by Edward Braun. London: Methuen, 1969.

Meyerhold, Vsevolod. *Schriften: Aufsätze, Briefe, Reden, Gespräche*. Berlin: Henschelverlag, 1979.

Miles-Brown, John. *Directing Drama*. London: Peter Owen, 1980.

Mitchell, Lee. *Staging Premodern Drama: a Guide to Production Problems*. Westport, CT and London: Greenwood Press, 1983.

Mitter, Shomit. *Systems of Rehearsal: Stanislavsky, Brecht, Grotowski, and Brook*. London and New York: Routledge, 1992.

Morrison, Hugh. *Directing in the Theatre*. New York: Theatre Arts Books, 1984.

Nelson, Richard and David Jones. *Making Plays: the Writer-Director Relationship in the Theatre Today*. Ed. Colin Chambers. London; Boston: Faber and Faber, 1995.

Nemirovich-Danchenko, Vladimir. *My Life in the Russian Theatre*. Boston: Little, Brown and Co., 1936.

————. *Retisenzii, ocherki, stati, intereiu, zametki, 1877-1942*. Moskva: Vseror. Teatralnoe ob-vo, 1980.

426

O'Neill, R. H. and N.M. Boretz. *The Director as Artist: Play Direction Today*. New York: Holt, Rinehart, and Winston, 1987.

Osiński, Zbigniew. *Grotowski and His Laboratory*. New York: PAJ Publications, 1986.

Osterwa, Juliusz. *Reduta i teatr*. Zebrali Zbigniew Osiński i Teresa Zabłocka. Wrocław: Wiedza o Kulturze, 1990.

Owen, Alice. *The Art of Play Directing: A Tentaive Bibliography*. Boston: Simmons College, 1943.

Page to Stage: Theatre as Translation. Ed. Ortrun Zuber-Skerritt. Amsterdam: Rodopi, 1984.

Pandolfi, Vito. *Regia e registi nel teatro moderno*. Bologna: Capelli, 1973.

Panovski, Naum. *Directing Poiesis*. New York: P. Lang, 1993.

Patterson, M. *Peter Stein: Germany's Leading Theatre Director*. New York: Cambridge University Press, 1981.

Piscator, Erwin. *The Political Theatre;* Translated, with chapter introductions and notes by Hugh Rorrison. London: Methuen, 1980.

Pizzato, Mark. *Edges of Loss: From Modern Drama to Postmodern Theory*. Ann Arbor: The University of Michigan Press, 1998.

Pleśniarowicz, Krzysztof. *Teatr śmierci Tadeusza Kantora*. Chotomów, Wydawnictwo Verba, 1990.

Production Notebooks. Ed. with an introduction by Mark Bly. New York: Theatre Communications Group, 1996.

Pryor, Nick. *Putting on a Play*. New York: Thomson Learning, 1994.

Purdom, Charles. *Harley Granville Barker, Man of the Theatre, Dramatist and Scholar*. Westport, CT: Greenwood Press, 1971.

Radishcheva, Olga. A. *Stanislavski i Nemirovich-Danchenko: Istorieia teatralnykh otnoshenii: 1897-1908*. Moskva: Artist, Rezhisser, Teatr, 1997.

Ratliff, Gerald Lee. *Playscript Interpretation and Production*. New York: Rosen Pub. Group, 1985.

Reinhardt, Max. *Leben für das Theater: Briefe, Reden, Aufsatze, Interviews, Gesprache, Auszuge aus Regiebuchern*. Berlin: Argon-Verlag, 1989.

Rodgers, James W. and Wanda C. Rodgers. *Play Director's Survival Kit: A Complete Step-by-Step Guide to Producing Theater in Any School or Community Setting;* graphics and illustrations by Russell Jones. West Nyack, NY: Center for Applied Research in Education, 1995.

Rose, Enid. *Gordon Craig and the Theatre: A Record and an Interpretation*. New York: Haskell House Publishers, 1973.

Roubine, Jean Jacques. *Théâtre et mise-en-scène, 1880-1980*. Paris: Presses Universitaires de France, 1980.

Rouché, Jacques. *L'Art théâtral moderne*. Paris: E. Cornely and Cie., 1910.

Rucker, Robert M. *Producing and Directing Drama for the Church*. Kansas City, MO: Lillenas, 1993.

Rudnitsky, Konstantin. *Meyerhold the Director*. Ann Arbor, MI: Ardis, 1981.

Saint-Denis, Michel: *Theatre: The Rediscovery of Style*. New York: Theatre Arts Books, 1960.

Savary, Jérôme. *La vie privée d'un magicien ordinaire*. Paris: Ramsay, 1985.

Saville, Jonathan. *From Script to Production*. Boston: Educational Associates, c1975.

Schecher, Richard. *Environmental Theatre*. New York: Hawthorn Book, 1973.

————. *Between Theater and Antopology*. Philadelphia: University of Pennsylvania Press, 1985.

Schiller, Leon. *Teatr ogromny*. Opracował Zbigniew Raszewski. Warszawa: Czytelnik, 1961.

Selden, Samuel. *First Principles of Play Direction*. Chapel Hill: University of North Carolina Press, 1937.

Semil, Małgorzata and Elżbieta Wysińska, *Słownik współczesnego teatru*. Warszawa: Wydawnictwa Artystyczne i Filmowe, 1980.

Shapiro, Mel. *The Director's Companion*. Fort Worth: Harcourt Brace College Publishers, 1998.

Sharoev, Ioakim. *Dramaturgieia massovogo deistva: Uchebnoe posobie po kursu "Rezhissura i masterstvo aktera"*. Moskva: Gos. in-t teatralnogo iskusstva im. A.V. Lunacharskogo, 1979.

Sharp, William L. *Language in Drama; Meanings for the Director and the Actor*. Scranton: Chandler, 1970.

Shyer, Lawrence. *Robert Wilson and His Collaborators*. New York: Theater Communication Group, 1989.

Sievers, Wieder David, Harry E. Stiver, Jr., and Stanley Kahan. *Directing for the Theatre*. Dubuque, IA: W. C. Brown, 1974.

Simonov, Ruben. *Stanislavsky's Protegé: Eugene Vakhtangov*. New York: DBS Publications, 1969.

The Stage Directions Guide to Directing. Ed. Stephen Peithman, Neil Offen. Portsmouth, NH: Heinemann, 1999.

Stanislavsky and America: An Anthology from the Tulane Drama Review. Ed. by Erica Munk, Introd. By Richard Schechner. New York: Hill and Wang, 1966.

Stanislavsky on the Art of the Stage. Translated with an introductory essay by David Magarshack. London and Boston: Faber and Faber, 1980.

Stanislavsky, Konstantin. *An Actor Prepares*. New York: Theatre Arts Books, 1936.

————. *Building a Character*. New York: Theatre Arts Books, 1949.

————. *Creating a Role*. New York: Theatre Arts Boks, 1961.

————. *My Life in Art*. New York: Theatre Arts Boks, 1948.

428

————. *Rezhisserskie ekzempliary K.S. Stanislavskogo, 1898-1930*. Moskva: Iskusstvo, 1980-1994.

Staub, August W. *Creating Theatre: The Art of Theatrical Directing*. New York: Harper and Row, 1973.

Strasberg, Lee. *A Dream of Passion: The Development of the Method;* Ed. By Evangeline Morphos. Boston: Little, Brown, 1987.

Strehler, Giorgio. *Per un teatro umato*. Milano: Giangiacomo Feltrinelli, 1974.

Styan, J. L. *Max Reinhardt*. Cambridge; New York: Cambridge University Press, 1982.

Tairov, Aleksandr. *Notes of a Director*. Coral Gables, FL.: University of Miami Press, 1969.

Taylor, Don. *Directing Plays*. Black; New York: Routledge: Theatre Arts Books, 1996.

The Theatre Team: Playwright, Producer, Director, Designers, and Actors. Ed. Jeane Luere and Sidney Berger. Westport, CT and London: Greenwood Press, 1998.

Thomas, James. *Script Analysis for Actors, Directors, and Designers*. Boston: Focal Press, 1992.

Timberlake, Craig. *The Bishop of Broadway: David Belasco*. New York: Library Publishers, 1954.

Tolmacheva, Galina. *Creadores del teatro moderno: los grandes directores de los siglos XIX y XX*. Mendoza: Editorial de la Universidad de Cuyo,1992.

Törnqvist, Egil. *Transposing Drama: Studies in Representation*. New York: St. Martin's Press, 1991.

Tovstonogov, Georgi A. *The Profession of the Stage-Director*. Moscow: Iskusstvo, 1972.

Tytell, John. *The Living Theatre: Art, Exile, and Outrage*. New York: Grove Press, 1995.

Vakhtangov, Eugeny: *Zapiski, Pisma, Stati*. Moscow: Iskusstvo, 1939.

Vaughan, Stuart. *Directing Plays: a Working Professional's Method*. New York: Longman, 1993.

Verdeil, Jean. *Le travail du metteur en scène: un exemple*, Lyon: ALEAS, 1995.

Volbach, Walther R. *Adolphe Appia, Prophet of the Modern Theater: A Profile*. Middletown, CT: Wesleyan University Press, 1968.

Walaszek, Joanna. *Teatr Konrada Swinarskiego*. Warszawa: Państwowy Instytut Wydawniczy, 1991.

Watson, Ian. *Towards a Third Theatre: Eugenio Barba and the Odin Teatret;* With a foreword by Richard Schechner. London; New York: Routledge, 1993.

Welker, David Harold. *Theatrical Direction; The Basic Techniques*. Boston: Allyn and Bacon, 1971.

Whitmore, Jon. *Directing Postmodern Theater: Shaping Signification in Performance.* Ann Arbor: University of Michigan Press, 1994.

Whitton, David. *Stage Directors in Modern France.* Manchester [England]: Manchester University Press, 1987.

Wiles, Timothy J. *The Theater Event: Modern Theories of Performance.* Chicago: University of Chicago Press, 1980.

Willett, John. *The Theatre of Bertolt Brecht.* New York: New Directions, 1959.

————. *The Theatre of Erwin Piscator.* New York: Holmes and Meier, 1979.

Williams, Simon. *Richard Wagner and Festival Theater.* Westport, CT and London: Praeger, 1994.

Wills, J. Robert. *Directing in the Theatre: A Casebook.* Metuchen, N.J.: Scarecrow Press, 1994.

Withers-Wilson, Nan. *Vocal Direction for the Theatre: From Script Analysis to Opening Night.* New York: Drama Book Publishers, 1993.

Witkowska-Lis, Hanna, ed. *Teatr Współczesny Wrocław 1948-1978.* Wrocław: Teatr Współczesny, 1978.

Wolford, Lisa. *Grotowski's Objective Drama Research.* Jackson: University Press of Mississipi, 1996.

Woods, Porter. *Experiencing Theater.* Englewood Clifs: Prentice-Hall, 1984.

Young, John Wray. *Directing the Play; From Selection to Opening Night.* Port Washington, NY: Kennikat Press 1972.

Zabka, Thomas and Adolf Dresen. *Dichter und Regisseure: Bemerkungen über das Regie-Theater.* Göttingen: Wallstein Verlag, 1995.

Zadek, Peter. *Das Wilde Ufer: Ein Theaterbuch.* Köln: Kiepenheuer and Witsch Verlag,1990.

Zakhava, Boris. *Vospomianieia; Spektakli i roli; Stati.* Moskva: Vseros. teatralnoe ob-vo, 1982.

Ziege, Felix. *Leopold Jessner und das Zeit-Theater.* Berlin: Eigenbroedler Verlag, 1928.

NAME INDEX

434

Sykała, Roman, 29, 31
Synge, John Millington, 143
Szajna, Józef, 6, 37
Szaniawski, Jerzy, 39, 60, 83, 101, 373, 398
Szczepańska, Nora, 68
Szletyński, Henryk, 69, 70
Szymanowski, Karol, 25

Śląska, Aleksandra, 60, 62
Świderski, Jan, 55, 75, 95

Tairov, Aleksandr, 10, 70
Terayama, Shuji, 11
Terry, Meghan, 137
Tetmajer-Przerwa, Kazimierz, 386
Tieck, Ludwig, 107
Tolstoy, Leo, 87
Tomaszewski, Henryk, 11
Tretiakov, Sergey, 44
Trzciński, Teofil, 107, 145
Tylor, Rich, 313

Uspienskaya, Maria, 32

Vakhtangov, Evgeny, 11, 70
Van Itallie, Jean-Claude, 137
Vane, Sutton, 34
Vasiliev, Anatoly, 11
Vega, Lope de, 272
Verhaeren, Emile, 151
Vilar, Jean, 11, 38, 76-78, 106, 313
Vinci, Leonardo da, 6, 152

Wagner, Richard, 107, 279, 403
Warren, Robert Penn, 55

Wajda, Andrzej, 11, 65, 267, 314
Wałęsa, Lech, 82
Wesker, Arnold, 75, 345
Wilde, Oskar, 272
Węgrzyn, Józef, 35
Wierciński, Edmund, 11, 36, 410
Wilder, Thornton, 59, 382, 393
Wilk, Andrzej, 99-100
Williams, Tennessee, 55, 75, 140, 163, 314, 342
Wilson, Robert, 6, 12, 106, 130, 131, 148, 242, 338, 403
Witkiewicz, Stanisław Ignacy (Witkacy), 36, 60, 261, 334, 393
Wojtyła, Karol, See John Paul II
Wolf, Friedrich, 44
Woszczerowicz, Jacek, 75, 141
Wyspiański, Stanisław, xiii, xix, 8, 9, 16, 24, 33, 36-37, 39, 44, 64, 71-72, 75, 83, 101, 119, 137, 149, 150, 161, 273, 398
Wyszyński, Stefan, 73

Young, Stark, 316

Zachwatowicz, Krystyna, 147
Zagórski, Jerzy, 36
Zamkow, Lidia, 152
Zawieyski, Jerzy, 36
Zelwerowicz, Aleksander, 10
Ziajski, Adam, 314
Zwieg, Arnold, 44

Żeromski, Stefan, 44, 87, 104
Żulinski, Anthony, 23-25, 31, 70, 414

PLAY INDEX

438

STUDIES IN THEATRE ARTS

"Shakespeare"

BY ANOTHER NAME

To my father,
George R. Anderson,
who has supported and believed in me
every step along the way

"Shakespeare"

BY ANOTHER NAME

The Life of Edward de Vere, Earl of Oxford,
The Man Who Was Shakespeare

MARK ANDERSON

FOREWORD BY SIR DEREK JACOBI

GOTHAM BOOKS

GOTHAM BOOKS
Published by Penguin Group (USA) Inc.
375 Hudson Street, New York, New York 10014, U.S.A.
Penguin Group (Canada), 10 Alcorn Avenue, Toronto, Ontario, Canada M4V 3B2
(a division of Pearson Penguin Canada Inc.); Penguin Books Ltd, 80 Strand,
London WC2R 0RL, England; Penguin Ireland, 25 St Stephen's Green, Dublin 2, Ireland
(a division of Penguin Books Ltd); Penguin Group (Australia), 250 Camberwell Road,
Camberwell, Victoria 3124, Australia (a division of Pearson Australia Group Pty Ltd);
Penguin Books India Pvt Ltd, 11 Community Centre, Panchsheel Park, New Delhi – 110 017, India;
Penguin Group (NZ), Cnr Airborne and Rosedale Roads, Albany, Auckland,
New Zealand (a division of Pearson New Zealand Ltd); Penguin Books (South Africa) (Pty) Ltd, 24
Sturdee Avenue, Rosebank, Johannesburg 2196, South Africa

Penguin Books Ltd, Registered Offices: 80 Strand, London WC2R 0RL, England

Published by Gotham Books, a division of Penguin Group (USA) Inc.

First printing, April 2005
1   3   5   7   9   10   8   6   4   2

"Ashbourne Portrait of Shakespeare": By permission of the Folger Shakespeare Library, Washington,
D.C.; "Wellbeck Portrait" of Edward de Vere: National Portrait Gallery, London; Photograph of Castle
Hedingham: By permission of Charles Bird; Sir William Cecil (later Baron Burghley): National
Portrait Gallery, London; Titian's *Venus and Adonis:* By permission of the Barberini Gallery, Rome;
Archivio Fotografico Polo Museale Romano; Anne Vavasour portrait: By permission of the
Company of Armourers & Brasiers in the City of London; photograph of Anne Cecil effigy: By
permission of Gerit Quealy; "Armada Portrait" of Queen Elizabeth: By kind permission of His
Grace the Duke of Bedford and the Trustees of the Bedford Estates (© His Grace the Duke of
Bedford and the Trustees of the Bedford Estates); "Tower Portrait" of Henry Wriothesley, 3rd Earl
of Southampton: By permission of His Grace the Duke of Buccleuch. "Droeshout Engraving
of Shakespeare": By permission of the Folger Shakespeare Library; *Shake-speare' Sonnets* title
page and dedication page & *Minerva Britanna* title page: By permission of the
Huntington Library, San Marino, Calif.

Gotham Books and the skyscraper logo are trademarks of Penguin Group (USA) Inc.

ISBN 1-592-40103-1

Printed in the United States of America
Set in Caslon Book BE   •   Designed by Sabrina Bowers
Maps by Compass Projections/Anita Karl and James Kemp

CONTENTS

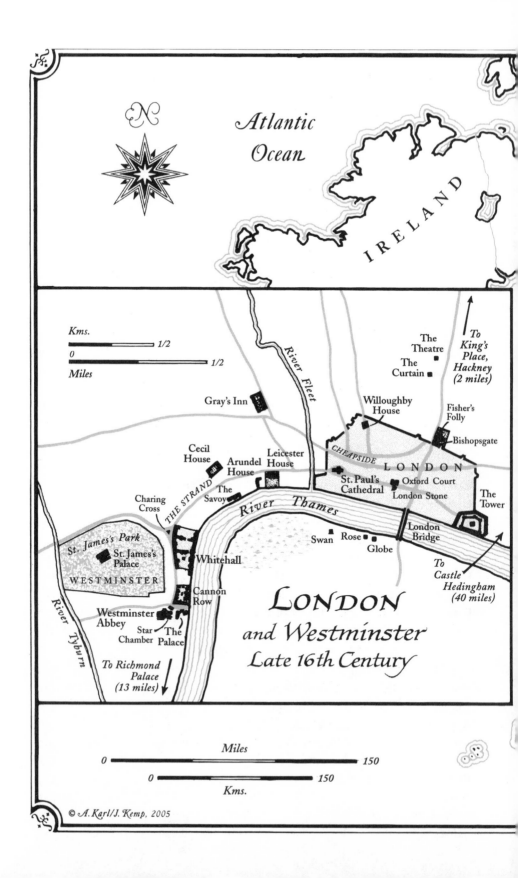

N

Atlantic
Ocean

IRELAND

Kms.

0   1/2

Miles

0   1/2

River Fleet

The
Theatre

The
Curtain

To
King's
Place,
Hackney
(2 miles)

Gray's Inn

Willoughby
House

Fisher's
Folly

Bishopsgate

Cecil
House

Arundel
House

Leicester
House

CHEAPSIDE

LONDON

St. Paul's
Cathedral

Oxford Court

London Stone

The
Tower

Charing
Cross

THE STRAND

The
Savoy

River Thames

Swan

Rose

Globe

London
Bridge

St. James's Park

St. James's
Palace

WESTMINSTER

Whitehall

To
Castle
Hedingham
(40 miles)

River Tyburn

Cannon
Row

Westminster
Abbey

Star
Chamber

The
Palace

LONDON
and Westminster
Late 16th Century

To Richmond
Palace
(13 miles)

Miles

0   150

0   150

Kms.

Venice

Ghetto

Campo San Geremia

Canal Grande

Rialto

Santa Maria Formosa

Piazza San Marco

San Giorgio dei Greci

FREZZERIA

Palazzo Ducale

Miles
0   1/4
0
Kms.

EUROPE
Late 16th Century

Atlantic Ocean

← Azores

Kms.
0   200
200
Miles

N

ENGLAND
London

Calais
Dunkirk

Bruges
Brussels

NETHERL

Paris

Langre

FRANCE

Lyon

Châteaus
Roussillon/
Tournon

PORTUGAL

SPAIN
Madrid

Cádiz

Mediterranea

© A. Karl/J. Kemp. 2005

HOLY ROMAN EMPIRE

DUCHY OF MILAN

REPUBLIC OF VENICE

Verona Padua

Milan

Mantua

Genoa

DUCHY OF MANTUA

Ferrara

DUCHY OF FERRARA

Venice (See inset)

KINGDOM OF HUNGARY

ILLYRIA

REPUBLIC OF GENOA

Florence

DUCHY OF TUSCANY

DUCHY OF URBINO

Ragusa

Siena

PAPAL STATES

Rome

KINGDOM OF NAPLES

Naples

ITALY

Miles

0 ____ 150

0 Kms. 150

Trápani

Palermo

Messina

Segesta

KINGDOM OF SICILY

DENMARK

Elsinore

HOLY ROMAN EMPIRE

BOHEMIA

Prague

Strasbourg

ITALY (See inset above)

Sea

Black Sea

Constantinople

OTTOMAN EMPIRE

Mt. Parnassus

Athens

Gulf of Lepanto

TIMELINE

Historical Events		Edward de Vere
	12 Apr. 1550	(Lord) Edward de Vere born, Castle Hedingham, Essex, to John de Vere, 16th earl of Oxford, and Margery, countess of Oxford.
Death of King Edward VI; accession of **July 1553** Queen Mary I.	**c. 1554**	Lord Edward's sister Mary born.
Mary I marries Prince Philip (later King Philip II). **July 1554**	**c. 1554–1562?**	Lord Edward under tutelage of Sir Thomas Smith, probably at Smith's estate of Ankerwicke, near Windsor.
Death of Mary I; accession of Queen Elizabeth I; **Nov. 1558** Sir William Cecil appointed principal secretary to Elizabeth.	**Oct. 1558**	Lord Edward entered Queen's College, Cambridge (recorded enrollment through Mar. '59).
Coronation of Queen Elizabeth I. **Jan. 1559**		
	Aug. 1561	Queen Elizabeth visits Castle Hedingham.
	Jul. 1562	Lord Edward contracted to marry into powerful Hastings family.
	Aug. 1562	Lord Edward's father dies; Lord Edward now 17th earl of Oxford and ward of state; moves to Cecil House, London, under guardianship of Sir William Cecil, principal advisor to Queen Elizabeth.
Elizabeth falls deathly ill with smallpox, names her **Oct. 1562** favorite, Robert Dudley, as lord protector of England if she should die.		
	1563	De Vere tutored by Anglo-Saxonist Laurence Nowell (who also signs his name on the *Beowulf* manuscript during this year).
Elizabeth raises Robert Dudley to earl of Leicester. **Sept. 1564**	**Sep. 1564**	De Vere receives bachelor's degree from Cambridge University.
	Sep. 1566	De Vere receives M.A. from Oxford University.
Lord Darnley, husband of Mary, Queen of Scots, **Feb. 1567** murdered.	**Feb. 1567**	De Vere enrolls in law school at Gray's Inn, London.
Mary, Queen of Scots, abdicates crown in Darnley **July 1567** murder scandal. Mary's infant son, James, is now officially King of Scotland.	**July 1567**	De Vere kills undercook at Cecil House in fencing accident.
Mary, Queen of Scots, flees for England; **May 1568** Elizabeth imprisons Mary.		
Earls of Northumberland and Westmoreland lead **Nov. 1569** Northern Rebellion against Elizabethan state.		
Pope Pius V declares Queen Elizabeth's reign **Feb. 1570** illegitimate.	**Early 1570**	De Vere recovers from illness at an inn in the town of Windsor.
	Apr. 1570	De Vere joins earl of Sussex in military campaign to suppress rebellion of Northern Earls in English border counties and southern Scotland.
Sir William Cecil raised to Baron (Lord) **Feb. 1571** Burghley.	**Apr. 1571**	De Vere sits in his first Parliament as member of House of Lords.
(De Vere's cousin) the duke of Norfolk **Sept. 1571** imprisoned for attempting to marry Mary, Queen of Scots, and depose Elizabeth.	**Dec. 1571**	De Vere married to his guardian's daughter Anne Cecil.
	Jan. 1572	De Vere publishes Latin preface to Latin edition of Castiglione's *Courtier.*
Thomas Howard, duke of Norfolk, executed **June 1572** for treason.		
Massacre of 10,000 French Protestants **Aug. 1572** (Huguenots), begun on St. Bartholomew's Day (Aug. 24) and continued across France into fall.	**c. 1573**	De Vere rumored to be Queen Elizabeth's lover.
	May 1573	De Vere's men assault father-in-law's servants on road to Rochester.
	June 1574	De Vere runs away to Lowlands; promptly recalled by queen.
	Feb. 1575	De Vere begins fourteen-month continental grand tour; attends coronation of French King Henri III at Rheims.

Historical Events	Date	Date	De Vere Events
		May 1575–Mar. '76	De Vere travels throughout Italy (and other lands), using Venice as a home base; (in England) daughter Elizabeth born in July.
		Apr. 1576	De Vere storms back to England, hearing rumors of his wife's infidelity.
The first public space for theater (The Theatre) opens north of London.	1577	Jan. 1577	The masque *A Historie of Error* performed at court for the queen, probably by de Vere, making self-deprecating jokes at his own jealous rage.
Elizabeth entertains marriage petition of French duc d'Alençon.	June 1578	c. 1578-'79	De Vere a founding member & patron of "Euphuist" school of poets.
Alençon arrives in England to press his case for marriage in person.	Aug. 1579	Sep. 1579	De Vere famously quarrels with Sir Philip Sidney at a royal tennis court.
Arrival of covert Catholic missionaries in England.	June 1580	1580	De Vere buys mansion Fisher's Folly, north of London, a bohemian retreat for Euphuist writers; de Vere has love affair with courtly belle Anne Vavasour.
		Dec. 1580	De Vere turns in Catholic traitors (and erstwhile comrades) Howard, Arundell & Southwell, who in turn spread malicious libels about de Vere.
Execution of Catholic missionary Edmund Campion.	Dec. 1581	Mar. 1581	Queen throws de Vere & Vavasour in Tower after Vavasour gives birth to illegitimate son Edward Veer; de Vere exiled from court.
Alençon marriage collapses; Elizabeth celebrated as "Virgin Queen."	Feb. 1582	Mar. 1582	De Vere & Vavasour's uncle duel, sparking intermittent family warfare.
		Spring 1583	De Vere leases Blackfriars Theatre in London; buries a (legitimate) infant son; re-admitted to court; travels with court to Oxford University.
Assassination of Dutch Protestant leader William of Orange.	July 1584	Apr. 1584	De Vere's daughter Bridget born.
		Dec. 1584	De Vere's troupe performs *The History of Agamemnon & Ulysses* at court, probably by de Vere, arguing for a commandership in Lowlands war.
		Aug. 1585	De Vere sent to Lowlands to join English officer corps.
		Oct. 1585	De Vere recalled to England.
Scots queen arrested for "Babbington Plot" to assassinate Elizabeth.	July 1586	June 1586	Queen grants de Vere £1000 annuity.
Mary, Queen of Scots, sentenced to death for treason.	Oct. 1586	Oct. 1586	De Vere sits on jury for Mary, Queen of Scots, trial.
Mary, Queen of Scots, executed.	Feb. 1587	May 1587	De Vere's daughter Susan born.
Spanish Armada launches from Lisbon for England.	May 1588	June 1588	De Vere part of early intercept force to engage Spanish Armada en route to England; de Vere's wife Anne, countess of Oxford, dies.
English naval forces engage, ultimately defeat Armada.	Aug. 1588	Dec. 1588	De Vere sells Fisher's Folly.
Puritan, anti-Anglican "Martin Marprelate" pamphlets circulate.	1588-'89	1589	*Arte of English Poesie* lists de Vere as court author whose works would be widely lauded if his "doings could be found out and made public with the rest."
Murder of French king Henri III; Henri of Navarre now King Henri IV.	July 1589	1590-'93	Marriage alliance between de Vere's daughter Elizabeth and the earl of Southampton promoted by Lord Burghley–and de Vere.
Robert Cecil (son of Lord Burghley) becomes Secretary of State.	Apr. 1590	Dec. 1591	De Vere makes over Castle Hedingham in trust to his three daughters.
		late 1591–early '92	De Vere marries Elizabeth Trentham of Rochester.
Playwright Robert Greene dies of overindulgence; posthumous pamphlet lambastes actor Will Shakspere as great literary pretender.	Sept. 1592	Sept. 1592	De Vere (as "Will Monox") joins Robert Greene and satirist Thomas Nashe on Greene's fateful day of drinking and overindulgence.
Playwright Christopher Marlowe murdered in Deptford tavern.	May 1593	1593	Nashe's pamphlet *Strange News* dedicated to de Vere (as "Gentle Mr. William").

Date	"Shakespeare" / literary & political events	Date	De Vere (Oxford) events
		Feb. 1593	De Vere's son and heir Henry (Lord Bolbec) born.
Summer 1593	Publication of poem *Venus & Adonis*, first work by "Shakespeare."		
1594	Publication of poem *Lucrece*–like *V&A*, dedicated to earl of Southampton.	1594	Pamphlet *Willobie His Avisa* published with character "Avisa" representing de Vere's wife Elizabeth; suggests scandalous affair between her and Southampton (as "H.W.") with de Vere (as "W.S.") satirically portrayed as egging Southampton on.
		Jan. 1595	De Vere's daughter Elizabeth marries William Stanley, earl of Derby.
June 1596	Earl of Essex leads successful raid of Spanish outpost at Azores.	1596-'97	De Vere, his wife, and son move to King's Place, Hackney.
July 1596	Sir Robert Cecil is made principal secretary to Queen Elizabeth.		
July 1597	Earl of Essex leads failed raid of Spanish fleet at Cádiz.		
Aug. 1598	Death of William Cecil, Lord Burghley.	1598	De Vere listed (along with "Shakespeare") as playwright in Francis Meres's literary and courtly who's-who *Palladis Tamia*.
1598	First publications of plays under the byline "Shakespeare." (Other than above poems, all previous publications had been anonymous).		
Mar.-Sept. 1599	Earls of Essex's and Southampton's failed campaign in Ireland.		
June 1600	Essex stripped of offices and placed under house arrest.	1600	De Vere seeks governorship of Isle of Jersey, to no avail.
Feb. 1601	Essex and Southampton rebel against Elizabeth (and Cecil) and lose. Essex and Southampton condemned for treason; Essex beheaded.	1602	De Vere's moribund troupe of actors, merged with Earl of Worcester's Men listed as performing at the Boar's Head Tavern.
Mar. 1603	Death of Queen Elizabeth I; accession of James VI of Scotland. Southampton released from Tower.		
July 1603	Coronation of King James I (de Vere performed ceremonial role).	July 1603	King James renews de Vere's £1000 annuity.
late 1604	The "good quarto" of *Hamlet* represents the last new Shake-speare work to appear in print, two brief periods (below) excepted.	June 24, 1604	De Vere dies at King's Place, Hackney; son Henry becomes 18th earl.
		1605	De Vere's daughter Susan marries Philip Herbert, earl of Montgomery.
		1607	De Vere's natural son Edward Veer knighted.
1608-'09	Spate of four new Shake-speare texts appear in print: *King Lear*, *Pericles*, *Troilus and Cressida*, and the *Sonnets*.	Apr. 1609	De Vere's widow given permission to sell King's Place, Hackney.
May 1612	Robert Lord Cecil dies.		
Nov. 1612	Henry Stuart, Prince of Wales, dies.		
1612	Henry Peacham's emblem book *Minerva Britanna* is published.		
		1615	Susan de Vere Herbert's brother-in-law the earl of Pembroke wins appointment as lord Chamberlain to King James–securing control of the future of the Shake-speare plays, to be shared between the two earls (as well as, one suspects, Susan).
Apr. 1616	Will Shakspere of Stratford dies; doggerel epitaph printed on gravestone in Trinity Church, Stratford; (sometime pre-1623) red-herring monument erected elsewhere in Trinity Church imploring viewers to "sieh [look there, at the gravestone, which is] all he hath writ."		
1619	Publisher William Jaggard publishes editions of ten Shake-speare reprints, two of which are falsely attributed.	1619	Publisher William Jaggard dedicates book to de Vere's daughter Susan and her husband, imploring them to pick the "fairest fruitages" and "bestow [them] how and when you list"–requesting access to unprinted Shake-speare texts.
1621	King James pursues marriage alliance with Spain for his son Prince Charles.		
June-July 1621	Anti–Spanish Marriage crusaders earl of Southampton and (18th) earl of Oxford arrested; Oxford thrown in Tower of London.	April 1622	18th earl of Oxford back in Tower; threats emerge of his execution.
1622	Shake-speare's *Othello* published, the first new work since 1609.	1622	Jaggard's shop begins hurried production of complete works of Shake-speare.
Oct. 1623	Spanish Marriage collapses; earl of Oxford released from Tower. Florentine courtly correspondent notes "All's well that ends well."	Nov. 1623	Publication of Shake-speare "First Folio" dedicated to anti–Spanish Marriage crusaders earls of Montgomery and Pembroke.

⁂

DRAMATIS PERSONAE

Chapter 1:
THE EYE OF CHILDHOOD [1550–1562]

EDWARD DE VERE, Lord Bolbec, [post-1562] seventeenth earl of Oxford, Lord Great Chamberlain of England (1550–1604)–A.k.a. "Pasquill Caviliero," "William Shake-speare."

JOHN DE VERE, sixteenth earl of Oxford, Lord Great Chamberlain of England (1516?–1562)–A.k.a. "Earl John," Lord Edward's father.

MARGERY (GOLDING) DE VERE, countess of Oxford (1525?–1568)–Lord Edward's mother.

SIR THOMAS SMITH, [1548–53, 1572–77] Secretary of State (1513–1577)–Lord Edward's tutor (c. 1554–1562).

"THE FIGHTING VERES": HORACE ("HORATIO") VERE, [post-1596] Sir Horatio (1565–1635), and **Francis Vere,** [post-1588] Sir Francis (1560–1609)–Lord Edward's revered military cousins.

MARY DE VERE, [post-1578] Mary Bertie (1554?–1624)–Lord Edward's sister.

KATHERINE DE VERE, Lady Windsor (1541?–1600)–Lord Edward's half-sister.

EDWARD TUDOR, [post-1548] King Edward VI of England (1537–1553).

MARY TUDOR, [post-1553] Queen Mary I of England (1516–1558).

ELIZABETH TUDOR, [post-1558] Queen Elizabeth I of England (1533–1603).

SIR ROBERT DUDLEY, [post-1564] earl of Leicester (1532?–1588)–Princess/Queen Elizabeth's lifelong favorite.

JOHN BALE (1495–1563)–Playwright, author of *King Johan,* employed by Earl John, perhaps the first playwright Lord Edward ever met.

SIR WILLIAM CECIL, [post-1571] Baron (Lord) Burghley (1520–1598)–Queen Elizabeth's principal advisor and spymaster; Lord Edward's guardian (1562–71), Lord Edward's father-in-law (1571–88).

HENRY HASTINGS, [post-1560] earl of Huntington (1535–1595)–Heir presumptive to English crown circa 1561, when he arranged a marriage match between one of his sisters and Lord Edward–a nuptial that never came to pass.

CHAPTER 2:
EVERMORE IN SUBJECTION [1562–1569]

LAURENCE NOWELL (1530–c. 1570)–Anglo-Saxon scholar; de Vere's tutor (1563).

ROBERT CECIL, [post-1591] Sir Robert, [post-1603] Baron Cecil, [post-1604] Viscount Cranborne, [post-1605] earl of Salisbury (1563–1612)–Grew up in Cecil House along with de Vere; [post-1571] de Vere's brother-in-law.

ARTHUR GOLDING (1536?–1606)–Classical scholar and antiquarian; de Vere's uncle; translator of Ovid's *Metamorphoses* (among other works); de Vere's tutor (?) c. 1563.

RICHARD EDWARDS (1525–1566)–Playwright and editor of poetry anthology *The Paradise of Dainty Devices* (published 1576), containing some of de Vere's earliest poetry.

EDWARD MANNERS, [post-1563] earl of Rutland (1549–1587)–Classmate of de Vere's from Cecil House; juror on Mary, Queen of Scots trial, 1586.

PHILIP SIDNEY, [post-1583] Sir Philip (1554–1586)–Courtier, poet, scholar, soldier, longtime de Vere rival.

GEORGE GASCOIGNE (1535?–1577)–Poet, playwright, author of enigmatic collection *Hundreth Sundry Flowres* (1573–75), to which de Vere may have contributed.

THOMAS BRINCKNELL (d. 1571)–Undercook at Cecil House killed by de Vere in fencing accident.

CHARLES TYRELL (d. 1570)–Horsemaster for Dudley family; married de Vere's mother, Margery, within a year of Earl John's death.

ANNE CECIL, [post-1571] countess of Oxford (1556–1588)–De Vere's foster sister after de Vere's 1562 move to Cecil House; married de Vere in 1571; de Vere accused Anne of cuckolding him in 1576, and the two were separated until 1582.

CHAPTER 3:
TREASONS AND VILE INSTRUMENTS [1569–1572]

THOMAS RADCLIFFE, third earl of Sussex, [post-1573] Lord Chamberlain (1527?–1583)–De Vere's military commander, mentor, and court advisor; likely one of de Vere's earliest theatrical producers (in his capacity as master of the Lord Chamberlain's Men).

MARY STUART, Queen of Scots (1542–1587)–Great-granddaughter of King Henry VII and heir presumptive (to many English subjects, at least) to the English throne.

"THE NORTHERN EARLS": CHARLES NEVILLE, [post-1564] earl of Westmorland (1543–1601), and SIR THOMAS PERCY, [post-1557] earl of Northumberland (1528–1572)–Rose up in 1569–70 in favor of Mary, Queen of Scots, and against Queen Elizabeth; de Vere participated in the suppression of the Northern Rebellion.

THOMAS HOWARD, [post-1554] fourth duke of Norfolk (1536–1572)–De Vere's cousin and the highest-ranking nobleman in Elizabethan England.

CHRISTOPHER HATTON, [post-1578] Sir Christopher, [post-1587] Lord Chancellor (c. 1540–1591)–One of Queen Elizabeth's favorites, whom she nicknamed "Lids," "Mutton," and "Sheep"; one of de Vere's rivals at court.

HENRI VALOIS, [post-1575] King Henri III of France (1551–1589)–Son of Catherine de Medici, aided his mother in the St. Bartholomew's Day Massacre of 1572.

PHILIP HAPSBURG, [post-1556] King Philip II of Spain (1527–1598)–Briefly married to Queen Mary Tudor (1554–58); Elizabethan England's greatest and longest-standing enemy.

FRANCIS WALSINGHAM, [post-1577] Sir Francis (c. 1532–1590)–English spymaster with international espionage networks to rival that of the Cecils.

ROWLAND YORKE (d. 1588)–De Vere's associate and servant (?); believed to have been the (double?) agent who whispered rumors of Anne Cecil's infidelities into de Vere's ear in 1576 that unleashed de Vere's jealousy and paranoia.

CHAPTER 4:
FOR MAKING A MAN [1573–1575]

THOMAS TWYNE (1543–1613)–Medical student de Vere patronized who published the book *A Breviary of Britain.*

THOMAS BEDINGFIELD (1545–1613)–Scholar and friend of de Vere's; translated the book *Cardanus's Comforte* into English at de Vere's command; retrieved de Vere from the Lowlands when the earl ran away there in 1574.

WILLIAM BYRD (1543?–1623)–Composer; recipient of de Vere's patronage; wrote "The Earl of Oxford's March"; defrauded of an estate de Vere had given him by one of de Vere's servants.

MILDRED (COOKE) CECIL (1526–1589)–William Cecil's wife; [post-1571] de Vere's mother-in-law.

GABRIEL HARVEY (1553–1631)–Cambridge scholar and pedantic pamphleteer; eulogized de Vere at a time (1578) when de Vere was hiring a private secretary; mocked de Vere afterward as an Italianate fop; traded pamphleteering jabs in 1590s with satirist Thomas Nashe [q.v.].

GEORGE BAKER (1540–1612)–Physician to de Vere and his wife; practitioner of new "Paracelsian" medicine; dedicated medical books to both de Vere and Anne.

DON JOHN OF AUSTRIA (1547–1578)–Bastard brother to Spain's King Philip II, military commander for Spanish and Catholic forces in Italy, the Lowlands, and the Mediterranean; de Vere may have met Don John amid the civil strife brewing in Genoa in 1575–76.

FRANÇOIS VALOIS, duc d'Alençon, [post-1576] duc d'Anjou (1554–1584)–Younger brother to King Henri III of France; longtime suitor for Queen Elizabeth's hand; de Vere allied with supporters of Alençon marriage match.

JOHAN STURMIUS (1507–1589)–Renowned classical scholar in Strasbourg; de Vere studied under Sturmius in 1575.

ORAZIO CUOCO (fl. 1575–76)–Venetian page whom de Vere hired in Venice and brought back with him to England.

VIRGINIA PADOANA (fl. 1575–76)–Venetian courtesan whom de Vere reputedly hired during his yearlong stay in Venice.

CHAPTER 5:
THE FABLE OF THE WORLD [1575–1578]

TITIAN (TIZIANO VECELLIO) (c. 1488–1576)–Venetian master painter whom de Vere may have met during his Venetian sojourn.

ALESSANDRO PICCOLOMINI (1508–1579)–Sienese playwright and author of comedy *The Deceived (Gl'Ingannati)*, staged in Siena every year on the twelfth night after Christmas.

ANTHONY MUNDAY (1560–1633)–Dramatist, poet, pamphleteer, translator, and de Vere's private secretary (on and off) from the 1580s onward.

HÉLÈNE DE TOURNON (d. 1577)–French noblewoman whom de Vere likely met on his return journey from Italy.

JAN CASIMIR (fl. 1576)–German duke who led an army toward Paris that de Vere encountered in 1576.

PRINCE WILLIAM OF ORANGE ("WILLIAM THE SILENT") (1533–1584)–Protestant defender of the faith in civil wars in the Lowlands.

CHARLES ARUNDELL (1540?–1587)–Catholic conspirator with whom de Vere had once coplotted but whom de Vere turned in to the authorities in 1580; Arundell viciously libeled de Vere for months thereafter; in 1584 Arundell (who had escaped to France) published and is the likely author of a similarly vicious screed against the earl of Leicester, *Leicester's Commonwealth.*

SEBASTIAN WESTCOTE (c. 1515–1582)–Leader of the Children of St. Paul's, a drama troupe that de Vere was affiliated with.

PEREGRINE BERTIE, [post-1580] Baron Willoughby de Eresby (1555–1601)–Swashbuckling soldier who wed de Vere's sister Mary in 1577; ambassador to the Danish court at Elsinore, 1582 and '85.

KATHERINE WILLOUGHBY, duchess of Suffolk (1519–1580)–Peregrine Bertie's mother; strong-willed woman who contrived to woo de Vere back to his wife by showing him the infant daughter Elizabeth, who de Vere claimed was not his.

WILLIAM HOWARD (1563–1640)–Youngest of the duke of Norfolk's three sons; de Vere attended Howard's wedding in 1577; Howard fought a protracted inheritance battle with his family and his wife's family (that of Elizabeth Dacre) that ended in 1600.

MARTIN FROBISHER (1535?–1594)–Navigator and adventurer; de Vere invested in Frobisher's attempts to find the fabled "Northwest Passage" to the Orient.

CHAPTER 6:
IN BRAWL RIDICULOUS [1577–1582]

HENRY HOWARD, [post-1604] earl of Northampton (1540–1614)–One of Catholic coconspirators (along with Charles Arundell) whom de Vere turned in in 1580; leveled malicious slanders at de Vere in order to discredit de Vere's testimony.

THOMAS NASHE (1567?–1601)–Satirist and pamphleteer; sometime compatriot (and secretary?) to de Vere; dedicated 1592 pamphlet *Strange News* to de Vere using moniker "Gentle Master William."

EDMUND SPENSER (c. 1552–1599)–Poet and author of *The Faerie Queene;* may have been one of the applicants for the job of de Vere's secretary c. 1578.

JOHN LYLY (1554–1606)–Playwright and novelist; author of the popular *Euphues* novels; de Vere's secretary.

ABRAHAM FLEMING (c. 1552–1607)–Amanuensis, author, editor, and de Vere's secretary.

WALTER RALEIGH, [post-1584] Sir Walter (1554–1618)–Explorer, author, and military commander; de Vere's courtly friend and foe throughout the 1580s, '90s, and early 1600s.

JEAN DE SIMIER (fl. 1579–1582)–The duc d'Alençon's charming nuptial negotiator to Queen Elizabeth in Alençon's absence; became a royal favorite unto his own.

FULKE GREVILLE, [post-1621] Lord Brooke (1554–1628)–Ally of Sir Philip Sidney's, sole witness to infamous "tennis court fight" between de Vere and Sidney in 1579; owner of King's Place, Hackney, after de Vere's widow sold it in 1609.

EDMUND CAMPION (1540–1581)–Jesuit missionary to England; arraigned for treason in a trial in which Anthony Munday [q.v.] was a witness.

SEBASTIAN, king of Portugal (1554–1578)–Portuguese king who had disappeared after leading a raid against Morocco; rumors abounded for years that Sebastian had survived and was returning to reclaim the Portuguese throne.

DON ANTONIO (1531–1595)–Pretender to the Portuguese throne whose cause many English nobles supported, in opposition to Philip II of Spain's uniting of the Portuguese and Spanish kingdoms in 1580.

THOMAS CHURCHYARD (1523?–1604)–Soldier, poet, and sometime servant to de Vere.

THOMAS WATSON (1556–1592)–Poet and compiler of *The Hekatompathia* (1582), a collection of sonnets dedicated to de Vere.

ROBERT GREENE (1558?–1592)–Pamphleteer, poet, playwright, and likely hanger-on at de Vere's 1580s bohemian pleasure garden Fisher's Folly.

ANNE VAVASOUR (fl. 1580–1621)–De Vere's mistress c. 1579–82.

THOMAS KNYVET (1546–1622)–Vavasour's uncle who challenged de Vere to a duel to right his niece's wronged honor; Knyvet's and de Vere's retainers battled in London street fights for more than a year afterward.

FRANCIS SOUTHWELL (fl. 1580)–Third Catholic coconspirator whom de Vere turned in in 1580s; issued a series of more tame libels against de Vere (compared to the flaming libels of Howard and Arundell).

EDWARD VEER, [post-1607] Sir Edward (1581–1629)–De Vere's natural son by Anne Vavasour [q.v.]; scholar, poet, and soldier.

SIR HENRY LEE (1533–1611)–Tiltyard champion who was Anne Vavasour's [q.v.] next known lover after de Vere.

CHAPTER 7:
FORTUNE'S DEAREST SPITE [1582–1585]

ROCCO BONETTI (fl. 1580s)–Italian fencing master who set up a fencing school at the Blackfriars, London; frequently accosted by de Vere's men.

"GASTRELL" AND "HORSLEY" (fl. 1582)–Two Londoners claiming to be de Vere's retainers who fought in the de Vere–Knyvet street brawls and were caught and arraigned for the transgression.

THOMAS EDWARDES (fl. 1587–1595)–Elizabethan poet who memorialized the de Vere–Knyvet street brawls in the envoy to his 1595 book *Narcissus.*

RICHARD MULCASTER (1532–1611) Master of the Merchant Taylors' Boys drama troupe, another company that de Vere likely used in 1583 to perform one of his courtly masques.

HENRY EVANS (fl. 1583–84)–Welsh scrivener and playmaster who, with John Lyly [q.v.], supervised dramatic troupes sponsored by de Vere in 1583 and '84.

FREDERICK, [post-1559] King Frederick II of Denmark and Norway (1534–1588)– De Vere's brother-in-law Peregrine Bertie [q.v.] visited Frederick at Castle Elsinore twice, in 1582 and '85, to invest the Danish king in England's Order of the Garter and to negotiate a commercial treaty with the monarch.

TYCHO BRAHE (1546–1601)–Danish astronomer whom Bertie [q.v.] visited with King Frederick II [q.v.] at Brahe's observatory.

GEORGE PEELE (1556–1596)–Playwright and poet with whom de Vere (and his servants John Lyly [q.v.] and Henry Evans [q.v.]) shared the Blackfriars playhouse in 1583.

ALBERT LASKI (fl. 1583)–Polish prince and general who visited Oxford University in 1583 as part of a courtly entourage that de Vere likely joined.

GIORDANO BRUNO (1548–1600)–Free-thinking Italian philosopher, also on hand during the 1583.

PHILIP HOWARD, [post-1580] earl of Arundel (1557–1595)–Eldest son of the executed duke of Norfolk [q.v.], like his younger brother William [q.v.] married to a Dacre (Anne Dacre); de Vere sat on the jury that condemned Howard for treason in his plotting for the success of the Spanish Armada–although Howard's death sentence was never carried out.

CHAPTER 8:
TO THY RUDDER TIED BY TH' STRINGS [1586–1589]

ANTHONY BABINGTON (1561–1586)–Catholic conspirator who was caught in a plot that would have deposed Queen Elizabeth and crowned Mary, Queen of Scots; Mary was also arraigned for the "Babington Plot" and found guilty of treason.

ELIZABETH DE VERE, [post-1595] countess of Derby (1575–1627)–De Vere's first daughter, whose paternity de Vere disputed in 1576; affianced c. 1590–93 to Henry Wriothesley, earl of Southampton.

BRIDGET DE VERE, [post-1599] Lady Norris of Rycote (1584–1620?)–De Vere's second daughter; initially affianced in 1598 to William Herbert (later earl of Pembroke).

SUSAN DE VERE, [post-1605] countess of Montgomery (1587–1629)–De Vere's youngest daughter, likely played a role in supervising the transfer of her father's manuscripts to her husband and brother-in-law the earl of Pembroke to be turned into the Shake-speare First Folio in 1623.

FRANCIS DRAKE, [post-1581] Sir Francis (1540–1596)–Circumnavigator and admiral; co-led the initial naval expedition to seek out the Spanish Armada before it reached English shores in early summer of 1588.

CHARLES HOWARD, [post-1573] Lord Charles, [1574–85] Lord Chamberlain, [1585–1618] Lord Admiral (1536–1624)–Legendary naval and military commander; co-led pre-Armada expedition in early summer 1588 with Sir Francis Drake [q.v.].

ANGEL DAY (fl. 1583–1595)–Author and secretary; dedicated his *English Secretary* to de Vere in 1586.

THOMAS LODGE (1558–1625)–Poet, playwright, and novelist and likely hanger-on at Fisher's Folly, lamenting the Folly's demise as a mythical place called "Silexedra."

CHRISTOPHER MARLOWE (1564–1593)–Poet, playwright, and spy; artistic peer to Shake-speare; killed by three fellow spies in a suspicious tavern brawl.

CHAPTER 9:
GENTLE MASTER WILLIAM [1589–1593]

HENRI DE LORRAINE, DUKE OF GUISE (1550–1588)–One of the French nobles vying for the crown (the "War of the Three Henries") with Henri of Navarre and Henri III. Assassinated in 1588; de Vere had sent servants to fight on Guise's behalf in 1577.

"MARTIN MAR-PRELATE" (fl. 1589–91)–Puritan pamphleteer, probably a pseudonym for Job Throkmorton, MP (1545–1601).

ROBERT DEVEREUX, [post-1576] earl of Essex (1565–1601)–Stepson to Robert Dudley, earl of Leicester [q.v.]; polarizing figure at court who led a faction that opposed the power of the Cecil family, especially Sir Robert [q.v.]; de Vere famously disliked Essex–but did not extend this ill feeling toward Essex's ally the earl of Southampton [q.v.]; Essex led a rebellion with Southampton in 1600 that resulted in his being tried for treason and beheaded.

HENRY WRIOTHESLEY, [post-1581] earl of Southampton (1573–1624)–Affianced to de Vere's eldest daughter, Elizabeth (she of the disputed paternity), c. 1590–93; later became close with de Vere's son, Henry, eighteenth earl of Oxford; Edward de Vere appears to have been besotted with Southampton–the "Fair Youth" of Shake-speare's *Sonnets;* de Vere sat on the jury that condemned Southampton (and Essex [q.v.]) to death for treason in the Essex Rebellion; Queen Elizabeth commuted Southampton's death sentence; Southampton later led the coalition of earls opposing King James's proposed Spanish Marriage alliance c. 1620–23.

JULIA PENN (fl. 1590)–Landlady whom de Vere owed for London flat that Thomas Churchyard (and other writers) rented out citing de Vere's promise to pay.

ELIZABETH TRENTHAM, [post-1592] countess of Oxford (1559?–1612)–De Vere's strong-willed and businesslike second wife.

JOHN (GIOVANNI) FLORIO (1553–1625)–Poet and Italian dictionary editor; de Vere may have contributed a sonnet (under the pen name "Phaeton") to Florio's 1591 *Second Fruits.*

THOMAS HOWARD, [post-1597] Baron Howard de Walden, [post-1603] earl of Suffolk (1561–1626)–Second son of executed duke of Norfolk.

WILLIAM SHAKSPERE (1564–1616)–Stratford-upon-Avon–native actor, broker, and entrepreneur; first noted appearance in London in 1592 by pamphleteer Robert Greene as a literary pretender; ultimately became known as the author of the plays and poems written by de Vere.

HENRY DE VERE, LORD BOLBEC, [post-1604] eighteenth earl of Oxford (1593–1624)–De Vere's son and heir by his second wife, Elizabeth; joined anti–Spanish Marriage coalition with the earls of Southampton [q.v.], Montgomery [q.v.], and Pembroke [q.v.], circa 1620–23.

CHAPTER 10:
THE SHARP RAZOR OF A WILLING CONCEIT [1593–1598]

ROBERT POLEY (fl. 1586–93)–Spy for Robert Cecil's network; murderer of Christopher Marlowe?

KING JAMES VI OF SCOTLAND, [post-1603] King James I of England (1566–1625).

MARY BROWNE WRIOTHESLEY, dowager countess of Southampton (fl. 1572–1594)–Henry Wriothesley's mother; remarried into Cecil faction in 1594 at a wedding that scholars suspect featured the debut of *A Midsummer Night's Dream.*

SIR THOMAS HENEAGE, [post-1589] vice-chamberlain of England (c. 1532–1595)–Mary Browne Wriothesley's second husband.

THE LORD CHAMBERLAIN'S MEN– "Shakespeare's troupe"; many first editions of Shake-speare plays advertise that the Lord Chamberlain's Men performed the text; Will Shakspere was exclusively associated with this troupe from 1594 onward; featured some of the best actors in the country (Richard Burbage, Will Kemp).

WILLIAM STANLEY, [post-1594] earl of Derby (1561–1642)–Court playwright who married de Vere's eldest daughter, Elizabeth de Vere [q.v.]; may have worked with de Vere in revising de Vere's courtly interludes from the 1570s and '80s into the "Shakespeare" canon.

NICHOLAS HILL (1570–c. 1610)–Pioneer in atomic philosophy; one of de Vere's secretaries during de Vere's final years.

CHAPTER 11:
BURIED BE [1598–1604]

HUGH O'NEILL, earl of Tyrone (1550?–1616)–Irish rebel whom the earls of Essex and Southampton led a force in 1599 to fight.

MARY SIDNEY HERBERT, countess of Pembroke (1561–1621)–Sister of Sir Philip Sidney [q.v.]; talented scholar and poet with whom de Vere was friendly; mother of William and Philip Herbert–de Vere daughters had been affianced to both, and both were later the patrons of the Shake-speare First Folio (1623).

FRANCIS NORRIS, [post-1600] Baron Norris of Rycote (1579–1622)–In 1599, married to Bridget de Vere [q.v.].

PIERCE EDMONDS (fl. 1600)–English officer with whom the earl of Southampton had become intimate during the Irish campaign.

BEN JONSON (1572–1637)–Satirist, poet, and playwright on friendly terms with Henry de Vere [q.v.]; railed against Will Shakspere as a "poet-ape" and a great pretender; hired in 1623 to work on the Shake-speare First Folio (1623).

ROBERT ARMIN (1563–1615)–Comic actor for Lord Chamberlain's Men beginning in 1599; wrote of serving his "Lord in Hackney"–de Vere.

THOMAS GREY, [post-1593] Lord Grey de Wilton (1575–1614)–Served under Essex and Southampton [q.v.] in Ireland; imprisoned for insubordination; sought revenge against Southampton in 1601 in London street brawl that prefigured the Essex Rebellion.

EDWARD SOMERSET, earl of Worcester, [post-1601] Master of the Horse (c. 1550–1628)–Ambitious courtier who, after the Essex Rebellion, amalgamated the moribund Earl of Oxford's Men into his troupe and rehearsed their courtly performances at the Boar's Head Inn in London.

꧁

FOREWORD

by Sir Derek Jacobi

A N ACTOR FACES ALMOST CONSTANT CRITICISM—ALL THE MORE SO
when one advocates that Edward de Vere wrote under the pen-name
"Shakespeare." Some of the more popular accusations today include charges
of the wildest eccentricity, outrageous snobbery, and downright heresy. It's
pointless, of course, to engage these unbecoming personal attacks. Fortu-
nately, serious academic debate is triumphing while orthodoxy continues its
retreat behind a facade of mind-numbing vilification. Herein, dear reader, you
will find a book that performs the important, often fraught, always contentious, but necessary service of turning the spotlight full on the breathtaking discrepancies and shining anomalies in the accepted version of the
creation of the Shakespeare canon.

So what does the Shakespeare authorship controversy mean for the poor
player that struts and frets his hour upon the stage? It means, in brief, that we
happy few have the opportunity at last to make contact with the original
fount of thought and reason, to comprehend the hand that wrote, the eye
that saw, the brain that forged, the heart that conceived, and the being that
transformed a monumental life into an immortal corpus of literature.

An actor's instincts and the evidence of a growing body of research convinces me that de Vere was—along with being a scholar, patron, and author
par excellence—an actor. The troupe kept by Edward de Vere's father had influenced his early childhood. De Vere's own troupe had nurtured those interests, and acting and stagecraft became intrinsic to his talents. Hence the
precise and very special observation of the mechanics and meaning of the
world of the theater are everywhere expressed in the plays, often as instinctive comments on more serious topics.

In *"Shakespeare" by Another Name,* Mark Anderson demonstrates the intense intellectual energy and attention to factual detail that are required to unravel what, to honest minds, is an obvious mystery. *"Shakespeare" by Another Name* presents the logical, valid, and excitingly precise arguments for recognizing that de Vere, like all writers, drew from his own experiences, interests, accomplishments, education, position, and talents, and that he invested his writing with universal truths, emotional reality, and recognizable humanity drawn from his own unique life. Just as de Vere uses theatrical phrase and metaphor naturally and easily, so, too, his wide-ranging education and ingrained knowledge of many subjects flow effortlessly through his writing. Contrast this with the lack of any evidence which places a pen in the hand of William of Stratford (except, of course, on a dubious monument!).

The great excitement of this seminal work is the precise relationship between de Vere's life and his art, unveiling many thrilling revelations of how much of himself de Vere put into his characters. This book, with fascinating specificity, suits "the action to the word, the word to the action." Innumerable instances of de Vere's experiences, his relationships, his travels, and his unusual circumstances find expression in his plays and poems. *"Shakespeare" by Another Name* is one of the very best whodunnits you will ever read.

The game's afoot!

Sir Derek Jacobi
London
February 2005

INTRODUCTION

"A human being is the best plot there is."
–John Galsworthy

E VERY AUTHOR'S LIFE TELLS A STORY. ACCORDING TO THE CON-
ventional biography, William Shakespeare was born in Stratford-upon-
Avon in 1564; he moved to London sometime in the late 1580s or early 1590s
and soon enjoyed great success as an actor and playwright, authoring some
37 or more plays, 2 epic poems, 154 sonnets, and assorted other verse that
have become the crowning works of the English language. He retired to his
hometown sometime around 1612, and he died in 1616. Seven years after his
death, the first edition of his collected plays appeared in print. Although no
authenticated portrait from his lifetime exists, the 1623 folio of Shakespeare's
works features the above image on its opening page.

Yet this image and this conventional story have confounded many great
minds over the years.

The novelist Henry James remarked in a 1903 letter to a friend that he
was "haunted by the conviction that the divine William is the biggest and
most successful fraud ever practiced on a patient world." In Sigmund Freud's
1927 essay "An Autobiographical Study," the founding father of modern psychology stated, "I no longer believe that William Shakespeare the actor from

Stratford was the author of the works that have been ascribed to him." Mark Twain published an entire book in 1909–*Is Shakespeare Dead?*–that tore the conventional Shakespeare biography to tatters. Walt Whitman told a confidant in 1888: "It is my final belief that the Shakespearean plays were written by another hand than Shaksper's [*sic*].... I do not seem to have any patience with the Shaksper argument: it is all gone for me–up the spout. The Shaksper case is about closed."

Doubts about the Shakespeare story emerged less than a century after the first conventional biography appeared. In 1709 the dramatist Nicholas Rowe first sketched out "Some Account of the Life, *&c.* of Mr. William Shakespear [*sic*]." In 1747, the antiquarian Joseph Greene came across a copy of Shakespeare's will and was singularly unimpressed, calling the document "so absolutely void of the least particle of that spirit which animated our great poet." In 1767, the theatrical impresario David Garrick launched the Shakespeare industry in Stratford-upon-Avon with a three-day jubilee that transformed the backwater Warwickshire town into the literary tourist mecca that Stratford has remained to this day. During the same year, Garrick's friend, the physician Herbert Lawrence, wrote an allegory, *The Life and Adventures of Common Sense,* accusing "Shakespear" of stealing other people's works. In 1786, the American statesman John Adams, upon visiting Stratford, echoed a growing skepticism of the validity of the Shakespeare story. "There is nothing preserved of this great genius which is worth knowing," Adams recorded in his personal travelogue. "Nothing which might inform us what education, what company, what accident, turned his mind to letters and the drama." Early in the next century, the novelist Washington Irving continued the thread of doubt with his own semiautobiographical account of a visit to Stratford. "The long interval during which Shakespeare's writings lay in comparative neglect has spread its shadow over his history," Irving wrote in his 1820 *Sketch Book of Geoffrey Crayon, Gent.* "And it is his good or evil lot that scarcely anything remains to his biographers but a scanty handful of conjectures."

Throughout the nineteenth and early twentieth centuries, Walt Whitman, Mark Twain, and Henry James had joined a chorus of doubters who all expressed the same grave reservation: The conventional biography of Shakespeare is simply wrong; the ghost of another man haunts the canon.

In 1920, this ghost materialized in a revolutionary work of investigative scholarship by the British educator J. Thomas Looney. Looney's *"Shakespeare" Identified in Edward de Vere, seventeenth Earl of Oxford* gained early converts such as Sigmund Freud and the actor and director Leslie Howard–both of whom proclaimed their conviction that the Elizabethan courtier Edward de Vere was "Shakespeare." In establishment circles of Shakespeare scholarship, however, Looney's book was met with a resounding harrumph. (Looney's detractors' most consistent critique was also their most effective: He has a funny name.)

De Vere (1550–1604) was a courtly poet and playwright who, as one literary critic in 1589 put it, would be recognized as perhaps the finest of his age "if [his] doings could be found out and made public with the rest." Although some sixteen to twenty youthful poems have been attributed to de Vere—some of notable quality, some not—none of his mature dramatic or poetic works have survived under his own name. The young de Vere was an active patron of literature and drama and a sponsor of theatrical troupes. And, this book proposes, de Vere added to and revised his early courtly masques and interludes, eventually transforming them into the plays and poems published under the byline "William Shakespeare."

"I think [the earl of] Oxford wrote Shakespeare," the filmmaker and leading Shakespearean actor and director of the first half of the twentieth century Orson Welles told an interviewer in 1954. "If you don't, there are some awful funny coincidences to explain away." In the half century since the screen legend uttered these prophetic words, countless scholars and investigators have compounded those "awful funny coincidences" to the point that every corner of the Shakespeare canon has now been found to contain snippets or passages from de Vere's life and times.

De Vere became entangled in a love affair that led to an interfamilial war–Elizabethan Montagues and Capulets. While traveling in France, de Vere suffered the devilish whisperings of his own IAGO, who ignited de Vere's jealousy over his wife's alleged infidelities. De Vere lived in Venice and went into debt borrowing from the local loan merchants. De Vere's first marriage produced three daughters who inherited their alienated father's family seat while he was still alive *(King Lear)*. He had a close but rocky relationship with Queen Elizabeth–whom he portrayed variously as the witty and charming OLIVIA *(Twelfth Night)*, the powerful vixen CLEOPATRA, the cloying VENUS, and the compromised CRESSIDA. De Vere's father-in-law was the historical prototype for POLONIUS; de Vere's brother-in-law was the original for PETRUCHIO; de Vere's sister the model for PETRUCHIO's KATE; his first wife for OPHELIA, DESDEMONA, and HERO (among many others); de Vere's second wife for PORTIA; his eldest daughter for MIRANDA; her husband for MIRANDA's FERDINAND.

Perhaps the most autobiographical play in Shakespeare is *Hamlet*, with multifarious connections to de Vere's life that are discussed in nearly every chapter of this book. For example, when de Vere was traveling through France at age twenty-six, he encountered a Teutonic prince who paraded his troops before de Vere's eyes. Soon thereafter, de Vere boarded a ship that was overtaken by pirates, and de Vere was stripped naked and left on the English shore. In Act 4 of *Hamlet*, in a sequence that is in no known source text for the play, HAMLET first witnesses the invading PRINCE FORTINBRAS's troops and then boards a ship that is overtaken by pirates, in an ordeal that leaves a humiliated HAMLET stripped naked on the Danish shore.

"Shakespeare," it turns out, was one of the most autobiographical authors who ever took pen to paper. To recognize this, one need only redefine "Shakespeare."

The best place to begin is with the name itself: Shake-speare.* The hyphen appears in many of the first publications of the plays and poems. Hyphenated phrases in an author's name often suggested a concealed author–in an age rife with political and religious intrigue, when picking the wrong alliance or offending the wrong official could mean imprisonment, torture, forfeiture of one's properties to the crown, or a death sentence. In the words of literary historians Archer Taylor and Frederic J. Mosher, "In the sixteenth and seventeenth centuries, the Golden Age of pseudonyms, almost every writer used a pseudonym at some time during his career." During the Elizabethan Age (the period spanning the reign of Queen Elizabeth I of England: 1558–1603), hyphenated pen names included "Martin Mar-prelate," a pamphleteer who railed at Anglican prelates; "Cuthbert Curry-knave," a satirist who savaged ("curried") his knavish pamphleteering opponents; and "Tom Tell-truth," a supposedly truth-spouting polemicist.

William Shake-speare is no exception. According to ancient Greek myth, the goddess Athena–divine protectress of learning and the arts–was born from the forehead of her father, Zeus, fully dressed and armed for battle. At birth, she is said to have shaken her spear, and authors looking back upon this legend associated her with the act of spear shaking. As a deft allusion to the classical goddess affiliated with the theater, "Shake-speare" was in fact a perfect pen name for a playwright.

Numerous candidates for the authorship of the Shake-speare canon have been suggested over the years, including Edward de Vere, Francis Bacon, Christopher Marlowe, the countess of Pembroke, Edward Dyer, the earl of Rutland, the earl of Derby, etc. The academic establishment has largely ignored the heretics, assuming that only the incumbent could have written the plays. But the Stratford native Will Shakspere–as the actor preferred to spell it–is not as inevitably "Shakespeare" as he first appears.

To begin with, no original playscripts exist. The greatest literary manhunt in history has yielded no manuscripts, no diaries, and no correspondence issuing from Will Shakspere's pen. The only known letter written to him, concerning a loan, was never sent. Despite the enormous economic incentive that

---

* This book will use two different spellings to distinguish between the man and the myth: *Shake-speare* with a hyphen will signify the author, who this book hypothesizes was Edward de Vere, earl of Oxford (1550–1604); *Shakspere* will be used for Will Shakspere (1564–1616), the Stratford-upon-Avon–born actor, theatrical entrepreneur, and hypothesized literary front man.

has existed for centuries to find any scrap of paper with Will Shakspere's handwriting on it, scholars have authenticated only a few signatures on legal documents written by other people and two words, *By me*, signed on his will. These scratchings are all that has ever been found from the pen of the man presumed to be the greatest literary genius in the Western world.

Then there is the matter of Will Shakspere's last will and testament. In it, the Stratford actor detailed his worldly possessions down to his silver gilt bowl and second-best bed. An interlineation in the will bequeaths money to three actor friends for mourning rings. But nowhere does Will Shakspere mention any literary or theatrical properties. No books, no manuscripts, no plays–the most precious things in a dramatist's life–and one is to believe that not a scrap of it merited mention in his will?

Since great writers are invariably great readers, a further question emerges: Where are Will Shakspere's books? Public libraries did not exist in Elizabethan England. Unless one had access to university libraries or other private collections, what was in your household was what you read. Approximately 150 books were printed in Elizabethan England per year. (By comparison, 40,000 books per year are printed today in the United States.) A vast majority of Elizabethan titles concerned matters of religion, law, or medicine. Assembling a library of more than a hundred volumes–especially a secular library containing plays, poems, and other works of fiction–was an impressive, time-consuming, and costly feat. Books were cherished commodities.

More than two hundred books survive from each of the libraries of the of the early seventeenth-century playwright Ben Jonson and poet John Donne. The Shake-speare plays and poems reveal that the author was a voracious reader–citing over two hundred books, some of which were untranslated works published on the Continent in Greek, Latin, French, Italian, and Spanish. Yet, scholars have never authenticated a single book, play, pamphlet, or broadsheet that ever belonged to Will Shakspere. Some Shake-speare plays, such as *Hamlet* and *Macbeth*, draw characters and story lines from unpublished manuscripts in private archives. But there is no explanation for how Shakspere could have gained access to restricted aristocratic family libraries.

The erudition on display in Shake-speare is wide-ranging and profound. Studies of the Shake-speare canon by lawyers, theologians, physicians, astronomers, philosophers, linguists, military tacticians, sailors, historians, botanists, literary scholars, musicians, and classicists conclude that Shake-speare manifests a ready knowledge of their respective fields. All find the author anywhere from competent to expert in these varied disciplines. The myth that Shake-speare had "small Latin and less Greek"–stemming from a misreading of a poem by Ben Jonson–has inhibited the natural conclusion of these studies: Shake-speare was one of the most learned and broadly educated authors in history.

Even if Will Shakspere had attended the Stratford Grammar School as a child, a supposition for which there is no evidence, it would not have provided him the kind of myriad-minded expertise one finds in abundance in Shake-speare. Will Shakspere's documented biography is extensive, but it is all commercial activities, lawsuits, and entrepreneurial ventures. It reveals no formal education, tutelage, or apprenticeship in his presumed craft.

Shake-speare's works also convey a familiarity with specialized knowledge of places and cultures that could not have been found in books or taught in school. The plays and poems reveal a well-traveled world citizen—one who had an intimate familiarity with Italian and French culture unattainable at second hand. Shake-speare sets as many plays in France and Italy as he does in England. *Henry V* contains a scene written entirely in courtly (and bawdy) French, while the characters and situations of *Love's Labour's Lost* reveal a familiarity with French manners, mannerisms, and courtly culture. Shake-speare knew that Florence's citizens were recognized for their arithmetic and bookkeeping *(Othello)*; he knew that Padua was the "nursery of arts" *(The Taming of the Shrew)* and that Lombardy was "the pleasant garden of great Italy" *(Taming of the Shrew);* he knew that a dish of baked doves was a time-honored northern Italian gift *(The Merchant of Venice)*. He knew Venice, in particular, like nowhere else in the world, save for London itself. Picayune Venetian matters scarcely escaped his grasp: the duke of Venice's two votes in the city council, for example, or the special nighttime police force—the *Signori di Notte*—peculiar to Venice, or the foreign city where Venice's Jews did most of their business, Frankfurt.

The cornerstones of the case for Will Shakspere as "Shakespeare," in fact, constitute one meager docket:

Greene's Groatsworth of Wit: In 1592, the playwright Robert Greene allegedly lashed out in print at Shakspere. Greene's posthumous pamphlet *Greene's Groatsworth of Wit* chastised someone nicknamed "Shake-scene" as an "upstart crow . . . an absolute *Johannes factotum*" who "supposes he is as well able to bombast out a blank verse as the rest" of London's top dramatists. Because Shakspere "supposes" that he was as capable a composer as his fellow playwrights, *Greene's Groatsworth* would appear to deliver crucial testimony that Shakspere was, in fact, an author—however much Greene did not like him.

A closer reading of *Groatsworth,* however, discredits Shakspere as a writer of any capacity. In Aesop's *Fables,* the crow was a figure that disguised itself in the plumage of other birds. A "*Johannes factotum*" in sixteenth-century usage was a braggart and vainglorious dilettante. And according to the *Oxford English Dictionary,* Elizabethans often used the word *suppose* to mean, "To feign, pretend; occasionally, to forge." Shakspere, *Greene's Groatsworth* suggests, was actually an impostor.

The Return from Parnassus: This anonymous comedy staged by students at Cambridge University in 1600 pokes fun at an oafish actor, the clown Will Kemp. Kemp is made to say, "Few of the university men pen plays well; they smell too much of that writer Ovid and that writer Metamorphosis." The joke here is that Kemp doesn't know the difference between an author (Ovid) and the title of his work *(The Metamorphoses)*.

In the next breath, Kemp says, "Why here's our fellow Shakespeare puts them all down!" With these words, Kemp glorifies the playwright "Shakespeare," a "fellow" actor. But the joke is on Kemp. A sophisticated Elizabethan university audience would understand that if Kemp doesn't know that "Metamorphosis" wasn't the name of a writer, he would have zero credibility to talk about the actor Shakspere as a writer.

Venus and Adonis* and *The Rape of Lucrece: These two Shake-speare poems from 1593 and '94 are dedicated to the earl of Southampton, a high-ranking Elizabethan courtier. Southampton is conventionally assumed–upon no further evidence–to have been Shakspere's patron. A number of scholars over the past two centuries have devoted countless man-hours to discovering other evidence of Southampton's patronage of Shakspere. They have found none. As will be seen in Chapter 9, the *Venus and Adonis* and *Lucrece* dedications actually make more sense coming from Edward de Vere's pen than from Shakspere's. For one, at the time of the dedications, Southampton was being considered as a possible husband for de Vere's daughter Elizabeth.

"Terence": In a pamphlet published in 1611, the poet John Davies described "Shake-spear" [*sic*] as "Our English Terence." Terence is known today to have been both an actor and a playwright.

However, this is not what many in the sixteenth and early seventeenth centuries believed. According to the essayists Cicero, Quintilian, and Montaigne, as well as a leading literary textbook of the Elizabethan Age, the actor Terence was actually a front man for one or more Roman aristocratic playwrights. Although most scholars today dismiss the possibility, many of Davies's learned contemporary readers would have recognized the allusion: Shakspere was an actor who pretended to be an author. The author Shake-speare was someone else altogether.

The Book and the Monument: Shakspere's funerary monument in Stratford-upon-Avon's Trinity Church, constructed sometime before 1623, ostensibly suggests he was a writer. (The statue is of a man using a pillow for a desktop, holding a quill pen over a blank piece of paper; the cryptic inscription beneath the statue reads, in part, "... all [that] he hath writ leaves living art but page to serve his wit"–although exactly what these words mean has long been a mystery and will be discussed later.) The first edition of the complete plays of Shake-speare in 1623 alludes to the Trinity Church bust ("... when time dissolves thy Stratford monument...") and to the river in

Shakspere's hometown ("...sweet swan of Avon..."). Together, the 1623 First Folio and the Stratford monument would appear to deliver prima facie evidence for Shakspere as Shake-speare.

However, both date to a period (circa 1623) when Edward de Vere's children and in-laws were waging a brutal campaign in the court of King James I against a controversial British royal marriage alliance with Spain. This book argues de Vere's children and in-laws used the works of Shake-speare as part of a propaganda war during the "Spanish Marriage Crisis" of the early 1620s—and that the Stratford monument and publication of the Folio constituted a last-ditch maneuver to preserve de Vere's literary legacy, even if it meant burying his identity.

And that's the whole of it. There are abundant additional references in sixteenth- and early seventeenth-century writings to Shake-speare's plays and poems, none of which connect to Shakspere of Stratford. There are also contemporary allusions to Shakspere's business investments and theatrical activities at the Globe Theatre and elsewhere. But these don't connect to Shake-speare the author.

So far as is known and can be proved, Shakspere never traveled anywhere beyond the roads connecting London to Stratford-upon-Avon. So far as is known and can be proved, he did not even attend Stratford Grammar School. So far as is known and can be proved, Shakspere never wrote a complete sentence in his life. Shakspere's wife and daughters were, like his parents and siblings, either illiterate or close to it.

"We are the reasoning race," Mark Twain wrote in *Is Shakespeare Dead?* "And when we find a vague file of chipmunk tracks stringing through the dust of Stratford village, we know by our reasoning powers that Hercules has been along there. I feel that our fetish is safe for three centuries yet."

Edward de Vere was a brilliant and troubled man with whom one might enjoy sharing a beer but loathe sharing a house. He was at times a cad and a scoundrel. He also was a notorious teller of tall tales. One of his contemporaries recorded a fable de Vere recited about his adventures in Italy: "In it [de Vere] glories greatly. Diversely hath he told it, and when he enters into it, he can hardly out, which hath made such sport as often have I been driven to rise from his table laughing."

Despite his tall tales, it was actually de Vere's truthfulness that ultimately necessitated his taking refuge behind the Shake-speare mask. De Vere spent nearly his entire life in Queen Elizabeth's court, portraying this world and its key figures unflinchingly. He skewered such powerful men as Sir Christopher Hatton (MALVOLIO in *Twelfth Night*), Sir Philip Sidney (SLENDER in *The Merry Wives of Windsor*; SIR ANDREW AGUECHEEK in *Twelfth Night*; MICHAEL CASSIO in *Othello*), Lord Robert Dudley (CLAUDIUS in *Hamlet*; JUSTICE SHALLOW in

The Merry Wives of Windsor), William Cecil, Lord Burghley (POLONIUS), the earl of Southampton (PATROCLUS in *Troilus and Cressida*), and the earl of Essex (CORIOLANUS). De Vere also exposed the court's dirty laundry, accusing Dudley of being a poisoner *(Hamlet)*, turning Cecil into a veritable pimp (PANDARUS in *Troilus and Cressida*), and even portraying the sacred Virgin Queen as a vain and fickle tease with a Jezebel streak (CLEOPATRA, GERTRUDE, CRESSIDA, VENUS). "Shakespeare" was a subterfuge that distanced the scandalous works from its primary subjects: the queen and her powerful inner circle of advisors. The "Shakespeare" ruse enabled de Vere to write till the end of his days in 1604. However, the bargain was a Faustian one, depriving de Vere of the immortality due him for his literary accomplishments and foisting upon the world a monumental myth.

The Shake-speare canon, informed by de Vere's life story, paints a vivid and complex picture. He was both a defender and critic of the state, a bohemian and a statesman, an outlaw and an enforcer of the law, a comic and a quintessentially tragic figure, a patron and an artist seeking patronage. He was an athletic figure with military aspirations who also was effeminate and inhabited a small frame.

But de Vere's most striking physical characteristic was his eyes. His extant portraits (two of which are pictured on the cover of this book and discussed in Appendix D) all find the sitter, eyebrows arched, fixing a piercing gaze out of the canvas and through the ages. Behind those windows lay the cagey intellect of a man who knew he knew too much.

USAGE NOTE

T HE INTRODUCTION HAS ALREADY EXPLAINED THE USAGE OF *Shakspere* (meaning the Stratford-upon-Avon–born actor and hypothesized front man) and *Shake-speare* (meaning the hypothesized author, Edward de Vere). Spelling has been modernized in the letters, poems, plays, and other documents quoted herein–except for a few instances in which retaining Elizabethan spelling adds useful color or character. Where available, original spelling is used in the notes. Inside the quotation marks, confusing Elizabethan syntax has been slightly updated with the addition of missing names, titles, articles, and conjunctions in square brackets. Glosses of antiquated words or phrases appear in square brackets in italic type.

A few other anachronisms and simplifications have been introduced to assist the reader in remembering family alliances and navigating a sea of shifting titles, names, and offices: The female leads in this story retain their maiden names after marriage. The subject of this biography will be referred to as "Lord Edward" while his father is still alive and, simply, "de Vere" once he becomes the seventeenth earl of Oxford. (De Vere's children will also be referred to using the surname "de Vere" as opposed to just "Vere." Although some American authors capitalize the *d*, this book retains the convention of keeping the honorific "de" in lowercase.) Queen Elizabeth's paramour and potential husband the French duc d'Alençon will be referred to throughout the book as "Alençon"–even though he held other titles (such as duc d'Anjou) later in his life. To help the reader keep track of the key players and their various offices and titles, this book's prefatory materials also feature a *Dramatis Personae* and time line.

In this book, the new year always begins on January 1. (In many, though maddeningly not all, original documents from the period, the year didn't change over till March 25.) Other than this modernization, all dates in this book remain "old style"–as heedless as Elizabethans were of the ten-day calendrical shift Pope Gregory XIII introduced in 1582.

Small caps will be used to distinguish the names of characters from the Shake-speare canon: FALSTAFF, HAMLET, PORTIA, etc.

CHAPTER 1

THE EYE OF CHILDHOOD

[1550–1562]

O N APRIL 12, 1550, IN THE PRIVATE APARTMENTS OF A BRITISH stone-walled medieval fortress, a lord and lady welcomed their heir into the world. If the boy survived, the child's father–John de Vere, sixteenth earl of Oxford–could henceforth rest assured that when he died, his own son would carry forward the title of seventeenth earl.

From the moment of christening at Castle Hedingham in the eastern county of Essex, Edward de Vere would be known as Viscount Bolbec. Lord Edward's high birth would place him in adulthood among kings and queens and the powerful men around them who ran the state. His fate was to be their gadfly and fool, a black sheep of this ancient and revered family. But nothing at the time of his birth would have led anyone to suspect that such a strange and ungainly future awaited.

This biography will proceed under the assumption that, by himself or in collaboration, Edward de Vere wrote under the name William Shake-speare. He is not the Shakespeare with whom we are familiar.

Edward de Vere's ancestors had, for four hundred years, played a leading role in the wars and politics of England. In an uninterrupted succession from the Norman Conquest onward, de Veres had served the crown as statesmen and military commanders. After 1142, de Veres also wore the coronet of the earldom of Oxford. The first earl of Oxford had supported Empress Matilda's (unsuccessful) claim to the throne against King Stephen; the second earl had served under King John; the third earl had taken up arms against John; the seventh earl led a naval fleet against the French at Calais and laid siege to Rheims. The ninth earl, the most infamous of his line, had been a consort and royal favorite of the homosexual king Richard II, and had forfeited his lands on Richard's fall. The eleventh earl had served Henry V at Agincourt. The twelfth earl had fought in the Wars of the Roses and was executed by King Edward IV.

The history of the fifteenth earl is intimately bound up with the history of Tudor England. The fifteenth earl had supported the divorce of King Henry VIII's queen Catherine and carried the crown for the coronation of Anne Boleyn, mother of the future queen Elizabeth. Edward de Vere himself was named after Henry's only son, England's king Edward VI. The 13-year-old king Edward sent a gilded chalice for Lord Edward's christening on April 17, 1550.

Infant mortality rates demanded that children be baptized soon after birth, lest they die in the nursery without being blessed by holy water–dooming their souls to limbo. Then again, limbo was just the sort of idolatrous belief that the reformist king Edward was working to abolish. When Henry VIII founded the Church of England in 1534, it was little more than a British denomination of Catholicism. Communion still assumed the physical transformation of wine into blood and bread into the body of Christ. Much of the Mass in Henry VIII's day was still read in Latin. Saints and sacraments of yore–blessing of the candles at Candlemas, releasing of the doves from the roof of St. Paul's on Whit Sunday–remained firmly in place. Henry's son, on the other hand, was a reformer. Edward VI set out to smash all remaining vestiges of Catholic beliefs. He enacted new laws to support Protestant reformers. He commissioned new books of homilies and a Book of Common Prayer; and in a bold stroke of radicalism, his government made English the primary language of the church service.

In the mid-sixteenth century, the ancient earldom of Oxford was a vestige of a bygone age. The earldom's seat was a place called Castle Hedingham in East Anglia, northeast of London, set on a hill near the river Colne. The river wound through East Anglia, past another de Vere estate at Earls Colne, and into the North Sea via Colchester. Hedingham had been built within the first century after the Norman Conquest (1066), when the family's ancestors came across the channel from their home in the Côtentin Peninsula of Normandy. William the Conqueror granted Castle Hedingham and thirteen other estates to the de Veres for their military service in helping the Normans overrun the Saxons. Castle Hedingham's central Norman keep–the one building that remains today–was a foreboding stone fortress roughly 60 feet on each side and 110 feet tall. Built to withstand the engines of a medieval siege, the keep sheltered five stories that included soldiers' quarters, a munitions room, and a banquet hall and armory beneath a twenty-one-foot-high Norman arch. Brick walls around the entire hilltop estate formed a first defense against attackers. Inside stood the keep, a stable and barnyard, a brewhouse, a granary, a chapel, a tennis court, lodgings, kitchens, and pantries. In its exemplary battle, the castle was besieged in 1216 by King John himself.

Edward de Vere's father owned some three hundred castles and mansions across England. But each of these medieval manors generated enormous bills as well as a dwindling supply of income. Many properties were forever in the red. Feudal estates had been ideal holdings to command in the centuries after the Conquest, when the government required its lords to provide armies for crusades and wars. The Tudors, on the other hand, needed money. Those who could generate a steady stream of income were the new men of the age. A keen business manager might have spent a career making the holdings of the earls of Oxford productive and profitable once again. But John de Vere, sixteenth earl of Oxford—or Earl John, as he was commonly called—was no businessman.

Personally, John de Vere seems to have been a man both boorish and cultured. His relationships with women can only be described as rocky. Earl John abandoned, but did not divorce, his first wife. One of his mistresses, to whom he may have been bigamously married, was beaten up by his in-laws and other associates. He abandoned a second mistress and left a woman to whom he was engaged, on the day before their wedding.

And yet Earl John was also a generous patron, sponsoring a dramatic troupe (the Earl of Oxford's Men) that featured some of the finest actors in England. According to the scholar and diplomat Sir Thomas Smith, "I think no man of England...could do so much and so readily with threatenings, imprisonments, and pains as my lord doeth here with the love that the gentlemen and the whole country beareth to him."

A story survives of Earl John hunting wild boar in France. His French companions were armed as if for war, while he was "no otherwise attired than as when he walked in his own private bedchamber, only a dancing rapier by his side." When the hunting party cornered the beast, Earl John dismounted and attacked the boar with his inferior blade—much to the consternation of his fellow hunters. "My lords," he replied to his astonished companions, "what have I done of which I have no feeling? Is it the killing of this English pig? Why, every boy in my nation would have performed it. They may be bugbears to the French: to us they are but servants."

Of Margery, Earl John's second wife and Lord Edward's mother, few records survive. What she thought about her husband's romantic history is unknown but probably not hard to guess. Countess Margery's two known references to her son, both found in letters written to the Secretary of State Sir William Cecil, appeared at a time when the young lord Edward had been moved out of the house. These missives give only passing mention of her child and do not request any information about his life or well-being. The countess, it appears, lived out the teachings of the sixteenth-century humanist Juan Luis Vives, whose popular book *Instruction of a Christian Woman* told mothers that "cherishing marreth the sons and it utterly destroyeth the daughters."

This skewed philosophy of mothering consistently appears as the norm in Shake-speare. Lord Edward would grow up to portray caring and nurturing

mother figures almost as emissaries from an alien world–loving LADY MAC-
DUFFS in a land where brutal LADY MACBETHS command center stage. A third
of the Shake-speare canon features no mothers whatsoever.

While the author named characters after other family and friends–his
cousins Horatio and Francis Vere, for instance, are known to eternity as *Hamlet*'s HORATIO and FRANCISCO–the name Margery gets only a passing mention, in *The Merchant of Venice*:

> LAUNCELOT I am LAUNCELOT, your boy that was, your son that is, your
> child that shall be.
> OLD GOBBO I cannot think you are my son.
> LAUN. I know not what I shall think of that.... I am sure Margery your
> wife is my mother.

At the time of Edward's birth, the sixteenth earl and his countess had one
other child, Katherine, from the husband's first marriage. Katherine was approximately nine years older than Edward. (Her exact birth date is unknown.)
She, too, never appears to have been close to her half-brother and would later
file a slanderous lawsuit against her sibling accusing him of being a bastard.
Sometime around Lord Edward's fourth year, his other sister, Mary, was born.

As Castle Hedingham was the family seat, it is safe to assume that no
small part of Lord Edward's early childhood was spent there. As a toddler
inside this ancient castle, Edward's formative years were probably quite
lonely ones, living with an indifferent mother and a distant, feudal lord of a
father. During the winter months, when the sixteenth earl's dramatic troupe
was not touring the provinces, the players would have stayed at the castle to
entertain the family and revel away the long, cold nights–while the troupe's
fool (some have suspected the otherwise unemployed jester from Henry
VIII's court Will Somers) would naturally have been a magnet for a precocious and lonesome child with a budding sense of verbal foolery. HAMLET's
heartfelt words over Yorick's skull certainly suggest an author reflecting on
his earliest days:

> Alas, poor Yorick! I knew him, HORATIO; a fellow of infinite jest, of most
> excellent fancy. He hath bore me on his back a thousand times, and now
> how abhor'd in my imagination it is! my gorge rises at it. Here hung
> those lips that I have kiss'd I know not how oft. Where be your gibes
> now, your gambols, your songs, your flashes of merriment that were
> wont to set the table on a roar?

By the great stone fireplace in this ancient Norman keep, the players and the
patriarch no doubt favored the young heir with tales of his ancestors' exploits.

Such accounts of de Vere family successes and failures would color how Lord Edward would later portray the story of England in the Shake-speare history plays. Shake-speare's histories reveal an acute sense of de Vere family legend: the Shake-speare canon rewrites English history not only to glorify the Elizabethan dynasty (the House of Tudor) but also to amplify some of the earls of Oxford's greatest accomplishments and paper over some of the earls of Oxford's greatest embarrassments.

Robert, the third earl of Oxford, living in the time of King John (1199–1216), had helped to force the monarch to sign the Magna Carta at Runnymede. There the earl was elected one of the Great Charter's twenty-five guardians. Excommunicated by the pope for insolence, the third earl committed treason when he joined a rebellion to hand the throne over to the French dauphin. In response, King John laid siege to Castle Hedingham—a military campaign that ended in the French dauphin returning to his home country and John retaining the throne. In Shake-speare's account of this era *(King John)*, the traitor third earl is never even mentioned.

On the other hand, the thirteenth earl of Oxford brought fame to the annals of family legend. He patronized leading men of letters, including the translator and printer William Caxton. The thirteenth earl also helped depose the Yorkist king Richard III in the storied battle of Bosworth. A stone bas-relief now thought to have hung in Castle Hedingham tells the tale of this battle, with an unhorsed Richard III—one can almost hear him crying, "My kingdom for a horse!"—grasping at his crown while a victorious Henry Tudor rides triumphantly with the earl of Oxford close at his side.

Shake-speare is hardly subtle about the esteem he accords this illustrious de Vere: In the Shake-speare *Henry VI* plays, the thirteenth earl becomes "valiant OXFORD" and "brave OXFORD, wondrous well belov'd." Shake-speare's *Henry VI* plays have the EARL OF OXFORD retreating from one battle only to take up arms against the Yorkists at Dorset. At the Battle of Tewksbury, "sweet OXFORD" determines the place where the enemies will be fought. In reality, the historical thirteenth earl of Oxford was neither at Dorset nor at Tewksbury—and was certainly not worthy of the undying praise Shake-speare heaps upon him. Shake-speare also poked fun at his own infatuation with his ancestor, inserting a gratuitous joke into *Henry V* about the thirteenth earl of Oxford's most inglorious moment—a friendly-fire incident that led to an embarrassing defeat at the Battle of Barnet.

In the winter of 1552–53, King Edward VI fell ill with what doctors now think was a virulent strain of pneumonia. On July 6, 1553, the prophecies of a long and illustrious Edwardian Age did not come to pass. The sixteen-year-old monarch had died. Next in line to the throne—after a botched attempt to crown the Protestant sympathizer Lady Jane Grey—was King Edward's half-sister Mary, as zealously Catholic as her brother was Protestant.

Mary hated her younger half-sister Elizabeth, who the new queen thought was just a bastard child of her father's strumpet Anne Boleyn. Elizabeth assured her elder half-sibling that she celebrated Catholic Mass with an honest and open heart. But, according to one eyewitness, Princess Elizabeth was also "very timid and trembled when she spoke" with Mary.

As England's Protestants had feared, "Bloody" Mary, as she would soon be known, wanted foremost to return England to the Roman faith. The tools of the Spanish Inquisition awaited the application of her reactionary zeal.

Smart courtiers who valued their lives and lands discovered in themselves a renewed love of Catholicism. Protestants-at-heart learned to keep their antipapist curses to themselves. Earl John was one of many nobles drafted into supervising Mary's burnings of Protestant heretics.

Sometime during Lord Edward's youth—when is not precisely known—the child was moved out of Castle Hedingham and into the household of Sir Thomas Smith. Former Secretary of State to the late king Edward, Smith was a Protestant friend of the family. According to a letter written years later between two of Smith's courtly colleagues, Smith had, at some point during Lord Edward's youth, made Lord Edward his "scholar." During Queen Mary's reign, Smith was otherwise unemployed, enjoying a prosperous country life at his riverside estate of Ankerwicke in Buckinghamshire, near Windsor Castle. Smith had also recently married into a family that owned an Essex estate named Hill Hall, a day's ride from Castle Hedingham.

Smith would later write to the Lord Treasurer of England that Lord Edward was "brought up in my house." By this statement, Smith likely meant that he home-schooled his young student at either Hill Hall or Ankerwicke. However, since Hill Hall was under construction during much of the 1550s, Smith's Buckinghamshire estate is the more likely site of a rigorous classical and Renaissance education for one precocious earl-in-waiting. The former statesman and Cambridge University regius professor of civil law may have felt that the task of tutoring a mere child was a demotion. But Smith's instruction of Edward de Vere would, in the end, prove to be an inestimably generous gift to the world of English letters.

Ankerwicke was a manor that overlooked the Thames and stood an hour's walk from Datchet Mead, Frogmore House, and the town of Windsor, all part of the local color that form the backdrop of Shake-speare's *Merry Wives of Windsor*. Although Ankerwicke was pulled down in the nineteenth century, inventories of the twenty-room domicile survive—detailing a comfortable but still modest household containing such curious items as a "picture in a table," "a hanging of cosmography," and three unidentified "painted pictures." In 1555, the forty-two-year-old Smith, who had recently served as provost of nearby Eton College, was settling into Ankerwicke with his new wife, Philippa Wilford, the childless widow of an Essex landowner.

The Smiths' marriage remained childless, too, although the husband had an illegitimate son, Thomas, three years older than Lord Edward, who may have spent some time in the family household. Disburdened of raising her own brood, Philippa Smith, in her early thirties at the time, was probably the closest the former Hedingham resident ever had to a caring mother figure in his life. When, as a young adult, Edward de Vere was recuperating from a deadly illness, he holed himself up amid surroundings that must have sparked childhood memories of a nurturing environment–the nearby town of Windsor.

Nurturing, however, would only have consumed a small portion of the day's agenda in the Smith household.

Education started early in those days. In one extreme example, the French essayist Montaigne was already fluent in Latin by the age of six. Nobles in particular were given little time to enjoy childhood. In the words of the handbook on upper-class child-rearing, Thomas Elyot's *Boke Named the Governour* (1531), "That infelicity of our time and country compelleth us to encroach somewhat upon the years of children, and especially of noblemen, that they may sooner attain to wisdom and gravity." What a student might today encounter in college was deemed appropriate for elementary-school-aged children.

Some of Lord Edward's earliest lessons were at the hands of a truly gifted educator. According to Smith's twentieth-century biographer Mary Dewar, "There is evidence that [Smith] was an outstanding teacher. Apart from his brilliant formal 'oratory' he held strong views on the techniques of teaching and thorough study. His recommendations to young students intending to apply themselves to the law in his inaugural lecture are formidable." One contemporary even compared Sir Thomas Smith to Plato.

The analogy was apt–and not just for Smith's tendency to surround himself with the brightest young minds. Intellectually, Smith was also an insatiable omnivore. In his biographer Dewar's words, "[Smith's] colleagues and students were always dazzled by his wide range of interests and impressed by his capacity to discuss any topic and pronounce learnedly in almost any field of study." One of Smith's students called Smith "the flower of the University of Cambridge." According to Smith's seventeenth-century biographer John Strype, Smith was "reckoned the best scholar [at Cambridge] University, not only for rhetoric and the learned languages, but for mathematics, arithmetic, law, natural and moral philosophy."

Lord Edward, as his "scholar," would have had access to Smith's library of hundreds of books. In 1566, Smith inventoried his collection at more than four hundred titles–quite sizable for its day–in theology, civil law, history, philosophy, mathematics, medicine, grammar, and literature. Nearly all these works were in foreign tongues. Smith was fluent in Latin, Greek, French, Italian, Spanish, and Hebrew; it's likely that the scholar introduced his student to these languages via the cornucopia of culture at his fingertips. Works by Livy, Tacitus, Virgil, Plutarch, Saxo Grammaticus, Edward Halle, Plato, Pliny, Homer, Ovid, Pindar, Aristophanes, Sophocles, Plautus, Petrarch, Dante, and Boccaccio lined Smith's bookshelves. Modern scholars have found all of these authors inspiring and informing the writings of Shake-speare.

In 1554, Smith was working on what would become an influential tract concerning international economics, "For the Understanding of the Exchange." Smith also interested himself in mathematics, geography, and astronomy and indulged these scientific instincts with projects (erecting sundials and constructing geographical globes) and experiments (he would conduct his own observations of the supernova of 1572). Smith's textbook on government and politics *De Republica Anglorum* would influence the Shake-speare history plays as well as *Measure for Measure* and *Julius Caesar.* Observations Smith recorded about Spanish pronunciation show up in *Love's Labors Lost.* Smith's fascination with horticulture, pharmacology, and medicine is shared by Shake-speare, who specialists in these fields say must have been an "expert gardener" and "an apothecary and a student of medicine." Smith did not shy away from heretical writings, either, carrying both Copernicus's revolutionary tract on cosmology *De Revolutionibus* and the complete works of Niccolò Machiavelli in his library.

At the center of Smith's universe, though, was the law. Legal studies represented to Smith an ideal playground for the true Renaissance intellect. The educator reserved contempt for lawyers who practiced as if the law were an isolated subject unto itself. Following Justinian's *Pandects,* the classic treatise interpreting Roman law, Smith believed legal training first required a mastery of subjects including philosophy, rhetoric, language, and history. One of Smith's later students, the Cambridge academic Gabriel Harvey, recorded in his journals his frustration at the reading Smith mandated before a student could even crack the spine on Justinian.

For nearly two centuries, eminent lawyers and judges have recognized in Shake-speare a fellow man of the craft, someone whose unerring legal allusions and metaphors betrayed an expertise that can only have come from years of study in the field. With Sir Thomas Smith as his earliest teacher, it is little wonder that Shake-speare used legal terminology, in the words of the nineteenth-century legal historian Richard Grant White, "as if it were a part of the language of his daily life, making no mistakes that can be detected by a learned professional critic."

Beyond the rigors of legal studies, Lord Edward would also have learned the forms of recreation that rounded out a gentleman's education. Chief among those were hawking and hunting. Commoners were traditionally prohibited from either hunting deer or keeping a bird of prey–although these prohibitions did not prevent hunting from becoming a popular Elizabethan sport. The arcane terminology of hunting and hawking–intentionally kept arcane to enforce the conventional class distinctions–serves as fodder in Shake-speare for vivid metaphors concerning love, marriage, death, war, and sex. The hunt and the law both represented worlds apart from the experience of many English subjects. Both would have become firsthand knowledge at Ankerwicke.

The year 1558 marked two major events in Edward de Vere's life: He began his brief university career, and his queen came to the throne. The two were probably connected. As a Protestant and a former Secretary of State, Smith expected that he would hold government office again under the Protestant Elizabeth. When Queen Mary was discovered to be suffering from cancer, Smith prepared to return to the seat of power. In October 1558, a month before Queen Mary's death, de Vere was enrolled at Smith's alma mater, Queens' College at Cambridge University. Men typically went to college in their early teens. As de Vere was only eight, he was entered as *impubes,* too young to take the university's oath of fidelity. Three months later, de Vere also enrolled at St. John's College, although he continued to reside at Queens' College.

De Vere's curriculum at Cambridge does not survive. Only one record– concerning the replacement of a broken windowpane in de Vere's Queens' College dormitory room–taunts the ages with its inconsequence.

The turbulence of a Catholic nation turned Protestant turned Catholic about to turn Protestant again was mirrored in the Cambridge University campus. Once the nation's wellspring of higher learning, Cambridge under Mary Tudor had become a reactionary government institution given over to despotism. To be admitted for a degree, Cambridge students in Queen Mary's day had to swear an oath of papal supremacy and condemn as "pestiferous heresies" the teachings of Martin Luther and his ilk. Two years before Edward de Vere's enrollment, the King's College scholar John Hullier was arrested for nonconformity and burned alive by the banks of the river Cam. In an even more ghastly display of Marian barbarity, the bodies of two recently deceased foreign Protestant professors had been exhumed, chained together, and publicly burned on the university's Market Hill.

Nonetheless, the eight-year-old's brief stay on campus was probably enlightened by Cambridge's one beacon of learning during the dark decade of the 1550s, Dr. John Caius. Caius was a cosmopolitan and moderate Catholic professor of medicine, who had studied anatomy under Andreas Vesalius at the University of Padua in that faraway Italian Renaissance utopia, the Republic of Venice. De Vere would later reencounter Caius once the doctor had been appointed court physician to the soon-to-be-crowned queen Elizabeth. Caius (d. 1573) would twice be memorialized by name in Shake-speare, both in the character of the French doctor in *Merry Wives of Windsor* and in the alias the EARL OF KENT assumes during his period of exile in *King Lear.*

Also in 1558, state records reveal the hiring of the tutor Thomas Fowle for de Vere. The post carried with it a handsome annuity of £10. Fowle was a hot-blooded Protestant, like Smith, although less distinguished in his erudition. Fowle's scholarly record and curriculum with de Vere do not survive, nor do accounts of his teaching style.

On November 17, 1558, cancer retrieved Bloody Mary from her missionary calling on this earth. The passing of Mary Tudor marked the third British royal death in nearly twelve years. The prospects for yet another short-lived Tudor monarchy tainted the enthusiasm that greeted the wan and frail-looking Elizabeth as she entered London six days later. The twenty-five-year-old queen consulted her astrologers for the most auspicious date to be crowned Elizabeth I of England, Ireland, and France. (England still hadn't come to grips with its loss of the last patch of French soil, Calais, earlier in the year.) Her Majesty waited until after the Christmas season had passed.

During December and January, foreign visitors to London could be forgiven for believing that the city was under siege. Cannon fire from the Tower and from specially equipped barges on the Thames punctuated the young queen's frequent visits throughout the city and Westminster. From Elizabeth's first days on the throne, she was no cloistered royal, sheltered from her subjects like a precious work of art. Elizabeth was a true politician, in the modern sense of the word, and she could win over a room or work a crowd like any of the best vote-seekers today.

Practically evey nobleman and -woman in the nation—and not a few of the thousands of English gentry, too—attended Queen Elizabeth's coronation and banquet on January 15, 1559. The eight-year-old Lord Edward undoubtedly made the pilgrimage with his fellow Cambridge students to Westminster sometime in early January. Earl John had claimed his ancestral right as Lord Great Chamberlain of England to serve as royal water-bearer, enabling Her Majesty to symbolically wash herself before and after the coronation feast. De Vere's mother, Countess Margery, served as one of the queen's numerous ladies-in-waiting at the Westminster Abbey service.

As if inaugurating the stylistic Renaissance her reign would usher in, Elizabeth had four complete outfits made for each portion of the day's proceedings. In her city processional gown, Her Majesty frequently stopped the royal train along the parade route to converse with subjects presenting Christian tableaux and allegories of time and justice. Elizabeth's remarkable gift for oratory is preserved in this, her first official day as monarch addressing her subjects. "I will be as good unto you as ever queen was to her people," she told the assembled crowds in London's Cheapside. "No will in me can lack. Neither, do I trust, shall there lack any power. And persuade yourselves that for the safety and quietness of you all, I will not spare, if need be, to spend my blood."

Her coronation service, complete with two costume changes, featured a monarch for the first time swearing the oath of office on an English Bible. Bowing to Catholic tradition, some of the ceremony was read in Latin. The archbishop also elevated the bread and wine into the body and blood of Christ. But, although she took communion, the Anglican Elizabeth withdrew herself behind a curtain during the elevation of the Host. The feast that followed, celebrating a newly crowned monarch resplendent in violet velvet, carried on from three P.M. till one o'clock the following morning.

As an introduction to the woman who, in concert with her chief ministers, would map out the terrain that Lord Edward would be navigating for the rest of his life, the festivities of January 15 must have been as overwhelming and exhausting as the voluminous accounts of the day that soon appeared in London booksellers' stalls.

The following fall, Queen Elizabeth gave Sir Thomas Smith, Earl John, and the queen's handsome favorite, Lord Robert Dudley, an assignment. She had already begun entertaining suitors for her hand in marriage, and the duke of Finland would soon sail to England to press the case for his elder brother Eric, king of Sweden. In early October of 1559, the group rode to Colchester to greet the duke. Lord Edward probably joined his tutor and father on the journey.

With the accession of Queen Elizabeth, Dudley had vaulted to a position of unrivaled power unlike any other during the whole of the Elizabethan age. He was also emerging as a serious candidate for Elizabeth's hand. Dudley's greatest hindrance at the time was the inconvenient fact that he was already married.

Dudley, Smith, and Earl John escorted the Swedish noble through Colchester, parading their train through the hilly town with all the ceremony befitting royalty. Hundreds rode in formation, with eighty men displaying gold chains and the tawny livery of the earls of Oxford. Following the train were two hundred more yeomen bearing an embroidered emblem of the blue boar, the earl of Oxford's heraldic badge, on their left shoulder. The columns of horses, men, and military hardware then set off for London, where the journey would end at Oxford House near London Stone.

Both court and Parliament were working to ensure that Elizabeth marry soon. All but perhaps Elizabeth herself hoped that, within a few years at most, a sensible husband—not the Master of the Horse Dudley—could be settled upon. Then the real business of running England could begin. And Elizabeth could concern herself with the proper role of queens: delivering heirs to the throne.

That Her Majesty would soon marry was taken as a given. The disastrous reign of Elizabeth's predecessor Mary only reinforced the prevailing prejudice that a woman was simply incapable of running a country by herself. As the Protestant polemicist John Knox wrote in 1558, "To promote a woman to bear rule, superiority, dominion, or empire above any realm, nation, or city, is repugnant to nature, contumely to God, a thing most contrary to his revealed will and approved ordinance; and finally, it is the subversion of good order, of all equity and justice." Quotations from the Bible and from Aristotle buttressed Knox's *ad feminam* attack, which was repeated in more muted tones by authors such as Thomas Becon and even Sir Thomas Smith.

However, Elizabeth confounded the pundits of her day. Her refusal to marry Sweden would be the first of many nuptial evasions.

When news arrived in 1561 that the still unmarried queen would be visiting Castle Hedingham in August, little in the eleven-year-old Edward's life could have been more exciting. For a few glorious days, all the power and stature belonging to this realm would be contained within the walls of his family's ancestral estate. His father would be the center of the court's attention.

The Elizabethan royal summer progress, of which the 1561 Hedingham visit played just one small part, was the queen's great annual outreach campaign. In July, Elizabeth would depart from the city—which during the summer became more subject to plague outbreaks anyway. Her Majesty would invite herself into the country seats of ten or fifteen noble families. The queen and the hundreds of retainers and courtiers that made up her royal household would take over their hosts' estates for several days of feasting, hunting, and entertainments. As one Puritan critic wrote, during the annual progress season Elizabeth was "entirely given over to love, hunting, hawking, and dancing, consuming day and night with trifles [*plays*].... He who invents most ways of wasting time is regarded as one worthy of honor." And it was the progress that made each of these diversions a full-time job that carried on into the fall.

More than three hundred carts, stretching down the road as far as the eye could see, trucked luggage and provisions from site to site.

At each stop, the queen would address and mingle with hundreds of locals from the surrounding shires. It appealed to her notorious vanity to be treated like an earthbound deity by a new phalanx of admirers every few days. Simply by visiting a household, she paid her host family a singular honor. However, each household also tried to outdo all others in extravagance. All parties thus conspired to maximize the estate-crushing magnitude of their burden. In her wake, Elizabeth often left behind a family whose purse had been ransacked. And the deer population in her hosts' parks, decimated by the wholesale slaughter that was the typical royal hunting party, might take years to restore.

Elizabeth's 1561 progress worked its way northeast from greater London and Havering into Chelmsford and to the city of Colchester–where Sir Thomas Smith, Earl John, and Lord Robert Dudley had met the Swedish embassy to England two years before. Britain's oldest recorded town, Colchester was once the capital of Roman Britain, with ruins dating back to the pre-Christian era.

On August 6–9, Queen Elizabeth and her roving train of opulence–which, one is tempted to suppose, included an eleven-year-old heir to the region's great earldom–descended upon Ipswich.

Although the Ipswich city fathers entertained the court with all the customary pageantry, the queen still lost her temper at her hosts. Her Majesty was shocked to find widespread "undiscreet behavior" among the ministers and readers at the colleges. There was, as one courtly correspondent lamented to the archbishop of Canterbury, a "great variety in [ad]ministration" of communion, including clerics giving the sacrament in their street clothes. "The ministers follow the folly of the people," the letter writer added, "calling it charity to feed their fond humor." Elizabeth was most shocked by the presence of women and children in the sacred spaces of the colleges and cathedral closes. Then and there she wanted to prohibit clergy from marrying altogether. But she was talked down to proclaiming an edict that only prohibited women from lodging at the universities. This measure would later come back to haunt the queen–and provide inspiration for the comedy *Love's Labor's Lost.*

Also at Ipswich, Elizabeth and her assembled throng took in one or more plays written by the former Carmelite monk John Bale. The Ipswich players, it is now thought, staged his history of the reign of King John. Bale's *King Johan* was a work of Protestant propaganda that had debuted before the court of Elizabeth's father twenty-five years before. Scholars have long noted Bale's likely influence on the Shake-speare play *King John,* even though Bale's *King Johan* was available only in manuscript and never, so far as is known, staged anytime after the early 1560s. If the young de Vere were not in the audience that night in Ipswich, he would at least have had access to Bale's manuscript, since Earl John had been one of Bale's longtime patrons.

King Johan purports to tell the history of England's legendary thirteenth-century king–a man most famous today for his reluctant signing of Magna Carta. However, *King Johan* in no small part is also about sixteenth-century England. Since King John's claim to the throne was often compared to Queen Elizabeth's, any play celebrating John's reign was, by extension, a public affirmation of Elizabeth's sovereignty.

The Protestant propaganda in Bale's *King Johan* is impossible to miss. Throughout the play, Bale's righteous, antipapist king opposes such transparently Catholic villains as Sedition, Dissimulation, Treason, Usurped Power (symbolizing the pope), and Private Wealth (a cardinal). Sedition and Dissimulation ultimately succeed in assassinating the king, but the noble hero Verity (Bale's tip of the hat to his patron) emerges to defend the king's good name and to help his colleague Imperial Majesty (the House of Tudor) carry John's anti-Catholic crusade forward. "He that condemneth a king condemneth God without doubt," says Verity. "...I charge you, therefore, as God hath charged me, to give to your king his due supremity—and exile the pope [from] this realm for evermore."

Though the play seems heavy-handed today, *King Johan* was in fact a groundbreaking piece of drama for its time. It departed from the traditional morality plays by dramatizing contemporary politics, drawing upon English history—not just biblical tales or folklore—as the playwright's polemical tool. It was also the first English play to cast a historical English king as a character onstage and to portray a tragic hero as a man of essential virtues, not just vice.

One can readily picture Bale, a learned and contentious sixty-five-year-old, greeting the heir to his patron's earldom. The eleven-year-old child had probably never met a playwright before this moment. The young de Vere would certainly have been impressed by the royal and courtly attention lavished upon the dramatist. Whether at Castle Hedingham or later, after he'd inherited the family's papers and manuscripts, de Vere could also have read Bale's other writings, including his history of a knight from King Henry V's day. Bale's *Chronicle of the Blessed Martyr Sir John Oldcastle* exhorts English authors to retell English history with a decidedly Protestant slant now that England has thrown off the yoke of Rome. "Set forth the English chronicles in their right shape," Bale urges his readers. De Vere would, in fact, grow up to do just this, crafting an entire epic of history plays that refocused and distorted English history so as to, as Bale puts it, discard old "Romish lies and other Italish beggaries." The most celebrated character from the Shakespeare history plays, SIR JOHN FALSTAFF, would be based in part on Oldcastle.

Also on hand during the August 1561 progress to Castle Hedingham was a man Sir Thomas Smith had known since his earliest days at Cambridge. Much to Smith's frustration, Sir William Cecil had advanced in government far beyond him. During Mary's reign, Cecil had helped to orchestrate Princess Elizabeth's survival and ultimate rise to power. While outwardly conforming to Catholicism—one contemporary called Cecil a "creeper to the cross"—Cecil had also maintained a secret correspondence with the princess, providing her with insider knowledge from the court and valuable counsel. As an administrator, Cecil proved to be an undisputed master. At times strategically savvy and sly as a fox, he could also be a maddeningly plodding and unoriginal thinker. But it was his keen instinct for political survival that made him Elizabeth's closest and dearest advisor and, as she put it, her "code of laws." The queen would keep this wily statesman, a man she would nickname "Sir Spirit," by her side until his dying day.

A crafty, scheming, and disarmingly politic man, Cecil at age forty had already become the most powerful man in England short of Elizabeth's favorite, Dudley. Earlier in the year, before his appearance at Castle Hedingham, Elizabeth had appointed Cecil to the coveted post of Master of the Court of Wards and Liveries. The court of wards was an institution set up to supervise the lands and wealth of underage heirs and to arrange their marriages. It was a plum of an assignment, since the Master of Wards had notorious leeway to tap into and otherwise manipulate some of the country's richest estates. The office had been profitable for Cecil's predecessor Sir Thomas Parry, and Cecil would harvest this cash farm to his own financial and political advantage.

At the time of the queen's Hedingham visit, Cecil's son Thomas was living in Paris. According to intelligence Cecil had gathered, Thomas was also gaining a reputation as a lout. As the elder Cecil wrote in a letter posted from Hedingham, he had learned that his child was becoming "sloth[ful] in keeping his bed, negligent and rash in expenses, careless in apparel, an immoderate lover of dice and cards; in study soon weary, in game never." De Vere would later caricature Cecil as *Hamlet's* officious and manipulative court counselor POLONIUS–who sends his spies to check on his wayward son LAERTES, living in Paris.

Sometime around or soon after the departure of the queen's train from Hedingham, Earl John began to negotiate with a family of royal lineage for marriage with Lord Edward. On July 1, 1562, Earl John and Henry Hastings, earl of Huntington, drew up a marriage contract. This agreement ensured that Edward, once he turned eighteen, could choose one of Henry Hastings's younger sisters–Mary or Elizabeth–to be his bride. The twenty-seven-year-old earl of Huntington was descended of royal blood from a brother to Richard III and was considered at the time the most likely inheritor of the throne should Queen Elizabeth die childless. Earl John had secured a step up in the world for his son, enabling Edward to marry into a potential future royal family of England.

At twelve, Edward was still two years shy of the legal age of consent for marriage contracts. The Hastings–de Vere deal was not legally binding in 1562. However, to ensure that the Hastings–de Vere marriage go through, the two patriarchs would only need to reaffirm the contract in April 1564, once Edward had reached the age of consent. If he played the courtly game right, Edward's children or grandchildren might someday look forward to sitting on the throne of England themselves.

But those royal progeny were not meant to be. Mary Hastings would, in fact, die years later, an unmarried woman. Yet this tall, lean and fair-haired beauty exerted enough of a sentimental tug on the author's heartstrings that he would later look fondly back upon her as one that got away, a love's labor lost. Hastings would later cause a scene at court when she publicly refused a marriage offer by the czar of Muscovy's envoy. The event gained so much notoriety that *Love's Labor's Lost* spoofs it. The play's wooing lords (FERDINAND, LONGAVILLE, BEROWNE, and DUMAINE) disguise themselves as ambassadors from Muscovy and try to win over the mistress MARIA (Mary Hastings) and her friends. But just as Mary Hastings dressed down the real-life Russians, in *Love's Labor's Lost* MARIA and her three friends rebuke the supposed Muscovites.

The Hastings daughters would constitute the final image of de Vere's childhood. Mary's eyes may have uttered "heavenly rhetoric" and she may have been the "empress of . . . Love"–to quote the infatuated suitor describing MARIA in *Love's Labor's Lost*. But the "vapor vow" to Mary/MARIA would soon be broken, though it was, as the forsworn suitor says, "no fault of mine." Only a month after Earl John had sealed the marriage contract with the Hastings family, a new and unexpected shock wave would shake the foundations of Lord Edward's world.

On August 3, 1562, at Castle Hedingham, Edward's father died. Earl John was forty-three years old. He'd prepared a will–his second known will–less than a week beforehand. Although this act might seem like hasty preparations for the hereafter, the historical record suggests Earl John was neither ailing nor on death's doorstep at the time. In late June, the sixteenth earl had accompanied his dramatic troupe on a tour to Ipswich and had adjudicated day-to-day business of the local government, collecting fees from the local "alehouses and tipling houses." The language of the earl of Huntington marriage contract also suggests the father of the presumptive groom anticipated a long life–stipulating provisions presuming a time when Earl John would have other male children of his own and even when he would become a grandfather.

Before his father's death, life was good with all the prospects only getting better. Lord Edward looked forward to his teenaged years, free from the burdens of labor, enjoying some of the finest opportunities the Elizabethan Age had to offer in learning and leisure.

But now, whether he wanted the title or not, the twelve-year-old Edward de Vere had become the seventeenth earl of Oxford. Because he was still in his minority, Lord Edward would now be under the administration of the royal Court of Wards and Liveries. His marriage would become a commodity to be bought or sold like property by Sir William Cecil, Master of the Court of Wards. With Earl John's death, the Hastings marriage deal was effectively over before it had even been made official. Any fantasies of marrying into a potential royal family of England were now just so much faerie dust.

The love's labor that de Vere had lost was not just Mary Hastings or her sister Elizabeth. It was also an entire alternate universe wherein de Vere had remained the master of his own fate into his young adulthood.

But how much had the twelve-year-old boy come to know the foreboding figure of his father? Behind the Shake-speare mask, he would twice portray Earl John's passing—in *All's Well That Ends Well* and *Hamlet*—as something that takes place before the play's action begins, an event that carries less significance in itself than it does in its aftermath. Edward knew his father in death, one suspects, as he did in life: a specter to be contemplated from a distance.

Edward, Countess Margery, and several trusted servants were brought in as executors of the sixteenth earl's will. Earl John left household items, livestock, several manors, and money to various friends, servants, family, and charities.

Earl John had also vested a "use" on his properties wherein he conveyed them in trust to the duke of Norfolk—a twenty-six-year-old nephew—and to the queen's favorite, Sir Robert Dudley. It was a legalistic trick sometimes used to avoid the possibility of a child losing his inheritance in the Court of Wards bureaucracy.

However, from a child's perspective, the "use" surely looked like trading one swindle for another. For in short order, records of the Court of Wards reveal that Dudley had been rewarded with "all . . . the lands . . . and all and singular there appertaining in the counties of Essex, Suffolk, and Cambridgeshire, late the inheritance of the Right Hon. John de Vere, earl of Oxford." In scarcely more than a year after Earl John's death, Edward's mother was complaining about Dudley's diversion of revenues from the farm income of Earls Colne to line his own pockets.

In 1562, Dudley was worrying other courtiers, since his wife, Amy Robsart, had recently been found dead at the bottom of a staircase. Dudley was now available to marry Elizabeth and become King Robert.

It doesn't take a paranoiac to piece together Dudley's gains derived from Earl John's death—both de Vere family properties and the nullifying of Edward's marriage match with potential royal significance—and wonder whether the usurper was also a murderer.

In *Hamlet* the theft of family inheritance and the murder of a father achieve tragic grandeur. Shake-speare's HAMLET is concerned, not only with the passing of his father, but also with his lost family properties. As HAMLET notes, "I can say nothing—no, not for a king upon whose *property* and most dear life a damned defeat was made" (emphasis added); the PRINCE later adds that his father was poisoned "for his estate."

Edward's noninheritance would be his first taste of the brutal and backstabbing world of the Tudor court. To survive, he, too, would learn the language of courtly realpolitik—a dialect that he would ultimately translate for the stage under the Shake-speare guise. This "riotous inn," this "palace of tongues," would be home for the rest of de Vere's life. And the author would soon enough find that "the art o' the court," in the words of a banished courtier in *Cymbeline,* is "as hard to leave as keep, whose top to climb is certain falling, or so slippery that the fear's as bad as falling."

Earl John's body lay at Castle Hedingham for twenty-two days as the family made funeral arrangements. Noble funerals were events of consequence and pomp, like a wedding, that required weeks of planning. Heralds from the Royal College of Arms were typically called in as freelance consultants–funerals were an important source of income for them–to plan the ceremony and prepare the many heraldic banners and badges that would festoon the church and adorn the liveries of the servants performing their various ceremonial duties. In the words of the diarist Henry Machyn, Earl John's funeral at the end of August, held probably at the parish church at Earls Colne, featured "three Heralds of Arms ... with a standard and a great banner of arms, and eight banner rolls, crest, target, sword, and coat armor, and a hearse with velvet and a pall of velvet and a dozen of scutcheons [*heraldic shields*] and with many mourners in black; and a great moan was made for him."

Three days after burying his father, de Vere prepared to leave the quiet world of country estates and hilltop luxuries behind. The knowledge he had absorbed after years of intensive schooling, under the likes of Sir Thomas Smith and Thomas Fowle, would now lie offstage. At the other end of his journey, as the child readied his train of servants to depart out of the Castle Hedingham gates, stood a world of power, mystery, and romance that the boy must have dreaded as much as he yearned for it.

His immediate future was now to serve as a ward of the crown, living in the household of that strange, officious man whom the boy had seen the year before spying on his own son. Sir William Cecil was to be the child's new foster father. The halcyon days of youth had come to an abrupt end. He would depict this moment, in its shocking starkness, in the opening lines of *All's Well That Ends Well*:

COUNTESS In delivering my son from me, I bury a second husband.
BERTRAM And I in going, madam, weep o'er my father's death anew;
    but I must attend His Majesty's command, to whom I am now in
    ward, evermore in subjection.

CHAPTER 2

EVERMORE IN SUBJECTION

[1562–1569]

O N THURSDAY, SEPTEMBER 3, 1562, THE LONDON DIARIST HENRY Machyn recorded that between five and six o'clock in the afternoon, the twelve-year-old earl of Oxford came riding out of Essex "with seven-score horse all in black through London and Cheap and Ludgate and so to Temple Bar." The child's parade was hundreds of feet long as it progressed over the drawbridge and through the arches of London's Aldgate, on the eastern side of the city. With 140 horsemen riding behind the youth bearing the colorless cast of mourning, de Vere took his entrance onto the worldly stage as the boy in black.

As his procession made its way into London, the first sensations that would have struck a child from the country were the swarming noise and the powerful smells. Elizabethan London was a loud and odiferous city, hemmed in by the Thames to the south and a wall in all other directions that was broken every quarter mile by gates–Aldgate, Bishopsgate, Moorgate, Cripple-gate, Aldersgate, Newgate, and Ludgate. The scents of a summer's worth of garbage and filth perfumed Aldgate Street as Londoners no doubt paused to observe such an opulent procession of mourning forging its way west. De Vere's train would in a matter of minutes have converged onto Cheapside, a wide thoroughfare and shopping district featuring vendors offering up everything from breads and puddings to live peacocks and apes. The commercial traffic and racket of haggling would have only taken on a more polyglot air as de Vere's parade headed down Paternoster Row near St. Paul's Cathedral. St. Paul's was London's largest church, and its yard was also the site of the city's booksellers, who hawked their literary wares in competition with hellfire preachers, and, often, public executions. Every day the courts were in session, men hung for their crimes–with pronounced traitors suffering the posthumous indignity of having their bloody heads displayed on pikes at London Bridge.

Down Fleet Street toward Temple Bar, de Vere approached a more affluent section of the city. As the road, which became the Strand, veered closer to the Thames, de Vere would have heard the echoes of the boatmen—the mass transit operators of their day—cry out, "Eastward ho!" and "Westward ho!" And as the river's path flowed closer to the Strand, the houses got richer. Leicester House, Arundel House, Somerset House: All these mansions abutted the Thames, eliminating any worries of waste disposal and, since they were upstream from London, (somewhat) clean water. De Vere's dark parade would have ended with a right turn off the Strand near an apartment complex called the Savoy. Situated behind the north side of this prosperous section of the Strand was the earl of Oxford's destination.

Cecil House, Sir William Cecil's estate at the edge of Covent Garden, was to be de Vere's new home. (Pulled down in the late seventeenth century, the former Cecil House grounds are now in the heart of the West End theater district—roughly where the Lyceum Theatre now stands.) As master of the Court of Wards, Cecil was now master of an underage aristocrat whose life and lands would never be wholly returned to him.

Although Cecil would later write of it disparagingly, Cecil House was hardly a property to be ashamed of. The philosopher John Locke, when he lived in the same house a century later, spent the most productive years of his middle age amid the greenery of the estate's spacious gardens, enjoying the intellectual climate of this prosperous neighborhood. When the twelve-year-old de Vere moved into Cecil House in the autumn of 1562, the grounds and gardens were being expanded.

One late Elizabethan writer spoke of Cecil House as "very fair ... raised with bricks, proportionately adorned with four turrets placed at the four quarters of the house; within, it is curiously beautified with rare devices and especially the oratory, placed in an angle of the great chamber." No further clues identify Cecil House's ornaments, although at the same time Cecil was also ordering busts of twelve Roman emperors, marble pillars, and other classically inspired artifacts and artworks for Burghley, his country estate in Stamford, Lincolnshire.

Gardens and libraries distinguished Cecil House. The master of the household afforded himself some of the finest and most extensive of both. For two decades, Cecil employed the noted horticulturalist John Gerard to design and maintain his numerous gardens at Cecil House and elsewhere. De Vere must have taken solace in Gerard's company, continuing the botanical education begun under that noteworthy pharmaculturalist Sir Thomas Smith. *Love's Labor's Lost* even uses Gerard's floral imagery from his pamphlet *Herbal: Or General History of Plants* to pinpoint the seasonal emergence of the cuckoo bird—associating the late spring "cuckoo" with the blooming of silver-white lady-smocks.

Then there was the library. The variety of books kept within Cecil House was truly astonishing for those fortunate few who enjoyed access. If the library of Sir Thomas Smith offered a broad-ranging introduction to the great works of Western culture, Cecil's library provided the encyclopedic resources for de Vere's graduate studies. Some 1,700 titles and 250 manuscripts lined the walls of this idyllic scholarly retreat. While the straightlaced Cecil paid little mind to contemporary plays and poetry, Cecil House's stock of classics and tomes from the Continent was something to behold. Scores of Shake-speare's primary sources can be found within its catalog, many of which were in the original Latin, Greek, French, Italian, and Spanish editions.

The physical environment would have been welcoming for an intellectually engaged young prodigy from the hinterlands of Essex.

But less than two months after de Vere arrived at court, the government faced a crisis. In October, Queen Elizabeth was diagnosed with smallpox. The deadly and disfiguring disease had only recently killed the countess of Bedford, so fears were heightened that, like Mary and Edward before her, Elizabeth would die young and childless, leaving behind a country without a clear line of succession. The queen's death would have introduced just the sort of royal discontinuity that civil wars were fought over. Factions had already begun to emerge for at least three rival claimants to the throne.

Lord Robert Dudley was making his own claims as well. In 1562, the usurping holder of many of de Vere's lands also came closest to marrying royalty. The previous January, the political tragedy *Gorboduc* had been staged for the queen as part of a propaganda campaign to promote Dudley as Her Majesty's future husband. Soon thereafter, a majority vote of the prestigious Order of the Garter had endorsed Dudley's marriage bid. And now that Elizabeth was flirting with the Grim Reaper, she wanted to name Dudley the lord protector of England–effectively rendering him executor of the throne in the event of Her Majesty's death.

This moment, with the prospect of Dudley as magistrate two months after Earl John's death, must have burned into de Vere's mind: "That it should come to this!" HAMLET muses in his opening soliloquy. "But two months dead, nay, not so much, not two."

Yet the child enjoyed few idle moments to ponder treacheries of state. Upon arriving at Cecil House, de Vere led a strictly regimented life. His lesson plan at Cecil House was

7:00–7:30	Dancing
7:30–8:00	Breakfast
8:00–9:00	French
9:00–10:00	Latin
10:00–10:30	Writing and drawing

Common prayers and so to dinner

1:00–2:00	Cosmography
2:00–3:00	Latin
3:00–4:00	French
4:00–4:30	Exercises with his pen

On holy days this timetable was to be modified so that the young earl would "read before dinner the Epistle and Gospel in his own tongue and the other tongue [*Greek*] after dinner. All the rest of the day [is] to be spent in riding, shooting, dancing, walking, and other commendable exercises, saving the time for prayer."

Historians who have studied the intellectual climate of Cecil House conclude there was nothing like it in its day. De Vere's new home was, says G.P.V. Akrigg, "the best school for boys to be found in Elizabethan England." Joel Hurstfield calls Cecil House "the best school for statesmen in Elizabethan England, perhaps in all of Europe." J. A. van Dorsten adds, "Cecil House was England's nearest equivalent to a humanist *salon*. . . . As a meeting place for the learned it had no parallel in early Elizabethan England."

And not just in its syllabus did de Vere's education prove worthy of such endorsements. The scholars and tutors who surrounded the young earl combined medieval traditions with the latest trends in Renaissance pedagogy. The superlative talent first hired to supervise de Vere's curriculum at Cecil House, Laurence Nowell, would introduce the child to the riches of the native English culture and language as well as a prized pearl from its literary history.

Nowell–often mistaken for a cousin of the same name who was dean of Lichfield Cathedral–was a cartographer and expert in pre-Norman England. Having learned of Nowell through a scholarly friend, Cecil hired the Saxonist and mapmaker for both his teaching and map-making skills. De Vere's daily afternoon studies in "cosmography" were undoubtedly supervised by Nowell, who was then creating the most detailed map of the British Isles ever drawn.

The map Nowell eventually drew, which today can be found at the British Library, is an impressive piece of Renaissance cartography. It was also the first map of the British landscape drawn from scratch since the fourteenth century. So far as is known, it was never copied or printed. Cecil was so impressed with the document that he filled the blank side of the map with his own copious handwritten notes and is said to have "carried this map always about with him." The map may also have inspired a series of cartographical jokes in *The Comedy of Errors* about maps of England, Ireland, and other nations.

However, cosmography was a more all-encompassing discipline than the name might imply. To the Renaissance imagination, cosmography was about cataloging all of the earth's cultures as well as the entire history of human civilization. Cosmography was history, sociology, economics, geology, astronomy, linguistics, English, comparative literature, geography, classics, and political science all in one. To the sixteenth-century French scholar François de Belleforest, cosmography meant "catalogs of lawmakers, philosophers, poets, orators, historians, nymphs, muses, sybils; also myths, oracles, rites, idols, marvels, and other prodigies surpassing nature...."

Cosmography was, in essence, a more wide-ranging version of what is called "social studies" today—an omnibus field of learning that relied heavily upon the specializations of the instructor teaching the course. Today, Nowell is widely recognized as a founding father of Anglo-Saxon studies. Nowell would go on to collect and edit Old English ballads and chronicles and compile the first Anglo-Saxon dictionary, the *Vocabularium Saxonicum*. And for at least part of the time Nowell was revolutionizing the field, he had a young intellectual prodigy at his side.

Nowell also had at his disposal perhaps the single most important Anglo-Saxon manuscript of all time. Sometime in 1563, the same year he was tutoring de Vere, Nowell signed his name in a volume of manuscripts containing the only known copy of *Beowulf*. In addition to *Beowulf*, the manuscript volume (the "Nowell Codex") contains handwritten accounts of such myths, oracles, and prodigies surpassing nature as "The Passion of Saint Christopher," an alliterative English poem based on the biblical figure Judith and "The Wonders of the East."

Beowulf was as inaccessible as the crown jewels to anyone outside of Cecil House. With an author whose childhood education would have exposed him to *Beowulf*, the ancient poem's influence on Shake-speare becomes not inexplicable but rather expected. Scholars have already ferreted out a few initial connections between the *Beowulf* saga and *Hamlet*. One may reasonably expect this trend to continue.

Beowulf and the original Hamlet myth ("Amleth") are cousins from the same family of Scandinavian folklore. Shake-speare uses both as sources for *Hamlet*. Once HAMLET kills his uncle CLAUDIUS, Shake-speare stops following "Amleth" and starts following *Beowulf*. It is Beowulf who fights the mortal duel with poison and sword; it is Beowulf who turns to his loyal comrade (Wiglaf in *Beowulf*; HORATIO in *Hamlet*) to recite a dying appeal to carry his name and cause forward; and it is *Beowulf* that carries on after its hero's death to dramatize a succession struggle for the throne brought on by an invading foreign nation.

Laurence Nowell's time as the young earl of Oxford's tutor was to be brief. In June 1563, at the completion of roughly one school year, Nowell wrote in Latin to his employer that he wanted to return to full-time research. He notified Cecil that he wished to map all of England and embark on new Anglo-Saxon scholarship. And then, using words whose meaning has long been debated, Nowell said, "I clearly see that my work for the earl of Oxford cannot be much longer required." Some may read this statement as a testament to de Vere's impossible temperament or Nowell's frustration at teaching a thirteen-year-old child unwilling to learn. However, Sir Thomas Smith expressed nothing but praise and admiration for de Vere as a student. More likely, Nowell meant simply that his student had already mastered more than what the Saxonist could reasonably expect to impart. Pure scholarship beckoned, and Nowell parted ways with his young scribe.

De Vere later memorialized his tutor Laurence as *Romeo and Juliet*'s learned FRIAR LAURENCE—a character that conflated Nowell with de Vere's other illustrious teacher, Sir Thomas Smith, who, like the friar, was notoriously adept at concocting tinctures and tonics.

In June of 1563, Sir William Cecil's second wife gave birth to her only surviving son, Robert. De Vere, an illustrious earl who had probably come to be the star of the household, now saw the attention shift from him. Robert Cecil would become one of the great Machiavellian figures in de Vere's life, a sly and complex character with whom his foster brother Edward would share a conflicted relationship until his final days.

Sometime during Robert's infancy, his nurse accidentally dropped him on the floor. The child would be indelibly marred by this accident—growing up stunted with a crookback and a hobbled gait. The hunchback, duplicitous usurper, and sympathetic victim of fate, would become a primal inspiration for Shake-speare's RICHARD III.

Also in June of 1563 de Vere's elder half-sister, Katherine, and her husband, Edward, Lord Windsor, threatened to file a lawsuit against de Vere and his sister Mary. Katherine had accused her half-brother of being a bastard and thus an illegitimate claimant to inherit Earl John's estates and riches. Katherine, it seems, believed that her father was already wed when he married Edward and Mary's mother, Margery.

Although the plaintiffs' allegations do not survive, a legal statement filed in Edward and Mary's defense does. The defendants' uncle Arthur Golding lodged the response on June 28, 1563. The plaintiffs, Golding noted, had petitioned the archbishop of Canterbury—the leading ecclesiastical authority in the land—to produce witnesses to prove that Edward and Mary were legitimate heirs to the de Vere estate.

Golding's defense was successful, but later in de Vere's life, the bastardy lawsuit would once more be unsuccessfully resurrected. Moreover, Queen Elizabeth would at least once call de Vere a bastard. It was rumored that for so besmirching his legitimacy, de Vere said he "would never love her and [would] leave her in the lurch one day." Twice in the Shake-speare canon, anxiety bubbles to the surface for a character being branded a bastard by a legitimate sibling. In *King Lear,* the bastard EDMUND spends most of the play conniving to disinherit his legitimate half-brother EDGAR from the earldom of GLOUCESTER. "Why bastard? Wherefore base?" asks EDMUND.

> When my dimensions are as well compact,
> My mind as generous, and my shape as true
> As honest madam's issue? . . .
> Fine word, *legitimate*!
> Well, my legitimate, if this letter speed
> And my invention thrive, Edmund the base
> Shall top the legitimate. I grow, I prosper:
> Now, gods, stand up for bastards!

In *King John,* PHILIP THE BASTARD gallops through his play like a Greek chorus, uttering most memorable speeches and immortal lines along the way. (Shake-speare inflates PHILIP's role immensely; the historical Philip the Bastard from the actual reign of King John was inconsequential.) At the beginning of *King John,* PHILIP is introduced to court via a disinheritance scheme not unlike the 1563 de Vere case. Into PHILIP THE BASTARD, the plum role in *King John,* de Vere poured his own bastard cauldron of angst, pride, wit, and fortune-snatching vainglory.

These plays came later in life, as the earl looked back on his questioned legitimacy–and on a bastard son he himself would father one day. Closer to the date of the actual lawsuit, de Vere also wrote a juvenile lyric, titled "Loss of Good Name," that may well have been inspired by his sister's accusations. The following excerpt sounds a familiar Shake-spearean alarum–albeit in an adolescent voice given to tub-thumping meter and alliterative excess:

> Help Gods, help saints, help sprites and powers that in the heav'n do dwell,
> Help ye that are aye wont to wail, ye howling hounds of hell;
> Help man, help beasts, help birds and worms, that on the earth do toil,
> Help fish, help fowl, that flock and feed upon the salt sea soil,
> Help echo that in air doth flee, shrill voices to resound,
> To wail this loss of my good name, as of these griefs the ground.

In the summer of 1563, after Nowell's departure, Cecil was in the market for tutors to advance de Vere's knowledge of French. On August 23, 1563, de Vere wrote a letter to Cecil in fluent French, wherein he diplomatically urged his foster father to mind his own business. The letter reveals a compositional sophistication beyond the author's thirteen years. As translated into English, de Vere wrote:

My very honorable sir:

Sir, I have received your letters, full of humanity and courtesy, and strongly resembling your great love and singular affection towards me, like true children duly procreated of such a mother, for whom I find myself from day to day more bound to Your [Lordship]. Your good admonishments for the observance of good order according to your appointed rules, I am resolved (God abiding) to keep with all diligence, as a thing that I may know and consider to tend especially to my own good and profit, using therein the advice and authority of those who are near me, whose discretion I esteem so great (if it suits me to say something to their advantage) that not only will they comport themselves according as a given time requires it, but will as well do what is more, as long as I govern myself as you have ordered and commanded. As to my curriculum, because it requires a long discourse to explain it in detail, and the time is short at the moment, I pray you affectionately to excuse me therefore for the present, assuring you that by the first passerby I shall make it known to you at full length. In the meantime, I pray to God to give you health.

Edward Oxinford

De Vere, who typically wrote out his title using the Old English "Oxenford" (or "Oxinford"), was in August 1563 clearly studying under a rigorous new curriculum. Who de Vere's new tutors were is uncertain. One likely candidate is the legal defender of de Vere's legitimacy, his uncle Arthur Golding. Golding was an extraordinary twenty-seven-year-old scholar employed by Cecil to supervise the day-to-day details of managing those de Vere family estates not held by Dudley. As Golding's modern biographer notes, "It has been assumed that [Golding] acted as tutor to his nephew Edward. No definite record has been found indicating such a connection which, however, would appear reasonable in view of the factor of relationship as well as the fitness of the one and the youth of the other." In addition, Cecil's household had recently acquired a second ward, the fourteen-year-old Edward Manners, third earl of Rutland; Golding's services as a tutor would have been doubly in demand.

If "Orders of the Earl of Oxford's Exercises" offer any guidance, Golding was probably teaching between nine and ten in the mornings and two and three in the afternoons. Latin was Golding's subject, and in 1563 he translated one of the greatest Latin poems ever written, Ovid's *Metamorphoses*. The poet Ezra Pound once pronounced, with characteristic hyperbole, that Golding's Ovid is "the most beautiful book in the [English] language."

Golding's edition of *The Metamorphoses* is also widely regarded by scholars of all persuasions as the single most influential source for Shake-speare, other than the Bible. The hundreds of interlocking parallels between Ovid (especially Golding's Ovid) and Shake-speare have been studied and discussed for centuries. As the eminent literary critic Sir Sidney Lee wrote, "The phraseology of Golding's translation so frequently reappears in Shakespeare's page . . . as almost to compel conviction that Shakespeare knew much of Golding's translation by heart."

It is a fascinating and likely connection: The boy who would become Shake-speare was being tutored by the man who translated Shake-speare's favorite nonbiblical work. Shake-speare quotes from every one of *The Metamorphoses*'s fifteen books, and there is hardly a single Shake-speare play or poem that does not owe character, language, or plot to Ovidian mythology.

De Vere's personal recollections of his uncle probably stretched back as far as the child could remember. Golding was de Vere's mother's half-brother, an Essex native who spent much of the 1550s and early '60s in and around the neighborhood of Castle Hedingham. Golding was a good friend of Sir Thomas Smith, and it may have been through Golding that Earl John first heard about Smith's talents as a tutor. De Vere hints at his maternal ties to Ovid's translator in *Titus Andronicus*. At a moment when *Titus*'s plot calls for a copy of Ovid to be brought onstage, the book is introduced by a school-aged Boy who notes, " 'Tis Ovid's *Metamorphoses*. My mother gave it me."

In 1564, Golding dedicated to his nephew his English translation of Justin's *Abridgement of the Histories of Trogus Pompeius*. This condensation of a longer history of the world was the sort of book that would appeal to a young student of cosmography. As Golding wrote,

> It is not unknown to others, and I have had experience thereof myself, how earnest a desire Your Honor hath naturally grafted in you to read, peruse, and communicate with others as well the histories of ancient times, and things done long ago, as also of the present estate of things in our days—and that not without a certain pregnancy of wit and ripeness of understanding.

This was the first of twenty-eight books dedicated to de Vere during his lifetime. Already, one discerns a thumbnail sketch resembling what would be expected of a young Shake-speare: a precocious intellect with an avid love for studying history coupled with a talent for mellifluous and witty retellings of that history. The Shake-speare canon resounds with echoes from the Justinian lessons Golding translated. *Henry VI, Part 1; Titus Andronicus; The Taming of the Shrew; Henry V;* and *The Winter's Tale* all cite characters, lessons, and plotlines that derive from *Trogus Pompeius*.

However, Golding's dedication also highlights what would become a significant difference of opinion between the scholar and his nephew. The purpose of history, Golding explained in his dedication, is to adduce "a variety and multitude of examples [that] tend all to one end—that is, the advancement of virtue and the defacing of vice." Golding held a Puritanical view of both history and contemporary affairs, while de Vere most certainly did not.

De Vere's juvenile poetry (the sixteen to twenty poems published in contemporary anthologies and/or found in Elizabethan manuscript collections that were signed either "Earle of Oxenford" or "EO") is noteworthy for its lack of moralistic or religious proselytizing. Whereas many of de Vere's contemporaries published pious or morally didactic verse–and Golding practically devoted a career to moralistic prose–the teenaged de Vere was already exploring such Shake-spearean themes as honor and revenge. These decidedly amoral interests can be seen in the "Loss of My Good Name" stanza quoted above or in another juvenile poem by de Vere that concludes:

> My heart shall fail and hand shall lose his force,
> But some device shall pay despite his due.
> And fury shall consume my careful course,
> Or raze the ground whereon my sorrow grew.
> Lo, thus in rage of ruthful mind refused,
> I rest revenged of whom I am abused.

Within a few years, Golding appears to have regretted that he had ever introduced his nephew to that libertine poet Ovid. In 1571, Golding dedicated a sober translation of John Calvin's commentaries on the Psalms to his nephew. This time, Golding's dedicatory preface takes on a tone that is almost scolding in its moralizing: "I beseech Your Lordship consider how God hath placed you upon a high stage in the eyes of all men," Golding wrote to de Vere. "... But if you should become either a counterfeit Protestant or a perverse papist or a cold and careless neuter (God forbid), the harm could not be expressed which you should do to your native country." To his Puritanical uncle, de Vere was, in the end, a wayward soul. Though Golding would outlive de Vere by two years, their paths diverged after the early 1570s.

Between 1564 and 1569, de Vere's studies go mostly unchronicled. That de Vere was studying during much of this period is likely, given his guardian's interest in education. Cecil believed that the nobility and gentry owed it to their country to study as diligently as possible in their teenaged years, for they would soon be representing England as generals, ambassadors, and functionaries of state. It was a point of pride to Cecil that his wards would become some of the most rigorously trained highborn men in all of Europe.

The years 1563–65 were also rife with plague, when those who could get out of the city did. During some of this period, de Vere was out of London. Perhaps the conceit of *Love's Labor's Lost*, wherein a clique of noble French youth sequester themselves at the KING OF NAVARRE's country estate to study for three years, is not so far-fetched. It was standard practice for aspiring professionals in their middle teens to pack off to the university, although noble students typically worked independently of Cambridge or Oxford. Their tutors were often some of the best the university had to offer, as in the case of Sir Thomas Smith. But even if a young aristocrat was affiliated with a university, as de Vere was at Cambridge in 1558, he rarely took a degree. A bachelor's degree was more of a professional certificate, relevant to middle-class life and careers, than it was any mark of prestige for the entitled classes.

One fact about de Vere's activities from this period does survive. From August 5 to 10, 1564, de Vere lodged at St. John's College, Cambridge University. De Vere, his housemate the earl of Rutland, de Vere's cousin the duke of Norfolk, and other prominent men at Elizabeth's court were to receive Master of Arts degrees from the university. Cecil himself, who had been chancellor of the university for the past five years, would also receive an M.A.

The queen was scheduled to participate in these celebrations. However, Elizabeth faced one small problem: She had furiously proclaimed at Ipswich in 1561 that no woman would ever be permitted to stay overnight at an English university or abbey. And yet here Her Majesty was, lodging at Cambridge University for five nights.

Her chroniclers kindly overlook this moment of royal hypocrisy. But Shake-speare does not. *Love's Labor's Lost,* a play in which the primary theme is oath breaking, takes Elizabeth to task for her 1561 proclamation. The sequestered scholars of *Love's Labor's Lost,* who have pledged not to fraternize with women, face a host of problems when the PRINCESS OF FRANCE (a stand-in for Queen Elizabeth) and her train pay a visit. The princess's loyal attendant BOYET (a lighthearted caricature of Cecil) announces the arrival of the royal entourage but is sent back to inform Her Highness that, essentially, no girls are allowed. The scholars, BOYET regretfully notifies the PRINCESS, intend "to lodge you in the field."

The shocked PRINCESS's repartee with her host the KING OF NAVARRE spoofs what Elizabeth *would* have faced had the Cambridge University officials actually held the queen to her 1561 edict. *Love's Labor's Lost*'s exchange certainly never happened in reality, but such an exchange also offered up the kind of ribbing that Elizabeth would have enjoyed.

KING Fair Princess, welcome to the court of Navarre.
PRINCESS Fair I give you back again; and welcome I have not yet: the
  roof of this court is too high to be yours, and welcome to the wide
  fields too base to be mine.
KING You shall be welcome, madam, to my court.
PRIN. I will be welcome, then: conduct me thither.
KING Hear me, dear lady; I have sworn an oath.

It was the thirty-year-old queen's first visit to a university, and her five-day stay was recorded at length by at least four contemporary chroniclers.

Cecil took great pains to arrange for lavish entertainments and spectacles to delight and stimulate Her Majesty and the court. As the bishop of London wrote in a July 1564 letter to the university officials, Elizabeth's visit would include "all manner of scholastical exercises–*viz.* with sermons both in English and Latin, disputations in all kinds of faculties, and playing of comedies and tragedies."

On the afternoon of Saturday, August 5, the queen and her entourage arrived at Cambridge and retired to their lodgings–Elizabeth at King's College with de Vere, Rutland, and Cecil up the street at Cecil's alma mater, St. John's. The following night, King's College Chapel was converted into a theater with, in the words of one contemporary account, "a great stage containing the breadth of the church from the one side unto the other that the chapels might serve for houses. In length, it ran two of the lower chapels full, with the pillars, on a side." Cecil and the other attendees, presumably including de Vere, entered with guards bearing torches. The guards stood by the stage, providing the only source of illumination for the play. The queen and her attendants then entered and took their seats, with Her Majesty watching the play from a special throne onstage. She was, after all, still the center of attention.

The following day was given over to public debates at St. Mary's Church on such topics as art, the superiority of monarchy to a republic, and the merits of simple over complicated foods. The evening's performance was Edward Haliwell's tragedy *Dido*. A marginally anti-Catholic play followed on Tuesday night, Nicholas Udall's drama about the biblical king Hezekiah and his destruction of idolatry. By the following evening, after another day of disputations and an extemporaneous speech of her own in Latin, Elizabeth was too worn out to enjoy any more entertainments. So she awarded honorary degrees to the fourteen-year-old de Vere and others the next morning and then decamped for the nearby priory of Hinchinbrook.

A troupe of players from the university, however, followed the queen's train. De Vere, who probably departed Cambridge with Elizabeth, would have watched as these presumptuous undergraduates overtook the massive convoy of horses and carts. The players begged Elizabeth to let them perform just one masque. After some pleading, she finally consented.

Perhaps emboldened by the mildly anti-Catholic Hezekiah play two nights before, the student players proceeded to lampoon a group of Catholic bishops who were then being held in prison. The play provoked such an uproar that the queen's chroniclers omit any mention of it. The tale survives only in the correspondence of the Spanish ambassador, who was in the business of reporting courtly scuttlebutt back to his king.

According to the ambassador, the students in the drama "came in dressed as some of the imprisoned bishops. First came the bishop of London carrying a lamb in his hands as if he were eating it as he walked along, and then others with devices [*props*], one being in the figure of a dog with the Host in his mouth."

Elizabeth was so outraged at this breach of civility that she stormed out of the performance. (In 1559, she had issued a proclamation outlawing any discussion of religion or politics on the popular—as opposed to courtly—stage.) The queen spared no words. The Spanish ambassador adds that "the men who held the torches, it being night, left them [*the rest of the court*] in the dark, and so ended the thoughtless and scandalous representations."

De Vere must have marveled at the visceral response a simple skit had produced. These players, ham-fisted though their farce was, had truly caught the conscience of the queen. Such an explosive response to a theatrical performance never happened again in Elizabeth's court. (Henceforth the queen's handlers would vet court dramas more carefully.) But once was enough, and *Hamlet* preserves this very moment of royal distemper:

OPHELIA The king rises. . . .
POLONIUS Give o'er the play.
KING Give me some light! Away!
POLONIUS Lights, lights, lights!

In 1565, de Vere and his housemate the earl of Rutland served as pages for a prominent Protestant wedding in London between Ambrose Dudley, earl of Warwick, and Anne Russell, daughter of the stalwart antipapist earl of Bedford. On the morning of Sunday, November 11, 1565, de Vere and Rutland escorted the bride from her guest suite at Westminster Palace to the queen's receiving room (her "great closet"). There, with the queen and her maids of honor in yellow satin trimmed with green velvet and silver lace, the ceremony began. Robert Dudley, the groom's purple-satin-bedecked younger brother, who had recently been named earl of Leicester, gave away the bride. According to a chronicle of the event, after the vows and benedictions, the wedding party then repaired to the council chamber to dine "at a long board well set with lords and ladies." For two days following, the wedding party held jousts and tournaments in honor of the nuptials.

The wedding celebration also featured plays and revels, supervised by Richard Edwards, director of the Children of the Chapel Royal. At the time, Edwards was also compiling a collection of court poetry and songs, and it was probably at this wedding that he met de Vere. Edwards's *The Paradise of Dainty Devices* would later be published containing eight of de Vere's youthful poems—signed "E.O." for Edward Oxford/Oxenford.

On the wedding night, Dudley's military colleagues celebrated with three volleys of cannon fire. However, the second volley splintered the cannon's barrel, killing the queen's chief master gunner, Robert Thomas. As one chronicler observed, the evening ended on a note of "great sorrow and lamentation."

In the first week of September 1566, at the end of an excessively hot summer, de Vere, Cecil, and ten other courtiers and diplomats arrived at Oxford University to receive master's degrees. As with the Cambridge diploma presented two years before, de Vere's Oxford M.A. was probably honorary. This degree did carry more academic weight, though, since Oxford had recently tightened its rules to ensure that a recipient's learning equaled or surpassed the requirements of the degree being conferred.

The queen had arrived at Oxford on August 31 for a six-day royal visit, culminating in the cap-and-gown ceremony on Friday, September 6. (Once again, she was violating her own prohibition against women lodging at the universities–and, once again, no one but Shake-speare would ever dare call her on it.) De Vere was awarded his M.A. at the refectory at Christ Church. One of the dons then launched into a Latin oration at the cathedral, which the queen slipped out of–from the heat as well as the exhaustion of attending so many academic disputations.

In all, Elizabeth's visit to Oxford was much like the Cambridge festivities two years before. Naturally, Oxford wanted to outdo its sister university. The university's purses were thus opened to present a festival of drama and debate that outstripped Cambridge's 1564 revels. Richard Edwards, whom de Vere had met at the Dudley-Russell wedding, was tapped to organize and stage the plays at Oxford.

As the English novelist Evelyn Waugh describes Elizabeth's 1566 Progress to Oxford,

> The visit lasted for six days. There were some lighter moments: a Latin play in Christ Church Hall, called *Marcus Geminus,* which the queen did not attend (the Spanish ambassador spoke so highly of it that she resolved to lose no more sport thereafter); an English play acted in two parts named *Palamon and Arcite,* at the first night of which the stage collapsed, killing three people and injuring five more; on the second night a pack of hounds was introduced into the quadrangle, which moved the young scholars, confined to the upper storeys, to such excitement that the queen expressed her fear that they would fall out of the windows; there were several elaborate dinners; but for the most part the entertainment was strictly academic; orations, sermons, debates, the presentation of Latin verses translated from the Hebrew, the conferring of honorary degrees.

The original texts of the plays presented at Oxford do not survive. However, several in attendance at the performances recorded plot summaries and a few excerpts of dialogue. Edwards is conventionally assumed to have been the author of these entertainments.

This assumption, however, needs to be reassessed. The surviving excerpts of *Palamon and Arcite* strongly resemble de Vere's early poetry. Also, Shake-speare's *The Two Noble Kinsmen* tells the same story with the same characters as *Palamon and Arcite*. The prologue to Shake-speare's *The Two Noble Kinsmen* suggests it was the author's first dramatic work ("new plays and maidenheads are near akin"), which it almost certainly would have been had it originated in de Vere's pen in 1566.

De Vere's academic load soon shifted from the world of cosmography, languages, philosophy, and physic to the common law. His legal training under Sir Thomas Smith and others would have centered around civil (i.e., Roman) law and perhaps some ecclesiastical law as well. Both of these legal fields were the province of the university and its tutors. But study of the common law, the day-to-day stuff that most citizens came into contact with, took place at the Inns of Court in London. And just as Cecil had definite plans for the tutors to be hired for de Vere, there was no second-guessing which law school de Vere would be attending: Cecil's alma mater, Gray's Inn, where Cecil would also send his own sons and his son-in-law Lord Wentworth. In February 1567, de Vere matriculated at Gray's Inn, around the same time as another young and charming prodigy–the frequent guest at Cecil House, Philip Sidney.

The distance from Cecil House to Gray's Inn was less than a mile, from the hubbub of the Strand to the bucolic northwestern outskirts of the city. Unlike law schools today, the Elizabethan Inns of Court provided both traditional legal training and a courtly finishing school, with revels and theatrical entertainments as part of the curriculum. Some of the finest English poets and playwrights of the late sixteenth and early seventeenth centuries had Inns of Court educations–including Francis Beaumont, John Ford, John Marston, Sir John Davies, Thomas Campion, and John Donne. And to that list may now be added the name Shake-speare.

Sometime between January of 1566 and March of 1567, the celebrated dramatist George Gascoigne staged two plays for the students at Gray's Inn: *Jocasta* and *The Supposes*. De Vere was related to Gascoigne by marriage, and the two may also have ridden into London together during de Vere's triumphal entrance onto the city scene in 1562. If de Vere had missed the original performance of Gascoigne's plays, he would have had ready access to the play manuscripts either via the school's archives or the author himself.

Jocasta was familiar stuff for an Inns of Court audience: a serious and stately tragedy with lengthy choruses and diatribes aplenty. However, Gascoigne's *Supposes* was more unusual for its law school audience. *The Supposes* was a groundbreaking piece of theater–considered today to be the first work in the genre of Elizabethan comedy. It was a play staged on a lavish budget with a vast assortment of costumes and props, drawing from the best of contemporary Italian comedy, featuring a strong female protagonist and a risqué plot. To the young de Vere, *The Supposes* would become every part as inspirational as John Bale's *King Johan* in 1561 or the royal "lights, lights, lights!" fiasco three years later. De Vere would pilfer a subplot from *The Supposes,* and arguably the entire theme of the play, for *The Taming of The Shrew.*

The Supposes and *Jocasta* were almost certainly performed in the Great Hall at Gray's Inn's ancient manor house. Although its inhabitants and their entertainments were illustrious, Gray's Inn was still something of a rowdy school. Both the floor of the Hall and of the chambers were strewn with rushes. And because of their unruliness, students were given silver cups and plates; since the administrators figured that the expense of glass or earthenware, "from constant breaking, [would] exceed the value of silver."

Moreover, it was at Gray's Inn that de Vere would find one of the sources for *Hamlet*–in the case of *Hales v. Petit.*

The judge and Gray's Inn alum Sir James Hales had become a Protestant cause célèbre for continuing to punish Catholics even after Mary Tudor had become queen. Tortured and imprisoned, Hales drowned himself in a stream near Canterbury in 1554. Since his death was a suicide, some of Hales's possessions (including his leases) had been forfeited to the crown. The crown had then turned around and leased one of Hales's forfeited leases to a man named Cyriack Petit. The Hales family, wanting their lease back, argued that they'd inherited Hales's possessions at the moment of his death, before the state deemed it a suicide. Thus Petit had no right to be living on land that the Hales family had already inherited.

The tortured language of both sides in this case reads like a skit from *Monty Python's Flying Circus.* The documented arguments on behalf of the Hales family: "Sir James Hales was dead, and how came he to his death? It may be answered, by drowning. And who drowned him? Sir James Hales. And when did he drown him? In his life-time: So that Sir James Hales being alive caused Sir James to die and the act of the living was the death of a dead man." The documented arguments on behalf of Petit: "The Forfeiture of the Goods and Chattels, real and personal, shall have relation to the Act done in the Party's Life-time, which was the Cause of his Death; and upon this the parts of the Act are to be considered.... The Act consists of three Parts. The first is the Imagination, which is a Reflection or a Meditation of the Mind.... The second is the Resolution.... The third is the Perfection.... And this Perfection consists of two Parts, viz, the Beginning and the End."

Such legalistic hairsplitting must have made for entertaining table talk among the Gray's Inn students. As a student from Hales's alma mater, de Vere enjoyed ready access to the *Hales v. Petit* docket. Moreover, the theme of the case—usurpation of family lands from a rightful heir—would certainly have resonated with the young earl, still disinherited from many of his own ancestral estates. When de Vere later wrote his masterpiece recalling the death of his father, he used *Hales v. Petit* to jab at a legal system that could strip a child of his rightful inheritance. *Hamlet's* GRAVEDIGGERS comically rehash the arguments of *Hales v. Petit* as they muse over OPHELIA's death:

> FIRST CLOWN Is she to be buried in Christian burial that willfully seeks her own salvation?
>
> SECOND CLOWN I tell thee she is ... the crowner hath sat on her and finds it Christian burial.
>
> FIRST How can that be, unless she drowned herself in her own defense?
>
> SECOND Why, 'tis found so.
>
> FIRST It must be *se offendendo;* it cannot be else. For here lies the point: if I drown myself wittingly it argues an act; and an act hath three branches: it is to act, to do, and to perform: *argal,* she drowned herself wittingly.
>
> SECOND Nay, but hear you, goodman delver—
>
> FIRST Give me leave: Here lies the water; good; here stands the man; good; if the man go to this water and drown himself, it is will he, nill he, he goes; mark you that? But if the water come to him, and drown him, he drowns not himself, *argal,* he that is not guilty of his own death shortens not his own life.
>
> SECOND But is this law?
>
> FIRST Ay, marry, is't; crowner's quest law.

Legal shenanigans of the contorted kind would soon enough be familiar terrain for de Vere. During the summer of 1567, the seventeen-year-old earl for the first time had a run-in with the law. Someone less politically connected could have been charged with murder.

On the evening of July 23, de Vere and a tailor named Edward Baynam were practicing their fencing moves in the backyard behind Cecil House. A third man, Thomas Brincknell, a cook from Cecil House, became involved. Here is what the coroner's inquest found:

> Along came Thomas Brincknell, drunk ... who ran and fell upon the point of the Earl of Oxford's foil (worth twelve pence), which Oxford held in his right hand intending to play (as they call it). In the course of which, with this foil Thomas (Brincknell) gave himself a wound to the front of his thigh four inches deep and one inch wide, of which he died instantly. This, to the exclusion of all other explanations, was the way he died.

Either de Vere was fencing with an unbated sword—unlikely in a practice bout—or his sword broke, a common enough occurrence even in modern fencing. He seems to have pierced Brincknell's femoral artery. The scene would have been gruesome. No Elizabethan doctor could have saved him, and death would have come within minutes.

The body of the cook, lying in a pool of blood, must have drawn the entire staff of Cecil House into the courtyard to witness what horrendous mischief that unruly teen had just caused.

Under a more modern criminal justice system, such a reckless adolescent might expect to face charges of criminal negligence (if he was using an unguarded blade) and wrongful death. He might expect to be tried as a juvenile and face either juvenile prison or a suspended sentence.

However, no such leniency was available in sixteenth-century English courts. From his legal training, de Vere no doubt knew that what he had just done would technically be classified as murder. And a murder conviction carried with it a mandatory death sentence. Since 1547, English courts had begun to outline the lesser crime of manslaughter—drawing the distinction between killing "of malice prepensed" and accidental death "through chance medley." But in the 1570s, manslaughter trials remained dangerous and uncharted waters. A man who killed someone accidentally could still hang.

There was one legal trick, though, that saved defendants caught in binds such as this. For centuries, the only form of voluntary homicide that courts were permitted to forgive was homicide committed *se defendendo,* in self-defense. So accidental killings were sometimes twisted into cases of self-defense. In this kind of trial, an accidental death could technically be written off as the deceased running upon the blade of the defendant's weapon. The defendant, it would be argued, did not so much attack the deceased as the deceased threw himself upon the defendant's sword. This in turn converted the crime into *felo-de-se*—suicide. The deceased was now the criminal. But the deceased was also, conveniently, dead.

The only drawback to this clever bit of contortionism was that the heirs of the deceased would have to contend with the economic and societal stigma of a suicide verdict. The deceased's estate would be forfeit, and he could not be buried in sanctified ground. On the other hand, the *felo-de-se* chicanery prevented a second wrongful death—an unnecessary hanging—from stemming from the first.

Agnes Brincknell, the cook's widow, must have cursed de Vere's very soul. Because of this thoughtless boy, she had lost a husband and had to turn to charity both for herself and her fatherless child. And now, because of some fancy lawyer's shady trickery, her husband's death was going to be ruled a suicide? Was there any justice?

Cecil would later record in his journals that he did all he could to "find the death of the poor man, whom [de Vere] killed in my house, *se defendendo*"– or, as *Hamlet*'s gravediggers invert the term, *se offendendo*.

The case of OPHELIA versus the river, as argued by GRAVEDIGGERS one and two, becomes an appellate court hearing for both the Brincknell coroner's inquest and *Hales v. Petit*. As with nearly all his crimes and misdemeanors, de Vere's acknowledgment of his rash and destructive behavior came later in life– in the form of words that are performed today on stages around the world.

On December 2, 1568, de Vere's mother died. She was buried at Earls Colne next to Earl John. Sometime in 1562 or '63, the recent widow had remarried to a man well below her station–a former horse-master for the Dudley family named Charles Tyrell. Even after settling down with her second husband, Countess Margery had remained distant. She politely passed along her greetings to her son in letters addressed to William Cecil, but these were gestures no more loving than what one might expect of casual acquaintances. The only record of de Vere's reciprocal indifference to his mother and stepfather appears years later when he reportedly told his cousin Henry Howard–perhaps jestingly alluding to a play he was then cooking up–that a specter of the couple had paid a visit to the earl one haunted night. "Charles Tyrell appeared to him with a whip after he was dead," Howard recalled. "And his mother [was] in a sheet [*shroud*] foretelling things to come." HAMLET's droll banter with his father's GHOST was undoubtedly a familiar psychological defense mechanism for the author.

History does not record if de Vere made the pilgrimage to his mother's funeral. Whether or not he did, de Vere would have wanted to get away from Cecil House, where the fourteen-year-old Philip Sidney was planning to spend the Christmas holidays. That would have been impetus enough. Cecil doted on Sidney–telling the child's father that Philip was one "in whom I take more comfort than I do openly utter . . . and so I do love him as he were mine own." Where de Vere was abrasive and full of attitude, Sidney was the charming, well-scrubbed young champ who was every girl's father's dream. Sidney and de Vere were as destined to become rivals as the fox and the hound.

Sidney was also ill during the winter of 1568–69, and his visit to de Vere's home may have been the vector that brought sickness into de Vere's life. As the queen would later remark in a letter to Sidney's father, "dispersed in the country" was a "universality of sickness partly by agues, partly by the plague."

Whatever his malady and however he got it, in 1569 de Vere was sick for months on end. Just at the moment when de Vere most needed nurturing, his mother–detached though she may have been–had died. The deaths of both of his parents at sensitive moments in de Vere's life probably played a substantial role in transforming the precocious child into the driven man of letters. The list of "eminent creators" in literature who had to learn to parent themselves–whether due to early parental death, such as August Strindberg, or parental lovelessness, such as Honoré de Balzac–is impressive. Eugene O'Neill's morphine-addicted mother was a cold and distant figure to him, and when he had to mother himself through a deadly bout with tuberculosis, it was the turning point that he later said made him a dramatist. Psychological studies of literary genius draw substantial emotional meaning out of this forced truce between superego and id.

Lying in his sickbed, de Vere might well have been shocked into early thoughts of his own mortality. Like George Bernard Shaw, whose bout with tuberculosis spurred a burning desire to marry, de Vere also began, during or soon after his illness, to cast his eyes about for a wife.

The girl nearest to de Vere was the thirteen-year-old Anne Cecil, who had herself suffered a recent brush with death when she came down with smallpox in 1566. Judging from both the historical records and her portraits in Shake-speare, Anne Cecil would have been a willing and likely attendant to the handsome young noble she had known since she was five. At thirteen, she was four years younger than de Vere. But she probably came as close to being a mother substitute for de Vere during his convalescence as did any adult woman in the Cecil household.

However, Anne's father–de Vere's guardian–had already begun to make marriage plans for his daughter. The charming and talented Philip Sidney was being groomed for Anne's hand in marriage as soon as the couple reached the age of consent. Sidney's uncle, Lord Robert Dudley (now earl of Leicester), saw a marriage between his fifteen-year-old nephew and Anne Cecil as an important political alliance. Leicester pressed hard for this nuptial union. However, Leicester needed to conceal the fact that Sidney had lands but little money to woo his bride with. The lengthy marriage contract, now in the Cecil family archives, details Sidney's modest income at the time, the modest financial gain he'd receive upon the death of his father–and the substantial boost in annual income ($£325$) Sidney would net when his mother passed away. Sidney also stood to gain in excess of another $£300$ annually if the marriage with Anne went through. On the other side of the bargaining table, the marriage contract stipulates that Anne had a $£700$ inheritance awaiting her.

The wedding never happened. But this didn't stop de Vere from lampooning the haggling. Substituting the characters ANNE PAGE for Anne Cecil, SLENDER for Sidney, and SLENDER's uncle SHALLOW for Sidney's uncle Leicester, Shake-speare's *Merry Wives of Windsor* plays out in comic detail precisely as outlined above.

SHALLOW (Leicester) backs his apathetic nephew SLENDER (Sidney) into wooing ANNE PAGE, who, like her prototype, is set to receive a $£700$ inheritance. But ANNE wants nothing to do with him. SLENDER admits to ANNE that

"Till my mother be dead . . . I live like a poor gentleman born." Two acts later, ANNE mutters to herself as she's summoned to speak with SLENDER:

> ANNE PAGE [*Aside*] This my father's choice.
> O, what a world of vile, ill-favor'd faults
> Looks handsome in three hundred pounds a year!

Sidney, so far as can be determined, was indifferent to marriage with Anne. As SLENDER tells ANNE PAGE, "I would little or nothing of you. Your father and my uncle hath made [the] motions."

De Vere may well have been jealous, especially as he watched Leicester use blood money, extracted in part from de Vere family properties, to win Anne's hand for Sidney.

At the same time, de Vere also heard the call of military service. The long and valiant line of earls of Oxford had distinguished themselves as leaders on the battlefields of legend. And now the Scottish borderlands were beginning to look like the place where the next generation of great men would be put to the test. Catholic nobles in northern England were rising up against the queen, threatening to spark a revolutionary war.

On November 24, 1569, de Vere wrote to Cecil, Anne's father, that his health was returning—something that the coming months would prove untrue. His letter to Cecil resounds with the voice of an eager adolescent, seeking his share of fame and glory:

> Sir, Although my hap hath been so hard that it hath visited me of late with sickness, yet thanks be to God through the looking to which I have had by your care had over me, I find my health restored. . . .
>
> At this present, desiring you if I have done anything amiss that I have merited your offence, impute [it] to my young years and lack of experience to know my friends. And Having no other means whereby to speak with you myself I am bold to impart my mind in paper, earnestly desiring your h[onor] that at this instant, as heretofore you have given me your good word, to have me see the wars and services in strange and foreign places, sith [*since*] you could not then obtain me license of the Queen's Majesty. Now you will do me so much honor as that by your purchase of my License I may be called to the service of my prince and country as at this present troublous time a number are. Thus leaving to importune at you with my earnest suit I commit you to the hand of The Almighty. By your assured friend this twenty fourth of November.
>
> EDWARD OXENFORD

CHAPTER 3

TREASONS AND VILE
INSTRUMENTS

[1569–1572]

W AR COAXED, BUT ILLNESS COMMANDED. THOUGH DE VERE MAY
have downplayed his malady to his guardian, some ailment in the first
quarter of 1570 caused William Cecil to remit £15 15s 4d (15 pounds, 15
shillings, and 4 pence) to "Riche the apothecary for potions, pills, and other
drugs for my lord's [*de Vere's*] diet in the time of his sickness." Cecil also noted
the "hire of a hothouse"–an Elizabethan sweat lodge, sometimes involving
chemical vapors such as mercury, that treated illnesses ranging from agues
and consumption to venereal disease.

De Vere consumed prodigious amounts of cash. In his first four years as
Cecil's ward he burned through more than £625 for apparel alone, including
rapiers and daggers–upwards of $150,000 in today's currency. And even during
the earl's winter of ill health, Cecil recorded de Vere's purchase of a cape and
riding cloth for £6 5s, three doublets (waist-length jackets with high collars)
for £12 13s, black velvet hose for £10 9s 2d, ten pairs of Spanish leather shoes
and three pairs of mules (slippers) for £1 5s, handkerchiefs and velvet and satin
for a Spanish cape for £15 10s 8d, and a rapier, dagger, and belt for £1 6s 8d.

De Vere lodged in a hired room in Windsor during his period of recovery.
The town of Windsor, thirty miles west of London on the right (south) bank
of the Thames, abutted the royal castle and park of the same name. A Windsor room-for-hire sets the scene for *The Merry Wives of Windsor*–the only
Shake-speare play removed from de Vere's familiar world of court and castle.
A ten-minute walk down the town's thoroughfare, Datchet Lane, leads a traveler toward Datchet Mead and the town of Frogmore. Near Datchet Mead,
according to local lore, a hunter named Herne had hanged himself on a big
oak tree. His ghost, naturally, haunted the woods. This local legend and these
local landmarks appear in *Merry Wives*.

An ailing de Vere would have remembered childhood days cavorting through Windsor, taking breaks from his studies at Sir Thomas Smith's estate of Ankerwicke, an hour's walk away. Memories would have been all de Vere had, though. Smith and his wife, Philippa, had long since left Ankerwicke as their primary residence. The couple had first served as ambassadors and emissaries in Paris (1562–67) and then relocated to the Smiths' newly renovated Essex estate, Hill Hall.

As de Vere lay in his rented room in Windsor, bumping his head on the low ceiling beams and sending his servant down to the local tapster to fetch cakes and ale, his convalescence would have been rendered more enjoyable by writing and by the new books that were coming into his library at the time. Cecil recorded that in the first quarter of 1570, de Vere purchased two unspecified "Italian books" as well as "a Geneva Bible gilt, a Chaucer, Plutarch's works in French, with other books and papers." Of the hundreds of books de Vere could have bought in 1570, the Geneva Bible, Chaucer, and Plutarch are three of only a handful of volumes central to the Shake-speare canon. Entire treatises have been written about Shake-speare's use of Plutarch and of Chaucer, while one could fill a bookshelf with the studies that have been published about Shake-speare and the Bible.

As it happens, de Vere's "Geneva" translation of the Bible (1569–70) has survived the ages and now sits in the climate-controlled vaults of the Folger Shakespeare Library in Washington, D.C. De Vere's many handwritten markings within the covers of his Geneva Bible–and their profoundly Shakespearean character–are the subject of Appendix A.

By the early spring of 1570, de Vere was healthy again and eager to "see the wars and services in strange and foreign places." On March 30, Elizabeth sent de Vere northward, £40 in hand, to serve as an officer in a military campaign then afoot. His orders were to "remain with my Lord of Sussex." Thomas Radcliffe, third earl of Sussex, had recently been appointed lord lieutenant of the North to stamp out the unrest that had been growing in the strongly Catholic region. The insurrectionists wanted to wed the former Scottish queen Mary to the duke of Norfolk, who was de Vere's first cousin.

Mary Stuart, Queen of Scots, was great-granddaughter to King Henry VII, making her a clear contender for the English throne. She'd abdicated the Scots crown to her son in 1567 because of a murder scandal. Mary's second husband died in 1567 under suspicious circumstances, and suspicions were only heightened when Mary wed the suspected murderer, the earl of Bothwell, soon thereafter.

At the time of de Vere's northward voyage in 1570, Mary Stuart had been imprisoned at the estate of Chatsworth, southeast of Manchester. Bothwell had long since fled the country and his erstwhile queen only to end up in a Danish jail. Mary had applied to the pope for a divorce from Bothwell, an act that would have freed her to wed the recent widower Norfolk. Naïvely,

Norfolk thought he could convince Queen Elizabeth that his marriage to the Catholic Mary Stuart would be beneficial for everyone–that he and Mary could then beget heirs to the English throne in case Elizabeth died heirless.

If Norfolk actually believed this line, he did not know his queen. Elizabeth kept a close tally on any marriage with royal overtones; the heir presumptive to the English throne marrying a man with a minor royal claim himself was simply not permissible. Even if Norfolk and Mary harbored only innocent intentions, the couple could still have inspired Catholic insurgents to stage a palace coup. Norfolk ultimately left Elizabeth's court in disgrace, finding solace in two renegade northern nobles, the earls of Westmoreland and Northumberland. These two malcontent earls–and their ambitious countesses–used the political discord Norfolk had generated at court to advance their own agenda of weakening the power of Sir William Cecil and his increasingly centralized Tudor state. (The countess of Westmoreland was also Norfolk's sister and, thus, de Vere's first cousin.) The earls of Westmoreland and Northumberland also found allies in Scottish lairds who had helped the English nobles stage raids across the border.

Sussex and his officers planned a conference to discuss strategy beginning on April 5, 1570, at Newcastle-upon-Tyne, and this was where de Vere probably headed–with a party of servants and soldiers who'd embarked northward as part of a nationwide mobilization.

The 270-mile journey from London to Newcastle takes approximately ten days by horse. De Vere would have passed by Kimbolton Castle (which sets the scene for part of *Henry VIII*) and the city of York and the forest of Galtres (settings for both *Henry IV* plays and *Henry VI, Part 3*). To a young man from the south, the northern landscape was indeed a "strange and foreign place." Probably all of de Vere's life had been spent within a one or two days' ride from the queen and her court. His journey to the Scots border counties, a region where Catholicism still swayed many hearts and where feudal fiefdoms still defined the political power structure, was really a journey into the England of centuries past.

The commander of the English forces was–unlike Westmoreland, Northumberland, and Norfolk–a decisive and expeditious man. The earl of Sussex had served both Catholic and Anglican monarchs with distinction, helping to suppress a rebellion that opposed a Spanish marriage during Queen Mary's reign and helping to establish English settlements in Ireland under Elizabeth. The forty-four-year-old Sussex served as a counterbalance to the earl of Leicester and would be promoting French marriage matches in the years to come, matches that stood to unseat Leicester as Her Majesty's favorite.

Because of Sussex's strategic vision and military prowess, the Scottish and Northern Rebellion was virtually over before de Vere arrived at the front lines in mid-April.

For de Vere, Sussex's lifelong rivalry with Leicester made him a natural ally—and his military might and power at court made him an attractive role model and mentor. De Vere passed his twentieth birthday (April 12, 1570) amid Sussex's entourage, as these victorious commanders reviewed their actions to date and pondered the campaign to come.

Five days later, on April 17, Sussex began a retribution campaign in southern Scotland. All who cared to see a Protestant monarch remain on the throne recognized that the citizenry needed to be awed, ensuring that they'd never harbor active English rebels again. "I trust," Sussex wrote in a letter to Cecil, "before the light of this morn be past to leave a memory in Scotland whereof they and their children shall be afraid to offer war to England." Sussex and his soldiers reportedly burned three hundred villages to the ground and sacked fifty Scottish castles. As de Vere was only recently recovered from illness, it's unlikely that he saw much action—although he may well have traveled across southern Scotland with the invading English soldiers during the various campaigns over the border during April, May, and June.

Elizabeth's maltreatment of the Catholic-sympathizing insurrectionists was to be the last straw. On April 27, the pope excommunicated Queen Elizabeth. The "papal bull" declared Elizabeth "to be deprived of her pretended title to the aforesaid crown and of all lordship, dignity, and privilege whatsoever." Loyal Catholics who wanted to depose the bastard Elizabeth were now given papal dispensation to use any means necessary to do so.

England needed a response. One means of getting back at Rome was as ancient as Rome itself: state-sanctioned propaganda. Books, while a substantial part of London culture, reached only the minority of the population who could read or afford these luxury items. The two primary vehicles for propagandizing the British public at large were the pulpit and the stage. Elizabeth's government availed themselves of both.

Vicars across England were required, every Sunday, to read state-composed sermons to their congregations. The Anglican authorities printed a book of twelve homilies in 1547 and another set in 1562–63. These homilies dealt with general topics such as salvation, misery, swearing, and perjury. However, one homily was published in direct response to the Scottish and Northern uprising. This text was unique in more ways than one. The anonymous *Homily Against Disobedience and Willful Rebellion* (1571) is a proto-Shake-spearean piece of prose—containing enough distinctive rhetoric and poetic flourishes to lead one to suspect the hand of a twenty-year-old Bard. The influence of the 1571 homily on Shake-speare has been widely chronicled. However, the possibility that it was actually written by Shake-speare has never before been suggested. Did de Vere record his theological reflections on rebellion for clergymen across the land to recite to their flocks?

Church attendance was mandatory for all English subjects, so 1571 may have been the year de Vere first experienced the rush of addressing the entire nation—not just the elites at court for whom he had heretofore written.

> ... What a perilous thing were it to commit unto subjects the judgment which prince is wise and godly and his government good, and which is otherwise—as though the foot must judge of the head, an enterprise very heinous and must needs breed rebellion. For who else be they that are most inclined to rebellion but such haughty spirits? From whom springeth such foul ruin of realms? Is not rebellion the greatest of all mischiefs?
>
> ... How horrible a sin against God and man rebellion is cannot possibly be expressed according unto the greatness thereof. For he that nameth rebellion nameth not a singular or one only sin as is theft, robbery, murder and such like; but he nameth the whole puddle and sink of all sins against God and man, against his prince, his country, his countrymen, his parents, his children, his kinfolks, his friends, and against all men universally; all sins, I say, against God and all men heaped together, nameth he that nameth rebellion.

Shake-speare's *Henry IV, Parts 1* and *2* (staged in the 1590s, if not earlier) would immortalize this view of the Scots uprising. The focal point of both these Shake-speare histories is the squelching of a fifteenth-century rebellion—a rebellion that didn't quite happen the way Shake-speare tells it. Shake-speare's mishmash of the history of the reign of King Henry IV, however, presents a compelling allegorical retelling of the civil war that Queen Elizabeth almost faced in 1569. The 1569 Northern Rebellion's Bishop of Ross provides key inspiration for the charismatic religious leader, the ARCHBISHOP OF YORK, who spurs the rebels on. As Shake-speare's HENRY IV laments

> For that same word, *rebellion*, did divide
> The action of their bodies from their souls;
> ... But now the bishop
> Turns insurrection to religion.

The nineteenth-century historian Richard Simpson concluded that the *Henry IV* plays depict the context of the Northern Rebellion so accurately that the author must have consulted with a firsthand observer. In fact, Simpson was half right. The author *was* a firsthand observer.

Recognizing Sir William Cecil's "circumspection, stoutness, wisdom, dexterity, integrity of life, providence, care, and faithfulness," Elizabeth made her Secretary of State a baron on February 25, 1571. Henceforth he would be known as William Cecil, Lord Burghley. "If you list to write truly, the poorest lord in England," the prosperous tycoon later wrote to a friend, with characteristic false modesty.

Cecil's brutal brilliance as a spymaster as well as diplomat, treasurer, and political advisor kept him a constant figure at Elizabeth's side no matter who else she fancied at the moment. That Burghley was also prolix, socially awkward, and lacking in wit's finer graces was, in Elizabeth's eyes, a bonus. She liked keeping unremarkable and colorless personalities close to her, so that her own courtly virtues could shine all the more brilliantly. Cecil possessed the right combination of drive, erudition, cunning, ruthlessness, pedantry, and conventionality to win him the queen's ear for a lifetime. He was also already enjoying the spoils of royal favor–building two palatial estates (Burghley and Theobalds) in addition to expanding Cecil House.

Cecil's investiture ceremony as Baron Burghley–which de Vere, Sidney, Rutland, and all the other Cecil House residents and regulars undoubtedly attended–took place in the Presence Chamber at Westminster. Elizabeth and her ministers read the Latin proclamation, draped the baron's cloak over Cecil's shoulders, and pronounced him *Très noble Seigneur Guilliaume Cecil, chevalier baron de Burghley.*

The newly entitled Lord Burghley was one of only two men in all of Elizabeth's forty-five-year reign elevated to the peerage without noble ancestry or a blood relationship to the queen. He was a nouveau riche who had been handed the key to an ancient order. This fact grated at de Vere's familial insecurities and brought out an unflatteringly snobbish conservatism. Watching the old nobility crumble around him arguably led the seventeenth earl of Oxford to over-identify with an aristocrat's most valued asset: the antiquity of his lineage. In part because he saw his writings as the dying expressions of a medieval way of life, Shake-speare was often strident in his feudalism–defending the very traditions of honor, name, and pedigree that his guardian and adopted family so besmirched. As Walt Whitman observed,

> Shakespeare . . . is not only the tally of feudalism, but I should say Shakespeare is incarnated, uncompromising feudalism in literature.

On April 2, 1571, Elizabeth summoned the third Parliament of her reign. It would be de Vere's first as a sitting member of the House of Lords. (He would be twenty-one, the age of legal adulthood, ten days later.) Both Houses needed to address debts from the northern campaigns as well as an ongoing war in Ireland. In his ancestral role as Lord Great Chamberlain of England, de Vere served in the ceremonial opening of Parliament, which began with a royal procession from St. James's Palace to Westminster Abbey. This parade featured fifty gentlemen pensioners bearing gilded battle-axes, followed by a cortege of knights, barons, judges, attorneys, lords spiritual and lords temporal, the archbishop of Canterbury, and the officers of state. The queen rode in her royal coach, followed by her favorite, Leicester. De Vere carried Elizabeth's train as she was then led into the House of Lords.

Elizabeth's previous two Parliaments (in 1563 and '66) had been contentious affairs, with ministers and MPs imploring her to marry or at least to name a successor. Such an act of self-demotion she refused to perform. The 1571 session, however, was united in its recognition of the Catholic threat from abroad, made manifest in the Northern Rebellion. God, one 1571 Parliamentarian said, had graced England with a "blessed bird," a rare phoenix. Elizabeth's image as the rising phoenix would remain with her for the rest of her reign.

Also passed by the House of Commons was a bill simply titled "Against Wednesdays." This proposed piece of legislation, which never survived its first reading in the House of Lords, would have rescinded a 1563 measure that Cecil had passed, mandating that all English subjects eat fish on Wednesdays. Cecil had cleverly devised this measure, nicknamed "Cecil's Fast," to build up England's fisheries and, as a consequence, its naval forces as well. HAMLET baits POLONIUS with the epithet "fishmonger." The word may crudely signify "pimp," but the implicit pun traces back to Cecil's Fast.

The following month, on May 7 and 8, 1571, de Vere competed in a knight's tournament at Whitehall. Dating from Henry VIII's years of voracious palatial development, Whitehall was a sprawling twenty-three-acre plot along the Thames north of Westminster that became, at its building in the 1530s, the largest royal palace in Europe. The tiltyard at Whitehall was a long and skinny field of grass behind the palace with a "barrier," a shoulder-high wooden jousting fence, stretching down the middle. Around the yard were wooden bleachers where onlookers paid eighteen pence for a seat. At the far end of the field stood the royal reviewing stand, where Elizabeth and her court looked down on the proceedings. Challenging knights would enter at the east gate and defending knights at the west. Upon entering they recited a formal chivalric challenge to the constable: "My name is Edward, Lord Oxford, and I am hither come armed and mounted to perform my challenge against ___ and acquit my pledges." De Vere rode in the costume of the Red Knight, an Arthurian legend from the ancient tales of the quest for the Holy Grail.

On either side of the barrier the opposing knights raced their ornately decorated steeds toward one another, bearing long lances made of soft wood. The joust included de Vere, Charles Howard—one of the generals in the recent northern campaign—and the queen's royal champion, Sir Henry Lee. Also riding the lists was a newly elected member of Parliament, Christopher Hatton, a charming and preening social climber who would soon be dancing his way into Elizabeth's affections and onto de Vere's bad side.

All participants in the two-day tourney, according to the chronicler John Stow, "did very valiantly. But the chief honor was given to the earl of Oxford."

De Vere had broken thirty-two lances and scored three direct hits ("attaints") on the head or chest.

At age twenty-one, the Lord Great Chamberlain of England had triumphed over an experienced general (the thirty-five-year-old Howard) and the president of the Society of Knights Tilters (the forty-one-year-old Lee). Brilliance and manifold talents, as well as rank and riches, certainly made Edward de Vere one of the country's most promising marriageable bachelors.

From his first days at Cecil House, the girl who had always been close by–and who had perhaps also tended to him during his illness–was his guardian's daughter, Anne Cecil. Anne had already come to be known at court as a young woman of great learning and decorum. In the words of twentieth-century literary historian Austin K. Gray,

> Anne Cecil was by nature as sedate and demure as [de Vere] was rash and heedless. If he was a songster, she was a bluestocking, and a pattern of wifely virtue to boot. As a maid of honor she had won the favor of the queen by her learning, her domestic accomplishments, and the general gravity of her demeanor. While other maids of honor philandered with the young nobles in the galleries of Richmond or made the palace melodious with madrigals and part-songs, Anne Cecil, it was observed, was always deep in some learned work or plying her needle or discoursing gravely with reverend signors in the embrasure of a window.

The two plays de Vere later wrote that most unambiguously recall his 1571 courtship with Anne–*The Merry Wives of Windsor* and *All's Well That Ends Well*–both place him as the groom of a higher caste than his prospective bride. They also tell conflicting stories, reflecting his varying perspectives on a tumultuous marriage. In *The Merry Wives,* the young and valiant groom (FENTON) eagerly and steadfastly woos the lovely young maid (ANNE PAGE), much to the consternation of her parents. The story ends happily ever after, with the young couple wedding in secret and the parents coming to accept the union only after the matrimonial bonds have been sealed.

On the other hand, in *All's Well,* the young and valiant groom (BERTRAM) is the pursued, not the pursuer. In *All's Well* the bride, HELENA, seeks and ultimately wins BERTRAM's hand, but not without first enduring five acts' worth of his kicking and screaming. BERTRAM objects to the match with HELENA because it constitutes what heralds called "disparagement"–marriage beneath one's rank in society. The play resolves this problem with a quick entitlement of HELENA's family and a harsh threat against the young man. The KING tells BERTRAM that he'd better marry HELENA or else

> ...I will throw thee from my care forever,
> Into the staggers and the careless lapse

> Of youth and ignorance, both my revenge and hate
> Loosing upon thee in the name of justice,
> Without all terms of pity.

This act of intimidation was a stupid tactic, since it could have enabled BERTRAM to annul the marriage. According to sixteenth-century English law, at least, if either the groom or the bride could claim they did not give their "free and unforced consent," the marriage could later be dissolved. Annulment was also technically available for any couple who did not consummate their marriage for two years after the wedding–or three years if the groom or bride left the country. BERTRAM pursues neither of these routes. The events of the coming months, however, would make it clear that de Vere knew these back channels of nuptial law well.

If *Merry Wives of Windsor* suggests boy gets girl, while *All's Well That Ends Well* says girl gets boy, which was the truth? Courtly correspondence during the summer of 1571 leans toward the latter conclusion. The earl of Rutland was then in Paris and wanted to know the latest news about his former Cecil House friends. At the end of July, Rutland received a letter from a colleague at court, who noted, "The earl of Oxford hath gotten him a wife–or at least a wife hath caught him; this is Mistress Anne Cecil; whereunto the queen hath given her consent, and the which hath caused great weeping, wailing, and sorrowful cheer of those that had hoped to have that golden day."

Another letter suggests a different cause. On August 15, Burghley wrote to Rutland about the upcoming de Vere–Anne Cecil marriage. With a prolixity befitting POLONIUS, Burghley noted that after the Sidney marriage arrangements had fallen apart, he preferred to wait till his daughter turned the ripe age of sixteen before marrying her off. But then, with a creepy wink and a nudge, Burghley acknowledges another marriage possibility that he does not name–perhaps Rutland had had his sights set on Anne too. Burghley wrote:

> I think it doth seem strange to Your Lordship [*Rutland*] to hear of a purposed determination in my lord of Oxford to marry with my daughter. And so, before His Lordship moved it to me I might have thought it, if any other had moved it to me but himself. For at his own motion I could not well imagine what to think, considering I never meant to seek it nor hoped of it. . . . Truly, my lord, after I was acquainted of the former intention of a marriage with Master Philip Sidney, whom always I loved and esteemed, I was fully determined to have of myself moved no marriage for my daughter until she should have been near sixteen. . . . Truly, my lord, my good will serves me to have moved such a matter as this in another direction than this, but having more occasion to doubt of the issue of the matter, I did forebear. And in mine own conceit I could have

as well liked there [*in that "another direction"*] as in any other place in England. Percase Your Lordship may guess where I mean, and so shall I, for I will name nobody.... And surely, my lord, by dealing with him [*de Vere*] I find that which I often heard of Your Lordship, that there is much more in him of understanding than any stranger to him would think. And for mine own part I find that whereof I take comfort in his wit and knowledge grown by good conversation.

"A purposed determination in my lord of Oxford to marry with my daughter." Here Burghley is being disingenuous. Without telling the outside world, Burghley had made marriage with his daughter extremely attractive to de Vere. Although unrecorded in Cecil's papers or in the state records, Spanish embassy correspondence avers that Burghley dangled a generous £15,000 dowry, four to six million dollars today, in front of de Vere's nose. (The word OPHELIA in Greek means either "profit" or "indebtedness." Anne had become both to the young free-spending and cash-strapped groom who came of age in her household.) De Vere may very well have originally loved Anne as *The Merry Wives of Windsor*'s FENTON does "sweet ANNE PAGE." But the treasure trove of a dowry and its subsequent disappearance from the records underscore the fact that marrying into the house of Cecil meant entering a world of political maneuvering and cutthroat gamesmanship. De Vere–headstrong though he was–was no match for a man whose grasp on the scepter of power never loosened. Many in Elizabethan England thought the country was becoming, as the agent provocateur William Herle reported, a "Regnum Cecilianum." De Vere merely lived under it.

The nuptials had been set for Burghley's estate at Theobalds in late September, but in the interim pressing matters of state had pushed the wedding date back. De Vere's cousin Thomas Howard, duke of Norfolk, had once again blundered his way onto treasonous terrain. Whereas, during the Northern Rebellion, Norfolk had managed to dodge the consequences, this time he would have nowhere to run.

On September 1, 1571, the "Ridolphi Plot" unfolded into plain view. Norfolk's secretary, bearing a bag of gold and a ciphered letter, had let his cargo slip into the hands of a suspicious tradesman, who notified the authorities of the incendiary materials he'd been given. The letter allegedly contained details of a conspiracy that involved an Italian banker named Ridolphi. Ridolphi, it was said, was financing and spearheading a campaign to launch a Spanish invasion of England from The Netherlands, while at the same time deposing Elizabeth and installing Norfolk and Mary, Queen of Scots, as the new king and queen of England. Sir Thomas Smith interrogated the go-betweens. Smith wrote to Burghley, "In my mind the matter being now so manifestly opened and the duke taken as it were επ αντοφωρω [*in the act*], it were very fit he were more safely kept."

On September 5, Norfolk was led to the Tower of London, where he would await a trial for treason. The circumstances surrounding the Ridolphi Plot have been fodder for numerous authors and historians, serving to populate their London of 1571 with various agents, double agents, heavies, dupes, and innocents. One likely scenario posits that Burghley, who had been trying for years to catch Mary and/or Norfolk red handed, had used his burgeoning spy network to frame the duo and rid England forever of the gravest threat to Elizabeth's throne that it would ever know. Another suggests that the foolish Norfolk was once again led astray by forces that he himself may not have fathomed–and England had Cecil's spies to thank that the Ridolphi Plot never made it off the drawing board.

In any case, at the very moment de Vere was preparing to wed, his prospective father-in-law had conducted a covert operation that would result in the last remaining duke in England being sacrificed at the altar of Elizabethan realpolitik. Wedding bells and funeral bells were about to be tolling simultaneously: the former for de Vere and his foster sister, the latter for his cousin as the by-product of a campaign led by his foster father. De Vere the groom was also de Vere the feudal sentimentalist and loyal cousin. His heart led him in two directions at once, yielding dark prospects for the months ahead.

De Vere married Anne Cecil at Westminster Abbey, on Sunday, December 16, 1571. According to one report, the event was a double wedding. Through a stroke of fate, de Vere also caught a glimpse of what his life might have been had his father not died in 1562. At the same place and time of his wedding, Elizabeth Hastings–one of the two sisters whom de Vere had long ago been contracted to marry–wed Edward Somerset, earl of Worcester. Irony glazed the meats on de Vere's wedding banquet plate.

As Anne Cecil recited her vows for the archbishop, the all-powerful lord Burghley looked down the bridge of his nose at this gadabout that his naïve daughter was about to call her husband.

Anne's wedding was, nevertheless, a big event for the family–as well as a prime opportunity for political maneuvering. Burghley was anxious to see that the treason case against Norfolk would not be softened into another clemency. Queen Elizabeth had rosewater blood for her peers in the upper ranks of the aristocracy, and if left to her own predispositions, Her Majesty was likely to believe that Norfolk had been duped. No outcome in Norfolk's case was certain. When better to press Burghley's case than at the wedding of his daughter, when the entire elite of the court would be gathering?

The wedding ceremony at Westminster Abbey, along with the subsequent feasting, feting, jousts, and tourneys, carried on with all the requisite pomp. Fawning verses to the groom, bride, and the bride's parents survive in the Cecil family archives at Hatfield House, telling the part of the story that Burghley would have wanted to preserve. Would that history had also preserved the frenetic arguments that must have shuttled back and forth between the groom's party contending that cousin Norfolk was framed and the bride's party claiming that extending mercy would only encourage the pernicious agents of Rome.

And then there was the fifteen-year-old bride herself, perhaps sitting in the royal reviewing stand outside Whitehall with the newlywed countess of Worcester (Elizabeth Hastings Somerset) and the queen, as chivalrous knights jousted for the honor of the fair maidens being wed. Anne and the two Elizabeths would have waved and thanked the resplendent cavilieros as they raced across the Whitehall green, recalling the values of an earlier age that were soon to be put on trial.

The overshadowing of Anne's wedding day by family tension and court politics would foreshadow her entire married life. Throughout her dismal years with Edward, Anne would be, much like OPHELIA, forever caught between an officious and insincere father and a bullheaded and melancholic lover.

The unsuspecting Anne Cecil de Vere would soon be facing a hurricane of a force and variability that neither she nor her unpredictable husband could have anticipated. Anne's consolation for her suffering would be literary immortality: Eyes yet unborn would forever see her slandered as HERO, castigated as OPHELIA, brutalized as DESDEMONA, raped as LUCRECE—but then courted as ANNE PAGE, vindicated as HELENA, beloved as JULIET (both in *Romeo and Juliet* and *Measure for Measure*), and posthumously worshiped as HERMIONE.

The queen put it off for months, but Norfolk's trial was finally set for January 16, 1572. Gossip had been circulating concerning de Vere's past attempts to rescue his cousin. One of Burghley's agents in the Lowlands reported the rumors he was hearing locally that de Vere "hath been a most humble suitor for [Norfolk]," and that Burghley's role in Norfolk's predicament had resulted in de Vere forsaking Anne's bed. Another piece of scuttlebutt suggested that de Vere had "rail[ed]" at Norfolk for "coming at the queen's commandment"—i.e., for surrendering himself to the authorities. And another still suggested that just around the time of his wedding to Anne, de Vere had made a "certain proposal...to some of his friends" presumably related to Norfolk's imbroglio. Whatever substance, if any, supported these rumors, it was clear that de Vere wanted his cousin to be sheltered from the storm that had been brewing since the unrest of 1569. Simply by being single, the highest-ranking nobleman in England, and unwilling to forswear any interest in marrying Mary, Queen of Scots, Norfolk was already a marked man—especially after having been smeared by association with the blundering Northern Rebellion.

Before the trial began, de Vere loosed one final arrow into the enemy lines. It was carefully selected from his quiver—one designed to remind queen, court, and country just how crucial the feudal nobility was to the proper functioning of the Renaissance state. The Italian philosopher Baldassare Castiglione's book of court etiquette, *Il Cortegiano,* had been translated into English a decade before. In the intervening years, *The Courtier* had become akin to holy writ for English gentlemen seeking to emulate the sophistication of continental court culture. But de Vere was aiming for a larger and more important readership than simply his fellow countrymen. He sponsored *The Courtier*'s translation into Latin—thereby rendering it accessible to urbane readers throughout Europe. In publishing Bartholomew Clerke's Latin edition of Castiglione, de Vere had achieved two important objectives that would further the case for his cousin. First, it would flatter Her Majesty's intellect—always useful for winning her heart. Second, it would recount for her in the tongue of learned society the crucial role of the aristocracy in the queen's world.

The first objective was a natural consequence of the text itself. No philosophical tract more closely approximated life under Elizabeth. Castiglione's court was one presided over by a woman and in which all authority ultimately rested in women. Castiglione's duchess was, like Elizabeth, a figure to be platonically admired by the men surrounding her and yet adored and idolized like a terrestrial goddess of love. The second objective—underscoring the necessity of earls and dukes in a world that was increasingly giving them the squeeze—emerges from the lessons Castiglione teaches. The prince in Castiglione's universe is no autocratic agent. Rather, it is the courtier who leads the prince "through the rough way of virtue," who "distill[s] into his mind goodness and teach[es] him continency, stoutness of courage, justice." According to Castiglione, the courtier is effectively "more excellent than the prince."

On January 5, 1572, de Vere wrote a fluent prefatory letter in Latin to Clerke's edition of *The Courtier.* As translated into English, de Vere's preface reads:

> ... For what more difficult, more noble, or more magnificent task has anyone ever undertaken than our author Castiglione? Who has drawn for us the figure and model of a courtier, a work to which nothing can be added, in which there is no redundant word, a portrait which we shall recognize as that of a highest and most perfect type of man? And so, although nature herself has made nothing perfect in every detail, yet the manners of men exceed in dignity that with which nature has endowed them; and he who surpasses others has here surpassed himself, and has even outdone nature, which by no one has ever been surpassed.

Naturally, an author and thinker who was so highly esteemed would seep into the very fiber of de Vere's writings. And to assert that Castiglione's influence pervades Shake-speare's works is no exaggeration. (Indeed, anyone seeking to understand Shake-speare as a thinker would be well advised to first become acquainted with de Vere's three great intellectual forebears: Plato, Ovid, and Castiglione.)

In publishing the philosophical case for a thriving aristocracy, de Vere was second to none. But in actually protecting Norfolk from the Elizabethan state's Machiavellian machinery, de Vere was about as obscurantist and ineffective as Norfolk himself. Norfolk's legal defense referred back to a statute from 1352, which said that the state had to demonstrate that the alleged traitor had conducted acts, such as trying to kill the monarch, that were already on the books as being treasonous. Norfolk's crimes, in other words, did not rise to the level of treason, as the law had previously defined the term. He was right, but this defense was far ahead of its time. The proviso of 1352 would have to wait till the seventeenth century before it was revived as a credible defense in a treason trial.

Norfolk's trial, said historian Wallace MacCaffrey, was "as much a trial of the Scottish queen as of the duke of Norfolk." It was a metaphor of the modern Renaissance state versus the medieval feudal order, a show of judicial force by Burghley and his agents assiduously guarding the queen from all threats, whether perceived or real. Little wonder, then, that de Vere was one of the few ranking peers who did not participate in this kangaroo court. He knew, just as did everyone else in the drafty Westminster Hall, that the outcome was predetermined before the first witness even took the stand. Lawyers would have to wait more than a century before an accused traitor could mount his own defense with his own sworn witnesses; in an Elizabethan treason trial, the job of the accused was essentially to look valiant as the state, wary of entrusting a jury with potentially conflicting testimony, presented its one-sided case. The only practical option for a sixteenth-century peer accused of treason was to await the guilty verdict and then pull all the political strings he and his family could to convince the sovereign to overturn his death sentence.

The tribunal quickly concluded, and the condemned was led back to the Tower to await his execution. De Vere worked on his father-in-law, and perhaps the queen as well, to issue a royal pardon. Elizabeth signed a warrant for Norfolk's execution at the end of January, but then, after hearing the pleas of Norfolk's mother the countess of Surrey and his brother Henry Howard, the queen rescinded it. February came and went, with another death warrant followed by a reprieve. In late March Elizabeth fell ill, perhaps from food poisoning, and for five days she feared she might die. This naturally frightened the wits out of her Privy Council, because a new king or queen could be called upon in only a matter of days. Parliament was convened. Although Elizabeth quickly recovered, the newfound urgency had not abated. Parliament returned to the unresolved issue of Mary, Queen of Scots, and revisited the question of the succession. Many MPs thirsted for Mary's as well as Norfolk's blood. Security, they said, could only be enjoyed if Mary was brought to the scaffold.

On April 9, the queen signed another warrant for Norfolk's execution. Two days later, at two in the morning, she presented Burghley with a note. The memo said she could not make her heart agree with her head. She had decided once again to countermand the execution.

Finally, the Protestant extremists in Parliament began to call for the head of Mary, Queen of Scots. This was one sacrifice Elizabeth was not prepared to make. But in turning down a second demand for blood, she had been backed into a corner with the first. At the very least, Her Majesty knew she must now feed a man they called "the roaring lion" to the Christians. The duke of Norfolk was told to prepare to meet his maker. On Saturday, May 31, the queen ordered that a scaffold be erected on Tower Hill. The next day, Elizabeth visited the Tower to ensure the preparations went smoothly. She did not visit with the condemned. Even though Burghley may well have engineered Norfolk's execution, Norfolk still made provisions for his three sons to be schooled at Cecil House.

On Monday at 7 A.M., as the morning sun cast long shadows across Tower Hill, the condemned was led to the execution block. Asked for his final words, Norfolk addressed the crowd assembled around the scaffold: "For men to suffer death in this place is no new thing, though since the beginning of our most gracious queen's reign I am the first, and God grant I may be the last." Norfolk's wish was not to come true. Tower Hill would be making more Elizabethan widows yet. With one decisive stroke of the executioner's ax, the head of Thomas Howard, fourth duke of Norfolk, fell to the ground. The bloody trophy was raised for the crowds to see.

While de Vere had attended parliamentary meetings in the Star Chamber on "the great matter touching the Queen of Scots," he had achieved nothing of substance regarding Norfolk's fate. De Vere had failed his cousin. All he had managed to secure out of Parliament or the queen was a seat on a minor committee in the House of Lords on "Triors of Petitions for England, Ireland, Wales, and Scotland." De Vere's conscience would nag him for years about his inability to save his cousin from the scaffold. The fate of Norfolk's three sons would remain on de Vere's mind for the rest of his life. Their ordeals would form the basis for *As You Like It*–a play about a deceased and nearly deified father, SIR ROWLAND DE BOYS, and the troubles his three surviving sons face in marriage, in inheritance, and in courtly life.

De Vere the poet and dramatist ultimately achieved the aesthetic justice that his earthly life seemed never to attain. The Lord Great Chamberlain of

England may have had noble intents. But, as the condemned Norfolk wrote to his children, de Vere was in the final analysis "too negligent of friends' causes, or he might do you more good than any kinsman you have."

Throughout her reign, Elizabeth was forever balancing and counterbalancing each action. Just as she was cracking down on any hint of Catholic uprisings—or, perhaps more accurately, not actively inhibiting Burghley and his associates from cracking down for her—she was also conducting propaganda campaigns designed in part to bolster her image as a tolerant friend of Catholicism.

This sovereign who famously refused to "make windows into men's souls" also championed the none-too-subtly Catholic tradition of the royal Order of the Garter. This elite society, given to elaborate ceremonies recalling archaic Romanist rites—celebrating the Catholic Saint George, introducing only nominal changes to an avowedly papist initiation service—was the most exclusive club in all of England. It consisted of the sovereign plus up to twenty-five "knights of the Garter" (KGs). Candidates could only be elected to fill the vacant seats of members who had died or otherwise been ousted. The members of the Order voted in new knights at their annual gathering in April. But Elizabeth had the final say, sometimes overruling the election results. In 1571, all ten members of the Order voted to admit the twenty-one-year-old de Vere. But the queen, who may have felt de Vere was too young for the honorary title, had exercised her veto. In 1572, when seven KGs voted to admit de Vere to the Order, Elizabeth opted instead to admit Viscount Hereford, who had received only four votes. Another courtier in 1572 who received a plurality of votes and was approved by the queen was de Vere's father-in-law.

Lord Burghley, Viscount Hereford, two other ranking peers, and the French duc de Montmorency, all gathered at Windsor Castle on June 17 for the Order of the Garter's induction ceremony. De Vere, pictured in a contemporary engraving of the Garter ceremony carrying the sword of state, headed up the rear of the procession, leading the queen into the Chapel of St. George and on to the Chapter House, where the exclusive club held their meetings and induction rites.

De Vere, outside the Order and outside the inner circle of Elizabeth's advisors, remained sidelined. His most pronounced concerns circa 1572—at least those that survive in the public records—are those of a disinherited noble trying to recoup his lost lands. In May, Elizabeth had awarded the twenty-two-year-old earl license to begin repossessing the estates that had been stripped away from him when his father had died. Even with a legal title in his hands, however, it still took years for any practical transfer of ownership to take place. The priory at Earls Colne, for instance, wouldn't officially revert to de Vere until May of 1588—nearly seventeen years after he had supposedly regained ownership. De Vere would fritter away countless hours of his adult life attempting to rescue the inheritance he had lost at age twelve. Both HAMLET and the Norwegian prince FORTINBRAS express the author's anxieties over such legal quagmires. "I have some rights of memory in this kingdom," the latter declares, "Which now to claim my vantage doth invite me."

De Vere's father-in-law, on the other hand, continued to follow the path of a rising star. In July of 1572, Queen Elizabeth appointed Burghley Lord Treasurer of England—a promotion that effectively rendered him, in the words of his twentieth-century biographer Conyers Read, "an elder statesman, sure of his position, sure of his influence, beyond the reach of envy or Court intrigue—a unique figure on the political scene." Burghley had, in short, secured the role of POLONIUS. Sir Thomas Smith, recently returned from France after conducting a successful peace treaty with the rival Catholic nation, assumed Burghley's job as Secretary of State. But even in that capacity, Smith was hamstrung by the wide-ranging influence of his predecessor. The new Lord Treasurer still retained the power and influence he wielded in his previous role. As Smith would later write to Burghley, "I well perceive Her Highness is disposed to sign nothing except [if] Your Lordship be here."

In August, the queen went on progress into Warwickshire. De Vere joined the courtly train as it carted its tonnage of festoonery northwest and into the midland countryside. She and her court spent a week in and around the city of Warwick. She occupied her time partly with Leicester at his Kenilworth Castle, and partly at Warwick Castle. The progress was, by any objective measure, once again a public relations triumph. Elizabeth continued to wow her subjects with humility and grace—even as the courtiers around her also saw a woman transfixed by her own vanity. Idealized by poets and admirers as an earthly VENUS, the real-life Elizabeth was coming into her own as adroit but coquettish, demure but wildly changeable CLEOPATRA. The Warwick town recorder recited a lengthy ode to the queen, full of flattery. Elizabeth responded with words that have since become legend: "Come hither, little recorder. It was told me that you would be afraid to look upon me or to speak boldly; but you were not so afraid of me as I was of you; and I now thank you for putting me in mind of my duty."

This was a signature moment from the life of a political genius. Histories of the Elizabethan Age recite this moment as a token of "Gloriana's" magnanimity and political savvy. Yet, while Elizabeth was one of the canniest sovereigns who ever lived, closer scrutiny of her words reveals her greatest blind spot. The queen actually thanked the recorder for something he hadn't given. He had never uttered any advice. But she heard his obsequious praise as if he'd offered words of counsel. The exchange may offer an inadvertent glimpse into how Elizabeth rationalized her own self-infatuation: *My subjects advise it of me.*

The exchange recalls another shining moment of regal egotism. Years before, in 1564, Elizabeth had sent a messenger to meet with Mary, Queen of Scots. Upon his return, she demanded of him whether she or Mary had prettier hair, who spoke more beautifully and fluently, who danced better, who was more talented, who was taller. When the thirty-one-year-old Elizabeth learned that Mary was actually taller, she snapped, "She is too high, for I myself am neither too high nor too low." De Vere would later memorialize such moments of Elizabethan vainglory in *Antony and Cleopatra*, when QUEEN CLEOPATRA eagerly demands a description of her rival OCTAVIA.

> CLEOPATRA Is she as tall as me?
> MESSENGER She is not, madam.
> CLEO. Didst hear her speak? Is she shrill tongu'd or low?
> MESS. Madam, I heard her speak; she is low voic'd.
> CLEO. ... What majesty is in her gait? Remember,
>   If e'er thou look'dst on majesty.

De Vere, like *Twelfth Night*'s FESTE, was becoming Her Majesty's "allowed fool." He capered and jested and was beginning to catch her eye with other spectacles too. During the same Warwick progress, de Vere also orchestrated an elaborate mock combat, once again revealing that his greatest talents in her service were those of the stage.

De Vere's youthful zeal got the better of him this time. On Sunday night, August 18, after she enlisted the country folk to watch her dance, Elizabeth repaired to a viewing stand that afforded her the best seat for the entertainment to come. De Vere ("a lusty gentleman," in the words of the chronicler) served as the general for a crew of other courtiers, who had assembled a fort representing the castle for one side in an incendiary war. Philip Sidney's good friend Fulke Greville played the general of the opposing force and fort. If de Vere ever enjoyed a HENRY V moment in his life, this was probably it: He led his two hundred soldiers into the breach several times over, each time charging with battering rams into the opposing castle. Each assault was accompanied by explosive flashes of fireballs lobbing into the sky, toward the opposing side. The pyrotechnical stage combat thrilled and amazed Elizabeth, although it was "terrible to those that have not been in like experiences, valiant to such as delighted therein, and indeed strange to them that understood it not."

The fireballs shot far and near and rolled down the hill into the Avon from the rocky eminence where Warwick Castle stood. Some flickering projectiles even flew away into the night, landing unannounced in the nearby town and suburbs. The flames that licked up from the floating embers in the river below served as footlights to the night's warfare—a battle so intense that several of the mock combatants sustained real injuries. As a grand finale, de Vere and his men launched a large "dragon" into the air. The incendiary missile shot out flames as it traveled toward the opposing embattlement and turned Greville's fort into an inferno. However, the dragon ultimately overshot its mark, spewing a fireball onto a neighboring house, which in turn spread the fire to several other nearby houses. De Vere and Greville then ended the night leading their men to rescue the families and douse the blazes. (As HAMLET laments, "I have shot my arrow o'er the house and hurt my brother.") While the courtiers managed to rescue most residents and residences, there were also two likely fatalities. When all was over, and the *mêlée flambée* was merely a smoldering memory, four other houses in the nearby town and suburbs had suffered smaller fires, while one had a hole in its roof "as big as a man's head." The queen, de Vere, Greville, and other combatants paid out £25 12s 8d to the victims of their militaristic foolery.

August 1572 was to be an incendiary month. For even as de Vere and his fellow courtiers were occupying themselves in fireworks of Shake-spearean proportions, Paris proved to be the greatest tinderbox in all of sixteenth-century Europe. On the feast of St. Bartholomew, August 24, the French royal family (the Catholic House of Valois) celebrated a marriage to the Protestant king of Navarre. However, renegade Catholics had just two days before attempted to assassinate a prominent Protestant leader, Admiral Gaspard de Coligny. Fearing a Protestant campaign of revenge for the botched killing, the Catholic leadership–led by the sinister dowager queen Catherine de Medici–launched a preemptive slaughter of the Protestant grandees there assembled, including the Huguenot admiral Coligny. The massacre may have originally been planned simply to snuff out the opposition leaders, but it quickly spiraled out of control. Before the blood stopped flowing, four thousand Protestants lay dead in Paris, with an estimated six thousand more across France. Catholic Europe celebrated the slaughter. King Philip II of Spain would call news of the St. Bartholomew's Day Massacre "one of the greatest joys of my life."

One Englishman in Paris at the time, a man who helped to shelter whatever Protestants he could find on the city's deadliest night, would be transformed by the events of St. Bartholomew's Day. Ambassador Francis Walsingham was hardened by the atrocities he had witnessed and would devote the rest of his life to winning the war of attrition against the heartless papists at any cost. In his remaining eighteen years as Burghley's fellow spymaster, Walsingham would turn out to be one of England's most valuable assets in the coming cold war against Rome.

Protestant England was stunned by the news of this wholesale bloodshed. Refugees began appearing on England's shores on August 27, and by early September the court was abuzz with furor over the horrific events of the previous fortnight. De Vere perhaps captured the moment's drama and pathos most poignantly in a letter that he dashed off to Burghley. The two may often have been at odds over matters at court, but they were both loyal to their Protestant queen. The St. Bartholomew's Day Massacre inspired the most admiring and heartfelt letter de Vere ever composed to his POLONIAL father-in-law:

> I would to God Your Lordship would let me understand some of the news which here doth ring dolefully in the ears of every man of the murder of the Admiral [Coligny] of France, and a number of noblemen and worthy gentlemen, and such as greatly have in their lifetime honored the Queen's Majesty, our Mistress; on whose tragedies we have a number of French *Aeneases* in this city that tell of their own overthrows with tears falling from their eyes–a piteous thing to hear, but a cruel and far more grievous thing we must deem it them to see. . . .
>
> And sith [*since*] the world is so full of treasons and vile instruments daily to attempt new and unlooked for things, good my lord, I shall affectionately and heartily desire Your Lordship to be careful both of yourself and of Her Majesty. . . .
>
> And blame me not, though I am bolder with Your Lordship than my custom is, for I am one that count myself a follower of yours now in all fortunes; and what shall hap to you I count it hap to myself. . . .
>
> Thus, my lord, I humbly desire Your Lordship to pardon my youth, but to take in good part my zeal and affection toward you, as one on whom I have builded my foundation either to stand or fall. And, good my lord, think I do not this presumptuously as to advise you that am but to take advice of Your Lordship, but to admonish you, as one with whom I would spend my blood and life, so much you have made me yours.

The correspondence continued. Burghley replied to de Vere's grateful missive more than once–although these letters do not survive. The Lord Treasurer was discovering how thankless his job could be and was probably desperate for relief. As Burghley once noted, when suitors came to his office seeking lands and leases, "if the party obtain [the grant], I am not thanked; if not, the fault (though falsely) is imputed to me." No doubt recognizing the strain of Burghley's new job, de Vere wrote from London on September 22, 1572, "We do hope, after this, you having had so great a care of the Queen's Majesty's service, you will begin to have some respect of your own health, and take a pleasure to dwell where you have taken pain to build." Anne, de Vere noted, had just departed for "the country"–whether to de Vere's country estate at Wivenhoe or to Burghley's country estate at Theobalds, he does not say. De Vere added that he was planning on joining her "as fast as I can get me out of town."

Clearly, St. Bartholomew's Day was still on the young courtier's mind, because he also petitioned Burghley to pressure the queen to let him join the foreign service. The massacre had stepped up international tensions, and no one now knew what might be coming next. "If there were any service to be done abroad, I had rather serve there than at home where yet some honor were to be got," de Vere wrote. "If there be any setting forth to sea, to which service I bear most affection, I shall desire Your Lordship to give me and get me that favor and credit that I might make one. Which if there be no such intention, then I shall be most willing to be employed on the seacoasts, to be in a readiness with my countrymen against any invasion."

As a military commander or foreign agent, de Vere might have dazzled others with his wit, intelligence, and grace. But, lest one forget, this was also a man who was impulsive, irresponsible, and prone to fly off the handle. In a circle of artists, writers, and scholars, he may have been nature's lodestar. But among an officer corps or a foreign court full of backbiting politicians, some of whom could well be intimidated by his brilliance or set off by his mercurial nature, de Vere would have been a lodestone for trouble.

In requesting a "setting forth to sea," the twenty-two-year-old was probably responding in part to the romantic tales of naval adventures then circulating in London. In May, the explorer Sir Francis Drake had set out toward Panama, to plunder the Spanish way station that stored tons of treasure accumulated by the conquistadores. (Drake would return the following summer with £20,000 worth of stolen booty and a reputation as an English privateer second to none.) The earl also was seeking any means he could to explore Italy—that cornucopia of art and culture that he had read and studied so much about.

However, none of these options would be coming his way anytime soon. De Vere was having a hard enough time keeping a stable and marginally sane household. By the end of October 1572, the earl and his countess had taken refuge at his Essex estate of Wivenhoe. This estate, recently returned to de Vere's portfolio, had been in the family since at least the middle of the fifteenth century. Commanding an eminence on the river Colne's estuary as it flows into the North Sea, Wivenhoe Hall was, according to one account, a large and sumptuous house "having a noble gatehouse with towers of great height that served as a seamark."

According to charges laid out in a brief memorandum written by Burghley, de Vere was living during his Wivenhoe days like a wild man on a spending spree. Hundreds of pounds were flowing out of de Vere's accounts. One of the earl's riotous servants, Rowland Yorke, was reportedly barring Anne from her husband's chamber, presumably at de Vere's command. During much of the 1570s, Yorke would be to de Vere what Leicester was to Queen Elizabeth—a man given practical carte blanche by the commanding authority figure to exercise his will, his whim, and his underhanded tricks.

Other servants were practically running a bordello. Burghley reports that two women were "gotten with child" with "men entertaining them in [the] chamber." Anne, Burghley notes, did not dare to object to this outrageous behavior because the servants were also on good terms with the master of the household. PRINCE HAL's pranks and transgressions with his low and lewd companions clearly had some basis in de Vere's reality. Only, the real-life inspiration was worse. Shake-speare's account has been sanitized for the ages.

Or has it? On the other hand, the earl steadfastly denied what would have been some truly reckless and destructive behavior. In a letter to Burghley on All Saints' Eve of 1572 (October 31, now known as Halloween), de Vere wrote

> Sith I have been so little beholding to sinister reports, I hope now, with Your Lordship's indifferent judgment, to be more plausible unto you than heretofore, through my careful deeds, to please you, which hardly, either through my youth, or rather misfortune, hitherto I have done.

Translation: Whatever you suspect, I didn't do it. De Vere noted that what he termed "backfriends" were spreading malicious rumors to undermine Burghley's opinion of the earl. With a manipulative spymaster on one side and a notorious delinquent on the other, it's impossible to know for certain who was distorting their side of the story more. The earl continues:

> Though perhaps by reason of my youth, your graver and severer years will not judge the same. Thus therefore hoping the best in Your Lordship, and fearing the worst in myself, I take my leave, lest my letters may become loathsome and tedious unto you, to whom I wish to be most grateful.

CHAPTER 4

FOR MAKING A MAN

[1573–1575]

IN 1573, EDWARD DE VERE RENTED TWO FLATS IN AN ELIZABETHAN
apartment complex near Cecil House, the Savoy, for two or more servants
then working with him. Two translators the earl was then patronizing, Thomas
Twyne and Thomas Bedingfield, make likely candidates for recipients of the
earl's free lodging.

Twyne was a medical practitioner (not yet MD) whose poetry, as one
twentieth-century critic put it, "ring[s] out with an eloquence that is as anachro-
nistic as it is noble." Newly married at the time, the thirty-year-old Twyne was
then working on two translations from Latin into English: one, *A Breviary of
Britain*, was a tract about the history and geography of England; the other
was the last three books of *The Aeneid*. A dedicatory letter Twyne wrote to de
Vere, published in *A Breviary of Britain*, records the earl's continued fascination with cosmography:

> Hereon, when Your Honor shall be at leisure to look, bestowing such re-
> gard as you are accustomed to do on books of geography, histories, and
> other good learning, wherein I am privy Your Honor taketh singular de-
> light, I doubt not but you shall have cause to judge your time very well
> applied.

Twyne's 1573 edition of *The Aeneid*–which he dedicated to Anne Cecil de
Vere's uncle, Sir Nicholas Bacon–contains introductory matter that is equally
revelatory. As a preface to the conclusion of Virgil's epic, Twyne attached a
brief biographical sketch of *The Aeneid*'s author. Virgil, Twyne noted, once
anonymously posted a few of his verses in a public forum in Rome; Augustus

Caesar was so enamored of the poetry that he demanded to know who wrote it. But before Virgil could step forward, a local hack named Batillus claimed *he* was the author. Batillus was rewarded generously for his supposed poetical efforts. Incensed, Virgil then posted a follow-up poem that read, in part:

> These verses I did make, thereof another took the praise.
> So you not for yourselves, poor birds, your nests do build in trees,
> So you not for yourselves, ye sheep, do bear your tender fleece,
> So you not for yourselves, your honey gather, little bees.

The honeybee, Virgil says, gathers its nectar for others to enjoy. A poem de Vere wrote in 1573 snatches this analogy—and then adds to it a haunting verse about those unrecognized authors who "take the pain to pen the book." Could he have known how prophetic his words would be?

THE EARL OF OXENFORD
To the Reader

> The laboring man that tills the fertile soil
> And reaps the harvest fruit, hath not indeed
> The gain, but pain, and if for all his toil
> He gets the straw, the lord will have the seed. . . .
>
> The mason poor that builds the lordly halls
> Dwells not in them, they are for high degree.
> His cottage is compact in paper walls
> And not with brick or stone, as others be.
>
> The idle drone that labors not at all
> Sucks by the sweet of honey from the bee
> Who worketh most, to their share least doth fall,
> With due desert, reward will never be.
>
> The swiftest hare, unto the mastiff slow
> Ofttimes doth fall, to him as for a prey.
> The greyhound thereby, both miss his game we know,
> For which he made such speedy haste away.
>
> So he that takes the pain to pen the book
> Reaps not the gift of golden goodly muse
> But those gain that, who on the work shall look
> And from the sour, the sweet by skill doth choose.

> For he that beats the bush, the bird not gets,
> But who sits still—and holdeth fast the nets.

De Vere had transformed Virgil's anxiety of anonymity into a manifesto, incorporating medieval notions of caste and the division of labor in the human and natural world. Dubious as the politics may be to modern eyes, de Vere's introductory stanzas were nevertheless expressions of a twenty-three-year-old aristocrat whose eyes were only beginning to open to his greater calling as a poet-philosopher to all humankind—not merely to his courtly peers. KING LEAR, raving on the heath, stripped of all regal trappings and exiled from his "lordly halls...for high degree," was still a long way off.

"The earl of Oxenford's" poem appeared in *Cardanus's Comfort,* translated into English by Thomas Bedingfield. Bedingfield dedicated the 1573 book to de Vere, and according to the book's title page, Bedingfield published the tome at de Vere's command. The Latin original for *Cardanus's Comfort (De Consolatione)* contains philosophical consolations for the melancholic soul written by the Italian philosopher, physician, and mathematician Gerolamo Cardano.

De Vere was probably attracted to Cardano for both his Renaissance mind and his outlandish character. Dubbed by his twentieth-century biographer Oystein Ore "the gambling scholar," Cardano applied his expertise in statistics to win at games of dice and cards. He had infamously cataloged the many ways to cheat at games of chance—such as marking cards and loading dice. He would, however, tolerate no flimflam when he was at the table. Cardano once told of a con artist he'd gambled with: "When I discovered that the cards were marked, I drew my dagger and wounded him in the face."

HAMLET certainly knew his Cardano. The Danish prince's "To be or not to be" soliloquy—with its melding of the themes of death, sleep, and travel to strange places—draws no small inspiration from the consolations of the "gambling scholar." Consider this excerpt from *Cardanus's Comfort:*

> What should we account of death to be resembled to anything better than sleep....But if thou compare death to long travel...there is nothing that doth better or more truly prophecy the end of life than when a man dreameth that he doth travel and wander into far countries.

De Vere commissioned *Cardanus's Comfort* along with the Latin translation of *The Courtier* probably in the thick of the duke of Norfolk fiasco, when the philosophical consolations of great Renaissance minds would have been just the kind of balm that the earl needed.

And then, after Norfolk's execution, de Vere sat on the stack of papers containing *Cardanus's Comfort.* For months and months, de Vere did nothing.

As Castiglione's *The Courtier* notes, a nobleman who is also a writer must "take care to keep them [*his literary works*] under cover . . . and let him show them only to a friend who can be trusted."

Such commandments of extreme secrecy may strike the modern reader as bizarre, but a nobleman publicizing his writings in the Elizabethan Age was considered neither worthy nor prestigious. Castiglione was hardly the only one who urged all self-respecting courtiers to hide their prose and poetry from the peering gaze of the public eye. As the poet Michael Drayton would observe one generation later, contemporary English literature had gotten to such a state that "verses are wholly deduced [*diverted*] to chambers; and nothing [is] esteemed in this lunatic age but what is kept in cabinets and must only pass by transcription."

Ultimately, however, de Vere decided to publish Bedingfield's manuscript—putting both his own and Bedingfield's names on the title page. Yes, de Vere was disregarding the sacred Castiglione's advice to keep one's writings "under cover." But as de Vere writes in his preface to *Cardanus's Comfort:*

> Whereby as you [*Bedingfield*] have been profited in the translating, so many may reap knowledge by the reading of the same, that shall comfort the afflicted, confirm the doubtful, encourage the coward, and lift up the base-minded man to achieve to any true sum or grade of virtue, whereto ought only the noble thoughts of men to be inclined.
>
> And because next to the more sacred letters of divinity, nothing doth persuade the same more than philosophy, of which your book is plentifully stored, I thought myself to commit an unpardonable error to have murdered the same in the waste bottoms of my chests. And better I thought it were to displease one than to displease many.

Between the ideals de Vere set forth in the Latin translation of Castiglione (1572) and the English translation of Cardano (1573), the earl had laid out his recipe for literary mischief. It was a recipe that he would follow for the rest of his life: Treat the court as if it were a theater and the theater as if it were a court; write, but only do so covertly; publish, but only do so in such a way that some Batillus might divert the public's eye. In no mean fashion, Castiglione's *Courtier* and *Cardanus's Comfort* represent Shake-speare's true birthplace, the site of the Bard's unheralded entrance onto the public stage.

Sometime in 1573 or '74, de Vere had graciously signed over a family estate called Battails Hall in Essex to the musician William Byrd. Byrd was at the time the organist at the Chapel Royal, and the earl seems to have been enamored of

Byrd's talents. As a composer, Byrd is considered today to be perhaps the finest of the entire Elizabethan Age. De Vere's bequest would transfer the manor's ownership to Byrd once the current elderly occupants had passed away. De Vere would joke about his gift in *All's Well That Ends Well,* in which the play's CLOWN jests, "I know a man that . . . sold a goodly manor for a song."

Yet, nothing was ever so simple in the earl of Oxford's household, especially when that household's servants appear to have been retained based on their recklessness and wild abandon. One retainer, a painter named William Lewyn, ultimately defrauded Byrd from Battails Hall via some shady legal trickery. (Byrd evidently took the loss with equanimity, later writing a piece of music titled "The Earl of Oxford's March" in honor of his sometimes heedless patron.) Another of de Vere's servants in 1573 hung for a murder he'd committed, an adulterous crime of passion that titillated London society.

Three more earl of Oxford servants were highwaymen. In May of 1573, Danny Wilkins, John Hannam, and "Deny the Frenchman" accosted two of Lord Burghley's servants in the Kent countryside east of London, on the road between Gravesend and Rochester. According to Burghley's retainers' account of the assault, de Vere's three men had lain in a ditch near the road. When the Lord Treasurer's men appeared, the "three calivers [*light muskets*] charged with bullets discharged at [them]." One of Burghley's men was so startled that his saddle's girth snapped and both he and the saddle fell to the ground. The three musketeers then hopped on their horses and raced back toward London. After the immediate danger had passed, Burghley's men turned around toward Gravesend and took up lodging in the town. In a letter they wrote to their master regarding this "determined mischief," they sought his protection. Their plea preserves Burghley's version of the story.

De Vere's version of the story appeared on the public stage. Much of the first two acts of Shake-speare's *King Henry IV, Part 1* concern an assault that FALSTAFF and three associates carry out in the Kent countryside. As *1 Henry IV* tells it, the crime takes place at Gad's Hill—a landmark on the road between Gravesend and Rochester. FALSTAFF et al. await the TRAVELERS and spring upon them. The TRAVELERS quickly flee the scene. As a mocking self-portrait of the author's swollen ego, FALSTAFF whines and wheezes through the entire escapade. The appearance of this episode in the Shake-spearean history of King Henry IV suggests an apology of sorts to Elizabeth and Burghley for the author's callow rebelliousness as a youth.

As the unhorsed FALSTAFF says,

> I'll starve ere I rob a foot further. And [if] 'twere not as good a deed as drink to turn true man and to leave these rogues, I am the veriest varlet that ever chewed with a tooth. . . . A plague upon it when thieves cannot be true to one another!

At this moment when de Vere's men were playing BARDOLPH, PETO, and POINS to his FALSTAFF, the historical records also reveal Queen Elizabeth drawing the earl of Oxford closest to her bosom. Perhaps something about de Vere as outlaw poet and reckless gadabout intrigued Her Majesty.

On May 11, 1573, a young courtier named Gilbert Talbot wrote to his father a gossipy correspondence stating:

> My lord of Oxford is lately grown into great credit, for the Queen's Majesty delighteth more in his personage and his dancing and valiant-ness than any other. I think [the earl of] Sussex doth back him all he can. If it were not for his fickle head he would pass any of them shortly. My lady Burghley, unwisely, has declared herself, as it were, jealous, which is come to the queen's ear, whereat she has been not a little offended with her. But now she is reconciled again. At all these love matters my Lord Treasurer [Lord Burghley] winketh and will not meddle in any way.

Burghley was certainly winking at more than one "love matter" at the time. As of 1573, Burghley still had not delivered on Anne's alleged £15,000 dowry.

During the same month as de Vere's men's assault on the road between Gravesend and Rochester, Burghley had hit upon a way to raise some quick and dirty cash. The Lord Treasurer was at the time negotiating with the Span-ish to facilitate a more friendly and open trade policy. To ensure that Spain got the best deal possible, Spanish agents were trying, in essence, to set up a bribe. The Spaniards had learned about Burghley's outstanding dowry debt.

On May 1, 1573, the Spanish agent Antonio de Gueras wrote to the Spanish governor of the Lowlands, the duke of Alva, about a "gratuity" for Burghley that the two had worked out. Such a backdoor payment would leave the Lord Treasurer's hands clean but would also eliminate a major headache in the form of a son-in-law with his hand extended. De Gueras ex-plained to Burghley that payment couldn't be arranged unless Burghley com-mitted to the deal. Burghley said he personally couldn't commit to the deal, explaining that "if his colleagues [at court] knew that he was getting a gratu-ity from His Majesty [the king of Spain], it would be his undoing and in no way would he accept it."

De Gueras pressed on, treading lightly:

> I said to [Burghley] I thought that if there was no stipend, that to help with the marriage of madam his daughter, who married the earl of Ox-ford, that perhaps milady his wife [Lady Burghley] would not refuse the demonstration of His Majesty's goodwill. And to this [Burghley] did not reply—but as admitting it, he laughed to himself. And at that same time, madam his wife entered and greeted me, asking me how I was and if

there were anything in which she could please me–from which I could consider that she was hoping for this gift, because other times she had not granted me such favors.

De Gueras's letter ends with a request that the king of Spain send 40,000 escudos (£15,000), "which is what [Burghley] offered to give in dowry to his daughter." De Gueras suggested that the payoff come by way of a strong ship to the Spanish garrison at the Flanders coastal town of Dunkirk. All that remained was for the "gratuity" to be picked up.

Burghley certainly wasn't about to make the journey. De Gueras suggested that one of the family's retainers bring the two chests of gold back to Lady Burghley, presumably for her to dispense to the groom. But, from Lord Burghley's perspective, there was no motive for anyone in his household to do anything more. Sending a trusted messenger across the Channel to pick up the money would have been reckless in the extreme. Burghley's rivals could well have found out about the Spanish bribe, which, as the Lord Treasurer himself observed, would have guaranteed his own ruin. And sending someone less than trustworthy to retrieve the treasure chests from the Lowlands meant giving that same someone a free pass to a lifetime's income, never to be seen or heard from again.

The most logical person for the job was de Vere. It was his money, after all. Thus, sometime in May of 1573, Burghley may have told his son-in-law about the arrangements he had made with de Gueras: You can have your £15,000, but there's a small hitch–you have to travel overseas and meet with Spanish agents to pick it up. A Spanish dowry fiasco may well explain the other strange events of that month. Did de Vere order his men to strike out at Burghley's retainers on the road between Gravesend and Rochester in retaliation? And was Lady Burghley's "jealousy"–as recorded in Gilbert Talbot's letter–actually not jealousy at all? At the time de Vere was making friendly with the queen, Lady Burghley's husband was allegedly arranging for a shipment of Spanish payola behind the queen's back. One slip of the tongue on de Vere's part, and the Cecil family could have been ruined.

On the other hand, why Burghley was "wink[ing] and would not meddle in any way" in his son-in-law's alleged dalliances with Elizabeth remains a more intriguing question. In the way that he "laughed to himself" about the payola offer, the Lord Treasurer's knowing winks recall nothing so much as the leering love broker PANDARUS in *Troilus and Cressida*. In Shake-speare's satire, PANDARUS unabashedly sets up an amorous rendezvous between the title characters, who represent de Vere and the queen.

At this moment of a potentially suborned dowry, a chiding mother-in-law, and a winking father-in-law, de Vere was also jealously guarding his fickle queen. Elizabeth never entertained just one favorite; she was forever playing her men off against one another. At the same time she was drawing de Vere close, Elizabeth was flirting with her Puritan captain of the bodyguard, Christopher Hatton. He was ten years older than de Vere, tall, handsome, and a good dancer—always a plus with the queen. Elizabeth nicknamed Hatton her "Lids," as in eyelids. She would also later dub him "Mutton" or "Sheep."

Hatton and de Vere were now rivals for the greatest prize in the Elizabethan court: Her Majesty's affections. The previous year, the court poet Sir Edward Dyer had written Hatton a letter of advice in winning the queen's heart. Dyer's letter, of which only a transcription survives today, speaks of a hated rival of Hatton's designated as "my lord of Ctm." There was no one in Elizabeth's court by that name or abbreviation. But scholars suspect this is a scrivener's misreading of "my lord Chamberlain" or "my lord of Oxon." About this mysterious "lord of Ctm," Dyer advises Hatton to

> [R]emember that you use no words of disgrace or reproach towards him to any; that he, being the less provoked, may sleep, thinking all safe, while you do awake and attend your advantages.
>
> Otherwise you shall, as it were, warden him and keep him in order; and he will make the queen think that he beareth all for her sake, which will be as a merit in her sight.

The game of one-upmanship was on.

Hatton fell sick in the summer of 1573 and traveled to the spa in Antwerp to seek a cure. During his absence from court, he wrote a series of gushing letters to the queen. Hatton had been gone from court only two days when he wrote, "I will wash away the faults of these letters with the drops for your poor Lids and so enclose them. Would God I were with you but for one hour. My wits are overwrought with thoughts. I find myself amazed." Ten days later, Hatton was still amazed: "This is the twelfth day since I saw the brightness of that Sun that giveth light unto my sense and soul. I wax an amazed creature. . . . Forget not your Lids that are so often bathed with tears for your sake." When de Vere got wind of these florid dispatches, it must have turned his stomach.

Lids's lachrymose musings would soon be spoofed in a collection of poetry that de Vere has long been suspected of writing, or at least contributing to. *A Hundred Sundry Flowers* (1573) is an anthology that offers up a century of poems written by authors using numerous Latinized noms de plume—called "posies." One such pseudonym is Fortunatus Infoelix, which, the court observer Gabriel Harvey claimed, is "lately the posy of Sir Christopher Hatton." *Flowers* also contains a short story, called "The Adventures of Master F.I." Both of these elements of *Flowers* together recite an embarrassing tale of an indelicate love affair between a suitor and his courtly maid. The whole package would have been a humiliating blow to "Lids," who most court-wise readers probably thought had written this unseemly and scandalous narrative.

Hatton was now the subject of an elaborate courtly prank. *Flowers* had a brief press run; it was promptly snatched up by the authorities.

In January of 1574, de Vere was making himself familiar with the Spanish agent who had arranged for Burghley's payoff. One of Burghley's servants, doubtless unaware of the "gratuity," wrote to his boss about de Vere's negotiations with de Gueras. Burghley's agent, Ralph Lane, said he thought de Vere spoke with de Gueras too much and too freely. In Lane's words, "A western Spanish storm may, with some unhappy mate at helm, steer [de Vere's] noble bark so much to the northward [toward Mary, Queen of Scots] that unawares he may wreck, as some of his noblest kind hath done, the more pity of their fault."

Yet, de Vere's most likely motive was simply to collect the £15,000 that was rightly owed him. De Vere wanted to hire a ship and set sail across the Channel, and neither the queen nor Burghley would let him. As an English earl at a time of heightened religious tensions in the Lowlands, he would have needed protection in wandering into a battle zone where Catholic agents could easily kidnap or kill him. Elizabeth, who did not know why de Vere was itching to cross the Channel and make his way to Flanders, would not let him go.

By March, when de Vere was lodging with the court at the archbishop of Canterbury's residence at Lambeth, the earl presented a proposal to the queen that she in turn refused out of hand. Although no record survives of the matter of de Vere's "suit," it is likely that de Vere was continuing to plea to go to Flanders.

In the words of the chronicler John Nichols:

> The young earl of Oxford, of that ancient and *Very* family of the *Veres*, had a cause or suit, that now came before the queen; which she did not answer so favorably as expected, checking him, it seems, for his unthriftiness. And hereupon his behavior before her gave her some offense. [Italics in original]

De Vere was frustrated with the queen's hardheaded ways. Soon enough, he would take matters into his own hands.

In early July of 1574, de Vere and a courtly colleague–Lord Edward Seymour–hired a ship and crossed the Channel anyway. On July 6, Spanish agents in the Low Countries reported that Elizabeth's court was "completely shaken and full of apprehension after the earl of Oxford . . . has, with my lord Edward brother of the earl of Hertford, passed incognito across the sea to Flanders." Two days later, the French ambassador to London, La Mothe Fénelon, reported to his superiors that the Elizabethan court was "rather troubled" over the perceived defection. The Catholic rebels in exile in the Lowlands took de Vere's actions as a sign for rejoicing. The defeated earl of Westmoreland, of Northern Rebellion fame, made plans to meet de Vere in Bruges. Their paths never crossed.

Sir Thomas Smith wrote to Burghley on July 13 that

> of my lord of Oxford . . . it is commonly said that he arrived in Calais and was there very honorably received and entertained–and from thence he went to Flanders. As far as I can yet perceive, Her Majesty's grief for him, or towards him, is somewhat mitigated.

According to rumors in Scotland, de Vere had made it as far as the city of Brussels via Bruges. (Dunkirk, where de Gueras had ordered the £15,000 to be shipped, was on the road between Calais and Bruges.)

While Smith did not know de Vere's true motives in running away to Flanders, Burghley understood the whole story and stood up for his son-in-law. As Burghley wrote on July 15 to one of de Vere's mentors–the Lord Chamberlain, earl of Sussex, "Howsoever [de Vere] might be, for his own private matters of thrift inconsiderate, I dare avow him to be resolute in dutifulness to the queen and his country."

The queen's rage at de Vere's actions may have been "somewhat mitigated," but she still displayed the Tudor fury that her subjects had come to fear. She dispatched Thomas Bedingfield–the courtier who had translated *Cardanus's Comfort* for de Vere–to retrieve these wayward nobles. In short order Bedingfield returned to England with his quarry. Nothing suggests de Vere had picked up any of his Spanish "gratuity"–if indeed this was the purpose of his mission.

By July 27, de Vere had returned to Dover. As the courtier Sir Walter Mildmay wrote on that day, "I trust his little journey will make him love home the better hereafter. It were a great pity he should not go straight, there be so many good things in him to serve his God and Prince." Once again, de Vere's "fickle head" was on the minds of court observers.

On August 3, the French ambassador, Fénelon, wrote back to Paris that the annual summer Progress continued on its way toward Bristol, with the queen "quite happy that the earl of Oxford has returned at her command, moreover that my lord Edward be staying." On the same day, Burghley wrote a typically prolix letter to the spymaster Sir Francis Walsingham, explaining and apologizing for de Vere's actions. In returning to court, Burghley said that de Vere was

> a mixture of contrary affections, although both reasonable and commendable. The one, fearful and doubtful in what sort he shall recover Her Majesty's favor because of his offense in departure as he did without

license; the other, glad and resolute to look for a speedy good end because he had in his abode so notoriously rejected the attempts of Her Majesty's evil subjects and in his return set apart all his own particular desires of foreign travel and come to present himself before Her Majesty, of whose goodness towards him he saith he cannot count.

Burghley also awkwardly requested that Walsingham greet "Lids" on behalf of his son-in-law. "Remember Master Hatton to continue my lord's friend, as he hath manifestly been and as my lord confesseth to me that he hopeth assuredly so to prove him," Burghley concluded.

Elizabeth, at least outwardly, forgave her wayward earl. However, in the words of an unsigned letter from August 7, "The desire of travel is not yet quenched in [de Vere], though he dare not make any motion unto Her Majesty that he may with her favor accomplish the said desire. By no means he can be drawn to follow the court, and yet there are many cunning devices used in that behalf for his stay."

By now, de Vere had probably had his fill of the Cecil family. The twenty-four-year-old earl disappeared from the court records for the rest of the summer Progress of 1574. However, on September 19–20, de Vere did show his face at a garden party being given at his father-in-law's estate, Theobalds. His wife, Anne, was there, too, and the couple doubtless erected the facade of a normal marital relationship. Also on the guest list was an elder who could tell plenty of cautionary tales for any Catholic-leaning nobles caring to bend their ear her way. Margaret, countess of Lennox, was mother to Lord Darnley, the murdered second husband of Mary, Queen of Scots. As a rumored recent collaborator with Mary's supporters in the Lowlands, de Vere must have seemed to Lady Lennox to be a child desperately in need of a few cautionary words to the wise.

Yet, a few minutes' scolding would have been a small price to pay. For Lady Lennox was also de Vere's likely entrée to a vault of jewels beyond valuation. Her family archives held a manuscript about the kings of Scotland that is the main source for Shake-speare's *Macbeth*. It was from this manuscript–not printed until the nineteenth century–that the author would draw his portrait of the scolding and brutal LADY MACBETH. This manuscript would provide the inspiration for the portrayal of LADY MACBETH's husband as a fatalist and a brooding and hesitant murderer. In all, Lady Lennox's family manuscript sketches out dozens of details, conversations, and vignettes–from MACBETH's hallucinations to his paralysis at the sight of a forest marching forward–that can be found nowhere else but in Shake-speare's Scottish tragedy. A dozen years later, the tale of an ancient Scottish regicide would hold topical currency in de Vere's mind; de Vere himself would be party to the execution of a Scots monarch. Lady Lennox's manuscript would someday inform his literary muse.

Burghley's Theobalds garden party provided an important point of connection for de Vere's bride too. Caught once again like OPHELIA between a duplicitous father and a headstrong lover, Anne soon tried to arrange a reconciliation with her husband. Sometime in the autumn she wrote to the officer in charge of the queen's household, the Lord Chamberlain, earl of Sussex. In this undated letter, Anne asked if he could reserve another room at Hampton Court, where the queen would be lodging beginning in October. The beset countess arranged these accommodations hoping that she could persuade her husband to resume sleeping with her. "The more commodious my lodging is, the willinger I hope my lord my husband will be to come thither, thereby the oftener to attend Her Majesty," Anne wrote.

The latter half of 1574 must have been exhausting for the countess. Anne had scarcely even shared a bed with her husband, who remained locked in a power struggle with her officious father. The queen's private doctor, Richard Master, would later recall that de Vere had vociferously protested that if Anne ever became pregnant, it was not by him. If de Vere had in fact never slept with his wife since their wedding day, he may have had annulment on his mind. Mary, Queen of Scots, once wrote in a letter to Queen Elizabeth that she'd heard that de Vere had not had sex with his wife "for fear of losing the favor which he hoped to receive by becoming your lover."

By December, Anne had fallen sick, and it looked briefly as if her malady might be fatal. Unable to digest anything, Anne was also unable to ingest any medicines that her doctors concocted for her. Yet, Sir Thomas Smith was still close to de Vere and to the Cecil family. Like *Romeo and Juliet*'s FRIAR LAURENCE, Smith had a knack for brewing up the right kind of potions at the right moments. As a friendly gesture to a young woman in need, Smith sent Anne a distillation (a "chemical water," as it was then called), which, said Smith's biographer John Strype, "if she took no other sustenance in three days, ... would nourish her sufficiently. And within twenty-four hours, [Smith] doubted not but [Burghley] would see great effects and peradventure some appetite to meat to begin to come to her within that space; adding that there was never any one yet but felt good by it."

Anne eventually recovered, and she had a polymath pharmacist to thank. Smith was one of a handful of physicians in the 1570s who practiced what was called Paracelsian medicine—a new, empirical approach to healing using chemical distillations and essences. Founded on the teachings of the early sixteenth-century German physician Paracelsus, it was the precursor to modern pharmaceutical science. The earl and countess's doctor, George Baker, dedicated two Paracelsian books to the couple—the first, in 1574, to de Vere; the second, two years later, to Anne. In 1580, the surgeon John Hester would dedicate another classic tract in the field of Paracelsian medicine to de Vere.

In the sixteenth century, Paracelsians were regarded as quacks and could scarcely find a fair audience among the learned in England, for whom the second-century Galenic theory of medicine was the presumptive gold standard—understanding the body as a balance of "humors" and recognizing only herbal tonics as worthy of the medical profession.

De Vere, patron of the alternative medicine of his day, would insert the Paracelsian controversy into *All's Well That Ends Well*. The Anne Cecil–inspired heroine, HELENA, is in fact Shake-speare's mouthpiece for the teachings of Paracelsus. When the Galenic doctors at the court of the KING OF FRANCE cannot heal the ailing monarch, HELENA presents the KING with a strange and wondrous Paracelsian distillation. He is cured instantly, much to everyone's shock.

All's Well's courtiers are dubious of Paracelsian cures, and the COUNTESS OF ROUSILLION voices the general skepticism of the day about these empirically derived potions:

> I say we must not
> So stain our judgment or corrupt our hope
> To prostitute our past-cure malady
> To empirics. . . .

Yet, by healing a patient whose ailment was impervious to Galenic medicine, HELENA effectively rebukes the Galenists for their backward-thinking ways.

Paracelsian chemical distillations—also called "simples"—appear in other Shake-speare plays too. For instance, both ROMEO and LAERTES use "simples" as poisons that they purchase from Paracelsian street vendors. And in a subtle joke on the hypocrisy of the sixteenth-century medical orthodoxy, CAIUS, the old Galenist of *Merry Wives of Windsor*, keeps some "simples" in his closet that he will not "for all the world" leave behind.

By New Year's Day of 1575, de Vere had returned to court and had disposable income at the ready. His New Year's gift to Her Majesty was one of the two most lavish presents given that year. ("Lids" gave the other.) De Vere's token to the queen was, according to her account books, "[a] very fair jewel of gold, containing a woman holding a ship of sparks of diamonds upon her knee, the same fully garnished with sparks of diamonds, four fair rubies, one large diamond, and sundry diamonds with three pearls pendant—and three small chains of gold set with sparks of diamonds."

Something certainly persuaded Elizabeth to give de Vere leave to cross the English Channel. Practicality undoubtedly played a role in dispatching de Vere: The new king of France, Henri III, had scheduled his coronation for February 15, 1575, and his marriage for two days later. Elizabeth, whom

Henri had once courted, would have needed an English delegate to attend the coronation–someone with enough clout in Catholic circles not to offend the French Catholic court. Furthermore, Venice had not yet sent an ambassador to England. The Italian city on the lagoon was still skittish about opening diplomatic relations with a Protestant realm, lest it offend the more fervent Catholic nations of Spain or the Papal States. At the time she sent de Vere overseas, Elizabeth required the attentions of a high-ranking courtier fluent in French and Italian for important diplomatic missions in Paris and Venice. Could it simply be coincidence that the queen gave de Vere license to travel to these two key cities at the same time she needed these tasks completed?

The French ambassador, La Mothe Fénelon, reported back to Paris on January 24 of a rumor he'd once heard that de Vere would be leading a military regiment across the Channel–perhaps to intervene in the Lowlands. However, Fénelon added, there had been a change in plans. Now de Vere was to spend a month in Paris. Fénelon noted that he thought de Vere was a devotee of both the French king and the Scots queen. He advised King Henri to treat de Vere as "the premier of the country's nobility" and that such courtesy would be recognized in England. Fénelon cryptically added that he'd learned that Don John of Austria–the powerful Spanish general–might have a job for the English earl to perform.

De Vere made out an indenture on January 30, ensuring that the bulk of the estates still in his possession would pass to his sister Mary and her heirs in the event of his untimely death overseas. De Vere and Anne were still childless, so he provided only for the "life interest of his countess." The indenture also included a schedule of the debts that de Vere had inherited from his spendthrift father and had run up himself–totaling a staggering £9,096, some $2.5 million in today's money.

By February 7, de Vere had left the country. If de Vere's retinue resembled the typical nobleman's traveling household, he would have had a groom who cared for the horses, and a couple of gentlemen to handle everything from secretarial duties to security. (Bandits were a constant danger on the open road, and keeping a few capable swordsmen at one's side was always advisable.) One servant handled the money and another performed such housekeeping duties as making beds and tending fires. The only known member of the group that departed with the earl from London was a retainer named Nathaniel Baxter. Two other servants (Ralph Hopton and William Lewyn, the painter who defrauded William Byrd out of Battails Hall) are known to have joined the travelers later in the trip.

De Vere and his entourage set sail across the brisk and choppy seas of the English Channel in late winter. Dover to Calais was the standard route to Paris in those days, and unless the tides or winds forced the ship to the more distant port of Boulogne, the newly constructed citadel of Calais would have greeted these Englishmen as their boat pulled into the harbor. Once the party had landed, a five- or six-day journey to the French capital city awaited. De Vere's harbinger would have ridden ahead as the party approached each town and sounded the earl's trumpet call ("tucket") to ensure that all gates were opened and all privileges of passage secured.

Their first stop, the French royal court at the Louvre, would serve to remind de Vere just how staid and comfortingly normal the Elizabethan court actually was. Henri III was a flamboyant monarch, equal parts *reine* and *roi.* During his nearly fifteen years on the throne, the king of France would often be referred to as *"elle"* and would regularly wear gowns, makeup, earrings, and perfume. Frequently seen with "Sa Majesté" were his *mignons,* young male favorites whom the king dressed as ladies of the night. Henri was also very much under the sway of his domineering mother, Catherine de Medici. Mother and son, along with Henri's late brother Charles, still had blood on their hands from the Protestant slaughter they had ordered on St. Bartholomew's Day in 1572–the same genocide to which de Vere had reacted so viscerally in the letter quoted in the previous chapter.

The coronation, at Rheims Cathedral ninety miles east of Paris, was an extravagant farce. Henri's younger brother, the duke of Alençon, tried to kidnap Henri en route and obtain the crown himself. The plot fizzled. (De Vere would have heard of Alençon already; the French duke and his mother had since 1572 been pressing Queen Elizabeth to consider Alençon for her husband.) Once at the cathedral, Henri famously had a conniption over his bride's hair. The wedding was only able to proceed when she agreed to let the groom do her hair himself.

During the celebrations surrounding the coronation and wedding, de Vere must have met Henri of Navarre (later King Henri IV), who was as dashing a man as Catherine de Medici's clan was craven. Henri of Navarre was, however, caught in a lifelong struggle with the infamous Florentine dynasty: Catherine de Medici was his mother-in-law. De Vere probably also met the fifty-one-year-old poet Pierre de Ronsard–still considered one of the finest sonneteers in any language–and Jacques Amyot, Henri III's former tutor. Amyot had translated Plutarch's *Lives of the Noble Grecians and Romans* into French (one of the books de Vere had bought during his convalescence in Windsor in 1570) and had served as French ambassador to Venice. De Vere and the sixty-two-year-old scholar would have shared much intellectual common ground, and Amyot would have regaled the traveling Englishman with suggestions of things to do and places to visit once in Venice.

King Henri himself had also recently returned from Venice. The city on the lagoon had so impressed Henri that he had hired a troupe of Venetian actors to perform at the celebrations surrounding his coronation and marriage. These actors played a new and sophisticated form of Italian comedy that is today called "commedia dell'arte." The celebrations at Rheims would be the first of numerous occasions at which de Vere could have acquainted himself with this fantastical new theatrical and literary medium.

One of the defining characteristics of the commedia dell'arte was the development of *maschere* (stock characters) that an audience could become familiar with, as today they might get to know a character on a television sitcom. To Venetian citizens, the commedia had become as popular and accessible as TV too. Italian literary dramatists, in turn, responded to the commedia's pop cultural appeal with new experiments in pastoral drama—a genre that melded comedy with tragedy.

When Henri III visited Venice in 1574, the French king became particularly enamored of the "wonderful Magnifico" *maschera* he saw on the Venetian stage. Henri demanded that Magnifico be part of the troupe that performed for him—and, one suspects, for de Vere as well—at the celebrations surrounding the royal coronation in Rheims.

Magnifico, also called Pantalone, was an old, miserly patriarch who headed, and could scarcely control, a riotous household. Often mocked, even by his servants, Pantalone was forever trying and failing to bridle his rebellious daughter. His avarice was notorious; he was always in a quandary about his ducats. Pantalone was typically portrayed as a Venetian merchant, carrying an unwieldy knife by his side that he used to threaten the many characters who taunted him. Jokes often came at the expense of Pantalone and his comedic foil, a doctor of law named Gratiano.

Pantalone's strong resemblance to SHYLOCK and the typical Pantalone plotline's resemblance to characters and situations in *The Merchant of Venice* are just the beginning of a long and underappreciated tradition of Shakespeare's indebtedness to the commedia dell'arte.

Throughout his monthlong Parisian stay, de Vere discharged his duty honorably in representing Elizabeth to Henri III. As the English ambassador, Valentine Dale, wrote to the Secretary of State, Sir Francis Walsingham, "Lord Oxford...has spoken with the king and queen his wife, and taken his leave with many great words of compliment; he used himself very moderately and comely and is well liked as a goodly gentleman." On the same day, Dale added that "My lord's device [*conversation; flair*] is very proper, witty, and significant."

Meanwhile, back in England, the curtain was rising on the most damaging episode yet of de Vere's career. Anne Cecil de Vere had become pregnant. When the queen learned of this news, she jumped out of her chair and proclaimed, "Indeed, it is a matter that concerneth my lord's joy chiefly. Yet I protest to God that next to them that have interest in it, there is nobody that can be more joyous of it than I am!" Elizabeth's unusual expression of enthusiasm underscores the deterioration of de Vere's marriage. Before leaving England, the earl had told the queen's doctor that if his wife became pregnant the father would have to have been somebody else. And now his wife was with child, while the earl was in a foreign court, acting every part the diplomat.

If de Vere harbored any early doubts about the child's paternity, he did not at first make them apparent. Indeed, he responded to the news of Anne's pregnancy by having his portrait painted and sending it to Anne along with two coach horses. A copy of this painting (the "Wellbeck Portrait") survives and now hangs at the National Portrait Gallery in London; the Wellbeck can also be seen (as a whole) on the back cover of this book and (in part) on the front cover as well. It shows a young clotheshorse, in a haughty French ruff, gilded doublet, and black velvet hat with a dandified feather tucked in the back. A gold-stitched black cape hangs confidently off his left shoulder. A wisp of a mustache droops over his tightly pursed lips, while his arched eyebrows give his dark and piercing eyes a hint of bemusement, bewilderment, or cynicism.

De Vere wrote to his father-in-law about Anne's pregnancy and about his plans for the coming months of travel. He mentioned his debts to creditors, casting serious doubt on the prospect that he'd ever gotten his hands on the £15,000.

On March 17, de Vere wrote from Paris:

> My Lord, your letters have made me a glad man, for these last have put me in assurance of that good fortune which your former mentioned doubtfully. I thank God therefore, with Your Lordship, that it hath pleased him to make me a father where Your Lordship is a grandfather; and if it be a boy I shall likewise be the partaker with you in a greater contentation. But thereby to take an occasion to return I am far off from that opinion; for now it hath pleased God to give me a son of mine own (as I hope it is), methink I have the better occasion to travel, sith whatsoever becometh of me, I leave behind me one to supply my duty and service either to my prince or else my country....
>
> I have found here this courtesy: The king hath given me his letters of recommendation to his ambassador in the Turk's court; likewise the Venetian ambassador that is here, known of my desire to see those parties, hath given me his letters to the duke and divers of his kinsmen in Venice, to procure me their furtherances to my journey, which I am not yet assured hold; for if the Turks come, as they be looked for, upon the coasts of Italy or elsewhere, if I may I will see the [military] service; if he cometh not, then perhaps I will bestow two or three months to see Constantinople and some part of Greece.

A month still remained before the Alps would be passable. So de Vere's train followed the rising sun out of Paris, tracing the footsteps of the queen's tutor, Roger Ascham, who nearly thirty years before had traveled first to the

door of the Strasbourg humanist scholar Johan Sturmius before finally heading
south to Venice. In the early spring of 1575, de Vere would study at the feet
of this sixty-eight-year-old intellectual guru. As a rhetorician and classicist,
Sturmius was one of the giants of his age. Ascham had noted that of all the
modern scholars who could be imitated, only Sturmius was one "out of
whom the true survey and whole workmanship [of antiquity] is specially to
be learned."

After departing Strasbourg, de Vere, too, would extol Sturmius. As one of
the earl's servants later reported to Sturmius, de Vere "had a most high opinion of you, and had made the most honorable mention of you." Upon returning to England, de Vere would brag that he "read the rhetoric lecture publicly in
sermons preached at Strasbourg."

The scholar's great influences were Cicero and Plato–Sturmius was in
fact known as the "German Cicero." And it was from Sturmius that Ascham
derived his own (distinctly Platonic) philosophy of drama: "The whole doctrine of comedies and tragedies is a perfect imitation, or fair lively painted picture, of the life of every degree of man." Such wisdom from the lips of the
Strasbourg master would certainly have been noted and filed away for future
reference.

With the early hints of summer's thaw came de Vere's first real opportunity
to cross over the Alps and into the region that had in no small part defined his
studies under Sturmius, Sir Thomas Smith, and, perhaps, Arthur Golding as
well. Ovid, Virgil, Cicero, Petrarch, Dante, Castiglione, Cardano: These were
all names that the twenty-five-year-old earl knew as words on a page, authors
who had described places and scenes, all of which still only existed for him
within the vellum covers of books. The Florence of Dante and Machiavelli,
the Urbino of Castiglione, the Sicily and Campania of Virgil, the Rome of the
innumerable ancients, the lionized cosmopolis of Venice, the fabled university
at Padua–where Smith had studied and lectured–were now all about to become more than just points on a map, poised to reveal their true identities as
might masqueraders at the end of an evening's entertainment.

After passing the falls at Basel, the shores of Lake Constance, and the deep
gorges of the Alps, de Vere's train at last looked up toward the stream tracing to
the Rhine's glacial source, Lake Toma. For a youth whose idea of mountains
was the rolling northland hills he had seen in 1570, the Alps must have been a
visual feast. As de Vere's retinue pulled into Andermatt, in what is now Switzerland, and he gazed up at the 10,400-foot peak of Pizzo Rotondo, words may
well have failed–at least for the moment. But his fortnight spent winding
through what is now Switzerland and eastern France surely came back to him
years later in Shake-spearean snapshots such as "far-off mountains turned into
clouds" and "were I tied to run afoot even to the frozen ridges of the Alps" and

"night's candles are burnt out, and jocund day stands tiptoe on the misty moun-taintops."

On the other side of the St. Gotthard Pass stretched the Lombardy Plain—a comparatively easy journey into Milan and what is now Italy. Although referred to collectively as Italy in de Vere's day, the boot-shaped peninsula was actually an assortment of principalities, republics, Spanish regimes, and ever-shifting alliances of foes and friends. Milan was a duchy unto itself, and—owing to its Spanish overlords and its fanatical Catholic bishop—de Vere avoided entering the confines of the city. "For fear of the inquisition, I dare not pass by Milan, the bishop whereof excerciseth such tyranny," he had written to Burghley the previous March. (An English noble would have had no problems passing through the greater duchy; he wanted only to avoid entering the city gates.)

Recuperating from their Alpine crossing, de Vere and his retinue probably rested for a night or two at St. Gregory's Well—a church and hostel just outside Milan's northeast gate. Spurred on by the allure of their Adriatic destination, the travelers would have followed local custom and continued the last leg of their trek via boat. The water route from Milan involved navigating first by canal, then by a network of rivers to Verona. The 120 miles between these two cities stretched out for one quiet week. However, as de Vere's ship approached Verona, the ride became more dangerous as waters began to surge with mock tides—due to the flooding of the river Adige that year. De Vere preserved this entire journey, in reverse, in *Two Gentlemen of Verona:* from the "tides" and shipwreck-causing spring surges of the Adige to "St. Gregory's Well" outside Milan's city gates to the forests northeast of town that meet "the rising of the mountain foot."

Once at Verona, de Vere was also within two days of Venice. The Venice of 1575 was the New York City of its day—a world financial center, fueling an ongoing explosion of learning, literature, theater, music, and art. The city nicknamed *La Serenissima* had, with the economic and artistic decline of its rival Florence, become perhaps the premier cultural capital of late sixteenth-century Italy. Reaching the shore of the Venetian lagoon sometime in mid-May of 1575, the *conte d'Oxfort* had finally arrived.

As the boatman guided the ferry toward its island destination through the lagoon's shallow waters, a metropolis unlike any other came into view. Looking beyond the *traghetti*'s port bow, just off Venice's northeastern shore, a traveler would have witnessed a strange parade of walnut logs from the Dalmatian Mountains being guided through the lagoon to a place somewhere beyond view. That somewhere was Venice's massive naval shipyard that, at its peak of production, could lay a hull in the morning and churn out a ship before sundown. Warships and merchant galleys swarmed in the waters near the Arsenal like a pack of foxhounds milling around before a hunt. The city itself, home to

150,000, was a complex patchwork of tenements and palaces, canals and bridges. One could catch glimpses of the city's nautical mazes as the ferry wound its way around the island's northwest tip and onto the central waterway, the Grand Canal. As the sun set over the mainland, lamplighters across Venice performed the nightly futility of pushing back the shadows that engulfed this many-cornered city. Black waters and narrow stone passageways swallowed up the dim beams of oil tapers that now burned at bridges, intersections, and from the bows of gondolas that shuttled up and down Venice's briny thoroughfares.

Once the party had landed and off-loaded their gear–perhaps at the French ambassador's residence, until suitable housing could be located–de Vere's retinue would have made its way to the Piazza San Marco. The earl would have had to present his papers of introduction from the Venetian ambassador in Paris to the duke *(doge)* and his court at the Palazzo Ducale, the city's central municipal building–one that was Parliament, Whitehall, and Westminster all under one vast, U-shaped roof. The Ducal Palace's state chambers exceeded even the opulence of Elizabeth's court. Allegorical statues, murals, and paintings by the likes of Tintoretto and Veronese covered every staircase, doorjamb, and square foot of ceiling of the palazzo.

If de Vere had arrived before May 11, his welcome to Venice would have been a choice seat at the characteristically Venetian ceremony known to locals as the "Marriage of the Sea" *(La Sensa)*. The eleventh of May, 1575, represented the fifth anniversary of the reign of Alvise Moncenigo, duke of Venice. The *Sensa* celebrated a symbolic union between the city and the Adriatic. The doge sailed onto the lagoon on his flagship, followed by a flotilla of state ships, galleys, and gondolas, to witness the ritual wedding. The doge's boat (the *Bucintoro*) boasted a gilded ebony deck, red velvet upholstery from bow to stern, polychrome statues, and gold-leaf oars inlaid with mother-of-pearl. For *La Sensa*, the *Bucintoro* was piloted to the mouth of the Adriatic, where the head priest of San Marco blessed the groom and bride. With a ceremonial flourish, the duke dropped his gold ring overboard, reciting the words *Desponsamus te, Mare, in signum veri perpetuique dominii.* ("We espouse thee, O Sea, as a sign of true and perpetual dominion.")

Had de Vere arrived too late to witness *La Sensa*, he still would have caught its outgrowth–the annual theatrical season, which lasted until July. By the 1570s, Venice had become perhaps the most vibrant theatrical community in all of Europe. Venetian entrepreneurs had recently constructed the first two public theaters in the city. Venice's first two professional thespian troupes had also recently formed, in 1568 and 1572. One can readily envision how, as this *aristocratico inglese* settled into his new hometown, he also began attending plays that would be meting out ideas, plots, characters, and inspiration for the rest of his life.

The theatrical mixture of high and low, refined and proletarian, comic and tragic, that graced Venetian stages at the time would present an aesthetic philosophy that would later be developed into the works of Shake-speare.

If de Vere had seen Pantalone in action at Henri III's coronation, he would have had ample opportunity to study the character in greater detail after arriving in Venice. Pantalone's valet was a clown called Arlecchino, anglicized as Harlequin. These characters might be joined onstage by the pedant, Il Dottore–who overplayed his skills and learning–or the braggart captain, Il Capitano, who was a ladies' man and swaggering military type long on talk and, secretly, a coward.

These and the commedia's many other Zannis joined a cast of lovers, tricksters, heroes, and villains in improvised productions that survive today primarily in the form of brief plot summaries. It is unknowable what plays de Vere saw in Venice, when the commedia literally spilled out into the streets and piazzas.

The best guide to this will probably remain the works of Shake-speare: along with the aforementioned resemblance between Pantalone and SHYLOCK, Il Capitano is FALSTAFF's Venetian prototype; *Cymbeline's* Italian counterpart is a commedia named *La Innocentia Revenuta; Love's Labor's Lost, Comedy of Errors,* and *Two Gentlemen of Verona* are full of commedia stock characters and story lines; and *Othello* and *The Tempest* transform the commedia into tragedy and pastoral.

The two public theaters in Venice in 1575 were some twenty minutes by foot or by gondola from Piazza San Marco and the Ducal Palace. Both theaters were on the other side of the Grand Canal from St. Mark's. One was just off the Rialto Bridge, the other was roughly where the Accademia Gallery stands today. What de Vere's commute to these performance spaces would have been like, of course, depends on where he lived.

A Venetian page the earl would hire, Orazio Cuoco, later reported that he had first met de Vere at the church of Santa Maria Formosa and that de Vere himself worshiped at "the Church of the Greeks" (San Giorgio dei Greci). Both of these churches lie within a five-minute walk from the Ducal Palace and St. Mark's Square. Since de Vere was still a courtier, albeit in a foreign court, he undoubtedly sought out lodgings close to the center of the Venetian courtly universe. One further clue about the possible site of de Vere's Venetian household comes from the Shake-speare canon: OTHELLO reports that his house lies somewhere he calls "the Sagittary." Sagittary is arguably an Anglophonic rendition of Vicus Sagittarius. Known more commonly as the Frezzeria, this street was less than fifty meters from St. Mark's and was a prominent commercial venue that had derived its name from the arrows that were originally sold in its shops.

⁓✦⁓

Such was, in all likelihood, de Vere's world on the south side of the city: home, church, state, and theater all within twenty minutes' walk of one another. The Rialto Bridge and piazza, known in *The Merchant of Venice* as SHYLOCK's main haunt, was mere minutes away from the Frezzeria. De Vere probably visited the Rialto regularly, since it was one of Venice's main shopping centers, where the city's Jews lent money to anyone with good credit, and vendors of all creeds sold anything from swords and lamps to wine and meats for the banquet table. In the middle of the piazza on the Rialto's eastern side stood a platform supported by the statue of a hunchback, *Il Gobbo*. This unlikely pedestal was the podium where Venetians came to hear public pronouncements from the government and to witness the punishment of its criminals. *The Merchant of Venice* immortalizes this piece of Venetian trivia in the family name of SHYLOCK's servant—GOBBO.

De Vere's activities and wanderings were, of course, not limited to Venice's south side. One anecdote points to a portion of de Vere's life elsewhere on the island. Virginia Padoana was a courtesan of Paduan origin, as her name implies. She lived in an apartment on the Campo San Geremia, a square just off Venice's Grand Canal near its northern entrance. An English traveler a dozen years later would list Padoana as one who "honoreth all our nation for my lord of Oxford's sake."

As a *courtesana,* Padoana belonged to a distinguished tradition unknown to England. In the words of one contemporary traveler, "Thou wilt find the Venetian courtesan (if she be a selected woman indeed) a good rhetorician and a most elegant discourser." Often schooled as poets, scholars, and musicians, courtesans in Venice carried out entire careers true to the first syllable of their appellation. Some courtesans had gained fame as composers, intellectuals, or authors. In 1575 the courtesan Veronica Franco had published her *Terze Rime,* an erudite poem that satirized traditional love lyrics.

In Padoana's neighborhood—two minutes' walk across the Canale di Cannaregio—was the Jewish Ghetto of Venice, an island the size of a modern office building in the middle of the Cannaregio section of the city. In 1516, the Venetian Senate had set aside an old foundry (*gheto* is Venetian for "foundry") as a residential area for the city's Jews to live. Venice was, in fact, an attractive destination. With the advent of the Spanish Inquisition, the Renaissance for European Jews meant as much a rebirth of violent persecution as it did any cultural reawakening. Simply by allowing Jews to live and work within its borders, Venice proved itself one of the more tolerant cities in all of Christendom.

Even so, Venetian Jews were not permitted anywhere outside the Ghetto's walls after sunset and had to wear special badges that encouraged discrimination against them. These *siman,* dating back to 1215, were at various periods in history a yellow circle on the sleeve, a yellow scarf, a yellow or red beret, or a black cap. Because medieval laws forbade trade unions from allowing Jews to join and the Torah was more forgiving of charging interest than were Christian traditions, Jews were in a position to become the city's primary bankers and loan agents. It became an uneasy marriage of convenience: The thriving Venetian mercantile economy needed Jewish capital; the Jewish community needed the relative tolerance of Venice.

A generation before de Vere moved to Venice, a prosperous subset of Levantine Jews had moved outside their walled island enclosure and expanded the Ghetto's borders to the edge of the Canale di Cannaregio. Hailing a gondola at the same spot to take him down the Grand Canal, de Vere probably met some of the city's financiers on their way to the Rialto Bridge and nearby square, their primary place of business. If de Vere's house was indeed on the Frezzeria, the Rialto Bridge was also his gondola's exit. With the city's biggest marketplace echoing into a distant din, the earl's gondolier would have guided the boat off Venice's main transportation artery and down the wave-lapped alleyways that led him home.

De Vere happened to be visiting Venice during a window that historians now reckon was the period of greatest tension between the Jews and the rest of the city. Four years before de Vere's arrival, Venice and its allies had won a crucial naval victory against the Turks, spelling the beginning of the end of Turkish military supremacy in the Mediterranean. The 1571 battle of Lepanto was, in the words of historian Fernand Braudel, "the most spectacular military event in the Mediterranean during the entire sixteenth century." The hard-fought victory was all the more pronounced in that only the year before, Venice had lost its last military garrison—the island of Cyprus—to the Turks.

Venetians met the news of Lepanto with citywide celebrations. All business was suspended, and shops across the lagoon closed their doors with explanatory notes in the window proclaiming, "For the death of the Turk." In response to the victory, the Venetian Senate in 1571 entertained a motion "to show some sign of gratitude toward Jesus Christ, our blessed defender and protector, by making a demonstration against those who are enemies of his holy faith, as are the Jews."

In their jingoistic fervor, some Venetians had imagined that somehow the Jews had secretly collaborated with the infidel Turks, rumors that led to an anti-Semitic retribution campaign. In the seasons that followed, the city buzzed with arguments back and forth about expelling the Jews once and for all. In 1573, one of Burghley's European spies wrote back that the richest Venetian Jews were trying to bribe their city's Senate into quiescence—a report that no doubt resounded with more pathos after de Vere had assessed the pitiful situation firsthand. In 1575, de Vere would have heard of (or perhaps even read) *The Vale of Tears,* a newly published Venetian Hebrew chronicle desperately arguing that Venice's Jews, if expelled, would only strengthen the Turkish forces by plying their trade for the infidels. Some Jews left Venice before any expulsion could be finalized.

Venice's Jews were ultimately never expelled, nor was the Ghetto ever closed. But the tensions had only begun to simmer down when de Vere first moved there.

De Vere centered his two Venetian plays around the contemporary events of Venetian life during the period he lived in *La Serenissima*. In *Othello*, military commanders lead their forces in far-flung campaigns at sea and on the island of Cyprus. In *The Merchant of Venice*, a normally tolerant mercantile state turns rabid with hatred of Jewish moneylenders–recalling Venice's darkest years of anti-Semitism, during the first half of the 1570s.

Now that he had established his base camp in Venice, Edward de Vere had three factors driving him onward: The plague was becoming an ugly fact of Venetian life by midsummer of 1575; those letters of introduction from King Henri III to the Turkish court were sitting on his desk unused; and the money he had brought with him to Venice was burning a hole in his purse.

The Turk had not invaded Venice, nor was there any imminent threat. In fact, the new sultan of the Ottoman Empire, Murad III, had just taken a Venetian wife–who was working to improve relations between the Turks and her native republic. Since de Vere would be traveling on a Venetian ship under the Venetian flag, the earl enjoyed ample opportunity to visit the Ottoman-occupied lands to the east, including Greece.

In his letter from Paris, de Vere had written to his father-in-law that if the seas were still peaceful, he would "bestow two or three months to see Constantinople and some part of Greece." On July 20 one of de Vere's servants, who had lagged behind the main party and had at the time only made it to Strasbourg, wrote back to Burghley that he was uncertain if de Vere had yet left for Greece–a second, independent declaration of de Vere's intent to explore the Hellenic region during the summer. Finally, in the autumn it would later be reported that de Vere had hurt his knee in a Venetian galley–confirming that a sea voyage played some part in the earl's summer itinerary. No other records have been discovered detailing de Vere's movements during the summer of 1575. But the evidence that remains is consistent with a Greek itinerary.

By worshiping in Venice at the "Church of the Greeks"–just two years old in 1575–de Vere had placed himself at the heart of a community of Greek exiles. The Ottoman Empire had been ruling much of Greece for more than a century in 1575, and the Turk's heavy taxation, Islamic culture, and corrupt government had spurred an exodus of Hellenes. The church of San Giorgio dei Greci provided sanctuary to Greek intellectuals, artists, and political and religious refugees seeking life away from the sultan's influence. Like all refugee groups, many still had family and friends back in the old country. There was, in other words, no better place in Venice than de Vere's church to find and join a group of travelers making their passage to Greece.

The 1,100-mile, fifteen-day voyage to Athens would have followed the Adriatic currents down the Illyrian (now Croatian) coastline. To someone accustomed to a life of stately homes and manors, passage down the Adriatic was a humbling ordeal. The Venetian galley recognized no class boundaries; all were equally put upon. Vermin and lice were no strangers to these voyages, and the travelers were unburdened by such modern conveniences as toilets, running water, or refrigerated food.

The galley's design had scarcely changed since the days of Marc Antony— two masts and dozens of oars rowed by both prisoners and sailors-for-hire. The rowers served not only as propulsion but also as potential soldiers should pirates make chase. Venetian "great galleys" relied upon sail power as much as possible and used their rowers only when the winds died down or when maneuvering near shore. In the words of one contemporary Spanish traveler, galley crews "are diligent in profiting by good fortune, lazy in a gale; in a storm they command freely and obey little; their god is their sea chest ... and their pastime is watching the passengers being seasick." The long days and nights on the open water would certainly have been a time for de Vere to acquaint himself with Venetians and foreigners alike—be they Jews or Christians or otherwise.

Upon leaving Venetian waters, within its first forty-eight hours under sail, the galley would have passed along a thirty-five-mile stretch of Hungarian coastline, the seafaring end of a kingdom then ruled by Rudolf II, king of Bohemia. This Bohemian corridor was a mere finger of land squeezed between the Holy Roman and Ottoman Empires. And yet, between 1575 and 1609, the king of Bohemia and Hungary did in fact command a small parcel of seacoast. *The Winter's Tale* acknowledges this little-known fact of Central European history by setting several scenes on the "seacoast of Bohemia." (Critics dating back to the seventeenth-century dramatist Ben Jonson have harped on *The Winter's Tale*'s Bohemian seacoast scenes as proof of Shake-speare's general ignorance of continental Europe. But the critics are in error.)

The Venetian galley would then most likely have followed the currents south, down what is now the Croatian coastline, snaking its way past an Adriatic archipelago and shores belonging almost entirely to the Turks. These were dangerous waters, with pirates aplenty on the seas and unwelcoming ports on the shore. However, Venetian ships could always count on at least one safe haven on their treks down the eastern Adriatic coast: the independent city-state of Ragusa.

Southbound Venetian galleys trekking past the Illyrian coastline regularly restocked in Ragusa and gave their passengers and crew a few days of rest and relaxation. This ancient city—now called Dubrovnik—had once been a Venetian colonial possession. At the time of de Vere's travels, Ragusa was a sovereign city-state, albeit one that had retained healthy commercial and cultural ties to its former colonial master. Judging from maritime insurance records, Venice–Ragusa voyages in the sixteenth century were commonplace.

Ragusa also contained a parcel of de Vere family history: In 1193 the crusading king Richard I "the Lion-heart" shipwrecked off the coast of Ragusa and, according to legend, built a cathedral in the city to thank God for his deliverance from disaster–then continued his journey inland and was captured. The first earl of Oxford helped to pay the king's ransom, while his brother, Robert de Vere, may have accompanied Richard on the crusade that ran aground in Illyria.

Walking through this unusual city, de Vere would have been struck by the eclectic influences that defined the coastal metropolis. As an independent nation on a coastline dotted with impoverished colonial possessions, Ragusa stood apart both culturally and economically. Later known as "the Slavonic Athens," this Illyrian city-state was a rich and prospering nexus of East and West, as revealed in its Slavic, Italian, and Ottoman influences in architecture, music, art, and literature. The city's literary scene–much of it in Latin and Italian–spawned its own school of poetry that drew upon Ragusa's polyglot culture. In the early seventeenth century, Ragusa was the first region outside Italy to have developed its own opera. In the words of the Italian humanist Ludovico Beccadelli, Ragusa was "the mirror of Illyria and its greatest glory." Unlike any other city on the Illyrian shores, in Ragusa de Vere would certainly have been safe to "beguile the time and feed his knowledge with viewing of the town...," seeing sights that "satisfied [the] eyes with the memorials and the things of fame that do renown this city" and enjoying music that is the very "food of love."

These quotes come from *Twelfth Night,* a play set in an unnamed Illyrian city. A shipwreck off this city's coast introduces a noble band of travelers who fall in love with the town–and a few of its more eminent residents. Two forgotten Croatian studies, published in 1957 and '64, recognized Ragusa as the setting for this Shake-spearean comedy of families lost and fables untold. Most scholars and directors today, however, still treat the setting of *Twelfth Night* as an imaginary coastal city on the Adriatic with no real-world counterpart. A pleasant surprise awaits them in Ragusa.

After several days for repairs and resupplying, Venetian galleys would have left the harbor and sailed past the barren and stony coastline, dotted with cypress and olive trees. The mountains around the harbor are networked with caves from which pirates and other criminals often staged raids on unsuspecting ships. In *Twelfth Night,* the countess OLIVIA castigates her boorish cousin SIR TOBY BELCH by noting that he is only "fit for the mountains and the barbarous caves, where manners ne'er were preached!"

The journey southward down the Illyrian coastline and into the Gulf of Corinth would have taken another two or three days, past the site of the Lepanto battle and toward the Greece of lore and legend. Two independent but converging sets of reasons make it likely that if his ship made it as far as Greece, de Vere did not tarry long there. First, the records that do exist of de

Vere's summer grand tour suggest a very tight itinerary. Second, the Shake-speare plays containing nominally Greek settings (*Comedy of Errors, A Mid-summer Night's Dream, Troilus and Cressida, Two Noble Kinsmen, Pericles,* and *The Winter's Tale*) offer little local color or firsthand knowledge of Greece–especially when compared to the author's vivid depictions of Venice, north-ern Italy, and even Illyria. In the words of the French critic Michel Grivelet, "The Greeks of classical antiquity do not bulk large in Shakespeare's work. The Athens of TIMON is hardly more essential to the play than that of THE-SEUS and HIPPOLYTA in *A Midsummer Night's Dream.* There are Greek names in other works and a visit to the Oracle at [Delphi] in *The Winter's Tale.* But they all belong to the nowhere world of romance."

The last snippet of Greek geography and legend, however, may have been the only Hellenic sight to have been seen by Shake-speare's own eyes. In Paris, de Vere had learned about his wife's pregnancy; the legendary Delphic Oracle was only a few miles offshore from the Gulf of Corinth, the shortest route from Venice to Athens. In both *Timon of Athens* and *The Winter's Tale,* the Oracle is treated as a touchstone for legitimacy–antiquity's great paternity test. De Vere's tragically untamed jealousy was still welling up in his blood in 1575. But if he was in the region, he may well have wanted to figure out how his wife had become pregnant. (If one is to believe the letter from Mary, Queen of Scots, to Elizabeth, de Vere hadn't slept with Anne in some time–perhaps never.) The Oracle had worked for the ancients; perhaps it could calm those demons. The home of the Muses, Mount Parnassus, may have been one stop on the earl's itinerary.

As eagles and white-tailed Egyptian vultures soared overhead, de Vere's party would have approached the Temple of Apollo, which stood amid a col-lection of holy rubble that had once been a centerpiece of the ancient Greek world. The Oracle was part of a complex of memorials under the craggy cliffs of Parnassus, where spring water emerged from the mountainside. The ancient historian Plutarch, a former high priest of the temple, recorded that the Oracle was read by a local seer who entered the Apollonian temple and inhaled intoxicating gases emanating from a fissure in the mountain rock. She (it was always a woman) would reach a state of trance, receive the divine message, and then emerge to deliver the prophecy. The Oracle invariably took the form of a riddle or deliberately vague utterance that could mean dif-ferent things to different hearers. *The Winter's Tale* satirizes this tradition. The play's MESSENGERS travel to Delphi and returned with a message that's as un-ambiguous as a jury's verdict: The child is legitimate, the protagonist's wife is chaste, and he was wrong to doubt her.

From Delphi, another four days' travel by land to the southeast would have taken the party to Athens–through the same forest that would later become the setting for the imaginary exploits of PUCK, BOTTOM, the KING AND QUEEN OF THE FAERIES, and four young Athenian lovers. Yet, unlike the economically and culturally vibrant city-state of Ragusa, Athens in 1575 was a hollow shell. Whereas ancient Athens had long ago stood as the very seat of culture, learning, and rationality, sixteenth-century Athens under Turkish occupation had lost its intellectual and cultural luster.

In *The Winter's Tale,* the route from the land of the Oracle leads directly to Palermo, Sicily—where records do survive of a de Vere visit. This sea voyage would have taken de Vere's party approximately ten days—with scarcely a glimpse of coastline for the first nine. And unless the crew had an appetite for danger, the trip would have terminated with a smooth ride along Sicily's southern coast, where the four-knot currents carry their cargo westward like a maritime conveyor belt. (The other sea route to Palermo involves navigating the rocky straits of Messina—immortalized in myth as Scylla and Charybdis.)

Officially, the island of Sicily was a Spanish territory, and so far as is known, de Vere had no letters of introduction or passage. But Sicily was also the most corrupt government in Italy. If a noble visitor had cash enough to bribe, he had all the papers he needed.

The natural port on Sicily's west coast was a once-flourishing town named Trápani—a likely landing place for de Vere's ship. De Vere and his party would have made the fifty-mile overland journey from Trápani to Palermo on horseback. The first major stop on the trail out of Trápani was Segesta, an ancient hilltop town where the beasts of burden could rest and water, and where the travelers could enjoy the most illustrious ancient ruin in the entire island kingdom. The temple and theater at Segesta have inspired noteworthy commentary from ancients such as Thucydides and Virgil to modern art critics and archaeologists. According to ancient lore, Aeneas built the temple at Segesta, to honor the goddess Venus, as he meandered through the Mediterranean after the Trojan War. Segesta was esteemed as one of the greatest monuments anywhere to the legendary ancestor of the Roman race.

Winding his way through the stony hills to Segesta, de Vere would have caught occasional glimpses of this uncompleted wonder of the ancient world, teasing his eye with its distant elegance. Upon arriving at the Parthenon-like shrine and the nearby classical theater, de Vere may have wondered why he had ever wanted to visit Greece at all. Segesta provided him with Hellenic splendor aplenty without engendering the vast expense, the disillusionment, and the lengthy and treacherous passage to the Aegean and back.

The Winter's Tale, in fact, contains a subtle joke based on just these doubts, suggesting that KING LEONTES's slack messengers to the Oracle at Delphi sneak away to Segesta instead and never even leave Sicily.

Once in Palermo, de Vere would have sought out Spain's official viceroy of Sicily, the duke of Sessa. The viceroy was a unique persona in Palermo: a generous patron, a lover of masques and tournaments, as well as an accomplished poet who surrounded himself with first-rate scholars and artists—an embodiment of Castiglione's ideal courtly figure.

Once in Palermo, ruled by a prince who loved the equestrian sports, de Vere organized an impromptu tournament in the city to joust for the honor of Her Highness Queen Elizabeth. According to an undated English eyewitness testimony from Palermo:

> One thing did greatly comfort me which I saw long since in Sicily, in the city of Palermo, a thing worthy of memory: Where the right honorable the earl of Oxenford—a famous man for chivalry at what time he traveled into foreign countries—being then personally present, made a challenge against all manner of persons whatsoever and at all manner of weapons as tournaments [and] barriers with horse and armor, to fight a combat with any whatsoever in the defense of his prince [*Queen Elizabeth*] and his country. For which he was very highly commended. And yet no man durst be so hardy to encounter with him, so that all Italy over, he is acknowledged the only chevalier and nobleman of England. This title they give unto him as worthily defended.

Such valor would certainly have impressed Sessa. It may have even yielded de Vere letters of passage to the other Spanish kingdoms where records reveal that he would later be traveling—Naples and Milan. Sessa had, in fact, only recently returned from the Spanish garrison at Naples. While at Naples, the viceroy had become enamored of a lame Spanish soldier who was gaining notice as a first-rate poet, Miguel de Cervantes.

Cervantes had served under the Spanish commander Don John at the 1571 naval battle of Lepanto—where an injury left the budding young novelist without the use of his left hand. Since June of 1575, Don John had been Cervantes's commanding officer in Naples. In late August or early September, Cervantes was in Palermo to visit with Sessa at his palace. The ambitious twenty-seven-year-old had been honorably discharged from his military service and was looking forward to shipping out to Spain. (Cervantes's voyage, however, would never reach its destination. His ship would instead be intercepted by Turkish pirates, leaving Cervantes a Christian slave for five hellish years.)

Had de Vere and Cervantes crossed paths during this brief window, it would have been at a formative moment in both of their careers. The closest their lifelines come to intersecting today is on the printed page: The late summer of 1575 presents the earl of Oxford at perhaps his most quixotic—thumping his chest in the Palermo square, offering to tilt against any comer who might dare to challenge the virtues of his fair Dulcinea on the English throne. And Cervantes was a notoriously good observer who would spend the rest of his life transforming his youthful adventures into novels and plays. No one has ever considered de Vere as one of Cervantes's early character inspirations. Yet, if de Vere's Sicilian exploits do ring with the mock bravado of FALSTAFF, perhaps future scholars will find in them snapshots of Don Quixote as well.

Continuing eastward out of Palermo would take de Vere on a four-day horseback ride to Messina. The Italian squadron of the Spanish fleet was based there. In 1571, the fleet had launched from Messina to victory at Lepanto. In 1575, Messina would have attracted an English lord with feudal sympathies, since the Spanish military was then preparing to intervene in a conflict about old ruling class versus new.

The independent Republic of Genoa, a city-state on the Italian Riviera, was being torn apart in 1575 by a feud then brewing among the city's elite. Genoa's old nobility *(nobili vecchi)*, aided by Spain and the pope, were trying to keep the city's upstarts out of power. Genoa's newer patricians *(nobili nuovi)*, aided by France, resented the *vecchi*'s monopoly of control. As a defender of the old guard himself, de Vere would have sympathized with the *vecchi,* and therefore with Spain.

The commander of the Spanish military mission to Genoa was King Philip II's bastard brother Don John. The Spanish generalissimo spent the summer shuttling back and forth between his garrisons of troops in Messina and Naples. De Vere may well have met Don John at Messina. This conclusion emerges not from the historical record, but rather from the Shake-speare play set in Messina, *Much Ado About Nothing.* Messina is where a scheming bastard brother named DON JOHN enters the action. Wars in a far-off region of Italy are on everybody's mind in *Much Ado,* and DON JOHN arrives in this Sicilian port city on the heels of a mission he and his band of Italian nobles have completed in these wars.

By the summer of 1575, Don John was growing frustrated with his Italian post. He wanted to be working on his own plans to attack the Turks at Tunis. (The pope had promised Don John that he could be crowned king of whatever city or country he took next.) Yet, to his chagrin, the don had been appointed to adjudicate what he saw as a petty Italian squabble. Don John was thus looking to delegate authority in the Genoan campaign. Rumors were spreading abroad that Don John's force consisted of fifteen thousand men in Milan, ready to march into Genoa and wage war for the *nobili vecchi.* The Spanish commander needed a few good men who could lead squadrons of troops into Genoa, should the situation devolve into the civil war that everyone feared. When the French ambassador, La Mothe Fénelon, had written, the previous January, that Don John had a job for de Vere, this was probably what Fénelon had had in mind.

Records exist of a monetary advance de Vere took out in Naples at some unspecified date in 1575 or '76. Perhaps the earl, preparing to shake a spear in

Genoa on behalf of the *nobili vecchi*, sought an infusion of cash to outfit him in all the trappings of a noble commander that Don John's assignment would have entailed.

That de Vere was in Genoa in 1575 at the time of the civil strife is a known fact–attested to by letters received in England by Lord Burghley from Italian bankers handling de Vere's money. But these sources do not say whether de Vere ever fought for the *nobili vecchi*.

Yet, according to scandalous Catholic rumors circulated in England, de Vere would later brag that he had been appointed to command thirty thousand men in defense of the *vecchi* in Genoa. The gossip, to be covered in greater detail in Chapter 6, further claimed that de Vere boasted of

> excellent orations he made–as namely in the state of Venice, at Padua, at Bologna, and diverse other places in Italy. And which pleased himself above the rest [*was the speech he made*] to his army, when he marched towards Genoa, which when he had pronounced it, he left nothing to reply, but everyone to wonder at his judgment, being reputed for his eloquence another Cicero and for his conduct a Caesar.

In truth, the Genoese *nobili nuovi* and *vecchi* never did come to blows. Negotiations settled the dispute before swords were drawn, so any initial troop deployments would only have been recalled. But if any of the outrageous allegations ever dished out by de Vere's contemporaries are to be credited, surely the most believable is the claim that the earl of Oxford was a man given to lengthy orations, hilarious fictions, and imaginative elaborations. De Vere was indeed "for his eloquence another Cicero," regardless of the extent of objective, historical truth found in the gossip.

De Vere would return from Italy with many tall tales that he would spin for his drinking buddies and fellow pub crawlers. The Catholic chatterboxes who recalled de Vere's supposed actions in Genoa said that the earl also boasted that he would have been made duke of Milan for his valiance on the battlefield were it not for one of Queen Elizabeth's agents in Italy who had interceded. There would be no Milanese dukedom for this Englishman. De Vere, it was said, loved to tell this story: "Diversely hath he told it, and when he enters into it, he can hardly out, which hath made such sport as often have I been driven to rise from his table laughing."

One of de Vere's colleagues in the Genoese Civil War That Almost Was was a nobleman who, in 1575, became the new duke of Genoa. The new duke's name was Prospero Fattinanti. The seeds of *The Tempest*–the protagonist of which, PROSPERO, is a deposed duke of Milan–may well lie scattered

on the Genoese and Milanese ground in the late summer of 1575. De Vere's
Italian adventures, both real and imagined, would serve as the raw materials
out of which grand and monumental works of fiction were ultimately made.

Edward de Vere's grand tour in the summer and early fall of 1575 was an
exhausting endeavor, both physically and financially. He had injured his knee
on one of his Venetian galley trips and returned to the city on the lagoon running a fever. He must have walked in the door of his Venetian flat yearning for
the creature comforts that he had otherwise enjoyed throughout his twenty-
five years. From the letters de Vere's bankers were sending Lord Burghley–
and the record of his cash advance in Naples–de Vere's prodigal lifestyle had
not abated since he had crossed the Alps. Over fourteen months of travel, the
earl spent £4,561, some $1.2 million in today's currency.

The nineteenth-century English historian Isaac Disraeli once recorded a
legend he'd read that in passing through Italy or Germany, de Vere's train had
encountered a beggar. The destitute man asked one of de Vere's servants if he
could spare a sixpence or shilling. "What dost [thou] say if I give thee ten
pounds?" the servant replied. "Ten pounds!" the beggar said. "That would make
a man of me!" So de Vere's servant gave the beggar ten pounds and entered into
de Vere's account books, "Item, £10, for making a man." According to this
story, de Vere "not only allowed [it], but was pleased" when he learned of this
encounter. Such singular talent for cash dispersal led economic historian
Lawrence Stone to term de Vere "the greatest spendthrift tourist of all."

De Vere had also returned to Venice in late September to discover that
the three packets of letters he had sent back to his wife and father-in-law during his grand tour had never made it past the Alps. The plague had hit Italy
too hard. Letter carriers were denied passage to points north. De Vere had,
however, received two postings from his father-in-law, one of which announced that his wife Anne had delivered a daughter, Elizabeth.

De Vere would wait until he could get closer to home to discover the true
story about a pregnant wife whom he'd supposedly never impregnated.

In September, de Vere sent a letter to Lord Burghley explaining why communication had been cut off during the grand tour. He noted that rest and quiet
were what he now desired most. De Vere also requested that a loan he had
taken out for five hundred crowns should be settled with the sale of his lands.
Like *As You Like It*'s melancholy courtier JAQUES, de Vere was one who had
"sold [his] own lands to see other men's."

In his September 24 letter posted from Venice, de Vere wrote to his father-
in-law:

My good lord . . . I have been grieved with a fever; yet with the help of
God now I have recovered the same and am past the danger thereof,
though brought very weak thereby and hindered from a great deal of

travel, which grieves me most, fearing my time not sufficient for my desire. For although I have seen so much as sufficeth me, yet would I have time to profit thereby.

Your Lordship seems desirous to know how I like Italy, what is mine intention in travel, and when I mean to return. For my liking of Italy, my lord, I am glad I have seen it, and I care not ever to see it anymore, unless it be to serve my prince or country. . . .

Thus thanking Your Lordship for your good news of my wife's delivery, I recommend myself unto your favor; and although I write for a few months more, yet though I have them, so it may fall out I will shorten them myself.

In his Italian adventures, de Vere had seen much, although his sickness had hindered him from seeing more. To appease Burghley, who might have worried that his son-in-law was turning Catholic, de Vere downplayed his love of Italy. De Vere told his father-in-law not to expect many more letters. No doubt he wanted to minimize his feigned acknowledgment of a child whose conception remained a mystery.

CHAPTER 5

THE FABLE OF THE WORLD

[1575–1578]

T HE FALL OF 1575 WAS A BAD TIME TO GET SICK IN VENICE. THE city was suffering an epidemic of the bubonic plague. Anyone who had come into contact with known or suspected plague victims was quarantined for up to forty days. Unemployment was rising, especially among those whose livelihoods depended upon crowds, such as schoolmasters, mountebanks, and tavern keepers. The Venetian textile industry had been temporarily shut down because the plague could be transmitted through infected bedding, clothing, and fibers. The city would soon be losing one quarter of its population. Church spires across the Veneto were all too often aglow with "lanterns of the dead"– an Italian funerary tradition that appears in *Romeo and Juliet.*

The plague of 1575–77 would ultimately claim the life of one of the most celebrated Venetians of his day, the artist Tiziano Vecellio (later anglicized as Titian). In 1575, however, this octogenarian great master was anything but ailing. Titian's studio at the island's northern edge, Ca' Grande, was churning out complex works at the time such as *The Allegory of the Battle of Lepanto* and *The Allegory of Religion.* Both of these paintings were commissioned by King Philip II of Spain and would inspire literary tributes by the Spanish playwright Lope de Vega.

In sixteenth-century Italy, Titian was an artistic celebrity comparable to Picasso in the twentieth century. Venetian society flocked to his bayside home, and noteworthy foreign visitors frequently paid their respects. When King Henri III of France had resided in Venice, he had called upon Titian at Ca' Grande. It is likely de Vere did as well.

One of Ca' Grande's guests describes a soiree at Titian's:

Here, before the tables were set out, because the sun, in spite of the shade, still made his heat much felt, we spent the time in looking at the lively figures in the excellent pictures, of which the house was full, and in discussing the real beauty and charm of the garden with singular plea-sure and note of admiration of all of us. It is situated in the extreme part of Venice, upon the sea, and from it one sees the pretty little island of Murano, and other beautiful places. This part of the sea, as soon as the sun went down, swarmed with gondolas adorned with beautiful women, and resounded with varied harmony and music of voices and instru-ments, which till midnight accompanied our delightful supper.

Titian had lived and worked amid the highest caste of Venetian society when the city-state was still a Mediterranean powerhouse to be reckoned with. The artist had met, and in many cases painted, some of most of the prominent European figures of the sixteenth century, from popes and cardi-nals to artists and philosophers to dukes and kings. As one contemporary noted, "There was almost no famous lord, nor prince, nor great woman, who was not painted by Titian." Titian had outlived most of his colleagues and contemporaries. To a young earl with a romantic attachment to the past, there would have been plenty to be learned at the master's table.

One painting alone–depicting a myth from Ovid's *Metamorphoses*–would fire the Shake-spearean imagination years later. Shake-speare's epic poem *Venus and Adonis* boldly revises the Ovidian myth in the same way that Titian does.

Whereas all classical sources of the Venus and Adonis fable depict the couple's affair as mutually passionate, Titian's *Venus and Adonis* portrays the former as a desperate vixen and the latter as a disinterested boy. On Titian's canvas, a grasping goddess of love clings to a willful youth who appears both-ered by the temptress embracing him. Titian's Venus nearly falls over herself to restrain Adonis from leaving. Similarly, Shake-speare's VENUS tries to hold the heedless boy numerous times, when finally, "On his neck her yoking arms she throws; she sinketh down, still hanging on his neck. He on her belly falls, she on her back." In the words of art historian Erwin Panofsky, "Shake-speare's words . . . sound like a poetic paraphrase of Titian's composition."

There were at least four replicas of Titian's *Venus and Adonis* elsewhere on the Continent by 1575–most notably, in the collection of the king of Spain. But the copy remaining in Titian's studio was distinctive. In Titian's copy and in Titian's copy only, Adonis wears a stylized form of a man's hat known as a bonnet. The other copies of the painting feature a bareheaded Adonis. Shake-speare's ADONIS wears a "bonnet [that] hides his angry brow."

Not only would Titian's *Venus and Adonis* inform de Vere's vision of the Ovidian myth, works by two of Titian's closest artistic colleagues (long dead in 1575) also loom large in Shake-speare. Plays by Titian's literary mentor Pietro Aretino provided character studies, language, situations, and ideas for more than a dozen Shake-speare plays and poems, while two plays and both of Shake-speare's epic poems *(Venus and Adonis* and *The Rape of Lucrece)* allude to works by Titian's friend Julio Romano.

Romano is, in fact, mentioned by name in Shake-speare. In *The Winter's Tale,* a painted statue of the wronged wife HERMIONE is compared to statuary by "that rare Italian master Julio Romano." This sentence has often been cited by orthodox academics to disprove Shake-speare's knowledge of Italian art; Romano is known today as a painter, not a sculptor.

Yet a northern Italian trip that de Vere took in the late fall of 1575 points him in a direction that would resolve this controversy. On November 27, de Vere wrote Lord Burghley from Padua. Just a day's journey from Padua was the city of Mantua, where de Vere's idol Baldassare Castiglione had lived and worked. Castiglione was buried in the church of Santa Maria delle Grazie, five miles outside Mantua's city walls.

Le Grazie was a popular sanctuary containing numerous life-size statues in colored wax of local dignitaries and religious leaders. Amid these lifelike effigies stands Castiglione's tomb, which also holds the remains of the philosopher's wife, Ippolita. Atop the tomb one finds a masterful sculpture of a risen Christ. The monument was designed and sculpted by Castiglione's friend Julio Romano.

Ippolita Castiglione had died nine years before her husband, and the tomb records the widower's heartrending sorrow:

> I live no longer, sweetest spouse, since Fate which tore you from me has taken my life with yours; but I shall live, when I am buried in the same grave with you, and my bones are joined with yours. To Ippolita Torelli, who was no less fair than she was chaste, and had hardly entered on the first years of her youth, this tomb is raised by her inconsolable husband, Baldassare Castiglione, A.D. 1520.

The Winter's Tale's comparison between HERMIONES's memorial statue and sculpture by Julio Romano is not a hallmark of Shake-speare's ignorance. It is de Vere's memory of a Mantuan tomb dedicated to a much-loved wife.

Visiting dignitaries to Mantua, such as an English earl, would have been put up as a guest of the local duke, Guglielmo Gonzaga. The Gonzagas had in 1575 reigned as dukes of Mantua for nearly 250 years. De Vere probably read tales from the family's own bookshelves about the strange and curious history of the Gonzaga dynasty. One Gonzaga—a cousin to Castiglione—had been accused of murdering the duke of Urbino by pouring poison in his ear. This is the same story HAMLET tells in his play-within-the-play, *The Mousetrap.* "His name's Gonzago [*sic*]," HAMLET tells his colleagues at court. "The story is extant and writ in very choice Italian."

The Gonzagas' monstrous five-hundred-room, fifteen-courtyard *palazzo ducale* contained a number of suites for distinguished guests. In 1575, one of the main guest rooms was the Appartamento di Troia. The *appartamento* contained frescoes of famous scenes from the Trojan War, painted and decorated by none other than Julio Romano. The mural is one busy work of art: on the ceiling, Mount Olympus and battles between the Greeks and Trojans; on the walls, Paris's judgment, the rape of Helen, Hecuba's dream, the forging of Achilles's arms, the building of the Trojan horse, and the deceitful Sinon's ploy to induce his countrymen to receive the horse.

Shake-speare's *Rape of Lucrece* describes just such a painting—202 lines of poetic elaboration upon a mural of epic proportions.

> At last she [LUCRECE] calls to mind where hangs a piece
> Of skillful painting, made for Priam's Troy;
> Before the which is drawn the power of Greece,
> For Helen's rape the city to destroy,
> Threat'ning cloud-kissing Ilion with annoy,
>   Which the conceited painter drew so proud,
>   As heaven (it seem'd) to kiss the turrets bow'd.

And so on. *The Rape of Lucrece* describes in vivid pictorial detail much of what Romano had set upon the *appartamento*'s walls.

As the year 1575 drew to a close, de Vere's purse was under siege too. On November 27, the earl wrote to his father-in-law from Padua not to inhibit any sales of his family lands in order to stem a rising tide of debts. "I shall desire Your Lordship to make no stay of the sales of my land," the earl commanded his father-in-law.

De Vere wrote his brief letter in haste, as the messenger was preparing to depart soon. The Alps would not have been passable this late in the year, so the envoy likely prepared an alternate route to Genoa or another western port city and then onward through France. The messenger would hardly have been the only emissary in the neighborhood who was departing for a thousand-mile journey. Padua was a city in touch with the world.

One of Italy's most celebrated college towns, Padua was home to a university that, thanks to its independence from the Catholic Church, drew scholars from all across the Occident and Orient. Christians, Arabs, Jews, Persians, and Turks all studied within this institution's hallowed walls; registration was optional; tuition was, except for the rich students, free. The university also housed a world-famous law school, an institution where Sir Thomas Smith had once trained. Its most celebrated professor in 1575 was a jurist named Ottonello Discalzio—a man who made regular trips to Venice to render his considered opinion in court cases that required outside consultation. Discalzio's many contributions to Venetian jurisprudence inspired the duke of Venice to appoint the professor to Venice's prestigious Order of San Marco. Discalzio was the real-life inspiration for *The Merchant of Venice*'s celebrated Padua University law professor BELLARIO, consulted to settle the case of SHYLOCK V. ANTONIO.

The Merchant of Venice describes the trip from Padua to Venice–by what PORTIA calls "the *tranect*, the common ferry." The river Brenta connected the inland university town to the Venetian Lagoon, and the seven-hour journey by horse-drawn ferry *(traquet* or *traghetto)* was one of the most scenic river rides in all of northern Italy. Riverside estates on the Brenta were home to numerous luxurious mansions; the Brenta was in fact known to locals as "the continuation of the Grand Canal" *(la continuazione del Canal Grande)*. PORTIA lives on the Brenta in an estate called Belmont. Belmont, she notes, is at a location ten miles from Venice and two miles away from a monastery. There is only one villa that meets these two geographic details: the luxurious Villa Foscari on the Brenta, two miles from the Ca' delle Monache (The Nuns' House). King Henri III had stayed at Foscari during his 1574 trip to Venice, as had de Vere's probable host in Mantua, Guglielmo Gonzaga. *The Merchant of Venice* mentions this latter fact, when PORTIA's assistant, NERISSA, recalls a recent visit to Belmont by "the marquis of Montferrat." One of Gonazaga's titles, in addition to duke of Mantua, was marquis of Montferrat.

De Vere's ferry ride down the Brenta would have passed the classically inspired Villa Foscari as the *traghetto* slowed down to round a wide curve on the riverbank. One nineteenth-century English traveler, on a similar ferry ride down the Brenta with Lord Byron, recorded the inspirational beauty the local vistas provided.

> [I] remarked [on] the moon reigning on the right of us and the Alps still blushing with the blaze of the sunset. The Brenta came down upon us, all purple–a delightful scene. . . .

One final trip into the heart of Italy remained before de Vere would cross the Alps once again. This time neither the river and canal networks of northern Italy nor the Adriatic afforded him the convenience of journey by water. Overland travel would be his only option as he ventured out to see "the rest of Italy"–as de Vere told one of his creditors. De Vere and his train pointed their horses and carts south toward Florence on December 12. The duchy of Tuscany was their destination. But first de Vere had to pass through the neighboring duchy of Ferrara.

This dukedom does not appear in Shake-speare. De Vere did not tarry long there. However, one of Ferrara's famous sons, Giraldi Cinthio, had published a collection of short stories, *Gli Hecatommithi* (1566), that would have been spiritual balm to a husband pondering his wife's sexual duplicity. The

Hecatommithi recites the tale of a jealous Moor and a wife he accuses of infidelity, a fair young wench named "Disdemona."

Reaching Florence from the Ferrara-Tuscany border takes less than a day on horseback. Once de Vere's train arrived in this thriving mercantile city, probably around December 16, he would have been welcomed by the new duke of the city-state, Francesco de Medici. Even more than his father before him, Francesco I was a despot whose reign marked an age of disorder and misrule in nearly every function of the government: The duke regularly hired assassins to kill supposed enemies; his court was a quagmire of fear and loathing; crime flourished throughout the city.

However, the Medici were also a philosophically and artistically enlightened clan, patrons, in no small part, of the Italian Renaissance. The city's walls could hardly contain its wealth of art and learning. On her cobblestone streets had walked Dante and Machiavelli. Florence was also known as a center of both banking and science. Because of this, inhabitants of rival city-states sometimes derided Florentines, as the Venetian IAGO castigates the Florentine CASSIO, as "bookish" and as "mathematician[s]." Florence was also home to the monastery of Santa Maria Novella, widely renowned for its perfumes and sweet oils. De Vere would return to England bearing perfumed gloves as gifts to the queen and others—perhaps purchased during his stopover in Florence. (Shake-speare's other Florentine, *Much Ado About Nothing*'s CLAUDIO, gives these same "sweet gloves" to his betrothed, HERO.)

Near Christmastime, de Vere headed south out of Florence. On his journey, he would have run across many travelers heading toward Rome. Fifteen seventy-five was a Jubilee Year. Pilgrims from across Europe, summoned by the pope, were converging upon the Vatican and the yet-unfinished St. Peter's Basilica. Many English Catholics made the 850-mile journey from London. Upon meeting in Rome, some of these English exiles would together vow to "convert" their homeland back to the Catholic faith—a pact that would be keeping Burghley and Walsingham's secret agents busy for years to come.

It was an auspicious time to be riding in the direction of Rome. As if to time-stamp the historical moment of Shake-speare's travels through Tuscany, HELENA in *All's Well That Ends Well* seeks out her wayward husband BERTRAM, in Florence, by disguising herself as a pilgrim on Jubilee.

HELENA says her Italian destination is "St. Jaques le Grand." These words have puzzled critics. The most famous holy site of this name is a cathedral in Galicia, Spain. HELENA's destination is often cited as one more example of Shake-speare's supposed ignorance of continental Europe, like the seacoast of Bohemia.

During de Vere's Tuscan visit, Rome had reached its capacity. Pilgrims had arrived at the Holy City only to find the gates shut in their face. Many travelers never made it any farther south than overflow sites near Florence. Two such locations were the shrines to St. James the Great ("St. Jaques le

Grand" in HELENA's native French) in the Tuscan towns of Pistoia and Prato. In disguising herself as a Jubilee pilgrim heading toward "St. Jaques le Grand," HELENA effectively states that she intends to wind up near Florence in order to track down her husband.

On January 3, 1576, de Vere wrote a letter to his father-in-law from the southern Tuscan town of Siena. This time de Vere had ample time to compose his thoughts. The earl's letter begins in the same way as his missive from Padua regarding the impatience of his creditors and the need to sell his lands. But then it evolves into a trilingual expression of frustration at Burghley's meddling and conniving. The Lord Treasurer had, no doubt wisely, advised de Vere not to sell so many of his estates to pay his debts. Family properties were de Vere's primary source of income. In hastily selling off his holdings, he was like a trust-fund kid cashing in on his principal–a short-term gain leading to long-term ruin. Yet the twenty-five-year-old earl was having what would truly be the time of his life in Italy, and money could not get in the way of his continued immersion in Italian life and culture.

De Vere explained to Burghley that he had no other choice but to sell his family properties:

[A]lthough to depart with land Your Lordship hath advised the contrary and that Your Lordship for the good affection you bear unto me could wish it otherwise, yet you see I have none other remedy. I have no help but of mine own, and mine is made to serve me and myself not mine. Whereupon till all such incumbrances be passed over and till I can better settle myself at home I have determined to continue my travel, the which thing in no wise I desire Your Lordship to hinder, unless you would have it thus: *Ut nulla sit inter nos amicitia.* [Latin: "There would be no friendship between us."] For having made an end of all hope to help myself by Her Majesty's service, considering that my youth is objected unto me, and for every step of mine a block is found to be laid in my way, I see it is but vain *calcitrare contra li busi* [Italian, citing Acts 9:5: "To kick against the pricks"], and the worst of things being known, they are the more easier to be provided for to bear and support them with patience.

The statement "mine is made to serve me and myself not mine"–my monies and lands serve me and not the other way around–lays bare both the writer's petulant mood and his egocentric attitude. And yet to write off de Vere's protestations as mere narcissism is to miss a further point as well: Since he'd inherited them, the earl's estates had indeed been mostly serving others–primarily, in the final analysis, the queen. And now he was a foreigner in a faraway, Catholic land, a foreigner whose reputation rested on having the money to maintain his position, a poet and playwright in the making who was gathering his subjects and learning his craft. No matter how bad a money manager the earl of Oxford was, he was in the right to point out that this was a very bad time for his checks to start bouncing.

De Vere continued:

> Wherefore for things passed amiss to repent them it is too late to help them, which I cannot but ease them that I am determined to hope for anything I do not, but if anything do happen *preter spem* [Latin: "Beyond hope or expectation"], I think before that time I must be so old as my son, who shall enjoy them, must give the thanks, and I am to content myself, according to this English proverb that it is my hap to starve like the horse, while the grass doth grow.
>   ... The 3rd of January. From Siena.
>   EDWARD OXENFORD

De Vere did not, so far as is known, have a son in 1575. One presumes that he writes in the hypothetical, looking forward to a time when he will have an heir. In the same paragraph as the "son" remark, de Vere also spells out a proverb that his counterpart quotes to Burghley's counterpart in *Hamlet*. As the Danish prince says to POLONIUS, "Ay, sir, but, 'As the grass grows...'– The proverb is something musty."

For a spendthrift such as de Vere, opportunities for extravagance could be found anywhere in Italy. But in early January in Siena, temptations leading to wantonness were even greater than normal. Whether by choice or by accident, de Vere had arrived in Siena at a time of revelry. This gorgeous Tuscan town was one of the most active theatrical cities in all of Italy outside of Venice, and the period from Christmas to Twelfth Night (January 5) was filled with celebrations, parties, and plays.

Upon arriving in Siena, de Vere would likely have met the man who stood at the center of the Sienese theatrical world in 1576. The sixty-seven-year-old Alessandro Piccolomini was a Sienese philosopher-playwright widely hailed as "the prince of comic writers." Piccolomini had previously written a book that was something of a companion to Castiglione–detailing the proper education of the ideal courtier. Piccolomini also headed a local drama club called the Academy of the Deaf and Daft (Accademia degli Intronati) that spearheaded their own style of commedia dell'arte. By the 1570s, Piccolomini's academy had taken the radical step of hiring actresses. (Typically, on both Italian and English stages, boys played all the female roles.) As fellow artistic innovators, courtly gentlemen, and renegade scholars, Piccolomini and de Vere had much in common.

Piccolomini's Academy observed a decades-long Sienese tradition of performing his comedy *The Deceived (Gl'Ingannati)* on Twelfth Night. De Vere's letter from Siena is dated two days before the Academy's annual theatrical revelry, so Piccolomini would probably have importuned the city's courtly English visitor to stick around long enough to watch the Academy's comic masterpiece.

The plot of *The Deceived* concerns a brother–sister set of twins; the sister falls madly in love with a nobleman who's wasting his affections on someone else. The sister then disguises herself as a male servant, who ferries love letters between the noble and his elusive paramour. The twin brother, supposedly dead, arrives on the scene and straightens out the mess by falling in love with the noble's paramour, while the twin sister snatches the noble for herself. This is also the plot of Shake-speare's *Twelfth Night*–a fact that was recognized as far back as the early seventeenth century. (Traces of Piccolomini's comedy have also been found in *Romeo and Juliet* and *Two Gentlemen of Verona*.) De Vere would transform the setting of Piccolomini's farce to Ragusa, but Shake-speare's *Twelfth Night* would proclaim its Sienese origins in everything from its story line to its very title.

De Vere's Siena stopover came at a time not just of revelry but also of reverence. With his visit falling in the midst of the Christmas-Epiphany season, it's reasonable to assume that de Vere at least made an appearance at church. The cathedral in Siena was, like the Palazzo Ducale in Mantua, a unique piece of architecture and design, situated on the highest prominence in this hilly town, with a zebra-striped exterior and an exquisite interior to match nearly any cathedral in Italy. One peculiar piece of art inside Siena's *Duomo* is a circular mosaic representing the proverbial Seven Ages of Man. In the words of art historian Samuel C. Chew,

> Familiar to Shakespearean scholars because it has been cited as a parallel to JAQUES's lines in *As You Like It*. . . . the Ages [in Siena's Duomo] are represented thus: Infantia rides upon a hobbyhorse, Pueritia is a schoolboy, Adolescentia is an older scholar garbed in a long cloak, Juventus has a falcon on his wrist, Virilitas is robed in dignified fashion and carries a book, Senectus, leaning upon his staff, holds a rosary, Decrepitas, leaning upon two staves, looks into his tomb.

As You Like It's world traveler JAQUES–a melancholic who "sold his lands to see other men's"–describes these same seven ages in a speech that famously begins, "All the world's a stage, and all the men and women merely players." JAQUES continues:

> . . . At first the infant,
> Mewling and puking in the nurse's arms.
> And then the whining schoolboy, with his satchel
> And shining morning face, creeping like snail

> Unwillingly to school. . . . Last scene of all,
> That ends this strange eventful history,
> Is second childishness and mere oblivion,
> Sans teeth, sans eyes, sans taste, sans everything.

After the drizzly January voyage from Siena back to de Vere's Venetian home, a new kind of commedia dell'arte awaited him. Venice's Carnival season–from December 26 to the beginning of Lent–represented the city's other great annual period of theatrical and comic activity. Venetians from the highest-born grandees to the lowest vagabonds donned masks and performed with one another in Carnival skits and masquerades.

The Venetian Carnival masque was a social equalizer unlike anything de Vere would ever see again, an opportunity for an English blueblood to interact with all walks of life without either the burdens or the baubles of his high caste. The experience evidently affected him. From *Much Ado*'s masked revels to HENRY V's camouflaged interviews with his own troops to ANTONY and CLEOPATRA's walking through the common streets incognito, disguise in Shakespeare frequently affords highborn characters the opportunity to descend in rank and stature and learn something about the worlds they normally cannot access.

One thread of seventeenth-century oral history, distorted by the telephone game of multiple retellings, provides a glimpse into de Vere's activity during the Carnival celebrations. A commedia dell'arte performed in Naples in 1699 would recount the exploits of one "Elmond, milord of Oxford." Since there was no lord of Oxford named Elmond and only one Edward before 1699, scholars presume that the seventeenth earl of Oxford is being spoofed in this interlude. It begins:

> The horse of milord of Oxford is faun colored and goes by the name of Oltramarin [*Beyond-the-Sea*]. Elmond carries a large sword. His color of costume is violet. He carries for device a falcon with a motto taken from Terence: *Tendit in ardua virtus* [Valor proceeds to arduous undertakings].

The Elmond character jousts with "Alvida, countess of Edenburg" and for his efforts is awarded the "horn of Astolf"–named after a marauder from the time of Charlemagne who once besieged Rome. Tempting as it may be to try to wring meaning out of this farcical scenario, one must also remember that it is a tale told by an idiot. The character who recites this story is a clownish pseudointellect (the "Dottore") who mangles every speech he gives. Ultimately, this anecdote reveals more about the Neapolitan commedia at the end of the seventeenth century than it does about de Vere's travels in Italy. All the same, one revealing fact can be discerned from the commedia: De Vere had made such an impression during his continental travels that his memory was still treading the boards more than a century after his departure.

Perhaps due to the howl of too many impatient creditors, de Vere had by the end of February 1576 decided to close down his Venetian home and return to England.

On the day before Fat Tuesday, March 5, 1576, de Vere and his train packed their bags and bade farewell to the city that had yielded up so many of its riches—and unburdened the earl of Oxford of so many of his. *La Serenissima* was gearing up for the explosive Mardi Gras celebrations that would take place the following night. But, perhaps to beat the post-Carnival rush, de Vere and his servants boarded the "tranect, the common ferry," and watched as Venice floated away like an unmoored ship. Now on the mainland, many days of travel awaited them as they prepared to cross the Lombardy Plain and make their way into the Alps a second time.

The one recorded Italian contact they made on the return journey was in the vicinity of Milan. This was the third known time de Vere had passed by Milan—the first was on his way into Italy and the second at the conclusion of his summer grand tour. An Englishman then in Milan, Francis Peyto, had earlier tried to insinuate himself into the earl of Oxford's company. Peyto had devised an intricate genealogy illustrating the family ties between English and Scottish royalty. Peyto sought a rich patron to pay him for it. The work was probably a piece of Catholic propaganda—because it would publicize family ties to the English throne that the Scots queen could parlay to her advantage. De Vere wanted no part in it. Peyto wrote to Burghley on March 31, 1576, that he'd tried to show

> the designment to my lord of Oxford if he had passed this way visible to any English eye, as he did not. I always desired to know His Lordship both for his own sake and for my country's sake and to that end made offer of myself in his first coming hither. But . . . at this new demand I was refused to be spoken with.

Peyto's unusual wording—not that de Vere never made it to Milan but that he'd "passed this way [in]visible to any English eye"—suggests de Vere had entered Milan incognito.

A few Shake-spearean allusions to sites and scenes inside the walls of Milan would suggest that the author had enjoyed some fleeting glances of the city and its residents. MARGARET in *Much Ado About Nothing* mentions a sumptuous gown owned by the duchess of Milan. (Even in the sixteenth century, Milan was recognized as a center of haute couture. Once he'd returned to London, de Vere was said to have joked that "the cobblers' wives of Milan are more richly dressed every working day than the queen [is] on Christmas Day.") SILVIA in *Two Gentlemen of Verona* speaks of "Friar Patrick's Cell" in Milan, which was indeed a real place where the Irish friar Patrick O'Hely stayed during a Milanese stopover in the summer of 1576.

Unlike the more independent Spanish-controlled kingdom of Sicily, which English tourists had an easier time traversing, Milan was a stronghold of Spain's imperial might. For more than a generation, Milan's leader had actually been a colonial governor, a foreigner appointed by the king of Spain. In honor of his predecessors, the governor still retained the honorary title of duke. At the time of de Vere's probable visit, a Spanish "duke"–Don Antonio de Guzmán, marquis of Ayamonte–did indeed rule the city. (This peculiar feature of Milanese life makes its way into *The Two Gentlemen of Verona:* Shake-speare's DUKE OF MILAN reveals his nationality when he addresses his colleagues using the Spanish honorific "Don.")

Had de Vere actually infiltrated the Spanish-controlled city, he would likely have skipped over the houses of the "duke" and the archbishop of Milan for lodgings in another Milanese household that would readily have opened its doors to a visiting patron of the arts. The sculptor and engraver Leone Leoni kept a palazzo in the city's center that was an architectural testament to its owner's creativity and individuality. Eight stone giants lean ominously out of the building's facade, divided into three neat stories in an almost Elizabethan-style frame. Inside, the sixty-seven-year-old artist, a close friend of Michelangelo, displayed his extensive collection of drawings, paintings, and plaster casts. One painting in Leoni's inventory, Correggio's mythological masterpiece *Io,* makes its way into Shake-speare. An unnamed LORD in *The Taming of the Shrew* describes a picture he's seen:

> We'll show thee Io as she was a maid,
> And how she was beguiled and surpris'd,
> As lively painted as the deed was done.

As the twentieth-century cultural historian A. Lytton Sells observes, "It is possible that Shakespeare is here simply inventing; but it is more natural to suppose that he is describing real pictures such, for example, as Correggio's *Io.*"

De Vere's departure from Milan at the end of March 1576 represents the last known instance that his feet touched Italian soil. Historical records establish that during his ten-month Italian sojourn, de Vere visited Venice, Padua, Milan, Genoa, Palermo, Florence, Siena, and Naples. In traveling between his known destinations, de Vere had probably also seen parts of Messina, Mantua, and Verona. Yet this list still leaves out more than a dozen significant Italian cities and city-states. These locations–including Turin, Parma, Bergamo, Livorno, Rimini, Bologna, Ravenna, Reggio, Modena, and the island states of Sardinia and Corsica–are the same parts of Italy that go unmentioned in the Shake-speare canon. (Rome is a special case, since de Vere's personal secretary, Anthony Munday, would spend three months touring and studying there in 1579.) As the literary scholar H. F. Brown points out:

> Shakespeare displays a knowledge of Venice and the Venetian dominions deeper than that which he appears to have possessed about any other Italian state. Omitting the references to Rome, which are just under four hundred in number, we find that the chief cities of Italy come in this order: Venice, with fifty-one references; Naples, thirty-four; Milan, twenty-five; Florence, twenty-three; Padua, twenty-three; and Verona, twenty.

Undoubtedly, plenty of Italian allusions in Shake-speare remain to be ferreted out–such as de Vere's Sienese stay on or near Twelfth Night and its relevance to the play *Twelfth Night.* However, as a rule, these references have so far clustered around the Italian ports of call on de Vere's itinerary. There is little cause to doubt that this trend will continue.

As with his journey into Italy, de Vere faced the Alps on his outbound voyage when the spring thaws made the mountains passable. Correspondence from one of de Vere's moneylenders reveals that he had sent baggage as well as some traveling money ahead to await him in Lyon. Connecting the dots between Milan and Lyon, the Mont Cenis pass northwest of Turin provides the most probable route over the Alps.

The terrain at Mont Cenis gradually ascends over six miles but becomes too steep and jagged on the French side to accommodate any mode of transportation more technologically advanced than a beast of burden. At the base of the mountain, carriages were typically broken down and lugged over the mountain on pack mules. The passengers either rode on the mule train or on straw chairs hoisted by porters. The porters, no strangers to snow squalls and bracing winds, charged as much as £5 per head ($1,300 in modern currency) for the six-day trek. Nearly two centuries later, when passage across Mont Cenis involved the same sleety ordeal, one English traveler marveled, "It was a great miracle that [the carriage] was not dash'd into ten thousand pieces."

Landing in France, de Vere's caravan would have faced the choice of traveling by land or by water. The easier route involved following Mont Cenis's mountain stream, the Arc, which leads into the river Isère. The Isère flows through Grenoble and St. Marcellin, where it joins the Rhône. Numerous castles fortified the Rhône's banks, where a French-speaking cosmopolitan earl had lodging aplenty to choose from. Staying with one's "cousins"–as aristocrats often referred to one another–was generally the preferred overnight option for a nobleman on tour.

Less than a day's journey up the Rhône from its junction with the Isère lies the hillside town of Tournon. A small medieval city with a renowned university and an active market of printers and publishers, Tournon-sur-Rhône was at its peak of activity in the sixteenth century. In 1576, Tournon was also a provincial seat where the local magistrate–Just-Louis, Lord Tournon, count of Roussillion–kept a number of prominent nearby châteaux for his family and his distinguished visitors. King Charles IX of France had stayed with the family in 1564, and his successor, Henri III, had lodged with them ten years later. The door of Count Roussillion's estates would have been open to the *comte d'Oxford* as he made a similar progress upstream.

As baggage, books, and provisions remained tied down in the barges parked at the riverbank, probably with one or more servants camped out nearby to guard against pillaging, de Vere would have enjoyed his first taste of the refined and noble life since he'd left Renaissance Italy behind. The spacious Château Tournon, practically carved out of the granite peak in the center of town, served as both fortress and villa to the Roussillion clan. The count of Roussillion's family used the Château Tournon for their primary residence and may have entertained their worthy visitor either there or in the commodious lodgings of the nearby Château Roussillion.

Also in the Roussillion household in 1576 was Just-Louis's unmarried youngest sister. Hélène de Tournon was a fetching young woman who drew the admiration of townsfolk and visitors alike. (A room devoted to her in the Château Tournon, the Salle Hélène de Tournon, remains to this day.) Hélène's mother, the dowager countess of Roussillion, also lived with the family and remained watchful over her youngest daughter and young son who now ruled over the region.

The tribulations of this family must have been notably dramatic. *All's Well That Ends Well* is partly based upon them. The plot of *All's Well* originates in a primary source text (Boccaccio's *Decameron*) and draws its motivating force from de Vere's life–particularly from his mistreatment of Anne Cecil de Vere. But the touching story of Hélène de Tournon also feeds into the tragicomic tale that *All's Well* tells.

To begin with, the name of *All's Well*'s mistreated wife, HELENA, has no other known source. *All's Well* also faithfully preserves Hélène de Tournon's family at the time of de Vere's passage up the Rhône: Shake-speare's play features both a DOWAGER COUNTESS OF ROUSSILLION and her son, the COUNT OF ROUSSILLION. De Vere would fuse *All's Well*'s three primary sources to create a self-consistent dramatic framework–changing the location referenced in Boccaccio's story from the French *province* of Roussillion to the Château Roussillion and changing the relationship between HELENA and the COUNT OF ROUSSILLION from sibling to betrothed.

Like Anne Cecil de Vere, Hélène de Tournon would be the victim of a haughty lover and ugly family politics. When de Vere made his way up the

Rhône River Valley in 1576, Hélène had just one more year to live; her death would soon become the scandal of the French court. She was in love with a French marquis who returned her affections. But the marquis's family was opposed to the match; they wanted him to become a priest. The marquis gave in, and at a courtly function where both would-be lovers were in attendance, he refused to acknowledge Hélène's presence. She swooned and, as the story goes, died of "mortal sorrow."

The story of Hélène de Tournon contributed to another play as well: Happening by chance upon her funeral, the marquis inquired who was being buried. Discovering that it was the young woman his cold heart had inadvertently killed, he fainted and fell from his horse. The marquis repented for his cruelty, and according to one eyewitness, "his soul, I believe, enter[ed] the tomb to beg pardon of her whom his indifferent neglect has put there." Some French historians have recognized in the obscure melodrama of this maiden from southern France a seed of inspiration for the graveyard scene in *Hamlet*.

The Upper Rhône Valley and parts south and west, the Languedoc, was a Protestant stronghold in an increasingly strife-riven Catholic France. Since the St. Bartholomew's Day atrocities in 1572, Catholic–Protestant wars had become a source of potentially revolutionary instability. In early 1576, the king of France's younger brother, the duke of Alençon, had forged a secret alliance with Protestant forces in France, Germany, and England and had secretly begun to advocate for a coup d'état. A cavalry division led by the German duke Jan Casimir had invaded the eastern provinces to assist Alençon in the uprising. As de Vere was returning home on his way north toward Paris, the entire country was bracing itself for bloody hostilities. De Vere's train came across Casimir's forces, who were then based in the eastern region of Langres. The earl's encounter with the invading German prince survives in a peculiar form—in an extended encomium to de Vere that appears in a play by the Jacobean dramatist George Chapman.

Chapman's tragedy *The Revenge of Bussy d'Ambois* (c. 1607) has been hailed as one of the first great tragedies of passion, containing "perhaps the finest celebration in our language of the philosophy of Stoicism." Chapman's stoic hero is a French noble named Clermont d'Ambois, who claims to have been present at the meeting between de Vere and Duke Casimir. Chapman imbues his semifictional protagonist with the most commendatory attributes—Clermont's "virtues [rank] with the best of th' ancient Romans"—so Clermont's panegyric to de Vere is rightly seen as high praise indeed:

> I overtook, coming from Italy,
> In Germany, a great and famous earl
> Of England, the most goodly fashion'd man
> I ever saw; from head to foot in form

> Rare and most absolute; he had a face
> Like one of the most ancient honor'd Romans
> From whence his noblest family was deriv'd;
> He was beside of spirit passing great,
> Valiant and learn'd, and liberal as the sun,
> Spoke and write sweetly of learned subjects,
> Or of the discipline of public weals;
> And 'twas the earl of Oxford; and being offer'd
> At that time by Duke Casimir, the view
> Of his right royal army then in the field,
> Refus'd it, and no foot was mov'd to stir
> Out of his fore-determin'd course.
> I [Clermont] wondering at it, ask'd for his reason,
> It being an offer so much for his honor.
> He, all acknowledging, said 'twas not fit
> To take those honors that one cannot quit [*repay*].

In other words, Duke Casimir wanted to show off his armies for the earl of Oxford; de Vere refused because he could not return the favor.

Clermont then goes on to describe de Vere's haughty treatment of an upstart English gentleman who was then traveling with Casimir–Sir John Smith. Smith had taken Casimir up on his offer to review the troops in the field. De Vere bristled with elitist rancor at what he considered Smith's presumptuousness:

> And yet [de Vere] cast it only in the way,
> To stay and serve the world. Nor did it fit
> His own true estimate how much it weigh'd,
> For he despis'd it; and esteemed it freer
> To keep his own way straight, and swore that he
> Had rather make away his whole estate
> In things that cross'd the vulgar, than he would
> Be frozen up still like a Sir John Smith,
> His countryman, in common nobles' fashions,
> Affecting as the end of noblesse were
> Those servile observations.

Duke Casimir, a widely heralded Teutonic prince only seven years older than de Vere, had since the early 1560s been a major player on the world stage. One senses a hint of envy in de Vere's refusal to let Casimir show off his military force. On this unlikely stage outside of Langres, France, de Vere was shown his own failure at the nobleman's art. The earl of Oxford had been raised to become the power-brokering prince that now, in the person of Casimir, was preparing to command the will of the king of France.

HAMLET's final soliloquy ("How all occasions do inform against me...") is inspired by the puzzlement mixed with envy that wells up in him upon seeing his rival FORTINBRAS's troops march in front of him. Young FORTINBRAS's army—in a scene that is not in any known source of *Hamlet*—heads out to face a futile but deadly conquest in Poland. The effect of this show of military might is to force HAMLET to a new resoluteness to right his wronged honor. As HAMLET says while reviewing FORTINBRAS's army

> Rightly to be great
> Is not to stir without great argument,
> But greatly to find quarrel in a straw
> When honor's at the stake.

Neither Danish prince nor English earl can change places with the Teutonic prince who has inspired this surge of envy. In the words of twentieth-century literary critic Moody E. Prior, "[HAMLET's] admiration for FORTINBRAS's action may move him, but it is not an example he can readily follow." At the moment when they see the massed troops, both HAMLET and de Vere recognize their own fates awaiting them.

By March 21, de Vere and his men had arrived in Paris, where the English ambassador notified Lord Burghley of the new guest in town. The forces the earl had seen in the fields of Langres were now part of a larger army that had begun prying a host of concessions out of the king. The king's brother, Alençon, had surrounded Paris with a semicircular formation of thirty thousand troops. To placate his bloodthirsty brother, Henri gave Alençon the additional title of duke of Anjou. Henri gave Casimir three million francs, the duchy of Étampes, and nine lordships in Burgundy. But the besieging forces were not so easily bought off. Alençon had already caused a stir at court by notifying his mother (Catherine de Medici) that someone had attempted to poison him.

The rumor was false, but the situation was becoming frantic. Alençon's forces had cut off all goods and foodstuffs going into and out of Paris. On March 31, Ambassador Valentine Dale wrote to the spymaster Walsingham, "The camp of Monsieur [Alençon] approaches. The king is unready. The strangers [*Casimir's army*] cannot abide to linger this matter. Lord Oxford is here attending his coming."

This would probably have been de Vere's second meeting with the duke of Alençon, whom he is likely to have met at King Henri III's coronation. De Vere's part in the actual negotiations, if he had any place at the table, was soon ended, however. Another month and a half of talks would ensue before Henri and his younger brother sat down to ratify "the Peace of Monsieur," the treaty that ended the French wars of religion. By that time, de Vere would be engaged in his own battles.

In mid-April, after fourteen months of travels across the Continent–and perhaps into Asia Minor–de Vere prepared his luggage for the final crossing of the English Channel. His Italian odyssey had at last come to an end. The earl's many chests and boxes contained, according to one account, a "great collection of beautiful Italian items."

Burghley later recalled that as early as April 4, an unnamed receiver (probably de Vere's servant Rowland Yorke) was beginning to infect the earl's mind against his wife, Anne. The questions of cuckoldry raised earlier in the Italian sojourn were beginning to surface again, although this time inspired by the divisive whispers of a third party. As Burghley noted in a memo to himself and posterity:

> [De Vere] wrote somewhat that by reasons of a man of his, his receiver, he had conceived some unkindness, but he prayed to me to let pass the same, for it did grow by the doubleness of servants.

De Vere, understanding the need to downplay to Burghley the divisive nature of the rumor, asked his father-in-law not to worry about it. This is not to say, however, that de Vere was not concerned. Thus it was with some anxiety that, on or around Good Friday, April 20, de Vere boarded his ship. There were other reasons to be anxious than he knew.

In the spring of 1576, Spanish forces on the high seas were on heightened alert. Catholic France was preparing to concede everything but the throne to Alençon's armies; Spanish commanders in the Lowlands were undoubtedly apprehensive about the shift in power that an Alençon victory in Paris represented. The diplomatic correspondence arising from what was about to happen is quoted at length elsewhere. But the most expressive account is, naturally, Shake-speare's:

> Ere we were two days old at sea, a pirate of very warlike appointment gave us chase. Finding ourselves too slow of sail, we put on a compell'd valor, and in the grapple I boarded them. On the instant they got clear of our ship, so I alone became their prisoner. They have dealt with me like thieves of mercy, but they knew what they did: I am to do a good turn for them.

Just as HAMLET's review of FORTINBRAS's troops leads directly to an ocean voyage overtaken by pirates, de Vere's meeting with Duke Casimir's army was soon followed by a Channel crossing intercepted by pirates. (Neither the encounter with FORTINBRAS's army nor HAMLET's brush with buccaneers appears in any of the play's sources—to the puzzlement of numerous literary critics.)

The "pirate[s] of very warlike appointment" boarded de Vere's ship, and they stripped it bare. De Vere's luggage was ransacked, and the pirates even took the clothes from the earl's back. De Vere was, as the French ambassador later reported to his superiors, "left naked, stripped to his shirt, treated miserably, his life [would have been put] in danger if he hadn't been recognized by a Scotsman." (HAMLET notes that the pirates had him "set naked on your kingdom.") The ordeal anguished both the Privy Council and Prince William of Orange of the Lowlands. The latter soon learned the identities of some of the perpetrators and clapped them in prison for their insolence. As the poet Nathaniel Baxter, who was part of de Vere's entourage, wrote of the episode in a book of poetry from 1606:

> Naked we landed out of Italy
> Enthrall'd by pirates, men of no regard
> Horror and death assail'd nobility,
> If princes might with cruelty be scarr'd.
> Lo, thus are excellent beginnings hard.

Landing at Dover on a vessel stripped by seafaring bandits, de Vere had stepped ashore into a swarm of questions about Anne's daughter's paternity. Rumors about the unknown father of Elizabeth de Vere had spread beyond the queen's presence chamber and the Lord Treasurer's privy chamber.

Burghley was managing the crisis with a shotgun approach. He had fetched his son Thomas from a hundred miles away to greet de Vere at Dover and learn the earl's mind. He had also sent Lord Henry Howard, Norfolk's brother and de Vere's cousin, to bear Burghley's and Anne's greetings to de Vere. Other messengers followed soon thereafter. Anne and de Vere's sister Mary took a coach to Gravesend to intercept de Vere on his way to London—or at least intercept any messengers bearing further news about the earl's arrival. Meanwhile, none of these busybodies seemed to appreciate the fact that the stripped and humiliated man had nearly met his maker—and now probably wanted nothing more than to meet a good tailor.

The scandal surrounding de Vere's wife required utmost discretion, not Lord Burghley's ham-fisted promotion and publicity campaign. Perhaps there was a misunderstanding at the root of it. Ales and sweet wines flowed liberally in an age when clean water was a luxury; a night of drunken marital sex in the autumn of 1574 was not out of the question. De Vere had played along with the game when circumstances left him no other choice—witness the husband's courtly expressions of joy about the progress of Anne's pregnancy in his letters home. Now that he'd returned, however, de Vere undoubtedly wanted to resolve the controversy with minimal fanfare. Burghley's insistence on an immediate and public display of affection might have been designed to make that impossible. It was at best surprisingly undiplomatic, a sort of banner by the quayside proclaiming, WELCOME HOME, DEAR CUCKOLD, with a welcoming committee asking de Vere to stand by it and smile for the camera.

In future years, de Vere would come down—albeit still tentatively—on his father-in-law's side. In perhaps the last Shake-speare play ever written, *The Tempest*, PROSPERO tells his daughter that her mother "was a piece of virtue and she said thou wast my daughter." Even *The Tempest*'s great magus must rely on hearsay when divining MIRANDA's paternity. But for de Vere to reach this state of resolution would require years.

Easter weekend was upon them, and an ailing Burghley suggested via messenger that de Vere take his lodgings at Cecil House. However, de Vere undoubtedly knew that once he entered Burghley's managed care, access to information about the previous seventeen months would be closely screened.

De Vere declined his father-in-law's invitation. This would mark the beginning of a period when de Vere openly questioned his daughter's paternity. His trusted servant Rowland Yorke offered an alternative that provided what must have seemed the most neutral space available on such short notice. Rowland's older brother Edward kept a house in London on Walbrook, near London Stone. As Burghley notes in one of his copious memos:

> I sent letters to him to entreat him to take my house for his lodging, whereof I had no answer. And yet I wrote twice by 2 several messengers. But my son [Thomas] sent me word that he found him [*de Vere*] disposed to keep himself secretly 2 or 3 days in his own lodging.... Then my son told me how [de Vere] did suddenly leave the barge and took a wherry [boat]—and only with Rowland Yorke landed about Yorke's House.

The Monday after Easter, April 23, Burghley wrote a pleading letter to the queen, full of less matter and more art. In this nearly incoherent piece of correspondence, he protested that he and his daughter were being grievously abused and that "in anything that may hereof follow, whereof I may have wrong with dishonesty offered me, I may have Your Majesty's princely favor to seek my just defense for me and mine." Sir Thomas Smith, solicitous of the latest news about his former student, wrote to Burghley two days later. Smith was then in the final stages of throat cancer, and his physical pain was only heightened by the emotional anguish he felt for the family. "I am sure it must very much grieve Your Honor seeing it grieveth me for the love I bear him [de

Vere], because he was brought up in my house.... What counselors and persuaders he hath so to behave himself I cannot tell."

Smith was not the only observer who felt that de Vere was being "persuaded." Burghley later logged in his diary that de Vere "was enticed by certain lewd persons to be a stranger to his wife," while Nathaniel Baxter–the same poet who would later write about being abducted by pirates–later lamented of his former patron:

> Only some think he spent too much in vain,
> That was his fault. But give his honor due;
> Learned he was, just, affable, and plain,
> No traitor but ever gracious and true.
> 'Gainst [the] prince's peace, a plot he never drew.
> But as they be deceived that too much trust
> So trusted he some men that prov'd unjust.

Rowland Yorke, the same unruly servant who had angered Anne in 1573 for barring her from de Vere's private chamber, was the most likely deceiver. If OTHELLO's blindness to the dishonesty of his "honest IAGO" is in any way autobiographical, de Vere and Yorke must have made a pitiful team of verbally poisoned and verbal poisoner. Rowland Yorke takes top honors as the most venal man who ever served the seventeenth earl–a real distinction, considering the Elizabethan rogues and hooligans who at one time or another wore the livery of the blue boar.

Yorke first gained notice on the side of the Catholic rebels in the Northern Uprising of 1569. Forgiven for his treason, three years later he fought with English Protestant forces in the Dutch wars of independence. Lieutenant Yorke (the very rank IAGO aspires to) inspired suggestive rhymes by his colleagues in arms about both his fearlessness on the battlefield and his lascivious conduct with young nuns. The seventeenth-century antiquarian William Camden recalled that Yorke was a "man of a loose and dissolute behavior and desperately audacious, famous in his time amongst the common hacksters and swaggerers as being the first that ... brought into England that bold and dangerous way of foining [*thrusting*] with the rapier in dueling." (IAGO brags that he had often "yerk'd ... [opponents] under the ribs.")

In the Lowlands in 1584, Lieutenant Yorke would try unsuccessfully to betray allied positions to Spain. Two years later he would try again, with astonishing results; he and another commander would sell out the English army for Spanish silver. (IAGO, a name not in any of *Othello*'s sources, may be taken from *Santiago*–St. James, the patron saint of Spain.) The strategic consequences of Yorke's sedition were, in the words of one historian, "dramatic in the extreme."

The Spaniards trusted this rabid bulldog no more than did the English.

Yorke died in 1588, reportedly by Spanish poison. Dutch patriots, still angry at his heartless treachery, would later exhume his body and hang it like a scarecrow.

The above crimes are known, chronicled, and uncontested. However, one likely malfeasance also merits attention: The man who double-crossed his very homeland for a bloodstained purse in 1586 also appears to have played the role of turncoat ten years before. At a time when de Vere's ear was being infected with allegations of his wife's misdeeds, Rowland Yorke's brother Edward was servant to the earl of Leicester. The libeler Charles Arundell–who never lacked for sensational material–in 1584 published a screed accusing the earl of Leicester of manifold crimes against his countrymen, God, and England. One such allegation reads that

> [Leicester] hath ever used to sow and nourish debate and contention between the great lords of England and their wives, in which he always showed himself a good practitioner and very diligent, knowing that according to the Italian proverb, *Nel mare turbato guadagna il pescatore,* in a troubled water the fisher gains most.... The same he attempted between the earl of Oxford and his lady, daughter of the lord treasurer of England, and all for an old grudge he bare to her father the said Lord Treasurer.

Recall that Edward Yorke's house is where de Vere and his dear and trusted servant first stayed upon returning from the Continent. Could the Yorke brothers merely have been agents of Leicester's plans to destroy the house of Cecil?

The evidence in the Shake-speare canon is mixed. Two plays feature duplicitous servants/associates (IAGO in *Othello* and IACHIMO in *Cymbeline*) acting as free and independent agents who drive their respective compatriots (OTHELLO and POSTHUMUS) into rage and jealousy against the compatriots's chaste and wrongly accused wives. These Rowland Yorke-like characters act alone. On the other hand, the jealousy subplot in *Much Ado About Nothing* originates in a conspiracy; *Much Ado*'s mischief is masterminded by DON JOHN, a military commander of the highest station. The historical sources for DON JOHN may include the actual Don John of Austria, but the character also contains more than a hint of the earl of Leicester too. *Much Ado* reveals that de Vere suspected Leicester of being the mastermind behind Yorke's treachery.

One week after returning, a discontented de Vere wrote to his father-in-law. De Vere's letter reads like HAMLET addressing POLONIUS about OPHELIA– if HAMLET had been counseled by IAGO. De Vere writes:

> Urged ... by your letters to satisfy you the sooner, I must let Your Lordship understand thus much. That is until I can better satisfy or advertise

myself of some mislikes, I am not determined as touching my wife to accompany her. What they are because some are not to be spoken of or
written upon as imperfections, I will not deal withal. Some that otherwise discontent me I will not blaze or publish until it please me. And last
of all I mean not to weary my life anymore with such troubles and mo-
lestations as I have endured nor will I, to please Your Lordship only, discontent myself....

This might have been done through private conference before and
had not needed to have been the fable of the world if you would have
had the patience to have understood me. But I do not know by what or
whose advice it was to run that course so contrary to my will or meaning—
which made her disgraced, the world raised suspicions openly that with
private conference might have been more silently handled, and hath
given me more greater cause to mislike.

The voice is firm and eloquent; the man, shaken and offended. It was one
thing to feel a private and personal sense of embarrassment at the countess of
Oxford giving birth to, for all de Vere could know, a bastard. De Vere, who
had himself been accused of bastardy, would have felt this shame acutely.
Such blots on the family, if properly stage-managed, could be handled with
minimal difficulties. Problems of doubtful legitimacy are hardly unheard of in
any aristocratic culture. However, as de Vere puts it, Burghley had made this
crisis "the fable of the world." And that was the action that had gone beyond
the pale.

The truth is that both parties had handled the imbroglio badly. Burghley
had insisted on an immediate, public acknowledgment of Anne's virtue and
Elizabeth de Vere's paternity. De Vere had refused to give it. Both men were
in crisis. Burghley was ill and anxious about his daughter's position. De Vere
was worn out by traveling and unnerved by his close escape from death. Neither Burghley nor de Vere had ever got on with the other, appreciated the
other's strengths, or been able to abide the other's failings. This moment was
the beginning of a decisive change in de Vere's life and fortunes.

Two days after sending the above letter, de Vere met Burghley face-to-
face. In a memo preserved for posterity, Burghley recorded the charges leveled at him. De Vere accused his father-in-law of corresponding directly with
de Vere's servants when they were in Italy, presumably to obtain clandestine
intelligence of their master's activities and whereabouts. He claimed Burghley
had at times stranded him without sufficient money and that Burghley had
shown his son-in-law's letter, presumably the one quoted above, to the queen
"of set purpose to bring him into Her Majesty's indignation." Finally, de Vere
charged Lady Burghley with trying to foment an internal civil war at Wivenhoe and furthermore of wishing de Vere dead.

Contrary to the accusation of tightfistedness, Burghley replies in defense that he'd advanced de Vere £2,700 "by the credit of the Lord Treasurer when the earl's money could not be had." Other points he does not refute, such as his alleged reading of de Vere's letter to the queen. Burghley also jots down notes to himself that suggest talking points for a confrontational conversation. "Mislikings—yea, hatreds—hath amongst many been purified in time," the old counselor writes. "[*Blank*] ought to content all his friends, except there be any that regard some present or future profit more than his own honor," reads one incomplete thought. The platitude-dispensing POLONIUS shines through. One of Burghley's chestnuts even appears to have registered with his son-in-law, although not exactly in the way the old Lord Treasurer had intended. "The greatest possession that any man can have," Burghley notes, "is honor, good name, good will of many and of the best sort." This was one bromide that did not find its way to POLONIUS's mouth. Instead, it is uttered by one of the utmost villains in all of Shake-speare.

> IAGO Good name in man and woman, dear my lord,
>   Is the immediate jewel of their souls.
>   Who steals my purse steals trash, 'tis something, nothing;
>   'Twas mine, 'tis his, and has been slave to thousands;
>   But he that filches from me my good name
>   Robs me of that which not enriches him,
>   And makes me poor indeed.

For such an autobiographical artist as the earl of Oxford, extreme agony and disturbance in life ultimately provided profound inspiration. The litany detailed over the past chapter and a half represents just a sampling of the many Shake-spearean resonances to be found in the most exhaustively chronicled twelve-month period in de Vere's life, from de Vere's arrival in Venice in the late spring of 1575 to his tumultuous return to London in the late spring of 1576.

De Vere would spend the rest of his life writing about the dramatic and traumatic events of his twenty-sixth year. It's even possible to define a "spirit of '76" subcategory within the larger Shake-speare canon, embodying portions of *The Comedy of Errors, Two Gentlemen of Verona, The Merchant of Venice, The Merry Wives of Windsor, Much Ado About Nothing, Twelfth Night, All's Well That Ends Well, Measure for Measure, Hamlet, Othello, Pericles, Cymbeline, The Winter's Tale,* and *The Rape of Lucrece.* Setting aside the Shake-speare English history plays, de Vere's twenty-sixth year of life enters into slightly less than half of the canonical works of Shake-speare.

De Vere's doubts were, in fact, founded in more than mere whims and suspicions. A recently discovered March 1575 letter from the queen's physician, Richard Master, to Burghley records that a distraught Anne had tried unsuccessfully to get the doctor to perform an abortion on her a week after her husband's departure for Italy.

> My lady [of Oxford] being here at Shrovetide [February 12–15, 1575] had dealt with me to prepare some medicines *ad menses promotiones* [to cause the menses to resume]. But I counseled her to stay awhile. Her Majesty asked me how the young lady did bear the matter. I answered that she kept it secret 4 or 5 days from all persons and that her face was much fallen and thin, with little color–and that when she was comforted and counseled to be gladsome and rejoice, she would cry, "Alas, alas! How should I rejoice, seeing he that should rejoice with me is not here, and to say truth, [I] stand in doubt whether he pass [judgment] upon me and it [*the pregnancy*] or not."

Four months into her pregnancy at the time she sought out Dr. Master, Anne was not ignorant of her condition. (If she thought her periods had ceased for a reason other than pregnancy, why would she have made the up-roar she did when Dr. Master counseled her to "stay awhile"?) When the doctor notes that she requested an emmenagogue–an agent to introduce menstruation–he is euphemistically dancing around the fact that Anne wanted him to concoct one or more abortifacients. Three possibilities thus emerge: Either de Vere was the father and Anne was convinced he wouldn't believe it, or she wanted an annulment of their marriage just as much as he evidently did, or de Vere's suspicions were correct.

Anne's private conference with Dr. Master was probably at least part of the incendiary information whispered into de Vere's ear in Paris that caused him to return home in such a huff. The author would mull over his wife's conclave with Dr. Master for years. De Vere's anxiety over its causes and consequences surfaces in *Hamlet.*

OPHELIA, in her distracted state, is often found singing bawdy songs and reciting tales of copulation. ("Young men will do't if they come to't;/By Cock they are to blame.") HAMLET's feigned madness includes a confrontation with OPHELIA's father containing the immortal lines

> HAMLET For if the sun breed maggots in a dead dog, being a good
> kissing carrion–Have you a daughter?... Let her not walk i' th' sun.
> Conception is a blessing, but as your daughter may conceive, friend,
> look to 't.

OPHELIA ultimately drowns beneath a white willow tree–whose flowers were a known abortifacient. Before meeting her watery fate, she distributes flowers and herbs to the Danish courtiers. At least four of OPHELIA's flowers were used as antifertility drugs in the sixteenth century: rosemary, violets, fennel, and rue. Rue was the most powerful abortifacient listed in contemporary herbal medicinal literature. OPHELIA gives rue to QUEEN GERTRUDE but also keeps some for herself.

> OPHELIA [*to GERTRUDE*] There's rue for you, and here's some for me.
> We may call it herb of grace a' Sundays. You may wear your rue with
> a difference.

Difference was a heraldic term, according to the *Oxford English Dictionary,* "used to distinguish a junior member or branch of a family from the chief line." For instance, the child of an earl would wear a mark of difference on his or her coat of arms. Wearing one's rue with a difference, on a symbolic level, could be read as a heraldic hint at an attempted abortion.

De Vere no longer knew whom he could trust. In *Cymbeline,* once the young husband POSTHUMUS becomes convinced of his wife's supposed infidelity, his next soliloquy begins by calling to mind "that most venerable man which I did call my father." De Vere's distant father, Earl John, probably did serve as a security blanket in the author's imagination—as that deified mental construction KING HAMLET is to PRINCE HAMLET.

But in the land of the living, de Vere appears to have rested his faith in a most dishonest man.

Rowland Yorke remains not only the likely immediate instigator of de Vere's crisis but also—if rumors of de Vere's bisexuality are to be believed—a possible channel for de Vere's sexual frustrations. As de Vere's marriage withered and shriveled, Yorke remained at his master's side. It is possible that some closer relationship, be it sexually charged or sexually sublimated, existed between the two men. Numerous modern scholars find OTHELLO and IAGO's deadly dance of lies and misplaced trust resonating with homosexual overtones.

Throughout the summer of 1576, de Vere continued to feud with his in-laws and live apart from his wife. Burghley continued scratching out memos and notes, which he retained in his family archives. Burghley reported that de Vere's unkindnesses seemed "grounded upon untrue reports of others," while these "same untruths are still continued in secret reports to others." The queen had been pleading with de Vere to reach a swift and peaceful resolution to a dispute that was beginning to consume the attentions of her chief advisor. On July 13, de Vere wrote another letter to Burghley from his "lodging at Charing Cross," in Westminster. Yorke House, near Charing Cross, appears to have been where de Vere now called home.

De Vere noted a verbal agreement he'd struck with Burghley to keep

Anne away from him for now and for her father not to press their case. But, de Vere notes, he'd learned that the day after making this deal, Burghley was about to break it. As in the letter from three months before, de Vere continues to sound the refrain of the abandoned child: I'm looking out for number one now. In de Vere's words:

> Now I understand that Your Lordship means this day to bring [Anne] to the court, and that you mean afterward to prosecute the cause with further hope. Now if Your Lordship shall do so, then shall you take more in hand than I have or can promise you. For always I have and will still prefer mine own content before others, and observing that wherein I may temper or moderate for your sake, I will do most willingly. Wherefore I shall desire Your Lordship not to take advantage of my promise till you have given me some honorable assurance by letter or word of your performance of the condition—which being observed, I could yield, as it is my duty, to Her Majesty's request and bear with your fatherly desire towards her. Otherwise, all that is done can stand to none effect.

The terms are now starker. De Vere had set forth his bottom line: "Always I have and will still prefer mine own content before others." Also, he would only compromise if the queen ordered him to. Burghley commanded untold political power over his son-in-law, but he could not command de Vere's actions.

De Vere may well have recognized that, in a court where stories commanded the queen's attention and the queen commanded ultimate power, de Vere's blossoming talent was his own road to power. As HAMLET warns POLONIUS:

> Good my lord, will you see the players well bestow'd? Do you hear, let them be well us'd, for they are the abstract and brief chronicles of the time. After your death you were better have a bad epitaph than their ill report while you live.

As de Vere lamented the life he had returned to, his laments of years past had only just appeared in print. The work of the late Richard Edwards, the director and choirmaster whom de Vere had met during his youth, had finally been issued. Edwards's 1576 verse anthology *The Paradise of Dainty Devices* was a best seller. It would go through at least eight editions into the seventeenth century. "E.O." was now a published lyricist, with eight song lyrics in *Paradise;* one was given two different musical settings.

All but two of de Vere's verses in *The Paradise* belonged to the genre known as the Complaint—a form he would ultimately master in the Shakespeare poem *A Lover's Complaint.*

Here is one early experiment in the form:

Not Attaining to His Desire, He Complaineth

I am not as I seem to be,
Nor when I smile, I am not glad.
A thrall, although you count me free,
I, most in mirth, most pensive sad.
I smile to shade my bitter spite
As Hannibal that saw in sight
His country soil with Carthage town
By Roman force, defaced down.

And Caesar that presented was
With noble Pompey's princely head,
As 'twere some judge to rule the case
A flood of tears he seemed to shed.
Although in deed, it sprung of joy,
Yet others thought it was annoy.
Thus contraries be used I find
Of wise to cloak the covert mind.

Aye, Hannibal, that smiles for grief,
And let you Caesar's tears suffice.
The one that laughs at his mischief,
The other all for joy that cries.
I smile to see me scorned so;
You weep for joy to see me woe.
And I a heart by love slain dead
Present in place of Pompey's head.

O cruel hap and hard estate
That forceth me to love my foe.
Accursed be so foul a fate,
My choice for to profix it so.
So long to fight with secret sore
And find no secret salve therefore.
Some purge their pain by plaint I find
But I in vain do breathe my wind.
          Finis. E.O.

De Vere wrote this poem when he was still a teenager; Richard Edwards had died in 1566, ten years before his *Paradise of Dainty Devices* was finally published. De Vere's teenaged soliloquy quarrels with fate, dissembles behind a courtly countenance, loves out of its proper sphere, and conspires with heartrending frustration. In his sometimes halting verse–lines are still padded with filler like "saw in sight"–the teenager had nevertheless set down the first hints of character sketches that would later mature into OTHELLO (comparing himself to a North African hero who "smile[s] to shade my bitter spite"), HAMLET and PRINCE HAL ("I am not as I seem to be"), BERTRAM ("Cruel hap . . . that forceth me to love my foe"), and ROMEO ("So long to fight with secret sore/And find no secret salve therefore").

When he first saw *The Paradise of Dainty Devices* in the bookstalls outside St. Paul's Cathedral sometime in 1576, de Vere probably shook his head at the sixteenth-year-old kid who had thought he knew adversity. The "howling hounds of hell"–to use another "E.O." clunker from *Paradise*–were now baying like never before. But this time he needed a medium more complex than song lyrics to, as the teenaged earl had put it, "cloak the covert mind."

Taking his cue from what he had witnessed in Venice and Siena, de Vere would begin to stage his complaints in the form of commedia dell'arte, transformed and translated for English audiences.

On a field north of the Bishopsgate entrance to the City of London, a team of entrepreneurs were just opening the first custom-built playhouse in England. Two brothers-in-law named James Burbage and John Brayne had erected an open-air building they called simply The Theatre. A men's troupe sponsored by the earl of Leicester took over The Theatre and began staging works for public audiences–which meant that propaganda favoring Leicester would be well represented at Elizabeth's play-loving court come Christmastime.

As in Venice, the season from the day after Christmas to Shrove Tuesday (Mardi Gras) was the high point of the Elizabethan theatrical calendar, when the troupes that had been conducting staged rehearsals all year would entertain Her Majesty at court. On the night of December 30, 1576, The Earl of Leicester's Men presented an interlude for the queen and the highest-ranking peers in England called *The History of the Collier*. In Elizabethan slang, *collier* meant "cheat" or "dirty trickster," so through this play Leicester was probably grilling his lifelong rival, Lord Burghley.

The play does not survive–indeed, most plays that were performed at Queen Elizabeth's court are now supposedly lost. All that remains is a record in the queen's royal payment books of the title of the play performed, the date and place where it was enacted, and the name of the troupe that played it. Yet, there may be more to a few of these records than first meets the eye. It is the contention of this book that de Vere wrote some of these "lost" courtly interludes. Then, during the 1590s and early 1600s, he–probably with the assistance and input of others in his immediate circle of family, secretaries, and friends–rewrote these plays for the public stage. These revised texts constitute the central part of what is today called the Shake-speare canon.

Much of Shake-speare is thus a palimpsest, popular dramas refashioned from works that were originally written for an elite audience in the 1570s and '80s.

The dramatic troupe that de Vere enjoyed closest access to is the children's company of choirboys from London's St. Paul's Cathedral. Under the supervision and direction of Sebastian Westcote, Paul's Boys had staged plays for the court since 1552, when Elizabeth was still a princess. And during the court revels season of 1575–76, for the first time in more than a decade, Westcote had the privilege of presenting multiple entertainments for the queen.

On the evening of New Year's Day, Westcote led his troupe in a play titled *A Historie of Error.* Here, one suspects, is an early prototype of Shakespeare's *The Comedy of Errors.* As the literary historian Allison Gaw observed, *The Comedy of Errors* "is certainly a rewriting of pre-Shakespearean material, which may, with fair assurance, be identified with *A Historie of Error* played before the queen at Hampton Court by the Children of Paul's on January 1, 1577."

Today, it is hard to imagine preteen actors bringing to life stage productions of professional quality. Yet, paradoxically, where modern society might see child actors as a burden that would severely inhibit a playwright's expressiveness, Elizabethan children's troupes enjoyed liberties that were simply unavailable to adult players.

Elizabethan authors had to carefully disguise their criticism of contemporary events or authority figures for fear of censure, imprisonment, or worse. One of the simplest ways to present controversial material was to use child actors. From the mouths of babes, some otherwise scandalous words enjoyed the protective cloak of presumed youthful innocence. An adult calling the queen of England a harlot or the Lord Treasurer a backstabbing Janus could be thrown in jail. But depending on the craftiness of the playwright, a child could say the same thing in front of the entire court and be applauded. "Children and fools speak truth" was a popular bromide of the time. Three plays enacted by Elizabethan children's companies cited this very proverb—reminding the audience the special license granted to a dramatist writing for boys.

In the case of *A History of Error,* de Vere was probably inviting controversy by dramatizing his own imbroglio with the house of Cecil. The crux of *The Comedy* (and, one suspects, *History*) *of Errors* is marriage into a powerful family—the chief "error" of the title—that never should have been. De Vere the misunderstood husband becomes ANTIPHOLUS OF EPHESUS, married to a "fond fool" of an impatient wife, ADRIANA.

The twist that turns this melodrama into comedy is that ANTIPHOLUS has a twin brother, whom he doesn't know exists. The freewheeling ANTIPHOLUS

OF SYRACUSE falls in love with ADRIANA's placid and idealized sister, LUCIANA. Mix-ups soon follow, leading down the path to pure farce. Almost every element of *The Comedy of Errors* plot is stolen from commedia dell'arte scenarios of mistaken identity. But, psychologically, the conceit is entirely de Vere's own. The author has performed an experiment he would repeat many times throughout his career: He has splintered himself into more than one character. *The Comedy of Errors'* two couples are, in fact, the author's and his wife's egos cut in half. (*LUCIANA* roughly translates to "the light one" and *ADRIANA* "the dark one": Anne Cecil as de Vere first saw her and as she had become.)

A journey at sea, like the one de Vere had taken starting in his twenty-fifth year, frames *The Comedy of Errors*. Not coincidentally, the brothers ANTIPHOLI are also twenty-five.

Errors was the author's first attempt at broaching the topic of his at times pathological behavior toward his wife and her family. It's comedy in denial, oblivious to its own predispositions; an appropriate subtitle would be *What, Me Jealous?* The play also represents de Vere's first staged attempt to cauterize and suture his own emotional wounds.

The evening of New Year's Day 1577 may have marked the first time Elizabeth truly recognized the talents of her temperamental courtier. If *History* is *Comedy*, it was also the first time Shake-speare got away onstage with what other playwrights could only dream of. De Vere held his satirical license aloft when he portrayed Queen Elizabeth as the fat kitchen wench NELL. Courtly flatterers often personified the queen as a goddess, sometimes going so far as to portray Her Majesty as England itself; NELL is jokingly anatomized as a map of England and its dominions.

ANTIPHOLUS OF SYRACUSE What's her name?
DROMIO OF SYRACUSE Nell, sir; but her name and three quarters, that's an "El" and three quarters [*syllables*], will not measure her from hip to hip.
ANT. In what part of her body stands Ireland?
DRO. Marry, sir, in her buttocks, I found it out by the bogs.
ANT. Where Scotland?
DRO. I found it by the barrenness, hard in the palm of the hand.
ANT. Where France?
DRO. In her forehead, arm'd and reverted, making war against her heir. . . .
ANT. Where stood Belgia, the Netherlands?
DRO. O, sir, I did not look so low.

A year in Italy had transformed de Vere, twenty-six-year-old chronic pain in the ass, into a chronic pain in the ass with an astonishing capacity for court comedy.

At Whitehall Palace on Shrove Tuesday (February 19), Westcote's boys capped the season with an encore performance for the court. The palace's 4,500-square-foot Great Hall was to be illuminated one last time during the 1576–77 theatrical season. The chandeliers bearing dozens of candles hung overhead, casting their beams both downward onto the stage and upward into the banqueting hall's great "marble heaven." The queen's account books list the title of Westcote's masque as *The History of Titus and Gisippus*, an ancient story of friendship. It is also known to be one of two principal source texts for Shake-speare's *Two Gentlemen of Verona*.

Two Gentlemen features two grooms readily recognized as alter egos of the author. It also features the daughter of the most powerful man in the land, a representation of de Vere's wife Anne. *Two Gentlemen* splits the author's ego down the middle and stages his marital strife as a love triangle plot borrowed from the commedia dell'arte.

Two Gentlemen is ostensibly a tale of courtly love and courtly friendship set at odds. The titular gentlemen, PROTEUS and VALENTINE, are close friends whose amorous interests begin to overlap. Scholarly commentary on this early Shake-speare play focuses primarily on the codes of Renaissance friendship and courtly love. However, the affair most curiously chronicled in *Two Gentlemen* involves neither woman nor man. Instead, the most unlikely love affair in the play is with the pen. PROTEUS and VALENTINE are each at their most virile and impressive as writers. The otherwise emasculated VALENTINE, for instance, briefly comes into his own when his beloved (SILVIA) asks him to compose verses. In so doing, VALENTINE makes a discovery: An author writes not for his lover's nor his friend's nor even his sovereign's contentment. He writes for himself.

> VALENTINE Please you, I'll write Your Ladyship another.
> SILVIA And when it's writ, for my sake read it over,
>   And if it please you, so; if not, why, so.
> VALENTINE If it please me, madam? What then?
> SILVIA Why, if it please you, take it for your labor;
>   And so good-morrow, servant.

VALENTINE's page, SPEED, watches this exchange and marks how fond a folly he has just witnessed. "O excellent device, was there ever heard a better," he asks, "That my master, being scribe, to himself should write the letter?"

Since the summer of 1577, de Vere's younger sister Mary had been on her own quest for self-definition. With her father now dead, the immediate decision of whom she would wed lay in the hands of her big brother. (The queen's consent was ultimately needed for any aristocratic marriage.) But Mary, as strong willed as her brother, had wedding plans of her own.

Mary had been advocating for a husband that neither her family nor her proposed husband's family nor the queen favored. Peregrine Bertie, later Lord Willoughby, was twenty-three years old, a well-known soldier and swashbuckler who did mostly as he pleased and had little time or patience for courtly etiquette. Courtiers to him were mere "reptilia," as he liked to call them. Bertie once observed that he was about as comfortable in their presence as a lion on a feather bed.

On the other hand, when it came to defending his honor, Bertie obeyed the courtier's rulebook to the letter. This tightly wound ball of temperament did not tolerate affronts from anyone short of royalty. In 1570, Bertie got into a heated tiff with the earl of Kent, stating, "I must prepare a rough wedge for a rough knot, for I cannot perceive . . . that many others have regard to small fire-sparks until they grow out into dangerous flames." In later years, during a military expedition to the Lowlands, a gout-stricken Bertie received a challenge from a Catholic lord. "Though he was lame of his hands and his feet," writes one chronicler, "yet [Bertie] would meet him with a rapier in his teeth"!

Bertie had taken a shine to Mary de Vere sometime during the first half of 1577. And the twenty-three-year-old woman returned her pugnacious paramour's affections. Known for her sharp tongue, Mary was a headstrong woman whose heart pumped choler, the same fiery stuff that ran through the veins of her proud brother.

But the earl of Oxford didn't like Bertie. And Bertie's mother, the duchess of Suffolk, disliked both Mary and her brother. The previous year there had been a rumored attempt to betrothe Mary to one of her brother's acquaintances (Gerald Fitzgerald, Lord Garrat), and on the other side of the aisle, the antipapist duchess of Suffolk had tried to arrange for her son to marry a nice girl from a stable Protestant family. But neither Mary nor her beau, Peregrine, would brook a match other than their own.

The mother of the (would-be) groom was distraught. She wrote two letters to Lord Burghley during the summer of 1577 expressing her anguish. In the first, dated July 2, she noted that she'd heard how de Vere had "used you [*Burghley*] and your daughter so evil that I could not require you to deal in it." The duchess also noted:

It is very true that my wise son has gone very far with my lady Mary Vere, I fear too far to turn. I must say to you in counsel what I have said to her plainly, that I had rather he had matched in any other place. . . . If she should prove like her brother, if an empire follows her [*even with a tremendous dowry*], I should be sorry to match so. She said that she could not rule her brother's tongue nor help the rest of his faults. . . . And seeing

that it was so far forth between my son and her, she deserved my goodwill and asked no more.

One can imagine Mary de Vere's frustration with her older brother. Bertie's
bullheadedness was matched only by the earl of Oxford's own temperamental streak. Try as she might, Mary had no way to "rule her brother's tongue."

All available indicators would seem to doom this unlikely match. Bertie
wrote a letter to Mary observing "how uncourteously I am dealt with by my
lord your brother, who, as I hear, bandeth against me and sweareth my death,
which I fear not, nor force not, but lest his displeasure withdraw your affections from me." Thankfully, de Vere and Bertie never took their quarrels beyond exchanging threats and puffing their chests. Throughout the autumn,
no matter what anyone else said or did, the Bertie–Vere marriage match
inched forward.

On October 28, amid Mary's nuptial negotiations, de Vere attended the
wedding of the duke of Norfolk's youngest son, William Howard, at the
Howard family property of Audley End in Essex. The adolescent Howard,
not even fourteen, had been promised to his child bride since just before Norfolk's beheading–an awkward arrangement all too familiar to de Vere. Since
the trauma of Norfolk's execution, de Vere probably cared more about the
betterment of Norfolk's fatherless heirs than he did about the baby Elizabeth
de Vere, an infant of dubious legitimacy.

Betterment, however, is not what William Howard was in for. The autumn air cooled a wedding party already chilled by the prospect of a child
bride, Elizabeth Dacre, approaching the altar without an inheritance. (Both
the Dacre and the Howard clans would squander many years fighting over
who would get what properties and titles.) The groom's eldest brother was
married to the bride's elder sister, so the coming years of litigious feuds would
be burdened by the squabbling of two pairs of siblings. As de Vere wished the
juvenile couple all the happiness that Norfolk would have wanted for his
youngest boy, he must also have said a little prayer for these innocent children who knew not what kind of whirlwinds they were summoning.

The trials of three orphaned sons, the eldest and youngest of whom
marry into the same family, would become the main plot of *As You Like It*–a
play that was probably finalized in 1600 when a battered William Howard finally emerged from behind an accumulated mountain of affidavits. Twenty-
three years after exchanging rings with his spouse, Will Howard in 1600
finally won the inheritance that should have transferred to him and his wife
on their wedding night. De Vere witnessed the whole soap opera, beginning
with the fateful "I do" on that October afternoon in 1577.

Another problematic wedding was probably the last thing de Vere wanted
to concern himself with. Both he and the queen refused to make a decision
about Mary and Peregrine's fate, as reflected in a November 1577 letter to the

earl of Rutland, which notes that "the marriage of the Lady Mary Vere is deferred until after Christmas, for as yet neither has Her Majesty given license
nor has the earl of Oxford wholly assented thereto." The 1577–78 revels season at court, for which most of the records are now lost, began with no resolution to either the earl of Oxford's troubled marriage or his sister's troubling
marriage proposal.

Moreover, those laying impediments to Mary and Peregrine's wedding
were now laying other plots. Peregrine's mother, a willful matriarch who was
as persevering as her son was stubborn, had by December hatched a plan to
intervene in the domestic dispute between Anne Cecil de Vere and her estranged husband. The duchess's method was both devious and simple. She
sought simply to bring the infant Elizabeth de Vere in plain view of the child's
erstwhile father. "I will bring in the child as though it were some other child
of my friend's, and we shall see how nature will work in him to like [her]–and
[we'll] tell him it is his own after," the duchess wrote to Lord Burghley. The
busybody duchess added, recognizing the mercurial nature of her prey, "I
would wish speed that [de Vere] might be taken in his good mood. I thank
God I am at this present in his good favor."

However, the duchess did not find her subject in his good mood. Her appeal to pathos did nothing to weaken de Vere's conviction that the infant
was a bastard. It was only years later, after the duchess was dead and gone
(and de Vere and Peregrine were fast friends), that the author paid homage
to the iron-willed wench who dared stand up to him and call him the megalomaniac he was. PAULINA in *The Winter's Tale*–a character found in none of
The Winter's Tale's sources–performs precisely the same futile errand that Peregrine Bertie's mother played in de Vere's life in December of 1577. PAULINA
presents LEONTES with his own daughter, in the face of his vicious and deadly
threats. And yet, with a doggedness characteristic of the Bertie family, PAULINA
refuses to acknowledge LEONTES's legitimacy as a ruler, as a husband, or even
as a sane individual.

> PAULINA I'll not call you tyrant;
>   But this most cruel usage of your queen
>   (Not able to produce more accusation
>   Than your own weak-hing'd fancy) something savors
>   Of tyranny, and will ignoble make you,
>   Yea, scandalous to the world.

De Vere was, when he ultimately wrote *The Winter's Tale*, clearly impressed by
this woman who had had no right to do what she did–but did it anyway simply because it was the right thing to do. Katherine (Bertie) Willoughby, dowager duchess of Suffolk, survives through the ages in *The Winter's Tale*'s PAULINA,
a character who, in the words of one critic, "is one of the rare women in

Elizabethan drama who actively defies the male authority and, in the world of romance at least, is allowed to survive."

The fall and winter of 1577 was an ominous time for a man to wed or to contend with a (seemingly) unfaithful wife. Astrologically hypersensitive as a society, most Elizabethans saw dire consequences in the comet that blazed across the sky from November through January 1578. Even the most careful and scientific observations of the comet, by a colleague of Johannes Kepler in Germany, still treated it as a "new and horrible prodigy" whose presence in the sky forecast great and bloody conflicts for the peoples of Earth.

So when Peregrine Bertie and Mary de Vere finally did win the battle of wills–they wed sometime between Christmas of 1577 and March of 1578–de Vere must have marveled at how prophetically the celestial fires above reflected the terrestrial conflagrations below. In coming to friendly terms with this bullish family that were now his in-laws, de Vere apparently began plotting a comedy that recounted the wooing and wedding of these two obstinate and most unlikely lovers. Peregrine Bertie became the soldier PETRUCHIO, while, probably in homage to Peregrine's equally shrewish mother, Mary de Vere became KATHARINA (KATE). And that same comet that shone on the couple's fiery courtship makes its own cameo appearance:

> PETRUCHIO Gentles, methinks you frown,
>   And wherefore gaze this goodly company,
>   As if they saw some wondrous monument,
>   Some comet or unusual prodigy?

The play is, of course, *The Taming of the Shrew*. Its first recorded performance in its Shake-spearean form was in London in June 1594. But this five-act comedy probably originated as a comedic masque at court at a time when the memory of this disputatious duo's rocky courtship was still fresh in everyone's minds.

The numerous parallels between de Vere's sister and brother-in-law and *The Taming of the Shrew*'s infamous couple leave little room for doubt as to the play's original biographical source. PETRUCHIO is a swashbuckler who proudly recounts how he has "in a pitched battle heard loud alarums, neighing steeds, and trumpets' clang" His florid style of speech, like Peregrine's, is "extempore, from my mother-wit." PETRUCHIO is a superlative swordsman–a man who seizes his bride and tells her he can shield her "against a million." Like Peregrine, PETRUCHIO "tells you flatly what his mind is" and disdains all ceremoniousness: *Shrew*'s wild-eyed groom abruptly departs before his own wedding reception begins, and when he and KATE attend her sister's wedding, it is only in "honest mean habiliments." Both Peregrine's and PETRUCHIO's weddings take place in a drunken haze: Five hundred gallons of wine flowed at Peregrine's nuptial bacchanals. PETRUCHIO debases the communion wine by proposing a toast before he partakes—a sacrilege one might expect of the bull-in-a-china-shop Peregrine and a zealously Protestant family like the Berties. And both Peregrine and PETRUCHIO rule their retainers with an iron fist.

Like her brother, Mary was known for her quick temper and harsh tongue. As PETRUCHIO says of KATE, so might Peregrine have said of his bride: "I am as peremptory as she proud minded. And where two raging fires meet together, they do consume the thing that feeds their fury." In a letter to the earl of Leicester, Peregrine's mother complains of her great grief at her son's "unlucky choice of a fair lady [foreign] to full manners." Mary, she claims, fumed that the duchess was out to kill her! These were, in the duchess's words, "wicked and most malicious slanders"—and since nothing ever became of these supposed plots, history sides with the duchess.

The newlyweds' household proved as much a tinderbox as KATE and PETRUCHIO's bridal suite. Soon after Peregrine and Mary's nuptials, Anne Cecil's brother Thomas wrote of the connubial pyrotechnics he had witnessed during a recent visit. Peregrine's mother, he said, had visited the couple "to appease certain unkindness, grown between her son and his wife." The writer gives no specifics to the nature of the couple's quarrel, but he does venture to predict the outcome: "I think my lady Mary will be beaten with the rod which heretofore she prepared for others." A more succinct plot summary of *The Taming of the Shrew* one could not hope to find. However, as with the resolution of *The Shrew*, "the early differences between the young couple were soon adjusted," one historian writes, "and [Mary] proved a most loyal, capable wife."

Mary and Peregrine's exploits are further staged to great comic effect in *Twelfth Night*. In fact, one can think of *Twelfth Night*'s SIR TOBY BELCH and his mate MARIA as PETRUCHIO and his "tamed" KATE a few years into their marriage. In MARIA's first scene onstage, she is greeted, "Bless you, fair shrew." The similarities are not merely nominal: like MARIA, lady-in-waiting to the unmarried but romantically entangled OLIVIA, Mary was a lady-in-waiting to Queen Elizabeth. Like both Mary and the "tamed" KATE, *Twelfth Night*'s MARIA is ultimately loyal to her man, inspiring BELCH to boast, "She's a beagle true bred and one that adores me."

SIR TOBY BELCH is a mischief-making, dueling, drinking, quarrelsome swordsman—an exaggeration of Peregrine Bertie's persona at court, but not by much. And Bertie's close friendship with Sir Philip Sidney is hilariously spoofed in BELCH and SIR ANDREW AGUECHEEK's bumbling and roistering camaraderie. The author portrays Sidney/AGUECHEEK considerably less sympathetically than he does Bertie/BELCH. AGUECHEEK feigns sophistication but can scarcely speak without malapropisms. BELCH gets into two swordfights—both of which are extensions of a duel that the cowardly AGUECHEEK has shirked. TOBY BELCH is a superior scholar, AGUECHEEK a shallow and dense carpet knight; BELCH is a cunning trickster, AGUECHEEK a "clodpole."

De Vere's new brother-in-law had become a prime source of comic inspiration. But Peregrine Bertie's most important role in de Vere's life was yet to come. Bertie would, in only a couple of years, serve as his brother-in-law's eyes and ears in a famous foreign court, on an honored assignment of the sort that would cause PETRUCHIO to stand at attention and BELCH to sober up–at least long enough to greet a new king before running off and getting drunk with him.

By the time of his twenty-eighth birthday, in April 1578, Edward de Vere was falling out of love with court life and intrigues. Perhaps the tempests that beset his marriage had pelted him too long. Perhaps the Italian Renaissance had awakened him to a new world of art and culture that the boorish, porridge-sopping homebodies at Elizabeth's court did not appreciate. Perhaps he just wanted to try his hand at something beyond royal flattery, the common currency of the Elizabethan courtier. The previous December, Peregrine Bertie's mother (now part of de Vere's extended family), had written in a letter to Lord Burghley that she'd learned "[de Vere] is about to buy a house here in London about Watling Street, and not to continue a courtier as he hath done."

Watling Street was a commercial thoroughfare in the center of London, home to numerous woolen clothes retailers ("drapers"). Many printers and publishers also hailed from this neighborhood, because St. Paul's Churchyard, the biggest bookselling area in London, was nearby. A couple of blocks to the northeast stood the "Long Shop" near the church of St. Mildred in the Poultry, where a young printer's assistant named Anthony Munday was learning his trade. Munday had signed on in 1576 for an eight-year-long apprenticeship; soon, however, Munday would be working for a literary earl with a flair for the dramatic.

Although de Vere's attendance on the queen and her "reptilia" may indeed have been waning at the time, de Vere the classical courtier–the liberal-minded man of munificence as defined by Castiglione–was well and thriving. Like TIMON OF ATHENS before his liquid assets ran dry, de Vere still understood no form of fiscal restraint. Increasing numbers of rogues and worthies swarmed around him, and de Vere funded them all with abandon. Perhaps the earl's single biggest financial venture came during this period.

At the time, there was an ongoing search for the Northwest Passage to the Pacific, an ice-free trade route to India and China. If such a thing had actually existed, investing in its exploration would have yielded great financial returns. It would also have been a geopolitical coup for England, as Spanish- and Portuguese-controlled territories in South America and Africa made southern passages to the Orient treacherous for English ships. De Vere performed his courtly role as venture investor in expeditions that, ideally, could enrich both his purse and England's economic and colonial future.

The expeditions did neither.

In March of 1577, Elizabeth appointed the merchant Michael Lok governor for life of a new corporation, the Cathay Company. Two months later Lok sent his admiral, Martin Frobisher, with three ships into the Meta Incognita (the unknown boundary), which Frobisher's team had initially explored the year before. The Meta Incognita is today in northeastern Canada, near the inlet to Hudson's Bay.

Frobisher's second expedition, in which de Vere did not invest, returned to English shores in September 1577 with two hundred tons of ore, which Lok thought contained gold. (It was only pyrite, fool's gold.) Frobisher's men had also captured two adult Eskimos and one infant and had brought them back to England to show to the queen. These North American aborigines did not survive long in London. But even after their death, their cadavers evidently continued to fascinate the English aborigines. In *The Tempest,* the Shake-speare play most concerned with the New World and the people in it, the clown TRINCULO marvels at Englishmen who "will not give a doit [*one eighth of a penny*] to relieve a lame beggar, [but] they will lay out ten to see a dead Indian."

In 1578, lured by the promise of both gold and golden waterways to the Pacific, investors lined up to finance another expedition to the northwest. With a mission plan that included establishing a base camp to continue mining and searching for an Oriental passage, Frobisher pitched an ambitious itinerary that appealed to the adventurer in de Vere. De Vere wrote a memo in fluent legalese to the team four days before they were to set sail.

> After my very hearty commendations understanding of the wise proceeding and orderly dealing for the containing of the voyage for the discovery of Cathay by the Northwest, which this bearer, my friend Mr. Frobisher, hath already very honorably attempted, and is now eftsoons to be employed for the better achieving thereof, and the rather induced as well for the great liking Her Majesty hath to have the same passage discovered, as also for the special good favor I bear Mr. Frobisher, to offer unto you to be an adventurer therein for the sum of £1,000 or more, if you like to admit thereof, which sum or sums upon your certificate of admittance, I will enter into bond, shall be paid for that use unto you, upon Michaelmas day next coming.

De Vere also bought out £2,000 of Lok's shares in the adventure, making his £3,000 bond the single largest investment in the enterprise.

Frobisher named his landing site Queen Elizabeth's Foreland and a prominent hill on the island Mount Oxford. Nearby inlets he dubbed Leicester Point and Hatton's Headland. The names didn't stick. Queen Elizabeth's Foreland is now known as Resolution Island in the Canadian province of Nunavut; Mount Oxford is now, appropriately, an unnamed eminence.

In more ways than one, the expedition was a failure. This time the ships faced powerful storms and massive ice floes, ruining the food stocks and pre-fabricated shelters they had brought to set up the explorers' outpost. They could do nothing but mine the ore, twelve hundred tons of which they returned to England. Some of this worthless rock can still be seen in Dartford on the Lower Thames, where Frobisher had set up smelting works to extract his quarry's ostensible riches. Frobisher and his investors soon discovered, however, that they were ruined.

Yet, all was not lost. De Vere would later use his humbling experience as failed financial speculator for his literary endeavors. In *The Merchant of Venice,* the munificent ANTONIO takes out a 3,000-ducat bond with the financier SHYLOCK—a name that is a tip of the hat to Michael Lok. But when ANTONIO discovers that his shipping ventures have proven disastrous, he has no choice but to default on his bond, setting in motion the Shake-spearean plot sequence that derives from other sources.

Though de Vere had been badly burned with his £3,000 bond—he was never, so far as is known, able to pay it all back—he would sink yet more money into Northwest Passage expeditions in 1584 and '85. These latter expenditures came at a time when de Vere was arguably developing the story line for *Hamlet.* With an addiction for investing in Frobisher-like enterprises, de Vere could certainly claim, as does the Danish prince, that he was "but mad north-northwest."

᭥

Closeups of the "Ashbourne Portrait of Shakespeare" and the "Wellbeck Portrait" of a twenty-five-year-old Edward de Vere (1575). The Ashbourne, four centuries old, first gained notice as a "Shakespeare" portrait in 1847. It has since been discovered to be an overpainted image of someone else. Although many orthodox scholars today believe the Ashbourne's original sitter to be a mayor of London named Hugh Hamersley, the strong resemblance to the Wellbeck argues another thesis: Beneath the "Shakespeare" veneer lies Edward de Vere. For more on the Ashbourne controversy, see this book's Appendix D.

Castle Hedingham in Essex, the ancient family seat where earls of Oxford had resided since c. 1140 and where Edward de Vere spent part of his youth.

An aerial view of sixteenth century London as seen from the west: Fleet River (aka "Fleet Ditch") is in the immediate foreground, with Ludgate and St. Paul's just beyond. In the distance, spanning the Thames, is London Bridge.

Sir William Cecil painted in the 1560s by or after a portrait painted by Arnold van Brounckhorst. In 1561, Cecil was appointed master of the queen's Court of Wards and Liveries; ten years later, Elizabeth would elevate him to the peerage, styling him the first Baron Burghley.

The tomb of Anne Cecil (d. 1588) and her mother Mildred Cecil, baroness of Burghley (d. 1589) at Westminster Abbey.

The copy of Titian's painting *Venus and Adonis* that was in Titian's Venice studio in 1575; Shake-speare's 1593 poem *Venus and Adonis* depicts the mythological couple in the same idiosyncratic terms as does Titian–from the desperate and clawing goddess to the heedless hunter wearing a "bonnet [that] hides his angry brow."

Henry Wriothesley, third earl of Southampton, as painted during his imprisonment in the Tower of London between 1601 and 1603. The Latin motto pictured near Southampton's left shoulder reads *In vinculis invictus*– "Unconquered though in chains."

Anne Vavasour, a gentlewoman of Her Majesty's Bedchamber, with whom Edward de Vere had a tempestuous extramarital affair from 1579-81.

The "Armada Portrait" of Queen Elizabeth I by George Gower presents a triumphal image in celebration of the victory of the English naval forces over the Spanish Armada in the summer of 1588. Over the ornately clad queen's left shoulder are the storm-tossed seas that the Spanish fleet (and, briefly, the English fleet as well) faced. To Her Majesty's right is an image of the victorious English navy, probably off the shores of Calais. Not coincidentally, Elizabeth's imperial crown rests below the latter image, while she confidently places her right hand on the globe, prefiguring her nation's increasingly global ambitions.

CHAPTER 6

IN BRAWL RIDICULOUS

[1577–1582]

I N THE 1570S, SPAIN, FRANCE, AND ENGLAND WERE LIKE THREE dancers trying to tango. Two countries would attempt a couple of steps together; then the third would cut in, leaving one or both of the original partners slighted. These brief political alliances, sometimes lasting only a few months, make for a dizzying courtly backdrop against which Edward de Vere led his life.

For Elizabeth and her chief ministers, the single most important factor that determined who allied with whom at any given moment was religion. Protestant hard-liners like Walsingham, Leicester, and Sidney were less likely to negotiate and promote deals with Catholic foreigners than were old-school feudalists like the earls of Sussex and Worcester and the duke of Norfolk's heirs and cousins. However, any of them could switch alliances, depending on the rewards they stood to reap—or the punishments they'd face if too strongly allied with the losing side.

De Vere's role in this game was shifting as well. Sometime in 1576 or '77, according to the French ambassador to England (Michel de Castelnau, seigneur de Mauvissière), the earl of Oxford had become a secret Catholic. As ambassador Mauvissière later recalled:

> On his return from Italy, [de Vere] made profession of the Catholic faith together with some of his relatives among the nobility and his best friends and had sworn, as he says, and signed with them a declaration that they would do all they could for the advancement of the Catholic religion.

One of de Vere's Catholic cohorts was Henry Howard, the late duke of Norfolk's younger brother. Howard, ten years older than de Vere, was a brilliant and learned man, having taught civil law at Cambridge. As a supporter of Mary, Queen of Scots, and her claims to Queen Elizabeth's job, Howard risked losing his head, like his brother. Yet the fact that Howard outlived nearly all of his contemporaries—he would die at the ripe age of seventy-four—speaks highly of his survival skills in a time of adversity. De Vere was won over by his canny and guileful cousin, a man nearly as smart and accomplished as Sir Thomas Smith—and an outspoken adherent of *The Courtier* to boot.

Another of de Vere's Catholic comrades was Howard's cousin Charles Arundell. Arundell's father had been executed for a conspiracy against the earl of Leicester's father. Arundell, raised with four siblings by a gallows widow, would carry his father's grudge and would ultimately find ample opportunity for sweet revenge.

Arundell would later tell two versions of why de Vere reconciled himself to the pope: to please a former schoolmaster—although the identity of this papist teacher has yet to be found—and to ease his conscience over an unspecified murder. The only murder (or, more accurately, manslaughter) that de Vere is known to have committed was the accidental killing of Thomas Brincknell in 1567. But a second homicide has also been proposed as the cause of de Vere's newfound religiosity, although his connection to it is considerably more tenuous.

In July of 1577, a London yeoman named William Weekes had killed William Sankey, one of de Vere's men. Weekes was arrested in Durham in November. The queen's Privy Council got involved, ordering the extrication of Weekes from Durham to London, where he was tried for murder, found guilty, and hanged. These are the known facts in the case. Arundell would later charge, however, that de Vere had hired Sankey to kill Rowland Yorke, and Henry Howard would add that de Vere had hired Weekes to kill Sankey—and that £100 of de Vere's money had been found on Weekes at the time of his arrest.

None of these convoluted charges can be verified beyond the cobwebs of conspiracy that Arundell and Howard's later testimony weave. Arundell and Howard cite witnesses who, so far as is known, were never summoned or deposed. The Privy Council's record concerning the Sankey murder case mentions nothing about de Vere's alleged involvement. And the allegation itself makes little sense, considering de Vere's continued closeness at the time to his "honest IAGO."

Whatever his reasons, the earl of Oxford was now engaged in the kind of backroom plotting that might liberate England from its heretic church but might also just as readily liberate de Vere's head from his body. Letters between Ambassador Mauvissière and King Henri III reveal that de Vere and his band of brethren planned to capture the French Protestant (Huguenot) prince Henry of Condé if he ever made it to England. The prince never did. De Vere may also have been the *"jeune seigneur"* to whom Mauvissière referred–a young lord who had offered to send a squadron of five ships to assist de Vere's cousins, Francis and Robert Vere, in fighting Huguenot forces in the Netherlands. This, too, never came to pass. The French ambassador quietly indulged de Vere's insurrectionist brainstorming without ever openly embracing it. In July of 1577, Mauvissière awarded de Vere a jewel as a token of his king's appreciation.

Not everyone was so tolerant. On June 13, 1577, Leicester wrote to Burghley:

> I am sorry my lord of Oxford should for any respect think any more of going over sea. I can but wish and advise him to take such advice in all things as were best and most honorable for him–and specially in his consideration toward Her Majesty and his country.

De Vere's misplaced evangelism stemmed in no small part from his frustration with Protestant hypocrisy and ineptitude, especially as practiced by Burghley and Leicester. As Howard would later testify:

> His Lordship suddenly replied again that touching the Protestants, he saw them practice other courses daily, where they ... [wed] Catholics, like good *Ave Maria* coxcombs, [and] were content to lay down their heads till they were taken off. And therefore for his own part he wished that for every one they [*Protestants*] lost, they might lose a thousand, till they learned to be wiser and took out another lesson.

Ever the temperamental sectarian, de Vere also squabbled with his priest, who refused to give him communion until the earl resumed living with his estranged wife.

Sometime in 1577 or '78, the earl of Oxford was looking to hire a secretary. De Vere, with increasing literary aspirations, needed one or more talented university graduates to help him find suitable source material and adapt these texts into plays for court performance. De Vere needed someone who knew his Boccaccio and his Ovid, someone adept with the Romance languages and a quill pen.

The luxury of a private secretary became more affordable with the royal favor recently bestowed upon him. On January 15, 1578, the queen, citing de Vere's "true and faithful service done and given to Us," awarded the stately Castle Rising to her fickle lord. If the queen was at all aware of de Vere's intrigues and conspiracies with the likes of Arundell and Howard, she played a very smart card. Castle Rising, alienated from the late duke of Norfolk's portfolio, was worth a handsome £250 a year. De Vere was hardly in a position financially to turn it down. But now he'd accepted blood money from the very estate that had been sacrificed, to his great anger, on the altar of Elizabethan politics. How could this "*Ave Maria* coxcomb" then turn around and cook up schemes against the government?

Rising was no mere trinket to be tossed away–especially as de Vere was hardly Her Majesty's favorite gentleman caller these days. Elizabeth and de Vere hadn't exchanged New Year's gifts since he had fallen out with his wife. (Countess Anne, on the other hand, continued to elicit the sympathies of queen and court–and continued to receive annual New Year's gifts from Her Majesty.) De Vere had not, in any official capacity at least, rendered "true and faithful service" to the crown. Yet, the queen had a sixth sense for recognizing and nurturing the talents of those around her. Elizabeth's grant may have been the first material encouragement the literary earl had ever received to continue writing and producing.

Another prime opportunity to produce more material–and to cast about for top-rate assistants–came that summer. Elizabeth's Progress of 1578 was to be, like her progresses to Cambridge and Oxford in 1564 and '66, filled with scholarship, learned debates, and theatrical diversions. She and her household first rested at the Cecil family estate of Theobalds in early July–where de Vere was almost certainly not. (He still had an agreement with Burghley about keeping his distance.) But de Vere did attend Her Majesty's court at the next stop: Audley End in Essex. This Howard family estate, where the earl had recently visited for the wedding of his once-removed cousin William Howard, was now in full regal splendor, while some of the nation's up-and-coming young writers and scholars from nearby Cambridge University would be showcasing their wares.

One of these was Gabriel Harvey, a contemporary of de Vere's and a fellow student of the recently deceased Sir Thomas Smith. (Smith had died of throat cancer the summer before, and Harvey had soon thereafter published a moving Latin eulogy to his teacher.) De Vere had known Harvey since at least their late teenaged years, when the earl had bestowed money and favors on him while studying at Christ's College, Cambridge. By 1578, Harvey had been appointed professor of rhetoric at Cambridge, and had gained a reputation as both a bright light and an argumentative blowhard. No doubt he had been encouraged in his egomania by Smith. "Gallant audacity is never out of countenance," Harvey once wrote, "but hath ever a tongue and a hand at will."

For the Audley End presentations, Harvey had prepared a series of lectures to be delivered to the prominent members of the court, the earl of Oxford included. Harvey was well aware of de Vere's literary interests and his need for a secretary.

Harvey also believed that men of rank and stature should perform actions "singularly worthy of most glorious and immortal fame." War was the traditional job of noblemen. Writing was a lesser task, for learned men and secretaries. Harvey's exhortation was brash and unsolicited. But Harvey said it anyway: You, milord, are wasting your time in pursuing a career based around poetry and the courtly stage. Between the lines, Harvey seems to have been putting himself forward for the job of de Vere's secretary.

The satirist Thomas Nashe would later nickname Harvey "Timothy Tiptoes" for his audacious rhetoric in his Audley End verses. Here is what Harvey wrote to de Vere, translated from the original Latin:

Thy splendid fame, great earl, demands even more than in the case of others the services of a poet possessing lofty eloquence. Thy merit doth not creep along the ground, nor can it be confined within the limits of a song. It is a wonder that reaches as far as the heavenly orbs.

...For a long time past Phoebus Apollo has cultivated thy mind in the arts. English poetical measures have been sung by thee long enough. Let that courtly epistle–more polished than even the writings of Castiglione himself–[*de Vere's 1573 Latin preface to Castiglione's Courtier*] witness how greatly thou dost excel in letters. I have seen many Latin verses of thine; yea, even more English verses are extant. Thou hast drunk deep drafts not only of the muses of France and Italy but hast learned the manners of many men, and the arts of foreign countries. It was not for nothing that Sturmius himself was visited by thee. Neither in France, Italy, nor Germany are any such cultivated and polished men. O thou hero worthy of renown, throw away the insignificant pen, throw away bloodless books and writings that serve no useful purpose. Now must the sword be brought into play. Now is the time for thee to sharpen the spear and to handle the great engines of war.... What if suddenly a most powerful enemy [*Spain*] should invade our borders? If the Turk should be arming his savage hosts against us? What though the terrible war trumpet is even now sounding its blast? Thou wilt see it all. Even at this very moment thou art fiercely longing for the fray. I feel it. Our whole country knows it. In thy breast is noble blood. Courage animates thy brow, Mars lives in thy tongue, Minerva strengthens thy right hand, Bellona reigns in thy body, within thee burns the fire of Mars. Thine eyes flash fire, thy will shakes spears. Who would not swear that Achilles had come to life again?

Will shakes spears. At the time Harvey uttered these words, a fourteen-year-old boy in Stratford-upon-Avon was still living in obscurity. The first opportunity Will Shakspere of Stratford would have to join London society–and, presumably, to come to the attention of literati such as Harvey–was still years away. It must be one of the great coincidences of Western literature that Harvey's

1578 encomium to de Vere would reference the very name the earl of Oxford would one day use to conceal his own writings.

More significant, though, is Harvey's statement that at age twenty-eight, de Vere had written "many Latin verses . . . [and] even more English verses"– in excess of the handful of published song lyrics then under his name. De Vere was already gaining a reputation among the intelligentsia as a courtier poet. Harvey must have felt that appealing to de Vere's military potential might curry favor. As was often the case in Harvey's life, he completely misread the situation. The earl of Oxford was unimpressed.

One former student of "Timothy Tiptoes" appears to have tossed his hat in the ring in 1578 as well. The poet Edmund Spenser–who would later earn his place among the greatest English poets with his *Faerie Queene*–was in 1578 preparing an extended literary work that, in the words of one Spenser expert, "serves as an advertisement of Spenser's qualifications for secretaryship."

Scholars have long recognized Spenser's *The Shepherd's Calendar* as an allegory depicting prominent Elizabethan figures such as Harvey, de Vere, Sir Philip Sidney, Leicester, and Queen Elizabeth. Contemporary critics recognized it as well. The 1579 publication of *The Shepherd's Calendar* is generally regarded as one of the more important milestones in the history of English letters. Missing from the conventional picture, however, is a compelling explanation of why Spenser wrote what he did when he did.

Spenser in 1578 was newly under the earl of Leicester's patronage. However, Leicester had no talent for literature, and *The Shepherd's Calendar* appears to be a book-length job application written for one or more prospective next employers, perhaps including de Vere. The *Calendar* revels in the secrets it conceals. It showcases Spenser's humanist education, his skills as a rhetorician, and his ability to be trusted with sensitive and intimate details, an essential quality in a secretary.

Neither Harvey nor Spenser got the job. De Vere would hire at least three men at this time or soon thereafter: the playwright John Lyly (affiliated with de Vere by 1582), the translator and playwright Anthony Munday (by 1579), and the amanuensis Abraham Fleming (by 1580).

As a friend and sometime employee of Leicester and the Sidney family, Spenser would have little cause to second-guess de Vere's choice of secretaries. De Vere would appear occasionally in Spenser's writings over the years, such as in a dedicatory sonnet written to the earl in *The Faerie Queene,* where de Vere may also appear as the character "Scudamore." However, Spenser remained an observer of the unfolding Shake-speare game from afar, as seen through the eyes of colleagues and patrons who happened to be Shake-speare's greatest and most long-standing courtly rivals.

Spenser moved on, but Harvey continued to stew over his lost opportunity. In 1580, Harvey published a plodding poem that lampooned a foppish Italianate Englishman who was clearly a caricature of de Vere. Harvey's unnamed nobleman was one of "valorous words," "frivolous deeds," "Tuscanish look," and "womanish works." Harvey labors over de Vere's effeminate appearance—a "forefinger kiss," "little apish hat," and a "large-bellied codpieced doublet." The Italianate fop, Harvey says with all the sarcasm he can muster, is "a diamond for nonce, a fellow peerless in England." For publishing such a nasty libel about a peer of the realm, Harvey would later be hauled before the queen's Privy Council to answer for his impudence. Ultimately, the matter burned out on its own. But de Vere would never trust or take Harvey seriously again, and that fact would stick in Harvey's craw for many years to come.

Around the time Gabriel Harvey delivered his speech at Audley End, in late July of 1578, two French ambassadors had joined the queen's progress to advocate for a most delicate matter. Their employer, François de Valois, duke of Alençon, had been lobbying on and off for six years to marry Elizabeth, and now his case was moving to the front and center of English politics. This was the same French lord who had amassed troops against his older brother (King Henri III of France) when de Vere was making his way home from Italy. Although he came from a strongly Catholic family and was only twenty-four (to Elizabeth's forty-four), Alençon had also shown enough animosity toward Spain and Catholicism to make him an attractive potential husband for Elizabeth. A new Anglo-French alliance was just one wedding ring away.

However, Alençon's mother, Catherine de Medici, was a major stumbling block to the young duke's chances. She was still widely reviled in England for her role in the 1572 St. Bartholomew's Day Massacre. Protestant patriots like the earl of Leicester and Sir Philip Sidney were opposed to the Alençon match. Gabriel Harvey spent part of his Audley End verses railing against "Machiavellians"—a code word for the Medici clan—and the "dark blood" they threatened to visit on the "white cliffs of the English."

Burghley, on the other hand, backed Alençon. The Lord Treasurer saw in this unlikely match the possibility of a crucial alliance that would keep both Spain and Mary, Queen of Scots, in check. The bleak choice he felt England now faced was either an Alençon marriage or eventual war with Spain. Time would ultimately prove him correct too. One additional deciding factor, unmentioned in Burghley's letters and memoranda at the time, must nevertheless have also made Alençon an attractive suitor: No husband of Elizabeth's would put up with the queen's longtime favorite, Leicester. Burghley's—and de Vere's—eternal rival would be tossed out as soon as the French marriage was finalized.

De Vere continued to anger and frustrate his father-in-law over his mistreatment of Anne, and yet these two men with so many differences did agree about one thing. They both stood against Leicester and Sidney and supported the wedding plans with Alençon. Since meeting Alençon in Paris two years before, de Vere had seen eye-to-eye with the short, pockmarked French lord. Drinking one night with a cadre of English Catholic ne'er-do-wells, including a young Walter Raleigh, Oxford reportedly bragged that Alençon had once offered him a salary of 10,000 crowns a year to move to France. (He also said the French have a knack for "crowning none but coxcombs.")

However, de Vere would only go so far in advocating for Alençon, whom Elizabeth would soon nickname her "frog." On August 14, on the way toward Norwich, the Spanish ambassador wrote home about an uncomfortable incident between de Vere and Alençon's envoys. "The queen sent twice to tell the earl of Oxford, who is a very gallant lad, to dance before [Alençon's] ambassadors, whereupon he replied that he hoped Her Majesty would not order him to do so as he did not want to entertain Frenchman," the Spanish ambassador reported. De Vere may have enjoyed dancing with the queen, but entertaining overgrown errand boys was a humiliation to which he was not prepared to subject himself.

De Vere's indifferent attitude toward the very suitors he ostensibly supported suggests another, more subtle move in the never-ending chess game of court politics. Modern psychological profiles of Elizabeth have pointed out that the queen's personal relationships were forever dogged by her overpowering fear of rejection. From an early age, this most unwanted princess had learned that survival meant playing coy with love and ultimately repudiating it altogether—before any potential lover had a chance to reject her. The Scots ambassador once told the queen, "I know your spirit cannot endure a commander," while the Spanish ambassador laid a-hundred-to-one odds that Elizabeth would dump Alençon before they ever reached the altar. De Vere may have felt secure enough in Elizabeth's permanently unmarried state to play politics with the Alençon match. In promoting Alençon, de Vere was preventing Leicester and Sidney from receiving the queen's attentions and largesse, a reward in itself, and currying favor with his powerful father-in-law.

The approaching court revels season of 1578–79 presented an opportunity for the earl of Oxford to present his perspective. Plays performed for the queen and her court would become de Vere's propaganda device—a semipublic space in which he could spell out his views and opinions about the powers and players at court.

The Lord Chamberlain's Men—headed by de Vere's mentor, the earl of Sussex—were slated to perform at court on December 28 and January 6. Again, the historical record for the 1578–79 season furnishes only the names of the troupes and the plays they performed. No playscripts exist. Nonetheless, these two performances by a company whose patron was closely affiliated with de Vere bore titles evocative of Shake-speare plays.

చ్రో

Before this veritable festival, Elizabeth had sent back to Paris the low-level envoys for whom de Vere would not dance. The queen had them tell Alençon that she would never marry someone she hadn't first seen in the flesh. Alençon's response was to prepare his negotiator Jean de Simier, who was more Don Juan than diplomat, for a journey to England in mid-January. The following summer, Alençon himself would make an incognito visit to Elizabeth. But the Lord Chamberlain's Men plays, staged between visits of French envoys, would appear before a primarily English audience. Therefore, any messages these plays conveyed could be more controversial and less diplomatic than when Simier and his entourage would be on hand. And diplomatic, it would appear, they were not.

Both performances would be staged at Richmond Palace. Built by the queen's grandfather, Henry VII, Richmond was one of Elizabeth's favorite retreats from nearby London. Behind Richmond's gabled and turreted walls, she would one day plan the naval campaign against the Spanish Armada and agree to the terms for peace in England's war against Ireland. In 1603, Her Majesty would breathe her last breath within this enormous monument to late medieval architecture.

England was in the midst of, according to the antiquarian William Camden, "a sharp winter, full of snows." But no mere forces of nature would shut down Elizabeth's cherished seasonal revels. On the Sunday after Christmas, December 28, 1578, Richmond's Great Hall shone with the radiance of hundreds of candles, projecting their beams out through the hall's large windows and onto the snowy orchard next door. De Vere would have joined the queen and her assembled court in the center of the chilly and cavernous hall, warmed by the charcoal fire glowing behind them. Portraits and statues commemorating Elizabeth's royal ancestors adorned the walls. And on the far end of the hall stood the dais where the Lord Chamberlain's Men enacted their play, titled *An History of the Cruelties of a Stepmother.*

A stepmother's cruelties are the centerpiece of Shake-speare's *Cymbeline.* *Cymbeline*'s matriarch is, in the words of one late twentieth-century critic, the "wicked stepmother, par excellence." *Cymbeline*'s convoluted story was cribbed in no small part from a book, *The Ethiopian History of Heliodorus,* that was dedicated to de Vere just one year before *The Cruelties of a Stepmother* was enacted. And the story *Cymbeline* tells makes a close fit with the characters and situations in de Vere's life circa 1578.

Cymbeline's plot concerns a contemptible old QUEEN's attempts to marry her stepdaughter IMOGEN off to a vainglorious dolt of a son CLOTEN. IMOGEN wants nothing to do with the foolish would-be groom and instead weds a heroic young nobleman named POSTHUMUS. However, POSTHUMUS's overweening problem is his irrational jealousy of his wife, stoked in no small part by an IAGO-like colleague named IACHIMO. De Vere dramatizes himself as

POSTHUMUS and his wife, Anne, as IMOGEN. *Cymbeline* is in part another look at the author's still-troubled marriage.

POSTHUMUS is an orphan. Like de Vere, POSTHUMUS was raised under the same roof as his wife. "It is your fault that I have lov'd POSTHUMUS. You bred him as my playfellow," IMOGEN petulantly tells her father. Also like the earl of Oxford, POSTHUMUS received a first-rate education in his adopted home. As one incidental character in the play reveals, "POSTHUMUS [gleaned] all the learnings that his time could make him the receiver of, which he took as we do air, fast as 'twas minister'd."

De Vere's/POSTHUMUS's mistrust toward his wife gets fobbed off once again on Rowland Yorke/IACHIMO. And thus, in this most basic reading of the play, the wicked stepmother stands none too subtly for a certain mother-in-law with whom de Vere was forever squabbling. (Lady Burghley had wanted Anne to marry Philip Sidney and probably never tired of saying as much.) *Cymbeline* shares the author's opinion of his mother-in-law when the play's court physician says of the QUEEN:

> I do not like her. She doth think she has
> Strange ling'ring poisons. I do know her spirit
> And will not trust one of her malice. . . .
> She is fool'd
> With a most false effect. And I the truer
> So to be false with her.

De Vere evidently had no qualms about airing his griefs with the Cecil family on the courtly stage. In late 1578, however, a courtly audience presented with a play entitled *The Cruelties of a Stepmother* would have understood that the title character represented Catherine de Medici, a conniving woman who would have become stepmother to England had Elizabeth married Alençon. De Medici, more than any other royal matriarch in Europe, fitted the profile laid out in *Cymbeline* of "a mother hourly coining plots." Here de Vere the truth teller is also de Vere the coy and crafty dramatist. He conceals his personal level of meaning within a contemporary political context. One can imagine de Vere taking perverse pleasure skewering de Medici and her doltish son, that rival for Elizabeth's affections, as *Cymbeline*'s corrupt QUEEN and her spotty child CLOTEN:

> That such a crafty devil as his mother
> Should yield the world this ass! A woman that
> Bears all down with her brain; and this her son
> Cannot take two from twenty, for his heart,
> And leave eighteen.

During the midst of the revels season, de Vere and Elizabeth resumed giving and receiving New Year's gifts. The earl graced Her Majesty with a "very fair jewel of gold, wherein is a helmet of gold and small diamonds." Elizabeth returned the favor with a gold basin, ewer, and a pair of pots. De Vere's sister Mary was also on hand that evening, receiving a royal gilt bowl for the "vale of open work with gold and spangles" that she presented to Her Majesty. Mary's husband, Peregrine Bertie, that hater of courtly "reptilia," was nowhere to be found—or if he was on hand, he had opted out of the New Year's traditions of polite society.

The following Tuesday, January 6, 1579, the Lord Chamberlain's Men presented the play *The History of the Rape of the Second Helen*. The title plays off the legendary rape of Helen—the implied "first Helen"—in the Trojan War, who Shake-speare depicts in *Troilus and Cressida*. In the Shake-speare canon, there's a second afflicted Helen. She appears in *All's Well That Ends Well*.

All's Well That Ends Well is yet another refiguring of de Vere's troubled relationship with his wife, including this unique twist: Sometime during de Vere's separation from Anne, the husband found himself faced with one of the most bizarre marital alibis ever concocted to explain how his wife's child was allegedly his.

According to Essex country lore, de Vere had in fact slept with his wife when he believed he was having sex with another woman. Or so de Vere was later told. De Vere "forsook his lady's bed," the Essex antiquarian Thomas Wright notes, "[but] the father of Lady Anne by stratagem contrived that her husband should unknowingly sleep with her, believing her to be another woman." Lord Burghley's meddling hand once again appears.

Anne or one of her servants had handed the perplexed husband this jaw dropper, and de Vere must have wondered to himself how it possibly could have transpired—and if any other rube in human history had been played like this before. Here is where having a secretary on hand must have come in handy. There was in fact ample historical and literary precedent for what is called "the bed trick." In the book of Genesis, a meddling father-in-law sneaks the bride's sister Leah into Jacob's bed. Chaucer turned the tables and made the wife the deceived party in "The Reeve's Tale." One also finds bed tricks in the ancient legends of King Arthur, and Giovanni Boccaccio's *Decameron* details eight different bed tricks. One of the bed-trick plots from Boccaccio, in fact, concerns a French province named Roussillion. And this became the central bed-trick story line through which the tale of Hélène of the Château Roussillion would be framed.

The tale of Hélène and Boccaccio's short story would provide the cover de Vere needed to speak his own set of troubling truths. De Vere's young life is as much an inspiration for *All's Well*'s BERTRAM as it is for HAMLET. BERTRAM loses his father and then is packed off to become a ward of court.

BERTRAM is married to the comely maid HELENA against his will. The groom protests that her family is beneath his social standing—and to rectify this heraldic wrong, the sovereign entitles HELENA's family. (Elizabeth, the reader will recall, ennobled the Cecil clan soon before Anne's marriage to de Vere.) BERTRAM forsakes his wife's bed and runs off to Italy. Then HELENA wins BERTRAM back by playing the same bed trick that Anne allegedly played on her recalcitrant husband.

By staging *The Rape of the Second Helen* for Elizabeth and her court on Twelfth Night of 1579, de Vere had arguably laid out for his friends and allies the conundrum that he'd recently been saddled with. One suspects the bed-trick alibi was as hard to believe then as it is today. And yet... what if? Could de Vere say for sure that he hadn't been bed-tricked? Perhaps he had been sexually promiscuous during the autumn before his continental adventure. (Double standards in marital relations were certainly the standard of the day—especially for the upper classes.) If so, how hard would it have been for the all-seeing Lord Treasurer to fool his son-in-law? In fact, de Vere highlighted a passage in his Bible about these very questions in the book of Ecclesiasticus:

> 18 A man that breaketh wedlock and thinketh thus in his heart: "Who seeth me? I am compassed about with darkness. The walls cover me. Nobody seeth me. Whom need I fear? The Most High will not remember my sins."
>
> 19 Such a man feareth the eyes of men and knoweth not that the eyes of the Lord are ten thousand times brighter than the Sun, beholding all the ways of men.

De Vere would later ruminate over these ideas in the epic Shake-speare poem *The Rape of Lucrece*—yet another mythical working out of his distressed marriage with Anne and the mystery daughter he could not account for. The poem's heroine, LUCRECE, thinks "not but that every eye can see/ The same disgrace which they themselves behold" and concludes:

> Make me not object to the telltale day.
> The light will show, charactered in my brow,
> The story of sweet chastity's decay,
> The impious breach of holy wedlock vow.

The question of Elizabeth de Vere's paternity would continue to simmer for years, even into his daughter's adulthood. The uncertainty over the bed trick, the true nature of Anne's character (innocent HERO or manipulated OPHELIA?) and the extent of his father-in-law's meddling in the couple's bedchamber remained an unanswered mystery. Lacking definite answers, de Vere was left to spend much of the rest of his life poetically and dramatically exploring every possible scenario behind Elizabeth de Vere's birth. Was de Vere deceived by a bed trick? *All's Well* and *Measure for Measure* consider such a stratagem. Could Anne have been raped and then have covered it up? *The Rape of Lucrece* and *Titus Andronicus* present this scenario. Was Anne actually unfaithful? *The Winter's Tale* sneaks in such a possibility. Was de Vere misled by a sinister servant? Well...yes. And that one certainty is laid out in full view in *Othello* and *Cymbeline*. Did de Vere act cruelly and heartlessly, no matter what Anne had or hadn't done? *The Winter's Tale* and *Othello* suggest he'd reached that conclusion by the end of his life.

De Vere also satirizes his own jealous obsessions. *The Comedy of Errors* and *The Merry Wives of Windsor* both poke fun at the jealous insanity the author recognized in himself. In the latter, de Vere casts himself as the wildly accusatory FORD–who, naturally, is at one point punningly labeled an "Ox." *Merry Wives* relentlessly mocks FORD for mistreating his innocent and cunning wife. (Perhaps this is why there is an oral tradition that the queen loved *Merry Wives* so much.) In one scene, FORD's English friend PAGE, his Welsh colleague EVANS, and his French doctor CAIUS all stand astonished at FORD's stubborn inability to recognize that his jealous accusations against his wife are utterly unfounded.

> PAGE Good Master FORD, be contented. You wrong yourself too much.
> FORD True, Master PAGE. Up, gentlemen, you shall see sport anon.
>   Follow me, gentlemen.
> EVANS This is fery fantastical humors and jealousies.
> CAIUS By gar, 'tis no the fashion of France. It is not jealous in France....
> EVANS If there be any pody in the house, and in the chambers, and in
>   the coffers, and the presses, heaven forgive my sins at the day of
>   judgment!
> CAIUS Be-gar, nor I too. There is no bodies.
> PAGE Fie, fie, Master FORD. Are you not asham'd? What spirit, what
>   devil suggests this imagination? I would not ha[ve] your distemper in
>   this kind for the wealth of Windsor Castle.
> FORD 'Tis my fault, Master PAGE. I suffer for it.

On January 22, 1579, the German prince Jan Casimir–the would-be FORTINBRAS whom de Vere had encountered on his way to Paris in the spring of 1576–arrived in England for a three-week court visit. He had come to win support for military and economic aid in The Netherlands. Elizabeth responded with ceremony. She personally invested the prince in the Order of the Garter and lavished upon him generous gifts and accommodations. But none of these trinkets of state mattered to the blunt and warlike prince. Casimir ultimately left England frustrated at the queen's noncommittal approach to international politics.

The newly arrived French ambassador, Jean de Simier, would have done well to recognize in Casimir's frustrations a forecast of his own. Elizabeth soon turned Alençon's ambassador against Alençon. By February 1579, Her Majesty was flirting with Simier himself, her *singe* (monkey), as she nicknamed him. And Simier gladly played *coq* to the queen's *coquette.* The whole spectacle, with a forty-five-year-old grand dame who imagined herself perennially seventeen, must have been slightly disturbing even to Alençon's supporters at court. For a man whose marital jealousies ventured far beyond the pale, de Vere may well have begun to feel twangs of jealousy over Elizabeth. He was, after all, still the young Casanova who had been rumored to be the queen's lover only five years before. It's hard to tell precisely where or when de Vere began drifting back toward the Protestant tradition in which he was raised. But one suspects seeds were already being sown by the time the "monkey" came a-courting for the "frog."

The following Shrovetide (March 1–3, 1579), de Vere and his cousins and in-laws performed in a masque for the court at Whitehall. The palace's Great Hall, or perhaps its more intimate Great Chamber, was the site of this interlude that did not impress the one audience member who recorded his reaction. "The device was prettier than it hap to be performed," the courtier Gilbert Talbot succinctly noted in a letter to his father. "But the best of it–and I think the best liked–was two rich jewels which was [*sic*] presented to Her Majesty by the two earls [of Oxford and Surrey]."

Shrove Tuesday (March 3) was undoubtedly the evening in question, since it was the only night of the three that featured a masque. The professional troupe performing that night was the Lord Chamberlain's Men, who presented the play *The History of Murderous Michael.* De Vere, Surrey, and associates handled the other item on the evening's bill, *A Moor's Masque.*

The History of Murderous Michael was probably later revised and reprinted (in 1592) as the anonymous Elizabethan drama *Arden of Feversham. Arden* is based on a true story about a wife who conspires to kill her husband with the treacherous assistance of a servant named Michael. *A Moor's Masque,* conversely, may have been an extremely rough version–a "masque" was then what one might today call a skit–of what later became Shake-speare's domestic tragedy about a husband who conspires to kill his wife with the goading of a servant named IAGO.

With this possible *Ur-Othello,* de Vere was again presenting courtly theatrics about his dysfunctional family life. Shake-speare was, it now appears, an obsessive man. One may rightly marvel how the earl of Oxford managed to keep poison out of his porridge and stray daggers out of his gut when he made pointed jab after pointed jab at the most powerful and dangerous family in the Elizabethan court: his in-laws.

In preparation for Alençon's visit, the queen needed to choose blue-blooded hostages to send to France as collateral to ensure Alençon's safe return. Elizabeth volunteered de Vere as well as two other *Moor's Masquers*. Although de Vere was ultimately never sent overseas in exchange for Alençon, the earl's gargantuan pride was probably sore from the slight. De Vere would later reflect on his experiences as conflicted royal nuptial advocate in *Twelfth Night.*

In this play, the author casts himself as the jester FESTE. The play's female ruler, OLIVIA, hears the marriage pleas of a suitor only through a series of messengers. She refutes the first messenger, and the suitor (DUKE ORSINO) responds with another, whom OLIVIA falls for. This is a direct parallel to the rebuked Alençon ambassadors in the summer of 1578, followed by the queen's "monkey" Simier.

Ultimately, *Twelfth Night's* DUKE shows up on OLIVIA's doorstep, just as Alençon finally met Elizabeth face-to-face in August of 1579. FESTE watches this from the wings, cracking wise all the while. (The fool is clearly wary of wedding bells. "Many a good hanging prevents a bad marriage," FESTE says.) However, FESTE also entertains the DUKE with a love song–perhaps de Vere's acknowledgment that he did his part in hosting and entertaining Alençon during a brief English visit in September of 1579.

OLIVIA presides over an unruly household that consists of key antagonists and protagonists in the author's life at court circa 1579. As noted previously, there's de Vere's sister Mary (MARIA), her roistering, cut-knuckle husband, Peregrine Bertie (SIR TOBY BELCH), and Bertie's dearest friend, Sir Philip Sidney (SIR ANDREW AGUECHEEK).

The "clodpole" AGUECHEEK's time onstage consists of one verbal pratfall after the next. The knight doesn't understand the meaning of the word *accost* or the French word *pourquoi*–and, in admitting as much, AGUECHEEK becomes the butt of a bawdy French double entendre about his sexual inexperience.

And yet, in *Twelfth Night* a conflicted portrait of AGUECHEEK emerges. The sympathetic BELCH holds AGUECHEEK near to his heart. BELCH speaks of AGUECHEEK as if he were the very ideal of Castiglione's courtier who "speaks three or four languages word for word without book." All of this certainly holds true of Sir Philip Sidney.

In 1579, the twenty-five-year-old Sidney was widely adored on the Continent as England's brightest light. Prince William of Orange proclaimed Sidney the most learned and promising statesman in all of Europe. And as a poet, Sidney stood out as a distinctive voice among a dull and generally speechless tribe. Had Sidney lived into his forties or fifties, the Elizabethan

Age might well have become known as the period that produced four time-less literary legends: Shake-speare, Spenser, Donne, and Sidney.

One of AGUECHEEK's lines speaks to a more substantive dispute de Vere had with Sidney. AGUECHEEK confides in BELCH that "I am a fellow o' the strangest mind i' th' world: I delight in masques and revels sometimes alto-gether!" With these words, Shake-speare unsheathes his sword against a liter-ary rival.

In 1579 the Puritan pamphleteer Stephen Gosson, sensing a potential kindred spirit, dedicated to Sidney a railing pamphlet *(The School of Abuse)* denigrating literature as the handmaiden of evil. But Sidney agreed only in one small part with Gosson. Sidney responded with a manuscript circulated at court and then, more than a decade later, printed for public consumption. Sidney's *Defense of Poesy* has been rightly hailed as one of the finest pieces of English Renaissance literary criticism. In it, Sidney gives the lie to the Pu-ritanical scolds who would condemn literary creation as unholy and devoid of moral value. Poetry, Sidney says, is not "an art of lies, but of true doc-trine; not of effeminateness, but of notable stirring of courage; not of abus-ing man's wit, but of strengthening man's wit; not banished, but honored by Plato."

However, Sidney goes on to concur with naysayers like Gosson who be-little the new breed of English plays. Sidney never names names, but his crit-icisms make it clear that the man who would become Shake-speare was clearly in his sights. One theatrical innovation that Sidney strenuously objects to is the compression of time and space itself—condensing the scope of entire lives into a two-hour play, or continually shifting moods and settings without explaining each step to the audience. Sidney, whose theatrical tastes are clearly not fit for the modern age, writes:

> Now you shall have three ladies walk to gather flowers, and then we must believe the stage to be a garden. By and by, we hear news of ship-wreck in the same place, then we are to blame if we accept it not for a rock.... While in the meantime two armies fly in represented with four swords and bucklers, and then what hard heart will not receive it for a pitched field?

De Vere shot back at Sidney in a Shake-spearean fashion. Shake-speare's *Henry V,* the final draft of which was undoubtedly written years after the author's personal quarrel with Sidney, contains a CHORUS that apologizes more than thirty times for its regular shifting of time, mood, and setting. Whenever the play hops over the English Channel or otherwise requires the audience to exercise their imagination, the CHORUS interjects a satirical note of explication for fussbudgets like Sidney who require everything to be laid out neatly. In glossing over the Battle of Agincourt, for instance, the CHORUS sarcastically responds to Sidney's above quote as follows:

> CHORUS And so our scene must to the battle fly;
>   Where–O, for pity!–we shall much disgrace
>   With four or five most vile and ragged foils
>   (Right ill dispos'd in brawl ridiculous)
>   The name of Agincourt.

Just as de Vere opposed Sidney on the printed page, so, too, he treated Sidney brusquely in real life. In September of 1579, less than a month after the completion of Alençon's seemingly successful mission to win Elizabeth's hand, de Vere and Sidney publicly quarreled. Alençon's adversaries were no doubt feeling particularly embattled at that moment, as it looked more likely than ever that the queen would accept the "frog's" hand in marriage. What retribution would lie in store if King François of England wanted payback? Sidney and his cohorts were on edge. The fight that resulted would become perhaps the single most notorious event in de Vere's life.

According to the sole witness who recorded his recollections, Sidney's friend Fulke Greville, Sidney was playing tennis–probably at Greenwich Palace–in the presence of sundry French nobles when de Vere entered the arena. The earl probably sensed hint of awkwardness colors the account of this event, as one of the leading Francophobes at court was entertaining some of Alençon's strongest allies and advocates. De Vere asked to join the game. Sidney first ignored de Vere and then, upon a second, more insistent request, Sidney responded in words that offended de Vere. (The eyewitness does not say what these words were.) De Vere, by now red in the face with both embarrassment and anger, insisted that Sidney stop playing immediately till they could settle the matter. Sidney did no such thing, in response to which de Vere branded Sidney a "puppy." More angry words were batted across the net, and Sidney ultimately left in a rage, preparing to fight a duel with de Vere. But the queen forbade it. Some of de Vere's adversaries would even suggest that he secretly planned to murder Sidney.

However, beyond the time frame and the identities of the key players, the actual course of events surrounding the tennis-court blowup remains obscure. The historical sources–de Vere's adversaries' account, Fulke Greville's eyewitness, and the works of Shake-speare–are strongly partisan on either side. De Vere's enemies make the earl of Oxford look like a petty criminal without a shred of honor, picking a quarrel with Sidney, shamelessly shirking a duel, and then lurking in the shadows to murder him. De Vere, on the other hand, avers that it was Sidney who was too cowardly to face his opponent man-to-man. (In *Twelfth Night*, SIR ANDREW AGUECHEEK is goaded into provoking a duel but then occupies several comic scenes trying ignominiously to wriggle his way out of it.)

De Vere also suggests that Lord Burghley was actually the primary figure responsible for stoking these fires. In *Hamlet,* POLONIUS recites to one of his servants a list of dirty tricks that can be used to discredit a courtier. One such deception, the old counselor notes, involves starting a smear campaign over a "falling out at tennis." The literary critic E. K. Chambers recognized that POLONIUS may be alluding here to the infamous Sidney–de Vere tennis court quarrel.

Moreover, the poet Edmund Spenser also suggests that Burghley pulled strings to turn the quarrel into a scandal. Spenser's poem *Muiopotmos* (1590), about a butterfly fluttering into a spider's web, has been recognized as an allegory about Burghley's machinations against Sidney in the tennis court dispute. As the Alençon negotiations came ever closer to being finalized, Burghley no doubt wanted to prevent both parties–Sidney the Alençon opponent and de Vere the loose cannon–from spoiling the negotiations. Wasting their time squabbling with each other would be one easy way of keeping both Sidney and de Vere away from the queen's bargaining table. Spenser mused:

> I sing of deadly dolorous debate
> Stirr'd up through wrathful nemesis despite
> Between two mighty ones of great estate
> Drawn into arms and proof of mortal might.

As the wet and dreary fall of 1579 dragged on, neither the Alençon marriage nor the de Vere–Sidney dispute reached any resolution. The queen kept de Vere under close supervision, mandating that he not leave his rented lodgings near the court at Greenwich. One of Sidney's continental friends, Hubert Languet, wrote him in November to say that the German prince Jan Casimir felt "great pain" for Sidney in his contentions with de Vere. "[Casimir] begs you to consider whether he can do anything to assist you, for he assures you that you shall not want his good offices," the correspondent notes. On January 27, 1580, the queen, who had already interceded to cool these hotheads down, took de Vere out for a walk in the orchard near Whitehall. According to the questionable testimony of Charles Arundell, on the same day de Vere sent Sidney two written challenges. (The challenges, if they ever existed, have not survived.) No further developments are known, other than the continuation of de Vere's house arrest.

*   ❧

De Vere and Sidney were well suited for each other's enmity. Both were exceptionally intelligent and well-educated young men wielding great worldly knowledge and literary talents. Both were also quick to anger and prone to carrying grudges. But in the ongoing war for the queen's continually distracted attentions, these two temperamental courtiers were both being outmaneuvered by an older man of more pedestrian bearing.

He was Sir Christopher Hatton, that same mawkish parliamentarian whom the queen had doted on since he'd danced his way into her heart in 1562. Since the royal flirtations cited in a previous chapter, "Lids" had slowly climbed the ladder of court advancement. In 1577, Hatton had been knighted, appointed vice chamberlain of England, and made a member of Her Majesty's Privy Council. He was no match for de Vere or Sidney in a war of wit or intellect. But he was charismatic, a smart politician, could dance a pretty galliard, and he still cut a handsome figure. Hatton was also a team player, whereas the earl of Oxford was all renegade.

In the spring and early summer of 1579, Hatton had joined with Leicester in opposing the Alençon marriage. With a Leicester alliance in place, de Vere now had double the cause to oppose Hatton. Leicester and Hatton flexed their power on the Privy Council to win a near-unanimous vote against the Alençon match. (With considerable political skill, Hatton also played both sides against the middle, condemning the anti-Alençon pamphleteer John Stubbs in Parliament and remaining on close terms with the French envoys.)

Throughout the Alençon affair, Hatton was still the dispenser of syrupy epistles to Elizabeth. "The writing of your fair hand, directed by your constant and sacred heart, do raise in me joy unspeakable," he gushed in a 1580 letter, signed "Your Majesty's 'Sheep' and most bound vassal." An undated letter the "Sheep" wrote was also probably penned around this time. Hatton wrote to his queen:

> You are the true felicity that in this world I know or find. God bless you forever. The branch of the sweetest bush I will wear and bear to my life's end. God doth witness I feign not. It is a gracious favor, most dear and welcome unto me. Reserve it to the "Sheep"—he hath no tooth to bite; where the "Boar's" tusk may both raze and tear.

The "Sheep" promised to adorn himself with a branch of rosemary or some other "sweet bush." This nonsensical piece of costuming would forever remind him of his beloved—and would also, no doubt, make him a laughingstock among everyone else at court. The tusk of Hatton's nemesis, a certain "Boar"—the animal on de Vere's heraldic crest—was evidently on the "Sheep's" mind too. And for good reason. According to perhaps the most tantalizing paper trail in de Vere's life, the earl was doing some noteworthy razing and tearing at the time.

This is one instance that an original play manuscript written by de Vere survived—for at least a century and a half, if not down to the present day. A comedy de Vere wrote around the time of Hatton's letter made its way into the collection of de Vere's sometime secretary and literary protégé Abraham Fleming. During the early eighteenth century, Fleming's archives transferred to the household of the antiquarian Francis Peck. Peck, an assiduous if disorganized scholar, published in 1732 a long list of documents he intended to bring into print soon. One of them was "a pleasant conceit of Vere, earl of Oxford, discontented at the rising of a mean gentleman in the English court, circa 1580." Peck died eleven years thereafter, never having gotten around to this "pleasant conceit," or indeed anything else from the Fleming vaults. No trace of Fleming's papers has surfaced since.

If someday the Fleming archive can be relocated, the "pleasant conceit" that nearly surfaced in the eighteenth century could well be one of the great leviathans of literary history. De Vere's "pleasant conceit discontented at the rising of a mean gentleman [*Hatton*] circa 1580" is arguably an early draft of *Twelfth Night*. As the first Shake-speare manuscript ever–no original notes or drafts of any Shake-speare play or poem has ever been found–this document would join the ranks of the Nowell Codex *(Beowulf)* as one of the priceless treasures of Western culture.

There are at least three reasons for equating an early *Twelfth Night* with Peck's "pleasant conceit by Vere, earl of Oxford . . . circa 1580."

The first is that de Vere and Hatton were notorious rivals circa 1580, and *Twelfth Night* mocks Hatton relentlessly: *Twelfth Night's* self-infatuated clod MALVOLIO is a barely concealed caricature of Queen Elizabeth's "sheep." SIR TOBY BELCH, for one, calls MALVOLIO a "rascally sheep-biter." Moreover, MALVOLIO happens upon a prank letter designed to make him look like an ass in front of the entire household. The letter is signed "The Fortunate Unhappy"–an English reversal of the Latin pen name (*Felix Infortunatus;* "the happy unfortunate") that Hatton used.

The second reason is that *Twelfth Night* refers to the 1580–81 English mission of the Jesuit priest Edmund Campion. Campion, who was one of de Vere's commencement speakers at Oxford University in 1566, had spent much of the 1570s preaching his message abroad, primarily in Prague. Campion had returned to England in 1580, however, at a time of heightened tensions. The pope had recently openly advocated for the assassination of Queen Elizabeth.

Upon the urging of the queen's more stringent antipapists (Burghley, Walsingham, Leicester, and Hatton), Campion was to be made an example. He was arrested in 1581 and tortured. His treason trial was a farce, even by the standards of the day: Racked so brutally that he couldn't even raise his right hand to be sworn as a witness, Campion was given all of two hours to work on his courtroom defense. He was even denied use pen, ink, or paper to compose his thoughts.

One of de Vere's secretaries, Anthony Munday, served as a witness at

Campion's trial. De Vere thus enjoyed unusual access to the facts surrounding Campion's case. In perhaps the most enigmatic scene in *Twelfth Night* (Act 4, Scene 2), MALVOLIO is thrown into a mock prison and denied pen, ink, and paper. The fool FESTE cross-examines MALVOLIO with his characteristically witty doublespeak, tossing off an aside about a "hermit of Prague who never saw pen and ink." FESTE then cross-examines MALVOLIO, who only wants what Campion couldn't have.

> MALVOLIO Good fool, as ever thou wilt deserve well at my hand, help
> me to a candle and pen, ink, and paper.... Fool, there was never man
> so notoriously abused. I am as well in my wits, fool, as thou art.
> FESTE But as well, then you are mad indeed if you be no better in your
> wits than a fool.

This scene presents Campion not as a character–MALVOLIO still represents Hatton and FESTE still represents de Vere–but rather as a point of contention. De Vere puts Hatton in Campion's shoes, expressing his discontent with a crooked system that could so heartlessly demolish a man in the name of religion.

The third reason for equating *Twelfth Night* with the "pleasant conceit of Vere, earl of Oxford," has to do with the geopolitical scene "circa 1580." *Twelfth Night* captures the mood of a brief moment on the international stage between 1578 and '80. During the 1570s, Spain commanded a strong but hardly invincible navy. However, in 1578 King Philip of Spain was handed a golden opportunity when King Sebastian of Portugal turned up missing in action after personally leading an idiotic crusade against Morocco.

If Philip secured the Portuguese throne, he could then consolidate his navy with Portugal's and turn his country into the undisputed military powerhouse of sixteenth-century Europe. Between 1578 and 1580, all eyes in Elizabeth's court were on Portugal and King Philip's attempts to secure the Portuguese crown. King Sebastian of Portugal had left no heir or clear line of succession, and to make matters worse, no one was even certain that Sebastian had died in 1578. On January 31, 1580, King Philip of Spain prevailed. The Portuguese kingdom and military were now to be under Spain's command. English strategists had, with one act of succession, seen their country's future. A Spanish armada launching a full-fledged invasion of England was suddenly not such a crazy idea.

Yet, if Sebastian washed ashore someday, he could rightfully seize the crown back from Spain and cripple the Spanish menace. Rumors persisted well after Spain's absorption of Portugal–indeed, well into the seventeenth century–that Sebastian was still alive and preparing to make his triumphant return. Many in Elizabeth's court had also championed the cause of Antonio, a pretender to the Portuguese throne. Antonio visited England in 1580 and '81 to muster support for his case as the rightful king of Portugal. Antonio found two supporters in Sidney (SIR ANDREW AGUECHEEK) and Hatton (MALVOLIO).

The story of *Twelfth Night* is in part the story of two friends, ANTONIO and SEBASTIAN, who are reunited when the latter washes ashore and into the action of the drama. SEBASTIAN is widely believed to have perished at sea, and he and his chum ANTONIO spend much of the play attempting to disentangle themselves from a series of misapprehensions that are the stock-in-trade of Shake-spearean comedy.

The "pleasant conceit of Vere, earl of Oxford, discontented at the rising of a mean gentleman in the English court, circa 1580," may, like the long-lamented King Sebastian, one day turn up and change the fate of every character in the ongoing drama of the legacy of Shake-speare.

Just north of the old London city walls, at the intersection of Houndsditch and Bishopsgate Street, a luxurious two-acre property stood out amid the surrounding real estate, with gardens and a bowling green skirting the central mansion. The palatial home, built by the goldsmith Jasper Fisher, was known to locals as Fisher's Folly or Mount Fisher. De Vere bought Fisher's Folly sometime in early 1580. One of de Vere's ancestors had probably occupied this land during the twelfth century, and now the seventeenth earl sank his ever more burdened purse into this money pit. The Folly, a long and luxurious house with its own private chapel, was set back from Bishopsgate behind a row of gardens and shade trees. The chronicler John Stow said that Queen Elizabeth once visited the mansion, although whether the royal stay occurred during de Vere's tenancy or the subsequent owner's is unknown.

Across the street from Fisher's Folly stood the notorious Bedlam insane asylum, where two to three dozen emotionally disturbed men and women from around London were held. Bedlam was closed to the public–although a curious lord would have been able to finagle a tour of the prisonlike grounds, if he were so curious. Bona fide OPHELIAS were there for the viewing. The man who was Shake-speare clearly had studied the "distracted" mind up close at some point in his life. *King Lear*'s EDGAR, feigning madness for the purpose of disguise, gives himself the folkloric name "Tom o' Bedlam"–perhaps in homage to the institution where the author observed psychosis in its most pronounced forms.

A third of a mile north of Fisher's Folly was a site of ascending importance to de Vere: London's commercial theaters. The Theatre and The Curtain were revolutionizing the local theatrical scene, as the Venetian and Sienese commedia dell'arte had been transforming theirs. Both London theaters, so far as can be determined today, resembled their architectural offspring that later cropped up on the Bankside of the Thames: the Globe, the Swan, and the Rose. The Curtain and The Theatre were round or polygonal structures with enclosed galleries surrounding an open yard with the stage at one end.

The location of the first two theaters was carefully chosen. Londoners had gathered for years in the adjoining Finsbury Fields to play, picnic, and sport. Finsbury's recreation grounds gave the new theaters a captive audience on any sunny summer's day. More important for their survival, the site of the theaters also lay on the grounds of a dissolved priory. Thus the properties fell under Elizabeth's jurisdiction and not the city's. Whereas London's Puritanical city fathers hated drama, Queen Elizabeth I was well known for her indulgence of players and their entertainments. She conveniently overlooked the plethora of vices—gambling, prostitution, thievery, and numerous other crimes—that took place within the public theaters' walls. The atmosphere inside the theaters was so rowdy that one could buy a ticket to a play and never hope to see a single moment of the show. A rogue could instead mill about, cut a purse or two, join in on the various games of dice and cards being played in the lobby, or even onstage, and then spend the winnings on a whore who might practice her trade at a nearby brothel or in one of the box seats.

By the time de Vere occupied Fisher's Folly in 1580, Londoners were heading daily by the hundreds to The Theatre and The Curtain, whenever the elements and the church calendar agreed. Up Bishopsgate Street and through the parks behind Bedlam, the joiners, the gentlemen, the alewives, the students, and the vagabonds all ventured. "I . . . saw such concourse of people through the fields," one pamphleteer wrote in 1589, "that I knew the play was done." Plays at the public theaters now were one thing all Londoners—save for a vocal minority of religious zealots—had in common. If de Vere hadn't recognized the potential of this new mass medium before, the crowds filing past his front yard garden every afternoon served as a diurnal reminder.

To the Puritans and hard-core moralists, though, the theaters were simply dens of iniquity and vice. No Christian nation, they said, should ever harbor such public haunts of sin and corruption. One popular polemicist, Stephen Gosson, drew a scatological comparison between the popular stage and the legendary fifth labor of Hercules. "Plays of themselves [are] as filthy as the stables of Augeas, impossible to be cleaned before they be carried out of England with a stiff stream," Gosson wrote in his 1581 diatribe *Plays Confuted in Five Actions*. "And the banishing of them [is] as worthy to be registered in the labors of Hercules as the conquering of the wild boar of Erymanthus that wasted the country round about."

Like Hatton's "boar" whose "tusk may both raze and tear," the historical identity of Gosson's boar is not hard to discern. De Vere was gaining notoriety by his involvement with the theater, and common pamphleteers—lacking the political power to challenge a nobleman by name—were crying foul.

Although de Vere had previously shown no interest in keeping his father's dramatic troupe going, by April of 1580 something had changed. During the winter or early spring of 1580, de Vere had taken over the Earl of Warwick's Men. His company, performing at The Theatre, was already causing a stir. On April 13, the Privy Council arrested two actors from the newly reorganized Earl of Oxford's Men for unspecified "committing of disorders and frays upon the gentlemen of the Inns of Court." (Whether these "disorders and frays" were of a physical or satirical nature, the Council recorder does not indicate.) This latest infraction prompted London's Lord Mayor to send an urgent letter to the queen's Lord Chancellor, begging him to shut down the theaters. "The players of plays, which are used at The Theatre... are a very superfluous sort of men and of such faculty as the laws have disallowed, and their exercise of those plays is a great hindrance to the service of God," the mayor wrote. "Therefore I humbly beseech Your Lordship... that the said players and tumblers be wholly stayed and forbidden as ungodly and perilous." The Lord Chancellor, bowing to his sovereign's tastes, did nothing.

Just days before, God had certainly sent a message to his true believers. An earthquake rattled the tankards around London during the late afternoon of April 6, when the day's plays were in progress. According to an eyewitness account recorded by de Vere's sometime servant Thomas Churchyard, some audience members in the lower galleries leaped to the yard below. Other playgoers "were so shaken, especially those that stood in the highest rooms and standings, that they were not a little dismayed, considering that they could no way shift for themselves." Puritan pamphleteers, such as Philip Stubbs, saw this as God's retribution for the theater's "devilish exercises." Conveniently left out of the pious polemics is the fact that only minor injuries were sustained at The Theatre and The Curtain, but two people were killed by falling stones in Westminster Abbey.

The first Elizabethan theatrical district was enjoying its first boom, and de Vere was living and working in the thick of it. The early seventeenth-century English playwright George Chapman arguably had de Vere in mind when he sketched out the roguish, almost FALSTAFFian character "Monsieur D'Olive" D'Olive, in a play of the same name (written circa 1604), delivers a resounding encomium to the principle of keeping an intellectually and artistically stimulating household.

> D'OLIVE Tush, man! I mean at my chamber, where we may take free
> use of ourselves; that is, drink sack and talk satire and let our wits run
> the wild goose chase over court and country. I will have my chamber
> the rendezvous of all good wits, the shop of good words, the mint of
> good jests, an ordinary of fine discourse; critics, essayists, linguists,
> poets, and other professors of that faculty of wit, shall at certain hours
> i'th' day resort thither. It shall be a second Sorbonne, where all doubts

> or differences of learning, honor, duellism, criticism, and poetry shall
> be disputed.

In the spacious galleries of Fisher's Folly, de Vere began to make his home "the rendezvous of all good wits." The homeowner had certainly hired two of London's more talented scribes.

Sometime between 1580 and 1582, de Vere had retained Anthony Munday and John Lyly as his private secretaries, servants who handled the earl's letters and personal papers and served as amanuenses for his writing projects. Munday and Lyly also occupied themselves cranking out poetry and prose for their master's consent and their own delight. And now, with the new mansion, the earl housed himself, his apprentices, and doubtless many other hangers-on, under the same roof. Fisher's Folly, one suspects, had become part literary mecca, part bohemian hangout, and part pulp factory.

Munday would use his apprenticeship to produce noteworthy–if not exactly immortal–literature. Munday's *Mirror of Mutability* (1579) is a narrative poem about the Seven Deadly Sins that experiments with blank verse and new forms of meter. Munday's *Zelauto* (1580) is a Homeric novel of worldly adventure that contains a variation on the plotline of *The Merchant of Venice*. Munday, newly returned from his own continental travels, dedicated both works to de Vere. He also collaborated with his employer on a poem that both laments and celebrates the life of the true Renaissance man.

The anonymous "Pain of Pleasure" (c. 1580), long assumed on little evidence to have been written by Munday, has recently been reattributed to de Vere by the literary scholar and novelist Sarah Smith. The "Pain of Pleasure," probably inspired by a similar poem by George Gascoigne, recites the many joys, pursuits, and vanities familiar to a well-rounded Renaissance courtier's life. "The Pain" extols the trappings of nobility (courtly love, opulence, well-bred horses and dogs, hunting, and hawking), the most laudable qualities of a man of the court (honor, erudition, beauty), the athletic prowess expected of him (fencing, climbing, wrestling, shooting, bowling, tennis, leaping, dancing), and the omnibus fields of learning he must command (medicine, law, astronomy, physiology, cosmography, philosophy, music, divinity). Each of these "pleasures" inspires between one and seventeen stanzas of poetic exposition. The author, it quickly becomes clear, writes about these diverse topics from firsthand experience. However, as the title implies, each "pleasure" exacts its price. Beauty and riches breed shallowness and avarice; sports and exercise lead to gambling and injury; a life spent feeding the mind also starves the soul; and so on.

"The Pain of Pleasure" offers a rare glimpse into the kind and quality of writing de Vere was doing at age thirty. He's still prone to molasses-mouthed alliteration ("As in such sort doth settle our delight,/ As doth our wits withdraw from wisdom quite."). He devotes too much verbiage to some things while shortchanging others. (The rich topic of music merits only two stanzas, while he overextends himself with 102 lines about hiking and climbing.) His pacing and meter feel forced at times. And yet, the fun he has with rhythm and language can be infectious. ("Lie here, lie there, strike out your blow at length,/ Strike and thrust with him, look to your dagger hand.") He's discovering his instinct for drama and pithy dialogue, as in this excerpt about an archery tournament: "'Tush,' says another, 'he may be excused,/ Since the last mark, the wind doth greater grow.'/ At last he claps in the white suddenly,/ Then: 'Oh, well shot!' the standers-by do cry." He's using the tension of his rhetorical formula—on the one hand, on the other hand—to draw the reader's interest. As Smith notes, the poem is no *Venus and Adonis*. But, she adds, "The poet of 'The Paine of Pleasure' can (just barely) be mentioned in Shakespeare's company."

Like Munday, John Lyly would use his tenure as de Vere's secretary to publish works that were probably collaborations with his boss. In 1579 Lyly wrote one of the first English novels ever, *Euphues: The Anatomy of Wit*. *Euphues* tells of an Italianate courtier's travels and his travails at love. Lyly dedicated *Euphues* to Thomas West, Baron Delaware. The following year, Lyly dedicated *Euphues*'s sequel *(Euphues and His England)* to de Vere. In Lyly's dedicatory epistle to de Vere, Lyly admits that in composing *Euphues*, he regularly visited "Homer's basin" to "lap up" the literary musings that his unnamed Homer cast off. *Euphues*, Lyly says, was sent

> to a nobleman to nurse, who with great love brought him [*Euphues*] up for a year, so that wheresoever he wander he hath his nurse's name in his forehead, where sucking his first milk he cannot forget his master.

Lyly's "Homer" appears to have been de Vere.

The Euphues novels reveal both Lyly's and his master's playful side. Often read as a straightforward romance or courtly book of manners, *Euphues* actually satirizes these very same traditions. In the words of literary historian Theodore L. Steinberg, *Euphues* is England's first "anticourtesy book." Although de Vere would continue to draw from Castiglione's *Courtier* for his own writings for the rest of his life, he, too, must have recognized that the sanctimonious tone and omniscient voice of the courtly advice genre was a satirical plum ripe for the picking. Thus Lyly created a parody, with de Vere's encouragement and perhaps even collaboration, using pompous and overblown language that is the hallmark of the "Euphuistic" style, making Lyly's protagonist an antithesis of Castiglione's ideal. Euphues, as painted by Lyly's brush, is boorish, misogynistic, bullheaded, insensate, arrogant, and deaf to others' advice but quick to dispense his own. One can readily imagine the late nights of laughter and invention that went into these novels as de Vere drove Lyly's parody-in-progress ever farther beyond the pale.

The formula worked. Lyly soon found himself sitting atop a two-volume franchise that London bookstalls continued to stock well into the next century. Lyly's employer also lent his support–and probably free lodging at Fisher's Folly–to the Euphuistic authors Thomas Watson and Robert Greene. Both of these authors would dedicate works to de Vere and, not coincidentally, publish books that would influence or even serve as sources for the Shake-speare canon.

De Vere would also toy with Euphuism in plays that recall his Fisher's Folly years: *Romeo and Juliet, Much Ado About Nothing, Love's Labor's Lost,* and *Twelfth Night* in particular. Shake-speare and Lyly were to become, at least in comedy, stylistic first cousins. Scholars have long recognized Lyly as perhaps the single most influential Elizabethan playwright for Shake-speare–in demonstrating how to mix wit with romance, in relying upon female perspectives and characters for comedy, in interspersing rustic with noble story lines. The voluminous scholarship on Lyly and Shake-speare certainly has recognized a crucial relationship between these two Elizabethan literary figures, but the influence flowed both ways. John Lyly may indeed have been the source of important ideas and innovations in Elizabethan literature. But it was in the context of Lyly's job as Shake-speare's private secretary.

One additional factor made Fisher's Folly an even more attractive buy for the earl of Oxford. Sometime in 1579, de Vere had begun seeing a younger woman, and Vere House–where his wife, Anne, had full access–could hardly have been a site for the couple's trysts. Her name was Anne Vavasour, and this nineteen-year-old courtly belle was just beginning a tempestuous life at court.

Vavasour was a tall and dark-haired country girl from the north, hailing from a family of genteel blood. (The term *vavasour* was a feudal rank between baron and knight.) Vavasour was cousins with de Vere's Catholic compatriot Charles Arundell, while her sister's mother-in-law was a Spenser, possibly of the same family as the poet. Her lean, equine features would soon be drawing the attentions of numerous courtly gentlemen–exciting the jealous rage of a queen who demanded that her maids of honor be bona fide vestal virgins.

Vavasour made a brilliant impression, dazzling courtiers with her beauty, poetic prowess, and wit. The girl's uncle, Thomas Knyvet, a groom of the queen's privy chamber, had introduced Vavasour to court and won her a place as gentlewoman of the queen's bedchamber. However, Vavasour's cousin Arundell, still part of de Vere's Catholic circle, was almost certainly the man who brought her into Shake-speare's orbit.

Of Vavasour's courtship with de Vere, four poems survive to attest to the infatuation and its aftermath. One poem, said to be "made by the earl of Oxford and Mistress Anne Vavasour," presents a commonplace pastoral conceit: A comely young wench wanders into the woods to think aloud about love. She asks advice of the trees and rocks, and the final syllable of each question echoes back to her with an answer.

> What wight [*man*] first caught this heart and can from bondage it
>   deliver? *Vere.*
> Yet who doth most adore this wight, o hollow caves? Tell me true!
>   *You.*
> What nymph deserves his liking best, yet doth in sorrow rue? *You.*

Walter Raleigh wrote some verses of advice to Vavasour, urging her to beware of this charming nobleman for whom she was falling:

> Many desire, but few or none deserve
> To cut the corn, not subject to the sickle.
> Therefore take heed, let fancy never swerve
> But constant stand, for mower's minds are fickle.
>   For this be sure, the crop being once obtain'd
>   Farewell the rest, the soil will be disdain'd.

In *Love's Labor's Lost,* Vavasour turns up as the choosy bachelorette ROS-ALINE. ROSALINE and her wooing lord (BEROWNE) trade echoing barbs in courtly combats of wit.

> BEROWNE My gentle sweet,
>   Your wit makes wise things foolish . . .
>   And rich things but poor.
> ROSALINE This proves you wise and rich, for in my eye–
> BER. I am a fool, and full of poverty.
> ROS. But that you take what doth to you belong,
>   It were a fault to snatch words from my tongue.

One wonders how many of ROSALINE's precious snipes were indeed snatched from the lips of the Yorkshire lass with a razor's tongue.

Another Shake-spearean heroine shares key traits–witty and combative, proud and reluctant to be wooed–with Vavasour. For centuries, critics have noticed ROSALINE's close kinship with *Much Ado About Nothing*'s witty protagonist BEATRICE. This is for good reason. *Much Ado*'s BEATRICE presents an even more candid glimpse into de Vere's affair with Vavasour.

BEATRICE is a sharp-witted lynx who, as her uncle explains, is engaged in "a kind of merry war" between herself and a vainglorious soldier named BENEDICK. The latter claims to be a lifelong bachelor, a state of marital purgatory that de Vere must have felt very much at home in by 1580. Just below the surface of BENEDICK and BEATRICE's sportive barbs is an adolescent flirtatiousness that one might expect to see in the teenaged Vavasour. For a thirty-year-old married nobleman with a four-year-old daughter, on the other hand, such shenanigans bespeak a man looking upon middle age and grasping at a fleeting opportunity to enjoy the carefree teenaged years he'd never had.

The affair almost exploded into an international incident in early 1580 when Vavasour became pregnant. So far as is known, Elizabeth, and indeed nearly everyone else at court, knew nothing.

De Vere, however, did partly confide in his cousin Henry Howard that he was in hot water. In late February of 1580, the two were walking along the terrace at Howard House—in London near Smithfield. Howard recalled:

> I began to deal with him about the trimming up of Fisher's Folly, and [it was] no great portion of His Lordship's wisdom considering the price. He told me that he was in hand with [Fisher's Folly] but some other should enjoy the pleasure. I demanded why, but he would not answer in a good while, till at the last he said he would deal plainly with me.
>
> "There is a cause," said [de Vere], not telling what it was, "that drives me to depart from hence. You are my cousin-german [*first cousin*] and most like of all men to be doubted and suspected for my going hence, considering your good devotion toward me. . . ."
>
> "Whither will you go, my lord?" said I.
>
> "To Spain," quoth he, "where I have promise to be well entertained."
>
> I told him that in my conceit this was the very worst course he could take, considering the jealousies between our states if ever he meant to return again. But if either debt or any such like cause should drive him hence, his best way were to bide in France, that if the [Alençon] marriage should after take effect, Monsieur [Alençon] might be witness of his good demeanor and be a means for his recovery.
>
> "But, my lord," said I, "what cause should make you lose this opportunity of benefiting both yourself and others, since you seem the likest man to wax great in Monsieur's favor if he come o'er? Else perhaps the queen will give you leave to travel, which is the surest way, because you may return at pleasure, and liberty is always acceptable."
>
> "God's blood!" said he. "Press me not about the cause, for it stands not now upon *quid est dialectica*, nor I will [*would?*] not tarry."

Quid est dialectica is Latin for "What is the logic?" De Vere, in his own mockingly formal way, told his cousin that if this crisis (the unnamed "cause") could actually be solved like a mathematical puzzle, he wouldn't be bothering with such extreme measures as fleeing to Spain. The "cause" was clearly something that could get him in trouble with the queen and with his in-laws. If his mistress carried their love child to term, he had no wish to stick around and see what devious punishments they would cook up for him. "There is not in the world a person more ingrateful than the queen," de Vere reportedly told Howard later in the same conversation.

De Vere just wanted to flee the country and deal with the consequences later. He claimed to have £15,000 "so bestowed as it should be safer much than if he carried it about him." (This may be the missing £15,000 dowry, perhaps still awaiting de Vere's pickup.) When Howard asked how de Vere would earn a living in Spain, de Vere replied that he "would find a better trade than the bearing of a white waster"—the staff he bore in his essentially pointless ceremonial role as Lord Great Chamberlain of England.

If Howard's account of the encounter is to be believed, around Easter of 1580, a new life overseas nearly ripped de Vere out of the England he was only beginning to transform with his pen and his patronage. It was, however, an alternate world he would never have to inhabit. Vavasour miscarried.

This is the same story that *Much Ado About Nothing* obliquely tells. Pregnancy and a dead or miscarried child is often in the background of BENEDICK and BEATRICE's words. BEATRICE's first line in the play is to inquire about BENEDICK:

BEATRICE I pray you, is *Signior Montanto* returned from the wars or no?

Signior Montanto translates to "Lord Upward Thrust." When writing verses in BEATRICE's honor, BENEDICK discovers that he can "find no other rhyme for *lady* but *baby*." And BEATRICE says that BENEDICK once lent his heart to her. "And I gave him use for it," she says. "A double heart for his single one." BEATRICE giving "use" to BENEDICK carries a sexual overtone, while the "double heart" she yielded up suggests the compounded interest of conception. BEATRICE and BENEDICK also refer several times to the labors of Hercules— penance that the ancient hero undertook for killing his own children. BEATRICE later notes, "I am not for him. Therefore, I will even take sixpence . . . and lead his apes into hell." This line comes from an old English ballad ("The Maid and the Palmer") wherein a maid leads an ape into hell by way of atoning for a dead illegitimate child.

Vavasour's miscarriage no doubt made for some very tense months in the spring and early summer of 1580. The April 1580 earthquake can only have added to the strain of de Vere's life spinning quickly out of control. ("I look for an earthquake, too, then," BENEDICK says.) Yet de Vere continued to play with fire. *Much Ado* hints at their extended temptation of the Fates: BEATRICE not only conceived a stillborn, the play suggests, but she hints that she's been inseminated again. Halfway through *Much Ado*, BEATRICE gets sick—she says she's "stuffed." In response to this, an attendant "pricks" BEATRICE with a thistle and gives the maid "distilled *carduus benedictus*." Other than making the obvious pun on her lover's name, the cure-all *carduus* potion had one special application for women. Renaissance doctors administered *carduus* to diagnose pregnancy.

Conception, as HAMLET notes, may well be a blessing, but not for a nineteen- or twenty-year-old lady-in-waiting to the queen. And this time around, the second pregnancy–Vavasour conceived in June or early July of 1580–continued past all modest means of concealment. Vavasour was growing round-bellied, and by the end of the year, there was little hope that the queen could be kept in the dark much longer. Broad farthingales and expansive skirts might, if one was creative and not a little bit lucky, hide the pregnancy. But once Vavasour went into labor, then what? The riverside parishes of Stepney and Whitechapel were home to numerous inns that served as anonymous birthing centers–places where mistresses of the well-heeled checked in to in the dark of night. But how could a young woman whose every move was monitored by a queen and a gossipy court conceal an actual childbirth? There was little hope de Vere and Vavasour's reputations would survive this incident intact.

All eyes at court were about to witness a new melodrama of de Vere's creation. Fearing, no doubt, that his and Vavasour's child was going to provide grief enough, de Vere decided to come clean on his secret Catholic dealings. For the previous four years, he'd been keeping close friends with his Catholic cousin Henry Howard and Howard's cousin Charles Arundell. The three of them, with an elusive figure named Francis Southwell, had, in their wilder moments, plotted insurrections and wild-eyed schemes to return the British kingdom to the Roman Catholic fold. To de Vere, at least, these complots evidently had about as much basis in reality as did his drunken yarns about imagined Italian battlefield adventures and damsels in distress. De Vere decided for once in his life to quit playing around. Conceiving secret Catholic plots in England circa 1580 was like holding a lit candle over an open barrel of gunpowder. Moreoever, by playing stool pigeon on his coconspirators, de Vere stood a chance to save his own neck in a treason trial that he must have feared he would soon face.

However, de Vere could have used some outside directorial advice when it came time to stage the confrontation scene. He hadn't prepared for the showdown; he was as disorganized as always; and he wore his desperation on his sleeve. On a Friday before Christmas 1580, in the Presence Chamber, de Vere dropped to his knees in front of the queen and confessed that he, Howard, Arundell, and Southwell had reconciled to Rome courtesy of a Jesuit priest whom the French ambassador had later sneaked out of England.

The sight of the earl of Oxford prostrating himself before the entire court must have brought a smile to Sir Christopher Hatton's typically humorless face. De Vere turned to the French ambassador, Mauvissière, to corroborate the story. Admitting complicity in these conspiracies would have been political suicide for Mauvissière, who shrugged his shoulders and told Elizabeth he had no idea what de Vere was talking about. As Mauvissière continues the story:

> On hearing this, the earl of Oxford once again threw himself on his knees before [Elizabeth] and implored her to urge me to tell her the truth. At the same time he begged me to do him the favor and recall a circumstance which touched him very closely. He reminded me that he had sent a message begging me to assist the said Jesuit [who reconciled de Vere and his friends] to return in safety to France and Italy, and that when I had done so he gave me his thanks. I replied clearly and unequivocally to the queen that I had no recollection whatever of this incident. The effect of my reply was that the earl was fairly put to confusion in the presence of [Elizabeth].

However embarrassing this moment was, the humiliation was only just beginning. On Christmas Eve and again on Christmas night, de Vere and Arundell met secretly by the maids' chamber at Westminster—where Vavasour also joined them in the shadows. De Vere tried to bribe Arundell into becoming a witness for the prosecution. Arundell would not budge. Vavasour brainstormed with her lover. Like *King Lear*'s scheming EDMUND, de Vere then tried to incite his near-kinsman to flee, a flight which he could use as a tacit admission of guilt. But nothing would become of the Christmas confab— except for Arundell's compromising revelation weeks later that de Vere had tried to buy him off.

The Privy Council issued writs for the arrest of Arundell and Howard, who sought sanctuary at the Spanish ambassador's residence. The ambassador (Bernardino de Mendoza) hid them. But when the refugees learned that they would simply be placed under house arrest, they turned themselves in. Hatton took custody of Arundell and Howard; Sir Francis Walsingham got Southwell.

De Vere, newly returned to the Anglican fold whence he had come, composed thirty-four questions to be put to Arundell and Howard. The interrogatories ranged from the pointed (Did you ever meet so-and-so or visit such-and-such a place?) to the broad sweeping (How much has the Catholic movement in England grown during your recusancy?). Among de Vere's memoranda are the following queries:

> *Item.* Whether do you know of any offer made to the earl of Oxford from Monsieur [Alençon] that if he [*de Vere*] would forsake the realm and live in France, Monsieur with the help of the king his brother would better house him and furnish him with better ability and revenue than ever he had in England. . . .

Item. What prophecies have you lately seen or heard which might concern the contempt, reproach, and overthrow of our most gracious sovereign whom our Lord God bless forever. . . .

Item. Whether Charles Arundell did not steal over into Ireland within these five years without leave of Her Majesty–and whether that year he was not [*sic*] reconciled or not to the church likewise. . . .

What began as a fact-finding operation, however, quickly devolved. The prisoners turned the investigation on its head. Arundell and Howard were, after all, now living in the custody of one of de Vere's long-standing rivals. Under Hatton's roof, the two cousins began what the Renaissance scholar D. C. Peck has called "a perverse sort of apprenticeship in defamation."

Believing that they were destined for the gallows, Arundell and Howard began flinging mud. Their target was de Vere. Arundell and Howard–and to a lesser extent the more subdued Southwell–churned out nearly one hundred pages of invective against de Vere, accusing him of being a liar, a murderer, an atheist, a pederast, a homosexual, an alcoholic, a practitioner of bestiality and necromancy, a traitor, a vile and unredeemable creature, and a "monstrous adversary . . . who would drink my blood rather than wine."

The Arundell Libels recount the numerous elaborate fictions that de Vere had been known to tell, especially when the ale or sweet wines flowed. Evidently, not only did de Vere love to spin wild yarns, but his audience loved to hear them too. "This lie is very rife with him," Arundell said of one of de Vere's elaborate Italian fictions, "and in it he glories greatly. Diversely hath he told it, and when he enters into it, he can hardly out, which hath made such sport as often have I been driven to rise from his table laughing."

Arundell and Howard's slanders are at once the most revealing and also the most misleading documents from the whole of de Vere's life. De Vere's two previous biographers–B. M. Ward and Alan H. Nelson–have taken polar opposite views on these troublesome papers. The former finds little of any historical value in the entire Arundell-Howard docket, other than as sidelights on a nasty catfight. Nelson, on the other hand, essentially treats the Libels as statements of documentary fact.

As it happens, though, history has conducted a control experiment. Only a few years after Arundell and Howard let fly against de Vere, a nearly identical defamatory screed was leveled at the earl of Leicester. The anonymous 1584 pamphlet *Leicester's Commonwealth* similarly charges Leicester with murder, conspiracy, incest, bigamy, lechery, and generally being "overwhelmed and defamed in all vice." Arundell is, in fact, the most likely author of *Leicester's Commonwealth*. Enmity to Leicester dating from Arundell's father's execution gives Arundell motive aplenty, and the style of writing and the intimate courtly knowledge the libel conveys all point strongly in Arundell's direction.

Historians treat the anti-Leicester libels as "gross and malevolent"; a "mass of misdemeanors and infamies"; and "not only scurrilous but dangerous, even treacherous." Yet, to quote D. C. Peck again, "in our investigations of individual charges, in this and the other libels against the earl [of Leicester], we find few to be entirely true, but few to be entirely false." The Elizabethan historian E. K. Chambers concluded that the bias of the anti-Leicester libels "is too strong to give . . . unsupported statements much credence."

So it goes with the Arundell–Howard Libels against de Vere. They cannot be wholly written off, but no responsible historian has cause to take them at face value either. Consider the Arundell Libels's most disturbing accusation against de Vere: pederasty and bestiality. De Vere, they said, "confessed buggery to William Cornwallis"; he "almost spoiled" his cook; he bragged that he "abused a mare" and "that when women were unsweet, fine young boys were in season." Similar charges would be leveled at the playwright Christopher Marlowe in 1593, just after his death. A strong antitheatrical bias colors both sets of libels: For these libelers, who hated drama, the only understandable motive for spending hours rehearsing theatrical troupes of men and boys would involve sex.

De Vere may well have engaged in any number of crazy or criminal acts. His vices may have been extreme, and perhaps he was bisexual in a culture that could only understand nonheterosexuals as perverts. The Arundell Libels are only as reliable a witness to the earl of Oxford's alleged wrongdoings as *Leicester's Commonwealth* is to the earl of Leicester's. Unless the Arundell Libels can ever be substantiated, they are best treated as they were four hundred years ago: as a compilation of malicious innuendo and hearsay. Instead, the truth must lie somewhere in between. One may provisionally accept some of Arundell and Howard's accusations (such as the many colorful anecdotes of de Vere's tall tales) and throw others out of court for lack of evidence.

As in Sherlock Holmes's "The Adventure of Silver Blaze," the fact that the dog did not bark may provide an important clue as well. De Vere would live on for another quarter century, and despite the named names and alleged witnesses that Arundell and Howard cite, no one ever pressed charges, no lawsuits came out of the libels, no investigations were called, no further accusations emerged, no other scandals arose.

Nevertheless, the queen was growing perturbed with the unbelievable accusations flying back and forth and the ignominy that fell on her court by association. *Much Ado About Nothing* was Shake-speare's response.

One of *Much Ado*'s subplots involves a malaprop-spouting constable named DOGBERRY. DOGBERRY and his fumblebum henchmen unearth a conspiracy central to the play's plotline–concerning the deception of the jealous groom CLAUDIO. The constable and his motley crew then conduct a comic interrogation of the perpetrators. DOGBERRY's scenes onstage are uproarious, yet they often strike readers as extraneous. Critics have offered little insight as to why Shake-speare created this comic diversion. One scholar speaks of "recognition of sure marksmanship directed at a well-defined satiric target," although who or what that target is goes unsaid. But DOGBERRY's satiric target is readily appreciated when one reads the Arundell Libels.

Arundell used conflicting numbering systems to enumerate de Vere's vices. As Arundell testifies:

> First, I will detect him of the most impudent and senseless lies that ever passed the mouth of any man.... His third lie which hath some affinity with the other two is of certain excellent orations he made.... The second vice, wherewith I mean to touch him though in the first I have included perjury in something [*sic*] is that he is a most notorious drunkard and very seldom sober ... thirdly I will prove him a buggerer of a boy ... fifthly to show that the world never brought forth such a villainous monster, and for a parting blow to give him his full payment, I will prove against him his most horrible and detestable blasphemy in denial of the divinity of Christ our Savior and terming the Trinity a fable ... that Joseph was a wittold [*cuckold*] and the Blessed Virgin a whore.
>
> To conclude, he is a beast in all respects and in him no virtue to be found and no vice wanting.

De Vere gave constable DOGBERRY the last word on this matter. "Marry, sir, [the accused] have committed false report," says *Much Ado*'s constable. "Moreover, they have spoken untruths, secondarily they are slanders, sixth and lastly they have belied a lady, thirdly they have verified unjust things, and to conclude, they are lying knaves."

Arundell elsewhere notes that de Vere "has perjured himself a hundred times and damned himself into the pit of hell." Or as DOGBERRY puts it, "Why, this is flat perjury to call a prince's brother 'Villain.' ... O villain, thou wilt be condemned into everlasting redemption for this!"

Divining Edward de Vere's close friends at court is, with the exception of his steadfast ally the earl of Sussex, never a trivial task. However, by mid-January of 1581, de Vere's chief enemies were now known to everyone. Previous tiffs and scuffles no doubt appeared in a new and less partisan light. With a bastard child on the way and two unscrupulous adversaries charting new frontiers in defamation, the Sidney tennis-court quarrel must have now seemed a trifle.

De Vere began to mend severed ties with Sidney. The late duke of Norfolk's eldest son, Philip Howard, had recently inherited the earldom of Arundel, and on January 22 the young Howard hosted a tilt in honor of his new

title. Arundel–not to be mistaken for the libeler Charles Arundell [*sic*]–
assumed the persona of a knight named "Callophisus" or "lover of beauty."
"Callophisus" and his minion "the Red Knight" (Sir William Drury) stood
their ground on the tilt field at Whitehall, armored and festooned in their
chivalric finery, offering to stand in defense of the honor of Queen Elizabeth.
De Vere and Sidney, among other allied comrades-in-arms, responded to the
call. Sidney, as the "White Knight," stepped forward, pretending not to know
which sovereign mistress "Callophisus" was fighting for. Sidney offered instead to combat the earl of Arundel in honor of his own "sovereign mistress
that royal virgin, that peerless prince, that Phoenix and paragon of the world
whom with all devotion I serve." To cheers and jeers from the royal reviewing stand and the capacity crowds filling the bleachers, Sidney made a valiant
attempt–but did not outscore the young and eager "Callophisus."

Sidney had left it to his former adversary to pick up the fallen standard. De
Vere's challenge was, in fact, one of the most elaborately conceived Elizabethan
tiltyard productions ever recorded. Like a nervous actor on opening night, de
Vere had watched his jousting predecessors from behind the curtain of a luxurious orange tawny taffeta tent in plain view of the crowds and the tiltyard. At
the appointed time, according to a contemporary account of the event,

> from forth this tent came the noble earl of Oxenford in rich gilt armor
> and sat down under a great high bay tree–the whole stock, branches,
> and leaves whereof were all gilded over that nothing but gold could be
> discerned.... After a sovereign sound of most sweet music, he mounted
> on his courser very richly caparisoned [*decked out*], when his page, as-
> cending the stairs where Her Highness stood in the window, delivered to
> her by speech his oration.

De Vere himself acknowledged Sidney's athletic prowess and courtly
worthiness–uncharacteristic words of praise that must have caused some
double takes in the queen's reviewing stand. De Vere said:

> But whereas he [*"Callophisus"*] vaunts himself to honor [the queen] above
> all ... this is so far beyond his compass, as the White Knight is above him
> in zeal and worthiness.... Wherefore as a friend to his [*Sidney's*] mind ...
> I mean to try my truth with no less valor than I have desire, not minding
> to disorder so noble a presence but rather to entertain the same with a
> longer abode by diversity and change of arms–and to join with this wor-
> thy White Knight, if the next day may be given to the sword.

For his own tiltyard *nom de guerre*, de Vere borrowed from the Norse legends of a great golden tree in the center of the universe (Yggdrasil), representing the sun. The earl of Oxford's page stood before the queen and recited

the following myth: Once upon a time there was a knight who had once lived in a verdant grove where the trees began to succumb to infections and worms. So he made his way out onto the plains. But the barren lands there were so harsh and unforgiving that the knight soon had to leave the plains too. This is when he first encountered the Yggdrasil. "This tree, fair knight, is called the Tree of the Sun," an old hermit told him, "whose nature is always to stand alone, not suffering a companion, being itself without comparison." The Tree of the Sun was so fair and beautiful that the knight could scarcely believe his eyes. So he kissed the ground and "swore himself only to be the Knight of the Tree of the Sun, whose life should end before his loyalty." The newly dubbed Knight went to sleep sheltered by the Yggdrasil's canopy and there dreamed that he saw "diggers undermining the Tree behind him." De Vere's page continued the tale:

> That Sun Tree suspecting the Knight to give the diggers aid might have punished him in her prison. But failing of their pretense and seeing every blow they struck to light upon their own brains, they threatened him by violence whom they could not match in virtue. . . .
>
> This he will avouch at all assays: himself to be the most loyal Knight of the Sun Tree, which who so gainsayeth, he is here pressed either to make him recant it before he run or repent it after, offering rather to die upon the points of a thousand lances than to yield a jot in constant loyalty.

In the Elizabethan cosmos, the Sun Tree symbolically represented Elizabeth. Assuming the persona of the Knight of the Sun Tree, de Vere was genuflecting before his sovereign, humbly asking her to forgive his recent transgressions. Yes, he had wandered from the grove where he was born (in other words, he had become disillusioned with the Anglican faith in which he was raised), he had spent time in the company of diggers (Arundell and Howard) who were trying to uproot the mighty Sun Tree. But the Sun Tree recognized that her Knight was steadfast and decided not to punish him. The diggers threatened the Knight, but he was unafraid. It was a pat story that obviously stretched the truth, but the man behind the Knight of the Sun Tree armor must have hoped that his queen would nevertheless buy it.

"And after the finishing of the sports," the account of the tournament concludes, "both the [gold-embossed] bay tree and the beautiful tent were by the standers-by torn and rent in more pieces than can be numbered." The crowd looted de Vere's props and scenery. The day ended in both tragedy and triumph—tragedy because crowds had gathered in the stands in such abundance that several were killed and several more injured when the bleachers collapsed. On the other hand, the Knight of the Sun Tree took top honors for the day. The queen presented de Vere with his prize.

What the prize was goes unrecorded, although it was probably comparable to what de Vere had won at the tilt ten years earlier: a "table of diamonds." Shake-speare's Sonnet 122 rhapsodizes over just such a trinket:

> Thy gift, thy tables, are within my brain
> Full character'd with lasting memory,
> Which shall above the idle rank remain,
> Beyond all date, even to eternity.

This may be the ultimate thank-you note for the queen's generosity at the tilt-yard.

Yet the Sun Tree was not in a forgiving mood. In the early spring of 1581, Queen Elizabeth finally learned of Vavasour's pregnancy. The queen's maid of honor gave birth on March 21. It was a boy, whom the mother named Edward Veer. The father's first impulse, prevailing rumors had it, was to flee—what was called a "jade's trick" of squirming out of the yoke that constrained him. (In *Much Ado*, BEATRICE uses these words to criticize BENEDICK.) Two days after the birth, Sir Thomas Walsingham noted in a letter:

> On Tuesday at night, Anne Vavasour was brought to bed of a son in the maiden's chamber. The earl of Oxford is avowed to be the father, who hath withdrawn himself with intent as it is thought to pass the seas. The ports are laid for him and therefore if he have any such determination, it is not likely that he will escape. The gentlewoman [on] the selfsame night she was delivered was conveyed out of the house and the next day committed to the Tower. Others that have been found in any ways parties to the cause have been also committed. Her Majesty is greatly grieved with the accident [*incident*], and therefore I hope there will be some such order taken as the like inconvenience will be avoided.

If de Vere ever managed to leave the country, his departure was swiftly followed by an enforced return. A family of international investors, the German Fugger dynasty, noted the scandal in one of their newsletters:

> The earl of Oxford ... is in the Tower for forgetting himself with one of the queen's maids-of-honor, who is in the Tower likewise. This in spite of his having a pretty wife, daughter of the [Lord] Treasurer. But he will not live with her.

The Jacobean Master of the Revels Sir George Buc would later write that for fathering this "base son," de Vere "was committed to the Tower and was [a] long time in [the queen's] displeasure."

༄

The royal opprobrium de Vere had brought on his head—for refusing to reconcile with his wife, for creating such a scandal with Messrs. Howard and Arundell, and for getting one of Her Majesty's maids of honor pregnant—spelled the beginning of a long, cold period away from the hearth of Queen Elizabeth's court. Once the queen had made her disillusionment with the earl of Oxford known, she had effectively declared open season on him. Although de Vere's fellow courtiers had regularly honored him with anywhere between four and eight votes for the prestigious knighthood of the Garter, after Elizabeth dumped him from her list of favorites, he couldn't inspire a single one of them to cast a ballot in his support.

De Vere remained imprisoned in the Tower of London for two and a half months after his attempt to escape the country. For a nobleman, time spent in the Tower meant confinement to a modest but still comfortable furnished space. A courtier, even in disgrace, was well fed, allowed access to his servants, and given plenty of wood and coal for the fireplace. He was allowed to take fresh air and to exercise on the Tower's battlements. A well-heeled prisoner could also receive visitors and enjoy conjugal visits with his spouse—a privilege one may presume that de Vere did not partake in. On the other hand it is safe to assume that his secretaries, Munday and Lyly, made regular visits to their incarcerated master.

One play probably written by de Vere suggests the Tower of London as its birthplace. The unpublished proto-Shake-spearean play *Sir Thomas More*— a manuscript primarily in Munday's handwriting—tells the story of King Henry VIII's famous counselor. More, most famous today for writing the book *Utopia,* tells the story of a loyal servant to Henry VIII who quells an insurrection and is later thrown in the Tower and executed. More, as portrayed in the play, is a spirited and genial courtier whose downfall comes not due to his own failings but rather to the fickle whims of the fates. *Sir Thomas More* is ultimately a cosmic tragedy about a courtier's loyalty to his monarch despite his own unfairly marred fortunes. MORE expresses his contempt for rebellion in stark terms that have been compared to the 1570 *Homily Against Disobedience and Willful Rebellion*—a homily that, as previously noted, may have come from de Vere's own pen. *Sir Thomas More* even castigates those who would try to flee their country.

> MORE Who will obey a traitor?
>   Or how can well that proclamation sound
>   When there is no addition but a rebel
>   To qualify a rebel? . . .
>   What country by the nature of your error
>   Should give you harbor? Go you to France or Flanders,
>   To any German province, Spain or Portugal,

Nay, anywhere that not adheres to England,
Why, you must needs be strangers....
Give up yourself to form, obey the magistrate,
And there's no doubt but mercy may be found if you so seek it.

Current scholarship shows that the *Sir Thomas More* manuscript was later re-visited and revised by at least five other hands. The original story upon which the alterations build, however, is universally agreed to be in Munday's hand-writing. It is thus suggested that Munday's foundation laying for *Sir Thomas More* came in the spring of 1581 in the Tower of London with a frenetic and clemency-seeking earl padding up and down his stony cell, reciting lines into the echoing air.

De Vere, who varying reports suggest paid anywhere from nothing to £2,000 in child support to Vavasour, was probably not seeing his mistress during his imprisonment. Vavasour was not only busy caring for the infant Edward Veer, she may also have started seeing another man—whether during her stint in the Tower or after her unspecified release date. The queen's tilt-yard champion Sir Henry Lee was, it has been argued, probably Vavasour's jailer. Lee and Vavasour would have a long and passionate love affair that be-gan as early as 1581—and would later land Lee in hot water just like de Vere before him. A manuscript poem thought by E. K. Chambers to have been written by Vavasour certainly would have made a fitting end to a fiery affair. The departing lover concludes:

> Thus farewell, friend, I will continue strange.
> Thou shalt not hear by word or writing ought.
> Let it suffice my vow shall never change;
> As for the rest, I leave it to thy thought.

On June 8, 1581, Elizabeth ordered de Vere released from the Tower, al-though he was to remain under house arrest for a month or more. Sometime in July, de Vere wrote his father-in-law a letter "touching my liberty." Eliza-beth had sent the earl a Dutch hat of black taffeta, indicating her acknowl-edgment of his freedom. De Vere thanked Burghley for having done whatever could be done while he was in the Tower. But, de Vere cautions, the queen would probably forget all about her newly released Lord Great Cham-berlain. He notes that the salacious slanders still being kicked out by Arundell and Howard—"the two lords," as de Vere calls them—would continue to sway Elizabeth against him unless certain powerful in-laws could continue to put in a good word. De Vere writes:

> Unless Your Lordship shall make some [move] to put Her Majesty in
> mind thereof, I fear, in these other causes of the two lords, she will

forget me. For she is nothing of her own disposition, as I find, so ready to deliver as speedy to commit—and every trifle gives her matter for long delay.

De Vere goes on to put in perspective the libels and rumors circulating about him. He as much confesses to a shadow of truth to these slanders but at the same time urges Burghley to recognize that they have been blown far out of proportion. "The world is so cunning," de Vere notes, "as of a shadow they can make a substance and of a likelihood a truth. And these fellows, if they be those which I suppose, I do not doubt but so to decipher them to the world, as easily Your Lordship shall look into their lewdness and unfaithfulness."

De Vere would later be vindicated when Arundell and Howard were implicated in the "Throckmorton Plot" on the queen's life in 1583—which would see the former take up exile in France and the latter end up in prison again. Both would again write scurrilous libels to try to extricate themselves from their continued troubles. But in the summer of 1581, de Vere still had to deal with the aftereffects of the Libels.

It was a lonely summer and fall that year, with neither mistress nor wife to turn to for comfort and succor. The emptiness of life outside court and outside his own family was clearly affecting him. De Vere distanced himself from Anne Vavasour and his son, Edward Veer, while at the same time applying to the Court of Wards to serve as foster father to a four-year-old Essex lad named Henry Bullock. By November, de Vere had been declined this wardship.

In December, de Vere started corresponding with his wife again. Copies of two letters from Anne to her wayward husband survive, dated December 7 and 12, 1581. The copies are written in Burghley's handwriting, with his own emendations and interlineations, indicating that they are drafts of a text the spymaster intended for his daughter to copy out in her own hand and sign. In the first letter, "Anne" takes note of "your favor that you began to show me this summer." "Her" words of protest—perhaps written as a collaboration between father and daughter—ring out with the studied eloquence of so many wrongfully accused Shake-spearean heroines:

My good lord, I beseech you in the name of that God, which knoweth all my thoughts and love towards you, let me know the truth of your meaning towards me, upon what cause you are moved to continue me in this misery, and what you would have me do in my power to recover your constant favor—so as Your Lordship may not be led still to detain me in calamity without some probable cause, whereof, I appeal to God, I am utterly innocent.

Five days later, she acknowledges the receipt of a letter in response (now lost). Anne says she's "most sorry to perceive how you are unquieted with the uncertainty of the world"–and adds the zinger "whereof I myself am not without some taste." She assures her husband that her father wishes only the best for him.

Finally, sometime in late December of 1581, de Vere and his wife made their peace. The Alençon marriage proposal was falling apart, but the earl and countess of Oxford were coming back together. Richard Madox, a court observer at Oxford University, wrote on March 3, 1582, that he'd learned "the earl [of Oxford] hath company with his wife since [last] Christmas and taken her to favor." The long-suffering Anne Cecil de Vere, countess of Oxford, had at last taken her long-erring husband back into her bed.

༖

CHAPTER 7

FORTUNE'S DEAREST SPITE

[1582–1585]

B Y JANUARY OF 1582, THE ALENÇON MARRIAGE WAS VIRTUALLY A
dead letter. Alençon, who had been in England since October, had not
given in to Burghley's increasingly untenable demands, including that France
give Calais back to England. At the same time, Burghley was also advocating
that Sir Francis Drake's recent plunder of Spanish treasure be returned to
Spain as a good faith gesture. The Lord Treasurer had begun to hedge his
bets. When Alençon embarked on his final journey to France, on February 7,
1582, Her Majesty was outwardly mournful and spoke of Alençon as her
"brother." Yet, in the confines of her chambers, she danced for joy that the
Alençon match had fallen through. But the end of the Alençon match also
spelled the end of hopes for an heir to the throne from Elizabeth.

It also spelled the end of the first Age of Elizabethan mythology. Poets,
playwrights, pamphleteers, and painters had to date portrayed their monarch
as a nubile and marriageable beauty, a heaven-sent Venus and a terrestrial
Minerva. (The latter-day belief that Elizabeth had sworn a vow of virginity
upon her accession in 1558 is a posthumous myth.) It was only in 1582, at the
collapse of the French marriage, that the cult of the Virgin Queen gained its
footing. Henceforth, Elizabeth would become an earthly manifestation of the
moon goddess Diana (a.k.a. Cynthia). By the close of the decade, Edmund
Spenser's portrayal of Elizabeth as the perpetually chaste Belphoebe would
represent the essence of the Virgin Queen's public image. The works of
Shake-speare, however, do not recognize this shift in propaganda. The Elizabeth of the author's imagination would remain the marriageable young
woman he had intimately known circa 1573–74.

Then again, Elizabeth circa 1582 had become about as foreign a figure to
de Vere as the prince of Siam. The Lord Great Chamberlain of England was

still on the outs with Her Majesty. One further complication would ensure he'd remain so for some time to come.

In early February, court observers recorded an unexpected aftershock stemming from de Vere's former affair with Vavasour. To redeem Vavasour's reputation, her family took to the sword. Two contemporary and all-too-terse reports survive of what Burghley would later colorfully term the "brabbles and frays" between the Vere and Vavasour clans. Vavasour's uncle Thomas Knyvet took charge of the operation. In the words of Walsingham's secretary (Nicholas Faunt) in a letter of March 17:

> In England of late, there hath been a fray between my lord of Oxford and Mr. Thomas Knyvet of the Privy Chamber–who are both hurt, but my lord of Oxford more dangerously. You know Mr. Knyvet is not meanly beloved in court, and therefore he is not like[ly] to speed [*come to*] ill whatsoever the quarrel be.

One of de Vere's servants was killed in the melee. Nothing else is known of this first skirmish in an interfamily war. Where this duel took place, for instance, is not known–certainly not where de Vere would later set it: "In fair Verona, where we lay our scene . . ."

The injury de Vere sustained from his sword fight with Knyvet did not immediately incapacitate him, as de Vere would remain able-bodied enough to ride in another tournament a few years later. However, near the end of his life de Vere would complain, both in his private letters and in the Shakespeare Sonnets numbered 37 and 89, of a debilitating lameness. ("Thus I made lame by fortune's dearest spite/Take all my comfort of my worth and truth.")

The result was that, as the historian Albert Feuillerat observed of the Vere–Vavasour war, "like another time in Verona, the streets of London were filled with the clamorous quarrels of these new MONTAGUES and CAPULETS." Soon after the duel, several men claiming to be employees of de Vere–Burghley would later deny they held any affiliation with the earl's household–began a campaign of attrition against Knyvet and others.

The Italian fencing master Rocco Bonetti was first on their list. Bonetti had in 1575 secured crown patents (injunctions) to protect himself from "the earl of Oxford's men." True-blue Englishmen saw Bonetti's Italian fighting style as cowardly, and no officially sanctioned English fencing school would teach it. So a few courtiers, including de Vere's brother-in-law Peregrine Bertie, imported Bonetti for private instruction. Since the Italian tutor took away business from the crown monopoly of English fencing schools, Bonetti was also seen as a threat. And the fact that he almost never stood up for himself only encouraged bullying. (On one of the two recorded instances Bonetti ever drew his sword in anger, he answered the challenge of an inebriated and unarmed boatman who still managed to "soundly [beat Bonetti] with oars and stretchers for his pains.")

In 1582 Bonetti had just returned from a self-imposed exile in Scotland. Now that the Bergamo native had returned to England, taking up residence in the western Ludgate section of London, Bonetti found that the ostensible earl of Oxford's retainers were still hectoring him. On April 16, Bonetti sought protection at the residence of the French ambassador, Mauvissière. "He tells me that he is threatened by the people of the earl of Oxford, which puts him in great trouble and despair of ever being able to live securely in this realm," the ambassador wrote to the spymaster Sir Francis Walsingham on April 16.

Bonetti's story excites mixed sympathies. After all, if the man were truly so adept at teaching the martial arts, it's hard to believe he was incapable of fending off a few common desperadoes. Still, Bonetti's reputation as a fencing instructor extraordinaire preceded him, and *Romeo and Juliet* pays tribute to the innovations in swordsmanship that Bonetti introduced to England. The play's sword-and-buckler and rapier-and-dagger fights are, in the words of the historian Charles William Wallace, "a mimetic resumé of changes in Elizabethan fencing wrought by Rocco." Bonetti had famously boasted that he could "hit any Englishman with a thrust upon any button," and this finds its way into *Romeo and Juliet* as well. MERCUTIO jests at Bonetti's expense when he compares TYBALT to

> MERCUTIO the very butcher of a silk button—a duelist, a duelist, a
> gentleman of the very first house, of the first and second cause. Ah,
> the immortal *passado*, the *punto reverso*, the hay!
> BENVOLIO The what?
> MER. The pox of such antic lisping, affecting phantasimes, these new
> tuners of accent.

Bonetti would, in just a few years' time, brush off his pugnacious tormenters and establish his own martial arts "colledge." This renegade school of defense, like the London theaters, was to be established on a former church property—a site where the city fathers had no jurisdiction. In 1584, Bonetti set up shop on the Blackfriars "liberty," a converted monastery in Central London nearby where Fleet Ditch meets the Thames.

Blackfriars was a poorly policed neighborhood where rogues and ne'er-do-wells such as "the earl of Oxford's servants" could conduct their mischief with relative impunity. On June 18, two ostensible de Vere retainers named Gastrell and Horsley took advantage of the Blackfriars' liberties to wreak some havoc. That day, Knyvet and four associates were walking through the narrow streets by the Blackfriars gatehouse when the two belligerents jumped the unsuspecting targets.

Sword clashed with pike clashed with fist. Little was visible to anyone but the inner circle gathered around the scrum. (Unlike the de Vere–Knyvet duel in February, this battle resulted in multiple arrests and depositions. Therefore, much more is known about it.) A din of shouts, cries, and exclamations reverberated through the narrow Blackfriars alleys as the afternoon sun cast heavy shadows on the gathering crowds. Arriving waves of boatmen and boat riders craned their necks over the spectators to see the action, and the early comers jumped in with their weapons drawn to get a piece of the action, keep the peace, or perhaps a little of both.

A lawyer named Roger Townshend shuttled back and forth that afternoon between representatives of the disputing families. De Vere had spent part of the afternoon with his sister Mary and her husband, Peregrine Bertie, at their house in the Barbican. In subsequent testimony, Townshend notes he'd heard rumors that de Vere and Bertie were planning to ambush Knyvet and his kin later that day. The rumor was untrue. (Or did de Vere or one of his minions hire Gastrell and Horsley to do the job for him? Or were the "servants" seeking revenge for other parties? The evidence is unclear.) So Townshend went to confront Bertie and de Vere to find out their story. When Townshend arrived at Bertie's house, he discovered Bertie enjoying a walk in his garden. Bertie said he and de Vere had heard that Knyvet and his party were planning to attack *them.* "Thereupon," Townshend notes, "my lord of Oxford himself (and also his men) was somewhat grieved at it."

Monday's tussle generated only bruises, cuts, and animosity. But four days later, on Friday, June 22, Gastrell and another man named Harvey set upon Knyvet's men again near the Blackfriars. Both Gastrell and Harvey sustained wounds in the skirmish, the latter, accidentally, at the hands of the former.

By the third street battle, the authorities were growing tired of vendettas. Something quieted the quarrelers down–for a time, at least. *Romeo and Juliet* begins at just this point, with the PRINCE OF VERONA breaking up another MONTAGUE–CAPULET melee with a new and wary resolve

> PRINCE Three civil brawls bred of an airy word
>   By thee, old CAPULET and MONTAGUE,
>   Have thrice disturb'd the quiet of our streets
>   And made Verona's ancient citizens
>   Cast by their grave-beseeming ornaments
>   To wield old partisans, in hands as old,
>   Canker'd with peace, to part your canker'd hate.
>   If ever you disturb our streets again
>   Your lives shall pay the forfeit of the peace.

These words were probably set down years later, as de Vere recollected the gladiatorial strife. If Lord Burghley is to be believed, the earl of Oxford had nothing to do with the Knyvet quarrelers beyond the original duel. However, the Shake-speare canon suggests something else. As ROMEO laments,

> Doth not [JULIET] think me an old murderer
> Now I have stain'd the childhood of our joy
> With blood remov'd but little from her own?

Romeo and Juliet retains an accurate–if dramatically embellished–chronology of fatalities: First come the three battles mentioned in the beginning of the play. Then, in a subsequent melee, a MONTAGUE falls. (A "slain" servant of de Vere's is buried eight months after the Blackfriars tussles.) Finally, before the armistice that concludes the play, the MONTAGUES fell one last CAPULET on Verona's bloodied streets. (A month after de Vere's man is slain, Burghley records the killing of one of Knyvet's servants.) As a last act, in 1585 de Vere himself was challenged to another duel; he did not answer and the war finally sputtered and died.

A decade later, the author Thomas Edwardes would, in his book *Narcissus* (1595), memorialize the de Vere–Knyvet violence–and the earl's attempts to distance himself from it. Edwardes's book contains an epilogue consisting of a set of laudatory verses about the great poets of the Elizabethan Age. The epilogue to *Narcissus* praises the work of such contemporary writers as Edmund Spenser, Christopher Marlowe, and Shake-speare.

But then Edwardes turns cryptic. Immediately after Edwardes's Shake-speare allusion (a tribute to Shake-speare's epic 1593 poem *Venus and Adonis*) appear a dozen lines about an unspecified nobleman with a "bewitching pen" who "should have been of our rhyme/The only object and the star." This superlative courtly author is, Edwardes implies, in disgrace, "in purple robes disdained"–who also "Differs much from men/Tilting under friaries." Translation: The disgraced courtier poet has distinguished himself from those who brawl and quarrel under the protection of converted friaries such as the Blackfriars.

The mystery poet is, in other words, recognizable as Edward de Vere. *Narcissus*'s Shake-speare commemorative verse and its de Vere commemorative verse, two adjacent sections of the same poem, are arguably one eighteen-line homage to the same person. Edwardes's *Narcissus* appears to be one stunning contemporary allusion to de Vere as Shake-speare.

After June's brabbles and frays, the remainder of 1582 was a quiet year. Expelled from court and low on money, de Vere was exiled as thoroughly as ROMEO is to Mantua. Book dedications, and with them requests for patronage, had slowed to a near standstill. During the banner years of 1579 and '80, when Fisher's Folly must have been a hive of activity, five books had been dedicated to de Vere–all of them proudly displaying full-page reproductions of the seventeenth earl of Oxford's coat of arms. These authors, including de Vere's secretaries Lyly and Munday, had showcased their affiliation as a prize-winning athlete shows off a trophy. The year 1581, on the other hand, saw just one book dedicated to de Vere, with no coat of arms; and this publication had nothing to do with creative literature or the liberal arts–it was merely a translation of the sermons of John Calvin by Thomas Stocker, someone who had grown up in the sixteenth earl of Oxford's household.

In 1582, however, the poet Thomas Watson had the courage to dedicate to de Vere a book of sonnets, *The Hekatompathia*–one of the most distinguished books of Elizabethan poetry that had yet been published. By throwing his lot in with the disgraced earl of Oxford, Thomas Watson was sharing his patron's disgrace; yet Watson had no qualms. Watson had written out a hundred sonnets and had given the manuscript to his patron to scrutinize. De Vere's approval ensured the work would be published. "For since the world hath understood (I know not how) that Your Honor had willingly vouchsafed the acceptance of this work and at convenient leisures favorably perused it, being as yet but in written hand," Watson wrote to de Vere in his dedicatory letter, "many have oftentimes and earnestly called upon me to put it to the press, that for their money they might but see what Your Lordship with some liking had already perused."

Unlike the authors of most contemporary over-the-top book dedications, Watson seems to have been guilty of understatement. De Vere did more than peruse the manuscript. Prefixed to every sonnet in Watson's book is an unsigned introduction that knowingly speaks of and sometimes even criticizes Watson. The comments quote and translate various lines of poetry and philosophy that each of Watson's sonnets references. Furthermore, Watson is always spoken of in the third person.

The breadth of mastery and depth of knowledge in these introductory comments is truly Shake-spearean. To bolster his literary arguments, Watson's unnamed critic offhandedly excerpts Seneca, Sophocles, Lucan, Theocritus, Horace, Martial, Xenophon, Pliny, Ronsard, Virgil, Homer, Petrarch, and Ovid. Obscure French, Italian, and Latin poets (Forcatulus, Fiorenzuola, Strozza, Tibullus, and Parabosco) are also quoted as matter-of-factly as someone might detail what he ate for supper last night. As C. S. Lewis observed about the *Hekatompathia*, "These notes are the most interesting part of the book." Even some orthodox scholarship has pointed to de Vere as the likely author of these glosses–which, if they were from de Vere's pen, would be Shake-speare's only known work of literary criticism.

The commentary in *The Hekatompathia* is generally illustrative, concise, and direct. When the commentator likes a sonnet, he says so. And when he doesn't, he doesn't mince words. In the gloss to Watson's Sonnet 41, for instance, the anonymous critic points out Watson's overuse of word repetition (technically called *reduplicatio*). To give an example, the critic quotes from memory from the German rhetorician Johannes Susenbrotus.

> This passion [*sonnet*] is framed upon a somewhat tedious or too much affected continuation of that figure in rhetoric which of the Greeks is called παλιλογι'α or 'αναδι'πλωσιζ, of the Latins *reduplicatio:* Whereof Susenbrotus (if I well remember me) allegeth this example out of Virgil:
>
> *Sequitur pulcherrimus Austur*
> *Austur equo fidens*

The definitive study of Shake-speare's classical learning, by T. W. Baldwin, devotes an entire chapter to Susenbrotus's wide-ranging influence on the Shake-speare canon. The erudition so casually on display in the commentary to Watson's sonnets reveals a mind that is finely tuned to literary nuance, rhetorical structure, and the most arcane of allusions. Sir Thomas Smith and the tutors of Cecil House would have been proud to claim the anonymous commentator as their former student. If the author of Watson's glosses were not de Vere, an additional Elizabethan literary genius still awaits the light of discovery.

Watson, whose influence on Shake-speare has been widely recognized, may be referring to de Vere in his Sonnet 71. In this poem, Watson addresses an otherwise unnamed "ancient friend" whom he calls "Titus." (*Ancient* here is probably used in the honorific or legal sense, meaning the friend is of an exalted or courtly rank.) Watson, newly distracted by a love affair, writes:

> Alas, dear Titus mine, my ancient friend,
> What makes thee muse at this my present plight,
> To see my wonted joys enjoy their end
> And how my muse hath lost her old delight?

Watson's nickname for his "ancient friend" would be particularly appropriate in 1582, since some have speculated that de Vere was working on a version of the play *Titus Andronicus* as his first response to the shame and scandal of his exile from court. Banishment plays an important role in the latter half of *Titus*. When the title character learns that his son Lucius has been exiled from Rome, for instance, Titus sees it as a good thing.

> Titus   O happy man! They have befriended thee.
>   Why, foolish Lucius, dost thou not perceive
>   That Rome is but a wilderness of tigers?

At the play's conclusion, as LUCIUS returns from banishment, he recites the catalog of woes faced by a man of the court blockaded from the life he once knew.

> LUCIUS [M]yself unkindly banished,
>   The gates shut on me and turn'd weeping out
>   To beg relief among Rome's enemies;
>   Who drown'd their enmity in my true tears,
>   And op'd their arms to embrace me as a friend. . . .
>   My scars can witness, dumb although they are,
>   That my report is just and full of truth.
>   But soft, methinks I do digress too much,
>   Citing my worthless praise: O, pardon me;
>   For when no friends are by, men praise themselves.

Exile and banishment also figure prominently in a second Shake-speare play that comments on the events of 1582. *Timon of Athens* charts the downward spiral of a man who cannot manage power, money, or responsibility. The title character, a prodigal patron and manic spendthrift, occupies the first half of the play running through his cash and the second half discovering the pain of desertion brought about by his destitute state. However, before TIMON's final and complete downfall, he faces some painful moments of reckoning with his faithful steward FLAVIUS. The wastrel master learns that his dwindling estates cannot pay his mounting debts—a gloomy fate that de Vere must have recognized was becoming all too probable.

> FLAVIUS O my good lord
>   At many times I brought in my accounts,
>   Laid them before you; you would throw them off,
>   And say you found them in mine honesty. . . .
>   My loved lord,
>   Though you hear now, too late!—yet now's a time—
>   The greatest of your having lacks a half
>   To pay your present debts.
> TIMON Let all my land be sold!
> FLAVIUS 'Tis all engaged, some forfeited and gone,
>   And what remains will hardly stop the mouth
>   Of present dues.

FLAVIUS, fearing TIMON's retribution, defends his actions as those of a true and steadfast retainer. "If you suspect my husbandry or falsehood," the steward tells TIMON, "Call me before the exactest auditors/And set me on the proof."

This is what John Lyly encountered in the summer of 1582. As de Vere faced more and more financial difficulties, he first sought to fix the financial blame on someone else, his trusted secretary. As with the countess of Oxford's alleged infidelities, it was only in retrospect that de Vere came to appreciate the selfless and loyal service of his own personal FLAVIUS. Sometime in July, Lyly wrote to Burghley begging that the Lord Treasurer intercede:

> It hath pleased my lord [Oxford] upon what color I cannot tell, certain I am upon no cause, to be displeased with me–the grief whereof is more than the loss can be.... This conscience of mine maketh me presume to stand all trials, either of accounts or counsel, in the one I never used falsehood, nor in the other dissembling.

Since Lyly was welcoming audits of his "accounts," the secretary was clearly also serving as the earl's bookkeeper.

As of October, de Vere had, like TIMON, cast himself out of the city gates. On October 2, he even made a rare appearance at his ancestral family seat, in the feudal role of lord of the manor of Castle Hedingham. (Records preserve de Vere's appearance in town to sign off on the creation of a butcher shop in the Castle Hedingham village.)

As the trip involved transporting his wife and the few servants he could still afford, de Vere probably split the sixty-mile trip from London to Hedingham into a two or three days' journey. Essex roads, still the boggy trails of sodden earth and thigh-deep ruts that de Vere knew as a child, were downright treacherous in the autumn. One nearly risked drowning in the gaping ruts that filled with water during the rainy season. The countess and her household's servants probably journeyed via coach, together with horse-drawn carts that carried luggage and provisions. The unsprung wagons would have painstakingly navigated through deep, sloshy channels of water, mud, and manure, while de Vere would have accompanied the train on horseback.

With little in London to draw them back, de Vere and Anne probably spent the rest of 1582 and perhaps the early part of 1583 at Hedingham. Without a court to attend or a court culture to keep up with, these days were probably much like the bucolic life under Sir Thomas Smith. Smith, now known only to eternity, had set the example of a country lord's duties: study, learn, explore, question, read, write, and, in the old master's words, "pass [one's] time now and then with hawking and hunting and now and then with looking on a book."

Away from the distractions of the Elizabethan court, almost eleven years after saying "I do," de Vere finally began to lead some semblance of a married life. By Christmas, the twenty-six-year-old countess of Oxford was once again pregnant.

৵

The months of solitude during the fall and winter of 1582–83 spawned at least one creative by-product: a comedy that recaps the offenses that had landed de Vere in the queen's displeasure. The play was an Italianate jape arguing that de Vere's missteps of 1576–81 were much ado about nothing.

De Vere does not show himself at his best, or his most political. His accusations of infidelity against his wife appear in *Much Ado* as the rash actions of a jealous groom (CLAUDIO) who unjustly rages against a chaste fiancée (HERO). This might begin to atone for the author's previous misbehavior toward his wife; *Much Ado* acknowledges that HERO was chaste and CLAUDIO was clearly in the wrong to doubt her. However, in the crucial matter of assigning blame, CLAUDIO is given a full pardon without ever apologizing. The agent of evil is the mischief maker (DON JOHN). "Yet sinn'd I not–but in mistaking," says CLAUDIO, and nobody disagrees.

Moreover, de Vere's extramarital affair with Anne Vavasour is alchemized into the story of a proud and witty soldier (BENEDICK) wooing an equally proud and witty maid (BEATRICE). Thomas Knyvet's challenge to de Vere spawns BEATRICE's wronged uncle's challenge: "Win me and wear me, let him answer me! Sir boy, I'll whip you from your foining fence, nay, as I am a gentleman, I will!" This may have made for an entertaining recap of recent courtly and amorous affairs. But, again, *Much Ado* offers up nothing to suggest the author's contrition. Instead, the audience enjoy themselves as the unlikely couple of BENEDICK and BEATRICE fall in love and rattle off countless jokes and quips to charm even an iron-hearted curmudgeon. It's a recipe for great romantic comedy. But it was horrible politics, if de Vere was also attempting to atone for his extramarital dalliances with his own BEATRICE.

Third, in *Much Ado* the Arundell–Howard Libels against de Vere become a series of outrageous allegations recorded by an incompetent constable (DOGBERRY). To take DOGBERRY's libels seriously is to accept the witness of an utter imbecile. Yet, as late as May of 1583, Elizabeth was considering reopening the investigation into the charges Arundell and Howard filed against de Vere. As spoofs of the Arundell Libels, the DOGBERRY Libels are timeless expressions of a timeless wit. But as a dramatic apology for the Arundell–Howard affair, DOGBERRY leaves much to be desired. On all three counts, *Much Ado About Nothing* insulted the intelligence and integrity of anyone–the queen in particular–who was angry at de Vere for his misdeeds.

De Vere gave it a shot all the same–or so the courtly records would suggest. On the night of Shrove Tuesday (February 12, 1583), the Merchant Taylors' Boys, one of the queen's favorite troupes, headed by Richard Mulcaster, appeared at Richmond Palace to stage a play. The text Mulcaster's boys performed does not survive, although the title does: *A History of Ariodante and Genevora*. The Italian legend of Ariodante and Genevora, from Ariosto's *Orlando Furioso*, is the source text upon which much of *Much Ado About Nothing* is based. Ariodante is the prototype for CLAUDIO, as Genevora is for HERO. *Ariodante and Genevora,* after successive rewrites, would ultimately have been published in 1600 as Shake-speare's *Much adoe about Nothing.*

De Vere appears to have argued for his reinstatement at court in a second play, which appears on the Revels calendar for the 1582–83 season. On Twelfth Night (January 5), the troupe of de Vere's ally and mentor the earl of Sussex presented the old chestnut *The History of Error.* (As noted in Chapter 5, Shake-speare's *Comedy/History of Errors* also tells the story of a jealous groom and unjustly accused spouse.) The apology that *The Comedy of Errors* makes for the author's errors in matrimony was an appropriate sentiment to convey to Her Majesty in early 1583, as she considered whether to allow her estranged earl to return to court. The split personality of *Comedy of Errors* protagonists–embodied as the twins ANTIPHOLUS OF EPHESUS and ANTIPHOLUS OF SYRACUSE–provides a metaphor for authorial regret: My marriage has been a mess, the author implies, because it united my bride with only one half of my whole self. As the DUKE OF EPHESUS observes of the twin brothers:

> One of these men is genius to the other:
> And so of these, which is the natural man,
> And which the spirit? Who deciphers them?

Between these two protoShake-speare texts, *The History of Error* and *Ariodante and Genevora,* the message sent to the queen in January and February of 1583 would have been plain: The misunderstandings that had led to the earl of Oxford's downfall were ultimately not his fault. The Arundell/DOGBERRY libels were preposterous on their face. Third parties deceived a noble CLAUDIO into slandering his chaste and fair HERO. And the BEATRICE love affair was just a fling that appealed to the wild side of the author's untamed personality, the ANTIPHOLUS OF SYRACUSE in him.

The queen, however, accepted no such message. De Vere remained exiled from court as the 1582–83 revels season drew to a close. Had he given even a hint of acknowledging some of his own shortcomings, Elizabeth's reaction might have been different. Instead, he did little more than confess that "mistakes were made." And that's no apology.

After the revels season, de Vere farmed out any remaining theatrical pleas for clemency to his secretary John Lyly–with whom de Vere had evidently settled his differences. For Lyly, de Vere rented the indoor theater at the Blackfriars, the same building outside of which the men professing to be de Vere's servants had attacked Thomas Knyvet and his minions. During the spring or summer of 1583, Lyly and the Welsh scrivener Henry Evans began holding open rehearsals of a troupe of boy players in front of paying crowds. Lyly–with de Vere as patron and overseer–worked on the text, while Evans rehearsed the children.

Unlike the public theaters near Fisher's Folly, the "private" theater of the Blackfriars served a more elite crowd. The theatrical space resembled a Tudor banquet hall, converted to house public performances with the rows of wooden bleachers across the floor and the modest stage at the far end. Admission prices were steeper and the plays' subject matter was typically courtly allegories and commentary intended for the queen's ear. Aspiring courtiers often sat onstage at the Blackfriars, the better to draw attention to themselves. The satirist Thomas Dekker would later jest, in a spoof of the courtly advice book, that all proper gallants who sat onstage should feign detachment. "You publish your temperance to the world, in that you seem not to resort thither to taste vain pleasures with a hungry appetite," he wrote, "but only as a gentleman, to spend a foolish hour or two, because you can do nothing else."

The literary team of de Vere, Lyly, and Evans was known for its poisoned pens and mastery of court gossip. As one correspondent wrote at the time, "Take heed and beware my lord of Oxenford's man called Lyly, for if he sees this letter he will put it in print or make the boys in Paul's play it upon a stage." With a touch of self-mocking irony, de Vere parrots these same anxieties in *Hamlet* when he has the prince's friend ROSENKRANTZ complain about "an eyrie of children, little eyases" who "so berattle the common stages... that many wearing rapiers are afraid of goose quills and dare scarce come thither." The Blackfriars–and the courtly stages where the workshopped Blackfriars plays ended up–was fast becoming the one place in high society where a gentleman did not want to hear his name or see his likeness.

Lyly was developing two plays at the Blackfriars in the spring of 1583. One, *Sappho and Phao*, was an allegory about a failed courtship of Venus–no doubt a nod to the recently concluded Alençon nuptial negotiations. Lyly's other production (titled *Campaspe*) was more of a gamble. It appears to have concerned de Vere's affair with Vavasour. But this time, instead of glorifying the amorous fling as a battle of wits à la *Much Ado About Nothing,* Lyly's drama portrayed de Vere as a detached statesman, Alexander the Great, who willingly gave up his paramour to another man.

Her Majesty would surely find de Vere more forgivable if he were portrayed as someone who had given Vavasour his blessing to pursue another lover. This ploy was true too: Vavasour had wasted little time in seducing the queen's tiltyard champion (and also her jailer at the Tower) Sir Henry Lee. Lee would become so besotted with Vavasour that he would have a suit of armor made with her initials engraved all over it.

If there was a hot ticket in London in 1583, *Campaspe* was it. For here, court observers knew, was an exiled courtier's dramatic plea for royal forgiveness–a second time around. *Ariodante and Genevora* may have failed to excuse de

Vere's extramarital dalliance, but Lyly's production gave de Vere the opportunity to argue that his scandalous affair with the temptress Anne Vavasour was now ancient history.

A family tragedy may have thawed Elizabeth's heart more than these plays. In the spring, the countess of Oxford delivered a son, the heir apparent to the earldom. However, at only two days old, the boy died. According to an epitaph credited to Anne and published the following year in a book written by the hack poet John Soowthern, the queen wept profusely over the boy's death. (As the plodding, meterless verse of the epitaph sounds the same as Soowthern's accredited poetry, Soowthern probably wrote the funereal verse and gave the countess the dubious distinction of its authorship.) The epitaph recalls a legend of the goddess Venus crying so greatly over the death of her beloved Adonis that flowers appeared where the goddess's tears struck the ground. In the words of the elegy, Queen Elizabeth "caused more silver to distill from her eyes than when the drops of her cheeks raised daisies."

Death had been a regular visitor to the de Vere household in the spring of 1583. In April, Anne's sister, Elizabeth, died. Anne's father, Lord Burghley, became so distraught that he left court, as the queen put it, "to wrestle with nature." Furthermore, the Lord Chamberlain earl of Sussex–de Vere's longtime mentor and military commander from the Northern Rebellion days– was dying. On April 20, Sussex made out his will and moved to his estate in Southwark to ease his passing into death.

To bury their son, de Vere and his wife held a private ceremony at Castle Hedingham. There in St. Nicholas's Church, just down the hill from the Norman keep, lies a monument to the fifteenth earl of Oxford. This is where de Vere and his countess buried their infant on May 9, 1583. The service at St. Nicholas's Church was probably an understated affair, as de Vere lacked the money for ceremony and the political connections for drawing noteworthy mourners. And with only three servants in de Vere's train, the boy's funeral banquet could hardly have been the feast that befitted the passing of an heir to England's oldest earldom.

For perhaps the first time in his life, de Vere entered St. Nicholas's Church and opened the family crypt. There in the chancel stood the imposing alabaster monument to his grandfather the fifteenth earl–a monument that by this time may also have contained the remains of the reinterred sixteenth earl as well. Into a tomb beneath the floor de Vere laid his son's remains among the bones of the infant's progenitors. In coming to St. Nicholas's Church to bury a son, the seventeenth earl of Oxford had unwittingly immersed himself in the presence of family ghosts.

Specters from beyond were not mere metaphors. A nearby de Vere family property in the Essex town of Earls Colne was reputed to be haunted. One seventeenth-century legend alleges that the ghost's visitations were announced by the bell in the nearby priory's tower ringing once, the cue that announces the presence of *Hamlet*'s ghost.

The spring winds must have seemed particularly chilly and foreboding on those starry nights at Hedingham. Astrological almanacs had forecast that the conjunction of Saturn and Jupiter would make 1583 a year of grave consequences. With a newly buried son and dismal prospects for advancement at court, de Vere would have scorned these distant lamps of doom overhead. Brought low by fortune's spite, the earl trod the same cold stone floors where his illustrious father's dramatic troupe had once entertained the queen, when he himself had been a child.

From atop the ancient castle's battlements, on a clear night, one could see across the Essex and Suffolk countryside for ten or more miles. From these brave walls, many earls of Oxford had surveyed towns that swore their fealty to the lord at Castle Hedingham. Now inhabiting the Norman castle that his father and mother had once called home, de Vere may have pondered long-dormant questions: What was Father like? How did he die? Why did Mother remarry so dishonorably? Why had marriage to Anne been so troubled? What had *really* happened with her first pregnancy? And why had she continued to sanction her father's spying on us?

The outlines of *Hamlet* are so pronounced within de Vere's life that one invariably illuminates the other. De Vere appears to have begun work on his masterpiece by 1583. (*Hamlet*'s GRAVEDIGGER explains that YORICK, the royal jester whom HAMLET once knew, had died twenty-three years anterior to the play's action; YORICK's likely inspiration, the famous royal jester Will Somers, whom de Vere would have known as a child, had died in 1560.) And as with the rest of his early works that matured into Shake-speare, de Vere would continue revising this play throughout his life.

If the earl could only get back into royal favor, he'd have the right troupe to play it too. In the spring of 1583, the best actors in London–including one of the Earl of Oxford's Men–merged to form a new company, the Queen's Men. Exiled from court when the troupe was founded, de Vere had no immediate access to them. But, ultimately, the Queen's Men performed early versions of plays that were later revised and published as Shake-speare's.

Upon returning to London sometime after his son's funeral, de Vere had two good reasons to visit his father-in-law. First, he needed more than ever to return to the queen's favor. And second, there were all those words, words, words to be found in Burghley's library. In addition to most of the other texts from which Shake-speare's plays are derived, two of *Hamlet*'s primary sources (the chronicle histories of Belleforest and Saxo Grammaticus) were to be found within Burghley's collection. Burghley's doppelgänger POLONUIS accosts HAMLET when the prince is reading a book; this kind of interaction would have been a regular occurrence at Cecil House.

Yet why write a play about Denmark, of all places–in 1583, of all times?

To begin with, it was the subject of current family table talk. De Vere never had the chance to see Denmark himself–although his German mentor, Sturmius, had once confided in Burghley his hopes that de Vere and his wife might visit Elsinore. Instead, de Vere would see the royal Danish court through the eyes of a family member. The previous summer, de Vere's brother-in-law Peregrine Bertie, who in 1580 inherited the title of Lord Willoughby de Eresby, had paid an extended visit to Elsinore. On a mission from the queen, Bertie traversed the North Sea in June of 1582 to invest King Frederick II of Denmark as a knight of the Garter.

Elizabeth needed the Danish king to stop harassing English ships as they passed through nearby seas. The English Muscovy Company was doing a brisk trade with Russia, and their business was greatly inconvenienced by levies exacted from them for using Danish sea lanes. So the queen sent her Lord Willoughby to induct the king into the Order of the Garter and to win a more favorable shipping treaty.

Bertie proved a fine match for the blustery monarch, and the two hit it off famously–although Bertie never did manage to change Frederick's mind on any of the seafaring matters he'd been sent to address. Between the 1582 voyage and a subsequent 1585 trip to Elsinore, Bertie spent five months in the castle that *Hamlet* immortalizes. Lord Willoughby's two embassies included royal feasts, hunting expeditions, and fireworks. Bertie chronicled his trip in a handwritten memoir circulated at Elizabeth's court. He no doubt also regaled friends and family with his exploits. The Danish king, pleased to be honored with Elizabeth's knighthood, feted Bertie with multiple nights of revelry that included grand speeches about Her Majesty and the Order of the Garter. "All which [were] performed after a whole volley of all the great shot of the castle discharged," Bertie notes. *Hamlet* chronicles this peculiarly Danish drinking ritual: "There's no health the king shall drink today but the great cannon to the clouds shall tell," says KING CLAUDIUS.

In his capacity as ambassador, Lord Willoughby met top Danish officials–including one courtier with the family name of Rosenkrantz and two surnamed Guldenstern. Bertie also visited the legendary astronomer Tycho Brahe at his observatory. Ten years before, Brahe had observed a supernova in the constellation Cassiopeia–the same bright "star that's westward from the pole" that *Hamlet's* guards on the Elsinore battlements notice. Brahe had also used his Danish observatory to make the most accurate observations ever of planetary conjunctions, oppositions, and retrograde motions. From this data, Brahe had concluded that the ancient geocentric theory of the universe was correct, that the Earth was indeed the celestial body around which everything else in the celestial spheres orbited. The Danish king touted his court astronomer's achievements, a fact that escaped neither Lord Willoughby nor his brother-in-law. *Hamlet's* KING CLAUDIUS denies the PRINCE's request to return to school by noting that it would be "retrograde

to our desire"; he says HAMLET's excessive mourning is in "peevish opposition" to the facts of life and a "fault to heaven"; he says that his new wife,
GERTRUDE, is "conjunctive" to his soul, and that he orbits her as a "star
moves not but in his sphere."

For providing such bountiful local color, de Vere ultimately gave his
brother-in-law a tip of the pen. *"Enter... English Ambassador"* the stage directions read as *Hamlet* draws to a close. With six dour lines to recite–one of
which is "ROSENKRANTZ and GUILDENSTERN are dead"–*Hamlet*'s ENGLISH AM-
BASSADOR to Elsinore is hardly an ample stand-in for the colorful Lord
Willoughby. Still, to those in on the joke at court, no further explanation was
necessary. PETRUCHIO had made his cameo.

Ultimately, it took more than staged entertainments to win de Vere back into
Her Majesty's good graces. The task required the intercession of a rising star
at court, one with a bright future ahead of him.

On May 11, 1583, at the end of the haunted week that began with the
burial of de Vere's son, a third party argued the earl of Oxford's case before
the queen. Walter Raleigh (later Sir Walter) put in a good word with Elizabeth about de Vere's reinstatement. Raleigh had ferried the challenges and
communications between Sidney and de Vere following their tennis-court
blowup. De Vere and Raleigh had also enjoyed moments of conviviality
during the Arundell–Howard years. But somehow, Raleigh had escaped
the ensuing Arundell–Howard scandals. In 1583, Raleigh was riding higher
than nearly anyone else at court. Six feet tall and with an athletic frame,
Raleigh wielded power with the queen that even de Vere's father-in-law did
not enjoy.

Elizabeth replied that she still harbored doubts about de Vere. In fact,
she said she was considering reopening legal proceedings against him for his
disloyalty to the crown. But by this, she told Raleigh, "she meant... only
thereby to give the earl [of Oxford] warning." Rumors were continuing to
spread about de Vere's alleged treacheries. The traitor Henry Howard was at
the time preparing to publish a pamphlet *(A Defensative Against the Poison of
Supposed Prophecies)* repeating accusations that de Vere owned prophetic books
relating to the succession of the English throne, which itself was considered an
act of treason. De Vere, never arraigned on these charges, would get the last
word: He mockingly quotes from Howard's libelous tract in the plays *Hamlet,
Macbeth, Antony and Cleopatra,* and *Henry VI, Part 1.*

Raleigh had seen satirical wounds cut into the reputations of Sir Christopher Hatton (MALVOLIO in *Twelfth Night*) and Sir Philip Sidney *(Twelfth Night*'s
SIR ANDREW AGUECHEEK and SLENDER in *The Merry Wives of Windsor).* Raleigh
must have wondered what would stop the literary earl from lambasting him.
In a letter to Burghley, Raleigh recalls the Greek legend of a man who nursed

back to health a snake that ultimately attacked its benefactor: "I am content, for your sake," Raleigh wrote, "to lay the serpent before the fire, as much as in me lieth, that having recovered strength, myself may be most in danger of his poison and sting." Raleigh's fears may have eventually been realized: The nouveau riche landowner, the florid and flattering Raleigh, does share these same qualities with the equally nouveau, florid, and flattering courtier OSRIC— whose main purpose in *Hamlet* is to deliver the challenge for a duel, the same role Raleigh had played in de Vere's life.

Raleigh's words in de Vere's favor apparently worked. On Saturday, June 1, 1583, de Vere and Elizabeth finally reconciled their differences. The reconciliation took place at the royal palace at Greenwich. The queen had just arrived from Cecil House, the Lord Treasurer's mansion on the Strand. "The earl of Oxford came to her presence," one eyewitness wrote, "and after some bitter words and speeches, in the end all sins are forgiven, and he may repair to the court at his pleasure. Master Raleigh was a great man, whereat Pondus [*Lord Burghley*] is angry for that he could not do so much."

De Vere's welcome back to court was bittersweet: On June 9, his mentor the earl of Sussex finally gave up the ghost. The widowed countess of Sussex lamented in a letter circulated at court about the "sea of sorrows" that she now faced, and that "were it not for the fear of God's revenge, I could with all heart redeem them with the sacrifice of my life." These morbid sentiments recall HAMLET's musing over suicide and taking "arms against a sea of troubles."

Sussex had for decades been the leading voice of opposition against Leicester's pernicious influence at court. At one point, in 1566, the Sussex and Leicester factions had been so well demarcated that Sussex's supporters wore yellow ribbons and Leicester's wore purple ribbons. As he lay on his deathbed, Sussex issued a grave warning about Leicester, whom he derisively called "the gypsy": "I am now passing into another world and must leave you to your fortunes and to the queen's graces," Sussex said. "But beware of the gypsy, for he will be too hard for you all. You know not the beast so well as I do." Sussex had been an outspoken isolationist, feeling that England had no business meddling in The Netherlands. But now that he was no longer able to oppose Leicester, the scales began to tip further toward English military interventionism. The role of counterbalancing Leicester's influence fell to Burghley—and to a lesser extent, to de Vere.

The earl of Sussex—the loyal subject, brave warrior, cunning courtier, chivalrous nobleman, and surrogate father to de Vere—presents the idealized paternal qualities that are projected onto the late KING HAMLET. "See what a grace was seated on this brow: Hyperion's curls, the front of Jove himself," the PRINCE observes. Leicester had taken over many of de Vere's lands upon Earl John's death in 1562—reminding a reader of CLAUDIUS's usurpation of HAMLET's inheritance upon KING HAMLET's death. No evidence suggests that Leicester poisoned Earl John, as CLAUDIUS did HAMLET SENIOR. But in 1584, Charles Arundell would publish a new set of libels, alleging that Leicester poisoned Sussex.

Scholars today treat *Leicester's Commonwealth* as a problematic and often unreliable source. Arundell claimed Leicester was a "rare artist in poison"–as reckless hyperbole as Arundell's more outrageous charges against de Vere. One nineteenth-century chronicler wrote, "[Leicester] was said to have poisoned Alice Drayton, Lady Lennox, Lord Sussex, Sir Nicholas Throgmorton, Lord Sheffield, whose widow he married and then poisoned, Lord Essex, whose widow he also married, and intended to poison, but who was said to have subsequently poisoned him–besides murders or schemes for murder of various other individuals, both French and English." Yet even if one disqualifies these accusations as so much vicious hearsay, the fact remains that rumors circulated during the 1580s that the death of Sussex originated in a vial borne by the "gypsy's" hands. Leicester, whose cruelty excited "extreme fear" among those at court who dared oppose him, was certainly considered a suspect in Sussex's demise. And for a lifelong opponent of Leicester, these suspicions may well have been good enough for the purpose of art. In making Leicester the contemptible poisoner CLAUDIUS of *Hamlet,* de Vere had given himself two poignant levels of contemporary metaphor–one (with the sixteenth earl of Oxford representing KING HAMLET) in which de Vere would raise the old issue of Leicester's usurpation of his inheritance, and the other (with the earl of Sussex representing the poisoned KING HAMLET) which anticipated Leicester's power grab after Sussex's demise.

Leicester was practically unavoidable during de Vere's first few days back in the Elizabethan court. Just one day after Sussex's passing–Monday, June 10–Leicester led the court on a trip to Oxford University. The Polish prince and general Albert Laski was in town, and as chancellor of Oxford University, Leicester had arranged for four days of revels honoring the distinguished guest.

The leading courtiers, scholars, and authors of the day would be feasting, debating, and attending new dramas directed and produced by de Vere's fellow Blackfriars playwright George Peele. For more than two years, de Vere had been persona non grata at every royal banquet, entertainment, progress, and hunt. Plays performed before the queen had become as remote from him as they were when de Vere had lived in Venice. And yet, less than a fortnight after returning to court, fate had handed de Vere the prospect of a four-day-long party full of fine food, learned discussions, and courtly drama. No record exists of de Vere's presence at Oxford during this celebration. But, given the circumstances, one may suppose that the thirsty would turn down water and the frostbitten warmth sooner than the man who was Shake-speare would have let this opportunity pass.

The party centered around one distinctive figure. The warlike prince Laski was a tall and loquacious man who had fought in dozens of battles throughout his military career, was fluent in numerous languages, and wore a long white beard nearly to his navel. Laski and his entourage stayed at Christ's Church College, and after two nights of fireworks and other entertainments, he and the court took in a new Latin play titled *Dido*. As the chronicler Raphael Holinshed noted, *Dido* was a "very stately tragedy . . . with Aeneas's narration of the destruction of Troy." The play, extant today in manuscript, was a bombastic spectacle, complete with a kennel of hounds and a simulated tempest with thunder, hail, fake snow, and rain–just the sort of theatrical hue and cry that a lifelong military man like Laski would have enjoyed. The general savored the play as if it were a fine delicacy.

Watching this play by torchlight at the college hall, de Vere may have marveled to himself at the unexpected overlaps between the classical melodrama being staged before his eyes and the Danish tragedy he was then beginning to sketch out in his mind. For in *Dido* one also finds the hero, Aeneas, haunted by his father's ghost. "How often is the sad shade of my father borne before my eyes, when quiet relaxes my limbs and a sweet sleep has overwhelmed my tired body?" muses the play's Aeneas. "How often does the sad shade of my father enter my bedchamber advising a hasty flight?"

Dido, an otherwise undistinguished university play that was never published or acted again, proved to be yet another creative spark. None of *Dido's* words are quoted in *Hamlet;* but the Danish tragedy suggests the author had seen this production. For when the troupe of players arrive at Elsinore, HAMLET instructs one of his actors to perform "Aeneas's tale to Dido." (The real-life CLAUDIUS, Leicester, had originally commanded its performance at Oxford.) Before loosing the PLAYER KING on Aeneas's speech, HAMLET explains that the Dido play he's thinking of "was never acted, or if it was, not above once. For the play, I remember, pleased not the million. 'Twas caviar to the general." (This final line is a pun on the fact that *General* Laski did indeed relish the play like caviar and that the Latinate university drama was too refined for the *general* multitudes.)

Also on hand during this four-day festival was the Italian philosopher Giordano Bruno. At the time, Bruno was staying with his mentor, patron, and host, the French ambassador, Mauvissière–the diplomat with whom de Vere shared a chequered past. Bruno was a native of Nola, a township in the kingdom of Naples, and was one of the most free-thinking intellects of his generation. Bruno also enjoyed one of the largest egos of his day, no minor accomplishment considering the competition in the Elizabethan court. The Nolan, as he referred to himself in his writings, took great pleasure in informing his readers just how important and magnanimous he was.

At Oxford, Bruno lectured the assembled crowds on "the immortality of the soul" and "the fivefold sphere." According to one eyewitness, the stocky Bruno rolled up his sleeves "like some juggler" and laid out his argument in

Latin infused with a thick Italian accent. The university professor who then debated Bruno rebuked and embarrassed the guest. "Have them tell you with what uncouthness and discourtesy that pig acted, and about the extraordinary patience and humanity of the Nolan, who showed himself to be a Neapolitan indeed, born and raised under a more benign sky," Bruno wrote in a pamphlet that recounts the Oxford fiasco.

Oxford University and Giordano Bruno were celestial bodies in opposition. The university preached the ancient geocentric theories of Aristotle and Ptolemy. Every object in the heavens, it was said, orbited the earth, and the earth occupied the center of the universe. All matter was composed of five elements: earth, water, air, fire, and the heavenly fifth element, "quintessence." Each element seeks out its rightful place in a hierarchy of five concentric spheres. Oxford students were forbidden to defy these teachings under the penalty of a hefty five-shilling fine ($75 in today's currency). The Nolan, on the other hand, would have nothing to do with the university's retrograde approach to scholarship. Instead, he touted the novel theory of Nicolas Copernicus, wherein the earth orbited the sun. Overturning the medieval order of a fixed universe with a tidy fivefold sphere, Bruno advocated three further heresies: that the stars, contrary to fixed Church doctrine, are free-floating objects in a fluid celestial firmament; that the universe is infinite, leaving no room for a physical heaven or hell; and that elements in the universe, called "monads," contain a divine spark at the root of life itself. Even the dust from which we are made contains this spark.

These notions prefigure a vast Newtonian cosmos, as well as an emerging field in present-day physics in which monads (renamed by the twentieth-century philosopher Alfred North Whitehead as "occasions of experience") are being reconsidered as a key concept in understanding the conscious mind. Bruno, in other words, was the forward-thinker he considered himself to be. After departing England, seeking an intellectual climate hospitable to his bold ideas, Bruno settled at the University of Wittenberg, a major center for the study of Copernican theory, where he taught for two years. Wandering further across Europe, Bruno was captured by the Inquisition. He was thrown into prison for seven years and then burned at the stake for his heresies in 1600.

As *Hamlet* reveals, de Vere was moved by Bruno's remarkable show at Oxford: Each of Bruno's tenets finds expression in the play. HAMLET, not coincidentally a student at Wittenberg, is Bruno's mouthpiece. To his fellow Wittenberg students ROSENKRANTZ and GUILDENSTERN, HAMLET recites the Nolan's theory of an infinite universe, although he admits he still finds the notion disturbing. ("I could be bounded in a nutshell and count myself king of infinite space, were it not that I have bad dreams.") In a poem he gives to OPHELIA, HAMLET wonders what the stars are made of and whether they are indeed fluid or fixed in place. ("Doubt thou the stars are fire/ Doubt that the sun doth move/ Doubt truth to be a liar/ But never doubt I love.") HAMLET

waxes existential over losing a comforting and familiar framework of five elements. ("This goodly frame the *earth* seems to me a sterile promontory, this
most excellent canopy the *air*, look you, this brave o'erhanging firmament,
this majestical roof fretted with golden *fire*, why, it appeareth nothing to me
but a foul and pestilent congregation of *vapors*." Emphasis added.) HAMLET
wonders about the essence underlying human life–the question that prompted
Bruno to postulate the existence of monads–and whether this divine spark can
indeed be found in inanimate matter. ("What a piece of work is a man, how
noble in reason, how infinite in faculties, in form and moving, how express and
admirable in action, how like an angel in apprehension, how like a god! the
beauty of the world; the paragon of animals; and yet to me, what is this quintessence of dust?")

In 1583, when hints of *Hamlet's* composition first begin to appear in de Vere's
life, the author had more impetus for hatred of Leicester than of Burghley.
The alleged poisoning of the earl of Sussex and old grudges of usurped family
properties, rekindled by recent trips to these properties, was exacerbated by
Leicester's pernicious influence at court. Burghley, on the other hand, had
proved himself to be one of de Vere's staunchest allies. De Vere wrote a letter
to his father-in-law on June 20, 1583, that smacks of genuine, if grudging, respect for his father-in-law. "I am in a number of things more than I can reckon
bound unto Your Lordship," he wrote to Burghley. "...I hope Your Lordship
doth account me now–on whom you have so much bound–as I am; so be you
before any else in the world, both through match–whereby I count my greatest stay–and by Your Lordship's friendly usage and sticking by me in this time
wherein I am hedged in with so many enemies."

But Burghley was still Burghley. On October 30, 1584, when de Vere wrote
to his father-in-law to plead for assistance in postponing some debts to the
crown, the son-in-law appended a hastily scribbled postscript. De Vere had just
learned that Burghley was interrogating de Vere's servants behind their master's
back: "I think [it] very strange that Your Lordship should enter into that course
towards me whereby I must learn what I knew not before, both of your opinion
and goodwill towards me," de Vere wrote to his father-in-law. "But I pray, my
lord, leave that course. For I mean not to be your ward or your child. I serve
Her Majesty, and I am that I am–and by alliance near to Your Lordship, but
free. And [I] scorn to be offered that injury to think I am so weak of government as to be ruled by servants or not able to govern myself."

This stinging rebuke to Burghley sounds like the Danish PRINCE addressing the manipulative busybody in his life, POLONIUS. Both HAMLET and de
Vere, at such a moment, could have dashed off Shake-speare's Sonnet 121, a
poem that expresses disgust and anguish over finding oneself the target of espionage. De Vere uses the same phrase in his October 30 letter as in Sonnet

121–a quotation from Exodus 3:14 ("I am that I am," God's words to Moses from the burning bush when asked His name).

121

'Tis better to be vile than vile esteemed,
When not to be receives reproach of being;
And the just pleasure lost, which is so deemed
Not by our feeling, but by others' seeing:
For why should others' false adulterate eyes
Give salvation to my sportive blood?
Or on my frailties why are frailer spies,
Which in their wills count bad what I think good?
No, I am that I am, and they that level
At my abuses reckon up their own:
I may be straight, though they themselves be bevel;
By their rank thoughts my deeds must not be shown;
   Unless this general evil they maintain,
   All men are bad and in their badness reign.

To Burghley, political survival was predicated on a continuous flow of information–however duplicitously that information was obtained. As far as the Lord Treasurer was concerned, anyone at court could and should be clandestinely monitored. Burghley "was the queen's puppeteer, pulling strings to a greater degree than Elizabeth ever knew," writes the historian John Guy. "To a large extent England was his fiefdom, governed by his 'assured' Protestant clique. He wasn't the power behind the throne but the power in front of it."

Newly minted lords, as was Burghley himself, commanded the same respect and the same scrutiny from Burghley as did someone whose ancestors had served the crown since the Conqueror. "Gentility is nothing but ancient riches," Burghley was fond of saying, and there was probably no aphorism in his repertoire that angered de Vere more–as it neglected the value of generations of honor and sacrifice.

HAMLET gives voice to this frustration in his "get thee to a nunnery" speech to OPHELIA. "Virtue shall not so inoculate our old stock but we shall relish of it," HAMLET says to the counselor's daughter. Such sarcasm about the prince's ancient lineage falls in the middle of a loaded exchange between a young woman forever caught in the middle and a strong-willed young man forever under somebody's thumb. As one literary critic described OPHELIA, "She never sees through her father or her brother and follows obediently to her fate. She permits herself to be used by everyone and in a sense thus justifies the smut of HAMLET's remarks." Any love shared between HAMLET and OPHELIA remains subjugated to the political realities of their life under the influence of POLONIUS. The same could be said of de Vere, Anne Cecil de Vere, and her prying father.

Just as Burghley relied on espionage in his public life, so was he often found hiding behind the arras in family matters. The troubled and compromised relationships between HAMLET, OPHELIA, and POLONIUS bear a tragic resemblance to the family triangle of de Vere, his wife, and her father.

De Vere's feudal heritage and upbringing ill prepared him for life among the upwardly mobile and the arrivistes who populated Gloriana's court. In the 1580s, one conspicuous vestige of the chivalric orders was the Accession Day tilts—jousts held in honor of the anniversary of the queen's accession to the throne, November 17. Although de Vere participated in at least three other court tournaments in his lifetime, November 17, 1584, was the only time in his life that history records the earl of Oxford's participation in the Accession Day celebrations.

The tiltyard at the fields of Whitehall was the site of this annual glance toward England's feudal past. Jousting knights entered the yard in pairs with trumpets sounding each jouster's tucket—their signature melody—as they rode toward the queen. Each combatant and his servants came attired in costume, some dressed as Irishmen, some as horses, some as savages. The servant would then mount the stairs to Elizabeth's box seat and deliver an oration and, should she so desire, dance a caper for her too.

A manuscript of Accession Day Tournament speeches and poems delivered to Elizabeth ("the Ditchley Manuscript") now sits in the British Library, and one anonymous oration thought to date from the 1584 tourney records a skit with multiple players. This theatrical script features two knights—"th' one following desire and innocency, th' other truth and constancy"—whose quarreling at the Temple of Peace had sent them into exile from their homeland. For their penance, the temple's high priestess instructed these wayward knights to travel to a land called "Terra Benedicta, where the rarest princess and most virtuous and greatest friend in the world to peace now holdeth the scepter."

As dusk approached, Leicester bade the riders to cease. The paying crowd milled about in the reviewing stands, and Elizabeth descended from her box to present the day's awards. For top honors, she singled out de Vere and the late duke of Norfolk's eldest son, Philip Howard, earl of Arundel (not Arundell the libeler). Both de Vere and his kinsman secured important recognition at the tournament from Her Majesty that salved their wounded reputations.

During this time of renewed favor, when the queen addressed de Vere on the floor of the House of Lords as "our most dear cousin Edward, earl of Oxford, Great Chamberlain of England," de Vere found a new assignment at Parliament. He was appointed to a committee in the House of Lords that considered petitions for adventurers seeking to explore the New World. Ten bishops and lords sat on this board, which undoubtedly helped facilitate the recently knighted Sir Walter Raleigh's ambitious plans to colonize the lands beyond the seas. (De Vere could dole out favors too.) Raleigh asked Her

Majesty to name his outpost in the New World. Since Elizabeth's final marriage proposal was now history, she knew that virginity–that trait that gave her an aura of the blessed mother of Christ–would forever remain the focus of her public image. The queen decided to name this new colony "Virginia."

In December 1584, de Vere would make a bid for an office of singular importance to the nation. It represented a departure for de Vere–but also one wholly in step with the overseas threats now facing the country.

These were ominous days for Protestant England. The newly united kingdoms of Spain and Portugal, grown rich from New World plunder, were eyeing England as a potential conquest. Aggravated by English pirate raids of Spanish galleons, Catholic Spain had practical as well as theological reasons for aggressive action against her foe. As early as 1583, Europe was already abuzz with talk of a Spanish Armada. Conflicting reports posited that the armada would invade Ireland to enlist insurrectionists or perhaps assail English raiders at sea. But whatever form Spain's military strike would assume, its shadow loomed ever larger.

By 1584, the gravest threat to Elizabeth came in the form of a united Catholic front using both native English conspirators and invading Spanish forces. The Catholic zealot Francis Throckmorton had been executed in 1584 for just such a scheme. Spain's ambassador to England, Bernardino de Mendoza, had been implicated in the Throckmorton plot and expelled from England. Elizabeth's political survival was literally a matter of life or death for her Protestant courtiers.

And if war is a quest to exploit an enemy's weaknesses, in 1584 England enjoyed one chance to exploit Spain's: The Netherlands. King Philip II had inherited the crown of the Lowlands and tried to micromanage the provinces' internal affairs from afar and to enforce his Catholicism on many Netherlanders who had already embraced Protestantism. Starting in the 1560s, Protestant Dutch forces had waged a bloody rebellion against its Spanish overlords. (In 1567, de Vere had sent his retainer Thomas Churchyard off to fight for the Protestants in the Netherlands.) Under the charismatic Prince William ("the Silent") of Orange, Dutch rebels had the potential to soak up Spanish resources and divert Spain from its plans to attack England. England could add to this diversion by abetting the Dutch rebel forces, if only the interventionists could convince the queen to do so.

Protestant patriots–including the earl of Leicester–supported William the Silent's campaign to overthrow Spanish forces in the Lowlands and lobbied the queen to give military and economic aid to the Dutch. And now that the earl of Sussex was dead and gone, little resistance remained to the notion of an English campaign in the Lowlands. To the maddeningly cautious queen, though, such decisions were best handled by procrastination. Advisors urged Her Majesty to take action before the illustrious general Don John joined the Spanish ranks; Elizabeth did nothing. Don John then joined the fight, scoring military victories against the rebels; Elizabeth did nothing. Dutch ambassadors made personal trips to the queen, arguing for the urgency of their cause; Elizabeth did nothing. A Portuguese assassin nearly killed Prince William, and with it the Lowlands' best chance of beating Spain; Elizabeth did nothing.

In March 1584, the German scholar Sturmius—whom de Vere had studied under during his continental travels in 1575—wrote to Elizabeth pleading for an English force to be sent to The Netherlands, led by "some faithful and zealous personage such as the earl of Oxford, the earl of Leicester, or Philip Sidney." Elizabeth still did nothing.

Then, on July 10, 1584, an assassin made his way into William the Silent's home at Delft and, catching the prince off-guard, fired at him with a heavy pistol at point-blank range. As William staggered into the arms of an aide, he reportedly cried out, "My God, have pity for my soul! My God, have pity for these poor people!" He died in a matter of minutes.

Spurred in part, no doubt, by regret for not having come to the prince's aid while he was alive, Elizabeth finally agreed to give the Lowlands the military aid they had long requested. She was greeted with an outpouring of gratitude. In fact, for a brief period, it was even thought that Elizabeth might rule over the Dutch as new subjects to the English crown.

However, a logistical question soon followed: Who would lead the ground forces against Spain? Who would assume the governorship of this possible English colony? Leicester was the leading choice. As early as 1577, pleas had come in to appoint the earl of Leicester commander of England's Dutch campaign. Yet, as Sturmius's letter shows, de Vere had become a contender for the job too.

This was a candidacy that de Vere took seriously. And in the Elizabethan court's Christmas revels of 1584, he gave his aspirations voice.

On the night of December 27, 1584, Henry Evans led Oxford's Boys in a performance before the queen and her court at Windsor Castle of a play called *A History of Agamemnon and Ulysses*. This text, like nearly all court plays of that time, was never printed or preserved. Yet even the orthodox scholar Albert Feuillerat thought that de Vere might be the author of this "lost" play.

This "lost" play was probably a draft of part of Shake-speare's dark satire *Troilus and Cressida*. *Troilus and Cressida* contains a heated dispute between AGAMEMNON and ULYSSES, which forms the intellectual core of the larger play. AGAMEMNON and ULYSSES, as portrayed in *Troilus and Cressida*, use language and rhetorical tricks such as Euphuism that were fashionable in the early 1580s. The AGAMEMNON and ULYSSES scenes in *Troilus and Cressida* suggest a 1584 context: AGAMEMNON notes that the Greek campaign against Troy has been going on for seven years; William the Silent's campaign against Spain had lasted since 1577.

Shake-speare's AGAMEMON and ULYSSES also argue over some of the very issues at stake in the Lowlands. The legendary figures of Agamemnon and Ulysses are Greek military leaders besieging the foreign city of Troy. In December of 1584, a play staged for Queen Elizabeth about the siege of Troy would readily have been seen as a representation of the siege of The Netherlands.

If *Agamemnon and Ulysses* was indeed an early draft of the AGAMEMNON and ULYSSES scenes from *Troilus and Cressida,* de Vere would have been arguing not only for military intervention but also for his leadership of the English forces–portraying himself as ULYSSES, a paragon of aristocratic and military ideals. As literary critic F. Quinland Daniels notes about Shake-speare's ULYSSES:

> Here we face a man of vigor and reason, and an exponent of order in all the Renaissance sense of the term, for these are Elizabethan men, for all their Greek names and the Trojan situation which is their vehicle.

On the other hand, Shake-speare's AGAMEMNON drags the audience through tiresome speeches and strained rhetorical devices. Daniels again:

> AGAMEMNON, we find, is a firm exponent of the British "endure" and "muddle through" philosophy. In him we have the "Colonel Blimp" prototype of World War II fame, a doughty figure who exalts persistence and "bulldog tenacity" but who is himself incapable of wile or strategy.... He is, we perceive, an emotionally motivated thinker and military "blowhard" whose mind works patly within its limitations, but who cannot entertain concepts which are outside those bounds.

Leicester/AGAMEMNON, Shake-speare argues, would be a foolish and simple-minded campaigner and a stale and predictable strategist.

De Vere once again stacked the deck. Just as *Ariodante and Genevora* provided pat alibis for the author's misbehavior, *Agamemnon and Ulysses* gave Elizabeth an overt choice for commander of her Lowlands campaign: the man who was ULYSSES. (In 1584, the complexity and subtlety that defined de Vere's mature literary voice were still only incipient.)

One chilly December night in 1584 found the queen and her court assembled at Windsor Castle, taking in this dramatic argument for military advancement–Shake-speare promoting himself to Queen Elizabeth as England's next generalissimo. In response to AGAMEMNON's affected discourse on disorder among the rank and file, ULYSSES effectively calls for order and sanity among the Protestant forces in the besieged Lowlands:

ULYSSES And look how many Grecian tents do stand
   Hollow upon this plain, so many hollow factions.
   When that the general is not like the hive
   To whom the foragers shall all repair,
   What honey is expected? Degree being vizarded,
   Th' unworthiest shows as fairly in the mask.
   The heavens themselves, the planets, and this center
   Observe degree, priority, and place,
   Insisture, course, proportion, season, form,
   Office, and custom, in all line of order.

ULYSSES's words eloquently express the feudal, royalist philosophy of a divinely ordered world. (These exhortations are philosophical companions to de Vere's 1573 prefatory poem to *Cardanus's Comfort* on the "idle drone" and the "halls of high degree.") To ULYSSES, the problem now facing the invading army is the anarchy and confusion bred by too much equality within a military hierarchy that should be precisely defined and obeyed.

As the author neared thirty-five, HAMLET represented de Vere's thinking at its most progressive—revealing his fondness for the novel ideas and ideals of Italian Renaissance thinkers such as Gerolamo Cardano and Giordano Bruno. However, ULYSSES represented de Vere at his most regressive—an old-school feudalist aghast at the egalitarian and permissive ideals practiced by the Dutch. The republican notions inspired by the Dutch uprising—which later came to fruition in the British, American, and French revolutions—were anathema to the royalist Shake-speare.

The queen, no less an exponent of medieval notions of royalty than de Vere, must have found an appeal in de Vere's rhetoric of rank and deference. Foolish though it would have been to appoint her court playwright as a general and colonial governor, Elizabeth would not acknowledge as much until the last possible moment. Such was the nature of her familiar ploy to pit multiple suitors against one another—and wait to see who survived the dreary and expensive waiting game.

A portrait of an unidentified thirty-four-year-old Elizabethan nobleman, believed in the nineteenth century to be of Shake-speare, survives today at the palace of Hampton Court, twelve miles southwest of London. The confident sitter, bearing the same tight-lipped and narrow-eyed piercing gaze that defines the known images of de Vere, proudly holds his right hand on a ceremonial sword. His gold-embossed doublet, ornate buckles and holsters, and lace neck and wrist ruffs project the image of a military officer with mighty aspirations. Infrared examination of this portrait by Charles Wisner Barrell in 1947 claimed to identify the sitter's sword with the Lord Great Chamberlain's Sword of State. Although a definitive study is still lacking, the supposition that de Vere struck a commanding pose for a court painter sometime in 1584 or early 1585–giving it to the queen as a reminder of his bid to become England's next four-star general–makes for a tempting theory indeed.

On July 10, 1585, the queen put Sir John Norris in temporary command of some seven thousand Englishmen for a military expedition to rescue the besieged city of Antwerp. She then signed the Treaty of Nonsuch on August 20, formally committing her country to aid their Dutch compatriots on the battlefield. England was no longer an observer in the Spanish conflict. Elizabeth had effectively entered into an open state of war with Spain.

The Treaty of Nonsuch killed any last-ditch hope of averting a Spanish naval attack on England. This abstract fact of international politics began to carry concrete meaning on the streets of London. Royal shipwrights, working the shipyards at Deptford and Woolwich on the south bank of the Thames near Greenwich, would see their customary workload increase sixfold. Between 1584 and '86, the Royal Navy's shipwrights would crank out as many warships (thirteen) as they had built and refurbished over the preceding eighteen years. *Hamlet* pays witness to these days of feverish military buildup when one of the Danish palace guards asks:

> Why [is there] such daily cast of brazen cannon
> And foreign mart for implements of war?
> Why such impress of shipwrights, whose sore task
> Does not divide the Sunday from the week?
> What might be toward that this sweaty haste
> Doth make the night joint-laborer with the day?

On August 24, Norris and his troops embarked across the Channel, and soon thereafter engaged Spanish forces at the Dutch city of Arnhem. Norris enjoyed modest success in battle, but the queen was still playing as conservatively as ever. She would later rebuke him for disobeying orders "to defend, not to offend." Meanwhile, amid such frustrations and mixed messages, de Vere received notice that he'd been appointed commander of the horse in the Lowlands theater of war.

De Vere's dramatic pleas, it seems, had worked! "AGAMEMNON" was stuck holding Her Majesty's hand in London, while "ULYSSES" had received the first of what he must have hoped would be a series of promotions. On August 28, de Vere's advance team landed at the North Sea port town of Flushing (Vlissingen). The next day, the Spanish ambassador Mendoza reported back to his king that de Vere had boarded a ship to cross the Channel and meet his retinue. Depending on the tides and prevailing winds, these crossings were sometimes an overnight journey. For an experienced ocean traveler like de Vere, the cramped and swaying accommodations would be familiar. The only factor that would have kept him awake at night was the anticipation and excitement of the new adventure unfolding before him.

Upon landing and greeting a grateful Dutch populace, de Vere began a progress up the coastline to The Hague, probably via Rotterdam and Delft. According to one historical account, similar English processions in the months to come would be greeted with "fifteen hundred musketeers and armed infantry and escorts of six to seven hundred, and in all of which the citizens thronged the processional route cheering and crying, 'God save Queen Elizabeth!'"

Such a welcome, perhaps more muted in tone, would have filled de Vere's breast with pride. At age thirty-five, he was finally fulfilling the earls of Oxfords' long and glorious tradition of military service to the crown. This was the kind of pomp and ceremony the Lord Great Chamberlain could revel in.

As commander, de Vere would be expected to bear much of the cost for his troops—although how this down-at-the-heels courtier could contemplate taking on such financial burdens is anybody's guess. He would also be expected to import with him a tucket, the musical logo used to distinguish one lord's soldiers from another's. Military musicians, playing single-valved trumpets, typically rattled out such ditties to rally the troops, cue them for various tasks (such as charging and retreating), and signify the unit's presence to allied commanders in the field. De Vere had long supported and remained friends with the composer William Byrd, the same man given and soon thereafter stripped of the Essex estate of Battylshall. Byrd's elaborate harpsichord piece, "The Earl of Oxford's March," full of flourishes and potential tuckets, was probably composed to honor de Vere's new military commission.

Upon arriving at The Hague on Friday, September 3–after a four-day journey from Flushing–de Vere met and dined with Lord Norris and the other superior officers. There the commanders surveyed the assembled troops and awaited further orders. (De Vere would later lard *All's Well That Ends Well* with names of various commanders in the Lowlands campaign.) Commands from London were slow in coming. No one had even been appointed to the generalship, the post for which the play *Agamemnon and Ulysses* had likely served as Shake-speare's application. De Vere had another problem as well: He had left behind no prominent advocates to continue pressing Her Majesty on his behalf. With Sussex now gone, the only ally de Vere had at court was Burghley. And the old counselor hardly had time to worry about promotions for his ingrate son-in-law.

Soon after de Vere had set sail for Flushing, the spymaster Francis Walsingham wrote to a Lowlands commander that Her Majesty was considering sending over "a nobleman" to serve as the commanding officer. Ouch. Walsingham used no name for this "nobleman," and in this case no names were needed. Leicester had visited and advocated for a Lowlands expedition for seven years. He had previously met with the martyred prince William and enjoyed the support of commanders in the field. The winds were not in de Vere's favor, however noble and lofty ULYSSES's speech may have been.

In October, the inevitable came to pass. De Vere was recalled home from the Lowlands—as OTHELLO would be from his wars—and Leicester and Sidney captured the key roles in the campaign. Much like HAMLET, de Vere suddenly found that he "lacked advancement."

Adding insult to injury, Spanish pirates had looted a boatload of de Vere's provisions and monies. As one officer wrote to Leicester on October 14, "The earl of Oxford sent his money, apparel, wine, and venison by ship to England. The ship was captured off Dunkirk by the Spaniards on that day, and a letter from Lord Burghley to Lord Oxford found by them on board. This letter appointed him to the command of the horse." Yet de Vere transformed his second experience with buccaneers into something useful: *Hamlet* contains not only an encounter with pirates but also an analogous plot twist involving suborned letters at sea.

Sidney would die from wounds received on the battlefield in 1586, while Leicester's disastrous two-year campaign would end in ruin, leaving the ailing AGAMEMNON drained and exhausted. Leicester would die a year after returning home. The Lowlands wars would drag on for more than sixty years, claiming the lives of thousands more soldiers. Had de Vere actually stayed on in the Lowlands in 1585, he might well have died there too. And England would have been robbed of the man who gave it language.

CHAPTER 8

TO THY RUDDER TIED
BY TH' STRINGS

[1586–1589]

PERHAPS INSPIRED BY ULYSSES'S ELOQUENT ADVOCACY OF THE FINEST courtly ideals, Elizabeth had at first fallen prey to her own bard's rhetoric. But when sober heads prevailed, she recognized that she'd handed de Vere the wrong assignment. The Virgin Queen had other designs for her earl of Oxford.

Once Elizabeth had sent troops to fight Spanish forces in the Lowlands, England was committed to armed conflict. Tax rates, which had remained stable since her accession, would double by the end of the decade and triple by 1593. Most of this increased cash flow would be streaming out to England's armies in Ireland and The Netherlands and to its incipient Royal Navy. Some of it, however, would be used on the home front.

Over the previous three years, the fifty-one-year-old privy councilor, Francis Walsingham, had been running the dramatic troupe the Queen's Men. But Walsingham didn't care about the artistic mission of his company. From his former post at the English embassy in Paris, Walsingham had seen the carnage of St. Bartholomew's Day 1572, when Catholics had murdered Protestants in the streets. The spymaster had made it his solemn and self-appointed task to ensure that England never witnessed such carnage. If it meant interrogating and torturing supposed subversives and keeping tabs on every Catholic-sympathizing household in the country, then so be it.

The Queen's Men's mission was political. Walsingham's new troupe applied the lessons of John Bale's *King Johan* (1562) on a nationwide scale: Recast the story of a long-gone monarch to advance the cause of Queen Elizabeth's reign; unite the British people against the scourge of Catholicism; wrap these lessons in a pretty package to entice the crowds. Walsingham recognized the propagandistic potential of the mass media of his age: the theater.

Queen's Men plays such as *The True Tragedy of Richard III* and *The True Chronicle History of King Leir* [*sic*] emphasized historical "truth." It was a particularly Elizabethan view of historical truth, one in which the facts of history meant little by themselves. History, to the English Renaissance mind and to the Queen's Men's dramatists in particular, was never just a study of the past. Instead, history became a passport to the present, affording new views on contemporary affairs as refracted through the lens of the past. History wasn't "was" as much as it was "is" and "should be."

Most scholars today assume the anonymous Queen's Men's plays *King Leir, The Famous Victories of Henry V, The True Tragedy of Richard III,* and *The Troublesome Reign of King John*–all of which were later published–served as sources for their respective Shake-spearean counterparts. But *source* is too timid a word for these texts. They are more likely to have been de Vere's first drafts, probably written in collaboration with secretaries and associates such as John Lyly and Anthony Munday.

In re-creating English history on the public stage as a means of popularizing Queen Elizabeth's church and state, de Vere was taking part in what the Elizabethan satirist and de Vere confidant Thomas Nashe later called "the policy of plays"–plays as political action and Tudor evangelism. Writing in 1592, Nashe in his pamphlet *Pierce Penniless* stood behind the use of the English stage as a propaganda tool in the ongoing war against Spain.

> There is a certain waste of the people for whom there is no use but war, and these men must have some employment still to cut them off.... If they have no service abroad, they will make mutinies at home. Or if the affairs of state be such as cannot exhale these corrupt excrements [*rowdy Londoners*], it is very expedient they have some light toys to busy their heads withal, cast before them as bones to gnaw on, which may keep them from having leisure to intermeddle with higher matters.
>
> To this effect, the Policy of Plays is very necessary–howsoever some shallow-brained censors (not the deepest searchers into the secrets of government) mightily oppugn them....

Nashe's comments appear in a section of his pamphlet in which the satirist rails against all forms of sloth. He explains, however, that theater is *not* a form of sloth, as Puritan would-be censors were claiming, but rather an expression of patriotism. The "Policy of Plays," as he called it, was a key strategy in the effort to maintain order and indoctrinate the populace. Nashe cites two successful examples of the Policy of Plays.

> How would it have joyed brave TALBOT [*from Shake-speare's* Henry VI, Part 1], the terror of the French, to think that after he had lain two hundred years in the tomb, he should triumph again on the stage–and

have his bones new embalmed with the tears of ten thousand spectators at least?...

All arts to [the Puritans] are vanity.... [T]ell them what a glorious thing it is to have HENRY THE FIFTH represented on the stage, leading the French king prisoner and forcing both him and the DAUPHIN to swear fealty.

The HENRY THE FIFTH to whom Nashe refers is likely from the Queen's Men's *The Famous Victories of Henry V.*

Correspondence from a six-day period during late June 1586 suggests that, beginning in 1586, de Vere was working for the state, and for his queen, in a new capacity.

On Thursday, June 21, Burghley wrote to the master of the Queen's Men to request if he'd spoken with the queen about an unnamed proposal concerning de Vere. "I pray you, send me word if you had any commodity to speak with Her Majesty to speak of My Lord of Oxford and what hope there is," Burghley wrote to Walsingham. "And if you have any [news], to let Robert Cecil understand [that] it [is] to relieve his sister, who is more troubled for her husband's lack than he himself." Anne was more worried about finances than her husband.

Four days later, de Vere wrote a letter to his father-in-law discussing a case he had before the queen—presumably the same case that Burghley had mentioned in his June 21 missive. De Vere's letter also makes clear that the master of the Queen's Men had insider knowledge about this "suit." The suit involved a considerable payout from the royal treasury. From the money that was yet to come, in fact, de Vere asked his father-in-law for a cash advance. De Vere wrote to Burghley:

My very good Lord—

As I have been beholding unto you divers times—and of late by my brother[-in-law] R. Cecil, whereby I have been the better able to follow my suit, wherein I have some comfort at this time from Master Secretary Walsingham—so I am now bold to crave Your Lordship's help at this present. For, being now almost at a point to taste that good which Her Majesty shall determine, yet am I as one that hath long besieged a fort and not [been] able to compass the end or reap the fruit of his travail, being forced to levy his siege for want of munition.

Strip away de Vere's florid military metaphor, and one finds a straightforward message: de Vere needed money. He continues:

Being therefore thus disfurnished and unprovided to follow Her Majesty, as I perceive she will look for, I most earnestly desire Your Lordship that

you will lend me 200 pounds till Her Majesty perform her promise. . . . I
would be loath to trouble Your Lordship with so much, if I were not
kept here back with this tedious suit from London. . . . I dare not, having been here so long and the matter growing to some conclusion, be
absent. I pray Your Lordship bear with me, that at this time wherein I am
to get myself in order I do become so troublesome. From the court this
morning.

Your Lordship's ever bounden
EDWARD OXENFORD

The day after de Vere wrote this letter, the queen "performed her promise."
On Sunday, June 26, Her Majesty affixed the seal of the Privy Council to
a royal warrant for a stunning £1,000 annual salary for de Vere. This annuity, comparable to $270,000 today, was to be split into quarterly payments
"during Our pleasure or until such time as he shall be by Us otherwise provided for to be in some manner relieved." She stipulated that the grant had
no strings attached: "Neither the said earl nor his assigns nor his or their
executors . . . shall by way of account, imprest, or any other way whatsoever
be charged towards Us." It was de Vere's money to be dispersed, she proclaimed, as he saw fit. For the rest of his life, de Vere would continue to
draw these quarterly payments, even into the reign of the next monarch,
King James I.

Although neither the seal nor the language of de Vere's annuity hints at
the queen's motives, the timing and the exorbitant amount of money give
pause. Just as the Queen's Men were beginning to ramp up their performance
schedule—enacting histories, some of which were prototypes, if not first drafts,
of Shake-speare plays—the queen had begun to ramp up her benevolence to
de Vere.

The average senior servant in Elizabeth's government had to make do
with no more than £50 per year. And even most exceptions to this rule only
made three-figure salaries: Her Majesty's lieutenant of the Tower, Sir Owen
Hopton, pulled in £100 annually. Edmund Tylney, Master of the Revels, net-
ted £200. Sir Robert Cecil, de Vere's brother-in-law, would soon be earning
£800 a year as he took over national security and espionage duties for his aging father. As the cash-starved government stared at the prospect of a long
war with Spain—one that would empty out the treasury in just ten years'
time—Elizabeth seldom gave direct gifts of money to the nobility, preferring
to give monopolies in goods and commodities like sweet wine or wool or tin.
The new monopolist could then earn out a comfortable living, all without
withdrawing a penny from the state's coffers.

Queen Elizabeth I would hand over the equivalent of nearly $5 million to
her Lord Great Chamberlain. The quid pro quos—whether stated or not—lurking
behind de Vere's annuity remain one of the more vexing unsolved problems

of his biography. Was Her Majesty intentionally buying him the time needed to develop what would become the Shake-speare history plays? Or was she subsidizing other related activities, such as his supervising a workshop of playwrights (*e.g.,* Munday and Lyly) who were themselves generating the Queen's Men's playscripts? Or was the queen just being exceptionally, inexplicably, generous?

Elizabeth the canny political strategist was also Elizabeth the master manipulator. In putting her flaky play-puppet on the public dole, the queen had effectively attached as many strings to his little marionette arms and legs as she needed. *The Comedy of Errors* acknowledges as much. Annual grants of £1,000, one learns, come with some very large strings attached. One of *The Comedy of Errors*'s two de Vere characters (ANTIPHOLUS OF EPHESUS) tells his servant to go out and buy some rope. The servant replies with a non sequitur that critics have scratched their heads over for centuries: "I buy a thousand pounds a year!" the servant says. "I buy a rope!"

In the words of literary scholar Seymour M. Pitcher:

> Others have gone beyond [de Vere biographer Bernard M.] Ward to suggest, with some plausibility, that the funds [behind de Vere's annuity] were intended "for the first organized propaganda. Oxford was to produce plays which would educate the English people—most of whom could not read—in their country's history, in appreciation of its greatness, and of their own stake in its welfare." In point of fact and time, a spate of chronicle plays did follow the authorization of the stipend. Is it not conceivable that they were produced with such subsidy? *The Famous Victories [of Henry V]* may have been one of the first plays—perhaps the very first—commissioned for the Queen's Men under this policy.

Under this scenario, the end products of the queen's £1,000 annuity were Shake-speare's *King John; Richard II; 1 and 2 Henry IV; Henry V; 1, 2, and 3 Henry VI; Richard III;* and *Henry VIII.* They were the culmination of a nuanced and sophisticated public relations campaign. Shake-speare's English history plays may contain de Vere's own snipes and personal vendettas— FALSTAFF's Gad's Hill robbery, RICHARD III's canny resemblance to Robert Cecil. But in toto they tell a story that is essentially a breathtaking apology for Tudor power and a timeless testament to English national pride—think of Laurence Olivier's film version of *Henry V* rallying the country at the height of the German blitz. Seldom has a government invested its money so well.

Just one month after the queen approved de Vere's £1,000 annuity, the Venetian ambassador to Spain reported back to his superiors that King Philip had been outraged to learn that theatrical troupes were making a mockery of him on the public stages in England. The ambassador wrote:

What has enraged him [*the king of Spain*] much more than all else and has caused him to show a resentment such as he has never displayed in all his life is the account of the masquerades and comedies which the queen of England orders to be acted at his expense.

Some English playwright was making an impression.

De Vere's secretary John Lyly would later write a courtly allegory, *Endymion,* thanking Elizabeth for her gracious annuity. The story of *Endymion* tells of a protagonist who has a secret love affair (read: Vavasour) that angers the moon goddess (read: Elizabeth). The moon puts Endymion to sleep, symbolizing de Vere's years of royal disfavor. But ultimately, she forgives her wayward swain and awakens him with a kiss, symbolizing the £1,000 annuity. Now revived like Rip van Winkle after his dormancy, Endymion exclaims:

Your Highness hath blessed me, and your words have again restored my youth. Methinks I feel my joints strong and these moldy hairs to molt—and all by your virtue, Cynthia, into whose hands the balance that weigheth time and fortune are committed!

In the mid–seventeenth century, a vicar from Stratford-upon-Avon named John Ward recorded some of the legends he'd heard about Will Shakspere—by then widely accepted as the author of the works of Shake-speare. In his private diaries, Ward recorded:

I have heard that Mr. Shakespeare ... supplied the stage with 2 plays every year and for that had an allowance so large that he spent at the rate of £1,000 a year, as I have heard.

The vicar never, however, wonders how "Shakespeare" could have paid out such a tidy sum as £1,000 per year: William Shakspere's cash estate never exceeded £350.

The year 1586 was an important crossroads for another prominent figure of the day. Since 1568, Mary, Queen of Scots, had been a captive of the Elizabethan state. The Scots queen had abdicated the Scottish throne in favor of her infant son, James, in 1567 and fled south in 1568, driven by a seamy murder scandal in which historians now suspect Burghley's agents played a crucial role.

Mary Stuart was a Catholic and, other than Queen Elizabeth herself, had arguably the best claim to the English throne. To English Catholics, the Scots queen was just one papally sanctioned assassination away from being crowned Queen Mary II of England—which might have ushered in Catholic–Protestant bloodshed such as Walsingham had witnessed in Paris in 1572.

Walsingham and Burghley had long been hoping for the day when Mary could be tried and executed for planning to overthrow Elizabeth—regardless of such sentimentalities as the truth of the charges. The evidence, the spymasters knew, needed to be so damning as to convince Elizabeth to sign the execution order. Elizabeth had resisted previous appeals to authorize Mary's death warrant when the duke of Norfolk allegedly planned to marry Mary and overthrow the Elizabethan state. Elizabeth's unwillingness was no mere exercise of judicial restraint. Mary was an anointed queen—God's messenger of divine order. Executing the queen of Scotland, tantamount to rebellion against heaven itself, would have set a dangerous precedent for the queen of England.

In January 1586, a brewer managed to smuggle secret letters to Mary via a watertight box inside a beer keg. The Scots queen soon opened a cryptographic correspondence with French conspirators who were planning to assassinate Elizabeth. The ringleader of the plot was a dashing young Derbyshire lad named Anthony Babington. However, the brewer, the couriers, and even a few of the French subversives were all on Walsingham's payroll. Mary was walking into Walsingham's trap.

In July, Babington wrote to Mary of his plans to "dispatch . . . the usurping Competitor" [Elizabeth]. Foolishly, the Scots queen wrote back. One of Walsingham's agents, recognizing the monumental significance of this piece of evidence, drew a picture of a gallows in the margin of Mary's reply. The Queen of Scots was caught at last. Babington was arrested on August 14 and tortured. He confessed to everything on August 18.

Now all that remained was to try Mary for treason. This meant assembling the nobility of England to pronounce judgment on the Queen of Scots. Before long, de Vere learned he would be a member of the jury.

Elizabeth had at the time just signed a deal with Mary's twenty-year-old son, King James VI, who had worn the Scots crown since his absent mother's hasty departure. Elizabeth had played on James's two weak points: He was broke and ambitious. The Virgin Queen gave James a £4,000 pension to ensure his loyalty to the Elizabethan state. It worked. Throughout the trial to come, James would make only nominal protests over the judicial murder of his mother. He knew if he sacrificed his mother, he stood a good chance of someday inheriting the English crown himself.

The Mary Stuart trial summoned forty-five jurors, two of whom were Catholic. They met first at the Star Chamber at Westminster on September 27 and reassembled on October 8. After much vacillation, Elizabeth had settled on the Northamptonshire castle of Fotheringhay as the site of the trial. She would not be present. Though they corresponded with each other for decades, the two cousin queens would never meet.

Couriers ferrying news back to London from Fotheringhay could make the trip in twenty-four hours, riding at speed. For de Vere and his fellow commissioners, trailing their carriages of baggage behind them, the muddy road through the crimson-and-amber autumn woods snaked on for some three days. The medieval fortress of Fotheringhay offered an appropriately cold and foreboding refuge for the task at hand. The castle's great room had been cleared of furniture save for five long benches, two of which straddled either side of an empty banquet table in the center. At one end of the echoing hall stood an empty throne, draped with the cloth of state. This would serve as Elizabeth's symbolic presence during the proceedings.

As quickly became clear, Mary scarcely had a leg to stand on. Raised and tutored in France, she neither knew nor had any access to lawyers who knew English jurisprudence. In 1584, Parliament had effectively passed a lynch law (the Act of Association), which stated that simply being privy to a plot against Elizabeth was treason. The act made clear that it applied to both English subjects and nonsubjects—a provision written with the Queen of Scots in mind. Like the duke of Norfolk and the martyr Edmund Campion, the defendant Mary would be simply the protagonist of a tragedy produced and directed by the state.

Despite all the factors working against her, Mary raised a spirited defense and impressed the jury. She said,

> I do not deny that I have earnestly wished for liberty—and done my utmost to procure it for myself. In this I have acted from a very natural wish. But can I be responsible for the criminal projects of a few desperate men, which they planned without my knowledge or participation?

Mary prayed that God might grant forgiveness to the commission for treating her "somewhat rudely." Before her final exit from the courtroom, she whispered a few words into Walsingham's ear and turned to face her accusers, saying, "May God keep me from having to do with you again." Before the commissioners could announce their preordained guilty verdict, Elizabeth ordered the jury to reconvene at the Star Chamber in Westminster.

Upon arriving in London, where the jury's pronouncement was made, the jurors learned that death had delivered one surprise verdict: Sir Philip Sidney had been injured in action in the Lowlands and, on October 17, had died from his wounds. The knight's body had been repatriated and would lie in state at London's Church of the Holy Trinity Minories for fifteen weeks—a royal distraction from the Mary Stuart debacle.

After months of weeping and procrastination, Elizabeth finally consented to Mary's execution—while still desperately trying to insulate herself from blame. On February 1, 1587, she commanded her secretary, William Davison, to bring her the death warrant. He did; she signed it, swearing Davison to utmost secrecy.

On the morning of February 9, news arrived from Fotheringhay that Mary had been executed the previous day. At the time, Elizabeth was at

Greenwich, preparing for a hunt. Unable to reach the queen before her hunting party departed, the courier instead told Burghley, who thanked the messenger for his service but was wise enough to let someone else deliver the news to Her Majesty. The event itself, Elizabeth soon learned, had been cursed. The executioner had not completed his bloody task with the first stroke of his blade; he had required two chops to cleave the royal neck. Many saw this as God's condemnation of the execution. In the words of one contemporary ballad:

> The ax that should have done the execution
> Shunned to cut off a head that had been crowned.
> The hangman lost his wonted resolution
> To quit a queen of noblesse so renowned.
> There was remorse in hangman and in steel
> When peers and judges no remorse could feel!

To make matters worse, Mary had worn a wig to her execution. When the axman tried to hoist the queen's severed head to display to the crowd, the head fell to the floor with a thump.

Elizabeth was distraught—and not just at the axman's bumbling. She disowned any responsibility for ordering the execution and laid all responsibility at secretary Davison's feet. Elizabeth had Davison fined an exorbitant 10,000 marks ($1.8 million in today's currency) and sentenced to prison in the Tower of London. The fine was later rescinded, but Davison spent a year and a half behind bars.

The commissioners must have marveled at the queen's gall. De Vere had probably thought *he* was being disingenuous in his comedies by blaming everyone else for his own jealousy and misbehavior. Yet Elizabeth's denial of basic reality was truly stunning. If she had signed the death warrant intending that it not be enacted, as she claimed, she must have realized that she had given Burghley, Walsingham, and all of Parliament exactly what they had wanted for years. None of them was going to ask twice. Yet, she sent a letter to the king of France expressing her sorrow for the horrible snafu of Queen Mary's death and confided in the Venetian ambassador her deep regret and anger. It was as if another woman altogether had signed the death warrant.

The Queen's Men would enact this same privy chamber melodrama on the public stage in *The Troublesome Reign of King John*. In this pre-Shakespearean play, KING JOHN orders that a younger, papally sanctioned claimant to the throne (PRINCE ARTHUR) be blinded with hot pokers. The KING's servant HUBERT reports back to the KING that by inadvertence the hot pokers have actually killed the PRINCE. KING JOHN then lashes out at HUBERT for having had the effrontery to follow orders.

KING JOHN Art thou there, villain? Furies haunt thee still,
  For killing him whom all the world laments.
HUBERT Why here's my lord Your Highness's hand and seal,
  Charging on life's regard to do the deed.
JOHN Ah, dull, conceited peasant—knowst thou not
  It was a damned execrable deed?
  Showst me a seal? Oh, villain, both our souls
  Have sold their freedom to the thrall of hell
  Under the warrant of that cursed seal.
  Hence, villain, hang thyself, and say in hell
  That I am coming for a kingdom there.

In a curious plot twist, HUBERT then informs JOHN that ARTHUR isn't actually
dead. But, to complete the circle, ARTHUR immediately thereafter dies in an
accident. None of this actually happened during the reign of the historical
King John.

  The Troublesome Reign of King John suggests KING JOHN (Elizabeth) actually didn't want to sanction the death of ARTHUR (Mary, Queen of Scots); the
Catholic heir to the throne was killed by accident. Shake-speare's *King John*
reenacts this same strange fiction. In both the anonymous Queen's Men's play
and the mature Shake-speare drama, KING JOHN's sidestepping of responsibility was a clever propagandistic trick. It revealed the inside story of Queen
Elizabeth's court; but it also allowed Her Majesty a convenient out. *King
John* blunted the criticism Elizabeth faced both at home and abroad for the
beheading of the Queen of Scots.

  In *King John*, de Vere put a spin on the royal lynching in which he'd
played a part. However, as his more personal moments reveal, he must have
also been quite disturbed by the Mary Stuart debacle. De Vere's Geneva Bible
contains several underlined verses that suggest how sacrosanct the life of an
anointed monarch was to him. In the book of I Samuel, de Vere underlined
the passage in which Samuel anointed David as King Saul's successor. (I
Samuel 16:13.) Later in the biblical story, King Saul jealously attempts to murder David. Given two chances to kill the corrupt Saul and seize the throne,
David makes it clear that he respects Saul's sacred office. In another marked
passage, David explains himself to his king. Here is the biblical passage from
I Samuel 24:10–11, with de Vere's original underlining.

> 10 <u>And David said to Saul, "Wherefore</u>
>   givest thou an ear to men's words that
>   say, '<u>Behold, David seeketh evil against
>   thee?</u>'
> 11 "<u>Behold, this day thine eyes have seen</u>
>   that the Lord had delivered thee this

day into mine hand in the cave, and some
bade me kill thee. But I had compassion
on thee, and said, 'I will not lay
mine hand on my master: For he is the
Lord's anointed.'"

De Vere, whose underlinings elsewhere in the biblical books of Samuel and
Kings reveal that he personally identified with the figure of the poet-king
David, evidently took his Old Testament lessons to heart. The darkest play in
the entire Shake-speare canon suggests de Vere was even more disturbed by
the Mary Stuart execution than was Elizabeth.

Macbeth would serve as the author's private answer to his own *King John*.
De Vere probably began it sometime in the heat of the Mary Stuart crisis and,
as he did with most of the Shake-speare canon, would spend the rest of his
life revising and reworking it. The Scots queen's ultimate fate haunts *Macbeth*,
a tragedy that begins and ends with an offstage beheading and the ritual display of the severed head.

Queen Elizabeth is the leading candidate for LADY MACBETH, the regicidal vixen who had bathed her country in the blood of an anointed Scots
monarch. As one of *Macbeth*'s nobles, MACDUFF, laments when he first sees
the body of the slain Scots king:

> MACDUFF Confusion now hath made his masterpiece:
>   Most sacrilegious murder hath broke ope
>   The Lord's anointed temple and stole thence
>   The life o' th' building.

And as an accomplice to the murder of Mary Stuart, de Vere was as much
MACBETH as any member of the jury. He and Elizabeth had arguably violated
Mary's rights twice over. The Stuart queen had been a royal guest in England;
according to Scots law, Mary had been in England under what was technically called "double trust." Naturally, *Macbeth* outlines this important but abstruse point of Scottish law:

> MACBETH He's here in double trust:
>   First, as I am his kinsman and his subject,
>   Strong both against the deed; then, as his host,
>   Who should against his murderer shut the door,
>   Not bear the knife myself.

Macbeth, with its nihilism and criticism of both Queen Elizabeth and
Queen Mary Stuart, was no propaganda piece for the Queen's Men to enact on
the public stage. In fact, no evidence exists of any performance of *Macbeth*

during the reigns of Queen Elizabeth I, King James I, or even King Charles I—save for one mention of a staging at the Globe Theatre on April 20, 1611. The Scots tragedy was probably written to excise the author's own personal demons. Once a monarch has been murdered, says MACBETH, what gives anyone or anything else a greater right to life?

> MACBETH   Had I but died an hour before this chance,
>   I had liv'd a blessed time; for from this instant
>   There's nothing serious in mortality:
>   All is but toys; renown and grace is dead,
>   The wine of life is drawn, and the mere lees [*sediment*]
>   Is left this vault to brag of.

As high-minded as he may have been in his writings, by the time of the execution of Mary, Queen of Scots, Edward de Vere was becoming a bitter man. One would not wish the fate of Anne Cecil de Vere on anyone. By late August of 1586, Anne was pregnant for the fifth time. (After the 1583 death of their one son, the infant Lord Bolbec, she had given birth to a second daughter, Bridget, on April 6, 1584, and a third daughter, Frances, sometime in 1585 or '86.) During the final month of Anne's pregnancy, in early May of 1587, de Vere had once again chided her for her father's perceived misdeeds. The earl had so insulted his wife this time that, according to her father, she had cried all night. The cause of such distemper in her moody and unpredictable husband was neither principled nor high-minded. De Vere simply thought Burghley was leaving his son-in-law out of his perceived share of the forfeited estates of the Babington traitors.

As Burghley lamented to Walsingham on May 5, 1587,

> No enemy I have can envy this match, for thereby neither honor nor land nor goods come to their [*his daughter and son-in-law's*] children, for whom being 3 already to be kept and a 4th like to follow, I am only at charge . . . for their sustenation [*sustenance*].
>
>   But if their father were of that good nature as to be thankful for the same, I would be less grieved with the burden.

On May 26, 1587, Anne delivered the couple's fourth daughter, Susan. In September of 1587, the couple's two- or three-year-old daughter Frances died and was buried north of London at the Church of All Saints, Edmonton.

De Vere now had no surviving sons and three daughters. According to both his wife and father-in-law, he could support none of his children financially. All costs and responsibilities for their upbringing fell upon his in-laws.

After the £1,000 annuity, the historical records of de Vere's life grow fewer. The corpus that would become Shake-speare was, one presumes, occupying ever greater portions of the author's time.

The record is blank for what was probably the most significant single event in de Vere's life since the death of his father: On June 5, 1588, evidently quite unexpectedly, Anne Cecil de Vere, countess of Oxford, died at the queen's palace at Greenwich. She was thirty-three years old. Anne's epitaph, printed on her tomb that stands to this day at Westminster Abbey, records that she had been "debilitated by a burning fever."

De Vere is nowhere listed as a mourner or as an attendant at his wife's funeral; no records survive to suggest what he was doing during the spring and early summer of 1588 or even if he were anywhere in the greater London area. His silence and apparent distance are made all the more remarkable by the effusion of memorial verse that Anne's death generated. At least twenty in memoriam tributes were written—in English, Latin, Greek, and Hebrew—by as many different authors. Furthermore, since Burghley was clearly distraught by the loss of his favorite daughter, several letters from peers and colleagues (including from Peregrine Bertie, Lord Willoughby) arrived at the Lord Treasurer's doorstep, expressing their condolences. Again, no letters from or to de Vere survive.

One obscure elegist, Wilfred Samonde, paid tribute to Anne's many virtues. He writes:

> For modesty, a chaste Penelope
> Another Grissel [Griselda] for her patience,
> Such patience as few but she can use,
> Her Christian zeal unto the highest God,
> Her humble duty to her worthy queen,
> Her reverence to her aged sire,
> Her faithful love unto her noble lord,
> Her friendliness to those of equal state,
> Her readiness to help the needy soul,
> His [God's] worthy volume had been altered
> And filled with the praises of our Anne,
>> Who as she liv'd an angel on the earth,
>> So like an angel she doth sit on high.

Samonde's praise is noteworthy for its analogy between Anne and the medieval figure Griselda. Griselda, according to the ancient legend, married a nobleman who treated her horribly; and she did nothing to fight it. Griselda simply endured. In an age that required women to bow to the whims of their husbands, however unreasonable they might be, Griselda was seen by some

Elizabethans as an example (perverse in the extreme by today's standards) for young girls to follow.

It was only through his creative work, in plays completed years after Anne was gone, that de Vere expressed what should have been plain to him while his wife was alive: He'd been married to a woman who had practically martyred herself for him. The figure of Griselda, although mentioned by name only once in the Shake-speare canon (in *The Taming of the Shrew*), nevertheless haunts most of the Shake-speare plays that grapple with the problems of de Vere's marriage to the Cecil clan: *Hamlet, Othello, The Winter's Tale, The Comedy of Errors, All's Well That Ends Well, Measure for Measure, Much Ado About Nothing, Cymbeline*, and *Two Gentlemen of Verona*. Literary scholarship is flush with comparisons between Griselda and the Anne Cecil–inspired heroines in these plays: OPHELIA, DESDEMONA, HERMIONE, LUCIANA, HELENA, ISABELLA, HERO, IMOGEN, and JULIA.

Some Griselda-like heroines die; others don't. But all represent aspects of the relationship between de Vere and his wife. HELENA presents Anne at her most ambitious and aggressive. OPHELIA stands for Anne as the pawn of her overbearing and omnipotent father. (One of the unpublished epitaphs to Anne, in fact, compares her to the legendary Anna Perenna, the Ovidian goddess who drowned herself in a brook—suggesting one possible source for OPHELIA's ultimate fate.) DESDEMONA becomes a channel into which the author focuses his most selfish and maliciously misled feelings of jealous rage.

On the other hand, three of Shake-speare's Cecilian heroines exist in a kind of limbo between living and dead: *Much Ado About Nothing, Cymbeline,* and *The Winter's Tale* all guide their Griselda characters (HERO, IMOGEN, and HERMIONE respectively) through a course that begins with suspicions of infidelity, follows with the heroine's counterfeit death, and ends with her apotheosis. All three stories effectively perform an emotional autopsy on a disastrous marriage, exploring the realms of the author's psyche that led him to such vile behavior toward his wife.

The simplest of these three Shake-spearean resurrection fables comes in *Much Ado,* wherein HERO's betrothed (CLAUDIO) unjustly accuses her of infidelity. To teach the groom a lesson, HERO is spirited away into hiding. Everyone else in the play is then told that CLAUDIO's emotional cruelty has killed HERO. The ghostly father who devises this scheme (FRIAR FRANCIS) explains his motives thus:

> She dying, as it must be so maintain'd
> Upon the instant that she was accus'd
> Shall be lamented, pitied, and excus'd
> Of every hearer; for it so falls out
> That what we have we prize not the worth

> Whiles we enjoy it, but being lack'd and lost,
> Why then we rack the value; then we find
> The virtue that possession would now show us
> Whiles it was ours.

As noted previously, an early draft of *Much Ado* may have been written and performed at court in 1583. But the hammer blow of Anne's death–and the rebuke it delivered to her wayward husband–probably caused de Vere to revisit the play sometime soon after June of 1588.

Cymbeline considers Anne Cecil more deeply. Taking her fate into her own hands, IMOGEN fakes death to bring her husband to his senses. But this time no acts of theatrical resuscitation can bring her back. As IMOGEN observes:

> The dream's here still. Even when I wake it is
> Without me, as within me; not imagin'd, felt.

Whether or not de Vere was ever in love with the flesh-and-blood Griselda he married, it appears he fell in love with his dramatic portrayals of Anne onstage. He was becoming a Pygmalion–the mythic sculptor described by Ovid who became so transfixed by the statue of a woman he'd created that she came to life and married him–but a Pygmalion whose love had gone from flesh to statue.

Pygmalion is, indeed, the root story of the last play that ritually resurrects Anne Cecil. *The Winter's Tale* fixates on the slandered wife HERMIONE's death and then revels over her rebirth. The play's jealous husband, LEONTES, presents de Vere in a brutally honest self-portrait–a tyrannical egomaniac who accuses his wife of infidelity and stubbornly refuses to hear any contrary arguments, even when the infallible Oracle at Delphi pronounces HERMIONE chaste.

LEONTES's jealous rage kills his spouse, at which point she becomes transformed into a painted statue. Painted statues were a frequent feature of Elizabethan funerary art; de Vere may have been thinking of the one most personal to him, on the lavish tomb in Westminster Abbey that Burghley had constructed for his daughter. On the Westminster Abbey monument, the painted figure of Anne lies recumbent. As LEONTES observes about HERMIONE's statue:

> The fixture of her eye has motion in't
> As we are mock'd with art.

Perhaps this was ultimately how Anne Cecil de Vere exacted revenge on her husband, by colonizing his very imagination and tormenting him–via his own pen–from beyond the grave.

In the summer of 1588, able-bodied Englishmen had more to do than wrestle with the demons of their past. The imminent invasion of England by Spain was becoming, in the words of historian De Lamar Jensen, "the worst-kept secret in Europe." Sir Francis Drake had stopped the Spanish fleet during the summer of 1587 with a search-and-destroy mission to the Spanish base at Cádiz. But by April of 1588, Drake and the lord admiral Charles Howard knew that Spain was going to try its luck again during the coming summer.

The combined force of Spain and Portugal's navies set their courses north and readied their cannons. In the Lowlands, a Spanish invasion force of twenty-three thousand men awaited the Armada to ferry them across the Channel. If the invasion succeeded, Elizabeth could be deposed by midsummer and English subjects could be pledging their allegiance to a Spanish-appointed Catholic puppet regime.

De Vere had been pressing his father-in-law for opportunities to show Elizabeth his mettle. The reason he was not near at Anne's death (June 5) and funeral (June 25) may well be because he was at sea.

Sir Francis Drake was to lead the English naval forces against the Armada. Ever the buccaneer, Drake intended to lead an English fleet south and stop the Armada before it could even leave Spanish waters—as he'd done the summer before at Cádiz. Gale-force winds and unseasonably strong rainstorms during the spring of 1588 prevented any venture into the open sea. However, on May 30, the weather finally broke long enough for Drake's fleet to set sail, to ambush the Armada during its northbound transit.

An English propaganda poem, published the following winter, celebrates the many worthies who participated in the eventual military victory against Spain. De Vere is given prominent placement. The poem's author ("I.L."– thought to be either John Lyly or the Protestant apologist James Lea) writes:

> When from the Hesperian bounds [*western shores*],
> with warlike bands,
> The vowèd foemen of this happy isle
> With martial men, drawn forth from many lands,
> 'Gan set their sail, on whom the winds did smile,
> The rumors ran of conquest, war, and spoil
> And hapless sack of this renownèd soil.....
>
> De Vere, whose fame and loyalty hath pierced
> The Tuscan clime, and through the Belgike [*Belgian*] lands
> By wingèd fame for valor is rehearsed,
> Like warlike Mars upon the hatches stands.
>> His tuskèd boar, 'gan foam for inward ire,
>> While Pallas filled his breast with warlike fire.

Later accounts of the Armada as written by the chroniclers Richard Hakluyt (1598–1600), John Stow (1615), and William Camden (1625) also list de Vere among the ranks of the "great and honorable personages" who took up arms against a sea of Spaniards.

If de Vere was part of Drake's first wave of naval forces, the voyage would probably have been the most stomach-turning encounter with the ocean in his life. The English fleet had on May 30 been lured out by a break in the weather only to find themselves blown around by the same tempests that were battering the Armada. "We endured a great storm (considering the time of year) with the wind southerly and at southwest for seven days," Drake would later write in a letter to Burghley. For a long week they fought the elements when they should have been preparing to fight the Spanish. The opening scene of *The Tempest* may have drawn its inspiration from the nautical adventure the English fleet experienced during the first few days of June 1588.

The Tempest begins onboard a ship in the midst of a rising gale. The ship's master, standing on the quarterdeck, calls out to the BOATSWAIN. "Fall to it yarely [*Step to it*] or we run ourselves aground!"

The BOATSWAIN orders the topsail hauled down–a move that experienced mariners know spells trouble, since that means the winds are becoming too stiff and changeable to be used for propulsion. As the topsail canvas comes thundering down, no one can hear a thing. Only the shipmaster's whistle can be made out over the rumbling din. "Tend to the master's whistle," the BOATSWAIN tells his crew.

The roar of the falling topsail and sudden change in the boat's inclination surprise the passengers belowdeck. One, ALONSO, emerges to ask what's going on.

The BOATSWAIN urges the inexperienced seaman back to his cabin before an unexpected surge sweeps him into the dark and foreboding ocean. Sensing more trouble ahead, the BOATSWAIN cries to his crew, "Down with the topmast! Yare! Lower, lower! Bring her to try with main-course!" Striking the topmast was an extreme measure practiced by Elizabethan mariners as a last-ditch attempt to reduce a ship's top-heaviness–especially when it was perilously close to shore. The BOATSWAIN then yells out, "Lower, lower!" Now with only the round-bellied mainsail driving the ship–and no hope of re-hoisting the topsail anytime soon–the BOATSWAIN has his crew turn the ship into the wind ("bring her to try") and move the creaking and groaning vessel away from the driving spray of the rocks that grow ever closer.

Two more outraged passengers emerge from belowdeck, cursing in their mortal fright. The BOATSWAIN tells the passengers that if they will not stay belowdeck, they had better prepare to put their shoulder into the ropes and masts with the rest of the crew. As Sir Francis Drake famously told one of his well-heeled passengers, "I must have the gentlemen to hale and draw with the mariner and the mariner with the gentlemen. What, let us show ourselves all to be of [one] company."

In the process of striking the topmast and coming about, however, the ship has been driven closer to the rocky shore. The BOATSWAIN shouts, "Lay her a-hold, a-hold!" He tries to put the ship on another tack, hoping the new direction may yield more sea room. A few tense moments pass as the mainsail flutters and cracks and then fills again. The ship lurches seaward. At last, a window of opportunity opens, if only briefly. The ship now needs as much forward power as quickly as can be tapped. The BOATSWAIN orders the foresail unfurled. "Set her two courses!" he commands.

The tension begins to dissipate as the shore's spray and spume grows fainter. "Off to sea again!" the BOATSWAIN exclaims. "Lay her off!" The BOATSWAIN, it would appear, has saved the ship from its near certain doom.

The pitch-perfect timing, virtuosic command of nautical vocabulary, and dramatic economy of *The Tempest*'s opening scene suggest that de Vere knew at first hand at least some of the seaborne danger he so masterfully dramatized.

Such scenes were to be the only catch of the English navy's May 30 fishing expedition. On June 6, the storm-beaten English fleet returned to Plymouth. As the landlubbing passengers recovered from their perilous journey, urgent news from London would have arrived informing de Vere that only the day before, his wife had suddenly died. This is the same situation HAMLET finds himself in, as he washes ashore from his nautical adventures to discover that OPHELIA has drowned. The Danish prince's manic response to his graveside discovery reminds one of de Vere's mercurial extremes. Suddenly, the cold embrace of death has made the bereaved lover discover how much he adored the deceased.

> HAMLET [to LAERTES] I lov'd OPHELIA. Forty thousand brothers
> Could not, with all their quantity of love,
> Make up my sum. What wilt thou do for her?
> ... Woo't weep, woo't fight, woo't fast, woo't tear thyself?
> Woo't drink up eisel [*vinegar*], eat a crocodile?
> I'll do it.

If de Vere had been part of Drake and Howard's first expedition, however, duty would have kept the earl close to fleet headquarters in Plymouth. There was still no sign of the Spanish Armada; the commanders knew they could still face the enemy at sea and prevent a Spanish invasion. During another break in the weather on June 19, they again sent the fleet out. This time, however, the headwinds were so strong that the ships returned to port only two days later.

Anne's funeral was fast approaching, but Drake and Howard wanted to make one last try. The day before the countess of Oxford's memorial service, on June 24, England's final hope of preemptively defeating the Spanish menace launched from Plymouth. Again, de Vere would have been a likely officer on this mission. The weather was more cooperative this time, but when no sign of Spanish galleons could be found by early July, the English commanders grew nervous that the Armada had somehow skirted around them and was heading toward an undefended English coastline. The risks of pressing any farther south were growing too great. Drake and Howard decided to turn the ships around and head back to port. They arrived at Plymouth on July 12. A week later, the Armada would be first sighted off the southernmost tip of Cornwall.

Here is where the conventional story of the Spanish Armada begins, but here is also where de Vere's role recedes into the background. The English fleet's three failed search-and-destroy expeditions were probably all of the naval warfare that the earl of Oxford saw during the Spanish Armada campaign. It is possible that de Vere took part in the first few days of engagement with the enemy, on July 20–22, when the Spanish fleet first plowed through the Channel in an ominous crescent-moon formation.

But that is all the calendar permits. For historical records reveal that de Vere had arrived at the English camp at Tilbury (east of London) on July 27 at the latest. And Tilbury was at least a four days' ride from Plymouth, where he would have disembarked.

On July 28, as the Armada was anchored off the coast of Calais, Leicester (at Tilbury) wrote to Walsingham (in London):

> Your other letter concerned my lord of Oxford who was with me as he went–and returned again yesterday by me with Captain Huntley in his company. He seemed only [that] his voyage was to have gone to my Lord Admiral [Howard]–and at his return, [de Vere] seemed also to return again hither to me this day from London, whither he went yesternight for his armor and furniture. If he come, I would know from you what I shall do. I trust he be free to go to the enemy [*to participate in close combat*], for he seems most willing to hazard his life in this quarrel.

Leicester's syntax is confusing, but it would appear that at some point de Vere had parted from Leicester's company to follow the command of Admiral Howard–during the aforementioned search-and-destroy missions, perhaps. Then, some time later, de Vere arrived at Tilbury. And from Tilbury, de Vere dispatched himself to London on the night of July 27 to fetch his armor and furniture. By being "free to go to the enemy," de Vere was evidently committed to lay down his life or be taken hostage if the situation merited.

On the night of July 28, English fireships dispersed the Spanish fleet, which then sailed northeast from Calais. Through a fortuitous combination of bad weather and bad timing, the Armada had failed to rendezvous with the Spanish armies planning to invade England. The Armada was—incorrectly, it turns out—expected to make landfall in Essex. Elizabeth gave her temperamental earl the assignment of commanding two thousand men in the Essex deep-water port city of Harwich.

However, de Vere soon wanted no part of it. He yearned to be on a war-ship chasing Spaniards. By August 1, he had returned to London, where he angered Leicester. Leicester wrote to Walsingham:

> Deliver to my lord of Oxford Her [Majesty's] gracious consent of his will-ingness to serve her. . . . She was pleased that he should have the govern-ment of Harwich and all those that are appointed to attend that place, which should be 2,000 men. [He has] a place of trust and of great danger.
>
> My lord seemed at the first to like well of it. Afterward, he came to me and told me he thought that place of no service nor credit, and therefore he would to the court and understand Her Majesty's further pleasure. . . .
>
> Also, make him know that it was of good grace to appoint that place to him, having no more [military] experience than he hath. . . . [I] for my own part being gladder to be rid of him than to have him but only to have him contented—which now I find will be harder than I took it. And [he] denieth all his former offers he made to serve rather than not to be seen to be employed at this time. . . .
>
> [P.S.] I am glad I am rid of my lord Oxford, seeing he refuseth this, and I pray you let me not be pressed any more for him, what suit so ever he make.

Leicester could only wish good riddance to an insubordinate commander who wanted no part of any military assignment that wasn't center stage.

The story of the Armada, now enshrined in myth, ends happily for England. But for de Vere, the tale of Spain's naval assault in the summer of 1588 is one that begins with his wife's death, follows with an inglorious retreat from a naval mission gone awry, and ends onshore with a clash of egos and military authority.

A tale from the ancient world suggests itself. From his copy of Plutarch's *Lives*, de Vere would have read about a celebrated Roman who had gone from losing a wife to forfeiting a naval battle. This ignominious loss at sea, Plutarch notes, came about because the Roman worthy had retreated before his fleet could engage the enemy. The ancient Roman's name was Marc Antony, and to make the tale more attractive for de Vere's pen, Antony's infamous relationship with an infamous queen provided ample opportunity to explore the two most complex and remarkable psyches at Queen Elizabeth's court.

Antony and Cleopatra represents Shake-speare at his most imaginative and adaptive. Whereas *Hamlet,* for instance, closely follows the contours of de Vere's life, *Antony and Cleopatra* represents a more evenhanded mixture of autobiography and ancient chronicle. It is opera before England had discovered the form. The escapism this play provided, one suspects, was what the author needed after losing the woman who was both his albatross and his emotional anchor: Anne Cecil de Vere.

ANTONY would be invested with all the taints and honors of the author who brought him to life. De Vere's willingness to "hazard his life in this quarrel," as reported by Leicester, suggests a man newly unmoored, giving himself over to the extremes of recklessness. De Vere's own mental disunity, even more disheveled than usual, translated into the erratic behavior of Shake-speare's tragic triumvir. CLEOPATRA would embody Elizabeth's own vain–and attractive–extremes.

Antony and Cleopatra begins with an introduction to the title characters. The first scene presents the bantering of the besotted ANTONY and the changeable CLEOPATRA. What appears in the play as idle chitchat no doubt represents a distillation of years of privy chamber encounters between de Vere and his queen. CLEOPATRA asks ANTONY about his inconvenient marriage (to the Roman Republican FULVIA).

> CLEOPATRA Excellent falsehood!
>   Why did he [ANTONY] marry FULVIA and not love her?
>   I'll seem the fool I am not. . . .
> ANTONY Let's not confound the time with conference harsh:
>   There's not a minute of our lives should stretch
>   Without some pleasure now.

Soon thereafter, breaking from Plutarch's version of the story, ANTONY is informed of the death of FULVIA via messengers from abroad. ANTONY's detached reaction to the news about FULVIA stands in contrast to HAMLET's discovery of OPHELIA's death.

> THIRD MESSENGER FULVIA thy wife is dead. . . .
> ANTONY There's a great spirit gone! Thus did I desire it:
>   What our contempts doth often hurl from us,
>   We wish it ours again. The present pleasure,
>   By revolution lowering, does become
>   The opposite of itself: She's good, being gone,
>   The hand could pluck her back that shov'd her on.

What most husbands might look upon as a horrific message to receive, ANTONY takes as a liberation. "My idleness doth hatch," he says, freed from the hindrance of his troubled and annoying marriage.

Weaving through a web of conflicted alliances, ANTONY soon realizes he has offended his fellow triumvir OCTAVIUS CAESAR. ANTONY prepares himself for war. Shake-speare's portrayal of the naval conflict that ensues, the Battle of Actium, has been compared to the infamous events of 1588. "The political contrast is striking," notes literary scholar Keith Rinehart. "Elizabeth staked her throne on a decisive sea battle—the fight with the Spanish Armada—and won; CLEOPATRA staked hers on the decisive Battle of Actium and lost." Before battle could be waged, CLEOPATRA turned her ship around and fled. ANTONY, "like a doting mallard," followed her. The word *mallard* puns on the actual commander who turned the pre-Armada search-and-destroy mission around: Drake.

Ultimately, what becomes significant for the play is not the military defeat but rather the transformation in ANTONY that his shameful retreat brings about. After Actium, ANTONY recognizes that his delusions of political and military leadership are merely fancy. ANTONY is not a leader; he is the led. This revelation may help to explain de Vere's act of effrontery at Harwich. He had finally recognized his own failure to be the military leader he'd been raised to become. His lot in life was not to lead armies or to wield the sceptres and orbs of power. It was probably a shameful realization, but it was also square with cold reality. Replace the word *Egypt* with *Elizabeth* in ANTONY's third-act epiphany, and one may have reached the emotional core of de Vere's drama as the bedraggled Spanish Armada sailed into the North Sea.

> ANTONY O, whither hast thou led me, Egypt? See
> How I convey my shame out of thine eyes
> By looking back what I have left behind
> 'Stroyed in dishonor....
>   Egypt, thou knewst too well
> My heart was to thy rudder tied by th' strings,
> And thou shouldst tow me after.

On November 24, de Vere joined a parade of nobles and military leaders through London in celebration of the defeat—or at least temporary setback—of Spanish forces. An anonymous ballad recounts the pomp and circumstance of the parade, including the earl of Oxford assuming his role as play master for the queen. After Her Majesty attended a sermon at Paul's Cross, de Vere opened the curtains ("windows") for the queen and presented his boy players from the old hospital at the Blackfriars Theatre. What interlude the troupe performed is not recorded.

[T]o lovely London fair our noble queen would go
And at Paul's Cross before her God her thankful heart would show;
Where prince and people did consent with joyful minds to meet
To glorify the God of heaven with psalms and voices sweet....

The lord marquess of Winchester bareheaded there was seen,
Who bare the sword in comely sort before our noble queen;
The noble earl of Oxford, then High Chamberlain of England,
Rode right before Her Majesty his bonnet in his hand....

And after by two noblemen along the church was led,
With a golden canopy carried o'er her head.
The clergy with procession brought Her Grace into the choir;
Whereas Her Majesty was set the service for to hear.

And afterwards unto Paul's Cross she did directly pass,
There by the bishop of Salisbury a sermon preachèd was.
The earl of Oxford opening then the windows for Her Grace
The children of the hospital she saw before her face.

During the amazing eight-year stretch from de Vere's affair with Anne Vava-sour to the defeat of the Spanish Armada, he had maintained his bohemian retreat to the northeast of the old London city gates. Fisher's Folly remained de Vere's folly through the end of 1588. The literary gristmill continued to churn. In 1587, Burghley wrote to Walsingham that de Vere's "lewd friends ... still rule him by flatteries." These lewd friends were a regular presence in de Vere's London life.

John Lyly's best-selling Euphues novels, widely imitated by other lead-ing London writers, had come to symbolize the wild life at Fisher's Folly. Among the wags and scribblers de Vere kept under his roof, the character Euphues represented a kind of collective identity for the Euphuists and other hangers-on at the Folly. According to the fables the Euphuists began publishing after de Vere had purchased Fisher's Folly, Euphues could be found at the "bottom of the mount of Silexedra." (Fisher's Folly was some-times also referred to as "Mount Fisher.") "Silexedra" came to be known, even to non-Euphuist writers such as Barnabe Riche, as a suburban place of study and a literary retreat.

One "Silexedra" regular was the hack writer Robert Greene, who in 1584 dedicated to de Vere a shameless piece of literary piracy called *Gwydonius*–a story cobbled together from one of Greene's earlier novels and the work of anthologist George Pettie. Greene's dedication praised de Vere as a worthy favorer and fosterer of learning [who] hath forced many through your excellent virtue to offer the first fruits of their study at the shrine of Your Lordship's courtesy.

Other Fisher's Folly frequenters were slightly less roguish than Greene. During the "Silexedra" years, de Vere's secretary, Anthony Munday, began translating an epic of French, Spanish, and Italian chivalric legends about a noble knight, Palmerin d'Olivia, and his son Primaleon. Munday trickled out publications of the Palmerin books into the first two decades of the seventeenth century. Some of Munday's translations were never published. As Munday wrote in his dedication of one of the Palmerin romances to de Vere:

If *Palmerin* hath sustained any wrong by my bad translation, being so worthily set down in other languages, Your Honor having such special knowledge in them I hope will let slip any faults escaped.

Since de Vere was fluent in Italian, French, and–if the above quote is to be believed–Spanish as well, Munday was covering his rear.

A related romance Munday translated *(Amadis de Gaule)* told of a hero named Florisel whose lover is substituted with a statue; the sculpture is so lifelike that Florisel mistakes it for the lifeless body of his beloved. The deception is later revealed, and Florisel and his lover are reunited. Combine *Amadis's* Florisel plot and the legend of Pygmalion and one has the makings for *The Winter's Tale.* Another of Munday's Englished romances became a source for *The Tempest.*

Then there was Angel Day. In 1586, Day dedicated a letter-writing guidebook to de Vere. In the preface to *The English Secretary,* Day notes he'd been working on this book for six years–from the first days of de Vere's Fisher's Folly tenancy. Day's preface also extols its patron, "whose infancy was from the beginning ever sacred to the muses."

The English Secretary celebrates the secretary in the Elizabethan sense of the word: a correspondent, a confidant, and a keeper of a powerful man's secrets. To illustrate his rhetorical points, Day printed sample letters. Some letters were real; others were clearly spoofs crafted by a razor wit.

In one of Day's obviously fictionalized letters, for instance, a reader can practically see the correspondent's bulging neck veins as the railing and abuse come pouring forth. It is the insult as raised to an art form–a peculiarly Shake-spearean art form:

An example of an epistle vituperatory, concerning also the person

SIR, the strangeness of an accident happening of late amongst us hath occasioned at this instant this discourse to come unto your hands. There was, if you remember, at your last being with me in the country, a man of great ability dwelling about a mile from me. His name was B., and if I fail not of memory therein, we had once at a dinner together....

You have not (I am sure) forgotten in so much as he was called the *hell* of the world, the *plague* of a common-weale, the *mischief* of men, and the *bondslave* of the devil. And no marvel, for what injury might be conceived that was not by him imagined?...I have wondered sithence with myself many times what soil it might be or what constellation so furious as affected their operations in production of so bad and vile a creature at the time when he was first put forward with living into the world. In the search whereof I have been the less astonished, insomuch as thereby I have grown in to some particular knowledge of his original and parents. His sire, I have understood, was a villain by birth, by nature, by soil, by descent, by education, by practice, by study, by experience; his dam the common sink of every rakehell's filthiness. [Emphasis in original.]

And on it goes, detailing in comic hyperbole the villainous villainy of this horrid man called "B." One can readily picture de Vere reciting these words as he's pacing back and forth one afternoon at the Folly, with one of his secretaries scratching out every word as it drops from de Vere's acid tongue–all to the great amusement of the rakehells who had gathered that day to soak up a few drops of the inspiration flowing as liberally as the ale.

As with the PRINCE HAL scenes in the *Henry IV* plays, the wild times and drunken escapades at the Folly were bound to last only so long. Euphues's Silexedra retreat was soon to be closed down for good.

In December of 1588, de Vere sold Fisher's Folly. Perhaps to make a clean break from his life under the House of Cecil, de Vere closed the shutters on his London pleasure palace and transferred the deed to a friend of the family, William Cornwallis.

The following year, Thomas Lodge published a book bemoaning the loss of Silexedra, *Rosalynde: Euphues's Golden Legacy, Found After His Death in His Cell at Silexedra*. The year after *Rosalynde*, Robert Greene followed suit with his novel *Menaphon: Camilla's Alarm to Slumbering Euphues in His Melancholy Cell at Silexedra*. As far as the former Euphuists were concerned, Euphues was by the end of the '80s either asleep or dead–and in any event, Silexedra was the site of his terminal torpor. Lodge would later reminisce about the Silexedra years in his novel *Euphues's Shadow*. In a prefatory epistle to the book, Lodge noted how "Euphues repent[ed] the prime of his youth misspent in folly and virtuously end[ed] the winter of his age in Silexedra."

Silexedra was no more. It was also no great joy for the new owners to move into. Cornwallis soon found himself in hot water. Burghley had been keeping close watch over de Vere's finances, since de Vere was anything but forthcoming with child support. And now that Anne was no longer part of the equation, Burghley had no further cause to remain on congenial terms with his former son-in-law. The Lord Treasurer would soon be suing de Vere for back debts, winning court orders to seize some of the earl's properties.

De Vere's sale of Fisher's Folly, however, had been a backroom deal over which Burghley had had no say. Burghley was angry, because he wanted more control over de Vere's finances. De Vere was undoubtedly upset, because he felt his money and portfolio were his business. Cornwallis was caught in the middle.

But Cornwallis and his wife persevered, and eventually the literary mecca of Silexedra was converted to their suburban home. One of de Vere's literary colleagues, the poet Thomas Watson, opted to stay on at the Folly and tutor the young Cornwallis daughter, Anne. It was to be an auspicious pairing.

Anne Cornwallis is known to posterity as the creator of a precious manuscript: She kept a commonplace book of contemporary poetry, probably as part of her schooling in literature and penmanship. Cornwallis's manuscript contains poems by such noted versifiers of the day as Sir Philip Sidney, Sir Walter Raleigh, and Sir Edward Dyer. The book includes four youthful verses written by de Vere, including two that are also associated with Anne Vavasour.

One handwritten transcription is an anonymous poem that begins:

> When that thine eye hath chose the dame,
> And stalled the deer that thou wouldst strike,
> Let reason rule things worthy blame,
> As well as fancy, partial like
> > Ask counsel of some other head
> > Neither unwise nor yet unwed.

> And when thou com'st thy tale to tell,
> Whet not thy tongue with filèd talk,
> Lest she some subtle practice smell–
> A cripple soon can spy a halt–
> > But plainly say thou lovs't her well,
> > And set thy person forth to sell.

The poem goes on for another seven stanzas of collegial advice in the fine art of wooing.

The verse Anne Cornwallis–or her tutor–wrote down later appeared in a 1599 poetic anthology titled *The Passionate Pilgrime By W. Shakespeare.* The ditty "When that thine eye hath chose the dame" in Cornwallis's commonplace book can be found today in any edition of the collected works of Shake-speare.

The commonplace book's transcription of "When that thine eye..." is the only extant sixteenth-century manuscript copy in the world of any Shakespeare work. The manuscript is now stored in the vaults of the Folger Shakespeare Library in Washington, D.C. The gold lettering on the spine of the book today reads "MSS. POEMS BY VERE EARL OF OXFORD &C."

De Vere's sale of Fisher's Folly represents the beginning of a new period in the earl's life. With the closing of Silexedra, de Vere built a new house near the town of Earls Colne in Essex. (He had already sold the manor at Earls Colne and the nearby estate at Wivenhoe.) Records reveal that de Vere hired a team of joiners to work on Plaistow House in Plaistow (or Plaiston) from 1588 to '96—a time when de Vere had little cash to spare. Presumably the earl was fixing up Plaistow in order to accommodate a single man and his servants and secretaries.

Like LEONTES in *The Winter's Tale* and CLAUDIO in *Much Ado About Nothing*, de Vere probably wanted time to think about his marriage, his irrational jealousies, and his ruinous treatment of his wife. In 1589 Thomas Lodge published an epic poem titled *Scilla's Metamorphosis*. Appended to this work were shorter verses, one of which sounds suspiciously like the godfather of the Euphuists as he decamped from the city:

> I will become a hermit now
> And do my penance straight
> For all the errors of mine eyes
> With foolish rashness filled.
>
> My hermitage shall placèd be
> Where melancholy's weight
> And none but love alone shall know
> The bower I mean to build....
>
> Of faintful hope shall be my staff
> And daily when I pray
> My mistress's picture placed by love
> Shall witness what I say.

A second de Vere estate, in the Avon River Valley in Warwickshire, makes an equally likely retreat for a widower looking to get away from his former cosmopolitan life. This second country house was called Bilton and by all accounts was a gorgeous piece of property. In the *History of the County of Warwick*, the nineteenth-century chronicler William Smith records his reflections on Bilton:

The situation is desirably retired, and the windows of the principal rooms command a fair respect...on the north side of the grounds is a long walk....In its original state, no spot could be better adapted to meditation, or more genial to his temper; the scenery round is bounded by soft ranges of hills, and the comely spire and Gothic ornaments of the adjacent village church impart a soothing air of pensiveness to the neighborhood.

In early 1589, the duties of earldom brought de Vere to London and Westminster at least briefly. The queen called a new session of Parliament on February 4, and as a member of the House of Lords, de Vere attended five days of the thirty-five-day session, including the opening ceremony. In a rare image from his later years, the earl of Oxford is pictured as part of a seventeenth-century engraving memorializing Queen Elizabeth's 1589 Parliament. Sir Christopher Hatton, the new Lord Chancellor of England, delivered the opening oration. Noteworthy in his absence was the earl of Leicester, who had died the previous September.

In April, after Parliament had adjourned, de Vere again became involved in the lives of the sons of his cousin, the late duke of Norfolk. The duke's eldest son, Philip Howard, earl of Arundel, had been held in the Tower of London since 1585 on charges of Catholicism and attempting to flee the country without the queen's permission. During the heat of the Spanish Armada battles in the English Channel, Arundel had been caught holding Mass. In an age of superstition, this was effectively conspiring with God and therefore an act of treason.

Now that the Spanish menace was safely gone, the queen wanted to clean house. Arundel's trial was set for April 4 in the Court of the Lord High Steward. De Vere joined twenty-two of his peers in Westminster Hall to witness the ruination of another Elizabethan Catholic noble—the same young man with whom de Vere had shared top honors at the Accession Day Tournament of 1584.

As in the trials of Mary, Queen of Scots, and his own father, Arundel's verdict was practically preordained. De Vere and his fellow peers watched the pro forma display of evidence. Attorney General Sir John Popham presented the jury with a curious "painted prophecy," a pictorial allegory that the state claimed was further proof of the earl of Arundel's papist and treasonous designs. It was described as "an emblem...wherein was painted on one side a hand shaking a serpent into the fire with this inscription, *If God be with us, who shall be against us?* and on the other side a lion rampant, his claws cut off, with this motto: *Yet a lion.*"

The treason verdict came in as expected, and a death sentence soon followed. However, Elizabeth never gave the execution orders. The eldest son of the executed duke of Norfolk was granted clemency, albeit the worst kind—clemency by royal inaction. Elizabeth simply never felt enough political pressure to do anything more about Philip Howard, who would remain in the Tower until his death in 1595.

As You Like It, portraying the travails of inheritance of the youngest Howard brother, William (ORLANDO DE BOYS), also gives voice to the eldest brother (OLIVER DE BOYS) as he faces his own fate. As dramatized in the play, OLIVER is nearly killed by a living embodiment of the very emblem entered into evidence in the Arundel trial—a serpent and a lion. However, ORLANDO rescues his eldest brother from the jaws of death.

De Vere watched the travails of the duke of Norfolk's boys with the interest of a cousin—and now of a juror too. If he hadn't been inspired before to dramatize the twisted story of Norfolk's three sons, the 1589 trial may have provided the impetus. Much of *As You Like It* takes place in the forest of Arden, near de Vere's estate of Bilton. Local oral tradition holds that *As You Like It* was actually written at Billesley, an estate just outside Stratford-upon-Avon owned by the family of de Vere's grandmother, Elizabeth Trussell. Perhaps on a journey from Bilton, visiting his relatives' extensive library at Billesley Manor, the lonely widower spent a few days and nights at a family estate among the books and histories that were his first love.

The year 1589 marks an important milestone not just in de Vere's life but also in the chronicles of the Elizabethan literary world. The anonymous 1589 book *The Art of English Poesie* was a guidebook to courtly writing and courtly writers that became the gold standard upon which literary criticism of the age was based.

In the midst of a lengthy discourse on the finer points of writing and surviving at court, *The Art* notes that a few highborn authors in Elizabeth's day have begun publishing their works, but not under their own names. The anonymous author of *The Art* explains:

> I know very many notable gentlemen in the court that have written commendably and suppressed it again—or else suffered it to be published without their own names to it, as if it were a discredit for a gentleman to seem learned.

Who these "very many notable gentlemen" were *The Art* does not state.

In 1589, a new voice on the scene mocked *The Art of English Poesie* for being such a tease about anonymous and pseudonymous courtly authors whom it refuses to name. In his print debut, the satirist Thomas Nashe wrote:

> Sundry other sweet gentlemen I know that have vaunted their pens in private devices and tricked up a company of taffeta fools with their feathers....

Nashe also made fun of the leading named dramatist of the day, Christopher Marlowe, whom he nicknames "English Seneca":

> English Seneca read by candlelight yields many good sentences.... If you entreat him fair in a frosty morning, he will afford you whole *Hamlets*–I should say, handfuls–of tragical speeches. But O grief!... The sea exhaled by drops will in continuance be dry, and Seneca let blood line by line and page by page at length must needs die to our stage.

In other words, Nashe cautioned Marlowe that filching plots from Seneca might allow him to create a *Hamlet* or two–Nashe here probably had Marlowe's tragedy *Tamburlaine* in mind. More important, Nashe's analogy shows that what would eventually become known as "Shakespeare's" *Hamlet* was already on the minds and pens of the London literati by the end of the 1580s.

Yet de Vere's writings were not slipping by in complete anonymity. *The Art of English Poesie,* in a separate chapter from the coy "I know very many notable gentlemen..." passage, notes:

> And in Her Majesty's time that now is are sprung up another crew of courtly makers, noblemen and gentlemen of Her Majesty's own servants, who have written commendably well–as it would appear if their doings could be found out and made public with the rest–of which number is first that noble gentleman Edward, earl of Oxford....
>
> Th'earl of Oxford and Master [Richard] Edwards of Her Majesty's Chapel [are the best] for comedy and interlude.

Just three years before de Vere received this praise, the critic William Webbe had written:

> I may not omit the deserved commendations of many honorable and noble lords and gentlemen of Her Majesty's court, which in the rare devices of poetry have been and yet are most excellent skillful–among whom the right honorable earl of Oxford may challenge to himself the title of most excellent among the rest.

De Vere's work was indeed beginning to be found out and made public with the rest.

Yet this was nothing any self-respecting "courtly maker" should aspire to–as Castiglione himself had asserted. And it was time for de Vere to be discreet and courtly. By 1589, Burghley had already begun to look around for a husband for de Vere's eldest daughter, Elizabeth, now age fourteen. Would the earl ruin his daughter's life by dragging her family's name through even more mud?

Would Elizabeth de Vere face the brutal marriage market as the daughter of a lowly and vulgar playwright–whose plays frankly discussed her mother and father's appalling marital history? Her father had once been one of the most esteemed and admired peers in all of England. The least he could do now was not make life for his children and their heirs any worse than it already was.

A few contemporary critics might have valued de Vere as "most excellent among the rest," but henceforth Hamlet's final words would be the earl's guiding philosophy about publishing under his own name: The rest is silence.

CHAPTER 9

GENTLE MASTER WILLIAM

[1589–1593]

IN 1589, ENGLAND COULD AT LAST TAKE A RESPITE FROM THE DYNASTIC ambitions of King Philip II and his expansionist house of Hapsburg. Sometime during this year, scholars now suspect that the Queen's Men staged the triumphal *True Tragedy of Richard the Third.* De Vere probably created the play in collaboration with Munday, Greene, or other former Fisher's Folly-ites. *The True Tragedy* includes a bit of special pleading for the earl of Oxford. ("Oxford ... will not wink at murders secretly put up, nor suffer upstarts to enjoy our rights.... Content thee, good Oxford, and tho I confess myself bound to thee for thy especiall care, yet at this time I pray thee hold me excused.") But its principal goal was to legitimize Queen Elizabeth and her house of Tudor by celebrating the Tudor regime's first victory–the deposition of Richard III by Henry Tudor in 1485.

In the play's concluding speech, "Worthy Elizabeth" is celebrated as

> ... the lamp that keeps fair England's light,
> And through her faith her country lives in peace:
> And she hath put proud Antichrist [*Catholic Spain*] to flight,
> And been the means that civil wars did cease.

The speech is classic Elizabethan propaganda. The line about "civil wars," however, was overhasty. Although the defeat of the Spanish Armada represented a serious setback for those hoping for a Catholic overthrow of Elizabeth, there were other troubles brewing elsewhere. Watchful English eyes had by 1589 already turned to France.

The 1584 death of Elizabeth's longtime suitor, the French heir presumptive duke of Alençon had left the French crown with a contested line of succession. Two other leaders had emerged to assume the mantle of French king-in-waiting, and by 1588, they had grown impatient with the wait. Henri, king of Navarre, was the Protestant (Huguenot) favorite; Henri, duke of Guise, the leading Catholic contender for the throne. Disillusioned with Henri III's ineffective and irresolute government, both factions were fighting against the king; even as England celebrated its victory against the Armada, just across the Channel the "War of the Three Henries" was raging.

The duke of Guise had come to prominence in 1576 when the Catholic faction in France blanched at the king's concessions to the Huguenots–the same uneasy peace de Vere had participated in brokering on his way home from Italy. Religion aside, Guise was an old-fashioned feudalist who despised Henri III's consolidation of power at the expense of the French nobility. During de Vere's years of flirtation with Catholicism, Guise had been able to count on his support. De Vere had in 1577 sent servants to France to fight on Guise's behalf, and according to the Arundell Libels, de Vere had proclaimed Guise "a rare and gallant gentleman [who] should be the man to come into Scotland, who would breech Her Majesty [Elizabeth] for all her wantonness."

So the news from France in December 1588 was doubly shocking. On December 23, by the king's orders, Guise was lured into a private antechamber at the royal château of Blois, where a squad of nobles surrounded him and stabbed him dozens of times. As a collective act of aristocratic assassination, the murder of Guise, like that of Julius Caesar, could conveniently not be pinned on any single individual. King Henri reportedly arrived on the crime scene soon afterward and protested the death with crocodile tears: "I no longer have any boon companion, now that the duke of Guise is dead."

Catholic France was outraged by Guise's murder. At his funeral, at Notre Dame on January 30, 1589, one observer noted that no king of France had ever been buried with so much honor. Revisionist histories of Guise's assassination soon began appearing in the French press, reporting "marvelous signs" and ominous apparitions on the eve of the assassination, portending the bloody mischief to come–again like the histories of Julius Caesar.

Now that one Henri had been eliminated, the "coxcomb" French king–as de Vere had once described Sa Majesté–allied with Henri of Navarre to crush what remained of the late Guise's Catholic League. But retribution awaited Henri III. In August of 1589, a fanatical monk stabbed the king. The man who'd ordered Guise's assassination had seen the dagger of tyrannicide turn on him. As JULIUS CAESAR's assassin BRUTUS foresees his own death:

> BRUTUS O, JULIUS CAESAR, thou art mighty yet!
>   Thy spirit walks abroad, and turns our swords
>   In our own proper entrails.

The comparison between Guise and CAESAR is no happenstance. As the literary historian John Bakeless notes, "the [French] Catholic party habitually referred to their champion, the duke of Guise, as 'Caesar,' and one of their partisans even drew up a laborious comparison between the two heroes which occupies four printed pages." Shake-speare's *Julius Caesar* immortalizes the martyred would-be king of France in a tragedy that begins where the French Catholic League's apologists leave off.

The Bard's Roman tragedy emphasizes the points of similarity between Guise and the historical Caesar, while downplaying the differences. Although the actual Julius Caesar led a long and extraordinary military and political career, the Shake-spearean version of his life concentrates only on the circumstances surrounding his assassination—the point where the parallels with Guise are strongest. As with the French murder, the party of assassins in Shake-speare's *Caesar* set their plans in motion in the early hours of the morning. ("O conspiracy,/ Sham'st thou to show thy dangerous brow by night/ When evils are most free?") Shake-speare's plotters pun on Guise's rank. ("I know no personal cause to spurn at him [CAESAR]/ But for the general. He would be crown'd.") And all parties observe the omens around them foretelling the regal death to come.

Julius Caesar triangulates between history, contemporary allegory, and imaginative fiction. An early draft of the Roman tragedy was likely completed in the wake of Guise's assassination: At least four English plays from as early as 1589 use distinctive lines (such as *"Et tu, Brute?"*) suggesting a borrowing from the Shake-spearean original.

Julius Caesar–probably reworked sometime during the 1590s–represents a maturation in de Vere's craftsmanship. No clear winners emerge from *Julius Caesar*'s bloody regicide. CAESAR has the familiar Shake-spearean (and de Verean) shortcomings of excessive pride and gullibility, while BRUTUS and his conspirators are about as sympathetic a set of villains as one can find in the canon. Perhaps it was de Vere's mixed religious, sentimental, and political alliances that prompted him to see the cases for all three points of view in the "War of the Henries." Or perhaps it took his liberation from the Manichaean life under the Cecils for de Vere to begin to appreciate the scales of gray in the world around him.

Immediately after Guise's death, French pamphleteers conducted a propaganda campaign that in part had led to the assassination of Henri III. Similarly in London, a pamphleteering campaign was emerging to challenge Elizabeth's legitimacy.

A pseudonymous Puritan zealot styling himself "Martin Mar-prelate" began in 1588 to publish pamphlets leveled at the prelates in the Anglican Church. Marprelate expressed growing distaste for the idea that the hierarchy of state-appointed bishops should control all aspects of the Church of England's religious service. It smacked too much of papism. Martin and his cohorts wanted, for starters, to eliminate the upper rung of Anglican bishops.

As in the civil strife across the English Channel, there were three factions in the Martin Marprelate war: Martinists, who hated Anglicans and the more moderate Protestants who put up with the Church of England's pseudo-Catholic rites; Anglicans and English patriots, content with the state church as it was, who just wanted the Puritans and Martinists to shut up; and Catholics, who thought all Protestants were heretics.

Martin Marprelate was an annoying and effective gadfly. He saw Anglicanism as the new church tyranny and himself the new iconoclast. It was not for nothing that he picked the name Martin. Like Martin Luther, Marprelate intended to destroy the authority structures of his state religion.

In the fall of 1588, Martin fired his first shot, a witty riposte to a recent fourteen-hundred-page book defending the doctrine of the Anglican Church:

> There [has] not been since the Apostles' time such a flourishing estate of a Church as we have now in England. Is it any marvel that we have so many swine, dumb dogs, nonresidents with their journeymen the hedge priests, so many lewd livers, as thieves, murderers, adulterers, drunkards, cormorants, rascals, so many ignorant and atheistical dolts, so many covetous popish bishops in our ministry, and so many and so monstrous corruptions in our Church and yet likely to have no redress?

Martin's tract was unlicensed, and Church authorities and state officials, such as Lord Burghley, were incensed that it could sneak its way into London bookstalls. No one knew who this rascally "Martin" was. (The author's identity, in fact, remained a mystery until well into the twentieth century, when a strong case was made that Martin Marprelate was a Puritan member of the House of Commons named Job Throkmorton.) Between October 1588 and the following September, the pseudonymous Martin and his coconspirators published seven devastating tracts.

When Thomas Cooper, bishop of Winchester, wrote a stern and humorless book in response to them, Martin took it as a demand for even more Marprelate pamphlets:

> Oh, brethren. There is such a deal of love grown of late I perceive between you and me that although I would be negligent in sending my 'pistles unto you, yet I see you cannot forget me.

The Elizabethan state clearly needed a more capable writer to reply to Martin.

Enter the pseudonymous pamphleteer "Pasquill Caviliero," one of at least a dozen writers who rose to the challenge of giving, as Pasquill called it, a "countercuff...to Martin." In his first pamphlet, published in August 1589, Pasquill replies:

> It is impossible for thee [Martin] to cast the religion of this land into a new mold every new moon. The whole state of the land perceives it well enough that to deliver up the prelacy to Martin is a canker more dangerous than...it is for the sheep to betray their shepherds to the wolf....
>
> Never brag in this quarrel of your five hundred brethren of credit and ability. Pasquill hath excellent ferrets to follow them in their own boroughs. And he can tell you that there is a common kind of affection which men of this age carry to such as you, whilst they have any service to put to you—like unto them that having somewhat to do with a confection of poison rejoice when they find it, yet they hate the malice of it and throw it out of the doors when their turn is served. Neither doubt I but that the same reckoning in the end will be made of you, which your favorers commonly make of their old shoes when they are past wearing: They barter them away for new brooms or carry them forth to the dunghill and leave them there.

Pasquill's rhetoric is clever; his pen is swift, and his voice is engaging and assured. Unlike his fellow hacks, he is also a man of high station. Pasquill writes about sitting as a justice in "divers of the courts, benches, sessions, that are held in this land in Her Majesty's name." He writes about hearing speeches in the queen's Star Chamber. He discusses the places he's visited in The Netherlands and Italy. And, most tellingly, Pasquill signs one of his pamphlets "from my castle and colors at London Stone."

London Stone, on Candlewick Street in the center of the city, was a famous landmark just outside the front door of Vere House. Edward de Vere had responded to the Martinist threat to queen and country by publishing literary works under the disguise of a pseudonym. Here was Shake-speare at war, in the final few years before the world would know him as Shake-speare.

Two months later, de Vere published a longer second pamphlet, *The Return of the Renowned Caviliero, Pasquill of England, from the Other Side of the Seas*. *The Return* presents a dialogue between Pasquill and his sidekick "Marforius" that reveals an ear tuned in to the nuances of character, vivid language, and dramatic pacing.

> MARFORIUS Speak softly, Caviliero! I perceive two or three [Martinists] lay their heads at one side, like a ship under sail, and begin to cast about you. I doubt [not but] they have overheard you....
>
> PASQUILL All the better for me. When I lack matter to talk of, I may resort hither to take up a little news at interest.

MARF. I marvel, Caviliero, that you press not the Martinists with much scripture. They are great quoters of commonplaces if you mark them.

PASQ. Therein they are like to a stale courtesan, that finding herself to be worn out of credit, borroweth the gesture of a sober matron which makes her to everyone that knows her the more abominable....

The Return of the Renowned Caviliero also shows the same elitist distrust of the commons that one finds in Shake-speare–as in the mob scenes in *Julius Caesar, 2 Henry VI,* and *Richard III.* Pasquill notes:

The chronicles of England–and the daily enclosures of the commons in the land–teach us sufficiently how inclinable the simpler sort of the people are to routs, riots, commotions, insurrections, and plain rebellions when they grow brain sick, or any new toy taketh them in the head. They need no...Martin to increase their giddiness....I would wish the whole realm to judge uprightly, who deserves best to be bolstered and upheld in these dangerous times, either they that have religiously and constantly preached obedience to Her Majesty's loving people, or they that with a mask of religion discharge them of their obedience?

Despite such appeals for obedience, Pasquill and his coterie won no new friends in the Privy Council or the archbishopric.

Puritans had been railing at players and playgoers for more than a decade. Now that Martin had made anti-Puritanism in vogue, the theaters struck back at Puritans and Martinists with a vengeance. Two anti-Martinist plays survive: Anthony Munday's *John a Kent and John a Cumber* and the anonymous *Knack to Know a Knave.* Many more are referred to by other writers of the period. Even troupes with a strong royal affiliation–the Queen's Men and Paul's Boys–propped up Martin only to whack him down and knock the stuffing out of him every afternoon.

The satirist Thomas Nashe–who was probably the model for Pasquill's sidekick Marforius–published his own anti-Martinist pamphlet, *An Almond for a Parrot,* which muses how much Martin lately has been "attired like an ape on the stage." De Vere's secretary John Lyly wrote in his anti-Martinist diatribe, *Pap With a Hatchet:*

Will they [the Martinists] not be discouraged for the common players? Would those comedies might be allowed to be played that are penned, and then I am sure he would be deciphered and so perhaps discouraged....

A stage player, though he be but a cobbler by occupation, yet his chance may be to play the king's part. Martin, of what calling so ever he be, can play nothing but the knave's part.

Lyly goes on to describe how he envisions mock hangings of the Martinists onstage.

The anti-Martinists went too far. The Anglican authorities were grateful for the backing that London's hack writers and playwrights gave them, but they were incensed at the scurrilous tone that had been taken. Although Martin himself had gone silent, other Puritan pamphleteers continued their literary campaign of attrition.

Elizabeth had maintained domestic tranquility by being conservative and moderate in all matters of church and state, and she was not about to change her policy for the sake of a bunch of railing actors and scurrilous playwrights. By 1590, in response to their anti-Marprelatism, Paul's Boys had been disbanded and the Queen's Men had been sent away from the city, to tour Ireland and Scotland. In his final work as "Pasquill Caviliero," *The First* [and only] *Part of Pasquill's Apology,* dated July 2, 1590, de Vere showed that he was likewise taking flak from both sides in the Marprelate war.

Pasquill takes on the Puritan pamphleteer John Penry, a man so outgunned it's hardly even fair. *Pasquill's Apology* is a forty-year-old de Vere at his most expressive, clever, deft, and spirited. More reflective than in his previous two pamphlets, Pasquill writes:

> Because that by the length of other men's frailties every man may take the measure of himself, I will carry my mouth in my heart and let them pass. And though there be a pad in the straw that must be roused, I have taken out this lesson from the wise: There is a time for speech and a time for silence.

The pseudonymous earl also notes that he's lately been spending more time in Warwickshire "than I mean to name." His Warwickshire estate at Bilton–and perhaps his grandmother's estate of Billesley, too–had no doubt been serving as his home away from home where he could collect his thoughts and reflect on his options for the years to come.

If de Vere wanted to continue with the literary and theatrical activities he'd practiced since returning from Italy, the strategies of the 1570s and '80s no longer applied. The 1590s was to be a new era in the history of the London theater. To adapt, de Vere would need a new approach.

By the end of 1590, the relationships, both good and bad, that had shaped de Vere's courtly world had practically vanished. The bodies were piling up as in the final act of a revenge tragedy. His parent figures and mentors–such as the earl of Sussex and Sir Thomas Smith–were dead; his wife: dead; his rivals Sir Philip Sidney and the earl of Leicester: dead; the shadowy spymaster of the Queen's Men Sir Francis Walsingham–a man nearly devious enough to cheat the grim reaper himself–dead. The only representative from the cabal of courtiers whom de Vere had once so loved to hate, Sir Christopher Hatton, would have less than a year to live.

The familiar power struggle that had rendered de Vere's marriage unbearable was now shifting with the advancing age of the seventy-year-old Lord Treasurer. Burghley's son, the twenty-seven-year-old Robert Cecil, was redefining the role of the house of Cecil. Stunted and round shouldered from a fall as an infant, the younger Cecil was a brilliant Machiavel who was beginning to eclipse his more nuanced and principled father. De Vere would soon pine for the days when the Lord Treasurer was the worst of his worries.

With so much of the court's old wood now cleared away, a new generation of saplings was emerging. Two of the leading figures among the new Elizabethan courtiers were the twenty-five-year-old Robert Devereux, earl of Essex, and a strapping sixteen-year-old, Henry Wriothesley, earl of Southampton. De Vere had watched both young lords as they were raised from childhood as royal wards in Burghley's household. Essex and Southampton had both come to know de Vere's three daughters Elizabeth (15), Bridget (6), and Susan (3)–probably better than their father knew them. Burghley was grooming Southampton as a marriage match for the fifteen-year-old Elizabeth.

In September 1590, Burghley met with Southampton's grandfather (Anthony Browne, Lord Montague) at Oatlands, a royal seat in Surrey. Southampton, more interested in spending time with his fellow ward Essex, had already told his guardian that he didn't want to concern himself with marriage until he was older. But nobody told Burghley what he could or could not do, and Burghley had the legal right to determine whom his ward would marry. The grandfathers of the prospective bride and groom met to discuss their strategy to sway the headstrong young buck.

While at Oatlands, Burghley received messengers informing him of yet another of de Vere's financial troubles. De Vere, still some £11,000 in debt (upwards of $2.5 million today), had already sold most of the estates his father had left behind in 1562.

De Vere's life was also being complicated at the time by a fiasco involving the soldier and poet Thomas Churchyard. Churchyard had been in de Vere's service on and off since the 1560s–de Vere had once sent him to the Lowlands to fight on his behalf. Now the septuagenarian poet had entered into a pricey lease with a London landlady named Julia Penn, who had apartments near St. Paul's Cathedral. De Vere had made a verbal agreement to cover Churchyard's rent, £100 per year (approximately $2,200 per month today). Churchyard moved in, and the first quarter's payment came due on March 25.

It soon became clear that de Vere would not meet the debt. In desperation, Churchyard sought refuge at a nearby house of worship. De Vere could now add "deadbeat tenant" to his list of vices. His rent problems with Julia Penn would be preserved in *Twelfth Night*. A few doors down from Churchyard's

apartment was the Church of St. Benet's of Paul's Wharf. De Vere would, in
his literary creation, make an unlikely association between coins due to servants and the clanging of St. Benet's church bells. In the first scene of *Twelfth
Night*'s Act 5, FESTE begs for three gold pieces. "The old saying is the third
pays for all," FESTE says. "The triplex, sir, is a good tripping measure. Or the
bells of St. Benet, sir, may put you in mind—one, two, three."

FESTE ultimately gets his cash; Churchyard did not. De Vere had other
things on his mind.

In 1590, Edmund Spenser published a dedicatory sonnet "To the right
honorable the earle of Oxenford, Lord High Chamberlain of England &c." in
the first edition of his epic allegory *The Faerie Queene*. Spenser notes that

> ... [t]h' antique glory of thine ancestry
> Under a shady veil is therein writ,
> And eke [*moreover*], thine own long living memory
> Succeeding them [*de Vere's ancestors*] in true nobility;
> And also for the love which thou dost bear
> To th' Heliconian imps [*Muses*]—and they to thee—
> They unto thee and thou to them most dear:
> Dear as thou art unto thyself.

Spenser had mastered the art of fine-tuned flattery. Spenser's friendship with
de Vere's rivals Sir Philip Sidney and the earl of Leicester gave the poet a distinctly one-sided view of the earl of Oxford. Spenser's dedication both praises
and underhandedly criticizes de Vere. The sonnet begins by recognizing how
the historical earls of Oxfords' heroics had been written "under a shady veil"—
alluding, one suspects, to the glaringly ahistorical glorifications of de Veres
appearing in Queen's Men's plays. Spenser then recognizes de Vere's blossoming poetic brilliance, while still sneaking a jab in at de Vere's notorious
narcissism.

The enigmatic figure de Vere presented evidently engaged Spenser's
muse. In another poem from 1591, *The Tears of the Muses*, Spenser writes of

> [T]hat same gentle spirit from whose pen
> Large streams of honey and sweet nectar flow,
> Scorning the boldness of such base-born men
> Which dare their follies forth so rashly show;
> Doth rather choose to sit in idle cell
> Than so himself to mockery to sell.

Spenser criticizes a vainglorious poet who sits quietly alone, pouring forth
honey from his pen but choosing to withhold it from public scrutiny and
mockery.

The year 1591 was the beginning of a strange and brutal decade for de Vere. Still under pressure to pay off his outstanding debts, the seventeenth earl of Oxford continued selling properties inherited from the sixteen distinguished lords who had come before him. By the end of 1592, de Vere would alienate every estate he'd inherited, as well as the properties he'd been granted over the years by the queen.

In May 1591, de Vere wrote to Burghley a long letter concerning his continued problems with money and untrustworthy servants. The queen had put the Welsh manor of Denbigh up for sale for £8,000. De Vere said he wanted to buy it. Denbigh would, he notes, generate £230 in annual rents. But as the Churchyard-Penn fiasco demonstrated, de Vere had no cash on hand. So he came up with a payment plan. De Vere rashly proposed to give up his annuity in exchange for a £5,000 one-time payment and an interest-free loan of £3,000. If de Vere's estimate of Denbigh's rental value is to be taken at face value—which would mean buyer's lust had clouded his vision—then if the deal went through, de Vere would have faced an annual revenue loss of £1000 – £230 = £760. Yet, de Vere was probably underestimating Denbigh's value as much as he could in order to make the best case possible for an easy sale. Considering the additional bargaining chip de Vere tossed in, he must have thought Denbigh was worth far more than he was letting on.

To his Denbigh proposal, de Vere offered up Castle Hedingham. Feeling remorse for not doing enough for his three daughters, de Vere wrote to Burghley that if the old man helped him acquire Denbigh, de Vere would sign over his Essex properties (worth £500–£600 in annual rents) to defray the cost of their upbringing. In this letter to Burghley, dated May 18, de Vere wrote:

> The effect hereof is I would be glad to have an equal care with Your Lordship over my children, and if I may obtain this reasonable suit of Her Majesty [*to buy Denbigh*], granting me nothing but what she hath done to others and mean persons—and nothing but that I shall pay for it—then those lands which are in Essex, as Hedingham, Brets, and the rest whatsoever, which will come to some £500 or £600 by year, upon Your Lordship's friendly help towards my purchases in Denbigh, shall be presently delivered in possession to you, for their use. And so much I am sure to make of these demesnes for myself.
>
> So shall my children be provided for, myself at length settled in quiet—and I hope Your Lordship contented, remaining no cause for you to think me an evil father, nor any doubt in me, but that I may enjoy that friendship from Your Lordship—that so near a match, and not fruitless, may lawfully expect.

De Vere apparently had his heart set on retiring to an ancient Welsh castle, never to darken any English courtier's doorstep again. Elizabeth, however, would hear none of it. De Vere was to remain in London; Denbigh would not become another financial mess under the earl of Oxford's reckless hand.

What should have been a trade became a gift: De Vere gave away Hedingham; Burghley did nothing in return. On December 2, de Vere signed over Castle Hedingham to Burghley in trust for the three de Vere girls. The original purpose of the bequest may have been to prove what a good father he could be. Its effect was that de Vere made a final surrender of his ancient family seat and had little left to support himself. The earl of Oxford had, through his own rashness and bad fortune, become a landless lord, a king sans castle. In a fit of desperate rage, de Vere razed and liquidated whatever he could from the Hedingham grounds. And he prepared himself for a humbling future wherein he would be beholden to his three daughters for a kingdom that had once been his.

Three years later, the Queen's Men would bring this story to the stage. *The True Chronicle History of King Leir* [*sic*] would present de Vere in his motley as a fond and foolish old man who had squandered his inheritance and independence. The Queen's Men's *Leir* describes the conflict de Vere must have felt between filial devotion and self-preservation.

> Leir Oh, what a combat feels my panting heart
> 'Twixt children's love and care of common weal!
> How dear my daughters are unto my soul
> None knows but He that knows my thoughts and secret deeds.
> Ah, little do they know the dear regard
> Wherein I hold their future state to come,
> When they securely sleep on beds of down.

Just as in de Vere's life, in the Queen's Men's version of the story, Leir is a recent widower, still bemoaning his loss. ("Wanting now their mother's good advice/Under whose government they have receiv'd/A perfect pattern of a virtuous life.") And the king's three daughters are all unmarried.

Published anonymously more than a decade later, *King Leir* is another early 1590s Queen's Men's text that is proto–Shake-speare in form and substance. The Queen's Men's *Leir* and Shake-speare's tragedy of *King Lear* contain characters and scenes found in no other sources, including Kent and Oswald, the King's wanderings, and the thunderstorm scene. The most noteworthy difference between *Leir* and *Lear* is that the former ends happily, with Leir and his daughter "Cordella" reconciling and Leir being returned to the throne. Chalk it up to wishful thinking that in the early 1590s, de Vere hoped he could still make amends with his alienated daughters and see some of his ancestral lands returned to his estate.

This does not necessarily mean, however, that the whole of *King Leir* had come from de Vere's pen. The authorship of *Leir*–like the authorship of *The*

True Tragedy of Richard III, The Famous Victories of Henry V, and *The Trouble-some Reign of King John*—is not easily arrived at. De Vere is arguably the master craftsman behind these Queen's Men's texts, but, as many paintings "by" Titian were actually executed in his Venetian shop by other artisans, de Vere may have supplied an outline, character sketches, and assorted speeches and lines, and left one or more of his "lewd friends" to fill in the blanks.

His contribution may well have varied from play to play. Several more years would remain before de Vere would be shunning his followers and secretaries and taking up the solitary task of rewriting his courtly and Queen's Men's entertainments for posterity.

De Vere needed someone who could manage a life that he could not, someone with enough intelligence to keep him away from his own account books, and with enough backbone to stand up to him. Moreover, the seventeenth earl needed a future eighteenth earl. He must have been terribly lonely, too. The prospect of a smart helpmeet—this time, a woman without such a powerful, nosy, and compromising father—was looking ever more attractive.

When Julia Penn pleaded with the earl of Oxford about the overdue rent, in March of 1591, the landlady indicated that she'd considered contacting a certain "virtuous gentlewoman" to settle the matter. In Penn's words:

> [G]ood my lord, deal with me in courtesy, for that you and I shall come at that dreadful day and give account for all your doing. My lord, I thought to have been a suitor to that virtuous gentlewoman, mistress Trentham, but I thought it not good (to do so) because I know not Your Lordship's pleasure. I would be loath to offend your honor in anything.

The "mistress Trentham" was Elizabeth Trentham, the eldest daughter of a wealthy Staffordshire landowner. Trentham, in her early thirties at the time, had been a maid of honor to the queen for at least ten years. She was known both for her beauty and her savvy.

De Vere must have been openly courting Trentham in March 1591, at the time of the Penn–Churchyard fiasco. By May, a touching and witty lyric to the earl's paramour was published in a pirated edition of love poetry called *Brittons Bowre of Delights.*

> Time made a stay when highest powers wrought
> Regard of love where virtue had her grace,
> Excellence rare of every beauty sought
> Notes of the heart where honor had her place;
> Tried by the touch of most approved truth,
> A worthy saint to serve a heavenly queen,

> More fair than she that was the fame of youth,
> Except but one, the like was never seen.

The first letter of each line spells out "Trentame," an Elizabethan alternate spelling of Trentham. Curtsying to Her Majesty in the final three lines, the author clearly understood how to flatter a courtly lady while still avoiding any disrespect to his queen. Since *Brittons Bowre* contained at least two other canonical poems by de Vere, scholars are inclined to give him this one as well.

Romantic notions a reader might have of passionate, heart-aflutter courtships, however, had little to do with the realities of the forty-one-year-old de Vere's life when he wooed "Trentame." Shake-speare in love was also Shake-speare deep in debt. De Vere would soon be applying unsuccessfully to Queen Elizabeth for a monopoly in wools, fruits, and oils.

De Vere was, at the time, failing to meet basic household expenses, such as paying servants. One retainer of de Vere's named Henry Lok had written to Burghley the previous year to complain that he had worked for de Vere "amost twenty years" but was still owed £80 ($20,000). Lok explains to the Lord Treasurer that he'd taken out loans and pawned items from his household ("chains and nails") to keep his head above water.

> I have bent myself wholly to follow the service of the honorable earl of Oxford, whose favor shown sometimes so graciously upon me that my young years were easily drawn thereby to account it. . . .
>
> I of late, indeed too late, resolved to stop the opinion of many, which thought me among the number of overmany greedy horse-leaches which had sucked too ravenously on his [de Vere's] sweet liberality. . . .

Lok was not, he claimed, one of those "horse-leaches" who were sucking de Vere's bank accounts dry.

But other servants were stealing. A Thomas Hampton had been caught skimming off the earl's rents, while another servant, Israel Amyce, had allegedly continued to hold properties that de Vere had already leased out to others. De Vere wrote Burghley on May 18, 1591, to thank him for exacting some discipline when he apparently could not:

> My lord, I do thank Your Lordship for the punishment of Hampton, whose evil doings towards me, being put in trust with my causes in law, I hope Your Lordship will think them sufficient to deserve your disgrace.

"Mistress Trentame" would change this. In July of 1591, Trentham's brother Francis and a partner (John Wooley) bought out the remainder of the property that was once Fisher's Folly "to be disposed of for the advantage of

Elizabeth, sister of the said Francis Trentham." The wedding vows hadn't even been uttered, and Trentham was already taking charge. She'd grown up in a household with at least three brothers—and even so, Elizabeth had still become the executor for her father's estate after his 1587 death. Extant letters of hers written years later, one to Robert Cecil and another to a judge named Sir Julius Caesar, reveal a sharp-minded, independent woman at ease with legal and business matters and not afraid to flex her muscles.

For once in his life, de Vere let good sense guide his heart. De Vere and Trentham wed sometime in November or December of 1591. Queen Elizabeth, who often objected to her courtiers spiriting away her maids of honor, offered no objections to this match. Her Majesty, too, probably recognized what a boon to her problematic and headstrong Lord Great Chamberlain this marriage would be. The queen gave wedding gifts to de Vere and the new countess of Oxford on December 27, 1591 (unspecified), and November 23, 1592 (a gilt bowl with a cover).

Trentham had remained single for a surprisingly long time; it was rare for an Elizabethan woman to wait until her thirties to marry. Yet this fact, too, reveals something of the bride's indomitable character. *The Merchant of Venice*'s brilliant, discriminating, and cagey PORTIA was probably modeled on the crafty woman with whom de Vere had fallen in love in 1591. BASSANIO, after all, courts PORTIA in part to climb his way out of debt.

> BASSANIO Gentle lady,
>   When I did first impart my love to you,
>   I freely told you all the wealth I had
>   Ran in my veins—I was a gentleman—
>   And then I told you true; and yet, dear lady,
>   Rating myself at nothing, you shall see
>   How much I was a braggart. When I told you
>   My state was nothing, I should then have told you
>   That I was worse than nothing.

Perhaps the most candid portrait of de Vere's second wife appears in an anonymously printed satirical 1594 poem called *Willobie His Avisa*. The identity of "Avisa," a young woman described as a "chaste and constant wife," has long been debated by scholars. But closer examination reveals that *Willobie*'s description of Avisa fits Elizabeth Trentham with stunning precision.

According to the poem, "Diana took the maid" Avisa into her service around the age of "full twenty year." Then, "ten years . . . tried this constant dame." Finally "Diana" gave her leave for Avisa to be wed. Elizabeth Trentham became a maid of honor to Queen Elizabeth at approximately the age of twenty, served Her Majesty in this capacity for ten years, and left to marry de Vere. *Willobie* notes that Avisa was born in western England, "where

Austin pitched his monkish tent." Trentham was born and grew up in the Austin (Augustinian) priory of Rocester in Staffordshire–to the northwest of London.

Finally, the book states that after her marriage, Avisa and her husband lived nearby to a noteworthy well and a castle or priory that had recently been "by brothers bought and sold." By the time of the poem's publication, the earl and countess of Oxford were living in the north London suburb of Stoke–Newington–nearby the Well of St. Agnes and The Theatre and the Curtain, on the site of a former priory that had been bought and resold by the actor James Burbage and his brother-in-law John Brayne.

Identifying Trentham as Avisa fills in a few sorely lacking biographical details about the woman who would stand by Shake-speare's side unto his dying day. *Willobie* notes that when Avisa was still single, she had been propositioned by a wealthy nobleman. But Avisa turned this suitor down, even after relentless courting. Avisa explains:

> Although I [will] be a poor man's wife,
> Yet then I'll laugh as well as you.
>> Then laugh as long as you think best
>> My fact shall frame you no such jest.

After marrying her unidentified husband, Avisa shuns the city life in modest country retirement. However, she is also frequently seen at The Theatre and the Curtain (the place nearby her house where the "Muses sing... [and] satyrs play") and at the nearby pub of St. George's Inn in Shoreditch. Avisa is quite an attractive woman, too; young men make frequent passes at her. But she is a constant wife who unswervingly resists temptation.

> And there she dwells in public eye,
> Shut up from none that list to see.
> She answers all that list to try,
> Both high and low of each degree:
>> But few that come but feel her dart
>> And try her well ere they depart.

One of Avisa's suitors is a man styled "Didymus Harco," which is probably a macaronic disguise for Thomas Howard, second son of the late duke of Norfolk. "Harco" tries to win Avisa's love with gold and trinkets, and he speaks in the legal language of jury trials. (De Vere had been one of the peers who had voted Howard's elder brother Philip guilty of treason. "Harco" may have wanted both the countess and the earl of Oxford to help press the queen to forgive Philip Howard.) "Harco" says to Avisa:

And though I be by jury cast
Yet let me live a while in hope,
And though I be condemned at last,
Yet let my fancy have some scope.

At one point, Harco shows up at Avisa's doorstep when her husband is not at home. The suitor leaves her with a letter pleading for her attentions and affections. Avisa will have none of it, or him. In her reply to Harco, Avisa explains that her husband is a homebody these days—in language suggesting that de Vere was at the time revisiting the play that would someday become Shake-speare's *Troilus and Cressida.*

No Helen's rape nor Trojan war
My loving mate hath forc'd away,
No Juno's wrath to wander far
From loving bed can make him stray
Nor stay at all in foreign land
But here I have him still at hand.

My sweet ULYSSES never stays
From his desired home so long
That I should need such rare delays
To shield me from intended wrong.
My chief delights are always nigh
And in my bosom sweetly lie.

My heart is fixed, since I did give
My wedlock faith to chosen friend.

De Vere had found an enviable match—a woman in whom he could place his brittle faith and a lover whose affections were deep and mutually felt. Both tortured and torturer in his first marriage, de Vere had been blessed in 1591 with a rewarding second marriage that must have felt like a warm and sturdy shelter for his storm-tossed soul.

Another of Avisa's suitors is an Italian named "Cavaliero"—who has been taken to represent the bombastic Italian pedant Giovanni Florio. This colorful figure, tutor to the earl of Southampton, was at the time on the hunt for a patron. Florio likely sought out the infamous erstwhile Italianate earl—perhaps during one of Avisa's afternoons at St. George's Inn and the theaters—to muster support for an Italian dictionary Florio was then preparing.

De Vere had little to offer any writer financially. However, prefaced to

Florio's 1591 book *Second Fruits* is a pseudonymous sonnet credited to one "Phaeton," who sounds much like the poet who honored "Trentame."

Phaeton to his friend Florio

Sweet friend, whose name agrees with thy increase,
How fit a rival art thou of the Spring!
For when each branch hath left his flourishing,
And green-locked Summer's shady pleasures cease,
She makes the Winter's storms repose in peace
And spends her franchise on each living thing:
The daisies sprout, the little birds do sing;
Herbs, gums, and plants do vaunt of their release.
So that when all our English wits lie dead
(Except the laurel that is evergreen)
Thou with thy fruits our barrenness o'erspread
And set thy flowery pleasance to be seen.
   Such fruits, such flow'rets of morality,
   Were ne'er before brought out of Italy.

De Vere was sometimes personified by Elizabethan wits as "the Spring" or its Latin form *Ver*. The unidentified Elizabethan who assumed the pen name Phaeton had clearly mastered the courtier's fine art of flattery. ("How fit a rival art thou of the Spring!") The Phaeton sonnet would be the last noncanonical published work by the man who would soon assume the most famous pseudonym the world would ever know.

By the time de Vere and his new wife had settled into their suburban home north of London in early 1592, the nearby Theatre and Curtain were no longer the only theaters in town. On the south bank of the Thames, a performance venue called the Rose was flourishing under the tenancy of two troupes, Lord Strange's Men—also called the Earl of Derby's Men—and the Lord Admiral's Men. A brilliant young playwright named Christopher Marlowe had transformed the Rose into the crown jewel of London literary society, presenting sensational blank-verse tragedies like *Tamburlaine, The Tragical History of Doctor Faustus,* and *The Jew of Malta.* Marlowe's dramas were direct and visceral, staging exciting plots of world conquest and bargains with the devil. The Cambridge-educated playwright's broad appeal owed both to his talent as a captivating plot-weaver and his innovation of casting aside the stilted format of rhyming verse that had distinguished the Queen's Men's style.

Yet, for all his iconoclasm, Marlowe was only building on the foundation his predecessors had laid. The Euphuist salon that Fisher's Folly had been from 1580–88 had helped to spawn a literary revolution. De Vere's associates and employees John Lyly, George Peele, and Robert Greene–now between the ages of thirty-two and thirty-eight–had become the elder statesmen of a clique of young and eager writers in their twenties. John Day, Michael Drayton, and Thomas Dekker had been or would soon be turning out plays, poems, and pamphlets that fueled a literary renaissance that would continue into the next century.

Only four years had passed between the closure of Fisher's Folly and de Vere and his wife's move to Stoke Newington, near his old neighborhood in the theater district. Yet those four years were a time of great change for the Elizabethan stage. With Oxford unable to fund them, the Earl of Oxford's Men and the Earl of Oxford's Boys would become a practical nonentity during the 1590s. (Only one record survives of "thearle of Oxfords players"– putting on a show in Kent in 1594–during this most revolutionary decade in the history of the English stage.) On the other hand, new troupes had formed. Companies of actors under de Vere's peers the Lord Admiral, the earl of Pembroke, the new earl of Sussex (brother of de Vere's mentor, who had died in 1583) and the Lord Strange/earl of Derby were enjoying great success both on the public and courtly stages. These companies–Strange's and the Admiral's Men in particular–had the best actors in England working for them. Players like Edward Alleyn (Admiral's), Will Kemp (Strange's) and Richard Burbage (Strange's) were transforming the public face of the theater.

With the continued commercial boom that the theaters were enjoying, a new form of celebrity was being forged. Like their thespian predecessors in ancient Rome and Greece and Renaissance France and Italy, English actors were beginning to eclipse the fame of celebrities in practically all other walks of life save for royalty and nobility. To spot an Alleyn or Burbage on the London streets was becoming an event worthy of a maiden's best swoon or a wag's best gawk.

Some writers took this emerging fact of life better than others. Robert Greene was the jealous sort. Actors, especially those who tried to improvise their own lines in the middle of his scripts, had been getting on his nerves. Greene had his own special reason to be bitter. He'd recently been caught red-handed trying to sell the same playscript to two different companies–the Lord Admiral's Men and the Queen's Men. So, during the plague-ridden summer of 1592, when the theaters were all closed, Greene brooded.

Sometime in early August, the satirist Thomas Nashe visited the city to meet Greene for an afternoon of drinking. Nashe would later publish his recollections of this day of roistering. In addition to Nashe and Greene, a third party joined these two scribblers for a steady diet of Rhenish wine and pickled herring. In a pamphlet that appeared the following year, Nashe notes, "I and one of my fellows, Will. [*sic*] Monox (hast thou never heard of him and his great dagger?) were in company with [Greene]."

Scholars have searched the documentary record for centuries for the identity of "Will. Monox." Nashe, it appears, was making up one more playful Euphuistic pseudonym. Monox, the pidgin-French "My Ox," in his role as the Lord Great Chamberlain of England, had as one of his ceremonial duties to bear the sword of state—a.k.a. "his great dagger."

The "Will." part will become clear presently.

On that August afternoon, drinking with de Vere and Greene, Nashe might have wanted to tell the man who had been "Pasquill" about the play Nashe had been working on. It was a comedy called *Summer's Last Will and Testament* that prominently featured a character named Ver or "the Spring." Ver is a monstrously prodigal character. "I tell you, none but asses live within their bounds!" Ver exclaims. Nashe was never one to play light or easy with his caricatures.

According to Nashe's account, Greene, Nashe, and "Monox" met at a London establishment called the Steelyard. Destitute though he may have been, Greene showed up at the bar wearing a lavish doublet and cloak worth a couple of pounds at least—hundreds of dollars in today's money. Nashe later joked that his friend's getup was "fair ... with sleeves of a grave goose-turd green."

If FALSTAFF, BARDOLPH, and POINS could have picked an Elizabethan den for their iniquity, the Steelyard would have been an appropriate choice. The Steelyard was home to the medieval German trading company the Hanseatic League. Dealers could often be found haggling over the price of everything from Norwegian falcons to Flemish linen. The bar's low-vaulted ceilings reverberated with their polyglot chatter. Specialties of the house included German ("Rhenish") wine and Northern European delicacies such as smoked ox-tongue, salmon, caviar, and pickled herring. One seventeenth-century visitor called the Steelyard the "Dutch magazine of sauce." The Steelyard was also as caste-free an atmosphere as one could find in Elizabethan London. Bishops and privy-chamber counselors mingled with the mercantile classes and cosmopolitan set.

Nashe and "Monox" returned to their domiciles after the day's drinking, dining, and bantering was done. But whether from food poisoning or just a life of overindulgence, Greene fell ill. He would die a month later, on September 3. Prolific to the end, the thirty-four-year-old pamphleteer apparently spent his final weeks composing two repentant pamphlets. "Many things I have wrote to get money, which I would otherwise wish to be suppressed," Greene wrote. "Poverty is the father of innumerable infirmities. In seeking to salve private wants, I have made myself a public laughingstock." A literary colleague, Henry Chettle, claimed to have collected some of Greene's deathbed papers, and *Greene's Groatsworth of Wit* appeared in London bookstalls in late September or early October of 1592.

Greene's Groatsworth of Wit is an important and controversial document in the history of English literature, because *Groatsworth* introduces the world to Will Shakspere of Stratford-upon-Avon.

Groatsworth begins with the tale of a transparently autobiographical character named Roberto, who is both a scholar and an author. Roberto, the reader learns, has inherited from his father only a worthless coin, a groat. Wallowing in self-pity, Roberto happens upon a garrulous country bumpkin. This unnamed traveler, Greene says, was once a puppet master and "country author" who put together morality plays in traveling carnival shows. But now, seven years after first entering show business, the puppet master has made the big time. He lives in the city; he hires others to write plays that he produces; he's a "gentleman player"; his wardrobe alone he estimates to be worth £200 (more than $50,000 today). He speaks of this wardrobe as his "share," implying that the garments are used for the theater. The player salts his speech with Latin phrases that he doesn't understand and bludgeons out a few lines of doggerel, of which he is overfond.

Greene then shifts the focus of *Groatsworth* from his "Roberto" parable to a rant. But it is clear that the country player is still on the pamphleteer's mind. In *Groatsworth's* closing jeremiad, Greene doles out unsolicited advice to Nashe, Marlowe, and another playwright, George Peele, lines quoted in practically every "Shakespeare" textbook ever printed:

> Base-minded men, all three of you, if by my misery you be not warned:...
> There is an upstart crow, beautified with our feathers, that with his tiger's
> heart wrapped in a player's hide supposes he is as well able to bombast out
> a blank verse as the rest of you. And being an absolute *Johannes factotum*
> [*braggart and vainglorious dilettante*] is in his own conceit the only shake-
> scene in the country.

The line "Tiger's heart wrapped in a player's hide" is a spoof on a catchphrase ("Oh, tiger's heart wrapped in woman's hide!") from an anonymous play that the Earl of Pembroke's Men were performing in 1592, *The True Tragedy of Richard, Duke of York*. This play was eventually revised and published as Shake-speare's *Henry VI, Part 3*.

Take the "Roberto" parable together with the above quote, and the message is as clear as Greene's convoluted rhetoric can make it: There is a country player, who's been in the business now for seven years, who buys up plays and puts them on London stages. This player, whom Greene nicknames "Shakescene," also owns a substantial wardrobe used in the plays he produces. He "supposes" he can crank out blank verse like the professional playwrights. However, in Elizabethan usage, the word *supposes* often meant "feigns" or "pretends." The great pretender, Greene says, is an "upstart crow"–probably referring to the crow from Aesop's fables, a bird that dressed itself up in other birds' feathers. In short, "Shake-scene" talks a good game, but according to Greene, he's a big phony. He'll hire a working writer, like Greene, to write a play–and then "Shake-scene" will smash it together with another script or just present it as his own. For scripts that advertised no owner or original author, such as those that came from de Vere's shop, it was all the more easy for "Shake-scene" to parade around dressed up in borrowed plumage.

So far as the documentary evidence reveals, William Shakspere of Stratford-upon-Avon was baptized in 1564, married in 1582, and sired a daughter, born in 1583, and twins born in 1585. After that, he disappeared from the historical record until 1592, when a "Willielmus Shackspere" loaned £7 to one John Clayton in London. The span between Shakspere's disappearance from Stratford records and the publication of *Greene's Groatsworth of Wit* is seven years–the same amount of time that Greene's proverbial "gentleman player" had been in show business.

If Greene is to be taken at his word, Will Shakspere had been touring around the provinces as a player and puppet master. Shakspere had cobbled together a few morality tales and had ultimately made his way to London. Considering Greene tags "Shake-scene" with a quote from a Pembroke's Men play, it stands to reason that Shakspere was in 1592 working as a producer-player-factotum for the Earl of Pembroke's Men.

During the winter and spring of 1592, Philip Henslowe, manager of the Rose Theatre, recorded the first known performances of anonymous plays he calls *Harey the VI* and *Harey of Cornwall*. *Harey the VI* is widely accepted to be Shake-speare's *Henry VI, Part 1*. *Harey of Cornwall* is probably Henslowe's shorthand for Shake-speare's *Henry V*–alluding to the popular scene in which the king interviews his troops on the eve of Agincourt under the assumed name of "Harry le Roy" of Cornwall. Subsequent entries in Henslowe's journals in 1593 mention the performance of a play called *Titus & Ondronicus*. Henslowe never noted who wrote these texts.

According to the title page of the first printed edition of *Titus Andronicus* (published anonymously in 1594), this early Shake-speare tragedy had been performed by Pembroke's Men in addition to Strange's/Derby's Men and Sussex's Men. De Vere, on familiar terms with each of these patrons, was apparently not particular about which companies produced his first few plays after he'd moved back into the theatrical district. De Vere would have had little control over a loudmouthed actor who might have enjoyed backstage boasts about how he'd written plays that, in truth, had come from a nobleman's shop.

Tom Nashe knew a good joke when he saw it. The idea that an uneducated and inexperienced provincial actor might claim he wrote an urbane, complex Roman historical tragedy like *Titus Andronicus* or a blatant aristocratic apologia like Shake-speare's *Henry VI*–material like this was a satirist's manna.

Styling de Vere as "Will. Monox" in 1592 may be the earliest published hint that the player William Shakspere had already paraded around in de Vere's feathers on the public stage. What ended years later in an avalanche that buried nearly every trace of Edward de Vere evidently began in 1592 with the trickle of a few pebbles. The Shake-speare canon, as it is known today, most likely existed in 1592 as an assortment of de Vere's courtly scripts and scenarios from the 1570s and '80s that called out to their creator for revision. And Will Shakspere had, as suggested by Robert Greene's deathbed diatribe, probably not done anything more extreme than brag to a few acquaintances or audience members about his handiwork on the likes of *Titus* or *Harey the VI.*

No one could have then known the curious course of events that would lead, in 1598 or early 1599, to the first publication of a de Vere play under the byline "William Shakespeare."

Before 1598, what are now recognized as Shake-speare's plays were all published anonymously. There was nothing in 1592 to indicate that de Vere's forthcoming literary output would be treated any differently than the scripts that had already been turned out for the Queen's Men: public performances and, eventually, anonymous publications.

Still, a joke is a joke. And Nashe was not one to turn down the temptation of his muse. The same pamphlet that contains the "Will. Monox" anecdote (*Strange News,* published in January 1593) is dedicated to a prolific poet whom Nashe nicknames: "Gentle Master William *Apis Lapis.*"

Nashe's "Gentle Master William *Apis Lapis*" is the same person as "Will. Monox." And, although it is rarely studied today, Nashe's *Strange News* is every bit as important to the biographical evidence of Shake-speare as is Robert Greene's "upstart crow" diatribe.

Whereas Greene introduces the world to the country player Will Shakspere, Nashe presents de Vere tricked up for the first time in the guise of a writer and wit named "William."

Apis is the name of a legendary ox from antiquity that the Egyptians worshiped. *Lapis* is a Latin adjective meaning "insensate" or "lacking empathy." To Tom Nashe, de Vere was a "stubborn old ox."

Nashe roasts "Gentle Master William" while he worships "William's" literary talents. De Vere is, Nashe says, "the most copious carminist [*poet*] of our time" but a "famous pottle-pot [*drunkard*] patron" who has spent "many pounds ... upon the dirt of wisdom."

Gentle Master William: ... [I]f your worship—according to your wonted Chaucerism—shall accept in good part, I'll be your daily orator to pray that that pure sanguine complexion of yours may never be famished with potluck, that you may taste till your last gasp and live to see the confusion of both your special enemies: small beer and grammar rules.

(Nashe loved to poke fun at things like "grammar rules," since his pamphleteering opponent Gabriel Harvey was a notorious pedant.)

Since de Vere doesn't have money, Nashe doesn't expect money for his dedication. Instead Nashe asks de Vere to use his influence to ensure that *Strange News* survives the journey from manuscript to printed book.

> I conjure thee to draw out thy purse and give me nothing for the dedication of my pamphlet.

> Thou art a good fellow, I know, and hadst rather spend jests than money. Let it be the task of thy best terms to safe-conduct this book through the enemy's country.

> Proceed to cherish thy surpassing Carminical [*poetic*] art of memory with full cups (as thou dost).... However I write merrily, I love and admire thy pleasant witty humor, which no care or cross can make unconversable. Still, be constant to thy content. Love poetry, hate pedantism.

> Thine entirely,
>   Tho. Nashe

The content of *Strange News* is mostly an arcane and, at times, hilarious rejoinder to Gabriel Harvey's pamphlets written against Nashe. In the midst of railing against Harvey, Nashe notes that the Cambridge pedant has angered de Vere. This, Nashe warns, is not something anyone in his right mind should do.

> Mark him [*de Vere*] well. He is but a little fellow, but he hath one of the best wits in England. Should he take thee in hand again—as he flieth from such inferior concertation—I prophesy that there would be more gentle readers die of a merry mortality, engendered by the eternal jests he would maul thee with, than there have done of this last infection [*plague*]. I myself ... enjoy but a mite of wit in comparison of his talent.

De Vere memorializes his friendship with Tom Nashe in *Love's Labor's Lost*—a comedy that also offers up a caricature of Will Shakspere.

As noted in previous chapters, this French court comedy is in part about the women who got away: Anne Vavasour (Rosaline), Mary Hastings (Maria), and even Queen Elizabeth herself (the Princess of France). But the final, Shake-spearean version of this multilayered comedy contains added touches that most scholars agree date to the period 1592–94.

It is the circa-1593 layer of *Love's Labor's Lost* that presents de Vere, Nashe, Harvey, and Shakspere of Stratford-upon-Avon–in fact, it is the most intimate account yet found of the relationship between the seventeenth earl of Oxford and Stratford Will. The interrelations among these four figures onstage are a doorway through which one can look into the public and literary life of de Vere and Will Shakspere at the very dawn of the Shake-spearean Age.

In addition to de Vere's courtly persona in *Love's Labor's Lost* (the noble wooer BEROWNE), de Vere also presents a clownish version of himself in the play: the failed, down-at-the-heels swashbuckler, the Spanish soldier DON ADRIANO DE ARMADO. This self-characterization probably served as a jesting allusion to the scandalous rumors that circulated in 1593 that "the erle of Oxford" had become so dissatisfied with the English government that he "wold easelye be movyd to folow the Spanish king" if only given the opportunity.

ARMADO is introduced to the audience of *Love's Labor's Lost* as

> ... [A] refined traveler of Spain,
> A man in all the world's new fashion planted
> That hath a mint of phrases in his brain,
> One who the music of his own vain tongue
> Doth ravish like enchanting harmony.

But, ARMADO soon confesses, he is "in love with a base wench." The dame, named JAQUENETTA, is his literary muse:

> I do affect the very ground, which is base, where her shoe, which is baser, guided by her foot, which is basest, doth tread.... Assist me, some extemporal god of rhyme, for I am sure I shall turn sonnet. Devise, wit; write, pen! For I am for whole volumes in folio!

ARMADO's page is MOTH, Tom Nashe writ in boldface. ARMADO calls MOTH a "most acute Juvenal"–the same Roman satirist to whom Nashe was most frequently compared. MOTH's lines spoof Nashe's writings: MOTH and his master trade rhymes about "the fox, the ape, and the humblebee"; Nashe's *Pierce Penniless* goes into an extended parable that uses the figures of a fox, an ape, and honeybees.

Love's Labor's Lost also pricks the pretensions of Nashe's nemesis Gabriel Harvey. The play's verbose pedant HOLOFERNES becomes Harvey hoist with his own petard. In their pamphlet war, Harvey and Nashe traded jabs over an obscure piece of Latin verse by the Mantuan poet Battista Spagnuoli. In Act 4, HOLOFERNES quotes precisely this verse.

Although Nashe could be devastatingly scurrilous and acid at times, de

Vere must have valued their unlikely friendship for the young man's outstanding wit. The destitute Spaniard ARMADO and his satirical page, MOTH, are almost always together, quipping and punning at each other all the while.

ARMADO Boy, what sign is it when a man of great spirit grows melancholy?
MOTH A great sign, sir, that he will look sad.
ARM. Why! Sadness is one and the selfsame thing, dear imp.
MOTH No, no; O Lord, sir, no.
ARM. How canst thou part sadness and melancholy, my tender Juvenal?
MOTH By a familiar demonstration of the working, my tough signor.
ARM. Why tough signor? Why tough signor?
MOTH Why tender Juvenal? Why tender Juvenal?

MOTH and HOLOFERNES, on the other hand, quibble with each other—a polite encapsulation of the pamphlet battles Harvey and Nashe would fight during the 1590s. ARMADO (de Vere) and HOLOFERNES (Harvey) are not friends, although they exchange erudite pleasantries with each other. Tellingly, ARMADO eggs both MOTH and HOLOFERNES on.

ARMADO [to HOLOFERNES] Monsieur, are you not lettered?
MOTH Yes, yes. He teaches boys the hornbook.... Ba! Most silly sheep with a horn. You hear his learning?
HOLOFERNES Quis, quis, thou consonant!...
ARMADO Snip, snap, quick and home! It rejoiceth my intellect: True wit!
MOTH Offered by a child to an old man, which is wit-old. [pun on wittol or cuckold]
HOL. What is the figure? What is the figure?
MOTH Horns.
HOL. Thou disputest like an infant. Go, whip thy gig.

Love's Labor's Lost also talks about Shakspere and the emerging Shakespeare ruse in the character of an ambitious country gentleman named COSTARD. In the play's first scene, the audience is told that COSTARD had once loved ARMADO's love object, JAQUENETTA—the author's muse. ARMADO is given custody of COSTARD, at which point the downtrodden Spaniard decides to set COSTARD free on the condition that he serve as a messenger to carry ARMADO's written epistles of love to the woman they have in common. Symbolically, this is nearly the whole story: De Vere uses his country clown as an envoy to satisfy the author's longing for the literary delights and public fame that he cannot himself taste.

ARMADO Fetch hither the swain. He must carry me a letter.

MOTH A message well sympathized: A horse to be ambassador for an ass. . . .

[*exit* MOTH; *reenters with* COSTARD]

ARM. Sirrah COSTARD, I will enfranchise thee.

COSTARD O! Marry me to one Frances! [*a proverbial prostitute*] . . .

ARM. By my sweet soul, I mean setting thee at liberty, enfreedoming thy person: Thou wert immured, restrained, captivated, bound.

COST. True, true, and now you will be my purgation and let me loose.

ARM. I give thee thy liberty, set thee from durance; and in lieu thereof, impose on thee nothing but this: Bear this significant to the country maid JAQUENETTA.

There is remuneration. For the best ward of mine honor is rewarding my dependents. MOTH, follow.

[*exit* MOTH]

COST. [*to himself*] Remuneration! O, that's the Latin word for three farthings.

There is no documentary record of de Vere and Shakspere ever meeting. COSTARD's banter with de Vere's personification in *Love's Labor's Lost* is the closest to such a record that has yet been found.

Love's Labor's Lost ends with a masque ("The Nine Worthies") that AR-MADO is asked to write for the court. COSTARD assumes the starring role in the skit. As COSTARD says of the character he plays in DON ARMADO's masque, so might it be said for Will Shakspere himself:

For mine own part, I know not the degree of the worthy. But I am prepared to stand for him.

The players of ARMADO's skit–including MOTH, HOLOFERNES, ARMADO, and COSTARD–are relentlessly heckled by the courtly audience. De Vere plays fair, throwing as many rhetorical rotten tomatoes at his own caricature, AR-MADO, as at the rest of his fellow thespians. The character who handles the tough crowd best, though, is COSTARD. He plays the audience like a pro; AR-MADO's skit is the one moment in *Love's Labor's Lost* where COSTARD really shines. When the actor playing Alexander the Great leaves the stage in tears, COSTARD jumps in to keep the show rolling.

COSTARD There, an't shall please you: a foolish mild man; an honest man, look you, and soon dashed! He is a marvelous good neighbor, faith, and a very good bowler. But, for Alexander–alas! you see how 'tis–a little o'erparted. But there are worthies a-coming will speak their mind in some other sort.

ARMADO and COSTARD compete for the same lowborn muse; COSTARD practically rings the curtain down with the revelation that ARMADO has gotten JAQUENETTA pregnant. ARMADO says that he will "right himself like a soldier" and "hold the plough for her sweet love": ARMADO will marry JAQUENETTA. But the public revelation of ARMADO's consorting with his muse still leaves the Spaniard embarrassed, so the hot-tempered ARMADO challenges COSTARD to a fight. COSTARD begins to roll up his sleeves. But MOTH steps in to break it up.

> MOTH [to ARMADO] Master, let me take you a buttonhole lower. Do
> you not see [COSTARD] is uncasing for the combat? What mean
> you? You will lose your reputation!

That the scrappy Tom Nashe would urge his ox not to scrap with Will Shakspere suggests a colorful scene. De Vere would grow angrier at Shakspere over the coming years. But, Nashe's doppelgänger suggests, a lord who started a fight with a COSTARD would lose his "reputation."

Perhaps the greatest irony in the entire Shake-speare fable in *Love's Labor's Lost* is that de Vere's reputation was already lost. It was Will Shakspere, COSTARD, who would restore it.

⌘

On February 24, 1593, Elizabeth Trentham gave birth to a baby boy. The earldom of Oxford now had an heir apparent, styled Lord Bolbec. Edward and Elizabeth named their son Henry.

Queen Elizabeth had called a new Parliament on February 19, and de Vere took his place in the House of Lords on opening day as well as on February 20 and 24. After his son was born, though, the boy's father would be missing in action until Parliament's closing day on April 10.

For a man in his forties, to sire a first legitimate son is a rite of passage and a reflection on mortality. In September of 1590, de Vere–staring down his fortieth winter–had written to Burghley that he was chronically ill. Now, three years later, his impoverished household was home to the next earl of Oxford. The boy's father must have felt pangs of shame as he rehearsed in his mind what he would say to his son once the child grew old enough to understand what an enormous inheritance, of money and good name, his father had squandered.

De Vere had another source of generational strain as well. His eldest daughter, Elizabeth de Vere (eighteen years old in 1593), had been matched with a boy she'd known since she was seven, a ward of state as Edward de Vere had once been. And in Henry Wriothesley's proposed marriage with de Vere's daughter–Burghley's granddaughter–de Vere saw his youth and disastrous first marriage alive again.

Henry Wriothesley, third earl of Southampton, was a charming and courtly lad, two years older than Elizabeth de Vere. As a young man under the watchful eye of Lord Burghley, he was well educated in all the trappings of nobility–from hawking and hunting to music and poetry. Burghley had been pushing for Southampton's marriage to Elizabeth de Vere as far back as 1590. But Southampton was uninterested in taking his foster sister as a wife.

In 1591, Burghley's secretary John Clapham had dedicated a Latin poem to Southampton titled *Narcissus*. Taking as its subject the cautionary Roman fable of self-love, Clapham's poem was a thinly veiled warning to the head-strong youth not to grow so fond of himself that he might offend Lord Burghley. Clapham's dedication to Southampton, also written in Latin, used the language of procreation to bring his point home. Translated into English, Clapham wrote:

> Whatever will be other people's opinion of me, all will be well with me, I hope, if you think this tender offspring–reborn, as it were, from the grave, although to many it could seem premature–deserving the patronage of your honor.

Clapham urged Southampton to marry Elizabeth de Vere and have a child.

In so many words, this is the essential argument of the first seventeen of Shake-speare's *Sonnets*. Since the early nineteenth century, many scholars have suspected that Southampton was the *Sonnets'* primary addressee–the "fair youth," as critics have dubbed the elusive creature. De Vere, as Shake-speare's *Sonnets* suggest, had more than a passing interest in Southampton.

2

> When forty winters shall besiege thy brow
> And dig deep trenches in thy beauty's field,
> Thy youth's proud livery, so gazed on now,
> Will be a tottered weed of small worth held.
> Then being asked where all thy beauty lies–
> Where all the treasure of thy lusty days–
> To say within thine own deep-sunken eyes
> Were an all-eating shame and thriftless praise.
> How much more praise deserved thy beauty's use,
> If thou couldst answer, "This fair child of mine
> Shall sum my count and make my old excuse"–
> Proving his beauty by succession thine.
>   This were to be new made when thou art old,
>   And see thy blood warm when thou feel'st it cold.

De Vere had squandered his own youth in jealous malcontent and bootless obstinacy. But he could at least pass along a legacy of lessons learned to a young man beginning to navigate the swift and changing waters in Elizabeth's court. De Vere must have thought that Southampton would make a fine husband for his daughter—and, someday, a fine father for their children too.

13

O! that you were yourself; but, love, you are
No longer yours than you yourself here live.
Against this coming end you should prepare,
And your sweet semblance to some other give.
So should that beauty which you hold in lease
Find no determination—then you were
Yourself again after your self's decease,
When your sweet issue your sweet form should bear.
Who lets so fair a house fall to decay,
Which husbandry in honor might uphold
Against the stormy gusts of winter's day
And barren rage of death's eternal cold?
　　O! none but unthrifts. Dear my love you know,
　　You had a father, let your son say so.

But as Shake-speare's "marriage sonnets" testify, de Vere had grown fond of this young Henry, not just as a potential son-in-law. The name de Vere and his countess chose for their own son, for his March 31, 1593, christening, was a first for the house of de Vere. Aubrey, Aubrey, Robert, Hugh, Robert, Robert, John, Thomas, Robert, Aubrey, Richard, John, John, John, John, John, Edward: The Christian names of the seventeen earls of Oxford had sometimes celebrated the reigning monarch, sometimes a family tradition. But the name Henry was a first. It could have been an homage to a king whom de Vere had never met, Henry VIII. It might also, however, have been a tribute to the young man whom Edward de Vere was courting on behalf of his daughter.

When de Vere was Southampton's age, a forty-two-year-old earl of Sussex had taken the wild-eyed de Vere under his wing, providing the lonely and orphaned youth with a father figure. It had been a stabilizing relationship that had changed and perhaps even saved de Vere's life. De Vere's deteriorating health in 1593 must have led him to suspect that he would not live long enough to guide his own son through the gauntlets of a courtier's life. But de Vere could pay back the debt he owed Sussex by playing father figure to another wayward ward under the Cecils' officious gaze—perhaps in hopes (hopes that would ultimately come true) that Southampton could in turn be there for the eighteenth earl of Oxford when the next generation of de Veres needed guidance and a strong ally at court.

The word *lover* is used in Shake-speare to connote both eros between a man and woman and to represent the love of a deep and profound platonic same-sex friendship, of a sort not uncommon in the Renaissance but lost to the modern age. Some such love seems to have existed from de Vere toward Wriothesley. This is not to say that there were no erotic or sexual feelings between the men. But any eros between the earls of Oxford and Southampton would have been only part of the emotion being felt and expressed. The *Sonnets* testify to the strength of that emotion; about its exact nature they are open to multiple interpretations.

De Vere's love for the youth who was still being groomed as his possible son-in-law could hardly be broadcast to the public at large. The Arundell–Howard libels had accused de Vere of homosexuality and pederasty; no matter what the relationship was between the older man and the younger, the poems could lead to scandal. Shake-speare's sonnets would be circulated, according to the courtly observer Francis Meres, "among [the author's] private friends" and would not be published until the next decade.

As a road map to his own failings and muddled achievements, de Vere wrote another poem that could be dedicated openly to Southampton. It was an epic poem, based in part on the Titian painting de Vere had probably seen at the great master's studio in Venice in 1575 or 1576. The story this poem told was, on the surface at least, an Ovidian narrative not unlike Clapham's *Narcissus*. The dedication read much like Clapham's dedicatory epistle, too–using procreative language to raise the topics of marriage and offspring. It read:

To the Right Honorable Henry Wriothesley, Earl of Southampton and Baron of Titchfield

Right Honorable: I know not how I shall offend in dedicating my unpolished lines to your Lordship, nor how the world will censure me for choosing so strong a prop to support so weak a burden. Only if your Honor seem but pleased, I account myself highly praised and vow to take advantage of all idle hours, till I have honored you with some graver labor. But if the first heir of my invention prove deformed, I shall be sorry it had so noble a godfather–and never after ear [*plant*] so barren a land, for fear it yield still so bad a harvest.

This dedication prefaced a poem titled *Venus and Adonis*, which was submitted to the highest censor in the land (the archbishop of Canterbury) and approved for publication on April 18, 1593. The London bookseller John Harrison published *Venus and Adonis* between late April and early June of 1593.

The poem itself is nearly twelve hundred lines long, retelling the ancient myth of the legendary proud hunter and the goddess of love. As in Ovid's original tale, the couple meet and fall in love, but Shake-speare's ADONIS prefers to spend his time in more manly pursuits. Despite VENUS's vehement protestations to the contrary, ADONIS runs off to hunt the wild boar. He is killed, and VENUS sequesters herself in mourning. As a piece of contemporary allegory, the poem portrays VENUS as the queen of England—as Spenser's recent epic poem *The Faerie Queene* portrayed his title character as Queen Elizabeth. ADONIS symbolically operates on two levels: one, with the author as ADONIS, as a fable of de Vere's own experiences with the terrestrial goddess on England's throne; the other as a cautionary story, with Southampton as ADONIS, of the mortal dangers of seeking and maintaining a place of favor in the fickle Elizabeth's eyes.

As a couple, VENUS and ADONIS are often compared to Shake-speare's ANTONY and CLEOPATRA. Both the goddess of love and the goddess of Egypt are shrewd, bullish, and changeable. And ANTONY, in the words of literary critic J. W. Lever, "is ADONIS ... allowed to grow up." The same petulance and overweening pride can be seen in ADONIS as in the warrior who fled from the Battle at Actium. But in ADONIS, the egotism is more childish and pronounced. It is, in essence, the difference between de Vere at age twenty-three, when he was the queen's favorite, and de Vere at age thirty-eight, when the Spanish Armada sailed.

Venus and Adonis is voyeurism raised to a high art. As Samuel Taylor Coleridge once observed, "You seem to be told nothing, but to see and hear everything." One can almost hear the "shhhhh" of a fellow voyeur, as unbelieving eyes peer from behind the bushes to witness new secrets unfold. VENUS tries and tries to get ADONIS to kiss her, and as in Titian's *Venus and Adonis,* ADONIS couldn't care less. VENUS assures her young lover that the flowers on the riverbank will not give away their secrets. The queen of love tells ADONIS:

> Be bold to play, our sport is not in sight.
> Those blue-vein'd violets whereon we lean
> Never can blab, nor know not what we mean.

She smothers him with a thousand kisses—a metaphor for the £1,000 annuity.

> To sell myself I can be well contented,
> So thou wilt buy, and pay, and use good dealing. . . .
>
> A thousand kisses buys my heart from me,
> And pay them at thy leisure, one by one.

VENUS's kisses are also the queen of love's best tool for censorship: She shuts ADONIS up with the "seal manual [of her] wax-red lips."

Her lips are conquerors; his lips obey,
Paying what ransom the insulter willeth;
    Whose vulture thought doth pitch the price so high
    That she will draw his lips' rich treasure dry.

The BOAR, the earls of Oxford's heraldic device, intervenes to steal ADONIS away from VENUS. VENUS says:

'Tis he, foul creature, that hath done thee wrong:
I did but act, he's author of thy slander....

But this foul, grim, and urchin-snouted boar,
Whose downward eye still looketh for a grave,
Ne'er saw the beauteous livery that [ADONIS] wore,
Witness the entertainment that he gave.

Venus and Adonis, decked out in its Ovidian finery, with plenty of stylistic distractions to keep the general public ignorant of its courtly message, was nevertheless de Vere's warning to Southampton: Queen Elizabeth is a seductress. Don't end up smothered in a thousand "kisses" a year, gagged and gored by courtly duties to your sovereign.

Venus and Adonis fast became a best seller. The esoteric levels of meaning may have been lost on many readers. But the buzz the poem created was still enough to keep it flying off the shelves, generating an average of one new printing per year in its first decade on the book stands.

Not everyone remained in the dark, however, about the veiled courtly layers beneath *Venus and Adonis*'s Ovidian surface. One Londoner, a street-corner ranter named William Reynolds, wrote a letter to Burghley in the summer of 1593 that spelled out the terms of *Venus and Adonis* in plain and graphic Elizabethan English:

Also within these few days, there is another book made of Venus and Adonis, wherein the queen represents the person of Venus—which queen is in great love (forsooth) with Adonis. And [she] greatly desires to kiss him. And she woos him most entirely, telling him [that] although she be old, yet she is lusty fresh and moist and full of love and life. (I believe a good deal more than a bushelful.) And she can trip it as lightly as a fairy nymph upon the sands. And her footsteps not seen. And much ado with red and white.

Red and white were the colors of the Tudor Rose, the emblem of the House of Tudor. Reynolds says, essentially, that *Venus and Adonis* is a work of pornography that stars Queen Elizabeth I of England. If Reynolds was right, following the story of *Venus and Adonis*, this then meant that the Virgin Queen was a grasping she-wolf and a desperate spinster. Reynolds was declared an insane man.

Within a fortnight of *Venus and Adonis*'s registration at the Stationer's Guild, Gabriel Harvey had already gotten wind of it. Hardly known for his discretion, although more cultivated in his exposition than Reynolds, Harvey shot off another volley in his ongoing literary war with de Vere's MOTH, Tom Nashe. Writing his pamphlet *Pierce's Supererogation* in the form of an open letter, Harvey closes his diatribe with the following exhortation:

> ...And so for this present, I surcease to trouble your gentle courtesies, of whose patience I have...in every part simply, in the whole tediously presumed under correction. I write only at idle hours that I dedicate only to *Idle Hours* [Harvey's emphasis]....
>   This 27 of April 1593. Your mindful debtor, G.H.

Harvey's closing words are a parody of *Venus and Adonis*'s dedication to Southampton. Probably courtesy of his network of scholars and ecclesiastical contacts, Harvey could quote *Venus and Adonis* just nine days after the archbishop had declared the poem fit for public consumption.

But in the same pamphlet, in which Harvey mimics *Venus and Adonis*'s dedication, he does more: He says that the author of *Venus and Adonis* is "Pierce Penniless." Discussing the great writers of his age, Harvey praises authors whom he genuinely loves, such as Sir Philip Sidney and Edmund Spenser. Then he sarcastically overpraises three authors with whom he's fed up: Robert Greene, Thomas Nashe, and "Pierce Penniless."

> Wit [did] bud in such as Sir Philip Sidney and M. [Edmund] Spenser—which were but the violets of March or the primroses of May. Till the one began to sprout in M. Robert Greene...the other to blossom in M. Pierce Penniless, as in the rich garden of poor Adonis. Both to grow in perfection in M. Thomas Nashe.

The *garden of Adonis* is an idiom meaning "a worthless toy" or "very perishable goods." *Venus and Adonis* is, Harvey suggests, a mere novelty, a trendy poetic trinket aimed at pleasing the younger crowd. With these words, Harvey registers his disapproval of the latest work of "Penniless."

Since *Pierce Penniless* was originally the title of a pamphlet written by Tom Nashe, Harvey sometimes called Nashe "Pierce Penniless." But Harvey also occasionally called *de Vere* "Pierce Penniless." Because Harvey mentions Nashe by name separately, Nashe cannot be "Pierce Penniless" in this case. Harvey is thus saying that the "Pierce Penniless" who wrote *Venus and Adonis* is de Vere.

This is direct contemporary testimony, and Harvey was in as good a position as anyone to know. But *Venus and Adonis*'s dedication to Southampton asserts the author is someone else:

> I leave it to your Honorable survey, and Your Honor to your heart's content, which I wish may always answer your own wish and the world's hopeful expectation.
>
> Your Honor's in all duty
William Shakespeare.

For the first time, the name "Shakespeare" has been given the legitimacy of print. William Shakespeare is the author of *Venus and Adonis*.

By using the disguise of another man's name, de Vere had protected himself from the fate of William Reynolds—a man who had uncovered just one facet of *Venus and Adonis*'s hidden meaning and was cast aside to the very fringes of society. *Venus and Adonis* represents the debut of the ruse that would enable de Vere to become Elizabethan England's most candid truth-teller. Following the recipe laid out in Castiglione's *Courtier* (1572) and *Cardanus's Comfort* (1573), de Vere had published his heart in *Venus and Adonis* using a Batillus—the "upstart crow" Will Shakspere—as the beard who would distract the public gaze from the regal truths to be found within.

Enter COSTARD, stage left.

CHAPTER 10

THE SHARP RAZOR OF A WILLING CONCEIT

[1593–1598]

I N 1593, ELIZABETH I CELEBRATED THE THIRTY-FIFTH ANNIVERSARY of her coronation. The sixty-year-old queen had now sat on the throne for as long as her predecessors Edward VI, Mary I, and Henry VII combined. Her father, Henry VIII, was the only Tudor who had reigned longer. The sickly young princess whom few could have expected to survive the 1560s had instead established herself as the greatest member of the dynasty that had ended the War of the Roses, founded the Anglican Church, spawned the English Renaissance, and laid the groundwork for the British Empire.

But the house of Tudor would end with Elizabeth, and the power she and Lord Burghley had once monopolized was beginning to slip from her grasp.

It was probably in everyone's best interests that Elizabeth continued to distract herself with the coquette games she'd perfected in the 1560s and '70s, when she could still bear a child. Courtiers and visiting dignitaries in the 1590s still had to pretend that Her Majesty was the most radiant star in the firmament. Any young man seeking royal preferment still was required to act as if he only had eyes for England's Eliza. She wore embarrassingly low-cut dresses, and because of her love for sweets, her teeth had begun to rot. Her Highness's breath stank. She often sucked on a perfumed silk handkerchief before seeing visitors. And yet, eternally the ingenue, Elizabeth batted her eyelashes and played adolescent love games with the boys around her.

Meanwhile, forward-looking courtiers had begun to prepare for the coming war for the crown. Without any clear line of succession, nothing under the royal sun could be taken for granted. Because of the deal he had consummated before the execution of his mother, Mary, Queen of Scots, King James

VI of Scotland seemed a likely–but far from certain–successor. The eighteen-year-old Arabella Stuart, who traced her descent from a sister of Henry VIII, enjoyed a claim nearly as strong as did the Scots king. Lady Arabella would remain a staple of English conspiracy mongers for years. A Spanish takeover remained a possibility, too, as King Philip II and his daughter, Infanta Isabella Clara Eugenia, descended from John of Gaunt, the same royal grandsire whose line included the English kings Henry IV, V, and VI.

Nevertheless, even if one set aside all other viable claimants and assumed that King James VI of Scotland would become the next king of England, he would still be a foreign prince arriving in London with a woefully incomplete household. Who among Elizabeth's favorites would remain in high standing? Who would be falling from grace? What newcomers would the next king lavish gifts upon and appoint to positions of power? Who would find themselves out in the cold altogether? For the whole of Queen Elizabeth's court–approximately one hundred nobles and privy chamber members and the five to six hundred others granted access "above stairs"–a genteel free-for-all was about to begin, one that would set the course for the rest of their careers.

The 1590s would go down in history as one of the more brutal decades in the English court's existence. Two essential factions defined the face of power in the waning years of the Elizabethan era: A ring of gentlemen, spies, and nobles clustered around Sir Robert Cecil (age thirty in 1593); and a cult of personality surrounding the earl of Essex, the late earl of Leicester's stepson. The younger Cecil had continued his rise to power on the connections and networks his father had established. Essex, upon his stepfather's death in 1588, had been both blessed and burdened as the queen's new Leicester incarnate. The Leicester–Cecil power struggle of old was continuing into the 1590s–under new management.

Robert Devereux, earl of Essex (age twenty-eight in 1593), ironically, had grown up under the same roof as had Robert Cecil. Essex had been a ward of court since 1576, in Lord Burghley's household. Essex had become good friends with his fellow ward the earl of Southampton, as well as with the de Vere daughters.

Robert Cecil had begun to augment his father's extensive espionage networks with his own cabal of agents and assassins. One of Cecil's more promising minions was an operative named Robert Poley, who had helped to engineer the downfall of Mary, Queen of Scots. With characteristic flair, Poley had apprehended the Scots queen's conspirators one fateful night in August 1586 during a dinner that he'd hosted for them at a London tavern. Poley wined and dined his unwitting prey–and then snatched them up like rats in a trap.

Now, between December of 1592 and March of 1593, Poley had spent more than two months "rydeing in sondrey places" in Scotland–no doubt conducting reconnaissance missions for his bosses, possibly communicating with James or his court. Poley's paymaster was Sir Thomas Heneage, a close adherent to the Cecil faction. If King James VI of Scotland was going to become King James I of England, such "rydeing" and knowledge gathering would be providing the intelligence necessary to keep the Cecil faction at the center of power into the next regime.

However communicating with Scotland concerning James's potential future on the English throne was treason; Elizabeth had forbidden discussion of her succession.

One particularly loose set of lips knew too much about Poley and his "rydeings." On May 30, 1593, at a tavern in Deptford, Poley had another dinner party. He and two agents under the employ of Sir Thomas Walsingham (the late Sir Francis Walsingham's cousin) feted a part-time agent who himself had been accused of carrying on correspondence with King James. The part-time agent had recently testified before the Star Chamber. He'd been released on bail pending further inquiries. His testimony might have exposed Poley and the Cecilian network for which he worked.

The dinner party was, like its predecessor in 1586, a convivial affair. There was a surprise ending too. By the time the bill had arrived, someone had started a fight, which ended with a dagger being lodged above the right eyeball of the part-time agent. There were no other witnesses to the homicide other than the three spies left standing.

The murdered part-time agent's name was Christopher Marlowe, the undisputed master of the London public stage at the time. A postmortem inquiry concluded that the four revelers had squabbled over the bar tab, and Marlowe had drawn the dagger that ended up killing him.

Some latter-day "Marlovians" have construed the dodgy inquiry as evidence of a conspiracy—that Marlowe had faked his own death so that he could move to Italy and, eventually, write the works of Shake-speare. Occam's razor, however, would suggest a simpler explanation: The murder was a hit job. None of the agents was ever punished because they were only carrying out the orders of powerful forces who could have been brought low had Marlowe lived long enough to complete his testimony for the Star Chamber.

In addition to being a secret agent, Marlowe was also the only serious literary competition Elizabethan England could offer Shake-speare. The careless youth and part-time spy had, in his tragically brief career, shown the potential of the public theaters as a canvas upon which masterpieces could be painted. De Vere had been raised to recognize courtly performances as the ultimate purpose of a courtier's theatrical endeavors. To de Vere, catching the conscience of the king had been the thing, the only thing. Yet Marlowe's *Tamburlaine, Doctor Faustus,* and *Edward II* reigned above all other works yet produced for the London stage in popularity and acclaim. Compared to the immediate and visceral appeal of Marlowe's plays, works by the

Euphuist-inspired playwrights and Queen's Men's contributors looked stilted and artificial.

After Marlowe's mellifluous voice had been silenced, the English theater could easily have gone back to the fawning courtly comedies of yesteryear. Such outmoded voices as John Lyly and George Peele were still around, and in the absence of anything better, they could be counted on to crank out more preening fluff. But Marlowe had shown the astonishing new directions that English drama could take–from the sea-spanning conquests of Oriental potentates to the inner dramas of historical English kings. It was now Shakespeare's torch either to dowse or to carry forward.

On February 6, 1594, the London printer John Danter registered "a booke intituled a Noble Roman Historye of Tytus Andronicus." It was the first published Shake-speare playscript, a blood-and-gore fest worthy of Marlowe's nightmarish vision. No hint of an author's name appeared anywhere in the book. The title page did announce, however, that the play had been performed by the troupes of de Vere's friends and colleagues the earl of Derby, the earl of Pembroke, and the earl of Sussex. On April 6, 1594, the theater manager Philip Henslowe recorded a performance, as previously noted, by the Queen's Men and Sussex's Men of the play *King Leare* [*sic*]. Three months later, Henslowe recorded two other troupes (the Admiral's Men and/or the newly formed Lord Chamberlain's Men) performing a play called *Hamlet*. Unknown forces, perhaps de Vere's new and settled married life, perhaps the impetus of Marlowe's death, had stoked de Vere's creative fires.

In 1594, the earl of Southampton faced a choice about the direction of his life. In refusing to marry Elizabeth de Vere, Robert Cecil's niece, Southampton risked alienating himself from a ruthless house that did not take kindly to being snubbed.

Southampton's widowed mother set the counterexample. On May 2, 1594, Mary Browne Wriothesley, dowager countess of Southampton, had married into the Cecil faction. Browne's new husband was Sir Thomas Heneage, the paymaster of Robert Poley. Heneage was also one of England's leading landholders. In addition to securing her family a place within the Cecil clan, Browne was also marrying a real estate tycoon active both in London and the provinces.

Browne was situating herself in a position of considerable comfort and power. If only her son would consider so smart an alliance.

Two of Heneage's provincial holdings, the forest of Waltham and Havering Park, had traditionally been owned by the earls of Oxford. De Vere had long yearned to repatriate these family properties. De Vere and Heneage had gone to law school together, at Gray's Inn, and had both taken degrees during the 1564 ceremonies at Cambridge University. De Vere no doubt wanted to maintain good ties with his aging classmate—especially since de Vere's ancestral properties were now just one bequest away.

Furthermore, an office Heneage held, the Vice Chamberlainship of England, also made his ring particularly attractive to kiss in 1594. As Vice Chamberlain, Heneage was second-in-command of a new theatrical troupe that was consolidating the best actors and theatrical professionals in the country under one organizational structure.

The Lord Chamberlain's Men would soon become the country's premier band of actors. The troupe employed one of the finest tragedians in the land, Richard Burbage. Will Kemp, an unsurpassed comic talent, had joined the company at its 1594 founding. The rosters of the Lord Chamberlain's Men further boasted a theatrical player-manager-shareholder-producer-entrepreneur from Stratford-upon-Avon. So far as the woefully incomplete Elizabethan theatrical records reveal, Will Shakspere was from 1594 onward exclusively associated with the Lord Chamberlain's Men. According to oral histories of the English stage, Shakspere played the role of the GHOST in *Hamlet*–a witty piece of casting, considering the ephemeral nature of the play's actual author.

If de Vere was not present at the wedding of Heneage and the dowager countess of Southampton, a new play of his probably was. For more than a century, scholars have suspected that *A Midsummer Night's Dream* was performed in celebration of the May 2, 1594, Heneage–Browne nuptials. And given Heneage's close relationship with the nascent Lord Chamberlain's Men, the company that performed at his wedding would have been Shakspere's troupe.

Several references in the play suggest that *A Midsummer Night's Dream* had its world premiere on the night before the marriage of Sir Thomas Heneage and Mary Browne Wriothesley. When THESEUS encounters the four young lovers in the forest, he says, "No doubt they rose up early to observe/The rite of May," suggesting that the action of the play occurs on and just after May Day. Other lines in *A Midsummer Night's Dream* mention the notoriously inclement weather of the spring of 1594 ("thorough this distemperature we see/ The seasons alter: hoary-headed frosts/ Fall in the fresh lap of the crimson rose"), and the presence of Venus in the morning sky, where the planet could be found in the late spring of 1594 ("yonder Venus in her glimmering sphere").

A Midsummer Night's Dream is primarily a romantic farce of magically mistaken identities. But the play's central plotline is bookended by a more sober tale of the marriage of a powerful and gallant figure (DUKE THESEUS) with a former mortal enemy (HIPPOLYTA). THESEUS, the dignified elder statesman, stands in for the senior Elizabethan official Heneage, and HIPPOLYTA, the matriarch of a rival faction, for Mary Browne Wriothesley. HIPPOLYTA's alliance with THESEUS represents a truce between unfriendly clans. For a recalcitrant earl of Southampton, the moral of the story would have been that of the *Sonnets:* that he, too, should marry into the Cecil clan. In *A Midsummer Night's Dream,* THESEUS in fact sounds the refrain heard in many Shakespeare sonnets, that the duty of a beloved youth is to make a copy of himself to preserve for future generations:

> THESEUS ... [E]arthlier happy is the rose distill'd
>   Than that which, withering on the virgin thorn,
>   Grows, lives, and dies in single blessedness.

When the text of *A Midsummer Night's Dream* was eventually published in 1600, the title page announced that Will Shakspere's troupe, the Lord Chamberlain's Men, had performed the play "sundry times." And the script contains a role that, like COSTARD, appears to have been tailor made for the company's Stratford-bred "upstart crow."

One of the subplots of *A Midsummer Night's Dream* concerns a theatrical troupe that features one garrulous, malaprop-spouting, limelight-grabbing ham at the center of the action. Thanks to the play's puckish magic, the star actor BOTTOM is transformed into an ass with whom the fairy queen TITANIA inappropriately falls in love.

BOTTOM briefly experiences the life of a royal consort. TITANIA, subject to an aphrodisiac spell, lavishes her carnal desires upon this amazed sir nobody. De Vere's own rumored days of flirtations and privy chamber sighs shared with the queen of England in 1573 must have seemed, two decades later, as strange as *A Midsummer Night's Dream*'s vision of a faerie queen tumbling in the hay with an ass.

> TITANIA Come sit thee down upon this flowery bed,
>   While I thy amiable cheeks do coy,
>   And stick musk roses in thy sleek smooth head,
>   And kiss thy fair large ears, my gentle joy.

Once the magic wears off, returning BOTTOM to his human form and TITANIA to fairy land, BOTTOM marvels:

> I have had a most rare vision. I have had a dream, past the wit of man to say what dream it was. ... Man is but a patched fool if he will offer to say what methought I had. The eye of man hath not heard, the ear of man hath not seen, man's hand is not able to taste, his tongue to conceive, nor his heart to report what my dream was.

If BOTTOM's "dream" is to be taken at face value, the real-life Faerie Queen (Elizabeth) had taken a shine to a blowhard actor and jack-of-all-trades from Stratford. Will Shakspere's star was rising.

If *A Midsummer Night's Dream* was meant to persuade Southampton to a Cecil marriage, it didn't work. On May 9, one week after the Heneage wedding, de Vere tried again. The London bookseller John Harrison published the sequel to *Venus and Adonis*–that "graver labor" that the 1593 best seller had promised. It was titled, simply, *Lucrece.*

The story of *Lucrece* (which after the sixth edition in 1616 was given the fuller title *The Rape of Lucrece*) was a tragic allegory about the downfall of the Roman monarchy. Like *Venus and Adonis, Lucrece* was an epic poem, dedicated to the earl of Southampton. It would be de Vere's second published warning to his fond and foolish potential son-in-law about the path he was choosing, the road that led away from the house of Cecil–and de Vere. *Lucrece*'s dedication to Southampton is as tautly constructed a piece of courtly innuendo as was the first dedication. It begins:

> *To the Right Honorable Henry Wriothesley, earl of Southampton and baron of Titchfield.*
>
> The love I dedicate to Your Lordship is without end; whereof this pamphlet without beginning is but a superfluous moiety.

Moiety is a legal term meaning one half. In other words, if a reader doesn't already understand what *Venus and Adonis* is saying, *Lucrece* will seem a pointless trifle. The dedication continues:

> The warrant I have of your Honorable disposition, not the worth of my untutored lines, makes it assured of acceptance. What I have done is yours, what I have to do is yours, being in part all I have, devoted yours. Were my worth greater, my duty would show greater; meantime, as it is, it is bound to Your Lordship, to whom I wish long life still lengthened with all happiness.
>
> Your Lordship's in all duty,
WILLIAM SHAKESPEARE

If de Vere's fiscal house were in any state of order, he would have had dowries and other material inducements to draw Southampton into a marriage contract. But bereft of even his ancestral seat Castle Hedingham, de Vere could only promise his devotion.

Whereas *Venus and Adonis* painted the world as it once was, circa 1573, when de Vere and England's omnipotent Queen Venus had been intimate with each other, *Lucrece* portrayed the more desperate state of the union circa 1594–when female power had waned and the House of Tudor was fading. During the queen's final years, the male grasp held the scepter of power. The birth of the Roman Republic depicted in *Lucrece* parallels the rise of the quasi-republican Regnum Cecilianum out of the ashes of the Tudor dynasty. The Cecils had practically become the winners, before the race had even reached its final lap. The Essex faction, such as it was, had only a vain, prancing whelp who had little appreciation for how brutal his courtly opponents could be.

But de Vere knew. He had lived under the Cecilian thumb for too long to be ignorant of his brother-in-law's plans for retaining power into the reign of the next king. This was the kind of knowledge that had probably killed Christopher Marlowe. And via the pseudonymous yarn-spinning of a Roman allegory, it was also the cautionary tale that Shake-speare would be relaying to his "patron."

LUCRECE is Elizabeth as the "Virgin Queen," a faithful and constant wife; in the later years of her reign, the queen often protested that she was married to the state. But the world of *Lucrece* is filled with ruthless male courtiers: TARQUIN, COLLATINE, OLD LUCRETIUS, and BRUTUS. These power brokers dominate the action of the poem. LUCRECE is little more than an observer in a world that she cannot control. One night, TARQUIN and company gather to boast about the chastity of their respective wives. But when these claims are put to the test, only COLLATINE's wife, LUCRECE, is discovered to be performing her spousal duties, spinning yarn and pining away the hours in modest observance of her husband's authority. Following the ancient tale of the historical Lucrece, TARQUIN grows jealous and entraps LUCRECE, raping her and fleeing.

Lucrece turns the tables on *Venus and Adonis,* from aggressive woman and submissive man to male dominator and female victim–from the autocratic control of a forceful queen to a male-dominated hierarchy of state power. The author had done what he could to warn the boy against offending the Cecilian new order.

But the warnings fell on deaf ears. On October 6, the earl of Southampton had reached the age of twenty-one, his majority. He could now say with complete legal authority what his inaction had previously only implied: He was not going to marry Elizabeth de Vere. For this dereliction of authority, Lord Burghley demanded Southampton pay an exorbitant fine of £5,000 ($1.3 million today).

The crazy scenario of the Shake-speare poems, steadfast refusals of marriage, and outlandish financial punishment would eventually make for some good comedy. At the turn of the century, as the Elizabethan Age became even more surreal, a clique of students at Cambridge University would stage a series of farces called *The Pilgrimage to Parnassus* and *The Return from Parnassus, Parts 1 and 2.* The college kids' plays offer one of the more candid views of court life as seen by a number of hip Elizabethan youth.

In the *Parnassus* plays, Southampton is satirized as a narcissistic courtly wannabe, "Gullio," who–in a sarcastic inversion of reality–hangs on every word written by Shake-speare. In one scene, Gullio recalls a recent visit he'd paid to the household of an unnamed earl who wanted to marry his daughter to Gullio. Instead, Gullio gave his hosts a modest tip.

> GULLIO The countess and my lord entertained me very honorably.
> Indeed, they used my advice in some state matters, and I perceived
> the earl would fain have thrust one of his daughters upon me. But I
> will have no knave priest to meddle with my ring! I bestowed some 20
> angels [£10] upon the officers of the house at my departure, kissed
> the countess, took my leave of the lord, and came away.

With *Venus and Adonis*, "Shakespeare" had become a best-selling author. *Lucrece* took longer to build momentum, but it, too, remained a solid seller for publisher John Harrison. The "graver labor" was reprinted seven times between 1598 and 1640.

Other writers around London soon tried to cash in on the phenomenon that *Venus and Adonis* and *Lucrece* had created. By September 1593 at the latest, Thomas Nashe had cranked out a pornographic spoof of *Venus* that he titled *The Choice of Valentines*. Nashe dedicated his manuscript to "Lord S."—no doubt Southampton—and made *Venus and Adonis*'s implicit sex as explicit as one could get. Nashe set his narrative in a brothel. *The Choice of Valentines*, not surprisingly, remained in manuscript form only—it was finally published in 1899.

In 1594, the Elizabethan dramatist Thomas Heywood published his own knock-off of *Venus and Adonis*, which he called *Oenone and Paris*. From the book's dedication "To the courteous readers" onward, it was clear which best seller Heywood was imitating, from the red and white of the Tudor Rose to the aggressive female assuring her lover that no one will know of their affair ("thy milk-white skin the pebbles shall not mark") to the silencing of the hero with a thousand kisses (a "thousand thanks" in *Oenone*). The following year, the poet-dramatist Michael Drayton produced his similarly Shake-spearean *Endymion and Phoebe*.

Drayton and at least four other poets in 1594—Richard Barnfield, John Dickenson, Sir William Harbert, and one anonymous elegist—also quoted from or otherwise referenced *Venus and Adonis* and *Lucrece*. Moreover, Harbert began to draw connections between the epic poems printed with the name "Shakespeare" attached to them and the plays, which had no such imprimatur.

The sieve was leaking. Shake-speare the officially recognized author of *Venus and Adonis* and *Lucrece* was beginning to become identified with the unofficially recognized "upstart crow" who'd been producing, acting in, and taking credit for various plays in the public theaters. If de Vere had ever thought the pseudonym Shake-speare could be isolated to just a couple of narrative poems, by 1594 he was being proven wrong.

Now that the two epic poems had demonstrated how many pounds and shillings could be made from the by-products of de Vere's pen, the marketplace began to take over. In 1594, Pembroke's Men's *Taming of A* [*sic*] *Shrew* and *The First Part of the Contention betwixt the two famous Houses of York and Lancaster* (later cleaned up and republished as Shake-speare's *Henry VI, Part 2*) were both published. Neither of these anonymous publications appears to have been approved or in any way supervised by the author.

Another play called *Locrine* was also registered for print in 1594, ultimately appearing on the book stands under the lucrative byline "W.S." Many scholars today suspect that the author of *Locrine* was Charles Tilney, a member of the Babbington conspiracy that had tried to install Mary, Queen of Scots, in 1586. The "W.S." on *Locrine's* title page merely *implied* Shake-speare's authorship enough to sell an otherwise worthless old manuscript.

This was all too much. De Vere wrote to his former father-in-law to complain about maltreatment in what he termed "my office." The nature of de Vere's government job remains an unsolved mystery. But the widespread abuse of the Shake-speare name in the first half of 1594 provides another suggestion that the "office" had something to do with the Shake-speare brand. On July 7, de Vere wrote to Lord Burghley:

> My very good Lord: If it please you to remember that about half a year or thereabout past, I was a suitor to Your Lordship for your favor, that whereas I found sundry abuses, whereby both Her Majesty and myself were in mine office greatly hindered, that it would please Your Lordship that I might find such favor from you that I might have the same redressed.
>
> At which time I found so good forwardness in Your Lordship that I thought myself greatly beholding for the same. Yet by reason at that time mine attorney was departed the town, I could not then send him to attend upon Your Lordship, according to your appointment. But hoping that the same disposition still remaineth towards the justness of my cause, and that Your Lordship to whom my estate is so well known & how much it standeth me on, not to neglect as heretofore such occasions as to amend the same may arise from mine office, I most heartily desire Your Lordship that it will please you to give ear to the state of my cause, and at your best leisure, admit either mine attorney or other of my counsel in law to inform Your Lordship that the same being perfectly laid open to Your Lordship, I may enjoy the favor from you which I most earnestly desire. In which doing I shall think myself singularly beholding in this, as I have been in other respects. This 7th of July 1594.
>
> Your Lordship's ever to command,
> EDWARD OXENFORD

De Vere's prose, thick with legalistic provisos, reveals a man looking to play whatever cards he held in his hand very cautiously. Both he and the queen, de Vere noted, had been "abused" in some fashion. Perhaps de Vere hoped he could get the seventy-three-year-old Lord Treasurer to help de Vere preserve some dignity and semblance of ownership over the writings that were slipping out of his grasp. Perhaps de Vere wanted to establish some more permanent relationship with the country's best theatrical company, the Lord Chamberlain's Men, or otherwise pull some strings to rein in a situation that had spiraled out of control.

The "abuse" only continued unabated, however. In September, a London printer named John Windet registered for publication the most revealing and damning text about de Vere since the Arundell Libels. (It would later be reprinted in a pirated edition in 1596 and then banned by the archbishop of Canterbury three years after that.) The book was titled *Willobie His Avisa: Or the True Picture of a Modest Maid and of a Chaste and Constant Wife*. Chapter 9 quoted from *Willobie's* revealing portrait of Elizabeth Trentham de Vere ("Avisa"). But one crucial portion of the *Willobie* story remains untold. And it is probably why *Willobie* became such a hot and controversial text.

The Avisa of the story, as noted previously, had become known around literary London for associating with all manner of gentlemen and riffraff at the St. George's Pub near The Theatre. According to the book, Avisa dismisses the men seeking attention and patronage there. *Willobie* celebrates Avisa for her steadfast devotion to her unnamed husband. None of this should have been any cause for uproar. Yet *Willobie* also mentions one further suitor for Avisa's hand, a suitor who is particularly insistent. The suitor is named "H.W." This initialed Englishman is "a headlong youth" who is given to "fantastical fits." He's nicknamed "Harry." And, to add to the clues that would identify the mystery suitor, H.W. had also recently "departed voluntarily to Her Majesty's services." All of these descriptions fit the headstrong and petulant Henry Wriothesley, earl of Southampton, who in 1590 had run away across the English Channel to Dieppe, where he was expecting his friend the earl of Essex to bring English forces in aid of King Henry IV of France. Elizabeth summarily snatched Harry—as he was known to his family—back from the brink of his militaristic pretensions.

Thus, if *Willobie* is to be believed, at precisely the same time de Vere was trying to interest Southampton in his daughter, Southampton was paying undue attention to "Avisa," de Vere's wife! As the narrator of *Willobie* explains:

> H.W., being suddenly infected with the contagion of a fantastical fit, at the first sight of A[visa], pineth a while in secret grief. At length not able any longer to endure the burning heat of so fervent a humor, [H.W.] bewrayeth the secrecy of his disease to his familiar friend W.S., who not

long before had tried the courtesy of the like passion–and was now newly recovered of the like infection.

The irony runs thick. De Vere (as "W.S.") had indeed "tried the courtesy of the like passion" for Avisa–he'd married her. But now the story suggests that "W.S." was feeling "newly recovered" from Avisa's love, which is perhaps the polite way of saying that "W.S." was becoming just as fond of "H.W." as he was of his spouse.

The narrator continues:

Yet finding his friend [H.W.] let blood in the same vein, he [W.S.] took pleasure for a time to see him bleed–and instead of stopping the issue, he enlargeth the wound with the sharp razor of a willing conceit, persuading him [H.W.] that he [W.S.] thought it a matter very easy to be compassed.... In viewing afar off the course of this loving comedy, [W.S.] determined to see whether it would sort to a happier end for this new actor [H.W.] than it did for this old player [W.S.]. But at length this comedy was like to have grown to a tragedy by the weak and feeble estate that H.W. was brought unto by a desperate view of an impossibility of obtaining his purpose.

So, in a farce of mixed-up intentions, *Willobie* has Southampton confessing his lust for the countess of Oxford ... to that old man of the stage, the earl of Oxford. And Southampton receives de Vere's amorous encouragement ... as de Vere's endorsement of the wooing of his own countess. *Willobie* even has de Vere play the role of trickster, encouraging Southampton's dalliances believing that his wife will not cheat on him with Southampton. This is the stuff of great comedy–and not a little embarrassment. Little wonder, then, that the next authorized version of *Willobie* had to wait until 1605, after de Vere was dead.

And like Nashe roasting de Vere as "Gentle Master William," *Willobie* offers further evidence that London literati in the early to mid 1590s knew de Vere's secret identity as "W.S."

The last third of *Willobie* features a brief exchange between H.W. and W.S. about the art of wooing and winning a woman, followed by H.W.'s fruitless pursuits of Avisa, who turns him down at every occasion.

Shake-speare's sonnets 40, 41, and 42 conclude the love triangle story. Presuming Southampton is the "fair youth" being addressed in these poems, as has often been argued by scholars of all persuasions, the meaning of these once enigmatic poems becomes clear. De Vere had discovered that Southampton and his wife had become scandalously close. (Depending on the timing of the affair, the paternity of Henry de Vere could thus have been cast into doubt.) But de Vere's admiration for Southampton, and his trust in his chaste Avisa, were enough to keep his once insane jealousy under control. De Vere had truly made a shift in his life: from jealous and paranoid doubter of his first wife to confident believer in the love of his second wife–even if she might have been briefly tempted by Southampton's charms.

40

Take all my loves, my love. Yea, take them all.
What hast thou then more than thou hadst before?
No love, my love, that thou mayest true love call.
All mine was thine, before thou hadst this more:
Then, if for my love, thou my love receivest,
I cannot blame thee, for my love thou usest.
But yet be blam'd, if thou this self deceivest
By willful taste of what thy self refusest.
I do forgive thy robbery, gentle thief,
Although thou steal thee all my poverty.
And yet love knows it is a greater grief
To bear love's wrong than hate's known injury.
     Lascivious grace, in whom all ill well shows,
     Kill me with spites, yet we must not be foes.

41

Those pretty wrongs that liberty commits,
When I am sometime absent from thy heart,
Thy beauty and thy years full well befits,
For still temptation follows where thou art.
Gentle thou art, and therefore to be won,
Beauteous thou art, therefore to be assailed;
And when a woman woos, what woman's son
Will sourly leave her till he have prevailed?
Ay me, but yet thou might'st my seat forbear,
And chide thy beauty and thy straying youth,
Who lead thee in their riot even there
Where thou art forced to break a twofold truth:
     Hers, by thy beauty tempting her to thee,
     Thine, by thy beauty being false to me.

42

That thou hast her, it is not all my grief,
And yet it may be said I loved her dearly;
That she hath thee is of my wailing chief,
A loss in love that touches me more nearly.
Loving offenders, thus I will excuse ye:

Thou dost love her, because thou know'st I love her,
And for my sake ev'n so doth she abuse me,
Suff'ring my friend for my sake to approve her.
If I lose thee, my loss is my love's gain,
And losing her, my friend hath found that loss;
Both find each other, and I lose both twain,
And both for my sake lay on me this cross.
    But here's the joy: My friend and I are one;
    Sweet flatt'ry, then she loves but me alone.

De Vere cannot have failed to anticipate at least some of Shake-speare's popular appeal. He'd first published an Ovidian kiss-and-tell poetic memoir about Queen Elizabeth at the height of her power and erotic appeal. Then he'd followed it up with a contemporary epic poem about sex, potency, and the continued ascent of the house of Cecil. Add to this a cluster of plays being performed around London with a loudmouthed actor and producer advertising himself as an author. And add to *that* a cluster of love sonnets—written to another man—being circulated in manuscript among the courtly class, and one has the makings of a guerrilla marketing campaign unlike any other in history.

Both of the official Shake-speare publications, *Venus and Adonis* and *Lucrece,* contained nuanced and circumspect dedications to Southampton. And as the Parnassus plays indicate, the university and literary set appreciated that Southampton's involvement in the Shake-speare enterprise had soon become its own comedy: The preoccupied and paternalistic author had gotten hung up on a dashing young star at court; the dashing young star at court was growing enamored of the "Shakespeare" plays and poems, not to mention the "Shakespeare" wife; the "Shakespeare" plays and poems, contrary to design, were leading the young star ever farther away from the author's daughter; the author's daughter was probably slinking away from the whole embarrassing scene; the whole embarrassing scene was making perfect fodder for farce.

Farce was how the strange year of 1594 ended too. On December 13, de Vere and Heneage's alma mater, Gray's Inn, sent out invitations for a blowout season of plays and entertainments to rival anything ever seen or staged before in England. With Her Majesty's blessing, the law students—potential courtiers of tomorrow, every one—established a faux princedom named after the manor house (Portpool) around which Gray's Inn was built.

On opening night, the "Prince of Purpoole" and his moot entourage had entertained and danced with so many noteworthy ladies of London that word of this new singles club soon disseminated around town. The following night of festivity, December 28, the stage and the halls of Gray's Inn were thronged with actual courtiers, pretend courtiers, and randy poseurs of all persuasions. This was no public-theater afternoon of russet jackets and modest kirtles. Like its royal counterpart at Whitehall, the court of Purpoole demanded ostentation. Some of London's finest doublets and gowns strode up and down the crowded Gray's Inn stage like the countless powdered gallants de Vere had seen in his visits to "Queen" Henri III's flamboyant court in Paris.

The stench of wall-to-wall sweat, perfumes, and aromatic herbs–soap and hot-water baths were a rarity even for the well-heeled–must have laden the heavy winter air that hung over the evening's overflow-capacity crowd at Gray's Inn. Actual peers of the realm, unaccustomed to crowds and tight spaces, pickled in their own sweet juices.

According to an anonymous scribe's account of the evening, an entourage from another nearby law school–Inner Temple–was so repelled by the mob scene that they left "discontented and displeased." The Inner Temple students missed a real show too. "After such sports, a *Comedy of Errors* . . . was played by the players," the chronicler notes. The evening, he adds, "was ever afterwards called 'The Night of Errors.'"

An unnamed "sorcerer or conjurer" received most of the blame. This "sorcerer" had ordered the construction of the stage at Gray's Inn; he'd invited much of the crowd that had horded into the makeshift theater; he'd also "foisted a company of base and common fellows to make up our disorders with a play of errors and confusions." So the "sorcerer" was brought before the prince of Purpoole. The mystery man pleaded that the entertainment was "nothing else but vain illusions, fancies, dreams, and enchantments." Purpoole ultimately accepted the "dream" defense and dismissed any outstanding mock charges that his court might have brought. Whether the "sorcerer" was the author de Vere or producer-actor Will Shakspere–DON ARMADO or COSTARD–is anybody's guess. But one of the two men behind the Shake-speare ruse appears to have been the instigator of Gray's Inn's "Night of Errors."

In early December of 1594, Elizabeth de Vere had convinced her family to accept her own choice of mate. As *Venus and Adonis* and *Lucrece* suggest, de Vere had advocated for Southampton's hand until the very last. But Burghley had urged his grandchild to try other bachelors too–the earl of Bedford, then the earl of Northumberland, whom the nineteen-year-old de Vere girl told her officious grandfather she "[could not] fancye." She "fancyed" another man–William Stanley.

William Stanley, a thirty-four-year-old courtier poet, was a younger brother to the theatrical patron and courtier poet Ferdinando Stanley, fifth earl of Derby, Lord Strange. The Stanley brothers were great-great-grandchildren of King Henry VII and thus lived on the outer fringes of royalty. Practically, this had meant nothing to William, the landless and untitled younger sibling–until in July 1594, when his older brother had died suddenly of a stomach ailment.

Ferdinando's marriage had produced two daughters and thus no heirs to the earldom. During the remainder of the year, the Stanley family remained on tenterhooks. Ferdinando Stanley's widow was pregnant. If she delivered a boy, by the laws of primogeniture the newborn would become the next earl of Derby. If the child was a girl, William Stanley would succeed.

The dowager countess of Derby gave birth to a daughter. Elizabeth de Vere would soon become the next countess of Derby.

Those "vain illusions, fancies, dreams, and enchantments" that the bride's father specialized in were pulled out for the girl's wedding. As the chronicler John Stow recorded:

> The 26 of January, William, earl of Derby, married the earl of Oxford's daughter at the court then at Greenwich, which marriage feast was there most royally kept.

Sunday the twenty-sixth would actually be the first of several nights of parties that would conclude eighty-five miles to the north at Burghley House in Lincolnshire, where four days later the wedding ceremony itself would be held. The groom's family was particularly sensitive to the astrological significance of the timing of events, so the service was scheduled to fall on the date of the new moon, January 30.

In the meantime, Queen Elizabeth bade farewell to her maid of honor in a soiree at Greenwich Palace on Sunday night. According to a letter posted to Robert Cecil as the plans were being laid for the party, at least one play had been prepared to entertain the many gentlefolk who would attend. A dance also closed out the night, with the queen entertaining an exiled Spaniard with her merry footwork.

A Midsummer Night's Dream was probably the play performed in the Great Chamber of Greenwich Palace on the evening of the twenty-sixth. Although the *Dream* had been used once before to celebrate another Cecil family wedding, events peculiar to William Stanley and Elizabeth de Vere's marriage get prominent mention in this play too. *A Midsummer Night's Dream* begins with the observation that "four happy days bring in another moon," while the play ends with a dance and a cast of faeries being sent off to bless "each several chamber . . . through this palace."

A Midsummer Night's Dream retells the story, in satirical form, of de Vere's obsession with one of his daughter's potential bridegrooms, while she remained fixated upon the man she would ultimately marry. The central love triangle of Elizabeth Vere and the earls of Southampton and Derby translate respectively into the trio of mixed-up lovers HERMIA, DEMETRIUS, and LYSANDER. HERMIA's doting father, EGEUS (de Vere), is embarrassingly enamored of DEMETRIUS

(Southampton), his choice for HERMIA's husband. Meanwhile, HERMIA (Lady Elizabeth) and LYSANDER (Derby) only have eyes for each other. De Vere's self-mocking side comes to light once again in the play's first scene:

> DEM. [*Southampton*]:
>   Relent, sweet HERMIA; and LYSANDER, yield
>   Thy crazed title to my certain right.
> LYS. [*Derby*]:
>   You have her father's love, DEMETRIUS:
>   Let me have HERMIA's. Do you marry him.
> EGEUS [*de Vere*]:
>   Scornful LYSANDER! True, he hath my love;
>   And what is mine my love shall render him;
>   And she is mine, and all my right of her
>   I do estate unto DEMETRIUS.
> LYS. I am, my lord, as well deriv'd as he,
>   As well possess'd; my love is more than his;
>   My fortunes every way as fairly rank'd.

EGEUS's description of his love for DEMETRIUS, in fact, sounds suspiciously like Shake-speare's fond descriptions of the "fair youth" of the *Sonnets*.

Bowing to the laws of romantic comedy, in the end the true lovers are united. LYSANDER marries HERMIA, just as Elizabeth de Vere won her Derby. DEMETRIUS winds up matched with a maiden who's infatuated with him. (Southampton would not be walking down the aisle for a few more years, but would ultimately make a love match.) And EGEUS stages a wedding masque for *A Midsummer Night's Dream*'s lucky couples.

On the actual night of the earl and his new countess of Derby's wedding, another masque was presented–this time by the poet John Davies. Davies's solemn "Masque of the Nine Muses" is nothing like the uproarious send-up of *A Midsummer Night's Dream*. Think of the *Dream* as a lighthearted entertainment crafted for de Vere's daughter's royal wedding shower. Davies, on the other hand, presented a carefully constructed homage to the newlyweds as seen through the eyes of the nine legendary Muses. History (Clio) honors the bridegroom who has been "raised by the heavens" into his earldom. Tragedy (Melpomene) recites the great military victories won by "Warlike Vere," the bride's father's cousin. Astronomy (Urania) unfolds the heavenly significance of the marriage day. And so on.

The January 30 wedding at Burghley House may have been de Vere's first visit since the completion of Burghley's country seat in 1587. Guests–a courtly who's who that included the queen herself–could relax in the house's drawing rooms and extensive libraries. The master of the household proudly displayed his rare books and maps, his coins and gems, and his marble busts of all the Caesars in Roman history. The mansion's vast courtyard, gardens, and even sprawling rooftop provided ample grounds for the wandering sort to explore the country seat of an English family unrivaled in their power.

De Vere's later reflection upon his eldest daughter's wedding would appear in *The Tempest*. In tribute to Derby's brother–the lamented Ferdinando, Lord Strange–the earl of Derby character in *The Tempest* is named FERDINAND. Puns on the word *strange* pepper the play's dialogue, while contemporary legends about Derby's extensive travels provide fodder for jokes about FERDINAND. *The Tempest*'s authorial character, PROSPERO, is initially unconvinced of FERDINAND's worthiness for the hand of his daughter, MIRANDA, who must play a waiting game. Ultimately, however, FERDINAND convinces PROSPERO. FERDINAND and MIRANDA wed, and PROSPERO stages a wedding masque for the newlywed couple.

PROSPERO's masque turns the tables on the bride and groom, presenting the story of a maid (Psyche) who must go to extreme lengths to please an exacting mother of the groom (Venus). PROSPERO later admits that he's asked a great deal of his potential son-in-law. But, he adds, the payment for FERDINAND's efforts is "a third of mine own life"–one of the author's three daughters.

> PROSPERO If I have too austerely punish'd you
>   Your compensation makes amends, for I
>   Have given you here a third of mine own life,
>   Or that for which I live.... All thy vexations
>   Were but my trials of thy love, and thou
>   Hast strangely stood the test.

Between the marriage of his eldest daughter and the midsummer of 1595, Edward de Vere was occupied with two troubles that shaped his final years: his declining financial state and his physical infirmities. Poverty was a condition he'd been raised to believe that only other, less fortunate souls experienced. But now that he had children to provide for, de Vere attempted to repair the fiscal damage wreaked during his reckless youth. The mining and commodities trading of tin would be de Vere's latest last-ditch scheme. De Vere scratched out more than a dozen letters and memoranda in 1595 to petition for a royal patent on the production of tin, and in the next few years he would continue to pursue it.

Tin, the element that, when alloyed with copper, makes bronze, was a precious national resource abundant in the southwestern tip of England, in the counties of Devon and Cornwall. These tin deposits had proved valuable for international trade from the days of the Roman Empire onward. Some scholars have suspected the presence of Cornish tin in the smelting fires of the ancient Greeks and Phoenicians.

By the first half of the sixteenth century, the tin mines were producing nearly two million pounds of metal per year. But in the 1590s, due to economic hard times and poor management, tin production fell by a third. De Vere was one of a handful of Elizabethan courtiers who recognized that Cornish tin could once again become an international commodity.

De Vere's "tin-mining letters" constitute the single most concentrated source of manuscript pages yet collected from his pen. Between March 9, 1585, and March 14, 1586, he wrote fifteen dated tin-mining letters and memoranda; no doubt some of his eight undated tin-mining documents come from this period as well. Taken as a whole, de Vere's careful and meticulous tin-mining letters are also strikingly out of character with his wastrel image. One suspects the influence of Elizabeth Trentham de Vere lurking behind the schedules and figures.

She didn't write the letters, though. Even when idling over the driest of managerial minutiae, de Vere still churned out curious images, phrasings, and metaphors. One characteristic feature of Shake-speare's rhetorical style is the extensive use of a classical figure called *hendiadys*–or, more plainly, the "two-in-one" construction. ("*Slings and arrows* of outrageous fortune"; "full of *sound and fury*"; "*abstract and brief* chronicles of the time"; "*wild and whirling* words") So, amid the tin filings and marginal calculations of de Vere's petitions, one finds the tin petitioner introducing such curious hendiadyses as "she shall never have any *sense or feeling* thereof ...”; "under *titles and mean-shows* into the hands of private persons..." and "he should effect his *cross and overthwart* towards me...."

The letters, though dry and legalistic, show a rhetorician's training, a characteristic delight in rare words, and a deft use of metaphors:

> Those matters which I allege and bring forth to be judged by you ... be so pondered that reason be not oppressed with a vain confidence in a light person, nor truth smothered up rather by false appearance than assisted by indifferent hearing, nor that Her Majesty's former trusts be now made the very instruments of her infinite loss.

And

> By the breach of this custom, many abuses creep in which are neither profitable to the realm nor to Her Majesty in especial.

And

> I find of [the queen] herself to have oftentimes sundry good motions and dispositions to do me good. Yet for want of such a friend as Your Lordship [Burghley] that may settle her inclination to a full effect, I

perceive all my hopes but fucate [*falsified, counterfeit*] and my haps to wither in the herb.

De Vere didn't get the job. The queen instead awarded supervisory roles in the "stannaries" to four other gentlemen of her court, including Sir Walter Raleigh.

De Vere's health was also failing. On March 25, 1595, he wrote to Burghley, apologizing for his inability to keep up with a man thirty years his senior.

When Your Lordship shall have best time and leisure if I may know it, I will attend Your Lordship as well as a lame man may at your house.

Three days later, he wrote to one of Burghley's servants that he could not visit the old Lord Treasurer because "I am not able nor fit to look into that place, being yet no better recovered." In seven other letters, dating from 1590 to 1602, de Vere complains of ill health, infirmity, or lameness. Shake-speare complains of lameness in Sonnet 37:

> I, made lame by fortune's dearest spite
> . . . am not lame, poor, nor despised,
> Whilst that this shadow doth such substance give . . .

and in Sonnet 89:

> Speak of my lameness, and I straight will halt,
> Against thy reasons, making no defense.

During the summer of 1595, de Vere reported to Burghley that his health continued to be "not so good" and that doctors were bloodletting to fight the maladies that plagued him. Sometime between October 1595 and '96, de Vere visited the western city of Bath. For two millennia the hot mineral springs at Bath had been used as cure-alls for ailing English subjects seeking to balance their uneven body fluids, or humors.

Shake-speare's Sonnets 153 and 154, the last two in the series, recount an Ovidian tale of a healing journey to this same site.

> ### 153
> [Cupid's] love-kindling fire did quickly steep
> In a cold valley fountain of that ground,
> Which borrowed from this holy fire of love,
> A dateless lively heat still to endure—
> And grew a seething Bath which men yet prove
> Against strange maladies a sovereign cure. . . .

> I sick withal the help of Bath desired,
> And thither hied, a sad distempered guest. . . .

By the late fall of 1595, rumors had begun circulating that de Vere had succumbed to the maladies that plagued him. Rowland Whyte, agent of Sir
Philip Sidney's younger brother Robert, wrote to his boss, "Some say my lord
of Oxford is dead."

These were days of strange rumors and chatters. In 1595, the poet George
Chapman wrote a proud and critical poem ("A Coronet for His Mistress's
Philosophy") that mentioned an unnamed poet-playwright whose "loose
feathers beautify" someone else. Because of its extensive allusions to Shake-
speare's *Sonnets* and other works, some orthodox scholars have suspected
Shake-speare was Chapman's critical target. However, none of them has addressed why Chapman seems to be suggesting—à la *Greene's Groatsworth of
Wit*—that the works of Shake-speare involve the use of an "upstart crow"
front man. Also during 1595, the poet Thomas Edwardes published his tribute to Shake-speare's *Venus and Adonis* (cited in Chapter 7) and the unnamed
nobleman poet who "differs much from men tilting under friaries"—de Vere
and his servants who had once fought Sir Thomas Knyvet's servants at the
Blackfriars.

Taken as a whole, the above squibs suggest that halfway through the final
decade of the sixteenth century, the London gossip mill was ruminating over
de Vere, his writings, and the country clown being beautified by the shadowy
feathers of his rhyme.

The year 1596 for Edward de Vere was more quiet.

The only record of de Vere's activities, other than a debt to a joiner that
he couldn't pay, are two brief letters in September to Robert Cecil, who had
recently been promoted to secretary of state. In the first letter, written on
September 6, de Vere put in his first sentence what was now in all likelihood
first in his life:

> The writing which I have is in the country, for I had such care thereof as
> I carried it with me in a little desk. Tomorrow or the next day I aim to
> go thither and so soon as I come home, by the grace of God, I will send
> it you.

The "writing" in this case was probably a letter or petition: One reader whom
de Vere certainly did *not* tap to proofread poems or plays was his former
brother-in-law. But if only that "little desk" could have been inventoried for
other papers, posterity might have cared more about it.

De Vere was also concerned about his newlywed daughter's lifestyle. The twenty-year-old girl was evidently living wildly and acting in a manner unbecoming to a noblewoman. Eleven days after writing the above letter, de Vere wrote again to Cecil:

> I am most earnest to desire you that you are her [*Elizabeth de Vere's*] uncle and nearest to her next to myself, that you will friendly assist her with your good advice. You know her youth and the place wherein she lives— and how much to both our houses it imports that she carry herself according to her honor. Enemies are apt to make the worst of everything. Flatterers will do evil offices, and true and faithful advice will seem harsh to tender ears.

De Vere entreated Cecil to give his eldest niece a guiding hand. The uneasy father continued:

> But sith my fortune hath set me so far off as I cannot be at hand in this her troublesome occasions, I hope you will do the good office of an uncle. And I commit unto you the authority of a parent in mine absence. Thus confounded with the small understanding of her estate and the care of her well-doing, I leave to trouble you any farther—most earnestly desiring you as you can get leisure to advertise me how her causes stand....

De Vere wrote the first of these two personal appeals from Cannon Row, his son-in-law's house. He was still trying to negotiate a contract that would guarantee his daughter £1,000 per year from her well-to-do husband. De Vere had stayed at Cannon Row in 1595 as well. Indeed, into the late 1590s, the historical record reveals traces of family ties retained between both father and daughter, stepmother and son-in-law.

Derby himself was recognized by contemporaries as an accomplished court poet and playwright. In 1599, a correspondent would note that de Vere's son-in-law "is busied only in penning comedies for the common players." A tantalizing possibility thus opens up. Although the Shake-speare canon speaks in one distinctive voice and concerns itself primarily with de Vere's life and affairs, one topic sorely in need of research is the possibility of de Vere–Derby collaborations on scenes or portions of plays–or perhaps touch-ups of de Vere's work after the author was dead. *The Tempest* or *A Midsummer Night's Dream,* concerning themselves as they do with Derby's marriage, make attractive candidates for attribution studies attempting to detect a trace of Derby's hand.

On April 23, 1597, five new royal knights of the Garter were elected at Windsor Castle, and an installation ceremony was set for the following month. De

Vere had once garnered a majority of votes for membership in the Order of the Garter himself, but by age forty-seven, he must have realized that he would never be appointed. Yet, as a courtier, de Vere was privy to the ceremonies and gossip surrounding the Order. *The Merry Wives of Windsor* recites inside jokes about one of the newly elected knights Garter in 1597, the German count Frederick of Mompelgard, duke of Würtemberg.

Mompelgard had made a nuisance of himself since his visit to England in 1592, pestering Elizabeth incessantly that he should be promoted to a Garter knighthood. De Vere had probably met the cloying German peer at Windsor Castle during that visit. In 1597, Elizabeth finally gave in. But she took advantage of a rule introduced during her father's reign that she didn't technically have to notify a Garter inductee that he was going to be inducted. So on April 23, St. George's Day, Elizabeth and her court hosted a feast and revels for the new knights of the Garter. All the inductees were there, except one. Somehow, through some oversight, Mompelgard had never received an invitation.

In *The Merry Wives of Windsor,* the HOST OF THE GARTER INN exchanges an otherwise throwaway line with BARDOLPH about a certain unnamed German duke:

> BARDOLPH Sir, the German desires to have three of your horses. The
>   duke himself will be tomorrow at court, and they are going to meet
>   him.
> HOST What duke should that be comes so secretly? I hear not of him in
>   the court.

Even in the late 1590s, de Vere was still adding offhand topical references to plays that he'd probably begun writing twenty years or more before.

In the same year, 1597, when the Lord Chamberlain's Men were casting about for a new theater to call home, Shakspere's troupe staged *The Merchant of Venice*. Taking its plotline from a fourteenth-century Italian book of short stories (unavailable in English), early drafts of *The Merchant of Venice* may have graced English stages as early as 1578. But, as with *Merry Wives*, de Vere also added an underplot relevant to current events in 1597. It was a specialized message for a crowd of specialists: lawyers and law students.

According to Elizabethan legal practice, if two parties were embroiled in a contract dispute, they could try it in the common law courts. The loser at common law could then take his claim to a separate legal system called the chancery (equity) courts. Both common law and chancery had jurisdiction over the case, and both could rule independently of each other. This naturally led to innumerable collisions and traumas, wherein each disputant held opposing legal judgments or decrees. The common law courts, firmly bound to centuries of precedent, were more strict and tended to render "letter-of-the-law" judgments; whereas equity courts, given more free reign by the crown, could answer appeals to higher principles like mercy and justice.

In January of 1597, de Vere's wife, Elizabeth, was served with a "supplication" for enforcing an outstanding bond. The bond concerned back wages de Vere had paid out to some gunners during the brief period when he was stationed in the Lowlands in 1585. The plaintiff in the lawsuit, named Thomas Gurlyn, in 1585 had promised to loan de Vere the money needed to pay out the gunners' salaries–stipulating that Gurlyn would then receive the government's reimbursement for the payroll. But neither the reimbursement nor Gurlyn's pledged loan had ever been paid, at least not in any form useful to de Vere. Gurlyn's 1597 case is a miasma of twelve years of payments promised and payments dodged. (Gurlyn originally promised de Vere £300; an undertreasurer named Sir Thomas Sherley owed Gurlyn £300; at de Vere's behest, Sherley didn't pay Gurlyn; Gurlyn then twice paid de Vere £200 ... out of de Vere's own accounts; Sherley finally paid Gurlyn £300; Gurlyn thereafter claimed de Vere owed *him* £100.) It was all a big mess, and Gurlyn had presented a petition to de Vere's wife–who had nothing to do with the dispute, but controlled the household's purse strings now.

Exasperated, on January 11 de Vere wrote to his former brother-in-law appealing for justice.

> Good Sir Robert Cecil, whereas my wife hath showed me a supplication exhibited to the lords of the [Privy] Council against her, I have longed both to yield thanks to you for your courtesy to her and myself in making her acquainted therewith–and also to advertise you how lewdly therein he [Gurlyn] behaves himself.... [C]onsider the date of his supplication, which signifieth five years ago, at what time I think she never knew the man.

De Vere was embarrassed by the legal quagmire his wife had been dragged into because of him. The letter continues:

> I do not doubt therefore but ... you will let him [Gurlyn] have his deserts according to his presumption....
>
> [I]f he hath had any cause to have complained, it should then have been against myself, as the same will complain. But his shifts and knaveries are so gross and palpable, that doubting to bring his parties and jugglings to light, he doth address his petition against her that is utterly ignorant of the cause.
>
> Thus desiring you to conceive how thankfully I take this honorable dealing with my wife and friendly care to me, I will the less set forth in words what I the more desire in deeds to show, if I were so happy as to find opportunity.

De Vere and his wife wanted the chance to present their case. If the venue was going to be a common law court, however, Gurlyn stood a fighting chance: If one wanted to split judicial hairs, Gurlyn did have a marginally feasible argument.

De Vere and his countess did ultimately prevail over Gurlyn. As Elizabeth Trentham de Vere reflected years later, after the death of her husband, "Thomas Gurlyn...[sued] for a debt pretended to be due unto him from the said late earl [and] was at the trial thereof overthrown upon manifest proof made of the satisfaction of that debt." But the idea of conflicting possible verdicts in common law and equity courts provided the inspiration to update an old Venetian chestnut.

The Merchant of Venice stages the core problems behind Gurlyn's frivolous "supplication." ANTONIO has taken out a loan from SHYLOCK in anticipation of money from overseas. When the money fails to come through, ANTONIO must default on his debt. ANTONIO and SHYLOCK square off in a Venetian court of law. Their trial scene is rich in legal terminology.

The case of *SHYLOCK v. ANTONIO* loosely parallels Gurlyn's 1597 case; it also debates the larger questions the Gurlyn case raises over Justice versus Mercy and common law verdicts versus chancery edicts. Abstruse as the issue sounds today, law versus equity was perhaps the leading judicial question of the age. As de Vere saw firsthand in 1597, the unsettled dispute between these conflicting modes of justice upset many lives and unjustly harassed many innocent people.

The verdict in the Gurlyn case, de Vere's pleading letter to Robert Cecil, and the story of *The Merchant of Venice* all deliver the same judgment: Letter-of-the-law verdicts corrupt justice; equity must carry the day. The Shake-speare canon's greatest legal mind, PORTIA, weaves arguments from both common law and chancery courts, arguing that strict and myopic reading of the law must yield to that quality that is "mightiest in the mightiest." PORTIA's immortal speech is, in part, a prayer for the relief of unjustly persecuted subjects at the hands of literalist and strict-constructionalist common law:

> PORTIA The quality of mercy is not strained;
>   It droppeth as the gentle rain from heaven
>   Upon the place beneath. It is twice blest;
>   It blesseth him that gives and him that takes.
>   'Tis mightiest in the mightiest; it becomes
>   The thronèd monarch better than his crown.

PORTIA is de Vere's most touching tribute to his adroit and talented wife. She had been dragged in as a third party to the Gurlyn dispute and ultimately had carried the day.

❧

Around this time, rumors had begun to spread that Elizabeth de Vere Stanley, countess of Derby, was having a love affair with the earl of Essex.

If the rumors were true, her infidelity would have been concern enough for her father; but her choice of bedmates would have been a slap in the face. De Vere harbored a grudge against Essex. In 1595, de Vere had written to Robert Cecil about a long-standing legal case before Lord Burghley concerning the possible inheritance of the forest of Waltham. Burghley had referred de Vere to the earl of Essex on the matter, but de Vere had flat out refused to deal with Essex. De Vere wrote to his brother-in-law:

> [Burghley] wisheth me to make means to the earl of Essex–that he would forbear to deal with it. [That is] a thing I cannot do in honor, since I have already received diverse injuries and wrongs from him [*Essex*]–which bar me from all such base courses.

At the time, though, Essex was on the rise. In the summer of 1596, Essex had launched a successful naval strike against the garrison at Cádiz, Spain's primary Atlantic port. Countess Elizabeth may not have been attracted to Southampton, but she took a fancy to his comrade-in-arms.

Before Essex and Southampton embarked on a raid of the Spanish fleet in the Azores in July of 1597, one rumor monger reported that Essex "laye with my lady of Darbe before he went." In the same month, Derby moved himself and his countess far away from the temptations of the court to the Stanley family's ancestral estate in Lancashire. Robert Cecil employed at least one agent working in Derby's household, keeping him informed of the latest bruit about the young couple. On August 9, one of Cecil's agents reported that Derby "is in such a jealous frame as we have had such a storm as is wonderful [*wondrous*]."

Cecil's niece would be protected. De Vere's daughter had, the agent noted, "by courtesy and virtue got the love of all here." So when Derby threw a tantrum over his wife's alleged infidelities, the household's servants stood on the bride's side. Cecil's agent wrote his master that

> They [Derby's servants] all went to my lord ... and told him that as they had served him and his father and been the same by them ... if he would hate her and [not] desist from this jealousy and bitterness to Her Ladyship and not dishonor himself, or else [*then*] they would hate him and bring her to my lord [Burghley] and you [Cecil].... My lady wanteth not friends, friends firm to our purposes, wise and experienced in this humorous house.

Two days later the earl of Cumberland, Derby's uncle, arrived on the scene and backed the countess as well. All in all, it was a successful show of Cecil's political muscle.

Within a week, Derby had his opportunity to save face. On August 20, Derby issued the following public statement:

> If anyone can say that I know my wife to be dishonest of her body or that I can justly prove it by myself or anyone else, I challenge him the combat of life. If anyone suppose any speeches of mine to have proceeded out of that doubt, he doth me wrong.

Burghley, Robert Cecil, and the Lord Admiral Charles Howard countersigned this challenge. De Vere did not. Two days later, Derby and his countess wrote to Cecil to express their newfound appreciation for each other. They signed the letter, "Your loving niece and nephew."

Even as the younger Cecil was taking over his father's political power, Southampton was moving farther away from the house in which he'd grown up. Southampton had lately been courting Mistress Elizabeth Vernon. Vernon was one of the queen's maids of honor—a vestal virgin so far as Her Majesty was concerned. Vernon was also Essex's cousin. The court observer Rowland Whyte had noted in 1595 that Southampton had "with too much familiarity" been pursuing Vernon. The clandestine courtship carried on into 1596 and '97.

In *A Midsummer Night's Dream,* Southampton's character (DEMETRIUS) ends the play paired with the infatuated young maid HELENA—after he escapes the externally enforced match with the daughter (HERMIA) of de Vere's self-mocking self-portrait (EGEUS). However, so far as the Cecil–Essex power game was concerned, *Midsummer Night's Dream* hedges its bets: DEMETRIUS ends up marrying HELENA (Vernon), but DEMETRIUS is also the only character in the play who's still under the influence of the love potion as the final curtain rings down. *A Midsummer Night's Dream* conceals the secret hope that the play's one remaining spell would be broken—and DEMETRIUS would break off his dangerous courtship with HELENA and offend the powerful Cecils no more.

In October 1597, Southampton and his commander, the earl of Essex, had returned from their mission to the Azores. The expedition's intent was both to weaken Spanish naval forces and to plunder the *flota,* the Spanish treasure fleet that carried its New World riches from Havana to Spain every year. Essex's Azores mission did neither. It did little more than squander a lot of money and time and further anger the Spanish. Essex, naturally, tried to cast his failure in a positive light. Rowland Whyte reported the first news from Essex's newly returned fleet after they'd made landfall during the last week of October:

> [Essex's fleet] had unfortunately missed the [Spanish] king's own ships with the Indian [*New World*] treasure and fell upon the merchant's fleet [instead]. Four of them he hath taken and brought home safe and sunk

many more. My lord of Southampton fought with one of the king's great men of war and sunk her.

In a bid to distract from his own disaster, Essex played up Southampton's minor achievement. Essex had also knighted Southampton during the voyage.

Elizabeth was now furious at her naval commander, so Essex sequestered himself in his house and claimed to be sick. Essex's sometime secretary Sir Henry Wotton later recalled that in times of trouble Essex was known to "evaporate his thoughts in a sonnet (being his common way)."

Essex was hardly a poet for the ages. What little verse of his that survives reveals Essex to be technically proficient and clearly learned–but incapable of and probably uninterested in divining such apolitical matters as the nature of truth, beauty, or the depths of the soul. Essex wrote sonnets for political reasons–to impress his queen and courtly colleagues and to advance his own causes. Upon returning from the Azores, Essex had, it appears, begun to write sonnets in praise of the mission's single success story: the earl of Southampton.

This conclusion emerges from Shake-speare's Sonnets 78–86, sometimes called the "Rival Poet series." Essex fits Shake-speare's description of the mysterious adversarial poet vying for the immortal beloved's attentions.

79

Whilst I alone did call upon thy aid
My verse alone had all thy gentle grace.
But now my gracious numbers [*sonnets*] are decayed,
And my sick Muse doth give another place.
I grant, sweet love, thy lovely argument
Deserves the travail of a worthier pen,
Yet what of thee thy poet doth invent
He robs thee of and pays it thee again.
He lends thee virtue, and he stole that word
From thy behavior; beauty doth he give
And found it in thy cheek; he can afford
No praise to thee but what in thee doth live.
    Then thank him not for that which he doth say,
    Since what he owes thee thou thyself dost pay.

80

O how I faint when I of you do write,
Knowing a better spirit doth use your name,
And in the praise thereof spends all his might,
To make me tongue tied speaking of your fame.
But, since your worth, wide as the ocean is,

> The humble as the proudest sail doth bear,
> My saucy bark, inferior far to his,
> On your broad main doth willfully appear.
> Your shallowest help will hold me up afloat,
> Whilst he upon your soundless deep doth ride;
> Or, being wracked, I am a worthless boat,
> He of tall building and goodly pride.
> > Then, if he thrive and I be cast away,
> > The worst was this: My love was my decay.

De Vere, fed up with a tempter who had already enticed his daughter away from his son-in-law's marriage bed, was not going to stand by as Essex pulled Southampton ever farther away. De Vere acknowledges Essex's prowess as a naval commander (his is "the proudest sail") and Essex's "tall building [*stature*] and goodly pride." Like the ailing de Vere, the newly returned Essex draws his inspiration from a "sick Muse." De Vere puns on Essex's family mottoes ("Virtue With Envy" and "Loyalty the Basis of Virtue") by noting that the Rival Poet "stole that word [*virtue*]/From thy behavior." De Vere also plays upon Essex's recently granted monopoly on cochineal, a red dye used in cosmetics. Portraits of Essex from this period show the sitter unabashed in his use of makeup on the face and lips. Sonnet 83 begins, "I never saw that you [*Southampton*] did painting need."

The concluding couplet to Sonnet 79 states de Vere's argument against Essex: You don't owe Essex any thanks or attention because of his praise of you; your plunder of the Spanish man-of-war was practically the only saving grace of the entire Azores mission.

Yet no mere words from de Vere's pen could convince Southampton to stay his outbound course. De Vere continues to chronicle Southampton's slippage into the Essex camp, a camp that was growing ever more paranoid. Essex's chief intelligence officer at the time was a scholar named Anthony Bacon, brother of the famous philosopher Francis. Sonnet 86 observes how the Rival Poet had lately been "gulled" with nightly intelligence briefings—a Latin pun on the name Bacon. (The gull family is called *laridae;* the Latin for *bacon* is *larida.*)

86

> Was it the proud full sail of his great verse,
> Bound for the prize of all too precious you,
> That did my ripe thoughts in my brain inhearse,
> Making their tomb the womb wherein they grew?
> Was it his spirit, by spirits taught to write
> Above a mortal pitch, that struck me dead?
> No, neither he, nor his compeers by night

Giving him aid, my verse astonishèd.
He, nor that affable familiar ghost,
Which nightly gulls him with intelligence,
As victors, of my silence cannot boast;
I was not sick of any fear from thence.
    But when your countenance filled up his line,
    Then lacked I matter, that enfeebled mine.

As the Christmas season of 1597 approached, the opposition between the Cecil and Essex factions grew deeper and the outlines starker. No doubt hoping to escape the intensifying courtly infighting, Southampton prepared to take flight, securing a two-year license from the queen for foreign travel. The next sonnet after the Rival Poet series, Sonnet 87, begins, "Farewell, thou art too dear for my possessing."

At this time, de Vere himself was also withdrawing even further from court life. The queen had summoned Parliament in October 1597, but de Vere assumed his place in the House of Lords only once during the entire four-month session, on December 14, 1597. It would be his last day ever as an MP.

Sometime in 1597, de Vere, his wife, and their four-year-old son packed their trunks and horse carts and moved to the suburban village of Hackney. Their new £3,300 home, King's Place (later Brooke House), would be held in a joint trust that included the countess, her brother Francis, and her cousin Ralph Snead. De Vere was kept out of the ownership circle, no doubt to insulate the family domicile from any more unexpected lawsuits or carping creditors.

King's Place, while spacious, was no Fisher's Folly or Castle Hedingham. The structure sat on a quarter-acre-sized footprint and was originally constructed for William Worsley, a fifteenth-century curate of St. Paul's Chapel. Worsley had adorned his residence with a holy painting of himself kneeling before St. Peter; he also decorated a nearby wall jamb with emblems of the Tudor Rose. Henry VIII's principal minister, Thomas Cromwell, had later occupied King's Place, as did the former Lord Chamberlain Henry Carey, Lord Hunsdon.

Lord Hunsdon had engraved his family arms and emblems on the ceiling of a long second-floor gallery that overlooked King's Place's courtyard on one side and the backyard gardens and lawn on the other. Ironically, in one of the rooms where de Vere would have prepared and revised plays to be handed off to the Lord Chamberlain's Men, the Lord Chamberlain's menagerie of heraldic horses, bulls, swans, and stags looked down from their overhead perches. Unable to afford his own rich engravings of boars, stars, and other earl of Oxford emblems, de Vere nevertheless left his own mark on the gallery space, temporary though it was. An early seventeenth-century inventory of

King's Place reveals that the great parlor was adorned with a blue-and-yellow military banner (a "hanging of blewe and yellow seigne"). Oxford blue and Reading tawny (yellow) were the heraldic colors of the house of de Vere.

In King's Place's "little parlor"–probably de Vere's private study–one noteworthy item caught the eye of the man conducting the house's inventory: "A story of the rich man and death." (The word *story* here refers to a now-antiquated definition, meaning a painting or sculpture that depicts a narrative or historical scene.) The independent American scholar Gerit Quealy has recently discovered an inventory at the National Portrait Gallery in London for a painting that is probably the "story" in question. The 51.5-by-50.5-cm panel presents a pictorial allegory of

> a rich young nobleman and old man holding a skull and prayer book facing each other across a table containing a rhyming morality verse, surmounted by a winged figure of Father Time flanked by four more tablets, containing further admonitory verses, a skull on the floor before them....
>
> It has been suggested that the figure of the young nobleman... bears a good resemblance to the [Wellbeck] portrait of Edward de Vere, 17th Earl of Oxford, dated 1575 in the National Portrait Gallery, London.

It's appropriate that the rooms at King's Place that posterity knows most about are the quiet rooms–the places of study, contemplation, and writing. King's Place was no "Silexedra" for its guest list. Afternoons would have been much quieter than the tavernlike atmosphere that had prevailed at the Folly. De Vere could no longer afford his extravagant 1580s lifestyle, but he was also no longer a man fleeing an unhappy marriage, and his deteriorating health would probably have made him a tankard-of-ale-with-supper sort of man. The roistering was only going on in his imagination.

By the time of the King's Place move, de Vere's former secretaries and close literary associates John Lyly and Thomas Nashe had plenty of troubles of their own to worry about. In 1597 Nashe was practically in exile. Never known for his propriety, Nashe and the rapscallion poet-playwright Ben Jonson had, in 1597, collaborated on a satire, *The Isle of Dogs,* so politically explosive that it shut the theaters down. *The Isle of Dogs,* "a lewd plaie... contaynynge very seditious and sclanderous [*sic*] matter," remains one of the great unknowns in the history of the Elizabethan theater. It was never printed, nor has it been preserved in any manuscript yet discovered. For his offense, Jonson was thrown in jail. Nashe fled to Great Yarmouth in Norfolkshire.

Lyly spent practically the entire 1590s applying for and never receiving the mastership of the revels. Lyly had married, had a son, and was living to the northwest of the London city wall, near Aldersgate. He disappears almost completely from the historical records during this period. Lyly might have been quietly continuing to serve in his secretarial post for his longtime employer—or not.

The same ambiguity plagues the late 1590s activities of de Vere's other longtime secretary, Anthony Munday. Munday, aged thirty-seven in 1597, remained on friendly terms with de Vere, although whether their relationship was simply collegial or more formal remains uncertain. What is known but hard to explain without de Vere is the fact that Munday published two English translations under the pseudonym "Lazarus Piot" in 1595 and '96. (In the biblical parable of Lazarus and the rich man, Lazarus is lame and sickly; *piot* is northland slang for "saucy chatterbox.") One of the two "Lazarus" publications represented part of Munday's ongoing project to Anglicize the continental Primaleon and Palmerin series of chivalric romances—a primary source for *The Tempest.* The other "Lazarus" translation, published in English in 1596, was Alexandre Sylvain's rhetorical guidebook *The Orator.* Sylvain's *Orator* recalls, among other tales, the legend of a Jew who insists upon a pound of flesh as his form of payment from a Christian debtor; another of Sylvain's tales concerns a ravished maid who demands first that her rapist be made her husband and then that he be sentenced to death—the same punishment advocated by the DUKE in *Measure for Measure.* The complete works of "Lazarus Piot," two books that inspired at least three Shake-speare plays, may still have come from Munday's pen. But as with the Euphues series, de Vere would have been the motivating force. Or perhaps "Piot" represents the combined efforts of a secretary and the man who had once employed him.

De Vere's only known secretary during his later years was the philosopher Nicholas Hill. Hill was ridiculed around London as the leading advocate of Democritus's atomic philosophy. The scientist and skeptic was just the sort of maverick thinker—like Nashe or the Paracelsian physician John Baker—whom de Vere indulged. *Romeo and Juliet* and *As You Like It* both toy with Hill's "atomies" as nature's unit of irreducible smallness, while PORTIA fuses Hill's atomism with a meditation on the immortality of the human soul:

> PORTIA There's not the smallest orb which thou behold'st
>   But in his motion like an angel sings,
>   Still quiring to the young-eyed cherubins;
>   Such harmony is in immortal souls.
>   But whilst this muddy vesture of decay
>   Doth grossly close it in, we cannot hear it.

Rude reminders of mortality were no mere poetic conceit at the time of de Vere's move to King's Place. "I have not an able body," he wrote in a letter to Robert Cecil in September 1597. De Vere must have known that he and his wife were settling in to the home in which he would die.

Yet, the grim reaper was preparing to harvest another crop much sooner. In the summer of 1598, Lord Burghley, age seventy-seven and suffering from painful attacks of the gout, took to his bed to ease his way into death. During the spring and early summer, Burghley had been negotiating for peace with Spain in the Lowlands, a position that the earl of Essex would hear nothing of. In one of his final acts on the Privy Council, Burghley had taken in his arthritic hand a Psalter and held up Psalm 55:23 to Essex: "The bloody and deceitful men shall not live out half their days." The queen, who had never known a time on the throne without her "Sir Spirit," came to Burghley's bedside and fed him with her own hand.

Burghley's climb to political dominance and steady accumulation of influence, titles, lands, and offices had been stunning in its magnitude. From the time of Henry VIII, William Cecil had advanced through a half century in government to become the preeminent nonroyal political power of his day. Life as Burghley's ward and son-in-law may have been a macabre game of duck and dodge. But practically all that de Vere now had, he owed to that fading nova of omnipotence. The very world the lame and despised de Vere now inhabited was in no small part Burghley's bequest. Burghley's private library, one of the greatest in Elizabethan England, had provided inspiration for the works of Shake-speare, and the tutors Burghley had hired for de Vere had shaped his thought and character.

The meddlesome Lord Burghley may be most notoriously commemorated in Shake-speare as POLONIUS, but let it not be said that de Vere could only speak ill of his guardian and father-in-law. *The Tempest*'s ailing sorcerer, PROSPERO–representing de Vere in his final days–has nothing but generous words for the play's kindly and doddering court counselor GONZALO. And PROSPERO remembers GONZALO for the most important gift anyone ever gave him–the written word.

> PROSPERO A noble Neapolitan, GONZALO,
>   Out of his charity . . . did give us–with
>   Rich garments, linens, stuffs, and necessaries
>   Which since have steaded much–so of his gentleness,
>   Knowing I lov'd my books, he furnish'd me
>   From mine own library with volumes that
>   I prize above my dukedom.

On August 4, the great Lord Treasurer breathed his last. "Serve God by serving of the queen; for all other service is indeed bondage to the devil," he implored his son Robert in his final handwritten letter. The queen had never been so bereaved. For months, she could not even hear the name of her faithful Sir Spirit without bursting into sobs.

The recent widower Robert Cecil had lost the closest confidant he would ever have. A profound religious faith had always anchored Burghley's moral beliefs. But the thirty-five-year-old Sir Robert had no such ethical bedrock on which to build his world. Religion was, like everything else in Robert Cecil's life, about power.

Lord Burghley's passing would effectively remove his son Robert's muzzle. Payback time was nigh.

In 1597, the play *Richard III* had first appeared in print. The analogy between Shake-speare's humpbacked usurper and the power-hungry Robert Cecil was hardly obscure and not hard to apprehend. Common libelers, for instance, were fond of comparisons between Cecil and Richard III. ("Richard [III] or Robin [Cecil], which was the worse?/ A crook't back great in state is England's curse," etc.) And although *Richard III* appears to have been printed without the author's permission, its appearance in London bookstalls could not have been more poorly timed for de Vere.

A tantalizing cover page for a circa-1597 manuscript of *Richard III*–and a number of other controversial works–has survived the centuries and now sits in the archives of Alnwick Castle in Northumberland. The manuscripts for which this page serves as the cover have all, however, been lost or destroyed. The one-page document is a list of seditious or surreptitiously obtained texts: *Richard III*, *Richard II* (treasonously depicting the deposition of a sitting monarch), Nashe and Jonson's *Isle of Dogs*, and the libelous *Leicester's Commonwealth*.

On this single surviving sheet, a scrivener, whose handwriting has never been identified, scratched out two words that would henceforth be seared into the flesh of every mature play from de Vere's pen. There on a single page, scattered amid sundry sentence fragments, quotes, and titles, are written the words "Willi...Sh...Sh...Shak...will Shak...Shakespe...Shakspeare...Shake-speare...william...william Shakespeare...William Shakespeare."

"Thence comes it," in the words of Sonnet 111, "that my name receives a brand." Robert Cecil's ex-brother-in-law, who had so tormented Cecil's sister, who had so skewered Cecil's father onstage, who had so debased the court with his lewd and scandalous plays, would finally be getting his just deserts. Will Shakspere, now devoting more time in the country to his newly purchased Stratford-upon-Avon mansion New Place, was about to become more famous than he could have imagined.

Lacking the approval of the state censors at the Stationer's Company, sometime in 1598 Cuthbert Burby–publisher of one of the "Lazarus Piot" books–presented posterity with the first dramatic publication under the Shake-speare byline. It was titled *A Pleasant Conceited Comedy Called Love's Labor's Lost...Newly corrected and augmented by W. Shakespere* [sic]. "Shakespeare" was no longer another short-lived pseudonym like "Pasquill Caviliero" or "Lazarus Piot." "Shakespeare" was now a poet *and* playwright.

In the fall of the same year, Burby published another book crucial to the genesis of Shake-speare. This one was approved by the state censors. The rector Francis Meres's *Palladis Tamia . . . : A Treasury of Divine, Moral, and Philosophical Similes and Sentences, Generally Useful* (1598) served as something of a *Farmer's Almanac* for the educated and well-to-do Londoner.

One chapter of *Palladis Tamia* gathers an assortment of sixteenth-century English literary criticism, drawing heavily from the anonymous 1589 book *The Art of English Poesie*–the one that praised de Vere's skills as a comic playwright and secret court poet. Meres makes slavish analogies between the ancients and the latter-day English writers. For instance:

> As the Greek tongue is made famous and eloquent by Homer, Hesiod, Euripides, Aeschylus, Sophocles, Pindarus, Phocylides, and Aristophanes and the Latin tongue by Virgil, Ovid, Horace . . . [*etc.*], so the English tongue is mightily enriched and gorgeously invested in rare ornaments and resplendent habiliments by Sir Philip Sidney, [Edmund] Spenser, [Samuel] Daniel, [Michael] Drayton, [W.] Warner, Shakespeare, [Christopher] Marlowe, and [George] Chapman.

In the words of Don Cameron Allen, the editor of the modern edition of Meres's treatise, *Palladis Tamia's* chapter on poetry is "pseudoerudition and bluff." Meres's compilation would never merit consideration today were it not for one additional fact: *Palladis Tamia* is the first book of literary criticism that mentioned Shake-speare as a dramatist.

> As the soul of Euphorbus was thought to live in Pythagoras, so the sweet witty soul of Ovid lives in mellifluous and honey-tongued Shakespeare: Witness his *Venus and Adonis,* his *Lucrece,* his sugared sonnets among his private friends, &c.
>
> As Plautus and Seneca are accounted the best for comedy and tragedy among the Latins, so Shakespeare among the English is the most excellent in both kinds for the stage: Witness for comedy *Gentlemen of Verona, Errors, Love's Labor's Lost, Love's Labor's Won, Midsummer Night's Dream, Merchant of Venice.* For tragedy: *Richard the 2, Richard the 3, Henry the 4, King John, Titus Andronicus, Romeo and Juliet.*

This list of eleven Shake-speare plays plus the mysterious *"Love's Labor's Won,"* like the "upstart crow" passage in *Greene's Groatsworth of Wit,* is in practically every Shake-speare textbook ever written.

Orthodox scholars treat the above passage as if it were a comprehensive listing of the entirety of the Shake-speare canon in 1598–as if plays that Meres did not mention must ipso facto have been written sometime after Meres's book was published.

Yet by 1598, the poet Michael Drayton had written at least nine works; Meres neglects to mention four of them. More generally, Meres was hardly in a position to make original observations about any author. Meres's treatise on poetry was only one small part of a seven-hundred-page book. As Meres's modern editor has demonstrated, Meres's classical quotes came from a quotation dictionary; his information about classical and neoclassical authors came from a schoolboy's textbook; practically every statement Meres made about an English author came from another critic; and Meres doesn't seem to have minded that inevitable clashes of opinion and fact arose from his multiple and conflicting sources.

One of Meres's lists proclaims "Edward, earle of Oxford" as first for comedy–just as he was cited in *The Arte of English Poesie*–while farther down "Shakespeare" is mentioned as another fine comic playwright. Thus it is often said that Meres disproves that de Vere could have been Shake-speare–because Meres implies that Shake-speare and de Vere were two different people.

Yet, even setting aside Meres's questionable authority, mistaking a pseudonym or literary alter ego for a distinct author is not an uncommon error in the history of literary criticism and accolades. Late nineteenth-century editors of *Who's Who*, for instance, wrote separate biographical entries for the authors William Sharp and Fiona Macleod, although they were the same person. The names Joseph Shearing, Marjorie Bowen, George R. Preedy, John Winch, and Robert Payne were all pseudonyms for Margaret Vere Campbell Long, and each of Campbell Long's bylines occasioned its own separate entry in publishers' lists or *Who's Who*. When Stephen King published his novel *Thinner* under the pseudonym Richard Bachman in 1984, one reviewer praised the work as "what Stephen King would write if Stephen King could write." In 1953, screenwriter Ian McLellan Hunter won the Academy Award for Best Story for the movie *Roman Holiday;* but McLellan Hunter was just a front man for the blacklisted screenwriter Dalton Trumbo.

In perhaps the most extreme example of confused literary identities in Western history, the Portuguese poet Fernando Pessoa (1888–1935) wrote under as many as seventy-five different pseudonyms in his lifetime. Some of his alter egos were literary critics who lambasted the work of some of his other alter egos. Pessoa had great, puckish fun with his sheaf of alternative identities– creating biographies for each. Pessoa's master poet "Alberto Caeiro" was born in Lisbon in 1889 and "committed suicide" in 1915. "Caeiro"'s disciple "Ricardo Reis" was two years older than "Caeiro," while "Caeiro"'s other disciple "Alvaro de Campos" was three years younger. These two critics often vehemently disagreed on the proper interpretation of the works of their late lamented master. "Reis" eventually gave up on literature, became a physician, and moved to Brazil.

ᶜᵚᵌ

In a series of books published in 1597 and '98, two scolding Elizabethan satirists named Joseph Hall and John Marston blasted a scurrilous poet whom they dubbed "Labeo." The problem with criticizing Labeo, Hall said, was that Labeo laughed at his detractors from behind a protective screen.

> Labeo is whip't, and laughs me in the face.
> Why?...
> Who list complain of wronged faith or fame
> When he may shift it to another's name?

Marston gives the reader a clue to Labeo's identity. Labeo, Marston notes, once wrote that "his love was stone: Obdurate, flinty, so relentless none." This is a quote from line 199 of *Venus and Adonis*. ("Art thou obdurate, flinty, hard as steel?")

"Labeo" is Shake-speare.

But if de Vere was laughing at anybody's attempts to criticize and unmask him, the mirth was just clown's-mirth, fool's-mirth. The *Sonnets,* the closest there is to Shake-speare's private diaries, reveal the complexity of the author's relationship to "Will." "Will" had taken over from Edward. "Will" was no longer de Vere's to control. "Will," a thing of his own creation, had taken over the very creatures of his brain. But mixed with the outrage and horror was some degree of fascination. De Vere had always been in love with the brink, the uncontrollable, the extreme. Now, one last time, it had found him.

De Vere probably wrote the following two salacious sonnets to the queen, sardonically cursing his fate as a politically compromised author, whose courtly exposés could only be published under the disguise of a common "Will":

135

> Who ever hath her wish, thou hast thy *Will,*
> And *Will* to boot, and *Will* in overplus;
> More than enough am I that vex thee still,
> To thy sweet will making addition thus.
> Wilt thou, whose will is large and spacious,
> Not once vouchsafe to hide my will in thine?
> Shall will in others seem right gracious
> And in my will no fair acceptance shine?
> The sea, all water, yet receives rain still,
> And in abundance addeth to his store;
> So thou being rich in *Will* add to thy *Will*
> One more will of ruin to make thy large *Will* more.
> > Let no unkind, no fair beseechers kill;
> > Think all but one, and me in that one *Will.*

136

If thy soul check thee that I come so near
Swear to thy blind soul that I was thy *Will*,
And will thy soul knows is admitted there;
Thus far for love, my love-suit sweet fulfill.
Will will fulfill the treasure of thy love,
Ay, fill it full with wills—and my will one.
In things of great receipt with ease we prove
Among a number one is reckoned none.
Then in the number let me pass untold,
Though in thy store's account I must one be.
For nothing hold me, so it please thee hold
That nothing me, a something sweet to thee.

    Make but my name thy love, and love that still
    And then thou lov'st me, for my name is *Will*.

[Emphases in original]

CHAPTER 11

BURIED BE

[1598–1604]

T HAT LOVELY BOY WHOM DE VERE HAD DOTED OVER—AND EVEN, AS suggested previously, forgiven for an affair with his wife—had been in Paris since February 1598. Southampton's mistress, Essex's cousin Elizabeth Vernon, had become visibly pregnant by the late summer. Southampton, enjoying a lusty bachelor's French vacation at the time, sneaked back into England in August (the same month Lord Burghley died) long enough to marry Vernon. Then Southampton returned to his wanton life in Paris. Sir Robert Cecil sent Southampton a letter on September 3, noting that the queen had learned about Southampton's clandestine marriage and demanded that he return to England immediately. Southampton, with heavy gambling debts in Paris, postponed his return.

The *Sonnets* chronicle de Vere's reaction to this sex scandal involving his beloved youth. "Thou didst forsake me for some fault," Sonnet 89 laments. Sonnet 92 taunts, "But do thy worst to steal thyself away"—dating, one suspects, to Southampton's brief return to England in August for a sub rosa marriage followed by a hasty departure. Sonnet 95 notes the "beauty of thy budding name"—a reference to Southampton's budding wife. The shameful Parisian escapades lamented in Sonnets 87–96 are then followed by Southampton's return to England and swift imprisonment on or around November 11, as described in Sonnet 97

97

How like a winter hath my absence been
From thee, the pleasure of the fleeting year!
What freezings have I felt, what dark days seen!
What old December's bareness everywhere!

> And yet this time removed was summer's time,
> The teeming autumn big with rich increase,
> Bearing the wanton burthen of the prime,
> Like widowed wombs after their lords' decease.
> Yet this abundant issue seemed to me
> But hope of orphans, and unfathered fruit;
> For summer and his pleasures wait on thee,
> And thou away, the very birds are mute;
>> Or if they sing, 'tis with so dull a cheer,
>> That leaves look pale, dreading the winter's near.

Sonnet 98 notes that Southampton was also absent "when proud-pied April, dressed in all his trim,/ Hath put a spirit of youth in everything." Southampton had indeed been missing from England and from de Vere's life during the spring, summer, and fall of 1598. The newlywed but as yet still abandoned countess of Southampton delivered a daughter on November 8– explaining the comparison to "widowed wombs." And the autumn of 1598 was indeed "teeming" twice over–both in that Southampton was now father to a newborn infant and that England's harvest that year had been unusually bountiful.

Southampton did not stick around England long after his November return. In April 1599, Southampton joined the officer corps leading troops into Ireland. Irish rebels, led by the earl of Tyrone, had won a decisive victory the previous year over occupying English forces at Armagh. The Irish populace, spurred on by Tyrone's upset victory, was soon bristling with rebellion. Only an extreme show of English force was going to keep Ireland an English territory. Southampton's friend Essex had at first balked at the opportunity to lead the Irish military expedition. His previous sorties to Cádiz and the Azores had left a power vacuum, which Robert Cecil and his minions were only too glad to fill. Every time Essex returned from an overseas mission, he was feted at a court in which he wielded less and less power. Yet, the temptation to serve once more as England's glorious soldier was too great. Southampton, it was rumored, would be Essex's second-in-command, serving as general of the horse.

De Vere held long-standing sympathies for the Irish rebels. The Arundell Libels of 1581 tell of de Vere's admiration for the Irish patriots Viscount Baltinglas and Nicolas Sanders–the latter of whom *Henry VI, Part 2,* jestingly memorializes as "Saunder Simpcox." And, as de Vere's previously quoted April 1595 letter to Robert Cecil shows, de Vere was also no friend of Essex.

De Vere must thus have felt torn. A mewling buccaneer-*cum*-nobleman named Essex was about to lead an expedition against a sympathetic Irish foe. If this had been the whole story, de Vere might well have gotten himself into trouble rooting for the Irish. But one factor made the 1599 Irish expedition a very different situation. Southampton would be in danger.

Around this time, Robert Bertie (son of Peregrine and de Vere's sister Mary) wrote his uncle an affectionate letter in French referring to de Vere's *"plus serieux affaires."* These *affaires* had been, one suspects, what the *Sonnets* would call "spending old words new"–rewriting his courtly and Queen's Men's interludes of years past.

Sometime during the first half of 1599, scholars concur that the Lord Chamberlain's Men performed Shake-speare's *Henry V* at the newly constructed Globe Theatre on the south bank of the Thames. *Henry V*–probably first written during the 1570s and later played by the Queen's Men as *The Famous Victories of Henry V*–expressed the public, propagandistic side of de Vere's feelings about the Essex expedition to Ireland. It was a prayer for the success of Essex's, and therefore Southampton's, mission.

The CHORUS to Shake-speare's *Henry V* notes:

> Were now the general of our gracious empress,
> As in good time he may, from Ireland coming,
> Bringing rebellion broached on his sword,
> How many would the peaceful city quit
> To welcome him!

And Londoners did indeed throng the streets to give the warriors a royal send-off. The largest army Queen Elizabeth had ever sent abroad made their way westward out of London through a gauntlet of cheering subjects. De Vere's mixed feelings must have made the farewell bittersweet.

But de Vere would again turn toward his muse to express his more private feelings about Essex in the Shake-speare play *Coriolanus*. The correlation between the historical Roman general Caius Marcius Coriolanus and the earl of Essex was not unheard of at the time. The Elizabethan prelate William Barlow would later famously compare Essex to Coriolanus in a sermon at Paul's Cross. (The play *Coriolanus* may well be what Essex was referring to when in 1600 he wrote to Elizabeth, "They print me and make me speak to the world, and shortly they will play me on the stage.")

Coriolanus is rarely performed today, in part because the protagonist, the least sympathetic in the Shake-speare canon, is so snobbish and unappealing. Audience members often find themselves disappointed in Shake-speare's story, because the play leaves them indifferent to whether the hero lives or dies. But *Coriolanus* is one of the more unjustly neglected works of Shake-speare. Once one appreciates that de Vere disliked the man who inspired CORIOLANUS, then the nature of the story turns upside down.

Read as a classical tragedy, wherein deadly human flaws lead a sympathetic protagonist into the inferno, *Coriolanus* is an artistic failure. However, if one instead reads *Coriolanus* as a darkly comic critique that intentionally strips all ennobling qualities from its hero, the play becomes a devilish satire of the entire genre of tragedy—and of Essex, in particular, as a man incapable of rising to tragic grandeur. "It is," George Bernard Shaw once quipped, "the greatest of Shakespeare's comedies."

Coriolanus recites the history, as recorded in Plutarch's *Lives,* of a military conqueror from the days of the Roman Republic. The title character is an arrogant general who leads a victorious force against a foreign uprising. The parallels between the plot of *Coriolanus* and Essex's Irish expedition and its aftermath are, in the words of the twentieth-century Shakespearean actor Robert Speaight, "unmistakable." Essex's haughtiness and irksome sense of infinite entitlement are sarcastically mirrored in the Roman soldier-statesman who berates a starving mob as

> CORIOLANUS ... dissentious rogues
>   That, rubbing the poor itch of your opinions,
>   Make yourself scabs.

CORIOLANUS's trusty aged friend MENENIUS recites the twisted moral of the play in the first scene.

> MENENIUS There was a time when all the body's members
>   Rebell'd against the belly. . . .
>   The senators of Rome are this good belly,
>   And you the mutinous members: For examine
>   Their counsels and their cares, digest things rightly
>   Touching the weal o'th'common, you shall find
>   No public benefit which you receive
>   But it proceeds or comes from them to you,
>   And no way from yourselves. What do you think,
>   You, the great toe of this assembly?

In Plutarch's original version of the Coriolanus story, the historical Menenius also recites a fable of the belly—but in a very different context. Here, as a patronizing jeremiad intended to quiet a crowd of starving Romans, MENENIUS's fable of the belly is gruesome. It's so cruel that it's comic for a self-satisfied patrician with a full stomach to tell a crowd of starving people that their problems will go away if they just "digest things rightly."

Shake-speare had found his late voice, that complex and contradictory amalgam of misanthrope and humanist. The earls of Essex and Southampton and the politics of Elizabeth's last years were proving to be almost as much of an inspiration for growth and great art as de Vere's hellish first marriage—no small accomplishment.

Sometime during May or June of 1599, de Vere's second child by Anne was married. Bridget de Vere, now age fifteen, had gone through nearly as many prospective grooms as had her older sister, the countess of Derby. Two years before, in 1597, Bridget had been engaged to a son of the Brooke family. Shortly thereafter, Bridget had been matched with William Herbert, son of Mary Sidney Herbert, countess of Pembroke. Mary, sister to the late Sir Philip Sidney, was a munificent literary patron and talented versifier with whom de Vere was friendly. One of de Vere's letters indicates he was keen on this match–he was very fond of the Herbert family and wrote that the prospective groom "hath been well brought up, fair conditioned, and hath many good parts in him." But Bridget's potential alliance with the Herbert clan had also fallen through.

Instead, Bridget's husband was to be the twenty-year-old aspiring politician Francis Norris, a hothead who would years later fight a duel with Peregrine Bertie junior "upon an old reckoning." The de Vere–Norris wedding was an understated affair due to the recent passing of Lord Burghley, who cast a long shadow in death as in life.

Soon after saying "I do," Norris raced off to the Continent and left his blushing bride behind. Bridget had wound up with a husband who, all too like her father, would become the absentee man in her life.

During the summer of 1599, word came from Ireland that Essex's mission was proving to be a disaster. Essex had been running through his supplies and cash like a spoiled child on holiday. Elizabeth quipped that she'd given her commander "a thousand pounds a day to go on progress."

Moreover, before Essex departed in the spring, the queen had rebuked him for attempting to appoint Southampton to the position of general of the horse. Her Majesty had made it clear, or so she thought, that Essex's best friend would be receiving no such promotion. But when the battalions disembarked onto Irish soil, Essex gave Southampton the generalship anyway.

That was a mistake. Queen Elizabeth may have become a parody of her youthful self by 1599. But behind that perfumed suck-handkerchief and beneath that powdered wig operated the same strategic genius that had led a nation from crisis and irrelevance to power and consequence. Elizabeth sent a rebuke across the Irish Sea, demoting Southampton. In response, the petulant Essex abolished the post of general of the horse altogether.

In August, although Essex expressed grand intentions of attacking the rebel earl of Tyrone at his Ulster stronghold, the only conquest the invading English army made was five hundred cows and sixty garrans (small Irish horses). The embarrassment continued into the fall. In September, Essex and Tyrone met in a secret conference at the ford of Bellaclynthe. The two commanders, who should have been leading forces against each other, instead agreed to a truce that allowed Tyrone to keep his rebel positions and prohibited the English from building any new forts or garrisons. It is difficult to understand how Essex could have felt good about this settlement. Tyrone was only biding time. Reinforcements were on their way from Spain to Ireland.

Elizabeth was, naturally, furious. When she learned of Essex's hastily brokered accord, she dispatched another blistering letter, reminding her commander that he had abused his authority once again. She noted that unless English garrisons could be stationed around Ireland, Essex had only thrown together a "hollow peace."

De Vere must have watched with wonder at Essex's astonishing devolution. The forty-nine-year-old earl of Oxford had come to know the many different flavors and varieties of royal shame and disapproval. But nothing de Vere had experienced compared with this. As recently as 1597, when Essex was still the celebrated hero of Cádiz, the clouds parted when he strolled through the courtly sky. But now, after having embarrassed himself in the failed Azores mission, having regularly disobeyed the queen's orders, and having led an Irish expedition that spewed money like a geyser, Essex was a body in free fall.

To make matters more interesting, the Elizabethan gossip William Reynolds reported at the time that, in the sexually charged environment of war, Southampton had begun to dote upon one Pierce Edmonds. Reynolds, who had served under Essex and Southampton in Ireland, said:

> Pierce Edmonds . . . ate and drank at [Southampton's] table and lay in his tent. The earl of Southampton gave him a horse. . . . The earl [of] Southampton would cole [*embrace*] and hug him in his arms and play wantonly with him.

Troilus and Cressida, which is perhaps Shake-speare's most murky and impenetrable play, presents a likely portrait of Southampton's situation in the form of two Grecian officers who are part of the force besieging the city of Troy. ACHILLES and his fellow commander PATROCLUS represent Shake-speare's one same-sex friendship, outside of OTHELLO and IAGO's troubled relationship, that is touched with intimations of homosexuality. Rather than fight and serve honorably with their fellow Grecians, ACHILLES and PATROCLUS prefer to while away the days in their tent, privately enjoying each other's pleasures. *Troilus and Cressida*'s railing satirist THERSITES spells out the rumors against ACHILLES and PATROCLUS

> THERSITES [to PATROCLUS] Thou art said to be ACHILLES's male varlet.
> PATROCLUS Male varlet, you rogue? What's that?
> THERS. Why, his masculine whore. Now the rotten diseases of the
>   south [*venereal diseases*] . . . take and take again such preposterous
>   discoveries!

PATRO. Why, thou damnable box of envy, thou, what means thou to curse thus?

THERS. Do I curse thee?

PATRO. Why, no, you ruinous butt, you whoreson indistinguishable cur, no.

THERS. No? Why art thou then exasperate, thou idle immaterial skein of sleeve silk, thou green sarsenet [*fine silk*] flap for a sore eye, thou tassel of a prodigal's purse, thou!

THERSITES calls PATROCLUS a varlet and a femme, and PATROCLUS makes no effort to refute the charge. He just returns the vitriol in kind.

Elizabethan authors had equated Essex with the legendary figure of Achilles at least four times in the preceding five years, so no doubt de Vere was displacing some of his resentment toward Southampton onto a man he already disliked. In *Troilus and Cressida*'s Greek officers' camp, then, Southampton's alleged sexual dalliances with a fellow officer become an accusation of degenerate and improper conduct against Essex himself. (One might read ACHILLES as Essex and PATROCLUS as Southampton or, alternately, ACHILLES as Southampton and PATROCLUS as Pierce Edmonds. Both interpretations would appear to be valid.)

In *Troilus and Cressida*, the idealized officer ULYSSES utters Shake-speare's most eloquent homage to the Elizabethan chain of being: nature's rank and degree for everything and everyone. So it is only fitting that ULYSSES is the one who sits ACHILLES down for a mentoring session about the fleeting nature of courtly favor. De Vere, who probably portrayed himself as ULYSSES in the 1584 court masque *Agamemnon and Ulysses,* knew this lesson from first-hand experience.

ACHILLES What, am I poor of late?
　　'Tis certain, greatness, once fall'n out with fortune,
　　Must fall out with men too. . . .
　　What, are my deeds forgot?
ULYSSES Time hath, my lord, a wallet at his back,
　　Wherein he puts alms for oblivion,
　　A great-siz'd monster of ingratitudes.
　　Those scraps are good deeds past, which are devour'd
　　As fast as they are made, forgot as soon
　　As done. . . .
　　For beauty, wit,
　　High birth, vigor of bone, desert in service,
　　Love, friendship, charity, are subjects all
　　To envious and calumniating Time.
　　One touch of nature makes the whole world kin.

Here, again, where ULYSSES serves as de Vere's mouthpiece, ACHILLES might be seen to represent Essex—although ULYSSES's caring and sage counsel makes it more likely that Southampton was the intended audience.

De Vere probably wrote his dark Trojan satire for a private performance before the court or a select subset of courtiers sometime in 1599. (Although the play was first published in 1609, its first recorded performance was not until 1679.) An anonymous 1599 play, *Histrio-Mastix* ("The player whipped"), spoofs *Troilus and Cressida*. *Histrio-Mastix* features a miniature love scene between two characters named Troilus and Cressida. As if to ensure that the identity of the playwright being burlesqued is entirely clear, the play's "Troilus" speaks of himself in the third person as someone who "shakes his furious spear."

Near the end of *Histrio-Mastix,* the play's character "Poverty" says:

> I scorn a scoffing fool about my throne,
> An artless idiot that like Aesop's dawe [*crow*]
> Plumes [*plucks*] fairer feathered birds. No, Poverty
> Will dignify her chair with deep divines.
> Philosophers and scholars feast with me.

"Poverty" respects philosophers and scholars but scorns an "artless idiot" and "scoffing fool" who disguises himself behind the feathers plucked from other birds. *Greene's Groatsworth of Wit* had said essentially the same thing about Will Shakspere in 1592.

Notice, too, that *Histrio-Mastix* mentions multiple "birds" from whom the "artless idiot" filches feathers. The dramatist and satirist Ben Jonson points to a similar conclusion—that Will Shakspere was stealing from writers other than de Vere. Jonson wrote an epigram circa 1599 about someone he calls a "poet-ape."

> Poor "poet-ape," that would be thought our chief,
> Whose works are even the frippery of wit,
> From brokage [*brokerage*] is become so bold a thief
> As we, the robbed, leave rage and pity it.
> At first he made low shifts, would pick and glean,
> Buy the reversion [*revision*] of old plays. Now grown
> To a little wealth and credit in the scene,
> He takes up all, makes each man's wit his own.
> And told of this, he slights it. "Tut, such crimes
> The sluggish, gaping auditor devours;
> He marks not whose 'twas first, and aftertimes
> May judge it to be his, as well as ours."
>   Fool! as if half-eyes will not know a fleece
>   From locks of wool, or shreds from the whole piece.

One might paraphrase Jonson's sonnet in modern English as follows: The man who many people think is England's finest author (Will Shakspere) is in fact a "poet-ape"—someone whose works are sloughed-off pieces of wit from one or more actual authors. The "poet-ape" began his career as a (play?) broker and then, emboldened, he became an out-and-out play-thief. We playwrights were mad, but we also pity the guy. He used to be sly and would cobble together bits and pieces of plays here and there. But now that he's prominent in the London theatrical scene, he takes an entire play and claims it as his own. When he's confronted with this, he responds that others may figure out who wrote it—or not. But what a fool he is! With one's eyes halfway closed, anyone can easily tell the difference between hanks of wool and a whole fleece, or between mere patches and an entire blanket.

What was Will Shakspere actually doing? There are no company records or playbills from the early days of the Globe, so there's no way of verifying what Will Shakspere said or did during public performances. If one takes Jonson's "Poet-Ape" sonnet literally, Shakspere claimed credit for texts or shreds of text that didn't have an author's name firmly attached. "Poet-ape" Shakspere may have provided publishers with cobbled-together texts for such "bad" Shake-speare quartos as the 1597 first edition of *Romeo and Juliet* and the 1603 first edition of *Hamlet* ("To be or not to be; Ay, there's the point. . . ."). Perhaps part of "poet-ape" Shakspere's job included patching incomplete de Vere scripts together with scenes that were handed off to other playwrights: For centuries critics have suspected other authors' contributions to such lesser Shake-speare plays as *Titus Andronicus, Pericles, Two Noble Kinsmen,* and *Henry VIII.*

In 1599, Ben Jonson wrote a comedy for the Lord Chamberlain's Men called *Every Man Out of His Humor.* Jonson promptly published the play the following year, thereby ape-proofing the text from Shakspere, who might want to "pick and glean" from Jonson's complete and indivisible creation. In a later edition of the play, Jonson advertised which of the Lord Chamberlain's Men performed which roles in his play. Notably missing from Jonson's cast list is Will Shakspere.

This is probably because Jonson savages Will Shakspere in *Every Man Out of His Humor. Every Man Out of His Humor* features a pitiful, buffoonish wannabe named "Sogliardo." Jonson, who prefaced his print edition of the play with descriptions of each character, anatomizes "Sogliardo" thus:

> So enamored of the name of a gentleman that he will have it, though he buys it. He comes up every term to learn to take tobacco and see new motions [*puppet plays*]. He is in his kingdom when he can get himself into company where he may be well laughed at.

In 1596, an application was submitted to London's College of Arms to buy Will Shakspere's father, John, a coat of arms. By 1599, the application had gone through, and Shakspere could style himself a gentleman. The college presented the country landholder with a heraldic crest and a new motto, Not without right *(Non sanz droit)*—sounding suspiciously like an underhanded joke on the part of the granting officer, implying that the arriviste is not *entirely* without a claim to the gentry.

Jonson satirically skewers Shakspere's newly purchased gentlemanhood. In the following scene from *Every Man Out of His Humor*, "Sogliardo" is Shakspere, "Carlo" is Jonson's jester, and "Puntarvolo" is a vainglorious knight and world traveler (who, given that he elsewhere parodies *Romeo and Juliet*'s balcony scene, is probably a spoof on de Vere):

SOGLIARDO [*Shakspere*] By this parchment, gentlemen, I have been so
toiled among the heralds yonder, you will not believe! They do speak
in the strangest language and give a man the hardest terms for his
money that ever you knew.

CARLO [*Jonson*] But have you arms, have you arms?

SOG. I'faith, I thank them. I can write myself gentleman now. Here's my
patent. It cost me thirty pound, by this breath.

PUNTARVOLO [*de Vere?*] A very fair coat, well charged and full of
armory.

SOG. Nay, it has as much variety of colors in it as you have seen a coat
have. How like you the crest, sir?

PUNT. I understand it not well. What is it?

SOG. Marry, sir, it is your boar without a head, rampant. A boar without
a head! That's very rare!

CAR. Ay, and rampant too! I troth, I commend the herald's wit. He has
deciphered him well: a swine without a head, without brain, wit,
anything—indeed, ramping to gentility....

PUNT. Let the word [*motto*] be "NOT WITHOUT MUSTARD." Your crest is
very rare, sir.

"Sogliardo"/Shakspere tells "Puntarvolo"/de Vere that the newly obtained crest contains "*your* boar without a head." This was no idle slip of the pen. With the Shake-speare ruse, de Vere's ancient heraldic crest had been turned into "a swine without a head" and handed over to Shakspere to parade around as his own.

Jonson's "poet-ape" and "Sogliardo" and the "artless idiot" of *Histrio-Mastix* provide just a sampler of the revelations about Shakspere and Shakespeare that appeared in London bookstalls and on London stages near the turn of the century. As society teetered on the brink of social revolution—with England still lacking an heir to the throne, the stilling of the sixty-six-year-old Elizabeth's heart could engender a nationwide religious and political upheaval in a matter of days—the market for explosive and outrageous books and plays mirrored the bizarre and unstable world in which English subjects now lived. New books of railing satires and epigrams had become so outrageous as to make the Nashe–Harvey pamphlet wars of the early 1590s look genteel.

Religious extremists and Puritanical versifiers saw Ovidian poetry such as the pornographic *Venus and Adonis*–which went through two separate editions in 1599 alone–as symbols of the decadence of modern life. Joseph Hall berated "Labeo" (the author Shake-speare) using words that one might associate with a scolding schoolteacher: "For shame! Write better, Labeo, or write none." Another unhinged scribbler was the bluntly named Thomas Bastard. In one of Bastard's epigrams (published in his 1598 collection *Chrestoleros*), no names were named, but Shake-speare is clearly his target: The author Bastard criticizes writes sinful works, is widely admired, and hides behind another man's identity.

> Thou, which deluding raisest up a fame
> And having showed the man, concealest his name,
> Which canst play earnest as it pleaseth thee
> And earnest turn to jest as need shall be,
> Whose good we praise, as being liked of all,
> Whose ill we bear as being natural,
> Thou which art made of vinegar and gall . . .
> Cease, write no more to aggravate thy sin.
> Or, if thou wilt not leave, now I'll begin.

Hall and Bastard were no doubt aware of Shake-speare's latest book. In 1599, *The Passionate Pilgrim by W. Shakespeare* was published, containing sonnets and other poems that revealed de Vere's innermost feelings toward Southampton–potentially perceptible, to the censorious at least, as homosexual feelings.

De Vere must have been angry with the publisher of *The Passionate Pilgrim* (William Jaggard) for sneaking compromising material into print under the Shake-speare imprimatur. Printing works intended for the public stage was one thing, but *The Passionate Pilgrim* was another altogether. De Vere's conflicting feelings about Southampton were certainly not meant to become the fable of the world, at least not during de Vere's lifetime. To add insult to injury, fifteen of *The Passionate Pilgrim*'s twenty poems–all said to be "by W. Shakespeare"–were actually written by other authors. This cobbling together of various surreptitiously obtained patches of verse may well be the handiwork of "poet-ape" Will Shakspere.

One of the poets anthologized in *The Passionate Pilgrim* was Thomas Heywood, a sometime servant to Southampton and a playwright who had worked with de Vere's son-in-law the earl of Derby. Heywood later reflected that his unwitting contributions to *The Passionate Pilgrim* were "not worthy his [*de Vere's*] patronage...so the author I know [was] much offended with Mr. Jaggard—that altogether unknown to him presumed to make bold with his name."

The book publishers, the satirists, and the epigrammatists had all gone too far. During the summer of 1599, the archbishop of Canterbury and bishop of London issued an edict banning Joseph Hall's satires, John Marston's satires, John Davies's epigrams, Thomas Nashe's satires, Gabriel Harvey's books, and many other topical works. All were to be recalled and burned. ("No satires or epigrams [will] be printed hereafter....No English histories [will] be printed except [if] they be allowed by some of Her Majesty's Privy Council....") *Willobie His Avisa*, which had recently reappeared in a pirated edition, was also recalled from London bookstalls.

The very archbishop whose patronage Tom Nashe had once enjoyed had now decreed that "All Nashe's books and Dr. Harvey's books be taken wheresoever they may be found and that none of their books be ever printed hereafter." One can imagine the down-and-out Nashe—who had alienated so many that no one stood up for him anymore, not even de Vere—watching the bonfire of books outside London's Stationer's Hall. As the flames licked into the summer sky, Nashe's life's work turned into anonymous ash. Nashe, who would die in obscurity three years later, must have wondered whether any of his merry jestings with "Gentle Master William" would escape the inferno.

De Vere must have wondered, too, as flames consumed the life's work of the unfortunate authors targeted in the Bishops' Ban, if his own degenerate, sex- and bloodstained works would ultimately survive the torches and press raids of the burgeoning Puritan movement. The fates of Nashe, Harvey, and their ilk issued de Vere a warning written in fire.

On September 24, Essex and Southampton had decided they were through dealing with the troublesome earl of Tyrone; they were through with receiving angry missives from the queen; they were through with her contradicting their orders. Despite specific instructions not to leave Ireland without Her Majesty's permission, Essex, Southampton, and a cadre of other discontented commanders departed for London, leaving their botched military campaign in charge of a junior officer, Sir George Carey, and the archbishop of Dublin.

The decision to desert his command while on active duty was quintessential Essex. He felt he was owed the opportunity to speak with Elizabeth in private, without any Cecilians whispering poisons in her ear. So Essex, not unlike de Vere in the heat of the Spanish Armada campaign, simply left his post. Essex showed up at the royal Nonsuch Palace four days later. He'd left his fellow travelers back in London, thinking it best to keep his controversial sometime general of the horse, Southampton, out of the picture.

It was midmorning when Essex arrived, and without taking time to wash up or change out of his mud-spattered clothes, the once unassailable CORIOLANUS burst into the queen's bedchamber while she was still in her dressing gown. Without her wig or her daily cake of makeup, Elizabeth must have looked as astonishing to the surprise visitor as she was astonished to see him. Still, the queen maintained her composure, listened to what Essex had to say, and bid him good-day.

She would never allow Essex in her presence again. In October the queen had her onetime favorite confined to the chambers of Yorke House. By December, Essex would be under censure by the Star Chamber and all but stripped of his nobility. His household of 160 servants dispersed to find new work.

The Cecil faction could now win the entire game if they could only complete Essex's ruin before his star rose again. De Vere must have feared for his beloved young favorite, damned by association.

During the autumn of 1599, with nothing else to do, Southampton and his friend the earl of Rutland—another former ward from Cecil House—spent their afternoons at the public theaters. (One correspondent wrote to Cecil, in October, that Southampton and Rutland "pass away the tyme in London merely in going to plaies every Day.") The chance diary entry of a Swiss tourist in London in September 1599 records that at the time one of the works onstage at the Globe was the old tragedy *Julius Caesar*—probably first written, as previously noted, about the duke of Guise's 1588 assassination. However, by 1599 de Vere was undoubtedly less interested in the blood sports of princes than in the political force of gravity: that ghostly impulse that tails a man's meteoric rise and drags him ever earthward.

Coriolanus continues to chart Essex's descent. For his haughty irreverence toward the people and the government, Rome's crestfallen general is eventually banished from the state. CORIOLANUS's response mingles de Vere's heartfelt devotion to the ancient feudal order with his satirical impulse to bring low a megalomaniac who had taken the privileges of rank too far.

> CORIOLANUS It is a purpos'd thing, and grows by plot
> To curb the will of the nobility:
> Suffer't, and with such as cannot rule,
> Nor ever will be rul'd....
> My nobler friends,
> I crave their pardons.
> For the mutable, rank-scented meinie [*mob*], let them
> Regard me as I do not flatter, and
> Therein behold themselves. I say again,
> In soothing them, we nourish 'gainst our senate

The cockle of rebellion, insolence, sedition,
Which we ourselves have plough'd for,
    sow'd, and scatter'd.

In Essex's disastrous return from Ireland–and its workings-through in *Coriolanus*–one can almost hear the crunching of gilded gears in de Vere's mind. In an abstract sense, Essex was the embodiment of all that Castiglione's *Courtier* celebrated: Essex could rightly boast of birth, wealth, valor, patronage, and courageous service to his prince. Yet Essex was also reaping the harvest of enmity his arrogance and overweening ambition had sowed.

Coriolanus is a bitter symphony in a minor key, scarcely pausing to lighten the mood with a comic interlude. And in its unstinting darkness, as Shaw rightly noted, *Coriolanus* is all comedy. Yet de Vere had experienced the same arcing trajectory from promising star to powerful young elite to dejected exile. De Vere probably drew inspiration from *Coriolanus* to retell the same story–but this time in autobiographical form.

Timon of Athens is Shake-speare's self-portrait as a downwardly mobile aristocrat. And thanks to some jokes about *Timon of Athens* that appear in a John Marston play from 1600 and a Ben Jonson play from 1601, it follows that Shake-speare's dark satire must have been staged and known to London audiences by 1600 at the latest. Marston and Jonson were probably riffing on *Timon* because it was then current news.

Timon's railing philosopher APEMANTUS encapsulates the theme of this play when he tells the title character:

APEM. The middle of humanity thou never knewest, but the extremity
    of both ends. When thou wast in thy gilt and thy perfume, they
    mock'd thee for too much curiosity; in thy rags thou know'st none–
    but art despis'd for the contrary.

Timon of Athens tells the story of de Vere's precipitous drop from finery to patches. TIMON begins the play as an admired and admirable lord, patronizing all worthy endeavors that come to his attention. He pays out generous grants to poets and painters. TIMON is the very mirror of Castiglionian nobility–not unlike *The Merchant of Venice*'s ANTONIO in both bounteousness and recklessness. Yet, when TIMON's credit slips, his impulse is all too familiar:

STEWARD My lov'd lord,
    Though you hear now (too late), yet now's a time:
    The greatest of your having lacks a half
    To pay your present debts.

TIMON Let all my land be sold!
STEWARD 'Tis all engag'd, some forfeited and gone,
   And what remains will hardly stop the mouth
   Of present dues. The future comes apace.

TIMON ends the play a bitter misanthrope, exiled from Athens, railing at the whole of humanity. In his jeremiads against everyone and everything, TIMON even recalls the first step of de Vere's downward spiral–the doubtful paternity of his first child by Anne Cecil de Vere. Shaking his dirty fist at a city that has spurned him, TIMON wants nothing more than to see everything laid to waste.

TIMON Spare not the babe
   Whose dimpled smiles from fools exhaust their mercy:
   Think it a bastard, whom the oracle
   Hath doubtfully pronounc'd the throat shall cut,
   And mince it sans remorse. Swear against objects.
   Put armor on thine ears and on thine eyes
   Whose proof nor yells of mothers, maids, nor babes,
   Nor sight of priests in holy vestments bleeding
   Shall pierce a jot. There's gold to pay thy soldiers.
   Make large confusion.

But the presence of one of England's greatest comedians on de Vere's doorstep come Christmastime would be a reminder that nothing was ever wholly good or bad for the earl of Oxford. Only the musing made it so.

The comic actor Robert Armin, who had just joined the Lord Chamberlain's Men the previous year, in 1600 published an otherwise disposable joke-book called *Quips Upon Questions* in which he made a most indisposable statement. In an introductory epistle, dated in late December 1599, Armin wrote that he was preparing to spend the holiday with an unspecified nobleman. "On Tuesday [Christmas Day 1599] I take my journey," Armin wrote, "to wait on the Right Honorable good my lord my master whom I serve in Hackney."

There were two known noblemen with established households in Hackney at the time, de Vere and Edward, Lord Zouche. Zouche was out of town in 1599 on diplomatic missions to Denmark and preparing to settle in to a new interim job as deputy governor of the island of Guernsey in the English Channel. The only "Right Honorable" lord whom Armin could have been serving in person in the borough of Hackney was de Vere.

Armin is famous today as one of Shake-speare's greatest clowns. Scholars suspect his first role was that of TOUCHSTONE in *As You Like It.* De Vere and Armin were probably working together during the holiday season of

1599–1600 to put the final touches on an old play about an old family to whom the author had long felt indebted.

As noted in previous chapters, *As You Like It* primarily concerns the legally entangled fortunes of the three sons of the executed duke of Norfolk (SIR ROWLAND DE BOYS, as the lamented patriarch is named in the play). In 1577, de Vere had attended the wedding of Norfolk's youngest son, William, to the heiress Lady Elizabeth Dacre.

And now, some twenty-two years after William Howard had pledged his love to the young Dacre girl, the light at the end of the tunnel *finally* appeared. At the time of Armin's visit to Hackney, Howard was approaching an agreement to purchase the rights to his wife's inheritance for the exorbitant fine of £10,000 (some $2.5 million today). De Vere, who himself never enjoyed his full inheritance, surely felt for his cousin. *As You Like It* was to be the present that celebrated small victories. It is–unlike *Troilus and Cressida, Coriolanus,* or *Timon of Athens*–an exuberant display of the author's still expert hand at creating comedy and romance, even amid the bitter disappointment of exile.

The unstoppable wit Armin, whose visits to King's Place must have recalled the riotous days of Fisher's Folly, probably joined his lord in the great study–beneath the carved wood ceiling figures of the Lord Chamberlain–and jested and parried back and forth as if it had been the 1580s all over again. Armin's character in *As You Like It,* TOUCHSTONE, was to play a crucial role both as the author's mouthpiece and as the comedic combatant in one of the most underappreciated scenes in the Shake-speare canon. *As You Like It,* Act 5, Scene 1, re-creates the COSTARD–DON ARMADO–JAQUENETTA triad from *Love's Labour's Lost* that burlesqued de Vere's strange relationship with his muse and with Will Shakspere. In *As You Like It,* de Vere's muse is named AUDREY.

This time around, though, Will Shakspere's character was not nearly as sympathetic a figure as COSTARD. De Vere was probably fed up with the Shake-speare ruse and wanted to unleash a literary assault upon the man who symbolized the whole rotten mess.

Armin was a rapid-fire comic whose humor delighted thousands of Londoners. But even he, a man who could work with dark material, must have been taken aback when handed the lines for TOUCHSTONE's confrontation scene with a simple country lad named WILLIAM.

The scene is full of the sort of sardonic comedy that was becoming de Vere's specialty: TOUCHSTONE wants to marry AUDREY, but WILLIAM wants to marry her too. Sparks fly. The setting is the forest of Arden, near de Vere's former property of Bilton, near his extended family's property of Billesley, and–most important–near Stratford-upon-Avon. TOUCHSTONE and AUDREY hire a priest to carry out the nuptials. The priest's name, SIR OLIVER MARTEXT, harkens back to the pamphleteer Martin Marprelate: De Vere tipped his hat to the role that the government's post-Marprelate crackdown played in bringing WILLIAM onto the scene.

TOUCHSTONE We shall find a time, AUDREY, patience, gentle AUDREY.

AUDREY Faith, the priest was good enough, for all the old gentleman's saying.

TOUCH. A most wicked SIR OLIVER, AUDREY, a most vile MARTEXT. But, AUDREY, there is a youth here in the forest lays claim to you.

AUD. Ay, I know who 'tis; he hath no interest in me in the world. Here comes the man you mean.

Enter WILLIAM

TOUCH. It is meat and drink to me to see a clown. By my troth, we that have good wits have much to answer for; we shall be flouting. We cannot hold.

WILLIAM Good ev'n, AUDREY.

AUD. God ye good ev'n, WILLIAM.

WILL. And good ev'n to you, sir.

TOUCH. Good ev'n, gentle friend. Cover thy head, cover thy head; nay, prithee be cover'd. How old are you, friend?

WILL. Five and twenty, sir.

TOUCH. A ripe age. Is thy name WILLIAM?

WILL. WILLIAM, sir.

TOUCH. A fair name. Wast born i' the forest here?

WILL. Ay, sir, I thank God.

TOUCH. "Thank God"—a good answer. Art rich?

WILL. Faith, sir, so so.

TOUCH. "So so" is good, very good, very excellent good; and yet it is not, it is but so so. Art thou wise?

WILL. Ay, sir, I have a pretty wit.

TOUCH. Why, thou say'st well. I do now remember a saying, "The fool doth think he is wise, but the wise man knows himself to be a fool."

Notice that TOUCHSTONE calls WILLIAM "gentle." The word in sixteenth-century usage meant not "docile" or "kindly" but rather someone of the next highest caste above yeoman. After the granting of Shakspere's coat of arms, as Ben Jonson's "Sogliardo" points out, Shakspere could indeed finally style himself a gentleman.

TOUCH. ...Do you love this maid?

WILL. I do, sir.

TOUCH. Give me your hand. Art thou learned?

WILL. No, sir.

TOUCH. Then learn this of me: To have is to have. For it is a figure of rhetoric that drink, being pour'd out of a cup into a glass, by filling the one doth empty the other. For all your writers do consent that *ipse* is he. Now, you are not *ipse*–for I am he.

Here is where the tone shifts. This is no longer comedy.

In Italian, "To have is to have" translates as *Avere è avere*: A Vere is a Vere. To make sense of TOUCHSTONE's "figure of rhetoric," one needs to turn to Plato's *Symposium,* wherein the transfer of knowledge from one person to another is contrasted to the pouring of a drink from one cup to another:

> My dear Agathon, Socrates replied as he took his seat beside him, I only wish that wisdom *were* the kind of thing one could share by sitting next to someone–if it flowed, for instance, from the one that was full to the one that was empty, like the water in two cups finding its level through a piece of worsted [*fine woolen fabric*]. If that were how it worked, I'm sure I'd congratulate myself on sitting next to you, for you'd soon have me brimming over with the most exquisite kind of wisdom.

Yet, Socrates says, wisdom does not have the properties of water. TOUCHSTONE concurs.

Finally, *ipse* is an emphatic pronoun in Latin, meaning "he himself." TOUCHSTONE suggests that there has been a confusion of identities: "You are not *ipse*–for I am he."

In plain English, then, TOUCHSTONE tells WILLIAM: Know this, kid. I am he himself, the author, a Vere. Don't think that just by being associated with me, you can drink in all the talent and wisdom in my head. You are only pretending to be me. You are not me. You never will be me.

WILLIAM is, naturally, flabbergasted at TOUCHSTONE's outburst. He replies:

WILL. Which he, sir?
TOUCH. He, sir, that must marry this woman [*my muse*]. Therefore, you clown, abandon–which is in the vulgar, "leave"–the society–which in the boorish is "company"–of this female–which in the common is "woman." Which, together is, "Abandon the society of this female"–or, clown, thou perishest; or, to thy better understanding, diest. Or, to wit, I will kill thee, make thee away, translate thy life into death, thy liberty into bondage. I will deal in poison with thee, or in bastinado, or in steel; I will bandy with thee in faction. I will o'errun thee with policy. I will kill thee a hundred and fifty ways. Therefore, tremble and depart!
AUD. Do, good, WILLIAM.
WILL. God rest you, merry sir. [*Exits*]

❧

As tension mounted between the real-life TOUCHSTONE and the real-life WILLIAM, the national mood itself was turning ugly. Essex was under house arrest and the threat of prosecution for his Irish escapades. Southampton and others began plotting for Essex's escape—and even for armed rebellion. But in April, Southampton left for Ireland to seek out the more placid atmosphere of a battlefield. During the summer he decamped Ireland to join the Protestants' army in the Lowlands. All the while, Essex was subject to occasional interrogations for his alleged treasons in cutting deals with the rebel earl of Tyrone.

Smart families, once strongly allied with Essex and his stepfather, began looking around for the nearest exit. One key booster of Essex and his cause during the 1590s, the powerful and titled Somerset family, during the summer of 1600 made a key marriage alliance with the Cecil faction. Edward Somerset, earl of Worcester, de Vere's contemporary, had served his sovereign honorably as ambassador to Scotland, knight of the Garter, and deputy Master of the Horse. Worcester had also bankrolled poetic tributes to the earl of Essex and stood by the troubled commander upon his stormy return from Ireland. But now, on June 16, 1600, Worcester married his son and heir Henry to Cecil's cousin Anne Russell.

De Vere was still trying to repair his ruined finances. In July, de Vere wrote to his former brother-in-law asking for the governorship of the isle of Jersey. Neither Cecil nor the queen appears to have taken his case seriously. Sending his letter from Hackney, de Vere wrote:

> Although my bad success in former suits to Her Majesty have given me cause to bury my hopes in the deep abyss and bottom of despair, rather than now attempt—after so many trials made in vain and so many opportunities escaped—the effects of fair words or fruits of golden opportunities, yet for that, I cannot believe but that there hath been always a true correspondence of word and intention of Her Majesty. I do conjecture that with a little help, that which of itself hath brought forth so fair blossoms will also yield fruit....
>
> And I know not by what better means or when Her Majesty may have an easier opportunity to discharge the debt of so many hopes—as her promises have given me cause to embrace—than by this which give she must, and so give as nothing extraordinarily doth part from her. If she shall not deign me this in an opportunity of time so fitting, what time shall I attend which is uncertain to all men unless in the graves of men there were a time to receive benefits and good turns from princes.

De Vere says, in effect, that he'd heard many promises from Elizabeth for a long time. But unless she advanced or appointed him to something soon, the only place he'd be able to enjoy his "benefits and good turns" was in his grave. His ailing body told him his days were few. The following year, de Vere would similarly make pitiful pleas for the presidency of Wales, which would also fall on deaf ears.

De Vere wasn't the only former favorite who no longer enjoyed access to offices and incomes. In September of 1600, the queen refused to renew Essex's monopoly on sweet wines–a financial mainstay in his household. Shakespeare's Sonnet 125 draws upon de Vere's, and now Essex's, inability to win this license to farm "compounds sweet" as a symbol of the futility of all royal office-seeking:

> Have I not seen dwellers on form and favor
> Lose all and more by paying too much rent
> For compound sweet, forgoing simple savor,
> Pitiful thrivers, in their gazing spent?

Also in 1600, Anthony Munday wrote a prefatory poem to a book that–like Francis Meres's *Palladis Tamia*–appears to separate de Vere from "Shakespeare." John Bodenham's 1600 quotation anthology *Belvedere* claimed to excerpt verse from contemporary authors including both "Edward, earle of Oxenford" and "William Shakspeare" [*sic*]. At first glance, Bodenham's list would appear to testify that "Shakespeare" and de Vere were two separate entities. And unlike the dismissable case of *Palladis Tamia*, one of de Vere's secretaries had given his tacit endorsement to the project.

Munday, however, may be absolved when *Belvedere* is put under the microscope. Detailed analysis of *Belvedere's* contents reveals that Bodenham's list of authors is a case of dressed-up hucksterism: Bodenham claims to anthologize famous authors of the day (King James VI of Scotland, John Davies, and George Peele) whose works are nowhere to be found in the book, while neglecting to list plenty of the lesser-known authors whom he actually does anthologize. *Belvedere's* list was, in short, a paradise of bylines that the editor could use to sell books. De Vere is mentioned for his title, Shake-speare because he was a best seller.

As seen by the occupant of the upstairs study at King's Place, *Belvedere* was only the latest reminder that the author was being bound and tied down on all sides, like Gulliver among the Lilliputians. One can begin to appreciate the bitter frustration articulated in Shake-speare's Sonnet 66:

> 66
> Tir'd with all these, for restful death I cry:
> As to behold desert a beggar born
> And needy nothing trimmed in jollity,

And purest faith unhappily forsworn
And gilded honor shamefully misplaced
And maiden virtue rudely strumpeted
And right perfection wrongfully disgraced
And strength by limping sway disablèd
And art made tongue tied by authority. . . .

Even in a remote London suburb like Hackney, courtly ears were still privy to courtly rumblings. Essex had lately been heard uttering such blasphemies as that the queen "being now an old woman . . . was no less crooked and distorted in mind than she was in body." The queen's godson Sir John Harrington, who'd been keeping tabs on the defrocked commander for his godmother since the Irish expedition, recorded a visit he paid to Essex's household in late 1600. Harrington wrote:

> [Essex] shifteth from sorrow and repentance to rage and rebellion so suddenly as well proveth him devoid of good reason or right mind. . . . He uttered strange words, bordering on such strange designs that made me hasten forth and leave his presence.

Another of Essex and Southampton's rash decisions in Ireland would come back to haunt them. During his brief tenure as general of the horse, Southampton had imprisoned an officer for insubordination. The shaming of that man, Thomas, Lord Grey de Wilton, turned a potential ally into a hardened enemy. On the evening of January 9, 1601, Lord Grey de Wilton and some of his henchmen ambushed Southampton as he rode through the London streets. In the ensuing melee, one of the attackers lopped off the hand of Southampton's houseboy.

Queen Elizabeth had Grey de Wilton thrown in the Fleet Prison for his lawlessness. But the signal was clear. Swords were coming unsheathed, and more blood would be spilled. Unless some very skilled mediator interceded, civil war would probably determine whether Essex's or Cecil's party remained standing.

Essex and his ragged and dwindling band had one last point in their favor: Much of the public at large still loved Essex for his military heroics during the mid-1590s. An effective coup d'état relies upon the support—or at least docility—of the masses. Essex now needed to rouse the rabble in his support.

Two years earlier, the lawyer John Hayward had published a controversial book, *The Life and Reign of Henry IV*, that told the history of the deposition of England's king Richard II. Hayward, a supporter of Essex and Southampton, had written a best-selling tract that none too subtly drew parallels between the corruption and misgovernment in Richard II's court and the abuses of

Elizabeth's. The historical king Richard II had been forced to abdicate the throne by the man who would become Henry IV; Hayward's polemic implied that a similar fate should befall the queen. Queen Elizabeth saw Hayward's book as incitement to revolution. He was tried for treason in the summer of 1600.

On February 6, 1601, Essex and Southampton pushed Hayward's historical parallel further by hiring the Lord Chamberlain's Men to perform Shakespeare's *Richard II* at the Globe. As it happens, Shake-speare's RICHARD II is actually de Vere through and through–a philosophical poet-king and proto-HAMLET whose origin probably dates back to the 1580s when the author was more politically engaged himself. But what motivated the February 6 performance of *Richard II*–containing an actual deposition scene, no less–was the equation of "Richard II" with Queen Elizabeth in the public's mind.

Elizabeth got the gist of the performance. "I am Richard [II]. Know ye not that?" she later asked the scholar William Lambarde. It is indicative that none of Elizabeth's officials tried to find or punish the author of the play *Richard II.* The queen and her interrogators knew de Vere's enmity toward Essex already, and neither needed to discover more about *Richard II*'s author, or inquire about his loyalty.

While de Vere's loyalty to Elizabeth was indeed true, the follow-up to the *Richard II* performance was tumultuous. On the evening of Sunday, February 8, de Vere–probably in Hackney with his wife and son–received word that the entire structure of English power had changed. In one swift and deadly day, Essex and Southampton had gambled everything and lost.

That morning, Essex and Southampton, along with some three hundred other nobles and remaining adherents to the Essex faction, had gathered at Essex House (formerly Leicester House) to discuss their next move. Cecil's spies had long since infiltrated the Essex House staff, however. The turncoats notified their superiors. The Lord Chief Justice, the Lord Keeper, and other privy councilors arrived at the Essex House gates asking the cause of such an assembly. Essex explained to them that plots had been laid against his life. Southampton recalled the recent unprovoked attack by Lord Grey de Wilton.

The officials responded that Lord Grey de Wilton had been punished and that if Essex had any specific information about specific plots, he should notify the proper authorities. This was not the response the insurgents were looking for. So Essex, Southampton, and a rabble of some two hundred men raced through the London streets to the sheriff's house. (Essex believed the sheriff of London to be on his side.) "For the queen! For the queen! A plot is laid for my life!" Essex shouted as the throngs made their way up Fleet Street toward Ludgate.

Once Essex and his men had arrived at the sheriff's house, however, they learned their supposed ally had fled for the lord mayor's house.

Essex was stuck in the middle of London leading a mob that now had no particular purpose. They marched back toward Essex House to regroup. But Cecil had already drawn in the net. The bishop of London, a man who owed his job to Cecil, had ordered that Essex's men be stopped in their tracks. A chain was placed across the street at the west end of St. Paul's, and armed guards ensured that neither Essex nor his men could proceed any farther.

Essex responded like the hothead he was, by fighting. In a matter of minutes, the ensuing violence left four men dead and many more wounded. And Essex had become the de facto commander of a rebel army inside the city gates of London.

Essex had handed Cecil everything the scheming spymaster had wanted. The game was now up.

Essex, Southampton, and other advisors were allowed to return to Essex House. They holed themselves up there for the rest of the day. By evening, a force led by the Lord Admiral, Lord Grey de Wilton, and others were besieging Essex House. Southampton tried to convince the Lord Admiral to send some of his men into Essex House as hostages to ensure safe passage to the queen's chambers, where Essex and Southampton could then have a private conference with Her Majesty. The Lord Admiral told them they were in no position to make any demands. The only acceptable option was unconditional surrender. After several tense hours, at 10 P.M., Essex, Southampton, and their cabal laid down their arms.

A treason trial was the next logical step. De Vere must have heard before the night's end that, as a member of the House of Lords, he would soon be sitting in judgment of his young, proud, dearly beloved, and grievously stupid Southampton.

On February 19, the trial of Essex and Southampton took place at Westminster Hall. For the event, the Hall had been arranged in the same spare layout as at the arraignment of Mary, Queen of Scots, at Fotheringhay. De Vere joined twenty-five other peers sitting on either side of the cavernous room. The canopy of state was set at the upper end, underneath which sat the Lord Treasurer, the Lord High Steward, and seven sergeants-at-arms.

The constable of the Tower and his assistants brought in the pair of prisoners. As the peers' names were called who would sit on the jury, Lord Grey de Wilton's name came up. Essex laughed and tugged Southampton by the sleeve. They both objected to the personal vendetta Lord Grey had against Southampton. The Lord Chief Justice informed the prisoners, however, that peers of the realm could not be excused from any jury.

The trial lasted from nine till six. Sir Francis Bacon, a onetime member of the Essex faction, headed the prosecution, which called upon such witnesses as the earl of Worcester, John Davies, and Sir Walter Raleigh. Essex scoffed when Raleigh swore his oath to tell the truth and nothing but the truth. When it was

Essex's turn to testify, he dropped a bombshell. Cecil, Essex claimed, had been advocating in secret for the Infanta Isabella Clara Eugenia of Spain. At this charge, Cecil approached the Lord Steward, dropped to his knees, and pleaded he be allowed to respond to this malicious fiction. Cecil asked Essex and Southampton to name any privy councilor to whom he had supposedly advocated the Spanish succession. They named no one. Further questioning revealed that Cecil had simply been seen reading a book that argued for the Spanish infanta's claim to the English throne. Cecil turned the moment around masterfully, addressing Essex:

> Your malice whereby you seek to work me into hatred amongst all men
> hath flowed from no other cause than from my affection to peace for the
> good of my country and your own inflamed heart for war, for the bene-
> fit of military men which may be at your beck.

The jury took only a half hour to find both Essex and Southampton guilty of high treason. De Vere had performed his duty as a peer to condemn his dear Southampton to death.

Essex said he was prepared to die, but he asked that the court spare the life of Southampton. In the *Sonnets,* many of which were evidently written to Southampton, de Vere later reflected upon his bizarre role as judge and jury against his beloved–from the first sessions to trial to the adversarial role de Vere played against himself in the jury room.

30
When to the sessions of sweet silent thought
I summon up remembrance of things past,
I sigh the lack of many a thing I sought,
And with old woes new wail my dear time's waste.
Then can I drown an eye, unused to flow,
For precious friends hid in death's dateless night ...

35
No more be grieved at that which thou hast done. . . .
All men make faults, and even I in this
Authorizing [*Avouching*] thy trespass [*revolt*] with compare [*compeer;*
    an aristocratic equal or rival],
Myself corrupting salving thy amiss,
Excusing thy sins more than thy sins are;
For to thy sensual fault I bring in sense–
Thy adverse party is thy advocate–
And 'gainst myself a lawful plea commence.
Such civil war is in my love and hate,

That I an accessory need must be
To that sweet thief [*the trial*] which sourly robs from me.

46

To [de]cide this title is empaneled
A quest of thoughts, all tenants to the heart;
And by their verdict is determined
The clear eye's moiety, and the dear heart's part.

Between seven and eight A.M. on Ash Wednesday, February 25, Essex was beheaded. Although the loss of Essex evidently meant little to de Vere, the loss it foreshadowed meant the world. In the Tower, Southampton had literally worried himself sick; fever and swelling threatened to take his life without the aid of any ax. (Sonnet 45 frets over the return of "swift messengers returned from thee/ Who ev'n but now come back again, assured/ Of thy fair health, recounting it to me.")

On March 13, the fellow Essex rebels Sir Gelly Merrick and Henry Cuffe were taken to the gallows at Tyburn and hanged, cut down while still alive, then drawn and quartered. On March 18, Sir Charles Danvers and Sir Christopher Blount were taken to Tower Hill and given the comparatively humane end of an ax chop to the neck.

De Vere recognized in Danvers's death an opportunity to make an ancestral claim to one of Danvers's forfeited properties. De Vere would be presenting legal briefs to Cecil and the queen for months to come that the Danvers property should be transferred to the earldom of Oxford. In the words of historian Lawrence Stone:

> After the Essex revolt there was a hectic rush for the spoils.... The earl of Oxford angled for Sir Charles Danvers's lands, Sir Robert Cecil grabbed John Littleton's horses, Lord Burghley [*Thomas Cecil, Robert's elder brother*] asked for those of the earl of Southampton.

Sir Robert Cecil had begun receiving petitions from Southampton's wife and mother to spare their beloved from the executioner's ax. One wonders, too, if some version of what became Shake-speare's Sonnet 94 was part of the pleading:

> They that have the power to hurt and will do none,
> That do not do the thing they most do show,
> Who, moving others, are themselves as stone,
> Unmovèd, cold and to temptation slow;
> They rightly do inherit heaven's graces,

And husband nature's riches from expense;
They are the lords and owners of their faces,
Others but stewards of their excellence.
The summer's flower is to the summer sweet,
Though to itself it only live and die,
But if that flower with base infection meet,
The basest weed outbraves his dignity.
>   For sweetest things turn sourest by their deeds;
>   Lilies that fester smell far worse than weeds.

The queen's execution orders had effectively eliminated the only real rival to the Cecils, the Essex faction. Leaving Essex's sidekick still standing would be a fitting coup de grace, ensuring that a living reminder and testament to Cecil's power would endure into the next regime.

Sometime on or around March 18, news arrived that Southampton's sentence had been commuted to life in prison in the Tower of London.

68

Before the golden tresses of the dead,
The right of sepulchers were shorn away.
To live a second life on second head–
Ere beauty's dead fleece made another gay.

Southampton had been spared, and Cecil had been instrumental in convincing the queen to pardon him. But Southampton was, in fact, not Southampton anymore. He'd been stripped of all his lands and titles. He was a commoner, plain old Henry Wriothesley.

69

Those parts of thee that the world's eye doth view
Want nothing that the thought of hearts can mend. . . .
>   But why thy odor matcheth not thy show,
>   The soil is this, that thou dost common grow.

The ensuing seven sonnets muse over de Vere's compromised literary fate and, with the fair youth now spared the death sentence, ponder the one fell messenger that de Vere knew would be visiting soon enough.

70

That thou art blamed shall not be thy defect. . . .
Thou hast passed by the ambush of young days.

71

No longer mourn for me when I am dead....
Nay, if you read this line, remember not
The hand that writ it, for I love you so....
Do not so much as my poor name rehearse,
But let your love ev'n with my life decay.

72

After my death, dear love, forget me quite...
Unless you would devise some virtuous lie....
My name be buried where my body is—
And live no more to shame nor me nor you.
    For I am shamed by that [*literary work*] which I bring forth
    And so should you, to love things nothing worth.

74

The prey of worms, my body being dead,
The coward conquest of a wretch's knife,
Too base of thee to be rememberèd.

76

Why write I still all one, ever the same,
And keep invention [*writing*] in a noted weed [*disguise*]?...
So all my best is spending old words new,
Spending again what is already spent.
    For as the sun is daily new and old,
    So is my love still telling what is told.

In 1601, the reverend and poet Charles Fitzgeffrey wrote a book of Latin poems and epigrams about friends, colleagues, and the celebrities of his day. In Fitzgeffrey's *Affaniae: Sive Epigrammatum...* (1601), the poet lauded the big names in contemporary English literature: Samuel Daniel, Michael Drayton, Ben Jonson, George Chapman, Thomas Nashe, John Marston, Edmund Spenser, and so on. Glaring in its absence, however, is even the slightest mention of Shake-speare.

However, Fitzgeffrey does include a series of couplets addressed to a writer he cryptically calls "the Bard." One couplet wonders about the state of the Bard's health and suggests that the Bard consider complete literary self-censorship. Another avers that the Bard is melodramatically crucifying himself—and rushing headlong toward posthumous publication. As translated into English, Fitzgeffrey's enigmatic couplets read:

To The Bard

Are you healthy, he who writes for the last generation? [*posterity?*]
Let "the letter" [*the* Sonnets?] never be handed over, O Bard. Be silent.

To The Bard

You have been cautious, saying, "I will publish verses after my death."
I would not so hurriedly crucify yourself, O Bard.

Fitzgeffrey may have gotten his hands on some of Shake-speare's *Sonnets*. He may not himself have known the identity of the sonneteer, but if he is referring to the *Sonnets*, he was the first of countless readers to puzzle over the riddles these poems pose. Evidently troubled by the political and/or homoerotic character of the verse, Fitzgeffrey advised that the sonneteer never "hand over" the poems to a printer: "Be silent."

In addition to being maddeningly opaque to every reader from Fitzgeffrey onward, the *Sonnets* mark the final drama in Shake-speare's Elizabethan career. De Vere owed back taxes and was still petitioning for hopeless causes like the forfeited estate of the Essex conspirator Sir Charles Danvers. But there were no more new and grand statements to be made on the political stage. The author was sick and getting sicker; the Cecil cabal was strong and getting stronger; and the queen was still stringing England along, refusing to name an heir.

Wriothesley's recent brush with death—and de Vere's moribund physical state—must have cast de Vere's world in drab, funereal colors. Elizabeth was reaching the end of her line too. The author had once upon a time known Her Majesty as a nubile VENUS, a consort and a lover, the most powerful woman in Europe, with the future of Britain in her blood. But what had become of their lives? De Vere had squandered his on "trifles"—in the self-effacing language of Sonnet 87. Elizabeth had led one of the most incredible lives of her age, but dynastically, her cause was now as hopeless as de Vere's. Elizabeth's mythic emblem in her twilight years was a phoenix rising from the ashes. Yet, without an heir, when mortal fire consumed Elizabeth, the phoenix would not be reborn.

In 1601, an unregistered book called *Love's Martyr* appeared on the London book market. The versifier Robert Chester had written a florid poem imagining the queen's sad state of mind after the loss of the earl of Essex. *Love's Martyr* also anticipated the arrival of a "New Phoenix"—a mythic emblem that would soon become associated with King James VI of Scotland, son of Mary, Queen of Scots. Cecil had been grooming James for the English throne for years. Cecil had unchecked access to Elizabeth's ear to determine who would be the future king of England—and who would be in power and who would not. Chester dedicated *Love's Martyr* to an up-and-comer in the Cecil faction, Sir John Salisbury.

Appended to *Love's Martyr* was a group of thematically related poems, including one by "William Shake-speare" [*sic*] that lamented the death of "Beauty" and "Truth." (De Vere's family motto was "Nothing Truer than Truth.") De Vere pictured himself as the lonesome TURTLE[DOVE] and his sovereign as a dimming and dying PHOENIX. Shake-speare's *Phoenix and the Turtle* is an anticipatory dirge, simultaneously harkening back to the author's youthful passion for his queen and looking ahead to their imminent deaths

Here the anthem doth commence:
Love and constancy is dead;
PHOENIX and the TURTLE fled
In a mutual flame from hence.

So they lov'd, as love in twain
Had the essence but in one:
Two distincts, division none;
Number there in love was slain.

Hearts remote, yet not asunder;
Distance and no space was seen
'Twixt this TURTLE and his Queen
But in them it were a wonder....

Whereupon it made this Threne [funeral song]
To the PHOENIX and the DOVE,
Cosupremes and stars of love,
As Chorus to their tragic scene....

Death is now the PHOENIX' nest,
And the TURTLE's loyal breast
To eternity doth rest.

Leaving no posterity:
'Twas not their infirmity,
It was married chastity.

Truth may seem, but cannot be;
Beauty brag, but 'tis not she;
Truth and Beauty buried be.

To this urn let those repair
That are either true or fair:
For these dead birds sigh a prayer.

༄

Perhaps as he mused in his "trifles" to Wriothesley over the power of his immortalizing pen, de Vere began to ponder the effect of burying his name where his body was. Shake-speare was a corpus of diminishing value to the world for which it was initially created—the court. At least one courtly Shake-speare revival, with halfhearted new topical additions, would amuse the aging queen in the first few years of the seventeenth century. (That throwback to 1580s rivalries, *Twelfth Night*, was staged once at Middle Temple Hall in 1602 and perhaps another time at court the year before.) But other courtly wits, such as Ben Jonson and Thomas Dekker, were generating new and brilliant allegorical comedies, histories, and tragedies for the court's delectation. Jonson, Dekker, et. al., would, naturally, be replaced someday, too, and the life cycle of disposable court dramas and dramatists would continue.

Yet the *Sonnets* reveal that de Vere knew his works would live on.

81

Your name from hence immortal life shall have,
Though I, once gone, to all the world must die.
The earth can yield me but a common grave,
When you entombèd in men's eyes shall lie.
Your monument shall be my gentle verse,
Which eyes not yet created shall o'er-read,
And tongues to be your being shall rehearse,
When all the breathers of this world are dead,
        You still shall live—such virtue hath my pen—
        Where breath most breathes, ev'n in the mouths of men.

The cover that Will Shakspere provided protected de Vere's writings by depoliticizing their meaning. Yet, despite the self-effacing nature of Sonnet 81, de Vere must also have hoped that the "Shakespeare" ruse would one day unravel, that "Shakespeare" would become a kind of Venetian Carnival mask, withholding the owner's identity from the thronging crowds until the chimes at midnight sounded—when the mask could finally be taken off.

Shake-speare's farewell quartet of plays—*Measure for Measure, King Lear, The Tempest*, and *Hamlet*—forestall dusty death long enough to eke out some concluding thoughts, reconsidering the paradox of an author's obliterated identity in spite of his works' unquestionable immortality. These four plays represent the author's ultimate message to the latter day, his time capsule buried five full fathoms deep, awaiting the indulgence of eyes and ears yet unborn.

Four passages in de Vere's Geneva Bible (with de Vere's underlining) encapsulate what would become Shake-speare's parting request to a darkening world:

13. Then I heard a voice from heaven saying unto me, "Write. Blessed are the dead, which hereafter die in the Lord. Even so saith the Spirit. For they rest from their labors, and their works follow them."

Revelations 14:13

10. For God is not [so] unrighteous that he should forget your work and labor of love. . . .

Hebrews 6:10

c. As the hope of the daylight causeth us not to be offended with the darkness of the night, so ought we patiently to trust that God will clear our cause and restore us to our right.

Psalm 38, footnote c (Geneva ed.)

9. I will bear the wrath of the Lord because I have sinned against him, until he plead my cause and execute judgment for me. Then will he bring me forth into the light, and I shall see his righteousness.

Michah 7:9

༉

Between February and May of 1601, de Vere presented his pleadings to Cecil for the presidency of Wales. The previous long-serving president of Wales–Henry Herbert, earl of Pembroke–had died in January. De Vere was fond of the Herbert family and had been a strong promoter of a marriage alliance between his own second daughter, Bridget, and Pembroke's son William. Now de Vere wanted Pembroke's old position.

As with de Vere's previous unsuccessful attempt at a diplomatic appointment–the governorship of the isle of Jersey in 1600–his letters reveal little grasp of the enormity of the task. Appeals to family ties are all the qualifications de Vere lists. (". . . None is nearer allied [to you] than myself, since of your sister, of my [late] wife, only you have received nieces.") The presidency of Wales was no idle monopoly or forest to be farmed for its resources. The previous president had spent practically the whole of his fifteen years in office at the Welsh presidential palace, Ludlow Castle in Shropshire, discharging the daily duties of a regal overseer to an entire nation.

De Vere must have imagined some kind of rule by proxy, wherein he could delegate all the actual duties of leadership. As it was, simply living in the suburb of Hackney, de Vere could scarcely make it to court to pay tidings to his all-powerful former brother-in-law. De Vere's excuse for not being at court more often, an observation that could hardly have helped his application, was that he was a "hater of ceremonies." If the lame, ailing, and friendless de Vere actually thought he stood a chance at becoming president of Wales, one in which ceremony played no small role, he was living in another world.

The other world that de Vere appears to have inhabited at that moment traces its source to his year abroad at the age of twenty-five. During de Vere's Italian sojourn, manuscripts circulated of the comedy *Epitia* by the Ferraran courtly novelist and playwright Giraldi Cinthio. Adapted from one of Cinthio's short stories, *Epitia* tells the tale of a strange Austrian emperor who decides one day to take leave of his office, transferring power to an underling. The underling is corrupt and hypocritical; all is restored to normality, but only after the figurehead has been toppled and the true original resumes his rightful place.

Measure for Measure is one of Shake-speare's most abstract and autobiographically haunted pieces of writing. The play borrows heavily from Cinthio's *Epitia*–from the cast list to the plot's outline to the drama's setting and tone. But to view *Measure for Measure* merely as a work of adaptation is to miss the point of the exercise. Perhaps more than any other work in the canon, *Measure for Measure* is a parable of the author's own unique predicament.

There is no COSTARD or WILLIAM in *Measure for Measure*. De Vere had satisfied his fascination with the front man in *Love's Labor's Lost* and *The Taming of the Shrew* and purged himself of his anger in *As You Like It* and the *"Will"* sonnets. The play's secret wellspring of comedy is the protagonist's compromised situation. Although *Measure for Measure*'s DUKE (de Vere) would appear to be in complete control of his surroundings, powers outside the scope of the play force him into disguise. It's no coincidence that the word *authority* appears in *Measure for Measure* more often than in any other Shake-speare play. De Vere had come to know more about the censoring power of authority than anyone else of his time.

Measure for Measure's DUKE is a tongue-tied playwright situated within his own creation. Wherever a simple resolution might naturally occur, thus prematurely ending the play, the DUKE jumps in and artificially extends the drama with an unnecessary bit of tension. The DUKE leaves a sex-crazed Puritan in charge of the state and remains in the city incognito, only to complicate matters for scene after inexplicable scene. Drawing from his grab bag of autobiographical favorites, de Vere has the DUKE throw in a "bed trick"–like the one his first wife played on him–while he saves another character from execution by the skin of his teeth–like the Southampton-*cum*-Wriothesley predicament de Vere had so recently sweated through.

If one tries to understand the DUKE as a rational ruler, *Measure for Measure* will be a jumble of inexplicables. But the brilliance of the comedy is in its conceit. *Measure for Measure* is tragicomedy beyond mere laughter and tears. *Measure for Measure* is, with de Vere restored as author, every bit as profound, as moving, and as transcendent as the Bard's tragedies. *Measure for Measure* is one of the greatest plays by Shake-speare, because *Measure for Measure* is also one of the greatest plays *about* "Shakespeare."

In the play's first scene, when the DUKE supposedly leaves Vienna–only to don a disguise and remain–he explains his hasty retreat:

> I love the people
> But I do not like to stage me to their eyes.
> Though it do well, I do not relish well
> Their loud applause and *aves* vehement,
> Nor do I think the man of safe discretion
> That does affect it.

Reprising a familiar theme from the Anne Cecil years, the disguised author sets a chaste and wronged wife (MARIANA) upon the state's unsuspecting deputy (ANGELO). ANGELO has sex with his long-ago betrothed MARIANA, although he thinks he's sleeping with another woman (ISABELLA). The DUKE watches the fireworks–as if he'd become detached enough from his own first marriage that he could set the Anne Cecil predicament on some other character's shoulders.

Ultimately, the wronged ISABELLA becomes the play's advocate for truth telling and mask removing. As de Vere would write in a letter to Cecil, "Truth is truth, though never so old, and time cannot make that false which was once true." Now ISABELLA practically recites these same words, mingled with de Vere's family motto, to the DUKE. The DUKE, in response, self-mockingly dismisses ISABELLA's pleadings.

> ISABELLA It is not truer he is ANGELO
>   Than this is all as true as it is strange.
>   Nay, it is ten times true. For truth is truth
>   To th'end of reckoning.
> DUKE Away with her! Poor soul.
>   She speaks this in the infirmity of sense!

As *Coriolanus* comically turns the formula of the tragic hero upside down, *Measure for Measure* expands the bounds of comedy to envelop the tragedy of a man's looming anonymity. Like the other three cornerstones in Shakespeare's farewell quartet, *Measure for Measure* presents an author coming to terms with his willed mask and his masked *Will*.

Measure for Measure was experimental theater as radical as the works of Eugene Ionesco or Samuel Beckett were in the twentieth century. One wonders if it was ever staged before its first known performance in 1738.

Ironically, the theatrical troupe with de Vere's name attached to it was not only not radical, it scarcely merits a footnote in the history of theatrical companies from the early 1590s onward: De Vere's fiscal and organizational ineptitude probably explains why the Earl of Oxford's Men was such a washout.

An anonymous slapdash comedy, *The Weakest Goeth to the Wall,* appeared in print in 1600 stating that it had been performed by the Earl of Oxford's Men. Since *Weakest* draws its source from the 1581 Christopher Hatton–subsidized book *Farewell to Military Profession,* the play reads like a cast-off from the Fisher's Folly years that one or more hangers-on at the Folly put together to amuse their patron. In 1601, another play, *The History of George Scanderbeg,* was registered for publication, with the stationer's entry stating that it was "lately played by the Right Honorable earl of Oxenford his servants." Unlike *Weakest, Scanderbeg* was never printed. Gabriel Harvey mentions *Scanderbeg* in one of his pamphlets and suggests that the play was probably Tom Nashe's attempt circa 1592 to cash in on the hype surrounding Christopher Marlowe's *Tamburlaine.*

These two plays, likely written by two or more de Vere secretaries or associates, are the whole of the Earl of Oxford's Men's known repertoire under de Vere's supervision. The Earl of Oxford's Men, however, did soon find a willing and capable supervisor. After the downfall of Essex, the earl of Worcester, the newly appointed Master of the Horse, was still optimistically climbing the Elizabethan courtly ladder. According to the rules of the courtly game, the highest flyers needed their own theatrical troupe to advocate their patron's pet causes during the annual Christmastime revels season. By 1602, Worcester's fledgling troupe had subsumed whatever remained of de Vere's company. On March 31, 1602, this newly amalgamated troupe applied for a permanent home at the Boar's Head Inn in London.

Had Worcester's enthusiastic takeover come at an earlier phase in de Vere's literary career, the history of Shake-speare might have been radically different. But Worcester assumed the newly consolidated company's leadership at the bitter end of de Vere's life. What use did a social climber like Worcester have for a backward-looking author who obsessed over such cheery topics as death, enforced anonymity, and a lifetime of wrong turns and bad decisions? While Worcester's Men thrived well into to the reign of King James I, one never sees a hint of de Vere's affiliation with them again.

On March 22, 1602, de Vere sent Cecil a fifth and final petition to receive the inheritance of the late Sir Charles Danvers's Wiltshire estate. De Vere claimed that Elizabeth had promised him the property but, as was her wont, was doing nothing to fulfill her promise. "I find by this waste of time that lands will not be carried without deeds," he snapped. And no judges or other functionaries of state would move forward without word from on high. "Then is my suit as it was the first day," de Vere lamented. The Danvers case proved as fruitless as his petitions for the isle of Jersey appointment, presidency of Wales, and various monopolies de Vere had attempted to secure during the previous decade.

Other than a legal entanglement with an old tenant and notices of more back taxes owed in Hackney, nothing else of note about de Vere slipped into the historical record for the rest of 1602. At the end of the year, the countess of Oxford exchanged New Year's gifts with Elizabeth.

By February 1603, Queen Elizabeth was dying. Since acceding to the throne in 1558, she'd superstitiously never taken off her coronation ring. By 1603, the ring had grown into her flesh. The ingrown piece of jewelry had to be sawn off her finger. Elizabeth was sensitive about symbols; as far as she was concerned, this portended a dissolution of her sacred union with the nation. A second ill omen came on February 24, when Elizabeth's closest personal friend died. Catherine (Kate) Carey, countess of Nottingham, had been installed as a maid of honor in 1558, had nursed Elizabeth through her nearly fatal bout with smallpox in 1562, and had been variously first lady of the bedchamber, mistress of robes, and mistress of jewels. Now robbed of her spiritual sister, Elizabeth began hinting at her own imminent death.

The question of the succession was on everyone's mind. According to an inquiry Cecil later spearheaded, on March 21, de Vere hosted a dinner party at King's Place where the topic was broached. De Vere's guest was another flighty and temperamental lord, the earl of Lincoln. De Vere and Lincoln talked into the night about the future of England and what the old nobility should do about it. De Vere no doubt regaled his guest with chivalric visions of succession by sword–involving spiriting a rightful heir to the throne over to France only to return with a conquering army. According to a secondhand account recorded by the commander of the Tower of London, Sir John Peyton:

> [De Vere and Lincoln] after dinner retired apart from all company [and] began, as the earl of Lincoln said, to discourse with him of the impossi-
> bility of the queen's life and that the nobility, being peers of the realm, were bound to take care for the common good of the state in the cause of the succession–in the which, himself (meaning the earl of Lincoln) ought to have more regard than others, because he had a nephew of the blood royal, naming my lord Hastings [Lincoln's nephew], whom he persuaded the earl of Lincoln to send for. And that there should be means used to convey him [*Hastings*] over into France, where he should find friends that would make him a party of the which there was a precedent in former times.

English kings-to-be had indeed been known to gather their forces across the Channel to mount an invasion. This "precedent" came both from recent history (as, described in *Richard III*) and from the English chronicles (such as informed *King Lear*).

Lincoln claimed that during the post-supper chatter, de Vere also began to rail against the legitimacy of the Scots king, James VI–a prince who practically every other noble in England had recognized would become King James I of England. But, as Peyton later explained to Cecil:

> I knew him [de Vere] to be so weak in body, in friends, in hability, and all other means to raise any combustion in the state as I never feared any danger to proceed from so feeble a foundation.

De Vere had set himself apart from practically every other English subject. So, alone on the hill, the old man howled.

On the other hand, Lincoln was probably the ultimate instigator of the illconceived earl of Hastings conspiracy—it was Lincoln's, not de Vere's, kinsman who was being put forward as an heir to the throne; Lincoln, not de Vere, had discussed the Hastings succession with the French embassy. Moreover, Peyton himself admitted that Lincoln was the sort who would blame someone else for his own mutterings or seditions: "His [*Lincoln's*] fashion is to condemn the world if thereby he might excuse himself," Peyton later wrote to Cecil.

By the week of March 20, 1603, it was clearly only a matter of days. Elizabeth was ill, could not eat, refused medicine, and refused to go to bed. "She saw things" when in bed, it was said. Cushions were laid on the floor where she rested instead. And still she would not address the question of her successor. She lost her voice sometime on the twenty-first or twenty-second. Dubious accounts exist of the queen privately informing Cecil—whether by word or by pantomime gestures—that James of Scotland had her dying blessing. In fact, it's just as likely that Elizabeth never named a successor and that the "Great Council" of peers, privy councilors, and bishops made the decision for her posthumously.

Between one and three A.M. on March 24, Sir Robert Carey heard from Elizabeth's private chambers the wails and sobs of the queen's ladies-in-waiting. Her Majesty had just died. Carey raced from Richmond Palace, where the queen's body now lay, to Westminster to await official orders from the Privy Council to make his way north to Scotland. By ten A.M., without any further instructions, Carey risked it. He posted 155 miles to Doncaster by nightfall—the longest recorded journey on horseback in England over a single day. On March 25, the nation's official harbinger to the future king James I of England had made it as far as Northumberland, and on the evening of March 26, Carey arrived at Holyroodhouse in Edinburgh, just as James was being seated for supper. Carey's land speed record—London to Edinburgh in less than sixty hours—would not be bested by any form of transportation until the early nineteenth century.

The Great Council issued a broadside proclamation announcing the impending arrival of King James I of England, Scotland, and Wales. De Vere neither signed the proclamation, nor was his name listed as a signatory on the proclamation's first imprint. However, de Vere's name appeared on subsequent reprints of the nation's declaration of King James I's legitimacy as heir to the throne.

News of the queen's death triggered a nationwide wave of mourning. At least thirty printed ballads, books, and broadsides quickly appeared in shops around London. One of these funerary tributes, Henry Chettle's *England's Mourning Garment,* mused over Shake-speare's silence at this most auspicious turning point in the nation's history. "Shepherd, remember our Elizabeth," Chettle wrote. "And sing her rape, done by that TARQUIN, death."

In the days that followed Elizabeth's death, a now leaderless state turned its eyes north toward a foreign king, raised on foreign soil. James's peaceful progress southward into England would signify the unification of two previously sovereign nations: England and Scotland. Such a smooth and seamless transition of power was a tribute to the political cunning of Sir Robert Cecil. Cecil had spent years working toward this moment, when his cabal would engineer the very succession of the monarchy—thereby ensuring themselves the leading positions of power in the new regime.

King James I was a politically shrewd man, albeit one with his own weaknesses and sore spots that aspirants for his favors would exploit in the years to come. One particularly sensitive subject was Elizabeth's execution of his mother. James may have acquiesced to his mother's judicial murder in 1586, but he would still harbor a lifelong resentment of the political compromise to which he had once agreed. Although Elizabeth was first buried in the grand sepulcher of Henry VII at Westminster, James eventually turned Elizabeth's funerary monument into a public symbol of his animosity toward his predecessor. At James's behest, Elizabeth's remains were later reburied in a new tomb. The king also had his mother reburied in Westminster, practically within spitting distance of Gloriana's statuary. Visitors to Westminster Abbey to this day can see Mary Stuart's ornate mausoleum on the south side of the Henry VII Chapel, while on the chapel's north side, half the size of the Scots queen's memorial, is the more modest tomb of Queen Elizabeth I. James's predecessor, perhaps the greatest monarch England has ever known, rests atop the remains of her Catholic rival and hated half-sister Mary Tudor.

Payback came in other, less superficial forms as well. One of James's first acts as king of England was to order the release of Henry Wriothesley and to restore the common rebel against the Elizabethan state to his former titles and appointments. Nineteen days remained between Southampton's release from the Tower of London (April 10, 1603) and the state funeral of Queen Elizabeth (April 28). As the scholar and author Hank Whittemore recently pointed out, the nineteen sonnets beginning with Sonnet 107 appear to present daily meditations that culminate in the interment of the house of Tudor.

107

Not mine own fears nor the prophetic soul
Of the wide world dreaming on things to come
Can the lease of my true love control:
Supposed as forfeit to a confined doom.
The mortal moon [*Elizabeth, associated with the moon goddess Diana*]
    hath her eclipse endured [*died*]....
My love looks fresh, and death to me subscribes,
Since spite of him I'll live in this poor rhyme.

109

O never say that I was false of heart,
Though absence seemed my flame to qualify....
    If I have ranged
Like him that travels [*King James*], I return again,
Just to the time, not with the time exchanged:
So that myself bring water for my stain.

The final line quoted above from Sonnet 109 involves a point of ceremonial arcana. As Lord Great Chamberlain of England, de Vere was heir to a tradition at the royal coronation that involved bringing water and towels to the monarch. Earl John had performed this office at Queen Elizabeth's coronation in 1558. Before and after King James's coronation feast, the seventeenth earl of Oxford would—with all its baptismal implications—wash the royal countenance. "Hater of ceremony" though he professed to be, de Vere applied for and received this ancestral water-bearing role for King James's coronation. In the context of Sonnet 109, de Vere writes of performing the same function for himself, cleansing his soul from the metaphorical "travels" (and travails) of his own life.

As the reactions to Southampton's release from his "confined doom" continue to flow, the sickly author reflects upon the shame of his lowly playwrighting profession and to the Shake-speare "brand" now stamped on his works.

110

Alas, 'tis true, I have gone here and there
And made myself a motley [*fool*] to the [*public's*] view,
Gored mine own thoughts, sold cheap what is most dear,
Made old offences of affections new.

111

Thence comes it that my name receives a brand,
And almost thence my nature is subdued

To what it works in. . . .
　　Pity me then, dear friend, and I assure ye,
　　Ev'n that your pity is enough to cure me.

115

Those lines that I before have writ do lie,
Ev'n those that said I could not love you dearer. . . .
But reck'ning time, whose millioned accidents
Creep in 'twixt vows and change decrees of kings . . .

De Vere's worsening state of health remained at the forefront of his thoughts too.

118

[S]ick of welfare, [I] found a kind of meetness
To be diseased ere that there was true needing.

119

What potions have I drunk of Siren tears,
Distilled from limbecks [*alchemical medicines*] foul as hell within . . .
How have mine eyes out of their spheres been fitted
In the distraction of this madding fever!

123

No, Time, thou shalt not boast that I do change. . . .
Thy registers [*the biblical "book of life"*] and thee I both defy,
Not wond'ring at the present nor the past. . . .
　　This I do vow, and this shall ever be,
　　I will be true despite thy scythe and thee.

The grim reaper hovered ever nearer to the author's head, even as final preparations for Elizabeth's state funeral fell into place.

　　The historical records are unclear whether de Vere attended Queen Elizabeth's funeral. He was granted forty yards of cloth for fashioning mourning garments for himself and his servants. De Vere's role in royal processions—such as one conducted for King James the following March—was to flank the canopy bearers. And if Sonnet 125 is to be believed, de Vere was indifferent to the whole undertaking. He states that it means nothing to him to perform such ceremonial duties as a canopy bearer, putting on a great show of outward mourning for the late queen, laying a foundation for funerary monuments that will ultimately be decimated by time anyway:

125

Were't aught [*anything*] to me I bore the canopy
With my extern the outward honoring,
Or laid great bases for eternity,
Which proves more short than waste or ruining...

Nostalgia is a kaleidoscope. At the dawn of the Jacobean Age, one disillusioned courtier was fixing his retrospective gaze into the viewfinder: The queen had certainly indulged her lordly fool; her £1,000 annuity never stopped, although it was also never enough. She was maddeningly opaque and fickle; she was amazingly brilliant and fascinating. She was tightfisted, two-faced, and a horrible tease. She was, in her day, perhaps the sexiest and most alluring woman de Vere had ever met in his life. She was a hag; she was a goddess. She was dead.

In a letter dated variously April 25 and 27–mere days before Elizabeth's funeral–de Vere wrote his first reflections upon the late queen's life for Cecil. The missive is an arresting departure. Reading de Vere's sixty other extant letters, nine tenths of which were written to his father- and brother-in-law, is mostly like watching a poker game. Cards are dealt, played, and held close. But rarely, if ever, does de Vere lay them all on the table. How could he? Every piece of information handed to either Cecil *père* or *fils* was potentially a nugget of power–a tip for the spy network, a piece of gossip to be seeded among the enemy, an innocent fact that might someday be transformed into a weapon.

But de Vere's April 1603 letter to "the ryght honorable my very good Brother in Lawe, Sir Robert Cecil, principall secretarie" is as candid a glimpse into the author's mind as he ever set on paper for his in-laws. De Vere first asked what he could do "concerning our duties to the King's Majesty." De Vere had recently been caught playing in the wrong playground; now was clearly a time for an excess of "oblation" toward the new monarch. To break the ice, de Vere then shared a candid anecdote about trying to keep up with Cecil, despite a state of deteriorating health:

For the attending or meeting of His Majesty, for by reason of my infirmity, I cannot come among you [at court] so often as I wish. And by reason my house is not so near ... either I do not hear at all from you or at least with the latest [news]. As this other day it happened to me, receiving a letter at 9 of the clock, not to fail at 8 of the same morning to be at Whitehall–which, being impossible, yet I hasted so much as I came to follow you into Ludgate, though through press of people and horses, I could not reach your company as I desired. But followed as I might.

De Vere's sketch of life at King's Place makes it clear that he had picked his domicile to put some distance between himself and the court. Yet, when the call to appear at Whitehall arrived at his doorstep, he couldn't *not* respond.

The letter now shifts its attention to the upcoming state funeral. De Vere writes:

> I cannot but find a great grief in myself to remember the mistress which we have lost–under whom both you and myself from our greenest years have been in a manner brought up. And although it hath pleased God, after an earthly kingdom, to take her up into a more permanent and heavenly state, wherein I do not doubt but she is crowned with glory ... yet the long time which we spent in her service, we cannot look for so much left of our days as to bestow upon another. ...
>
> In this common shipwreck, mine is above all the rest–who least regarded, though often comforted, of all her followers, she hath left to try my fortune among the alterations of time and chance: either without sail, whereby to take advantage of any prosperous gale; or with[out] anchor to ride till the storm be overpast.

De Vere's April 1603 letter to Cecil pines for a familiar Elizabethan courtly landscape, however flawed and corrupt it may have been. To stress his point about the extremes of his fortunes, de Vere draws analogies to gales and shipwrecks. Maritime metaphors were ready at hand.

In the fall of 1575, when de Vere had been in his "greenest years" in Genoa, the visiting English earl had mustered troops alongside a leading Genoese patrician named Prospero Fattinanti–or so libels of Charles Arundell *et al.,* claim he claimed. Lord Prospero became the duke of Genoa soon after the city's civil-war-that-almost-was, while Lord Oxford allegedly bragged that he was almost made duke of Milan, were it not for Queen Elizabeth's intercession.

In 1603, as de Vere looked back upon a lifetime of misfires and should-haves, the glory of his former Genoese comrade-in-arms must have summoned up a sympathetic image of a Castiglionian courtier standing tall for the ancien régime. A world that Lord Prospero fought for and won in 1575 was a world that de Vere no doubt realized was dying just as surely as he.

As previously noted, de Vere's on-and-off secretary Anthony Munday had for years been working on translating a series of continental chivalric romances about a knight named Primaleon and his progenitors. The third book in the Primaleon series tells of a magician who controls an "enclosed island"; the magician spirits Primaleon, a prince, and other assorted characters to his island and manipulates their surroundings so as to resolve conflicts and bring lovers together. Munday's literary mining expeditions in the *Primaleon* vein paid generous dividends for his former employer: *Primaleon, Book III,* served as the source for Shake-speare's play of PROSPERO and his enchanted, "uninhabited" isle.

Generations of scholars have debated where this island could be–the Bermudas, the Azores, somewhere in the Mediterranean, the island Cuttyhunk off the coast of Massachusetts, etc. But they've missed the joke. Just as *The Tempest* is a surreal recasting of the events of the final years of de Vere's life, so the play's setting is naturally a surrealist vision of the island he called home. *The Tempest*'s "uninhabited island" is England.

The Tempest was Shake-speare's redrawing of the Elizabethan map, using *Primaleon* as a set of guideposts. Mislabeled as a romance, *The Tempest* is actually a fantastical and even dangerous satire that recounts the tales of, as noted in Chapter 10, the late Lord Burghley (GONZALO), de Vere's daughter Elizabeth (MIRANDA), and her husband the earl of Derby (FERDINAND). The plotlines these characters follow are hardly controversial–especially that of GONZALO, who represents de Vere's most sentimental recollections of his former guardian and father-in-law.

However, what makes *The Tempest* an explosive play is its burlesque of the Essex Rebellion and its key players. In 1605 the dramatist Samuel Daniel was hauled before the Privy Council to answer for the crime of dramatizing the 1601 uprising. Daniel's colleague Fulke Greville destroyed one of his plays, *Cleopatra,* out of fear that he, too, would be charged with representing the Essex Rebellion onstage.

The Tempest presents Shake-speare's final word on the horrid mistakes that Essex, Southampton, and company had made. To insulate himself from the woes of Daniel and Greville, de Vere turned the uprising into what he probably had seen it as all along: a grotesque.

The ringleader of *The Tempest*'s rebellion is a deformed subhuman named CALIBAN. Just as Essex had once had a rumored tryst with Elizabeth de Vere, so CALIBAN is said to have almost "violated" MIRANDA. CALIBAN's gross and vile nature is in part a manifestation of de Vere's dislike of Essex. But more than mere spite motivates the characterization of CALIBAN. *The Tempest*'s "man–monster" was probably also the author's satirical response to utopian visions of the "noble savage"–as most famously put forward by the sixteenth-century French philosopher Michel de Montaigne.

CALIBAN's coconspirators, in a comic apology for the other participants in the Essex Rebellion, are simple clownish drunkards who are little more than along for the ride. In Shake-speare's version of the 1601 mutiny, CALIBAN and crew try to sneak into PROSPERO's cell and steal some of his magic. But PROSPERO and his puckish muse, ARIEL, hound the rebels into a cage. After the insurgents have been tracked down and imprisoned, the play's puppet master says to ARIEL:

> PROSPERO Let them be hunted soundly. At this hour
>   Lies at my mercy all mine enemies.
>   Shortly shall all my labors end, and thou
>   Shalt have the air at freedom. For a little [while]
>   Follow, and do me service.

The suppression of the rebellion represents the culmination of PROSPERO's career as a magical creator and manipulator.

After arranging for the rebels' pardon (CALIBAN does not face Essex's mortal fate) *The Tempest*'s sorcerer reflects on his tremendous career as resuscitator of long-dead figures, such as the many monarchs and nobles who populate Shake-speare's history plays. Yet PROSPERO also knows that he has little life left in him to continue his art.

> PROSPERO   Go, release them [*the rebels*], ARIEL.
>   My charms I'll break, their senses I'll restore....
>   [T]he strong-bas'd promontory [*cliff*]
>   Have I made shake, and by the spurs pluck'd up
>   The pine and cedar. Graves at my command
>   Have wak'd their sleepers, op'd, and let 'em forth
>   By my so potent art. But this rough magic
>   I here abjure [*give up*] ... I'll break my staff,
>   Bury it certain fathoms in the earth,
>   And deeper than did ever plummet sound
>   I'll drown my book.

The self-silencing theme continues into *The Tempest*'s epilogue, in which PROSPERO walks onstage solus and addresses the audience directly. De Vere knew that the recognition of his authorship of Shake-speare would rely on those eyes and ears yet unborn who would read and watch his plays. PROSPERO's epilogue is Shake-speare's great redemption song–pleading with posterity to take him at his word. He asks for future generations' "indulgence," in both the word's secular usage and in the Catholic sense of escape from Purgatory–in this case, a Purgatory of forced anonymity.

> [R]elease me from my bands
> With the help of your good hands.
> Gentle breath of yours my sails
> Must fill, or else my project fails,
> Which was to please. Now I want
> Spirits to enforce, art to enchant,
> And my ending is despair,
> Unless I be reliev'd by prayer,

Which pierces so that it assaults
Mercy itself and frees all faults.
As you from crimes would pardon'd be,
Let your indulgence set me free.

The only kind of indulgence that would greet the earl of Oxford in 1603 came from an unexpected source to the north.

On May 7, de Vere sent Cecil (soon to be Robert Lord Cecil, baron of Essendon) a letter arguing for the restoration of the de Vere family's properties of Waltham Forest and Havering House in Essex. De Vere noted that his ancestors had owned the estate "almost sithence [*sic*] the time of William Conqueror." And it was only the pernicious whim of Henry VIII that had stripped his family of Waltham and Havering. Elizabeth had once assured de Vere that Waltham and Havering would be restored to the earldom of Oxford. "But so it was," de Vere told his former brother-in-law, "she was not so ready to perform her word as I was too ready to believe it." Having written numerous similar pleas for offices and appointments in the past, de Vere must have anticipated that his words would fall on deaf ears–just as they had throughout the previous four decades.

Yet, on July 18, King James granted de Vere his wish. Waltham and Havering were now his.

The following week, on July 25, de Vere ceremonially washed the king at the coronation dinner and, "hater of ceremonies" though he was, participated in the coronation service at Westminster.

James kept the benevolence flowing. On August 2, the newly crowned monarch extended de Vere's £1,000 annuity. This was no mere pro forma exercise. Consolidating the account books of two national treasuries to make one impoverished nation, James could just as easily have cut de Vere off. Instead, the king extended his predecessor's benevolence, as if presenting a peace offering. De Vere had never known such swift royal remuneration in his life.

A thank you to this very generous monarch was in order.

During August, James and his court were on an inaugural progress throughout the western and southern counties of England. They'd reached the city of Salisbury on August 26. Tantalizing secondhand evidence exists of a letter from de Vere's friend the dowager countess of Pembroke to her son William Herbert, earl of Pembroke–who was then, presumably, on progress with the king. The literary patroness and poet commanded her son to return home and bring the king with him. *As You Like It,* she noted, was about to be performed on the grounds of Wilton House. And, the dowager countess reportedly assured her son, "we have the man Shakespeare with us."

Sure enough, according to the royal chronicler John Nichols, "On the twenty-ninth and thirtieth of August, the Royal Party were entertained at Wilton." The man *Shakspere* was part of the newly incorporated King's Men (formerly the Lord Chamberlain's Men), and the King's Men were touring the provinces during the summer of 1603, since the London stages had been closed for the plague. The question remains unanswered, however, whether the dowager countess was referring in her letter to the actor who inspired WILLIAM or the man who created WILLIAM. The Wilton performance of *As You Like It,* in either case, would have been a fitting introduction to Shakespeare for the new king: love put to the test, family feuds, exiled courtiers, high hilarity, and an author's standoff with a country clown.

De Vere's youngest daughter, Susan, was evidently on friendly terms with her lame and impoverished father around this time. She signed a letter dated only "1603" to Cecil from Hackney–presumably King's Place. The girl wrote her uncle to request permission to borrow some money to visit Queen Anne, "knowing my charges [*expenses*] would be more than ordinary." Lady Susan came by her propensity for borrowing naturally.

As de Vere's one remaining single daughter, the sixteen-year-old girl faced the aristocratic marriage market with a distinct disadvantage: Her father had nothing to offer for a dowry. During the previous summer, the poet and pardoned Essex rebel John Davies–who had previously written a masque to celebrate Elizabeth de Vere's wedding–had said as much in considerably more loaded language. Davies had written a masque for a group of noble young ladies, including Susan de Vere, to perform at court during the summer of 1602. As part of the show, each masquer was given a gift accompanied by a witty couplet. Susan was given nothing. Davies's epigram for her read:

> Nothing's your lot. That's more than can be told.
> For Nothing is more precious than gold.

What in the early seventeenth-century was "more than can be told" can today be told in one word: CORDELIA.

As the youngest of de Vere's three daughters, Susan de Vere was a clear prototype for *King Lear*'s dowerless child:

LEAR What can you say to draw a third more opulent than your sisters?
  Speak.
CORDELIA Nothing.
LEAR Nothing?
COR. Nothing.
LEAR Nothing will come of nothing. Speak again.
COR. Unhappy that I am, I cannot heave
  My heart into my mouth. I love Your Majesty
  According to my bond, no more nor less. . . .

LEAR But goes thy heart with this?
COR. Ay, my good lord.
LEAR So young and so untender?
COR. So young, my lord, and true.
LEAR Let it be so. Thy truth then be thy dow'r!

CORDELIA's banter with her father plays like a baroque minuet upon the de Vere family motto: Nothing truer than truth.

While CORDELIA's story is well known, the play's EDMUND–EDGAR subplot is underappreciated. Onto the original father–daughter plot of *King Leir*–a Queen's Men's text that no doubt originated with de Vere and his secretaries–de Vere grafted a story from Sir Philip Sidney about a deceiving bastard son who disinherits his legitimate half-brother through treachery. EDMUND and EDGAR's battle for possession of their father's true rights parallels what must have been one truly tempestuous internal struggle going on in de Vere's mind as he prepared himself for the grave–and wondered how his children and, ultimately, posterity would perceive him.

The bastard of *King Lear*, EDMUND, tricks his gullible father (the EARL OF GLOUCESTER) into doubting the truth of GLOUCESTER's own legitimate son (EDGAR) by means of a letter, a written text.

GLOUCESTER. What paper were you reading?
EDMUND Nothing, my lord.
GLO. No?... The quality of nothing hath not such need to hide itself.
  Let's see. Come, if it be nothing, I shall not need spectacles.

Lear's symphony of "nothing" continues.

EDMUND then convinces his trusting brother to flee on the false pretense that EDGAR has somehow acted offensively toward their father. To escape detection, EDGAR disguises himself as a madman.

EDGAR Whiles I may 'scape
  I will preserve myself and am bethought
  To take the basest and most poorest shape
  That ever penury, in contempt of man,
  Brought near to beast. My face I'll grime with filth,
  Blanket my loins, elf all my hairs in knots,
  And with presented nakedness outface
  The winds and persecutions of the sky....
  That's something yet. EDGAR I nothing am.

EDGAR meets up with the disheveled and distracted LEAR, who becomes convinced that EDGAR is a "philosopher" and a "learned Theban." EDGAR winds up guiding a blinded GLOUCESTER, who naturally only gains his vision for the truth after he loses his physical sight.

Yet, as the tides begin to turn and EDMUND and his fellow villains begin to lose the power they've usurped, EDGAR casts aside his feigned monstrosity. "Men must endure their going hence even as their coming hither," EDGAR observes. "Ripeness is all."

A letter written by EDGAR issues a challenge to single combat with ED-MUND. Finally, as EDGAR and EDMUND meet for their duel, EDGAR conceals his face behind a helmet. When a HERALD instructs EDGAR to identify himself to the crowd, the anonymous combatant replies:

> EDGAR Know, my name is lost.
> By treason's tooth bare-gnawn and canker-bit,
> Yet am I noble as the adversary
> I come to cope.

EDMUND falls, and EDGAR reveals himself to the world. EDGAR the true conquers EDMUND the false, and though his name was "lost," EDGAR is ultimately brought forth into the light.

In January 1604, even as the first steps were being taken for a project that would become the King James Bible, de Vere returned to the work that began when his life effectively began—at the age of twelve, upon the death of his father and his arrival at the lion's den of Cecil House.

The Tempest may have been the last play the author created from start to finish. But *Hamlet* must be another one of the last works de Vere touched: The final scene, if nothing else, appears to date from that brief period, from August 1603 onward, when King James had won over a once-reluctant de Vere. In the person of his Danish prince, de Vere gives an ex post facto nod to the legitimacy of the Scots regime. As HAMLET lies dying, he explains to his confidant HORATIO—in words reminiscent of Beowulf's instructions to his beloved Wiglaf—that the prince from the kingdom to the north (FORTINBRAS) should inherit the throne.

> HAMLET I cannot live to hear the news from England.
> But I do prophesy th' election lights
> On FORTINBRAS. He has my dying voice. . . .
> FORTINBRAS For me, with sorrow, I embrace my fortune.
> I have some rights of memory in this kingdom,
> Which now to claim my vantage doth invite me.

Although the invading warrior FORTINBRAS does not represent King James as HAMLET so thoroughly represents de Vere, the closing lines of Shake-speare's greatest play are de Vere's peace offering to a monarch who had treated him with respect.

On January 30, 1604, de Vere wrote a businesslike letter to James to thank him again for his generosity in restoring Waltham and Havering to his otherwise ruined estate, to report on a survey he'd ordered of the lands, and to advocate for the prosecution of a poacher, Sir John Gray. The simple fact that de Vere could write to the king directly without going through an intermediary on the Privy Council—verboten under the Tudors—was a harbinger of the many changes the Stuarts would be ushering in. Had de Vere lived a few more years into James's regime, his fortunes might well have been better secured.

But that did not happen. Instead, de Vere attended one state function and then simply dropped from sight. On March 15, 1604, de Vere joined a parade of peers escorting the new king through London. A lame, poor, and despised earl of Oxford marched within a pike's length from King James, who was borne aloft, sheltered beneath a canopy. The Earl Marshal—Edward Somerset, earl of Worcester—carried the Sword of State, marching next to de Vere. Four days later, James called his first Parliament. De Vere and his peers were summoned to the House of Lords; de Vere never appeared. More money was owed, this time to a joiner who claimed to have worked on Fisher's Folly and Plaistow House, which went unpaid.

On June 18, de Vere transferred custody of the forest of Essex to his son-in-law Lord Norris and his cousin Sir Francis Vere.

On June 24, the earl of Oxford died of unknown causes—no doubt of the maladies that had long plagued him. De Vere was buried in the churchyard of St. Augustine at Hackney on July 6. De Vere's half-cousin Percival Golding later wrote a brief eulogy to the deceased.

Edward de Vere, only son of John, born the 12th day of April 1550, earl of Oxenford, high chamberlain, Lord Bolbec, Sandford, and Badlesmere, steward of the forest in Essex, and of the Privy Council to the King's Majesty that now is. [*De Vere was not, so far as can be determined today, a member of King James's Privy Council.*] Of whom I will only speak what all men's voices confirm: He was a man in mind and body absolutely accomplished with honorable endowments.

During the eighteenth century, the Church of St. Augustine at Hackney was razed, and the present St. John-at-Hackney was erected in its place. Golding also reported that "Edward de Veer ... lieth buried at Westminster [Abbey]." This curious claim has never been corroborated. De Vere's corpse appears to have been lost to the ages. De Vere's corpus, on the other hand, still awaits its final verdict.

> HAMLET I am dead, HORATIO. Wretched queen, adieu!
> You that look pale, and tremble at this chance,
> That are but mutes or audience to this act,
> Had I but time—as this fell sergeant Death,
> Is strict in his arrest—O, I could tell you—
> But let it be. HORATIO, I am dead.
> Thou livest. Report me and my cause aright
> To the unsatisfied. . . .
> O God, HORATIO, what a wounded name,
> Things standing thus unknown, shall I leave behind me!
> If thou didst ever hold me in thy heart,
> Absent thee from felicity awhile,
> And in this harsh world, draw thy breath in pain
> To tell my story.

EPILOGUE

[1604–1623]

A N AIR OF MYSTERY SURROUNDS EDWARD DE VERE'S JUNE 24, 1604, death. He left no will; there is no record of any funeral. But for the elegies referred to in Chapter 11, there were no memorials.

One possible reason for the hush-hush nature of de Vere's passing has been suggested: suicide. Had the ailing earl taken his own life, the law mandated that some of his possessions–including, perhaps, manuscripts–should be forfeited to the crown. A suicide's survivors would thus be ill advised to draw any attention to the deceased. Those with political clout would no doubt pull whatever strings they could to paper over the legal quagmire.

Equally mysterious was the other event that took place on June 24. On the evening of de Vere's death, King James rounded up the earl of Southampton and assorted former Essex Rebellion cohorts. As Nicolo Molin, the Venetian ambassador to England, wrote to his superiors in letters posted June 26 and July 4:

> On Sunday night [June 24], by order of the king and [Privy] Council, the earl of Southampton, Baron Danvers, and five others were arrested and each one confined in a separate house. Yesterday morning [June 25], after undergoing several examinations, they were set at liberty....

> [*Molin continues on July 4*]
> The reason for Southampton's arrest was the slanderous charge preferred against him by unknown enemies that he plotted to slay several Scots who were much about the person of the king. On his release, he went to the king and declared that if he knew who the slanderer was he would challenge him to combat. But as he did not, he could only appeal to His Majesty. The king gave him fair words but nothing else as yet.

According to Sir Anthony Weldon's 1650 retrospective history of the Jacobean court, the king acted on the urging of Sir Robert Cecil–now Lord Salisbury–who had "put some jealousies into the king's head."

King Henri IV of France, the former king of Navarre, marveled to his English ambassador in a letter dated July 14:

> I find it strange that [King James] dissatisfies at once the Catholics and Puritans, that he so lightly jailed and then released the earl of Southampton and the other persons designated in your specified letters.

King James's strange behavior–and his malleability at the hands of Cecil and others–would be the subject for much gossip in the years to come.

Sometime during the latter half of 1604 an ornate print edition of *Hamlet* appeared, the title page of which said it was "newly imprinted and enlarged to almost as much again as it was according to the true and perfect copy." A printer's device incorporating the royal coat of arms graced the top of the first page of the play's text. The 1604 "good quarto" of *Hamlet* was to be as regal a funereal send-off for Shake-speare as the closing scene of the Danish tragedy. After the 1604 *Hamlet* quarto was published, the rest was indeed silence.

Excepting a brief spate noted below, no new Shake-speare plays would appear in print between 1604 and the months leading up to the 1623 First Folio. The Shake-speare canon contains no unambiguous references to literary sources or events after 1604. Although Shake-speare waxes poetic about a number of pre-1604 scientific discoveries (including William Gilbert's 1600 theory of geomagnetism and "Tycho's Supernova" of 1572), no new science appears in Shake-speare after de Vere's death (including a supernova that appeared in October 1604 and Johannes Kepler's groundbreaking 1609 study of the orbit of the planet Mars). Although some pre-1604 reprints of Shake-speare plays had advertised that they were "newly corrected" by the author, after 1604 Shake-speare stopped correcting his published works too.

The documentary evidence for post-1604 composition of the Shake-speare canon is vanishingly small–arguably nil. After de Vere's death, the Shake-speare factory had all but closed down. (For more on the multiple layers of post-1604 Shake-spearean silence, see Appendix C, "The 1604 Question.")

The King's Men would continue performing Shake-speare plays through the remainder of the decade and into the next, from *King Lear* and *Julius Caesar* at court to *Cymbeline* and *The Winter's Tale* at the Globe Theatre. But these performance records give no indication when these plays were written. No doubt in a gesture of gratitude for James's kind treatment of the Essex conspirators, one overnight house arrest notwithstanding, Southampton staged *Love's Labor's Lost* for James and the court during the Christmas revels season of 1604–05.

De Vere's ghost was scarcely allowed a moment's rest. Brokers and play buyers would have been eager to get their hands on the late author's unpublished and unstaged works. Friends of the family and de Vere's professional colleagues were in an ideal position to access the priceless papers to be found at King's Place in Hackney.

In a satire published in 1604, Anthony Munday's friend Thomas Middleton mused over this very scenario. In Middleton's 1604 *Black Book*, Lucifer returns to earth after receiving Pierce Penniless's letters.

> No sooner was *Pierce Penniless* breathed forth, but I, the light-burning sergeant, Lucifer, quenched my fiery shape and whipped into a constable's nightgown, the cunningest habit that could be, to search tipsy taverns, roosting inns, and frothy alehouses.

One of the characters Lucifer runs across in his wanderings is a destitute FAL-STAFFian lieutenant married to a prostitute named Audrey. (Recall AUDREY was the name of the country muse whom TOUCHSTONE marries in *As You Like It*.) Lucifer discovers the lieutenant and his dear Audrey sleeping.

Middleton describes the abject and pitiful state of the rogue officer, not unlike HAMLET in his antic disposition: "In a pair of hoary slippers, his stockings dangling about his wrists [*sic*], and his red buttons like foxes out of their holes..." The disturbed lieutenant can hardly contain his anger at being raised from what he calls his "first sleep."

> "Why, master constable," [the lieutenant exclaims,] "dare you balk us in our own mansion, ha? What! Is not our house our coal harbor [*sanctuary*], our castle of come-down and lie-down? Must my honest, wedded punk here, my glory-fat Audrey, be taken napping and raised up by the thunder of bill men? Are we disannulled of our first sleep and cheater of our dreams and fantasies?...
>
> "Come you to search an honest bawdy-house, this seven and twenty years in fame and shame? [*twenty-seven years before, 1577, marked the first full year of de Vere's post-Italy downward spiral*] Go to, then, you shall search. Nay, my very boots too. Are you well now? The least hole in my house too. Are you pleased now?"

The lieutenant—who expresses his desire to bring his tales of woe and destitution to the stage—ends up trying to borrow money from the devil. Lucifer returns the playwright-lieutenant's rage with interest. The demon from the netherworld exclaims:

After many such inductions to bring the scene of his poverty upon the stage, he [*the lieutenant*] desired me, in cool terms, to borrow some forty pence of me. I, stuffed with anger at that base and lazy petition... replied to his baseness, "Why, for shame!"

Even the grave could not stop de Vere's friends and colleagues from joking about the literary earl's never-ending need to borrow money.

The first sign of posthumous life in the Shake-speare publishing world came in late 1607. A book publisher named Nathaniel Butter secured a version of the text of *King Lear*. The London Stationer's Office registered *Lear* for publication in November. Sometime the following year, the printer Nicholas Okes ushered Shake-speare's great tragedy onto the London book market.

Leaks often precede a burst, and the 1608 first edition of *Lear* was just such a leak. The dowager countess of Oxford and her fifteen-year-old son, the eighteenth earl of Oxford, no longer needed the suburban isolation from court that King's Place had afforded her late husband. The young earl was like his father as a teenager. Henry de Vere needed to be in the center of the courtly universe, establishing a name for himself and beginning to climb the ladder of royal preferment.

On April 1, 1609, Elizabeth Trentham de Vere was given royal permission to sell the King's Place house and grounds, which included 270 acres of land. In June, she sold King's Place plus two hundred acres for £4,980, making herself a handsome £1,680 profit. The new homeowner of King's Place, Sir Fulke Greville, was a courtier, a scholar and—as if the gods of courtly rivalries had arranged the deal themselves—the fawning biographer of Sir Philip Sidney. Greville would make King's Place his greater London residence, and his heirs would hand the property down the family line for the next two centuries. Greville later renamed his domicile Brooke House, after a barony granted him by King James.

As with any move, a relocating family consolidates and packs some things and jettisons others. The period 1608–09 is both the period during which King's Place was being cleaned and prepared for new owners and the one posthumous window (before the 1622–23 production of the First Folio) during which new Shake-speare works appeared in print.

A pilfered copy of *Pericles* made its way in 1609 into the hands of the publisher and bookseller Henry Gosson, whose quarto of the play became so popular it went through two editions in its first year. During the same year, the printer George Eld came out with a controversial edition of *Troilus and Cressida*. Eld first printed this play with a front-page advertisement that the King's Men had performed the play at the Globe Theatre. Before the year was out, however, Eld had issued a corrected version of the play quarto that disowned any affiliation with any theatrical company–attaching a preface that stated, disingenuously, that the text had never been enacted before. ("Eternal reader, you have here a new play, never staled with the stage, never clapper-clawed with the palms of the vulgar . . .")

Nevertheless, whatever trouble *Troilus and Cressida* caused, Eld was still having a banner year. In 1609, Eld would also print one of the most pondered-over books in literary history. On May 20, the publisher Thomas Thorpe registered with the Stationer's Company "A Booke called Shake-speares sonnettes."

Here is the title page:

SHAKE-SPEARES

S O N N E T S.

Neuer before Imprinted.

AT LONDON
By *G. Eld* for *T. T.* and are
to be folde by *Iohn Wright*,dwelling
at Chrift Church gate.
1 6 0 9.

The book dedication, from the book's publisher to a "Mr. W.H." appeared on page two.

The identity of the *Sonnets'* dedicatee–and the meaning of the twelve-line salutation–has puzzled scholars and writers over the centuries. Oscar Wilde's short story, "The Portrait of Mr. W.H.," hypothesizes that the mystery dedicatee was Willie Hughes, "a wonderful boy actor of great beauty." Other candidates put forward have included William Herbert (earl of Pembroke), Henry Wriothesley (earl of Southampton) with the initials reversed, William

Hathaway, William Harte, and Sir William Harvey. The nineteenth-century sleuth D. Barnstorff even suggested "William himself."

Three clues can be gleaned from the dedication and title page above that might identify "Mr. W.H.":

· He is on familiar terms with Thomas Thorpe and/or George Eld and perhaps has worked with one or both of them before.

· He was in 1609 "setting forth" on an "adventure" that inspires Thomas Thorpe to wish him "that eternity promised by our ever-living poet." The eternity *Shake-speare's Sonnets* speaks of, in the first seventeen sonnets especially, is settling down and having children. Mr. W.H., in other words, appears to have recently been married.

· He's the "only begetter" of *Shake-speare's Sonnets*–probably using a now-antiquated sense of the word "beget," meaning "to get or acquire, usually by effort."

The first clue points to a poem written by the duke of Norfolk's eldest son, Philip Howard, *A Four-Fold Meditation* (1606). Howard was convicted for treason in 1589, by a jury on which de Vere sat. Howard was never executed; he died in the Tower of London in 1595. George Eld printed *A Four-Fold Meditation,* which one "W.H." appears to have acquired for him. In a preface to *Four-Fold Meditation,* "W.H." writes that Howard's poems had "long...lien in

TO. THE .ONLIE. BEGETTER. OF.
THESE . INSVING . SONNETS.
Mr. W. H. ALL .HAPPINESSE.
AND .THAT. ETERNITIE.
PROMISED.

BY.

OVR. EVER-LIVING. POET.

WISHETH.

THE . WELL-WISHING.
ADVENTVRER . IN.
SETTING.
FORTH.

T. T.

obscurity, and haply [perhaps] had never seen the light, had not a mere accident conveyed them to my hands."

As for the second clue, the Hackney parish registers record the marriage of one William Hall in August of 1608, less than a year before the publication of *Shake-speare's Sonnets*. There was also a William Hall who wrote commendatory verses to his cousin Anthony Munday–de Vere's secretary–in Munday's 1579 book *The Mirror of Mutability*. If these two William Halls were the same, or even simply related, the third clue may solve the riddle.

De Vere and his second wife, as noted in Chapter 10, had heard pleas by Philip Howard's brother Thomas in the early 1590s, no doubt to assist the family in obtaining royal clemency for the convicted Philip. Knowing that poetry provided a fast track to winning de Vere's sympathies, Thomas may well have given a manuscript copy of Philip's poetic lamentations to the literary earl. Thus one suspects *A Four-Fold Meditation* among de Vere's books and papers at the time of his death in 1604.

Who better, then, to enjoy the "mere accident" of being handed *A Four-Fold Meditation* than the kinsman of de Vere's private secretary? As the preface to the book would imply, Hall turned around and sold the manuscript to George Eld.

Three years later, a newly married Hall (he's "*Mr. W.H.*" now) enjoyed the providence of a far greater "mere accident" as the de Vere family was moving out of King's Place. Munday's kinsman acquired, no doubt with some effort, de Vere's *Sonnets*. The same channels landed the manuscript in Eld's hands, and a publisher grateful beyond measure wrote a gushing preface dedicating the book to Hall, wishing the newlywed "all happinesse" for his nuptial adventures ahead and that Hall's marriage be blessed with many children.

In 1612, another puzzle concerning de Vere's posthumous legacy appeared in the London bookstalls. And this one was unmistakably designed as a puzzle.

The courtly observer Henry Peacham's book *Minerva Britanna* was a multilingual tour de force of Renaissance cryptography. *Minerva* belonged to a genre known as the "emblem book," a collection of allegorical engravings accompanied by explanatory poems. Emblem books used anagrams, pictograms, and other arcane methods of encoding secret messages to conceal everything from secrets of state to bawdy jokes. In the sixteenth century, scores of emblem books were published in Italy, France, Germany, Spain, and The Netherlands. But Peacham was one of the first to introduce the emblem book to English eyes.

Here is the title page:

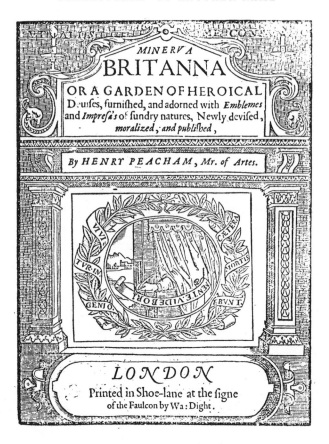

Four clues identify the subject of Peacham's title page engraving:

- Consider the title: *Minerva of Britain.* Minerva was the Roman counterpart to the spear-shaking Greek goddess Athena. Presented in the context of the rest of Peacham's title page, one might translate *Minerva Britanna* as "England's spear-shaker."
- The Latin inscriptions tell de Vere's story. Two candles burn at the top of the page, surrounded by the words, "I consume myself for others in a similar way." *(Ut aliis me consumo.)* Just as the tapers give of themselves to illuminate their surroundings, the mystery subject dissipates itself. Winding scrolls surrounding the central image read, "One lives by means of his genius. The rest will belong to death." *(Vivitur ingenio. Caetera mortis erunt.)*
- The central engraving features a hidden man's hand writing from behind a theatrical curtain. The title page emblem would appear to be about a disguised playwright.
- Lastly, the hand from behind the curtain writes on a scroll the words "By the mind, I will be seen." *(Mente videbor.)* The hidden playwright appears to be adding the letter *i* to *videbor.* However, there is no Latin word

"*videbori.*" Yet "*videbori*" makes a perfect anagram of the sentence—and would also make sense of the stray period between the two words. Unscramble "*MENTE.VIDEBORI,*" and one Latin phrase makes all the pieces of the puzzle fit together: *TIBI NOM. DE VERE.* Or in English: "Thy name is de Vere."

Peacham knew de Vere's secret, and when Peacham's courtly etiquette book *The Compleat Gentleman* came out years later, the puzzlemaster presented an exhaustive list of the great Elizabethan poets. At the top of Peacham's list was "Edward, earle of Oxford." Nowhere in Peacham's 1622 book—or in any of his revised editions that appeared over the ensuing four decades—does Peacham mention Shake-speare. Peacham must have understood that doing so would be a redundancy.

Minerva Britanna had appeared on the London book market during the midst of a turbulent year. In May of 1612, the forty-eight-year-old Sir Robert Cecil, Baron Salisbury, Viscount Cranbourne, breathed his last. Six months later, the great and celebrated hope for the future of Protestant England, Prince Henry, King James's eighteen-year-old son, unexpectedly died of typhoid fever.

England was in mourning for months. In the nine years since Queen Elizabeth's death, King James I had proved himself to be little more than a place holder for some great monarch to come. By all signs, Henry, Prince of Wales, would have been that monarch: brilliant, erudite, well trained as a military man, an enthusiastic patron of the creative arts, an unrepentant but still accommodating moderate Protestant, a decisive man of high morals. Had Prince Henry lived to assume his place on the throne, it's likely that post–seventeenth–century world history would be unrecognizable today.

Instead, Henry's corrupt younger brother Charles eventually inherited the crown and so enraged Parliament and the population at large in the 1640s as to spark the English Civil War—a conflagration that resulted in Charles's beheading in 1649 and in which Oliver Cromwell's Puritan revolution shut down all the theaters.

This sociopolitical turbulence during the early seventeenth century would be responsible in no small part for continuing the Shake-speare ruse past the lifetimes of the author and his contemporaries.

During these days of funerals and funereal tributes, an ailing dowager countess made out her last will and testament. In her November 1612 will, Elizabeth Trentham de Vere—who had devoted the eight years after her husband's death to restoring the earldom of Oxford to some semblance of solvency—requested that her body be buried "in the Church of Hackney . . . as near unto the body of my said late dear and noble lord and husband as may be." She further willed "that there be in the said Church erected for us a tomb fitting our degree and of such charge as shall seem good to mine executors hereafter named."

On January 6, 1613, two letters from correspondents at court noted the passing of the dowager countess of Oxford—one of them stating that her fatal malady was "this new disease," probably meaning typhoid fever. The Hackney parish registers record Elizabeth Trentham de Vere's burial on January 3. Her exact date of death is unknown.

One of the countess's greatest accomplishments after her husband's death was the repatriation of Castle Hedingham. Yet Edward's son, Henry de Vere, was to be the last of his lineage to own the ancestral Essex estate, a family seat that had been in the Vere family since the days of William the Conqueror. After the eighteenth earl's death, in 1625, Castle Hedingham would pass to his wife, Diana Cecil—great-granddaughter to William Cecil, Lord Burghley.

During the Christmas revels season of 1612–13, King James celebrated a Protestant marriage match that distracted from the mourning for Prince Henry. On December 27, 1612, a sixteen-year-old princess Elizabeth Stuart accepted a marriage offer made by her contemporary Frederick, elector Palatine—soon to be Frederick V, king of Bohemia. The ensuing months before the couple's April departure, including their February 1613 wedding, featured a stunning twenty court performances by the King's Men. The works of that great Anglican apologist of yesteryear, Shake-speare, served as a centerpiece of the King's Men's repertory for the anti-Catholic crusader and his bride. Works performed included the War of the Henris redux *Julius Caesar,* the Bohemian-flavored opera *The Winter's Tale,* and the post-Elizabethan satire *The Tempest.*

Elizabethan nostalgia had already become a cottage industry. In 1615, one such sentimentalist, the prolific scribbler Richard Brathwait, published a satire *(Strappado for the Devil)* about the glory years of Queen Elizabeth and the inferior literary works being published under King James. Brathwait wrote:

> Yea, this I know I may be bold to say,
> Thames ne'er had swans that sung more sweet than they.
> It's true I may avow it, that ne'er was sung,
> Chanted in any age by swains so young,
> With more delight than was perform'd by them,
> Prettily shadow'd in a borrowed name.
> And long may England's thespian springs be known.

In so many words, Brathwait blew Shake-speare's cover. Translated into contemporary English:

> Let me tell you: London never saw writers more gifted than the ones I saw during the reign of Queen Elizabeth. And never were there more

delightful plays than the ones performed by youth [*probably the children's companies*] whose author wrote under a borrowed name.

Sometime around 1613, Will Shakspere is conventionally believed to have retired from London and returned to his hometown to lead a country burgher's life. In 1614, "Mr. Shakspeare" is listed as a landowner in Stratford. In 1616, he drew up his will. He died on his fifty-second birthday, April 23, 1616.

The epitaph on Shakspere's gravestone inside Stratford-upon-Avon's Trinity Church is an embarrassing piece of mock-Gothic doggerel. To quote Mark Twain:

> So far as anyone *knows and can prove,* Shakespeare of Stratford wrote only one poem during his life. This one is authentic. He did write that one–a fact which stands undisputed; he wrote the whole of it; he wrote the whole of it out of his own head. He commanded that this work of art be engraved upon his tomb, and he was obeyed. There it abides to this day. This is it:
>
> > Good friend, for Jesus' sake forbear
> > To dig the dust enclosed here.
> > Blessed be ye man that spares these stones,
> > And cursed be he that moves my bones.
>
> ... He was probably dead when he wrote it. Still, this is only conjecture. We have only circumstantial evidence. Internal evidence.

Nearby Shakspere's gravestone, on the north wall of Trinity Church, stands a monument to Shakspere that constitutes–together with the prefatory material to the 1623 First Folio of Shake-speare–the strongest case ever made that Shakspere wrote Shake-speare. No records exist of the construction of the Stratford monument. The first notice of Shakspere's monument appears in 1623, in prefatory verses by Leonard Digges in the Shake-speare Folio ("When that stone is rent/And time dissolves thy Stratford monument ...").

The monument contains a cryptic engraved epigram, a reproduction of the Shakspere coat of arms, and two cherublike figures who sit atop a ledge that shelters a bust of Shakspere. Shakspere's likeness rests his arms on a pillow, upon which sits a blank piece of paper. Shakspere grasps at a quill pen with his right hand and gazes emptily out into space. The bust has been the subject of much witty chatter throughout the ages. As Twain wrote:

> The bust too–there in the Stratford Church. The precious bust, the priceless bust, the calm bust, the serene bust, the emotionless bust, with the dandy moustache, and the putty face, unseamed of care–that face which

has looked passionlessly down upon the awed pilgrim for a hundred and fifty years and will still look down upon the awed pilgrim three hundred more, with the deep, deep, deep, subtle, subtle, subtle expression of a bladder.

The Shakspere monument's eight-line epitaph, at first glance, would appear to support the conclusion that Shakspere was Shake-speare. But the epitaph, like the monument itself, is a red herring. The first line, written in Latin, states that Shakspere was "A Nestor in judgment, a Socrates in genius, a Virgil in art." All three analogies—inapt for Shake-speare—fit the "upstart crow" Shakspere capably. In Homer's *Iliad*, Nestor is both a garrulous storyteller and a self-appointed spokesman for his people. Shakspere, one supposes, manifested the judgment of Nestor in regaling theatergoers with rambling tales of his fictional literary talents. Socrates is never known to have written a word; some of his contemporaries, most notably Plato, wrote *about* him. Praising Shakspere's "Socratic genius" and "Nestor-like judgment" tells the learned admirer that Shakspere was a talker, not a writer. Finally, a "Virgil in art" can just as readily be read as a "Virgil in artifice." Virgil, as previously noted, had an infamous run-in with an impostor (Batillus) who tried to claim credit for one of Virgil's poems. Furthermore, many Renaissance readers believed that Virgil composed his great works possessed by a holy spirit, that Virgil's ghost was the true author of *The Aeneid*.

The English portion of Shakspere's epitaph is more vexing than the Latin. It concludes with a convoluted sentence that contains the only potential reference to Shakspere as a writer: "Sieh [*German: 'look there'*] all that he hath writ leaves living art but page to serve his wit." The phrase "Look there [at] all that he hath writ" sounds more sarcastic than honorific. And the imperative "Look *there*" would seem to point the viewer across the Trinity Church chapel to Shakspere's burial marker with the "Good friend for Jesus sake forebear..." verse engraved on it.

What this perplexing sentence, then, says is "Look there at that doggerel Shakespere wrote: All his wit leaves a living corpus of works that adds up to a single page." A second reading turns on the meaning of *art* as "contrivance" or "ruse," *page* as "servant," and *wit* as "a witty person": "Look there at the one thing Shakspere wrote: The rest lives on as the ruse that is but a servant to the wit whom Shakspere stood for."

The English section of Shakspere's epitaph—the authorship of which is unattributed—famously begins, "Stay, passenger. Why goest thou by so fast? Read if thou canst, whom envious death hath placed within this monument Shakespeare." These three sentences, in fact, point to the obscurantist handiwork of the same Latinate satirist who crafted the scandalous *Isle of Dogs* with Thomas Nashe and who would in 1623 oversee the Shake-speare First Folio. Ben Jonson's known epitaphs written in memory of other notables of his day include such lines as "Wouldst thou hear what man can say in a little? Reader, stay," and "If, passenger, thou canst but read, stay," and "Stay, view this stone; and if thou beest not such, read here a little, that thou mayst know much."

What remained was the myth. De Vere had left behind a corpus of work that now rested in the hands of his progeny. And as *King Lear* had prophesied, the youngest daughter proved true to her father's life and legacy.

In December of 1604, six months after her father's death, Susan de Vere had married into the Herbert family—headed up by the literary legend Mary Sidney Herbert, dowager countess of Pembroke. Edward de Vere had tried and failed to marry his second daughter, Bridget, into the Herbert clan. But, soon after Susan's father passed away, Susan made the family tie her father could not. Two days after Christmas of 1604, the seventeen-year-old Susan married Sir Philip Herbert (later earl of Montgomery) in an elaborate wedding.

The Herberts were the premier literary aristocratic family in the early seventeenth century. And in this great English Renaissance household, young Susan (b. 1587) revealed how much of her father's love of letters and learning she'd inherited. Susan had performed in Jacobean courtly masques and had been the subject of literary tributes by leading writers such as Nathaniel Baxter, John Ford, Aemilia Lanyer, and Joshua Sylvester. Susan admired John Donne's preaching and once requested a copy of his sermons for further study. Anthony Munday, in his ongoing project to translate the Palmerin–Amadis de Gaule romances into English, sought out the latter-day CORDELIA for her assistance in tracking down obscure literary sources. She found for him, he later wrote, "such books as were of the best editions." One dedication to Susan and her husband stands out in particular. In 1619, the London printer and bookseller William Jaggard dedicated to the noble couple a book called *The Ancient Treasury (Archaio-Ploutus)*, an anthology of folklore and customs of the English, Italian, Spanish, and Gallic cultures.

Also in 1619, Jaggard had been hurriedly issuing a series of ten Shakespeare reprints—two of which, *The Yorkshire Tragedy* and *Sir John Oldcastle*, were falsely advertised as being written by Shake-speare. Jaggard was an ambitious man who by 1619 was evidently positioning himself to become the de facto printer of Shake-speare's works. To do this, Jaggard needed access to the vault of unpublished Shake-speare plays. Susan de Vere Herbert, countess of Montgomery, would be the solution to Jaggard's problem.

Here is where Jaggard turned on the charm. His florid dedication to *The Ancient Treasury* began:

To the most Noble and Twin-like pair of truly honorable and complete perfection: Sir Philip Herbert . . . earl of Montgomery . . .

As also to the truly vertuous and noble countess his wife, the lady Susan, daughter to the Right Honorable Edward Vere, earle of Oxenford, Viscount Bolbvec, Lord Sandford and of Baldesmere and Lord High Chamberlain of England, &c.

Jaggard dedicated almost as much ink listing Susan's father's titles and offices as he did those of either of his dedicatees. Already, one senses his agenda. He invited his patrons to "enter into a spacious forest," where he said Lady Susan

> ... may meet with a fair bevy of queens and ladies, at diverse turnings as you walk. And every one will tell you the history of her life and fortune (rare examples of virtue and honor) as themselves can best, truly and plainly discourse unto you. Some other also you shall see, sadly sitting under yew and cypress trees, with garlands of those leaves wreathed about their heads, sighing out their divers disasters: whom your noble nature cannot choose but commiserate, as grieving to see a scratch in a clear skin and a body beautified by nature, to be blemished by unkind destiny.

Jaggard's words offer up a simple first layer of meaning: *Please, my lord and lady, enjoy reading this book.* But Jaggard was also making a secondary and far more important appeal. He noted:

> ... an orchard stands wide open to welcome you, richly abounding in the fairest fruitages: not to feed the eye only, but likewise to refresh the heart, inviting you to pluck where and while you please and to bestow how and when you list.

The fruits of the orchard that Jaggard appealed to his dedicatees to "bestow how and when you list" was not money or political influence, it was manuscripts.

For the next couple of years, Jaggard's pleas would lie unanswered. But, as the independent American researcher Peter W. Dickson recently discovered, international religious politics soon changed the equation.

Since assuming the throne, King James had proven himself a protector of the Anglican faith–from sponsoring a confrontational 1604 religious conference that resulted seven years later in the King James Bible, to stubbornly driving a congregation of Puritan nonconformists to found a colony at Plymouth, Massachusetts, in 1620. Yet, the king once confessed, he had a "cunning for to make dispute." Since 1604, James had also entertained offers for a marriage alliance with Spain.

The unapologetically Protestant prince Henry would not consent to any such surrender of his nation's faith. (The offered terms of marriage inevitably had involved some form of England's reconciliation with Catholicism.) However, now that a more corruptible Prince Charles carried the title of prince of Wales, James listened more closely to the overtures of the underhanded and charming Spanish ambassador Don Diego Sarmiento de Anuña, Count Gondomar.

Gondomar had enjoyed a close friendship with James's homosexual lover, George Villiers, marquis (later duke) of Buckingham. (In letters to James, Buckingham made no pretense about his evidently rapturous intimacy with royalty, signing one letter "Your Majesty's humble slave and dog," threatening in another to grab "hold of your bedpost . . . never to quit it," longing in yet another to have "my dear dad and master's legs soon in my arms.") Buckingham and Gondomar made a formidable team at court. Buckingham, as the sexual favorite of the sovereign, had become the Jacobean equivalent of the earl of Leicester in Queen Elizabeth's court. Gondomar, with his friend Buckingham sharing the most intimate pillow talk with the king, had a perfect messenger for unfettered access to the royal ear.

Soon after James had dismissed Parliament in 1621, the king, Buckingham, and Gondomar moved forward with the resolve of marrying Prince Charles to the Spanish Infanta Doña María. But just because James and his entourage were working to turn Protestant England into Rome's slave and dog didn't mean that the rest of the court was about to roll over. The faction opposed to the Spanish Marriage was headed by four earls, all of whom were affiliated by blood, marriage, or authorial fascination to the seventeenth earl of Oxford. The anti–Spanish Marriage coalition would transform English politics circa 1621–23 into the kind of nasty partisanship not seen since the Essex–Cecil split at the end of Elizabeth's reign. Leading the charge were the eighteenth earl of Oxford, Susan de Vere's husband the earl of Montgomery, her brother-in-law the fourth earl of Pembroke, and the "fair youth" of Shake-speare's *Sonnets*, the third earl of Southampton.

Both sides in this war would be using the printed word as weapons of mass propaganda. On the king's side was the power of state censorship–His Majesty had previously warned Parliament that he would tolerate no "meddl[ing] with any thing concerning . . . our dearest Son's match with the Daughter of Spain." The king's supporters also had a few propagandistic arrows that they would loose before the whole affair was over. But the anti–Spanish Marriage alliance had one item that gave them the advantage in firepower: Shake-speare.

৵৵

The first shot was fired in 1621.

In March, Southampton had nearly come to blows with Buckingham on the floor of the House of Lords. Ostensibly, they were only squabbling over matters of parliamentary procedure. But the bitter enmity between these two foes was thinly veiled. The forty-seven-year-old Southampton hated Buckingham for his unmatched royal influence and for his toady obeisance to Ambassador Gondomar and to Spanish national interests.

Forces of the Holy Roman Empire had recently ousted James's daughter, Elizabeth, and her husband, King Frederick V, from Bohemia, and James and Buckingham displayed no interest in returning these Protestant heroes to power. Both Southampton and the eighteenth earl of Oxford had fought in Germany and the Lowlands for the Protestants, and now that Catholic forces had won a major victory, the two Henries were not about to give up the battle.

But Buckingham was powerful enough to ensure that Southampton and the eighteenth earl did not get their way and, moreover, that they cooled their heels. In June, Southampton was arrested for plotting mischief with members of the House of Commons and was placed in the custody of the dean of Westminster. The following month, after the eighteenth earl had vociferously expressed his hatred of the proposed Spanish Marriage, he was thrown in the Tower of London.

In the fall of 1621, after both prisoners had been released, the first new Shake-speare play in fourteen years was registered for publication. It was *Othello,* the story of an insecure leader who is played like a marionette by a sinister villain, IAGO—whose name happens to be identical with that of the patron saint of Spain. Although the seventeenth earl of Oxford had written the play decades earlier to vent his frustrations over a completely different situation in a completely different court, the contemporary relevance was hard to miss. As OTHELLO says of IAGO, so might the Protestant patriots have hoped their king would say of the Spanish ambassador: "Demand [of] that demidevil/Why he hath thus ensnar'd my soul and body."

The title page of the first edition of *Othello* (1622) states it was "written by William Shakespeare." De Vere's family stuck with the cover story they'd inherited. Too much of their own lives hung in the balance to play games with their father's compromised identity.

In December, probably as a token gesture, Buckingham gave Henry de Vere command of *The Assurance,* a patrol boat that guarded English shores from Dutch and Spanish pirates. *The Assurance* soon intercepted a Dutch frigate, and Oxford was dressed down for interfering with Dutch commerce. With characteristic de Vere lip, the twenty-eight-year-old lord Henry uttered his contempt for Buckingham, saying he wished that someday justice might actually flow from a king, not from his errand boy.

By April of 1622, Henry de Vere was back in the Tower of London. And this time the stakes were high. In May Gondomar wrote back to his Spanish sovereign, "I told King James to arrest this man and put him in the Tower in a narrow cell so that no one can speak to him. I have a strong desire to cut off his head, because he is an extremely malicious person and has followers."

One fourth of the anti–Spanish Marriage coalition was, if Gondomar could have his way, effectively now on death row. Southampton, Edward de Vere's son-in-law the earl of Montgomery, and Montgomery's brother the earl of Pembroke knew they had to take action. By the end of 1622, Prince Charles and Buckingham were preparing to go to Spain and finalize the marriage deal.

Edward de Vere had written practically nothing that treated Catholicism or Spain kindly. Once he'd been played for a sucker by his Catholic coconspirators, Henry Howard and Charles Arundell in 1580, de Vere no longer had a problem putting Elizabethan church and state above his erstwhile interest in Catholicism. With the exception of *Romeo and Juliet*'s FRIAR LAURENCE–who was himself based on de Vere's strongly Protestant tutors Sir Thomas Smith and Laurence Nowell–no papist authority figure in Shake-speare is treated with respect or dignity.

If the Spanish Marriage went through, Protestant England could have become as much a historical curio as Mary Tudor's brief reintroduction of Catholicism in 1553–58. The royal policy of publication under a Catholic regime would necessarily have changed to reflect the new religious order; a pro-Anglican, anti-Spanish, Tudor apologist playwright of old would have had no place in this world. Under a Spanish-controlled puppet state, *The Tragoedy of Othello, The Moore of Venice* (1622) [*sic*] would probably have been the last work of Shake-speare that London booksellers could have offered to the buying public.

Still unpublished in any form, pirated or not, were *The Comedy of Errors; The Taming of the Shrew; The Two Gentlemen of Verona; As You Like It; Twelfth Night; All's Well That Ends Well; Measure for Measure; Henry VI, Part 1; King John; Henry VIII; Julius Caesar; Macbeth; Antony and Cleopatra; Coriolanus; Timon of Athens; Cymbeline; The Winter's Tale; The Two Noble Kinsmen;* and *The Tempest.*

William Jaggard's 1619 appeal to Susan de Vere Herbert and her husband, the earl of Montgomery, began to look more and more attractive. She probably felt that as the most literary sister of de Vere's three daughters, it was up to her to do something about her father's works. And if Prince Charles's marriage went through, Susan de Vere Herbert might never have such a chance again.

Around the same time Henry de Vere was thrown in the Tower, Jaggard's presses started rolling with the first quires of what would become the "First Folio of Shakespeare." Jaggard undertook this monumental project without registering the previously unpublished plays with the Stationer's Company, the state's censors.

With Gondomar's vendetta hanging over the eighteenth earl of Oxford and with the future of English Protestantism in the balance, the Folio's masters treaded lightly. The unveiling of the author's identity would have to wait for less politically tumultuous times. Jaggard's collection would not be the *Comedies, Histories and Tragedies of Edward de Vere*. Susan's husband and her brother-in-law served as patrons to what was to be entitled *Mr. William Shakespeares Comedies, Histories & Tragedies, Published according to the True Originall Copies.*

The King's Men's playwright Ben Jonson, a friend to the Herberts and to Henry de Vere, was hired to edit and oversee the Folio. Jonson would write two prefatory poems attached to the Folio as well as, some scholars have concluded, the Folio's dedication to Pembroke and Montgomery and a preface "To the great variety of readers"—two prose tracts that are signed by the King's Men's players John Heminges and Henry Condell. One suspects that around this time the family also hired Jonson to write the quizzical epitaph engraved onto Shakspere's Trinity Church monument in Stratford-upon-Avon.

The First Folio of Shake-speare would stand as nostalgic testimony to the immortal brilliance of the reign of Queen Elizabeth—a period celebrated for its relative peace and prosperity and for its Protestant defiance of Catholic Spain. King James, who loved the Shake-speare plays and often had his King's Men perform them for him at court, should by all rights have been front and center in the First Folio. Yet in the Folio's prefatory materials, the king is practically a nonentity—there is only one passing mention of "our James." Instead, the Folio heaps praise upon the earls of Pembroke and Montgomery, two courtiers who at the time were vociferous opponents of the crown and the Spanish marriage.

The Folio's dedicatory epistle to Pembroke and Montgomery reads:

To the most noble and incomparable pair of brethren ...

There is a great difference [of opinion] whether any book choose his patrons or [his patrons] find them. This hath done both. For so much were Your L[ordships] likings of the several parts when they were acted, as before they were published, the volume asked to be yours. We have but collected them and done an office to the dead, to procure his orphans guardians.

As the first months of 1623 thawed into a spring of grave uncertainty, James's minions must have gotten wind of the earls of Pembroke and Montgomery's pet project. In April, a history of the Roman emperor Nero was registered, as the Stationer's Office scribe noted, "by His Majesty's special command." Edmund Bolton's *Nero Caesar* was to be the pro–Spanish Marriage propaganda in presumptive response to the Shake-speare Folio.

Nero Caesar was a rewrite of ancient history that, contrary to historical evidence, claimed that English civilization had never flourished more than when ancient Rome had ruled during the first four centuries of the Christian era. (Roman historians such as Tacitus actually stated just the opposite, that Rome had corrupted the ancient Britons. But historical accuracy was not *Nero Caesar*'s intent.) The book, dedicated to Buckingham, was a shoddy attempt at preempting the Protestant agitprop that would be coming out beneath the "Shakespeare" byline. English subjects, *Nero Caesar* implied, needn't worry about Rome (read: Spain) returning to its shores. A period of even greater prosperity, under King Charles and his Spanish queen, was just around the corner.

In May and June of 1623, new papist-inspired chapels were being designed at St. James's Palace, and roads from the port town of Southampton were being repaired to ease the transit of the presumptive new Anglo-Spanish princess. But in Madrid, despite all the feasting and feting, the negotiations stalled. Each side demanded too many conciliations; neither was ready to compromise. By September, it was clear to the negotiators in Madrid that a marriage alliance between England and Spain was simply not going to happen. A broken and unsuccessful prince Charles and the duke of Buckingham returned to English shores in October.

The vast majority of Londoners celebrated the collapse of the marriage deal as a victory. Bonfires were lit in the streets, and Londoners reveled as if the Spanish Armada had been defeated again. Broadsides and pamphlets rushed into print praising the return of an empty-handed prince. Oxford and Cambridge Universities printed collections of poems and orations celebrating the prince's repatriation, sans Spaniard alliance.

On November 8, once the entire Shakespeare Folio had been printed, William Jaggard finally presented the book to the London Stationer's Company to be registered. The First Folio of Shakespeare, priced at £1 ($165 in today's currency), had a press run of approximately 750 copies. The first recorded purchase was on December 5. Over the next nine years, it sold well enough to justify a second edition, the 1632 Second Folio of Shakespeare. Some 238 copies of the First Folio survive to this day.

On December 30, Henry de Vere was released from the Tower. Within a matter of days he married the Elizabethan lord Burghley's great-granddaughter Diana Cecil and staged a public reconciliation scene with Buckingham. As a Florentine correspondent, Amerigo Salvetti, reported of the détente between the earl of Oxford and the duke of Buckingham, "All's well that ends well."

Within two years, Southampton and his son James, Lord Wriothesley, would be dead. The eighteenth earl of Oxford would be dead. All three served their country to the last, fighting with their Protestant allies on the battlefields of the Lowlands. In 1625, the king of England succumbed too. A Scots physician to James later circulated a scurrilous tract alleging that Buckingham and his mother had poisoned the king. And so Charles I embarked on a twenty-four-year voyage that would result in the English Civil War.

"This figure that thou see'st here put, It was for gentle Shakespeare cut," Ben Jonson wrote in his preface "To the Reader" on the first page of the 1623 First Folio of Shakespeare. Jonson's "To the Reader" poem appears opposite Martin Droeshaut's famous engraving, pictured on the first page of the Introduction.

But Jonson's poem says that no engraving, no matter how perfectly executed, could contain the "wit" and "life" found in Shakespeare's works printed within. To understand Shakespeare, Jonson says, pay no mind to the superficial, the image, the cover story. The author's words tell all.

> ... [T]he [En]graver had a strife
> With nature to outdo the life.
> O, could he but have drawn [Shake-speare's] wit
> As well in brass, as he hath hit
> His face, the print would then surpass
> All that ever was writ in brass.
> But since he cannot, reader, look:
> Not on his picture but his book.

So what becomes of the Shake-speare canon with Edward de Vere as its author? How does the experience of Shake-speare change for a reader, a performer, a director, and an audience member?

First, the plays and poems become more integrated. The works of Shake-speare become the *work* of Shake-speare. *All's Well That Ends Well* is no longer a single, enigmatic "problem comedy" but rather more of a darkly comic prelude to *Hamlet*–one that branches into *Measure for Measure* and *Richard II* as well. *Much Ado About Nothing* becomes a failed apology for de Vere's misdeeds chronicled in *Romeo and Juliet* and *The Winter's Tale*. The jealousy of OTHELLO represents the tragic extreme of a wide spectrum that terminates in MASTER FORD of the comedy *The Merry Wives of Windsor,* KING LEAR's anxiety echoes de Vere's over his three daughters, while *As You Like It* ponders the fate of de Vere's cousin's children–the three sons of the executed duke of Norfolk. De Vere's expression of bemusement and fascination with Will Shakspere in *Love's Labor's Lost* becomes a tempest of fury in *As You Like It.*

Second, the boundaries between comedy, history, and tragedy become more porous. TOUCHSTONE's rage at the country clown WILLIAM in *As You Like It* is not so much comedy as bitter tragedy–brought about by the angst of an author who realizes his name will be lost. *Coriolanus* is not so much tragedy as bitter comedy–understanding that the same historical figure (the earl of Essex) inspired CORIOLANUS as inspired the "Rival Poet" of the *Sonnets.* *King John* and *Macbeth* become two sides of the same royal conundrum that de Vere and Queen Elizabeth faced in the execution of Mary, Queen of Scots. PROSPERO's final plea to be released from his bonds, although often performed today with a smile and a curtsy, is one of the most tragic scenes in the whole of the Shake-speare canon.

Third, Shake-speare becomes a venturesome cosmopolitan and a true citizen of western Renaissance Europe. No longer does a jaunt to London and a bus ride to Stratford-upon-Avon suffice in apprehending the terrain and cultures that directly inspired Shake-speare. From the north-country shires de Vere explored in the Northern Rebellion campaign of 1570 to the East Anglian lands of his childhood and ancestry to the royal castles and estates surrounding London to the Oxbridge academic settings of his youth to the Channel-side sites of his departures for Spanish Armada campaigns and continental adventures ... Shake-speare's England is practically the whole of England. And England isn't even the half of it. Shake-speare's continental European settings derive from de Vere's own travels: the regal surroundings of the Louvre and Rheims, the magnificent bustle of Venice's Rialto and St. Mark's Square, the sheltered Alpine gorges of the Rhine, the ancient halls of the universities of Strasbourg and Padua, the Tuscan byways of Siena and Medici-era Florence.

Fourth, the artistic arc of Shake-speare's career charts a course from preening and prancing young champion to a betrayed and jealous middle-aged skeptic to a resigned and bitter old man. Early Shake-speare is like early Mozart: precocious in the extreme, ostentatious in his genius, and unstoppable in his inventiveness. But late Shake-speare is more like late Beethoven: angry and intransigent, alienated and disturbed. Beethoven, banished from his art because of his deafness, had by the end of his career become what one musicologist described as a "lonely prince of a realm of spirits." These words also fit an ailing Edward de Vere as he pondered the dimming candle of his life knowing his epitaph would effectively be, in the words of Sonnet 72, "My name be buried where my body is."

Finally, it may be said that Shake-speare's development as a writer traced his development as a human being–stripping away the snobbish trappings of his blue-blood upbringing and outgrowing his spoiled, egomaniacal behavior as a youth. The literary by-products of his personal development, littered along the highway of his life, provide milestones. *The Comedy of Errors* and *Much Ado About Nothing* reveal an overgrown adolescent unwilling to shoulder responsibility for his own actions. *Twelfth Night* and *The Taming of the Shrew* present a keen observer gaining his foothold on humanity by charting the foibles and follies of the Elizabethan courtly "reptilia," a class to which he knew he belonged.

Writing ultimately became a cathartic exercise performed not for his sovereign or for his peers but rather for himself–his own mechanism for psychological and spiritual salvation. De Vere vented his jealous rage against his first wife in *Othello* and *The Winter's Tale;* he may have tamed his inner demons and acknowledged his wary acceptance of her only after her death, as expressed in HAMLET's graveside lamentations over OPHELIA's stony corpse. What had once been a green-eyed monster then became a strange satyr–half adoration, half admiration–that he loosed upon his second wife, Elizabeth Trentham de Vere (PORTIA) and his eldest daughter's onetime fiancé the earl of Southampton (the "Fair Youth" of the *Sonnets* and BASSANIO of *Merchant of Venice,* among others). And as suggested by Sonnets 40–42, the anonymous 1594 poem *Willobie His Avisa* (*not* written by de Vere) and *The Merchant of Venice* (wherein ANTONIO enables his fair youth BASSANIO to woo PORTIA), de Vere may even have countenanced a romantic affair between his second wife and his dashing "Fair Youth."

Lacking a satisfactory chronology of Shake-speare–so much of which is now, without more definitive evidence, thrown into a temporal limbo involving early drafts in de Vere's twenties and thirties and final drafts in his forties and early fifties–one cannot say for certain which plays constitute the true "end point" of Shake-speare. Final drafts of *King Lear* and *Hamlet,* for instance, surely date from de Vere's closing years. And *The Tempest* is one of the few plays–perhaps the only one–that appear to have been wholly conceived and composed during the fifteen-month period between Queen Elizabeth's death and de Vere's own.

The "late style" of artistic development, as defined by the critics Theodor Adorno and Edward Said, may provide a valuable guideline for reassessing Shake-speare's ultimate accomplishments as an artist. For it was the more humanized, humbled, and unfettered de Vere of his forties and fifties who revised much, if not all, of his youthful canon–the entirety of which was then published in the quartos of the 1590s and 1600s and, posthumously, in the First Folio of 1623. Traces of "late style" may yet be found in bits and patches in much of Shake-speare. As Said noted, an artist in his or her "late style"

> has the power exactly to render disenchantment and pleasure without resolving the contradiction between them. What holds them in tension, as equal forces, straining in opposite directions, is the artist's mature subjectivity, stripped of hubris and pomposity, unashamed either of its fallibility or of the modest assurance it has gained as a result of age and exile.

In the final analysis, repatriating Edward de Vere's life to the Shake-speare canon provides motivation behind the characters and plots, charts an artistic path intrinsic to the flawed but fascinating life of the artist, uncovers new levels of autobiographical meaning in the greatest works of English literature, and replaces the incomprehensible mystery of a deified genius with a comprehensible–if still incomparable–man who, for all his failures, became the very breath and soul of the English-speaking world.

APPENDIX A

EDWARD DE VERE'S GENEVA BIBLE

AND SHAKE-SPEARE

T HE THESIS OF THIS BOOK, THE "OXFORDIAN" PROPOSITION THAT
Edward de Vere was Shake-speare, is a theory built upon circumstantial
evidence. There is no single "smoking gun" document that leads one inex-
orably to the conclusion that de Vere wrote *Hamlet, King Lear,* the *Sonnets,* etc.
Instead, one builds the case upon a series of facts and observations that, when
put together like pieces of a puzzle, produce an overall picture that becomes
difficult to deny.

The most important single new piece of Oxfordian evidence is Edward de
Vere's copy of the English translation of the Bible produced and printed in
1569–70 by English exiles based in Geneva. De Vere's "Geneva Bible"–now in
possession of the Folger Shakespeare Library in Washington, D.C.–is sumptu-
ously bound in a crimson velvet cover with silver medallions on the front and
back bearing heraldic images from de Vere's family crest of a boar capped with
a coronet and a quartered shield with a star in the upper left quadrant. The Bible
contains 1,028 handwritten underlinings and marginal notes. Expert handwriting analysis of the marginal notes supports the reasonable conclusion that not
only did de Vere own and read this Bible, he wrote the marginalia in it too.

Between 1990 and 2000, Roger Stritmatter–now an assistant professor of
English at Coppin State College in Baltimore, Maryland–conducted a study of
the marginal notes in de Vere's Bible that formed the basis of Stritmatter's Ph.D.
dissertation at the University of Massachusetts, Amherst. Of the 1,028 markings in the de Vere Bible, 568 appear in the Old Testament, 156 appear in the
New Testament, 15 appear in a hymnal of Psalms appended to de Vere's copy
of the Geneva Bible, and 289 appear in a set of marginally canonical biblical
texts–rarely studied or read by most laypeople today–called the Apocrypha.

Stritmatter discovered that approximately one out of every four of the marked passages in de Vere's Bible appears in Shake-speare. The parallels range from the thematic–sharing a motif, idea, or trope–to the verbal–using names, phrases, or wordings that suggest a specific biblical passage.

While the Shake-speare canon as a whole contains hundreds of biblical allusions, there are only eighty-one biblical verses referenced four or more times in Shake-speare. These eighty-one biblical excerpts comprise what Stritmatter calls the "Shakespeare Diagnostic" set of verses. Shake-speare knew and evidently loved these passages from Scripture more than any others. He probably took note of many if not all of these verses somewhere in his collection of Bibles.

Shake-speare clearly knew more than one edition of the Bible, too. Shake-speare's plays and poems contain language that points to verses from an earlier edition of the Geneva Bible, from the Bishop's Bible of 1568, and from one or more other English, Latin, and other vernacular translations as well.

De Vere's letters reveal his familiarity with the Italian Bible, when he wrote to his guardian and father-in-law Lord Burghley that "I see it is but vain *calcitrare contra li busi*"–quoting an Italian translation of Acts 9:5. De Vere also bought and shipped home a Greek edition of the New Testament during his tour of Italy in 1575–76.

De Vere's 1569–70 Geneva Bible thus appears to have been just one of his multiple copies of the Good Book. So one would not reasonably expect the markings in de Vere's 1569–70 Geneva Bible to subsume the whole of de Vere's biblical consciousness.

Nevertheless, the overlap between the "Shakespeare Diagnostics" and the de Vere Bible markings is substantial. De Vere marked 30 of the 81 Shake-speare Diagnostic verses (37 percent) in his 1569–70 Geneva Bible.

For comparison, Stritmatter also assembled a control set of Diagnostic verses for three of Shake-speare's contemporaries: Francis Bacon, Christopher Marlowe, and Edmund Spenser. The same rules applied. The works of Francis Bacon refer to 101 biblical verses four or more times. Just two of those Bacon Diagnostic verses are marked in de Vere's Bible (2 percent). The overlap between Spenser's Diagnostic verses and the markings in de Vere's Geneva Bible is 5.4 percent. The overlap between Marlowe's Diagnostic verses and the de Vere Bible is 6.8 percent.

Statistics, however, tell only a small part of the story to be found within those crimson velvet covers bearing the arms of the earls of Oxford. The markings in de Vere's Geneva Bible also exhibit a continued interest in a series of themes, six of which will be briefly considered below.

1) The primacy of an anointed king. Four of the historical books of the Old Testament (I and II Samuel, I and II Kings) recite the central Judeo-Christian precedent underlying the divine right of kings: The grace of God alone gives the monarch the mandate to rule a nation. In Protestant England, the scriptural basis for monarchy had an important corollary. The selection and coronation of a king or queen by birthright stood in contrast to the practice in Catholic countries, where the pope–the "bishop of Rome" as Protestant polemicists called him–often intervened to pick a leader most compatible with Roman interests. According to the founding doctrine of the Anglican Church, just as God chose David to rule Israel, so God chose the Tudors to rule England. Any pope who said otherwise (such as Pius V in 1570) was contravening God's will.

The signifier of God's political choice was the anointing of a monarch. Once the archbishop of Canterbury dabbed holy oil on the head of a king or queen during the coronation ceremony, the Lord's vote had effectively been cast. Regicide–the killing of God's anointed–was considered a crime against heaven itself.

David's story, again, set the precedent. The prophet Samuel had chosen and anointed David to become the next king of Israel. But Saul, the sitting king at the time, grew jealous. The faltering Saul tried and failed to kill David. David later happened upon a sleeping Saul. A spear stood nearby. Israel's future king had the opportunity to bury the spear in Saul's heart. David, however, did not do so. (Each of the biblical passages below contains a facsimile of de Vere's original underlining.)

> 11 "Behold, this day thine eyes have seen that the Lord had delivered thee this day into mine hand in the cave and come bade me kill thee," [David states.] "But I had compassion on thee and said, 'I will not lay mine hand on my master [Saul]: For he is the Lord's Anointed.'"
> *–I Samuel 24:11*

Later, after a servant had helped a terminally wounded Saul to commit suicide, David ordered the servant to be executed.

> 14 And David said unto him, "How wast you not afraid to put forth thine hand to destroy the Anointed of the Lord?"
> *–II Samuel 1:14*

One finds in Shake-speare the same fascination with the divine primacy that anointment confers upon a prince. When RICHARD II is stripped of his crown, he reminds the rebels who depose him that

> RICHARD Not all the water in the rough rude sea
>   Can wash the balm off from an anointed king.

When King DUNCAN's body is discovered in *Macbeth*, MACDUFF exclaims:

> MACDUFF Most sacrilegious murder hath broke ope
>   The Lord's anointed temple!

And when a corrupt LEONTES instructs his henchman CAMILLO to poison the King of Sicilia, POLIXENES, in *The Winter's Tale*, CAMILLO takes the high road originally traveled by David:

> CAMILLO I must be the poisoner
>   Of good POLIXENES, and my ground to do't
>   Is the obedience to a master; one
>   Who, in rebellion with himself, will have
>   All that are his [*in rebellion*] too. To do this deed,
>   Promotion follows. [*Even*] If I could find examples
>   Of thousands that had struck anointed kings
>   And flourished after, I'd [*still*] not do't.

2) **The Neoplatonic cluster.** During the Italian Renaissance, authors and thinkers such as Marsilio Ficino and Pico della Mirandola revived and expanded upon the philosophy of Plato. These "Neoplatonists"–and their pre-Christian predecessors–upheld a series of propositions, three of which are reflected in the markings in de Vere's Bible: that all things and events in the cosmos follow ideal patterns and precedents that provide the answers to life and the universe; that even the smallest things contain within them a microcosm of all other things; and that the human senses can only perceive fallen and outward appearances–a subject's inner quintessence always contains the greater beauty.

As an example of what Stritmatter calls de Vere's "Neoplatonic cluster" of markings, consider the final item on the above list: inner truth versus outward show. The discrepancy between appearance and reality is probably the greatest unifying theme in the entire Shake-speare canon. De Vere, whose body was short and feeble, lighted upon one manifestation of the don't-judge-a-book-by-its-cover precept in the first book of Samuel:

> 7   But the Lord said unto Samuel, "Look not on his countenance nor on
>   the height of his stature, because I have refused him. For God seeth
>   not as man seeth. For man looketh on the outward appearance, but
>   the Lord beholdeth the heart."
>   –*I Samuel 16:7*

De Vere also underlined a set of Neoplatonic passages in Paul's letters to the Corinthians:

<u>18</u> Flee fornication. Every sin that a man doeth is without [*outside*] the body. But he that commiteth fornication sinneth against his own body.

<u>19</u> Know ye not that your body is the temple of the Holy Ghost, which is in you, whom ye have of God? And ye are not your own.

<u>20</u> For ye are bought for a price. Therefore glorify God in your body and in your spirit. For they are Gods.

–I Corinthians 6:18–20

<u>16 Therefore</u> we faint not, but though our outward man perish, yet the inward man is renewed daily–

<u>17 For</u> our light affliction, which is but for a moment, causeth unto us a far [more] excellent and eternal weight of glory,

<u>18 While</u> we look not on the things which are seen but on the things which are not seen, for the things which are seen are temporal, but the things which are not seen are eternal.

–II Corinthians 4:16–18

Instances of the same Neoplatonic ideal in Shake-speare include GLOUCESTER's admonition to the PRINCE OF WALES in *Richard III*:

> Nor more can you distinguish of a man
> Than of his outward show, which, God he knows,
> Seldom or never jumpeth [*accords*] with the heart;

TROILUS's description of CRESSIDA as one

> Outliving beauty's outward with a mind
> That doth renew swifter than blood decays;

and FALSTAFF's inquisition of SHALLOW in *Henry IV, Part 2*:

> Will you tell me, Master SHALLOW, how to choose a man? Care I for the limb, the thews [*strength*], the stature, bulk, and big assemblance of a man? Give me the spirit, Master SHALLOW.

Ultimately, though, enumerating a list of Neoplatonic quotations does a disservice to the concept itself. The most prominent example of the "hidden inner truth" substrate in Shake-speare *is* Shake-speare. Four centuries have shined their light on the Bard's outward show–Will Shakspere of Stratford. De Vere must have taken some solace in the Apostle's assurance that someday, "though our outward man perish, yet the inward man is renewed daily."

3) **Sin.** The Greek word used for *sin* in the New Testament, *hamartia,* is also the word Aristotle uses in his *Poetics* to describe the fatal flaw of a character that drives the action of a tragedy forward. Edward de Vere was fascinated with sin. He marked fifty-three verses in his Bible concerning the subject and wrote the index word *sinne* an additional eight times in the margin.

De Vere marked a passage in Ezekiel, for instance, on the noninheritability of sin:

> 20 The same soul that sinneth shall die. The son shall not bear the iniquity of the father, neither shall the father bear the iniquity of the son. But the righteousness of the righteous shall be upon him, and the wickedness of the wicked shall be upon himself.
> *—Ezekiel 18:20*

Both MACDUFF (in *Macbeth*) and LUCRECE flip Ezekiel's words upside down:

> MACDUFF … Sinful MACDUFF!
>   They [*his children*] were all struck for thee. Naught that I am:
>   Not for their own demerits, but for mine,
>   Fell slaughter on their souls.

> [LUCRECE] … [H]ere in Troy, for trespass of thine eye,
>   The sire, the son, the dame and daughter, die.
>   Why should the private pleasure of some one
>   Become the public plague of many moe?
>   Let sin alone committed, light alone
>   Upon his head that transgressed so.

De Vere underlined another verse in Ezekiel on the sins of the ancient city of Sodom:

> 49 Behold, this was the iniquity of thy sister Sodom: Pride, fullness of bread [*gluttony*] and abundance of idleness was in her and in her daughters. Neither did she strengthen the hand of the poor and needy.
> *—Ezekiel 16:49*

HAMLET seizes upon Ezekiel's language in describing the state of his father, KING HAMLET, at the time of KING HAMLET's death:

> HAMLET [CLAUDIUS] took my father grossly, full of bread.

In the Genevan book of Paul's Letter to the Romans, de Vere corrected a typographical error by inserting a missing pronoun–suggesting more than a passing interest in the Apostle Paul's Neoplatonic conception of sin:

> 20 Now if $_\wedge$^{i} do that I would not, it is no more I that do it but the sin that dwelleth in me.

HAMLET emends the Apostle's words by suggesting that HAMLET was not the party responsible for his own actions. It was his "sin," his feigned madness.

> HAMLET Was't HAMLET [who] wrong'd LAERTES? Never HAMLET!
> ...Who does it, then? His madness. If 't be so,
> HAMLET is of the faction that is wronged.
> His madness is poor HAMLET's enemy.

4) The weapons in God's armory. De Vere highlighted a series of passages in his Geneva Bible revealing a Neoplatonic belief in the superiority of spiritual munitions over mere military matériel such as swords and shields. "[The] weapon of [the] godly is praier" de Vere wrote in the margin adjacent to the Apocryphal verse Wisdom 18:21.

QUEEN MARGARET in *Henry VI, Part 2,* and BOLINGBROKE in *Richard II* voice the same belief:

> MARGARET [KING HENRY's] champions are the prophets and the
> apostles,
> His weapons, the holy saws of sacred writ,
> His study is his tilt-yard....

> BOLINGBROKE To reach at victory above my head,
> Add proof unto mine armor with thy prayers,
> And with thy blessings steel my lance's point,
> That it may enter MOWBRAY's waxen coat.

The spiritual-armor theme continues in another set of verses in Wisdom, in which de Vere underlined the final passage:

> 17 He shall take his jealousy for armor and shall arm the creatures to be
> revenged of the enemies.
> 18 He shall put on righteousness for a breastplate and take true judg-
> ment instead of an helmet.
> 19 He will take holiness for an invincible shield.
> 20 He will sharpen his fierce wrath for a sword and the world shall fight
> with him against the unwise.
> *–Wisdom 5:16–20*

And again in Paul's first epistle to the Thessalonians:

> 5 Ye are all the children of light and the children of day. We are not of the night, neither of the darkness.
> 6 Therefore, let us not sleep as do others. But let us watch and be sober.
> 7 For they that sleep, sleep in the night. And they that be drunken are drunken in the night.
> 8 But let us [who] are of the day be sober, putting on the breastplate of faith and love and of the hope of salvation for an helmet.
> *–I Thessalonians 5:5–8*

Both de Vere's personal letters and the works of Shake-speare reveal the sentiment expressed in the above biblical markings: embracing the ability to arm or adorn oneself with abstract qualities such as righteousness or justice or holiness. As de Vere wrote in his 1573 preface to the book *Cardanus's Comfort*:

> In mine opinion as it beautifieth a fair woman to be decked with pearls and precious stones, so much more it ornifieth a gentleman to be furnished in mind with glittering virtues.

Thirty years later, de Vere wrote his brother-in-law Robert Cecil:

> Nothing adorns a king more than justice, nor in anything doth a king more resemble God than in justice....

Such extended Neoplatonic metaphors appear frequently in Shake-speare, from KING HENRY VI's observation

> KING What stronger breastplate than a heart untainted!
>   Thrice is he arm'd that hath his quarrel just;
>   And he but naked, though lock'd up in steel,
>   Whose conscience with injustice is corrupted.

... To ISABELLA's reminder in *Measure for Measure*

> ISABELLA Not the king's crown, nor the deputed sword,
>   The marshal's truncheon, nor the judge's robe
>   Become them with one half so good a grace
>   As mercy does.

On the other hand, anyone familiar with de Vere's militaristic pretensions from the 1560s through the '80s knows that there's another side to the transcendent qualities being celebrated in the above words.

De Vere was no holy pacifist. He was, rather, a wolfish earl born and bred, with a lifetime of unfulfilled yearnings for military glory and honor. In classic Shake-spearean contradiction, de Vere's biblical notes also reveal an abiding interest in the worldly details of physical weaponry from biblical battles.

In King David's later years, the Israelite army faced the Philistines and their allies in a series of minor battles—chronicled in II Samuel 21. De Vere underlined seemingly trivial details about the weapons of Israel's adversaries. A Hittite giant named Ishbi-Benob wanted to fight David one-on-one but was instead killed by one of David's officers. Ishbi-Benob was armed with a spear with a head that "weighed 300 shekels of brass." De Vere underlined the weight of Ishbi-Benob's spearhead.

Another warrior David's army faced was "Goliath the Hittite" (not to be confused with the Hittite's infamous gargantuan brother of the same name whom David had slain years before). Goliath the Hittite, according to the account in II Samuel, carried a spear "the staff . . . [of which] was like a weaver's beam." De Vere underlined the dimensions of Goliath the Hittite's weapon too. One of David's soldiers, named Elhanan, killed Goliath the Hittite.

Note that in both cases, the armament on which de Vere fixated was the spear.

FALSTAFF seizes upon the confusion between the Geneva Bible's two Goliaths when, in *The Merry Wives of Windsor*, he brags, "I fear not Goliath with a weaver's beam!" The joke here is that, to those who don't know their biblical history exceptionally well, FALSTAFF seems to brag that he is so valiant that he would face off against the very same giant whom David famously killed. But those who know their Old Testament trivia—or at least have access to de Vere's Geneva Bible, which highlights such trivia—understand that the cowardly FALSTAFF is just cleverly sneaking through a biblical loophole. In fact, Shake-speare's rotund braggart is simply saying that he's not afraid to battle the *other* Goliath, the same pipsqueak who was killed off in the span of less than a sentence by one of King David's foot soldiers.

5) The heavenly duty of mercy. In the gutter straddling the fiftieth chapter of the Old Testament book of Jeremiah, de Vere wrote the index word *mercy*. The story de Vere annotated concerns an angry God rebuking the kingdom of Israel's oppressors. The king of Babylon and his country will be punished, God says. And when that glorious day comes, He adds, even the sinful will ultimately be forgiven. In *The Merchant of Venice*, PORTIA calls out to SHYLOCK for such heavenly mercy, becoming of kings and God alike, in her immortal plea

> The quality of mercy is not strained.
> It droppeth as the gentle rain from heaven
> Upon the place beneath. It is twice blest:
> It blesseth him that gives and him that takes.

'Tis mightiest in the mightiest, it becomes
The thronèd monarch better than his crown....
It is an attribute to God himself;
And earthly power doth then show likest God's
When mercy seasons justice. Therefore, Jew,
Though justice be thy plea, consider this,
That in the course of justice, none of us
Should see salvation. We do pray for mercy,
And that same prayer doth teach us all to render
The deeds of mercy.

PORTIA's pleading also borrows from a scriptural source marked in de Vere's Bible. In the Apocryphal book of Ecclesiasticus, de Vere underlined the verse numbers attached to the following words:

1 He that seeketh vengeance shall find vengeance of the Lord—and he will surely keep his sins.
2 Forgive thy neighbor the hurt that he hath done to thee, [and] so shalt thy sins be forgiven also, when thou prayest.
3 Should a man bear hatred against man and desire forgiveness of the Lord?

—Ecclesiasticus 28:1–3

The act of praying for forgiveness, PORTIA says, guides us to be forgiving as well. In drawing her lesson from the above verses, PORTIA is also proving herself an adept biblical scholar. Ecclesiasticus 28:1–3 is a key pre-Christian teaching—one that SHYLOCK would be most amenable to—that calls for the kind of unconditional and reciprocal mercy that the defendant ANTONIO needs in his legal case against the Jew.

PROSPERO also draws upon Ecclesiasticus's call for prayer as a precondition for mercy and redemption. In his closing remarks to the audience, *The Tempest*'s great magician asks for the audience to pray for his freedom—a plea from an exiled author to restore him to his greatest dukedom, the canon of his own writings.

EPILOGUE
PROSPERO [R]elease me from my bands
    With the help of your good hands!
    Gentle breath of yours my sails
    Must fill or else my project fails,
    Which was to please. Now I want
    Spirits to enforce, art to enchant,
    And my ending is despair,

Unless I be reliev'd by prayer,
Which pierces so that it assaults
Mercy itself and frees all faults.
As you from crimes would pardon'd be,
Let your indulgence set me free.

6) The scriptural precedent for the discovery of a man's secret works.

As discussed in Chapter 11, a cluster of verses in de Vere's Bible yearn for the day a neglected and forgotten sinner can be finally brought forth into the light.

9 I will bear the wrath of the Lord because I have sinned against him, until he plead my cause and execute judgment for me. Then will <u>he bring me forth into the light, and I shall see his righteousness.</u>
—Micah 7:9

11 Though men mourn for their body, yet the wicked name of the ungodly shall be put out.
—Ecclesiasticus 41:11

c. <u>As the hope of the daylight causeth us not to be offended with the darkness of the night, so ought we patiently to trust that God will clear our cause and restore us to our right.</u>
—Psalm 38, footnote c (Geneva ed.)

1 Take heed that ye give not your alms before men, to be seen of them—or else ye shall have no reward of your Father which is in heaven.
2 Therefore when thou givest thine alms, thou shalt not make a trumpet to be blown before thee, as the hypocrites do in the synagogues and in the streets, to be praised of men. Verily I say unto you, they have their reward.
3 But when thou doest thine alms, let not thy left hand know what thy right hand doeth.
4 That thine alms may be in secret—and thy Father that seeth in secret, he will reward thee openly.
—Matthew 6:1–4

10 For God is not [so] unrighteous that he should forget your work and labor of love....
—Hebrews 6:10

14 Do all things without murmuring and reasonings
15 That ye may be blameless and pure and the sons of God without

rebuke, in the midst of a naughty and crooked nation, among whom
ye shine as lights in the world.
–Philippians 2:14–15

5 He that overcometh shall be clothed in white array and I will not put
his name out of the Book of Life. But I will confess his name before
my Father and before his Angels.
–Revelations 3:5

13 Then I heard a voice from Heaven saying unto me, "Write. Blessed
are the dead, which hereafter die in the Lord. Even so," saith the
Spirit. "For they rest from their labors, and their works follow them."
–Revelations 14:13

The image derived from this collection of de Vere Bible markings is that
of a time capsule–involving an identity that must be buried for a time with the
promise of eventually being rediscovered and brought back into the world.

De Vere knew he was no saint. As HAMLET says, "I could accuse me of
such things that it were better my mother had not borne me." According to de
Vere's underlined verses in Micah and Ecclesiasticus, the sinner's identity will
be subsumed. But even the acerbic Micah allows for the fact that after one has
endured God's wrath–however long the ordeal–God will then bring a sinner
back "into the light." The underlined Genevan footnote to Psalm 37 stresses
the patience and trust in God's divine plans and that in due time He will "clear
our cause and restore us to our right."

The New Testament's view about secret works is more reassuring. There
Christ himself, as part of his Sermon on the Mount, says that the path of the
godly is to do one's great service to mankind in secret.

The anonymous Epistle to the Hebrews adds that God "is not so unjust
that he should forget your work and labor of love." In the founding documents of the Anglican Church, in fact, these words so flew in the face of prevailing dogma–that works are insufficient by themselves in impressing the
Lord–that church members were specifically enjoined to "pay no attention"
to them. Anyone who matriculated at Cambridge or Oxford University, as de
Vere did, would have had to sign his name to such a prohibition.

De Vere's "secret works" eschatology concludes in two underlined passages
from the book of Revelations. John the Divine assures posterity that a man's
name will *not* be blotted from the "Book of Life." Later, a voice from heaven
tells John to write–as the voice of HAMLET's ghost tells his son to write. To
combine the prophetic words of Micah with those of John, the dead's "works"
will one day follow them into the light. The "indulgence" PROSPERO seeks–the
long-overdue recognition of an author alienated from his own canon–cannot
be far behind.

APPENDIX B

THE SHAKE-SPEARE APOCRYPHA

T HE FOLLOWING NON-SHAKE-SPEARE PLAYS, POEMS, AND MISCEL-
laneous tracts were all, so far as can be determined, written during the
lifetime of Edward de Vere, earl of Oxford (1550–1604), and all reveal at least
the possibility of de Vere's hand in their authorship. Some are anonymous or
dubiously or tenuously attributed to another author and, for biographical or
stylistic reasons, appear "de Verean" in character and form; some are attributed to authors close to de Vere's orbit (such as his secretaries John Lyly or
Anthony Munday) and may either be wholly the product of de Vere's pen
and simply published under the other man's name or instead may be the collaborative by-product of de Vere and one or more associates.

In nearly every case, the background scholarship and attribution studies
necessary to prove or disprove de Vere's authorship are either incomplete or
have simply not been undertaken yet. As with the Shake-speare canon itself,
no single "smoking gun" connects these works with de Vere. Instead, the
same process of aggregating circumstantial evidence awaits the scholar hoping to add to the Shake-speare canon.

If current scholarly awareness and interest in de Vere provides any pre-
diction of future activity, within the next decade one can imagine that the
Complete Works of Shake-speare will resemble a broad and polyglot array of
texts—poetic, dramatic, and otherwise—that reveal the complete life cycle of
an author from precocious schoolboy to courtly poet-playwright-patron to
conscience-catching court dramatist to masked and anonymous man subsumed by the Shake-speare myth.

In the coming years, further study will no doubt reveal that some of the
following texts were, in fact, not written by de Vere. On the other hand, as a
starting point for further investigation, this list will just as certainly be found to

contain at least a few new streams of nectar flowing from the pen of the man who was Shake-speare.

PLAYS

[Publication dates below do not indicate composition dates, which more likely are from the 1570s or '80s.]

Edmund Ironside (n.d.)
Thomas of Woodstock (n.d.)
The Troublesome Raigne of John King of England (1591)
The Chronicle History of King Leir (1605)
The Famous Victories of Henry V (1600)
The True Tragedy of Richard III (1594)
The Taming of A Shrew (1594)
The Boke of Sir Thomas More (n.d.)

POETRY COLLECTIONS AND SHORT VERSE

Anthony Munday, *The Paine of Pleasure* (1580)
George Gascoigne, *Hundreth Sundrie Flowers* (1575–76) [portions thereof?]
"Phaeton" sonnet in John Florio's *Second Fruits* (1591)
"Trentame" poem in *Brittons Bowre of Delights* (1591)
Poems by "Ignoto" in *England's Helicon* (1600)
"Praise of a Contented Mind" poem appended to *Willobie His Avisa* (1594)

FICTIONAL OR HISTORICAL PROSE

John Lyly's *Euphues* novels (1580, 1588), Anthony Munday's *Zelauto* (1580) [possible collaborations with de Vere's secretaries]

TRANSLATIONS

Ovid's *Metamorphoses,* tr. Arthur Golding (1562–63) [student–teacher collaboration?]
Apuleius's *Golden Asse,* tr. William Adlington (1566)
English translations by "Lazarus Piot" [collaboration with Anthony Munday?]: *Amadis de Gaule* (1596); *The Orator* (1596)

MISC.

Prose introductions to the sonnets in Thomas Watson's *Hekatompathia* (1581)

Some of the sample letters in Angel Day's *The English Secretary* (1586)

The Homily on Disobedience and Willful Rebellion (1571)

"Pasquill Caviliero" pamphleteering replies to "Martin Marprelate": *A Countercuffe Given to Martin Junior*... (1589); *The Returne of the Renowned Cavaliero*... (1589); *The First Part of Pasquils Apologie* (1590)

APPENDIX C

"THE 1604 QUESTION"

IT IS OFTEN OBJECTED THAT EDWARD DE VERE, EARL OF OXFORD, could not have written the works of Shake-speare because many Shake-speare plays were allegedly written after 1604, the year de Vere died. However, upon closer examination, chronological evidence supports rather than refutes the theory that de Vere wrote Shake-speare. After 1604, the London stages and bookstalls appear to have been reviving bits and patches of a *posthumous* Shake-speare canon.

Because no original Shake-speare manuscripts exist, and because no other records provide an unequivocal date of composition of the Shake-speare works, what remains is a host of scholarly suppositions—some better founded in historical fact than others. Will Shakspere (1564–1616) is conventionally assumed to have written the Shake-speare canon from his late twenties through the end of his forties (c. 1592–1613). The progression of Shake-speare plays from stylistically "early" (such as *The Comedy of Errors*) to "late" (such as *The Tempest*) is thus folded into the span of Will Shakspere's assumed career as liquid plastic is poured into a mold. Orthodox scholars then point to the assorted plays that convention places after 1604, which in turn, they claim, present conclusive proof that de Vere could not have been Shake-speare. This is circular reasoning.

There is no such thing as a "standard" chronology of Shake-speare. *The Riverside Shakespeare*, a textbook used in many classrooms today, dates eleven plays to sometime after 1604: *King Lear, Macbeth, Antony and Cleopatra, Coriolanus, Timon of Athens, Pericles, Cymbeline, The Winter's Tale, The Tempest, Henry VIII,* and *The Two Noble Kinsmen.* On the other hand, some orthodox scholarship yields the now-heretical conclusion that Shake-speare stopped writing in 1604. Alfred Harbage's Pelican/Viking editions of Shake-speare (1969; 1977) provide a range of dates for the likely composition of each of the plays: Only *The Tempest* and *Henry VIII* fall beyond 1604. And the nineteenth-century German literary historian Karl Elze dated both of these plays to the period 1603–04, theorizing that *Henry VIII* was originally written in early 1603 to celebrate the seventieth birthday that Queen Elizabeth never lived to see, while *The Tempest*, Elze concluded, "would at latest fall to the year 1604."

One eighteenth-century scholar, unaware of the significance of the year 1604, flatly stated what the above amalgam of scholarship implies. In *Memoirs of the Life and Writings of Ben Jonson* (1756), W. R. Chetwood concludes on the basis of performance records that "at the end of that year [1603] or the beginning of the next, 'tis supposed that [Shake-speare] took his farewell of the stage, both as author and actor."

Below are the methods scholars use to determine the dates of Shake-speare works, followed by an examination of the three strongest cases for post-1604 composition: *Macbeth, Henry VIII,* and *The Tempest.* Each play and each method, in fact, reinforce the conclusion Chetwood innocently put forward in 1756 and that has been ignored–in orthodox scholarly circles, at least–ever since.

One unassailable fact establishes the latest possible date by which a Shake-speare play must have been written: the year of first publication.

The 1593 epic poem *Venus and Adonis* was Shake-speare's print debut. During the ensuing decade, new Shake-speare plays and poems appeared in print, on average, twice per year. Then, in 1604, Shake-speare fell silent.

The silence was broken twice. The first break came in 1608–09 when de Vere's widow, Elizabeth Trentham de Vere, was preparing to move out of King's Place in Hackney, the house that she had shared with her late husband during his final years. Four new Shake-speare works (*Pericles, King Lear, Troilus and Cressida,* and the *Sonnets*) were printed during this period. The second window began with the publication in 1622 of the debut edition of *Othello* and culminated the following year in the publication of the thirty-seven plays (eighteen of which had never been printed before) that constitute the 1623 "Shakespeare First Folio."

The early history of *reprints* of Shake-speare plays and poems also points to 1604 as a watershed year. Some Shake-speare texts appear, by their shoddy nature, to have been cobbled-together versions of actors' playscripts or transcriptions from live performances by an audience member, Elizabethan equivalents of a video camcorder smuggled into a movie theater. Other Shake-speare texts–responding to these pirated editions–appear genuine, boasting on their title pages that they contain the author's revisions and corrections.

The title page of the second edition of *Romeo and Juliet* (1599), for instance, states that it has been "newly corrected, augmented, and emended," while the third edition of *Richard III* (1602) notes that it has been "newly augmented." The title page of the second edition of *Hamlet* (1604) states that the ensuing text has been "newly imprinted and enlarged to almost as much again as it was, according to the true and perfect copy."

After 1604, the "newly correct[ing]" and "augment[ing]" stops. Once again, the Shake-speare enterprise appears to have shut down.

Shake-speare draws upon contemporary scientific events and discoveries through the end of the sixteenth century. Yet Shake-speare is mute about science that appeared after de Vere's June 1604 death. A 1572 supernova in the constellation Cassiopeia becomes in *Hamlet* "... yond same star that's westward from the pole [making] his course to illume that part of heaven." William Gilbert's theory of geomagnetism (published in 1600) inspires a geomagnetic metaphor in *Troilus and Cressida* ("As true . . . as iron to adamant, as earth to the center"). Yet a spectacular supernova in October 1604–appearing nearby a celestial conjunction of Mars, Saturn, and Jupiter–occasions no mention in Shake-speare, nor does Johannes Kepler's revolutionary 1609 study of planetary orbits.

Shake-speare's source texts are also consistent with the proposition that the author was born in 1550 and died in 1604. Shake-speare's chief source texts appear at a frequency of seven to eight per decade from the 1560s through the end of the 1590s. Then, excepting two publications in 1603, the final curtain rings down. In Geoffrey Bullough's eight-volume *Narrative and Dramatic Sources of Shakespeare,* the twentieth-century literary scholar locates only one post-1604 Shake-speare source text that Bullough claims had more than just a "possible" or "probable" influence on the Bard. Bullough's single post-1604 "source," for *The Tempest,* will be discussed below.

The spotty record of Shake-speare performances provides less reliable conclusions about dates of composition. Shake-speare plays were performed for private audiences such as the students at Gray's Inn in 1594 *(The Comedy of Errors)* or Middle Temple Hall in 1602 *(Twelfth Night)*. In November 1611, *The Winter's Tale* was enacted for King James at court. None of these recorded performances, however, indicate the plays were newly written at the time. Yet scholars today assume as much in all three cases.

As this book proposes, the first version of *The Comedy of Errors* probably dates to 1577, when the Children of Paul's performed an otherwise lost courtly interlude for Queen Elizabeth called *A History of Error.* The first version of *Twelfth Night* was likely the manuscript cataloged during the eighteenth century as "[a] pleasant conceit of Vere, earl of Oxford, discontented at the rising of a mean gentleman in the English court circa 1580"–and, subsequently, lost. *The Winter's Tale,* which presents de Vere's self-flagellating reflections over his jealous mistreatment of his first wife, would appear upon internal evidence to stem from the period after her 1588 death. But de Vere probably never intended the searing autobiographical portrait of *The Winter's Tale* to be performed during his lifetime–not unlike the restrictions Eugene O'Neill placed upon his uncompromising family exposé *Long Day's Journey into Night.*

One performance record does point to 1604 as a speechless moment in Shake-spearean history. When the King's Men appeared at court during the winter of 1604–05, Queen Anne requested that the company perform some Shake-speare that she hadn't already seen. They told her they could not fulfill her request. So the King's Men staged the old standby *Love's Labor's Lost* instead.

Shake-speare's alleged references to seventeenth-century historical events as well as seventeenth-century Londoners' references to Shake-speare provide a hotly contested set of clues about dates of composition. Three plays in particular have been the site of pitched scholarly battles over whether the man who was Shake-speare died in 1616 or 1604.

Macbeth: The first recorded performance of Shake-speare's Scots tragedy was at the Globe Theatre in 1611. (The next known staging of *Macbeth* after that was in 1664.) However, for once, conventional scholarship supposes an earlier date of composition than what the scattershot performance records might imply. In Act 2, Scene 3, a drunken PORTER answers the knocking at MACBETH's castle door with the line

> Faith, here's an equivocator, that could swear in both the scales against either scale; who committed treason enough for God's sake, yet could not equivocate to heaven. O, come in, equivocator!

These words, along with other references to equivocating throughout *Macbeth,* led historians to a controversial Catholic policy of church-sanctioned duplicity, known as the Doctrine of Equivocation. Equivocations and equivocators gained notoriety around London in March 1606 during the celebrated trial of Father Henry Garnett, when he cited the Doctrine of Equivocation against an accusation of trying to blow up Parliament. (The defeat of the "Gunpowder Plot" is celebrated to this day in England on Guy Fawkes Day, November 5.) Because of the play's multiple allusions to equivocation, *Macbeth* is thus conventionally dated to c. 1606.

However, equivocation was hardly a novel concept in 1606. In a 1583 tract, *A Declaration of the Favorable Dealing of Her Majesty's Commission Approved for the Examination of Certain Traitors and of Tortures Unjustly Reported To Be Done Upon Them For Matters of Religion,* Edward de Vere's father-in-law, Lord Burghley, mused over Catholics who, when tortured, used "hypocritical and sophistical speech" to evade their torturers' questions. In 1584, a Spanish prelate named Martin Azpilcueta first formally laid out the Doctrine of Equivocation, which was disseminated across the Continent and into England. A 1595 trial of the English Catholic martyr Robert Southwell raised the issues central to Azpilcueta's thesis: that God-fearing papists could with clear conscience lie to Protestant inquisitors. While it is true that Garnett popularized the topic of equivocation in London in 1606, *Macbeth* makes no allusions to equivocation that can be tied to the Gunpowder Plot trial specifically.

This book hypothesizes that the regicidal anxiety expressed in *Macbeth* stems from de Vere's role as a juror who condemned Mary, Queen of Scots, to death in 1586. So, in fact, the wider context of the play would suggest that Burghley's 1583 treatise and Azpilcueta's 1584 formulation of the Doctrine of Equivocation were the more likely wellspring for the jestings of *Macbeth*'s PORTER scene.

Henry VIII: On June 29, 1613, the Globe Theatre burned to the ground during a performance of Shake-speare's *Henry VIII*. At least six independent eyewitness accounts of the fire exist. Two of these six—July 1613 letters written by the poet Sir Henry Wotton and the London merchant Henry Bluett—refer to the play as being "new."

It is indeed possible that in 1613 *Henry VIII* was new to the general theatergoing public. De Vere may well have left an incomplete *Henry VIII* manuscript behind at the time of his death only to be touched up in 1613 by other hands and debuted on the Globe stage.

Yet there's also no reason to treat the audience members Wotton and Bluett as expert witnesses either. In December 1663 the London diarist Samuel Pepys also referred to *Henry VIII* as being "new."

Before the twentieth century, when the Oxfordian theory forced the 1604 Question, many of the leading lights of eighteenth- and nineteenth-century Shake-speare scholarship placed the composition of *Henry VIII* to before 1604. Scholars such as Samuel Johnson, Lewis Theobald, George Steevens, Edmund Malone, and James Orchard Halliwell-Phillipps recognized the absurdity of dating such a Tudor apologist play as *Henry VIII* to the reign of King James, who never forgave the Tudors for having beheaded his mother. With characteristic polite understatement, Malone wrote of *Henry VIII*:

> It is more likely that Shakspeare [*sic*] should have written a play, the chief subject of which is the disgrace of Queen Catharine, the aggrandizement of Anne Boleyn, and the birth of her daughter [Elizabeth] in the lifetime of that daughter, than after her death: at a time when the subject must have been highly pleasing at court, rather than at a period when it must have been less interesting.

The Tempest is often portrayed as the silver bullet that kills the Oxfordian theory—because of parallels alleged between *The Tempest* and accounts of a

1609 wreck of the English ship the *Sea-Venture* off the Bermuda coast. PROS-
PERO's sprite ARIEL notes how he had once traveled "at midnight to fetch dew
from the still vex'd Bermoothes"—interpreted, somehow, to mean that the
shipwreck must have been in the Bermudas. Yet the Bermudas were not just a
string of islands in the Atlantic Ocean; "The Bermudas" was also the nickname of a neighborhood in Westminster near Charing Cross. If, as proposed
earlier, *The Tempest*'s "uninhabited island" is a grotesque of England, PROS-
PERO's servant recalling an errand he'd once made to fetch "dew from the still
vex'd Bermoothes" could simply be the author's jesting recollection of a favorite part of town in which to buy distilled liquor.

Regardless, the 1609 Bermuda shipwreck produced a flood of recollections written by the survivors (circulated in a manuscript written by William
Strachey and published in a 1610 pamphlet by Sylvester Jourdan) that orthodox scholars compare at length to the plot and dialogue of *The Tempest*. Strachey writes of "great strokes of thunder," while two characters in *The Tempest*
use the term *thunder-stroke;* Strachey writes that his crewmates "purposed to
have cut down the main mast"; *The Tempest*'s BOATSWAIN cries out, "Down
with the topmast!"; Strachey's account of the survivors has them splitting into
two parties; *The Tempest* has two parties of survivors plus FERDINAND.

Those without an a priori need to dash Edward de Vere on the rocks,
however, have found the Strachey-*Tempest* parallels less than overwhelming.
In *The Sources of Shakespeare's Plays* (1978), the literary scholar Kenneth Muir
notes:

> The extent of verbal echoes of [the Bermuda] pamphlets has, I think,
> been exaggerated. There is hardly a shipwreck in history or fiction
> which does not mention splitting, in which the ship is not lightened of
> its cargo, in which the passengers do not give themselves up for lost, in
> which the north winds are not sharp, and in which no one gets to shore
> by clinging to wreckage.

Muir also points to thirteen thematic and verbal parallels between *The Tempest*
and St. Paul's account of his shipwreck at Malta in the Acts of the Apostles
chapters 27–28—and this over just two pages of Scripture compared to the
114 pages of Strachey and Jourdan.

Perhaps the single most impressive Strachey-*Tempest* similarity is Strachey's detailed account of St. Elmo's fire and ARIEL's description of the heavenly light-show he provided for the storm-tossed mariners

> . . . now on the beak,
> Now in the waist, the deck, in every cabin,
> I flam'd amazement: Sometime I'd divide,

And burn in many places; on the topmast,
The yards and boresprit, would I flame distinctly
Then meet and join.

Yet Strachey was not the only seaman of his day to marvel at St. Elmo's fire, a continuous electric spark often seen in thunderstorms around ships' masts and church spires—essentially a neon light without the glass. In 1600, in a collection of nautical tales and discoveries published in London, the voyager Robert Tomson noted:

> ...in the night, there came upon the top of our mainyard and mainmast, a certain little light, much like unto the light of a little candle... this light continued aboard our ship about three hours, flying from mast to mast and from top to top. And sometime it would be in two or three places at once.

And if de Vere had himself endured the stormy adventures of the pre-Armada reconnaissance expeditions in June of 1588, as discussed in Chapter 8, he would probably have needed no reference texts to write convincingly about such a phantasm, such a thing as dreams are made on.

APPENDIX D

THE "ASHBOURNE PORTRAIT"

OF SHAKE-SPEARE

T HE FRONT COVER IMAGE OF THIS BOOK FEATURES A SPLIT-SCREEN comparison between two portraits: One (on the left) is the *Mona Lisa* of Shake-speare images, the "Ashbourne Portrait of Shakespeare" now owned by the Folger Shakespeare Library in Washington, D.C. The other (on the right) is the "Wellbeck Portrait" of Edward de Vere, seventeenth earl of Oxford, a copy of a now-lost original painted in 1575 when de Vere was in Paris. The Wellbeck presently hangs at the National Portrait Gallery in London. As a visual metaphor for the overall story of this book—that de Vere and Shake-speare are inseparable—superposing the Wellbeck and Ashbourne is attractive for both its eye-catching and provocative nature.

However, the cover image also masks a detective story in and of itself. To assert, as this book's cover implicitly does, that de Vere was the original sitter of the Ashbourne Portrait, is to welcome no small amount of controversy—even apart from the Shake-speare authorship controversy.

On March 8, 1847, the English schoolmaster Clement Usill Kingston wrote a letter to the portraiture expert Abraham Wivell announcing the discovery of a painting of Shake-speare. Kingston's letter is the first officially recognized notice of what is now called the Ashbourne Portrait, named after Kingston's Derbyshire hometown and the grammar school where he taught. "I am perfectly aware of the numerous deceptions and frauds of every possible kind which are practiced upon the unwary connoisseur," Kingston wrote. "... I will warrant every portion of the picture to have been painted at the same period.... I will warrant my picture to be purchased in its original state, and that the canvas, etc., is peculiarly of the period in which Shakespeare lived; that it has never been retouched since it was painted."

Kingston explained to Wivell where he'd learned of the portrait: "A friend in London sent me word that he had seen a portrait of Shakespeare, that he was positive it was a genuine picture. . . . I immediately wrote back requesting him to secure me the prize."

The prize was worldwide recognition as the "discoverer" of what remains to this day the finest and most exquisitely rendered portrait of the Bard. The Ashbourne sitter wears a black doublet, delicate wrist and neck ruffs, and a gold-embroidered costume dagger belt. His left hand clasps a glove with crimson gauntlet, while the thumb sports a signet ring. The right hand holds an ornate book with red silk tie-ribbons. And—in a gesture that Dutch and Flemish artists often used to signify that the sitter was either a medical man or a deep thinker and philosopher—the Ashbourne sitter rests his right forearm on a skull.

Gold lettering in the upper-left quadrant of the portrait notes that the sitter is age forty-seven in the year 1611—fitting Will Shakspere of Stratford-upon-Avon. In a detailed 1910 examination of the painting for *Connoisseur* magazine, the art historian M. H. Spielmann observed that there were at least two different kinds of gold paint being used on the Ashbourne canvas. "Whether or not [the gold paint used in the lettering] is a later addition is an open question," Spielmann observed. "But the fact must not be lost sight of that the color of it corresponds to that of the book-cover gold and that of the thumb ring, and is in sharp contrast to that on the belt and glove."

In 1940, the optics expert and Shake-speare researcher Charles Wisner Barrell published an article in *Scientific American* asserting that in fact the Ashbourne had been modified from its original state. The Ashbourne Portrait of Shake-speare, Barrell said, was actually an overpainted image of Edward de Vere, seventeenth earl of Oxford. Using X-ray and infrared photography of the Ashbourne, Barrell concluded that the gold paint of the lettering was a later addition, discovering what he claimed was an artist's monogram "CK" and an overpainted coat of arms (featuring three griffins) of Edward de Vere's second wife, Elizabeth Trentham de Vere. Barrell did a rubbing of the daub of paint on the Ashbourne sitter's thumb ring, revealing a concealed image of a boar's head—a heraldic device of the earls of Oxford.

Barrell examined "CK" monograms by the sixteenth-century Dutch portrait painter Cornelius Ketel and concluded that the "CK" on the Ashbourne was probably Ketel's signature. Ketel had, during his residency in England from 1573 to '81, painted many of the Elizabethan nobility. One of Ketel's contemporaries noted that Ketel had "made a portrait of the duke of Oxford (Edward de Vere). [*sic*]" Recent work by the independent art researcher Barbara Burris confirmed that the style of the Ashbourne painting is consistent with known examples of Ketel's portraits.

Ketel's portrait of de Vere next turns up at Wentworth Woodhouse in south Yorkshire—a vast estate thirty-five miles northeast of Ashbourne that belongs to a family line descended from Edward de Vere's great-granddaughter Henrietta Maria Stanley, countess of Strafford. The 1695 will of Countess Henrietta's husband mentioned among the family heirlooms a portrait of the "earl of Oxford my wife's great-grandfather at [full] length" In 1721, the artist George Vertue recorded that a large portrait of the earl of Oxford painted by Cornelius Ketel had been in the possession of the countess of Strafford of Wentworth Woodhouse–no doubt the same portrait mentioned in the 1695 will.

However, after Vertue's mention of the Ketel portrait, the painting disappears from the historical record. A 1782 inventory of Wentworth Woodhouse no longer lists the heirloom Ketel portrait of the earl of Oxford. On the other hand, the 1782 inventory does list in the mansion's main dining room a heretofore unnoticed, unframed three-quarter-length portrait of "Shakespear."

The fact that the Ashbourne today (as well as the inventory listing of the 1782 "Shakespear" portrait) is at three-quarters length and that the Ketel of de Vere was at full length–meaning head-to-toe–has confounded some scholars. But internal Folger documents obtained by Burris reveal that when the Folger Shakespeare Library performed its restoration on the Ashbourne in 1979, the Ashbourne was found not, in fact, to have any original edges; the Ashbourne had at some time been trimmed down from a larger size.

Finally, Burris sent a copy of an 1848 woodcut of the Ashbourne (presenting an image of the painting as close as possible to its original and unrestored state) to the Victoria and Albert Museum in London. Burris's study of sixteenth- and seventeenth-century English men's fashions had led her to conclude that the Ashbourne sitter's costume dated to the period when Cornelius Ketel was painting in England (1573–81). Susan North, Textiles and Dress curator at the V & A, responded to Burris's query:

> I would agree that the dress does not appear to date from 1611.... The general shape of the doublet with close fitting sleeves and a waistline dipping only slightly below its natural place in front corresponds with men's dress of the 1570s.... Regarding your comments on the [Ashbourne's] wrist ruffs, I agree that these go out of fashion in the 1580s.

In summary, then:

- The Ashbourne Portrait of Shake-speare was originally a larger portrait and has subsequently been painted over at least once–to obscure family-identifying heraldic emblems and to add year and age information consistent with the supposition that the Ashbourne sitter was Will Shakspere of Stratford-upon-Avon.
- The signet ring on the Ashbourne sitter's thumb and the coat of arms are consistent with the original Ashbourne sitter having been Edward de Vere.
- The Ashbourne sitter's costume dates it to the period of Cornelius Ketel's residency in England, when Ketel painted the "duke of Oxford."

- A full-length portrait of de Vere by Ketel, tracked to Wentworth Wood-house in the early eighteenth-century, has since gone missing. However, late eighteenth-century Wentworth Woodhouse records reveal a previously un-accounted-for three-quarters-length portrait of "Shakespear."
- The three-quarters-length Ashbourne Portrait appears, by its "CK" mono-gram and its style, to have been painted by Ketel.
- Given the above, along with the similarity of the facial features of the Ashbourne sitter with the 1575 Wellbeck portrait of Edward de Vere, the evidence would appear to be overwhelming that the Ashbourne Portrait of Shake-speare is in fact an overpainting of the otherwise missing Cor-nelius Ketel portrait of Edward de Vere (c. 1580).

However, while a few orthodox scholars provisionally accepted Barrell's 1940 findings in favor of de Vere as the Ashbourne sitter, the Folger rejected the at-tribution. In a 1993 article in the Folger Shakespeare Library's journal *Shake-speare Quarterly*, the art historian William L. Pressly conceded that Barrell was correct insofar as the Ashbourne was an overpainted portrait of someone else.

But the original sitter of the Ashbourne, according to Pressly, was Sir Hugh Hamersley (1565–1636), lord mayor of London from 1627 to '28. In fa-vor of the Hamersley attribution, Pressly makes three claims:

- Restoration of the Ashbourne conducted by Folger-appointed conserva-tors in 1979 revealed that the final digit of the 1611 date concealed a painted-over "2." Thus, the Folger contends, the original inscription would have read that the sitter was age forty-seven in 1612–Hamersley's age.
- The 1979 restoration also uncovered the coat of arms that Barrell's 1940 *Scientific American* viewed with X-ray and infrared photography. The re-stored Ashbourne coat of arms, Pressly claims, contained three ram's heads and a scroll with a partially obliterated family motto, the only letters of which that could be read were the final four: "... MORE." Hamersley's coat of arms contained three rams' heads, and his family motto was *Honor et amore*. (Yet, Folger internal documents reveal that in 1979 even the Fol-ger's own restoration expert, Peter Michaels, was unable to find the "... MORE." In addition, the "ram's heads" are hardly an unambiguous like-ness; what to Pressly appear to be rams can just as readily be seen as the griffins that Barrell pointed out in his original *Scientific American* article.)
- Pressly was unable to find any boar insignia on the Ashbourne thumb ring or any "CK" monogram. X-rays taken for the Folger at the National Gallery of Art in the late 1940s, Pressly notes in his *Shakespeare Quarterly* article, "do not reveal a 'CK'" And, in any event, Pressly claimed, "on stylistic grounds, even though the painting is in poor condition, one can confidently state that Ketel never touched this canvas."

Yet in a 1993 catalog of Folger Paintings, Pressly notes that the "CK" monogram is "only faintly visible" in these same X rays. He supposes that the monogram "stood for Clement Kingston [who first bought the Ashbourne in 1847], who could not resist initialing his handiwork, even though he had to cover up the letters with overpainting."

One undisputed portrait of the Ashbourne's supposed original sitter, Hugh Hamersley, does exist. It is today in the collection of the London Haberdashers Company. The likeness of Hamersley features a longer face, a pointier and longer nose, lower lips, bushier eyebrows, larger eyes, and more diagonal chin line than that of the Ashbourne (and Wellbeck) sitter.

Thus, to accept the Ashbourne as an overpainted portrait of Hugh Hamersley is to endorse an unclothed emperor:

Who painted the Ashbourne? If it's Hamersley, the artist is unknown—and the "CK" monogram was painted onto the canvas (and then inexplicably hidden beneath another layer of paint) by a schoolmaster who bought the portrait in the mid–nineteenth-century. If it's de Vere, the artist is, on solid historical and stylistic evidence, Cornelius Ketel.

What is the Ashbourne's provenance? If it's Hamersley, the pre-1847 provenance is unknown. If it's de Vere, the Ketel portrait would have passed down through the family line of his first daughter, Elizabeth de Vere, whose granddaughter the countess of Strafford had it in her collection of heirlooms at her family's estate at Wentworth Woodhouse as late as 1721. Sometime before 1782, the full-length portrait was cut down to three-quarter length. (Conservators sometimes trim away part of a damaged canvas in order to save the rest of the painting, not unlike a surgeon amputating a limb.) Then—for reasons unknown—the portrait slipped into the public marketplace in the mid–nineteenth century and ended up in the nearby town of Ashbourne as a bona fide portrait of "Shakespeare."

When was the Ashbourne overpainted? If it's Hamersley, the date of overpainting is unknown. If it's de Vere, the date is also unknown–but the 1611/12 on the overpainted canvas provokes suspicion that the Ashbourne ruse was perpetrated at the behest of one or more of de Vere's daughters in (perhaps panicked) response to the family and national crises then unfolding. As noted in the Epilogue, in 1611–12, the Protestant savior and heir to the English throne Prince Henry Stuart died, the girls' uncle Robert Cecil died, their stepmother, Elizabeth Trentham de Vere, died, and Henry Peacham's *Minerva Britanna* was published, cryptically announcing on its title page a concealed playwright whose "name is de Vere."

Why does the Ashbourne sitter look so much like Edward de Vere? Because it was Edward de Vere.

AUTHOR'S NOTE

IN THE SUMMER OF 1993, I FIRST LEARNED ABOUT AN UNDERCURrent of dissent among accomplished scholars and writers who, over the past two and a half centuries, have doubted the conventional biography of "Shakespeare." I was astonished. Here was perhaps the greatest author who had ever lived, and legendary figures in their own right say he actually wrote nothing? Was this the biggest case of mistaken identity in history? What had haunted the likes of Henry James, Sigmund Freud, Mark Twain, and Walt Whitman so much? Why had I never heard of this before?

I was just out of graduate school, having completed a master's degree in astrophysics–concluding seven years of academic training (including a B.A. in physics) that centered around applications of deductive and inductive reasoning. Having concentrated on theoretical physics, I was most interested in what makes a theory work, what kinds of evidence support a theory, and what kinds of evidence modify or negate a theory.

Moreover, I was beginning a career as a freelance investigative journalist, creative writer, and arts (particularly music) critic. The Shake-speare question enabled me to engage all of these interests.

As I began researching the issue, I found that the Shake-speare question was also considered a heresy in the church of English letters. I recall early encounters with otherwise reasonable people who became irrational and redfaced with anger when the words "*earl of Oxford*" were uttered in concordance with "Shakespeare." This unfortunate fact of life remains unchanged today.

When I began my investigative journey in 1993, I was an outsider, a stranger to the field. Yet the outsider has a perspective that can also be a valuable asset. In his 1979 book *Studies in Intellectual Breakthrough,* the social historian Charles David Axelrod observes:

Coming from the outside, and therefore open to a wider world than is the full-fledged member, the stranger can more easily remain unshackled by "sacred" tradition.... Inquiry of the sort invoked by the stranger involves the capacity to question, even to violate, what has already been accumulated and accepted within the community.

Axelrod's insight, in essence, describes the eighty-five-year history of the "Oxfordian" movement. Outsiders have contributed much of the scholarship that forms the foundation of *"Shakespeare" by Another Name*. Some of the "outsider" books that were critical to the development of my thinking about Edward de Vere were the pioneering work *"Shakespeare" Identified in Edward de Vere, seventeenth Earl of Oxford* (J. Thomas Looney, 1920) as well as *Hidden Allusions in Shakespeare's Plays* (Eva Turner Clark, 1931), *The Man Who Was Shakespeare* (Eva Turner Clark, 1937), *This Star of England* (Dorothy and Charlton Ogburn Sr., 1952), *The Mysterious William Shakespeare* (Charlton Ogburn Jr., 1984), *The Shakespeare Controversy* (Warren Hope and Kim Holston, 1992), *Shakespeare: Who Was He?* (Richard Whalen, 1994), *Alias Shakespeare* (Joseph Sobran, 1996), and *Edward de Vere's Geneva Bible* (Roger Stritmatter, 2001).

I was also often surprised at the amount of orthodox scholarship that actually supported the entirely unorthodox conclusion that de Vere was Shakespeare. A glance through the endnotes of this book will confirm that just as often as I was drawing from Oxfordian research in writing the text, I was also quoting some of the leading orthodox scholarship.

"Shakespeare" by Another Name draws liberally from the Shake-speare works in describing de Vere's life from its earliest moments onward: Simply because a Shake-speare play or poem is quoted or mentioned at any given point in de Vere's life does not mean this book assumes the final version of the Shake-speare play or poem was written by then. Reevaluating the chronology of composition of the entire Shake-speare canon is a task exceeding the scope of this book. It is assumed that the Shake-speare canon began in earliest form as de Vere's lyrics, short poems, and courtly masques in the 1560s, '70s, and '80s—and in the 1590s and early 1600s, de Vere and perhaps other collaborators revised these early texts into the mature Shake-speare plays and poems as they exist today. Exceptions to this rule of thumb, no doubt, will be discovered as Oxfordian research continues to widen its scope. It is hoped that a complete and viable Oxfordian chronology of composition of the Shake-speare canon can be arrived at over the next decade; in the meantime, however, "When was that written?" will remain one of the most important unanswered questions for any Shake-speare play.

A glance at the endnotes will also reveal the dual-layered nature of *"Shakespeare" by Another Name*. This book is foremost a popular biography of Edward de Vere as Shake-speare. Thus, by design, the reader can easily make it through *"Shakespeare" by Another Name* without ever having to consult a single endnote.

Yet, to tell the unorthodox story of *"Shakespeare" by Another Name,* I some-times had to disassemble various orthodox theories and interpretations and then fit the pieces back together with de Vere as Shake-speare. In some cases, this re-quires paragraphs of explication—just to write a phrase or sentence in the main-body text. The lengthy endnotes are there for the readers who want to see more specifically how I arrived at my conclusions.

The Introduction presented the basic arguments against Will Shakspere as Shake-speare. Recommended books that present a more complete refutation of Shakspere as Shake-speare include Mark Twain's *Is Shakespeare Dead?* (1909, which Oxford University Press reprinted in 1996) for its sheer wit and page-turning pleasure; the nearly twelve hundred pages of G. G. Greenwood's *The Shakespeare Problem Restated* and *Is There A Shakespeare Problem?* (John Lane/The Bodley Head, 1908 and 1916) for their breadth and scholarly mag-nitude; and Diana Price's *Shakespeare's Unorthodox Biography: New Evidence of an Authorship Problem* (Greenwood Press, 2001) for some of the latest schol-arly views on the authorship controversy.

Compiling eighty-five years of the most relevant Oxfordian research for this book—some unpublished, some published in obscure journals and books, some my own discoveries—makes an overwhelming case that, I've long felt, needed only to be assembled into one popularly accessible package. I have found that the pieces of the puzzle fit together so fully and completely that I didn't need to divert the story to make arguments.

In writing this book, I knew that if the Oxfordian theory did not in fact hold up, the narrative would reveal its own internal fallacies. Time and again, I discovered instead that the explanatory and revelatory power of the Oxford-ian solution to the Shake-speare problem is its own best advocate. But let the reader be the ultimate judge.

You don't need a degree in Elizabethan history or English literature to know whether *"Shakespeare" by Another Name* has identified its man. All you need is an open mind and a sense of curiosity about one of the greatest mys-teries in the history of Western literature.

FREQUENTLY CITED SOURCES

In the endnotes, the following abbreviations will be used.

AKRIGG=G.P.V. Akrigg. *Shakespeare and the Earl of Southampton*. London: Hamish Hamilton, 1968.

ALLUSION BOOK=C. M. Ingleby, ed. *The Shakspere* [sic] *Allusion-Book: A Collection of Allusions to Shakspere from 1591 to 1700, Originally Compiled by C. M. Ingleby, Miss L. Toulmin Smith and by Dr. F. J. Furnivall, With The Assistance of the New Shakspere Society: Re-Edited, Revised and Re-Arranged, With An Introduction by John Munro (1909) and Now Re-Issued With A Preface By Sir Edmund Chambers*. 2 vols. London: Oxford University Press, 1932.

ARBER=Worshipful Company of Stationers and Newspaper Makers. *A Transcript of the Company of Stationers of London, 1554–1640 A.D.* Edited by E. Arber. 5 vols. London: Privately printed, 1875–77.

BREWER'S=Ebenezer Cobham Brewer. *Brewer's Dictionary of Phrase and Fable,* revised and enlarged. New York: Harper & Brothers, n.d.

BREWSTER=Eleanor Brewster. *Oxford and His Elizabethan Ladies*. Philadelphia: Dorrance & Co., 1972.

BULLOUGH=Geoffrey Bullough. *Narrative and Dramatic Sources of Shakespeare*. 8 vols. New York: Columbia University Press, 1957–75.

CAMPBELL & QUINN=O. J. Campbell and Edward G. Quinn, eds. *The Reader's Encyclopedia of Shakespeare*. New York: Thomas Y. Crowell Co., 1966.

CHAMBERS/ES=E. K. Chambers. *The Elizabethan Stage*. 4 vols. Oxford: Clarendon Press, 1923.

CHAMBERS/WS=E. K. Chambers. *William Shakespeare: A Study of Facts and Problems*. 2 vols. Oxford: Clarendon Press, 1930.

CHILJAN=Katherine V. Chiljan, ed. *Book Dedications to the Earl of Oxford.* Privately published, 1994.

CLARK=Eva Turner Clark. *The Man Who Was Shakespeare.* New York: Richard R. Smith, 1937.

CSP=Great Britain, Public Record Office. *Calendar of State Papers.* London: Her Majesty's Stationery Office.

COMPLETE PEERAGE=George Edward Cokayne, Vicary Gibbs, H. A. Doubleday, Duncan Warrand, Howard de Walden, eds. *The Complete Peerage.* 13 vols. London: St. Catherine's Press, 1910–59.

DE VERE SOCIETY NEWSLETTER=Newsletter of the (U.K.) De Vere Society [http://www.deveresociety.pwp.blueyonder.co.uk]

DEWAR=Mary Dewar. *Sir Thomas Smith: A Tudor Intellectual in Office.* London: University of London, Athlone Press, 1964.

DNB=*The Dictionary of National Biography.* Oxford: Oxford University Press, 1917, 1975, 2004.

EB/1911=*Encyclopaedia Britannica,* 11th edition. New York: Encyclopedia Britannica Co., 1910.

ELIZ. JOURNALS=G. B. Harrison. *The Elizabethan Journals: Being a Record of those things most talked about during the years 1591–1603.* 3 vols. in one. New York: Macmillan Co, 1939.

ELIZABETHAN REVIEW=Scholarly authorship journal (1993–1999) [http://www.jmucci.com]

FELDMAN/AMENDMENTS=Bronson Feldman. "Amendments to Bernard Mordaunt Ward's *The Seventeenth Earl of Oxford.*" *The Bard* 4 (1984), 53–67.

FELDMAN=Bronson Feldman. *Hamlet Himself.* Philadelphia: Lovelore Press, 1977.

FEUILLERAT=Albert Feuillerat, ed. *Documents Relating to the Office of the Revels in the Time of Queen Elizabeth.* Louvain: A. Uystpruyst, 1908.

FOWLER=William Plumer Fowler. *Shakespeare Revealed in Oxford's Letters.* Portsmouth, N.H.: Peter E. Randall, 1986. [http://ruthmiller.com]

HOLLAND/SHAKESPEARE OXFORD=H. H. Holland. *Shakespeare, Oxford and Elizabethan Times.* London: Denis Archer, 1933.

HOLLAND/OXFORD GLASSES=H. H. Holland. *Shakespeare Through Oxford Glasses.* London: Cecil Palmer, 1923.

HURSTFIELD=Joel Hurstfield. *The Queen's Wards: Wardship and Marriage under Queen Elizabeth I.* London: Longmans, Green & Co., 1958.

KAWACHI=Yoshiko Kawachi. *Calendar of English Renaissance Drama, 1558–1642.* New York: Garland Publishing, Inc., 1986.

KITTLE/DE VERE=William Kittle, *Edward de Vere, 17th Earl of Oxford, and Shakespeare.* Baltimore: Monumental Printing Co., 1942.

KITTLE/GASCOIGNE=William Kittle, *G. Gascoigne: April 1562 to Jan. 1, 1578, Or, Edward de Vere, Seventeenth Earl of Oxford.* Washington, D.C.: W. F. Roberts, 1930.

LIBEL = "Arundell Libels" as transcribed by and following the numbering system of Alan H. Nelson, online at socrates.berkeley.edu/~ahnelson; computer printouts in the Edward de Vere Collection at Concordia University, Portland, Ore; and the Massachusetts Center for Renaissance Studies at the University of Massachusetts, Amherst.

MAY = Stephen W. May, ed. "The Poems of Edward de Vere, Seventeenth Earl of Oxford, and of Robert Devereux, Second Earl of Essex." *Studies in Philology* 77:5 (Early Winter 1980).

MAY/ECP = Steven W. May. *The Elizabethan Courtier Poets: The Poems and Their Contexts.* Asheville, N.C.: Pegasus Press, 1999.

McKERROW = Ronald B. McKerrow. *The Works of Thomas Nashe, edited from the original texts.* 5 vols. London: Blackwell, 1958.

MILLER/FLOWRES = George Gascoigne. *A Hundreth Sundrie Flowres, from the Original Edition of 1573.* Edited by B. M. Ward and Ruth Loyd Miller. Jennings, La: Minos Publishing Co., 1975; first ed. 1926. [http://ruthmiller.com]

MILLER/HASP = Eva Lee Turner Clark. *Hidden Allusions in Shakespeare's Plays: A Study of the Early Court Revels and Personalities of the Times.* Edited by Ruth Loyd Miller. New York/London: Kennikat Press, 1974; first ed. 1931. [http://ruthmiller.com]

MILLER/LOONEY = J. Thomas Looney. *"Shakespeare" Identified in Edward de Vere, Seventeenth Earl of Oxford–and–The Poems of Edward de Vere.* 2 vols. Edited by Ruth Loyd Miller. New York/London: Kennikat Press, 1975; first ed. 1920. [http://ruthmiller.com]

NELSON = Alan H. Nelson. *Monstrous Adversary: The Life of Edward de Vere, 17th Earl of Oxford.* Liverpool, U.K.: Liverpool University Press, 2003.

NICHOLS = John Nichols. *The Progresses and Public Processions of Queen Elizabeth.* 3 vols. New York: Burt Franklin, 1966; first ed. 1823.

OED = *The Oxford English Dictionary.* Oxford: Oxford University Press, 1971, 1989.

OGBURN/TMWS = Charlton Ogburn Jr. *The Mysterious William Shakespeare: The Myth and the Reality.* McLean, Va.: EPM Publications, 1992; first ed. 1984.

OGBURNS/TSOE = Charlton Ogburn Sr. and Dorothy Ogburn. *This Star of England.* New York: Coward-McCann, 1952.

PECK/COMMONWEALTH = D. C. Peck, ed. *Leicester's Commonwealth: The Copy of a Letter Written by a Master of Art of Cambridge (1584) and Related Documents.* Athens, Oh.: Ohio University Press, 1985.

PRICE = Diana Price. *Shakespeare's Unorthodox Biography.* Westport, Conn.: Greenwood Press, 2001.

PMLA = *Publications of the Modern Language Association.*

READ/BIBLIO = Conyers Read. *Bibliography of British History, Tudor Period, 1485–1603.* 2nd ed. Totowa, N. J.: Rowman and Littlefield, 1978; first ed. 1933.

READ/CECIL =Conyers Read, *Sir William Cecil and Queen Elizabeth*. London: Jonathan Cape, 1965; first ed. 1960.

READ/BURGHLEY=Conyers Read. *Lord Burghley and Queen Elizabeth*. New York: Alfred A. Knopf, 1955.

RES=Review of English Studies.

SCHRICKX=W. Schrickx. *Shakespeare's Early Contemporaries*. Antwerp: De Nederlandsche Boekhandel, 1956.

SHAHEEN=Naseeb Shaheen. *Biblical References in Shakespeare's Plays*. Newark, N.J.: University of Delaware Press, 1999.

SH. ENG.=Sidney Lee and C. T. Onions, eds. *Shakespeare's England: An Account of the Life and Manners of His Age*. 2 vols. Oxford: Clarendon Press, 1916.

SHAKESPEARE MATTERS=Newsletter of the Shakespeare Fellowship (U.S.) [http://www.shakespearefellowship.org]

SHAKESPEARE OXFORD NEWSLETTER=Newsletter of the Shakespeare Oxford Society [http://www.shakespeare-oxford.com]

SH.Q=Shakespeare Quarterly.

SMITH/ET=Lacey Baldwin Smith. *Elizabeth Tudor: Portrait of a Queen*. Boston: Little, Brown & Co., 1975.

STATE TRIALS=T. B. Howell, ed. *A Complete Collection of State Trials and Proceedings for High Treason and other Crimes and Misdemeanors*. 21 vols. London: T. C. Hansard, 1816.

STONE=Lawrence Stone, *The Crisis of the Aristocracy, 1558–1641*. Nonabridged edition. Oxford: Clarendon Press, 1965.

STOPES=Charlotte Carmichael Stopes. *The Life of Henry, Third Earl of Southampton, Shakespeare's Patron*. Cambridge: Cambridge University Press, 1922.

STOW=John Stow. *The Survey of London*. Edited by Valerie Pearl. London: Everyman's Library/Dent, 1987; first ed. 1598.

STRITMATTER=Roger Stritmatter, "The Marginalia of Edward de Vere's Geneva Bible: Providential Discovery, Literary Reasoning and Historical Consequence." Ph.D. Diss., University of Massachusetts, 2001. [http://shakespearefellowship.goemerchant7.com]

STRYPE=John Strype, *The Life of the Learned Sir Thomas Smith, Kt. D.C. L.* Oxford: Clarendon Press, 1820.

VAN DREUNEN=Elizabeth Appleton Van Dreunen, *An Anatomy of the Marprelate Controversy, 1588–1596: Retracing Shakespeare's Identity and That of Martin Marprelate*. Renaissance Studies, Vol. 5. Lewiston, N.Y.: Edwin Mellen Press, 2001.

V. ANDERSON=Verily Anderson. *The De Veres of Castle Hedingham*. Lavenham, Suffolk: Terence Dalton, Ltd., 1993.

WALLACE=Charles William Wallace. *The Evolution of English Drama Up to Shakespeare*. Berlin: G. Reimer, 1912.

WARD=B. M. WARD. *The Seventeenth Earl of Oxford, 1550–1604: From Contemporary Documents.* London: John Murray, 1928.

WHITTEMORE=Hank Whittemore. *The Monument: Shakespeare's Sonnets by Edward de Vere, 17th Earl of Oxford.* Marshfield Hills, Mass.: Meadow Geese Press, 2005.

NOTES

INTRODUCTION

p. xxv, Galsworthy quote: "Some Platitudes Concerning Drama," from *The Inn of Tranquility* (New York: Charles Scribner's Sons, 1924), 193.

p. xxv, James quote: Henry James to Violet Hunt, August 26, 1903, in *The Letters of Henry James,* ed. Percy Lubbock (New York: Charles Scribner's Sons, 1920), 1:424–5; discussion of James's convictions in Warren Hope and Kim Holston, *The Shakespeare Controversy: An Analysis of the Claimants to Authorship and Their Champions and Detractors* (Jefferson, N.C.: McFarland & Co., 1992), 61–5.

pp. xxv–vi, Freud quote: Freud goes on to say, "Since reading *Shakespeare Identified,* by J. Thomas Looney, I am almost convinced that the assumed name conceals the personality of Edward de Vere, earl of Oxford." [Freud, *Autobiography,* tr. James Strachey (New York: W.W. Norton & Co., 1935), 130.] This statement–and indeed practically all of Freud's Oxfordian endorsements–have been expurgated by disciples eager to paper over Father Freud's heretical beliefs vis à vis Shakespeare. On the story of the censorship of Freud's convictions about Edward de Vere, cf. MILLER/LOONEY, 2:264–73.

p. xxvi, Whitman quote: Horace Traubel, *With Walt Whitman in Camden* (New York: Rowman and Littlefield, 1961), 1:234, 239.

p. xxvi, Rowe's Accounts: S. Schoenbaum, *Shakespeare's Lives* (Oxford: Clarendon Press, 1991; first ed. 1970), 86ff.

p. xxvi, Herbert Lawrence: OGBURN/*TMWS,* 125–7; Schoenbaum, op. cit., 92–3.

p. xxvi, Adams quote: John Adams, "Notes on a Tour of English Country Seats &c. . . . April 1786," in Hope and Holston, op. cit., 151.

p. xxvi, Irving quote: Washington Irving, "Stratford-on-Avon," in *Selected Writings of Washington Irving,* ed. William P. Kelly (New York: Modern Library, 1984), 281.

p. xxvi, Looney's early converts: Hope & Holston, op. cit., 123ff.; MILLER/LOONEY, 2:264–73; Charles Boyle, *To Catch The Conscience of the King: Leslie Howard and the 17th Earl of Oxford* (Northampton, Mass.: Oxenford Press, 1993).

p. xxvi, Looney's name: "The best trained and most highly respected professional students of Shakespeare in the colleges and universites of England and America contemplated the seemingly seamless argument presented in *"Shakespeare" Identified* and quickly discovered a flaw in it. The book was written by a man with a funny name. They found their arguments against Looney where they had found their arguments in favor of William Shakspere–on a title page." Hope & Holston, op. cit., 116; on the history of J. Thomas Looney's writing of *"Shakespeare" Identified* and the reception it received, Hope and Holston, 90–138, MILLER/LOONEY, 1:647–57.

p. xxvii, "... with the rest": This quote appears in the anonymous 1589 book of Elizabethan literary criticism, *The Arte of English Poesie*–and the precise meaning of the line "if his doings could be found out and made public with the rest" has been the subject of no small amount of debate: cf. Terry Ross, "What Did George Puttenham Really Say About Oxford: And Why Does it Matter?" http://shakespeareauthorship.com/putt1.html; Roger Stritmatter, "A Matter of Small Consequence" and Andy Hannas, "'The Rest' is not silence" *The Ever Reader* 3 (1996) http://www.everreader.com/everrea3.htm.

p. xxvii, De Vere's youthful poetry: Steven W. May, *The Elizabethan Courtier Poets: The Poems and Their Contexts* (Asheville, N.C.: Pegasus Press/University of North Carolina at Asheville, 1999), 269–70.

p. xxvii, De Vere as theatrical patron,: On the recorded theatrical activities of the Earl of Oxford's Men, cf. NELSON, 239–48, 391–3.

p. xxvii, Welles quote: Quoted in Cecil Beaton and Kenneth Tynan, *Persona Grata* (New York: Putnam, 1954), 98.

p. xxvii, ... on the Danish shore: For discussion and citations on de Vere's FORTIN-BRAS/pirate adventure, cf. Chapter 5.

p. xxviii, "... Golden Age of pseudonyms ...": Archer Taylor and Fredric J. Mosher, *The Bibliographical History of Anonyma and Pseudonyma* (Chicago: University of Chicago Press, 1951), 85.

p. xxviii, Mar-prelate: "Martin Marprelate" often spelled his name without a hyphen too. Examples of a hyphenated "Mar-prelate" include *The just censure and reproofe of Martin Junior, Wherein the rash and undiscreete headlines of the foolish youth is sharply meete with and the boy hath his lesson taught him, I warrant you, by his reverend and elder brother Martin Senior, sonne and heir unto the renowmed* [sic] *Martin Mar-prelate* ... (1589) and "Pasquill Cavaliero's" first published words: "Valiant Martin ... thy father Mar-prelat was a whelpe of that [heretical] race." in *The Works of Thomas Nashe*, ed. Ronald B. McKerrow (London: A. H. Bullen, 1904-10), 1:59.

p. xxviii, Spear shaking: The spear-shaking epithet also applies to Athena's Roman equivalent, Minerva. Roger Stritmatter, "The Not-Too-Hidden Key to *Minerva Britanna*," *Shakespeare Oxford Newsletter* 36:2 (Summer 2000), reprinted at http://www.shakespearefellowship .org/virtualclassroom/MinervaBritanna.htm. In addition to the allusions Stritmatter cites, here are several more which equate Minerva/Pallas/Athena with spear shaking: "Pallas ... shaked her speare at [Vulcan] and threatened his sauciness." (footnote by "E.K." in Edmund Spenser's *The Shepeardes Calendar* [1579], October eclogue, 186–94); "Cast off these loose vailes and thy armour take. /And in thy hand the speare of Pallas shake" (Ovid's *Art of Love,* tr. Thomas Heywood (1625), Book I, ll. 904–5); "[Minerva] held a golden Speare, which the people oft thought the goddesse had shaken." (Kingsmill Long, *Barclay His Argenis* [1625], Book I, Chap. XX, sig I2).

p. xxviii, ... affiliated with the theater: Athena was also goddess of Athens, classical birthplace of the theater. Lee Hall, *Athena: A Biography* (Reading, Mass.: Addison Wesley, 1997), 31ff.

p. xxviii, Alternate Shake-speare candidates: Sources for the respective alternative Shake-speare theories include **Marlowe:** Calvin Hoffman, *The Murder of the Man Who Was "Shakespeare"* (New York: Grosset & Dunlap, 1955); **Dyer:** Alden Brooks, *Will Shakspere and the Dyer's Hand* (New York: Charles Scribner's Sons, 1943); **Derby:** Abel LeFranc, *Under the Mask of William Shakespeare,* tr. Cecil Cragg (Braunton, UK: Merlin Books, Ltd., 1988; first French ed. 1918); **Rutland, Bacon, the Countess of Pembroke:** John Michell, *Who Wrote Shakespeare?* (London: Thames & Hudson, 1996).

p. xxviii, Spelling of "Shakspere": The name "Shakespeare" was spelled in more than thirty different variants by contemporaries (cf. H. Cutner, "The Spelling of 'Shakespeare,'" *Shakespearean Authorship Review* 5 [Spring 1961], 6–7). However, in the words of Gary Taylor, "'Shakspere'... seems to have been his [*the Stratford actor's*] own preferred spelling." (*Reinventing Shakespeare: A Cultural History from the Restoration to the Present* [New York and Oxford: Oxford University Press (paperback), 1989], 414.)

p. xxix, Shakspere's signatures: Even the six signatures are on shaky ground. The documentary historian Jane Cox concluded, "It is obvious at a glance that these signatures... are not the signatures of the same man." (*Shakespeare in the Public Records*, ed. David Thomas [London: Her Majesty's Stationer's Office, 1985], 33; Peter R. Moore, "The Demolition of Shakspere's Signatures," *Shakespeare Oxford Society Newsletter* 30:2A [Spring 1994]: 1.)

p. xxix, ... in the Western world: It is often claimed that 147 lines of prose and verse on folios 8ª, 8ᵇ, and 9ª of the *Booke of Sir Thomas Moore* playscript (Harleian MS 7368) are also in Shakspere's hand. However, when W. W. Greg produced his definitive *English Literary Autographs 1550–1650* ([London: Oxford University Press, 1932]: "Part I–Dramatists"), he deliberately left out the supposed Shakspere additions to *Moore*, noting, "I have not considered it generally advisable to include hands known only from the writer's signature, since this is of very uncertain value as a guide to a man's ordinary writing. I have avoided the controversial subject of Shakespeare's hand...."

This book subscribes to the point of view presented by Samuel A. Tannenbaum (*Problems in Shakspere's Penmanship, Including a Study of the Poet's Will* [New York: The Century Co./Modern Language Association of America, 1927], 179–211) when he concluded, "The weight of the evidence is overwhelmingly against the theory that in folios 8 and 9 of *The Booke of Sir Thomas Moore* we have a Shakspere [*sic*] holograph." For more on this contentious topic, cf. Sir George Greenwood, *The Shakspere Signatures and "Sir Thomas More"* (London: Cecil Palmer, 1924).

p. xxix, Books per year in Elizabethan England: There are 1,014 different English books from the 1560s that have survived the centuries; during this same period, the Stationer's Register records 1,005 manuscripts approved for publication. Similar data exists for the 1570s. (Cyndia Susan Clegg, *Press Censorship in Elizabethan England* [Cambridge: Cambridge University Press, 1997], 17–18).

p. xxix, ... religion, law, or medicine: Edith L. Klotz, "A Subject Analysis of English Imprints for Every Tenth Year from 1480 to 1640." *Huntington Lib. Quarterly* 1 (1937/8), 417–9.

p. xxix, Jonson's library: David McPherson, "Ben Jonson's Library and Marginalia: An Annotated Catalogue" *Studies in Philology* 71:5 (December 1974), 1–106.

p. xxix, Donne's library: Geoffrey Keynes, *A Bibliography of Dr. John Donne, Dean of St. Pauls* (Oxford: Clarendon Press, 1973).

p. xxix, ... in private archives: cf. the discussion of the *Beowulf* MS. in Chapter 2 and Margaret, countess of Lennox's, *Buik of Croniclis of Scotland* MS in Chapter 4.

p. xxix, ... ready knowledge of their respective fields: What follows is nowhere near a comprehensive bibliography–only a sample. **Law:** William L. Rushton, *Shakespeare a Lawyer* (London: Longmans, 1858); George Greenwood, *Shakespeare's Law and Latin* (London: Watts & Co., 1916), Edward J. White, *Commentaries on the Law in Shakespeare* (St. Louis: F. H. Thomas Law Book Co., 1913); Cushman K. Davis, *The Law in Shakespeare* (Washington, D.C.: Washington Law Book Co., 1883). **Theology:** SHAHEEN; Richmond Noble, *Shakespeare's Biblical Knowledge* (New York: Octagon Books, 1970; 1935 first ed.); Roland Mushat Frye, *Shakespeare and Christian Doctrine* (Princeton, N.J.: Princeton University Press, 1963). **Medicine:** Charles Woodward Stearns, *Shakespeare's Medical Knowledge* (New York: D. Appleton, 1865); Aubrey C. Kail, *The Medical Mind of Shakespeare* (Balgowlah, NSW: Williams and Wilkins, 1986). **Astronomy:** Cumberland Clark, *Shakespeare and Science* (New York: Haskell House, 1970). **Philosophy:** William John Birch, *An Inquiry into the Philosophy and Religion of Shakspere* [sic] (London: C. Mitchell, 1848); Bertram Emil

Jessup, *Philosophy in Shakespeare* (Eugene: University of Oregon Press, 1959). **Linguistics:**
Jane Donawerth, *Shakespeare and the Sixteenth Century Study of Language* (Urbana: University of Illinois Press, 1984); Sister Miriam Joseph, *Shakespeare's Use of the Arts of Language*
(New York: Columbia University Press, 1947). **Military studies:** Duff Cooper, *Sergeant
Shakespeare* (London: Hart Davis, 1949); Paul A. Jorgensen, *Shakespeare's Military World*
(Berkeley: University of California Press, 1956). **Naval art and science:** A. F. Falconer, *A
Glossary of Shakespeare's Sea and Naval Terms Including Gunnery* (London: Constable,
1965); A. F. Falconer, *Shakespeare and the Sea* (New York: F. Ungar Publishing Co., 1964).
History: Beverly Ellison Warner, *English History in Shakespeare's Plays* (New York: Longmans, Green, 1894); William Hudson Rogers, *Shakespeare and English History* (Totowa, N.J.:
Littlefield, 1966); F. S. Boas, *Aspects of Classical Legend and History in Shakespeare* (London:
H. Milford, 1943). **Botany:** Leo H. Grindon, *The Shakespeare Flora* (Manchester: Palmer &
Howe, 1883); Alan Dent, *World of Shakespeare: Plants* (Reading: Osprey, 1971). **Literary
scholarship:** Stephen Orgel and Sean Keilen, eds., *Shakespeare and the Literary Tradition*
(New York: Garland Publishing, 1999); **Music:** E. W. Naylor, *Shakespeare and Music* (New
York: Da Capo Press, 1965); F. W. Sternfeld, *Music in Shakespearean Tragedy* (London: Routledge & Kegan Paul, 1963). **Classical studies:** Charles Martindale, *Shakespeare and the Uses of
Antiquity* (New York: Routledge, 1990); Robert S. Miola, *Shakespeare and Classical Tragedy*
(Oxford: Clarendon Press, 1992); Robert S. Miola, *Shakespeare and Classical Comedy* (Oxford:
Clarendon Press, 1994).

    p. xxix, ... misreading of a poem by Ben Jonson:

> ... [H]ow far thou didst our Lyly outshine
> Or sporting Kyd or Marlowe's mighty line.
> And though *thou hadst small Latin and less Greek*
> *From thence to honor thee,* I would not seek
> For names, but call forth thund'ring Aeschylus,
>   Euripedes and Sophocles to us.... [*emphasis added*]

Ben Jonson, "To The Memory of My Beloved, the Author, Mr. William Shakespeare and
What He Hath Left Us." *Mr. William Shakespeare's Comedies Histories & Tragedies* (the "First
Folio") London (1623).

    Jonson's phrase *small Latin and less Greek* has, in fact, been stripped of its original context. As the above excerpt shows, Jonson leads into his famous quote by comparing Shakespeare with contemporary English authors. But Jonson suggests that this comparison
instead reveals how far Shake-speare outshines all of his theatrical peers. To Jonson, Latin
and Greek drama represented the pinnacle of artistic expression. So, he says, although he
can draw small Latin and less Greek *from thence* (from the list of English playwrights) to
honor Shake-speare, Jonson does not seek for names of playwrights with which to make
ample comparisons to Shake-speare. Instead, Jonson calls forth the great Aeschylus, etc.
The entity that had "small Latin and less Greek" was Shake-speare's contemporaries–
meaning Jonson felt there was little of classical or enduring value in Lyly, Kyd, and Marlowe. Jonson was *not* talking about Shake-speare's book-learning or skills as a classical
scholar–although given the subterfuge evident elsewhere in the First Folio, as will be discussed in the Epilogue, it's not surprising that Jonson twisted his words so elegantly as
to facilitate such a misreading. (Andrew Hannas, "From Thence to Honor Thee," unpublished MS.)

    p. xxx, Shake-speare plays in France and England: **England:** *King John, King Richard
II, King Henry IV, Parts 1 and 2, King Henry V, King Henry VI, Parts 1, 2, and 3, King Richard
III, King Henry VIII, Merry Wives of Windsor, King Lear, Cymbeline, As You Like It* (14); **Italy
or France (wholly or partly):** *Henry V* (counted in both lists), *Love's Labour's Lost, The Two
Gentlemen of Verona, Much Ado About Nothing, The Merchant of Venice, The Taming of the*

Shrew, All's Well That Ends Well, The Winter's Tale, Romeo and Juliet, Othello (Act I), *A Midsummer Night's Dream, Coriolanus, Titus Andronicus, Julius Caesar* (14).

p. xxx, Shake-speare and France: Sidney Lee, *The French Renaissance in England* (Oxford: Clarendon Press, 1910), 423–27; Émile Montégut in *A New Variorum Edition of Shakespeare: Love's Labour's Lost,* ed. Horace Howard Furness (New York: Dover Publications, 1964; 1904 first ed.), 374–5; Abel LeFranc, *Sous le Masque de "William Shakespeare": William Stanley, VIe comte de Derby*... (Paris: Payot & cie., 1918–19), Chapter 7. (LeFranc argued that the earl of Derby, whom LeFranc believed was Shake-speare, traveled extensively in France and spent much time at the French court. The playwright earl of Derby was also, after 1595, de Vere's son-in-law.)

p. xxx, Shake-speare and Venice: Ernesto Grillo, *Shakespeare and Italy* (Glasgow: Robert Maclehose and Co., 1949); "Shakespeare" in A. Lytton Sells, *The Italian Influence in English Poetry* (London: George Allen & Unwin Ltd., 1955), 188–211; R. L. Eagle, "Shakespeare and Italy," *Nineteenth Century and After* 93 (January/June 1923), 860; Bart Edward Sullivan, "Shakspeare and the Waterways of North Italy" *Nineteenth Century and After* 64 (July/December 1908), 215; Georg Brandes, *William Shakespeare: A Critical Study* (London: Heinemann, 1914), 113–18; John W. Draper, "Shakespeare and the Doge of Venice," *Journal of English and German Philology* 46:1 (January 1947), 75–81; Karl Elze, *Essays on Shakespeare* (London: Macmillan & Co., 1874), 254–315.

p. xxx, Robert Greene: Controversy also exists over the authorship of *Groatsworth;* some suspect Henry Chettle wrote it (e.g., MILLER/LOONEY, 2:340–54). As D. Allen Carroll concludes (*Greene's Groatsworth of Wit,* D. Allen Carroll, ed. [Binghamton, N.Y.: Medieval and Renaissance Texts and Studies, 1994], 80–83, 117–29), "The evidence suggests that Chettle had much more to do with the book than he admitted and more than has been generally realized since then. Exactly how much more is impossible to tell."

p. xxx, ... in print at Shakspere: Later in 1592, Henry Chettle–who prepared Robert Greene's pamphlet in question *(Greene's Groatsworth of Wit)* for publication and may have even secretly written it–apologized for *Groatsworth.* Chettle explains in his tract (titled *Kind-Hearts Dream*) that two of the three "divers play-makers" addressed in *Groatsworth* took offense. Those three "play-makers" are widely believed to have been Christopher Marlowe, Thomas Nashe, and George Peele. Which two of the three playwrights were the offended parties is less certain. And yet, many orthodox commentators to this day continue to assert that because they *assume* Will Shakspere to have been a playwright, somehow Chettle must have been addressing Will Shakspere in his apology. Therefore, Chettle is seen as delivering crucial evidence that Will Shakspere was a playwright. Dogs sometimes perform a similar trick with their tails.

The Oxfordian researcher Robert Detobel (unpublished MS., 2004) has arrived at markedly different conclusions concerning both *Groatsworth* and Chettle's apology; he adduces evidence that Shakspere was not the "upstart crow" player at all but that Greene's "Shake-scene" was rather the actor Edward Alleyn. The debate over these controversial texts continues–even within Oxfordian circles.

p. xxx, ... London's top dramatists: "Base-minded men all three of you, if by my misery you be not warned ... [T]here is an upstart crow, beautified with our feathers, that with his tiger's heart wrapped in a player's hide [*] supposes he is as well able to bombast out a blank verse as the best of you; and being an absolute *Johannes factotum* is in his own conceit the only 'shake-scene' in a country."

Greene's Groatsworth of Wit Bought With a Million of Repentance, ed. D. Allen Carroll (Binghamton, N.Y.: Medieval and Renaissance Texts and Studies, 1994), 84–85.

[* "O tiger's heart wrapped in a woman's hide" *2 Henry VI,* 1.4.137.]

p. xxx, ... plumage of other birds: Other mythological crows had more innocuous occupations. For instance, Horace's crow was a plagiarist. Diana Price (PRICE, 45–57) dissects Greene's rhetoric at length, concluding that the most likely interpretation of the entire Greene passage is one excoriating Shakspere as a heartless theatrical paymaster who only *pretended* he could write.

p. xxx, ... claimed he could do: As D. Allen Carroll (op. cit., 134) notes, "*Factotum* did not then mean what it does now: 'a man-of-all-work, a servant who does odd jobs about the place' (*OED, Factotum*, 1c) It meant, instead, 'A person of boundless conceit, who thinks himself able to do anything, however much beyond the reach of real abilities.'"

p. xxx, "... occasionally to forge": *OED* definition 12, first attested usage, 1566; Jonathan Dixon, "The 'Upstart Crow' Supposes," *Shakespeare Oxford Society Newsletter* 36:1 (Spring 2000), 7.

p. xxxi, Kemp quote: Anon., *The Return from Parnassus, Part 2, or the Scourge of Simony* (c. 1600), 4.3.15–19.

p. xxxi, They have found none: Charlotte Carmichael Stopes, the author of the definitive biography of Southampton (STOPES) devoted no small portion of her professional career to finding anything that would link Henry Wriothesley, earl of Southampton, with Will Shakspere. As Louis P. Bénézet writes, "After thirteen years of research through the letters and records of the Wriothesley family, she had to confess that there was in them not one word relating to the man who had made the young earl's name immortal by dedicating to him *Venus and Adonis* and *Lucrece*. She remarked to B. M. Ward, 'My life has been a failure,' and confessed to another prominent Oxfordian that she was beginning to doubt the whole Stratford story." (Bénézet, "Look in the Chronicles," *Shakespeare Fellowship Newsletter* (US) 4:3 [April 1943], 28.)

p. xxxi, "Our English Terence": John Davies (of Hereford), *The Scourge of Folly* (London, 1611), Epigram 159; PRICE, 62–7. This epithet, like Greene's "upstart crow" passage, has long been misread. Today Terence is known as a Roman playwright who produced many popular comedies. By 1611, of course, Shake-speare had become famous not for comedies but for his great tragedies such as *Othello, Hamlet, Macbeth,* and *King Lear.* Davies, we are told, memorialized the *author* Shake-speare in 1611 with a comparison to a comic playwright. This comparison would have been woefully out of date—something like paying tribute to Orson Welles in the 1940s (after *Citizen Kane* and *The Magnificent Ambersons* had gained him worldwide acclaim) as merely a producer of radio adaptations of H. G. Wells. Davies's analogy of "Shake-spear" to Terence is much more likely to have been about the actors/front men who only claimed to have been authors.

p. xxxi, ... Roman aristocratic playwrights: *EB/*1911 entry on Terence; Roger Ascham, *The Schoolmaster (1570),* Lawrence V. Ryan (Ithaca, N.Y.: Cornell University Press, 1967), 143–44.

p. xxxi, ... sometime before 1623: The first reference to the Stratford-upon-Avon funerary monument appears in the First Folio of Shake-speare (1623).

p. xxxi, "... but page to serve his wit": For a fuller, more critical discussion of the Stratford monument, cf. the Epilogue and PRICE, 153–67.

p. xxxii, ... for Shakspere as Shake-speare: On the self-destructing nature of the First Folio evidence, cf. the Epilogue and PRICE, 169–94; OGBURN/*TMWS,* 208–39.

p. xxxii, ... burying his identity: For discussion and citations on the "Spanish Marriage Crisis" and the solidification of the Shake-speare ruse in 1623, cf. the Epilogue.

p. xxxii, ... sentence in his life: Mark Twain (*Is Shakespeare Dead?* In *1601 and Is Shakespeare Dead?* [Oxford: Oxford University Press, 1996; 1909 first ed.], 35–36) records an important caveat to this fact—quoted in the Epilogue.

p. xxxii, Twain quote: Twain, op. cit., 131.

p. xxxii, "... rise from his table laughing": Charles Arundell (circa January 1581) in PRO SP12/151[/45], ff. 100-2 (LIBEL 4.3[1.2])

p. xxxiii, ... inhabited a small frame: On de Vere's physical size: "You hath courtly incensed the earl of Oxford. Mark him well. He is but a little fellow, but he hath one of the best wits in England." Thomas Nashe, *Strange News* (1592), in *The Works of Thomas Nashe*, ed. Ronald B. McKerrow (Oxford: Basil Blackwell, 1958), 1:300–1. For discussion of the "Mark him well" passage and its applicability to de Vere, cf. Chapter 9; on de Vere's effeminacy: cf. discussion in Chapter 6 of Gabriel Harvey's lampoon of de Vere as a foppish Italianate gentleman.

USAGE NOTE

p. xxxv, On using "de Vere" rather than "Oxford": Most books refer to Edward de Vere, seventeenth Earl of Oxford, as either "Oxford" or "Lord Oxford." This book will instead refer to him as "de Vere" for two reasons. First, mention of "Oxford" for most readers implies the famous university, a distracting and irrelevant association. However, the more important reason is an aesthetic one: De Vere, this book contends, has become known to posterity as "William Shakespeare." De Vere's titles and aristocratic rank meant everything in Elizabethan society. In the present day, however, the most important title he carries bar none is also the one bereft of rank.

CHAPTER ONE

p. 2, April 17, 1550: BL MS. Add. 5751A, f. 283, cited in NELSON, 20.

p. 2, . . . language of the church service: Simon Schama, *A History of Britain* (New York: Hyperion, 2000), 307–21.

p. 2, . . . peninsula of Normandy: Clements R. Markham, *The Fighting Veres* (Boston: Houghton, Mifflin & Co., 1888), 3.

p. 2, lodgings, kitchens, and pantries: From a 1592 survey of Hedingham, "made by order of the lord high treasurer. Burghleigh," Severne Majendie, *An Account of Hedingham Castle* (London: T. Smith, n.d.), 24.

p. 3, . . . and other associates: Huntington Library EL5870 19–20 January 27E1 (1585); transcription of deposition of Richard Enews and William Walforth. NELSON, 15–16, 18–19.

p. 3, Smith quote: Letter from Sir Thomas Smith to Sir William Cecil, October. 1, 1559: CSP Dom., Eliz. vii, 2. Cited in COMPLETE PEERAGE, 10:248.

p. 3, Earl John quote: Gervase Markham, *Honor in His Perfection;* quoted in WARD, 10.

p. 3, . . . references to her son: One, dated April 30, 1563, is reprinted in WARD, 21–22; the other, dated October 11, 1563, is reprinted in Gwynneth Bowen, "What Happened at Hedingham and Earls Colne?" *Shakespearean Authorship Review* 24 (Spring 1971), 4–5. Both are addressed to Sir William Cecil.

p. 3, Vives quote: Richard Hyrde, tr. T. Berthelet (London, 1529), fol. m4ᵛ.

p. 3, . . . norm in Shake-speare: Mary Beth Rose ("Where Are the Mothers in Shakespeare?: Options for Gender Representation in the English Renaissance," *SH.Q* 42:3 [Autumn 1991], 291–314) isolates three schools of thought about mothers and children. The first is represented by the above Vives's quote. The final two are slightly more liberated views, recognizing both the mother's role as lifelong nurturer and her right to outline her own approach to child rearing–including writing books on the subject. "Shakespeare participates overwhelmingly in the first construction in his representation of mothers," Rose writes, "rarely experimenting with the second and ignoring the third." (313)

p. 4, . . . no mothers whatsoever: Rose, op. cit., 291–2.

p. 4, . . . your wife is my mother: *Merchant of Venice,* 2.2.84–93.

p. 4, . . . Mary was born: While no documents record Mary de Vere's birth date, a January 28, 1554, codicil to Earl John's will does not mention Mary, implying that she had not been born yet. NELSON, 23.

p. 4, Will Somers: HOLLAND/*SHAKESPEARE OXFORD*, 79; MILLER/*HASP*, 666.

p. 4, ... table at a roar: *Hamlet*, 5.1.184–91.

p. 5, ... greatest embarrassments: Daniel L. Wright, " 'Vere-y Interesting': Shakespeare's treatment of the earls of Oxford in the history plays." *The Shakespeare Oxford Newsletter* 36:1 (Spring 2000), 1, 14–21; Clive Willingham ("Professor Daniel Wright, Ph.D.–'Vere-y Interesting...': A Response." Unpublished MS. circulated on ElizaForum email Listserv [January 2004]) presents the antithesis to Wright's thesis–a synthesis of which might be summarized as follows: Immature Shake-speare (e.g., *Henry VI, The Famous Victories of Henry V*) played games with the author's ancestors; mature Shake-speare (e.g., *Richard II, Henry V*) did not concern itself with such chest-thumping, sophomoric pranks.

p. 5, ... John retaining the throne: COMPLETE PEERAGE 10:210–3.

p. 5, ... never even mentioned: Robert, ninth earl of Oxford, is also a Vere ancestor–onetime favorite of Richard II–absent in Shake-speare's *Richard II*. (Wright, "Vere-y" op. cit., 15–16) However, Willingham (op. cit.) points out, "Richard II reigned from 1377 to 1399, some twenty-two years. Robert [the] 9[th earl] was a major figure for only about four of those years, betwen 1384 and 1387, and accordingly he is not essential to the play, the action of which commences a decade after he fled into exile, and five years after he had died."

p. 5, William Caxton: Samuel Moore, "Patrons of Letters in Norfolk and Suffolk, c. 1450 II," *PMLA* 28:1 (1913), 79–105; 86–87.

p. 5, ... tale of this battle: The sculpture is presently at Stowe School in Buckinghamshire. Linda B. McLatchie, "De Vere and the Battle of Bosworth," *Shakespeare Oxford Newsletter* 29:4 (Fall 1993), 4–7.

p. 5, "...wondrous well belov'd": *Henry VI, Part 3*, 5.1.1, 4.8.17.

p. 5, ... nor at Tewksbury: As a counterpoint to this, Willingham (op. cit.) notes, "If OXFORD's presence at Tewkesbury is not credible, because it didn't happen, equally incredible is Shakespeare's portrayal of CLARENCE, who shines through *Richard III* like a martyr destined for sainthood rather than the historically treacherous character that he was."

p. 5, ... Shake-speare heaps upon him: Wright, "Vere-y" op. cit., 17–19.

p. 5, ... Battle of Barnet: The mind that inhabited the character of FALSTAFF could not have strutted his ancestors across the stage so shamelessly without also mocking his own pretensions. The mockery, in this case, comes at the expense of the one humiliating battlefield incident in the thirteenth earl of Oxford's career: At the Battle of Barnet in 1471, fog on the battlefield led the Lancastrian earl of Warwick to confuse the star of the house of Vere with the sun of the house of York. Because he mistook stars for suns, Warwick accidentally led his troops to fire upon Oxford's forces and, in the process, helped to doom the fate of his king. While Shake-speare's account of Barnet politely glides over the earl of Warwick's historic "friendly fire" incident, elsewhere de Vere does sneak in a self-mocking jibe about the thirteenth earl's embarrassment at being attacked by his own allies. In *Henry V*, one of the French nobles asks, "The armor that I see in your tent tonight, are those stars or suns on it?" (*Henry V* 3.7.74; Richard Desper, "Stars of Suns," *Shakespeare Oxford Newsletter* 28:2 [Spring 1992], 3–4.) Although the question is wholly out of place in the play, it is fully in keeping with the fun that Shake-speare had in boosting the importance of his family in the history of England.

p. 5, ... strain of pneumonia: Recent scholarship (Jennifer Loach, *Edward VI* [New Haven: Yale University Press, 1999], 162) suggests King Edward died of acute bilateral bronchopneumonia.

p. 6, Princess Elizabeth and Mary: Jasper Ridley, *Elizabeth I: The Shrewdness of Virtue* (New York: Fromm Publishing, 1989; 1987 first ed.), 51.

p. 6, ... burnings of Protestant heretics: *Acts of the Privy Council* 1554-5, p. 104; 1555, pp. 141, 148; Christopher Paul, private communication (August 2004).

p. 6, Lord Edward and Sir Thomas Smith: Two letters point unquestionably to Smith's extended tenure as de Vere's tutor: On April 25, 1576, Smith wrote William Cecil, extending his best wishes to young Edward "for the love I beare hym, bicause he was brought vp in my howse." On August 3, 1574, Cecil wrote to Sir Thomas Walsingham, "I dout not but Mr. Secretary Smith will remembre his old love towardes the Erle whan he was his scollar." (NELSON, 25) No records of payments to Smith survive, however. (Stephanie Hopkins Hughes, "'Shakespeare's' Tutor: Sir Thomas Smith," *The Oxfordian* 3 (2000), 19–44; Hughes, *Shakespeare's Tutors: The Education of Edward de Vere* (Portland, Ore.: Privately published, 2000).)

However, by process of elimination, one concludes that Smith must have "brought vp" de Vere "in my howse" for some extended period during the years 1554–62. Between 1562 and '66, Smith was living in Paris as ambassador and envoy to the French court. In 1567, Smith was still performing diplomatic missions to France and, with his burden of courtly duties, would scarcely have had time to tutor a precocious young child as well. (Mary Dewar, *Sir Thomas Smith: A Tudor Intellectual in Office* [London: University of London, Athlone Press, 1964], 88–128.) By 1566–67, de Vere was clearly leading a young courtier's life in Cecil House, with letters to Cecil, parliamentary records, and even the killing of an undercook in Cecil House demonstrating that the young Edward de Vere could not have been "brought vp" under Smith's care from this period onward. Dewar (77) hypothesizes that de Vere was moved to Smith's household in 1554. Stephanie Hopkins Hughes has begun the research necessary to fill in the blanks in de Vere's early childhood. ("Report on Smith research" on the Edward de Vere Studies Conference [now Shakespeare Authorship Studies Conference] Listserv, shakespeare@list.cu-portland.edu [June 11, 2004].) However, Hughes has, at the time of this writing, been unsuccessful in nailing down any more of the whens and wheres of de Vere's youth spent as Smith's "scollar."

p. 6, . . . from Castle Hedingham: DEWAR, 67–9, 77.

p. 6, . . . earl-in-waiting: *Pace* DEWAR (77) and NELSON (25), who presume that Hill Hall was the site of de Vere's tutoring under Sir Thomas Smith's guiding hand; Hughes ("Report," op. cit.) has discovered that Hill Hall "appears to have been under construction during the years when he would have been with Smith."

p. 6, . . . "painted pictures": "The inventory exists in a private notebook of Smith's, now in possession of Queens' College, Cambridge. It is printed in A.W. Lipscombe, *History of Buckinghamshire* (1847), iv. 595–6" Dewar, 68, fn. 1; also in the inventory is "a christening robe for a child"–perhaps that of the child boarder in this otherwise childless household?

p. 7, . . . in the family household: DNB entry under "Smith, Sir Thomas (1513–1577)."

p. 7, . . . wisdom and gravity: Sir Thomas Elyot, *The Boke Named the Governour*, ed. S. E. Lehmberg (London: J.M. Dent, 1962; 1531 first ed.), 17; cited in Hughes, op. cit.

p. 7, Dewar quote: DEWAR, 15.

p. 7, comparison between Smith and Plato: Richard Carew, *Treatise on the Excellency of the English Tongue* (1595); quoted in DEWAR, 17.

p. 7, second Dewar quote: DEWAR, 14.

p. 7, . . . flower of the University of Cambridge: Quote from Richard Eden; cited in DEWAR, 14.

p. 7, ". . . natural and moral philosophy: John Strype, *The Life of the Learned Sir Thomas Smith, Kt., Doctor of Civil Law, Principal Secretary of State to King Edward the Sixth and Queen Elizabeth*, revised ed. (Oxford: Clarendon Press, 1820), 18.

p. 7, . . . grammar, and literature: Strype, *Smith*, op. cit., 274–81; quoted in Hughes, op. cit.

p. 7, Edward Halle: One copy of Edward Halle's 1550 *Chronicle* history of the Wars of the Roses has long been suspected of being Shake-speare's personal copy of Halle, because of the correspondence between Shake-speare's history plays and the book's many handwritten marginal notes. (Alan Keen and Roger Lubbock, *The Annotator* [New York: Macmillan, 1954].) However, the connection between this book and the Stratford actor Will Shakspere is tenuous at best, relying on paleographical similarities between Shakspere's extant signatures (the only Shakspere holograph available) and the secretary script in the marginal notes. However, one owner of this book was, on the evidence of his handwriting, a schoolboy named Edward. (The signature *Edward* appears twice in this book. (210–11) Could "The Annotator" of this book have in fact been Shake-speare a.k.a. Edward de Vere? Nina Green (*Edward de Vere Newsletter* Nos. 32–34, 1991) has published some suggestive preliminary findings, although a more definitive attribution study is still wanting.)

p. 8, . . . informing the writings of Shake-speare: Hughes, "Shakespeare's Tutor," op. cit., 32.

p. 8, "For the Understanding of the Exchange: M. Dewar, "The Memorandum 'For the Understanding of the Exchange': Its Authorship and Dating," *The Economic History Review,* New Series, 17:3 (1965), 476–87.

p. 8, supernova of 1572: "Tycho's Supernova" of 1572 would later make a famous appearance–as the star referenced in the first scene in *Hamlet;* Donald W. Olson, Marilyn S. Olson, and Russell L. Doescher, "The Stars of *Hamlet,*" *Sky and Telescope* 96:5 (1998), 67–73.

p. 8, Smith's textbook on government and Shake-speare: Gordon Ross Smith ("A Rabble of Princes," *Journal of the History of Ideas* 41:1 [January–March 1980], 34) finds in Thomas Smith's *De Republica Anglorum* (written c. 1562) precepts about tyranny explored in Shake-speare's history plays; John W. Dickinson ("Renaissance Equity and *Measure for Measure,*" *SH.Q* 13:3 [Summer 1962], 290) highlights in *De Republica* a discussion of the chancellor's court of equity germane to the portrayal of equity in *Measure for Measure;* Wayne A. Rebhorn ("The Crisis of the Aristocracy in *Julius Caesar,*" *Renaissance Quarterly* 43:1 [Spring 1990], 80) considers Smith's analogy between the class structure of ancient Rome and that of Elizabethan England–and recognizes in *De Republica* (and William Harrison's *Description of England*) the fundamental principle behind *Julius Caesar*'s allegory.

p. 8, Spanish pronunciation in *Love's Labour's Lost:* Gustav Ungerer, "Two Items of Spanish Pronunciation in *Love's Labour's Lost,*" *SH.Q* 14:3 (Summer 1963), 245–51.

p. 8, ". . . a student of medicine": Jules Janick, *Horticulture* (November 1977), cited in OGBURN/TMWS 438 and Hughes, *Shakespeare's Tutors,* op. cit., 134; CHAMBERS/WS, 1:23.

p. 8, . . . language and history: DEWAR, 14.

p. 8, . . . spine on Justinian: Too busy to do the required reading, Harvey admitted that he had not completed all the work required "for my better profiting in the civil law." *The Letter Book of Gabriel Harvey, A.D. 1573–1580,* ed. Edward Long John Scott (Westminster: Camden Society, 1884), f. 96, p. 176.

p. 8, Shake-speare's legal knowledge: Mark Andre Alexander, "Shakespeare's Knowledge of the Law: A Journey Through the History of the Arguments," *The Oxfordian* 4 (2001), 51–120; reprinted online at http://www.shakespearefellowship.org/virtualclassroom/Law.

p. 8, White quote: Richard Grant White, "William Shakespeare, Attorney at Law and Solicitor in Chancery," *The Atlantic Monthly* [July 4, 1859], 104.

p. 9, prohibitions concerning hunting and hawking: Roger B. Manning, *Hunters and Poachers: A Social and Cultural History of Unlawful Hunting in England, 1485–1640* (Oxford: Clarendon Press, 1993), 4.

p. 9, Shake-speare's knowledge of hunting and hawking: Even the commonplace can inspire an offhand comparison to the chase. As a greyhound overtakes ("cotes") a hare, so ROSENKRANTZ reports that he "coted" the players on the way to Elsinore. As a falconer sews ("seels") his bird's eyelids shut, so ANTONY observes that "the wise gods seel our eyes," while DESDEMONA might "seel her father's eyes up close as oak." As an injured falcon's wing is splinted ("imped"), so *Richard II*'s EARL OF NORTHUMBERLAND hopes to "imp out our drooping country's broken wing." As a hawk gets distracted from its quarry ("checks"), so *Twelfth Night*'s VIOLA fears that the clown FESTE will "check at every feather that comes before his eye." Unlike Ben Jonson, a middle-class playwright who demonstrates his own inexperience with birds of prey and the hunt, Shake-speare reveals his manifest ease with these highborn pursuits. OGBURN/*TMWS,* 263–9; J. W. Fortescue, "Hunting" in *Sh's Eng,* 2:334–40; Maurice Pope, "Shakespeare's Falconry" *Shakespeare Survey* 44 (1992), 131–43.

p. 9, . . . oath of fidelity: De Vere was enrolled at St. John's College "impubes"–meaning that he was too young to take the oath of fidelity to his alma mater, a ceremony reserved for those ages fourteen and older. John Venn and J. A. Venn, *Alumni Cantabrigienses* (Cambridge: Cambridge University Press, 1922), 10 vols. Vol. 1, pt. 1, p. vi.

p. 9, . . . reside at Queens' College: NELSON, 24.

p. 9, . . . dormitory room: NELSON (24) reprints the Queens' College record for March 1559 for the repair in *cubiculo Domini Bulbecke.*

p. 9, Marian barbarity at Cambridge: J. Bass Mullinger, *A History of the University of Cambridge* (London: Longsmans, Green & Co., 1888), 101–12; Christopher Haigh, *English Reformations: Religion, Politics, and Society under the Tudors* (Oxford: Oxford University Press, 1993), 233.

p. 9, Dr. John Caius: Mullinger, op. cit., 110–11.

p. 10, "Caius" in Shake-speare: Lord McNair, "Why Is the Doctor in *The Merry Wives of Windsor* Called Caius?" *Medical History* 13:4 (October 1969), 311–39; Stewart Robb, "Shakespeare and Cambridge University" *Baconiana* (1949), 151; Dr. Caius will also be discussed in Chapter 2.

p. 10, Thomas Fowle: Fowle would remain on the earl of Oxford's paybooks for another four years. PRO WARD 8/13, m.519, cited in NELSON, 25; discussed by Nina Green on Phaeton e-mail Listserv (http://www3.telus.net/oxford/phaeton.html; 13, 28 & 29 June and 5 July 2004); Christopher Paul (Phaeton email Listserv June 29, 2004) also points out CECIL PAPER 146/1, which records payments to Thomas Fowle in 1563/4 (£20), 1565/6 (£20), 1566/7 (£10), 1567/8 (£10), 1568/9 (£10), 1570/1 (100 s.).

p. 10, on January 15, 1559: Paul Johnson, *Elizabeth I* (New York: Holt, Rinehart & Winston, 1974), 67–9.

p. 11, ". . . to spend my blood": Ibid.; NICHOLS 1:38–60.

p. 11, Queen Elizabeth's coronation: Johnson, op. cit., 68–9.

p. 11, . . . rode to Colchester: Smith wrote a letter to Sir William Cecil from Colchester during Earl John's visit. CSP Dom. Eliz., vol. vii, no. 2.

p. 11, Dudley as candidate for Elizabeth's hand: In only a matter of months, rumors would begin to circulate in the countryside that he had gotten the queen pregnant. F. G. Emmison, *Elizabethan Life: Disorder* (Chelmsford, UK: Essex City Council, 1970), 41.

p. 11, . . . on their left shoulder: SP Dom (1559) 7/2, 5, 72; SP For (1559) 5; John Stow, *The Annals of England* (London, 1580), 34, cited in FELDMAN 15.

p. 12, Knox quote: John Knox, *The First Blast of the Trumpet Against the Monstrous Regiment of Women* (1558), from *The Political Writings of John Knox,* ed. Marvin A. Breslow (London: Associated University Presses, 1985), 42.

p. 12, . . . even Sir Thomas Smith: Constance Jordan, "Woman's Rule in Sixteenth-Century British Political Thought," *Renaissance Quarterly* 40:3 (Autumn 1987), 421–51.

p. 12, Puritan criticism of progresses: Lacey Baldwin Smith, *Elizabeth Tudor: Portrait of a Queen* (Boston: Little, Brown, 1975), 66–7; "Trifle" *OED* definitions 1–4.

p. 13, . . . pre-Christian era: R. E. Mortimer Wheeler, Philip G. Laver, "Roman Colchester," *The Journal of Roman Studies* 9 (1919), 139–69.

p. 13, . . . at the colleges: Diarmaid MacCulloch, John Blatchly, "Pastoral Provision in the Parishes of Tudor Ipswich," *Sixteenth Century Journal* 22:3 (Autumn 1991), 457–74; 465.

p. 13, "... to feed their fond humor": Sir William Cecil to Matthew Parker, August 1561; *Correspondence of Matthew Parker,* eds. John Bruce and Thomas Thomason Perowne (Cambridge: Parker Society Publications (v.33) Cambridge University Press, 1853), 148–9.

p. 13, inspiration for *Love's Labour's Lost:* Hastings MSS. Religious 1561–1691 L5A7, August 9, 1561; cited in Ruth Loyd Miller, "Oaths Forsworn in *Love's Labour's Lost*" public presentation, Shakespeare Oxford Society, Double Tree Inn, Pasadena, Calif. (October 27, 1990).

p. 13, Ipswich players staged *King Johan:* In 1879, John Payne Collier first adduced evidence that Bale's *King John* was performed at Ipswich for Queen Elizabeth in August 1561, cf. Jesse W. Harris, "John Bale" *Illinois Studies in Language and Literature* 25:4 (1940), 104; *John Bale's King Johan,* ed. Barry B. Adams (San Marino, Calif.: Huntington Library, 1969), 20–24; *King John by John Bale,* ed. John Henry Pyle Pafford (London: Malone Society, 1931), xix–xxiii.

p. 13, Bale's influence on Shake-speare: James H. Morey, "The Death of King John in Shakespeare and Bale," *SH.Q* 45:3 (Autumn 1994), 327–31; "Curiously enough, however, Bale's influence is reflected in [the anonymous play] *The Troublesome Raigne [of King John]* and in William Shakespeare's *King John,* even though the authors of these dramas probably never heard of Bale or his play." Harris, op. cit., 93–94.

p. 13, ... if the young de Vere were not in the Ipswich audience: "Before Bale's death, at an advanced age, in 1563, Archbishop Matthew Parker and [Sir William] Cecil were aware of the value of Bale's work and were involved in efforts to retrieve Bale's manuscripts from various sources (B. M. Lansdowne MS, Pt. 1, no. 6, Art. 81). Undoubtedly 'Shakespeare' saw Bale's manuscript plays, and undoubtedly he saw them through the eyes of Edward de Vere, who owned many of them, in the Library at Cecil House." Ruth Loyd Miller, LOONEY/MILLER, 2:469–81 fn. (N.B.: It is a supposition that de Vere ever owned any of Bale's manuscripts, albeit a reasonable one.)

p. 13, Earl John as Bale's patron: "Bale's heading to the catalog of fourteen plays in the *Anglorum Heliades* (1536) states that he composed them especially for Master John Vere, the earl of Oxford. Apparently the statement is inclusive and means that all fourteen of the plays were written for the earl of Oxford." Jesse W. Harris, "John Bale: A Study of the Minor Literature of the Reformation," *Illinois Studies in Language and Literature* 25:4 (1940), 68.

p. 13, King John's claim to throne compared to Elizabeth's: *The Life and Death of King John,* ed. A. R. Branmuller. The Oxford Shakespeare (London: Oxford University Press, 1989), 58–61.

p. 13, ... affirmation of Elizabeth's sovereignty: Shake-speare's *King John,* on the other hand, begins with the same premise and offers, by way of moral instruction, a lesson to Queen Elizabeth on the pitfalls awaiting a sovereign with an already precarious claim to the throne. As will be pointed out in subsequent chapters, the characters CONSTANCE and PRINCE ARTHUR form a tidy (if still imperfect) parallel to Mary, Queen of Scots, and her son, James VI–and *King John* offers another prophecy about the horrors that inevitably follow an act of regicide. (This and *Macbeth* were arguably written with the trial of Mary, Queen of Scots, in mind; a trial for which the author sat on the jury.)

p. 14, "... this realm for evermore: ll. 2350–60; *John Bale's King Johan,* 138.

p. 14, ... virtues, not just vice: Carole Levin, "A Good Prince: King John and Early Tudor Propaganda," *Sixteenth Century Journal* 11:4 (Winter 1980), 30; Adams, op. cit., 63–4.

p. 14, ... Bale urges his readers: Harris, op. cit., 116.

p. 14, ... other Italish beggaries: Ibid.; Daniel Wright, *The Anglican Shakespeare: Elizabethan Orthodoxy in the Great Histories* (Vancouver, Wash.: Pacific-Columbia Books, 1993).

p. 14, FALSTAFF based on Oldcastle: Douglas A. Brooks, "Sir John Oldcastle and the construction of Shakespeare's authorship" *Studies in Eng. Lit., 1500–1900* 38:2 (1998), 333ff.; The historical figure after whom Falstaff was named–Sir John Fastolf–was no stranger to de Vere either. The twelfth earl of Oxford was friends with Fastolf, and correspondence between the two men survives to this day (*The Paston Letters, 1422-1509 A.D.*, ed. James Gairdner [Westminster: Archibald Constable & Co., 1900], 184–5)–at least some of which was likely in the papers of the earls of Oxford that de Vere inherited upon his accession to the earldom.

p. 14, "Sir Spirit": READ/*BURGHLEY*, 276.

p. 15, . . . financial and political advantage: J. Hurstfield, "The Profits of Fiscal Feudalism, 1541-1602," *The Economic History Review* 8:1 (1955), 53–61.

p. 15, ". . . in game never": FELDMAN 11–12; *READ/CECIL* 212–16, 227; *CSP Dom.* (1561) xix, 26; xx, 20, 41; *CSP Dom.* (1562) xxii, 17, 49; xxiii, 24.

p. 15, POLONIUS spies on LAERTES: *Hamlet*, 2.1.1–15.

p. 15, Hastings marriage agreement: "Oaths Forsworn," op. cit.; Claire Cross, *The Puritan Earl, The Life of Henry Hastings, Third Earl of Huntington, 1536-1595* (New York: St. Martin's Press, 1966), 29–30.

p. 15, E. of Huntington's claim to throne: *DNB* entry for Henry Hastings, third Earl of Huntington (1535–1595).

p. 15, . . . not legally binding in 1562: "'The lawful age to contract matrimony by the laws ecclesiastical,' wrote an Elizabethan lawyer, 'is when the man is of the full age of fourteen years and the woman of twelve. If before this year any contract be made it is not to be accounted matrimony but spousation.' Until the age of consent, the contract was not binding." Hurstfield, op. cit., 135.

p. 16, Hastings refuses Tsar of Muscovy: Cross, 29–30; Hastings refused the offer of Ivan the Terrible's ambassador in March of 1583. The ambassador wrote back to the tsar that "Mary Hastings is tall, slender, pale faced, has gray eyes, fair hair, a straight nose, and long tapered fingers." Kathy Lynn Emerson, *Wives and Daughters: The Women of Sixteenth Century England* (Troy, N.Y.: Whitson, 1984), 106.

p. 16, MARIA rebukes Muscovites: *Love's Labor's Lost*, 5.2.264–5.

p. 16, Quotes about MARIA: 4.3.56, 61–the epithet "Empress of my Love" is a direct allusion to Mary Hastings, too, since after 1583 Mary Hastings became known at court by the nickname "the empress of Muscovia." ("Oaths Forsworn," op. cit.; *DNB* entry for Francis Hastings, second earl of Huntington [1514?–1561].)

p. 16, "no fault of mine": 4.3.71–2. Longaville's sonnet to Maria was also reprinted in *The Passionate Pilgrim* (1599).

p. 16, Earl John *not* ailing in summer 1562: *Pace* NELSON, 30: "[I]t is clear that he [Earl John] saw death coming."

p. 16, Earl John's activities in June 1562: Ipswich tour: FELDMAN 7; adjudication: Essex Records Office Q/SR 6/25 Sessions Rolls, Midsummer 1562, "Divers persons with their pledges and securities for keeping 'lez Alehouses and Tipling-houses' taken before John, Earl of Oxford..." in Nina Green, Carl Caruso and Christopher Paul, "Post Mortem on John de Vere, 16th Earl of Oxford," *Shakespeare Oxford Newsletter* 40:2 (Spring 2004), 8–9.

p. 16, . . . 16th earl would become a grandfather: PRO C54/626, June 2, 1562, Indenture of the 16th Earl of Oxford (on socrates.berkeley.edu/~ahnelson) in Green, Caruso & Paul, op. cit.

p. 17, Earl John's "use": PRO C. 54/626, No. 45; cited in Bowen, op. cit., 2, 11 fn. 4.

p. 17, Court of Wards and Liveries records: PRO WARDS 8/13 f. 521; cited in Bowen, op. cit., 7.

p. 17, . . . to line his own pockets: Lansdowne MSS., 6. 34; cited in Bowen, op. cit., 4–7; Dudley, historians now know, was just a middleman; he ended up primarily as a conduit for streaming the de Vere family revenues to the queen. (Daphne Pearson, "Did Lord Edward 'send his patrimony flying'?" *De Vere Society Newsletter* [UK] 3:3 [May 1999], 16).

p. 17, HAMLET concerned with loss of family property: "There is a consistent and coherent pattern of legal allusions [in *Hamlet*] to defeated expectations of inheritance, which applies to every major character. The allusions run the gamut from points of common knowledge by landowners or litigants, to technical subtleties only lawyers would appreciate, but their common theme is disinheritance and the way it can occur." J. Anthony Burton, "An Unrecognized Theme in *Hamlet*: Lost Inheritance and Claudius's Marriage to Gertrude." *The Shakespeare Newsletter* 50:3, No. 246 (Fall 2000), 71, 76, 78, 82; 50:4, No. 247 (Winter 2000/2001), 103, 104, 106.

p. 17, ". . . fear's as bad as falling": *Cymbeline*, 3.3.46-8.

p. 18, site of Earl John's funeral: Bowen points out (op. cit.) that Earl John's will specifies that he is to be buried at Earls Colne. Today, his remains lie in the tomb of the fifteenth earl of Oxford at St. Nicholas's Church in Castle Hedingham. Bowen narrows down the time frame in which Earl John's remains were reburied at Castle Hedingham as "between 1572, when Edward de Vere was granted possession of his estate at Castle Hedingham–though not apparently Earls Colne Priory–and 1592, when the plan of the Castle was made for Lord Burghley." ("What Happened at Hedingham and Earls Colne? Part 1," *Shakespearean Authorship Review* 23 [Summer 1970], 4). For the purposes of argument, it will be assumed in Chapter 7 that Earl John had been interred in his final resting place at Castle Hedingham by 1583.

p. 18, Machyn's account of Earl John's funeral: *The Diary of Henry Machyn*, ed. John Gough Nichols, (London: Camden Society, 1848), cited in WARD, 14.

CHAPTER TWO

p. 19, Machyn's account of seventeenth earl of Oxford's trip to London: *The Diary of Henry Machyn*, ed. John Gough Nichols (London: Camden Society, 1848), 291.

p. 19, . . . was the Earl of Oxford's destination: The previous paragraphs' description of Elizabethan London comes from Gamini Salgado, "London–Flower of Cities All," in *The Elizabethan Underworld* (Sutton Publishing, Gloucestershire (1997; 1992 first ed.), 1–36; H. W. Brewer and Herbert A. Cox, *Old London illustrated: London in the XVIth Century*, eighth ed. (London: The Builder House, n.d.), Adrian Prockter, Robert Taylor, and John Fisher, *The A to Z of Elizabethan London* (London: Harry Margary/Guildhall Library, 1979).

p. 20, Cecil would later write of it disparagingly: READ/*BURGHLEY*, 121.

p. 20, . . . this prosperous neighborhood: *EB*/1911 16:845, entry on John Locke. During much of the seventeenth century, Cecil House was known as Exeter House, after Thomas Cecil, earl of Exeter (son of William Cecil, Lord Burghley). One of the intellectual roundtables Locke held at Exeter House prompted him to write, years later, his famous *Essay Concerning Human Understanding*.

p. 20, . . . elite of Westminster and London: Henry B. Wheatley, "Cecil House" *London Past and Present* (London: John Murray, 1891), 1:343; F.H.W. Sheppard, ed., "The Parish of St. Paul, Covent Garden," *Survey of London* (University of London, 1970), 21–22.

p. 20, ". . . of the great chamber": Norden's *Middlesex*, Harl. MS 570; cited in Wheatley, op. cit.

p. 20, On Burghley, Stamford, Lincolnshire: Reginald Blomfield, *A History of Renaissance Architecture in England, 1500–1800* (London: George Bell & Sons, 1897), 1:31.

p. 20, Gerard and Shake-speare: OGBURN/*TMWS*, 437–8; quoting Tom Prideaux, "The Garden Talk of William Shakespeare," *Horticulture* 55:11 (November 1977), 24-7. Gerard's pamphlet first appeared in print in 1597, making him the likely borrower–unless the author had heard this analogy directly from Gerard's lips years before.

p. 21, Cecil House library: Eddi Jolly, "'Shakespeare' and Burghley's Library: *Bibliotheca Illustris: Sive Catalogus Variorum Librorum*," *The Oxfordian* 3 (2000), 3–18.

p. 21, . . . from the hinterlands of Essex: Some Oxfordians even argue that de Vere was already publishing his work pseudonymously–Arthur Brooke's narrative poem *Romeus and*

Juliet was first published in 1562. *Romeus* was, as the name might indicate, a primary source for *Romeo and Juliet.* OGBURN/*TMWS* 449–51.

p. 21, Factions vying for the throne: Neville Williams (*All The Queen's Men: Elizabeth I and Her Courtiers* [London: Cardinal, 1972], 78) cites Lady Catherine Gray, the earl of Huntington (of the de Vere marriage match mentioned in Chapter 1), and the countess of Suffolk and her son Lord Darnley.

p. 21, Propaganda promoting Dudley: Henry James and Greg Walker, "The Politics of *Gorboduc,*" *The English Historical Review* 110:435 (February 1995), 109–121.

p. 21, O.G. endorsed Dudley marriage: BL Add. MS 48023, fo. 363, cited in James and Walker, op. cit., 112. It was in no small part due to Cecil's meddling behind the scenes that Dudley never did make it to the altar with Elizabeth. Susan Doran, "Why Did Elizabeth Not Marry?" in *Dissing Elizabeth* (Durham, N.C.: Duke University Press, 1998), 44–45.

p. 21, Dudley as possible Lord Protector: Neville Williams, op. cit., 78.

p. 21, "not so much, not two": *Hamlet,* 1.2.138–9.

p. 21, De Vere's lesson plan: SP Dom. Eliz., 26.50 in WARD, 20; de Vere's lesson plan is often quoted today in biographies and histories of the period to illustrate the rigors of education for the Elizabethan upper classes.

p. 22, "the other tongue": READ (*BURGHLEY,* 125) presumes Cecil to have meant Greek in this passage—a supposition strengthened by the fact that de Vere's doctor would later write in a book dedication that de Vere could "both read and understand the same [books] in the first tongues wherein the [Greek] authors have written." George Baker, *Oleum Magistrale* (1574); quoted in CHILJAN, 30. The volume includes a translation of the Greek anatomist Galen—a source for *All's Well That Ends Well* (cf. Richard K. Stensgaard, "*All's Well That Ends Well* and the Galenico-Paracelsian Controversy," *Renaissance Quarterly* 25:2 [Summer 1972], 173–88).

p. 22, De Vere's lesson plan, ctd.: SP Dom. Eliz., 26.50, quoted in WARD, 20. This curriculum appears in the section of state papers dated 1562. "When 'any hard place' was encountered in the Gospel, 'commentary' was ordered from Master Frith and later from Laurence Nowell. Frith was Richard Frith, dancing master of Blackfriars." (FELDMAN/ *AMENDMENTS,* 54.)

p. 22, On a Cecil House education: HURSTFIELD, 255; AKRIGG, 25.

p. 22, Cecil House as salon: Van Dorsten ("Literary Patronage in Elizabethan England: The Early Phase," in van Dorsten, *The Anglo-Dutch Renaissance: Seven Essays* [Leiden: E. J. Brill, 1988], 61, 64) makes these remarks as a to rebuttal Conyers Read, who claimed that Cecil cannot "justly be regarded as a patron of the arts, except architecture." (READ/*CECIL,* 11.)

p. 22, On the two Laurence Nowells: "It was undoubtedly the antiquary and not the dean of Litchfield who was tutor in June of 1563 to Edward de Vere, the earl of Oxford, then a ward of Sir William Cecil, principal secretary to the queen." Retha M. Warnicke, "Note on a Court of Requests Case of 1571" *English Language Notes* 11:4 (June 1974), 250–6; Andrew Hannas, "In Defense of Edith Duffey: Which Nowell Tutored Oxford?" *Shakespeare Oxford Newsletter* 29:1A (Winter 1993), 3. The confusion between the two Nowells is widespread and found in many scholarly sources, including the *DNB.*

p. 22, Nowell's map: Brit. Lib. Add. MS 62540; Peter Barber, "A Tudor Mystery: Laurence Nowell's Map of England and Ireland," *The Map Collector* 22 (1983), 16–21; *Early Maps of the British Isles, A.D. 1000–A.D. 1579,* ed. G. R. Crone (London: Royal Geographical Society, 1961), 9–10, plate 17.

p. 22, Cartographical jokes in Shake-speare: *Comedy of Errors,* 3.2.71–164; Bernhard Klein, "Partial Views: Shakespeare and the Map of Ireland," *Early Modern Literary Studies* 4:2, special issue 3 (Sept. 1998), 5.1–20; http://purl.oclc.org/emls/04-2/kleipart.htm

p. 23, "…marvels and other prodigies surpassing nature"; Gerald Strauss, "A Sixteenth-Century Encyclopedia: Sebastian Münster's *Cosmography* and its Editions." *From*

The Renaissance to the Counter-Reformation: Essays in Honor of Garrett Mattingly, ed. Charles H. Carter (New York: Random House, 1965), 152.

p. 23, Nowell as Anglo-Saxon scholar: "I begin with the acceptance of Laurence Nowell as the father of Anglo-Saxon studies in Renaissance England." R. J. Schoeck, "Early Anglo-Saxon Studies and Legal Scholarship in the Renaissance," *Studies in the Renaissance* 5 (1958), 102.

p. 23, Nowell's Anglo-Saxon dictionary: "Laurence Nowell's *Vocabularium Saxonicum,*" ed. Albert H. Marckwardt (Ann Arbor: University of Michigan Press, 1952).

p. 23, Contents of Nowell Codex: The "Wonders" contains a series of striking cartoons of fantastical beasts, including a sketch of a man with his head beneath his shoulders–the same "anthropophagi" that OTHELLO recalls encountering in his oriental adventures. (Cotton Vitellius A XV, fol. 102v.; *Othello* 1.3.144–5) Furthermore, the medieval scholar Peter J. Lucas concludes that the final lines of the Judith poem were penned by someone "circa 1600" who was imitating the medieval scribes. (Peter J. Lucas, "The Place of *Judith* in the *Beowulf* Manuscript," *Review of English Studies* 41:164 (1990), 472). It is tempting to see in these copied lines the hand of a mischievous teenaged earl of Oxford studying the forms of Old English script–perhaps, when his instructor was not looking, during one of those daily "Exercises with his pen"? This hypothesis could someday be tested by comparing the chemical composition of the ink in the "Judith" addendum to the ink in de Vere's August 1563 letter (written in French) to Sir William Cecil–and to the chemical composition of the ink in Laurence Nowell's June 1563 letter (written in Latin) to Cecil.

p. 23, Connections between *Beowulf* and *Hamlet*: E.g., Edward B. Irving, *Rereading Beowulf* (Philadelphia: University of Pennsylvania Press, 1989), 25–50; a more tenuous possible connection between *Beowulf* and *Julius Caesar* is discussed in John W. Velz and Sarah C. Velz, "Publius, Mark Antony's Sister's Son," *SH.Q* 26:1 (Winter 1975), 69–74.

p. 23, . . . same family of Scandinavian folklore: Kemp Malone, *The Literary History of Hamlet: I. The Early Tradition* (Heidelberg, Germany: Carl Winters Universitätsbuchhandlung, 1923).

p. 23, . . . by an invading foreign nation: (On "Amleth," cf. BULLOUGH, 7:60–79) In Beowulf's words (*Beowulf*, tr. Burton Raffel [Amherst: University of Massachusetts Press, 1971; 1963 first ed.], ll. 2,799–2,808):

> . . . Take
> What I leave, Wiglaf, lead my people,
> Help them; my time is gone. . . .

And in HAMLET's dying plea (*Hamlet*, 5.2.343–54):

> . . . HORATIO, I am dead,
> Thou livest. Report me and my cause aright
> To the unsatisfied. . . .

In the words of Renaissance scholar Andrew Hannas ("Ignoto," "Beowulf, Hamlet, and Edward de Vere," *Shakespeare Oxford Newsletter* 26:2 [Spring 1990], 3–6): "Both Beowulf and HAMLET are concerned not just about their own names and stories–which Wiglaf and HORATIO will report–but also over the fate of the kingdom, the succession to the throne. Both lands either are or soon will be overrun by a foreign power. And oddly, the puzzling slipping of time: The aging of Beowulf bears a curious resemblance to the passage of time in which HAMLET appears in Act 5 to have aged from a prince in early manhood to an ostensible thirty years of age." [Beowulf's aging (1.2200 et. seq.); HAMLET's aging: (5.1.142–57)]

p. 23, Nowell quote: Lansdowne MSS, 6.54; WARD, 20 (Nowell's original letter is in Latin, tr. by Ward).

p. 24, ... tinctures and tonics: Stephanie Hopkins Hughes, "'Shakespeare's' Tutor: Sir Thomas Smith (1513-1577)," *The Oxfordian* 3 (2000), 38-40.

p. 24, ... marred by this accident: Sir Theodore Mayerne (Henry Ellis, *Original Letters, Illustrative of English history*..., second ser [London: Harding & Lepard, 1827], 3:246, in P. M. Handover, *The Second Cecil: The Rise to Power, 1563-1604, of Sir Robert Cecil, Later First Earl of Salisbury.* [London: Eyre & Spottiswoode, 1959], 5) diagnosed Robert Cecil's deformed spine as originating from a fall from his childhood nurse's arms; some historians today question this diagnosis.

p. 24, ... primal inspiration for Shake-speare's RICHARD III: The tradition of a hunchback Richard III–who, at most, had a minor case of "Sprengel's deformity"–is largely a piece of Tudor propaganda, dating back to Sir Thomas More. However, Shake-speare emphasizes the profound and intimate psychological connection between his peculiar deformity and his evil and usurping nature: "I, that am curtail'd of this fair proportion, cheated of feature by dissembling nature, deform'd ... am determined to prove a villain and hate the idle pleasures of these days." (1.1.18-31)

p. 24, Earl John and Margery Golding's wedding: Hank Whittemore, "Oxford's Metamorphoses," *Shakespeare Oxford Newsletter* 32:4 (Fall 1996), 12-13; V. ANDERSON, 148-52; Louis Thorn Golding, *An Elizabethan Puritan*, (New York: Richard R. Smith, 1937), 22-4, 235-6.

p. 24, ... legitimate heirs to the de Vere estate: PRO SP12/29[/8], ff., 11-12; translated in Golding, op. cit., 38-39. Arthur Golding wrote that on June 28, 1563, Edward and Mary de Vere were *"minorem quatordecem annorum,"* which the latter-day Golding mistranslates as stating that Edward and Mary were both minors aged fourteen. However, Christopher Paul ("The 'Prince Tudor' Dilemma," *The Oxfordian* 5 [2002], 53-4) points out that the correct translation should in fact be that Edward and Mary were "younger than fourteen years" on June 28, 1563.

p. 24, "... would leave her in the lurch one day": PRO SP12/151 [/46] ff. 103-4; cited in Percy Allen, *The Plays of Shakespeare and Chapman in Relation to French History* (London: Denis Archer, 1933), 155.

p. 25, EDMUND's speech: *King Lear* 1.2.6-22; *King Lear*'s bastard subplot derives in no small part from a book that Thomas Underdowne would dedicate to Edward de Vere in 1569, Underdowne's translation of Heliodorus's *Aethiopian History.* (Samuel Lee Wolff, *The Greek Romances in Elizabethan Prose Fiction* [New York: Columbia University Press, 1912], 312-13, 366).

p. 25, historical Philip the Bastard ... was inconsequential: Julie C. Van de Water, "The Bastard in *King John*," *SH.Q* 11:2 (Spring 1960), 137-46.

p. 25, ... not unlike the 1563 case: Like EDMUND, *King John*'s BASTARD also utters a memorable paean to opportunism. ("Since kings break faith upon commodity, gain be my lord, for I will worship thee!") But then, by the fourth act, PHILIP matures into a veritable English patriot who proves himself a true subject to the crown and selfless deputy of the king. *King John*, 2.1.597-98; Van de Water, op. cit.

p. 25, "... as of these griefs the ground": Quoted in OGBURN/*TMWS* 431; for further possible parallels to the 1563 bastardy lawsuit, cf. *The Tempest* 1.2 and MILLER/*HASP*, 586-9.

p. 25, de Vere's knowledge of French: STRYPE, 19.

p. 26, de Vere's first letter: English translation from FOWLER, 1; Original French from WARD, 21:

MONSIEUR TRÈS HONORABLE:
Monsieur j'ay reçu voz letters, plaines d'humanité et courtoisie, et fort resemblantes à votre grand amour et singulier affection envers moi, comme vrais enfants devement procrées d'une telle mere pour laquelle je me trouve de jour en jour plus tenu à v.h. [votre honneur] vos

bons admonestements pour l'observation du bon ordre selon vos appointements. Je me délibère (Dieu aidant) de garder en toute diligence comme chose que je cognois et considère tender especialment à mon proper bien et profit, usant en celà l'advis et authorité de ceux qui sont auprès de moi, la discretion desquels j'estime si grande (s'il me convient parler quelquechose à leur avantage) qui non seulement ils se proteront selon qu'un tel temps le requiert, ains que plus est feront tant que je me gouverne selon que vous avez ordonné et commandé. Quant à l'ordre de mon etude pour ce qu'il requiert un long discours à l'expliquer par le menu, et le temps est court à cette heure, je vous prie affectueusement m'en excuser pour le present, vous assurant que par le premier passant je le vous ferai savoir bien au long. Cependant je prie à Dieu vous donner santé.

EDWARD OXINFORD [*sic*]

It should be noted that the quality of de Vere's education in French is attested to by his use of accents, which were not in widespread usage at the time. Roy Wright, personal communication (2003); Ferdinand Brunot, *Histoire de la Langue Française, Des Origines à Nos Jours* (Paris: Librairie Armand Colin, 1967), Tome II, le XVIe siècle.

p. 26, "...the youth of the other": Louis Thorn Golding, *An Elizabethan Puritan: Arthur Golding, the translator of Ovid's "Metamorphoses" and John Calvin's "Sermons"* (New York: Richard R. Smith, 1937). 29; "Golding served as tutor to his nephew Edward, the seventeenth earl [of Oxford], during the years in which he was a ward of court to Lord Burghley at Cecil House." Mark Archer, "The Meaning of 'Grace' and 'Courtesy': Book VI of the *Faerie Queene*," *Studies in English Literature, 1500–1900* 27:1 (Winter 1987), 17.

p. 26, Pound quote: Ezra Pound, *ABC of Reading* (New York: New Directions, 1960; 1934 first ed.), 127.

p. 26, Ovid and Shake-speare: Jonathan Bate's *Shakespeare and Ovid* (Oxford: Clarendon Press, 1993) contains a comprehensive bibliography of the history of scholarship on Ovid's influence on Shake-speare (271–83).

p. 27, Lee quote: Sidney Lee, "Ovid and Shakespeare's Sonnets," *Quarterly Review* 210 (April 1909), 458.

p. 27, *The Metamorphoses* and Shake-speare: Shake-speare's next most frequently cited classical author, Virgil, only crops up one fourth as often as does Ovid. John Frederick Nims, "Introduction," (Ovid's) *Metamorphoses. The Arthur Golding Translation, 1567* (New York: Macmillan, 1965), xx; in OGBURN, 443.

p. 27, Golding's relationship to de Vere: Golding, *Puritan*, op. cit., 24.

p. 27, *Titus Andronicus* quote: *Titus Andronicus*, 4.1.42–3. Some Oxfordians believe that de Vere translated *The Metamorphoses*, and Golding only signed his name to it (cf. OGBURN/*TMWS*, 446; Michael Brame and Galina Popova, *Never and For Ever* [Vashon Island, Wash.: Adonis Editions, 2003]). In favor of this theory one might add the enigmatic note by Edward Dowden that de Vere "was said by Coxeter to have translated Ovid...but no one has ever seen his Ovid." (G.M.B[owen]., "A Shakespeare Allusion Continued?" *Shakespearean Authorship Review* 7 [Spring 1962], 12.) Nevertheless, the present biography concurs with the above to the following extent: The intimate involvement of de Vere in "Golding's" translation of *The Metamorphoses*–in some form–is extremely likely. The extent to which "Golding's Ovid" was really de Vere's Ovid is a subject for further research.

p. 27, Golding's dedication to de Vere: CHILJAN, 6–7.

p. 27, twenty-eight books dedicated to de Vere: CHILJAN, 3.

p. 27, Justinian and Shake-speare: Charles Wisner Barrell, "Arthur Golding: The Uncle of Edward de Vere," *Shakespeare Fellowship News-letter* 1:6 (October–November 1940), 3–4.

p. 28, re "E.O.": NB: "E.O." may have stood for either "Earle of Oxenford" or Edward Oxenford/Oxford.

p. 28, ...lack of moralistic or religious proselytizing: For the canonical and "possible" de Vere juvenilia, cf. MAY and MAY/*ECP,* 269–86. Nearly a third of all mid-sixteenth-century verse was either moralistic or pious, while none of de Vere's verse could be classified under such rubrics. Steven W. May, "The Earl of Oxford's Poetry in Context," presentation at the Sixth Annual Edward de Vere Studies Conference, Concordia University, Portland, Oregon, 12, April 2002.

p. 28, "Loss of My Good Name": MAY, 33.

p. 28, Golding quote: CHILJAN, 15; Golding also urges de Vere to become one with the Psalms: "And David . . . exhorteth you by his own example . . . to talk of [the Psalms] afore kings and great men, to love it, to make your songs of it, to remember it night and day, to count it sweeter than honey, to take it as an heritage, and to make it the joy of your heart." (Ibid.) This, under his Shake-spearean guise, de Vere would do.

p. 28, . . . mostly unchronicled: As Christopher Paul has found (HMC Cal. Salisbury MSS, Vol. 13, p. 107, 6pp. [146.1]), Thomas Fowle continued to draw an average £10 per year between 1562/3 and 1569/70. Whether Fowle was being paid for services rendered in the present tense or rather for tutorial services previously rendered (i.e., during the 1550s and early '60s) is an open quesiton.

p. 28, Plague in London: The plague hit London in 1563 and was in such towns as Exeter and Bristol as late as 1565. Paul Slack, *The Impact of Plague in Tudor and Stuart England* (London: Routledge & Kegan Paul, 1985), 61, table 3.3.

p. 29, . . . rarely took a degree: STONE, 688–9.

p. 29, oath-breaking: Judith Perryman, "'The Words of Mercury': Alchemical Imagery in *Love's Labour's Lost,*" in *The Spirit of the Court,* ed. Glyn S. Burgess and Robert A. Taylor (Cambridge: D. S. Brewer, 1985), 246–53; Frances A. Shirley, *Swearing and Perjury in Shakespeare's Plays* (London: Allen & Unwin, 1979).

p. 29, *Love's Labor's Lost* excerpt: *Love's Labor's Lost,* 2.1.90–105; Ruth Loyd Miller, "Oaths Forsworn in *Love's Labor's Lost,*" op. cit. When this drama was first performed is not known. However, Katharine E. Eggar ("Turberville's Tragical Tales," *Shakespeare Fellowship News-Letter* [UK] [April 1954], 6–7) argues that George Turberville's *Tragical Tales* (1569) is redolent with *Love's Labor's Lost* parallels, suggesting an early draft of the play may have been performed by this time. (I disagree with Ms. Eggar that de Vere was necessarily the author of the *Tragical Tales;* it's just as possible that Turberville was simply alluding to a court play that he had seen or heard of.) Also, as Eva Turner Clark argues (MILLER/*HASP,* 167–251), an early draft of *Love's Labor's Lost* was probably performed for the queen in 1578, when the French personages in the play would have been au courant, given the French marriage negotiations going on at the time.

p. 29, . . . at least four contemporary chroniclers: NICHOLS, 1:149–89; F. S. Boas (*University Drama in the Tudor Age* [Oxford: Clarendon Press, 1914], 90), discusses the four contemporary accounts of the queen's Cambridge visit.

p. 30, Bishop of London quote: F. S. Boas, *University Drama in the Tudor Age* (Oxford: Clarendon Press, 1914), 91.

p. 30, on King's College Chapel: *Ibid.*

p. 30, Debates at St. Mary's Church: John Caius (1510–1573) was, according to his *DNB* entry, one of the presenters at the disputations. He was a notorious figure about court, serving as the queen's physician until he was dismissed in 1568 on charges of Catholicism. He was almost certainly the inspiration for the DR. CAIUS of *Merry Wives of Windsor.* (Lord McNair, "Why Is the Doctor in *The Merry Wives of Windsor* Called Caius?" *Medical History* 13:4 [October 1969], 311–39; Stewart Robb, "Shakespeare and Cambridge University," *Baconiana* [1949], 151.) Caius may also have treated de Vere when he was sick and laid up in a Windsor inn in early 1570 (cf. Chapter 3).

p. 30, Edward Haliwell's *Dido:* Although the text does not survive, scholars conclude it was probably a Senecan adaptation of Virgil. As will be seen in Chapter 7, William Gager produced an alternate version of the Dido tragedy for the court at Oxford University in

1583. Either or maybe both are likely being alluded to when HAMLET has his PLAYER KING rehearse a speech from "Aeneas's tale to Dido." (2.3.420–520.)

p. 31, Proclamation against religious or political discussion on stage: John N. King, "Queen Elizabeth I: Representations of the Virgin Queen," *Renaissance Quarterly* 43:1 (Spring 1990), 43.

p. 31, Spanish ambassador quote: Boas, 382–5.

p. 31, *Hamlet* quote: *Hamlet*, 3.2.259–64; Tom Goff, "For If The Queen Like Not the Comedy," *Shakespeare Oxford Newsletter* 26:1 (Winter 1990), 14–19; Hank Whittemore, "1564: The Education of Young Shakespeare," *Shakespeare Matters* 1:3 (Spring 2002). NB: At least two Stratfordian commentators recognize the parallels between the 1564 Hinchinbrook incident and *Hamlet*'s "Lights, lights, lights!" vignette–although neither has any explanation why the presumptive author from Stratford-upon-Avon (b. 1564) would learn about or dramatize such an obscure moment of court history. Roland Mushat Frye, *The Renaissance Hamlet: Issues and Responses in 1600.* (Princeton, N.J.: Princeton University Press, 1984), 134; G. K. Hunter, *John Lyly; The Humanist as Courtier* (London: Routledge & Kegan Paul, 1962), 148–9.

p. 31, Nuptial jousts and tournaments: J. H. Wiffen, *Historical Memoirs of the House of Russell, in two volumes* (London: Carpenter & Son, 1833), 1:426–30.

p. 31, Chronicle of A. Dudley's wedding: NICHOLS, 1:199.

p. 32, Hot summer: Cornelius Walford, "The Famines of the World: Past and Present," *J. Stat. Soc. London* 41:3 (September 1878), 478.

p. 32, On an Oxford M.A.: *The Complete Works of John Lyly*, ed. R. Warwick Bond, 3 vols. (Oxford: Clarendon Press, 1902), 1:8.

p. 32, Queen's visit to Oxford: It should be noted that William Adlington's translation of Apuleius's *Golden Asse* was dated September 18, 1566, from University College, Oxford. This classical novel of bawdry is an important source for Shake-speare (e.g., D. T. Starnes, "Shakespeare and Apuleius," *PMLA*, 60:4 December 1945), 1021–50; J.J.M. Tobin, *Shakespeare's Favorite Novel: A Study of the* Golden Asse *As Prime Source* (New York: University Press of America, 1984). The coincidence between de Vere's trip to Oxford in early September 1566 and the appearance, in mid-September, of "Adlington"'s translation of Apuleius certainly deserves further research.

p. 32, ... so many academic disputations: NICHOLS, 1:215–6.

p. 32, Oxford visit v. Cambridge visit: Both were originally on the agenda for 1564, but the plague prevented Elizabeth from realizing the second half of her academic itinerary for two more years.

p. 32, Waugh quote: Evelyn Waugh, *Edmund Campion* (Oxford: Oxford University Press, 1980; first ed. 1935), 9. One of the stars of the academic disputes was the subject of Waugh's biography. Campion will resurface in the early 1580s, when de Vere alludes to Campion's predicament circa 1580 in *Twelfth Night*.

p. 32, Plot summaries of Oxford entertainments: NICHOLS, 1:206–47; W. Y. Durand, "*Palaemon and Arcyte, Progne, Marcus Geminus,* and the Theater in Which They Were Acted, as Described by John Bereblock (1566)," *PMLA* 20:3 (1905), 502–28; Hyder E. Rollins ("A Note on Richard Edwards," *RES* 4:14 [April 1928], 204–6) also located a scrap of *Palamon and Arcite*, Emily's song after the death of Arcite.

p. 33, *Palamon and Arcite* v. de Vere's early poetry: Katherine Chiljan, "Oxford and *Palamon and Arcite:* Could this 1566 play actually be an early work by Edward de Vere?" *Shakespeare Oxford Newsletter* 35:1 (Spring 1999), 10–13.

p. 33, *Two Noble Kinsmen & Palamon:* Both plays recall Chaucer's "Knight's Tale."

p. 33, ... originated in de Vere's pen in 1566: Ibid. *The Two Noble Kinsmen* prologue also enigmatically notes that "we perceive our losses fall so thick," words that sound like an honorific bow to the loss of life at *Palamon and Arcite*'s 1566 premiere.

When *Two Noble Kinsmen* first appeared in print in 1635, it was credited as being coauthored by Shake-speare and the seventeenth-century dramatist John Fletcher. It has long been argued that Fletcher was the author of much of Acts 2–4, concerning a subplot involving a jailer's daughter (e.g., Theodore Spencer, *"The Two Noble Kinsmen," Modern Philology* 36:3 [February 1939], 255–76). As Chiljan writes, "It's most unlikely that Fletcher's subplot about the daughter of Palamon and Arcite's jailer–a poor imitation of OPHELIA– was part of the original play, as it had almost no relation to the main plot. One can only conjecture that the first and last acts of Shakespeare's original version had survived, and that later Fletcher filled in the rest. Fletcher rode on the coattails of Shakespeare before– as late as 1611 he wrote a sequel to *Taming of the Shrew* called *The Woman's Prize, or the Tamer Tamed*." (10)

p. 33, Civil law taught at university: Craig R. Thompson, *Universities in Tudor England* (Ithaca, N.Y.: Cornell University Press, 1959), 13.

p. 33, de Vere and Sidney at Gray's Inn: J. A. van Dorsten, "Mr. Secretary Cecil, Patron of Letters," in van Dorsten, *The Anglo-Dutch Renaissance: Seven Essays* (Leiden: E. J. Brill, 1988), 37; READ/CECIL, 436–7.

p. 33, On Elizabethan Inns of Court: *Gesta Grayorum*...(1594), ed. Desmond Bland (Liverpool: Liverpool University Press, 1968), xxv.

p. 33, ... may now be added the name Shake-speare: F.J.M. Marrian (*Shakespeare at Gray's Inn* [London: private press, 1967]) even supposed that the Stratford Shakspere attended Gray's Inn in 1579 under the pseudonym "William Rich," a protégé of Robert Lord Rich. Marrian points out that *Polimanteia* (1595) and Hall's *Satires* (1597) both suggest a university- and/or Inns-of-Court–educated Shake-speare–and on that score Marrian is right. (Peter R. Moore, "Stratfordians Prove the Bard Had a University Education," *Shakespeare Oxford Newsletter* 30:4 (Autumn 1994), 1–3; Mark Andre Alexander, "Shakespeare's 'Bad Law,'" *Shakespeare Oxford Newsletter* 35:4 (Winter 2000), 1, 9–13). Marrian just has the wrong Shake-speare.

p. 33, Gascoigne and de Vere in 1562?: WARD, 15.

p. 33, ... school's archives or the author himself: As Katherine Duncan-Jones (*Sir Philip Sidney: Courtier Poet* [New Haven, Conn.: Yale University Press, 1991], 48) points out, "Two plays by [the earl of] Oxford's kinsman George Gascoigne, the comedy *Supposes* and the tragedy *Jocasta*, were performed at Gray's Inn sometime in 1566. They may belong either to the New-Year-to-Shrovetide festivities in 1565–6 or those of 1566–7; Gascoigne seems to have spent time at Gray's Inn in both years. Sidney's presence at their performance is highly probable."

p. 33, On *Jocasta*: It has, nevertheless, been suggested that a speech of HOTSPUR's (*1 Henry IV*, 1.3.201) owes a debt to *Jocasta*–and perhaps the Euripidean original too. John Pentland Mahaffy, *A History of Classical Greek Literature* (New York: Macmillan & Co., 1895), 1:366 fn; Felix E. Schelling, "Three Unique Elizabethan Dramas," *Modern Language Notes* 7:5 (May 1892), 130.

p. 34, On *The Supposes*: Sidney Lee, *The French Renaissance in England* (Oxford: Clarendon Press, 1910), 419–21.

p. 34, Inspiration of *The Supposes*: David Bevington, "Cultural Exchange: Gascoigne and Ariosto at Gray's Inn in 1566," in *The Italian World of English Renaissance Drama*, ed. Michele Marrapodi (Newark: University of Delaware Press, 1998), 25–40; Cecil S. Seronsy, "'Supposes' as the Unifying Theme in *The Taming of the Shrew*," *SH.Q* 14:1 (Winter 1963), 15–30.

p. 34, Where *Jocasta* & *Supposes* performed: In 1594, Gray's Inn also played host to a production of *The Comedy of Errors*.

p. 34, On Gray's Inn: A. Wigfall Green, *The Inns of Court and Early English Drama* (New Haven, Conn.: Yale University Press, 1931), 34; Robert J. Blackham, *Wig and Gown: The Story of The Temple, Gray's, and Lincoln's Inn* (London: Sampson, Low, Marston & Co., 1932), 84–7, 144–5.

p. 34, Arguments in *Hales v. Petit:* J. J. Dwyer, "The Poet Earl of Oxford and Gray's Inn," *Shakespeare Fellowship Quarterly* 8:1 (Summer 1947), 21–25; Edmund Plowden, *Les Commentaires ou les Reportes*...London, Luke Wilson (1571, part 1; 1987, part 2), 259a; "*Hamlet, Hales v. Petit* and the Hysteresis of Action," *ELH* 60:1 (Spring 1993), 17–55, 29.

p. 34, ... table talk amongst the Gray's Inn students: *Hales v. Petit* is still cited today, as a common-law precedent dictating that "the imagination of the mind to do wrong, without an act done, is not punishable." Fred J. Abbate, "The Conspiracy Doctrine: A Critique," *Philosophy and Public Affairs* 3:3 (Spring 1974), 301.

p. 35, *Hales v. Petit* as jab at legal system: "[*Hales v. Petit*] stated a rare but important rule by which the inheritance of real property could be defeated, or at least delayed indefinitely." J. Anthony Burton, "An Unrecognized Theme in *Hamlet:* Lost Inheritance and Claudius's Marriage to Gertrude," *The Shakespeare Newsletter* 50:3, No. 246 (Fall 2000), 71, 76, 78, 82; 50:4, No. 247 (Winter 2000/2001), 103, 104, 106.

p. 35, Brincknell post-mortem inquiry: PRO KB9/619(part 1)/13, cited and translated in NELSON, 47.

p. 36, On the nature of Brincknell's death: Private communication with Dr. Joseph Lex, Department of Emergency Medicine, Temple University Hospital, Philadelphia (February 18, 2004).

p. 36, Definition of "manslaughter": Jeremy Horder, *Provocation and Responsibility* (Oxford: Oxford University Press, 1992), 9–20.

p. 36, The deceased was also, conveniently, dead: Luke Wilson, op. cit., 37; NELSON, 48.

p. 37, Cecil and *Se defendendo* verdict: WARD, 124.

p. 37, De Vere's mother's death: NELSON, 49.

p. 37, Howard quote: (LIB-3.1/3) in NELSON, 58; this document is part of the problematic "Arundell Libels" file, to be discussed in Chapter 6.

p. 37, Sidney at Cecil House: James M. Osborn, *Young Philip Sidney, 1572–1577* (New Haven, Conn.: Yale University Press, 1972), 16.

p. 37, Cecil quote on Sidney: Ibid.

p. 37, "... partly by the plague": The queen to Sir Henry Sidney, August 19, 1570, reprinted in Jean Robertson, "*Young Philip Sidney: 1572–1577* (review)," *Modern Philology* 71:4 (May 1974), 419.

p. 38, On Strindberg and Balzac: Theodore Lidz, "August Strindberg: A Study of the Relationship Between His Creativity and Schizophrenia," and E.C.M. Frijling-Schreuder, "Honoré de Balzac–A Disturbed Boy Who Did Not Get Treatment," in *The Literary Imagination: Psychoanalysis and the Genius of the Writer,* ed. Hendrik M. Ruitenbeek (Chicago: Quadrangle Books, 1965).

p. 38, On O'Neill: Ron Halsted, "Washed Up in Windsor" (unpublished MS, 2003); Philip Weissman, "O'Neill's Conscious and Unconscious Autobiographical Dramas," in *Creativity in the Theater: A Psychoanalytic Study* (New York: Basic Books, 1965), 113–45.

p. 38, ... forced truce between superego and id: FELDMAN, 105–7; Michael Howe, "The Expertise of Great Writers," in *Genius Explained* (Cambridge: Cambridge University Press, 1999), 157–75; Kay Redfield Jamison, "Mood disorders and patterns of creativity in British writers and artists," *Psychiatry* 52 (May 1989), 125–34; Felix Post, "Verbal Creativity, Depression, and Alcoholism: An Investigation of One Hundred American and British Writers," *British Journal of Psychiatry* 168 (1996), 545–55.

p. 38, On Shaw: Weissman, "Shaw's Childhood and *Pygmalion*," *Creativity in the Theater*, op. cit., 161.

p. 38, Cecil–Sidney marriage negotiations: Hatfield MSS. 1/415 in J. Thomas Looney, "The Earl of Oxford as Shakespeare," *The Golden Hind* 1–2:1–8 (October 1922–July 1924), in MILLER/LOONEY, 2:168–76. The precise numbers are detailed in MILLER/LOONEY, 2:172–4: "On the day of marriage, Sidney should have an income of £266. 13s. 4d. (400 marks) yearly. As lay rector of Whitford, in Flint, he already had £80 a year; so that, after all charges against the living had been met, his total immediate income would be something over *three hundred pounds a year*. At his father's death [Sidney] was to receive an increase of only £147. 16s. 7d. a year; whilst at his mother's death an increase of £325. 14s. 3d." On Anne's side: "'If Anne's younger brother or brethren shall die without issue, A.C. shall have, in reversion, after the death of her father and mother, £200 lands and also a dwelling house within thirteen miles of London meet for a gentleman of £500 lands' (an inheritance, therefore, of exactly *seven hundred pounds*)." (emphasis in original.)

    p. 38, Parallels between *Merry Wives* and Cecil–Sidney marriage negotiations: *Merry Wives of Windsor*, 1.1.50–8, 250–4; 3.4.31–3; on ANNE PAGE's "grandsire" and Anne Cecil's grandfather, cf. MILLER/LOONEY, 2:173–5; when Robert Dudley became earl of Leicester in 1564, the earldom had lain dormant for three hundred years. This fact would explain why SHALLOW brags that he "can write himself a gentleman . . . [since] any time these three hundred years." ([1.1.6–13]; Burris, op. cit.; J. Thomas Looney/Ruth Loyd Miller, "The Sidney-Cecil-Oxford Triangle and *The Merry Wives of Windsor*," MILLER/LOONEY, 2:161–76; OGBURN/*TMWS*, 488; OGBURNS/*TSOE*, 741–2).

    p. 39, Sidney indifferent to marriage: Duncan-Jones, *Sidney*, op. cit., 51.

    p. 39, "Your father and my uncle hath made [the] motions": *Merry Wives*, 3.4.60–2.

    p. 39, De Vere's 24 November 1569 letter: FOWLER, 19. This letter marks the first instance of a peculiar signature form de Vere used–dubbed "the crown signature" for its iconic representation of a crown or earl's coronet strung between the "Edward" and "Oxenford." Ruth Loyd Miller, "Oxford's 'Crown' Signature: An Enigma Awaiting Time's Solution, with the Enigma Solved," unpublished MS (1998); Diana Price, "Rough Winds Do Shake: A Fresh Look at the Tudor Rose Theory," *The Elizabethan Review* 4:2 (Autumn 1996), 14–16; Elisabeth Sears, *Shakespeare and the Tudor Rose* (Marshfield Hills, Mass.: Meadow Geese Press, 2002), 190.

CHAPTER THREE

    p. 40, Payment to "Riche the apothecary": SP Dom Add., 19.38, quoted in WARD, 32–33.

    p. 40, On Elizabethan "hothouses": "Let a man sweat once a week in a hothouse and be well rubbed and froted [*sic*], with a plump juicy wench, and sweet linens: He shall ne'er ha' the pox." Ben Jonson, *Every Man Out of His Humor* (1599), 3.3; "Nor in the winter breathes with you a man/ Without his hothouse, bath or warming pan/ Where here with us, nature doth order keep/ We drink until we sweat, sweat until we sleep." Robert Tofte, "The First Satire of Ariostos" (1611), ll. 65–68; "Fain, as rich men's heirs would be of their gouty dads: that's the hothouse, where your parties are sweating." Thomas Dekker, *Westward Hoe* (1607), 5.1. (*Hothouse* was also a term for a brothel, leading to such commonplace puns as the above.)

    p. 40, De Vere's expenses in 1562–66: SP Dom Eliz., 42.38, quoted in WARD, 32.

    p. 40, On "mules": WARD transcribes the word as "Moyles." Compare J. Heywood's *Proverbs & Epigrams* (1562): "Thou wearest . . . Moyles of veluet to saue thy shooes of lether."

    p. 40, Where de Vere lodged during his sickness: That it was a Windsor room for hire where de Vere stayed is also revealed by Cecil's ledgers (SP Dom. Eliz., 42.38; WARD, 32–3). In one entry for the first quarter of 1570, Cecil mentions de Vere's "diet in the time of his sickness," another mentions de Vere's "being sick at Windsor," while another entry records a payment of £30/16/- for "house rent" and other expenses "in the time of his said diet" to one William Bishop. (There were two William Bishops then living in the town of Windsor.) *House* often meant "inn" (*OED*, definition 2c), although which Windsor "house" de Vere stayed at is a subject for further research. Barbara Burris, "A Room in the Garter Inn," Unpublished MS (2003).

p. 40, Local lore in *Merry Wives:* Burris, op. cit.; *The Merry Wives of Windsor,* ed. T. W. Craik, The Oxford Shakespeare (Oxford: Clarendon Press, 1989), 1–6.

p. 41, On Smith c. 1570: Mary Dewar, *Sir Thomas Smith: A Tudor Intellectual in Office* (London: University of London Athlone Press, 1964), 121.

p. 41, De Vere writing in 1570: We know that de Vere at least enjoyed a lively correspondence with the queen's astrologer John Dee in 1570, for in 1592, when he was charged with sorcery, his defense included a list of the many nobles he had come to know over the years. He mentioned, "the honourable the earl of Oxford, his favourable letters, anno 1570" (*A Compendious Rehearsal,* cited in WARD, 50).

p. 41, Book purchase for de Vere in 1569/70: The Italian books were purchased from William Bishop, the others from the stationer William Seres. In the third quarter of 1570, Cecil notes another purchase from William Seres of "Tully's and Plato's works in folio." WARD, op. cit. Tully is twice referenced in Shake-speare (*2 Henry VI,* 4.1.136; *Titus Andronicus,* 4.1.14). The correspondences between Plato and Shake-speare have been studied in such books as John Vyvyan's *Shakespeare and Platonic Beauty* (London: Chatto & Windus, 1961). (Shake-speare was also, as will be noted below, greatly influenced by the continental Renaissance neo-Platonist movement.)

p. 41, Shake-speare and Plutarch and Chaucer: **Plutarch:** *Shakespeare's Plutarch,* ed. Mary Ann McGrail, special issue of *Poetica: An International Journal of Linguistic-Literary Studies* (Tokyo: Shubun International, 1997); Vivian Thomas, *Shakespeare's Roman Worlds* (New York: Routledge, 1989). The French edition of Plutarch was translated by Jacques Amyot and published in 1559. Sir Thomas North then faithfully translated Amyot's French in an English edition published in 1579; it has long been assumed that North's edition of Plutarch was the one Shake-speare used. (And de Vere may well have had a copy of North too.) But no scholar that I am aware of has examined whether Amyot and/or Plutarch's original Greek were also part of Shake-speare's library. **Chaucer:** Ann Thompson, *Shakespeare's Chaucer: A Study in Literary Origins* (New York: Barnes & Noble, 1978); E. Talbot Donaldson, *The Swan at the Well: Shakespeare Reading Chaucer* (New Haven, Conn: Yale University Press, 1985).

p. 41, Shake-speare and the Bible: See the bibliographies in STRITMATTER; Naseeb Shaheen, *Biblical References in Shakespeare's Plays* (London: Associated University Presses, 1999); and Steven Marx, *Shakespeare and the Bible* (Oxford: Oxford University Press, 2000).

p. 41, De Vere's orders: S.P. Dom. Add., 19.37, quoted in WARD, 40.

p. 42, Agenda of Northern earls: Mark Charles Fissel, *English Warfare: 1511–1642* (London: Routledge, 2001), 134–6.

p. 42, Northern earls' allies in Scotland: WARD, 35–50.

p. 42, Sussex's April 1570 conference: Fissel, op. cit.

p. 43, Sussex's letter to Cecil: WARD, 48; Christopher Hibbert, *The Virgin Queen: Elizabeth I, Genius of the Golden Age* (Cambridge, Mass.: Perseus Books, 1991), 180.

p. 43, Sussex's scorched-earth campaign: Fissel, op. cit.

p. 43, Campaigns over Scots border in April–June 1570: Fissel, op. cit.; Thomas Churchyard, "The siege of Edenbrough Castell in the xv yeer of the raigne of our soueraigne Lady Queen Elizabeth," from *The Firste Parte of Churchyardes Chippes* (1575).

p. 43, On Elizabethan literacy: The literacy rate of Elizabethan England has never been reduced to a single, accepted number. David Cressy (*Literacy and the Social Order: Reading and Writing in Tudor and Stuart England* [Cambridge: Cambridge University Press, 1980], 124, 146, 169–70) notes a substantial but irregular drop in illiteracy across England during the period. In London and Middlesex, for instance, illiteracy among tradesmen and craftsmen dropped from forty-one percent to thirty percent between 1580 and 1610. Women were, given the few educational opportunities they enjoyed, far more likely to be illiterate than men.

p. 43, On de Vere's possible authorship of the *Homily Against Disobedience and Willful Rebellion*: The *Homily Against Disobedience and Willful Rebellion* was also a sermon rooted in its time—holding to the medieval ideal of a regimented universal order, as ordained by God, with the prince and the upper crust of society at the top of the pyramid and the lower castes of society naturally existing in their proper place—below. (cf. E.M.W. Tillyard, *The Elizabethan World Picture* [New York: Macmillan, 1944].) The 1571 homily was, by today's more enlightened standards, a collection of elitist rhetorical flourishes that would be no great feather in de Vere's cap, were he the author. Yet to posit de Vere's authorship of the 1571 homily is not inconsistent with his authorship of Shake-speare—a canon often misread today as being variously Marxist, antiestablishment, anticlass, or antielite. As Walt Whitman wrote in *November Boughs*, "The [Shake-speare] comedies (exquisite as they certainly are) bringing in admirably portray'd common characters, have the unmistakable hue of plays, portraits, made for the divertissement only of the elite of the castle, and from its point of view. The comedies are altogether nonacceptable to America and Democracy."

Shake-speare the universally accessible poet and enlightened moral and spiritual philosopher should not be mistaken for Shake-speare the political polemicist. Follow the political teachings of the Shake-speare canon—or the 1571 homily, for that matter—and one is on the road to feudalism.

p. 43, The *Homily on Disobedience . . .* and Shake-speare: A partial survey of allusions to the *Homily Against Disobedience and Willful Rebellion* in Shake-speare: **Shake-speare in general:** James Sutherland and Joel Hurstfield, *Shakespeare's World* (New York: St. Martin's Press, 1964), 35–37; Janet Clare, "'Greater Themes for Insurrection's Arguing': Political Censorship of the Elizabethan and Jacobean Stage," *RES*, new series, 38:150 (May 1987), 169 (and citations in fn. 1). **Richard II:** Donald M. Friedman, "John of Gaunt and the Rhetoric of Frustration," *ELH* 43:3 (Autumn 1976), 279–8; Janet Clare, "The Censorship of the Deposition Scene in *Richard II*," *RES*, new series, 41:161 (February 1990), 93; **Julius Caesar:** Paul N. Siegel, "Leontes a Jealous Tyrant," *RES*, new series, 1:4 (October 1950), 302, fn. 3; **Henry VI, Part 1:** Ronald Levao, *Renaissance Minds and Their Fictions: Cusanus, Sidney, Shakespeare* (Berkeley: University of California Press, 1985), 292; **Henry VI, Part 3:** Siegel, op. cit.; **Henry V:** *Henry V*, ed. Andrew Gurr, New Cambridge Shakespeare (Cambridge: Cambridge University Press, 1992), 4.1; **Henry IV, Part 1:** Barbara Hodgdon, ed. *The First Part of King Henry the Fourth: Texts and Contexts* (Boston: Bedford Books, 1997), Chapter 2, "Civic Order and Rebellion"; **Macbeth:** Arthur Kirsch, "Macbeth's Suicide," *ELH* 51:2 (Summer 1984), 270; Irving Ribner, "Political Doctrine in *Macbeth*," *SH.Q* 4:2 (Apr. 1953), 205; **Coriolanus:** Thomas Clayton, "Old Light on the Text of *King Lear*," *Modern Philology* 78:4 (May 1981), 350–1.

p. 44, Excerpt from *Homily:* Reprinted in Sutherland and Hurstfield, op. cit., 37–39; The homilist's "puddle and sink" is a figure of rhetoric known as *hendyades*—a figure central to both de Vere's writings under his own name and under the Shake-speare pen name (e.g., "*slings and arrows* of outrageous fortune"); for a review of hendyades and Shake-speare, cf. Brian Vickers, "Rhetoric: The Shakespearean 'Hendyades'" in *"Counterfeiting" Shakespeare* [Cambridge: Cambridge University Press, 2002], 163–88).

The homilist also rails about how rebels are "the most greatest unthrifts that have most lewdly wasted their own goods and lands, those that are over the ears in debt." The irony of this utterance will only become more apparent in the coming chapters if the homilist was indeed de Vere.

p. 44, Date of *Henry IV* plays: A juvenile version of both *Henry IV* plays plus *Henry V* survives in the Elizabethan play *The Famous Victories of Henry V.* Seymour M. Pitcher (*The Case for Shakespeare's Authorship of 'The Famous Victories'* [New York: State University of New York Press, 1961]) convincingly argues for its canonization. OGBURN/*TMWS*, 423–5, summarizes the argument for de Vere's authorship of *The Famous Victories* as early as the

1570s. Ramon Jimenez ("*The Famous Victories of Henry V:* Key to the Authorship Question?" *Shakespeare Oxford Society Newsletter* 37:2 [Summer 2001], 7) has published a more extensive case for same.

p. 44, Northern Rebellion and *Henry IV* plays: Lily B. Campbell, *Shakespeare's "Histories": Mirrors of Elizabethan Policy* (San Marino, Cal.: Huntington Library, 1958), 229–38.

p. 44, *Henry IV* excerpt: *2 Henry IV,* 1.1.194–201.

p. 44, Shake-speare must have consulted with Northern Rebellion eyewitness: Richard Simpson, "The Political Use of the Stage in Shakespeare's Time" and "The Politics of Shakespeare's Historical Plays," *The New Shakspere* [*sic*] *Society's Transactions* (1874), 371–441.

p. 44, Cecil quote: Thomas Wright, *Queen Elizabeth and Her Times* (London: H. Colburn, 1838), 1:391, cited in *DNB;* on Burghley's riches, cf. READ/CECIL, 352.

p. 45, Elizabeth's preference for unremarkable personalities as her advisors: SMITH/*ET,* 89.

p. 45, Cecil's investiture ceremony as Baron Burghley: READ/*BURGHLEY,* 33.

p. 45, ... or a blood relationship to the queen: Henry Lord Compton (1538–89) was the other. STONE, 98.

p. 45, Whitman quote: Walt Whitman, *The Complete Writings of Walt Whitman: Prose* (New York: G. P. Putnam's Sons, 1902), 2:277; Felix E. Schelling, *Shakespeare and 'Demi Science': Papers on Elizabethan Topics* (Philadelphia: University of Penn. Press, 1927), 85.

p. 45, Opening of 1571 Parliament: WARD, 51–3.

p. 46, Agenda of 1571 Parliament: J. E. Neale, *Elizabeth I and Her Parliaments: 1559–1581* (New York: W. W. Norton & Co., 1958), 177–87.

p. 46, Bill "Against Wednesdays": Neale, op. cit., 225.

p. 46, On "Cecil's Fast": James Anthony Froude, *English Seamen in the Sixteenth Century* (New York: Charles Scribner's Sons, 1895), 23; Parliament eventually eliminated "Cecil's Fast" in 1584, READ/*BURGHLEY,* 304.

p. 46, 1571 Tournament at Whitehall: This was, at least, the price paid at the 1584 Accession Day Tournament, as detailed by the German correspondent Lupold von Wedel, whose account is reprinted in *Queen Elizabeth and Some Foreigners,* ed. Victor von Klarwill, tr. T. H. Nash (London: John Lane, 1928), 330–2.

p. 46, Protocol for tournaments: Adapted from WARD, 58: Alan Young, *Tudor and Jacobean Tournaments* (London: Sheridan House, 1987).

p. 46, De Vere as Red Knight: In Chretien de Troyes's *Conte du Grael* (c. 1190), the hero Perceval slays the Red Knight; however, Perceval dons the Red Knight's armor, making a latter-day combatant in the armor of the Red Knight a stand-in for Perceval himself. (George M. Harper, "The Legend of the Holy Grail," *PMLA* 8:1 [1893], 90; Roy Bennett Pace, "The Death of the Red Knight in the Story of Perceval" *Modern Language Notes* 31:1 [January 1916], 53–55.) The Red Knight appeared in at least one other tournament that de Vere participated in, on January 22, 1581, although the role of the Red Knight was played that time by Sir William Drury. (Marshall W. S. Swan, "The Sweet Speech and Spenser's (?) [*sic*] *Axiochus,*" *ELH* 11:3 [September 1944], 168.)

p. 46, Score of 1571 Tournament: Stow, *Annals,* 669, cited in WARD, 56; Ashmole MSS, 837, f. 245, cited in FELDMAN/*AMENDMENTS,* 56.

p. 47, Gray on Anne Cecil: Austin K. Gray, "The Secret of *Love's Labour's Lost,*" *PMLA* 39:3 (September 1924), 585.

p. 47, Plays that recall 1571 courtship: To this list one could certainly add elements of *Hamlet, Much Ado About Nothing, Cymbeline, Romeo and Juliet,* and *Measure for Measure.*

p. 47, On "disparagement": Margaret Loftus Ranald, "'As Marriage Binds, and Blood Breaks': English Marriage and Shakespeare," *SH.Q* 30:1 (Winter 1979), 79–80; HURSTFELD, 141.

p. 47, *All's Well That Ends Well,* 2.3.159–65.

p. 48, On Elizabethan marriage law: Ranald, op. cit., 80.

p. 48, "E of O hath gotten him a wife...": Lord [Oliver] St. John, Baron Bletsoe to Rutland. Cal. Rutland MSS July 28, 1571, quoted in WARD, 61–2.

p. 48, Burghley letter to Rutland: Cal. Rutland MSS August 15, 1571, quoted in READ/BURGHLEY, 127–8.

p. 49, On Anne's dowry: Antonio de Guaras to the duke of Alva, May 1, 1573, reprinted in *Relations Politiques des Pays-Bas et de L'Angleterre, Sous le Règne de Philippe II,* ed. Le Baron Kervyn de Lettenhove (Brussels: Académie Royale des Sciences, etc., 1888), 6:723; this letter will be discussed at greater length in the next chapter.

p. 49, Origin of name OPHELIA: Ophelia's name is of Greek origin, although critics are unable to settle on which word it derives from. In his 1861 study *Der Hamlet,* Professor A. Gerth claims that it's a transcription of the Greek noun ωφελεια which means either "help/aid/succor" or "profit/advantage." On the other hand, the noun οφειλεια–which could also be transcribed "Ophelia"–means "indebtedness." Mark K. Anderson, "Ophelia's Difference, or, 'To Catch the Conscience of the Counselor,'" *Shakespeare Oxford Newsletter* 35:4 (Winter 2000), 17.

p. 49, *"Regnum Cecilianum"*: READ/BURGHLEY, 319–20.

p. 49, Wedding plans: NICHOLS, 1:291, fn. 1; WARD, 63.

p. 49, Smith letter to Burghley: Neville Williams, *Thomas Howard, Fourth Duke of Norfolk* (London: Barrie and Rockliff, 1964), 212.

p. 50, Burghley framed Norfolk?: Ronald Pollitt, "'Refuge of the Distressed Nations,' Perceptions of Aliens in Elizabethan England," *The Journal of Modern History* (On Demand Supplement) 52:1 (Mar. 1980), D1015; Francis Edwards, *The Marvellous [sic] Chance: Thomas Howard, Fourth Duke of Norfolk, and the Ridolphi Plot, 1570–72* (London: Rupert Hart-Davis, 1968).

p. 50, Norfolk was a dupe?: Williams, op. cit.

p. 50, Date of de Vere's marriage: Memo from George Golding (de Vere's auditor), reprinted in NELSON, 74; a letter from Burghley to Walsingham (December 19) suggests December 19 as the marriage day.

p. 50, Double-wedding?: NELSON, 74–5.

p. 51, Wedding verses in Cecil archives: Hatfield MSS (Cal. XIII, 109), reprinted in WARD, 64.

p. 51, Anne forever caught like OPHELIA: On Shake-speare's long-standing problems with women, as slowly resolved in his canon of plays, cf. Shirlee Nelson Garner "Male Bonding and the Myth of Women's Deception in Shakespeare's Plays" in *Shakespeare's Personality,* ed. Norman H. Holland, Sidney Homan, and Bernard J. Paris (Berkeley: University of California Press, (1989) 135–50); Roger Stritmatter, "Shakespeare's *Missing* Personality" (book review), *The Elizabethan Review* 1:2 (Fall 1993), 65–74.

p. 51, Rumors in Lowlands: John Lee to Burghley, March 18, 1572, reprinted in *Relations Politiques,* op. cit., 6:343.

p. 51, De Vere had "railed" at Norfolk: SP Dom. Eliz., 151.46–49, quoted in WARD, 67.

p. 51, De Vere's "certain proposal": *Correspondence... de la Mothe Fénelon,* quoted in WARD, 66; Edwards (op. cit., 403, fn. 5) notes that this evidence "is, surely, too vague to use as proof even of the rumor [of de Vere's alleged escape plots]."

p. 52, *The Courtier's* resemblance to Elizabethan court: "It is surprising how fully Elizabeth, both in her accomplishments and in her policies, met Castiglione's standards for the ideal prince." E. C. Wilson, *England's Eliza.* (New York: Octagon, 1966; 1939 first ed.), 259, fn. 63; Raymond B. Waddington, "Elizabeth I and the Order of the Garter," *Sixteenth Century Journal* 24:1 (Spring 1993), 104–6.

p. 52, ... like a terrestrial goddess of love: Waddington, op. cit.

p. 52, Courtier "more excellent than a prince": Castiglione's *The Courtier,* translated by Thomas Hoby (1561), cited in Joan Simon, *Education and Society in Tudor England* (Cambridge: Cambridge University Press, 1966), 340.

p. 52, De Vere's preface to *The Courtier:* Translation in WARD, 80–3.

p. 53, Shake-speare and Castiglione: What follows is a breviary of recent scholarship that isolates allusions to and reflections of Castiglione in Shake-speare: **Shake-speare in general:** John Vyvyan, *Shakespeare and Platonic Beauty* (London: Chatto & Windus, 1961); Curtis Brown Watson, *Shakespeare and the Renaissance Concept of Honor* (Princeton, N.J.: Princeton University Press, 1960); *All's Well:* Lisa Jardine, "Cultural Confusion and Shake-speare's Learned Heroines," *SH.Q* 38:1 (Spring 1987), 6–7; *Antony and Cleopatra:* Leonard Barkan, "The Beholder's Tale," *Representations* 44 (Autumn 1993), 154–7; *As You Like It:* Judy Z. Kronenfeld, "Social Rank and the Pastoral Ideals of *As You Like It,*" *SH.Q* 29:3 (Summer 1978), 337; *Coriolanus:* Linda Bradley Salamon, "The Courtier and The Scholemaster," *Comparative Lit.* 25:1 (Winter 1973), 23; *Hamlet:* W. B. Drayton Henderson, "Hamlet as Castiglione's Ideal Courtier," *PMLA* proceedings 43 suppl. (1928), xxxix; Donald K. Hedrick, "'It is No Novelty for a Prince to be a Prince,'" *SH.Q* 35:1 (Spring 1984), 74; *2 Henry IV:* Edward I. Berry, "The Rejection Scene in *2 Henry IV,*" *Studies in English Literature 1500–1900* 17:2 (Spring 1977), 208; *Henry V:* Robert Berkleman, "Teaching *Henry V,*" *College English* 13:2 (November 1951), 94; *Julius Caesar:* Robert C. Reynolds, "Ironic Epithet in *Julius Caesar,*" *SH.Q* 24:3 (Summer 1973), 332; *Measure for Measure:* George L. Geckle, "Shakespeare's Isabella," *SH.Q* 22:2 (Spring 1971), 167; *Merchant of Venice:* Maurice Hunt, "Ways of Knowing in *The Merchant of Venice,*" *SH.Q* 30:1 (Winter 1979), 90; *Much Ado:* Mary Augusta Scott, "The Book of the Courtyer: A Possible Source of Benedick and Beatrice," *PMLA* 16:4 (1901), 475–502; Lodwick Hartley, "Claudio and the Unmerry War," *College English* 26:8 (May 1965), 611; B. K. Lewalski, "Love, Appearance, and Reality: Much Ado About Something," *Studies in English Literature, 1500–1900* 8:2 (Spring 1968), 239; Richard Desper, "Remarks on Castiglione's *Il Cortegiano* as Applicable to the Authorship Question," *Shakespeare Oxford Newsletter* 35:2 (Summer 1999), 23, 27; *Othello:* "*Othello* as an 'Assay of Reason,'" *SH.Q* 24:2 (Spring 1973), 201; Viviana Comensoli, "Music, *The Book of the Courtier,* and OTHELLO's Soldiership," in *The Italian World of English Renaissance Drama,* ed. Michele Marrapodi (Newark, N.J.: University of Delaware Press, 1998), 89–105; *The Tempest:* Mary Chan, *Music in the Theater of Ben Jonson* (Oxford: Clarendon Press, 1980); *Timon:* W. M. Merchant, "Timon and the Conceit of Art," *SH.Q* 6:3 (Summer 1955), 252; *Troilus and Cressida:* Carolyn Asp, "Th' Expense of Spirit in a Waste of Shame," *SH.Q* 22:4 (Autumn 1971), 347; *Twelfth Night:* Keir Elam, "The Fertile Eunuch," *SH.Q* 47:1 (Spring 1996), 25; J. D. Schuchter, "Shakespeare's *Twelfth Night* I.iii.42," *Explicator* 29:1, no. 3; Desper, op. cit. *The Winter's Tale:* Chan, op. cit.

p. 53, De Vere's intellectual forebears: De Vere's early exposure to Ovid was chronicled in the previous chapter. His early exposure to Plato is recorded in Cecil's account books for the third quarter of 1570: "To William Seres, stationer, for Tully's and Plato's works in folio," op. cit., from WARD, 33.

p. 53, On proviso of 1352: Samuel Rezneck, "The Early History of the Parliamentary Declaration of Treason," *The English Historical Review* 42:168 (Oct. 1927), 508, fn. 1; STATE TRIALS 1:1027.

p. 53, "... as of the Duke of Norfolk": Wallace MacCaffrey, *The Shaping of the Elizabethan Regime* (Princeton, N.J.: Princeton University Press, 1968), 426.

p. 53, ... in this kangaroo court: Ibid., 424.

p. 53, ... before the first witness took the stand: Francis Edwards ("Topical Allusions in *The Winter's Tale*–II," *The Bard* 1:2 [1976], 47–64) argues that Norfolk's last stand serves as part inspiration for HERMIONE's defense in the treason trial brought against her by her husband, LEONTES.

p. 53, On the one-sidedness of treason trials: The Treason Act of 1696 was the ground-breaking law that changed this ugly precedent: "In permitting accused traitors to call sworn witnesses, the Act seemingly abandoned the ancient aversion to conflicts in oaths and marked the beginning of the end of medieval trial procedure." George Fisher, "The Jury's Rise as Lie Detector," *Yale Law J.* 107 (1997), 575–713.

p. 54, MPs calling out for Mary's head: MacCaffrey, op. cit., 428–34.

p. 54, Norfolk's address: Paul Johnson, *Elizabeth I* (New York: Holt, Rinehart & Winston, 1974), 187.

p. 54, De Vere's committee seat in Parliament: CLARK, 273.

p. 54, Norfolk's three Sons and *As You Like It*: John W. Draper, "*As You Like It* and 'Belted Will' Howard" *Review of English Studies* 12:48 (Oct. 1936), 440–44.

p. 55, De Vere "... too negligent of friends' causes: Williams, op. cit., 230; on a related note, NELSON (80) reprints Norfolk's instructions to his son Philip Howard: "I hope when I am gone nature will so work in them [*my kinsmen*] that they will be in good will to you, as heretofore they have been to me. Amongst whom I will begin as high as I unworthy dare presume, with my cousin Oxford."

p. 55, ... none-too-subtly Catholic tradition of the Order of the Garter: The Order of the Garter began under Elizabeth's reign emphasizing its Catholic trappings. (Roy Strong *The Cult of Elizabeth* [Berkeley: University of California Press, 1977], 165–7, 185) However, "By the close of [Elizabeth's] reign this old Catholic order was made to represent something different, a band of fiercely Protestant knights bound in unison to defeat the dragon of St. George, now reidentified as the pope, the Beast of the Apocalypse."(165)

p. 55, ... the Catholic St. George: "St. George" in *The Catholic Encyclopedia*, vol. 6 (New York: Robert Appleton Co., 1909).

p. 55, Queen admitted Viscount Hereford to O.G.: Hereford had recently distinguished himself as a military leader in quelling the Northern Rebellion. De Vere had performed no such service for the state. Peter R. Moore, "Oxford, the Order of the Garter, and Shame," *Shakespeare Oxford Newsletter* 32:2 (Spring 1996), 1, 8–11.

p. 55, De Vere, pictured in a contemporary engraving of the O.G. ceremony: Marcus Gheeraedts the Elder's engraving of the Garter Procession dates from 1576. The most proximate Garter Procession to this date was in May 1575, when de Vere was in Italy. It may, then, naturally be objected that de Vere is not depicted in this engraving. However, the engraving is also a tableau of nearly two dozen individuals who were never in the same room together in their lives, let alone in a single procession of the Order of the Garter. As Roy Strong notes, the engraving "is typically Elizabethan in its total indifference to the unities of time and space. The procession is selective: officials who should be there are omitted, foreign Knights who would not have been there are inserted, train- and canopy-bearers surrounding the queen are dispensed with." (Op. cit., 172.) The fact that "a nobleman" (whom Strong does not identify) is indeed depicted carrying the sword of state before Elizabeth–de Vere's ceremonial duty as Lord Great Chamberlain of England–strongly suggests that Gheeraedts had indeed included de Vere in this picture. The arched eyebrows and pursed-lip expression of the sword bearer also resemble the extant portraits of de Vere. (Burris, op. cit.) Finally, the cartouche below the unidentified sword-bearer's picture reads (as translated into English by Arthur M. Hind): "This place is always supplied by a nobleman being not of the order of the garter, to carry the sword." (Hind, *Engraving in England in the Sixteenth and Seventeenth Centuries: Part I, The Tudor Period* [Cambridge: Cambridge University Press, 1952], 111.) Gheeraedts' son would later paint a portrait of de Vere.

p. 55, ... where the exclusive club held their meetings: *The Merry Wives of Windsor* memorializes the author's participation in the final the Order of the Garter installation ceremony at Windsor Castle. In *Merry Wives,* 5.5.56–71, the bawdy hostess, MISTRESS QUICKLY, transforms herself into the "Faerie Queen," who then instructs her pages to

> Search Windsor Castle, elves, within and out;
> Strew good luck, ouphs, on every sacred room...

And nightly, meadow faeries, look you sing,
Like to the Garter's compass, in a ring:
Th'expressure that it bears, green let it be,
More fertile fresh than all the field to see;
And *Honi soit qui mal y pense* write
In em'rald tufts, flowers purple, blue, and white.

Honi soit qui mal y pense ("Evil be to him who evil thinks") is the motto of the Order of the Garter. QUICKLY's speech here instructs her servants to prepare the castle for a Garter knighthood installation. After 1572, Garter installations were no longer held at Windsor. (Raymond B. Waddington, "Elizabeth I and the Order of the Garter," *Sixteenth Century J.* 24:1 [1993], 107–8.)

p. 55, . . . stripped away from him when his father had died: Craig Huston, "Edward de Vere," *Shakespearean Authorship Review* 19 (Spring 1968), 2–3, and "Correspondence" 20 (Autumn 1968), 18–19.

p. 55, Priory at Earls Colne: Murdin's *Burghley State Papers*, 788, cited in Gwynneth Bowen, "What Happened at Hedingham and Earls Colne?" *Shakespearean Authorship Review* 24 (Spring 1971), 9; the Earls Colne Priory has a long and complicated history both in and out of de Vere's hands: Daphne Pearson, "Robin Hood's Pennyworth: The De Vere–Harlackenden Lawsuits," *The Elizabethan Review* 7:1 (Spring 1999), 4–32.

p. 56, *Hamlet* expressing anxiety over inheritance: *Hamlet* 5.2.394–5, cited by J. Anthony Barton, "An Unrecognized Theme in *Hamlet*," *The Shakespeare Newsletter* 50:3, No. 246 (Fall 2000), 76.

p. 56, On Burghley as "elder statesman": READ/*BURGHLEY*, 85.

p. 56, Smith's lament to Burghley: cited in READ/*BURGHLEY*, 102.

p. 56, Elizabeth's progress into Warwickshire: NELSON, 84: During July, de Vere had lodged–along with Rutland, Leicester, Hatton, Burghley, and other members of the court– at Burghley's mansion, Theobalds, during the queen's visit there. She'd also visited Havering-atte-Bower, a former family estate that de Vere would later be filing petitions to have returned to his portfolio. King James I would ultimately grant Havering (at least in part) to de Vere on July 18, 1603. Even then, however, Havering remained property of the crown, as part of Queen Anne's dower. (Christopher Paul, private communication, [June 2004].)

p. 56, Elizabeth's speech to Warwick town recorder: NICHOLS 1:315–6.

p. 56, Inadvertent glimpse into Elizabeth's psyche: Mary Thomas Crane, " 'Video et Taceo': Elizabeth I and the Rhetoric of Counsel," *Studies in English Literature, 1500–1900* 28:1 (Winter 1988), 6.

p. 57, Elizabeth on Mary Stuart's height: *The Memoirs of Sir James Melville of Halhill, 1535–1617*, ed. A. Francis Steuart (London: George Routledge & Sons, 1929), 95–7.

p. 57, Elizabeth memorialized as CLEOPATRA: On initial similarities between Elizabeth and CLEOPATRA: Keith Rinehart, "Shakespeare's Cleopatra and England's Elizabeth," *SH.Q* 23:1 (Winter 1972), 81–6; on the complexity of the character: Dolora G. Cunningham, "The Characterization of Shakespeare's Cleopatra," *SH.Q* 6:1 (Winter 1955), 9–17.

p. 57, *Antony and Cleopatra*, 3.3.11–18; cited in Rinehart, op. cit., 81–3.

p. 57, De Vere and Fulke Greville's mock combat: Greville is not named as such, but his role is inferred from the fact that he is listed as the other noble who rescued the family from the flaming house at the end of the night; since he was also Sidney's close friend, and Sidney and de Vere were rivals at court, it further stands to reason that Greville would have taken the opposing side in the mock combats. Sidney himself was in Paris at the time, a visit sadly timed for the courtier to witness sixteenth-century Europe's most notorious slaughter–about which, more momentarily.

p. 57, Pyrotechnical combat amazed Elizabeth: NICHOLS, 1:319–20.

p. 58, *Hamlet,* 5.2.243–4.

p. 58, Fatalities from the mock combat: WARD (71) and OGBURN (*TMWS* 505) both conclude that de Vere and Greville managed to save the couple ("with difficulty rescued") in the first house that caught fire. The chronicle of the evening, however, suggests that the couple died: "It happened that a ball of fire fell on a house at the end of the bridge, wherein one Henry Cowper, otherwise called Myller, dwelled, and set fire on the same house, the man and wife being both in bed and in sleep, which burned so, as before any rescue could be, the house and all things in it utterly perished, with much ado to save the man and woman." (NICHOLS, 1:320) The chronicler does say that all "things" in the house had perished in the fire, without specifying what happened to the residents. But, *pace* WARD and OGBURN, the chronicler leaves only a little room to doubt that the people in the first house did not survive. The chronicler's emphasis is on the valiant effort to save the couple and not the actual saving of the couple.

p. 58, De Vere's St. Bartholomew's Day Massacre letter: Harleian MSS 6991.5, as reprinted and delineated into verse form in OGBURN/*TMWS,* 506.

p. 59, Burghley's thankless jobs: SMITH/*ET,* 77.

p. 59, "... dwell where you have taken pain to build": De Vere to Burghley, September 22, 1572; Lansdowne MSS 14.84, reprinted in FOWLER 97.

p. 60, De Vere's intent to set "forth to sea": Ibid.

p. 60, ... de Vere would have been a lodestone for trouble: Some independent researchers, such as W. Ron Hess, have speculated that de Vere spent much of his adult life in the foreign service—in a cloak-and-dagger spy network that infiltrated Catholic, Spanish, and other anti-English alliances across Europe. W. Ron Hess, *The Dark Side of Shakespeare: An Iron-Fisted Romantic in England's Most Perilous Times,* 3 vols. (New York: Writers Club Press, 2003).

p. 60, Description of Wivenhoe: *A Glimpse into Wivenhoe's Past,* cited in Barbara Westerfield, "A Light on Wivenhoe," *Shakespeare Oxford Newsletter* 23:3 (Summer 1987), 3–4; also, according to the *Victoria History of the County of Essex* (Vol. X: *Lexden Hundred,* ed. Janet Cooper [Oxford: Oxford University Press, 2001]), "the manor house, Wivenhoe Hall, built just northwest of the church circa 1530, had a tower gateway used as a sea mark in the sixteenth century."

p. 60, Charges laid out in memorandum by Burghley: CP, xiv, pp. 19–20 (179/134), reprinted in NELSON 81.

p. 61, De Vere's Oct. 31, 1572, letter: Lansdowne MSS 14.85, reprinted in FOWLER 107.

CHAPTER FOUR

p. 62, On the Savoy: The Savoy would, in the nineteenth century, be transformed into a theater, the first building lit by electricity, wherein Gilbert and Sullivan premiered many of their operettas. It is now a luxury hotel.

p. 62, ... two or more servants working for him: In 1573, de Vere remitted £10 11s 8d for "part rent of two tenements within the hospital." W. J. Loftie, *Memorials of the Savoy* (London: Macmillan & Co., 1878), 125; cited in WARD, 84.

p. 62, On Twyne & Bedingfield: G. K. Hunter (*John Lyly: The Humanist as Courtier* [London: Routledge & Kegan Paul, 1962], 46–7) notes that de Vere would later rent one apartment in the Savoy for his secretary John Lyly up to and perhaps including the year 1578; Robert Detobel (private communication [July 2004]).

p. 62, Twyne's Poetry: Conrad H. Rawski, tr., *Petrarch: Four Dialogues for Scholars* (Cleveland: Press of Western Reserve University, 1967), 15; less praiseful is the *DNB,* which states in its entry for Twyne that "he inclines to dullness both in prose and verse."

p. 62, *Breviary of Britain:* Twyne's *A Breviary of Britain* introduced the term *British Empire* into the language. David Armitage, "Making the Empire British: Scotland in the Atlantic World, 1542–1707," *Past and Present* 155 (May 1997), 40–1.

p. 62, Twyne's dedication to de Vere: CHILJAN, 25.

p. 63, ... hack named Batfillus: PRICE, 55–6; Mark K. Anderson, "The Upstart Crow's Other Plumage," *Shakespeare Oxford Newsletter,* 36:4 (Winter 2001), 20–21, 28.

p. 63, Virgil's poem: "The Lyfe of Virgill" in *The Whole XII Bookes of the Æeneidos of Virgill,* tr. Thomas Phaer and Thomas Twyne (London: Wyllyam How, 1573), B3ᵛ.

pp. 63–4, De Vere's *Cardanus's Comfort* poem: "The Earle of Oxenforde To the Reader" in *Cardanus's Comfort* (1573), cited—with discussion of de Vere's biblical allusions, especially those underlined in his 1570 Geneva Bible—in Roger Stritmatter, "The Biblical Origin of Edward de Vere's Dedicatory Poem in Cardan's *Comforte,*" *The Oxfordian* 1 (1998), 53–61; 56.

p. 64, Cardano as "gambling scholar": Playing the games of chance and beating them at any cost is an ongoing theme of *Hamlet.* As the Danish prince himself says, "I'll win at the odds." The one explicit game of chance in the play, the duel between HAMLET and LAERTES, is laid out with mathematical precision—perhaps in homage to Cardano. As the court lackey OSRIC spells out the terms of the swordfight:

"The KING, sir, hath laid, sir, that in a dozen passes between yourself and him, LAERTES shall not exceed you three hits. He hath laid on twelve for nine."

For LAERTES to win the contest, in other words, he must score three hits in a row within the first dozen passes. The odds the KING lays, "twelve for nine," translate to 9 out of $(12+9)$ or $9/21$, which in decimals is 0.4286. In fact, using modern statistics, the actual odds—presuming HAMLET and LAERTES are swordsmen of equal skill—turn out to be $1815/4096$, or 0.4431. The odds THE KING lays down are only 3 percent off the rigorous, mathematical value. Not bad for an age before most of the tools of statistics had even been invented! (Evert Sprinchorn, "The Odds on HAMLET," *The American Statistician* 24:5 (Dec. 1970), 14–7.)

De Vere had evidently studied his Cardano. Although talk of odds can be found in much Elizabethan literature, only *Hamlet* and a pamphlet written by the Elizabethan author Robert Greene use the science of probability with any mathematical accuracy. (D. R. Bellhouse and J. Franklin, "The Language of Chance," *The International Statistical Review* 65:1 [April 1997].)

p. 64, Cardano's response to a con artist: From Cardan's *Autobiography,* cited in Ore, op. cit., 129.

p. 64, *Cardanus's Comfort* (1573), quoted in Charles Wisner Barrell, "The Playwright Earl Publishes 'Hamlet's Book,'" *Shakespeare Fellowship Quarterly* 7:3 (July 1946), 40.

p. 65, Baldessar Castiglione, *The Book of The Courtier,* tr. Charles S. Singleton (New York: Anchor Books, 1959), 70.

p. 65, Drayton quote: Michael Drayton, *Poly-Olbion* (1613), cited in Steven W. May, *Henry Stanford's Anthology* (New York: Garland Publishing, Inc., 1988), v–vi.

p. 65, De Vere's preface to *Cardanus's Comfort:* "To my louinge frende Thomas Bedingfeld Esquyer, one of her Maiesties gentlemen Pentioners" in *Cardanus's Comfort* (1573); Gwynneth Bowen ("Oxford's Letter to Bedingfield and 'Shake-speare's Sonnets,'" *Shakespearean Authorship Review* 17 [Spring 1967], 6–12) plumbs the Shake-spearean dimensions of de Vere's letter, citing striking parallels between de Vere's language and the language of the Shake-speare Sonnets 1, 5, 9, 52, 54, and 147.

p. 65, ... the court as if it were a theater and the theater as if it were a court: As Wayne A. Rebhorn (*Courtly Performances: Masking and Festivity in Castiglione's* Book of the Courtier [Detroit: Wayne State University Press, 1978], 23) notes, the quintessential courtier in Castiglione's eyes is essentially "a performer who produces beautiful spectacles continually for an appreciative audience. In this view, the court becomes a great theater; an individual's actions, really acting; and the ideal courtier, the star of stars."

p. 65, De Vere gave Byrd an estate: "About the year 1573 or 1574, the earl of Oxenford made a lease for 31 years of the manor of Battylshall in the County of Essex to W. Byrde one of the gent. of her Maties Chapple to take place at the death of Aubreay Veare Esquire [Edward de Vere's uncle] or at the death of his Lawful wife," *PRO Dom. Eliz.* 157.26, reprinted in Edmund H. Fellowes, *William Byrd* (London: Oxford University Press, 1948), 3; *All's Well That Ends Well,* 3.2.8–9.

p. 66, ... recklessness and wild abandon: When de Vere was out of the country, in 1575, his men were still up to no good. The Italian fencer Rocco Bonetti–who, as will be seen in a coming chapter, makes a cameo appearance in *Romeo and Juliet*–twice petitioned the queen for "protection against 'the people of the earl of Oxford.'" Bonetti ultimately took refuge in Scotland for a period until the unruly servants had simmered their tempers down to a rolling boil. Jay P. Anglin, "The Schools of Defense in Elizabethan England," *Renaissance Quarterly* 37:3 (Winter 1984), 409.

p. 66, Byrd defrauded out of estate: Fellowes, op. cit., 3–6.

p. 66, Another of de Vere's servants a murderer: NELSON, 89–92; Arthur Golding published an account of the murder, a factual recitation that offered "a plain declaration of the whole matter." *A Brief Discourse on the Late Murder of Master George Saunders* (1573) was Golding at his most Puritanical and sanctimonious. Golding urges the reader not to succumb to excessive curiosity or vindictiveness in the story of this homicide. Instead, he calmly recounts the events and concludes by unfolding the scaffold speeches of the condemned. These tales, Golding notes, should lead the reader to "use the example to the amendment of [his] life." (*A briefe discourse of the late murther of master George Saunders...* London (1573), STC 11985, cited in Leanore Lieblein, "The Context of Murder in English Domestic Plays, 1590–1610," *Studies in English Literature 1500–1900* 23:2 [Spring 1983], 186–7.)

Seven years later, de Vere's secretary Anthony Munday would amend the record for his employer, who was then under new storm clouds of controversy. Munday dedicated *A View of Sundry Examples Reporting Many Strange Murders [and] Sundry Persons Perjured...* (1580) to two of de Vere's more prosperous servants and signed his own preface, "A. Munday, servant to the right honorable the earl of Oxenford." [Anthony Munday, *A VIEW of sundry Examples. Reporting many straunge murthers, sundry persons peruired, Signes and tokens of Gods anger towards vs...* (1580), reprinted in *John a Kent and John a Cumber,* ed. J. Payne Colier, [London: Shakespeare Society, 1851], 79–80; ibid.] Tales of the Saunders murder would continue to live on as the primary source for the anonymous play *A Warning for Fair Women* (1599).

p. 66, Three of de Vere's servants highwaymen: Maurice Dennis, aka "Deny the Frenchman," may reappear in de Vere's biography in 1584, when one "John Soothern" dedicates the book *Pandora* to de Vere. Charles Wisner Barrell ("Who Was 'John Soothern'?" *Shakespeare Fellowship Newsletter* 4:6 [October 1943], 71–5) makes a plausible case that Dennis was indeed the mysterious "Soothern."

p. 66, Plea of Burghley's servants: S. P. Dom. Eliz. 91.36, reprinted in B. M. Ward, "*The Famous Victories of Henry V*: Its Place in Elizabethan Dramatic Literature," *The Review of English Studies* 4:15 (July 1928), 285–6.

p. 66, Kent robbery scene in *1 Henry IV*: The "Gad's Hill" robbery scene of *1 Henry IV* also takes place in the anonymous Elizabethan play *The Famous Victories of Henry V,* which, as will be seen in Chapter 8, was almost certainly written by de Vere–perhaps in collaboration with one or more of his secretaries. Stories of the historical Prince Hal's escapades include tales of robberies he committed too. (Cf. *The First English Life of King Henry the Fifth written in 1513 by an anonymous author...,* ed. Charles Lethbridge Kingsford

[Oxford: Clarendon Press, 1911], xiv–xv, xxix, 17, 19.) De Vere just embellished upon these tales with his own servants' dissolute prank that took place on the road between Gravesend and Rochester.

p. 66, FALSTAFF quote: *1 Henry IV* 2.1.21–8; for those so inclined–a "Vere" pun-alert sounds with these lines.

p. 67, Gilbert Talbot letter: The letter also contained court gossip about the earl of Leicester's flirtations with the queen and other women at court. "All these love matters" that Burghley winked at concerned both de Vere and Leicester. Talbot Papers, Vol. F, fol. 79, no. 74. Gilbert Talbot to the earl of Shrewsbury, May 11, 1573, in Edmund Lodge, *Il-lustrations of British History . . .*, Vol. 2 (London: John Chidley, 1838), 16–21; Christopher Paul, private communication (August 2004).

p. 67, Anne's alleged £15,000 dowry: If Burghley had paid £15,000 to de Vere from the Lord Treasurer's own meticulously detailed accounts, one may reasonably assume that record of such an enormous transaction would have survived.

p. 67, Burghley's negotiations with Spain: England had four years previously given os-tensible safe haven to a convoy of Spanish ships filled with gold–after which Elizabeth conveniently returned the pay ships to their owners emptied of their treasure. In essence, the queen had found a Spanish wallet and returned it to Spain without the cash. Naturally, this angered Spain nearly to the point of declaring war, and in 1572–73 the onus fell upon Burghley to renegotiate friendly economic relations with King Philip II. Burghley was thus thrust into a delicate situation, seeking favorable trade with a rich nation while still main-taining a firm stance against a Catholic enemy. And in Burghley, Spain sought someone who could tiptoe through this minefield while still keeping Spain's best interests at heart.

p. 67, Spain had learned about dowry debt: A memo by Burghley from 1576 (NEL-SON, 148) notes that de Vere's marriage "hath cost the Lord Tresorer from the begynning above v or vj M powndes [=£5000–6000]." Of course, technically, the Spanish dowry–if it did indeed come through–didn't cost Burghley a penny. In any event, the murky details behind the Spanish dowry arrangement and Burghley's role therein will require more re-search.

p. 67, ". . . if his colleagues knew that he was getting a gratuity . . .": Antonio de Guaras to the duke of Alva, May 1, 1573, reprinted in *Relations Politiques des Pays-Bas et de L'Angle-terre sous le Règne de Philippe II,* ed. Le Baron Kervyn de Lettenhove, 8 vols. (Brussels: F. Hayez, 1888), 721–4; KITTLE/*GASCOIGNE,* 53; Mark K. Anderson and (Roy Wright) Tekas-tiaks, "Burghley's Bribe; De Vere's Dower?" *Shakespeare Matters* 3:1 (Fall 2003), 25–7.

p. 68, 40,000 escudos: According to Arthur Dimock and Ro. Cecyll ("The Conspiracy of Dr. Lopez," *The English Historical Review* 9:35 [July 1894], 450–1, fn. 15), in 1593 "50,000 crowns or gold escudos [is] worth £18,800." This conversion rate yields the rela-tion 40,000 escudos = £ 15,040.

p. 68, . . . the leering love-broker PANDARUS: Shake-speare's *Troilus and Cressida* would appear to offer up reminiscences of de Vere's surreal days of royal affection. (To this tale of royal love's labor lost, de Vere would also graft on a separate vignette about the wars in the Lowlands circa 1585–a vignette discussed in Chapter 7.) The sardonic tragicomedy of *Troilus and Cressida* presents the most debased and unflinching sex scene staged in all of Shake-speare's plays. The scene (Act 4, Scene 2) is played out by the same strange triad–TROILUS, his changeable love CRESSIDA, and the broker who winketh at their every dal-liance, her leering uncle PANDARUS. Although the basic story of this trio comes down from Homer, Boccaccio, and Chaucer, the context in Shake-speare is clearly Elizabethan. In the words of one nineteenth-century German critic, "We see from the portraits of CRESSIDA, PANDARUS . . . that the intention is not to satirize Greek antiquity, but the evils of the day under the cloak of an old Greek saga." The Stratfordian biographer Frank Harris recog-nizes in CRESSIDA the same woman who served as the prototype for CLEOPATRA. And as Stratfordian critic Keith Rinehart points out, "[Queen] Elizabeth may well have been used as the living model for Shakespeare's splendid portrait of CLEOPATRA." (Augustus E. Ralli, quoting Hermann Freiherr von Friesen [*Altengland und Wm. Sh.*, 1874], *A History of Shakespearean Criticism, Vol. 1.* [Oxford: Oxford University Press, 1932], 556; Frank Harris, *The Man Shakespeare and His Tragic Life-Story* [London: Frank Palmer, 1911], 302, cited in OGBURN/*TMWS*, 519; Keith Rinehart, "Shakespeare's Cleopatra and England's Elizabeth," *SH.Q* 23:1 [Winter 1972], 81.)

p. 69, Elizabeth's pet names for Hatton: Eric St. John Brooks, *Sir Christopher Hatton: Queen Elizabeth's Favorite* (London: Jonathan Cape, 1946), 99–100; Brooks notes (100) that the earliest known use of "Sheep" as a nickname for Hatton was in 1579.

p. 69, Dyer to Hatton: Harleian MSS, 787, f. 88, reprinted in Nicolas, op. cit., 17–19; Nicolas footnotes "my Lord of Ctm." with the line "Query Oxford?"

p. 69, De Vere's role in *A Hundred Sundry Flowers*: B. M. Ward presented a flawed but valiant first attempt at piecing together the *A Hundred Sundry Flowers* puzzle in his 1926 edition of the text ([*London*: Etchells & Macdonald, 1926]; reprinted by Ruth Loyd Miller, ed. [Jennings, La.: Minos Publishing Co., 1975]) and a subsequent article ("Further Research on *A Hundred Sundry Flowers,*" *RES* 4:13 [January 1928], 35–48). Ward's argument, unfortunately, featured an acrostic supposedly "keyed in" to one of the poems that contained the name "Edward de Vere." This acrostic, when taken apart by more careful hands (Fredson Thayer Bowers, "Gascoigne and the Oxford Cipher," *MLN* 52:3 [March 1937], 183–6), allowed the veritable baby to be thrown out with the bathwater all too easily.

After a back-and-forth with W. W. Greg in *The Library* (Greg, op. cit.; letters, *The Library* 8 [1927], 123–30), the state of affairs was such that W. M. Pigman III could state in his recent edition of *Flowers* (Oxford: Clarendon Press, 2000), xlv) that Ward's "speculations" had been "disposed of." However, the most convincing evidence for de Vere's participation in *Flowers* in some manner remains the extensive biographical connections between de Vere, Gascoigne, Christopher Hatton, George Turberville, and the pseudonymous editors and authors of both editions of *Flowers*–as discussed in Miller (op. cit., 35–108) and OGBURN (*TMWS*, 508–18).

p. 69, Hatton's posy: Harvey's handwritten marginal note in his copy of *The Posies of George Gascoigne* (1575), cited in G. C. Moore Smith, *Gabriel Harvey's Marginalia* (Stratford-upon-Avon: Shakespeare Head Press, 1913), 166; Ward/Miller, *A Hundred Sundry Flowers*, op. cit., 17.

p. 69, Adventures of "F. I." could be seen as about Hatton: Brooks, op. cit., 104–110; Ward/Miller, *Flowers*, op. cit.; In 1577, a student of the common law named John Grange published a rebuttal to *A Hundred Sundry Flowers/The Posies of George Gascoigne*. This text tells of a love affair between "Sir N.O." and a mistress "A.O." The tales of Grange's *Golden Aphroditis*, while not perfect parallels, are certainly suggestive of the tribulations of "[Ned] Oxenford" and "Anne Oxenford" in the 1570s. Robert S. Knapp ("Love Allegory in John Grange's *Golden Aphroditis*," *English Literary Renaissance* 8:3 [Autumn 1978], 256–70) discusses the text, albeit without ever recognizing the potential parallels to de Vere and his wife.

p. 70, Lane on de Vere: Hatfield MSS CP 2/68, reprinted in FELDMAN/*AMENDMENTS*, 57, discussed in KITTLE/*GASCOIGNE*, 56–57.

p. 70, De Vere's "suit": NICHOLS, 1:388–9.

p. 70, Fénelon's report on de Vere: M. de Swevengehm et Jean de Boisschot à Requesens, July 6, 1574, reprinted in *Relations Politiques...*, op. cit., 7:204; Le Mothe Fenelon to Catherine de Medici, July 8, 1574, reprinted in *Recueil des Dépêches, Rapports, Instructions, et Mémoires des Ambassadeurs de France en Angleterre et en Écosse Pendant le XVIe Siècle*, ed. Charles Purton Cooper (Paris, 1840), 6:177; cited by KITTLE/*GASCOIGNE*, 61; translations by Mark Anderson.

p. 71, De Vere in Low Countries: Cal. S.P. Dom. Add. Edward Woodshaw to Lord Burghley, September 3, 1574, reprinted in WARD, 94.

p. 71, Burghley letter to Sussex: Cal. S.P. Foreign, Sir Thomas Smith to Lord Burghley, July 13, 1574, reprinted in KITTLE/*GASCOIGNE*, 62.; Cal. S.P. Foreign, Henry Killigrew to Sir Thomas Walsingham, July 18, 1574, reprinted in WARD, 93; Cotton MSS, Titus B.2.298, Lord Burghley to the earl of Sussex, July 15, 1574, reprinted in WARD, 94.

p. 71, Mildmay's report: Sir Walter Mildmay, July 27, 1574, cited in Thomas Wright, *Queen Elizabeth and Her Times* (London: H. Colburn, 1838), 507, WARD, 94.

p. 71, Fénelon's dispatch re de Vere's return: La Mothe Fénelon to Catherine, de Medici, August 3, 1574, *Recueil des Dépêches*, op. cit., 6:204.

pp. 71-2, Burghley's letter to Walsingham: S.P. Dom. 98.2, Lord Burghley to Sir Thomas Walsingham, August 3, 1574, reprinted in WARD, 95–6.

p. 72, Anonymous report on de Vere: Unknown (Walsingham?) August 7, 1574, Cal. S.P. Dom. 98.5, reprinted in WARD, 97.

p. 72, De Vere at Theobalds garden party: Hatfield MSS 8.144, cited in WARD, 97.

p. 72, Lady Lennox's MS and *Macbeth:* The MS, *Buik of Croniclis of Scotland* by William Stewart was first reprinted in 1858 (ed. William B. Turnbull [London: Longman, Brown, Green, Longmans and Roberts]). The other putative source for *Macbeth* was Holinshed's *Chronicles*. As C. C. Stopes notes, "In every case in which Stewart differs from Holinshed, Shakespeare follows Stewart!" ("The Scottish and English Macbeth," in *Shakespeare's Industry* [London: G. Bell and Sons, 1916], 102); Richard Whalen, "Shakespeare in Scotland: What did the author of *Macbeth* know and when did he know it?" *The Oxfordian* 6 (2003), 55–70; Lilian Winstanley, *Macbeth, King Lear, and Contemporary History* (New York: Octagon Books, 1970; 1922 first ed.); Arthur Melville Clark, *Murder Under Trust: The Topical Macbeth* (Edinburgh: Scottish Academic Press, 1981).

p. 73, Anne's letter: Colchester MSS, 150 (undated; Ward concludes from the placement of the letter that it dates from 1574 and, since the queen lodged at Hampton Court on October 1, almost certainly from the fall of that year), reprinted in MILLER/LOONEY, 1:488; WARD, 97–98.

p. 73, De Vere's protestations: Lansdowne MSS 19.83, reprinted in WARD, 114.

p. 73, Letter from Mary, Queen of Scots: Undated letter from Mary Stuart to Queen Elizabeth, reprinted and tr. in Frederick Chamberlin, *The Private Character of Queen Elizabeth* (New York: Dodd, Mead & Co., 1922), 167.

p. 73, Smith's "water" for Anne: STRYPE, 160.

p. 73, George Baker book dedicated to Edward and Anne: George Baker *Oleum Magistrale* (1574; STC 1209), *The Newe Jewel of Health* (1576; STC 11798), discussed in Gustav Ungerer, "George Baker: Translator of Aparico de Zubia's Pamphlet on the 'Oleum Magistrale,'" *Medical History* 30 (1986), 203–11.

p. 73, John Hester book to de Vere: Leonardo Fioravanti, *A Short Discourse . . . Upon Surgery*, tr. John Hester (1580); On Hester: Harry B. Weiss, "Thomas Moffett, Elizabethan Physician and Entomologist," *The Scientific Monthly* 24:6 (June 1927), 561; Paul H. Kocher, "The Idea of God in Elizabethan Medicine," *J. Hist. Ideas* 11:1 (January 1950), 14; On Fioravanti–and his influence on *Hamlet:* Gordon W. O'Brien, "*Hamlet* IV.iv.26–29," *SH.Q.* 20:1 (Winter 1969), 89–90.

pp. 73-4, On Paracelsians: "[Paracelsus was] the Luther of medicine, the very incarnation of the spirit of revolt. At a period when authority was paramount and men blindly followed old leaders, when to stray from the beaten track in any field of knowledge was a damnable heresy, [Paracelsus] stood out boldly for independent study and the right of private judgment." William Osler, *The Evolution of Modern Medicine* (New Haven, Conn.: Yale University Press, 1921), 135.

p. 74, Paracelsianism in *All's Well That Ends Well*: De Vere must have relished the irony of setting a play about a monarch who cannot be healed at the court of France: Since the ninth century, legend held that the oil French kings were anointed with gave them magical healing powers, allowing them to cure their own subjects of rare ailments and afflictions. David A. Powell, *"Le Sacre des Rois..."* (review), *The French Review* 61:6 (May 1988), 996.

p. 74, HELENA's cure: HELENA's medicine rids the KING of a fistula—a gaping wound that was commonplace for plague victims. It's probably no coincidence that the 1574 Paracelsian book that Baker dedicated to de Vere deals with curing this kind of ailment. (Richard K. Stensgaard, *"All's Well That Ends Well* and the Galenico-Paracelsian Controversy," *Renaissance Quarterly* 25:2 [Summer 1972], 173–88; Ungerer, op. cit., 210.)

p. 74, *All's Well*, 2.1.118–21; discussion in Stensgaard, op. cit., 182.

p. 74, De Vere's New Year's gift: NICHOLS, 1:412.

pp. 74-5, Why de Vere crossed the Channel: According to the seventeenth-century gossip John Aubrey, de Vere left the country out of his embarrassment at breaking wind in front of the queen. (John Aubrey, *Aubrey's Brief Lives*, ed. Oliver Lawson Dick [Ann Arbor: University of Michigan Press, 1957; first ed. 1949], 305.) Aubrey never let the facts get in the way of a colorful story; his biographical sketches of sixteenth- and seventeenth-century luminaries are today considered about as historically reliable as a supermarket tabloid.

p. 75, On Henri III's coronation: Richard Roe, private communication (2002); Urban T. Holmes Jr., "The Background and Sources of Remy Belleau's *Pierres Precieuses*," *PMLA* 61:3 (September 1946).

p. 75, On Venetian embassy: KITTLE/ *GASCOIGNE*, 69.

p. 75, Fénelon's dispatch re de Vere's departure: La Mothe Fénelon to Henri III, January 24, 1575, reprinted in *Recueil des Dépêches...*, op. cit., 6:360–1.

p. 75, De Vere's indenture: Essex Record Office D/DRg2/25, reprinted in NELSON, 119–20.

p. 75, £9,096: I here use the conversion rate given by the Economic History Services (eh.net) of $265 per Elizabethan pound in 1586.

p. 75, De Vere's departure date: Edward to Nathaniel Bacon, February 7, 1574/5, cited in NELSON, 121.

p. 75, Hopton and Lewyn joined de Vere's party: NELSON, 121.

p. 76, De Vere's landing in France: Richard Paul Roe, "The French Connection," presented at the Shakespeare Oxford Society annual meeting, October 17, 1992, Cleveland, Oh.

p. 76, Henri III, "Sa Majesté": Bonnie Bullough, Vern L. Bullough, *Cross Dressing, Sex, and Gender* (Philadelphia: University of Pennsylvania Press, 1993), 104; Kira Hall, Anna Livia, *Queerly Phrased: Language, Gender, and Sexuality* (Oxford: Oxford University Press, 1997), 140.

p. 76, De Vere and Amyot: Roe, "The French Connection," op. cit.

p. 76, *commedia dell'arte*: Like the word *Renaissance*, *commedia dell'arte* is a term that was invented long after the thing it describes first came into being. Secular Renaissance Italian comedy based on stock characters and wild situations was first called "commedia dell'arte" in 1750. Nevertheless, it is a useful and descriptive term that this book will retain. Richard Andrews, *Scripts and Scenarios: The Performance of Comedy in Renaissance Italy* (Cambridge: Cambridge University Press, 1993), 170.

p. 77, Henri III and the *commedia*: Ibid., 83.

p. 77, On Pantalone: John Robert Moore, "Pantaloon as SHYLOCK," *Boston Public Library Quarterly* 1 (1949), 33–42.

p. 77, Shake-speare and the *commedia*: On SHYLOCK, cf. Moore—with commentary on Pantalone's household (LORENZO, LAUNCELOT, JESSICA) at Richard Andrews, "Shakespeare, Molière, et la Commedia dell'Arte," tr. Catherine Richardson, in *La Commedia Dell'Arte, Le Théâtre Forain, et Les Spectacles de Plain Air En Europe: XVIe-XVIIIe Siècles*, ed. Irène Mamczarz (Paris: Klincksieck, 1998), 15–27.

p. 77, Dale's dispatch: Cal. SP Foreign, Valentine Dale to Sir Francis Walsingham, March 7, 1575, cited in KITTLE/ *GASCOIGNE*, 70.

p. 77, "device": OED "Device" definitions 1–5 (now obsolete); as an alternate reading of these words, B. M. Ward ("*The Famous Victories of Henry V:* Its Place in Elizabethan Dramatic Literature." *The Review of English Studies* 4:15 [July 1928], 270–94) and OGBURNS (*TSOE,* 83) think *device* meant "play" and suspect that Valentine Dale was commenting, perhaps, on de Vere's *Famous Victories of Henry V.*

p. 77, Elizabeth's protestations: Lansdowne MSS, 19.83, reprinted in WARD, 114.

p. 78, De Vere's letter from Paris: Hatfield MSS, 8.24, reprinted in FOWLER, 163–4.

p. 78, Ascham's itinerary: Walter Alexander Raleigh, *Some Authors: A Collection of Literary Essays* (Oxford: Clarendon Press, 1923), 61–2.

p. 79, Ascham on Sturmius: Roger Ascham, "*The Scholemaster*" (1570), in *Elizabethan Critical Essays,* ed. G. Gregory Smith (Oxford: Clarendon Press, 1904), 20.

p. 79, Letter to Sturmius: William Lewyn to Sturmius, September 8, 1576. (Lewyn was the same painter and de Vere retainer who would be usurping the estate in Essex that de Vere had willed to the composer William Byrd.) Zurich letters, second series (1845), reprinted in WARD, 105.

p. 79, De Vere's boast re Strasbourg: PRO S.P. 12.151.46 ff, 103–4 NELSON, 205; this is one of the problematic "Arundel Libels," dealt with further in Chapter 6.

p. 79, Ascham's philosophy of drama: Brian Vickers, "The Power of Eloquence and English Renaissance Literature" (review), *Modern Philology* 92:4 (May 1994), 511; Marvin Theodore Herrick, *The Poetics of Aristotle in England* (New Haven, Conn.: Yale University Press, 1930), 18.

pp. 79–80, De Vere's crossing of the Alps: I presume here that de Vere crossed the Alps at the St. Gotthard Pass: "The way usually taken by travelers coming down the Rhine valley into Italy ... No document has so far been found proving that he ever visited Munich, Bohemia, or crossed the Brenner Pass (the alternate route into Italy)." Noemi Magri, "No Errors in Shakespeare: Historical Truth and *The Two Gentlemen of Verona,*" in *Great Oxford* (Kent, UK: Parapress, Ltd., 2004), 66–78.

pp. 79–80, Shake-speare's Alpine vistas: *Midsummer Night's Dream,* 4.1.193, *Richard II,* 1.1.63–4, *Romeo and Juliet,* 3.5.9–10; as cited in OGBURN/*TMWS,* 543.

p. 80, De Vere's Italian itinerary: Edward de Vere's movements from his April/May 1575 arrival in Venice from Strasbourg to his March 1576 departure from Venice have been reconstructed in five discrete steps, beginning with the itinerary as laid out in NELSON, 121–57, and summarized at http://socrates.berkeley.edu/~ahnelson/ITALY/Itinerary .html (The books, records, and MS collections from which each step derives will be cited as each step is encountered in the main-body text.) **ONE (Arrival):** *St. Gotthard Pass, Lombardy Plain, Verona, Padua, Venice:* the most likely itinerary, given his expressed desire to avoid Milan; **TWO (The Grand Tour):** *Hiring a ship bound for the Aegean:* presumed, given de Vere's March 1575 letter expressing intent to "bestow two or three months to see Constantinople and some part of Greece," William Lewin's July 1575 letter (from Strasbourg) stating that he doesn't know if de Vere had *yet* left for Greece, de Vere's possession of the requisite letters of introduction for Greece and Constantinople (de Vere's March 1575 letter), his disappearance from Italian records between May and September; *Ragusa (Dubrovnik):* likely port of call for a Venetian ship in the Adriatic on its way into the Aegean; *Constantinople/Greece:* cf. above; *Sicily/Palermo:* likely Italian destination for ship traveling from Aegean; de Vere's presence in Palermo [n.d.] is recorded by Edmund Webbe (1591); *hiring a ship bound for Genoa:* presumed, de Vere unlikely to have traveled in Naples (Spain) or Papal States without proper papers; *Genoa:* Clemente Paretti's September 1575 letter; Benedetto Spinola's October 1575 letter; *Milan:* Benedetto Spinola's 1575 letter; *(Mantua?), Verona, Padua:* presumed; intervening cities between Milan and Venice; **THREE (Veneto and environs):** *Padua:* de Vere letter, November 1575; *Verona, Mantua:* presumed, readily accessible nearby cities requiring little to no extra paperwork to enter;

FOUR ("The Rest of Italy"): *Florence:* Pasquale Spinola's December 1575 letter; *Siena:* de Vere's January 1576 letter; FIVE (**Departure**): *Milan (outskirts):* Francis Peyto's March 1576 letter; *Rhône valley:* presumed, since (according to Benedetto Spinola's March 1576 letter) de Vere's baggage was waiting for him in Lyons.

p. 80, De Vere avoiding Milan: FOWLER, 163.

p. 80, ... avoid entering the city gates: Magri, op. cit.

p. 80, Water route from Milan: As Magri points out (13), in 1575 a journey from Milan to Verona was readily accomplished by an uninterrupted boat ride: from the Martesana Canal to the Adda River to the Po to the Castagnaro River (a tributary broken off from the Adige due to flooding) to the Adige.

p. 80, Flooding of Adige: Archivo di Stato, Verona, Archivo Commune, Processi B, 140, n. 702, cited in Magri.

p. 80, De Vere's journey preserved in Shake-speare: Magri, op. cit.; Such specific geographical details as "St. Gregory's Well"–referenced by PROTEUS at 4.2.81–are not in any known source text for *Two Gentlemen of Verona*. Moreover, the "Well" was torn down sometime after the plague of 1576. (18–19.)

p. 81, *Sensa* of May 11, 1575: Duke Alvise Moncenigo May 11, 1570–74 June 1577; D. S. Chambers, *The Imperial Age of Venice, 1380–1580* (London: Thames & Hudson, 1970), 208.

p. 81, ... inlaid with mother of pearl: Pál Kelemen, *El Greco Revisited* (New York: Macmillan, 1961), 49.

p. 81, "We espouse thee, O Sea...": Edward Muir, *Civic Ritual in Renaissance Venice* (Princeton, N.J.: Princeton University Press, 1981), 119–34.

p. 81, Venetian post-*Sensa* theatrical season: Ibid., 121.

p. 81, Venice's professional theatrical troupes: The first public theater in Venice, based on the Roman style, was built in 1565 by Vasa Palladio; the city's first troupes were the Gelosi (1568) and the Confidenti (1572); Anya Peterson Royce, "The Venetian Commedia: Actors and Masques in the Development of the Commedia dell'arte," *Theatre Survey* 27:1/2 (1986), 69–87.

p. 82, ... into the streets and piazzas: Many *commedia scenari* MSS date from the early seventeenth century. However, this does not mean that these *scenari* were not around in some form during de Vere's time in Venice. Robert Henke ("Pastoral as Tragicomic in Italian and Shakespearean Drama" in *The Italian World of English Renaissance Drama: Cultural Exchange and Intertextuality,* ed. Michele Marrapodi and A. J. Hoenselaars [London: Associated University Presses, 1998], 282) points out, for instance, that "as Ferdinando Neri argued in 1913, several commedia dell'arte pastoral scenarios dated between 1618 and 1622, but they surely represented a form of theater long in place, strikingly replicating characters, plot, and notorious neoclassical unities of *The Tempest.*" (*Scenari delle maschere in Arcadia* [S. Lapi: Città di Castello, 1913].)

p. 82, Il Capitano and FALSTAFF: *cf.* SHYLOCK note above; for a brief bibliography on Shake-speare and the *Commedia,* cf. fn. at Clubb, op. cit., 256–7.

p. 82, *Cymbeline* and the *commedia*: F. D. Hoeniger, "Two Notes on *Cymbeline,*" *SH.Q.* 8:1 (Winter 1957), 133.

p. 82, Other Shake-speare comedies and the *commedia*: Frances A. Yates, *A Study of Love's Labour's Lost* (Cambridge: Cambridge University Press, 1936); William C. Carroll, *The Great Feast of Language in* Love's Labor's Lost (Princeton, N.J.: Princeton University Press, 1976); O. J. Campbell, *"Love's Labor's Lost* Re-Studied" and *"The Two Gentlemen of Verona* and Italian Comedy," in *Studies in Shakespeare, Milton and Donne* (New York: Macmillan and Co., 1925); K. M. Lea, *Italian Popular Comedy: A Study in the Commedia dell'-Arte, 1560–1620 with Special Reference to the English Stage,* 2 vols. (New York: Russell & Russell, 1962; 1934 first ed.), 2:434.

p. 82, *Othello* and *The Tempest* and the commedia: Barbara Heliodora C. de Mendoça, "*Othello:* A Tragedy Built on a Comic Structure," in *Aspects of* Othello, ed. Kenneth Muir and Philip Edwards (Cambridge: Cambridge University Press, 1977); Henry David Gray, "The Sources of *The Tempest,*" *Modern Language Notes* 35:6 (June 1920), 321–30.

p. 82, Location of Venice's theaters: Vasa Palladio built the first public theater in 1565 at the Campo di Carità; the second public theater was constructed shortly thereafter in the Corte Micheiela at San Cassiano. Royce, op. cit., 73–4.

p. 82, Orazio Cuoco met de Vere at Santa Maria Formosa: Robert Detobel (private communication, August 2004) notes that from 1570 onward, one family worshiping at Venice's Santa Maria Formosa church was that of Gaspare Ribeiro–whom the historian Brian Pullan ("The Inquisition and the Jews of Venice: The Case of Gaspare Ribeiro, 1580–81," *Bull. of the John Rylands Lib.* 62 [1979–80], 207–31) calls "a curiously SHYLOCK-ian figure" who, though not Jewish, was a miserly merchant "of international scope," had gotten into trouble over a usurious loan of 3,000 ducats, and lost a daughter who converted to Catholicism upon marrying a northern Italian nobleman.

p. 82, De Vere and the "Church of the Greeks": "The Venetian Inquisition Inquiry Regarding Orazio Cuoco (1577)," tr. Noemi Magri, in *Great Oxford* (Kent, UK: Parapress, Ltd., 2004) 45–49.

p. 82, *Vicus Sagittarius:* Violet M. Jeffrey ("Shakespeare's Venice," *MLR* 27 [January 1932], 24–35) first drew the connection between *Othello's* "Sagittary" and Venice's Frezzeria. I am indebted to Noemi Magri for her research, assistance, and her study, shared via private communication (May 6, 2001), of *cinquecento* Venetian administrative documents attesting to the likelihood that the street Frezzeria would likely have been written in Latin in de Vere's lease–and thus would have been known to him by the Latinized form of the name.

p. 83, On *Il Gobbo:* Karl Elze, "The Supposed Travels of Shakespeare," in *Essays on Shakespeare* (London: Macmillan & Co., 1874), 281; James Morris, *The World of Venice* (New York: Pantheon Books, 1960), 220–1.

p. 83, Virginia Padoana: *Sir Stephen Powle of Court and Country: Memorabilia of a Government Agent for Queen Elizabeth I . . . ,* ed. Virginia F. Stern (Selinsgrove, Pa.: Susquehanna University Press, 1992), 83, cited–along with Venetian records proving Padoana's profession–in NELSON, 138–9. Nelson also points to a 1606 poem by Nathaniel Baxter, published in Philip Sidney's *Ourania* and dedicated to de Vere's daughter Susan, which Nelson cites as proof that de Vere caught a venereal disease in Venice. (137–8) However, both Frank M. Davis and Christopher Paul have definitively refuted Nelson's claim that "Hopping Helena" was a reference in any way to VD. Davis, " 'Her Warbling Sting'–Music, Not Malady: Refuting Alan Nelson's Thesis on Nathaniel Baxter's 1606 Poem," *Shakespeare Oxford Newsletter* (Summer 2001), 3–4; Paul, "Oxford, HAMLET, and the Pirates: The Naked Truth," *The Shakespeare Oxford Newsletter* 40:1 (Winter 2004), 1–5.

p. 83, ". . . most elegant discourser": Tomas Coryat, *Crudities* (1611), reprinted in Cathy Santore, "Julia Lombardo, 'Somtusoa Meretrize': A Portrait by Property," *Renaissance Quarterly* 41:1 (Spring 1988), 50.

p. 83, . . . first syllable of their appelation: Albert Frederick Sproule ("A Time Scheme for *Othello*" *SH.Q* 7:2 [Spring 1956], 217–26) notices that *Othello,* too, preserves these entirely Venetian social and sexual distinctions in the character Bianca–listed as a "courtezan" in the earliest quartos of *Othello.*

p. 83, Veronica Franco: In the words of feminist historian Margaret F. Rosenthal, "[The courtesan's] search for male patronage resembles, in the most general sense, the self-prostitution of the male courtier as well: Just as for the courtier, verbal expertise was essential to a courtesan's social advancement." (Rosenthal, "Veronica Franco's *Terze Rime* [1575]: The Venetian Courtesan's Defense," *Renaissance Quarterly* 42:2 [Summer 1989],

234); cf. also Lynne Lawner, *Lives of the Courtesans: Portraits of the Renaissance* (New York: Rizzoli, 1987).

p. 83, on the Ghetto: The history of the Ghetto here recounted comes primarily from Umberto Fortis, *The Ghetto on the Lagoon,* revised ed., tr. Roberto Matteoda (Venice: Storti Edizioni, 1987).

p. 84, The Rialto: The Rialto is, of course, the backdrop against which SHYLOCK conducts his moneylending business, e.g., *Merchant of Venice,* 1.3.20, 39, 108; 3.1.1, 48; Jay L. Halio, *Understanding the Merchant of Venice* (Westport, Conn.: Greenwood Press, 2000), 29–31.

p. 84, Period of greatest tension in Ghetto: "The time of greatest tension, however, was during the 1570s, particularly after the Battle of Lepanto in 1571." Fortis, 53.

p. 84, The Battle of Lepanto: Fernand Braudel, *The Mediterranean and the Mediterranean World in the Age of Philip II,* tr. Siân Reynolds (New York: Harper Colophon, 1973; first ed. 1949), 2:1088.

p. 84, "For the death of the Turk": Horatio F. Brown, *Venice: An Historical Sketch of the Republic* (London: Rivington, Percival & Co., 1895), 369.

p. 84, Venetian Senate's 1571 motion: Reprinted in Benjamin Ravid, "The Socioeconomic Background of the Explusion and Readmission of the Venetian Jews, 1571–1573," in *Essays in Modern Jewish History: A Tribute to Ben Halpern,* ed. Frances Malino and Phyllis Cohen Albert (Rutherford, N.J.: Fairleigh Dickinson University Press, 1982), 42.

p. 84, *The Vale of Tears:* Ibid., 49–51.

p. 85, 1570s setting for both *Merchant of Venice* and *Othello:* Isaac Reed (*The plays of William Shakespeare in twenty one volumes,* ed. Samuel Johnson, George Steevens, Isaac Reed [London: J. Nichols & Son, 1813]) points out that "we learn from [*Othello*] that there was a junction of the Turkish fleet at Rhodes, in order for the invasion of Cyprus, that it first came sailing towards Cyprus, then went to Rhodes, there met another squadron and then resumed its way to Cyprus. These are real historical facts which happened when [the Turk] Mustapha, Selymus [II]'s general, attacked Cyprus in May 1570, which therefore is the true period of this performance." Cf. also "Of Arms and Beards: The Loss of Cyprus and the Myth of Venice" in David C. McPherson, *Shakespeare, Jonson, and the Myth of Venice.* (Newark, Del.: University of Delaware Press, 1990), 75–90. Emrys Jones ("*Othello,* 'Lepanto,' and the Cyprus Wars" *Shakespeare Survey* 21 [1968], 47–52) supposes that, since Will Shakspere of Stratford couldn't have been to Venice to learn firsthand about Lepanto and the military struggles leading up to it, he must therefore have read it in King James's poem "Lepanto." Why the Stratford Shakspere would care about any of this is, as with all Stratfordian scholarship, a whimsy as mysterious as his presumed genius.

p. 85, . . . letters of introduction to the Turkish court: It has been suggested (Richard Roe and Silvia Moretti, private communication [1991]) that perhaps Henri III gave de Vere letters of passage to Constantinople to enable de Vere to deliver letters to the French embassy there. However, this book only follows de Vere's hypothesized itinerary as far as Greece; it does not speculate about a trip to Constantinople–although such an addition to the itinerary hardly seems implausible, given de Vere's expressed wishes and the time and money he had at his disposal.

p. 85, Murad III's wife: Kelemen, op. cit., 51; Murad III ultimately sired, by numerous wives and concubines, at least 103 children. *Henry IV, Part 2,* tips its hat to the succession problem the sultan faced. (John W. Draper, "The Date of *Henry IV*?" in *Stratford to Dogberry: Studies in Shakespeare's Earlier Plays* [Pittsburgh: University of Pittsburgh Press, 1961], 166–7.)

p. 85, . . . if de Vere had left for Greece: William Lewyn letter to Burghley, Cal. S. P. Foreign, 1575–7, p. 80, quoted in WARD, 106.

p. 85, De Vere's injury in a galley: "... [H]is Lordship hurt his knee in one of the Venetian galleys, but all is past without further harm." Clemente Paretti to Lord Burghley, September 23, 1575, Hatfield MSS, 2.114, quoted in WARD, 106.

p. 85, Evidence consistent with Greek itinerary: A more tenuous but nevertheless suggestive connection comes in Gabriel Harvey's 1593 pamphlet *Pierce's Supererogation*. In it, as VAN DREUNEN argues (215–59; 404), Harvey praises de Vere as someone Harvey calls "Entelechy." (This nom de guerre joins several others that Harvey uses to describe his noble playwrighting colleague.) In the pamphlet, Harvey writes, "Nimble Entelechy hath been a stranger in some countries, albeit a renowned citizen of Greece and a free denizen of Italy, Spain, France, and Germany." (*The Works of Gabriel Harvey D.C.L.,* ed. Alexander Grosart, 3 vols. [Private printing, 1884], 2:105–6.) As for the "free denizen of ... Spain" claim, Harvey may be referring to de Vere's travels in the Spanish states of Naples and Milan—or he may be referring to another as-yet-undiscovered trip that de Vere took sometime before 1593.

p. 85, ... an exodus of Hellenes: Apostolos E. Vacalopoulos, *The Greek Nation, 1453–1669,* (tr. Ian and Phania Moles, New Brunswick, N.J.: Rutgers University Press, 1976), 49–52.

p. 86, ... should pirates make chase: *The Age of the Galley: Mediterranean Oared Vessels Since Pre-Classical Times,* ed. Robert Gardiner (London: Naval Institute Press, 1995), 123–4.

p. 86, Words of one Spanish traveler: The traveler was Cervantes. William Byron, *Cervantes: A Biography.* (New York: Paragon House Publishers, 1988), 116.

p. 86, *The Winter's Tale's* Bohemian seacoast: Rudolph II was crowned king of Bohemia in 1572 and king of Hungary in 1575. (He would the following year become Holy Roman Emperor.) Rudolph II ruled from Prague, the seat of Bohemia. At the time, the kingdom of Hungary extended to the Adriatic coast. *EB/*1911 "Rudolph II," 23:817; Eric Cochrane, *Italy 1530–1630* (London: Longman, 1988), xii–xiii; Jaroslav Krejcir, Ing. Stanislav Sojak, *Czech History: Chronological Survey,* Jan Mynarik, tr. (Dubicko, Czech Republic: Infoa, n.d.), 51–3; "The Golden Age of Padua," *Shakespearean Authorship Review* 11 (Spring 1964), 16–18. Critical brickbats over *The Winter's Tale* and its "seacoast of Bohemia" date back to the time of Ben Jonson (who was probably cracking a joke that subsequent generations of critics did not get: In the play, Bohemia metaphorically represents England, which, of course, has *plenty* of coastline). On the long history of "seacoast of Bohemia" criticism, cf. *The Winter's Tale, A New Variorum Edition,* ed. Horace Howard Furness (New York: J. B. Lippincott Co., 1898), 139–141 fn. 5; Derek Sayer, *The Coasts of Bohemia: A Czech History* (Princeton, N.J.: Princeton University Press, 1998), 5. (Thanks to Joe Eskola for assistance in researching this note.)

p. 86, Venice-Ragusa voyages: Trading vessels traveling from Dubrovnik paid the cheapest insurance rates available (2–3 percent) if they traveled to Venice–or to one of four other Italian ports on the other side of the Adriatic from Dubrovnik. F. W. Carter, "The Commerce of the Dubrovnik Republic," *The Economic History Review,* new series, 24:3 (August 1971), 391–2.

p. 87, Robert de Vere in Illyria: On the shipwreck: *DNB* entry for Richard I; Francis W. Carter, *Dubrovnik (Ragusa): A Classic City-State* (London: Seminar Press, 1972), 458. On the de Vere family's role: V. ANDERSON, 35.

p. 87, "Slavonic Athens": Carter, op. cit., 446–523.

p. 87, Beccadelli on Ragusa: Carter, op. cit., 500; J. Torbarina, "The Setting of Shakespeare's Plays," *Studia Romanica et Anglica Zagrabiensia* 17–18 (July–December 1964), 47–8.

p. 87, Croation scholarship on *Twelfth Night*: Rudolf Filipovic, "Shakespeareova Ilirija," *Filologija,* JAZiU, Zagreb, 1 (1957), 123–38, cited in Torbarina, op. cit., 31–54.

Other than the initial spadework above, published in Croatia, no scholars (that this biographer has found) have recognized or expanded upon the discovery of *Twelfth Night's* Ragusan setting. The prerequisite to date for setting *Twelfth Night* in Ragusa has been a willful suspension of disbelief: It would have been practically impossible for the untraveled and unlettered Shakspere of Stratford to know or, more to the point, care one whit about this obscure Adriatic city state.

Also, *Comedy of Errors*, 1.1.92–3 ("Two ships from far, making amain to us,/ Of Corinth that, of Epidaurus this") appears to reference a map of Ragusa; As R. A. Foakes points out, "It seems that Shakespeare ... knew some such map of the ancient world that ... shows another Epidaurus (later Ragusa, now Dubrovnik), north of Epidamnum on the Adriatic coast." (*The Comedy of Errors*, [The Arden Shakespeare], ed. R. A. Foakes [London: Methuen & Co., 1962], xxx–xxxi.)

p. 87, ... no real-world counterpart: John W. Draper, "Shakespeare's Illyria," *Review of English Studies* 17:68 (October 1941), 459–60.

p. 87, Torbarina, op. cit., 53; *Twelfth Night*, 4.1.48–9.

p. 88, "... nowhere world of romance: Clifford Leech, "Shakespeare's Tragic Fiction," *Proceedings of the British Academy* 59 (1973), 168; Michel Grivelet, "Racine's 'Dream of Passion,'" *Shakespeare 1971: Proceedings of the World Shakespeare Congress, Vancouver, August 1971* (Toronto: University of Toronto Press, 1971), 145.

p. 88, *Timon of Athens*, 4.3.122–3.

p. 88, The Oracle at Delphi: In 2001, geologists discovered a fault line running through the temple and, with it, the source of intoxicating natural gas that the Oracle's seer inhaled. Philip Ball, "Oracle's Secret Fault Found," *Nature* (July 17, 2001); J. Z. de Boer, J. R. Hale, and J. Chanton, "New Evidence of the Geological Origins of the Ancient Delphic Oracle," *Geology* 29 (2001), 707–10.

p. 88, *Winter's Tale's* satire: Roger Stritmatter, private communication (2003).

p. 88, ... the same forest: The only patch of "forests and uncultivable land" adjacent to Athens lies directly west of the city. Peter Levi, *Atlas of the Greek World* (New York: Facts on File, 1980), 12.

p. 89, ... lost its ... luster: The traveler "Dousa" quoted in Vacalopoulos, op. cit., 174.

p. 89, ... Oracle leads directly to Palermo: One tidbit suggesting that de Vere had in fact made it all the way to Constantinople in 1575 comes from Ben Jonson's play *Every Man Out of His Humor*. The de Vere-like character "Puntarvolo" notes that during a "year of jubilee" (1575 was a jubilee year) he is "determined to put forth some five thousand pound to be paid me five for one upon the return of myself, my wife, and my dog [*sic*] from the Turk's court in Constantinople." (Act 2, Scene 1)

p. 89, Record of de Vere's Palermo visit: In addition to the record cited below, WARD (275) points out that a ferry scene in John Lyly's play *Sappho and Phao* (1.1) references detailed and accurate local geography in Sicily. Lyly, however, had not been to Sicily; he could, however, readily have inserted all the Sicilian local color he would desire courtesy of his boss, the earl of Oxford.

p. 89, Ten days: Here we take Shake-speare's word for it: *The Winter's Tale* says the round trip from Palermo to Delphi was twenty-three days–further assuming one day spent in transit from ship to the Oracle, one day consulting the Oracle, and one day returning to the ship.

p. 89, ... maritime conveyor belt: Magri, op. cit. A few of the findings of Richard Roe, detailing the lack of errors in Shake-speare's detailed knowledge of Italy, are detailed in Mark K. Anderson, "Richard Roe on Shakespeare and Italy," *Shakespeare Matters* 1:4 (Summer 2002), 24–5, 28.

p. 89, Sicily's corruption: In historian Dennis Mack Smith's words, sixteenth-century Sicilians' "capacity for false witness and bribery was notorious. Not only were they uncouth and ill bred, but they concentrated selfishly on their own good without consideration for the common weal. They had not the slightest interest in other countries." (Smith, *A History of Sicily: Medieval Sicily, 800–1713*, 3 vols. [London: Chatto & Windus, 1968], 2:119.)

p. 89, Trapani: Mack Smith, op. cit., 2:140.

p. 89, Commentary on temple at Segesta: Keith Rutter, "Sicily and South Italy: The Background to Thucydides Books 6 and 7," *Greece and Rome,* second series, 33:2 (October 1986), 153–4; Tenney Frank, "Vergil's Res Romanae," *The Classical Quarterly* 14:3/4 (July–October 1920), 159; Margaret Guido, "Segesta" in *Sicily: An Archaeological Guide* (New York: Frederick A. Praeger, 1967), 64–72; the eclectic art critic Milton C. Nahm (*The Artist as Creator: An Essay of Human Freedom* [Baltimore: Johns Hopkins University Press, 1956]) places the temple at Segesta on a similar artistic footing with Beethoven and the *Mona Lisa.*

p. 89, Aeneas and Segesta: Modern archaeological studies, such as that conducted by Alison Burford ("Temple Building at Segesta" *Classical Quarterly,* n.s. 11:1 [May 1961], 87–93), naturally question the founding mythology of Segesta. F. C. Penrose ("On the Orientation of Certain Greek Temples...," *Philosophical Transactions of the Royal Society of London* 190 [1897], 63) points to astronomical evidence that Segesta was originally dedicated to Jupiter. However, a sixteenth-century visitor to Segesta would, of course, only have been privy to the myth.

p. 89, ... one of greatest monuments to Aeneas: William Flint Thrall, "Vergil's *Aeneid* and the Irish *Imrama:* Zimmer's Theory," *Modern Philology* 15:8 (December 1917), 85; C. M. Bowra, "Aeneas and the Stoic Ideal," *Greece and Rome* 3:7 (October 1933), 9.

p. 89, *Winter's Tale's* messengers stop at Segesta?: LEONTES, KING OF SICILY, sends MESSENGERS from his court at Palermo to the Oracle at Delphi. LEONTES's envoys ride away and out of the action of the play. Some twenty-three days later their ostensible return is announced. However, in the next scene (3.1), the two envoys appear onstage alone. They seek fresh horses, indicating that they're still in transit to Palermo. They say they don't like how the KING is mistreating the QUEEN–and suggest they want to do something about it. They also describe an unnamed temple. "The climate's delicate, the air most sweet," says one MESSENGER to the other. "Fertile the isle, the temple much surpassing the common praise it bears."

This scene fits awkwardly at best into the action of the play; it's often cut from modern productions of *The Winter's Tale.* Yet ... the temple the first messenger describes cannot be Delphi, since Delphi was not on any "isle," fertile or otherwise. On the other hand, Segesta stood near a posting station, where overland travelers from Trapani could indeed obtain fresh horses. (Richard Roe, private communication [2002]; Anderson, "Richard Roe, on Shakespeare and Italy," op. cit., 24–25. *Dorastus and Fawnia,* Robert Greene's putative "source" of *The Winter's Tale*–more likely Greene's novelization of an early version of de Vere's play–garbles this joke and treats Delphi as if it really were on an island.)

The author, in other words, is playing a sneaky gag. All but the most experienced Sicilian travelers will read the MESSENGERS' conversation as a throwaway description of the temple at Delphi. But the select few who are in on the joke will instead recognize the hanky-panky the servants are playing: They've either come to this *Sicilian* temple to tamper with the oracle they collected at Delphi or, perhaps, they've just been hanging out in Trapani for twenty-three days and never even left Sicily to begin with. *The Winter's Tale's* MESSENGER scene feeds into an undercurrent running throughout the Shake-speare canon that the author never fully satisfied his doubts over the paternity of his first child. Cf. William B. Bache (*Design and Closure in Shakespeare's Major Plays: The Nature of Recapitulation.* [New York: P. Lang, 1991], 348–49) for other reasons, within the play itself, to doubt the veracity of the Oracle.

p. 90, ... eyewitness testimony from Palermo: Edmund Webbe's sighting of de Vere in Palermo is recorded in a book Webbe published in 1590 (*Edward Webbe, Chief Master Gunner, His Trauailes*). Edward Arber's edition of Webbe's travelogue ([London: Alex Murray & Son, 1869], 4) can only narrow down Webbe's Palermo stop to sometime between 1571 and 1580. It has been pointed out (Richard Roe, private communication

[2002], citing S. Salmone-Marino, "La Congregazione dei Cavaliere d'Armi e le Pubbliche Giostre in Palermo nel Secolo XVI," *Nuove effemeridi Siciliane* 3:5 [1877], 136–7) that the only recorded tilt in Palermo during the period de Vere was known to be in Italy was on January 27, 1576. (There was also a tilt in honor of Don John of Austria on Feburary 12, 14, and 17, 1572–a tempting possibility, given the character of DON JOHN in *Much Ado About Nothing.*) However, it may fairly be pointed out in response (Noemi Magri, private communication [2003]) that Webbe says he only saw de Vere issue a *challenge* to meet anyone on the tiltyard–a challenge to which no one responded. It would be extremely unlikely, at an actual tilt, that such a challenge would go unmet. More likely, de Vere made this challenge at a time other than those recorded in *Nuove effemeridi Siciliane.*

This book hypothesizes that Webbe's account of de Vere concerns de Vere's grand tour during the summer and early autumn of 1575–and not during any subsequent travels through Italy. By January of 1576, the plague was epidemic in Palermo (Magri), so it's unlikely that de Vere would have visited the city during his other known excursion into southern Italy, in early 1576.

p. 90, ... worthily defended: Arber, *Webbe,* op. cit., 32.

p. 90, Miguel de Cervantes: Byron, op. cit., 179.

p. 90, Cervantes in Palermo: Byron, *Cervantes,* op. cit., 183–4.

p. 91, ... resented the *Vecchi's* monopoly of control: Robert W. Carden, *The City of Genoa* (London: Methuen, 1908), 57.

p. 91, Don John in Messina and Naples: Charles Petrie, *Don John of Austria* (London: Eyre & Spottiswoode, 1967), 246, 253–4.

p. 91, DON JOHN in *Much Ado About Nothing:* From here, the plot is all about de Vere in England later in his life; Messina and DON JOHN only provide the backdrop.

p. 91, Don John's force in Milan: William Stirling-Maxwell, *Don John of Austria,* 2 vols. (London: Longmans, Green & Co., 1883), 2:44. Stirling-Maxwell discounts the veracity of these rumors.

p. 91, Monetary advance de Vere took out in Naples: Benedetto Spinola to Lord Burghley, March 23, 1576: "I think [de Vere's] action strange in not having had a larger supply of money: Of the 1,800 scudi with which he provided himself at Naples and other places in Italy he is now taking only 800 and for the other 1,000 scudi he wants to have letters of exchange for Lyons." As translated from the Italian by G. Bowen in an Editor's Note to G. Lambin, "Shakespeare in Milan," *Shakespeare Fellowship News-Letter* (UK) (Autumn 1957), 5. Shake-speare's familiarity with Naples is hardly extensive–nothing like the author's intimate familiarity with Venice, for instance. Nonetheless, in *Othello* (3.1.4) the CLOWN observes correctly that Neapolitans "speak in the nose," suggesting at least that the author was familiar with the Naples accent.

p. 92, De Vere was in Genoa at the time ... : Clemente Paretti to Lord Burghley, September 23, 1575 (op. cit.; WARD, 106) "[M]y lord's ... now last coming Genoa ..."; Benedetto Spinola to Burghley, October 6, 1575 (*Cal. S.P. Dom.* 105.50, quoted in G. M. Bowen, "Oxford *Did* Go to Milan," *Shakespearean Authorship Review* 4 [Autumn 1960], 20–21) "I feel ... very sorry that, when [de Vere] stayed in Genoa at the time of those discords, he could not have been given all the attention and affection, which would have been extended to him by my brothers and relations, all of whom were away from Genoa."

p. 92, "... for his conduct another Caesar": This testimony (PRO SP 12/151[/145], ff. 100–2, LIBEL 4[1.2] & [1.3]) is part of the problematic "Arundell Libels" docket.

p. 92, De Vere nearly made Duke of Milan?: "[Y]f my Lord [Charles? Henry?] Howard had not in the Quenes name callid him a waye by letter, he [*de Vere*] had bin governer of Millayne [*Milan*]." NELSON, 205; As Milan was occupied by Spain at the time, the Spanish governor of Milan was given the courtesy title of "duke of Milan."

p. 92, ... no Milanese dukedom for this Englishman: NELSON, 205.

p. 92, De Vere loved to tell the story: Libel [1.2], op. cit.

p. 92, Prospero Fattinanti: Claudio Costantini, *La Repubblica di Genova* (Torino: UTET Libreria, 1986), 128–9, 137–8; I am indebted to Noemi Magri for the translation.

p. 93, De Vere and the beggar: This anecdote has been misprinted in *John Aubrey's Brief Lives,* cf. "Secret History of Edward Vere, Earl of Oxford" in Isaac Disraeli, *Curiosities of Literature* (New York: T. Crowell, 1881), 3:200–3. (NB: not all editions of Disraeli's *Curiosities* contain this "Secret History.")

p. 93, De Vere "greatest spendthrift tourist": STONE 701.

pp. 93–4, De Vere's Sept. 24, 1575 letter: De Vere to Lord Burghley September 24, 1575, Hatfield MSS CP 160/74–5; reprinted in FOWLER, 181–2.

CHAPTER FIVE

p. 95, Venetian textile industry and the plague: Brian Pullan, "Wage-Earners and the Venetian Economy, 1550–1630," *The Economic History Review,* n.s., 16:3 (1964), 409.

p. 95, Plague losses in Venice: O. J. Benedictow, "Morbidity in Historical Plague Epidemics," *Population Studies* 41:3 (November 1987), 424; John Martin, "Salvation and Society in Sixteenth Century Venice: Popular Evangelism in a Renaissance City," *The Journal of Modern History* 60:2 (June 1988), 232.

p. 95, "Lanterns of the dead": *Romeo and Juliet,* 5.3.83–4; As Michael Olmert points out, *Lanternes des Morts* could be found in graveyards in Italy as well as France, Germany, Austria, Switzerland, and parts of Eastern Europe. However, they were never imported into England. ("Tale of a Churchyard Sleuth," *Archaeology* 43:2 (March/April 1990), 80, cited in Linda B. McLatchie, "Could Shaksper Have Known of 'Lanternes des Morts'?" *Shakespeare Oxford Newsletter* 26:2 [Spring 1990], 2).

p. 95, Titian in 1575: E. Tietze-Conrat, "Titian's Workshop in His Late Years," *The Art Bulletin* 28:2 (June 1946), 76–88.

p. 95, Titian's late works: Frederick A. De Armas, "Lope de Vega and Titian," *Comparative Literature* 30:4 (Autumn 1978), 345.

p. 95, Titian's celebrity: Bruce Cole, *Titian and Venetian Painting, 1450–1590* (Boulder, Colo.: Westview Press, 1999), 215.

pp. 95–6, Soirée at Titian's: Letter written by Francesco Priscianese (1540), tr. and reprinted in J. Crowe and G. Cavalcaselle, *The Life and Times of Titian,* 2 vols. (London: J. Murray, 1881), 2:40.

p. 96, Contemporary remark on Titian: Giorgio Vasari, *Le vite de piu eccellenti pittor, scultori, e architettori, Gaetano Milanesi,* ed. G. C. Sansoni (Firenze, 1878), 7:450; cited and tr. in *Titian: Prince of Painters,* ed. Susanna Biadene (Munich: Prestel-Verlag, 1990), 101.

p. 96, Works in Titian's studio in 1575: Titian's *Death of Actaeon,* for instance, remained unfinished at the master's death in 1576, while his *Flaying of Marsyas* was also painted sometime during the artist's final few years. Cole, op. cit., 177, 192.

p. 96, Classical sources of *Venus and Adonis:* A. Lytton Sells, *The Italian Influence in English Poetry.* (London: George Allen & Unwin, Ltd., 1955), 191–2.

p. 96, "... paraphrase of Titian's composition": Erwin Panofsky, *Problems in Titian, Mostly Iconographic* (New York: New York University Press, (1969), 153; a history of criticism comparing Titian's and Shake-speare's *Venus and Adonis* can be found at John Doebler, "The Reluctant Adonis: Titian and Shakespeare," *SH. Q* 33:4 (Winter 1982), 486, fn. 9; sources Doebler overlooks include Lytton Sells, op. cit.; David Rosand, "Ut Pictor Poeta: Meaning in Titian's Poesie," *New Literary History* 3:3 (Spring 1972), 536–40; and S. Clark Hulse, "Shakespeare's Myth of Venus and Adonis," *PMLA* 93:1 (January 1978), 98–99.

p. 96, ADONIS's "bonnet": Noemi Magri ("The Influence of Italian Renaissance Art on Shakespeare's Works; Titian's Barberini Painting: The Pictoral Source of *Venus and Adonis,*" in *Great Oxford* [Kent, UK: Parapress., Ltd., 2004], 79–90) traces the only original *Venus and*

Adonis wherein Adonis wears a cap to the inventory of Titian's studio at the time of the artist's death (August 27, 1576). This *Venus and Adonis* now hangs at the National Gallery of Palazzo Barberini in Rome. (Later, inferior copies of *Venus and Adonis*, not by Titian, exist with a becapped Adonis—such as those now found in the collections of the Galleria dell'Accademia of Venice and at the Picture Library of Dulwich College, London. The only *Venus and Adonis* in England during the sixteenth century was Philip II's copy when he was Mary Tudor's husband. Philip brought his *Venus and Adonis* back to Spain with him after her 1558 death.)

    p. 96, Aretino and Shake-speare: Elmer Edgar Stoll (*Shakespeare Studies, Historical and Comparative in Method*. New York: Macmillan & Co., [1927], 274) compares Aretino's character Giudeo (from the 1526 play *Marescalo*) to SHYLOCK; John M. Lothian ("Shakespeare's Knowledge of Aretino's Plays," *MLR* 25 [1930], 415–24) points out parallels to *Two Gentlemen of Verona, Twelfth Night, Love's Labor's Lost, As You Like It, Much Ado, 1 Henry IV, Winter's Tale, All's Well, Julius Caesar, Henry V, Romeo and Juliet,* and *Venus and Adonis;* John M. Steadman, "Shakespeare's Sonnet 130 and Aretino's *Ragionamenti,*" *Notes & Queries,* n.s., 13:4 (April 1966), 134–5; C. C. Ruggerio, "La fama dell'Aretino in Inghilterra e alcuni suoi influssi su Shakespeare," *Rivista de Letterature Modern e Comparate* 29:3 (September 1976), 182–203.

    p. 97, Shake-speare and Romano: On Titian and Romano's friendship, cf. Cole, op. cit., 124; *Winter's Tale,* 5.2.106; *Love's Labor's Lost:* MILLER/HASP, 239–42; *Venus & Adonis/ Rape of Lucrece:* B. R. Saunders, "A Note on the Origin of *Venus and Adonis,*" *Shakespeare Fellowship News-Letter* (UK) (November 1945), 6; H. Amphlett, "Shakespeare and the Palazzo del Te," *Shakespeare Fellowship News-Letter* (UK) (Spring 1956), 2–3; Michael Delahoyde, "Edward de Vere's *Rape of Lucrece*" (presented at the Edward de Vere Studies Conference, Portland, Ore. April 13, 2003; unpublished MS.); Noemi Magri, "Italian Renaissance Art in Shakespeare: Giulio Romano and *The Winter's Tale*" in *Great Oxford* [Kent, U.K.: Parapress, Ltd., 2004] 50–65.

    p. 97, De Vere's letter from Padua: In December 11, though, he was back in Venice and preparing for a longer trip. Thus any trips the earl took in the late autumn would have stayed close to his Venetian home base.

    p. 97, Castiglione's monument: The statue is a three-dimensional rendering of the main subject of Raphael's legendary painting *The Transfiguration;* Romano was Raphael's student. Julia Cartwright, *The Perfect Courtier: Baldassare Castiglione, His Life and Letters, 1478–1529,* 2 vols. (New York: E. P. Dutton & Co., 1927), 2:426–31.

    p. 97, Inscription on tomb: Ibid., tr. Julia Cartwright.

    p. 97, On the duke of Mantua: Judith Dundas, "Mocking the Mind: The Role of Art in Shakespeare's *Rape of Lucrece,*" *Sixteenth Century Journal* 14:1 (Spring 1983), 16; if one day documentary proof can be adduced for de Vere's visit to Mantua, further treasures await in the city's Palazzo Te, where equine murals by Romano may have inspired similar images in *Venus and Adonis* and where a "giant dwarf" (referred to in *Love's Labor's Lost*) can be found in the Palazzo's "Hall of Giants." Dwyer, op. cit.; Magri, op. cit.; John Hamill, "The Ten Restless Ghosts of Mantua," *Shakespeare Oxford Newsletter* 39:3 (Summer 2003), 1, 12–16; Karl Elze, "The Supposed Travels of Shakespeare," *Essays on Shakespeare,* tr. L. Dora Schmitz (London: Macmillan & Co., 1874).

    p. 97, On the Gonzagas and the duke of Urbino: Giovanni Paccagnini and Maria Figlioli Paccagnini, *Palazzo Ducale of Mantua,* tr. Paul Blanchard (Milan: Edizioni Electa Spa, 1986; 1974 first ed.), 18–20.

    pp. 97–98, *Appartamento di Troia:* Renato Berzaghi, *The Palazzo Ducale in Mantua,* tr. David Stanton (Milan: Electa, 1992), 58; William Farina, private communication (August 18, 2003).

    pp. 97–98, *Lucrece* and the Appartamento: J. J. Dwyer, "Italian Art in the Poems and Plays of Shakespeare" (Colchester, UK: Benham & Co., Ltd., 1946); Delahoyde, op. cit.

p. 98, . . . set on the *Appartamento's* walls: "The problem remains obscure; but, basing ourselves only on established facts, we may be allowed to suppose that the passage in *Lucrece* which comprises 202 verses (vv. 1366-1568) was founded on Giulio Romano's pictures [in the Appartamento di Troia] and that Shakespeare took certain additional details from Virgil." Lytton Sells, op. cit., 194.

p. 98, "Make no stay of the sales of my land": Hatfield MSS, 2.122, reprinted in FOWLER, 196.

p. 98, University of Padua: H. Amphlett, "The Golden Age of Padua: Lecture by Miss G. Cimino," *Shakespearean Authorship Review* 11 (Spring 1964), 16-18.

p. 98, Ottonello Discalzio and BELLARIO. Hermann Sinsheimer, *Shylock: The History of a Character* (New York: B. Blom, 1963), 97; T. Elze, *Shakespeare Jahrbuch* 13 (1878), 149, cited in *The Merchant of Venice, New Variorum Edition*, ed. Horace Howard Furness (New York: Dover Publications, Inc., 1964; first ed. 1888), 458-9.

p. 99, *traghetto*: Violet M. Jeffery, "Shakespeare's Venice," *Modern Language Review* 27 (January 1932), 28-35.

p. 99, The location of Belmont: PORTIA "My coach . . . stays for us / At the park gate, and therefore haste away/ For we must measure twenty miles today"; "There is a monast'ry two miles off . . ." *Merchant of Venice*, 3.4.82-4, 24-32; Magri ("Belmont," op. cit., 7-8) points out that twenty miles must be the *round-trip* distance between Venice and Belmont—Portia travels to Venice *and back* during the day in question, and it would have been impossible for her to travel forty miles by coach and boat and conduct all the business PORTIA conducts in the play. Belmont must therefore have been ten miles from Venice.

p. 99, *Merchant of Venice*, 1.2.109-10.

p. 99, Marquis of Montferrat: *Magri,* "Belmont," op. cit.

p. 99, Byron and the Brenta: Lord Broughton, Lady Dorchester, *Recollections of a Long Life, Vol. 2* (London: John Murray, 1910), 77.

p. 99, De Vere's desire to see rest of Italy: Pasquale Spinola to Burghley, December 11, 1575; NELSON, 131.

pp. 99-100, Cinthio's *Hecatommithi*: *Othello's* source text is a real problem for Stratfordians. Cinthio's tale of "Disdemona" and her jealous husband is unmistakably Shakespeare's source. (BULLOUGH, 7:193-252.) But no known edition of this tale appeared in English until 1753; a French translation of the *Hecatommithi* was published in 1584. If Shakspere were the author, one has to suppose that either he somehow got a copy of this obscure foreign book and *furthermore* was competent enough in French or Italian to be able to read it. Or, "just possibly there was a contemporary English translation or adaptation which has disappeared." (*Othello* [The Arden Shakespeare], ed. M. R. Ridley [London: Methuen & Co., Ltd, 1958], xv.)

Giraldi Cinthio also adapted one of his *Hecatommithi* stories into a play, *Epitia* (circa 1573), which resembles *Measure for Measure* more closely than any other known source, as detailed in Madeleine Doran, *Endeavors of Art: A Study of Form in Elizabethan Drama* (Madison: University of Wisconsin Press, 1954), 385-9. (De Vere would not have had the opportunity to meet the actual Ferraran playwright, who had died in 1573.) *Epita* remained unpublished and unperformed until 1583—although it would have been available to de Vere in manuscript in 1575, either in Ferrara or in the courtly and literary circles the English earl frequented in Venice. (Mary Lascelles, *Shakespeare's Measure for Measure* [London: The Athlone Press, 1953], 13.)

p. 100, Florence in 1575: Bennett A. Cerf, Donald S. Klopfer, G. F. Young, *The Medici* (New York: Modern Library, 1933), 600-3.

p. 100, The Florentine CASSIO: John W. Draper, "Shakespeare and Florence and the Florentines," *Italica* 23:4 (December 1946), 287-93.

p. 100, . . . perfumes and sweet oils: *Much Ado*, 3.4.62-3; T. F. Thiselton Dyer, *Folk-*

Lore of Shakespeare (New York: Harper & Bros., 1884), 538; Grace M. Ziegler, "The Diurnal Use of Perfumes and Cosmetics," *The Scientific Monthly* 34:3 (March 1932), 236.

p. 100, "sweet gloves": *Much Ado*, 3.4.62.

p. 100, Jubilee of 1575: Cf. Rocho Masini's account of the 1575 pilgrimage to Rome, reprinted in *Gregory Martin: Roma Sancta (1581)*, ed. and tr. George Bruner Parks (Rome: Edizioni di Storia e Letteratura, 1969), 270.

p. 100, English exiles in Rome: Michael L. Carrafiello, "English Catholicism and the Jesuit Mission of 1580–1581," *Hist. Journal* 37:4 (December 1994), 765.

p. 100, Shrines to St. James the Great: Georges Lambin, *Voyages de Shakespeare en France et en Italie* (Geneva: Librairie E. Droz, 1962), 34, tr. Talmadge Gartley Wilson and W. Ron Hess, reprinted in Hess, *The Dark Side of Shakespeare* (Lincoln, Neb.: Writers Club Press, 2002); Colin Morris, *The Papal Monarchy: The Western Church from 1050 to 1250* (Oxford: Clarendon Press, 1989), 313.

p. 101, Pistoia and Prato's shrines: The nearby town of Altopascio was technically the overflow site; the "St. Jaques" shrines in Pistoia and Prato were the prominent holy sites nearby; Altopascio was also an overflow site for the 1600 Papal Jubilee; ibid.

p. 101, De Vere in Siena: It is tempting to suppose that de Vere had made it to Rome for Christmas. However, supposition is all there is at the moment.

pp. 101–2, De Vere's Siena letter: Hatfield MSS, 8/12–13, reprinted in FOWLER, 204.

p. 102, ... looking forward to a time when he would have an heir: Some have argued that de Vere had by 1576 already sired an illegitimate son by Queen Elizabeth–and that this child was ultimately raised to become the third earl of Southampton, to whom Shakespeare's *Venus and Adonis* and *Rape of Lucrece* are dedicated. (E.g. FOWLER; OGBURNS/TSOE; WHITTEMORE; Elisabeth Sears, *Shakespeare and the Tudor Rose* [Marshfield Hills, Mass.: Meadow Geese Press, 2002]; in response, cf. Christopher Paul, "The Prince Tudor Dilemma: Hip Thesis, Hypothesis, or Old Wives Tale?" *The Oxfordian* 5 (2002), 47–69, and citations therein). While the hypothesis might begin to explain the seemingly royal and dynastic language of the *Sonnets* and such scenes as *Midsummer Night's Dream's* KING and QUEEN OF THE FAERIES arguing over their "changeling child," the historical evidence is still wanting that would bolster the "Prince Tudor" theory of Southampton's parentage. Thus the "PT" issue, as it is often abbreviated, remains highly speculative and has been a source of bitter and divisive controversy throughout much of the history of the Oxfordian movement.

p. 102, *Hamlet*, 3.2.358.

p. 102, Theatrical scene in Siena: Eric Cochrane, *Italy, 1530–1630* (New York: Longman, 1988), 62.

p. 102, Piccolomini as "prince of comic writers":*The Plays and Poems of George Chapman*, ed. Thomas Marc Parrott (London: George Routledge & Sons, 1914), 732.

p. 102, ... detailing the proper education of a courtier: Piccolomini's *Courtier*-like book was entitled *De la Institutione di tutta la vita de l'homo nato nobile;* Jane A. Bernstein, *Music Printing in Renaissance Venice: The Scotto Press, 1539–1572* (Oxford: Oxford University Press, 1998), 23.

p. 102, Academy of Deaf and Daft: Richard Andrews, *Scripts and Scenarios: The Performance of Comedy in Renaissance Italy* (Cambridge: Cambridge University Press, 1993), 91–2.

p. 102, ... hiring actresses: Keir Elam, "The Fertile Eunuch: *Twelfth Night*, Early Modern Intercourse and the Fruits of Castration" *SH. Q* 47:1 (Spring 1996), 21.

p. 102, *The Deceived*: Piccolomini and other lesser authors of the Academy have variously been accredited with writing *Gl'Ingannati*. Jackson I. Cope, *Secret Sharers in Italian Comedy: From Machiavelli to Goldoni* (Durham, N.C.: Duke University Press, 1996), 49.

p. 102, ... on Twelfth Night: William Farina, "Twelfth Night in Siena," *Shakespeare Oxford Newsletter* 39:1 (Winter 2003), 5–6; BULLOUGH, 2:271.

p. 103, Also the plot of Shake-speare's *Twelfth Night*: On February 2, 1601/2, John Manningham, a student at London's Middle Temple, recorded his observation that "a play called *Twelve Night or What You Will*...[was] most like and neere to that in Italian called *Inganni* [*sic*]." (Diary *of John Manningham,* ed. John Bruce (February 2, 1601/2 entry) [Westminster: J. B. Nichols & Sons, 1868], 18.) This may be a mistake for "Ingannati" or it may be bona fide–there was a play by Nicolo Secchi of the name Manningham records, cf. sources cited below.

p. 103, Piccolomini and other Shake-speare plays: Peter Alexander, *Shakespeare's Life and Art* (London: J. Nisbet, 1939), 135–6; O. J. Campbell, "*The Two Gentlemen of Verona* and Italian Comedy," *Studies in Shakespeare, Milton and Donne* (New York: Macmillan & Co., 1925), 49–63; Hanna Scolnicov, "*Romeo and Juliet* and the Scenic Convention of the Piazza," *'Divers Toyes Mengled': Essays on Medieval and Renaissance Culture* (Tours: Université François Rabelais, 1996).

p. 103, Description of mosaic in Siena's cathedral: Samuel C. Chew, *The Pilgrimage of Life* (New Haven: Yale University Press, 1962), 150–1; Christopher Paul, "This Strange Eventful History: Oxford, Shakespeare, and the Seven Ages of Man," *The Shakespeare Oxford Newsletter* 38:3 (Summer 2002), 1, 12–15, 24.

pp. 103–4, JAQUES's "all the world's a stage" speech: Chew, op. cit.; Edgar I. Fripp, *Shakespeare, Man and Artist,* 2 vols. (London: H. Milford, 1938), 2:533–4; Paul (op. cit.) further points out that Geoffrey Fenton's *Golden Epistles* (1575)–dedicated to de Vere's wife, Anne–also discusses the ages of man "and whether there be five or seven of them."

p. 104, Venice's Carnival theatrical season: Anya Peterson Royce, "The Venetian Commedia: Actors and Masques in the Development of the Commedia dell'Arte," *Theatre Survey* 27:1/2 (1986), 70.

p. 104,...Carnival skits and masquerades: Ibid.

p. 104, "Elmond, milord of Oxford: Andrea Perrucci, *Dell'Arte Rappresentative Premeditata ed all'Improviso* (Naples, 1699), cited in Julia Cooley Altrocchi, "Edward de Vere and the *Commedia dell'Arte*," *Shakespearean Authorship Review* 2 (Autumn 1959), and NELSON, 140.

p. 104, Description of Naples *Commedia*: Reprinted and tr. in NELSON, 140; Nelson's attempts to distort the records of de Vere's Italian travels into a year-long cruise of sexual perversion and, in the present example, to construe this Neapolitan masque as a "Rabelasian characterization...of a sexual adventurer" are, as Nelson himself later writes about de Vere (258), "endued with a hypocrisy, a pettiness of mind, and a lack of mental control that reveal far more about the accuser than the accused."

p. 104, "horn of Astolf": J. I. Mombert, *A History of Charles the Great (Charlemagne)* (London: D. Appleton, 1888), 43.

p. 104, Anecdote unrevealing about de Vere in Italy: Noemi Magri, private communication (June 14, 2003).

p. 105, Peyto to Burghley: Francis Peyto to Lord Burghley, March 31, 1576, cited in "Editor's Note" to G. Lambin, "Shakespeare in Milan," *Shakespere Fellowship News-Letter* (UK) (Autumn 1957), 5.

p. 105, Few Milanese scenes suggestive of firsthand knowledge: The Milanese allusions make up a meager lot, however, compared to Shake-speare's allusions to Venice. As Sidney R. Homan writes, "Milan, as it is referred to in [*The Tempest*], has even less claim to reality than [PROSPERO's] island." "*The Tempest* and Shakespeare's Last Plays: The Aesthetic Dimensions," *SH.Q.* 24:1 (Winter 1973), 75.

p. 106, De Vere's jest about Queen Elizabeth's dress: PRO S.P. 12/15 ff. 103–4, cited in NELSON, 205.

p. 106, "Friar Patrick's Cell": The "Friar Patrick" allusion in *TGV* occasioned a lengthy debate in Oxfordian journals between 1957 and '61 between Georges Lambin (who believed William Stanley, earl of Derby, wrote Shake-speare) and Gwynneth Bowen. (*Shakespeare Fellowship News-Letter* [UK] [Autumn 1957], 5; [Spring 1958], 11; *Shakespearean*

Authorship Review 1 [Spring 1959], 8–11; 2 [Autumn 1959], 24; 3 [Spring 1960], 23; 4 [Autumn 1960], 20–1; 5 [Spring 1961], 9–11; 23; 6 [Autumn 1961], 24.) The upshot is that "Friar Patrick" O'Hely could not have visited Milan anytime before de Vere's return to England in April 1576. Unmentioned in this debate, however, is the fact that de Vere's private secretary Anthony Munday visited Milan in 1579 (Anthony Munday, *The English Roman Life,* op. cit., xv) and therefore was the likely conduit of this piece of Milanese geographical trivia to de Vere.

p. 106, DUKE of MILAN using honorific "Don": Noemi Magri, "No Errors in Shakespeare: Historical Truth and the *Two Gentlemen of Verona,*" *De Vere Society Newsletter* (UK) 2:12 (May 1998), 15–19.

p. 106, Leone Leoni's palazzo: James Fergusson, Robert Kerr, *History of the Modern Styles of Architecture, Vol. 1* (New York: Dodd, Mead & Co., 1891), 166.

p. 106, *Taming of the Shrew* Ind.2.54–6; **Allusion:** Lionel Cust, "Painting, Sculpture, and Engraving," in *SH. ENG.* 2:9; Dwyer, op. cit., 11; **Provenance:** Cecil Hilton Monk Gould, *The Paintings of Correggio* (Ithaca, N.Y.: Cornell University Press, 1976), 275. Spain's king Philip II is said to have given Leone Leoni the painting. Leoni's acquisition thus dates from sometime between 1556 (when Philip II was crowned) and 1584 (when *Io* was reported to be in Leoni's collection).

p. 106, "... such, for example, as Correggio's *Io*": Lytton Sells, op. cit., 192.

p. 106, De Vere probably in Mantua, Verona, and Messina: I have left out of the present book, but still consider likely, the possibility that de Vere also visited Pisa, Urbino, and Rome.

p. 107, Anthony Munday in Rome: Anthony Munday, *The English Roman Life,* ed. Philip J. Ayres (Oxford: Clarendon Press, 1980), xv.

p. 107, Shake-speare's allusions to Venice, Naples, Milan, etc.: H. F. Brown, *Studies in the History of Venice* (London: John Murray, 1907), 2:160.

p. 107, De Vere sent luggage to Lyon: WARD, 112; NELSON, 134.

p. 107, $1,300 in modern currency: Cf. note on £10 in Chapter 4.

p. 107, English traveler's account of Mt. Cenis: The traveler was the *voiturier* of the legendary Shake-spearean actor David Garrick. E. S. Bates, *Touring in 1600: A Study in the Development of Travel as a Means of Education* (Boston: Houghton Mifflin, 1912), 334; Carola Oman, *David Garrick* (London: Hodder and Stoughton, 1958), 233.

p. 108, Tournon-sur-Rhône in 1576: Juliette Thiébaud, *Tournon-sur-Rhône: A Feudal Town,* tr. Eliane Monteil (Tournon, France: privately published, n.d.).

p. 108, Visitors to Tournon: Lambin, *Voyages de Shakespeare,* op. cit., 30; Juliette Thiébaud, "La Fin des Tournon et de la Baronnie," in Albin Mazon, *Notes Historiques sur Tournon et Ses Seigneurs* (Dolmazon: Le Cheylard, 1993), 322.

p. 108, Châteaus Tournon and Roussillion: Interview with Juliette Thiébaud, tr. Catherine Dougados (28 August 1998).

p. 108, from province of Roussillion to Château Roussillion: Lambin, op. cit., 25–40; Boccaccio sets his country scenes in the southern French *province* of Roussillion; no such castle is mentioned. *All's Well* sets its country scenes at the Castle Roussillion; no such province is mentioned. Shake-speare's description of Roussillion is accurate–so long as he's describing the castle, not the French province of the same name. In Act 5 of *All's Well,* for instance, the audience learns that Roussillion is "four or five" overnight stops from the city of Marseilles–a fact that is true about the château but incorrect about the province.

p. 109, Eyewitness account of Hélène's funeral: Marguerite de Valois, *Les Mémoires de la Reine Marguerite* (Paris, 1628), 220–2, cited in Lambin, op. cit., 27; this 1628 report was the first known publication of Hélène de Tournon's story, appearing in French five years after the complete works of Shake-speare had been published.

p. 109, Inspiration for *Hamlet*?: Lambin, op. cit., 26–8; Thiébaud, op. cit., 320.

p. 109, Protestant strongholds in France: Richard S. Dunn, *The Age of Religious Wars: 1559–1715* (New York: W. W. Norton & Co., 1979; 1970 first ed.), 36.

p. 109, Casimir in Langres: James Westfall Thompson, *The Wars of Religion in France, 1559–1576* (Chicago: University of Chicago Press, 1909), 522.

p. 109, De Vere encountered Casimir: *Pace* NELSON (126), de Vere encountered Casimir with a substantial army of troops in the field–this was on de Vere's homeward journey in the spring of 1576 and *not* on his journey to Italy in the spring of 1575. The spring of 1576 is when Casimir did indeed command twenty thousand men in eastern France, ready to pounce on Henri III's forces. The fact that Chapman says the encounter took place in Germany takes a backseat to the historical reality of Casimir's military expeditions. (Note, too, that a plausible reading of the passage is that Chapman says *de Vere* was "coming from Italy.")

p. 109, Chapman's hero a stoic: Hardin Craig, "Political Theory in the Plays of George Chapman" in *Essays in Dramatic Literature* (Princeton, N.J.: Princeton University Press, 1935), 32; John Press, *The Chequer'd Shade: Reflections on Obscurity in Poetry* (London: Oxford University Press, 1958), 28.

pp. 109–10, Portrayal of Clermont: George Chapman, *The Revenge of Bussy D'Ambois*, 2.1.259; Curtis Brown Watson, *Shakespeare and the Renaissance Concept of Honor* (Princeton, N.J.: Princeton University Press, 1960), 174.

p. 110, Clermont's description of de Vere and Casimir: Chapman, op. cit., 3.1; Richard Whalen ("On Looking into Chapman's Oxford," *The Oxfordian* 5 [2002], 119–31) discusses these lines in light of Aristotle's conception of the "great-souled man."

p. 110, Casimir major player on world stage: Casimir had allied with princes such as William of Orange in disputes across the Continent. In March of 1576, Casimir commanded twenty thousand troops that forced Henri III to reconsider his backhanded treatment of the Huguenots. In a little more than a month, this German prince's troops would be crossing France to wreak havoc elsewhere. Thompson, op. cit., 521–3; Paul van Dyke, *Catherine de Medici* (New York: Scribner's, 1922), 199.

p. 111, ... FORTINBRAS's troops march in front of him: There are more parallels between *The Revenge of Bussy D'Ambois* and *Hamlet* than just this encounter between de Vere and Casimir. Chapman's play tells the tale of the ghost of a murdered kinsman and a protagonist delaying a deed of revenge. And Clermont's final soliloquy before he commits suicide is nearly a direct paraphrase of HAMLET's "To be or not to be." (*Hamlet*, ed. G. R. Hibbard [London: Oxford University Press, 1998], 16, 240 fn. 68; Elmer Edgar Stoll, *Art and Artifice in Shakespeare: A Study in Dramatic Contrast and Illusion* [Cambridge: Cambridge University Press, 1933], 116; CAMPBELL AND QUINN, 106.)

Note also that, as Peter R. Moore demonstrates ("*Hamlet* and Psalm 8," *Neophilologus* 82 [1998], 487–98), a paraphrase of Psalm 8 written by de Vere's uncle the earl of Surrey is also a primary source for this soliloquy.

p. 111, Moody E. Prior, "The Thought of HAMLET and the Modern Temper," *ELH* 15:4 (December 1948), 272; *Hamlet*, 4.4.53–6; n.b. HAMLET's "How all occasions do inform..." soliloquy does not appear in either the first edition (Q1, 1603) or the complete works (F1, 1623) edition of *Hamlet*. Paul Werstine, "The Textual Mystery of *Hamlet*," *SH.Q.* 39:1 (Spring 1988), 20–3.

p. 111, Alençon's forces surrounding Paris: Van Dyke, op. cit., 198.

p. 111, Dale letter to Walsingham: Cal. S.P. Foreign, 1575–77, 709, cited in NELSON, 135; Nelson does not, however, apparently appreciate (or at least provide any hint of) the extreme circumstances behind this letter or that "Monsieur"–the standard French title for the younger brother of the king–was Alençon.

p. 112, "... beautiful Italian items": PRO 31.3.27, ("Baschet Transcripts"), cited in NELSON, 137; Christopher Paul ("Oxford, HAMLET, and the Pirates: The Naked Truth," *The Shakespeare Oxford Newsletter* 40:1 [Winter 2004], 5, fn. 3) translates the original French *hardes* in this document as "items" according to the 1571 *Dictionarie French and English* (STC 6832), which states that *hardes* meant "stuff, implements."

p. 112, Burghley's April 1576 memo: Salisbury MS, 2.68, 83, 114, 131, cited in MILLER/LOONEY, 2:395; WARD (118) sees April 4 as the day a "bomb" exploded in de Vere's life. However, as Bronson Feldman notes, "Captain Ward was apparently overfond of bomb-shells. We have no evidence in the available records of any explosion of April 4, 1576.... Cecil alone is Ward's source for the 'sudden change' of April 4, and the old statesman's word is scarcely more reliable than Lord Harry Howard's." (FELDMAN/AMENDMENTS, 59.)

p. 112, When de Vere boarded his ship: De Vere's arrival at Dover was April 20: NELSON, 137.

p. 112, Diplomatic scuttlebutt surrounding de Vere's brush with pirates: NELSON, 135–7.

p. 112, Shake-speare's account of pirate encounter: *Hamlet,* 4.6.15–22.

p. 113, Neither pirate encounter nor FORTINBRAS episode in *Hamlet*'s sources: William Witherle Lawrence, "HAMLET's Sea-Voyage," *PMLA* 59:1 (March 1944), 45–70; Martin Stevens, "HAMLET and the Pirates: A Critical Consideration," *SH.Q.* 26:3 (Summer 1975), 276–84; Karl P. Wentersdorf, "HAMLET's Encounter With the Pirates," *SH.Q.* 34:4 (Winter 1983) 434–40; William Witherle Lawrence, "HAMLET and Fortinbras," *PMLA* 61:3 (September 1946), 673–98; Paul Werstine, op. cit., 20–3.

p. 113, De Vere "left naked": Mauvissière to Catherine de Medici, April 21, 1576, cited in NELSON, 137.

p. 113, *Hamlet,* 4.7.43–4; Christopher Paul, "Naked Truth" op. cit., 1–5.

p. 113, Punishments for the pirates: NELSON, 136–7.

p. 113, Baxter's account of pirate episode: Nathaniel Baxter, *Sir Philip Sidneys Ourania* (1606), STC 1598, sig. A3v; Paul, op. cit.

p. 114, De Vere's welcoming party: Salisbury MS, 2.131–2, cited in READ/*BURGHLEY*, 134.

p. 114, Burghley's memo re Yorke House: Salisbury MS, 2.131–2, cited in READ/*BURGHLEY*, 134.

p. 114, Burghley's plea to Elizabeth: 23 April 1576 letter to Queen Elizabeth, unsigned (but in Burghley's hand), reprinted in READ/*BURGHLEY*, 136.

pp. 114–15, Smith's letter to Burghley: BL Harley MS, 6992[/21], f. 41v, cited in NELSON, 145; Smith's and Burghley's April 1576 ailments discussed in STRYPE, 144 and DEWAR, 186.

p. 115, Baxter's lament: Baxter, op. cit., B3, reprinted in NELSON, 430.

p. 115, Yorke's rank: Julia Genster, "Lieutenancy, Standing in and *Othello,*" *ELH* 57:4 (Winter 1990), 785–809.

p. 115, Suggestive rhymes about Yorke: George Gascoigne, *Gascoigne's Voyage into Hollande* (1572), cited in MILLER/LOONEY, 2:396; C. T. Prouty, "Gascoigne in the Low Countries and the Publication of *A Hundreth Sundrie Flowres,*" *RES* 12:46 (April 1936), 141.

p. 115, "Foining with the rapier": William Camden, *The History of the Most Renowned and Victorious Princess Elizabeth* (London, 1675), reprinted in MILLER/LOONEY, 2:398.

p. 115, IAGO's brag: *Othello,* 1.2.5; A. Bronson Feldman, "*Othello* in Reality," *American Imago* 11 (1954), 168; Peter R. Moore points out (private communication [September 2004]) that IAGO's "yerk[ing]" maneuver would undoubtedly have been with a dagger, not with a longer blade (as in the case of Yorke) such as a rapier. Note, too, that IAGO's "yerk" puns on Rowland Yorke's surname.

p. 115, IAGO and St. James: Eric Griffin ("Un-Sainting James: Or, *Othello* and the 'Spanish Spirits' of Shakespeare's Globe," *Representations* 62 [Spring 1998], 68) points out that IAGO's compatriot's name, RODERIGO, was also that of Spain's epic hero, from *El Cid Campeador.*

p. 115, "dramatic in the extreme": Albert J. Loomie, *The Spanish Elizabethans: The English Exiles at the Court of Philip II* (New York: Fordham University Press, 1963), 138–40.

p. 116, Yorke's body gibbeted: *DNB* entry "Rowland Yorke (*d.* 1588)."

p. 116, Allegations against Leicester: This charge was published only in the French edition of *Leicester's Commonwealth* (1585) and did not appear in England until 1641. *Leicester's Commonwealth: The Copy of a Letter Written by a Master of Art of Cambridge (1584) and Related Documents*, ed. D. C. Peck (Athens, Oh.: Ohio University Press, 1985), 242–3; Feldman "*Othello,*" op. cit., 158.

p. 116, Historical sources for DON JOHN: Both Leicester and Anne Cecil died in the same year, 1588. In *Much Ado*, DON JOHN's flight from the play is coincident with the reported death of HERO, the play's Anne Cecil-like heroine. As Leicester was de Vere's catchall enemy for numerous offenses throughout his life, from the death of Earl John to the usurpation of the Vere family lands to the infection of his own mind against Anne, so DON JOHN "seems eager to claim even more culpability than he deserves. [DON PEDRO] drags him around on a leash, like a pet CALIBAN, so that DON JOHN may receive blame for the trouble which . . . is orchestrated by DON PEDRO's practices." Harry Berger Jr. "Against the Sink-a-Pace," *SH.Q.* 33:3 (Autumn 1982), 311.

pp. 116–7, De Vere's letter upon returning: Salisbury MS, 2.132, reprinted in FOWLER, 248–9.

p. 117, De Vere's charges against Lady Burghley: Salisbury MS, 13.128 (146/11), reprinted in NELSON, 146–7.

p. 118, Burghley on "good name": Salisbury MS, 2.144–5 (160/115), reprinted in NELSON, 147.

p. 118, *Othello,* 3.3.155–61.

pp. 118–9, Richard Master to Burghley: Technically, the letter itself has long been known, but the key passage has only recently come to light: Dr. Richard Master to Burghley, CSP Foreign, 1575–77, No. 368, in NELSON, 121–3; WARD (114) reprints part of this letter but *elides* the crucial portion in which Master speaks of Anne seeking an abortion. Nelson prints the passage but passes over Master's astonishing revelation without a word of commentary.

p. 119, ". . . whether he pass upon me and it or not": Ibid.

p. 119, Anne's request for abortifacient?: On the use of emmenagogues and abortifacients in the sixteenth century, cf. John M. Riddle, *Eve's Herbs: A History of Contraception and Abortion in the West* (Cambridge, Mass.: Harvard University Press, 1997), 126–66.

p. 119, "By cock they are to blame": 4.5.62.

p. 119 "friend look to 't": *Hamlet,* 2.2.181–6; Mark K. Anderson, "Ophelia's Difference, or, 'To catch the conscience of the counselor,'" *Shakespeare Oxford Newsletter* 35:4 (Winter 2000), 17–19, 24.

p. 120, On rue as abortifacient: Robert Painter, Brian Parker, "Ophelia's Flowers Again," *Notes & Queries* 41 (March 1994), 42–4; I would like to thank Christopher Paul for drawing my attention to this article.

p. 120, Symbolism of "rue with a difference": *Hamlet,* 4.5.181–3; Anderson, op. cit.

p. 120, *Cymbeline,* 2.4.155–6.

p. 120, rumors of de Vere's bisexuality: NELSON, 213–18.

p. 120, OTHELLO and IAGO's deadly dance with homosexual overtones: Feldman, "*Othello*" op. cit.; "Psychoanalytic Criticism: IAGO as Latent Homosexual," in Stanley Edgar Hyman, *IAGO: Some Approaches to the Illusion of His Motivation* (New York: Atheneum, 1970); Robert Rogers, "Endopsychic Drama in *Othello,*" *SH.Q.* 20:2 (Spring 1969), 212; Arthur L. Little Jr. "'An Essence That's Not Seen': The Primal Scene of Racism in *Othello,*" *SH.Q.* 44:3 (Autumn 1993), 316–20; Patricia Parker, "Fantasies of 'race' and 'gender': Africa, *Othello,* and Bringing to Light" in *Women, 'Race,' and Writing in the Early Modern Period,* ed. Margo Hendricks and Patricia Parker (New York: Routledge, 1994).

p. 120, "grounded upon untrue reports of others": Salisbury MS, 1.474, reprinted in WARD, 124–5.

p. 121, De Vere's July 13, 1576, letter: Salisbury MS, 9.15, reprinted in FOWLER, 266.

p. 121, *Hamlet,* 2.2.522–6.

p. 121, De Vere in *Paradise of Dainty Devices*: A sixteenth-century handwritten annotation in the Bodleian copy of the 1578 printing of *Paradise* (STC 12507) notes that one of "E.O."'s lyrics had been set to two separate musical scores. The annotation beneath E.O.'s "A Lover Rejected, Complaineth" reads "This song is twyse set."

p. 122, "... But I in vain do breathe my wind": Poem [78], ibid., 71; n.b., according to the *OED*, in archaic British pronunciation forms *wind* has a long *i*. (Tekastiaks, private communication [October 4, 2003].)

p. 123, Date of *Paradise of Dainty Devices*: "H.D."'s epistle "To the Right Honorable Syr Henry Compton" notes the collection was "penned by diuers learned Gentlemen, and col[lec]ted togeather through the treuell of one, both of woorship and credite [*Edwards*], for his priuate vse: who not long since departed this lyfe." *The Paradise of Dainty Devices (1576–1606)*, ed. Hyder Edward Rollins (Cambridge, Mass.: Harvard University Press, 1927).

p. 123, ... called simply The Theatre: The timbers from this building would be recycled in 1598 to build the Globe.

p. 123, Definition of "collier": *OED*, definition 3.

p. 124, Dramatic troupe de Vere enjoyed closest access to: Seven years hence, after Westcote's death, de Vere and his entourage would briefly take over Paul's Boys. One of de Vere's theatrical servants from the 1580s (Henry Evans) was also one of Westcote's closest friends. (Charles T. Prouty, *Studies in the Elizabethan Theatre* [Hamden, Conn.: Shoe String Press, 1961], 152.) Furthermore, Westcote was a notorious Catholic at a time when de Vere was also infamously flirting with Catholicism. (Harold Newcomb Hillebrand, "Sebastian Westcote, Dramatist and Master of the Children of Paul's," *J. Eng. and Ger. Philology* 14 [1915], 568–84; NELSON, 164–73.)

p. 124, *Comedy* and *Historie of Error(s)*: Allison Gaw, "The Evolution of *The Comedy of Errors,*" *PMLA* 41:3 (September 1926), 664.

p. 124, Special licence granted boys' troupes: M. P. Tilley, *A Dictionary of the Proverbs in England in the Sixteenth and Seventeenth Centuries* (Ann Arbor: University of Michigan Press, 1950), C-328; cf. John Lyly, *Endymion*, 4.2.101–2; John Marston, *Jack Drum's Entertainment*, 3.221; Edward Sharpham, *Cupid's Whirligig*, p. 32, ll. 32–33. Cited in Michael Shapiro, *Children of the Revels* (New York: Columbia University Press, 1977), 41, fn. 15.

p. 124, The "error" of the title: A. Bronson Feldman, "Shakespeare's Early Errors," *Int. J. of Psycho-analysis* 36:2 (April 1955), 116–17.

p. 124, "fond fool" of an impatient wife: ANTIPHOLUS OF EPHESUS becomes so put upon that he patronizes a courtesan when he's locked out of his own house–a dramatic confession of the Venetian courtesan that de Vere had hired while overseas.

p. 125, *Comedy of Errors* and the *commedia dell'arte*: K. M. Lea, *Italian Popular Comedy: A Study in the Commedia dell'Arte, 1560–1620, with Special Reference to the English Stage*, 2 vols. (New York: Russell & Russell, 1962; 1934 first ed.), 2:434.

p. 125, Translations of ADRIANA and LUCIANA: Feldman, op. cit., 119.

p. 125, Age of the brothers ANTIPHOLI: At least, this is one of ANTIPHOLUS's *two* ages. Careful scholars have long noted the bizarre discrepancy in *The Comedy of Errors* that elsewhere ANTIPHOLUS's age is said to be thirty-three. (CHAMBERS/*WS*, 1:309.) Once again, this should come as no surprise. In 1583 (when de Vere was thirty-three), *A History of Error* was performed a second time at court. [*] When compiling the play for publication in the 1590s or 1600s, de Vere or one of his compositors evidently overlooked the protagonist's multiple ages–a mixup that inadvertently reveals the play's multiple layers of composition.

[*]FEUILLERAT (350) transcribes the 1583 title as "A historie of fferrar." (Feuillerat and Chambers [*WS* 1:309] dispute any connection with *The Comedy of Errors;* Collier [1:240], Bullough [1:3], William J. Rolfe [*C of E* 1894, 14] and D. Nichol Smith [*18th C. Essays on Sh.,* 306] all recognize a possible thread connecting "fferrar" with Shake-speare's early

play.) "A historie of fferrar" was enacted on January 6, 1582/3. Three months later De Vere turned thirty-three. The 1583 performance of *Error/Fferrar* is also discussed in Chapter 7.

p. 125, De Vere's attempts to cauterize his own wounds: Feldman, op. cit., 121–2.

p. 125, NELL as Queen Elizabeth: Roger Stritmatter, private communication (1994).

p. 125, Portraying Elizabeth as England itself: Leah S. Marcus, *Puzzling Shakespeare: Local Reading and Its Discontents* (Berkeley: University of California Press, 1988), 64.

p. 125, On NELL: NELL resembles Shake-speare's later portrait of Elizabeth as the aggressive manhuntress VENUS. James Schiffer, in *Venus and Adonis: Critical Essays*, ed. Philip C. Kolin (New York: Garland Publishing, 1997), 7.

p. 125, *Comedy of Errors*, 3.2.108–44; the allusion to France suggests either an allusion to the Fifth Civil War of 1575 (HOLLAND/*OXFORD GLASSES*, 27) or the armed resistance to Henry of Navarre in 1589. An allusion, not quoted here, to Spain's "whole armadoes of carrects," suggests that this extended gag was polished up and perhaps added to sometime after the 1588 invasion of the Spanish Armada.

p. 126, Sources for *Two Gentlemen of Verona*: FEUILLERAT 270, 461; on the history of the Titus story, cf. Ralph M. Sargent, "Sir Thomas Elyot and the Integrity of *The Two Gentlement of Verona*," *PMLA* 65:6 (December 1950), 1171–3.

p. 126, *Two Gentlemen* and the *commedia*: On *Two Gentlemen*'s indebtedness to the *commedia*: John W. Draper, *Stratford to Dogberry: Studies in Shakespeare's Earlier Plays* (Pittsburgh: University of Pittsburgh Press, 1961), 15.

p. 126, Commentary on *Two Gentlemen*: *Two Gentlemen of Verona: An Annotated Bibliography*, ed. D'Orsay W. Pearson (New York: Garland Publishing, 1988).

p. 126, *Two Gentlemen of Verona*, 2.1.122–7.

p. 127, . . . as a lion on a feather bed: Sir Robert Naunton, *Fragmenta Regalia, or Observations on the late Queen Elizabeth, Her Times and Favourites*, ed. Edward Arber (Southgate, London: English Reprints, 1870), 37; C. H. Parry, *A Memoir of Peregrine Bertie, Eleventh Lord Willoughby de Eresby* (John Murray, London 1838), 303–4.

p. 127, Bertie's tiff with the earl of Kent: Curtis Brown Watson, *Shakespeare and the Renaissance Concept of Honor* (Princeton, N.J.: Princeton University Press, 1960), 86; John Strype, *Annals of the Reformation and Establishment of Religion and other Various Occurrences in the Church of England During Queen Elizabeth's Happy Reign* (Oxford: The Clarendon Press, 1824), 4:589.

p. 127, ". . . with a rapier in his teeth": Parry, 89.

p. 127, De Vere's initial nuptial plans for his sister: February 16, 1577, letter from Thomas Screven to the earl of Rutland; Rutland MSS, 1.115, reprinted in NELSON, 172.

pp. 127–8, ". . . and asked no more": Salisbury MSS, 13.146, reprinted in Goff, 310.

p. 128, Bertie to Mary: Ancaster MSS, 4, cited in Goff, 15; this letter is undated but, given the context, undoubtedly dates from the months of Mary's and Peregrine's courtship.

p. 128, De Vere at William Howard's Wedding: NELSON, 176; on Audley End: Zillah Dovey, *An Elizabethan Progress: The Queen's Journey into East Anglia, 1578* (Madison, N.J.: Fairleigh Dickinson University Press, 1996), 33.

p. 128, Howard boys and *As You Like It*: John W. Draper, "*As You Like It* and 'Belted Will' Howard," *RES* 12:48 (October 1936), 440–44.

p. 129, Marriage of Mary de Vere deferred: Cal. Rutland MSS, I. 115, reprinted in WARD, 153.

p. 129, Duchess's stratagem, told to Burghley: Goff, 312–4.

p. 129, On PAULINA: Stephen J. Lynch, *Shakespearean Intertextuality: Studies in Selected Sources and Plays* (Westport, Conn.: Greenwood Press, 1998), 97.

p. 129, . . . the same futile errand Peregrine Bertie's mother played: BREWSTER, 65–8.

p. 129, PAULINA quote: *WT* 2.3.116–121; Peter B. Erickson ("Patriarchal Structures in *The Winter's Tale*." *PMLA* 97:5 [October 1982], 821–3) points out that LEONTES almost goads PAULINA into performing a maternal role to him; like LEAR, LEONTES's outrageous egomania stems in no small part from a burning and unfulfilled need to be mothered.

p. 130, PAULINA "defies male authority": Carol Hansen, *Woman As Individual in English Renaissance Drama: A Defiance of the Masculine Code* (New York: Peter Lang, 1993), 114.

p. 130, Comet of 1577–78: The new celestial object inspired more than a hundred tracts across Europe, marveling at the heavens' fiery visitation. C. Doris Hellman, "A Bibliography of Tracts and Treatises on the Comet of 1577," *Isis* 22:1 (December 1934), 41–68.

p. 130, "new and horrible prodigy": Michael Maestlin, *Observatio et Demonstratio Cometae* (Tübingen, 1578); quoted and translated in Andrew Dickson White, *A History of the Warfare of Science with Theology in Christendom* (New York: D. Appleton and Co., 1928), 1:185.

p. 130, Date of Peregrine and Mary's wedding: WARD, 154.

p. 130, ... in homage to Peregrine's equally shrewish mother: Joan Hartwig ("The Tragicomic Perspective of *The Winter's Tale*" *ELH* 37:1 [March 1970] 13) even recognizes in PAULINA–Peregrine's mother's doppelgänger from *The Winter's Tale*–a hint of the "shrew" character type.

p. 130, "Some comet or unusual prodigy?": *Taming of the Shrew* 3.2.93–96; HOLLAND/OXFORD GLASSES 31. Holland further points out that the "wondrous monument" in this quote is probably the London Bridge's old stone tower on the north end, which in January 1578 was being torn down, making room for a new edifice that the surveyor John Stow called a "beautiful and chargeable piece of work." (John Stow, *The Survey of London*, ed. H. B. Wheatley [London and Melbourne: Everyman's Library, 1987; first ed., 1912], 56.)

p. 130, First recorded performance of *Shrew*: Here I join Eric Sams (*The Real Shakespeare* [New Haven, Conn.: Yale University Press, 1995], 136–45) in assigning the anonymous *Taming of A* [sic] *Shrew* (first published by Peter Short for Cuthbert Burby in 1594) to Shake-speare. Sams dates *A Shrew* to circa 1587.

p. 130, ... still fresh in everyone's minds: The probable debut of the first draft of *Shrew* came on New Year's Day of 1579, when Sebastian Westcote's Children of Paul's performed a play for the queen called *A Moral of the Marriage of Mind and Measure*. MILLER/HASP 102–109.

p. 130, "... trumpets' clang": *Shrew*, 1.2.204–5.

p. 130, "mother-wit": *Shrew*, 2.1.264.

p. 130, "against a million": *Shrew*, 3.2.238.

p. 130, "flatly what his mind is": *Shrew*, 1.2.76–77.

p. 130, "honest mean habiliments": *Shrew*, 4.3.170.

p. 130, 500 gallons of wine at Peregrine's wedding: Hatfield MSS, Cal. II. 205, shows that soon after the wedding, the duchess of Suffolk paid for two tuns of wine (one tun is 2 butts, 4 hogsheads, or 252 gallons) for Peregrine and Mary Bertie.

p. 131, ... with an iron fist: PETRUCHIO fires his tailor in a flurry of epithets, saying, "Away, thou rag, thou quantity, thou remnant, or I shall so bemeet thee with thy yard as thou shall think on prating whilst thou liv'st!" (4.3.111–13). Among Peregrine's papers at Grimsthorpe Castle, Lincolnshire, is a detailed list of regulations he drew up for his servants wherein he threatens that he will "not fail to extirpe and root out such bad members as otherwise might offend and infect the rest." (*Report on the Manuscripts of the Earl of Ancaster, preserved at Grimsthorpe* [Dublin: J. Falconer, 1907], 6–7.)

p. 131, "... the thing that feeds their fury": *Shrew*, 2.1.131.

p. 131, "[foreign] to full manners": Cecilie Goff, *A Woman of the Tudor Age* (London: John Murray, 1930), 315.

p. 131, "... beaten with the rod ... she prepared for others": Salisbury MSS., reprinted in Goff, 315.

p. 131, Mary proved a loyal wife: Goff, 317.

p. 131, ... a few years into their marriage: SIR TOBY BELCH marries the lady of the household, MARIA, during the action of the play, and thus it would seem to enact the period around 1578, when Peregrine and Mary wed. Yet, as presented in Chapter 12, the larger context of *Twelfth Night* concerns events of the early 1580s. As often happens in Shake-speare, time is out of joint in *Twelfth Night*–and the dramatist's main concern appears to be one of appropriateness to his text, not unfaltering chronological precision.

p. 131, "Bless you, fair shrew": *Twelfth Night*, 1.3.47; MILLER/*HASP*, 367.

p. 131, Mary: The only time MARIA introduces herself in the play (1.3.54), she calls herself "Mary."

p. 131, lady-in-waiting to Queen Elizabeth: Violet A. Wilson, *Queen Elizabeth's Maids of Honor and Ladies of the Privy Chamber* (London: John Lane/The Bodley Head, 1922), 138–47.

p. 131, ". . . one that adores me": *Twelfth Night*, 2.3.179–80.

p. 131, AGUECHEEK is a dense carpet knight: *Twelfth Night*, 2.3.1–14.

p. 131, "clodpole": *Twelfth Night*, 3.4.190.

p. 132, De Vere "not to continue a courtier": Goff, 312–4.

p. 132, Where Anthony Munday was learning his trade: Julia Celeste Turner, *Anthony Mundy: An Elizabethan Man of Letters* (Berkeley: University of California. Press, 1928), 6.

p. 133, The unknown boundary: NELSON (187) translates *Meta Incognita* as "unknown land"; Robert Detobel ("List of Errors in [Nelson's] Chapter 34 About Northwest Passage" [unpublished MS, 2004]), however, points out that the *Oxford Latin Dictionary*'s definition 4 of *meta* ("boundary, limit") is more apt, given that George Best (*The three voyages of Martin Frobisher;* Hakluyt Society publications ([New York: B. Franklin, 1963 reprint], 31) writes, "Hir Majestie named [the land] very properly *Meta Incognita*, as a mark and *bounds utterly hitherto unknown....*" [Emphasis added.]

p. 133, Frobisher's second expedition: *Pace* NELSON, 186; Detobel (op. cit.) points out that de Vere came in *after* Frobisher's second expedition–i.e., during the third. S.P. Colonial, East Indies, 54. Dom. Eliz., cxix, No. 44.

p. 133, Only pyrite: Nelson's account of the Northwest expeditions is problematic and historically inaccurate (Detobel, op. cit.); for a more accurate accounting, see, for example, Ernest S. Dodge, *Northwest by Sea* (Oxford: Oxford University Press, 1961), 75–77.

p. 133, "ten to see a dead Indian": *The Tempest*, 2.2.133; Jane Ashelford, "Shakespeare and the 'Dead Indian,'" *The Bard* 2:3 (1979), 95–99.

p. 133, . . . searching for an Oriental passage: NELSON (187) mistakenly conflates the 1577 expedition's mission (mining with little opportunity to explore, cf. Dodge, 75–77) with the more open-ended 1578 mission (Dodge, 80) that did indeed offer up the promise of establishing a camp to seek out the fabled Northwest Passage. Nelson's conclusion that de Vere had "either . . . bought into the fictional [*sic*] cover for Frobisher's third [i.e., 1578] expedition or that he allowed himself to be deceived as to its true purpose" is without merit.

p. 133, de Vere's legal letter to voyagers: S.P. Dom, 149.42, cited in WARD, 238–9, NELSON, 187.

p. 133, De Vere's £3,000 bond: WARD, 236–43.

p. 133, Mount Oxford: Vilhjalmur Stefansson, *The Three Voyages of Martin Frobisher* (London: The Argonaut Press, 1938), 64; In 1980, Charlton Ogburn Jr. ("Locating Mount Oxford," *Shakespeare Oxford Society Newsletter* 16:1 [Winter 1980], 5–10) traces his tracks in trying to discern what names Frobisher's geographical sites go by today.

p. 134, Frobisher's smelting works: Ann Savours, *The Search for the North West Passage* (New York: St. Martin's Press, 1999), 9.

p. 134, . . . derives in part from Michael Lok: The Hebrew word for "cormorant" (*shallach*) was often used of usurers. (*The Merchant of Venice* [The Arden Shakespeare], ed. John Russell Brown [London: Methuen & Co., 1969; 1955 first ed.], 3 fn.) Thus the possible etymological formula Shallach+Lok=SHYLOCK.

p. 134, ... derives from other sources: Less than a year after the £3,000 fiasco, de Vere may already have begun to vent his frustrations with master Lok on the London stage: In 1579, a Puritanical pamphlet appeared in London railing about a new play called *The Jew*. The pamphlet noted that *The Jew* was about "the greed of worldly suitors and the bloody mind of usurers"—a fair plot summary of *The Merchant of Venice*.

Stephen Gosson, *School of Abuse* (1579). As Hermann Sinsheimer notes of Gosson's plot summary, "This might be taken to refer to *The Merchant of Venice*, especially when it comes from the pen of a Puritan.... Since Shakespeare has also connected the story of several suitors with the story of a usurer, there can be little doubt that *The Jew* served him in some respect of a model." (*Shylock: The History of a Character* [New York: B. Blom, 1963], 58.) Or perhaps *The Jew* was simply Shake-speare's first draft. Discussion of this plus a possible second allusion to a c. 1580 *Merchant of Venice* can be found in CHAMBERS/*WS* 1:373-4. An intriguing alternate interpretation is in Gwynneth Bowen's "*The Merchant of Venice*: A Living Source," *Shakespearean Authorship Review* 20 (Autumn 1968), 15-16. Cf. also note in Chapter 4 on Gaspare de Ribeiro, whom de Vere may have met at Venice's Santa Maria Formosa church.

p. 134, ... never, so far as is known, able to pay it all back: NELSON, 188; Nelson further presumes that de Vere was behind a riot on November 20, 1578, when Frobisher and forty men accosted Lok. (188.) Nelson gives no basis to support this conclusion, however. NELSON also fails to point out (Detobel, op. cit.) that a majority of Frobisher's investors, including Lord Burghley, never paid their tab in full.

CHAPTER SIX

p. 135, Political alliances at court: A.M.F. Robinson's "Queen Elizabeth and the Valois Princes," *The English Historical Review* 2:5 (January 1887), 40-77.

p. 135, De Vere as secret Catholic: Here I follow D. C. Peck's preferred spelling of "Charles Arundell"—which helps to keep him straight from Philip Howard, earl of Arundel. PECK/*COMMONWEALTH*.

p. 135, Mauvissière's recollections re de Vere's Catholicism: J. A. Bossy, "English Catholics and the French Marriage, 1577-81," *Recusant History* 5 (1959), 2-16; NELSON, 167.

p. 136, Henry Howard's survival skills: WARD, 116-7; *DNB* entry for Henry Howard, (later) earl of Northampton (1540-1614).

p. 136, On Howard: NELSON, 55.

p. 136, Arundell's stories of de Vere's reconciliation: Arundell says that de Vere sought out "some learnid man" [Protestant clergyman] because he was "greveid in conscience about the killing of [*blank*] as it semed, abowte a five year since...." (NELSON, 167.) This statement dates from December 1580. It is unclear whether the five-year period about which Arundell speaks is to be measured from the date of the libel (i.e., the unspecified killing took place sometime circa 1575) or from the date of de Vere's reconciliation (i.e., the unspecified killing took place sometime circa 1571). Even in Nelson's Al Capone–like version of de Vere's life, no murders from either of these dates can be pinned on him. So the "abowte" becomes the key word—smudging out the date Arundell could be speaking of to anytime from the late 1560s to the late 1570s.

p. 136, ... considerably more tenuous: NELSON, 174-6.

p. 136, Privy Council's involvement in Sankey murder: *Acts of the Privy Council*, ed. John Roch Dasent (London: Eyre & Spottiswoode, 1964), 10:103; NELSON, 174.

p. 136, De Vere's closeness to his "honest" IAGO: One is reminded *King Lear*'s trustworthy KENT (in disguise as the servant "CAIUS") who recognizes the pernicious influence of the villainous servant OSWALD and takes it upon himself to kill OSWALD. Might de Vere's man Sankey have seen what evil Rowland Yorke was doing and opted to kill Yorke of his own volition? Such a scenario would make more sense of Howard's claim that "Wekes confessed with what violence he had been sette [on] by my lord [of Oxford] after he [Weekes] had wounded him [Sankey] to the death without eyther cause ore courage." (NELSON, 174.) Howard here says that de Vere was *angry* at Weekes for killing Sankey–which in turn leaves open the question of whether *Yorke* was actually the one who hired Weekes to snuff out the loyal de Vere manservant who had tried to kill him (i.e., Yorke).

p. 137, De Vere as "jeune seigneur"?: Bossy, op. cit., 3; Nina Green ("Phaeton: John Bossy on Oxford," on Phaeton e-mail listserv http://www3.telus.net/oxford/phaeton.html [May 22, 2002]).

p. 137, Mauvissière awarded de Vere a jewel: Henri III to Castelnau de la Mauvissière, July 12, 1577, *Mémoires de Michel de Castelnau, seigneur de la Mauvissière,* ed. J. Le Labourer (Brussels, 1731), 3:520, cited in Bossy, op. cit., 3.

p. 137, Leicester letter to Burghley: Bossy, op. cit., 12, fn. 6; NELSON, 169.

p. 137, Howard's testimony: Undated Howard deposition, BM Cotton Titus C, vi, f. 5, cited in Bossy, 2–3.

p. 137, De Vere squabbling with priest: NELSON, 168.

p. 137, Queen's grant of Castle Rising: Patent Roll 1165. m. 34.20 Eliz (1578), cited in WARD, 149. Nelson (178), naturally, downplays the significance of this grant. He does not address Ward's argument (149–51) that Elizabeth lavished lands and titles only on those who worked hard on her behalf. Other than de Vere's service as courtly dramatist, no one has ever offered an alternative theory as to what Elizabeth was in fact rewarding.

p. 138, Queen and de Vere hadn't exchanged New Year's gifts...: NICHOLS, 2:1–2, 52–53, 65–91.

p. 138, Anne's gifts from queen: NELSON, 179–80, NICHOLS, 2:83. In 1577/8, Elizabeth and Anne exchanged gifts. In 1576/7, Anne gave Elizabeth a jewel pendant (NICHOLS, 2:52); Elizabeth's gifts are not recorded. Presumably the queen reciprocated Anne's kindness.

p. 138, Debates and diversions on 1578 Progress: Zillah Dovey, *An Elizabethan Progress: The Queen's Journey into East Anglia, 1578* (Madison, N.J.: Fairleigh Dickinson University Press, 1996).

p. 138, Harvey's eulogy of Smith: As SCHRICKX points out (96), Harvey's conduct at Smith's funeral was as insensate as his speech at Audley End: "In August 1577 occurred the death of Sir Thomas Smith and Harvey attended the funeral, on which occasion he fell foul of an insinuation from Dr. Andrew Perne, master of Peterhouse; Perne had called Harvey a fox for having induced Sir Thomas's widow to present him with some rare manuscripts."

p. 138, De Vere bestowing favors on Harvey at Cambridge: "In the prime of [de Vere's] gallantest youth, he bestowed angels [gold coins worth ~half pound] upon me in Christ's College in Cambridge and otherwise vouchsafed me many gracious favors at the affectionate commendation of my cousin [*sic*] Master Thomas Smith, the [illegitimate] son of Sir Thomas...." Gabriel Harvey, *Four Letters...* (1592), ed. G. B. Harrison (London: Bodley Head, John Lane, 1922), 34, cited in WARD, 158–9. Harvey matriculated at Christ College June 28, 1566, and earned his B.A. in 1569–70. (*DNB.*)

p. 138, Harvey quote re "gallant audacity": G. C. Moore Smith, *Gabriel Harvey's Marginalia* (Stratford-upon-Avon: Shakespeare Head Press, 1913), 157.13.

p. 139, Harvey quote re "immortal fame": David Perkins, "Issues and Motivations in the Nashe-Harvey Quarrel," *Philological Quarterly* 39:2 (April 1960), 229–31.

p. 139, "Timothy Tiptoes": "The time was when this Timothy Tiptoes made a Latin oration to Her Majesty." Thomas Nashe, *Strange News* (1592), in MCKERROW, 1:276–7.

p. 139, ... translated from the original Latin: Harvey appears to have burlesqued his Audley End speech in his own letter book, although the meaning of his words remains opaque: *The Letter-book of Gabriel Harvey, A.D. 1573–1580...*, ed. Edward John Long Scott (Westminster: Camden Soc. Publications, Nichols & Sons, 1884), 99; I would like to thank both Derran Charlton and Robert Detobel for bringing this verse to my attention.

p. 139, "... thy will shakes spears": The relevant Latin for this passage is *vultus tela vibrat*. WARD (158), overlooking the plural, translates these words as "thy countenance shakes a [*sic*] spear"; Thomas Hugh Jameson ("The *Gratulationes Valdinenses* of Gabriel Harvey" [Ph.D. diss., Yale University, 1938]) translates the same three words as "your glance shoots arrows." (NELSON [181] uses Jameson's translation.) However, according to Thomas Elyot's standard Latin-English dictionary of 1538 and 1559, "*Vultus* of old writers is taken for 'will.'" And Arthur Golding's edition of Ovid's *Metamorphoses* (8.459–60) translates *tela* as "boarspeare," while F. J. Miller's Loeb edition (1916, rev. G. P. Goold 1977) of the same passage from Ovid (8.341–42) translates *tela* as "spears." Andrew Hannas, "Gabriel Harvey and the Genesis of 'William Shakespeare,'" *Shakespeare Oxford Society Newsletter* 29:1B (Winter 1993), 1–8; Andrew Hannas, private communication (November 20, 2003).

p. 140, Harvey's encomium to de Vere: Gabriel Harvey, *Gratulationis Validienensis* (1578) *Liber Quartus*, translated (except for the *vultus tela vibrat*, cf. above note) in WARD, 157–8.

p. 140, ... the very name ... to conceal his own writings: Naturally, a chicken-or-egg question emerges as to whether Will Shakspere was selected as a front man in part because his name could so perfectly be molded into a clever pun, not only to Harvey's encomium but also to the Greek goddess associated with the theater (Pallas), who as it was shown in the Introduction, was often known by her signature spear-shaking. This is one dilemma that will have to wait for more evidence to emerge before any conclusions can be drawn.

p. 140, Spenser's work advertising his secretarial qualifications: Richard Rambuss, "The Secretary's Study: The Secret Designs of *The Shepheardes Calender*," *ELH* 59:2 (Summer 1992), 313.

p. 140, *Shepherd's Calendar* as courtly allegory: Paul E. McLane, *Spenser's Shepheardes Calender: A Study in Elizabethan Allegory* (Notre Dame, Ind.: University of Notre Dame Press, 1961). LOONEY (1:286–8) and OGBURN (622–3) believed that Spenser's character "Willie" was a de Vere doppelgänger. Roger Stritmatter (unpublished MS [1996]) has put forward an alternate interpretation that Spenser's Cuddie ("the perfect pattern of a poet") is in fact the most de Vere–inspired character in *The Shepheardes Calender*. McLane also believes (61–76) that the briar of Spenser's February eclogue stands for de Vere. If both interpretations are true, Spenser would have been playing both sides–fawning over de Vere's poetic talents in the Cuddie episodes and denigrating de Vere in favor of Leicester in the briar/oak episode.

p. 140, Contemporary critics recognized it as well: The anonymous author of the 1589 treatise *The Art of English Poesie*, for instance, noted that Spenser devised his book "not of purpose to counterfeit or represent the rustical manner of loves and communications, but under the veil of homely persons and in rude speeches to insinuate and glance at greater matters, and such perchance had not been safe to have disclosed in any other sort." Three years earlier, the critic William Webbe also noted *The Shepherd's Calendar*'s thinly veiled allegorical designs: "There is also much matter uttered somewhat covertly," Webbe wrote, "especially the abuses of some whom he would not be too plain withal." *The Arte of English Poesie*, ed. G. D. Willcock & A. Walker (Cambridge: Cambridge University Press, 1936), 38–9; William Webbe, *A Discourse of English Poetrie* in *Elizabethan Critical Essays*, ed. G. G. Smith (Oxford: Clarendon Press, 1904), 1:262–4; McLane, op. cit., 5–6.

p. 140, *Calendar* publication as milestone moment in English literature: Frank Kermode, *English Pastoral Poetry* (London: G. G. Harrap, 1952), 41.

p. 140, *Calendar* showcases Spenser's secretarial qualifications: Rambuss, op. cit., 328.

p. 140, Secretaries de Vere hired: G. K. Hunter, *John Lyly: The Humanist as Courtier* (London: Routledge & Kegan Paul, 1962), 47; Julia Celeste Turner, *Anthony Mundy: An Elizabethan Man of Letters* (Berkeley: University of California Press, 1928), 12–13; NELSON, 223, 239.

p. 140, "Scudamore": MILLER/*FLOWRES,* "A Note on 'L'Escu D'Amour' and 'Scudamore' in Spenser's *Faerie Queen,*" between pp. 34 and 35.

p. 140, "...a diamond for nonce...": Quotes from Gabriel Harvey's *Three Proper and Witty Familiar Letters* [to Edmund Spenser] (1580), cited in WARD, 189–90; VAN DREUNEN, 339–45.

p. 141, Harvey called before Privy Council: Harvey's lampoon inspired one wiseacre at Oxford University named William Withie to scratch out a satire of Harvey's "vile, arrogant English versifying" and of the litigious fiasco it brought about. Warren B. Austin, "William Withie's Notebook: Lampoons on John Lyly and Gabriel Harvey," *RES* 23:92 (October 1947), 297–309.

p. 141, Alençon: As noted in Chapter 5, Alençon had been given the additional title duc of Anjou in 1576; this book, for the sake of continuity, will continue to refer to François Valois as "Alençon."

p. 141, "Machiavellians": T. H. Jameson, "The 'Machiavellianism' of Gabriel Harvey," *PMLA* 56:3 (September 1941), 645–56.

p. 141, "...white cliffs of the English": Harvey, *Gratulationes,* op. cit., 2.8.9–12, cited in Jameson, 649.

p. 141, Bleak choice England faced: READ/*BURGHLEY,* 222.

p. 142, French crown "none but coxcombs": D. C. Peck, "Raleigh, Sidney, Oxford, and the Catholics, 1579," *Notes and Queries,* n.s., 25 (1978), 429; it is unclear whether de Vere's 10,000-crown boast and his "none but cockscombs" jest were uttered on the same night or not. They have been conflated for the purpose of narrative. Both come from the Arundel Libels (cf. below) and have been provisionally accepted as genuine, since both are consistent with de Vere's character as a rowdy drinker and witty braggart.

p. 142, "...he did not want to entertain Frenchmen": *Cal. S.P. Spanish* (1568–'79), 607.

p. 142, ...humiliation he would not subject himself to: One is tempted to recognize a parallel here with OBERON's tacit refusal of QUEEN TITANIA's invitation to dance in *Midsummer Night's Dream,* 2.1 (Skiles Howard, *The Politics of Courtly Dancing in Early Modern England* [Amherst: University of Massachusetts Press, 1998], 73–4).

p. 142, Queen's coyness with love games: Larissa J. Taylor-Smither, "Queen Elizabeth I: A Psychological Profile," *Sixteenth Century Journal* 15 (1984), 47–72; Susan Doran, "Why Did Elizabeth Not Marry?" in *Dissing Elizabeth: Negative Representations of Gloriana* (Durham, N.C.: Duke University Press, 1998), 30–59.

p. 142, Spanish ambassador's odds: Lacey Baldwin Smith, *Elizabeth Tudor: Portrait of a Queen* (Boston: Little, Brown, 1975), 122, 182.

p. 142, Lord Chamberlain's Men performances: The Lord Chamberlain's Men performed a third time during the 1578–'79 season. Their March 3, 1579, performance will be considered in the next section.

p. 143, Queen had sent envoys back to Paris: Katherine Duncan-Jones, *Sir Philip Sidney, Courtier Poet* (New Haven, Conn.: Yale University Press, 1991), 158–9.

p. 143, Elizabeth and Richmond: Stephen Pasmore, *The Life and Times of Queen Elizabeth I at Richmond Palace* (Surrey: Richmond Local History Society, 1992); *The Letters of Queen Elizabeth I,* ed. G. B. Harrison (New York: Funk & Wagnalls, 1968; 1935, first ed.), 296–301.

p. 143, "full of snows": William Camden, *Annals* (London: Thomas Harper, 1635), 390.

p. 143, Richmond's Great Hall: It is also possible that the Richmond performances were held in the palace's Great Chamber—both were used for royal entertainments at various times, although the first recorded performance in the Great Chamber was in 1588/9. John H. Astington, *English Court Theatre 1558–1642* (Cambridge: Cambridge University Press, 1999), 60–1.

p. 143, *Cruelties of A Stepmother:* WALLACE, 207.

p. 143, "wicked stepmother *par excellence*": "Rosalie L. Cole, "'Nature's Above Art in that Respect': Limits of the Pastoral Pattern," in *Shakespeare's Romances,* ed. Harold Bloom and Mirjana Kalezic (Philadelphia: Chelsea House, 2000), 100.

p. 143, *Heliodorus* as source for *Cymbeline:* It is widely believed that Thomas Underdowne's *Aethiopian Historie* dates from 1569, not 1577 (see, for example, MILLER/HASP, 98). However, Samuel Lee Wolff persuasively argues (*The Greek Romances in Elizabethan Prose Fiction* [New York: Columbia University Press, 1912], 238) that a more likely publication date for the first edition of this book is 1577, as was first suggested in the *Athenae Oxonienses*. On *Cymbeline's* debt to the *Aethiopian History,* cf. Carol Gesner, "*Cymbeline* and the Greek Romance: A Study in Genre," in *Studies in English Renaissance Literature,* ed. Waldo F. McNeir (Baton Rouge: Louisiana State University Press, 1962), 105–31.

p. 143, *Cymbeline* circa 1578: Robert Detobel ("The Date of *Cymbeline,*" unpublished MS., 2004) points out that the performance of the masque *The Rare Triumphs of Love and Fortune* at Windsor Castle on December 30, 1582–long thought to be an obscure source of *Cymbeline*–is, in fact, more likely an imitation of an early draft of *Cymbeline,* thus dating a prototype version of the Shake-speare play to before 1582.

p. 144, *Cymbeline,* 1.2.75–6; 1.1.42–5.

p. 144, Lady Burghley wanted Anne to marry Philip Sidney: Duncan-Jones, op. cit., 53; the Sidney character in *Cymbeline* (CLOTEN) is portrayed as a son of the QUEEN (Mildred Cecil) by a former husband. Anne's parents did indeed consider young Philip as all but a child of theirs. As William Cecil once wrote of Sidney, "I do so love him as he were mine own." (James M. Osborn, *Young Philip Sidney, 1572–1577* [New Haven, Conn.: Yale University Press, 1972], 16.)

p. 144, *Cymbeline,* 1.6.33–44.

p. 144, De Vere evidently had no qualms about airing his griefs . . . : However, when it would come time to officially attribute the play to a real-life playwright, when *Cymbeline* was first printed in the "Shakespeare" Folio in 1623, such catty characterizations of the great Cecil matriarch would constitute one more reason for the gambit that gave posterity Will Shakspere of Stratford-upon-Avon as putative author. The scions of William and Mildred Cecil have continued to hold positions of power and prestige in British society up to the present day: As will be argued in the Epilogue, some forward-thinking members of the Cecil–Vere clan circa 1623 recognized the artistic importance of preserving literary works like *Cymbeline,* but also of doing so in a way that minimized the sting of the temperamental author's sometimes venomous words.

p. 144, Catherine de Medici as "stepmother": The parallels between *Cymbeline* and the Alençon courtship are discussed at length in MILLER/HASP, 79–101, and OGBURN/TMWS, 607–10.

p. 144, . . . skewering de Medici and her doltish son: The final version of *Cymbeline* was certainly written years after the Alençon marriage had collapsed. Thus he was ultimately freed from any partisan commitments to play "pro" or "con"–and, as Shake-speare, he laid bare his feelings about the de Medici clan.

p. 144, *Cymbeline,* 2.1.57–61.

p. 145, New Year's gifts 1579: NICHOLS, 2:249–75.

p. 145, Peregrine Bertie absent from New Year's festivities: It has been suggested (MILLER/HASP, 102–9) that the Children of Paul's performance of a play titled *A Morall of the marryage of Mynde and Measure* on January 1, 1578, may have been an embryonic version of *The Taming of The Shrew* and/or the anonymous proto-Shake-spearean play published in 1594 titled the *Taming of A* [sic] *Shrew*. Since the travails of an unlikely royal wedding were clearly on all courtiers' minds, a marriage farce would certainly have been an ideal follow-up to *The Cruelties of a Stepmother*. And few highborn courtships in the history of Elizabethan England offered as much comedic potential as did the 1577 coupling of the hot-blooded Mary de Vere and the shrew-taming Peregrine Bertie.

p. 145, "by stratagem contrived that her husband should unknowingly sleep with her...": Thomas Wright (*The History and Topography of the County of Essex* [1836], 1:516) continues, "...and she [*Anne Cecil de Vere*] bore a son [*sic*] to him in consequence of this meeting." Anne delivered a daughter, Elizabeth. Cited in MILLER/LOONEY, 1:234. Charles Wisner Barrell ("He Is Dead and Gone, Lady," *The Shakespeare Fellowship Newsletter* 4:2 [February 1943], 14) discovered at least one of Wright's sources in Francis Osbourne's *Traditional Memoirs of the Reigns of Q. Elizabeth & King James I*. Osbourne was a horsemaster in the household of Susan de Vere, Edward and Anne's youngest daughter (b. 1587). Neither Wright's nor Osbourne's telling of this tale gets every fact straight: Wright claims the unlikely union produced a son; Osbourne says the bed trick produced Susan and not Elizabeth Vere. However, there is only one disputed paternity in Edward de Vere's first marriage, that of the daughter Elizabeth. And the bed tricks in Shake-speare (*All's Well, Measure for Measure, Cymbeline* and *Two Noble Kinsmen*) reveal that this unusual ploy remained on the dramatist's mind for the rest of his life. (Marliss C. Desens, *The Bed-Trick in English Renaissance Drama* [Newark: University of Delaware Press, 1994], 35).

p. 145, Bed tricks in Western literature: Desens, op. cit., 20–30; the story of Jacob and Leah comes from Genesis 29:15–28 and is not marked in Edward de Vere's 1569 Geneva Bible.

p. 145, French province named Roussillion: The province of Roussillion, in southwestern France, is a separate entity from the Château Roussillion, where Hélène and her family resided.

p. 146, Ecclesiasticus 23:18–19 in Edward de Vere's Geneva Bible (1568–70), now owned by the Folger Shakespeare Library (Folger shelf mark 1427). Hand underlining in original.

p. 146, *The Rape of Lucrece* 745, 806–9; Roger Stritmatter, "A New Biblical Source for Shakespeare's Concept of 'All Seeing Heaven.'" *Notes and Queries,* n.s., 46:2 (June 1999), 207–9.

p. 147,...sneaks in such a possibility: Cf. discussion of the Temple of Segesta in Chapter 4.

p. 147, The queen and *Merry Wives:* Karl J. Holzknecht, *The Backgrounds of Shakespeare's Plays* (New York: American Book Co., 1950), 26.

p. 147, *Merry Wives of Windsor,* 3.3.166–218.

p. 148, Casimir left England frustrated at the queen: H. R. Fox Bourne, *Sir Philip Sidney* (New York: G. P. Putnam's Sons, 1891), 172–4; Duncan Jones, op. cit., 157–60.

p. 148, "Monkey" came courting for the "frog": Indeed, according to Peter van der Merwe (*Origins of the Popular Style: The Antecedents of Twentieth-Century Popular Music* [Oxford: Oxford University Press, 1989], 194) the African-American folk/blues song "Froggy Went A-Courtin'" traces its origins back to a Jacobean lyric about "The Marriage of the Frog and the Mouse," which, as Duncan Jones points out (op. cit., 160–1) appears to have been brought out as a popular expression of outrage over Alençon's courtship of Elizabeth.

p. 148, "device was prettier than it hap to be performed": March 5, 1579, letter from Gilbert Talbot to his father, the earl of Shrewsbury. Edmund Lodge, *Illustrations of British History* (London, 1791), 2:209, cited in OGBURN/*TMWS,* 617.

p. 148,...the other item on the evening's bill, *A Moor's Masque:* WALLACE, 207; Gilbert Talbot was almost certainly responding to the "device" in which the two earls participated–i.e., *A Moor's Masque*. The correspondent did not set down any thoughts or reflections on *Murderous Michael*.

p. 148, *Arden of Feversham*: Some seventeenth- and eighteenth-century scholars thought *Arden* was written by Shake-speare. Indeed, if de Vere's hand is to be found in it at all, the play may represent a new type of Shake-spearean text hitherto unappreciated: the author's youthful collaborations and plays from the 1570s, later revised by other hands. (W. W. Greg argues ["Shakespeare and *Arden of Feversham*," *RES* 21:82 (April 1945), 134–6] that although Edward Jacob is generally thought to have been the first to attribute *Arden* to Shakespeare [1770], Edward Archer may have beaten Jacob to the punch by more than a century. For modern stylistic arguments for de Vere's (at least partial) authorship of *Arden*, cf. MILLER/HASP, 252–97.)

p. 149, pointed jab after pointed jab at … his in-laws: Ultimately, though, both *Othello* and *Cymbeline* fob the jealous groom's reactionary behavior off on a dastardly servant–IAGO and IACHIMO: Rowland Yorke, in other words. So even when de Vere was at his most accusatory toward his wife and in-laws, he also gave them convenient alibis–in this case, the duplicity of a venal servant.

p. 149, Elizabeth volunteered the *Moor's Masquers*: Mendoza to the king of Spain, April 8, 1579. *CSP Spanish 1568–79*, 662, cited in NELSON, 190.

p. 149, Hosting and entertaining Alençon: NELSON, 202–3; FESTE's song is about a lover who is "slain by a fair cruel maid." Alençon would die unmarried and alone in 1584, forever forestalled by the perennially indecisive Elizabeth.

p. 149, AGUECHEEK the butt of a bawdy double-entendre: Gustav Ungerer, "SIR ANDREW AGUECHEEK and His Head of Hair," *Shakespeare Studies* 16 (1983), 101–33; AGUECHEEK is also portrayed as prodigal and quarrelsome–two stones that de Vere could hardly cast easily from inside his own monumental glass house. And AGUECHEEK's chicken-heartedness and thickheadedness are harped on from his first to his last scene onstage. "SIR ANDREW, as a coward and gull, was despicable," notes John W. Draper. "But SIR TOBY had the respect of all the characters in the play, and so presumably of the audience." (Draper, "OLIVIA's Household," *PMLA* 49:3 [September 1934], 803.)

p. 149, … the very ideal of Castiglione's courtier: *Twelfth Night* 1.3.25–44; J. D. Schuchter ("Shakespeare's *Twelfth Night* 1.3.42," *The Explicator* 29:1 [September 1970]) translates SIR TOBY BELCH's line "*Castiliano vulgo;* for here comes SIR ANDREW AGUECHEEK" as "Here comes the common (i.e., homegrown, English) version of *The Courtier.*"

p. 150, Sidney on poetry: Sidney, "Defense of Poesy," in *Sir Philip Sidney, Selected Prose and Poetry*, ed. Robert Kimbrough (New York: Holt, Rinehart & Winston, 1969), 144.

p. 150, De Vere in Sidney's sights: Ramon Jimenez, "In Brawl Ridiculous: Philip Sidney, Oxford, and the Battle of Agincourt," *Shakespeare Oxford Newsletter* 38:2 (Spring 2002), 1, 12–15.

p. 150, Sidney, "Defense," op. cit., 148.

p. 150, … time, mood, and setting: Jimenez, op. cit.

p. 151, "And so our scene must to the battle fly": *Henry V* 4.Chorus.48–52; In the words of critic Sharon Tyler ("Minding True Things: The Chorus, the Audience, and *Henry V*," in *Themes in Drama 9*, ed. James Redmond [Cambridge: Cambridge University Press, 1987], 76) "It is tantalizing, but pure speculation, to see Shakespeare deliberately taking up the artistic gauntlet flung by Sidney." Jimenez makes a persuasive case that Sidney's digression on drama in the *Defense of Poesy* stems in no small part from the knight's responses to the apocryphal Shake-spearean play *The Famous Victories of Henry V*.

p. 151, … the sole witness who recorded his recollections: Reprinted in the *Life of the Renowned Sir Philip Sidney* by Fulke Greville (1652 first ed.), cited in WARD, 164–171.

p. 151, Probably at Greenwich Palace: Duncan-Jones, *Sidney*, op. cit., 164.

p. 151, De Vere branded Sidney a "puppy": Sidney ruminated over the "puppy" epithet in his *Arcadia*. A. Bronson Feldman, "OTHELLO in Reality," *American Imago* 11 (1954), 166.

p. 151, The queen forbade it: According to Fulke Greville (op. cit.), Queen Elizabeth forbade the duel, arguing that degree had to be respected and Sidney, whose knighthood was still four years off, could not challenge an earl. WARD, 170.

p. 151, . . . he secretly planned to murder Sidney?: This suggestion appears in the Arundel Libels, as reprinted in NELSON, 199–200.

p. 151, . . . beyond the time frame and identities of the key players: Walter Raleigh (later Sir Walter) was one such actor in this quarrel. The *DNB* entry on Raleigh says that the explorer carried a challenge from de Vere to Sidney; Sidney accepted but de Vere never took it up. Instead, de Vere planned to assassinate Sidney in secret, a plan that Raleigh declined to participate in, thus provoking de Vere's anger. The only evidence for this foiled would-be conspiracy is the problematic witness of the Arundel Libels. (NELSON, 199–200.)

p. 151, De Vere's enemies make him look like a petty criminal: This point of view is handily summarized in NELSON, 193–200.

p. 152, Chambers recognizes Sidney–de Vere quarrel in *Hamlet: Hamlet,* ed. E. K. Chambers, rev. Walter Morris Hart. Arden Shakespeare (Boston: D. C. Heath & Co., 1917), 2.1.59, p. 170; Roger Stritmatter, private communication (2001).

p. 152, *Muiopotmos* as allegory of Sidney–de Vere quarrel: Viola Blackburn Hulbert, "A New Interpretation of Spenser's *Muiopotmos,*" *Studies in Philology* 28 (1928), 128–48.

p. 152, De Vere sent Sidney two written challenges: NELSON, 197–99, 229–30.

p. 153, Hatton played both sides against the middle: Hatton rode with Simier and Elizabeth on a barge in July when a would-be assassin fired his pistol at the entourage. The shot hit six feet wide of the queen, piercing the wrist of a nearby rower. In the aftermath, Simier–who suspected Leicester was behind the plot–strategically leaked compromising information about Leicester to the queen, crippling the anti-Alençon cause. (Leicester had in 1578 secretly married the widow of the earl of Essex. Simier's sources for the information he leaked to Elizabeth were Charles Arundell and Henry Howard (they of the Libels to be discussed below.) PECK/*COMMONWEALTH,* 19, 57, fn. 64.)

p. 153, "Your Majesty's 'Sheep'": This was a new nickname for old "Lids." The first instance of the nickname "Sheep" seems to be 1579, when Hatton settled a sheep-stealing incident in Hertfordshire. (Brooks, op. cit., 100.)

p. 153, Hatton's letter to Elizabeth: Hatton to Elizabeth, undated letter, cited in Brooks, op. cit., 280. (Brooks, comically, misreads the word *tusk* for *tush.*) This missive is commonly dated to 1573. However, Brooks (98–100, 177) argues that it more likely dates from c. 1580. The sickness Hatton alludes to in the letter could, for instance, be the sickness that befell his entire household staff in 1580 (177).

p. 154, "Pleasant conceit of Vere, Earl of Oxford . . .": "Francis Peck's *Desiderata Curiosa* (1732), [Vol.] 1. A the end of Volume 1, Peck promises six books soon to be printed, 'Now ready for the press,' under various subjects. The following is given as the subject for Liber II, No. XXIII: 'A pleasant Conceit of Vere Earl of Oxford, discontented at the Rising of a mean Gentleman in the *English* Court, *circa* MDLXXX. *MS. Manu. Flemingi.*' The 'pleasant conceit,' however, is not referred to in the volume which follows." CLARK, 289, fn. 6.

MS. Manu. Flemingi means the MS collections of Abraham Fleming (*DNB* entry for Fleming, Abraham [1552?–1607]). In 1580 Fleming dedicated a translation of St. Paul's Letter to the Ephesians (STC 13058) to Anne Cecil de Vere (NELSON, 223, 239). Gerit Quealy (private communication, September 2004) notes that none of the items Peck advertised for his projected Volume 2 of *Desiderata* ever made it into print. She adds that according to an unpublished MS on the life of the antiquarian John Nichols written by Alan Broadfield (c. 1977), Peck's Leicestershire glazier brother had "ignorantly" destroyed what was to be Peck's Volume 2.

p. 154, MALVOLIO as caricature of Hatton: MILLER/*HASP,* 364–76.

p. 154, "Rascally sheep-biter": *Twelfth Night* 2.5.7; "Sheep-*biter*" was Elizabethan slang for a thief; fn. in Variorum Shakespeare *Twelfth Night,* ed. H. H. Furness (Philadelphia: J. B. Lippincott Co., 1901), 152; labeling Hatton with the epithet "thief" certainly was an appropriate criticism, since in 1576 Hatton had swindled the Bishop of Ely out of a spacious church property in London. The site of this former church property today is called Hatton Garden (Brooks, op. cit., 145–52).

p. 154, "The Fortunate Unhappy": *Twelfth Night*, 2.5.159; Gabriel Harvey, *Gratulationes Valdinenses* (London, 1578), liber iv; "Ad honoratissimum...Christophorum Hattonum...de suo symbolo *Foelix Infortunatus [The Happy Unfortunate]*"; WARD, 130–44; Brooks, op. cit., 107.

p. 154, Pope had recently advocated for Elizabeth's assassination: "No other Pope of the counter-reformation is more completely the child of his age than Gregory XIII [1572–1585]." Arnold Oskar Meyer, *England and the Catholic Church Under Queen Elizabeth*, tr. J. R. McKee (London: Routledge & Kegan Paul, Ltd., 1967), 269–72.

p. 154, Campion denied use of pen, ink, or paper: Even into the 1590s, an English citizen could be arrested just for owning a copy of the Campion-inspired poem "Why Do I Use My Paper, Ink, and Pen?" *The Arundel Harington Manuscript of Tudor Poetry*, ed. Ruth Hughey (Columbus: Ohio State University Press, 1960), 2:64; "Poems Relating to Campion" in *Ballads from Manuscripts, Vol. II, Part II*, ed. W. R. Morfill (Hertford: The Ballad Society/Stephen Austin & Sons, 1873), 157–91.

p. 155, FESTE's aside about "hermit of Prague": "FESTE *Buenas Dias*, SIR TOBY. For as the old hermit of Prague that never saw pen and ink [i.e., Edmund Campion] very wittily said to a niece of King Gorboduc [Queen Elizabeth?], 'That that is is.'" (*Twelfth Night*, 4.2.15–16.) C. Richard Desper, "Allusions to Edmund Campion in *Twelfth Night*," *The Elizabethan Review* 3:1 (Spring/Summer 1995), 37–47. To Desper's interpretation of "niece of King Gorboduc," one might add the fact that one of the two authors of the play *Gorboduc*, Thomas Norton, was the rackmaster who so brutally tortured Campion. (Brooks, op. cit., 206.)

p. 155, *Twelfth Night*, 4.2.82–92.

p. 155, *Twelfth Night* and international political scene circa 1580: Although nominally set in the days of the Roman Republic, Philip Massinger's *Believe as You List* (1631)–perhaps a takeoff on *Twelfth Night's* subtitle, *What You Will?*–stages the imagined exploits of Don Sebastian, king of Portugal. *Believe as You List* in *Philip Masinger, The Mermaid Series*, ed. Arthur Symons (London: T. F. Unwin, 1893), Volume 2; Anon., "*Twelfth Night* and Massinger's *Believe as You List*," *Shakespeare Fellowship News-Letter* (UK) (May 1944), 7.

p. 155, Sebastian preparing to make triumphant return: Mary Elizabeth Brooks, *A King for Portugal: The Madrigal Conspiracy, 1594–95* (Madison: University of Wisconsin Press, 1964); Alexandrino P. Severino, "Fernando Pessoa: A Modern *Lusiad*," *Hispania* 67:1 (March 1984), 52–3.

p. 156, *Twelfth Night* the story of ANTONIO and SEBASTIAN: MILLER/*HASP*, 380–81.

p. 156, ...a series of misapprehensions that are the stock-in-trade of Shake-spearean comedy: Sidney soon grew weary of Antonio's presence. (Harris Nicolas, *Memoirs of the Life and Times of Sir Christopher Hatton, K.G.* [London: Richard Bentley, 1847], 202–3.) *Twelfth Night* gives voice to Sidney's frustrations with the Portuguese pretender by having SEBASTIAN and ANTONIO duel with SIR ANDREW AGUECHEEK–and, since he can never resist a good swordfight, SIR TOBY BELCH.

The play also equivocates on the Alençon marriage by making DUKE ORSINO (Alençon) lose his marriage bid with OLIVIA (Elizabeth)–to the dead Portuguese king. SEBASTIAN and OLIVIA ring down the final curtain of *Twelfth Night* as a married couple. The author had recognized that his Queen would only settle her mind on a husband if that husband was also a complete fantasy. This would serve as Shake-speare's ultimate statement on the French marriage for which he ostensibly advocated.

p. 156, Mount Fisher: George Saunders to Richard Bagot, May 15, 1593, "...here at Mount Fisher, also called Fisher's Folie, without Bishopsgate," cited in Margaret Sefton-Jones, *Old Devonshire House by Bishopsgate* (London: The Swarthmore Press, 1923), 98. (N.B.: In the seventeenth century, Fisher's Folly was renamed Devonshire House.)

p. 156, De Vere's ancestors once occupied this property: Sefton-Jones, 64–7.

p. 156, . . . sank his ever more burdened purse: Mark Fortier describes another squandered de Vere real estate investment circa 1580: "Equity and Ideas: Coke, Ellesmere, and James I," *Renaissance Quarterly* 51:4 (Winter 1998), 126off.

p. 156, Elizabeth once visited Fisher's Folly: STOW, 149.

p. 156, On Bedlam: By the end of the century, as Bedlam expanded and budgets shrank, the managers began exhibiting the patients to a gawking public like animals in a zoo. Ken Jackson "Bethlem and Bridwell in the *Honest Whore* Plays," *Studies in English Literature, 1500–1900* 43:2 (2003), 395ff.; Patricia Allderidge, "Management and Mismanagement at Bedlam, 1547–1633," in *Health, Medicine, and Mortality in the Sixteenth Century,* ed. Charles Webster (Cambridge: Cambridge University Press, 1979), 141–64.

p. 156, De Vere had clearly studied the "distracted" mind up close: Sarah Smith, *Chasing Shakespeares* (New York: Atria Books, 2003), 182–4.

pp. 156–7, On the architecture of The Theatre and Curtain: Joseph Quincy Adams, *Shakespearean Playhouses* (Boston: Houghton Mifflin Co., 1917), 77.

p. 157, A rogue could mill about, cut a purse or two . . . : Gamini Salgado, *The Elizabethan Underworld* (London: Sutton Publishing, Ltd., 1995; first ed. 1977), 28.

p. 157, "I knew the play was done": *Tarlton's Newes out of Purgatory,* ed. J. O. Halliwell (London: The Shakspeare Society, 1844), 105.

p. 157, Plays "as filthy as the stables of Augeas": Stephen Gosson, Epistle dedication to Sir Francis Walsingham in *Playes Confuted in Fiue Actions . . .* (London: Thomas Gosson, 1581), 9; Arthur F. Kinney, "Stephen Gosson's Art of Argumentation in *The Schoole of Abuse,*" *Studies in Eng. Lit. 1500–1900* 7:1 (Winter 1967), 41–54.

p. 158, Privy Council arrested two of Oxford's Men: "[13 April] Robert Leveson and Larrance Dutton, servantes unto the Erle of Oxford, were committed to the Mareshalsea for committing of disorders and frayes appon the gentlemen of the Innes of Courte." *Acts of the Privy Council,* ed. John Roche Dasent (London: Eyre & Spottiswoode, 1890–1964), 9:445, cited in NELSON, 240.

N.B.: Leve[n]son may appear in the historical record again on January 19, 1583: "Vpon saterday last I was occupied all the daye in the exãiacon of one levenson and of his confederats and of sundrie Roberies & suche like / This levenson is a dangerus Ruffen / he haith misvsed my lo. of Oxenford wth words of indignitie." William Fleetwood to Lord Burghley, Lansdowne MS 37, f. 10, art. 5, reprinted in *Malone Society Collections, Part II* (Oxford: Horace Hart, 1908), 161.

p. 158, Players to be "forbidden as ungodly and perilous": CHAMBERS/*ES,* 4:279, cited in NELSON, 239–40.

p. 158, "Devilish exercises": Thomas Churchyard, *A Warning for the Wise* (London, 1580), B2, and Philip Stubbes, *The Anatomie of Abuses* (London, 1583), P3^v–4, cited in NELSON, 242.

p. 158, Two people killed by falling stones in Westminster: Turner, *Anthony Munday,* op. cit., 38.

p. 158, "Monsieur D'Olive": On D'Olive's resemblance to de Vere: Robert Brazil and Barboura Flues, ElizabethanAuthors.com; on D'Olive's FALSTAFF-like qualities: Elmer Edgar Stoll, *From Shakespeare to Joyce: Authors and Critics; Literature and Life.* (Garden City, N.Y.: Doubleday, Doran & Co., 1944), 233.

pp. 158–9, D'Olive speech: Brazil and Flues, op. cit.; Chapman, *Monsieur D'Olive,* 1.1, in *The Works of George Chapman, Plays,* ed. Richard Herne Shepherd (London: Chatto & Windus, 1874), 117.

p. 159, Munday and Lyly as amanuenses: If an original early de Vere/Shake-speare manuscript someday surfaces, such as the Fleming archive noted above, the first test should probably be whether it is in Lyly's or Munday's handwriting. De Vere may well have made a few corrections and emendations, but scratching out a longhand copy of what the master recites is just what a secretary was paid to do. (In his destitute final years, de Vere employed fewer servants and, one presumes, secretaries; so an original manuscript from later in life might well have come directly from the author's pen.)

p. 159, On *Mirror of Mutability*: Louis R. Zocca, *Elizabethan Narrative Poetry* (New York: Octagon Books, 1970), 42–3; Willard Farnham, "The Progeny of *A Mirror for Magistrates*," *Modern Philology* 29:4 (May 1932), 400–1.

p. 159, On *Zelauto*: Anthony Munday, *Zelauto: The Fountaine of Fame, 1580*, ed. Jack Stillinger (Carbondale: Southern Illinois University Press, 1963), vii–xxvii; Julia Celeste Turner, *Anthony Mundy: An Elizabethan Man of Letters* (Berkeley: University of California Press, 1928), 32–4.

p. 159, "Pain of Pleasure" reattributed: Sarah Smith, "A Reattribution of Munday's 'The Paine of Pleasure,'" *The Oxfordian* 5 (2002), 70–118.

p. 159, . . . inspired by a similar poem by Gascoigne: George Gascoigne, "The Grief of Joy" (1577), cf. Smith, "Paine," op. cit., 79–80.

p. 160, "(just barely) be mentioned in Shakespeare's company": Ibid. 86, 93.

p. 160, *Euphues* tells of courtier's travels and travails: Euphues also pleads for Lyly's advancement at court. R. W. Maslen, *Elizabethan Fictions* (Oxford: Clarendon Press, 1997), 220.

p. 160, *Euphues* sent "to a nobleman to nurse . . .": John Lyly, epistle dedication to de Vere in *Euphues and His England (1580)*, in *The Complete Works of John Lyly*, ed. R. Warwick Bond (Oxford: Clarendon Press, 1902), 2:4–5.

p. 160, Lyly's "Homer" was de Vere: WARD, 184–7.

p. 160, *Euphues* as anticourtesy book: Theodore L. Steinberg, "The Anatomy of *Euphues*," *Studies in Eng. Lit., 1500–1900* 17:1 (Winter 1977), 29.

p. 160, De Vere would continue to draw from *The Courtier*: Cf. Chapter 4, footnote on HAMLET's baiting of POLONIUS and its relation to Castiglione.

p. 160, . . . the hallmark of the Euphuistic style: The German scholar Friedrich Landmann, not quite getting the joke, notes, "I consider transverse alliteration in parisonic antithetical or parallel clauses as the indispensable criterion of the presence of Euphuism." (*Euphues* [Henninger: Heilbronn, 1887], xv.)

p. 160, Characterization of Euphues: Steinberg, op. cit., 27–38.

p. 161, *Euphues* continued to sell into the next century: Bond, op. cit., 1:100–5.

p. 161, . . . influence or even serve as sources for the Shake-speare canon: On the dedications: WARD, 194–98; On the influences: BULLOUGH, 8:118–22, 156–98; Jonathan Bate, *Shakespeare and Ovid* (Oxford: Clarendon Press, 1994), 85; Edgar I. Fripp, *Shakespeare, Man and Artist, Vol. I* (London: H. Milford, 1938), 323; Albert W. Feuillerat, *Venus and Adonis, Lucrece, and the Minor Poems* (New Haven, Conn.: Yale University Press, 1927), 178.

p. 161, Toying with Euphuism in plays that recalled the Fisher's Folly years: Morris P. Tilley, "A Parody of *Euphues* in *Romeo and Juliet*," *MLN* 41:1 (January 1926), 1–8; Bond, op. cit., 1:150–75; W. L. Rushton, *Shakespeare's Euphuism* (New York: AMS Press, 1973; first ed. 1871).

p. 161, . . . interspersing rustic with noble story lines: Hunter, *Lyly*, op. cit., 298–349.

p. 161, Anne Vavasour, age nineteen: NELSON, 231, citing E. K. Chambers (*Sir Henry Lee* [Oxford: Clarendon Press, 1936], 151, fn. 4) give Vavasour's probable age as nineteen; PECK (*COMMONWEALTH*, 271) and Josephine Waters Bennett ("Oxford and *Endimion*," [*sic*] *PMLA* 57:2 [June 1942], 356) both report Anne's age in 1580 as fifteen.

p. 161, On term *vavasour*: F. R. Coss, "Literature and Social Terminology: The Vavasour in England," in *Social Relations and Ideas, Essays in Honor of R. H. Hilton* (Cambridge: Cambridge University Press, 1983), 109–50.

p. 161, Vavasour's sister's mother-in-law a Spenser: CLARK, 69–70.

p. 161, Queen who demanded that her Maids of Honor be virgins: Alison Wall, "For Love, Money, or Politics? A Clandestine Marriage and the Elizabethan Court of Arches," *The Historical Journal* 38:3 (September 1995), 518.

p. 161, . . . her beauty, poetic prowess, and wit: On Vavasour's three known manuscript poems (one or more of which may have been written or cowritten by de Vere): Chambers, *Lee,* op. cit., 152–4; Arthur F. Marotti, *Manuscript, Print, and the English Renaissance Lyric* (Ithaca, N.Y.: Cornell University Press, 1995), 57–9, 164; On Edmund Spenser's possible infatuation with Vavasour, cf. CLARK, 69–72; as Clark notes (70–1), Gabriel Harvey confirms that the Christian name of Spenser's "Rosalind" is "Anne" in his *Three Proper and Wittie, familiar letters . . .* to Spenser (1580).

p. 161, Four poems attest to the affair and its aftermath: To the three Vavasour-related poems Chambers notices, Elizabeth Story Donno also adds the following verse by Sir John Harrington, "Of Lelia" (a feminization of Laelius, the Latinized name by which her later lover, Sir Henry Lee, was known).

Of Lelia

When lovely *Lalia* was a tender girle,
Sha hapt to be deflowred by an Earle;
Alas, poore wench, she was to be excused,
Such kindnesse oft is offered, seld refused.
But be not proud; for she that is no Countesse,
And yet lies with a Count, must make account this,
   All Countesses in honour her sermount,
   They have, she had, an honourable Count.

Sir John Harington's A New Discourse of a Stale Subject Called the Metamporphosis of Ajax (1596), ed. Donno (New York: Columbia University Press, 1962), 59, fn. 28; I would like to thank Christopher Paul for drawing my attention to this verse.

p. 162, Poems to and about Vavasour: Raleigh's poem and Vere/Vavasour "echo" poem: Chambers, *Lee,* op. cit., 151–3.

p. 162, Vavasour as ROSALINE: *Romeo and Juliet,* which, as will be seen below, is also in no small part about the Vavasour affair, features a young courtly beauty, who never appears onstage, named ROSALINE. However, to complicate matters, in *Romeo and Juliet,* Vavasour is portrayed as both JULIET *and* ROSALINE.

p. 162, *Love's Labor's Lost,* 5.2.374–82.

p. 162, ROSALINE's kinship with BEATRICE: Two nineteenth-century critics to point out the resemblance between BEATRICE and ROSALINE are Augustine Skottowe and F. J. Furnivall. Augustus E. Ralli, *A History of Shakespearean Criticism, Vol. 1* (Oxford: Clarendon Press, 1932), 169, 497.

p. 162, BEATRICE as candid glimpse into Vavasour affair: One Oxfordian interpretation of Shake-speare's *Sonnets,* which this biographer does not quite find persuasive, holds that Vavasour was the original for the *Sonnets'* "dark lady." Charles Wisner Barrell, "'Shake-speare's' Own Secret Drama," *Shakespeare Fellowship Newsletter* (US) 3:1 (December 1941), 1–5; 3:2 (February 1942), 13–17, 23–24; 3:3 (April 1942), 25–33; 3:4 (June 1942), 45–52; 3:5 (August 1942), 57–65; 3:6 (October 1942), 69–77.

p. 162, In late February of 1580: Nelson dates the time of this conversation between February 16, 1580 (Ash Wednesday), and February 24, 1580, since Howard mentions it took place during Lent and later mentions the ailing condition of "myne old lord of Arundell" (d. February 24). LIBEL-3.2/2.2@11.

p. 162, "'To Spain,' quoth he": BL Cotton Titus C.6, ff. 7–8, LIBEL-3.2/2.2.

p. 164, "the bearing of a white waster": Ibid.

p. 164, Vavasour miscarried: The only record of this pregnancy, the troublesome Arundell Libels (NELSON, 231–2), does not specify what happened beyond the fact that de Vere had impregnated Vavasour. However, the timing of subsequent events leads Nelson to conclude (232) that Vavasour a) did not carry the child to term and b) it was not an abortion.

p. 164, "Lord Upward Thrust": Dobranski, op. cit., 233–50.

p. 164, BEATRICE's "use" and "double heart": On "use": Hugh M. Richmond, *Shakespeare's Sexual Comedy: A Mirror for Lovers* (Indianapolis: Bobbs-Merrill, 1971), 185; "double heart": Dobranski, op. cit., 238.

p. 164, . . . penance . . . for killing his own children: Dobranski (op. cit., 234–6) also notes that BENEDICK twice offers to perform Herculean labors of his own. He first burlesques Hercules by asking his commanding officer (DON PEDRO) to assign him any task, just so long as it will keep him from seeing BEATRICE. ("I will fetch you a toothpicker from the furthest inch of Asia," etc.) Later, to right the wronged maid HERO, BENEDICK pledges to undertake any labor in BEATRICE's service.

I would add to Dobranski's list BEATRICE's line "What should I do with him [BENEDICK]? Dress him in my apparel and make him my waiting gentlewoman?" (2.1.30–1.) This is clearly an allusion to the mythical Queen Omphale, who dressed Hercules in women's apparel and made him her maidservant.

p. 164, . . . ape into hell by way of atoning for a dead illegitimate child: Dobranski (op. cit., 242) also notes that some versions of the "apes into hell" legend have virgins doing the escorting–although that would hardly explain why BEATRICE makes such an obscure allusion: to brag about her virginity?

p. 165, *Carduus* to diagnose pregnancy: *Much Ado*, 3.4.49–73; Dobranski, op. cit.

p. 165, Stepney and Whitechapel as anonymous birthing centers: David Cressy, *Birth, Marriage, and Death: Ritual, Religion, and the Life-Cycle in Tudor and Stuart England* (Oxford: Clarendon Press, 1997), 77–8.

p. 165, . . . elusive figure named Francis Southwell: NELSON, 56–7.

p. 166, Mauvissière on de Vere's being "put to confusion": John Hungerford Pollen and William MacMahon, *The Ven. Philip Howard, Earl of Arundel* (London: Catholic Record Society, 1919), 29–30, translated in WARD, 209.

p. 166, . . . a flight which he could use as a tacit admission of guilt: NELSON, 252–3.

p. 166, Refugees turned themselves in: Pollen and MacMachon, op. cit., 30–1; WARD, 209–10; NELSON, 253–4.

pp. 166–7, De Vere's interrogatory memos: NELSON, 254–8. The *Monstrous* biographer projects onto de Vere's interrogatories the claim that they're "endued with a hypocrisy, a pettiness of mind, and a lack of mental control that reveal far more about the accuser than the accused."

p. 167, "Apprenticeship in defamation": PECK/*COMMONWEALTH*, 21.

p. 167, One hundred pages of invective against de Vere: NELSON, 489–91.

p. 167, ". . . been driven to rise from his table laughing": PRO SP12/151[/45], ff. 100-2 (LIBEL 4.3[1.2]).

p. 168, . . . all point strongly in Arundell's direction: PECK (*COMMONWEALTH*) presents a comprehensive case for Charles Arundell's authorship of the *Commonwealth*–whether that is to the exclusion of other pamphleteers remains an open question.

p. 168, ". . . not only scurrilous but dangerous": J. E. Neale, *The Age of Catherine de Medici and Essays in Elizabethan History* (London: J. Cape, 1958), 152; Chester Penn Higby and B. T. Schantz, *John Lothrop Motley: Representative Selections* (New York: American Book Co., 1939), 317; Arthur F. Kinney, *"Leicester's Commonwealth . . ."* [review] *Renaissance Quarterly* 40:3 (Autumn 1987), 566.

p. 168, "Few to be entirely true, but few to be entirely false": PECK/*COMMONWEALTH*, ix; Chambers, *Sir Henry Lee*, op. cit., 160.

p. 168, ". . . fine young boys were in season": LIBEL-4.2/6, NELSON, 213–4.

p. 168, Strong antitheatrical bias colors libels: Joseph A. Porter, "Marlowe, Shakespeare, and the Canon of Heterosexuality," and Stephen Orgel, "Nobody's Perfect: Or Why Did the English Stage Take Boys for Women?" in *Displacing Homophobia: Gay Male Perspectives in Literature and Culture*, ed. Ronald R. Butters, John M. Clum, Michael Moon (Durham, N.C.: Duke University Press, 1989), 15–18, 128–9.

p. 168, *Lingua* as response to Arundell Libels: G. C. Moore Smith ("Notes on some English University Plays," *MLR* 3 (1927), 146–8; added to by M. P. Tilley, "The Comedy *Lingua* and Du Bartas' *La Sepmaine*," *Modern Lang. Notes* 42:5 [May 1927], 297–9) points out that the anonymous University play *Lingua* (first printed in 1607) makes an extended allusion to Queen Elizabeth's 1578 visit to Audley End. However, neither Smith nor Tilley can make sense of the line that the 1578 stop was "a little before the excoriation of Marsayas." As the only participant in the Audley End revels who was soon to be practically flayed alive, de Vere fits the description of the mythical satyr Marsayas perfectly.

p. 169, "...marksmanship directed at a well-defined satiric target": John A. Allen, "DOGBERRY," *SH.Q.* 24:1 (Winter 1973), 36.

p. 169, "To conclude, he is a beast in all respects...": MILLER/*HASP*, 549–52; Percy Allen, *"Much Ado About Nothing–A Burlesque of the Oxford-Howard-Arundel Quarrel." Shakespeare Fellowship News-Letter* (UK) (April 1950), 4–5; Peter R. Moore, "The Lame Storyteller, Poor and Despised," *Shakespeare Oxford Society Newsletter* 31:3 (Summer 1995), 17–18.

p. 169, *Much Ado*, 5.1.210–14.

p. 169, "Condemned into everlasting redemption for this": MILLER/*HASP*, 549–52.

p. 170, Arundel distinct from Arundell: e.g., Marshall W. S. Swan ("The Sweet Speech and Spenser's (?) *Axiochus*," *ELH* 11:3 [September 1944], 161–81) falls into this trap.

p. 170, "Phoenix and paragon of the world whom with all devotion I serve": B. L. Lansdowne MS 99, fol. 263a, in Alan Young, *Tudor and Jacobean Tournaments* (London: Sheridan House, 1987), 149.

p. 170, Account of tiltyard spectacle: *Plato, Axiochus... Hereto is annexed a speech spoken at the tryumphe at White-hall by the page to the earle of Oxenforde* (1592), repr. in NELSON, 262–4; Young, op. cit., 93–5.

p. 170, "...join with this worthy White Knight": Charles Wisner Barrell, "Queen Elizabeth's Master Showman Shakes a Spear in Her Defense," *Shakespeare Fellowship Quarterly* (US) 8:1 (Spring 1947), 4–14.

pp. 170–1, *Yggdrasil*: Thomas A. Sebeok, *Myth: A Symposium* (Philadelphia: American Folklore Society, 1955), 47–9; Paul C. Bauschatz, *The Well and the Tree: World and Time in Early Germanic Culture* (Amherst: University of Massachusetts Press, 1982).

Robert Detobel (private communication [September 2004]) points to an alternate possible original for de Vere's Knight of the Sun Tree: Diego Ortuñez de Calahorra, "Espejo de Principes," book 1, tr. by "M.T." (Margaret Tyler) and published as *The Mirrour of Princely deedes and knighthood: wherein is shewed the worthinesse of the Knight of the Sunne, and his brother Rosicleer....* Thomas East, London (1578) ff. 179.

p. 171, "...to yield a jot in constant loyalty": Swan, op. cit., 169; *Axiochus*, op. cit.

p. 171, "...rent in more pieces than can be numbered": Ibid.

p. 171, Bleachers collapsed: Raphael Holinshed, *Chronicles* (London: J. Johnson [etc.], 1808), 4:434, cited in Swan, op. cit., 168.

p. 172, "Table of diamonds": Harleian MSS 6064.87, reprinted in MILLER/LOONEY, 2:54.

p. 172, Ultimate thank-you note for queen's generosity: Julia Colley Altrocchi (reprinted in MILLER/LOONEY, 2:54–6) suggests an interesting but unconfirmed scenario to explain the whole of Sonnet 122: Shake-speare seems to be apologizing to the recipient of this sonnet (Elizabeth?) for "giving them [the tables] from me." Could de Vere have turned around and handed his prize to Vavasour, inciting the queen's rage–and inspiring this apologia of a sonnet?

p. 172, "Jade's trick": Dobranski, op. cit., 236, 244–45.

p. 172, Sir Thomas Walsingham's letter: Huntington Library HA13066, reprinted in NELSON, 266.

p. 172, De Vere in Tower "for forgetting himself...": *The Fugger News-Letters, second series...*, ed. Victor von Klarwill, tr. L.S.R. Byrne (New York: G. P. Putnam's Sons, 1926), 55.

p. 172, Buc on de Vere's fathering "base son": Sir George Buc, hand annotation in Mill, *Catalogue of Honour* (1610), cited by J.E.N.[eale?], "Short Notices," *The Eng. Historical Review* 53:209 (January 1938), 163.

p. 173, De Vere's lack of votes for Order of the Garter: Peter R. Moore, "Oxford, the Order of the Garter, and Shame," *The Shakespeare Oxford Newsletter* 32:2 (Spring 1996), 1, 8–11; NELSON, 269. As Moore points out, to his credit Burghley "always voted for Oxford as his first choice among English 'princes'... even during his separation from his wife."

p. 173, Tower of London as one play's birthplace: Fran Gidley, Shakespeare in Composition: Evidence for [the Earl of] Oxford's Authorship of *The Book of Sir Thomas More,*" *The Oxfordian* 6 (2003), 29–54.

p. 173, ... fickle whims of the fates: Irving Ribner, *The English History Play in the Age of Shakespeare* (Princeton: Princeton University Press, 1957), 212–3.

p. 173, ... compared to the 1570 *Homily*: Ibid.

pp. 173–4, *Sir Thomas More*, fol. 9ʳ, ll. 116–147 (cited in *The Riverside Shakespeare*).

p. 174, ... later revisited and revised by at least five other hands: Some Stratfordians have argued that one of the hands in the *Sir Thomas More* MS is Shakspere of Stratford's. However, this book subscribes to the point of view presented by Samuel A. Tannenbaum (*Problems in Shakspere's Penmanship, Including a Study of the Poet's Will* [New York: The Century Co./Modern Lang. Ass'n of America, 1927], 179–211) when he concluded, "The weight of the evidence is overwhelmingly against the theory that in folios 8 and 9 of *The Booke of Sir Thomas Moore* we have a Shakspere [*sic*] holograph." Cf. also a similar note in the Introduction.

p. 174, Munday's foundation laying for *Sir Thomas More* in 1581 in the Tower?: Sarah Smith (*Chasing Shakespeares* [New York: Atria, 2003], 205–6) suggests a March–July 1581 time frame for the composition of *Sir Thomas More*.

p. 174, Varying reports of de Vere's child support payments: NELSON, 266; Alison Weir, *The Life of Elizabeth I* (New York: Ballantine, 1998), 261.

p. 174, Sir Henry Lee as Vavasour's jailer: Josephine Waters Bennett, "Oxford and *Endimion,*" *PMLA* 57:2 (June 1942), 364.

p. 174, Lee would land in hot water like de Vere before him: Chambers, *Lee,* op. cit., 160ff.

p. 174, "As for the rest, I leave it to thy thought": Ibid., 154.

p. 174, ... to remain under house arrest for a month or more: Chambers, *Lee,* op. cit., 156.

p. 174, Elizabeth's gift of a Dutch hat: NELSON, 272.

p. 175, De Vere's letter "shadow they can make a substance": Lansdowne MSS 33.6, reprinted in Fowler, 283–4.

p. 175, De Vere's attempted 1570 wardship: Katherine Chiljan, "The Wardship of Henry Bullock," *The Shakespeare Oxford Newsletter* 34:3 (Fall 1998), 4; NELSON, 276–7.

p. 175, Letter written by "Anne": Lansdowne MSS 104/64; I would like to thank Christopher Paul for pointing out the fact that these MSS are in Burghley's hand with his own corrections to the text.

p. 175, "I am utterly innocent": Lansdowne MSS 104.63, reprinted in WARD, 226.

p. 176, Her father wishes only the best for him: Lansdowne MSS 104.64, reprinted in WARD, 226–7.

p. 176, De Vere "hath company with his wife since Christmas": BL MS Cotton Appendix 47, f. 7v, reprinted in NELSON, 280.

Chapter Seven

p. 177, Danced for joy over collapse of Alençon marriage: READ/*BURGHLEY,* 269–70.

p. 177, Virginity vow in 1558 a posthumous myth: John N. King, "Queen Elizabeth I: Representations of the Virgin Queen," *Renaissance Quarterly* 43:1 (Spring 1990), 36–7.

p. 177, . . . the essence of the Virgin Queen's public image: King (58ff) pinpoints Spenser's *Shepheardes Calender* (1579) as a turning point, wherein both marriageable monarch and Virgin Queen reside. Spenser's imitator Thomas Blenerhasset (*A Revelation of the True Minerva* [1582]) would become the first of the new breed of Virgin Queen propagandists. Ivan L. Schulze, "Blenerhasset's *A Revelation,* Spenser's *Shepheardes Calender,* and the Kenilworth Pageants," *ELH* 11:2 (June 1944), 85–91.

p. 178, Account of "fray" between de Vere and Knyvet: Nicholas Faunt to Anthony Bacon. Lambeth Palace MS 647, f. 123, cited in NELSON, 280.

p. 178, ". . . these new MONTAGUES and CAPULETS": *"Comme autrefois à Véronne, les rues de Londres furent emplies par les clameurs querelleuses de ces nouveaux Montagues et Capulets."* Albert Feuillerat, *John Lyly: Contribution à l'Histoire de la Renaissance en Angleterre* (New York: Russell & Russell, 1910; 1968 repr.), 126.

p. 178, Burghley's later denials: Letter of March 12, 1582, Burghley to Hatton, reprinted in Harris Nicolas, *Memoirs of the Life and Times of Sir Christopher Hatton* (London: Richard Bentley, 1847), 321–24; NELSON (285), naturally, cannot take the otherwise sacrosanct Burghley at his word when the Lord Treasurer steps in to defend his son-in-law.

p. 178, Bonetti's injunctions against de Vere's men: Jay P. Anglin, "The Schools of Defense in Elizabethan London," *Renaissance Quarterly* 37:3 (Winter 1984), 409.

p. 179, ". . . soundly beat him with oars and stretchers for his pains": J. D. Aylward, "The Inimitable Bobadill," *Notes and Queries* 195 (January 7, 1950), 2–4, 28–31.

p. 179, Bonetti lived in Ludgate: K. T. Butler, "Some Further Information about Rocco Bonetti," *Notes and Queries* 195 (March 4, 1950), 96.

p. 179, Mauvissière to Walsingham re Bonetti: *CSP Foreign* 1583, no. 249, cited in NELSON, 287.

p. 179, ". . . mimetic resumé of changes in Elizabethan fencing": WALLACE, 188.

p. 179, *Romeo and Juliet,* 2.4.23–29; Joseph Quincy Adams, *Shakespearean Playhouses* (Cambridge, Mass: The Riverside Press, 1917), 195.

p. 180, . . . keep the peace, or perhaps a little of both: Gwynneth Bowen, "Touching the Affray at the Blackfriars," in MILLER/LOONEY, 2:85–94; NELSON, 280–2.

p. 180, De Vere "was somewhat grieved at it": John Hungerford Pollen and William MacMahon, *The Venerable Philip Howard, Earl of Arundel* (London: Catholic Record Soc., 1919), 33–6.

p. 180, *Romeo and Juliet,* 1.1.87–93; 3.3.93–5.

p. 181, Killing of Knyvet's servant one month after de Vere's man falls: Guildhall Library MS 4515; BL MS Add. 15891, ff. 53–54v., cited in NELSON, 283–4.

p. 181, De Vere did not answer duel challenge: Letter from Thomas Vavasour to de Vere, January 19, 1585, Lansdowne MSS 99.93 (WARD, 229, NELSON, 295–6). Vavasour, possibly a brother to Anne, writes out a series of bombastic accusations: "Is not the revenge taken of thy victims sufficient, but wilt thou yet use unworthy instruments to provoke my unwilling mind? Or dost thou fear thyself, and therefore hast sent thy forlorn kindred, whom as thou has left nothing to inherit so thou dost thrust them violently into thy shameful quarrels? . . . [U]se not thy birth for an excuse, for I am a gentleman, but meet me thyself alone and thy lackey to hold thy horse." The background to this letter is sorely lacking–although it is clear that Vavasour accuses de Vere of sending unspecified relatives to cause more mischief with the Vavasours. Just who those relative(s) is/are and what (s)he/they were doing remains to be uncovered.

p. 181, Thomas Edwardes's *Narcissus* excerpt:

Adon *[is]* deafly masking thro,
Stately troupes rich conceited,
Shew'd he well deserved to
Loves delight on him to gaze
And had not love her selfe intreated,
Other nymphs had sent him baies.

Eke [Likewise] in purple roabes distaind,
Amid'st the Center of this clime,
I have heard saie doth remaine,
One whose power floweth far,
That should have bene of our rime
The onely object and the star.

Well could his bewitching pen,
Done the Muses objects to us
Although he differs much from men
Tilting under Frieries,
Yet his golden art might woo us
To have honored him with baies.

–Thomas Edwardes, *L'Envoy* to *Narcissus* (1595). Reprinted in *The Shakspere [sic] Allusion Book*, ed. C. M. Ingleby, L. Loutmin Smith, F. J. Furnivall, John Munro (London: Oxford University Press, 1932), 1:26–27. *"Adon"* here has long been accepted as a personified allusion to Shake-speare, via his epic poem *Venus and Adonis*. (Edwardes refers to other authors, such as Christopher Marlowe and Edmund Spenser, by the names of their characters too.)

p. 181, ... unspecified nobleman poet: Charles Wisner Barrell, "Rarest Contemporary Description of 'Shakespeare' Proves Poet to Have Been a Nobleman," *The Shakespeare Fellowship Quarterly* 9:1 (Spring 1948), 1–7.

p. 181, "Tilting": For usages of *tilt* meaning swordfight, cf. *Romeo and Juliet*, 3.1.160 and *Othello*, 2.3.174.

p. 181, Translation: I am grateful to Roger Stritmatter for decoding these enigmatic lines and kindly sharing his translation of them. (Unpublished manuscript, 2001.)

p. 182, ... proudly displaying de Vere's coat of arms: CHILJAN, 3: Anthony Munday, *Mirror of Mutability* (1579); Munday, *Zelauto* (1579); Geffrey Gates, *Defense of Military Profession* (1579); John Lyly, *Euphues and His England* (1580); John Hester, *Discourse on Surgery* (1580).

p. 182, Translation of the sermons of John Calvin: Thomas Stocker, *Diverse Sermons of Master John Calvin* (1581): "...I would shew some piece of my humble duty unto Your Honor ... in respect of being sometimes, as then very young, brought up in your L. father's house." CHILJAN, 60.

p. 182, Watson's dedicatory letter: Thomas Watson, *The EKATOMΠAΘIA, or Passionate Centurie of Love* (N.d., registered March 1582), "To the Right Honorable My *Very Good* Lord Edward de Vere..."

p. 182, "Notes are the most interesting part of the book": C. S. Lewis, *English Literature in the Sixteenth Century, Excluding Drama* (Oxford: The Clarendon Press, 1954), 483; on the other hand Eric Lewin Altschuler and William Jansen ("Poet describes stars in Milky Way before Galileo," *Nature* 428 [April 8, 2004], 601) point out that Watson's Sonnet 31 is the first known description of the Milky Way as discrete stars–even predating Galileo's discovery of same.

p. 182, De Vere as likely author of *Hekatompathia* glosses: John Payne Collier (1849), cited in *Thomas Watson, Poems*, ed. Edward Arber (London: Privately published, 1870), 9.

p. 183, *Hekatompathia* gloss excerpt: Watson, *EKATOMΠΑΘΙA*. Publications of the Spenser Society, Manchester (1869), 55; Virgil excerpt from *The Aeneid,* 10.180-1: "Then follows Astyr, of wondrous beauty–Astyr, relying on his steed...," tr. H. Rushton Fairclough. Loeb Classical Library (London: William Heinemann, 1918), 183.

p. 183, Susenbrotus's influence on Shake-speare: T. W. Baldwin, *William Shakspere's [sic] Small Latine & Lesse Greeke* (Urbana: University of Illinois Press, 1944), 2:138–75.

p. 183, Watson's influence on Shake-speare: What follows are only a few examples of many: *The Sonnets and A Lover's Complaint,* ed. John Kerrigan (London: Harmondsworth, 1986) 19–20; William Minto, *Characteristics of English Poets from Chaucer to Sidney* (Edinburgh: W. Blackwood & Sons, 1874), 204; Virgil K. Whitaker, *Shakespeare's Use of Learning* (San Marino, Calif.: Huntington Library, 1953), 118; Edgar I. Fripp, *Shakespeare: Man and Artist* (London: H. Milford, 1938), 323.

p. 183, Meaning of *ancient: OED* definitions II.9, III.5, III.7.

p. 183, De Vere working on version of *Titus Andronicus?*: OGBURNS/*TSOE*, 343–58.

pp. 183-4, *Titus Andronicus,* 3.1.52-4, 5.3.104-18; OGBURNS/*TSOE*, op. cit., 351–8.

p. 184, "...set me on the proof": *Timon of Athens,* 2.2.137-161; Charles Wisner Barrell, "John Lyly as Both Oxford's and Shakespeare's 'Honest Steward,'" *The Shakespeare Fellowship Quarterly* 9:3 (Autumn 1948).

p. 185, Lyly as de Vere's bookkeeper: Barrell, "Lyly"; cf. NELSON (288–9) on further evidence of Lyly as de Vere's accountant.

p. 185, De Vere's signing off on creation of butcher shop in Hedingham village: PRO S.P. 12/155[/61], f.111, cited in NELSON, 289.

p. 186, Rash actions of jealous groom (CLAUDIO) unjustly raging against HERO: *Much Ado* also portrays the father of the wronged maid as a Burghley-like character (LEONATO is a "white bearded fellow" with a leading role in the government and a tendency to insinuate himself into conflicted relationships with the de Vere doppelgängers) who joins the jealous groom in accusing the chaste fiancée of infidelity. However, this twist in the plot shows de Vere going one step too far: So far as is known, Burghley never took the earl's side in proclaiming Anne's infidelity.

p. 186, Agent of evil is the mischief maker: DON JOHN's henchmen are also the authors of the DOGBERRY-recorded libels. Indeed, as the play suggests, the same real-life malefactors–led by Henry Howard–both helped to inflame the jealousy that drove de Vere from his wife Anne in 1576 and issued the voluminous libels that were the cause of such trouble for de Vere in the early 1580s. These same figures inspire the vicious IAGO too. Joyce E. Sexton (*The Slandered Woman in Shakespeare* [Victoria, B.C.: University of Victoria Press, 1978]) examines the interlinkages between the two slanderers DON JOHN and IAGO– and points out further connections to *Cymbeline's* IACHIMO.

p. 186, "Yet sinn'd I not–but in mistaking": Neither of *Much Ado*'s two sources nor any of the other contemporary analogues to the Ariodante tale so fully exonerate the jealous groom. In every version but Shake-speare's, the CLAUDIO character shoulders at least some of the blame for his irrational acts of jealousy against his wrongfully accused fiancée. (Kerby Neill, op. cit., 102-107.)

p. 186, "...whip you from your foining fence": *Much Ado,* 5.1.83-4. "Foining fence" is a parrying or defensive move in fencing. Thus ANTONIO tells CLAUDIO that in a duel he'd have the boy on the run. Note that, in typical Shake-spearean fashion, the historical duel between de Vere and Knyvet is creatively altered to suit the dramatic circumstances: ANTONIO (Knyvet) challenges CLAUDIO (de Vere) to a duel for slandering HERO (Anne Cecil)– and not, as it actually happened, for any tryst with ANTONIO's niece BEATRICE (Vavasour). In this play, ANTONIO is uncle of both BEATRICE and HERO. Thus both of de Vere's romantic interests are conveniently rendered cousins, simplifying the plot for him but probably complicating his life by offending the Cecils, for portraying them as kin to de Vere's mistress's unruly family.

p. 186, Elizabeth was considering reopening the investigation: NELSON, 290.

p. 186, On the Merchant Taylors' Boys: Richard Mulcaster, headmaster of the Merchant Taylors' School, was a leading educator and literary figure in Elizabethan London. Mulcaster had been Edmund Spenser's teacher and was an early and staunch advocate of vernacular literature in England. De Vere and Mulcaster were aesthetic and philosophical kindred spirits. Ellwood P. Cubberley, *The History of Education* (Boston: Houghton Mifflin, 1920), 433; *Ovid's Metamorphoses,* tr. Arthur Golding, ed. Madeleine Forey (Baltimore: Johns Hopkins University Press, 2002), xi.

p. 186, *Much Ado* based on legend of Ariodante and Genevora: "*Much Ado* is a play of two interlocking plots, one tragicomic, the other comic. The story of BEATRICE and BENEDICK is usually more interesting to modern readers than that of HERO and CLAUDIO [Genevra and Ariodant in Ariosto], but the latter is the core around which the other was wound, and to trace the provenance of the HERO-CLAUDIO actions throws light on Shakespeare's conception of his play and also his manner of blending sources." Geoffrey Bullough, *Narrative and Dramatic Sources of Shakespeare* (New York: Columbia University Press, 1958), 2:62. There is a second source of the jealous-lover story, in Matteo Bandello's 1554 novella *La Prima Parte de le Novelle.* (Bullough, 2:112–134.) However, *pace* Allison Gaw (*PMLA* 50:3 [September 1935], 720–1), Bandello's influence is only superficial. "It is clear that, although [Shake-speare] took most of his externals from the [Bandello] version, he drew upon the [Ariodante and Genevora] version for the larger elements of the conflict–the type of love, the degree of proof, and the punishment of evil." (Kerby Neill, "More Ado About CLAUDIO: An Acquittal for the Slandered Groom," *Shakespeare Quarterly* 3:2 [April 1952], 106.)

p. 187, Earl of Sussex's men presented *History of Error:* "The doggerel in [*Comedy of Errors*] Act III.i, etc., has been taken to show that the play revised an earlier work, maybe the lost *The historie of Error* play by Paul's in 1577 or 'A historie of fferrar' played by Sussex's men in 1583." BULLOUGH, 1:3.

p. 187, *Comedy of Errors* tells story of jealous groom and unjustly accused spouse: Chapter 5; A. Bronson Feldman, "Shakespeare's Early Errors," *Int. J. of Psycho-analysis* 36:2 (April 1955), 114–33; CHAMBERS/*WS*, 1:309.

p. 187, DUKE OF EPHESUS's observation: Feldman, op. cit., 116; *Comedy of Errors,* 5.1.332–5.

p. 188, "... to spend a foolish hour or two, because you can do nothing else": Thomas Dekker, *The Gull's Hornbook* (1609), cited in Michael Shapiro, *Children of the Revels* (New York: Columbia University Press, 1977), 71.

p. 188, "... make the boys in Paul's play it upon a stage": December 1584 letter to Sir Roger Williams, transcribed in F. P. Wilson, "An Ironicall Letter," *Modern Language Review* 15 (1920), 82; G. K. Hunter, *John Lyly: The Humanist as Courtier* (London: Routledge & Kegan Paul, 1962), 74–6.

p. 188, *Hamlet,* 2.2.315–319.

p. 188, Lyly's drama about statesman who gave up his paramour: The analogy between de Vere and Alexander the Great was not uncommon in the 1580s. In 1582, Thomas Watson published the poetry collection *Ekatompathia* with a dedication to de Vere that, in Watson's words, "fitlie compare[s] your Honors person with *Alexanders,* for excellencie." And Angel Day dedicated *The English Secretary* to de Vere in 1586, saying that if he were as good as Apelles at painting, "I should neither faint to present a discourse to Alexander nor to tell a tale to a philosopher." (Watson also uses the trope of Apelles.) CHILJAN, 63, 73. The present interpretation of *Campaspe* has never, to this biographer's knowledge, been suggested before.

p. 188, Lee's suit of armor with Vavasour's initials engraved on it: E. K. Chambers (*Sir Henry Lee* [Oxford: Clarendon Press, 1936]) notes that Lee and Vavasour became involved sometime between 1581 and 1590, most likely on the earlier end of this period. (Josephine

Waters Bennett, "Oxford and *Endymion*," *Publications of the Modern Language Association* 57[1942], 364.) As Bennett argues, Lyly also writes about Lee and Vavasour's relationship in his play *Endymion*.

p. 189, Two days old: The young countess of Oxford bewailed her son's "two daies" of life in "Foure Epytaphes made by the Countes of *Oxenford*, after the death of her young Sonne, *the Lord Bulbecke, &c.*" Printed in John Soowthern, *Pandora* (1584).

p. 189, ". . . when the drops of her cheeks rained daisies": Ibid., "Idall, for Adon, neu'r shed so many teares . . ." ll. 5–7; Peter R. Moore, private communication (August 2004).

p. 189, "To wrestle with nature": READ/BURGHLEY, 276.

p. 189, . . . buried their infant on May 9, 1583: WARD, 232.

p. 189, . . . alabaster monument to the fifteenth earl: "Why should a man whose blood is warm within/Sit like his grandsire, cut in alabaster?" *Merchant of Venice*, 1.1.83–4; MILLER/*HASP*, 330.

p. 189, . . . likely contained the remains of the sixteenth earl as well: William Addison, *Essex Worthies* (London: Phillimore, 1973), 190.

p. 189, Into a tomb beneath the floor . . . : Charles Bird, private communication (November 2002).

p. 190, Legend of ghost's visitations announced by the bell ringing once: *The Essex Countryside* 12:93 (October 1964), as cited in Gwenneth Bowen, "What Happened at Hedingham and Earls Colne?" *Shakespearean Authorship Review* 24 (Spring 1971), 10.

p. 190, . . . 1583 a year of grave consequences: Caroll Camden, Jr., "Elizabethan Almanacs and Prognostications" (Pt. 2), *The Library* 12 (1931), 194–207.

p. 190, One could see across the Essex and Suffolk countryside for ten or more miles: H. Ranger, *Castle Hedingham: Its History and Associations* (Halstead: R. L. Hughes, 1887), 14.

p. 190, Will Somers as YORICK's likely inspiration: *Hamlet*, 5.1.166–175; MILLER/*HASP*, 665–6. Orthodox scholarship has not advanced a likely candidate for Yorick's original. Yet, "no Elizabethan fool captured the imagination both of his contemporaries and of posterity as did Will Somers, who must indeed have been one of the most lovable of court-fools." (Enid Welsford, *The Fool* [London: Faber & Faber, 1935], 170.) Whether via his father's troupe or through connections at court, de Vere as a child evidently knew Somers—witness the de Vere doppelgänger "Ver" in de Vere's secretary Thomas Nashe's play *Summer's Last Will and Testament* (1592), a play in which Will Somers and Ver clown around as if they were old buddies.

In addition, literary allusions in *Hamlet* suggest an early 1580s milieu. *Hamlet*, for one, features allusions to de Vere's own poetry from the 1570s and '80s (cf. *The Poems of Edward de Vere*, ed. Ruth Loyd Miller, in Looney, *"Shakespeare Identified,"* third ed. [Port Washington, N.Y.: Kennikat Press, 1975], 1:572–82). And *Hamlet* cites numerous literary texts written by others in the early 1580s: e.g., *Hamlet*, 1.3.59–72=John Lyly's *Euphues* (1580); *Hamlet*, 1.3.115=Stephen Gosson's *Apology for the School of Abuse* (1580); *Hamlet*, 2.2.236–244= Stephen Batman's *Doom: Warning All Men to Judgement* (1581); *Hamlet*, 2.2.350–354= Stephen Gosson's *School of Abuse* (1579); Thomas Lodge's *Defense of Poetry, Music, and Stage Plays* (1580); Stephen Gosson's *Plays Confuted in Five Actions* (1582); *Hamlet*, 3.2.23–26=*Plays Confuted in Five Actions* (1582); *Hamlet*, 3.2.212=Anonymous, *History of Love and Fortune* (1582); *Hamlet*, 4.3.9–10=*Euphues* (1580); *Hamlet*, 4.5.23–26=*Plays Confuted in Five Actions* (1582); *Hamlet*, 4.5.175=Various, *A Handful of Pleasant Delites* (1584). (HOLLAND/SHAKESPEARE OXFORD, 60–80).

p. 190, . . . continue revising this play throughout his life: There are three editions of *Hamlet*: The 1603 first edition ("First Quarto" or Q1), the 1604 second edition ("Second Quarto" or Q2), and the 1623 edition published in the complete works of Shake-speare (Folio or F). The title page of Q1 states that the version of *Hamlet* it retails is one that has been acted in the "City of London; as also in the two Universities of Cambridge and

Oxford." It is, in other words, a touring version of the play for the general public. Thus, many of the court in-jokes (as will be seen below) are excised from it. (However, in-jokes that the audience might get are kept: Hamlet's extended allusion to William Gager's *Dido*, performed at Oxford University in June 1583 (cf. below) remains in Q1.) Stylistically, Q1 is laughably inferior to Q2 and F. (For instance, Q1's famous soliloquy begins "To be or not to be; aye, here's the point. To die, to sleep, is that all? Aye, all.") Q1 would appear to originate in one or more actors' memorial reconstruction(s) of the text.

In 1589, Thomas Nashe wrote of "whole Hamlets of tragical speeches" in his preface to Robert Greene's *Menaphon*. This is taken by orthodox scholars to be an allusion to some *other* Elizabethan play titled *Hamlet*. (This fictitious play is today given the official-sounding name of the *"Ur-Hamlet."*) Yet the only reason for this theoretical shell game is chronology: If the Stratford player were the actual author, it would have been practically impossible for him to have turned out *Hamlet* before 1589. He hadn't even appeared in London by that point.

The scholarship needed to piece together the real story behind these three competing versions of *Hamlet*–Q1, Q2, and F–has yet to be done. For the present purposes, Q1 will be treated as actors' memorial reconstructions of an early touring text and Q2 and F will be considered later revisions of the play, replete with court in-jokes and all.

p. 190, . . . most of the other texts from which Shake-speare's plays are derived: Eddi Jolly, " 'Shakespeare' and Burghley's Library: *Bibliotheca Illustris: Sive Catalogus Variorum Librorum,*" *The Oxfordian* 3 (2000), 3–18.

p. 190, Chronicle histories of Belleforest: As Bronson Feldman points out (*Hamlet Himself* [Philadelphia: Lovelore Press, 1977], 28), Belleforest's *Histoires Tragiques* was published in Lyons, the fifth volume of which came out in 1576. De Vere was in Lyons on his way to Paris in March of 1576. It's entirely plausible that he picked up a copy of this volume for himself on his way through town.

p. 190, . . . were to be found within Burghley's collection: The primary source for *Hamlet* is in the twelfth-century book *Historia Danica* by Saxo Grammaticus. There was a French analogue to this tale which appeared in Belleforest's *Histoires Tragiques* (1576). Possible sources include Erasmus's *In Praise of Folly* and Seneca's *Troas* and *Agamemnon*. All were in the library at Cecil House. (Catalogue of library of Lord Ailesbury. British Library 821.i.8.(1.), microfilm; cited in Eddi Jolly, op. cit.) Contrary to popular critical belief, however, there was no *"Ur-Hamlet,"* which conventionally is assumed to have been Shake-speare's other source. The *"Ur-Hamlet"* was nothing more than his own first draft(s). Cf. above.

p. 191, Sturmius confides his hope that de Vere would visit Elsinore: Sturmius to Burghley, December 4, 1577, *Cal. S.P. For.* (1577), 349–50, cited in FELDMAN, 30. Sturmius first notes that he hopes Burghley and his wife might "bring from our Queen presents to the King of Denmark's wife." Then, noting the importance of well-educated wives who themselves can be part of a diplomatic mission to a foreign court, Sturmius adds, "As I write this I think of the Earl of Oxford, for I believe his lady speaks Latin also."

p. 191, The previous summer: B. M. Ward (234) incorrectly lists the year of Willoughby's first embassy to Elsinore as 1583.

p. 191, "... to the clouds shall tell": *Hamlet* quotation from Q1, corresponds to 1.2.125–126; Cotton MSS Titus C VII 229.

p. 191, . . . with the family name of Rosenkrantz and two surnamed Guldenstern: The guest list of a banquet that Willoughby attended features the names Georgius Rosenkrantz, Petrus Guldenstern, and Axellus Guldenstern; Cotton MSS. Titus C VII 224. n.b. in Q1 the courtiers are named "Rossenkraft" and "Guilderstone"–one more point in favor of Q1 being a memorial reconstruction of the play.

p. 191, Tycho Brahe's supernova: Donald W. Olson, Marilynn S. Olson, Russell L. Doescher, "The Stars of *Hamlet,*" *Sky & Telescope* (November 1998).

p. 191, *Hamlet*'s use of cosmological language: Peter Usher, "Shakespeare's Cosmic World View," *Mercury* 26:1 (January–February 1997), 20–23; all of the here-listed astronomical (and therefore geocentric) utterances of the king except one–"fault to heaven"– are missing in Q1. For the likely reason, cf. extended *"Ur-Hamlet"* note above.

p. 192, "She meant ... only thereby to give him warning": Edward Edwards, *The Life of Sir Walter Raleigh* (London: Macmillan and Co., 1868), 2:21–22.

p. 192, Books relating to succession were considered treason: Henry Howard, *A defensative against the poison of supposed prophesies* ... (1583) STC 13858; 116^v and 120–120^v (page numbers from 1620 reprint, STC 13859); Josephine Waters Bennett, "Oxford and *Endimion*," *PMLA* 57 (1942), 357, fn. 16.

p. 192, Mockingly quoting from Howard's *Defensative* in Shake-speare: C. G. Harlow, "The Authorship of *1 Henry VI* (Continued)," *Studies in English Literature, 1500–1900* 5:2 (Spring 1965), 269–81.

p. 192, De Vere having spoken of Raleigh as upstart courtier: Robert Naunton, *Fragmenta Regalia,* ed. Edward Arber (London: Southgate, 1870; reprinted from the third ed., 1653), 47.

p. 193, " ... myself may be most in danger of his poison and sting": Edwards, *Life of Raleigh,* 2:22.

p. 193, "Pondus is angry ...": Cal. Rutland MSS; reprinted in WARD, 233.

p. 193, Countess of Sussex letter: Harris Nicholas, op. cit., 345–6; FELDMAN, 40–41.

p. 193, Sussex's supporters wore yellow; Leicester's wore purple: Margaret P. Hannay, *Philip's Phoenix: Mary Sidney, Countess of Pembroke* (Oxford: Oxford University Press, 1990), 29–30.

p. 193, "You know not the beast so well as I do": Robert Naunton, *Fragmenta Regalia,* ed. Edward Arber (London: Southgate, 1870; 1653 first ed.), 30.

p. 193, Sussex had been an outspoken isolationist: Simon Adams, "Eliza Enthroned? The Court and Its Politics," *The Reign of Elizabeth I,* ed. Christopher Haigh (Athens: University of Georgia Press, 1985), 67.

p. 193, "Hyperion's curls, the front of Jove himself": FELDMAN, 77–78; 87.

p. 193, On the death of Earl John: For the background of Earl John's death and the potential *motives* for Leicester to kill Earl John, cf. Christopher Paul (with additional commentary by Nina Green and Carl Caruso), "Post Mortem on John de Vere, sixteenth Earl of Oxford," *Shakespeare Oxford Newsletter* 40:2 (Spring 2004), 8–9.

pp. 193–4, Leicester poisoned Sussex?: *Leicester's Commonwealth,* ed. D. C. Peck (Athens, Ohio: Ohio University Press, 1985; 1584 first ed.), 85.

p. 194, Arundell claimed ... : PECK/*COMMONWEALTH,* 25–31, makes the case for Arundell's authorship of *Leicester's Commonwealth.*

p. 194, "Rare artist in poison": *Fragmenta Regalia,* 43–44.

p. 194, List of persons Leicester alleged to have poisoned: John Lothrop Motley, *History of the United Netherlands* (New York: Harper, 1898), 1:368.

p. 194, Leicester excited "extreme fear": William Tresham to Sussex, January 27, 1582, cited in Alan Kendall, *Robert Dudley, Earl of Leicester* (London: Cassell, 1980), 191.

p. 194, Making Leicester the poisoner CLAUDIUS of *Hamlet:* On the connections between Claudius and Leicester, cf. Georg Brandes, *William Shakespeare* (London: William Heinemann, 1924), 364.

p. 194, No record exists of de Vere's attendance at Oxford [in 1583]: The bill of accounts (transcribed in "A University Entertainment in 1583," *The Oxford Magazine* [November 16, 1911], 85–6) represents the only record this biographer has been able to find for the Laski visit. These account books provide no record of the courtiers in attendance during the four-day university visit.

p. 194, The thirsty would turn down water ... : One other piece of evidence suggests that de Vere joined the court at Oxford from June 10–13, 1583: On June 20, de Vere wrote to his father-in-law to plead for financial assistance for one of Oxford University's top administrators: John Lord Lumley, the university's High Steward. De Vere had recently been briefed about Lumley's case–he writes about how loan payments to the Queen were then crippling the administrator. (WARD, 245-6) Both the information and motivation behind this letter are easily explained if de Vere had attended Oxford's big event. What better source is there for de Vere's letter than a conversation with Lumley himself?

p. 195, "... with Aeneas's narration of the destruction of Troy": *Holinshed's Chronicles of England, Scotland, and Ireland* (London: J. Johnson, 1807-8), 4:508.

p. 195, *Dido* manuscript: The MS is reproduced in photofacsimile in the Renaissance Latin Drama in England series (ed. J. W. Binns [Hildesheim/New York: George Olms 1981]) and in transcript with English translation (ed. J. W. Binns) in *Humanistica Lovaniensia* 20 (1971), 167-254.

p. 195, General savored the play like a delicacy: Frederick S. Boas, *University Drama in the Tudor Age* (Oxford: Clarendon Press, 1914), 183-191.

p. 195, *Dido's* Aeneas's father "advising a hasty flight": Binns, *Humanistica Lovaniensia*, op. cit., 214.

p. 195, The Danish tragedy suggests the author had seen this production: Technically, there was one other known drama about the Carthage Queen during the Elizabethan reign–performed at Cambridge University in 1564, when de Vere and a number of other courtiers got their (probably honorary) degrees. Boas, op. cit., 94; Tom Goff, "For if the Queen Like Not the Comedy," *Shakespeare Oxford Newsletter* 26:1 (Winter 1990), 14.

p. 195, " 'Twas caviar to the general": "The Player's Speech is so presented as to make it a visual image of the slaughter of a king by a remorseless avenger." (Arthur Jonhston, "The Player's Speech in *Hamlet,*" *Shakespeare Quarterly* 13:1 [Winter 1962], 27). Both HAMLET's description of *Dido* and the player's speech–albeit in truncated form–appear in Q1. (Interestingly, Q1 HAMLET says *Dido* was not acted "above twice," leading to the question of whether Gager revived his drama at Oxford anytime after the Laski command performance.) As speculated above, the reason the *Dido* references were kept in Q1 at all may be because allusions to the university drama were something that Oxford audiences would have understood and appreciated. However, the pun about the "general" does not appear. Q1 reads "It pleased not the vulgar; it was caviary to the million."

pp. 195-6, Bruno on the soul and the fivefold sphere: Giordano Bruno, *The Ash Wednesday Supper,* trans. Edward A. Gosselin and Lawrence S. Lerner (Hamden, Conn.: Archon Books, 1977), 187.

p. 196, Account of Bruno's presentation in thick Italian accent: Reprinted in Robert McNulty, "Bruno at Oxford," *Renaissance News* 13:4 (Winter 1960), 302-3.

p. 196, "Have them tell you ... about the extraordinary patience of the Nolan": Ibid.

p. 196, "Monads" contain a divine spark at the root of life: Dorothea Waley Singer, "The Cosmology of Giordano Bruno (1548-1600)," *Isis* 33:2 (June 1941), 187-96.

p. 196, Monads reconsidered in studies of conscious mind: Stuart Hameroff, "Fundamental [*sic*] Geometry: The Penrose-Hameroff 'Orch OR' Model of Consciousness," in *The Geometric Universe: Science, Geometry, and the Work of Roger Penrose,* ed. S. A. Huggett, L. J. Mason, K. P. Tod, S. T. Tsou and N. M. J. Woodhouse (Oxford: Oxford University Press, 1998), 136.

p. 196, De Vere moved by Bruno's remarkable show: One of de Vere's secretaries, Nicholas Hill, would become one of Bruno's most outspoken advocates in England. Daniel Massa, "Giordano Bruno's Ideas in Seventeenth Century England," *Journal of the Hist. of Ideas* 38:2 (April-June 1977), 228.

p. 196, Each Bruno tenet expressed in *Hamlet:* Hilary Gatti, *The Renaissance Drama of Knowledge: Giordano Bruno in England* (London: Routledge, 1989). Some may object that the complete list of points debated by Bruno at Oxford in 1583 is unknown. (E.g., Ernan McMullin, "Giordano Bruno at Oxford," *Isis* 77:1 [March 1986], 85-94) However, this point is immaterial, since the contents of the 1580s version of *Hamlet* are also subject to speculation.

p. 196, "... were it not that I have bad dreams": *Hamlet,* 2.2.254–6.

p. 197, "... congregation of vapors": *Hamlet,* 2.2.298–303. N.B.: Only the Bruno-inspired rhetoric of HAMLET's letter to OPHELIA (cf. below) made it into Q1. For the likely reason, cf. long note above. Peter R. Moore ("*Hamlet* and Surrey's Psalm 8," *Neophilologus* 82 (1998), 497–98) reveals that HAMLET's speech here also owes something to the paraphrase of Psalm 8 written by de Vere's uncle, the earl of Surrey.

p. 197, "... this quintessence of dust": *Hamlet,* 2.2.303–8; HAMLET's interrogation of Bruno's monad theory can also be found in his graveyard banter with HORATIO (*e.g.,* "Why may not imagination trace the noble dust of Alexander, till 'a find it stopping a bunghole?" 5.1.203–4).

p. 197, "I am that I am ...": FOWLER, 320–1.

p. 197, POLONIUS: In Q1 of *Hamlet,* POLONIUS is named "Corambis" (*cor ambis,* "double hearted")–a pun on the Cecil family motto *Cor Unum Via Una* (one heart, one way). The name POLONIUS is also fraught with meaning, since Burghley was nicknamed "Pondus" (cf. June 2, 1583, letter quoted above). Also, as HAMLET mouths Giordano Bruno's philosophies, so Polonius stands in opposition as the pedants Bruno faced down–one of whom, in Bruno's dialogues, was named Pollinio. (Gatti, op. cit., 131.) *Also,* as Andrew Hannas points out ("Gabriel Harvey and the Genesis of 'William Shakespeare,'" *Shakespeare Oxford Society Newsletter* 29:1B [Winter 1993], 1–8; 6), the pedant whom Socrates mocks in the *Gorgias* was named Polos.

p. 198, Quotation from Exodus 3:14: This verse is *not* marked in de Vere's Geneva Bible–yet the "I am that I am" passage is in one of his personal letters, in his own handwriting. This example is important to bear in mind in interpreting the de Vere Bible: One mustn't assume merely because de Vere makes a biblical allusion (whether in his personal letters or in Shake-speare) that therefore the corresponding verse must have been marked in his Geneva Bible.

p. 198, "He wasn't the power behind the throne but the power in front of it": John Guy, "Why Starkey Is Wrong About Elizabeth," *The Sunday Times,* November 11, 2001.

p. 198, "... thus justifies the smut of HAMLET's remarks": Myron Taylor, "Tragic Justice and the House of POLONIUS," *Studies in English Literature, 1500–1900* 8:2 (Spring 1968), 281.

p. 199, This annual glance toward England's feudal past: Details from the 1584 Accession Day Tournament come from the German correspondent Lupold von Wedel, whose account is reprinted in *Queen Elizabeth and Some Foreigners,* ed. Victor von Klarwill, tr. T. H. Nash (London: John Lane, 1928), 330–2.

p. 199, "Terra Benedicta...": "The Ditchley MS," British Museum Additional MS 41499B, 34–35. E. K. Chambers provides a calendar of the MS in Appendix D of his biography *Sir Henry Lee* (Oxford: Clarendon Press, 1936), 268–75. Chambers supposes, based on the proximity of this speech to a poem dated November 17, 1584, that the "Temple of Peace" speech also dates to the Accession Day Tournament of 1584. (272.)

The earls of Oxford and Arundel, both of whom participated in this tournament, were both still climbing out of the shadow cast upon them for falling out of royal favor. The two knights in this speech seem also to be paying penance for a recent falling-out. Arundel–the Duke of Norfolk's son, not the traitor Charles Arundell whom de Vere had squealed on–and de Vere, I suggest, may have been the two knights of this speech.

p. 199, "Our most dear cousin Edward Earl of Oxford...": Original text in Latin; CLARK, 273.

p. 199, ... considered petitions for adventurers seeking to explore the New World: Sir Simonds D'Ewes, *The Journals of All the Parliaments During the Reign of Queen Elizabeth* (1682); reprinted in CLARK, 273.

p. 200, Rumors as early as 1583 of a Spanish Armada: De Lamar Jensen, "The Spanish

Armada: The Worst-Kept Secret in Europe," *The Sixteenth Century Journal* 19:4 (Winter 1988), 623.

p. 200, In 1584: Since 1578, Elizabeth's onetime fiancé the French duke of Alençon had reigned as the Protestant Lord Protector of The Netherlands. However, in June of 1584, the Protestant forces were left leaderless when the thirty-year-old Alençon suddenly died, sending the queen into a period of protracted mourning for her dearly beloved "brother." (This may be the source of OLIVIA's mourning for her brother in *Twelfth Night.*)

p. 201, A Portuguese assassin nearly killed Prince William: The March 17, 1582, assassination attempt against Prince William of Orange finds a possible analogy to the assassination in Shake-speare's *Julius Caesar.* (Both happened at or around the Ides of March; both were heralded by prophecies [a comet appeared in the heavens in the spring of 1582], both Prince William and CAESAR had once been offered the crown and refused). De Vere, out of royal favor at the time of the assassination, may nevertheless have covertly staged a first draft of *Caesar* to rouse the Queen out of inaction over the assassination attempt–which the prince survived only after weeks of medical trauma that it was assumed he would not survive. Eva Turner Clark (*Hidden Allusions in Shakespeare's Plays*) points out allusions in *Caesar* that suggest the play's possible 1582 genesis. However, she unconvincingly links this play to a recorded court performance by Sussex's Men in January 1583 of *"A History of fferrar"*–almost certainly a revived *History of Error,* i.e., an early draft of *The Comedy of Errors.* cf. Chapter 9 for an alternate historical reading of *Julius Caesar.*

p. 201, Sturmius pleading for English force to be sent to Lowlands: *Calendar of State Papers Foreign* (1583–4), 404; reprinted in Ward, 250.

p. 201, William the Silent's assassination: C. V. Wedgwood, *William the Silent* (New York: W. W. Norton & Co., 1968; 1944, first. ed.), 250.

p. 201, Elizabeth might rule over the Dutch as new subjects to the English crown: R. C. Strong and J. A. van Dorsten, *Leicester's Triumph* (London: Oxford University Press, 1964), 3.

p. 201, Pleas to appoint Leicester commander of Dutch campaign: Strong, op. cit., 7.

p. 201, *Agamemnon and Ulysses:* Feuillerat, op. cit., 365; In *The Merry Wives of Windsor,* de Vere spoofed his Welsh children's playmaster Henry Evans as the Welsh children's playmaster *Hugh* EVANS. Note also that the real-life Evans, in the present context, staged a children's drama for de Vere at Windsor Castle. In the final act of *Merry Wives,* EVANS leads a troupe of children in a fairy masque whose centerpiece song is a close cousin to a fairy song that appears in Lyly's play *Endymion.* (*Merry Wives,* 5.5.99–102/*Endymion,* 4.3.33–37) In the play, EVANS is portrayed as a mischievous pedant–mediocre in his scholarship (his thick Welsh accent is the source of numerous jokes and malaprops) but distinguished as a trickster. Two chief scenes in *Merry Wives* find Evans doing both things for which de Vere's tenure at the Blackfriars was notorious–dueling and putting on children's plays.

p. 201, De Vere as author of this "lost" play: "I firmly believe that *Agamemnon and Ulysses* (though I agree it might have been a 'probable subject for Lyly,' as indeed it might have been for any other dramatist of that time), is one of Oxford's lost comedies." Feuillerat, op. cit., 471.

p. 201, Dispute between AGAMEMNON and ULYSSES forms core of larger play: Camille Slights ("The Parallel Structure of *Troilus and Cressida,*" *Shakespeare Quarterly* 25:1 [Winter 1974], 42–51) dissects the parallelism between *Troilus and Cressida's* titular plot of love and betrayal and the plotline that plays out in the Greek camp, including the AGAMEMNON and ULYSSES thread. As Slights notes, "The war story and the love story are not closely linked narratively." (48.) However, the scenes between AGAMEMNON and ULYSSES (most notably in 1.3) "constitute one of the dominant parallel patterns in the dramatic design, enlarging the scope of the satire and providing the intellectual and ethical context of the characters' behavior." (43.)

p. 201, Language and rhetorical tricks that were fashionable in the 1580s: F. Quinland

Daniels, "Order and Confusion in *Troilus and Cressida* I.iii," *Shakespeare Quarterly* 12:3 (Summer 1961), 287.

p. 202, William the Silent's campaign lasted since 1577: *Troilus and Cressida*, 1.3.12; "In 1577, all of the [Lowlands] provinces joined the Union of Brussels, shelving religious disputes and pledging to fight Spain until Philip restored their privileges and withdrew his troops. William was recognized as their military commander." Richard S. Dunn, *The Age of Religious Wars, 1559–1715* (New York: W.W. Norton & Co., 1979), 44.

p. 202, On ULYSSES: Daniels, 288.

p. 202, On AGAMEMNON: Daniels, 287–88, 290.

p. 202, *Troilus and Cressida*, 1.3.79–88.

p. 203, Republican notions in Dutch uprising seeded later revolutionary wars: Gordon Griffiths, "The Revolutionary Character of the Revolt of the Netherlands," *Comparative Studies in Society and History* 2:4 (July 1960), 452–72.

p. 203, Hampton Court Portrait: A definitive identification of the Hampton Court Portrait's sitter needs to be done. Charles Wisner Barrell's attribution study was only reported in the *Chicago Tribune* ("Infra-Red Peers into Mystery of Shakespeare," by John Astley-Cock [May 30, 1947]). A summary of Barrell's findings, along with a reproduction of the Hampton Court portrait, is reprinted in MILLER/LOONEY, 2:410.

p. 204, ... makes for a tempting theory indeed: Suggested by A. Bronson Feldman, "OTHELLO in Reality," *American Imago* 11 (1954), 160–1.

p. 204, Royal Navy's shipwrights' increased workload: David Loades, *The Tudor Navy: An Administrative, Political, and Military History* (Hants, UK: Scolar [*sic*] Press, 1992), 193.

p. 204, *Hamlet*, 1.1.75–81.

p. 204, Elizabeth rebuked Norris: "Sir John Norris" entry in the *DNB*.

p. 204, De Vere appointed Commander of the Horse in the Lowlands: This appointment is recorded secondhand in a letter from Thomas Doyley to the earl of Leicester on October 14, 1585. NELSON, 298.

p. 205, De Vere had crossed the Channel to meet his retinue: WARD, 252.

p. 205, "God save Queen Elizabeth!": Strong, op. cit., 37.

p. 205, Byrd stripped of Battylshall estate: Edmund H. Fellowes, *William Byrd* (Oxford: Clarendon Press, 1948), 3–5.

p. 205, Possible military origins of "Earl of Oxford's March": I am indebted to Sally Mosher (private communication, 2002) for lending her expertise on the question of Byrd's original purpose in composing "The Earl of Oxford's March."

p. 205, Names of Lowlands commanders in *All's Well That Ends Well:* "The captains of the Florentine army mentioned by PAROLLES appear to have many of their names based on those of the leaders in Flanders in 1586:

Guiltian	William or Roger Williams
Lodovice	Lewis
Jacques	Jacobzoon
Vaumond	de Warmond
Corambis	Sir Thomas Cecil
Gratii	Sir Philip Sidney

"The two latter [i.e., Cecil and Sidney] were the Governors of two of the towns in Flanders, and the names are suggestive of the Cecil and Sidney mottos." HOLLAND/OXFORD GLASSES, 113.

p. 206, Consider sending over "a nobleman": Cotton MSS, Galba C., VIII., 113, reprinted in WARD, 253.

p. 206, OTHELLO recalled home from his wars: *Othello,* 3.3.349–54; "OTHELLO, too, was replaced in command by one he resented: CASSIO." OGBURN/*TMWS,* 685.

p. 206, Spanish pirates looted boatload of de Vere's provisions: NELSON, 297–99.

p. 206, "This letter appointed him to the command of the Horse": Thomas Wright, *Queen Elizabeth and Her Times* (London: H. Colborn, 1838), 2:266; quoted in Ward, 254.

CHAPTER EIGHT

p. 207, Increased cash flow for military spending: Bernard M. Ward, "Shakespeare and the Anglo-Spanish War, 1585–1604," *Revue Anglo Americaine* (December 1929), in MILLER/LOONEY, 2:454–61; E. P. Cheyney, *A History of England from the Defeat of the Armada to the Death of Elizabeth* (New York: Longmans, 1926), 2:225–33.

p. 207, Walsingham heedless of artistic mission of Queen's Men: Scott McMillin and Sally-Beth MacLean, *The Queen's Men and Their Plays* (Cambridge: Cambridge University Press, 1998), 24–8.

p. 207, Walsingham recognized propagandistic potential of theater: Paul Whitfield White, "Playing Companies and the Drama of the 1580s: A New Direction for Elizabethan Theatre History?" *Shakespeare Studies* (2000), 265ff.

p. 208, Queen's Men's plays emphasizing "truth": McMillin & MacLean, op. cit., 32–36.

p. 208, History became a passport to the present: Irving Ribner, "The Tudor History Play: An Essay in Definition," *PMLA* 69:3 (June 1954), 591–609; Lily B. Campbell, *Shakespeare's "Histories": Mirrors of Elizabethan Policy* (San Marino, Calif.: The Huntington Library, 1947), 55–84.

p. 208, All of which were later published: G. M. Pinciss, "Thomas Creede and the Repertory of the Queen's Men 1583–1592," *Modern Philology* 67:4 (May 1970), 323; McMillin and MacLean, op. cit., 88–9.

p. 208, . . . sources for their respective Shake-spearean counterparts: BULLOUGH, 3:237–48; 4:1–24; 7:269–308; Seymour M. Pitcher, *The Case for Shakespeare's Authorship of "The Famous Victories"* (New York: SUNY Press, 1961).

p. 208, *Source* is too timid a word for these texts: Eric Sams (*The Real Shakespeare: Retrieving the Early Years, 1564–1594* [New Haven: Yale University Press, 1995], 146–53) makes a case that *Troublesome Raigne* and *King John* represent, respectively, immature and mature Shake-speare. On the other hand, E.A.J. Honigmann (*Shakespeare's Impact on his Contemporaries* [Totowa, N.J.: Barnes & Noble Books, 1982], 78–88) and Brian Boyd (*"King John* and *The Troublesome Raigne,"* *Philological Quarterly* 74:1 [1995], 37ff.) argue that Shake-speare's *King John* may in fact have been a source for *Troublesome Raigne.* Perhaps, in this scenario, *Troublesome Raigne* was a "dumbed down" provincial touring version of the more sophisticated Shake-spearean text.

p. 208, Probably written in collaboration with Munday and Lyly: The case for de Vere's authorship of a portion of the Queen's Men's repertory–perhaps in collaboration with his secretaries John Lyly and Anthony Munday–begins with the following observations: *The Troublesome Reign of King John* uses a source text that de Vere and very few others in England had any access to. ("Mrs. Martin Le Boutillier," *Bale's Kynge Johan* and the *Troublesome Raigne,"* *Modern Language Notes* 36:1 [January 1921], 55–7.) *The Famous Victories of Henry V,* as noted in earlier chapters, inserts the story of de Vere's men's confrontation with Burghley's men at or near Gad's Hill in 1572. And *The Famous Victories* and *True Tragedy of Richard the Third* glorifies the earl of Oxford character (based on the historical eleventh and thirteenth earls of Oxford, respectively) in a glaringly ahistorical way (Pitcher, op. cit., 184–5; on the thirteenth earl of Oxford's ahistorical role in *The True Tragedie of Richard the Third,* cf. Chapter 9.) This suggests that if the author wasn't Edward de Vere, it was somebody in his employ.

p. 208, "Policy of plays is very necessary": Thomas Nashe, *Pierce Penniless* in *The Works of Thomas Nashe,* ed. Ronald B. McKerrow (Oxford: Basil Blackwell, 1958), 2:211–12; G. B. Harrison, *Elizabethan Plays and Players* (Ann Arbor: University of Michigan Press, 1956), 99–100.

pp. 208–9, "...brave TALBOT, the terror of the French": Ibid., 212–3.

p. 209, De Vere was working for the state in a new capacity: Note also that in his 1593 pamphlet *Pierces Supererogation*, Gabriel Harvey refers to a man he nicknames "The Ass"—whom Elizabeth Appleton van Dreunen (VAN DREUNEN, 215ff.) has identified as de Vere. Harvey writes,

> Marvel not...that so many singular learned men have labored [over] the com-
> mendation of the Ass: He it is, that is the godfather of writers, the superintendent
> of the press, the muster-master of innumerable bands, the general of the great field:
> He and Nashe will confute the world!

(*The Works of Gabriel Harvey, D.C.L.*, ed. Alexander B. Grosart [New York: AMS Press, 1966; first ed. 1884], 2:79–80.)

It is a matter for future study to determine precisely what Harvey meant when he claimed that "The Ass" was a "superintendent of the press." Against the interpretation of *superintendent* as supervisor or censor, one must also weigh the fact that, in the words of Oxfordian researcher Robert Detobel, "The censors of the press are always explicitly named in the entries of the Stationer's Register. There is not a single trace in the Stationer's Register and the Court Books to support such a view." (Detobel, private communication [August 2004].)

p. 209, "...more troubled for her husband's lack than he himself": June 21, 1586, Burghley to Walsingham, in Cal. S.P. Dom., transcribed by Francis Edwards and reprinted (in part) in Derran Charlton, "Some Documents in the Case of Shakespeare's Authorship," *De Vere Society Newsletter* 3:2 (Feb. 1999), 6–7.

p. 209, Four days later: NELSON, 300. N.B.: previous scholars (e.g., WARD, 251; FOWLER, 342) had misread the letter's date as being June 24, *1585*.

pp. 209–10, "...till Her Majesty perform her promise": Lansdowne MSS 50.22, reprinted in FOWLER, 342.

p. 210, Comparable to $270,000 today: According to Economic History Services (www.eh.net), £1,000 in 1586 had the same purchasing power as £176,000 in 2002.

p. 210, No strings attached: PRO S.P. 12/190[/47], ff. 97–98, in WARD.

p. 210, Neither the seal nor the language hints at queen's motives: WARD (260) may have overreached when he wrote that the language of Elizabeth's Privy Seal warrant was made out following "the usual formula made use of in the case of secret service money." **On the seal:** Leonard W. Labaree and Robert E. Moody, "The Seal of the Privy Council," *The English Historical Review* 43:170 (Apr. 1928), 200; **On the language:** WARD cites, as his comparative example of secret service annuities, the queen's Privy Seal grant to Walsingham. But Conyers Read (*Mr. Secretary Walsingham and the Policy of Queen Elizabeth* (Cambridge: Harvard University Press, [1925], 2:370) notes, "A great deal of money was drawn from the treasury under such vague warrants as these."

p. 210, Queen's Men ramping up performance schedule: McMillin and McLean (op. cit., 175–88) track all the recorded performances of the Queen's Men. Between the troupe's first recorded performance in June of 1583 and de Vere's June 1586 £1,000 grant, the Queen's Men made forty-four known performances (and an additional eleven that fall sometime during the period of October 1585–November 1586)—an average of between fourteen and eighteen performances per year; during the next three-year period (June 1586–June 1589), the Queen's Men performed eighty-one known times (with an additional sixteen that may or may not fall into this date range)—making for an average of between twenty-seven and thirty-two performances per year.

p. 210, No more than £50 per year: Christopher Hibbert, *The Virgin Queen: Elizabeth I, Genius of the Golden Age* (Cambridge, Mass.: Perseus Books, 1991), 121.

An apocryphal story comes down to us about the poet Edmund Spenser, who received an annuity of £50. Burghley thought this grant excessive. "What! All this for a rhyme?" he reportedly asked the queen. She is said to have testily replied, "Then give him what is reason." (W. Forbes Gray, *The Poets Laureate of England: Their History and Their Odes* [New York: E. P. Dutton & Co., 1915], 15.)

p. 210, Took over espionage duties for his aging father: WARD (257–60; 357) presents a detailed comparison of de Vere's annuity with many other Elizabethan government salaries and onetime payments.

p. 210, Empty out the treasury in just ten years' time: SMITH/*ET,* 202.

p. 210, Without withdrawing a penny from the state's coffers: By the end of her reign, Elizabeth faced a scandal in Parliament for the excesses of her monopoly system. Hibbert, op. cit., 249–50; J. E. Neale, *Queen Elizabeth* (New York: Harcourt Brace & Co., 1934), 383–4; William Hyde Price, *The English Patents of Monopoly* (Cambridge, Mass.: Harvard University Press, 1913), 6–25.

p. 211, Or was the queen just exceptionally generous?: After de Vere died in 1604, his second wife, Elizabeth Trentham, would write to Robert Cecil begging his help in continuing the pension. Trentham wrote: "Your Lordship may truly inform His Highness that the pension of a thousand pounds was not given by the late queen to My Lord for his life, and then to determine. But to continue until she might raise his decay by some better provision." (CP, xvi, p. 258 [189/147], in NELSON, 302, 427.) Her late husband, she claims, had used his cash primarily to prop up his overburdened estates. Clearly de Vere and Queen Elizabeth had not entered into any official written agreement that could have contradicted Trentham's statement; the queen meant it when she said no one would need to answer for how de Vere spent the money.

p. 211, "I buy a rope": *The Comedy of Errors,* 4.1.21–2; STRITMATTER, 39.

p. 211, Quote on *Famous Victories* as "organized propaganda": Pitcher, op. cit., 186–7.

p. 211, Shake-speare history plays as culmination of £1,000 annuity: To this list of canonical history plays, one might also add the anonymous history plays that may also have come from de Vere/Shake-speare's pen: The Queen's Men's plays noted above, [*Thomas of*] *Woodstock, Edward III,* and *Edmund Ironside.*

p. 211, Breathtaking apology for Tudor power: "Each of the Shakespeare histories serves a special purpose in elucidating a political problem of Elizabeth's day and in bringing to bear upon this problem the accepted political philosophy of the Tudors." (Campbell, op. cit., 125.)

"Shakespeare imparts the Reformation tenets of the Anglican faith to his audience and establishes himself as an apologist for both the Tudor monarchy and the Church of England, setting himself (at least through his drama) firmly against the detractors, critics, and opponents of absolute monarchy and Anglican theology." (Daniel L. Wright, *The Anglican Shakespeare: Elizabethan Orthodoxy in the Great Histories* [Vancouver, Wash.: Pacific-Columbia Books, 1993], 20.)

p. 212, ". . . which the Queen of England orders to be acted at his expense": OGBURN/*TMWS,* 692.

p. 212, *Endymion* as thank-you for gracious annuity: Josephine Waters Bennett, "Oxford and [John Lyly's] *Endimion,*" *PMLA* 57:2 (June 1942), 354–69; Edward S. LeComte, *Endymion in England: The Literary History of a Greek Myth* (New York: King's Crown Press, 1944), 66–71.

p. 212, Read: Vavasour: The parallels between *Endymion*'s story of Tellus and her jailer and Vavasour and her jailer, Sir Henry Lee, are overwhelming. Waters Bennett, op. cit., 365; LeComte, op. cit., 79–83. (LeComte generally agrees with Waters Bennett's interpretation, noting, "Despite gaps in the evidence at certain points, [Waters Bennett's] interpretation meets all the requirements better than any other" [79].)

p. 212, Endymion's exclamation: *Endymion,* 5.3.188–91.

p. 212, Shakspere's cash estate never exceeded £350: Whittemore, op. cit., 29–30; CAMPBELL and QUINN, 936.

p. 212, Burghley's agents played crucial role in murder scandal: On the damning testimony of Holinshed's *Chronicles* and Burghley's evident role in the Mary Stuart–Darnley–Bothwell affair, cf. John Guy, *Queen of Scots: The True Life of Mary Stuart* (Boston: Houghton Mifflin, 2004).

p. 213, All on Walsingham's payroll: READ/*BURGHLEY*, 342–3.

p. 213, Elizabeth gave King James (VI) £4,000 pension: Helen Georgia Stafford, *James VI and the Throne of England* (London: D. Appleton-Century Co., 1940), 9; Rosalind K. Marshall, *Queen of Scots* (Lanham, Md.: Bernan-Unipub, 1987), 192.

p. 213, Stood a good chance of someday inheriting the English crown himself: *King James's Secret: Negotiations between Elizabeth and James VI relating to the execution of Mary Queen of Scots, from the Warrender Papers* (London: Nisbet & Co., 1927).

p. 213, Forty-five jurors: STATE TRIALS, 1:1166–7, lists forty-six, summoned to Elizabeth's commission to try Mary Stuart; one is the earl of Leicester, who was still in the Lowlands at the time. A contemporary engraving of the trial at the British Library pictures forty-four commissioners.

p. 213, The two cousin queens would never meet: Act 3, Scene 4, of Friedrich von Schiller's *Maria Stuart* imagines a hypothetical meeting between Elizabeth and Mary in the garden at Fotheringhay and has been called "one of the most brilliant and effective scenes of his entire dramaturgy." (Albert William Levi, "Literary Truth," *J. of Aesthetics and Art Criticism* 24:3 (Spring 1966), 378–9.)

p. 214, Provision written specifically with the Queen of Scots in mind: Jayne Elizabeth Lewis, *The Trial of Mary Queen of Scots: A Brief History with Documents* (New York: Bedford/St. Martin's, 1999), 19–21, 91–3.

p. 214, "May God keep me from having to do with you again": Marshall, op. cit., 197–8.

p. 214, Sidney's body in state for fifteen weeks: Sidney's body was returned to London on November 1, 1586, and his state funeral was held the following February 16, eight days after Mary Stuart's execution. NICHOLS, 2:483–94.

p. 215, "When peers and judges no remorse could feel": Anon., Poetical Miscellanies XVII, "On the execution of Mary Stuart," in *Early English Poetry, Ballads, and Popular Literature of the Middle Ages,* ed. James Orchard Halliwell (London: Percy Society, 1845), Vol. 15, p. 38; Pitcher, op. cit., 187–8.

p. 215, The head fell to the floor with a thump: Garrett Mattingly, *The Armada* (Boston: Houghton-Mifflin Co., 1959), 5.

p. 215, $1.8 million in today's currency: One mark was two thirds of a pound (Jeffrey L. Singman, *Daily Life in Elizabethan England* [Westport, Conn.: Greenwood Press, 1995], 35), and according to Economic History Services (www.eh.net), £6,666 in 1586 had the same purchasing power as £1,170,000 in 2002.

p. 215, Davison spent 1.5 years behind bars: READ/*BURGHLEY*, 366–70.

p. 215,. . . as if another woman had signed the death warrant: Mattingly, op. cit., 16–28.

p. 216, "That I am coming for a kingdom there": Anon., *The Troublesome Raigne of Iohn, King of England* (1591), ll. 1713–23, in BULLOUGH, 4:118; on *The Troublesome Raigne's* relationship to Shake-speare's *King John,* cf. Honigmann, op. cit.

p. 216, Shake-speare's *King John* reenacts same strange fiction: Richard Simpson, "The Politics of Shakespeare's Historical Plays," *Transactions of the New Shakspere [sic] Society* 1:2 (1874), 399–402; Evelyn May Albright, "Shakespeare's *Richard II* and the Essex Conspiracy," *PMLA* 42:3 (September 1927), 686–7; Campbell, op. cit., 160–2.

pp. 216–17, De Vere's Geneva Bible reveals sanctity of anointed king: STRITMATTER, 115–24.

p. 217, De Vere identified with figure of poet-king David: STRITMATTER, 107–14.

p. 217, Would spend the rest of his life revising and reworking it: As A. S. Cairncross notes about *Macbeth,* "Nothing in the [play's] internal allusions proves, on examination, to be inconsistent with a date about 1588–90." "A Note on *Macbeth*," in *The Problem of* Hamlet: *A Solution* (London: Macmillan & Co., 1936), 173–5.

Macbeth's fascination with witches and sorcery, for instance, may date from the time of the celebrated Scots witch trials of the early 1590s or of King James VI's trip to Denmark in 1590, after which it was alleged that witches had conjured up the storms that sank one of the king's ships. Deborah Willis, *Malevolent Nurture: Witch-Hunting and Maternal Power in Early Modern England* (Ithaca, N.Y.: Cornell University Press, 1995), 117–45; Lilian Winstanley, *Macbeth, King Lear, and Contemporary History* (New York: Octagon Books, 1970; 1922 first ed.), 104–15.

On a post–Essex rebellion revision to *Macbeth*, cf. D.W.T.C. Vessey, "Notes on the Dating of *Macbeth*," *Shakespearean Authorship Review* 17 (Spring 1967), 1–5.

p. 217, The ritual display of the severed head: *Macbeth* begins with the title character's beheading of the traitor MACDONWALD; it ends with MACDUFF's beheading of MACBETH. Marjorie Garber, "MACBETH: The Male Medusa," in *Shakespeare's Ghost Writers: Literature as Uncanny Causality* (New York: Methuen, 1987), 104–5.

p. 217, "Stole thence the life o' th' building": *Macbeth*, 2.3.79–82; Roger Stritmatter, "There's Not the Smallest Orb, But in His Motion Like an Angel Sings: A Report on the Geneva Bible of Edward de Vere, the Seventeenth Earl of Oxford" (Northampton, Mass.: Privately published, 1996), 73–5.

p. 217, "Not bear the knife myself": *Macbeth*, 1.7.16–20; Whalen, op. cit., 64; Clark, op. cit., 46. As Clark points out, the "double-trust" concept, introduced in 1587, only existed in Scots law.

p. 217, No propaganda piece for the Queen's Men to enact on the public stage: In the words of William C. Carroll, supposing Shake-speare wrote *Macbeth* for James would thus require one to assume the king to have been a "royal spectator of a royal bloodbath, whose own right of succession to the English throne was … questioned." (*Macbeth: Texts and Contexts*, ed. William C. Carroll [Boston: Bedford/St. Martin's, 1999], 2, 5); as Richard F. Whalen notes, "It strains belief to suggest that an English actor/playwright would celebrate the new Scottish king of England by writing a gloomy, violent, bloody tragedy depicting the assassination of a Scottish king that is instigated by witches. … There is no documentary evidence that James ever saw the play, read it, or even heard about it, much less felt celebrated." (op. cit., 56.)

p. 218, Staging of *Macbeth* on April 20, 1611: CAMPBELL and QUINN, 485.

p. 218, "The mere lees is left this vault to brag of": *Macbeth*, 2.3.91–6.

p. 218, "I would be less grieved with the burden": CSP Foreign 1586–7, p. 407, in WARD, 285, NELSON, 303–4.

p. 218, Frances was buried north of London … : Parish Register of All Saints, Edmonton in WARD, 286, NELSON, 306.

p. 219, Anne "debilitated by a buring fever": NELSON, 309.

p. 219, De Vere's activities in spring and early summer of 1588: NELSON (308) points out that a letter from Robert Cecil to Burghley on March 1, 1588 ("I have written to the Earl of Oxford and pray that my lady his wife may send it to him") suggests de Vere was in touch with Anne as late as the end of February.

p. 219, … or even if he were in London: "The mourners [at an aristocratic funeral] had to be of the same sex as the deceased, which meant, of course, that no one could act as a mourner for their own spouse. … The ironic situation therefore arose where, at its worst, most of the official mourners had little regret for the passing of the deceased, while the truly bereaved were excluded from any major part in the ceremony." Clare Gittings, *Death, Burial, and the Individual in Early Modern England* (Beckenham, Kent: Croom Helm, 1984), 175–77.

Anne Cecil's funeral had at least six male attendees (NELSON, 309), and Anne's mother's funeral in 1589 had at least three men in attendance; Lord Burghley is, obeying the above diktat, not recorded as a mourner at his wife's funeral. (Pauline Croft, "Mildred

Lady Burghley: The Matriarch," in *Patronage, Culture, and Power: The Early Cecils* (New Haven, Conn.: Yale University Press, 2002), 294; Pauline Croft, H-ALBION listserv communication [March 26, 2004].)

However, as will be seen below, there may be more to the story of the earl of Oxford's absence from his wife's funeral than either his dislike of her or a presumed deference to custom.

p. 219, In English, Latin, Greek, and Hebrew: In addition to the poems quoted below, I am notified by Christopher Paul (private communication [March 22, 2004]) of the existence of another nineteen epitaphs to Anne Cecil de Vere, by a separate authors, in the British Library's Lansdowne Manuscript collection. (Lansdowne, 104/78 ff. 195–214); NELSON (476, fn. 14) also cites Cotton Julius, 10, ff. 112–15v., which is mostly a copy of the Lansdowne MS (C.P., private communication [April 3, 2004].)

One Latin eulogy, by the university wit John Hoskyns, is discussed in Baird W. Whitlock, *John Hoskyns, Serjeant-at-Law* (Washington, D.C.: University Press of America, 1982), 64–9, and is reprinted (but not translated) in *The Life, Letters, and Writings of John Hoskyns, 1566–1638*, ed. Louise Brown Osborn (New Haven, Conn.: Yale University Press, 1937).

On June 25, 1588, the printer John Charlwood also registered "An epitaphe vupon the life and Death of the Countesse of OXON [*i.e., Oxford*]." So far as is known, this epitaph was never published. ARBER, 2:230.

p. 219, "So like an angel she doth sit on high": Hatfield MSS 277.8 in WARD, 288, and NELSON, 310–11.

p. 219, Comparison between Anne and Griselda: NELSON, 311.

p. 220, An example for young girls to follow: On the history of Griselda and the ways authors subverted the gruesome tale, cf. Harry Keyishian, "Griselda on the Elizabethan Stage: The Patient Grissil of Chettle, Dekker, and Haughton," *Studies in English Lit. 1500–1900* 16:2 (Spring 1976), 253–61; Judith Bronfman, "Griselda, Renaissance Woman," in *The Renaissance Englishwoman in Print: Counterbalancing the Canon*, ed. Anne M. Haselkorn and Betty S. Travitsky (Amherst: University of Massachusetts Press, 1990), 211–23.

p. 220, Comparisons between Griselda and Anne Cecil–inspired heroines in Shakespeare: Griselda and...DESDEMONA: James L. Calderwood, *The Properties of* Othello (Amherst: University of Massachusetts Press, 1989), 34; Hugh L. Grady, *Shakespeare's Universal Wolf* (Oxford: Oxford University Press, 1996), 110; Joan Lord Hall, *Othello: A Guide to the Play* (Westport, Conn.: Greenwood Press, 1999), 141; LUCIANA: Karl J. Holzknecht, *The Backgrounds of Shakespeare's Plays* (New York: American Book Co., 1950), 257; Ruth Vanita, "'Proper' Men and 'Fallen' Women: The Unprotectedness of Wives in *Othello*," *Studies in English Lit. 1500–1900.* 34:2 (Spring 1994), 355; IMOGEN: Hallett Smith, *Shakespeare's Romances* (San Marino, Calif.: Huntington Library, 1972), 36; Carol Hansen, *Woman as Individual in English Renaissance Drama* (New York: Peter Lang, 1993), 179; E. C. Pettet, *Shakespeare and the Romance Tradition* (London: Staples Press, 1949), 167, fn. 2; JULIA: Robert M. Smith, "Interpretations of *Measure for Measure*," *SH.Q.* 1:4 (October 1950), 216; OPHELIA: E. Ritchie, "Women and the Intellectual Virtues," *International J. of Ethics* 12:1 (October 1901), 74; ISABELLA: William G. Meader, *Courtship in Shakespeare* (New York: King's Crown Press, 1954), 209; David L. Stevenson, "Design and Structure in *Measure for Measure*: A New Appraisal," *ELH* 23:4 (December 1956), 258; HERMIONE: Carol Hansen, op. cit., 117; Lois Josephs, "Shakespeare and a Coleridgean Synthesis: CLEOPATRA, LEONTES, and FALSTAFF," *SH.Q.* 18:1 (Winter 1967), 19; HELENA: William Witherle Lawrence, *Shakespeare's Problem Comedies* (New York: Macmillan Co., 1931), 49; Edgar I. Fripp, *Shakespeare, Man and Artist* (London: H. Milford, 1938), 2:607; David Foley McCandless, *Gender and Performance in Shakespeare's Problem Comedies* (Bloomington: Indiana University Press, 1997), 46; Francis G. Schoff, "CLAUDIO, BERTRAM, and a Note on Interpretation,"

SH.Q. 10:1 (Winter 1959), 18; Lisa Jardine, "Cultural Confusion and Shakespeare's Learned Heroines: 'These are old paradoxes,'" *SH.Q.* 38:1 (Spring 1987), 12.

p. 220, Anne Cecil compared to Anna Perenna:

> *Anna soror soror Anna suae charissima Elisae*
> *Dum fugit hostiles per {mare/freta} fratis [=fratris?] opes:*
> *Itala naufragio felici littora tangit*
> *Et potitur Latia numen et exul humo*
> *Invenit et nomen, templum invenit, invenit aras,*
> { *Pigmalionaeae sic nocuere minae*
> { *Pigmalionaeis nuper abacta minis*
> *Sors ea Phoenissae:*

Osborn, op. cit.; Christopher Paul, private communication (March 22, 2004); Andrew Hannas, private communication (March 22, 2004).

p. 220, One possible source for OPHELIA's ultimate fate: On the 1579 drowning of Katherine Hamlet, cf. FELDMAN, 30-1.

p. 220, "... Possession would now show us whiles it was ours": *Much Ado,* 4.1.214-22; Maurice Hunt, "Comfort in *Measure for Measure,*" *Studies in Eng. Lit. 1500–1900* 27:2 (Spring 1987), 225-6.

pp. 220-1, ... may have been written and performed at court in 1583: Allison Gaw ("Is Shakespeare's *Much Ado* a Revised Earlier Play?" *PMLA* 50:3 ([September 1935], 720-1) propounds two unconvincing reasons to disbelieve any connection between *Ariodante and Genevora* and *Much Ado*:

1. Shake-speare's play is closer to the story in Matteo Bandello's twenty-second *Novella* (1554) than to Ariosto's story of Ariodante and Genevora from the fifth canto of *Orlando Furioso* (1516). But this argument assumes that there was one and only one version of the "Shakespeare" play. As an alternate scenario, one could just as well propose that the first version of the Shake-speare story (c. 1583) drew from the Ariodante and Genevora legend. And then, when the death of the heroine became a relevant part of the tale (i.e., after the author wanted to incorporate Anne's 1588 death into his play), Shake-speare switched over to Bandello's story as his primary text. Bandello, after all, includes the death of the heroine in his version of the tale.

2. Richard Mulcaster's children of the Merchant Tailor's School (who performed the 1583 *Ariodante and Genevora* at court) had no connection to the London theatrical environs where Will Shakspere of Stratford-upon-Avon presumably worked. Of course, this presupposes Shakspere as the author. And such presuppositions are just what this book proposes to eliminate.

p. 221, IMOGEN fakes death to bring her husband to his senses: The similarity between HERO's and IMOGEN's faked deaths is noted in D. E. Landry, "Dreams as History: The Strange Unity of *Cymbeline,*" *SH.Q.* 33:1 (Spring 1982), 72, and Richard Wincor, "Shakespeare's Festival Plays," *SH.Q.* 1:4 (October 1950), 225, fn. 7.

p. 221, *Cymbeline,* 4.2.307-8; D. E. Landry, op. cit., 72-3.

p. 221, *Winter's Tale* fixates on HERMIONE's death: "The play has, in fact, been criticized for making it too abundantly clear that HERMIONE is dead." James Edward Siemon, "But It Appears She Lives: Iteration in *The Winter's Tale,*" *PMLA* 89:1 (January 1974), 16, fn. 10.

p. 221, ... infallible Oracle pronounces HERMIONE chaste: As noted in Chapter 4, however, even at his most self-critical, de Vere still built himself a trapdoor that allowed for the possibility that Anne/HERMIONE had indeed cuckolded him; the Oracular assurance of HERMIONE's chastity may in fact have been forged. (Cf. Chapter 4.)

p. 221, She becomes transformed into a painted statue: As noted in Chapter 5, HERMIONE's statue is explicitly compared to the work of "that rare Italian master, Julio Romano"—probably alluding to Romano's painted statue at the tomb of Castiglione outside Mantua, and the young wife who was so prematurely ripped from the arms of *The Courtier's* author.

p. 221, "As we are mock'd with art": *Winter's Tale,* 5.3.67–8; Peter Berek, "'As We Are Mock'd with Art': From Scorn to Transfiguration," *Studies in Eng. Lit. 1500–1900* 18:2 (Spring 1978), 289–305.

p. 222, "Worst-kept secret in Europe": De Lamar Jensen, "The Spanish Armada: The Worst-Kept Secret in Europe," *Sixteenth Century Journal* 19:4 (Winter 1988), 623.

p. 222, Gale-force winds prevented any venture into open sea: Climatologists now recognize the remarkable storms during the summer of 1588 as a precursor to the "Little Ice Age" that would descend upon Europe in the coming century. Hubert H. Lamb, "Climatic Variation and Changes in Wind and Ocean Circulation: The Little Ice Age in the Northeast Atlantic," *Quaternary Research* 11 (1979), 16; Lloyd D. Keigwin, Woods Hole Oceanographic Institute, private communication (March 24–26, 2004).

p. 222, The weather finally broke long enough for Drake's fleet to sail: Harry Kelsey, *Sir Francis Drake: The Queen's Pirate* (New Haven, Conn.: Yale University Press, 1998), 320–1.

p. 222, "I.L." Armada poem: *An answer to the untruths published and printed in Spain in glory of their supposed victory achieved against our English Navy . . . by "I.L."* (London, 1589), in WARD, 291; NELSON, 313.

p. 223, Who took up arms against a sea of Spaniards: Richard Hakluyt, *Principal Navigations* (1598–1600), STC 12626a, p. 599; John Stow, *The Annals of England* (1615), STC 23338, p. 746a; William Camden, *Annales The True and Royall History of Elizabeth Queene of England* (1625), STC 4497, 3:277, in NELSON, 312.

p. 223, "We endured a great storm": Sir Francis Drake to Lord Burghley, June 6, 1588, *Cal. MS of the Marquis of Bath* (Dublin: H.M. Stationery Office, 1907), 2:28.

p. 223, "Fall to it yarely or we run ourselves aground!": *The Tempest,* 1.1; The nautical commentary in this and the paragraphs to follow comes from Rex Clements, "Shakespeare as Mariner," *Shakespeare Fellowship News-Letter* (UK) (Autumn 1956), 4–8.

p. 223, Striking the topmast: Clements (ibid.) points out that there were actually two topmasts onboard most Elizabethan ships, but only one (the "mainmast") could be struck.

p. 224, "Show ourselves all to be of company": ibid.; V. de Sola Pinto, *The English Renaissance, 1510–1688* (New York: The Cresset Press, 1938), 60.

p. 224, The BOATSWAIN has saved the ship from doom: It is only at this point, after the nautical crisis has been averted, that PROSPERO uses his magic to founder the ship.

p. 224, Storm-beaten English fleet returned to Plymouth: Kelsey, op. cit., 321.

p. 224, HAMLET washes ashore from his adventures to discover of OPHELIA's death: In December 1579, a Warwickshire girl named Katherine Hamlet drowned in the Avon River. An inquest was held the following February. Orthodox scholars make much of the connections between her drowning and OPHELIA's drowning—supposing that a tradesman from Stratford-upon-Avon would have heard about her in the local lore. Perhaps so. However, the Earl of Oxford's men toured Warwickshire every year from 1580 to 1585, which makes them just as likely to have heard about this drowning—and during this period, de Vere also kept an estate called Bilton in Warwickshire near the Avon. Feldman, op. cit., 30–31.

p. 224, "Eat a crocodile? I'll do it": *Hamlet,* 5.1.268–77.

p. 224, The ships returned only two days later: Kelsey, op. cit., 321.

p. 225, . . . in an ominous crescent-moon formation: M. J. Rodríguez-Salgado, *Armada, 1588–1988* (London: Penguin Books/National Maritime Museum, 1988), 233–51; note that dates in this source are new style. One must subtract ten days to obtain the date of each event as it appeared on the English calendar.

The "mortal moon" of Sonnet 107 and "terrene moon" of *Antony and Cleopatra*, 3.13.154, have variously been argued to represent the moon-shaped initial battle formation of the Spanish Armada. While I do not accept the former argument (Sonnet 107 almost certainly refers to Elizabeth's 1603 death), the latter is more believable. Cf. Donald E. Stanford, "Robert Bridges and Samuel Butler on Shakespeare's Sonnets: An Exchange of Letters," *SH.Q.* 22:4 (Autumn 1971), 330.

p. 225, Tilbury at least four days' ride from Plymouth: After July 22, the English fleet appears heavily engaged with the enemy in the Channel, and a trip to shore to permit a nobleman to ride to London seems unlikely. Rodríguez-Salgado, op. cit., 237-9.

p. 225, "He seems most willing to hazard his life in this quarrel": PRO S.P. 12/213[/55], f. 92v, in NELSON, 316.

p. 225, . . . during the aforementioned search-and-destroy missions, perhaps: NELSON (316) claims that Lord Admiral Howard was in London, but in fact throughout late July, Howard's and his command ship *The Ark Royal* were with the English fleet in hot pursuit of the Armada (Rodríguez-Salgado, op. cit.).

p. 226, Armada expected to make landfall in Essex: Colin Martin and Geoffrey Parker, "If the Armada had landed," in *The Spanish Armada* (New York: W. W. Norton & Co., 1988), 265-77.

p. 226, "I am glad I am rid of my Lord Oxford": PRO S.P. 12/214[/1], ff. 2-3, in NELSON, 317-18; WARD, 292.

p. 226, Story of Armada . . . ends happily for England: Recent scholarship by Jerry Brotton of London's Royal Holloway College has discovered that Sir Francis Walsingham may deserve as much credit as Drake in defeating the Armada: During the summer of the Armada, the Turkish fleet was splitting the attentions and resources of Spain's navy–and this was likely a result of back-channel deals made between Walsingham's agents and the Turks. (John Ezard, "Why We Must Thank the Turks, Not Drake, for Defeating the Armada," *The Guardian* [UK], www.guardian.co.uk [June 1, 2004].)

p. 227, Erratic behavior of Shake-speare's tragic triumvir: Lawrence Edward Bowling, "Antony's Internal Disunity," *Studies in Eng. Lit. 1500-1900* 4:2 (Spring 1964), 239-46.

p. 227, CLEOPATRA would embody Queen Elizabeth: Keith Rinehart, "Shakespeare's Cleopatra and England's Elizabeth," *SH.Q.* 23:1 (Winter 1972), 81-6.

p. 227, ". . . Should stretch without some pleasure now": *Antony and Cleopatra*, 1.1.40-55; ANTONY's line "Tonight we'll wander through the streets and note / The qualities of the people. Come my queen, / Last night you did desire it" offers a colorful potential glimpse into de Vere and Elizabeth's life: Had they sneaked out from the palace one night to race through the streets in common disguise?

p. 227, ANTONY informed of death of FULVIA via messengers from abroad: Ray L. Heffner Jr., "The Messengers in Shakespeare's *Antony and Cleopatra*," *ELH* 43:2 (Summer 1976), 154-5.

This dramatic embellishment seconds the above supposition that de Vere played some role in the English navy's pre-Armada advance missions between May 30 and July 12–and was therefore away from London at the time of Anne Cecil's death and funeral.

p. 227, "The hand could pluck her back that shov'd her on": *Antony and Cleopatra*, 1.2.114-24; ANTONY's friend ENOBARBUS presents an even more cold-blooded assessment of FULVIA's passing ("Why, sir, give the gods a thankful sacrifice . . .," 1.2.159ff.), on which cf. Elkin Calhoun Wilson, "Shakespeare's ENOBARBUS," in *Joseph Quincy Adams Memorial Studies*, ed. Giles E. Dawson, James G. McManaway, and Edwin E. Willoughby (Washington, D.C.: Folger Shakespeare Library, 1948), 391-408; L. T. Fitz, "Egyptian Queens and Male Reviewers: Sexist Attitudes in *Antony and Cleopatra* Criticism," *SH.Q.* 28:3 (Summer 1977), 297-316.

p. 228, "My idleness doth hatch": Arthur H. Bell, "Time and Convention in *Antony and Cleopatra,*" *SH.Q.* 24:3 (Summer 1973), 257.

p. 228, A web of conflicted alliances: ANTONY remarries to CAESAR's sister OCTAVIA (as in Plutarch)–and, as will be seen in the next chapter, de Vere also forges a convenient marriage alliance that yields practical (in his case monetary) benefits.

p. 228, "CLEOPATRA staked hers on ... Actium and lost": Rinehart, op. cit., 85.

p. 228, ANTONY is not a leader; he is the led: Paul Yachnin, "Shakespeare's Politics of Loyalty: Sovereignty and Subjectivity in *Antony and Cleopatra,*" *Studies in Eng. Lit. 1500–1900* 33:2 (Spring 1993), 353-4.

p. 228, "Thou shouldst to me after": *Antony and Cleopatra,* 3.11.51-1, 56–8; Donald C. Freeman, "'The Rack Dislimns': Schema and Metaphorical Pattern in *Antony and Cleopatra,*" *Poetics Today* 20:3 (Autumn 1999), 455.

p. 229, "The children of the hospital she saw before her face": Anon., "A joyful ballad of the Royal entrance of Queen Elizabeth into the City of London, the 24th of November in the thirty-first year of Her Majesty's reign, to give God praise for the overthrow of the Spaniards," in WARD, 293-4; Charles Wisner Barrell "New Milestone in Shakespeare Research," *Shakespeare Fellowship Quarterly* 5:4 (October 1944), 64-5.

An alternate reading of "children of the hospital" could be that de Vere helped to re-create a fabled encounter with the children of the hospital of St. Dunstan's (of the west) from the ceremonies surrounding Elizabeth's 1558 coronation. A. L. Rowse, *An Elizabethan Garland* (London: Macmillan, 1953), 17; *ES,* 1:132.

p. 229, "Lewd friends ... still rule him by flatteries": Burghley to Walsingham, May 13, 1587, in NELSON, 305; WARD, 286.

p. 229, "Bottom of the mount of Silexedra": John Lyly, *Euphues and His England* (dedicated to de Vere), in *The Complete Works of John Lyly,* ed. R. Warwick Bond (Oxford: Clarendon Press, 1902), 2:228.

The meaning of the place-name "Silexedra" has long been puzzled over; the hypothesis that "Silexedra" was Fisher's Folly is original to the present book. In Latin *exedra* means "a hall for conversing or disputing in" (*A Latin Dictionary, Founded on Andrews's Edition of Freund's Latin Dictionary,* ed. Charlton T. Lewis and Charles Short [Oxford: Clarendon Press, 1980], 682), while *sil* is a rare word meaning "ochre" and *silex* means "flint." So it would appear that *silexedra* is a descriptive name for a center of disputations–as Fisher's Folly must have been–with distinctive flint masonry or ochre coloring. (*OED;* Roy Wright–Tekastiaks, private communication [2000].)

p. 229, "Mount Fisher": George Saunders to Richard Bagot, May 15, 1593: "... here at Mount Fisher, also called Fisher's Folie, without Bishopsgate," cited in Margaret Sefton-Jones, *Old Devonshire House by Bishopsgate* (London: The Swarthmore Press, 1923), 98.

p. 229, ... a suburban place of study and literary retreat: Barnabe Riche (*The Second Tome of the Trauailes and aduentures of Don Simonides* ... [London: Robert Walley, 1584], 91, 113, 115) writes of his encounter with Euphues after he had "come from the Mount Silexedra into the city." According to Riche, Silexedra was a place where Euphues could "muse ... on [his] studies."

p. 229, On *Gwydonius*: Robert W. Dent, "Greene's *Gwydonius:* A Study in Elizabethan Plagiarism," *Huntington Lib. Q.* 24 (1961), 151-62.

p. 230, "... at the shrine of Your Lordship's courtesy": Robert Greene, *Gwydonius* (1584) in CHILJAN, 71.

p. 230, Some Munday translations never published: Gerald R. Hayes, "Anthony Munday's Romances of Chivalry," *The Library,* 4th ser., 6 (1926), 57-81.

p. 230, "I hope will let slip any faults escaped": Antony Munday, *Palmerin d'Oliva* (1588) dedication to de Vere, in WARD, 200-1.

p. 230, ... one has the makings of *The Winter's Tale:* Hayes, op. cit., 58; BULLOUGH, 8:133.

Robert Greene's 1588 novel *Pandosto* is typically assumed to be a source for *The Winter's Tale* (BULLOUGH, 8:115–55); however, given Greene's tendency to plagiarize, it is just as likely that de Vere began musing over the elements of *The Winter's Tale* at Fisher's Folly and Greene snatched the story from de Vere and rushed it into print. A similar case could be made with the hack Thomas Lodge–again, as a probable regular of Fisher's Folly, Lodge may well have heard *The Winter's Tale* recited by the master of the household. Lodge's 1592 novel *Euphues Shadow*–a title that itself suggests the book owes a debt to de Vere–contains a subplot about a slandered wife named "Eurimone" (a near-homophone for HERMIONE) who dies and is transformed into a painted statue. Lodge compares the jealous husband to Pygmalion. *EVPHVES SHADOW, The Battaile of the Sences* in *The Complete Works of Thomas Lodge,* ed. Edmund W. Gosse (New York: Russell & Russell, Inc., 1963; 1883 first ed.), 2:68–70.

p. 230, One of Munday's romances source for *The Tempest:* Gary Schmidgall, "*The Tempest* and *Primaleon:* A New Source," *SH.Q.* 37:4 (Winter 1986), 423–39.

p. 230, Day dedicated letter-writing guidebook to de Vere: On display for the first time in Angel Day's 1586 edition of *The English Secretary* is a coat of arms for de Vere with several new crests and standards–on the possible heraldic significance thereof, cf. Barbara Burris, "Oxford's New Coat of Arms in 1586: If Heraldry Is a Statement About Ancestry, What Was de Vere Saying?" *Shakespeare Matters* 2:4 (Summer 2003), 20–3.

p. 230, "... whose infancy was from the beginning ever sacred to the muses": Angel Day, *The English Secretorie* (1586), epistle dedication to Edward de Vere, in CHILJAN, 73.

p. 230, Keeper of a powerful man's secrets: Richard Rambuss, "The Secretary's Study: The Secret Designs of the *Shepheardes Calender,*" *ELH* 59:2 (Summer 1992), 313–35.

p. 230, Clearly spoofs crafted by a razor wit: "One of [Day's letters] is identified (56ff.) as 'Mr. R. Bowes, a member of Sir George Carey's embassy to Scotland,' writing a description of political events in Scotland addressed to Lord Hunsdon. This is almost certainly Sir Robert Bowes, born about 1535 and died in 1597, who was at his death Elizabeth's ambassador to Scotland." Sarah Smith, "*The English Secretorie,* or Shakespeare's Letters: Angel Day and the Background of *The English Secretorie*" (Unpublished MS, 2003).

pp. 230–1, The common sink of every rakehell's filthiness: Ibid.; *The English Secretary,* ed. Evans, 42–3.

p. 231, On *Rosalynde: Lodge's "Rosalynde" Being the Original of Shakespeare's "As You Like It,"* ed. W. W. Greg (London: Chatto & Windus, 1907).

p. 231, "... virtuously end[ed] the winter of his age in Silexedra": "Philautus to his Sonnes liuing at the Courte," in *EVPHVES SHADOW, The Battaile of the Sences,* in *The Complete Works of Thomas Lodge,* op. cit., 2:8.

p. 232, Burghley suing de Vere for back debts: Joel Hurstfield, "Lord Burghley as Master of the Court of Wards: 1561–98," *Trans. Royal Hist. Soc.,* 4th ser., 31 (1949), 106–7; Burghley would also never again cast a ballot for de Vere for the Order of the Garter.

p. 232, Cornwallis caught in the middle: On the disputes and strings pulled to transfer Fisher's Folly to the Cornwallis family, cf. NELSON, 319–20.

p. 232, "And set thy person forth to sell": "William Shakespeare," "When as thine eye hath chose the dame" (#18) in *The Passionate Pilgrim,* in *The New Cambridge Shakespeare: Poems,* ed. John Roe (Cambridge: Cambridge University Press, 1992), 255–6.

p. 233, "MSS. POEMS BY VERE EARL OF OXFORD &C": Ruth Loyd Miller, "The Cornwallis–Lysons Manuscript at Folger Shakespeare Library Contains the Earliest Copy of Any Portion of 'Shakespeare's' Works Known to Exist, Pre-Dating *Venus and Adonis* by Several Years, Circa 1585–90, and Links Shakespeare and Edward de Vere," in MILLER/LOONEY, 2:369–94; Arthur F. Marotti, "The Cultural and Textual Importance of Folger Ms. V.a.89," *Eng. Manuscript Studies 1100-1700,* 11 (2002), 70–92.

p. 233, De Vere hiring joiners to work on Plaistow/Plaiston: NELSON, 320–1, and references therein.

p. 233, "My mistress' picture...shall witness what I say": "Sundrie sweete Sonnets written by the same Gent. [*Thomas Lodge*]," #4 in Lodge, *Scillaes Metamorphosis* (1589), in *The Complete Works of Thomas Lodge*, ed. Gosse, op. cit., 1:43; cf. also CLARK, 148–51.

N.B.: Lodge may very well have written this poem, as advertised–but this book only supposes that the *subject* of the poem is a certain retiring earl who might in 1589 have had a guilty conscience about the treatment of his "mistress" and might have wanted to "do [his] penance straight"–as the works of Shake-speare suggest the author did upon the death of his own HERMIONE/HERO.

An anonymous poem, first printed in 1591 in *Brittons Bowre of Delights* B⁴ᵛ–C¹, also suggests de Vere as a subject or possible author:

> Like to an *Hermit* poore in place obscure,
> I meane to spende my dayes in endlesse doubt:
> To waile such woes as time cannot recure,
> Where none but loue shall euer finde me out....

The Phoenix Nest (1593), ed. Hyder Edward Rollins (Cambridge, Mass.: Harvard University Press, 1931), 167–8.

p. 233, On Bilton: Bilton was left as a jointure to Margery, countess of Oxford, in 1562 upon the death of her husband, the sixteenth earl of Oxford (de Vere's father). She died in 1568. It presumably passed into her son's hands upon her death. (Charles Wisner Barrell, "'Shake-speare's' Unknown Home on the River Avon Discovered," in MILLER/LOONEY, 2:355–69, and at www.sourcetext.com.)

p. 234, "...soothing air of pensiveness to the neighborhood": William Smith, *History of the County of Warwick* (1830), 177, in MILLER/LOONEY, 2:364–5.

p. 234, De Vere attended five days of 1589 Parliament: NELSON, 321.

p. 234, De Vere pictured in engraving of 1589 Parliament: Charles Wisner Barrell, "Newly Discovered Oxford-Shakespeare Pictoral Evidence," *Shakespeare Fellowship Quarterly* 5:2 (April 1944), 24–7.

p. 234, Arundel's trial set for April 4: Colin Rhys Lovell, "The Trial of Peers in Great Britain," *The American Hist. Rev.* 55:1 (October 1949), 75–7.

p. 234, *"Yet a lion"*: STATE TRIALS, 1:1249–64, Rene Graziani, "Elizabeth at Isis Church," *PMLA* 79:4 (September 1964), 385; Emma Marshall Dekinger, "The 'Impressa' Portrait of Sir Philip Sidney in the National Portrait Gallery," *PMLA* 47:1 (March 1932), 34, fn. 82.

p. 234, Treason verdict came in as expected: Lovell (op. cit., 75) points to only three acquittal verdicts in British court trials of peers–none of which happened during Elizabeth's reign.

p. 235, ORLANDO rescues his eldest brother from jaws of death: *As You Like It*, 4.3.98–120.

p. 235, On Billesley: J. Shera Atkinson, "The Manor of Billesley," *Shakespeare Fellowship News-Letter* (UK) (September 1953), 8–9; *Shakespeare Cross-Examination*, ed. Tappan Gregory (Chicago: Cuneo Press, 1961), 57.

p. 235, Among the books and histories that were his first love: That de Vere had begun work on a version of *As You Like It* by the end of 1589 is strongly suggested by another publication that appeared in London bookstalls the following year. In 1590, the Euphuist and likely Fisher's Folly regular Thomas Lodge appears to have plagiarized de Vere once again. As Greene had novelized *The Winter's Tale* in 1588, so Lodge in 1590 published a novella called *Rosalynde*. Lodge's Euphuistic pastoral is today considered the "source" of *As You Like It*. [BULLOUGH 2:143–256] But, again, the chain of cause and effect may have been reversed. An early *As You Like It* from the 1580s–perhaps simply recited and transcribed during the wild Euphuist years at Silexedra—was more likely Lodge's source. As an underhanded tribute to the true source of *Rosalynde,* Lodge subtitled his book *Euphues' Golden Legacy, Found After His Death in his Cell at Silexedra.* (*Lodge's 'Rosalynde,'* op. cit.)

p. 235, . . . the gold standard upon which literary criticism of the age was based: On the debts of the overrated Francis Meres's *Palladis Tamia* (1598) to *The Arte of English Poesie,* cf. Don Cameron Allen, "Francis Meres's Treatise 'Poetrie': A Critical Edition," *Univ. of Illinois Studies in Lang. and Lit.* 16:1 (Feb. 1931), 396ff.; on Shake-speare's intimate knowledge of *The Arte,* cf. William Lowes Rushton, *Shakespeare and the Arte of English Poesie* (Liverpool: Henry Young & Sons, 1909).

p. 235, ". . . as if it were a discredit for a gentleman to seem learned": *The Arte of English Poesie by George Puttenham [sic],* ed. Gladys Doidge Willcock and Alice Walker (Cambridge: Cambridge University Press, 1936).

p. 235, ". . . tricked up a company of taffeta fools with their feathers": Nashe, ed. Harrison, op. cit., 17; STRITMATTER, 38.

p. 236, ". . . at length must needs die to our stage": Thomas Nashe, "To the Gentlemen Students of both Vniuersities" in *Menaphon, by Robert Greene, and Margarite of America, by Thomas Lodge,* ed. G. B. Harrison (Oxford: Basil Blackwell, 1927), 9. On Marlowe as the likely inspiration for the epithet "English Seneca," cf. A. P. Rossiter, *English Drama from Early Times to the Elizabethans* (London: Hutchinson's University, 1950), 156–7; J. W. H. Atkins, *English Literary Criticism: The Renascence* (London: Methuen & Co., [sic] 1951) 234; also cf. the following note.

p. 236, Nashe probably had *Tamburlaine* in mind: John W. Cunliffe, "Nash and the Earlier *Hamlet,*" *PMLA* 21:1 (1906), 195, fn. 1.

p. 236, *Hamlet* already on minds and pens of literati by end of 1580s: Orthodox scholarship attempts to explain away Nashe's statement by supposing the existence of a now-lost alternate version of *Hamlet.* The *"Ur-Hamlet,"* as scholars conventionally call it, was written by Author Unknown. Then Shake-speare presumably filched from Author Unknown's work when writing the canonical *Hamlet* sometime after the turn of the century.

For Stratfordian arguments for a Shake-spearean *Hamlet* circa 1589, cf. Eric Sams, *The Real Shakespeare: Retrieving The Early Years, 1564–1594* (New Haven: Yale University Press, 1995), 121–4.

p. 236, ". . . of which number is first that noble gentleman Edward Earl of Oxford": Willcock and Walker, op. cit., 61–3; Willcock and Walker have also determined that the chapter naming the "courtly makers" was inserted at the last minute (xlvii–xlviii, cv–cvi).

p. 236, ". . . the title of most excellent among the rest": William Webbe, *A Discourse of English Poetrie* (1586), in *Elizabethan Critical Essays,* ed. G. Gregory Smith (Oxford: Oxford University Press, 1959; first ed. 1904), 1:243.

CHAPTER NINE

p. 238, *True Tragedy of Richard the Third:* Lewis F. Mott ("Foreign Politics in an Old Play" *Modern Philology,* 19:1 [August 1921], 65–71) argues persuasively that allusions to détente with the Turk (September 1589) and to putting Spain to "flight" in the closing speech of *The True Tragedy of Richard the Third* leave little room for this play being composed and staged any time *other* than 1589. By the summer of 1590, relations with the Turks had again soured and England was preparing itself for another Spanish invasion.

On the other hand, Ramón Jiménez presents an alternative Oxfordian chronology for *The True Tragedy,* arguing that it was the second drama from a teenaged Edward de Vere's pen in 1564. (*The Famous Victories of Henry V,* Jiménez argues, was the first.) Jiménez adduces topical allusions to events of the 1560s in *True Tragedy.* Jiménez, "*The True Tragedy of Richard the Third:* Another Early History Play by Edward de Vere," *The Oxfordian* 7 (2004).

p. 238, "Content thee good Oxford":

OXF. Oxford did never beare so base a minde
   He will not winke a murthers secretly put vp,
   Nor suffer vpstarts to enioy our rightes....
RICH. My Lord of Oxford, you as your second selfe,
   Shall haue the happie leading of the reare,
   A place I know which you will well deserue....
   Content thee good Oxford, and tho I confesse myself bound to thee for thy
   especiall care, yet at this time I pray thee hold me excused...," etc.

The True Tragedy of Richard the Third..., ed. Barron Field (London: The Shakespeare Soc., 1844), 56–7.

p. 238, Celebration of "Worthy Elizabeth": Mott, op. cit., 65.

p. 239, Guise the old-fashioned feudalist: Jean-Marie Constant, *Les Guise* (Paris: Hachette, 1984); James Eastgate Brink, *"Les Guise"* [review], *The Am. Hist. Rev.* 90:2 (April 1985), 423–4.

p. 239, "...who would breech Her Majesty for all her wantonness": NELSON, 169–71, 256.

p. 239, On December 23: December 13 as it would have appeared on the (O.S.) English calendar.

p. 239, Murder of Guise could not be pinned on any single man: "This had also been a Roman solution to end Julius Caesar's tyranny." Orest Ranum, "The French Ritual of Tyrannicide in the Late Sixteenth Century," *Sixteenth Century J.* 11:1 (Spring 1980), 65–6.

p. 239, "I no longer have any boon companion...": *"Je n'ai plus de compagnon, puisque le Duc de Guise est mort."* Ibid.

p. 239, No king of France had ever been buried with such honor: Pierre de L'Estoile, *Mémoires-Journaux*, ed. Édouard Tricotel (Paris: Librarie des bibliophiles, 1888), 3:243, in Mary Elizabeth Brown, "Henry of Guise," (honors thesis, Smith College, Northampton, Mass., 1933), 68.

p. 239, Like the histories of Julius Caesar: David A. Bell, "Unmasking a King: The Political Uses of Popular Literature under the French Catholic League, 1588–89," *Sixteenth Century J.* 20:3 (Autumn 1989), 377.

p. 239, *Julius Caesar*, 5.3.94–6.

p. 240, Laborious comparison between Guise and Caesar: John Bakeless, *Christopher Marlowe: The Man in his Time* (New York: William Morrow & Co., 1937), 295; also cf. Paul H. Kocher, "Contemporary Pamphlet Backgrounds for Marlowe's *The Massacre at Paris*," *MLQ* 8 (1947), 155.

p. 240, "When evils are most free?": *Julius Caesar*, 2.1.77–9.

p. 240, "He would be crown'd": *Julius Caesar*, 2.1.11–12.

p. 240, ...suggesting a borrowing from the Shake-spearean original: William Wells, *"Alphonsus, Emperor of Germany," Notes and Queries* 180 (October 5, 1940), 236–40.

p. 240, Propaganda campaign led in part to assassination of Henri III: David A. Bell, op. cit., 371–86.

p. 241, "...so many monstrous corruptions in our church and yet likely to have no redress?": Martin Marprelate [Tract 1], *[A]n epitome of the first Book of that right Worshipful volume written against the Puritans in the defence of the noble clergy*..., ed. J. D. Lewis at http://www.anglicanlibrary.org. On the hyphenated name "Mar-prelate," cf. note in the Introduction.

p. 241, Job Throkmorton: Leland H. Carlson, *Martin Marprelate, Gentleman: Master Job Throkmorton Laid Open in His Colors* (San Marino, Calif: Huntington Library, 1981).

pp. 241–2, ...one of at least a dozen writers: The anti-Martinist tracts of "Pasquill" join at least twenty other screeds written against Martin during the period 1588–90; Carlson, op. cit., 53–74; Joseph Black, "The Rhetoric of Reaction: The Martin Marprelate Tracts (1588–89), Anti-Martinism and the Uses of Print in Early Modern England," *Sixteenth Cent. J.* 28:3 (Autumn 1997), 707–25.

p. 242, "They barter them away for new brooms or carry them forth to the dunghill…": "Pasquill Caviliero," *A Countercuff giuen to Martin Iunior: by the venturous, hardie, and renowned Pasquill of England, Caualiero* (1589), in McKerrow, op. cit., 1:62–3.

p. 242, "From my castle and colors at London Stone": McKerrow, op. cit., 1:80, 114, 136.

p. 242, Publishing literary works under the disguise of a pseudonym: The works of "Pasquill" have traditionally been attributed to the satirist Thomas Nashe. But the editor of Nashe's complete works, R. B. McKerrow (op. cit., 5:50) notes that "further study [has] led me to suspect–indeed, to feel almost certain–that Nashe had nothing to do with them." Donald J. McGinn ("Nashe's Share in the Marprelate Controversy," *PMLA* 59:4 [December 1944], 952–84) argues persuasively that Nashe did participate in the anti-Martinist fray by writing the 1590 tract *An Almonde for a Parrot.*

Cf. VAN DREUNEN (and the earlier Elizabeth Appleton, *Edward de Vere and the War of Words* [Toronto: Elizabethan Press, 1985], 4 vols.) for the attribution of the "Pasquill" canon to de Vere.

pp. 242–3, Pasquill–Marforius dialogue: "Pasquill Caviliero," *The Returne of the renowned Caualiero Pasquill of England, from the other side of the Seas…* (1589), in McKerrow, op. cit., 1:82–3.

p. 243, "… or they that with a mask of religion discharge them of their obedience?": Ibid., 1:81–2.

p. 243, *John a Kent and John a Cumber:* N.B.: Many scholars have mistakenly dated *John a Kent* to 1596; I. A. Shapiro ("The Significance of a Date," *Shakespeare Survey* 8 [1955], 100–5) reveals that the *John a Kent* manuscript actually reads "1590." K. E. Eggar, "Anthony Munday's 'John a Kent,'" *Shakespeare Fellowship News-Letter* (UK) (Autumn 1955), 6–7.

p. 243, *Knack to Know a Knave:* Mary Grace Muse Adkins, "The Genesis of Dramatic Satire against the Puritan, as Illustrated in *A Knack to Know a Knave,*" *RES* 22:86 (April 1946), 81–95.

p. 243, Many more are referred to by other writers of the period: *ES* 1:294–5; Scott McMillin and Sally-Beth MacLean, *The Queen's Men and their Plays* (Cambridge: Cambridge University Press, 1998), 53–5; E.N.S. Thompson, *The Controversy Between the Puritans and the Stage* (New York: H. Holt, (1903), 197–204; Michael Shapiro, *The Children of the Revels* (New York: Columbia University Press, 1977; 1967 first ed.), 177–8.

p. 243, Pasquill's sidekick Marforius: VAN DREUNEN, 13.

p. 243, *An Almond for a Parrot:* McGinn, op. cit.

p. 243, "Attired like an ape on the stage": McKerrow, op. cit., 3:354.

p. 243, "Martin… can play nothing but the knave's part": John Lyly, *Pap With a Hatchet* (1589), in *The Complete Works of John Lyly,* ed. R. Warwick Bond (Oxford: Clarendon Press, 1902), 3:408.

p. 244, Paul's Boys had been disbanded: Hillebrand, op. cit., 143ff.

p. 244, Queen's men sent away from the city: McMillin & MacLean, op. cit., 53–5, 168.

p. 244, "There is a time for speech and a time for silence": McKerrow, op. cit., 1:123.

p. 244, More time in Warwickshire "than I mean to name": McKerrow, op. cit., 1:122.

p. 245, Grandfathers of bride and groom met to discuss their strategy: STOPES, 35–8.

p. 245, £11,000 in debt: NELSON, 334.

p. 245, De Vere had sold most of the estates his father had left behind: Although de Vere's debts were indeed staggering, such devastation was not uncommon for Elizabeth's favorites. Multitudinous seas of red ink also filled the books of Sir Francis Walsingham, who died with arrears of £27,324; the earl of Leicester died owing £35,087 to the queen; and Sir Christopher Hatton's jaw-dropping £42,139 debts to the crown would soon be driving the dancing Puritan to an early grave. Lawrence Stone, "The Anatomy of the Elizabethan Aristocracy," *The Economic Hist. Rev.* 18:1/2 (1948), 17, 44.

p. 245, Soldier and poet: Churchyard was anything but a distinguished versifier–C. S. Lewis calls Churchyard's best poetry "not quite contemptibl[e]." (*English Literature in the Sixteenth Century, Excluding Drama* [Oxford: Clarendon Press, 1954], 264.)

p. 245, De Vere could not meet the debt: A letter from Thomas Churchyard to Julia Penn (undated) and Penn's plea to de Vere are preserved in Lansdowne MSS 68.113, 114, and reprinted in WARD, 301–2; NELSON, 329.

p. 246, "The bells of St. Benet, sir, may put you in mind": Charles Wisner Barrell, "New Milestone in Shakespearean Research . . . ," *Shakespeare Fellowship Quarterly* 5:4 (October 1944), 59–60; *Twelfth Night*, 5.1.33–6; A. E. Daniell, *London City Churches* (London: Archibald Constable, 1907), 139–41.

p. 246, "Dear as thou art unto thyself": Edmund Spenser, "To the right honorable the Earle of Oxenford, Lord High Chamberlain of England &c.," in *The Faerie Queene* (1590), in *The Poetical Works of Edmund Spenser*, ed. J. C. Smith and E. de Selincourt (Oxford: Oxford University Press, 1926), 410.

Spenser memorializes thirteen other men (Sir Christopher Hatton, Burghley, Northumberland, Essex, Ormond, the Lord Admiral, Hunsdon, Lord Grey, Buckhurst, Walsingham, Sir John Norris, Sir Walter Raleigh) and two other women (the Countess of Pembroke and Lady Carew) at court. Since Spenser had been exchanging verses with Raleigh during their years together in Ireland, Spenser also praises Raleigh's poetic talents.

p. 246, "Doth rather choose to sit in idle cell . . .": Edmund Spenser, *Tears of the Muses* (1591) in *Works*, op. cit., 482; WARD, 359–69; H. Amphlett (*Who Was Shakespeare? A New Enquiry*. William Heinemann, Ltd., London [1955], 140–2) notices a possible additional allusion to de Vere in Spenser's *Faerie Queene*, Book 6, Cantos 5–6:

> [I]n all battles [he] bore away the bays.
> But being now attacked with timely age,
> And weary of this world's unquiet ways,
> He took himself unto this hermitage
> In which he lived alone, like careless bird in cage.

p. 247, De Vere would alienate every estate he'd inherited: NELSON, 193.

p. 247, ". . . underestimating Denbigh's value as much as he could in order to make the best case possible for an easy sale": Peter R. Moore, private communication (September 2004).

p. 247, De Vere offered up Castle Hedingham: On a September 8, 1590, letter from de Vere to Burghley and the sordid details of the problems surrounding Castle Hedingham–involving leasing the castle to a man named Henry Bellingham, who died and whose widow and son squabbled over possession thereof–cf. NELSON, 324–5.

p. 247, De Vere's May 18, 1591, letter: Lansdowne MSS, 68.6, in WARD, 305–6; NELSON, 331–4.

p. 248, De Vere razed and liquidated whatever he could from the Hedingham grounds: Severne Majendie, *An Account of Hedingham Castle* (London: H. T. Smith, n.d.); NELSON, 335.

p. 248, Three years later: Donald M. Michie (*A Critical Edition of "The True Chronicle History of King Leir And His Three Daughters Gonorill, Ragan, and Cordella,"* ed. Donald M. Michie [New York: Garland Publishing, Inc., 1991], 4–6) considers the date of *Leir*, pointing out that the one known performance of *Leir* was on the sixth and eighth of April 1594, at the Rose Theatre in London, presented by "the Quenes men and my lord of Susexe to geather."

p. 248, A fond and foolish old man who had squandered his inheritance and independence: The full title of *Leir* does not lie; the ancient chronicles of Geoffrey of Monmouth tell a cautionary tale of a doting and aged King Leir who bequeaths the kingdom to his three daughters, Gonorilla, Reagu, and Cordeilla. (Wilfrid Perrett, *The Story of King Lear from Geoffrey of Monmouth to Shakespeare* [Berlin: Mayer & Müller, 1904]; BULLOUGH 7:311). As will be seen in the coming chapter, a 1603 law case that probably prompted a revision of *Leir* features a youngest daughter named Cordella or, in some documents, Cordelia. Like Gabriel Harvey's "Will shakes spears" encomium in 1578, this fact remains one of history's strange coincidences.

p. 248, "When they securely sleep on beds of down": *Leir,* scene 3, ll. 4–34, in Michie, op. cit.

p. 248, "A perfect pattern of a virtuous life": *Leir,* scene 1, ll.10–12, in Michie, op. cit.

p. 248, ... proto–Shake-speare in form and substance: Peter Alexander (*Shakespeare* [New York: Oxford University Press, 1964], 230–3) argues that the Queen's Men's *King Leir* is in fact an early work from Shake-speare's pen.

p. 248, ... and the thunderstorm scene: KENT's equivalent in *Leir* is named Perillus; OSWALD's is Skalliger. A. S. Cairncross, *The Problem of Hamlet: A Solution.* (London: Macmillan & Co., 1936), 159.

The verbal parallels are considerable too: *Leir:* "Poor soul, she breeds young bones"; *Lear:* "Strike her young bones, you taking airs, with lameness"; *Leir:* "But he, the mirror of mild patience, puts up all wrongs and never gives reply"; *Lear:* "I will be the pattern of all patience; I will say nothing"; *Leir:* "The heavens are just and hate impiety"; *Lear:* "The gods are just, and of our pleasant vices make instruments to plague us"; *Leir:* "Ah, cruel Ragan, did I give thee all"; *Lear:* "I gave you all." (*Leir,* ed. Michie, op. cit., 26–34.)

p. 248, Leir being returned to the throne: Robert Adger Law, "*King Leir* and *King Lear:* An Examination of the Two Plays," in *Studies in Honor of T. W. Baldwin* (Urbana: University of Illinois Press, 1958), 117–18.

p. 249, Left one or more of his "lewd friends" to fill in the blanks: Robert Adger Law, for instance (op. cit., 112–24), recognized the stylistic thumbprint of the Euphuist hack Robert Greene in *King Leir's* lines, a possibility well within the bounds of reason, even with de Vere at the center of the authorship circle.

p. 249, "I would be loath to offend your honor in anything": PRO PROB 11/89, ff. 394–5v in NELSON, 329.

p. 249, In her early thirties at the time: Elizabeth Trentham's birth date is not recorded. Pauline K. Angell, examining Staffordshire records, concluded that Trentham was probably "born in 1559 or shortly after." ("Light on the Dark Lady: A Study of Some Elizabethan Libels," *PMLA* 52:3 [September 1937], 656, fn. 19.)

p. 249, Maid of honor to the queen for at least ten years: The first mention of Trentham as a member of Elizabeth's train appeared in 1581, during events surrounding the courtship of the Duke of Alençon. Violet Wilson, *Queen Elizabeth's Maids of Honor* (London: J. Lane, 1922), 134; ibid.

p. 249, Known both for her beauty and savvy: J. Farnham to Roger Manners (April 5, 1582), "Mistress Trentham is as fair, Mistress Edgcumbe as modest, Mistress Radcliff as comely, and Mistress Garrat as jolly as ever." Cal. Rutland MSS 1.134 in WARD, 307; NELSON, 336–7; on Trentham's business sense, cf. below.

p. 250, "Except but one, the like was never seen": *Brittons Bowre of Delights, 1591,* ed. Richard Jones and Hyder Edward Rollins (Cambridge, Mass.: Harvard University Press, 1933), 17; Bronson Feldman, "The Secret Verses of Edward de Vere," *The Bard* 3:3 (1982), 102–3.

p. 250, Scholars are inclined to give him this one as well: *Brittons Bowre,* op. cit., xiii–xviii, 72–3; Feldman, op. cit. The verse was also signed "Trentame." Undoubtedly the signature indicates the subject of the poem, not its author.

p. 250, License to import wools, fruits, and oils: Lansdowne MSS, 108[/14], ff. 25–26, July 1592, in NELSON, 337–8.

p. 250, "... which had sucked too ravenously on his sweet liberality": PRO S.P. 12/234, ff. 8–9, Henry Lok to Burghley, November 6, 1590, in NELSON, 325–7.

p. 250, Lok not "horse-leach" who sucked de Vere's accounts dry: Lok also disavowed any responsibility for de Vere's failed investment in the ventures of his uncle Michael Lok–the Cathay Company governor who organized the 1578 Northwest Passage expedition.

p. 250, De Vere to Burghley, "... think them sufficient to deserve your disgrace": Lansdowne MSS, 68.6, in WARD, 305–6, NELSON (including discussion of related debts and servants' misdeeds), 330–4.

pp. 250–1, "... sister of the said Francis Trentham": CSPD, addenda 1580–1625, p. 520, in NELSON, 335; Nelson points out that this property would be burdened with disputed claims of ownership for many years to come.

p. 251, Trentham executor for father's estate: Angell (op. cit., 663), citing private correspondence with B. M. Ward.

p. 251, Not afraid to flex her muscles: The letters reveal Trentham dealing with tenant problems (WARD, 337–8) and maximizing the benefit of her husband's £1,000 annuity. (NELSON, 427).

p. 251, Queen's wedding gifts to de Vere and Trentham: PRO E403/2559, f. 341; BL MS Add. 5751A, ff. 225–25v, in NELSON, 336–7.

p. 251, PORTIA modeled in part on Trentham: There are also elements of Queen Elizabeth in PORTIA, as in PORTIA's courtship of the PRINCE OF MOROCCO and the queen's similar flirtation. Gustav Ungerer, "PORTIA and the PRINCE OF MOROCCO," *Shakespeare Studies* 31 (2003).

p. 251, BASSANIO courts PORTIA to climb out of debt: J. Anthony Burton, "An Unrecognized Theme in *Hamlet:* Lost Inheritance and Claudius's Marriage to Gertrude," *The Shakespeare Newsletter* 50:3, no. 246 (Fall 2000), 76.

p. 251, "That I was worse than nothing": *The Merchant of Venice,* 3.2.251–9.

pp. 251–2, *Willobie His Avisa*'s description of Avisa fits Trentham: Avisa also signs her name with the motto "Alway [*sic*] the same"–an English translation of Queen Elizabeth's motto, *Semper eadem.* One suspects the author of *Willobie* (almost certainly *not* de Vere, for reasons propounded below) intended two Elizabeth T.'s to be his allegorical subject: the first level lampoons the goings-on of a most curious countess named Trentham, the second level lampoons the many suitors who courted a queen named Tudor.

p. 252, Nearby the Well of St. Agnes and the Theatre and the Curtain: This is only a sampling of the connections between "Avisa" and Elizabeth Trentham: Angell, op. cit., 652–74; T. W. Baldwin and Pauline K. Angell, "Light on the Dark Lady" (correspondence), *PMLA* 55:2 (June 1940), 598–602.

p. 252, "My fact shall frame you no such jest": "Avisa" to "Nob." in *Willobie His Avisa (1594),* ed. G. B. Harrison (London: John Lane/The Bodley Head, 1926), 53–4.

> See'st yonder house, where hangs the badge
> Of England's Saint? [St. George] When captains cry
> 'Victorious land!' to conquering rage,
> Lo, there my hopeless help doth lie....

Willobie, op. cit., 46, p. 121; Angell, op. cit., 662.

p. 252, Nearby pub of St. George's Inn in Shoreditch: *Willobie,* op. cit., 1.19–21, p. 26; Angell, op. cit., 660.

p. 252, "Try her well ere they depart": Without the benefit of the Elizabeth Trentham attribution, G. B. Harrison (op. cit., 221–2) originally guessed at Thomas Howard just by noticing the etymological resemblance to "Didymus Harco."

p. 252, Macaronic disguise for Thomas Howard: By the time of de Vere and Trentham's marriage, the thirty-year-old Howard had just completed command of a naval privateer mission to the Spanish outpost in the Azores. He had returned to England with cargo-loads full of Spanish treasure, but his fleet had betrayed one of its ships to Spanish pursuers. Howard was condemned as a coward, albeit one made rich with Spanish loot. (ORLANDO DE BOYS: "My brother JAQUES he [OLIVER] keeps at school, and report speaks goldenly of his profit." *As You Like It*, 1.1.5–7; Anthony Wolk, "The Extra JAQUES in *As You Like It*," *SH.Q.* 23:1 (Winter 1972), 101–5; *ELIZ. JOURNALS*, 1:62–9.)

p. 252, Tries to win Avisa's love with gold and trinkets: *Willobie*, op. cit., 38.1–3, p. 103.

p. 253, "Yet let my fancy have some scope": In 1591, Thomas Watson's friend Abraham Fraunce equated tales of Helen and Troy with stories of Endymion—suggesting that Lyly's allegory circa. 1588 of de Vere as Endymion continued to have currency into the 1590s:

> Let come fayre *Helene, Troys* tribulation
> Or braue *Edymions* sweete speculation

(Fraunce, *The Countesse of Pembrokes Yuychurch* [1591], sig. F4.) Note that *OED* definition 3a of *speculation* is "A spectacle or a sight; a spectacular entertainment or show" (first attributed usage 1440).

p. 253, At the time revisiting the play that would someday become *Troilus and Cressida: Willobie*, op. cit., 41.3–5, p. 111.

p. 253, "My wedlock faith to chosen friend": Arthur Acheson, *Shakespeare's Lost Years in London, 1586–1592* (London: B. Quartich, 1920), 193; Angell, op. cit., 663.

p. 253, Bombastic Italian pedant Giovanni Florio: "Phaeton to his friend Florio," in John Florio, *Second Fruits;* reproduced and discussed in Alden Brooks, *Will Shakspere and the Dyer's Hand* (New York: Scribner's, 1943), 145–8; Joseph Sobran, "The Phaeton Sonnet," *Shakespeare Oxford Newsletter* 32:3 (Summer 1996), 12–14.

p. 254, "Were ne'er before brought out of Italy": On Thomas Nashe's portrait of de Vere as "VER" in Nashe's play *Summer's Last Will and Testament* (1592), cf. STRITMATTER, 26–7.

p. 254, "The Spring" or its Latin form *Ver*: On the scholarly tradition of attributing the "Phaeton" sonnet to Shakespeare, cf. William Minto, "An Unrecognized Sonnet by Shakespeare," in *Characteristics of English Poets* (Edinburgh: William Blackwood, 1885), 371–82; examples of modern Stratfordian scholarship attributing "Phaeton" to Sh. include Robert Giroux, *The Book Known as Q* (New York: Atheneum, 1982), 120–4; Peter Levi, *The Life and Times of William Shakespeare* (New York: H. Holt, 1989).

p. 254, Suburban home north of London in early 1592: The first record of de Vere's residence with his new wife appears in February 1593–indicating they were living in Stoke-Newington. (NELSON, 343,) Given the lack of alternative lodgings between December 1591 and February 1593, it stands to reason that this is where they moved after the wedding.

p. 255, During this most revolutionary decade in the history of the English stage: NELSON, 391.

p. 255, Greene caught trying to sell same script to two different companies: "Aske the Queens Players if you sold them not *Orlando Furioso* for twenty Nobles [a unit of currency], and when they were in the country, sold the same play to the Lord Admirals men for as much more. Was not this plaine Conny-catching Maister R.G.?" Anon., *Defence of Cony-Catching* (1592), in SCHRICKX, 21.

p. 256, "Will. Monox": Nashe, *Strange News* (1593) in McKerrow, op. cit., 1:287; only a few paragraphs before Nashe discusses "Monox," he's alluding to Harvey's hexameter libel against de Vere. Ibid., 4:173.

Curiously, in one copy of *Strange News* (STC 18377b) the phrase "*Will Monox* (hast thou heard of him and his great dagger?)" has been redacted by some censorious reader over the centuries.

p. 256, *Ver*'s speech:

> VER Troth, my lord, to tell you plain, I can give you no other account. *Nam quæ habui, perdidi:* What I had, I have spent on good fellows. In these sports you have seen, which are proper to the spring and others of like sort (as giving wenches green gowns, making garlands for fencers, and tricking up children gay) have I bestowed all my flowery treasure and flower of my youth.
>
> WILL SUMMER [*named after an actual mid-sixteenth-century English court jester*] A small matter. I know one spent, in less than a year, eight and fifty pounds in mustard—and another that ran in debt in the space of four or five year about 14,000 pounds in lute strings and gray paper!...
>
> VER I tell you, none but asses live within their bounds!

Thomas Nashe, *Summer's Last Will and Testament* (1592), ll. 225–242 in McKerrow, op. cit., 3:240–1; STRITMATTER, 26–7.

p. 256, Greene, Nashe, and "Monox" met at the Steelyard: Although Nashe doesn't say where the convivial gathering took place, the Steelyard cellar is the most likely location, given both its immediate proximity to Greene's lodgings and its widespread notoriety as a den whose menu prominently featured both Rhenish wine and herring. Cf. Reinhold Pauli, "The Hanseatic Steelyard in London," from his *Pictures of England* (Cambridge: Macmillan and Co., 1861), tr. E. C. Otté.

In Pauli's words, "The Baltic itself yielded large quantities of its fish, more especially the herring, which had not then been found in any other waters." (160) He also traces the history of this German marketplace and how "six hundred years ago, Henry II granted to the men of Cologne the right of selling their Rhenish wine within the walls of their own factory [i.e., the Steelyard]" (162). The literary association with Rhenish wine and the Steelyard approached a commonplace, e.g., "Let us go to the Steelyard and drink Rhenish wine" (Nashe, *Pierce Pennilesse*), "I come to invite you to meet him this afternoon at the Rhenish winehouse in the Steelyard" (Thomas Dekker and John Webster, *Westward Ho!*), "The good man was made drunk at the Steelyard at a beaver of Dutch bread and Rhenish wine" (John Ford, *The Queen*), "Who would let a citizen...breathe upon her varnish for the promise of a dry neats tongue and a pottle of Rhenish at the Steelyard" (Thomas Nabbes, *The Bride*).

Finally, Nashe's literary nemesis Gabriel Harvey all but places Nashe's "fatal banquet" in the Steelyard ("Stilliard") in his 1593 pamphlet *Pierce's Supererogation.* Harvey begins one poem about Nashe with the words "So long the Rhennish furie of thy braine, / Incenst with hot fume of a Stilliard Clime..." Three stanzas later, Harvey puns on *Greene's Groatsworth of Wit* with the lines "So soone five Penniworth of thy groser witt/ (Yet thou art witty, as a woodcock would be)/ More then autenticall, hath learn'd to gett/ Thy Muse intitled, as it truly should be." Harvey, *Works,* ed. Alexander Grosart (New York: AMS Press, 1966; orig. ed. 1884), 2:345.

p. 256, "Grave goose-turd green": *Strange News,* McKerrow, op. cit., 1:288.

p. 256, The "Dutch magazine of sauce": James Shirley, *The Lady of Pleasure* (1637), 5.84.

p. 256, The mercantile classes and the cosmopolitan set: Pauli, op. cit.

p. 256, Two repentant pamphlets: The authorship of Greene's repentance pamphlets is an enigma in itself; for arguments in favor of attributing the pamphlets to Greene, cf.

Harold Jenkins, "On the Authenticity of *Greene's Groatsworth of Wit* and *The Repentance of Robert Greene*," *RES* 11:41 (January 1935), 28–41; on reasons to be dubious of Greene's authorship, cf. *Greene's Groatsworth of Wit*..., ed. D. Allen Carroll (Binghamton, N.Y.: Medieval and Renaissance Texts and Studies, 1994), 1–33.

p. 256, "Made myself a public laughingstock": *Greenes Vision* (1593) reprinted in *The Life and Complete Works in Prose and Verse of Robert Greene*, ed. Alexander B. Grosart, (New York: Russell & Russell, 15 vols. 1881–86; repub. 1964), vol. 12, p. 195.

p. 256, Late September or early October of 1592: On Chettle's possible authorship of *Groatsworth,* cf. Carroll, op. cit., 1–31.

p. 257, *Groatsworth* introduces the world to Will Shakspere: Even on this point, scholars disagree. The Oxfordian researcher Robert Detobel protests that *Groatsworth* has nothing to do with Will Shakspere; the pamphlet, he argues, instead lambastes Edward Alleyn. (Detobel, "The Letter in *Greene's Groatsworth of Wit:* Revisited–Why Chettle Should Have Used More Discretion, 'Especially in this Case'" [Unpublished MS, 2004]); also cf. the Marlovian scholar A. D. Wraight's *Christopher Marlowe and Edward Alleyn* (Chichester: Adam Hart, 1993).

p. 257, Roberto, who is both a scholar and author: This is a greatly condensed version of the summary and arguments found in PRICE, 45–57 and 95–109.

p. 257, Advice to Nashe, Marlowe, and George Peele: *Groatsworth,* ed. Carroll, op. cit., 82–5; 117–31.

p. 257, *Johannes factotum:* Carroll, op. cit., 134; cf. similar note in the Introduction.

p. 257, "There is an upstart crow...": Ibid., 83–5.

p. 257, Spoof on a catchphrase: *True Tragedy of Richard Duke of York ... as it was sundrie times acted by the Right Honorable the Earle of Pembrooke his seruants* (printed 1595), B2^v; *Groatsworth,* ed. Carroll, op. cit., 84, fn. 5.

p. 257, As clear as Greene's convoluted rhetoric can make it: Later in 1592, Henry Chettle–who prepared *Greene's Groatsworth of Wit* for publication and may have even secretly written it–apologized for *Groatsworth.* Chettle explains in his tract (titled *Kind-Hearts Dream*) that two of the three "divers play-makers" addressed in *Groatsworth* took offense. Those three "play-makers" are widely believed to have been Christopher Marlowe, Thomas Nashe, and George Peele. (*Greene's Groatsworth of Wit,* ed. D. Allen Carroll [N.Y: Medieval and Renaissance Texts and Studies, Binghamton, 1994], 80–83, 117–29. Which two of the three playwrights were the offended parties is less certain.) And yet, many orthodox scholars to this day continue to assert that because they *assume* Will Shakspere to have been a playwright, somehow Chettle must have been addressing Will Shakspere in his apology. Therefore, Chettle is seen as delivering crucial evidence that Will Shakspere was a playwright. This blatant example of circular reasoning has been left out of the present discussion for obvious reasons.

p. 257, *Supposes* means "feigns" or "pretends": *OED* definition 12, first attested usage, 1566; Jonathan Dixon, "The 'Upstart Crow' Supposes," *Shakespeare Oxford Society Newsletter* 36:1 (Spring 2000), 7.

pp. 257–8, Bird that dressed itself in other birds' feathers: Other mythological crows had more innocuous occupations. For instance, Horace's crow was a plagiarist. Diana Price (PRICE, 45–57) dissects Greene's rhetoric at length, concluding that the most likely interpretation of the entire Greene passage is one excoriating Shakspere as a heartless theatrical paymaster who only *pretended* he could write.

p. 258, "Shackspere" loaned John Clayton £7: For a concise, unembellished documentary life of William Shakspere, cf. PRICE, 14–19; Robert Detobel (unpublished MS, 2004) argues that the 1592 Clayton lawsuit establishes that the Shakspere being named in the case was in fact outside of the country at the time of the suit.

p. 258, If Greene is to be taken at his word: PRICE, 95–109.

p. 258, Shakspere working for Pembroke's Men: Shakspere's theatrical affiliations pre-1594 are a subject of much speculation. For arguments in favor of his working with Pembroke's Men, cf. *ES,* 2:128–34; Eric Sams, *The Real Shakespeare* (Conn: Yale University Press, New Haven, 1994), 114–15; Scott McMillin, "Casting for Pembroke's Men: The *Henry VI* Quartos and *The Taming of A Shrew,*" *SH.Q.* 23:2 (Spring 1972), 141–59.

p. 258, "Harry le Roy" of Cornwall: *Henslowe,* op. cit., 16–17; on the possibility that Henslowe's recorded 1592 performance of "Harry of Cornwall" is actually Shakespeare's *Henry V,* cf. *Henry V,* 4.1.35–50; Charles Wisner Barrell, "Shakespeare's *Henry V* Can Be Identified As 'Harry of Cornwall' in Henslowe's Diary," *Shakespeare Fellowship Quarterly* 7:4 (October 1946), 49–54.

p. 259, "Gentle Master William *Apis Lapis*": Charles Wisner Barrell, "Milestone," op. cit.

p. 259, *Apis Lapis* same person as "Monox": In 1944, Barrell established beyond a reasonable doubt that Nashe spoofed de Vere as "Gentle Master William." Barrell's argument has yet to be refuted. (Op. cit.; an online version of Barrell's article is linked to at www.shakespearebyanothername.com.)

p. 259, Meaning of *Apis* and *Lapis:* "*Apis* . . . a man whome the Egyptians honored for theyr chiefe god. Also an oxe, whom they woorshypped. . . ."; "*Lapis* . . . a negligent persone that bestyreth hym not in dooyng a thyng." Sir Thomas Elyot, *Bibliotheca Eliotae (1548),* ed. Lillian Gottesman (Delmar, N.Y.: Scholars Facsimiles and Reprints, 1975); Mark K. Anderson and Tekastiaks, "Revisiting 'Apis Lapis,'" *Shakespeare Oxford Newsletter* 34:4 (Winter 1999), 19, 24.

p. 259, "Stubborn old ox": Nashe adds a second jab to his satirical punch in the "Gentle Master William *Apis Lapis*" moniker. The proper form of address to an earl is "my lord" or "good my lord." Addressing the insensate aristocratic ox as "gentle master" indicates that Nashe was playing games with caste. Nashe clearly had a middle-class "William" in mind. One suspects the sobriquet "gentle master William" had already started making the rounds among de Vere's literary friends and drinking buddies by late 1592–by the time it had become clear that a player named William with high-flying ambitions was trying to attach his name to work that had come from de Vere's desk.

p. 260, "I myself . . . enjoy but a mite of wit in comparison of his talent": Nashe, *Strange News* in McKerrow, op. cit., 300–1. The quote begins "All you accuse him [Lyly] to have courtly incensed the Earl of Oxford against you. Mark him well. . . ."
Nashe's "All you" alludes to Harvey and his brothers.
The "Mark him well . . ." passage from *Strange News* has had a curious history. Some scholars (e.g., G. K. Hunter, *John Lyly: The Humanist as Courtier* [London: Routledge & Kegan Paul, 1962], 42) have assumed that the man with "one of the best wits in England" was Lyly. But the logical antecedent to Nashe's "Mark him well" is "the Earl of Oxford," not Lyly. Furthermore, the wit in question also "flies from . . . inferior concertation" with Harvey–i.e., the wit is of a higher caste than Harvey. This fact alone eliminates Lyly from consideration.

p. 260, Most scholars agree this dates to the period 1592–94: cf. *Love's Labor's Lost,* The Arden Shakespeare, ed. R. W. David (1968; first ed. 1951), xxiii–xxvii. One further revision of the play must have occurred in 1597 or '98, as the title page of the first edition of *Love's Labor's Lost* (printed in 1598 or early '99) says it was "performed before Her Highness this last Christmas."

p. 261, De Vere "wold easelye be movyd to folow the Spanish king": The quote comes from a September 1593 interrogation of an English prisoner named George Dingley. PRO S.P. 12/243[/11], ff. 18–19; copy ff. 20–21 in NELSON, 339.

p. 261, "Doth ravish like enchanting harmony": *Love's Labor's Lost,* 1.1.163–6.

p. 261, "I am for whole volumes in Folio!": *Love's Labor's Lost,* 1.2.54, 157–75.

p. 261, Nashe compared to Juvenal: e.g., In his *Groatsworth of Wit,* Robert Greene calls

Nashe "young Juvenal." MOTH is also labeled a "half-penny purse of wit" and a "pigeon-egg of discretion"–takeoffs on the title of a 1592 pamphlet by Nashe *(Pierce Penniless)* and Gabriel Harvey's nickname for same *(Nashe's Penniworth of Discretion)*. Charles Nicholl, *A Cup of News: The Life of Thomas Nashe* (London: Routledge & Kegan Paul, 1984), 212–3.

p. 261, Figures of a fox, an ape, and honeybees: Ibid.; Donald J. McGinn, "The Allegory of the 'Beare' and the 'Foxe' in Nashe's *Pierce Pennilesse*," *PMLA* 61:2 (June 1946), 431–53.

Further arguments in favor of Nashe as the prototype for MOTH can be found in Michael Baird Saenger, "Nashe, MOTH, and the Date of *Love's Labour's Lost*," *Notes and Queries* 243 (September 1998), 357–8; Frances A. Yates, *A Study of* Love's Labour's Lost (Cambridge: Cambridge University Press, 1936), 73–82.

p. 261, Skewering the pretensions of Gabriel Harvey: HOLOFERNES is, in fact, Gabriel Harvey with a few sarcastic twists. Like his teacher Sir Thomas Smith before him, Harvey was an outspoken advocate for orthographic reform–spelling words exactly as they sounded. In *Love's Labor's Lost*, though, the man who writes in an idiosyncratically phonetic style is ARMADO. And HOLOFERNES becomes the overblown critic of Harvey's pet fancy; e.g., "I abhor such fanatical phantasimes, such insociable and point-devise companions; such rackers of orthography as to speak 'dout,' fine, when he should say 'doubt.' . . . This is abhominable, which he would call 'abominable.' It insinuateth me of insanie."

(Both Nicholl (op. cit., 217) and M. C. Bradbrook ["St. George for Spelling Reform!" *Sh.Q.* 15:3 (Summer 1964), 135, fn. 13] present this as an argument for HOLOFERNES's *not* being a portrait of Gabriel Harvey. The notion that HOLOFERNES simply burlesques Harvey evidently did not occur.)

Whereas Harvey greeted de Vere and the entire Elizabethan court at Audley End in 1578 with a salutation from ancient Greek *("Chaere!")*, ARMADO greets HOLOFERNES using a similar silly affectation. But HOLOFERNES doesn't get it.

ARMADO Chirrah!
HOLOFERNES *Quare* 'Chirrah,' not 'Sirrah'?

Of course, HOLOFERNES can't ask a simple question in English. He lords his Latin–and his grammar rules–over everyone. (*Gabrielis Harveii* χαιρε *[chaere] vel Gratulationis Valdinensis Liber Primus* [1578], cited in Nicholl, op. cit.; Nicholl misses the joke here, however, arguing that ARMADO must therefore be Harvey.)

p. 261, verse by Battist Spagnuoli: *"Facile precor gelida quando pecus omne sub umbra Ruminat"*: *Love's Labor's Lost*, 4.2.90; cf. fn. in Arden ed., op. cit.

p. 262, "Why tender Juvenal? Why tender Juvenal?": *Love's Labor's Lost*, 1.2.1–18.

p. 262, Pamphlet battles between Harvey and Nashe: VAN DREUNEN, 215–35; "The quarrel between Nashe and the Harveys [Gabriel and his brothers John and Richard] seems in its origin to be an offshoot of the well-known one between Edward de Vere, Earl of Oxford and Sir Philip Sidney in 1579." McKerrow, op. cit., 1:73.

p. 262, "Go whip thy gig": *Love's Labor's Lost*, 5.1.43–60.

p. 262, . . . in the character of an ambitious country gentleman named COSTARD:/ Sometime during or before 1594, the Earl of Pembroke's Men performed the anonymous play *The Taming of A [sic] Shrew*. This text is arguably a rough draft of similarly titled Shake-speare play [Sams, op. cit., 136–45]

The Taming of A Shrew's rustic, CHRISTOPHER SLY, is a generic and two-dimensional figure compared to the witty and stage-wise COSTARD. SLY's job in the play is to get drunk, fall asleep, and then be the subject of a trickster nobleman's prank. The nobleman gives over his household to serve as SLY's temporary fiefdom, while the nobleman himself pretends to be SLY's page. The central story of the comedy, involving a shrewish maid and her taming husband-to-be, is then performed before the rustic's eyes. During the rest of the play, the drunken SLY wakes up occasionally, utters a few jocular words, and then passes out again. ("Am I not Don Christo Very?" SLY at one point punningly asks of his hosts in the House of [de] Very.)

It is tempting to suppose that the role of SLY was expressly written with Shakspere in mind. If so, then de Vere would soon be learning that he was not just dealing with some anonymous simp. Will Shakspere may not have penned the Shake-speare canon. But Will Shakspere was also not the country-bred naif that SLY makes him out to be.

p. 263, "MOTH, follow": *Love's Labor's Lost*, 3.1.47–129.

p. 263, The closest to such a record that has yet been found: *Love's Labor's Lost* also portrays the author as the courtier BEROWNE wooing the Anne Vavasour-like ROSALINE. Little wonder, then, that the script next calls for COSTARD to run into BEROWNE and receive a similar assignment. BEROWNE dispatches COSTARD to ferry a love letter to ROSALINE, to which COSTARD responds, "I will do it sir, in print!" (3.1.161–6.)

p. 263, COSTARD assumes the starring role: ARMADO's masque is, in fact, a takeoff on an actual skit about the nine worthies written for the Elizabethan court. The skit exists only in an undated manuscript, a document that now rests at the Folger Shakespeare Library in Washington, D.C. On evidence of its halting and choppy verse, the Elizabethan *Nine Worthies* skit likely did not come from de Vere's pen. (Even when the content of his juvenile rhymes was bad, the earl's poetic meter still ticks like a metronome.) On the other hand, de Vere would have been privy to the *Nine Worthies* manuscript–and, indeed, probably originally saw it staged for his sovereign.

The undated "nine worthies" skit is one of numerous entries in the commonplace book of the London scrivener Thomas Trevelyon. (Folger MS V.b.232.) Trevelyon completed the book in 1608, so all that can be said of the date of the masque is that it must be earlier than 1608–probably by decades. John L. Nevinson, "A Show of the Nine Worthies," *SH.Q.* 14:2 (Spring 1963), 103–7.

A second resemblance between Elizabethan court masque and *Love's Labor's Lost* has also been pointed out for *The Marriage of Wit and Science,* presented by Sebastian Westcote and the Children of Paul's–the children's troupe closest to de Vere–at Shrovetide of 1567/8. Trevor Lennam, " 'The Ventricle of Memory': Wit and Wisdom in *Love's Labour's Lost*," *SH.Q.* 24:1 (Winter 1973), 54–60.

p. 263, ARMADO's skit where COSTARD really shines: The role that COSTARD performs is Pompey the Great. Pompey was *not* one of the legendary nine worthies, but de Vere probably gave COSTARD the part anyway as a joke at ARMADO's expense; the historical Pompey's first great conquest was Spain. *EB/1911,* 22:56.

One of the other worthies in ARMADO's masque–Hercules, whom MOTH plays–was also not one of the original "nine worthies." However, as C. J. Sisson points out (*New Readings in Shakespeare* [Cambridge: Cambridge University Press, 1956], 121), Hercules was included in at least one Elizabethan courtly rendition of the "nine worthies" story, "as may be seen in the Documents of the Revels for 1558."

p. 263, "Worthies ... will speak their mind in some other sort": *Love's Labor's Lost,* 5.2.575–81.

p. 264, "You will lose your reputation!": *Love's Labor's Lost,* 5.2.692–4.

p. 264, ... missing in action until Parliament's closing day: NELSON, 343.

p. 265, Burghley pushing for Southampton marriage to Elizabeth de Vere as far back as 1590: Cal. S.P. Dom. 1581–90, p.680, in AKRIGG, 32.

p. 265, "If you think this tender offspring ... deserving the patronage of your honor": John Clapham, "EPISTOLA" in *Narcissus* (1591), in Charles Martindale and Colin Burrow, "Clapham's *Narcissus:* A Pre-Text for Shakespeare's *Venus and Adonis?*" *Eng. Lit. Renaissance* 22:2 (1992), 157.

p. 265, The "fair youth," as critics have dubbed him: e.g., *The Sonnets of Shakespeare,* ed. Raymond Macdonald Alden (New York: Houghton Mifflin Co., 1916), 467–8; AKRIGG;

Robert Giroux, *The Book Known as Q: A Consideration of Shakespeare's Sonnets* (New York: Atheneum, 1982); A. L. Rowse, *Shakespeare's Southampton: Patron of Virginia* (New York: Harper & Row, 1965); Martin Green, *Wriothesley's Roses in Shakespeare's Sonnets, Poems, and Plays* (Baltimore: Clevedon Books, 1993).

p. 267, Titian painting de Vere probably saw: Noemi Magri, "The Influence of Italian Renaissance Art on Shakespeare's Works; Titian's Barberini Painting: The Pictoral Source of *Venus and Adonis*," *De Vere Society Newsletter* (UK) (January 2001), 1–11. Cf. also Chapter 5.

p. 267, London bookseller John Harrison published: Stratfordian mythology to the contrary, *Venus and Adonis,* and *The Rape of Lucrece* after it, were published not by Richard Field (Shakspere's presumptive friend from Stratford-upon-Avon) but rather by John Harrison. Field was only the printer. G. G. Greenwood, *Is There a Shakespeare Problem?* (London: John Lane, The Bodley Head, 1916), 569–70.

p. 267, Between late April and early June of 1593: As Joseph Quincy Adams notes (*A Life of William Shakespeare* [Boston: Houghton Mifflin, 1923], 152) A copy of *Venus and Adonis* was purchased in June 1593 for 6 pence.

p. 268, ANTONY "is ADONIS... allowed to grow up": Philip C. Kolin, "Venus and/or Adonis Among the Critics," in *Venus and Adonis: Critical Essays,* ed. Philip C. Kolin (New York: Garland Publishing, 1997), 8.

p. 268, Told nothing but see and hear everything: Samuel Taylor Coleridge, "Shakespeare's *Venus and Adonis*," in *Critical Essays,* op. cit., 70.

pp. 268–9, "Witness the entertainment that he gave": *Venus and Adonis,* ll. 124–6, 513–8, 549–52, 1005–6, 1105–8; Roger Stritmatter, "Shakespeare on Mt. Parnassus: Irony, Paradox, and Authorship in *Venus and Adonis*," presented at the seventeenth Annual Shakespeare Oxford Society conference, Boston (October 1993).

p. 269, "And much ado with red and white": Lansdowne MSS 99.81–7 in Leslie Hotson, "Two Shakespearean 'Firsts,'" in *Shakespeare's Sonnets Dated and Other Essays* (London: Rupert Hart-Davis, 1949), 141–7; Katherine Duncan-Jones, "Much Ado With Red and White: The Earliest Readers of Shakespeare's *Venus and Adonis* (1593)," *RES* 44:176 (November 1993), 479–90.

p. 270, "I write only at idle hours that I dedicate only to *Idle Hours*": Gabriel Harvey, *Pierce's Supererogation* (1593), in *Gabriel Harvey (1550?–1631) Works,* ed. Alexander B. Grosart (New York: AMS Press, 1966; 1884 first ed.), 2:330–1.

p. 270, "Both to grow to perfection in M. Thomas Nashe": Harvey, *Pierce's Supererogation,* op. cit., 2:50. The full quote about Greene reads, "... till the one began to sprowte in M. Robart Greene, as in a sweating Impe of the euer-greene Laurell; the other to blossome in M. Pierce Pennilesse...." What Harvey means by the "sweating Impe of the euer-greene Laurell" I do not know.

p. 270, "Worthless toy" or "very perishable goods": BREWER'S, 12. A latter-day pamphlet war broke out in 2002–3 over Harvey's *Penniless* remarks and their purported implications for the Shake-speare authorship question, about which cf. Mark K. Anderson and Roger Stritmatter, "The Potent Testimony of Gabriel Harvey," *Shakespeare Matters* 1:2 (Winter 2002), 26–29; Terry Ross, "No, Harvey did NOT say Oxford wrote *V & A*," Usenet: humanities.lit.authors.shakespeare (February 20, 2002); Anderson with Stritmatter, "Ross's Supererogation," *Shakespeare Matters* 1:3 (Spring 2002), 28–31; Anderson, "More on Pierce Penniless," *Shakespeare Matters* 2:2 (Winter 2003), 26–8.

p. 270, Trendy poetic trinket aimed at pleasing the younger crowd: In his copy of Chaucer's works, Harvey in fact wrote in the margin, "The younger sort take much delight in Shakespeare's Venus and Adonis; but his Lucrece, and his tragedy of Hamlet, Prince of Denmarke, have it in them to please the wiser sort. 1598." *ALLUSION BOOK,* 1:56; Ross, op. cit.; "Ross's Supererogation," op. cit.

p. 270, Harvey sometimes called de Vere "Pierce Penniless": VAN DREUNEN, 215–35.

CHAPTER TEN

p. 272, Elizabeth and the perfumed handkerchief: John Guy, "The 1590s: The second reign of Elizabeth I?" in *The Reign of Elizabeth I: Court and Culture in the Last Decade*, ed. John Guy (Cambridge: Cambridge University Press, 1995), 3–4.

p. 273, Conspiracies swirled around Lady Arabella for years: *EB/1911* entry on Arabella Stuart (1575–1615); Joel Hurstfield, "The Succession Struggle in Late Elizabethan England," in *Elizabethan Government and Society* (London: Athlone Press, 1961), 369–96.

p. 273, Poley and the Scots queen conspiracy: Ethel Seaton, "Marlowe, Robert Poley, and the Tippings," *RES* 5:19 (July 1929), 280.

p. 273, "Rydeing in sondrey places": Eugenie de Kalb, "Robert Poley's Movements as a Messenger of the Court, 1588 to 1601," *RES* 9:33 (January 1933), 14–17.

p. 274, Heneage, an adherent of the Cecil faction: The paymaster of "Roberte Poolye"'s missions to Scotland is listed as "Mr. vicechamberleyne" (ibid., 16); Sir Thomas Heneage was Vice Chamberlain from 1588 to his death in 1595 (WARD, 373); Natalie Mears, "*Regnum Cecilianum?* A Cecilian perspective of the court" in *The Reign of Elizabeth I*, op. cit., 49.

p. 274, Murdered part-time agent: Marlowe's murder remains an unsolved mystery. This book follows the hypothesis presented by Bronson Feldman ("The Marlowe Mystery," *The Bard* 3:1 [1980], 44–6): "I believe that Marlowe was slain to prevent him from telling the Privy Council, perhaps from the Bridewell rack, about Robert Poley's transactions with the court of the Scots. Marlowe knew too much, and could not be trusted to stay mute about Poley's journeys to the north, made in obedience to his employers who looked to Edinburgh for preferment–'fruitful wits' (to use Marlowe's phrase in *Hero and Leander*) who 'discontent run into regions far.' Poley's main master was Sir Robert Cecil."

p. 275, Henslowe recorded performance of *Hamlet*: *Henslowe's Diary, second ed.*, ed. R. A. Foakes (Cambridge: Cambridge University Press, 2002; first ed. 1961), 21; the *Hamlet* text here discussed is assumed by scholars today to be the missing "Ur-*Hamlet*" written by Thomas Kyd or some other unknown author. There is no need for this unsupported supposition. The *Hamlet* being performed on June 9, 1594, was, this book asserts, Shakespeare's–albeit undoubtedly in a rough and inferior state compared to the version published in 1604.

p. 275, Heneage a leading landholder: Heneage held this wealth of properties in his capacity as the chancellor of the vast holdings of the duchy of Lancaster. (*DNB* entry for Sir Thomas Heneage [d. 1595].) Although the *DNB* does not list Cecil as one of his allies, Natalie Mears's comprehensive survey of the Cecil faction in the late-Elizabethan court (op. cit., 49) does. On the bizarre "kingdom within a kingdom" that was the Elizabethan duchy of Lancaster, cf. Richard Dutton, "Shakespeare and Lancaster," *SH.Q.* 49:1 (Spring 1998), 4–8.

p. 275, De Vere and Heneage at Gray's Inn and Cambridge: The *DNB* notes Heneage was admitted to Gray's Inn in 1565; Heneage was also created M.A. at Cambridge in 1564, along with de Vere.

p. 276, Shakspere as the GHOST in *Hamlet*: Sidney Lee, *Shakespeare and the Modern Stage* (New York: Charles Scribner & Sons, 1906), 27.

p. 276, Heneage-Browne nuptials: e.g., STOPES, 75; A. L. Rowse, *William Shakespeare: A Biography* (London: Macmillan & Co., 1963), 204–11; John Dover Wilson, "Variations on the theme of *A Midsummer Night's Dream*," in *Shakespeare's Happy Comedies* (London: Faber & Faber, 1962), 202–4–and references therein.

p. 276, World premiere of *A Midsummer Night's Dream*: *MND*, 1.1.9–10, 2.1.88–117, 3.2.61; William B. Hunter, "The First Performance of *A Midsummer Night's Dream*," *Notes and Queries*, n.s., 32 (March 1985), 45–7; Hunter, "Performance and Text: the Evidence of *A Midsummer Night's Dream*," *American Notes and Queries* 11:1 (Winter 1998), 7–12.

p. 276, "The rite of May": *MND*, 4.1.131–3; Wilson, op. cit., 202.

p. 276, Marriage of THESEUS to HIPPOLYTA: *A Midsummer Night's Dream* provides little back-story for the ancient Greek figure of Hippolyta, the Amazonian queen, that would reveal her former rivalry with Duke Theseus; however, the tale of "Palamon and Arcite"/*Two Noble Kinsmen* does emphasize Hippolyta and Theseus's ancient enmity. (CAMPBELL AND QUINN, 362) Perhaps relevant to the present circumstance is the fact that Philip Henslowe records an entry for a new ("ne") play titled "palamon & a⸢sett" on September 17, 1594 (Foakes, op. cit., 24).

p. 277, "Grows, lives, and dies in single blessedness": *MND*, 1.1.76–8; Rowse, op. cit., 205.

p. 277, BOTTOM transformed into an ass with whom TITANIA falls in love: BOTTOM's "dream" becomes a fantastical restaging of *Taming of the Shrew*'s SLY being tricked into the trappings of a nobleman.

p. 277, "Nor his heart to report what my dream was": *MND*, 4.1.1–4, 203–12; BOTTOM's words are a comic inversion of a famous verse from the Apostle Paul. (I Corinthians 2.9: "We preach as it is written: Things which the eye hath not seen, and ear hath not heard...") The Apostle then goes on to extol the Holy spirit for searching the "bottom of God's secrets"–a phrase that probably provided the source of the character's name. (Thomas B. Stroup, "BOTTOM's Name and His Epiphany," *SH.Q.* 29:1 [Winter 1978], 79–82.)

In de Vere's 1569 Geneva Bible, none of I Corinthians chapter 2 is underlined. On the other hand, one would not expect the 1569 edition to contain the underlining, since the 1569 edition of I Corinthians offers up a more mundane translation ("the deepe things of God") in place of the more evocative "bottom of God's secrets" found in the 1559 Geneva edition.

p. 278, De Vere could only promise his devotion: A sonnet, later published as Shakespeare's Sonnet 26, said essentially the same thing as the *Lucrece* dedication.

pp. 278–9, *Lucrece* parallels the rise of quasi-republican Regnum Cecilianum: For those of the anti-Cecil faction, "*Regnum Cecilianum* or 'Cecil's Commonwealth' was a phrase which had been frequently used." J. E. Neale, *The Age of Catherine de Medici and Essays in Elizabethan History* (London: J. Cape, 1958), 166.

p. 279, ... out of the ashes of the Tudor dynasty: "The key to Burghley isn't deference to monarchy, but quasi-republicanism.... He was the queen's puppeteer, pulling strings to a greater degree than Elizabeth ever knew. To a large extent England was his fiefdom, governed by his 'assured' Protestant clique. He wasn't the power behind the throne but the power in front of it." John Guy, "Why Starkey Is Wrong About Elizabeth," *The (London) Sunday Times* (November 11, 2001).

p. 279, LUCRECE is Elizabeth as "Virgin Queen": Peter Erickson, "Refracted Images of Queen Elizabeth in *Venus and Adonis* and *The Rape of Lucrece*," in *Rewriting Shakespeare, Rewriting Ourselves* (Berkeley: University of California Press, 1991), 31–56.

p. 279, ... to a male-dominated hierarchy of state power: Erickson, op. cit., 42–3.

p. 279, Fine of £5,000: AKRIGG, 39.

pp. 279–80, ... hangs on every word written by Shake-speare: e.g.

GULLIO Marry, I think I shall entertain those verses which run like these:

> Even as the sun with purple colored face
> Had ta'en his last leave on the weeping morn, etc.

O, sweet Mr Shakespeare! I'll have his picture in my study at the court!

The Three Parnassus Plays, ed. J. B. Leishmann (London: Nicholson & Watson, 1949), 80–2, 185; Pierce Butler, *Materials for the Life of Shakespeare* (Chapel Hill: University of N.C. Press, 1930), 88–93.

p. 280, GULLIO quote: *First Part of Return from Parnassis,* ll. 1101–12, op. cit. Naturally, in mocking two earls, a countess, and the all-powerful House of Cecil, the students needed to tread lightly. So they gave the character "Ingenioso" (based on Thomas Nashe) the task of uttering the follow-up disclaimer: "I thinks he means to poison me with a lie! Why, he is acquainted with ne'er a lord except my Lord Coulton [a Cambridge tailor]–and for countesses, he never came in the country where a countess dwells!"

p. 280, "Graver labor" reprinted seven times between 1598 and 1640: *The Poems,* The Arden Shakespeare, ed. F. T. Prince (London: Methuen, 1960), xii–xiii.

p. 280, *The Choice of Valentines:* Contemporary allusions in Nashe's *Choice* date it to between August 1592 and September 1593. Alan Armstrong, "The Apprenticeship of John Donne: Ovid and the Elegies," *ELH* 44:3 (Autumn 1977), 440, fn. 11.

p. 280, "Lord S." as Southampton: STOPES, 57–9; G. R. Hibbard (*Thomas Nashe: A Critical Introduction* [Cambridge: Harvard University Press, 1962], 56) also points out a verbal echo between Nashe's dedication to "Lord S" and Spenser's dedication to de Vere in *The Faerie Queene.*

p. 280, Finally published in 1899: The *Parnassus* plays would suggest that Nashe was on familiar terms with Southampton; in 1594 the satirist did go to print with a publicly accessible adventure novel, *The Unfortunate Traveler,* that he also dedicated to Southampton.

p. 280, From "To the courteous readers" onward: "Gentlemen: To make a long preamble to a short suit were folly, and therefore (in brief) thus: Here you have the first fruits of my endeavors and the maidenhead of my pen–which, how rude and unpolished it may seem in your eagle-sighted eyes, I cannot conceive, and therefore, fearing the worst, I have sought in some sort to prevent it. . . ." ("To the Courteous Readers," in T.H., *Oenone and Paris* (1594), ed. Joseph Quincy Adams [Washington, D.C.: Folger Shakespeare Library, 1943], 3.)

p. 280, "A thousand thanks": *Oenone,* ll. 399, 459.

p. 280, Drayton and at least four other poets in 1594: John Dickenson, *Arisbas: Euphues in His Slumbers* (1594, containing a dedication to Edward Dyer speaking of both "idle hours" and a graver labor to come); W. Har., *Epicedium;* Michael Drayton, *The Legend of Mathilda, the Chast;* Richard Barnfield, *The Affectionate Shepherd;* John Weever, *Epigrammes in the Oldest Cut and Newest Fashion.* The latter three can be found in the ALLUSION BOOK, 1:14–24.

p. 281, Pembroke's Men's *Taming of A Shrew and First Part of the Contention . . .*: Charles Wisner Barrell, "Exploding the Ancient Play Cobbler Fallacy: Contemporary Evidence Proving Shakespeare Himself Chief Victim of Play Pirates," *Shakespeare Fellowship Quarterly* 7:1 (January 1946), 3–7.

p. 281, None approved or supervised by the author: On Shakspere as the reporter responsible for the Shake-speare "bad quartos," cf. Alden Brooks, *Will Shakspere and the Dyer's Hand* (New York: Charles Scribner's Sons, 1943), 85–8.

p. 281, Author of *Locrine* as Charles Tilney: *Locrine* was, according to an annotation made by the courtier Sir George Buc in a *Locrine* quarto, written by Buc's late cousin Charles Tilney. CAMPBELL AND QUINN, 461–2; E. K. Chambers (*ES,* 4:26–7) suspects one of the "University Wits" (e.g., Robert Greene, George Peele) wrote *Locrene.*

p. 281, De Vere letter July 7, 1594: Lansdowne MSS, 76.74 in FOWLER, 484–5.

p. 281, Elizabeth snatched Henry back: Pauline K. Angell, "Light on the Dark Lady: A Study of Some Elizabethan Libels," *PMLA* 52:3 (September 1937), 652–74; STOPES, 39–40; G. B. Harrison, "An Essay on *Willobie His Avisa,*" in *Willobie His Avisa,* ed. Harrison (London: John Lane/The Bodley Head, 1926), 213–20.

p. 283, "H.W. was brought unto by a desperate view of an impossibility of obtaining his purpose": *Willobie,* ed. G. B. Harrison, ibid., 115–6.

p. 283, *Willobie* even has de Vere play the role of trickster: "Ingenioso's" (Nashe's) exchange with "Gullio" (Southampton) in *The Return from Parnassus,* cited above, takes on a new light with the revelations of *Willobie:* e.g., "For countesses, he never came in the country where a countess dwells!"

p. 283, London literati knew de Vere's secret identity as "W.S.": *Willobie* also contains the following prefatory verse "In praise of *Willobie his Auisa*":

> Yet TARQUYNE pluckt his glistering grape
> And Shake-speare [*sic*], paints poore LUCRECE rape.

Willobie, ed. Harrison, op. cit., 19; ALLUSION BOOK, 1:9–13.

p. 283, Who turns him down at every occasion: W.S.'s counsel is a spoof of a Shakespeare poem that was later published in the poetic miscellany *The Passionate Pilgrim*. It also is one of the poems that Anne Cornwallis, resident of Fisher's Folly after de Vere sold the property, transcribed in her commonplace book.

p. 285, The continued ascent of the House of Cecil: Tossed in with *Lucrece's* latter-day political commentary was also de Vere's old obsession about his wife's first pregnancy, the one that gave birth to Southampton's would-be bride; the late Anne Cecil de Vere, too, was probably more than a little bit LUCRECE in the author's mind. As noted in Chapter 5, after she is raped LUCRECE occupies many stanzas describing a painting of Troy that was inspired by the Salle du Troy in Mantua, where de Vere would have stayed during his probable stopover in this northern Italian town. Lines 1,520–68 concern the betrayal of Sinon, who convinced the Trojans to accept the infamous Horse. LUCRECE compares herself to Troy. As Conyers Read notes (READ/*BURGHLEY,* 96–7), at least one other Elizabethan poet had compared Lord Burghley to Sinon.

p. 285, Gray's Inn season of plays to rival anything staged in England: "So far as we know, nothing ever had equaled the revels of that year...." James M. Beck, "How Lawyers Worked and Played in Tudor Times," in *May It Please the Court* (New York: Macmillan & Co., 1930), 119.

p. 285, Established a faux princedom: *Gesta Grayorum 1688,* Malone Society, ed. W. W. Greg (Oxford: Oxford University Press, 1914).

p. 286, Evening called "the Night of Errors": It has been pointed out (R. H. Robertson, "Resemblances Between the First 14 Lines of *Love's Labour Lost* [*sic*] and the Speeches of the Six Counsellors in the Christmas Revels known as *Gesta Grayorum,*" *Baconiana* 3:16 [1920], 32) that the revels also provided a springboard from which Shake-speare could launch into his own jests.

p. 286, "Disorders with a play of errors and confusions": *Gesta Grayorum,* op. cit., 23; J. J. Dwyer, "The Poet Earl of Oxford and Gray's Inn" *Shakespeare Fellowship Quarterly* 8:2 (Summer 1947), 24–5.

p. 286, Purpoole ultimately accepted the "dream" defense: Beck, op. cit., 128.

p. 286, "...she [could not] fancye": A. W. Titherley, *Shakespeare's Identity: William Stanley, 6th Earl of Derby* (Winchester: Warren & Son, Ltd., 1952), 27.

p. 287, "Marriage feast was there most royally kept": John Stow, *Annales,* p. 768 (listed under 1595) in John Dover Wilson, "Variations on the theme of *A Midsummer Night's Dream*" in *Shakespeare's Happy Comedies* (London: Faber & Faber, 1962), 205, fn. 2.

p. 287, Wedding ceremony held at Burghley: David Wiles (*Shakespeare's Almanac:* A Midsummer Night's Dream, *Marriage and the Elizabethan Calendar* [Cambridge: D. S. Brewer, 1993], 143–7) corrects E. K. Chambers and successive scholars who have taken Stow's testimony at face value. Wiles demonstrates that the wedding itself had, *pace* Chambers, not happened on January 26. Instead, the party repaired to Burghley House for the ceremony on January 30. There were postnuptial celebrations on the thirty-first. Queen Elizabeth departed Burghley on February 1. For this book, I posit that *A Midsummer Night's Dream* was performed on the night of the twenty-sixth, but there is no ruling out the possibility that the play could have been enacted on any of the nights of the festivities.

p. 287, Sensitive to astrological significance of timing of events: Wiles (op. cit., 143) points out that William Stanley was a patron of the astrologer John Dee, while William's mother "had a reputation as one who consulted with 'wizards and cunning men.'"

p. 287, One play had been prepared . . . : Cal. Salisbury MS 99/January 1594/5, in J. R. Brink, "The Masque of the Nine Muses: Sir John Davies's Unpublished *Eithalamion* and the 'Belphoebe-Ruby' Episode in *The Faerie Queene*," *RES*, n.s., 23:92 (November 1972), 445–7.

p. 287, Entertaining an exiled Spaniard with her footwork: E. K. Chambers, "The Occasion of *A Midsummer Night's Dream*," in *Shakespearean Gleanings* (London: Oxford University Press, 1944), 61–7; Wiles, op. cit., 145.

p. 287, Great Chamber of Greenwich Palace: On the allusions that suggest a performance for the January 26, 1594/5 Vere-Derby wedding, cf. Dover Wilson, op. cit., 204–5; CHAMBERS/*WS*, 1:358–9; Titherley, op. cit., 71–5; Wiles, op. cit., 143–55; William B. Hunter Jr., "Appendix: The Date and Occasion for *A Midsummer Night's Dream*," in *Milton's Comus: Family Piece* (Troy, N.Y.: Whitson Publishing Co., 1983), 95–101; E. K. Chambers, "The Occasion of *A Midsummer Night's Dream*," in *Shakespearean Gleanings* (Oxford: Oxford University Press, 1944), 61–7.

p. 287, Bless "each several chamber . . . through this palace": *Midsummer Night's Dream*, 1.1.1–4, 5.1.387–406, Wiles, op. cit.; E.A.J. Honigmann, *Shakespeare: The "Lost Years"* (Manchester: Manchester University Press, 1985), 150–4.

p. 288, "My fortunes every way as fairly rank'd": *MND*, 1.1.91–101.

p. 288, DEMETRIUS winds up with a maiden infatuated with him: Note that DEMETRIUS is the only character who ends the play with PUCK's faerie spell still cast over him.

p. 288, EGEUS stages a wedding masque: EGEUS is only the playmaster in the 1623 Folio text of *MND*. In the 1600 quarto of *MND*, the incidental character PHILOSTRATE acts in EGEUS's stead as the revels master. (Hunter, "Performance," op. cit.; Barbara Hodgson, "Gaining a Father: The Role of EGEUS in the Quarto and the Folio," *RES* 37 [1986], 534–42). This is one of a number of reasons to suspect a *third* performance of *MND*–for the wedding of the daughter of the Lord Chamberlain (Elizabeth Carey). (For other reasons, cf. Dover Wilson and Wiles, op. cit.) In this ultimate version of *MND*, PHILOSTRATE would serve as a gentle caricature of the father-of-the-bride, the patron of the troupe that staged *MND*.

p. 288, Davies . . . paid homage to the newlyweds: It's no coincidence that one of the masques EGEUS offers up in celebration of the wedding of his daughter with LYSANDER is "the thrice three Muses." (5.1.52–5.) In a moment of characteristic Shake-spearean wit, THESEUS opts not to see the "thrice three Muses" skit, because he suspects "that is some satire, keen and critical."

p. 288, History *(Clio)*, Tragedy *(Melpomene)*, etc.: Sir John Davies, "Epithalameon for the Marriage of Lady Elizabeth Vere and William Stanley, Earl of Derby," in *The Poems of Sir John Davies*, ed. Robert Krueger (Oxford: Oxford University Press, 1975), 202–7; Wiles, op. cit., 146–55; Warren Hope, "John Davies's Sonnets for the Marriage of Elizabeth Vere and William Stanley," *Shakespeare Oxford Society Newsletter* 17:3 (Summer 1981), 5–9.

In 1592, Thomas Nashe noted that one of the things "Gentle Master William" (aka de Vere) held "most precious" was "John Davies's *Soul*"–i.e., Davies's poem on the immortality of the soul, *Nosce Teipsum*. (Charles Wisner Barrell, "A New Milestone in Shakespearean Research," *Shakespeare Fellowship Quarterly* 5:4 [October 1944], 64, fn. 37.)

pp. 288–9, . . . explore the country seat of an English family unrivaled in their power: Lady Victoria Leathem, *Life at Burghley: Restoring One of England's Great Houses* (Boston: Little, Brown & Co., 1992), 77.

p. 289, Jokes about FERDINAND:

PROSPERO [to FERDINAND] I'll manacle thy neck and feet together;
    Sea-water shalt thou drink; thy food shall be
    The fresh-brook mussels, wither'd roots, and husks
    Wherein the acorn cradled.

(*The Tempest*, 1.2.462–5.)

> The [fourth] Earl of Derby ... had two sons of noble race....
> The youngest was called Sir William Stanley....
> [He traveled to Greenland] where he endur'd more misery.
> For three months there was nothing but dark,
> And there Sir William was forc'd to want.
> He fed there on nothing but roots....

(*Sir William Stanley's Garland* (1814 ed.) stanzas 1–36, reprint and commentary in W. Ron Hess, *The Dark Side of Shakespeare* (New York: iUniverse, 2003), 2:406–23.)

    p. 289, FERDINAND convinces PROSPERO: Before PROSPERO will consent to his daughter's marriage, FERDINAND must first "remove some thousands of ... logs and pile them up." (De Vere was during the 1590s advocating for the return of his family's ancestral property of Waltham Forest; one wonders if FERDINAND's "wooden slavery" sequence in *The Tempest* is the author's acknowledgment that the earl of Derby had helped him lobby for the Waltham arboretum.)

    p. 289, "I have given you here a third of mine own life": *The Tempest*, 4.1.110–22; 4.1.1–7; the "third of mine own life" line has puzzled scholars for centuries, since technically PROSPERO only has one daughter. (Cf. the three pages of commentary devoted just to the word *third* in the New Variorum *Tempest*, ed. Horace Howard Furness [London: J. B. Lippincott & Co., 1892], 187–9.) But the autobiographical nature of the Shake-speare texts sometimes solves such enigmas in the blink of an eye.

    p. 289, Cornish tin in the smelting fires of ancient Greeks and Phoenicians: Ernest S. Hedges, *Tin in Social and Economic History* (London: Edward Arnold Ltd., 1964), 1–12.

    p. 290, Tin production fell by a third: George Randall Lewis, *The Stannaries: A Study of the English Tin Miner* (Cambridge: Harvard University Press, 1907), 41, 253–5.

    p. 290, Wrote seventeen dated letters and memoranda and eight undated ones: Using Nelson's indexing system (NELSON, 487–9), de Vere's "tin-mining" letters and memoranda will hereafter be referred to as LL-51 through LL-77 and can be read in full (in their original spelling) on Nelson's Web site, socrates.berkeley.edu/~ahnelson. (Two additional tin-mining letters, dated June 1599, are also in the present docket.)

    p. 290, "Two-in-one" construction: e.g., George T. Wright, "Hendiadys and *Hamlet*," *PMLA* 96 (1981), 168–93.

    pp. 290–1, "My haps to wither in the herb": Tin-mining letters LL-72, LL-76, LL-54, LL-60, LL-60, LL-65, op. cit.

    p. 291, Including Sir Walter Raleigh: Lewis (op. cit., 145–6) points to Sir Bevis Bulmer, Raleigh, and "Brigham and Wemmes" as Elizabethan holders of the tin patents.

    p. 291, "Being yet no better recovered": LL-53 and LL-55, op. cit.; Peter R. Moore, "The Lame Storyteller, Poor and Despised," *Shakespeare Oxford Newsletter* 31:3 (Summer 1995), 17–22.

    p. 291, Ill health, infirmity, or lameness: Letters dating from September 1590, March 1595, August 1595, September 1597, October 1601, November 1601, January 1602, April 1603; Moore, op. cit.

    p. 291, Bloodletting to fight maladies that plagued him: NELSON, 357.

    p. 291, Visited the western city of Bath: The visit is recorded in the register of the town's chamberlain, who presented his noble guest a gift of capons, chickens, pigeons, and sugar. Bath Record Office, Chamberlain's Account Roll No. 35 (1595–6) in NELSON, 358; in the same record, Bath's chamberlain also noted providing comestible gifts to Margaret Clifford, countess of Cumberland (1560?–1616).

p. 292, "Thither hied a sad distempered guest": Andrew Werth ("Shakespeare's 'Lesse Greek,'" *The Oxfordian* 5 [2002], 16–18) points out, "All past and present orthodox scholars who have sought the origin of [Sonnets 153–4], among them Katherine Duncan-Jones, A. L. Rowse, Stephen Booth, and G. Blakemore Evans, agree that the source of both is [Constantine Cephalas's] *Greek Anthology*. However . . . scholars cannot point to a translation, since the first complete one (in Latin, by Lubinus) was not published until 1603 (in Heidelberg). . . . If the inability of scholars to find the man from Stratford in the first 152 sonnets has supplied his claim to *Shakespeare's Sonnets* with a coffin, these last two may provide the nails."

p. 292, "Some say my Lord of Oxford is dead": West Kent County Record Office U1475/12/22 in NELSON, 354.

p. 292, The use of an "upstart crow" front man: George Chapman, "A Coronet for His Mistresse Philosophie," in *The Poems of George Chapman*, ed. Phyllis Brooks Barlett (Oxford: Oxford University Press, 1941), 83–6; for Stratfordian commentary, cf. Arthur Acheson, *Shakespeare's Sonnet Story* (London: B. Quaritch, 1922), 272–87; for Oxfordian commentary, cf. Percy Allen, *The Case for Edward de Vere, Seventeenth Earl of Oxford as "William Shakespeare"* (London: C. Palmer, 1930).

p. 292, Also during 1595: Around this time, John Davies (who had written the masque of the nine Muses for Elizabeth de Vere's wedding) published a poem about dancing which he called *Orchestra*–also containing possible allusions to de Vere as Shake-speare. D.W.T.C. Vessey, "An Early Allusion to Shakespeare?" *The Shakespeare Authorship Review* 19 (Spring 1968), 4–11; Warren Hope, "The Singing Swallow: Sir John Davies and Shakespeare," *The Elizabethan Review* 1:1 (Spring 1993), 21–39.

p. 292, Once fought Knyvet's servants at the Blackfriars: One possible further allusion to de Vere/Shake-speare in 1595 comes in John Trussell's *The First Rape of Fair Helen* (1595). This poet, a cousin of de Vere's hailing from the family that owned Billesley Manor in Stratford-on-Avon, addressed a sonnet to someone near and dear. (Trussell writes of "our friendship and our amity.") Since *Helen* is indebted to *Lucrece,* some scholars have suspected that Trussell's poem is addressed to Shake-speare. Cf. M. A. Shaaber, "*The First Rape of Fair Helen* by John Trussell," *SH.Q.* 8:4 (Autumn 1957), 407–48.

p. 292, Joiner that he couldn't pay: NELSON, 361.

p. 292, "By the grace of God, I will send it you": CP 44/63, September 6, 1596, in FOWLER, 514; NELSON, 360 (LL-26).

p. 293, "As you can get leisure to advertise me how her causes stand": CP 44/101, September 17, 1596, NELSON, 360–1 (LL-27).

p. 293, Family ties retained between father and daughter, stepmother and son-in-law: WARD, 319–21.

p. 293, "Busied only in penning comedies for the common players": Cal S.P. Dom. 271.34,35 in WARD, 321.

pp. 293–4, An installation ceremony was set for the following month: Knights Garter elected April 23, 1597: Frederick, Count of Mompelgard and Duke of Würtemberg (invested at Stuttgart November 6, 1603); Thomas Howard, first Lord Howard; George Carey, second Lord Hunsdon; Chalres Blount, eighth Lord Mountjoy; Sir Henry Lea. *The Knights of England,* ed. William Arthur Shaw (London: Heraldry Today, 1971; 1906 first ed.), 1:29.

p. 294, De Vere once garnered majority of votes for O.G. himself: Peter R. Moore, "Oxford, the Order of the Garter, and Shame," *The Shakespeare Oxford Newsletter* 32:2 (Spring 1996), 1, 8–11.

p. 294, Didn't technically have to notify a garter inductee . . . : *The Merry Wives of Windsor,* The Arden Shakespeare, ed. H. J. Oliver (London: Methuen, 1971), xlvii.

p. 294, De Vere still adding topical references in the 1590s: The punch line at Würtemberg/Mompelgard's expense is left to the French doctor CAIUS: "It is tell-a-me dat you make grand preparation for a Duke de *Jamanee*. By my trot, der is no Duke that the court is know, to come!"

When *The Merry Wives of Windsor* was later printed in quarto (in 1602), the title page read that the Lord Chamberlain's Men performed the play "before Her Majesty and elsewhere." Given the precise nature of the jests at the "Duke de *Jamanee*"'s expense–and the specific references in the play to Windsor Castle and Garter Knighthood inductions–the site for Shakspere's troupe's royal command performance of FALSTAFF's romantic comedy is not hard to guess. The location, conveniently, was in the play's very title. (*Merry Wives,* 5.5.56–71.)

p. 294, Shakespere's troupe staged *The Merchant of Venice*: The late 1590s draft of *The Merchant of Venice* (title page: "divers times acted by the Lord Chamberlaine his servants") can be dated with more precision than most Shake-speare texts: It was registered on July 22, 1598 (and mentioned by Francis Meres in his 1598 book *Palladis Tamia*), and contains a reference to the "wealthy *Andrew* docked in sand" (1.1.27)–an allusion to the Spanish ship *St. Andrew,* run aground in July 1596. David Grote, *The Best Actors in the World: Shakespeare and His Acting Company* (Westport, Conn.: Greenwood, 2002), 49.

p. 294, *Merchant* may have graced stages as early as 1578: In 1578, the Puritan pamphleteer Stephen Gosson railed about the play "The *Iew*...showne at the Bull...representing the greedinesse of worldly chusers, and the bloody mindes of Usuerers." (BULLOUGH, 1:445–9.)

p. 294, Higher principles like mercy and justice: Mark Edwin Andrews, *Law Versus Equity in* The Merchant of Venice (Boulder: University of Colorado Press, 1965), xi–xv; Stephanie Hopkins Hughes, "Oxford's Legal Education." Presentation at the First Shakespeare Fellowship Conference, Cambridge, Mass.: October 19, 2002.

p. 295, Gurlyn–Sherley–de Vere payments promised and payments dodged: NELSON, 361–7.

p. 295, "His shifts and knaveries are so gross and palpable...": CP 37/66(b), January 11, 1597, de Vere to Robert Cecil (LL-28 in NELSON, 361–7).

p. 296, Gurlyn did have a marginally feasible argument: Technically, Gurlyn had advanced de Vere £400 and received £300 in return. Never mind that Gurlyn had "paid" de Vere with de Vere's own money. Other than the fact that Gurlyn was blatantly in the wrong in any abstract moral sense, he had a case.

p. 296, "Overthrown upon manifest proof made of the satisfaction of that debt": PRO REQ 2/388/28 in NELSON, 366–7.

p. 296, Trial scene rich in legal terminology: Andrews, op. cit.; Maxine MacKay, "*The Merchant of Venice:* A Reflection of the Early Conflict Between Courts of Law and Courts of Equity," *SH.Q.* 15:4 (Autumn 1964), 371–5; J.D.E., "Shakespeare and the Legal Process: Four Essays," *Virginia Law Review* 61:2 (March 1975), 390–433; Charles Spinosa, "SHYLOCK and Debt and Contract in *The Merchant of Venice,*" *Cardozo Studies in Law and Literature* 5:1 (Spring 1993), 65–85, *esp.* 82, fn. 3.

p. 296, Law versus equity a leading judicial question of the age: Ironically, a seventeenth-century case with its origins in some 1580 investments of de Vere's would become a landmark ruling in the equity-versus-common-law dispute. Mark Fortier, "Equity and ideas: Coke, Ellesmere, and James I," *Renaissance Quarterly* 51:4 (1998), 1255ff.

p. 296, PORTIA uses both common law and chancery law arguments: for a detailed exposition of the legalistic bobsled run PORTIA leads the court–between chancery and common law and back again–cf. Andrews, op. cit., and MacKay, op. cit.

p. 296, "The quality of mercy is not strained": *The Merchant of Venice,* 4.1.182–7; this speech also draws from an annotated verse from de Vere's Geneva Bible in Jeremiah chapter 15, about which cf. Appendix A.

p. 296, She had ... ultimately carried the day: SHYLOCK, on the other hand, represents no single individual so much as an amalgamation of the many bottom-liners de Vere had encountered throughout his fiscally volatile life–including actual Venetian moneylenders and the Northwest Passage financier Michael Lok.

Although the composition of the published draft of *The Merchant of Venice* can be tightly dated to between July 1596 and July 1598, no records exist of any of *The Merchant of Venice*'s performances during this period. (The first recorded performance was by the King's Men at Whitehall on February 10, 1605. CAMPBELL & QUINN, 525.) However, with its actionable arguments appropriate for the finest of Elizabethan legal minds, it would have been surprising indeed had not at least one performance of *The Merchant of Venice* been given for the lawyers and law students at the Inns of Court. (Andrews [op. cit.] argues extensively for an Inns of Court performance of *Merchant of Venice* in 1597 or early 1598.)

p. 297, The countess of Derby was having an affair with Essex: Paul E. J. Hammer, *The Polarisation of Elizabethan Politics: The Political Career of Robert Devereux, 2ⁿᵈ Earl of Essex, 1585-1597* (Cambridge: Cambridge University Press, 1999), 321.

p. 297, "I have already received diverse injuries and wrongs from him": CP 31/106; April 24, 1595, de Vere to Robert Cecil (Nelson LL-23) in NELSON, 350-2.

p. 297, Essex "lay with my lady of Darbe": Cecil MS 55/45 in Hammer, op. cit.

p. 297, The latest bruit about the young couple: Peter R. Moore ("The Fable of the World, Twice Told, Part II," *Shakespeare Oxford Society Newsletter* 27:4 [Fall 1991], 5–9) adduces evidence that Derby's servants Sir Edward Fitton and Edward Mylar/Miller both worked for Cecil. Moore has subsequently learned (private communication, [September 2004]) that "Fitton" and "Mylar" were misreadings of the same name.

p. 297, "My lady wanteth not friends ...": HMC Salisbury 9/7, p. 339, in Moore, op. cit., 6.

p. 297, Cumberland backed the countess as well: HMC Salisbury 9/7, p. 344, in Moore, op. cit., 7.

p. 298, "If anyone suppose any speeches of mine proceeded out of that doubt ...": CP, xiv, p. 20 (179/140), in NELSON, 367-8.

p. 298, "Your loving niece and nephew": HMC Salisbury 9/7, p. 363, in Moore, op. cit., 7.

p. 298, "With too much familiarity" pursuing Vernon: Whittemore, op. cit.; AKRIGG, 48.

p. 298, Courtship carried on into 1596–97: In 1597, a twenty-two-year-old Leicestershire man named William Burton dedicated a translation of an ancient Greek romance called *The Loves of Clitophon and Leucippe* to Southampton. (*The Loves of Clitophon and Leucippe, Translated from the Greek of Achilles Tatius by William Burton ...*, ed. Stephen Gaselee and H.F.B. Brett-Smith [Stratford-upon-Avon: Oxford Basil Blackwell, 1923].) Burton's story tells of two half-siblings betrothed against their will. (Southampton and Elizabeth Vere, having grown up as foster-siblings in the same household, made practically as incestuous a match as Edward de Vere and Anne Cecil.) Clitophon and Leucippe escape their match made in hell, however, and end up marrying whom they choose. Only one copy of *Clitophon* has survived the centuries. ("It is difficult to account for the virtual disappearance of the book...." Ibid., xix.) The potential contemporary political implications of Burton's work merit further investigation.

p. 298, Essex Azores mission did neither: AKRIGG, 60.

pp. 298–9, "Southampton fought with one of the King's great Men of War and sunk her": Rowland Whyte, Esq., to Sir Robert Sidney, October 28, 1597, in Arthur Collins, *Letters and Memorials of State* (1746), 2:72 (repr. New York: AMS Press, 1973) in Peter R. Moore, "The Rival Poet of Shakespeare's Sonnets," *The Shakespeare Oxford Society Newsletter* 27:4 (Fall 1989), 8–12.

p. 299, Essex "evaporat[ing] his thoughts in a sonnet": Sir Henry Wotton, *Reliquae Wottonianae...*, 3rd ed. (London: T. Roycroft, 1672), 165, in Moore, op. cit.

p. 299, Probably uninterested in divining such apolitical matters: Steven W. May, *The Elizabethan Courtier Poets: The Poems and Their Contexts.* (Asheville, N.C.: Pegasus Press, 1999), 138–9.

p. 299, The mission's single success story: Southampton: Ironically, the Wotton quote above (not specifically pertaining to the aftermath of the Azores expedition) speaks of Essex writing sonnets to the queen at a time when Southampton had been "almost superinduced into favour."

p. 299, Vying for the immortal beloved's attentions: Peter R. Moore (op. cit.) was the first, so far as I am aware, to discover the manifold connections between Shake-speare's "Rival Poet" and the earl of Essex. The present section summarizes Moore's groundbreaking work.

p. 300, Essex pulled Southampton ever farther away: Essex was an inferior poet to de Vere, but this is inconsequential to de Vere's argument: What matters is not the abstract quality of the Rival Poet's verse but the fact that the Rival Poet is using poetry to draw Southampton away from de Vere.

p. 300, Essex family mottoes: *Virtutis comes invidia* and *Basis virtutum constantia;* Moore, op. cit.

p. 300, Unabashed in his use of makeup: "There are two portraits of Essex in the National Portrait Gallery in London, both believed to have been painted around 1597.... During the early part of [1597], Essex should have had something of a tan left over from his several months at sea during the summer of 1596. During the latter part of 1597, Essex should have been bronzed by his voyage to the Azores. However, the standing portrait shows Essex with a ghastly pallor; his face has obviously been painted white, and his lips have probably been carmined as well. The head and shoulders portrait shows him with lips of a bright, artificial red, unquestionably carmined, and a face that is not quite as pallid as in the other portrait, but that is far too pale for a man who had been making summer voyages to the latitude of southern Spain." Moore, op. cit., 11.

p. 300, Latin pun on the name Bacon: "As any crossword puzzle fan knows, the Latin for 'familiar ghost' is *Lar* or *Laris,* usually encountered in its plural form *Lares:* the Latin for 'ghost' or 'specter' is *larva.* The Latin for 'gull' is *larus;* the modern scientific name for the gull family is *Laridae.* The Latin for 'bacon' is variously *laridum, lardum,* or *larida.*" Moore, op. cit., 11.

pp. 300-1, "Was it his spirit, by spirits taught to write": As Moore notes (op. cit.), Essex's friends Anthony Bacon, Henry Cuffe, Lord Henry Howard, and Francis Bacon had all been known to assist Essex in his writing.

p. 301, Factions grew deeper and the outlines starker: In something as complex as Elizabethan court politics, there are always caveats. Many factionalists on either side maintained alliances across the widening gap between Robert Cecil and the earl of Essex. According to the French ambassador, for instance, Burghley and Essex had "great respect for one another and render[ed] strange charities to each other." (André Hurault, sieur de Maisse, *A Journal of All That Was Accomplished by Monsieur de Maisse...,* ed. G. B. Harrison and R. A. Jones [London: The Nonesuch Press, 1931], 114, in Hammer, op. cit., 342.)

p. 301, "Farewell, thou art too dear for my possessing": Sonnet 87 is the site of a heated debate on the Oxfordian interpretation of the *Sonnets.* Hank Whittemore and Bill Boyle (WHITTEMORE; William Boyle, "With the *Sonnets* Now Solved... Is the Debate Resolved?" *Shakespeare Matters* 3:4 [Summer 2004], 1, 11–15) claim that the correct interpretation of Sonnet 87, as Boyle argues, "really hinges on... one word–*misprision*" and that this word strongly points to the context of Southampton being spared a death sentence after the 1601 Essex Rebellion. Roger Stritmatter and Lynne Kositsky, on the other hand ("Response to Whittemore and Boyle," *Shakespeare Matters* 4:1 [Fall 2004]), counter that "this is a sonnet about emotional leave-taking. It appears at first as if the poet is abandoning his relationship with the addressee, but it soon becomes clear that *the addressee is actually relinquishing the poet*. . . . To accept the meaning supplied by Boyle and Whittemore requires us to ignore the obvious context (with its extensive monetary metaphors) of the sonnet [87] itself."

Southampton did take his leave of the author on the heels of the "Rival Poet" episode adduced in this chapter: to travel overseas in 1598. On this, cf. below and Peter R. Moore, "Dating Shakespeare's Sonnets 78 to 100," *The Shakespeare Oxford Society Newsletter* 26:1 (Winter 1990), 11–13.

p. 301, His last day ever as an MP: NELSON, 369.

p. 301, Moved to Hackney: architectural studies: Ernest A. Mann, *Brooke House, Hackney* (Committee for the Survey of Memorials of Greater London, 1904); F.H.W. Sheppard, op. cit.; inventory: *Ayscough's Catalogue No. 103, Sloan Roll* 31, in B. R. Ward, *The Mystery of "Mr. W.H."* (London: Cecil Palmer, 1923), 85–8; The building does not, however, stand today; severe damage to Brooke House during the London blitz caused the municipal government to tear it down in 1954.

p. 301, King's Place held in a joint trust: F.H.W. Sheppard, *Parish of Hackney (Part 1): Brooke House, a Monograph*. Survey of London, vol. 28 (London: Athlone Press, University of London, 1960), 61.

p. 301, Lord Chamberlain's heraldic menagerie looked down from overhead: Sheppard, op. cit., 67–70, plates 7 and 28.

p. 302, "Hanging of blewe and yellow seigne": Mann, in Ward, op. cit., 86; (*OED* entry under *senye;* Ward has "seige," but no usages of the word or its variants make sense in the context of a blue and yellow "hanging"; *seigne* is an attributed variant of *senye*.)

Sheppard questions the inventory's connection to Brooke House (80, item 3); however, the aptness of an (Oxford) blue and (Reading tawny) yellow wall hanging in a room dominated by heraldic emblems of the lords Hunsdon render it unlikely to be written off as mere happenstance.

p. 302, Definition of *story*: Mann, in Ward, op. cit., 86; *OED* definition II 8.

p. 302, Pictorial allegory of "rich young nobleman": National Portrait Gallery 1983 inventory of "A Vanitas Morality, English School." The painting was sold to an as-yet-undetermined buyer. I am grateful to Gerit Quealy for sharing her unpublished research on this painting (private communication, 2004).

p. 302, Never printed nor has it been preserved in any MS yet discovered: G. R. Hibbard, *Thomas Nashe: A Critical Introduction* (London: Routledge & Kegan Paul, 1962) 234–5.

pp. 302–3, Lyly had married and was living near Aldersgate: Warwick Bond (*The Complete Works of John Lyly* [Oxford: Clarendon Press, 1902], 1:43, 72) reprints baptismal records and taxes from 1596–1600 for Lyly in the ward of St. Bartholomew the Less, near Aldersgate; on Lyly's petitions, cf. Bond, 1:64–71.

p. 303, Munday and de Vere, friends or still in working relationship?: "Evidently the drama was not the chief bond between Mundy and the earl of Oxford, for their friendship continued long after Anthony had ceased to sign himself His Lordship's 'servaunt.'" Celeste Turner, *Anthony Mundy: An Elizabethan Man of Letters* (Berkeley: University of California Publications in English, 2:1 1928), 42.

p, 303, Two books under pseudonym "Lazarus Piot": *The second booke of Amadis de Gaule . . .*, tr. "Lazarus Pyott," (London: C. Burbie, 1595); *The orator . . .*, tr. "Lazarus Piot" (London: Adam Islip, 1596); I would like to thank Derran Charlton and Robert Detobel for pointing out the existence of the "Lazarus Piot" oeuvre (private communications, June 15–16, 2004.)

p. 303, *Piot* northland slang for "saucy chatterbox": *OED (piet, pyet, pyot)* definitions 3 ("Applied to a talkative or saucy person") and 4b ("Like a magpie; chattering").

p. 303, A primary source for *The Tempest*: Gary Schmidgall, "*The Tempest* and *Primaleon*: A New Source," *SH.Q.* 37:4 (Winter 1986), 423–39.

p. 303, Same punishment advocated in *Measure for Measure*: Jane Freeman, "'Fair Terms and a Villain's Mind': Rhetorical Patterns in *The Merchant of Venice,*" *Rhetorica* 20:2 (Spring 2002), 149–72; *The Merchant of Venice,* ed. Jay L. Hallio (New York: Oxford University Press, 1998), 20; Christy Desmet, *Reading Shakespeare's Characters: Rhetoric, Ethics and Identity* (Amherst: University of Mass. Press, 1992), 199–200, fn. 31.

p. 303, Two books that inspired at least three Shake-speare plays: A fourth Shake-speare play that "Lazarus Piot" influenced, *Pericles,* is discussed in Lorraine Helms, "The Saint in the Brothel: Or, Eloquence Rewarded," *SH.Q.* 41:3 (Autumn 1990), 319–32.

p. 303, De Vere as likely motive force behind works of "Piot": Despite a widespread belief that Lazarus Pyott/Piot was a separate individual (e.g., CHAMBERS/*WS,* 1:374), Celeste Turner Wright ("'Lazarus Pyott' and Other Inventions of Anthony Mundy," *Philological Quarterly* 42:4 [October 1963], 532–41) presents the definitive case that "Pyott" was indeed a pseudonym. She writes, "Anthony Mundy, versatile Elizabethan, will here (as in the nineteenth century) be identified with 'Lazarus Pyott,' whom most present-day scholars regard as a separate writer."

p. 303, Philosopher Nicholas Hill: DNB entry on Nicholas Hill (1570?–1610) cites Anthony À Wood (*Athenae Oxon.,* 2:86) as the authority for Hill's service to de Vere. Hill took his B.A. in May 1592 and then became a fellow of his college, making 1592 or '93 the earliest possible as a de Vere employee. Hill also lived under the patronage of the earl of Northumberland–which does not necessarily rule out serving as de Vere's secretary at the same time. Hill dedicated a book to his son Laurence, *Philosophia Epicurea,* in Paris in 1601, by which point he was presumably out of de Vere's service.

p. 303, Advocate of Democritus's atomic philosophy: "... those Atomi ridiculous/ Whereof old Democritus and Hill Nicholis/ One said, the other swore, the world consists." Ben Jonson, "Epigram 134" in DNB/Hill, op. cit.

p. 303, "This muddy vesture of decay doth grossly close it in": Jonathan Gil Harris, "Atomic Shakespeare," *Shakespeare Studies* (2002), 47ff.; *Merchant of Venice,* 5.1.60–5.

p. 303, De Vere's letter in September 1597: PRO S.P. 12/264[/111], ff. 151–51A, Sept. 8, 1597 (LL-29), in NELSON, 369.

p. 304, Burghley took to bed to ease his way to death: READ/Burghley, 544–6.

p. 304, The tutors Burghley had hired for de Vere had shaped his thought and character: Eddi Jolly, "'Shakespeare' and Burghley's Library: *Bibliotheca Illustris: Sive Catalogus Variorum Librorum,*" *The Oxfordian* 3 (2000), 3–18.

p. 304, "Knowing I lov'd my books, he furnish'd me ...": *The Tempest,* 1.2.161–8.

p. 304, The great Lord Treasurer breathed his last: Robert Cecil's elder brother Thomas inherited the title second Baron Burghley upon his father's death.

p. 305, No such ethical bedrock on which to build his world: Pauline Croft ("The Religion of Robert Cecil," *The Hist. Journal* 34:1 [1991], 773–96) points out that in contrast to his father, "Cecil has nothing that can be described as a unitary religious vision." Cecil's ecclesiastical outlook shifted with the tides.

p. 305, Payback time was nigh: WHITTEMORE; Acheson, *Davenant,* op. cit., 80–1.

p. 305, Analogy between Richard III and Robert Cecil: Lily B. Campbell, *Shakespeare's "Histories": Mirrors of Elizabethan Policy* (San Marino, Calif.: Huntington Library, 1947), 306–34; Margaret Hotine, "*Richard III* and *Macbeth*–studies in Tudor tyranny?" *Notes and Queries* 236 (1991), 480–6; Michelle O'Callaghan, "'Talking Politics': Tyranny, Parliament, and Christopher Brooker's *The Ghost of Richard the Third* (1614)," *The Hist. Journal* 41:1 (March 1998), 111–3; Pauline Croft ("The Reputation of Robert Cecil," *History Today* 43 (November 1993), 41ff.) points out that Shake-speare's *Richard III* was frequently reprinted until 1612, the year of Cecil's death–at which point publication of the play ceased for ten years.

p. 305, Libelers' comparisons between Richard III and Cecil: Ibid.; Croft, "The Reputation of Robert Cecil: Libels, Political Opinion, and Popular Awareness in the early Seventeenth Century," *Trans. Roy. Hist. Soc.* (1991).

p. 305, *Richard III* appears to have been reprinted without the author's permission: D. L. Patrick, *The Textual History of* Richard III (Stanford University Press, 1936). encapsulated in *King Richard III,* The Arden Shakespeare, ed. Anthony Hammond (London: Methuen, [1981], 3–10) argues that *Richard III* Q1 was a memorial reconstruction by actors and did not come from the author's papers.

p. 305, In the archives of Alnwick Castle: "The Northumberland Manuscript" in Clara Longworth Chambrun, *Shakespeare Rediscovered by Means of Public Records* (New York: C. Scribner's Sons, 1938), 267–80. Chambrun points out that E.K. Chambers (*WS,* Appendix B) assigns authorship of the MS to one "Adam Dyrmonth"–solely upon the fact that these words are part of the verbal tossed salad of this problematic document. A real attribution study is wanting.

p. 305, List of seditious or surreptitiously obtained texts: Lecture summary by David Vessey of a talk by Gwynneth Bowen, *Shakespearean Authorship Review* 21 (Spring 1969), 12–15.

p. 305, "Willi ... Sh ... Shak ... Shakspeare ...": ALLUSION BOOK, 1:40–1.

p. 305, Cuthbert Burby: *The second booke of Amadis de Gaule*..., tr. "Lazarus Pyott" (London: C. Burbie, 1595).

p. 306, This one approved by state censors: Robert Brazil, "Edward de Vere and the Shake-speare Quartos (Part I)," *The Shakespeare Oxford Newsletter* 35:2 (Summer 1999), 1, 16–17, 19.

p. 306, *Farmer's Almanac* for the Well-to-do Londoner: J. C. Shepherd, *Shakespeare's Double Image,* excerpted in *The Shakespeare Oxford Society Newsletter* 27:3 (Summer 1991), 1–3.

p. 306, Praised de Vere's skills as comic playwright and secret court poet: Don Cameron Allen, "Francis Meres's Treatise 'Poetrie': A Critical Edition," *Univ. of Ill. Studies in Lang. and Lit.,* 16:1 (February 1931), 54–5.

p. 306, "Warner, Shakespeare, Marlowe, and Chapman": Ibid., 73.

p. 306, "Pseudoerudition and bluff": "Francis Meres can no longer be considered either a thorough classical scholar or a keen critic, and even his historical data may now be questioned with justice." Ibid., 60.

p. 306, Quote from Meres: Ibid., 76.

p. 307, Meres neglects to mention four of them: *DNB* entry for Michael Drayton; Robert Detobel, Edward de Vere Studies Conference Listserv posting [DEVERE] (March 7, 2003).

p. 307, Meres doesn't seem to have minded ... : Allen, op. cit., 31, 50, 56–60.

p. 307, On front men throughout modern history: OGBURN/*TMWS,* 195–6; Mark Singer, "What Are You Afraid Of?: Terror is Stephen King's Medium ..." *The New Yorker* (September 7, 1998), 61; Dan Georgakas, "Hollywood Blacklist" from *Encyclopedia of the American Left,* ed. Buhle, Buhle, and Georgakas (Urbana: University of Illinois, 1992).

For more general discussion on the pervasiveness of pseudonyms in literary history, cf. Archer Taylor and Frederic J. Mosher, *The Bibliographical History of Anonyma and Pseudonyma* (Chicago: University of Chicago Press, 1951), especially references in 83, fn. 13.

p. 307, On Fernando Pessoa: Alex McNeil, "What's in a 'Nym," *Shakespeare Matters* 2:2 (Winter 2003), 16–20; *Always Astonished: Selected Prose by Fernando Pessoa,* tr. and ed. Edwin Honig (San Francisco: City Lights Books, 1998).

p. 308, "When he may shift it to another's name?": Joseph Hall, *Virgidemarvm* (books 1–3: 1597; books 4–6: 1598) in *The Collected Poems of Joseph Hall, Bishop of Exeter and Norwich,* ed. A. Davenport (Liverpool: Liverpool University Press, 1949), Lib. II, Sat. I (p. 21, ll. 1–2); Lib. IV, Sat. I (p. 50, ll. 37–44); John Marston, "The Authour in prayse of his precedent Poem," in *The Metamorphosis of Pigmalions Image and Certaine Satyres* (1598), in *The Poems of John Marston,* ed. Arnold Davenport. (Liverpool: Liverpool University Press, 1961), 65, ll. 29–30.

On attempts to identify the mystery writer (some of which conclude that "Labeo" was Shake-speare): *Poems of Joseph Hall,* op. cit., lix–lx; S. H. Atkins, "Who was 'Labeo'?" *Times Literary Supplement* (July 4, 1936), 564, with replies by J. D. Parsons (July 11, 1936), 580, A.G.H. Dent (July 18, 1936), 600, and S. H. Atkins (July 25, 1936) 616; Fred W. Manzo, "Who Was Joseph Hall's Labeo?" *The Elizabethan Review* 3:2 (Autumn 1995), 53–9; Patrick Buckridge, "What Did John Marston Know About Shakespeare?" *The Elizabethan Review* 4:2 (Autumn 1996), 24–40; Sanford M. Salyer, "Hall's Satires and the Harvey-Nashe Controversy," *Studies in Philology* 25 (1928), 149–70.

pp. 308–9, *Will* sonnets: Shake-speare does play with a preestablished convention (e.g., Sir Thomas Wyatt, Song 133, "The Ballad of Will," in *Sir Thomas Wyatt, the Complete Poems,* ed. R. A. Rebholz [London: Penguin, 1978], 168), which the *Will* Sonnets turn into a sardonic lament of a man coming to terms with his compromised identity.

CHAPTER ELEVEN

p. 310, Demanded that he return to England immediately: Sir Robert Cecil to Southampton, September 3, 1598, in STOPES, 122–3.

p. 310, Sonnet 89 laments: Peter R. Moore, "Dating Shakespeare's Sonnets 78 to 100," *Shakespeare Oxford Newsletter* 26:1 (Winter 1990), 11–13.

For an alternate chronology of these sonnets, involving Southampton's involvement in the Essex Rebellion, cf. WHITTEMORE; William Boyle, "With the *Sonnets* Now Solved... Is the Debate Resolved?" *Shakespeare Matters* 3:4 (Summer 2004), 1, 11–15; Hank Whittemore, "1601: 'Authorize Thy Trespass with Compare...'" *Shakespeare Matters* 3:4 (Summer 2004), 1, 16–21.

p. 310, On or around November 11: Moore, op. cit.; STOPES, 130–2.

p. 311, Autumn of 1598 was "teeming" twice over: Moore, op. cit.; STOPES, 131; Peter Ramsey, *Tudor Economic Problems* (London: V. Gollancz, 1963), 116.

p. 311, "Saunder Simpcox": Charles Wisner Barrell, "The Secret of Shakespeare's Irish Sympathies: Once Again Lord Oxford's Own Personality Speaks Through the Plays," *The Shakespeare Fellowship News-Letter* (June 1941), online at www.sourcetext.com; MILLER/HASP, 321–9.

p. 311, De Vere might have gotten himself in trouble rooting for the Irish: For a fanciful but not entirely inaccurate assessment of Shake-speare's Irish sympathies, cf. T. F. Healy, "Shakespeare Was an Irishman," *The American Mercury* 50:201 (September 1940), 24–32.

p. 312, *"Plus serieux affaires":* Robert Bertie to de Vere (March 3, 1599), in WARD, 333; NELSON, 374–5; OGBURN/*TMWS,* 749.

p. 312, The newly constructed Globe Theatre: The first quarto of *Henry V* (1600) notes that the play was "sundry times played by the Right Honorable the Lord Chamberlaine his Seruants"; the hopeful lines about the "General" returning from "Ireland" dates the composition of this speech to Essex and Southampton's March 1599 departure and their September 1599 inglorious return to England. *King Henry V,* The Arden Shakespeare, ed. John H. Walter. (London: Methuen & Co., 1970), xi.

p. 312, Prayer for the success of Essex's and therefore Southampton's mission: Ramón Jiménez (" 'Rebellion broachèd on his sword': New Evidence of an Early Date for *Henry V,*" *Shakespeare Oxford Newsletter* 38:1 [Winter 2002]) presents an alternative scenario, adducing evidence for a circa. 1583–84 version of *Henry V*–in which the CHORUS's lines about Ireland refer to England's response to the Desmond Rebellion of 1579–83.

p. 312, *Henry V* 5. Chorus. 30–4; *DNB* entry for Devereux, Robert.

p. 312, More private feelings about Essex in *Coriolanus:* Paul A. Jorgensen (*Shakespeare's Military World* [Berkeley: University of California Press, 1956], 292–314) avers that *Coriolanus*'s deviations from Plutarch "are not made in the direction of greater resemblance to Essex." However, Jorgensen also assumes that Shake-speare (i.e., Shakspere), as a lowly writer seeking to ingratiate himself with Southampton, would necessarily have painted a flattering portrait of Essex as CORIOLANUS. This assumption simply does not hold with de Vere, an Essex antagonist, as author.

p. 312, William Barlow compared Essex to Coriolanus: ". . . Coriolanus, a gallant young but discontented Roman, who might make a fit parallel for the late Earle, if you read his life." William Barlow, *A Sermon Preached at Paules Crosse on the First Sunday in Lent, Martij 1. 1600[/1]* (London, 1601), sigs. C3ʳ⁻ᵛ, in Brents Stirling, *The Populace in Shakespeare.* (New York: Columbia University Press, 1949), 137, fn. 90.

Assorted other parallels between CORIOLANUS and Essex make Shake-speare's comparison apt: Upon returning from his Irish campaign, Essex compared his English detractors to dogs; CORIOLANUS denounces his Roman detractors as "you common cry [i.e., pack] of curs" (3.3.120.) Paul D. Green, "Spenser and the Masses: Social Commentary in *The Faerie Queene,*" *J. of Hist. of Ideas* 35:3 (July–September 1974), 394; cf. also Willet Titus Conklin, "Shakespeare, *Coriolanus,* and Essex," *[University of Texas] Studies in Eng.* 11 (September 1931), 42–7; John Guy, "The 1590s: The Second Reign of Elizabeth I?" in *The Reign of Elizabeth I,* ed. John Guy (Cambridge: Cambridge University Press, 1995), 17, fn. 32.

Note also that *Coriolanus,* 5.4.44, exults in CORIOLANUS's expulsion of the Tarquins–as court-savvy readers of *Rape of Lucrece* recognized, the Tarquins represented the House of Cecil.

p. 312, "Shortly they will play me on the stage": Essex to Elizabeth, 1600, in G. B. Harrison, *The Life and Death of Robert Devereux, Earl of Essex* (New York: Henry Holt & Co., 1937), 261.

p. 312, CORIOLANUS is snobbish and unappealing: One does not find nearly as probing a character study of vice or folly in *Coriolanus* as one finds in, say, *Richard III.* "[CORIOLANUS's] inward conflicts are veiled from us. The change that came when he found himself alone and homeless in exile is not exhibited. The result is partly seen in the *one soliloquy in this drama,* but the process is hidden." (Emphasis added.) A. C. Bradley, *A Miscellany* (London: Macmillan & Co., 1929), 77–8.

p. 313, "The greatest of Shakespeare's comedies": in Oscar James Campbell, *Shakespeare's Satire* (Oxford: Oxford University Press, 1943), 198–9–upon whose insightful analysis of *Coriolanus* the present analysis is based.

p. 313, "Unmistakable": Robert Speaight, "Shakespeare in Performance," *SH.Q.* 36:5 (1985), 537.

p. 313, "Make yourself scabs": *Coriolanus,* 1.1.168–70.

p. 313, "You, the great toe of this assembly": *Coriolanus,* 1.1.95–154.

p. 313, Problems will go away if they just "digest things rightly": James Holstun, "Tragic Superfluity in *Coriolanus,*" *ELH* 50:3 (Autumn 1983), 485–8.

p. 314, Bridget had been engaged to a son of the Brooke family: March 16, 1597, letter from Rowlany Whyte to Robert Sidney in NELSON, 367.

p. 314, ". . . hath many good parts in him": De Vere to Lord Burghley, September 8, 1597 (LL-29), in NELSON, 369.

p. 314, "Upon an old reckoning": The duel between Peregrine Bertie the younger and Francis Norris was in the autumn of 1613; two years later, Norris fought Bertie's brother Robert Bertie, Lord Willoughby–a skirmish that resulted in the death of one of Willoughby's servants. *DNB* entry for Norris, Francis (1579–1623).

p. 314, Understated de Vere–Norris wedding: April 28, 1599, letter from the countess of Bedford to Robert Cecil in NELSON, 376.

p. 314, Norris raced off to the Continent: August 1599 letter from countess of Bedford to Robert Cecil in NELSON, 379.

p. 314, "A thousand pounds a day to go on progress": J. E. Neale, *Queen Elizabeth* (New York: Harcourt Brace & Co., 1934), 357.

p. 314, Essex abolished the post of General of the Horse: AKRIGG, 87.

p. 314, English conquest of cows and garrans: AKRIGG, 89.

p. 315, "Hollow peace": AKRIGG, 93.

p. 315, "Play wantonly with him": February 13, 1601, letter of William Reynolds to Robert Cecil in AKRIGG, 181–2. On the context of Reynolds's remarks, cf. Katherine Duncan-Jones, "Much Ado with Red and White: The Earliest Readers of Shakespeare's *Venus and Adonis,*" *RES*, n.s., 44: 176 (November 1993), 484–6.

p. 315, Intimations of homosexuality: The fuel that burns so brightly between OTH-ELLO and IAGO may indeed be repressed homosexual desire, but even their twisted relationship is never explicitly spelled out in sexual terms. On other homosocial (if not sexual) relationships in Shake-speare, cf. John Franceschina, *Homosexualities in the English Theatre: From Lyly to Wilde* (Westport, Conn.: Greenwood Press, 1997), 49–51.

pp. 315–6, "Tassel of a prodigal's purse, thou!": *Troilus and Cressida,* 5.1.14–33.

p. 316, Elizabethan comparisons between Essex and Achilles: Hugh Platt, *The Iewell House of Art and Nature* (1594); V. Saviolo, *V. Saviolo His Practise* (1595); *Seaven Bookes of the Illiades* (containing two mentions of Essex as Achilles), tr. George Chapman (1598), in E.A.J. Honigmann, "Shakespeare Suppressed: The Unfortunate History of *Troilus and Cressida,*" in Honigmann, *Myriad-minded Shakespeare* (New York: St. Martin's, 1998 second ed.), 115; also cf. *Troilus and Cressida,* The New Arden Shakespeare, ed. David Bevington (London: Thomson Learning, 2001; 1998 first ed.), 11–19.

p. 316, "One touch of nature makes the whole world kin": *Troilus and Cressida,* 3.3.74–175.

p. 317, Probably wrote Trojan satire for private performance: William R. Elton (*Shakespeare's Troilus and Cressida and the Inns of Court Revels.* [Aldershot, U.K.: Ashgate, 2000]) is only the latest of numerous Stratfordian critics to argue that *Troilus* was written for a private (Inns of Court, in this case) performance; Eric S. Mallin ("Emulous Factions and the Collapse of Chivalry," in *Shakespeare and the End of Elizabethan England* [Berkeley: University of California Press, 1995], 25–61) recognizes in *Troilus and Cressida* a caricature of the late-Elizabethan court.

p. 317, First recorded performance in 1679: The first state of Q1, *The Historie of Troylus and Cresseida* (1609), advertises that "it was acted by the Kings Maiesties seruants at the Globe." However, this title page was canceled and a new edition was issued with a preface stating that the play was "never stal'd with the stage, neuer clapper-clawd with the palmes of the vulger." The first recorded performance of *Troilus* was the adaptation *Troilus and Cressida, or Truth Found Too Late,* by John Dryden in 1679. CAMPBELL & QUINN, 890–7; Michael Dobson, *The Making of the National Poet: Shakespeare, Adaptation and Authorship, 1660–1769* (Oxford: Clarendon Press, 2001; first ed. 1992), 73–6.

p. 317, "The player whipped": *Histrio-Mastix* is typically dated to 1599, but Philip J. Finkelpearl ("John Marston's *Histrio-Mastix* as an Inns of Court Play: A Hypothesis," *Huntington Lib. Q.* 29:3 [1966], 223–34) presents a strong case that the play was in fact an Inns of Court entertainment from the 1598–99 revels season.

Conventionally attributed to John Marston, *Histrio-Mastix* has recently been shown by Roslyn L. Knutson ("*Histrio-Mastix:* Not by John Marston," *Studies in Philology* 98 [2001], 359–77) to be of unknown authorship.

p. 317, "Shakes his furious spears": Author unknown, *Histrio-Mastix,* in Richard Simpson, *The School of Shakespeare [sic]* (New York: J.W. Bouton, 1878). 2:39, l. 273.

p. 317, "Philosophers and scholars feast with me": Author unknown, *Histrio-Mastix,* 6.1.7–11, discussed in Alden Brooks, *Will Shakspere and the Dyers' Hand* (New York: Scribner's, 1943), 72.

p. 317, "From locks of wool, or shreds from the whole piece: Ben Jonson "Epig. 56, On Poet-Ape," in *Ben Jonson, Poems,* ed. Ian Donaldson (London: Oxford University Press, 1975), 31.

Naturally, one also needs to keep in mind that the term *poet-ape* is not original to Jonson. (E.g., Philip Sidney: "The cause why [poetry] is not esteemed in Englande is the fault of the Poet-apes, not Poets." *Elizabethan Critical Essays,* ed. G. G. Smith [Oxford: Clarendon Press, 1904], 1:205) However, Jonson clearly has a specific "ape" in mind—Jonson's epigram has charted out the "ape's" entire career path, "from brokage ... making low shifts ... now grown to a little wealth and credit in the scene," etc. In other words, Jonson is using a poetic term-of-art to skewer a single individual: i.e., Will Shakspere.

p. 318, Translation of "On Poet Ape": I used John Michell's paraphrase of "On Poet-Ape" (*Who Wrote Shakespeare?* [London: Thames & Hudson, 1996], 71) as a starting point for my own adaptation of Jonson's words.

p. 318, Other authors in lesser Shake-speare plays: The British literary scholar Brian Vickers recently conducted stylistic tests that attributed certain scenes and acts of each of these plays to the Elizabethan and Jacobean playwrights George Peele, George Wilkins, and John Fletcher (Vickers, *Shakespeare, Co-Author* [New York: Oxford University Press, 2002]).

p. 318, Jonson's complete and indivisible creation: "The title page of *Every Man Out of His Humour* (1600) offers not a theatrical but a reading experience, 'Containing more than hath been Publickely Spoken or Acted.' Available only in print, the 'real' play, Jonson suggests, is the one that he composed. ... The title page distances the play from the stage and, in the process, from the other play-quartos, generally assumed ephemeral: against expectation, it declares the play to be literature." Richard Barbour, "Jonson and the Motives of Print," *Criticism* 40 (1998), 499ff.

p. 318, "Motions [*puppet plays*]": Nicolaas Zwager, "Motions," in *Glimpes of Ben Jonson's London* (Amsterdam: Swets & Zeitlinger, 1926), 159–81.

p. 318, "... where he may be well laughed at": In 1599, Shakspere had settled in to his country manor of New Place in Stratford—so it's particularly curious that Jonson spoofs "Sogliardo" as a part-time Londoner, one who "comes up every term ... to see new motions."

p. 319, Parodies *Romeo and Juliet's* balcony scene: I would like to thank Roger Stritmatter for pointing out the hilarious (and mock-Shakespearean) exchange between "Puntarvolo" and his serving lady à la *Romeo and Juliet's* balcony scene in *Every Man Out of His Humor,* 2.1.

p. 319, "Your crest is very rare, sir": Ben Jonson, *Every Man Out of His Humour,* 3.1, in Arthur Huntington Nason, *Heralds and Heraldry in Ben Jonson's Plays, Masques, and Entertainments* (University Heights, New York, 1907), 92–4; MILLER/LOONEY, 2:44–51; PRICE, 68–77.

p. 320, Mirrored the bizarre and unstable world in which English subjects now lived: Hannah Betts, "'The Image of this Queene so quaynt': The Pornographic Blazon 1588–1603," in *Dissing Elizabeth: Negative Representations of Gloriana,* ed. Julia M. Walker (Durham, N.C.: Duke University Press, 1998), 169ff.

p. 320, "Or, if thou wilt not leave, now I'll begin": Thomas Bastard, *Chrestoleros* (London: Richard Bradocke for I.B., 1598), 28; KITTLE/DE VERE, 143.

p. 321, "Presumed to make bold with his name": Thomas Heywood, "To my approued good Friend Mr. Nicholas Okes," in *An Apology for Actors* (1612), ed. Richard H. Perkinson (New York: Scholars' Facsimiles and Reprints, 1941); Joseph Quincy Adams, "Shakespeare, Heywood, and the Classics," *Modern Lang. Notes* 34:6 (June 1919), 339; *DNB* entry for Thomas Heywood (d. 1650?).

p. 321, Archbishop's ban on Nashe and Harvey: Richard A. McCabe, "Elizabethan Satire and the Bishop's Ban of 1599," *The Yearbook of Eng. Studies* 2 (1981), 188–93; Lynda E. Boose, "The 1599 Bishops' Ban, Elizabethan Pornography, and the Sexualization of the Jacobean Stage," in *Enclosure Acts: Sexuality, Property, and Culture in Early Modern England,* ed. Richard Burt and John Michael Archer (Ithaca, N.Y.: Cornell University Press, 1994), 185–200.

p. 322, "Pass away the tyme in London merely in going to plaies": WHITTEMORE; AKRIGG, 96.

p. 322, First written about the duke of Guise's assassination: A Thomas Platter diary entry on September 21, 1599, records the performance of a tragedy, *"Vom Ersten Keyser,"* at the Globe; CAMPBELL & QUINN, 411.

pp. 322–3, *Coriolanus*, 3.1.37–70.

p. 323, Essex the embodiment of Castiglione's *Courtier*: Ray Heffney, "Essex, the Ideal Courtier," *ELH*, 1:1 (April 1934), 7–36.

p. 323, Jokes about *Timon of Athens* in Marston and Jonson plays: Orthodox scholarship dates *Timon of Athens* to approximately four years after de Vere's 1604 death. However, John Marston's 1600 play *Jack Drum's Entertainment* contains a series of topical allusions to *Timon of Athens* as well as the line "Come, come, now I'le be as sociable as Timon of Athens." (Fo. B4ʳ.) Although there was also a MS play from the period titled *Timon* (reprinted by the Malone Society in 1980), J. C. Bulman points out that this MS *Timon* play also refers to the Seven Stars Inn, which opened in 1602. ("The Date and Production of *Timon*," *Sh. Survey* 27 [1974], 111–27.) Thus in a 1600 play Marston cannot be referring to the MS *Timon;* he must be referring to Shake-speare's play of the same name. (Sandra Billington, "Was *Timon of Athens* Performed Before 1604?" *Notes and Queries* 45 [1998], 351–3.)

Also, as Robert Detbel points out ("The Testimony of Ben Jonson in Redating *The Tempest, Othello,* and *Timon of Athens*," *Shakespeare Oxford Newsletter* 40:2 [Spring 2004]), Jonson's 1601 satire *The Poetaster* (Act 2, Scene 2) features a character (Albius) who says of a piece of dialogue he's just recited, "I got that speech by seeing a play last day." Albius's quotation comes from Shake-speare's *Timon of Athens*, 1.2.155–59.

p. 323, "Art despis'd for the contrary": *Timon of Athens*, 4.3.301–5.

pp. 323–4, "The future comes apace": *Timon of Athens*, 2.2.142–8.

p. 324, "Make large confusion": *Timon of Athens*, 4.3.120–9.

p. 324, *Quips Upon Questions*: "Clunnyco de Curtanio Snuffe," *Quips Upon Questions* (London: W. Ferbrand, 1600). Frederic Ouvry (Private edition, London, 1875) attributed *Quips,* upon John Payne Collier's suggestion, to John Singer. However, since T. W. Baldwin ("Shakespeare's Jester," *MLN* 39 [December 1924]), scholars have generally accepted the attribution to Armin, e.g., CHAMBERS/ES, 2:300.

p. 324, "My Lord my master whom I serve in Hackney": "To the Right Worthy Sir Timothie Trunchion, *alias* Bastinado," in Robert Armin, *Quips Upon Questions*, ed. Frederic Ouvry (London, 1875), A2ʳ⁻ᵛ; Abraham Feldman, "Shakespeare's Jester–Oxford's Servant," *The Shakespeare Fellowship Quarterly* 8:3 (Autumn 1947), 39–43.

N.B.: I had originally suspected that "Sir Timothy" might be a *nom de jeste* for de Vere. However, in Armin's opening dedicatory sentence alone, Armin notes that "Sir Timothy" was "Right worthy (but not Right Worshipful, whose birth or grouth [was] in the open fieldes)." Armin also addresses "Sir Timothy" as if the latter had stayed behind in London when Armin went off to Hackney to "waite on the right Honorable good Lord my Maister." ("Say I am out of towne, and hear not their ribald mockes.") Considering that *bastinado* is one of the verbs TOUCHSTONE threatens WILLIAM with (cf. below) and that Truncheon is a "fragment of a spear" (*OED* 1b) and Armin refers to "Sir Timothy" as "euer my part-taking friende," could Armin's "Sir Timothie" in fact be Will Shakspere?

p. 324, Two noblemen with established households in Hackney: NELSON, 414.

p. 324, Zouche's whereabouts at turn of century: *DNB* entry for Edward Zouche, eleventh Baron Zouche of Harringworth (1556?–1625).

p. 324, Armin's first role in *As You Like It*: Charles S. Felver, *Robert Armin, Shakespeare's Fool: A Biographical Essay* (Kent, Oh.: Kent State University Bulletin, 1961), 39–48.

p. 325, SIR ROWLAND DE BOYS as he is named in the play: John W. Draper, *"As You Like It* and 'Belted Will' Howard," *RES* 12:48 (October 1936), 440–44.

p. 325, The present that celebrated small victories: In favor of this theory is the fact that *As You Like It* was registered on August 4, 1600, but was "to be staied." It was never printed until the 1623 First Folio; as evidence that earlier versions of *As You Like It* existed, one can point to the possible allusions to this play in Anthony Munday's *Downfall of Robert Earl of Huntington* and *Death of Robert Earl of Huntington* and Robert Greene's *Orlando Furioso*. CAMPBELL & QUINN, 41, 570; SCHRICKX, 66; Julia Celeste Turner, *Anthony Mundy: An Elizabethan Man of Letters* (Berkeley: University of California Press, 1928), 117.

p. 325, De Vere's muse named AUDREY: Roger Stritmatter points out (private communication, 2002) that in Ben Jonson's *A Tale of a Tub* (c. 1633) there is a similar character named "Awdrey" who's being carted around to see whom she will marry. She marries a yeoman from the country called "Turf." Jonson, *A Tale of a Tub*, ed. Florence May Snell (London: Longmans, Green & Co., 1915), 4.5.8off. at p. 75; also p. 165, fn. for 4.5.86.

p. 327, *Avere è avere:* Alex McNeil, "*As You Like It*: Is TOUCHSTONE *vs.* WILLIAM the first authorship story?" *Shakespeare Matters* 2:3 (Spring 2003), 1, 14–22.

p. 327, "I only wish that wisdom...[could be shared] by sitting next to someone": Plato's *Symposium*, in *The Collected Dialogues of Plato,* tr. and ed. Edith Hamilton and Huntington Cairns (Princeton, N.J.: Princeton University Press, 1961), 530; Louis E. M. Alexis, "Plato and Clown WILLIAM," *The Shakespeare Oxford Society Newsletter* (Summer 1975), 19–22.

p. 328, Southampton's plots: AKRIGG, 97–99.

p. 328, Worcester married his son and heir to Anne Russell: "One senses Worcester deliberately shifting his alliance away from the Essex circle and gravitating toward Sir Robert Cecil." Roy Strong, "The Queen: *Eliza Triumphans*," in *The Cult of Elizabeth* (Berkeley: University of California Press, 1977), 28.

p. 328, "To bury my hopes in the deep abyss and bottom of despair...": Hatfield MSS CP 251/28 (LL-30) in FOWLER, 540–1, NELSON, 394.

p. 329, Sweet wines monopoly a mainstay for Essex: Laura Hanes Cadwallader, *The Career of the Earl of Essex from the Islands Voyage in 1597 to His Execution in 1601* (Philadelphia: University of Pennsylvania Press, 1923), 71–2.

p. 329, "Pitiful thrivers, in their gazing spent": WHITTEMORE, commentary on Sonnets 26, 125.

p. 329, "By penning gigs for a country clown": John Lane, *Tom Tell-Troths Message and His Pens Complaint.* Excerpted from a compendium of "Tom Tell-Troth" pamphlets, ed. Frederick J. Furnivall. New Shakspere Society, London. Series VI, No. 2 (1876), 118; Mark K. Anderson, "The Upstart Crow's Other Plumage," *Shakespeare Oxford Newsletter* 36:4 (Winter 2001), 20–21, 28.

p. 329, Condemned to writing behind the mask of a country clown: Nicholas Breton's *Pasquils Fooles-Cap* (1600) may also hint at the Shake-speare ruse when he writes:

> Hee that doth hit vpon a printed booke,
> And findes a name neere fitting to his owne,
> And of his owne poore wit hath undertooke
> The ground of all hath from his humor growne,
> When euery Bird is by her feather knowne,
> > *Pasquill* doth tell him that poor *Aesop's* [mag]*Pie*
> > Will show him how his *Wit* hath gone awry.

Jean Robertson, "Nicholas Breton's Pasquil Books," *RES* 17 (1941), 85.

p. 329, *Belvedere* excerpted verse from both "Oxenford" and "Shakspeare": *Bodenham's Belvedere: Or Gardern of the Mvses, reprinted from the original edition of 1600* (Manchester: The Spenser Society, 1875).

Pace W. Ron Hess ("Was Anthony Munday's 1600 *'Bel-vedére or the Garden of the Muses'* Relevant to 'The Shakespeare Enterprise'?" in *The Dark Side of Shakespeare* [New

York: iUniverse, 2003], E.1–54), the most comprehensive scholarship on *Belvedere* to date (Charles Crawford, "Belvedere, or The Garden of the Muses," *Englische Studien* 43 [1910–11], 198–228) argues that John Bodenham was the "real begetter of these miscellanies, and that he, therefore, is responsible . . . for the bulk of the matter . . . and that 'A.M.' or Anthony Munday, played but a minor part in arranging the materials" (200, 213).

p. 329, One of de Vere's secretaries had given his tacit endorsement to the project: Curiously, Munday may tie in to the Meres story in some as yet unappreciated way too: Citing a quarrel between the printer Cuthbert Burby and Francis Meres, Celeste Turner Wright ("'Lazarus Pyott' and Other Inventions of Anthony Mundy," *Philological Quarterly* 42:4 [October 1963], 540) concludes, "There is now evidence that Meres was Mundy's personal friend and obtained from him much information about the theatrical world."

p. 329, Bodenham neglects to list lesser-knowns: "Very little attention need be bestowed on the list of authors mentioned in the preface [to *Belvedere*], for it is not only inaccurate and misleading, but seems to have been drawn up at random. Special mention is made of the poems of King James, the earl of Surrey, Henry Constable, Sir John Davies, and George Peele, but although I have spent much time in examining the works of these authors, I have failed to find in them a single passage that can be said to have been used in *Belvedere*. On the other hand, the preface makes no mention of Thomas Bastard, Samuel Brandon, Ch. Fitzgeoffrey, B. Griffin, E. Guilpin, John Lyly, Thomas Middleton, Mathew Roydon, and R. Southwell; yet much material was derived from some of these authors, especially from John Lyly, S. Brandon, and Southwell. These omissions from *Belvedere* of matter which should be in it, and the failure to mention the authors whom I have found in the book, go to show that the list in the preface is inaccurate." Crawford, op. cit., 200–1.

p. 330, "Designs that made me hasten forth and leave his presence": J. E. Neale, *Queen Elizabeth* (New York: Harcourt, Brace & Co., 1934), 371; Lytton Strachey, *Elizabeth and Essex: A Tragic History* (New York: Harcourt, Brace & Co., 1956; 1928 first ed.), 236–7.

p. 330, *The Life and Reign of Henry IV*: Some Londoners thought Essex was the author of *The Life and Reign of Henry IV,* which contained a dedication to Essex that was later removed. *DNB* entry for Hayward, Sir John (1564?–1627).

p. 331, Tried for treason in summer of 1600: Richard Dutton, "Buggeswords: Samuel Harsnett and the Licensing, Supression, and Afterlife of Dr. John Hayward's *The First Part of the Life and Reign of King Henry IV,*" *Criticism* 35:3 (1993), 305ff.; Rebecca Lemon, "The Faulty Verdict in *The Crown v. John Hayward*," *Studies in Eng. Lit. 1500–1900* 41:1 (2001), 109ff.

p. 331, Queen knew de Vere's enmity toward Essex already: "In 1601 depositions were taken from Sir Gilly Merrick, who arranged for the production of [Shake-speare's *Richard II* in February 1601], from the actor Augustine Phillipps and others–but from none was any enquiry made to its authorship. Phillipps, a fellow actor of Shaksper's, who left him a bequest in his will, merely calls it 'the play of King Rychard,' without any indication that he knew who wrote it. Nor did the authorities enquire it of him. If they had known Will Shaksper to be the author, would they not have requested from his friend some information about him?" D.W.T.C. Vessery, "Some Early References to Shakespeare," *Shakespearean Authorship Review* 11 (Spring 1964), 8–9.

p. 332, Bishop of London owed his job to Cecil: Bancroft, Richard (1544–1610) *DNB* entry; P. M. Handover, *The Second Cecil: The Rise to Power (1563–1604) of Sir Robert Cecil, later first Earl of Salisbury* (London: Eyre & Spottiswoode, 1959), 152–3.

p. 332, Essex, Southampton, et al., laid down their arms: G. B. Harrison, *The Elizabethan Journals* (New York: Macmillan Co., 1939), 3:144–9; WHITTEMORE, commentary to Sonnet 26.

p. 333, "For the benefit of military men which may be at your beck": Harrison, op. cit., 158.

p. 333, Essex asked court to spare Southampton: Harrison, op. cit., 155–60.

p. 333, ... to the adversarial role de Vere played against himself in the jury room: What follows is adapted from WHITTEMORE, whose approach to the *Sonnets* is considerably more global in scope (cf. Boyle, "With the *Sonnets* now solved ..." op. cit.)–seeing in much of it a "daily diary" beginning with the night of the Essex Rebellion (Sonnet 27; February 8, 1601) and ending, somewhat arbitrarily, on Sonnet 87 (April 9, 1601); then on a more infrequent basis carrying through to Queen Elizabeth's death (Sonnet 105; March 24, 1603) to Southampton's last night in the Tower (Sonnet 106; April 9, 1603) to Elizabeth's funeral (Sonnets 125–6; April 28, 1603).

I am grateful to Hank Whittemore for sharing his at-the-time unpublished MS on the *Sonnets* and for the many engaging discussions I have had with Whittemore, and Bill and Charles Boyle, over their theory. However, I still find Whittemore's comprehensive thesis lacking in corroborative historical evidence–and as yet unable to integrate the additional layers of the *Sonnets* that this book discusses, such as the connection between *Willobie His Avisa*, Elizabeth Trentham, and Sonnets 40–42; the Earl of Essex and the "Rival Poet" series (Sonnets 78–86); and the Southampton–Paris–Elizabeth Vernon scandal during the summer of 1598 (Sonnets 87–100). The enigmatic nature of Shake-speare's *Sonnets* persists, even with Edward de Vere as the author–although the mystery diminishes from the absolutely impenetrable quality of the *Sonnets* with Shakspere of Stratford as presumed author, to a set of testable alternatives, open to further literary/historical analysis and evidence. (For one comprehensive counterpoint to WHITTEMORE, et al, see Roger Stritmatter and Lynne Kositsky, "Response to Whittemore and Boyle," *Shakespeare Matters* 4:1 [Fall 2004].)

p. 333, "Authorizing thy trespass with compare": *Authorize: OED* def. 4 (*Obs.*); *trespass: OED* def. 2 ("*Law* In a wide sense, Any violation or transgression of the law; *spec.* one not amounting to treason, felony, or misprision of either"); *compare: OED* def. 1 ("compeer") (*Obs.*).

p. 334, Fever threatened to take Southampton's life: AKRIGG, 131–2; WHITTEMORE, op. cit.

p. 334, De Vere made ancestral claim on Danvers's properties: R. Ridgill Trout ("Edward de Vere to Robert Cecil," *Shakespearean Authorship Review* 17 [Spring 1967], 13–16) points out that "the interest of Oxford in seeking the Danvers estates was not mere selfish desire to build up his own estate. The Veres had been connected with the [Danvers] family for many years through the Latimer, Cornwallis, Neville, and other families. The Vere 'mollet' held a prominent place in the quartering of the Danvers arms."

p. 334, De Vere's briefs arguing for Danvers property: NELSON, 398–407 (LL-34, -38, and -50); FOWLER, 593–738; WARD, 337; Nina Green also posted recent discoveries of additional documents in the Danvers case to the Phaeton newsgroup (http://www3.telus.net/oxford/phaeton.html) on September 19, 2004.

Sonnet 52 may be commenting on the Danvers case:

> So am I as the rich whose blessèd key
> Can bring him to his sweet up-lockèd treasure,
> The which he will not every hour survey
> For blunting the fine point of seldom pleasure....
> So is the time that keeps you as my chest
> Or as the wardrobe which the robe doth hide
> To make some special instant special blest,
> By new unfolding his imprisoned pride.

p. 334, Lord Burghley [Thomas Cecil] asked for the those of the earl of Southampton: STONE, 414.

p. 334, Cecil had begun to receive petitions to spare Southampton: AKRIGG (128–30) records the petitions to Cecil and the importance of Cecil in the decision to spare Southampton's life.

p. 334, Was Sonnet 94 part of the pleading?: On Sonnet 94 and the marked passages in de Vere's Geneva Bible, cf. STRITMATTER, 140–5.

p. 335, Southampton's sentence commuted: AKRIGG (131) writes that the decision to spare Southampton's life came sometime on, or soon before, March 25.

p. 335, Cecil instrumental in convincing the queen to pardon Southampton: Robert Detobel points out (private communication, September 2004) that the genuflecting tone in de Vere's two extant letters to Robert Cecil in May 1601–some two months after Southampton had received his pardon–suggest a great favor that Cecil has done on de Vere's behalf. Conventionally these letters ([=32] arguably dated to May 1601 and [=33] May 11, 1601, at http://socrates.berkeley.edu/~ahnelson/llperson.html) are thought merely to concern another of de Vere's fruitless attempts at office seeking–in this case the presidency of Wales. However, de Vere never received this office. Part of his gratitude expressed in these missives may also concern the pardon Cecil had achieved for Southampton in March.

p. 336, "Why write I still all one, ever the same": Charlton (Sr.) and Dorothy Ogburn point out (OGBURNS/*TSOE,* 892–3): " 'Still all one' is a pun on Southampton's motto: *Ung par tout, tout par ung.* And 'Ever the same' is, literally, the motto on [Queen] Elizabeth's armorial badge: *Semper eadem.*"

p. 336, *Affaniae: Sive Epigrammatum . . .:* Alexander B. Grosart's *Poems of the Rev. Charles Fitzgeoffrey (1593-1636)* (Private publication, 1881) includes excerpts and translations from the *Affaniae.* However, Grosart does not consider or reprint the "BARDVM" (or "VERVM") epigrams discussed below.

p. 336, A writer he cryptically calls "The Bard": Query: Could Fitz-Geffry be the ultimate origin of this nickname, now commonplace, for Shake-speare?

p. 337, "I would not so hurriedly crucify yourself, O Bard": Charles Fitz-Geffry, *Affaniae: Sive Epigrammatum Libri Tres Ejusdem Cenotaphia* (Oxoniae: Josephus Barnesius, 1601), Short Title Catalog [STC] (2nd ed.) 10934.

IN BARDVM/ Cavisti dicens, Edam post funera versus,/ Optarem properam ne tibi *Bardi* crucem. (p. 24); AD BARDVM/ Sanus es, ad seram qui scribis posteritatem?/ Tradetur nunquam litera, *Barde,* sile. (p. 76)

A third, yet more enigmatic, "BARDVM" epigram suggests Fitzgeffrey suspects "The Bard" of literary thievery or plagiarism: IN BARDVM/ Scribere te reptim semper tua carmina dicis:/ Verum est; ex alijs omnia, Barde, rapis. (p. 16) ("You say that you always write your poems hurriedly./ [It] is true; from others all things, O Bard, you snatch.")

I would like to thank Roy Wright-Tekastiaks and Roger Stritmatter for their assistance in translating these most curious couplets.

p. 337, May not himself have known the sonneteer: A series of epigrams Fitzgeffrey wrote "AD HILARIVM VERVM" might suggest the epigrammist did know who wrote the *Sonnets.* However, the data is presently inconclusive, as a scholarly study of *Affaniae: Sive Epigrammatum . . .* –even just a complete English translation of same–is sorely lacking.

p. 337, De Vere still petitioning for Danvers's estate: In 1600–01, de Vere defaulted on a £20 tax debt (NELSON, 396); the extensive "Danvers Escheat" file of de Vere letters and papers, largely passed over for reasons of space in this book, are considered at length in, e.g., NELSON, 398–407 (LL-34, -38, and -50); FOWLER, 593–738.

p. 337, No more new and grand statements to be made on the political stage: NELSON (339–42) also summarizes a controversy over a grammar school in Earls Colne over which the earls of Oxford had control–a controversy that involved mediations and legal actions in 1601-2. In postings to the "Phaeton" newsgroup (http://www3.telus.net/oxford/phaeton.html), Nina Green counters Nelson's charges that de Vere was a reckless or irresponsible superintendent to the school. (Green, "Phaeton: Oxford and Earls Colne grammar school" [May 18–19, and June 10, 2004].)

p. 337, Elizabeth's mythic emblem was phoenix: "It would be impossible to list all the references to Elizabeth as Phoenix: T. Churchyard, *Challenge* (1593), is almost solely devoted to this conceit. Vennard, in his *Miracle of Nature* (1601), describes the queen as 'the onley phenix of our daies.' But the symbol is a commonplace of the era." D.W.T.C. Vessey, "Southampton, Essex, and Shake-speare: Some Notes," *Shakespearean Authorship Review* 15 (Spring 1966), 13, fn. 18.

p. 337, Poem imagining the queen's state of mind after loss of Essex: Anthea Hume, "Love's Martyr, 'The Phoenix and the Turtle' and the Aftermath of the Essex Rebellion," *RES*, n.s., 40:157 (February 1989), 48–71.

p. 337, "New Phoenix" as King James VI: Hume (op. cit., 54–5) cites three examples from 1603–5 from John Legat, Joshua Sylvester, and an anonymous balladeer–all equating King James with a new "Phoenix" who emerges from Elizabeth's flames.

p. 337, Chester dedicated *Love's Martyr* to Sir John Salisbury: On Salisbury, and an interpretation of *Love's Martyr* in which Salisbury is allegorized as the "Turtle," cf. Thomas P. Harrison, "*Love's Martyr*, by Robert Chester: A New Interpretation," *Univ. of Tex. Studies in Eng.* 30 (1951), 66–85.

p. 338, "For these dead birds sigh a prayer": Some Oxfordians have put forward the supposition, as has been noted previously, that Wriothesley was "in sleep a king" to de Vere because Wriothesley was, they hypothesize, a son of Queen Elizabeth, perhaps by de Vere himself. On the royalist implications of *The Phoenix and The Turtle*, cf. William Plumer Fowler, "Shake-speare's 'Phoenix and Turtle': An Interpretation" (with supplementary exegesis by Dorothy Ogburn) (Portsmouth, N.H.: Peter E. Randall, 1952 and 1986).

p. 339, *Twelfth Night* at Middle Temple Hall: On the performance of *Twelfth Night* at Middle Temple Hall on February 2, 1602 (recorded by the diarist John Manningham), cf. Anthony Arlidge, *Shakespeare and the Prince of Love: The Feast of Misrule in the Middle Temple* (London: Giles de la Mare, 2000); on the possible performance of *Twelfth Night* on Twelfth Night of 1601, cf. Leslie Hotson, *The First Night of* Twelfth Night (London: Rupert Hart-Davis, 1954).

p. 339, Shake-speare's farewell quartet of plays: For a continuously revised and revisited canon of works such as Shake-speare, it is naturally somewhat artificial to isolate any four plays as the author's "final" statement.

For instance, Daniel Wright ("No Catholics Allowed: Deciphering Reformation Rhetoric and Iconography in *Henry VIII*," presentation at the first annual Shakespeare Fellowship Conference, Cambridge, Mass. [October 19, 2002]) has suggested that *Henry VIII*–a play that revisionistically stacks the deck to argue Queen Elizabeth's legitimacy–was begun circa 1602–3 as a seventieth birthday present for Elizabeth. She, however, died before reaching this milestone. So the unfinished MS awaited other hands for its completion when *Henry VIII* appeared as a "new" play in 1613 at the Globe Theatre.

Furthermore, Act 5 of *Antony and Cleopatra*–with its departures from Plutarch concerning the burial of CLEOPATRA–may have also been a posthumous tribute to/jab at Elizabeth. (Cf. Julia M. Walker, "Reading the Tombs of Elizabeth I," *ELR* 26 [1996], 525–7.)

p. 340, Revelations 14:13, . . . Michah 7:9: STRITMATTER, 213–20.

p. 340, "Only you have received nieces": Hatfield MSS CP 18/80 (LL-32) in NELSON, 397–8; FOWLER, 577; Nelson provisionally dates this letter to May 1601, Fowler to March.

p. 340, "Hater of ceremonies": NELSON (LL-33), transcribed on socrates.berkeley .edu/~ahnelson

p. 341, Transferring power to an underling: Madeleine Doran, *Endeavors of Art: A Study of Form in Elizabethan Drama* (Madison: University of Wisconsin Press, 1954), 385–9. (For more on Cinthio, his works, and Shake-speare, cf. the notes to Chapter 5.)

p. 341, *Measure for Measure* as autobiographically haunted: The following analysis of *Measure for Measure* owes much to Roger Stritmatter's study of the play, the numerous insights he has helpfully shared with the present author over the years, and his chapter "Smallest Things in *Measure for Measure*" (STRITMATTER, 157–71).

p. 341, *Authority* appears most often in *Measure for Measure:* STRITMATTER, 157.

p. 341, "Their loud applause and *aves* vehement": Measure *for Measure,* 1.1.67–72.

p. 341, "Truth is truth, though never so old...": De Vere to Cecil, May 7, 1603, Hatfield MS 99/161 in FOWLER, 771.

p. 341, "She speaks this in the infirmity of sense!": *Measure for Measure,* 5.1.43–68.

p. 341, First known performance in 1738: The courtly-revels accounts for December 26, 1604, list a "Mesur for Mesur by Shaxberd"–an entry that Samuel A. Tannenbaum (*Shakspere Forgeries in the Revels Accounts* [New York: Columbia University Press, 1928]) established was a nineteenth-century forgery. Other seventeenth-century adaptations–William Davenant's *The Law Against Lovers* (1662) and Charles Gildon's *Measure for Measure or Beauty the Best Advocate* (1699)–sanitized *Measure for Measure* by stripping the play of its "low-life" or other seemingly immoral elements. (CAMPBELL & QUINN, 510.)

p. 341, Scarcely merits footnote in history of Elizabethan theatrical companies: There is only one performance record for the Earl of Oxford's Men (in Kent in 1594) during the 1590s. NELSON, 391.

p. 343, *Weakest's* source was *Farewell to Military Profession:* The source for *The Weakest Goeth to the Wall, As it hath bene sundry times plaide by the right honourable Earle of Oxenford, Lord great Chamberlaine of England his seruants* (1600), is the first ("Sappho, Duke of Mantona") of eight novellas in Barnabe Rich's collection *Riche His Farewell to Militarie Profession* (1581). Jill L. Levenson, *A Critical Edition of the Anonymous Elizabethan Play* The Weakest Goeth to the Wall (New York: Garland Publishing, 1980), 21; Levenson suggests Dekker, Chettle, Munday, and Webster as *possible* authors or contributors to *Weakest.* She does not consider the possibility of 1580s-era authors.

p. 343, "Lately played by the Right Honorable Earl of Oxenford his servants": July 3, 1601, entry in stationer's register: "the true historye of George Scanderbarge as yt was lately playd by the right honorable the Earle of Oxenford his servantes." In NELSON, 391.

p. 343, *Scanderbeg* probably Nashe's attempt to cash in on *Tamburlaine:* George Skanderbeg was a rebel leader of Christians in Albania attempting to free his people from the Turks. Marlowe's *Tamburlaine* also advocates war against Turkey. To quote Bronson Feldman ("The Marlowe Mystery," *The Bard* 3 [1980], 8):

> When the Cambridge pedant Gabriel Harvey wrote his cryptic obituary on Marlowe, "Gorgon," he associated the poet with "Scanderbegging," as though the word would summon to his readers' thought the strut and thunder of the Marlovian line.... Then he recalled a close friend of the dramatist, in whom he pretended to see the successor to the dead arts-master: "Have you forgot the Scanderbegging wight?" It is plain from the context of "Gorgon" that the wight Harvey had in view was Thomas Nashe. Perhaps Nashe was the author of *The History of George Scanderbeg,* evidently in imitation of Marlowe's epic tragedy.

p. 343, Newly amalgamated troupe applied for permanent home at Boar's Head: NELSON (391–2) reprints the March 31, 1602, application for Oxford/Worcester's men to play at the Boar's Head. For crucial historical context, missing in Nelson's account, cf. Andrew Gurr, *The Shakespearean Playing Companies* (Oxford: Clarendon Press, 1996), 317–36.

p. 343, Never a hint of de Vere's affiliation with troupe again: By 1604, Worcester's Men had even become the troupe of the next queen of England, Queen Anne–wife to King James. Gurr, op. cit., 322.

p. 343, "Then is my suit as it was the first day": Hatfield MSS CP 85/103 (LL-38) in FOWLER, 707–8; NELSON, 406–7.

p. 344, Countess of Oxford exchanged New Year's gifts with Elizabeth: NELSON, 407–9.

p. 344, Portended a dissolution of her union with the nation: Jarissa J. Taylor-Smither, "Elizabeth I: A Psychological Profile," *16ʰ C. Journal* 15 (1984), 70–1.

p. 344, Elizabeth began hinting at her own imminent death: Kathy Lynn Emerson, *Wives and Daughters: The Women of Sixteenth Century England* (Troy, N.Y.: Whitston, 1984), 41–2; J. E. Neale, *Queen Elizabeth*, op. cit., 391; Park R. Honan, *Shakespeare: A Life* (Oxford: Oxford University Press, 1998), 296.

p. 344, "There should be means used to convey him over into France...": PRO S.P. 14/4/14, ff. 28–9, in NELSON, 407–18, discussed in Peter R. Moore's review of Nelson, below.

p. 345, "I never feared any danger to proceed from so feeble a foundation": Ibid.

p. 345, "His fashion is to condemn the world if thereby he might excuse himself": Peter R. Moore, "Demonology 101: Alan Nelson's *Monstrous Adversary*," *Shakespeare Oxford Newsletter* 40:1 (Winter 2004), 16–17 online at http://www.shakespearefellowship.org/Reviews/moore-nelson.htm; PRO S.P. 14/4/14, f. 27, transcribed by Nina Green and posted online at http://www3.telus.net/oxford/list.html.

p. 345, Likely that "Great Council" made decision for Elizabeth posthumously: Cf. Paul Johnson (*Elizabeth I: A Biography* [New York: Holt, Rinehart & Winston, 1974], 436) for arguments against the authenticity of the accounts of Elizabeth's naming James in secret to Cecil.

p. 345, Carey's land speed record not bested until early nineteenth century: Jasper Ridley, *Elizabeth I: The Shrewdness of Virtue* (New York: Fromm, 1989; 1987 first ed.), 334.

p. 346, De Vere's name appeared on subsequent reprints: NELSON, 407–18.

p. 346, "Sing her rape, done by that Tarquin, death": CHAMBERS/*WS*, 2:189; Chettle here refers to TARQUIN in Shake-speare's *Lucrece*.

p. 346, Elizabeth's final resting place atop her half-sister's coffin: Walker, "Tombs of Elizabeth," op. cit.

p. 346, Daily meditations culminating in the interment of the House of Tudor: WHITTEMORE, commentary to Sonnets 107–25.

p. 347, Applied for and received this ancestral water-bearing role for James's coronation: "[De Vere] also asks that (he should have the same privileges) as his ancestors (who) from time immemorial served the noble progenitors of our Lord the King with water before and after eating the day of the Coronation, and had as their right the basins and towels and a tasting cup." SP Dom, James I (July 7, 1603), in WARD, 346.

N.B.: De Vere's onetime ceremonial role should not be confused with the royal office of the Ewery; cf. Nina Green, "Oxmyths," www3.telus.net/oxford.

p. 348, "To be diseased ere that there was true needing": The famous Sonnet 116 ("Let me not to marriage of true minds admit impediments...") probably originally dates to the period circa 1590–4, when Southampton was considering marrying Elizabeth de Vere.

p. 348, "In the distraction of this madding fever": Sonnets 121 and 122 also may originate to earlier periods: Sonnet 121 (*"I am that I am..."*) harkens back to de Vere's power struggles with Burghley; Sonnet 122 ("Thy gift, thy tables, are within my brain") may refer, as previously noted, to the "tables" of diamonds de Vere once received as a tournament prize from the queen—that he had perhaps turned around and regiven to Anne Vavasour? (MILLER/LOONEY, 2:54–6)

p. 348, The biblical book of life: On de Vere's interest in the biblical figure of the "book of life," cf. STRITMATTER, 125–32.

p. 348, Granted forty yards of cloth for mourning garments: NELSON, 418.

p. 348, De Vere's role in royal processions: *Pace* NELSON (424), during King James I's procession through London on March 15, 1604, de Vere ("The Lord Great Chamberlaine on the left hand") is recorded marching next to the Earl Marshall and before King James, beneath a canopy. John Nichols, *The Progresses, Processions, and Magnificent*

Festivities of King James the First (London: J. B. Nichols, 1828), 1:326. I would like to thank Christopher Paul (private communication, July 2004) for pointing out this fact of early Jacobeana.

p. 348, Means nothing to him to be canopy bearer: STRITMATTER (119–24) argues that de Vere *was,* in fact, a canopy bearer for Queen Elizabeth on at least some royal ceremonial occasions.

p. 349, "Which proves more short than waste or ruining": For varying interpretations of Sonnet 125, cf. STRITMATTER (119–24); WHITTEMORE; Stephen Booth (op. cit., 426–30); and Gwynneth Bowen, "Coronation Sonnet," *The Shakespeare Fellowship News-Letter* (UK) (Spring 1956), 7–9; (Autumn 1956), 10–11; (Spring 1957), 11–12.

p. 349, Reading de Vere's sixty other extant letters: As noted in NELSON (487–9) and on socrates.berkeley.edu/~ahnelson, de Vere's extant correspondence consists of forty-four personal letters and seventeen "tin-mining" letters–all but six of which (LL-12, LL-41, LL-44, LL-60, LL-67, LL-68) were written to either Lord Burghley or Robert Cecil. There are eleven memoranda, eight of which concern de Vere's tin-mining petitions. Finally, there is also a sheaf of accusations and memoranda surrounding the 1580–1 "Arundell Libels." Sarah Smith points out (private communication, July 2004) that one might also add to this number a yet-to-be-determined quantity of letters in Angel Day's 1586 *The English Secretary* that were probably also written by de Vere–as discussed in Chapter 8.

p. 350, "She hath left to try my fortune among the alterations of time and chance": De Vere to Cecil, 25, 27 April 1603 (LL-39) in NELSON, 418–9.

p. 350, Leading Genoese patrician named Prospero Fattinanti: Claudio Costantini, *La Repubblica di Genova.* UTET Libreria, Torino (1986) 128–9, 137–8; I am indebted to Noemi Magri for the translation; cf. Chapter 4 for more on the story of Duke Prospero.

pp. 350–1, Source for the play of the "uninhabited" isle: Gary Schmidgall, "*The Tempest* and *Primaleon:* A New Source," *SH.Q.* 37:4 (Winter 1986), 423–39; on the entire series of chivalric romances Munday translated, cf. Gerald R. Hayes, "Anthony Munday's Romances of Chivalry," *The Library,* 4th ser., 6 (1926), 57–81.

p. 351, The "uninhabited island" is England: As a literary precedent, one might cite George Chapman's *The Shadow of Night* (1594), which contains a fantastical but unnamed "fruitful island." Roy Battenhouse notes ("Chapman's *The Shadow of Night:* An Interpretation," *Studies in Philology* 38 [1941], 604), "[Chapman's] ravaged 'fruitful island' is probably to be understood specifically as England."

p. 351, Using *Primaleon* as a set of guideposts: *The Tempest* has long been a red-herring argument used against Oxfordians–since it was supposedly written after the year of de Vere's death (1604), de Vere could not have been Shake-speare. Yet, not even Stratfordians can agree upon the proper date of the play. As the New Variorum *Tempest* points out (ed. Horace Hoard Furness [London: J. B. Lippincott & Co., 1892], 306) such respected scholars as Hunter, Knight, Dyce, and Elze all dated *The Tempest* to the period 1596–1604; for an overview of the arguments for dating *The Tempest* (and indeed, the whole of the Shakespeare canon) to pre-1604, cf. Appendix C, "The 1604 Question"; Peter R. Moore, "The Abysm of Time: The Chronology of Shakespeare's Plays," *The Elizabethan Review* 5:2 (Autumn 1997), 51–3; Joseph Sobran, "1604: The Critical Year," in *Alias Shakespeare: Solving the Greatest Literary Mystery of All Time* (New York: The Free Press, 1997), 143–62; STRITMATTER, 481–6; OGBURN/*TMWS,* 388–90.

p. 351, Fulke Greville destroyed one of his plays about the Essex Rebellion: Michael Shapiro, *Children of the Revels: The Boy Companies of Shakespeare's Time and Their Plays* (New York: Columbia University Press, 1977), 95–6; Annabel Patterson (*Censorship and Interpretation: The Conditions of Writing and Reading in Early Modern England* [Madison: University of Wisconsin Press, 1984], 58) also notes that Ben Jonson was accused of representing the Essex Rebellion in his 1603 play *Sejanus.*

p. 351, CALIBAN "violated" MIRANDA: *The Tempest,* 1.2.347.

p. 351, Montaigne's "noble savage": Von Horst Oppel, "Die Gonzalo-Utopie in Shake-speares 'Sturm,'" *Deutsche Vierteljahrsschrift für Literatur Wissenschaft und Geistesgeschichte* 28 (1954), 194–220 in Dean Ebner, "*The Tempest:* Rebellion and the Ideal State," *SH.Q.* 16:2 (Spring 1965), 161–73.

p. 351, CALIBAN's clownish coconspirators: One anomaly that would argue against CALIBAN representing Essex is the close association between PROSPERO and CALIBAN—closer than de Vere appears ever to have been with Essex (e.g., 1.2.257–374). However, this might simply reflect the fact that both the author and Essex were raised and educated in Cecil House. I have elsewhere suggested ("PROSPERO's Travels: Toward A New Reading of *The Tempest,*" unpublished MS; presented at the Twentieth Annual Shakespeare Oxford Society Conference, Minneapolis, Minn. [October 1996]) that CALIBAN could, alternately, represent a grotesque of Southampton. Of course, *The Tempest's* "man–monster" may just as well represent a composite of *both* Essex and Southampton.

p. 352, "I'll drown my book": *The Tempest,* 4.1.262–6; 5.1.30–57.

p. 353, Baron of Essendon: Robert Cecil was created Baron Cecil of Essendon on May 13, 1603: John Nichols, *The Progresses, Processions, and Magnificent Festivities of King James the First...* (London: J. B. Nichols, 1828), 1:119.

p. 353, "She was not so ready to perform her word as I was too ready to believe it": Hatfield MSS 99/161 (LL-40) in NELSON, 420–1; FOWLER, 770–1.

p. 353, Participated in coronation service at Westminster: NELSON, 423; G. B. Harrison, *A Jacobean Journal: Being a Record of Those Things Most Talked of During the Years 1603–06* (New York: Macmillan Co., 1941), 49–50; Nichols's *Progresses,* op. cit., 1:230.

p. 353, "We have the man Shakespeare with us": The account of the missing letter appears in the nineteenth-century antiquarian William Cory's journals during a visit to Wilton House, viz., "Aug 5. The house ([Cory's hostess] Lady Herbert said) is full of interest:... we have a letter, never printed, from Lady Pembroke to her son, telling him to bring James I from Salisbury to see *As You Like It;* 'we have the man Shakespeare with us.' She wanted to cajole the king in Raleigh's behalf–he came." *Extracts from the letters and journals of William Cory,* ed. Francis Warre-Cornish. (Oxford: Privately printed, 1897), 168.

Note that, although the original letter is lost and undated, two facts strongly suggest that Cory's quoted excerpt refers to James's August 29–30, 1603, visit to Wilton: 1) James arrived at Wilton via Salisbury and 2) Raleigh was in trouble, causing the dowager countess to want to "cajole the king" on his behalf. In fact, 1) James's previous recorded stop before Wilton was in Salisbury on August 26 and 2) in July 1603, Raleigh had been arrested for his alleged involvement in a conspiracy known as the "Main Plot." Raleigh stood trial on November 17. (This argument is inspired by–and differs slightly from–an article by David Roper ("We have the man Shakespeare: Edward de Vere and the lost letter of Wilton," *Shakespeare Matters* 2:3 [Spring 2003], 1, 8–13) which, however, concludes that de Vere was in residence at Wilton during the autumn of 1603, and this was the time that the dowager countess wrote about "the man Shakespeare.")

p. 353, Royal party entertained at Wilton: Nichols, *Progresses,* op. cit., 1:254; Roper, op. cit.

pp. 353–4, Shakspere part of newly incorporated King's Men: For an Oxfordian spin on the founding of the King's Men, cf. Sarah Smith, *Chasing Shakespeares* (New York: Atria Books, 2003), 275–9.

p. 354, "My charges would be more than ordinary": "Lady Susan" to Robert Cecil, 1603. CP 15, p. 391 (206/6) in NELSON, 422.

p. 354, "Nothing is more precious than gold": NELSON (406) mistakenly attributes authorship of this epigram to the Middle Temple diarist John Manningham. In fact, as Warren Hope points out ("*Lear's* CORDELIA, Oxford's Susan, and Manningham's Diary," *The Elizabethan Review* 5:2 [Autumn 1997], 123–5; online at www.jmucci.com/ER/articles/lear.htm),

Manningham was merely recording couplets written by John Davies (later Sir John Davies; as distinct from John Davies of Hereford) for his courtly masque during the summer of 1602 welcoming Queen Elizabeth to Harefield. Davies's text for this masque was later published in the second edition of Francis Davison's *Poetical Rhapsody* (1608).

p. 354, One word: CORDELIA: Davies's witty epigram may have referred to the Queen's Men's play *King Leir*–the one with the happy ending. Like *King Lear*, *Leir* contains a dowry scene with the patriarch and a stubborn youngest daughter offering up nothing when asked to flatter for her inheritance.

pp. 354-5, "Thy truth then be thy dow'r": *King Lear*, 1.1.85-108.

p. 355, Grafted a story from Sidney about treacherous bastard son: BULLOUGH, 7:283-6; Wilfrid Perrett, *The Story of King Lear from Geoffrey of Monmouth to Shakespeare* (Berlin: Mayer & Müller, 1904).

As noted previously, de Vere began, in the early 1590s, with the ancient British tale of a king who divides his lands among his three daughters–inspired, no doubt, by de Vere's forced dispersal of Castle Hedingham among his three Cecil children. This initial version, complete with happy ending, became the circa. 1594 Queen's Men's play *King Leir*.

p. 355, "If it be nothing, I shall not need spectacles": *King Lear*, 1.2.30-45.

p. 355, EDGAR disguises himself as a madman: Robert Cecil owned a Catholic "book of exorcisms" from circa. 1598 onward that EDGAR uses extensively in his rantings as "Tom o' Bedlam." However, these "exorcisms" were also published in the spring of 1603 as Samuel Harsnett's *Declaration of Egregious Popish Impostures*. Gwynneth Bowen, "Hackney, Harsnett, and the Devils of *King Lear*," *Shakespearean Authorship Review* 14 (Autumn 1965), 2-7; F. W. Brownlow, *Shakespeare, Harsnett, and the Devils of Denham* (Newark, N.J.: University of Delaware Press, 1993), 21-22.

p. 355, "EDGAR I nothing am": *King Lear*, 2.3.5-21.

p. 356, James had won over a once-reluctant de Vere: Naturally, questions emerge over the alternate versions of *Hamlet* printed in the authorial Q2 of the play (printed in 1604) and the version printed in the First Folio (F) of 1623. Both Q2 and F contain clearly Shake-spearean dialogue and scenes that are unique to each. (Cf. Bernice W. Kliman and Paul Bertram, eds., *The Three-Text Hamlet*, 2nd ed. [New York: AMS Press, 2003].) Could these be "alternate cuts" of the same master text? (Kenneth Branagh's 1996 movie adaptation of *Hamlet,* for instance, used practically every word from Q2 as well as F.) Could de Vere's children and editors have "recut" the play for F? FELDMAN (72-3) offers one Oxfordian scenario, involving a c. 1600–01 edition of Q2 and a c. 1604 edition that was published in F.

p. 356, Now to claim my vantage doth invite me": *Hamlet*, 5.2.354-90; Stuart M. Kurland, "*Hamlet* and the Scottish Succession?" *Studies in Eng. Lit. 1500-1900* 34:2 (1994), 279ff.; N.B.: The HAMLET of Q1 (1603) does not give his blessing to FORTINBRAS's arrival and accession to the Danish throne–although the Q1 FORTINBRAS does still stake a claim ("I have some rights of memory to this kingdome/ Which now to claime my leisure doth inuite mee...").

p. 357, Prosecution of a poacher, Sir John Gray: NELSON claims (424), "Oxford, as was his wont, demands exemplary punishment." The full story of Sir John Gray is considered in Christopher Paul, "A Monument Without a Tomb: The Mystery of Oxford's Death," *The Oxfordian* 7 (2004).

p. 357, Harbinger of the changes the Stuarts would be ushering in: De Vere to King James, January 30, 1604, in NELSON, 424; Susan Campbell, "The Last Known Letter of Edward de Vere Brought to Light" *Shakespeare Oxford Newsletter* 36:1 (Spring 2000), 4-6.

p. 357, Edward Somerset, earl of Worcester: According to G.P.V. Akrigg (*Jacobean Pageant: Or, the Court of King James I* [Cambridge: Harvard University Press, 1962], 27), between James's coronation and 1621 (when James conferred the Earl Marshaldom upon Thomas Howard, earl of Arundel), "King James gave occasional special appointments to the earl of Worcester to serve as Earl Marshal when some ceremony required the presence of one."

p. 357, Marching next to de Vere: Nichols (*Progresses of King James,* op. cit., 326; *pace* NELSON, 424) notes that in the royal procession of March 15, 1604, "The Lord Great Chamberlaine on the left hand" flanked the earl Marshal, who carried the Sword of State.

p. 357, Joiner went unpaid: NELSON (424–5) presents variant accounts of the collecting joiner, Edward Johnson, in which either Johnson gets "40 shillings at a time" from the countess or de Vere reports that Johnson is a scam artist to whom the family owes nothing. "The said Earle . . . would cause him to be laid by the heeles yf ever he came more to him about anie such matter."

p. 357, Transferred custody of forest of Essex: WARD, 187, as NELSON, notes (425), "without particulars."

p. 357, No doubt of the maladies that long plagued him: Some Oxfordian accounts preserve the myth that the burial registers record de Vere dying of "ye plague" (beginning with WARD, 347, fn. 1, and re-reported uncritically over the ensuing decades). No such evidence exists. (Paul Altrocchi, "Did Edward de Vere Die of 'Ye Plague'?" Presentation at the Sixth Annual Edward de Vere Studies Conference, Concordia University, Portland, Ore: [April 12, 2002]; NELSON, 425–6).

p. 357, De Vere not a member of the Privy Council: NELSON, 431.

p. 357, "A man in mind and body absolutely accomplished . . .": Harleian MSS, in WARD, 348.

p. 357, "Lieth buried at Westminster": NELSON, 431, WARD, 370–1.

pp. 357-8, De Vere's corpse appears to have been lost: Christopher Paul ("Monument," op. cit.) considers at length the mystery surrounding de Vere's death, missing tomb, and legacy he bequeathed to his heirs.

EPILOGUE

p. 359, There were no memorials: Christopher Paul ("Monument without a Tomb: The Mystery of Oxford's Death," *The Oxfordian* 7 [2004], 6–68) notes the absence of mention of de Vere's passing in the writings of the court chroniclers John Chamberlain, Dudley Carleton, and William Camden, among others.

p. 359, Suicide: Christopher Paul (op. cit.) considers this possibility; Robert Detobel ("The Suicide Hypothesis" [Unpublished MS, 2004]) treats it at greater length.

p. 359, "The king gave him fair words but nothing else as yet": Cal. State Papers Venetian 1603-7, 10:165-8, in Christopher Paul, "A Midsummer Night's Drama" (Unpublished MS, 2004).

p. 360, "Put some jealousies into the king's head": Sir Anthony Weldon, *The Court and Character of King James* (1650) STC 1272, in Paul, "Drama," op. cit.

p. 360, ". . . other persons designated in your specified letters": Pierre Paul Laffleur de Kermaingant. *L'Ambassade de France en Angleterre sous Henri IV . . .* (Paris: Firmin-Didot et cie, 1895), 239, tr. in Paul, "Drama," op. cit.

p. 360, "According to the true and perfect copy": "The Second Quarto (Q2) was printed . . . in 1604, and evidently late in the year, since of the seven extant copies, three are dated 1604, the others 1605." *Hamlet,* The Arden Shakespeare, ed. Harold Jenkins (London: Routledge, 1992; 1982 first ed.), 14.

p. 360, Royal coat of arms graced the top of the first page: The head title of Q2 of *King Lear* (1619; falsely dated to 1608) also appears under ornament with royal arms. CHAMBERS/*WS,* 1:464.

p. 360, 1604 quarto of *Hamlet* a funereal send-off: The First Folio edition of *Hamlet* contains numerous alterations–both cuts and additional lines. (cf. *The Three-Text Hamlet: Parallel Texts of the First and Second Quartos and the First Folio,* 2nd ed., ed. Bernice W. Kilman and Paul Bertram [New York: AMS Press, 2003].) One of three possibilities suggests itself: Either de Vere had an "alternate cut" of *Hamlet* that became F, the Folio text; or Q2/F dates to an earlier period (e.g., FELDMAN [72–3] dates Q2 to 1600–1), with F/Q2 as the author's final version; or F represents the editorial intercession of other hands, such as de Vere's playwriting son-in-law the earl of Derby.

p. 360, No unambiguous references to literary sources or events after 1604: On *The Tempest* and the Strachey Letter (1609) cf. Peter R. Moore, "*The Tempest* and the Bermuda Shipwreck of 1609," http://www.everreader.com/tempdate.htm and Appendix C, "The 1604 Question."

p. 360, No new science appears in Shake-speare from after de Vere's death: Eric Lewin Altschuler, "Searching for Shakespeare in the Stars," http://xxx.lanl.gov/abs/physics/?9810042.

p. 360, Shake-speare stopped correcting his published works too: Robert Brazil, "Edward de Vere and the Shake-speare Quartos" (Parts I and II), *Shakespeare Oxford Newsletter* 35:2 (Summer 1999), 1, 16–17, 19; 35:3 (Fall 1999), 1, 10–14; Brazil also notes (Elizaforum listserv, http://www.elizabethanauthors.com/about.htm [June 28, 2004]) a few curious anomalies not in the above articles: The 6th ed. of *Lucrece* (1616) claims it's "newly revised"–scholars do not think these revisions are authorial; Q3 of *The Passionate Pilgrim* (1612) claims it's "newly corrected and augmented By W. Shakespeare"–however, one of the two extant copies of Q3 omits the ascription to Shakespeare. (*The Poems,* The Arden Shakespeare ed. F. T. Prince [London: Methuen, 1960], xxii; *The Whole Contention* (1619) claimed to be "newly corrected and enlarged" but simply repackaged old Shake-speare plays. "My main argument holds," Brazil concludes. "*Authentic* contemporary merchandising references to improved or augmented texts by the author, which were in fact provided by the real Shakespeare-Author, end with *Hamlet,* 1604."

p. 360, King's Men would continue performing Shake-speare into the next decade: This book follows the lead of Samuel A. Tannenbaum (*Shakspere [sic] Forgeries in the Revels Accounts.* [New York: Columbia University Press, 1928]) in rejecting the 1604/5 and 1611/2 alleged accounts of court performances of "Shaxberd" plays such as *"Mesur for Mesur"* and *"Marthant of Veins."* This is a minority opinion in mainstream scholarly circles today: Alfred Edward Stamp (*The Disputed Revels Accounts* [London: Oxford University Press, 1930]) presents the opposing argument for the veracity of these records.

p. 361, *Love's Labor's Lost* staged during Christmas revels season of 1604–05: "Burbage ys come & sayes there is no new playe that the quene hath not seene, but they have revyved an olde one, cawled *Loves Labore Lost,* which for wytt and mirthe he says will please her excedingly. And thys ys apointed to be played to morowe night at my Lord of Southampton's." Walter Cope to Robert Cecil, 1604. *The Third Report of the Royal Commission on Historical Manuscripts* (London, 1872), 3:3, 148, in Roslyn Lander Knutson, *The Repertory of Shakespeare's Company, 1594–1613.* (Fayetteville: University of Arkansas Press, 1991), 111.

p. 361, Munday's friend Thomas Middleton: David M. Bergeron ("Thomas Middleton and Anthony Munday: Artistic Rivalry?" *Studies in Eng. Lit. 1500–1900* 36:2 [1996], 461ff.) dispenses with the long-standing misperception that Middleton and Munday were rivals rather than collaborative colleagues.

p. 361, Middleton's *Black Book:* Middleton's *Black Book* was registered March 22, 1604, three months before de Vere's death. However, as seen in Chapters 10 and 11, de Vere had already begun to write about his own death (as the "Turtle[dove]" in *The Phoenix and the Turtle*) in 1601. Middleton didn't need an official obituary notice in early 1604 to recognize that the disguised nobleman author would soon be departing this sphere of tears.

p. 361, "To search tipsy taverns, roosting inns, and frothy alehouses": Middleton, *The Black Book,* in *The Works of Thomas Middleton,* ed. Alexander Dyce (London: Edward Lumley, 1840), 5:513.

p. 361, Married to a prostitute named Audrey: I would like to thank Roger Stritmatter for pointing out the Oxfordian implications of Middleton's *Black Book.*

Alexander Dyce, the editor of the nineteenth-century scholarly edition of *The Black Book,* notes the similarity between Middleton's Audrey and the wench of the same name in *As You Like It.* Middleton, *Black Book,* op. cit., 5:517, fn. y.

p. 361, "'Are you pleased now?'": Ibid., 5:516-7; Dyce cannot make sense of why Lucifer would want to search the Lieutenant's house, so he adds to the word *house* the footnote "Qy. 'hose'?"

p. 362, "'Why, for shame!'": Ibid., 5:518.

p. 362, Stationer's Office registered *Lear* in November: The publisher John Busby was a coregistrant of *King Lear* with Nathaniel Butter, but only Butter's name appears on the play quarto. CAMPBELL & QUINN, 427-8.

p. 362, Permission to sell King's Place house and grounds: F.H.W. Sheppard, *Survey of London: Parish of Hackney (Part 1) Brooke House: A Monograph* (London: Athlone Press, University of London, 1960), 61-2; NELSON, 432.

p. 362, Handsome £1,680 profit: Sheppard, op. cit., 62.

p. 362, Two editions in its first year: CAMPBELL & QUINN (268) conclude that "Gosson's *Pericles* is one of the 'stolne and surreptitious copies' referred to by Heminges and Condell in the Preface to the First Folio (1623)."

Pericles itself, however, did not appear in the Folio–about which, cf. Charles Boyle, "Why *Pericles* was not included in the First Folio," *Shakespeare Oxford Newsletter* 35:4 (Winter 2000), 6-8.

p. 362, Controversial first edition of *Troilus and Cressida: Troilus and Cressida* was registered for publication twice: First on February 7, 1603, by the publisher James Roberts ("to print when he hath gotten sufficient aucthority for yt. The booke of Troilus and Cresseda as yt is acted by my lo: Chamberlens Men"). Roberts evidently did not get "sufficient aucthority." Then on January 28, 1608, the booksellers and publishers Richard Bonion and Henry Walley registered the play, which they published using George Eld's presses. (*Troilus and Cressida,* The Arden Shakespeare, ed. Kenneth Palmer [London: Methuen, 1982], 1.)

p. 363, Stating, disingenuously: Even if *Troilus and Cressida* had not been enacted, as the first-state title page claims, by the King's Men at the Globe, James Roberts's February 7, 1603, entry (ibid.) states that *Troilus and Cressida* had been "acted by my lord Chamberlen's Men."

p. 363, "Never clapper-clawed with the palms of the vulgar": *Troilus and Cressida's* second-state quarto preface (titled "A neuer writer, to an euer reade...") also claims of the author, "...and when hee is gone and his commedies out of sale"–implying that Shakespeare was still alive when the preface was composed. On this point, Peter W. Dickson ("Was the *Troilus and Cressida* Preface written in 1602-1603?" *Shakespeare Oxford Newsletter* 35:3 [Fall 1999], 19) observes:

"The reader should know that, of the fourteen Shakespearean comedies in the First Folio, eight were never printed prior to 1623. Among the remaining six, *The Taming of the Shrew* was printed in 1607 but anonymously. Among those five comedies with Shakespeare on the title page, only one was printed after 1600: *The Merry Wives of Windsor,* registered for publication on January 15, 1602.

"The inescapable conclusion–which has awesome implications for the authorship debate–is that the *Troilus and Cressida* 'Never writer...' preface must have been composed in 1602-1603 when those 'commedies' were still available, and while Oxford was still alive."

pp. 363-4, Candidates for "Mr. W.H.": Edward Hubler, "Shakespeare's Sonnets and the Commentators," in *The Riddle of Shakespeare's Sonnets,* ed. Hubler (New York: Basic Books, 1962), 11-13; David Joseph Kathman, "Mr. W.H.," *The Oxford Dictionary of National Biography* (2005).

p. 364, Three clues that might identify "Mr. W.H.": The following takes its lead from the work of Oxfordian researcher B. R. Ward (*The Mystery of "Mr. W.H."* (London: Cecil Palmer, 1923])–a book that today needs to be corrected for advancing two improbable arguments:

1. Ward accepts the attribution of *A Fovre-Fold Meditation* to Robert Southwell; H.J.L. Robbie ("The Authorship of *A Fourefold Meditation,*" *RES* 5:18 [April 1929], 200–2) makes a more persuasive case that the *Meditation* was written by the earl of Arundel, as at least two contemporary MSS of the poems state.

2. Ward presumes the family of Lord Vaux to have lived at King's Place before de Vere; F.H.W. Sheppard (*Brooke House,* op. cit., 80) points out that there is no evidence for this claim.

p. 364, Ever-living: The phrase *ever-living* was often used to refer to the dead. (MILLER/LOONEY, 2:211–14; Peter R. Moore, "The Lame Storyteller, Poor and Despised," *Shakespeare Oxford Newsletter* 31:3 [Summer 1995], 21–22; *PMLA* reprints a debate on this subject: "Our Ever-Living Poet," *PMLA* 102:5 [October 1987], 838–41). Thorpe's statement, though frequently quoted by Stratfordian scholars, would thus appear to confirm that Shake-speare was dead in 1609. (Will Shakspere was still alive in 1609.)

p. 364, *Beget* meaning "to acquire, usually by effort": Orthodox scholars who accept this attribution include Edmonds and Robbie (op. cit.), Alfred W. Pollard (*Shakespeare's Fight with the Pirates and the Problems of the Transmission of His Text* [Cambridge: Cambridge University Press, 1920], 31) and Sir Sidney Lee (*A Life of William Shakespeare* [New York: Macmillan & Co., 1927 new ed.], 681.)

p. 364, *A Four-Fold Meditation*: Robbie, op. cit.

p. 365, "... had not a mere accident conveyed them to my hands": "To the Right Worshipfull and Vertuous Gentleman, Mathew Saunders, Esquire, W.H. wisheth, with long life a prosperous achieuement of his good desires," in *A Fovre-Fovld Meditation ... By R.S.* (1606), ed. Charles Edmonds (London: Elkin Mathews, 1895). Edmonds accepts the attribution of the *Meditation* to Southwell, about which cf. the above note and H.J.L. Robbie, op. cit.

p. 365, Marriage of William Hall in Hackney in August 1608: "William Hall and Magery Gryffyn were joyned in matrymonye on the 4th Aug. 1608." B. R. Ward, op. cit., 21–2.

p. 365, *Mirror of Mutability:* Celeste Turner, *Anthony Mundy: An Elizabethan Man of Letters* (Berkeley: University of California Press, 1928), 5, fn. 4; 26; Hall's verses on Munday appear in Munday's *Mirror of Mutabilitie* (1579), a book that is dedicated to de Vere.

p. 365, If these two William Halls ... were even simply related: There was also a London printer working in 1609 named William Hall. (R. B. McKerrow, *A Dictionary of Printers and Booksellers in England, Scotland, and Ireland and Foreign printers of English Books 1557–1640* [London: Bibliographical Soc., 1910], 121). However, I share E. K. Chambers's skepticism here (CHAMBERS/*WS*, 1:566): "There is some unconscious humor in the notion of Thorpe's dedicating the volume to a printer whom he had not employed." If William Hall the printer had gotten his hands on such a hot commodity as Shake-speare's *Sonnets,* why did he not publish this moneymaker himself?

p. 365, Royal clemency for the convicted Philip [Howard]: Recall the discussion of "Didymus Harco" and *Wilobie His Avisa* in Chapter 10.

p. 365, Wishing the newlywed "all happinesse": Note, too, that "Mr. W.H. ALL. HAPPINESSE ..." can also be read as "Mr. W. HALL. HAPPINESSE ..." CHAMBERS /*WS,* 1:566.

p. 365, Hall's marriage be blessed with many children: As to the odd layout and punctuation of Thorpe's dedication, Rollett (op. cit.) offers a curious–if still incompletely resolved–solution. The dedication is laid out like three inverted pyramids: The first stands six lines of print tall; the second measures two; the third measures four. (Notice that "Edward de Vere" has 6, 2, and 4 letters.) Using 6-2-4 as a cipher key, one first reads the sixth word, then the second word after that, then the fourth word after that, then the sixth word, and so on. The result: "THESE SONNETS ALL BY EVER THE FOURTH." Positing "EVER" as an abbreviation for E. Vere, only one question remains: What the devil does "Ever the fourth" mean?

p. 365, Peacham was one of the first to introduce emblem book to England: Alan R. Young, *Henry Peacham* (Boston: Twayne Publishers, 1979), 34–59; for an exhaustive list of English and Continental emblem books published between 1564 and 1616, cf. Henry Green, *Shakespeare and the Emblem Writers* (New York: Burt Franklin, 1870), 84–118.

p. 365, Spear-shaking Greek goddess Athena: Roger Stritmatter, "The Not-Too-Hidden Key to *Minerva Britanna*," *Shakespeare Oxford Newsletter* 36:2 (Summer 2000), reprinted at http://www.shakespearefellowship.org/virtualclassroom/MinervaBritanna.htm. Cf. also the Athena/Minerva note in the Introduction.

p. 365, "The rest will belong to death": Noemi Magri, "The Latin Mottoes on the Title-Page of H. Peacham's *Minerva Britanna*." *De Vere Society Newsletter* (UK) 3:3 (May 1999) 4–6; Magri, Letter to the editor, *Shakespeare Oxford Newsletter* 35:1 (Spring 1999), 21–2.

pp. 366-7, "Thy name is de Vere": John Astley-Cox, "The Latin Anagram on the Title-Page of Peacham's *Minerva Britanna:* A Footnote on an Important Oxford-Shakespeare Discovery," *Shakespeare Fellowship Quarterly* 8:3 (Autumn 1947), 36–9. Stritmatter ("Not-Too-Hidden Key . . ." op. cit.) discovers a series of erudite jokes throughout the whole of *Minerva Britanna* based upon the fact that the title page's scroll both contains the letter *i* and doesn't contain the letter *i*.

p. 367, Peacham clearly understood that doing so would be a redundancy: Revised editions of Peacham's *Compleat Gentleman* (originally published in 1622) that continue to list "Edward Earle of Oxford" as the greatest poet of the Elizabethan era (and never mention Shake-speare) appeared in 1627, 1634, and 1661. In the words of Louis P. Bénézet, "Could the inhabitants of Lilliput ignore Gulliver?"

Louis P. Bénézet, "The Remarkable Testimony of Henry Peacham," *Shakespeare Fellowship Quarterly* 6:4 (October 1945), 54–6; Peter W. Dickson, "Henry Peacham on Oxford and Shakespeare," *Shakespeare Oxford Newsletter* 34:3 (Fall 1998), 1, 8–18; John Rollett, Letter to the editor, *Shakespeare Oxford Newsletter* 34:4 (Winter 1999), 21.

p. 367, Restoring the earldom of Oxford to some solvency: NELSON'S coverage (Chapter 85, pp. 431–42) of de Vere's posthumous legacy–constrained, as *Monstrous Adversary* forever is, to documentary minutiae–is one of the book's most incomplete and erroneous chapters. Christopher Paul ("Monument . . . ," op. cit.) provides a more thorough documentary accounting of the events of 1604 and thereafter.

p. 368, Her exact date of death is unknown: NELSON, 440–1; curiously, Trentham also bequeaths "vnto my dombe man yearelie duringe his life [blank] powndes, to bee paide him by my Executors . . ." (PRO PROB11/121, ff. 74-5ᵛ, transcribed by Alan Nelson, at http://socrates.berkeley.edu/~ahnelson/oxdocs.html; Robert Detobel, private communication [July 2004].) Shake-speare's wife leaves no indication as to the identity of her "dombe man."

p. 368, Diana Cecil–great-granddaughter to William Cecil, lord Burghley: On January 1, 1624 (*n.s.*), Henry de Vere (1593-1625) m. Diana Cecil, 2ⁿᵈ dau. to William Cecil, 2ⁿᵈ Earl of Exeter. (*COMPLETE PEERAGE*, 10:254-6.) "[Henry's] widow (Diana Cecil) held the Castle and estate as her jointure till 1655, when at her death it became the sole property of Elizabeth Trentham, wife of Bryan Cockayne, second Viscount Cullen. In this family the castle remained till the year 1713, when it was purchased . . . by Robert Ashhurst, second son of Sir William Ashhurst, through whom by female descent it came to the present owner." Severne Andrew Ashurst Majendie, *Hedingham Castle and the De Veres* (London: H.

T. Smith, 1796), 23; H. Ranger (*Castle Hedingham: Its History and Associations* [Halstead: R. L. Hughes, 1887], 44) traces Hedingham's ownership down to his day to "James Ashurst Majendie, born April 17, 1871, heir to the estate."

Perhaps the most curious piece of post–de Vere history of Castle Hedingham is recorded in John Gower's *Pyrgomachia...: The Castle Combat* (1635), in which a fictional siege upon Hedingham is poetically described (Roger Stritmatter, private communication [1996]). Whether Gower touches on the castle's history vis-à-vis Shake-speare is a subject for future research.

p. 368, Soon to be Frederick V, king of Bohemia: Frederick V was to be known as "The Winter King" for his brief reign from 1619–20, when he lost Bohemia in the Battle of White Mountain.

p. 368, The King's Men performed *The Winter's Tale* and *The Tempest:* On the pre-1604 nature of *The Winter's Tale* and *The Tempest,* cf. the 1604 appendix.

p. 368, Elizabethan nostalgia as cottage industry: Curtis Perry, "The politics of nostalgia: Queen Elizabeth in early Jacobean England," in *The Making of Jacobean Culture* (Cambridge: Cambridge University Press, 1997), 153–87.

p. 368, Prolific hack writer Richard Brathwait: As he fondly recalled in his memoirs, published when he was fifty years old, Richard Brathwait considered himself something of a late-Elizabethan Tom Sawyer. Brathwait remembered the moment when for the first time he felt entitled to be called, as he put it, "an author! One of the wits!" He found inspiration in the great literary works of his day. "A long winter night seemed but a Midsummer night's dream," he wrote of those long-gone years. As a religious man of the country at the half-century mark, Brathwait in his memoirs harbored mixed emotions about his wild London youth and the lusty plays and poems he'd once written. "What wanton measures have I writ for the nonce," he mused, "to move a light courtesan to hug my conceit– and next [to] her *Venus and Adonis,* or some other immodest toy–to lodge me in her bosom?" ("Richard Brathwait Reflects on the Past," in *Female and Male Voice in Early Modern England: An Anthology of Renaissance Writing,* ed. Anne Lake Prescott, Betty S. Travitsky [New York: Columbia University Press, 2000], 10–12.)

p. 368, "And long may England's thespian springs be known": Richard Brathwait, *A Strappado for the Divell* (London, 1615). "Upon the Generall Sciolists or Poettasters of Britannie. A Satyre," ll. 85–93.

p. 369, He died on his fifty-second birthday, April 23, 1616: "[Shakspere:] A Concise Documentary Life," in PRICE, 14–19.

p. 369, "We have only circumstantial evidence. Internal evidence": Mark Twain, *Is Shakespeare Dead?: From My Autobiography* (New York: Harper & Bros., 1909), 36–7, 48.

p. 369, No records exist of the construction of the Stratford monument: The closest one has to a paper trail on the monument is the seventeeth-century antiquarian Sir William Dugdale's diary, which states, "Shakespeares and John Combes Monum^ts, at Stratford sup Avon, made by one Gerard Johnson." CAMPBELL & QUINN, 396.

p. 369, Prefatory verses by Leonard Digges: On Digges's connections to de Vere, cf. Richard F. Whalen, "Cross-examining Leonard Digges on his Stratford Connections," *The Shakespeare Oxford Newsletter* 37:1 (Spring 2001), 1, 13–15.

p. 369, Shakspere grasps at a quill pen: On the complex and controversial history of the Stratford monument's quill pen, paper, and pillow, cf. PRICE, 153–61.

pp. 369–70, "Deep, deep, deep, subtle, subtle, subtle expression of a bladder": Twain, *Is Shakespeare Dead?,* op. cit., 131–2.

p. 370, "A Nestor in judgment, a Socrates in genius, a Virgil in art": JVDICIO PYLIVM. GENIO SOCRATEM, ARTE MARONEM. TERRA TEGIT, POPVLVS MAERET, OLYMPVS HABET. (*The earth encloses, the people mourn, Olympus holds.*) PRICE, 161–2.

p. 370, All three analogies are inapt for Shake-speare: PRICE, 161–2; OGBURN/*TMWS,* 213–5.

p. 370, All three analogies fit Shakspere capably: I would like to thank Robert Detobel for sharing his perspectives on the Stratford monument and for sharing David Roper's unpublished MS "IUDICIO PYLIUM GENIO SOCRATEM," both of which have informed my commentary.

p. 370, Nestor as garrulous storyteller and self-appointed spokesman for his people: Kenneth John Atchity, *Homer's Iliad: The Shield of Memory* (Carbondale, Illinois: Southern Illinois University Press, 1978), 148.

p. 370, Virgil's ghost was the true author of *The Aeneid:* Craig D. Kallendorf, *Virgil and the Myth of Venice: Books and Readers in the Italian Renaissance* (Oxford: Oxford University Press, 1999), 118–9; Edward Kennard Rand, *The Magical Art of Virgil* (Cambridge, Mass.: Harvard University Press, 1931), 9.

p. 370, "Sieh": There is no English word *sieh*, nor does *sieh* appear as an alternate spelling anywhere in the *OED*. As Roper points out (op. cit.) the German word *sieh* ("look there") may provide the solution. Scholars typically assume that *sieh* is simply a mistake for *sith,* an archaic form of *since.* (PRICE, 164.) However, a Dutch engraver (Gheerart Janssen, cf. CAMPBELL & QUINN, 396) would have known the meaning of *sieh* and would not have been likely to insert a "mistake" into his work that makes this otherwise impenetrable sentence comprehensible. Moreover, Ben Jonson (argued below to have been the author of the epigram) demonstrated in his *English Grammar* (1640) a capable knowledge of German. (Alice Vinton Waite, "Ben Jonson's *Grammar,*" *Modern Lang. Notes* 24:5 [May 1909], 138.) Jonson was infamous for inserting esoteric levels of meaning into his writings, and his line "read if thou canst..." sounds like a taunt from a man who was playing a multilingual joke on the "passengers" who tried to decipher the epigram.

p. 370, "... all that he hath writ leaves living art but page to serve his wit": The punctuation, which confuses the meaning for modern readers more than it assists, has been excised. Here is the English portion of the Stratford monument's epitaph in its entirety:

STAY PASSENGER, WHY GOEST THOV BY SO FAST,
READ IF THOV CANST, WHOM ENVIOVS DEATH HATH PLAST
WITH IN THIS MONVEMENT SHAKESPEARE: WITH WHOME,
QVICK NATVRE DIDE WHOSE NAME DOTH DECK Y^S [*THIS*] TOMBE,
FAR MORE, THEN COST: SIEH ALL, Y^S [*THAT*] HE HATH WRITT,
LEAVES LIVING ART, BVT PAGE, TO SERVE HIS WITT.

OBIT ANO DO^I 1616
AETATIS 53 DIE 23 AP^R

pp. 370–1, Ben Jonson monuments exhorting "passenger" to "stay": Ben Jonson, "Epitaph on Elizabeth, L.H.," "An Epitaph on Henry, Lord La Warr/To the Passer-by," and "Epitaph on Cecilia Bulstrode," in *Ben Jonson,* ed. Ian Donaldson (Oxford: Oxford University Press, 1985), 272, 387, 442; Nina Green, "Did Ben Jonson Write the Inscription for the Shakespeare Monument in the Church at Stratford-on-Avon?" *Edward de Vere Newsletter* 9 (November 1989), online at http://www3.telus.net/oxford/newsletters.html.

p. 371, Susan de Vere married Sir Philip Herbert in 1604: Cal. S.P. Venetian 1603–7, 10:206–7; Norman Egbert McClure, *The Letters of John Chamberlain* (Phila.: Am. Philosophical Soc., 1939), 1:198–9; Maurice Lee Jr., *Dudley Carleton to John Chamberlain 1603–1624: Jacobean Letters* (New Brunswick, N.J.: Rutgers University Press, 1972), 66–9; Christopher Paul, "Monument" op. cit.; Re the Revels accounts detailing performances of plays such as "*Mesur for Mesur* [by] *Shaxberd,*" this book follows the lead of Tannenbaum, (op. cit.) in rejecting them as forgeries; cf. above note on *Shakspere Forgeries in the Revels Accounts.*

p. 371, Aemilia Lanyer: Stephanie Hopkins Hughes argues that that Aemila Lanyer was de Vere's "dark lady" of the Sonnets: "New Light on the Dark Lady," *The Shakespeare Oxford Newsletter* 36:3 (Fall 2000), 1, 8–15.

p. 371, "Such books as were of the best editions": Michael Brennan, *Literary Patronage in the English Renaissance: The Pembroke Family* (London: Routledge, 1988), 157; Robert Detobel (private communication [2004]).

p. 371, Anthology of folklore and customs of English, Italian, Spanish, and Gallic cultures: Roger Stritmatter (*Shakespeare Oxford Society Newsletter/Shakespeare Oxford Newsletter* 26:2 [Spring 1990], 1, 26A:3 [Summer 1990], 5–7; 34:3 [Fall 1998], 18–19) was the first to discover the importance of the *Arkaio-Ploutos* dedications and their relation to the Shake–speare First Folio.

p. 371, Falsely advertised as being by Shake-speare: One play, *The Yorkshire Tragedy,* was in the repertory of the King's Men; the other, *Sir John Oldcastle,* was written by Anthony Munday and colleagues for another company. W. W. Greg (*The Shakespeare First Folio* [Oxford: Clarendon Press, 1955], 11–14) analyzes the texts of "the Collection of 1619" and concludes "Only *The Merchant of Venice, King Lear,* and *A Midsummer-Night's Dream* could make any claim to represent the plays as Shakespeare wrote them." (12)

No doubt to stake a claim on copyright of the texts, at whatever cost, five of the plays from Jaggard's 1619 "collection" were falsely backdated to 1600 (*Sir John Oldcastle, A Midsummer-Night's Dream, The Merchant of Venice*) and 1608 (*King Lear, Henry V*). William J. Neidig, "The Shakespeare Quartos of 1619," *Modern Philology* 8 (1910), 145–65; "False Dates on Shakespeare quartos," *Century Mag.* (October 1910), 912–9; Greg, *Folio,* op. cit.

pp. 371–2, "To the most Noble and Twin-like pair...Sir Philip Herbert [and]...Susan [de Vere]": *Arkaio-Ploutos: Containing Ten following Bookes to the former TREASVRIE OF AVNCIENT AND MODERNE TIMES.* William Jaggard (London, 1619), "To the most Noble and Twin-like paire..." in Stritmatter, "Bestow how, and when you list...." *Shakespeare Oxford Newsletter* 34:3 (Fall 1998), 18–19.

p. 372, "Bestow how and when you list"–i.e., manuscripts: Stritmatter, op. cit.

p. 372, International religious politics soon changed the equation: What follows in this epilogue derives mainly from Peter W. Dickson's groundbreaking work on the "Spanish Marriage Crisis" and the Shake-speare First Folio, first presented in 1998 symposia in Washington, D.C., at the Library of Congress's Office of Scholarly Programs and reported on in the *Shakespeare Oxford Newsletter* 34:1 (Spring 1998), 2; 34:2; (Summer 1998), 1, 4–7; 34:3 (Fall 1998), 1, 8–13; 34:4 (Winter 1999), 14–15, 23; 35:1 (Spring 1999) 8–9, 24; 35:2 (Summer 1999), 7, 28; 35:3 (Fall 1999), 15, 23–24.

p. 372, "Cunning for to make dispute": Perry, *Making of Jacobean Culture,* op. cit., 177–8.

p. 372, James had, since 1604, entertained Spanish marriage offers: *Narrative of the Spanish Marriage Treaty,* ed. and tr. Samuel Rawson Gardiner (London: Camden Soc., 1844; reprint by AMS Press, New York 1968), 103ff.

p. 373, James's homosexual lover, George Villiers: Michael B. Young, *King James and the History of Homosexuality* (New York: New York University Press, 2000), 15ff.

p. 373, "My dear dad and master's legs soon in my arms": Young, op. cit., 46–7.

p. 373, Infanta Doña Maria: Little did James, Charles, Buckingham, and Gondomar know that at his death in 1621 King Philip III confided in his son (the soon-to-be-crowned King Philip IV) that he never intended to marry the Infanta Doña Maria to Charles; the Spanish were just using the marriage match to string the English along. Martin Hume, *The Court of Philip IV: Spain in Decadence* (New York: G. P. Putnam's Sons, 1907), 51–2, fn. 1.

p. 373, "Our dearest Son's match with the Daughter of Spain": "There is no more striking exhibit of these conditions [of state censorship and its response by writers and publishers] than the Spanish Marriage crisis in the early 1620s." Annabel Patterson, *Censorship and Interpretation: The Conditions of Writing in Early Modern England* (Madison: University of Wisconsin Press, 1984, 2nd ed.), 83–7.

p. 374, Both Southampton and eighteenth earl of Oxford arrested: *DNB* entries for "Vere, Henry de, eighteenth Earl of Oxford (1593–1625)," and "Wriothesley, Henry, third Earl of Southampton (1573–1624)."

p. 374, "Why he hath thus ensnar'd my soul and body": Peter W. Dickson, "1622 *Othello* Cracks a Frozen Shakespeare Market," *Shakespeare Oxford Newsletter* 35:3 (Fall 1999), 15, 23; W. Boyle (reporting on the work of Peter W. Dickson, referenced above), "Shakespeare's Son on Death Row?" *The Shakespeare Oxford Newsletter* 34:2 (Summer 1998), 6–7.

p. 374, "An extremely malicious person and has followers": Gondomar to King Philip IV of Spain (May 16, 1622), reprinted (tr. by Juan Manuel Perez) in "Shakespeare's Son on Death Row?" op. cit., 4.

p. 375, One fourth of anti–Spanish Marriage coalition on death row: Also during May, Henry's half-brother Sir Edward Veer (son of Anne Vavasour) wrote his imprisoned sibling an affectionate letter, implying that family ties had been maintained over the years. "My Lord, upon confidence that this letter shall find your Lordship a free man, or at least have the favor to have access unto you, I have written these few lines," Master Veer began, signing his missive, "Your Lordship's affectionate brother and humble servant." Harleian MSS 1581/30/160 in Christopher Paul, op. cit., 28.

p. 375, Treatment of papist figures in Shake-speare: Daniel L. Wright, *The Anglican Shakespeare: Elizabethan Orthodoxy in the Great Histories* (Vancouver, Wash.: Pacific-Columbia Books, 1993); Peter W. Dickson, "Bardgate: Was Shakespeare a Secret Catholic?" *The Oxfordian* 6 (2003), 109–27.

p. 375, Jaggard's presses started rolling with First Folio: Dickson (op. cit.) points out that Charlton Hinman (*The Printing and Proof-Reading of the First Folio of Shakespeare* [Oxford: Clarendon Press, 1963], 1:342–65) establishes through careful bibliographic research on all extant copies of the Folio and the works also being produced in William Jaggard's shop that the production dates of the Folio closely align with the period of Henry de Vere's imprisonment: late 1621/early 1622 to November 1623.

p. 375, Jaggard started printing before getting approval from Stationer's Company: On November 8, 1623, Isaac Jaggard and Edward Blount registered the sixteen Shake-speare plays that had not been printed before (Hinman, op. cit., 1: 24–30). Curiously, Jaggard still tried to drum up interest in his project among book collectors. The English reprint of the 1622 Frankfurt Book Fair catalog includes "Playes, written by M. *William Shakespeare,* all in one volume," among a list of books to be printed between April and October 1622. Peter W. M. Blayney, *The First Folio of Shakespeare* (exhibition catalog) (Washington, D.C.: Folger Library Publications, 1991), 7–8.

p. 375, Jaggard's shop surreptitiously printing Folio while issuing other books: Hinman, op. cit., 1:16–23.

p. 376, Jonson a friend to Herberts and to Henry de Vere: As Ruth Loyd Miller points out ("The Earl of Oxford's Gift to Ben I: Books from Shakespeare's Library?" [privately published MS, 1988]), a three-volume book of Plato in the Chetham Library, Manchester (*Platonis, opera quae extant omnia . . .* [Paris, 1578]) was once owned by Ben Jonson. But Jonson's title-page inscription in each of the three volumes states that the books were given to him by Henry de Vere, eighteenth earl of Oxford.

p. 376, Jonson hired to edit and oversee Folio: On Jonson's probable role as mastermind behind the Folio, cf. OGBURN/*TMWS*, 219–36.

p. 376, Two tracts signed by John Heminges and Henry Condell: On Jonson's probable authorship of the Heminges and Condell tracts, cf. W. W. Greg, op. cit., 17–21, 26–27 (Note E).

p. 376, Jonson wrote quizzical Stratford-upon-Avon monument inscription?: Jonson would write much about his role as chief fraudster of the Shake-speare First Folio, and his literary colleagues would jest with him about the same too. Oxfordians have focused a surprisingly small amount of attention on the smoking gun that is the Jonson canon–and the wits known as the "Tribe of Ben" who surrounded Jonson. For starting points, cf. Edwin Reed, *Francis Bacon Our Shake-speare* (London: Gay & Bird, 1902), 214–17 (on Jonson's

candid discussion of the Shake-speare Folio in his *Time Vindicated*); W. Lansdown Goldsworthy, *Ben Jonson and the First Folio* (New York: Haskell House, 1972) (on Jonson's discussion of same in his *The Staple of News*), and Percy Allen's response to Goldsworthy
("Oxford as Water-Bearer," *Shakespeare Fellowship News-Letter* [UK] [November 1945],
4–5); Alden Brooks, *Will Shakspere and the Dyer's Hand* (New York: Scribner's, 1943),
359–63 (on Francis Beaumont's poem "To Mr. B.J.," which jests with Jonson for "writ[ing]
the grin" on Shake-speare).

p. 376, King practically a nonentity in Folio materials: Ben Jonson, "To the memory
of my beloved, the author...": "*And make those flight upon the bankes of* Thames, / *That so
did take* Eliza, *and our* Iames!" Technically, there is also a pro forma mention of the king in
the Folio's dedication to Pembroke and Montgomery: "To the most noble and incomparable pair of brethren William, Earle of Pembroke, &c. Lord Chamberlaine to the *Kings most
Excellent Maiesty* and Philip, Earle of Montgomery, &c. Gentleman of his Maiesties Bed-
Chamber...." (Emphasis in original.) But this is even more of a slap in the face, given that
James is noticed only in the context of a list of titles held by his opponents.

p. 376, Folio heaps praise on two anti–Spanish Marriage ringleaders: On the Herbert
brothers' remarkable attempts to have and hold the office of the Lord Chamberlaincy,
even when it required refusing greater and higher-paying jobs, cf. Gwynneth Bowen, "The
Incomparable Pair and The Works of William Shakespeare," *Shakespearean Authorship Review* 6 (Autumn 1961), 3–8.

p. 376, Edmund Bolton's *Nero Caesar* as pro–Spanish Marriage agitprop: A. A. Bron-
ham and Zara Bruzzi (*The Changeling and the Years of Crisis, 1619–1624* [London: Pinter
Publishers, 1990], 37–78) establish that Thomas Middleton and William Rowley's play *The
Changeling* (c. 1623) also strongly advocated against the Spanish Marriage.

p. 377, Roman historians said that Rome had corrupted ancient Britons: Malcolm
Smuts, "Court-Centered Politics and the Uses of Roman Historians, c. 1590–1630," in *Cul-
ture and Politics in Early Stuart England,* ed. Kevin Sharpe and Peter Lake (Stanford, Calif.:
Stanford University Press, 1993), 39–40.

p. 377, A period of even greater prosperity, under a Spanish queen, was around the
corner: As I have noted elsewhere (Mark K. Anderson, "*Nero Caesar:* The First Folio's
Straight-Man," *Shakespeare Oxford Newsletter* 36:2 [Summer 2000], 5, 24) *Nero Caesar* only
made it into print after the Spanish Marriage had collapsed. However, the MS had been
submitted to James in January 1623 (n.s.) and registered three months later, at a time when
the Spanish Marriage was still being negotiated. Why James's faction sat on the MS until
after the marriage deal collapsed is a subject for future research: Perhaps James was waiting to release the book coincident with an announcement of Prince Charles's forthcoming
marriage to the Spanish Infanta–an announcement that never came.

p. 377, Preparations for presumptive Anglo-Spanish princess: Henry Ettinghausen,
Prince Charles and the King of Spain's Sister–What the Papers Said (University of Southampton, UK, from a lecture dated February 28, 1985), 12.

p. 377, Celebrations at collapse of Spanish Marriage: Ettinghausen, op. cit., 15–16.

p. 377, First Folio registered only after it had been printed: Hinman, op. cit., 1:362.

p. 377, Priced at £1: Blayney, (op. cit., 25–26) points out that prices varied: Three
copies of the First Folio cost £10 (=20s.), but another copy went for 15s. Copies of the
Second Folio of Shakespeare in 1632 were sold for anything between 6d. and £1 2s.

p. 377, $165 in today's currency: According to Economic History Services
(http://www.eh.net) £1 in 1623 had the same purchasing power as £105.53 in 2002; this
converts to approximately $165.

p. 377, First recorded purchase on December 5: Sir Edward Dering recorded his purchase of two copies of the First Folio on December 5, 1623, for £2. Blayney, op. cit., 25.

p. 377, Some 238 copies survive to this day: CAMPBELL & QUINN, 230.

p. 377, "All's well that ends well": Thomas Cogswell, *The Blessed Revolution: English Politics and the Coming of War, 1621–24* (Cambridge: Cambridge University Press, 1989), 101.

p. 377, Allegations that Buckingham and his mother had poisoned James: James Holstun, "'God Bless Thee, Little David!': John Felton and his Allies," *ELH* 59:3 (Autumn 1992), 518.

p. 379, "Lonely prince of a realm of spirits": Wendell Kretschmar on Beethoven in Edward Said, "Thoughts on Late Style," *London Review of Books* 26:15 (August 5, 2004), 3.

p. 380, *Late style* as defined by Theodor Adorno and Edward Said: Adapted from Edward Said, "Thoughts on Late Style," op. cit., 3, 5–7; Said, "The Rage of the Old," *The Observer (UK)* (August 1, 2004); Theodor W. Adorno, *Beethoven: The Philosophy of Music,* ed. Rolf Tiedemann, tr. Edmund Jephcott (Stanford, Calif.: Stanford University Press, 1998), 123–61. Said says little of Shake-speare in his commentary, only noting the conventional myth that the Bard's final works contain "a spirit of reconciliation and serenity"–a myth to which this book certainly does not subscribe. The late Said's posthumous book on "late style," the *London Review* notes, is forthcoming.

p. 380, "… unashamed either of its fallibility or of the modest assurance it has gained as a result of age and exile": Said, "The Rage of the Old," op. cit.

Appendix A

p. 381, On de Vere's Geneva Bible: On October 6, 1925, the Leicestershire bookseller Bernard Halliday sold the Geneva Bible in question to the American entrepreneur Henry Clay Folger. Halliday's receipt (Stritmatter, 50) states, "Bible, Geneva 1570, silver binding, arms of Earl of Oxford … £25." In 1570, the royal Court of Wards recorded the purchase of a gilt-edged Geneva Bible for de Vere. ("To William Seres, stationer, for a Geneva Bible gilt, a Chaucer, Plutarch's works in French, with other books and papers … £2/7/10," S.P. Dom. Add. 19/38 in Ward, 33.)

p. 381, De Vere's Bible at the Folger: Folger shelf mark 1472.

p. 381, De Vere wrote the marginalia in his Bible: According to an April 20, 2000, forensics report issued by the certified document examiner Emily J. Will of Raleigh, North Carolina: "After thorough examination of all the documents presented in this case, it is my expert opinion that it is highly probable that Edward de Vere, seventeenth Earl of Oxford, is the author of the … questioned annotations. It is the limitations of the questioned materials, rather than any significant difference between the known and questioned writing, which prevents an unqualified opinion." Stritmatter, 429–68.

p. 381, Study of de Vere Bible as Ph.D. thesis: The study was published in 2000 as Stritmatter's Ph.D. dissertation in comparative literature for the University of Massachusetts, Amherst. This appendix is based upon Stritmatter's dissertation (Stritmatter), upon his 1996 interim report (Stritmatter, *There's Not the Smallest Orb But in His Motion Like an Angel Sings … : A Report on the Geneva Bible of Edward de Vere, the Seventeenth Earl of Oxford* [Northampton, Mass.: Privately printed, 1996]), the article I wrote on Stritmatter's work for *Harper's* magazine (Anderson, "Thy Countenance Shakes Spears," *Harper's* 298:1787 [April 1999], 46–9), and upon the collaborative work I have conducted over the past decade with Stritmatter on his de Vere Bible research.

p. 381, Breakdown of where in the Bible the markings fall: These numbers were derived from the data presented in Stritmatter, 345–428; a slightly different set of numbers can be gleaned from David Kathman's independently tabulated summary of the de Vere Bible markings on his Web site at http://shakespeareauthorship.com/oxbib.html.

p. 382, "Shakespeare Diagnostics": Stritmatter, 265–300.

p. 382, Allusions pointing to an earlier Geneva edition: Cf. note in Chapter 10 on the relationship between Bottom and I Corinthians 2:9, citing Thomas B. Stroup, "Bottom's Name and His Epiphany," *Sh.Q.* 29:1 (Winter 1978), 79–82.

p. 382, Other editions of the Bible Shake-speare used: Naseeb Shaheen, "Which Version [of the Bible] Shakespeare Used," in *Biblical References in Shakespeare's Plays* (Newark, N.J.: University of Delaware Press, 1999), 38–48.

p. 382, De Vere purchase of Greek New Testament: de Vere to Burghley, January 3, 1576, in FOWLER, 203–47; STRITMATTER, 54; WARD, 108–9.

p. 382, Library de Vere had access to from age twelve: Eddi Jolly, "'Shakespeare' and Burghley's Library: *Bibliotheca Illustris: Sive Catalogus Variorum Librorum*," *The Oxfordian* 3 (2000), 3–18.

p. 382, One needn't expect this Bible to contain all of de Vere's biblical knowledge: As STRITMATTER points out (72), five biblical allusions in de Vere's letters and juvenile poems–Exodus 3:14, II Esdras 8:33–38, Matthew 7:3, Matthew 10:26, and Acts 9:5–*are* unmarked in de Vere's 1569–70 Geneva Bible.

"This would seem to provide certain verification," Stritmatter notes, "of the impression given above on less definite grounds, such as the wear and correction patterns of the De Vere Bible, that the annotator took mental notice of many Bible verses not marked in this particular copy of his Geneva Bible."

p. 382, Thirty of 81 diagnostic verses marked: Widen the net slightly, and the overlap between de Vere's biblical usage and Shake-speare's favorite verses is 60.5 percent: Three of the "Shakespeare Diagnostic" verses also appear as allusions in de Vere's personal letters (Ecclesiasticus [*sic*] 11:27, Matthew 7:3–4, and Matthew 10:26), while another sixteen are either thematically similar to verses marked in de Vere's Bible or appear within a few verse numbers from de Vere Bible markings. STRITMATTER, 261–3.

p. 382, Overlap with Bacon, Marlowe, and Spenser: STRITMATTER, 315–44, also examines control data for Michel de Montaigne and François Rabelais.

p. 382, On de Vere Bible statistics: STRITMATTER's Appendix C (James P. McGill, "Statistical Observations Related to the Marked Verses in the de Vere Bible," pp. 301–5) has since been modified and partially retracted–cf. McGill, "Re: Debate on Oxford's Bible" (November 6, 2002) on the Usenet group humanities.lit.authors.shakespeare.

p. 382, Thematic parallels: The six themes here considered are only a small subset of the thematic and narrative connections between the de Vere Bible and Shake-speare. No mere appendix can do the subject justice–it deserves a book of its own.

p. 383, Facsimile of de Vere's underlining: In many cases, when de Vere underlined the words in a particular verse, he underlined only to the end of the first or last line, although the thought continues on subsequent or previous lines. For instance, a strict facsimile of II Samuel 1:14 as it appears in de Vere's Bible would read:

> *Psal. 105,15* 14 <u>And Dauid said vnto him,</u> * How wast
> y^u not afraied, to put forthe thine hand
> <u>to destroy the Annointed of the Lord?</u>

Since the present reprint contains different margins and line wrapping than the de Vere Bible, some of the underlined passages may appear to begin and end in otherwise inexplicable places.

pp. 383–4, Anointed king examples: *Richard II*, 3.2.55, *Macbeth*, 2.3.67–8, *Winter's Tale*, 1.2.351–60.

p. 384, On the Neoplatonists: Ficino and Mirandola were merely latter-day proponents of an ancient school of philosophy. Neoplatonism traces back at least to the third century A.D., cf. Thomas Whittaker, *The Neo-Platonists: A Study in the History of Hellenism* (Cambridge: Cambridge University Press, 1928).

p. 384, Neoplatonic beliefs: Cf. STRITMATTER, 93–4, 107–13, 157–71, on the Neoplatonic verses not discussed here.

p. 384, Appearance versus reality in Shake-speare: Herbert J. Coursen, *Christian Ritual and the World of Shakespeare's Tragedies* (Lewisburg, Penn.: Bucknell University Press, 1976), 150, in STRITMATTER, 94.

p. 384, De Vere's body short and feeble: In his 1592 pamphlet *Strange News,* Thomas Nashe writes of de Vere, "Mark him well: He is but a little fellow, but he hath one of the best wits in England." On this quote and the widespread misconception that Nashe is speaking of Lyly, cf. Chapter 9 and related endnotes.

p. 385, Neoplatonic examples: *Richard III,* 3.1.9–11; *Troilus and Cressida,* 3.2.196–7; *Henry IV, Part 2,* 3.2.257–60; STRITMATTER, 95–7.

p. 386, On *hamartia:* STRITMATTER, 147; "... The tradition of using the English 'sin' for *hamartia* seems now so firmly established as to render any attempt to change it merely a cause for confusion." Christopher Bryan, *A Preface to Romans* (Oxford: Oxford University Press, 2000), 101; *"Hamartia"* in Richard H. Palmer, *Tragedy and Tragic Theory: An Analytical Guide* (Westport, Conn.: Greenwood Press, 1992), 23.

p. 386, Index words in margin of Bible: In the four centuries since the de Vere Bible's original purchase, the book has been rebound at least once. This means, as any bookbinder knows, its three unbound edges have been cropped at least once. Thus the outer parts of marginal notes are sometimes lost to the binder's knife. Three full marginal notations of "sinne" remain in the de Vere Bible today (Isaiah 59:11, Amos 5:11–12, Baruch 1:13). The other five today read only "si" or "ne." (Isaiah 29:19–20, 43:24, 63:11; Jeremiah 14:20; Baruch 1:17.) [STRITMATTER, 147, 441.]

p. 386, Sin examples: *Macbeth,* 4.3.223–7; *Lucrece,* 1476–84; STRITMATTER, 152.

p. 386, "Full of bread": STRITMATTER, 174, following upon the lead of Naseeb Shaheen (*Biblical References in Shakespeare's Tragedies* [Trenton, N.J.: University of Delaware Press, 1987], 104), points out that the word *bread* in the antipapist Geneva translation of Ezekiel 16:49 has a polemical purpose—which the more compromising Great Bible of 1539 and Bishop's Bible of 1568 paper over by translating Sodom's sin as "fullness of meat." Sodom's "fullness of bread" is a translator's jab at what the Genevan exiles thought was a Catholic superstitiousness about and overreliance upon Holy Communion.

HAMLET describes his father being killed when he was "full of bread" as a way of saying that his father had not received Catholic Last Rites and thus was doomed to Purgatory. However, his use of the pugnacious language of the Genevan Ezekiel 16:49 suggests that the Danish prince was also sneaking in an antipapist message.

p. 387, "Weapon of godlie is praier": STRITMATTER, 53; the note has been cropped in the book's subsequent rebindings over the centuries so that it now reads simply

pon of)
       } praier
dly is)

However, the full marginal note is readily reconstructed from the context of the adjacent verse, which speaks of "... the weapons of [a man's] ministracion, euen prayer...."

pp. 387–8, Godly weapon examples: *2 Henry VI,* 1.3.57–9; *Richard II,* 1.3.72–5; STRITMATTER, 53.

p. 389, Ishbi-Benob's spear: II Samuel 21:16, STRITMATTER, 100.

p. 389, On Goliath the Hittite: *Pace* STRITMATTER (100), who may have overlooked the footnote to "Goliath the Hittite" in de Vere's Geneva Bible (II Samuel 21:19, fn. P). The footnote reads: "That is, Lahmi, the brother of Goliath, whome Davide slewe, *I Chro.* 20, 5."

The Goliath of infamy was a Philistine; his Hittite brother was named Lahmi. However, the Geneva translators renamed Lahmi "Golliath the Hittite." Cf. "Elhanan" and "Lahmi" in Joan Comay, *Who's Who in the Old Testament* ... (New York: Bonanza Books, 1971), 107, 250.

p. 389, Goliath the Hittite's spear: "... Goliath the Hittite: *the staffe of whose speare was like a weauers beame.*" II Samuel 21:19; STRITMATTER, 100.

p. 389, "... weaver's beam": On FALSTAFF's amalgamation of II Samuel 21:19 and Job 7:6, cf. STRITMATTER, 101.

pp. 389–90, PORTIA on mercy: *Merchant of Venice,* 4.1.184–9, 195–202.

p. 390, On Ecclesiasticus 28:1–3: "Christians have sometimes thought that the words on forgiveness in the Lord's Prayer ('Forgive us the wrong we have done, as we have forgiven those who have wronged us' Matt. 6:12) were peculiarly Christian and that the later frequent encouragement to forgive others in Jewish writings was due to Christian influence.... However, Ben Sira's words in 28:2–4 (especially in verse 2 [*the one Portia quotes*]) show that this relation between human and divine forgiveness existed in Jewish teaching two centuries before Christ was born." John G. Snaith, *Ecclesiasticus: Or the Wisdom of Jesus Son of Sirach* (Cambridge: Cambridge University Press, 1974), 139–40.

p. 391, Micah 7:9: STRITMATTER, 213–20.

pp. 391–2, Philippians 2:14–15: On a discovery of a new biblical citation in *Merchant of Venice* that this underlining afforded, cf. STRITMATTER, 66.

p. 392, "Better my mother had not borne me": *Hamlet,* 3.1.124.

p. 392, Jesus's command to do one's works in secret: These same verses, in fact, come up elsewhere in the British history of disguised authorship. The early sixteenth-century biblical translator, William Tyndale, cited the same Christian teaching when he explained his motive for anonymously publishing his controversial English rendition of the New Testament:

"The cause why I set my name before this little treatise and have not done it in the New Testament is that then I followed the counsel of Christ, which exhorteth men (Matt vi) to do their good deeds secretly, and to be content with the conscience of well-doing and that God seeth us; and patiently to abide the reward of the last day which Christ hath purchased for us; and now would I fain have done likewise, but am compelled otherwise to do." Matthew Tyndale, *The Parable of the Wicked Mammon* (1527), reprinted in Brooke Foss Wescott, *A General View of the History of the English Bible* (London: Macmillan, 1872).

p. 392, The prohibition at Cambridge and Oxford Universities: "Article XIIA. *Of Good Works.* Good works, which follow after justification, can put away our sins, and spring out of the strenuous application of our willpower. Yet although the performance of such works is a necessary condition of our salvation, God is in no way bound to accept them, however many we may perform, and may capriciously choose to reject them and send us to hell. Pay not attention to the text in Hebrews 6, quoted in the communion service, 'God is not unrighteous, that he will forget your works and labor that proceedeth of love.'"

This comes from "The Thirty-Nine Articles of Religion, formulated and approved by Convocation in 1562 and incorporated in the Book of Common Prayer authorized by Parliament in the Acts of Uniformity of 1559 and 1662; required to be subscribed by all matriculants at Oxford and graduates of Cambridge." Richard Nash, "Benevolent Readers: Burnet's Exposition and Eighteenth-Century Interpretation of the Thirty-Nine Articles." In *Eighteenth-Century Studies* 25:3 (Spring 1992), 353–4.

APPENDIX B

p. 394, *Edmund Ironside:* Eric Sams (*Shakespeare's Edmund Ironside: The Lost Play* [Aldershot, Hants, U.K.: Wildwood House, 1986]) makes a compelling case for attribution to Shake-speare, while Donald W. Foster (review of *Edmund Ironside* in *SH.Q.* 39:1 [Spring 1988], 120–3) presents some compelling evidence to attribute it to Robert Greene. It could, in fact, be both—another of, one suspects, many collaborations from the Fisher's Folly days.

p. 394, *The Paine of Pleasure:* Sarah Smith, "A Reattribution of Munday's *The Paine of Pleasure,*" *The Oxfordian* 5 (2002), 70–118.

p. 394, *Hundreth Sundrie Flowres:* For arguments on behalf of de Vere's authorship of at least part of *Flowres,* cf. *A Hundreth Sundrie Flowres,* ed. Bernard M. Ward and Ruth Loyd Miller (Port Washington, N.Y.: Kennikat Press, 1975; first ed. 1926).

p. 394, "Ignoto": On this and other possible other miscellanies from de Vere's pen, cf. Bronson Feldman, "The Secret Verses of Edward de Vere," *The Bard* 3:3 (1982), 94–104.

p. 394, *Golden Asse:* It should be noted that William Adlington's translation of Apuleius's *Golden Asse* was dated September 18, 1566, from University College, Oxford. This classical novel of bawdry is an important source for Shake-speare (e.g., D. T. Starnes, "Shakespeare and Apuleius," *PMLA* 60:4 [December 1945], 1021–50; J.J.M. Tobin, *Shakespeare's Favorite Novel: A Study of the* Golden Asse *as Prime Source* [New York: University Press of America, 1984]). The coincidence between de Vere's trip to Oxford in September 1566 and the appearance, at the same time, of "Adlington"'s translation of Apuleius certainly deserves further research.

p. 394, "Lazarus Piot": Despite a widespread belief that Lazarus Pyott/Piot was a separate individual (e.g., CHAMBERS/*WS* 1:374), Celeste Turner Wright ("'Lazarus Pyott' and Other Inventions of Anthony Mundy," *Philological Quarterly* 42:4 (October 1963), 532–41) presents the definitive case that "Pyott" was indeed a pseudonym. She writes, "Anthony Mundy, versatile Elizabethan, will here (as in the nineteenth century) be identified with 'Lazarus Pyott,' whom most present-day scholars regard as a separate writer."

APPENDIX C

p. 397, 1604, the year de Vere died: Some of the following appendix is adapted from Mark Anderson and Roger Stritmatter, "Shakespeare Authorship FAQ" (1995), at http://www.shakespeare-oxford/com/faqfina3.htm; a good supplementary overview can also be found at Peter R. Moore, "The Abysm of Time: The Chronology of Shakespeare's Plays," The *Elizabethan Review* 5:2 (Autumn 1997), 24–60.

pp. 397–8, Harbage's dating of plays: *The Complete Works | William Shakespeare,* ed. Alfred Harbage (New York: Viking Press, 1977, 1969 first ed.).

p. 398, Elze's dating of plays: Karl Elze, "The Date of *The Tempest*" and *"King Henry VIII,"* in *Essays on Shakespeare,* tr. L. Dora Schmitz (London: Macmillan & Co., 1874), 1–29; 151–92.

p. 398, Chetwood on 1604: W. R. Chetwood, *Memoirs of the Life and Writings of Ben Jonson, Esq.* (Dublin: Chetwood, 1756; 1970 reprint by Garland Press, New York), 20.

p. 398, Shake-speare fell silent: Peter Dickson adds ("*Othello* [1622] cracks a frozen Shakespeare market," *Shakespeare Oxford Newsletter* 35:3 (Fall 1999), 15, 23–4) that except for the death of a publisher and subsequent estate sale, ownership of Shake-speare quartos never changed hands after 1603 either—until the 1622–23 buildup to the Shake-speare First Folio.

p. 398, On the *Sonnets*: The dedication to the *Sonnets* praised Shake-speare as "our ever-living poet." The epithet *ever-living* was rarely, if ever, used to honor a living person. MILLER/LOONEY 2:211–14; Peter R. Moore, "The Lame Storyteller, Poor and Despised," *The Shakespeare Oxford Newsletter* 31:5 (Summer 1995), 21–2.

p. 399, Correcting of texts stops in 1604: The Shake-speare quartos that advertise authorial revisions or alterations: *Love's Labor's Lost,* Q1 (1598); *Henry IV, Part 1,* Q2 (1599); *Romeo and Juliet,* Q2 (1599); *Richard III,* Q3 (1602), *Hamlet,* Q2 (1604). Robert Brazil, *The Mystery of the Shakespeare Publications: A Search for the Truth* (New York: Private publication, 2003), online at ShakespeareResearch.com; also: Brazil, "Edward de Vere and the Shake-speare Quartos," *Shakespeare Oxford Newsletter* 35:2 (Summer 1999), 1, 16–17, 19; 35:3 (Fall 1999), 1, 10–14. Cf. also similar fn. in Epilogue.

p. 399, On 1572 supernova: *Hamlet,* 1.1.38–40; Donald W. Olson, Marilynn S. Olson, and Russell L. Doescher, "The Stars of *Hamlet,*" *Sky & Telescope* (November 1998), 68–73.

p. 399, On pre- and post-1604 science: Eric Lewin Altschuler, "Searching for Shakespeare in the Stars" (1998) arxiv.org/abs/physics/9810042.

p. 399, Shake-speare's sources from 1560s through 1603: Joseph Sobran (*Alias Shakespeare: Solving the Greatest Literary Mystery of All Time* [New York: Free Press, 1996], 156-7) charts Shake-speare's top fifty-three sources, six of which must be supposed to have been read in Italian, French, or Spanish. Seven date from before 1550; three from the 1550s; eight from the 1560s; eight from the 1570s; four from the 1580s; ten from the 1590s.

p. 399, Bullough's list of sources: BULLOUGH; Tom Bethell, "The Case for Oxford," *The Atlantic Monthly* 268:4 (October 1991), 46.

p. 399, *The Winter's Tale* at court: CAMPBELL AND QUINN, 854-9, 950-1; Dr. Simon Forman's diary also records his attendance at a performance of *The Winter's Tale* at the Globe on May 15, 1611, although scholars such as Samuel Tanenbaum and Sydney Race have charged that the Forman diary is a forgery. (CAMPBELL AND QUINN, 240.)

p. 399, "Pleasant conceit . . . ": Cf. Chapter 6 for the discussion of Francis Peck's 1732 catalog of forthcoming reprints from the collection of the Elizabethan scrivener (and sometime de Vere secretary) Anthony Fleming–reprints that never saw the light of day.

p. 400, The King's Men and *Love's Labor's Lost*: January 1605 letter from the Chamberlain of the Exchequer to Robert Cecil, in Peter Quennell, *Shakespeare: A Biography* (Cleveland: World Publishing Co., 1963), 299.

p. 400, *Macbeth* in 1611 and 1664: Simon Forman's *Bocke of plaies* records a performance of *Macdobeth* [*sic*] at the Globe on April 20, 1611; after that it is known that Samuel Pepys saw *Macbeth* at least nine times between 1664 and 1669. CAMPBELL AND QUINN, 485.

p. 400, Equivocation in *Macbeth*: Frank L. Huntley, "*Macbeth* and the Background of Jesuitical Equivocation," *PMLA* 79:4 (September 1964), 390.

p. 400, *Macbeth*'s conventional date: Henry Paul, *The Royal Play of Macbeth* (New York: Octagon, 1971).

p. 400, Burghley on equivocation: William Cecil, Lord Burghley, *A Declaration of the favourable dealing of her Maiesties Commission appointed for the Examination of certaine Traitours, and of torture unjustly reported to be done upon them for matters of religion* (London, 1583), STC 4901 in Huntley, op. cit., 394.

p. 401, Southwell's trial: A. E. Malloch; Frank L. Huntley, "Some Notes on Equivocation," *PMLA* 81:1 (March 1966), 145-6.

p. 401, 1586 context of *Macbeth:* Subsequent English allusions to equivocating Catholic traitors from the 1590s and early 1600s should not be ruled out as sources for later revisions of *Macbeth*, either, e.g., William O. Scott, "MACBETH's–And Our–Self-Equivocations," *SH.Q.* 37:2 (Summer 1986), 161-2.

p. 401, Jestings of PORTER scene: Richard Whalen ("Shakespeare in Scotland: What did the author of *Macbeth* know and when did he know it?" *The Oxfordian* 6 [2003], 55-70) dismisses other, more suppositional arguments for dating *Macbeth*'s composition after 1604. One popular (but bizarre) theory, unsupported by any documentary evidence, is that *Macbeth* celebrated King James's survival from the Gunpowder Plot. However, Whalen notes, the Gunpowder Plot "was allegedly a plot by a gang of Roman Catholic radicals–none of whom was in any position to take power–to massacre the whole government of Great Britain . . . in broad daylight. . . . In contrast, MACBETH, ambitious to gain the throne, stabs his guest, KING DUNCAN, in the night while he sleeps alone in his bed. The two regicides could hardly have been more different."

See also Chapters 4 and 8 for further discussion of the likely back-story to de Vere's composition of *Macbeth*.

p. 401, Eyewitness accounts of Globe fire: R. A. Foakes edition of *Henry VIII* (Arden Shakespeare [London: Methuen, 1957], xxviii) mentions four accounts of the July 1613 Globe Theatre fire: by Sir Henry Wotton, Thomas Lorkin, Edmund Howes, and John Chamberlain. Since then, another letter (by Henry Bluett) and an anonymous contemporary ballad about the Globe fire have also been discovered. (Maija Jansson Cole, "A New Account of the Burning of the Globe," *SH.Q.* 32 (1981), 352; H. R. Woudhuysen, "*King Henry VIII* and *All Is True,*" *Notes and Queries,* n.s., 31 [June 1984], 217–8.)

p. 401, *Henry VIII* by multiple authors: Brian Vickers (*Shakespeare, Co-Author: A Historical Study of Five Collaborative Plays* [Oxford: Oxford University Press, 2002], 333–433) concludes that more than half of *Henry VIII* is written in the style of the King's Men's dramatist John Fletcher.

p. 401, No reason to bow to inexpert authority of Wotton and Bluett: Eva Turner Clark notes (MILLER/*HASP,* 889) that the actor Edward Alleyn listed among his costumes during "the early part of his career" (sometime around or before 1592) a "Harry VIII gown" and "Cardinall's [Wolsey's?] gown."

p. 401, Pepys and *Henry VIII*: Samuel Pepys's diary entry for December 26, 1663, in Foakes, op. cit. xxix.

p. 401, Malone on *Henry VIII*: Elze, op. cit., 153–4; *The Plays and Poems of William Shakspeare* [*sic*], ed. "The Late Edmund Malone" (London: Privately printed, 1821), 2:389–90.

p. 402, *The Tempest* and a 1609 shipwreck: David Kathman ("Dating *The Tempest*" at http://shakespeareauthorship.com/tempest.html) presents a comprehensive list of parallels between the accounts of the 1609 shipwreck in the Bermudas and *The Tempest;* Peter R. Moore ("*The Tempest* and the Bermuda Shipwreck of 1609," *Shakespeare Oxford Newsletter* 32:3 (Summer 1996), 6, at http://www.everreader.com/tempdate.htm) presents the counterargument to Kathman's attempts at debunking the Oxfordian theory of pre-1604 composition of *The Tempest.*

p. 402, "Bermoothes": *The Tempest,* 1.2.266–9.

p. 402, "Bermudas" a neighborhood outside London: Richard Whalen, *Shakespeare: Who Was He?* (Westport, Conn.: Praeger, 1994), 169, fn. 10, has a brief bibliography of the controversy over *The Tempest*'s "Bermoothes" and notes that the introductory map in David Riggs's *Ben Jonson: A Life* (Cambridge, Mass.: Harvard University Press, 1989) pictures "The Bermudas" just east of Charing Cross.

p. 402, Strachey and *The Tempest*: Kathman, op. cit.

p. 402, Muir on *The Tempest*: Kenneth Muir, *The Sources of Shakespeare's Plays* (New Haven: Yale University Press, 1978), 280, in Moore, op. cit,

p. 402, *The Tempest* and Acts of the Apostles: Muir, op. cit., in Moore, op. cit.

pp. 402–3, *The Tempest* and St. Elmo's Fire: *The Tempest* 1.2.196–201.

p. 403, Account of St. Elmo's Fire in 1600: Robert Tomson in Richard Hakluyt's *The Principal Navigations, Voyages, Traffiques and Discoveries, Vol. III* (London, 1600), 450, in Moore, op. cit.

APPENDIX D

p. 405, Kingston's account of portrait: M. H. Spielmann, "The Ashbourne Portrait of Shakespeare," *Connoisseur* (January–April and May–August 1910) in MILLER/LOONEY, 2:411.

pp. 405–6, Where Kingston learned of portrait: William L. Pressly, "The Ashbourne Portrait of Shakespeare: Through the Looking Glass," *SH.Q.* 44:1 (Spring 1993), 54–72; 56.

p. 406, Wrist and neck ruffs: Barbara Burris, "Ashbourne Story III: Close Review of the Painting's Restoration Reveals a History of Deception and Destruction," *Shakespeare Matters* 1:3 (Spring 2003), 1, 10–22.

p. 406, Forearm on skull: Spielmann (op. cit.) puzzles over the skull, noting that its presence in a portrait either signified death or disease or it indicated "that the sitter is a doctor, a medical professor, or a philosopher. This symbolic allusion is frequently seen in Dutch and Flemish pictures."

p. 406, Spielmann and the gold paint: Spielmann in MILLER/LOONEY, 2:414; Subsequent analysis of the gold paint by the Canadian Conservation Institute (Marie-Claude Corbeil and Jeremy Powell, "Scientific Examination of *The Ashbourne Portrait of Shakespeare/Sir Hugh Hamersley* for the Folger Shakespeare Library," Canadian Conservation Institute [October 11, 2002], 5) concludes, "The inscription, thumb ring, embroidery on the gauntlet, and most of the design on the book cover were painted using the same golden yellow paint, confirmed in the case of the inscription to contain lead-tin yellow. There are no indications that this paint is a later addition, especially considering that it was used in so many parts of the composition. This contradicts [Charles Wisner] Barrell's statements that the inscription was a later addition and that the thumb ring 'has been treated to a daubing of the thick orange gold already mentioned.'"

Barbara Burris, however, disputes the Canadian Conservation Institute's conclusion that Hamersley was the likely Ashbourne sitter (Burris, "Back to the Ashbourne," *Shakespeare Matters* 4:1 [Fall 2004], 21), noting that their "limited technical examination is nothing more than a cherry-picking exercise to verify the Folger's foregone conclusions."

p. 406, Boar's-head ring: Charles Wisner Barrell, "Identifying 'Shakespeare,'" *Scientific American* 162:1 (January 1940), 4–8, 43–45.

p. 406, Ketel's portrait of de Vere: Comment of Karel van Mander in Barrell, op. cit., 45.

p. 406, Ashbourne style consistent with Ketel: Burris, "Ashbourne III," op. cit., and Burris, "The Ashbourne Portrait: Part II: Costume Dating Debunks Folger's Hamersley Claim," *Shakespeare Matters* 1:2 (Winter 2002), 1, 17–21; Barrell, op. cit., 8, also compares Cornelius Ketel's "CK" monograms with the "CK" monogram on the Ashbourne.

p. 406, "At [full] length": This record and the 1782 inventory below were first discovered by English archival researcher Derran Charlton. Mark K. Anderson, "An Interview with Derran Charlton," *Shakespeare Matters* 3:2 (Winter 2004), 28; "Pictures and plate, etc., at Wentworth Woodhouse listed by Wiliam, Earl of Strafford, in his will. 9 September, 1695" (Wentworth Woodhouse Muniments D.1493); Barbara Burris, private communication (November 2004).

pp. 406–7, Portrait mentioned in 1695 will: Barrell, op. cit., 45; George Vertue, *Notebooks* (Oxford: Oxford University Press/ The Walpole Society, 1930–35), 1:91, in Burris, "Ashbourne III," op. cit., 12.

p. 407, 1782 inventory of "Shakespear" portrait: "A list of pictures extracted from an inventory of the goods, plate, etc., of Charles, Marquis of Rockingham, 1782" (abstract from the Wentworth Woodhouse Muniments at Archives); Barbara Burris, private communication (November 2004).

p. 407, No edges on Ashbourne: "... Original edges: none," Peter Michaels, initial examination of condition of Ashbourne painting before restoration (February 1979), Folger Shakespeare Library internal Ashbourne files, acquired with the Folger's permission by Barbara Burris; Barbara Burris, private communication (November 2004).

p. 407, Curatorial opinion on costume style: Letter from Susan North, head of Textiles and Dress for the Victoria and Albert Museum to Barbara Burris, March 30, 2001, in Burris "Ashbourne II," op. cit., 18.

p. 408, Similarity of facial features between Ashbourne and Wellbeck: Some might object that during the period it was not unheard of to have the same portrait sitter sit in for two or more different people. However, the Wellbeck portrait of de Vere dates from Paris in 1575, while–disputed date of the portrait aside–the Ashbourne was most likely painted in London.

p. 408, A few scholars accepted Barrell's findings: Oscar James Campbell ("Shakespeare Himself," *Harper's* 181 [July 1940], 172–85) accepts Barrell's attribution of the Ashbourne as an overpainted portrait of Edward de Vere but concludes that it is irrelevant to the larger Shake-speare authorship question.

p. 408, Pressly conceded overpainting of someone else: Pressly, "Looking Glass," op. cit., 54–6.

p. 408, Hamersley original sitter: To add another layer of complication, Pressly's article was preceded by more than a decade by a statement in the *Shakespeare Oxford Society Newsletter* by the Oxfordian organization's executive vice president, Gordon C. Cyr ("Portrait Identified: *Ashbourne* Sitter *Not* Oxford, New Findings Show," *Shakespeare Oxford Society Newsletter* 15:3 [Summer 1979], 1–6), wherein Cyr–who had been made privy to part of the *Ashbourne* restoration process, then ongoing–accepted the attribution of Hamersley as the original *Ashbourne* sitter, not de Vere. Cyr has since retracted this statement (Gordon C. Cyr, "'Smile and smile, and be a villain,'" *Shakespeare Matters* 1:3 [Spring 2002], 9), stating that because of Burris's new work on the *Ashbourne,* "I no longer believe that the *Ashbourne* sitter was Hamersley.... I now believe that the sitter–on Barrell's and Burris's evidence–is probably [the Earl of] Oxford at about age thirty or thereabouts, painted 1579–1583."

p. 408, *Honor et Amore:* Pressly, op. cit., 64–6.

p. 408, "...MORE": "Unfortunately, all of the lettering which must have been on the band below [the Ashboure's overpainted coat of arms] was obliterated." Peter Michaels to Ann Skiff (June 18, 1979) in Folger Ashbourne file, op. cit.; Barbara Burris, private communication (November 2004).

p. 408, Rams versus griffins: Barbara Burris, "The Coat of Arms and the Composite Sketch," *Shakespeare Matters* 1:3 (Spring 2002), 17; Burris, "A History of Alterations to the Coat of Arms," *Shakespeare Matters* 2:1 (Fall 2002), 12–13.

p. 408, "Ketel never touched this canvas": Pressly, op. cit., 61; Pressly cites no authority on Ketel or Dutch portraiture to back up his claim.

p. 409, Pressly on "CK" monogram: William Pressly, "The Ashbourne Portrait of Shakespeare/Sir Hugh Hamersley," in *A Catalogue of Paintings in the Folger Shakespeare Library, "As Imagination Bodies Forth,"* ed. William L. Pressly (New Haven: Yale University Press, 1993), 300.

p. 409, Likeness of Hamersley: The portrait of Hugh Hamersley is reproduced in Pressly, op. cit., 67, and Barbara Burris, "What Did Hamersley Look Like?" *Shakespeare Matters* 1:3 (Spring 2002), 18.

p. 409, Ashbourne overpainting from circa. 1612: Barbara Burris, private communication (November 2004).

AUTHOR'S NOTE

pp. 411–2, On inquiry and "the stranger": Charles David Axelrod, *Studies in Intellectual Breakthrough: Freud, Simmel, Buber.* (Amherst: University of Massachusetts Press, 1979), 5.

p. 412, Influential books on de Vere and Shake-speare: Bibliographical details about these books can be found in the Frequently Cited Sources section and in the endnotes.

p. 412, Amount of orthodox scholarship that supports Oxfordian thesis: Alan H. Nelson's 2003 "documentary biography" of Edward de Vere, *Monstrous Adversary: The Life of Edward de Vere, seventeenth Earl of Oxford* (NELSON) was published roughly halfway through the writing of this book. I soon found that, while overtly antithetical to the Oxfordian thesis, Nelson made discoveries that often added new and unexpected layers to the story of de Vere as Shake-speare. Nelson, for instance, was the first to discover that de Vere was indeed lame in the final years of his life, confirmation of the deteriorating state of health of the author of Shake-speare's Sonnets 37 and 89 ("I, made lame by fortune's dearest spite..."). This fact was first published on Nelson's Web site (http://socrates.berkeley.edu/~ahnelson/authorsh.html) in 1995 and discussed in Peter R. Moore, "The Lame Storyteller, Poor and Despised," *The Elizabethan Review* (Autumn 1995), and *The Shakespeare Oxford Newsletter* 31:3 (Summer 1995), 17–22. As discussed in Chapter 6 of this book, NELSON also adduces evidence that de Vere's mistress Anne Vavasour had in 1580 probably had a miscarriage by him—explaining a jesting allusion BEATRICE makes about BENEDICK in *Much Ado About Nothing* concerning a dead illegitimate child.

NELSON is the second biographer of de Vere (third if one counts Eva Turner Clark's *The Man Who Was Shakespeare* [New York: Richard R. Smith, New York 1937]). The first biographer, B. M. Ward (*The Seventeenth Earl of Oxford 1550–1604* [London: John Murray, 1928], hereinafter WARD) took the opposite tack to Nelson. Ward, an Oxfordian whose biography nevertheless does not pursue the Shake-speare authorship question, sometimes overlooked or defensively portrayed unflattering aspects of de Vere such as his foul temper, his mistreatment of his first wife, his prodigality, etc. As Peter R. Moore writes, "Nelson, who with some justice refers to Oxford's first biographer, B. M. Ward, as a hagiographer (250), pushes much further in the opposite direction, so much so that his study of Oxford may well be dubbed demonography." (Moore, "Demonography 101: Alan Nelson's *Monstrous Adversary*," *Shakespeare Oxford Newsletter* [Winter 2004], online at http://www.shakespearefellowship.org/Reviews/moore-nelson.htm.)

꿍

ACKNOWLEDGMENTS

Foremost in my thanks is Roger Stritmatter, who throughout this project in all its forms has been an insightful and generous guide, advisor, reader, and mentor. His brilliant Ph.D. thesis on De Vere's Geneva Bible, the first doctoral dissertation to openly advocate for de Vere as Shake-speare, was a key inspiration in taking on a project of the magnitude of *"Shakespeare" by Another Name*.

I also am fortunate to have an agent, Stephanie von Hirschberg, who has provided steadfast guidance and expert assistance on a project that, at times, must have seemed a long way from its final state. Our subrights agent Jennifer Weltz has helped develop *"Shakespeare" by Another Name* for foreign language publication and other new markets. Thanks also to Gerit Quealy who first put me in touch with Stephanie and who has kindly helped throughout the various stages of researching, writing, and promoting *"Shakespeare" by Another Name*.

Thanks are due to many people who provided input as I researched, wrote, re-researched, and re-wrote. Over the past twelve years, in this book's multiple incarnations, I have been kindly helped by Charles Beauclerk, Charles Bird, Bill Boyle, Charles Boyle, Barbara Burris, Robert Brazil, Lydia Brontë, Derran Charlton, Michael Delahoyde, Peter W. Dickson, Catherine Dougados, Michael Dunn, William Farina, Nina Green, Ronald Halstead, John Hamill, Andrew Hannas, W. Ron Hess, Isabel Holden, Stephanie Hopkins Hughes, Merilee Karr, Lloyd D. Keigwin, Lynne Kositsky, Jonathan Lazear and The Lazear Agency, Jennifer B. Lee, Joseph Lex, Hiram Morgan, Laura McDonnell, Noemi Magri, Roger Manning, Sally Mosher, Charlton Ogburn Jr., Michael Pisapia, Thomas Regnier, David Richardson, Alan Robinson, Richard Paul Roe, Elisabeth Sears, Randall Sherman, Juliette Thiébaud,

Dick Teresi, Richard F. Whalen, Hank Whittemore, Miryam Williamson, Clive Willingham, Geraldine Wind, Daniel Wright, Roy Wright Tekastiaks, and the many members of and participants in the Shakespeare Fellowship, the Shakespeare Oxford Society, the De Vere Society (UK), and the annual Shakespeare Authorship Studies Conference/Edward de Vere Studies Conference. Others outside of Gotham Books who have graciously helped in the promotion and publicity campaign for this book include Chris Collingwood, Stephen Eldredge, Timothy Holcomb, Randall Sherman, Earl Showerman, Christine Stevens, Brad Thayer, and Eileen Winnick.

I've left a few names off the above lists, as the following people should really be thanked twice over—once for lending their research expertise and once for their magnanimous gift of reading early drafts of the manuscript and providing numerous corrections and suggestions: Robert Detobel, Ramon Jimenez, Peter R. Moore, Christopher Paul, and Sarah Smith. This book also benefited from the insights and advice of both expert and lay readers whom I sought out for their feedback on the manuscript's accessibility and comprehensibility. Their input has greatly improved *"Shakespeare" by Another Name*: Jonathan Alberts, Mark Andre Alexander, George R. Anderson, Janice Cincotta, Burl Gilyard, Joe Eskola, Malcolm Hooper, Luke Jaeger, Stephanie Kraft, and Megan Schneider.

A decade spent researching this book has certainly taught me the tremendous value of a good research library. For nearly all of the digging that *"Shakespeare" by Another Name* demanded, I have looked first to the Five College Library system in western Massachusetts (especially the Hillyer, Josten, Neilsen, and Young Memorial Libraries at Smith College; the Frost Memorial Library at Amherst College; the Williston Memorial Library at Mt. Holyoke College; and the DuBois Memorial Library at the University of Massachusetts, Amherst) and to the Forbes and Jones Public Library (in Northampton and Amherst, respectively). The helpful staff at these institutions have provided immeasurable assistance and guidance. I am similarly grateful to the staffs of the Babbidge Memorial Library (University of Connecticut), the Bodleian Library, the British Library, the Butler Library (Columbia University), the Dinand Memorial Library (Holy Cross College, Worcester, Massachusetts), the New York Public Library, the Shain Memorial Library (Connecticut College), the Sterling Memorial Library (Yale University), and the Widener and Houghton Memorial Libraries (Harvard University).

My editor, Brendan Cahill, and the editorial, production, design, and promotion team at, or affiliated with, Gotham Books/Penguin Group USA (including Sabrina Bowers, Hector DeJean, Anita Karl, Jim Kemp, Robert Kempe, Melanie Koch, Ray Lundgren, Joseph Mills, Rachelle Nashner, Patrick Mulligan, Craig Schneider, and Susan Schwartz) have been helpful and gracious throughout the long process of converting what began as a pitch plus assorted sample chapters into a unified and cohesive story. Moreover, what impressed me first about Gotham continues to impress me to this day: The vision that both Brendan and publisher William Shinker articulated on our first meeting in August of 2002. It was clear then that they understood the scope and challenge of this book, and the ensuing seasons have only reinforced my initial gut feeling that this is a team that gets what *"Shakespeare" by Another Name* is about.

Finally, I remain ever grateful to my friends and family who have endured many a Shake-spearean spiel over these now-twelve years and, throughout, have responded with curiosity and interest that have, in turn, helped to fuel this journey. My wife Penny Leveritt deserves all the accolades the printed word can provide for her emotional support, editorial contributions, and unfaltering commitment to helping this project through from the earliest versions of sample chapters and book proposals to the final push for images and final-draft text to the road that lies ahead: promoting, publicizing, and reporting Edward de Vere's cause aright to the unsatisfied.

INDEX

NOTE:

Names in SMALL CAPS refer to characters from the Shake-speare canon.